Also by the Library of Congress

The Library of Congress Civil War Desk Reference
(edited by Margaret E. Wagner, Gary W. Gallagher, and Paul Finkelman)

THE LIBRARY OF CONGRESS

WORLD WAR II
COMPANION

★   ★   ★

THE LIBRARY OF CONGRESS

WORLD WAR II COMPANION

✶ ✶ ✶

Edited and with an Introduction by David M. Kennedy

Margaret E. Wagner, Linda Barrett Osborne,
Susan Reyburn, and Staff of the Library of Congress

Simon & Schuster
NEW YORK   LONDON   TORONTO   SYDNEY

SIMON & SCHUSTER
Rockefeller Center
1230 Avenue of the Americas
New York, NY 10020

First Simon & Schuster hardcover edition October 2007

SIMON & SCHUSTER and colophon are registered trademarks of Simon & Schuster, Inc.

For information about special discounts for bulk purchases,
please contact Simon & Schuster Special Sales at
1–800–456–6798 or business@simonandschuster.com

Designed by Publications Development Company of Texas.

Manufactured in the United States of America

10   9   8   7   6   5   4   3   2   1

Library of Congress Cataloging-in-Publication Data

Wagner, Margaret E.
    The Library of Congress World War II companion / edited and with an
introduction by David M. Kennedy ; Margaret E. Wagner, Linda Barrett
Osborne, Susan Reyburn and staff of the Library of Congress.
        p.   cm.
Includes bibliographical references and index.
1. World War, 1939–1945.   2. World War, 1939–1945—Sources.
3. History, Modern—20th century.   I. Kennedy, David M.   II. Osborne, Linda
Barrett, date.   III. Reyburn, Susan.   IV. Library of Congress.   V. Title.
D743.W24 2007
940.53—dc22   2007024647
ISBN-13: 978-0-7432-5219-5
ISBN-10: 0-7432-5219-5

ACKNOWLEDGMENTS

Development of a volume with the scope and complexity of *The Library of Congress World War II Companion* requires the dedicated effort of many people. Those who contributed directly to the creation of this book are acknowledged on page xxv—as are the individuals from the Library of Congress Veterans History Project who helped us find, select, and reproduce material from the uniquely valuable VHP World War II collections. The editors and contributors to this volume would also like to thank, for their advice and assistance, Beverly Brannan, Jan Grenci, Ellen Kays, Lewis Wyman, Phil Michel, and Helena Zinkhan from the Library's Prints and Photographs Division; and Domenico Sergi and Jade Curtis from LC's Information Technology Services. Specialists in many of the other Library divisions we visited in search of material—including the Geography and Map, Manuscript, and Rare Book and Special Collections divisions—were unfailingly helpful; and a special doff of our caps to the staff of the Loan Division, who monitored the flow of books, pamphlets, and other material from the stacks to the Publishing Office, and back again. We are also grateful for the help and support provided by people outside the Library: Mary Duby Carlson, Robert Conte, Betty Hensel, Michelle Krowl, Madelon Gail Lucky, Bruce and Kathy Porter, Gerard Quinn, Ken and Diane Reyburn, Virginia Shefferly, Eric Sollinger, Bob Wear, Inge Wehling, and Charles Wilkinson. Thanks to Sonya Porter for graciously allowing us to reprint excerpts of her husband Harold Porter's letters archived at the Dwight D. Eisenhower Presidential Library.

The Library of Congress Publishing Office was "home base" for this challenging project, and we are intensely grateful for the solicitude, support, good humor, and excellent advice of our Publishing Office colleagues Blaine Marshall, Myint Myint San, Evelyn Sinclair, and Vincent Virga. At Simon & Schuster, our publishing partner for this grand endeavor, the expert hand of our patient yet gently insistent editor, Bob Bender, was crucial in giving the book its final shape. His assistant, Johanna Li, kept track of the million-and-one details involved in preparing the book for publication and was ever prompt in answering our many queries. We salute you all!

To all those who served and sacrificed for the Allied cause

CONTENTS

INTRODUCTION
DAVID M. KENNEDY

World War II ended an era in the history of warfare. That era had opened with Napoleon Bonaparte's reliance on the *levée en masse* to replace France's relatively small regular fighting force with a vast citizen army. It continued through the Union's demonstration of the military importance of a deep civilian economic base in the American Civil War. It culminated in the twentieth century's two world wars, which pitted against one another the huge, lavishly equipped conscript forces of fully mobilized advanced industrial states in protracted contests of attrition.

All those conflicts were wars of quantities and endurance. Their outcomes were largely determined by the sheer size of armies—and, increasingly, economies—and by the ability of the combatant states to sustain their armed forces in the field for long periods.

That kind of warfare came to a catastrophic climax in World War II. Fittingly, in a conflict that turned on matters of scale, the numbers tell much of the grisly story. More than fifty nations declared formal belligerency, and few neutrals escaped the effects of the war's violent upheavals. The struggle went on for nearly six years in Europe and by one manner of reckoning even longer in Asia. It consumed over one trillion dollars of the planet's wealth. More than 100 million men took up arms. The war claimed some 60 million lives. And for perhaps the first time in the sorry annals of warfare, a majority of the dead were civilians, including the 6 million Jewish victims of Adolf Hitler's Holocaust, a cruelly systematic scheme of mass murder that gave rise to a chilling neologism, *genocide*.

The United States, late to the fighting and far removed from the major battlefronts, suffered few civilian deaths, but took some 16 million men and several thousand women into service, more than 400,000 of whom lost their lives. And America's economic engagement in the war was nothing short of prodigious. Forty percent of wartime production in the United States went to satisfy the ravenous appetites of the American and Allied armed forces, yielding 5,777 merchant ships, 1,556 major warships, 299,293 aircraft, 634,569 jeeps, 88,410 tanks, 2,383,311 trucks, 6.5 million rifles, and more than 40 billion bullets.

The ultimate reasons for war on such a horrendous scale no doubt lay in what Sigmund Freud called man's cruel determination to play the wolf to man. But its proximate causes can be traced to the troubled aftermath of World War I (1914–1918), in particular, to the thwarted yearnings of three states—Italy, Japan, and Germany—to enlarge their spheres in the world, by violent means if necessary; indeed, in the case of Germany's Hitler, by violent means if possible. Of those three, Japan and Germany proved capable of working the worst mischief. And of those two, Germany was by far the more formidable adversary. As President Franklin Delano Roosevelt said once the war came, "Defeat of Japan does not defeat Germany," whereas "defeat of Germany means defeat of Japan." Accordingly, the cornerstone of American, British, and Soviet strategy in the war was the "Germany-first" doctrine. All other decisions respecting priorities, timing, the allocation of resources, theaters of operation, and force configuration built on that foundational premise.

Japan's aspirations were incubated as early as the nineteenth century. With remarkable purposefulness following the Meiji Restoration of 1868, Japan transformed itself in less than two generations from an insular feudal fiefdom into a robust modern industrial society. Its ambitions and its prowess alike were on display in the Russo-Japanese War of 1904–1905—the first time in modern history that a European power suffered defeat by a non-Western state. Japan's response to the onset of the Great Depression—itself largely a product of the international economic distortions occasioned by World War I—had been to invade the Chinese province of Manchuria, install a puppet government, and dispatch half a million Japanese colonists to develop the region's industrial and agricultural resources.

Some historians date the beginning of World War II to the Japanese incursion in Manchuria in 1931; others cite the full-scale Japanese invasion of the Chinese heartland in 1937 as the war's moment of origin. But Japan's military adventurism had as yet only regional implications. Arguably, Japan might have been appeased, and its provocations confined to one corner of Asia, by some recognition of its stake in China—noxious as that might have been to recognized norms of international behavior, not to mention to the Chinese.

But *world* war came only when Europe, too, plunged into the maelstrom with Germany's invasion of Poland in September 1939. In the context of Europe's disruption, Japanese cupidity expanded to include Southeast Asia, the Dutch East Indies, the Philippines, and India. The conflicts in Asia and Europe now fatefully merged, leading in 1940 to a formal alliance among Japan, Germany, and Italy—thereafter known as the "Axis powers"—and eventually to Japan's attempt to shield its imperial project in Asia from American interference with a daring attack on the United States naval base at Pearl Harbor, Hawaii. With that act, and America's immediately subsequent entry into the war, virtually the entire planet was wreathed in violence.

Unlike Japan, Germany was never appeasable. Throughout the 1920s, Hitler built his National Socialist German Workers' (Nazi) Party out of the septic sludge of anti-Semitism and smoldering grievances over the vindictive settlement inflicted on Germany in the Treaty of Versailles that concluded World War I. The Great Depression visited especially severe privations on the German people, giving ex-soldier Hitler the chance to avenge his bitter resentment over Germany's military defeat in 1918. Appointed chancellor in 1933, Hitler turned the Reichstag into his personal instrument, dissolved the trade unions, muzzled the press, and declared the Nazis the only legal political party in the Reich. In the Nuremberg Decrees of 1935, he stripped Germany's half-million Jews of their citizenship, excluded them from the professions and military service, and banned marriage between Jews and Aryans.

Hitler also began to rearm Germany, at first surreptitiously, then brazenly in 1935 when he announced plans to create a 36-division German army, and more brazenly still in 1936 when he marched thirty-five thousand troops into the Rhineland, flagrantly violating the Versailles Treaty's prohibition on militarizing the buffer zone that separated France and Germany. Banking on the pusillanimity of the other European states and scarcely taking notice of the distant and apparently indifferent Americans, Hitler annexed Austria in early 1938. A few months later, he absorbed the Sudeten region of Czechoslovakia into the Reich, a deed meekly accepted by the other powers in the notorious Munich Pact, and a prelude to the conquest of the entirety of Czechoslovakia in March 1939. Italy meanwhile attacked Ethiopia in 1935, and the following year Germany and Italy together openly supported fellow-fascist Francisco Franco's successful military revolt against the left-leaning Republican government in Spain.

Hitler savored these mostly bloodless victories, but full-scale war was what he wanted. On September 1, 1939, he got it, pouring thousands of German troops across the Polish border. They employed the fearsome new tactic of *blitzkrieg* ("lightning war"), which sought to achieve quick and relatively inexpensive military success through the shock effect of swift and deep penetration by heavily armored columns. Britain and France declared war on Germany, but they proved unable to help Poland, also invaded from the east by the Soviet Union and quickly conquered and partitioned by the two aggressors. The following spring, Hitler unleashed blitzkrieg on Denmark, Norway, the Netherlands, Luxembourg, Belgium, and France, all of which crumpled ingloriously before the German onslaught. On July 10, 1940, he commenced aerial bombardment of Britain, preparatory to an anticipated amphibious invasion. Foiled in that objective by the fiery defiance of newly installed British Prime Minister Winston Churchill, and by the legendary resistance of the Royal Air Force, Hitler turned eastward again in June 1941 with a massive invasion of his erstwhile partner in aggression, the Soviet Union, opening what was to become until its conclusion the war's principal fighting front, sweeping first eastward, then westward over immense stretches of terrain and engaging millions of German and Soviet troops. Here for the first time blitzkrieg failed. Stalemated on the endless Soviet steppes, Hitler was now forced to fight the kind of war he had hoped to avoid—a lengthy battle of attrition requiring full mobilization and deep drafts of manpower and matériel.

Americans long watched these events with a lack of concern born of ancient habits of isolationism. The United States had grown to maturity on a remote continent with no powerful neighbors to fear, breeding in Americans the dangerous illusion that the world's troubles had no bearing on their own fate. The disappointing fruits of Woodrow Wilson's intervention in the European war in 1917 only reinforced the venerable wisdom that America's interests were best served by remaining aloof from the conflicts that seemed to convulse other societies with tragically metronomic regularity. In the two decades after World War I, Americans had virtually washed their hands of the international system. They spurned membership in the League of Nations, helped to strangle world trade by erecting the highest tariffs in their history, disrupted international capital flows by insisting that the Europeans repay their World War I-era debts, imposed sharp limits on immigration for the first time, and applauded when Congress enacted five successive "Neutrality Acts" in the 1930s, a decade that may be fairly described as the highwater mark of American isolationism.

Yet some Americans, notably President Franklin D. Roosevelt, early sensed the dangers that German Nazism and Japanese militarism posed for the United States. From 1935 forward, Roosevelt tried, sometimes hesitantly, but with notable consistency, to educate his countrymen about the gathering international peril. The United States could not survive, he said at Charlottesville, Virginia, in June 1940,

> as a lone island in a world dominated by the philosophy of force. Such an island may be the dream of those who still talk and vote as isolationists. Such an island represents to me . . . the nightmare of a people lodged in prison, handcuffed, hungry, and fed through the bars from day to day by the contemptuous, unpitying masters of other continents.

Roosevelt promised to "extend to the opponents of force the material resources of this nation." Along with the Germany-first doctrine, that pledge defined the essence of America's grand strategy in the war—a strategy Roosevelt later described as making the United States "the great arsenal of democracy."

The Japanese attack on Pearl Harbor on December 7, 1941, provided the occasion for America's formal entry into the war, which by then had been raging for several years in both Asia and Europe. But Japan remained for the United States only a secondary foe. Germany was the principal enemy, the one whose victory could most seriously threaten the United States.

Well before Pearl Harbor, Roosevelt had begun to implement America's grand strategy for the defeat of Germany by securing passage of the Lend-Lease Act. In March 1941, Congress initially appropriated some $7 billion in Lend-Lease aid for Britain—a sum that roughly equaled the entire federal budget in each year of the New Deal decade of the 1930s. A grateful Churchill called Lend-Lease "the most unsordid act in the history of any nation." Hitler thought it tantamount to a declaration of war.

In many ways, it was. The United States had now massively and unequivocally committed the resources of its behemoth economy—long slumbering through the Depression, but still possessed of enormous latent strength—to the struggle against the Axis powers. Before the war ended in 1945, the United States spent over $350 billion to fight it—more than the amount spent by Britain and the Soviet Union combined—including $50 billion in Lend-Lease aid.

The United States also mustered a 90-division army, a powerful navy organized around the new technology of aircraft carriers, and a huge long-range bomber fleet, dedicated to the novel doctrine of "strategic bombing," whose principal objective was not to attack the enemy's fighting forces in the field, but to cripple the enemy's economy and crush its citizens' morale by attacking its civilian heartland.

The United States configured its economy as well as its armed forces to serve its preferred war-fighting doctrine. It brought America's great industrial and scientific strength to bear, first for the defeat of Germany, then Japan, at the least possible cost in American lives. Relative to population, its land forces were far smaller, and its air and naval arms significantly larger, than those of any other belligerent. More than 400,000 Americans made the ultimate sacrifice, but U.S. war deaths were proportionately about one-third of Britain's, and less than one-sixtieth of the Soviet Union's. Some 24 million Soviet citizens perished, two-thirds of them civilians. Reflecting on those numbers, Soviet leader Joseph Stalin bitterly commented that the United States chose to fight with American money and American machines, but with Russian men—a cynical but not altogether inaccurate assessment.

The United States husbanded its human and material resources carefully and, whenever possible, tried to withhold them from battle until they enjoyed overwhelming superiority. The Americans fought mainly a naval war in the broad expanse of the Pacific, where they allocated a minor fraction of their overall effort, and in the main theater of Europe fought principally from the air until late in the war, launching their major ground attack (enshrined in American memory as *D-Day*, June 6, 1944), almost five years after Germany's invasion of Poland and less than a year before Germany's surrender in May 1945. Japan conceded defeat three months later, following the destruction of Hiroshima and Nagasaki by atomic bombs that only the United States had been capable of commanding the resources to build in time for use in the war. (The basic science of nuclear weaponry was widely understood among physicists the world over, but all other powers save Britain, which cooperated closely with the United States, were compelled to abandon or severely curtail their nuclear-weapons programs as too expensive.)

Meanwhile, the United States achieved on the home front something that few societies at war have ever managed to accomplish, and no other in World War II: it grew its civilian economy even while fighting history's most costly conflict. Elsewhere, the war exacted a horrific price not only in lives but in standards of living. Both the Soviet and British civilian economies shrank by nearly a third. Americans, by singular contrast, were better off during the war than they had been in peacetime, the beneficiaries of a 15 percent expansion in the production of consumer goods. It was here that the engines of growth that propelled the American economy through the following half-century of unprecedented prosperity were first ignited. And it was in the booming wartime economy, too, that old prejudices about women in the workforce and the role of blacks in the larger society came under serious assault—laying the groundwork for the feminist and civil rights revolutions that were such conspicuous features of the postwar landscape. Small wonder that Americans came to remember it as "the good war," one in which they had managed victory in a just cause even while enriching themselves in the process, and opening new paths to individual opportunity and social justice.

At the war's conclusion, Winston Churchill declared that the United States then stood "at the summit of the world"—an indisputable truth given the unconditional surrender of its foes, the utter desolation of much of Europe and Asia, and the impoverishment of its allies. If by the question "Who won World War II?" one means who paid the greatest price in blood and treasure to defeat the Axis powers, the answer is surely the Soviet Union. But if one means which country reaped the greatest advantages from the war's outcome, the answer is unambiguously the United States. And in stunning contrast to its behavior after World War I, the United States now became, not merely a participant, but the virtually unchallenged leader of the postwar international system. It founded and funded the United Nations, the successor body to the discredited League of Nations, and welcomed its headquarters on American soil. It built the scaffolding on which the postwar global economy flourished by creating new institutions like the International Monetary Fund, the World Bank, and the General Agreement on Tariffs and Trade (the predecessor of the World Trade Organization). The Marshall Plan of 1947 and the North Atlantic Treaty Organization in 1949 together provided the capital and the security guarantees that underwrote the economic recovery and eventual political integration of the historically warring Old World. Little of this would have been predictable from the vantage point of 1940, the last full peacetime year in the United States, when it remained a militarily weak, economically stricken, and politically isolationist country. World War II thus takes its rightful place among the great transformational events in American history, alongside the Revolution and the Civil War.

The atomic bombs that ended the war also closed the long chapter in military history that Napoleon had inaugurated a century and a half earlier.

The advent of nuclear weapons revolutionized warfare. Its future would turn on technology, not numbers. Its outcomes would be decided not on the traditional battlefield where armies had clashed since time immemorial, but in cities held hostage by weapons of mass destruction, and eventually by "asymmetric warfare" waged by terrorist bands against the very nations that had so conclusively demonstrated their capacity to marshal such massive human and economic resources in World War II. There will almost certainly never be another war like it.

Drawing on the thousands of books, diaries, letters, maps, and photographs in the unmatched collections of the Library of Congress, and on the peerless expertise of the Library's researchers and writers, *The Library of Congress World War II Companion* is at once a definitive source for specific information about the war and a collection of captivating narratives about why and how it was waged, and with what consequences. Like *The Library of Congress Civil War Desk Reference*, this volume addresses not only the major questions of politics, diplomacy, strategy, tactics, and intelligence-gathering, but also less-explored subjects such as the technological changes induced by the war, the organization and characteristics of the armed forces of the major belligerents, the war's impact on daily life in belligerent countries, the role of the media, war crimes, the treatment of prisoners of war, the war's challenges to civil liberties, and the complex and often morally tortured choice between resistance and collaboration. The United States receives special emphasis, but the volume honors the conflict's character as a *world* war with rich coverage of events in all major belligerent countries and in all corners of the globe. Liberally laced with quotes and eyewitness accounts and featuring more than 160 illustrations, *The Library of Congress World War II Companion* is an incomparable resource for understanding the events and the people—from political leaders to ordinary GIs, from spies to slave laborers—involved in the greatest conflict in human history.

PREFACE

"The suggestion of Vice President Henry A. Wallace that our Bill of Rights will have to be defended by a Bill of Duties if our democratic liberties are to endure will be the subject of a roundtable seminar," the Library of Congress announced in January 1943. For more than five savage years, the fires of war had spread around the globe, finally, at the end of 1941, engulfing the United States. The regimentation of society, the burning of books and suppression of free speech, massacres of innocents, slave labor, and the abomination of the Nazi death camps loudly proclaimed the nature of the Axis governments that had ignited this bitter conflagration. To defeat them, Americans joined many millions of people worldwide in subscribing to an unwritten Bill of Duties: to preserve, protect, and defend their lives, their families, their nations, and their right to participate in deciding their own destinies. The United States, the "Arsenal of Democracy," was again at the heart of a struggle to assure that government of the people, by the people, for the people would not perish from the earth.

The Library of Congress World War II Companion is a chronicle of Axis aggression and of the Allied millions, on the home front and the battlefield, who defeated it at such terrible cost in blood and destruction. In the book's twelve chapters, readers will find not only a detailed outline of eight years of battlefield and home-front events, but a rich and telling mosaic of heroism, venality, ingenuity, arrogance, wrenching sacrifice, appalling crimes, and the many kinds of courage of which people are capable. Quotations from leaders of both warring alliances and eyewitness accounts from "ordinary" soldiers and civilians lace through this epic account and constantly remind us that armies and political cabinets, production lines and guerrilla bands, are not remote monolithic entities but associations of human beings.

Several of the quotations included herein were drawn from the growing collections of the Library of Congress Veterans History Project (VHP), which collects and preserves personal narratives, correspondence, and visual materials of U.S. veterans from World War I to the present. Established in the year 2000—the Library's two-hundredth birthday—VHP is a relatively new component of what is now the largest library in the world; the Library's collections include more than 130 million items in all media and in more than 400 languages. Within these vast collections are millions of items pertaining to World War II—including the papers of Allied government and military figures (such as diplomat Averell Harriman and USAAF commander Henry "Hap" Arnold); Adolf Hitler's library; Axis and Allied maps; Japanese propaganda pamphlets and an international array of wartime books, posters, photographs, drawings, films, and radio broadcasts; declassified intelligence reports; and postwar analyses of the conflict. Many of these items are now directly available to people around the world via the Library's Web site, at http://www.loc.gov.

World War II also forms part of the Library's institutional memory. While remaining open to the public, the wartime Library served Congress, the Roosevelt administration, and researchers from more than 50 government agencies around the clock; supported such programs as the Committee on Defense Information; and hosted war-related exhibitions, discussions, and lectures. In January 1942, as some Library staff began leaving to join the military, then Librarian Archibald MacLeish announced that Nobel Laureate Thomas Mann, "Whose devotion to . . . democracy led him to self-imposed exile from Nazi Germany," was joining the staff as consultant in literature. The Library also sheltered "refugee" cultural materials from foreign institutions in the path of Axis armed forces. Most proudly, the Library supervised the safekeeping of this nation's precious founding documents, the Declaration of Independence and the U.S. Constitution—a story you will find on page 181 of this book.

In 1822, the principal architect of the Constitution, James Madison, wrote: "Knowledge will forever govern ignorance; and a People who mean to be their own governors, must arm themselves with the power which knowledge gives." Madison's words, now inscribed on the façade of the Library's James Madison Memorial Building, resonated throughout the dark years between 1937 and 1945. I commend to you this exploration of the greatest war in human history, drawn from the collections of this institution dedicated to keeping the torch of knowledge alight.

JAMES H. BILLINGTON
The Librarian of Congress

ABOUT THIS BOOK

T*he Library of Congress World War II Companion* considers the world's greatest conflict from the beginning of full-scale combat in Asia in July 1937 through the Japanese surrender in August 1945, and also includes, in its beginning and concluding chapters, discussions of the causes of the war and its aftermath. The volume's division into thematic chapters, each covering a particular aspect of the war, allows readers to move through the chapters consecutively, or concentrate on material of particular interest. Chapter 1 concludes with a general overview of Allied, Axis, and neutral nations—including information on parts of the globe rarely treated in general histories of the conflict—and also provides definitions for certain terms used throughout the book.

Because the war was so widespread and complex, no aspect of it can be considered in complete isolation from others. Therefore, in many cases, chapter topics overlap: those seeking information on home-front activities will find relevant material in Chapters 2 ("Wartime Politics"), 3 ("Mobilization"), 8 ("War Crimes and the Holocaust"), 9 ("The Underground War"), and 12 ("Aftermath")—in addition to Chapter 11 ("War on the Home Front"). Those interested in strategy and tactics will find relevant information in Chapters 2, 4 ("Military Leadership and Organization"), and 5 ("Instruments of War")—as well as in Chapters 6 and 7, which are devoted to military operations. To provide maximum assistance to readers, the book includes a Table of Contents and a comprehensive Index.

The Library of Congress World War II Companion is not only a book of facts, figures, and descriptions of events. People planned the war, fought it, and endured its ravages. Thus, the book includes first-person accounts and quotations as well as many sidebars on unusual wartime experiences—from "silking" spiders to extending "hospitality" to enemy diplomats. Each chapter concludes with a list of "Principal Sources and Further Reading," to assist readers who wish to delve deeper into this unparalleled event that convulsed the globe and shaped the world in which we now live.

CONTRIBUTORS

The Library of Congress World War II Companion
Edited and with an Introduction by David M. Kennedy

Project Coordinator/Editor, Library of Congress
Margaret E. Wagner

Principal Writers
Margaret E. Wagner
Linda Barrett Osborne
Susan Reyburn
  with Alan Bisbort
      Sharon Hannon
      Anjelina Keating

Picture Editor
Athena Angelos

Editorial Consultant
Richard Slovak

Contributors
Stephen J. Ackerman
Sarah Ifft
Catherine Osborne
Nicholas Osborne
Jesse Rhodes
Colin Wambsgams

Research
Aimee Hess
Joanne Lipson
Wilson McBee
Nancy Mensch

Director of Publishing, Library of Congress
W. Ralph Eubanks

The contributors to this book wish to extend special thanks to Neil Huntley, Rachel Mears, and Eileen Simon of the Library of Congress Veterans History Project (VHP), Robert Patrick, director, for guiding our research through VHP's extraordinary World War II collections. We urge readers of this volume to visit the Veterans History Project Web site at http://www.loc.gov/vets.

The World at War

Part I: Prelude

"You live in interesting times," the French poet Paul Valéry told a graduating class in Paris in 1932. "Interesting times are always enigmatic times that promise no rest, no prosperity or continuity or security. Never has humanity joined so much power and so much disarray, so much anxiety and so many playthings, so much knowledge and so much uncertainty."

Valéry spoke three years after the New York stock market crashed, opening the way to the Great Depression; one year after Japanese and Chinese troops fought for control of Manchuria; the same year famine struck the Soviet Union when communist-instituted collective farming failed to produce adequate crops; and a year before Adolf Hitler was named chancellor of Germany and a concentration camp for dissidents opened at Dachau. Economic depression, territorial expansion, the growing strength of communism and fascism: these were indeed interesting times. Political and social turmoil marked the period between World War I and World War II.

The events of the interwar years had their roots in the nineteenth century. Industrialization, expanding technologies, empire building, the search for resources and markets, nationalistic rivalries, the growth of mass political participation, and emerging and existing ideologies including Marxism and capitalism, had created conflicts within and between countries well before 1914. Not only did these interlocking issues reach a crescendo in World War I, they remained unresolved when it ended. In geographic scope, monetary cost, death tolls (estimates range between 10 and 13 million troops), and the use of modern military technology, World War I was unparalleled. Soldiers and refugees returned to bombed-out cities and villages. Clothing, housing, and food were in short supply. Famine and the

1918–1919 influenza epidemic killed an additional 50 million people, some 500,000 of them in the United States.

The war had far less impact on the American homeland and economy. The United States had not entered the war until April 1917, three years after it began. The country did lose some 116,516 troops from battle deaths and other causes and had incurred expenses, including loans to its allies, totaling more than $7 billion—plus some $3 billion in postwar loans to Allied countries and newly formed nations. But no battles took place on U.S. territory, civilians were not killed, and American soldiers were not worn out from years of fighting. In fact, the disruption to European empires and economies and their reliance on U.S. funding actually helped the United States replace Britain as the leading financial power in the postwar world.

Despite its economic influence, and a desire to expand trade, the United States pursued a strongly isolationist postwar foreign policy in its political commitments. The conservative Republican Congress that was elected in 1918 repudiated not only the relatively progressive domestic aims of President Woodrow Wilson, but also his championing of the League of Nations. In 1920, Republicans reclaimed the White House with the election of Warren G. Harding on the platform of a "return to normalcy"—steering clear of foreign entanglements and concentrating on the business of the United States.

Treaty of Versailles

The most prominent of the six treaties that ended World War I was the Treaty of Versailles, drawn up between the Allied powers—including Britain, France, Italy, Japan, and the United States—and Germany. (Separate treaties were signed with the other belligerents.) It was signed on June 28, 1919, and eventually ratified by every country involved except the United States. (Russia did not participate in formulating or signing the treaty.)

Germany lost European territory to Belgium, Denmark, Poland, and France; a corridor separated East Prussia from the rest of Germany; and Danzig (Gdansk) on the Polish coast became a free city with its own constitution, but under the protection of the League of Nations. Alsace-Lorraine (in the southwest corner of Germany), with its iron fields, was ceded to France, which also had the right to the coal mines in Germany's Saar Basin. Germany lost all its colonial territories; they became mandates of Britain, France, and Japan. The left bank of the Rhine River was to be occupied by the Allies for fifteen years.

On May 27, 1919, German delegates at the Trianon Palace Hotel listen to a speech by French premier Georges Clemenceau on the terms of the Treaty of Versailles.

In addition, reparations were to be paid to the Allies based on Article 231 of the treaty: "The Allied and Associated Governments affirm and Germany accepts the responsibility of Germany and her allies for causing all the loss and damage to which the Allied and Associated Governments and their nationals have been subjected as a consequence of the war imposed upon them by the aggression of Germany and her allies." The war guilt article also accused Kaiser Wilhelm II of crimes against international morality.

Germany was prohibited from having a draft, several types of weapons, and a military or naval air force. Numbers of personnel and equipment in the army and navy were drastically reduced. Austria and Germany could not be unified without unanimous permission from the League of Nations. France and Italy particularly desired this restriction because they feared the two Germanic nations would unite to become the single most powerful country in Europe, as their close alliance had made them before World War I.

Versailles' harsh terms toward Germany have often been blamed for fueling antagonisms that erupted into World War II. The Allies rejected German attempts to negotiate and forced the German government to accept every stipulation exactly as presented to them, including the despised war

THE LEAGUE OF NATIONS

The Covenant of the League of Nations stated that it was formed "in order to promote international co-operation and to achieve international peace and security." The original members of the League were those thirty-two countries that had signed the Treaty of Versailles. The United States never actually became a member, since Congress failed to ratify the treaty. Thirteen additional neutral countries in South America, Europe, and the Middle East were specifically invited to join the League in the Annex to the Covenant. Thus it began with forty-three members. Significantly, Germany, Austria, Hungary, Turkey, and the Soviet Union were not initially asked to join, which affected League intentions and policy as a global institution.

The League granted authority to Britain, France, and Japan to administer the former German colonies and territories of the Ottoman Empire in behalf of the people, until they could govern themselves. Although the Covenant called for the mandatories to support fair labor practices, legal justice, and "freedom of conscience and religion," for the people living in these mandates, the system seemed little different from the claiming and control of colonies that was a hallmark of the prewar period.

Although Article 10 of the Covenant called on the members to "respect and preserve as against external aggression the territorial integrity and existing political independence of all Members," none was prepared to provide troops to defend another country. But the League of Nations did deal with issues of housing, health, and education; sought to protect women and children; worked to abolish slavery and forced labor; helped to rebuild Austria, Hungary, and Bulgaria; and provided help to millions of refugees, including Russians, Greeks, and Armenians. In its humanitarian work, it was a beacon of hope to many people throughout the world.

guilt clause. Adolf Hitler's National Socialist German Workers' (Nazi) Party exploited these circumstances to arouse hatred in the German people as the Nazis rose to power.

The Treaty of Versailles also failed to resolve the underlying tensions that had preceded World War I. Versailles did not settle the struggle among countries worldwide for economic and military domination or secure the principle of self-determination for every political group and culture. It did not end conflict between communist, democratic, and later fascist ideologies; colonial and nationalist forces; and ethnic and religious groups. Rather, the treaty—and the political infighting that occurred as the various Allies negotiated terms—confirmed that control of empires, trade and resources, labor and agriculture, government and society, and defense and security were more on the minds of political leaders of every stripe than the often-expressed goals of peace and respect for all nations. This, in turn, reinforced the view of American isolationists. General Tasker Bliss, chief of the American military delegation at the Versailles negotiations, observed, "What a wretched mess it all is. If the rest of the world will let us alone, I think we had better stay on our side of the water and keep alive the spark of civilization."

Post-Versailles: The State of the World

The globe looked markedly different after World War I. Not only imperial Germany, but the Austro-Hungarian and Ottoman empires fell. Since newly communist Russia did not participate at Versailles, territory taken by Germany from Russia under the terms of the Brest-Litovsk Treaty concluded between the two countries on March 3, 1918, was now used to enlarge or create eastern European states: Estonia, Latvia, Lithuania, Finland (which had declared its independence in 1917), a reconstituted Poland, Czechoslovakia, and Yugoslavia. The political boundaries drawn after World War I trapped some ethnic populations within countries where a majority of the population had a different background (for example, Germans in Czechoslovakia), breeding interethnic conflict.

After the League mandate system added Palestine, the Transjordan, Tanganyika, and joint control with France of the Cameroons and Togoland to the British empire, Britain governed 23.9 percent of the world. Although Britain was in debt to the United States for some $4.3 billion, maintaining the empire, despite enormous cost, was one of its chief concerns, as well as maintaining naval supremacy and the balance of power on the European continent.

France, with the addition of Lebanon, Syria, and its share in Africa, governed 9.3 percent of the world. The country had borrowed $3.4 billion from the United States and had lost more men than any of the other Allies—except Russia. Most of the fiercest and prolonged fighting had taken place on French soil. France's paramount concern during the interwar years was security, which called for retaining the upper hand in relation to Germany.

While Britain and France acquired large mandates, Italy increased its territory by only 8,900 square miles and, perhaps more insulting, received no mandate over former German colonial territory. Not only its government, but its people were bitter and frustrated with the treaty's terms.

Japan had taken little active part in World War I, although it had been an Allied power in the hopes of expanding its territory. It made inroads into China during the war; this heightened tensions with the United States, a primary advocate of maintaining an "open door" to Chinese markets. On November 2, 1917, however, in the Lansing-Ishii Agreement, Japan and the United States agreed, "The United States recognizes that Japan has special interest in

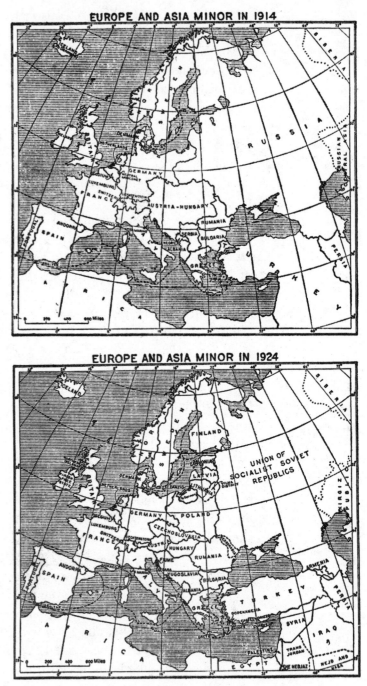

EUROPE AND ASIA MINOR IN 1914

EUROPE AND ASIA MINOR IN 1924

These maps show the boundaries of European and Middle Eastern countries in 1914, when World War I began, and in 1924, after the Treaty of Versailles went into effect.

China, particularly in the part to which her possessions are contiguous." Thus, the Japanese were angry when they met stiff opposition from the United States over territorial provisions and the Japanese desire to include the principle of racial equality in the Covenant of the League of Nations. Nonetheless, Japan received mandates for the formerly German-owned islands it had occupied. Although it had gained significant power, Japan would continue to be treated as an unequal partner by Europe and the United States, provoking anger and resentment that contributed to the policies leading up to World War II.

In Germany, Kaiser Wilhelm II went into exile on November 10, 1918, and a republican government was elected on January 19, 1919, a coalition of socialist, centrist, and democratic parties that convened in the town of Weimar. It was this government that was finally forced to accept the terms of the Treaty of Versailles because, with Germany's resources exhausted and its population weak and malnourished, the country was in no position to resume a war. However, this fact was little understood by the German people. Thus, many considered the acquiescence of the Weimar Republic a cowardly betrayal, placing the republic in a precarious position. After the first reparations payment of £50 million in 1921, the already deflated value of the mark dropped precipitously.

Ultranationalist and communist groups proved to be disruptive forces in Germany. Then, in 1923, French and Belgian troops occupied the Ruhr Valley, Germany's primary industrial region, claiming that Germany had failed to make its reparations payment. This tended to enrage—and to a certain extent unite—Germans of all views. The government ordered Ruhr workers to passively resist and printed enormous amounts of paper money to pay the workers, which sent inflation skyrocketing. An international committee finally formulated the Dawes Plan to stabilize German currency (see "Debt," p. 26).

Having made a separate peace with Germany (the Treaty of Brest-Litovsk), Russia took no part in drawing up the terms of Versailles. By February 1919, more than a half million White (anti-Bolshevik) Russians were engaged in a civil war with the Reds (Bolsheviks). The Whites were ultimately defeated in 1920, leaving Russia in Bolshevik hands.

Taking advantage of the end of the Ottoman Empire, Greek forces invaded Turkey in 1921. Mustapha Kemal (later Kemal Atatürk) finally defeated Greece in 1923, declared a Turkish Republic, and introduced modernizing reforms. Under the terms of the peace treaty of Lausanne that settled the Turkish-Greek conflict, an exchange of Turkish and Greek nationals living in Greece and Turkey respectively, took place.

French soldiers carry goods from a shop in Dortmund after they occupy the Ruhr, Germany's main industrial region, in 1923.

In China, Sun Yat-sen established the Kuomintang (KMT), or National People's Party (Nationalists), in 1912; he established a nationalist government at Canton in 1916, while rival war lords still vied for power. Extreme social and political instability continued into the 1920s. China was outraged that Versailles allowed Japan to take over the Chinese territory that had belonged to Germany, including Shantung, a peninsula southeast of Peking. In 1921, a Chinese Communist Party formed, allying itself with the Kuomintang in 1923. In 1927, Chiang Kai-shek, who headed the Kuomintang after Sun's death, purged the communists from his party, initiating a long civil war.

In the United States, the conservative Republican Congress that won election in 1918 set the tone and agenda in the 1920s. Liberals, who had hoped that labor reforms and business regulations instituted during the war would continue to create a more equal society, found themselves battling up-hill. In a country relatively unscathed by combat, traditional underlying divisions and tensions remained in relation to race, gender, and the workplace. War industries had created many new opportunities and, by 1920, one third of a million African Americans had relocated to Northern industrial centers, a change that sparked anti-black riots. Although women had also reinforced the wartime workforce, in 1920, women constituted a smaller percentage of the workforce than they had in 1910. Nonetheless, women, whom Wilson had called "vital to the winning of the war," were granted the right to vote in 1920.

World War I also changed the United States' standing as a world economic power. By 1919, it was a net creditor instead of a debtor to other countries. It had loaned $10 billion to foreign governments; nearly half that amount went to Britain. However, unlike Britain, which had been the nineteenth-century center of world finance, the United States did not pump enough money into the world economy to significantly stimulate global economic growth. By reserving most funds for domestic investment and by insisting that the cash-strapped Allies repay their debts, American fiscal policies and practices contributed to the economic instability and eventual worldwide depression of the interwar period.

Although politically, the United States wanted no more involvement in European and other international conflicts, it did have international aspirations. In the 1920s, Republican administrations under presidents Warren G. Harding (1921–1923) and Calvin Coolidge (1923–1929) sought to make the United States preeminent in trade and naval power, competing with both Britain and Japan; sought economic concessions, particularly in Asia; supported open-door trade policies in China; opposed Japanese expansion in China; and opposed the spread of communism—attitudes that would affect the course of events leading to World War II.

Communism versus Fascism

The clashes between communists and fascists in the 1920s and 1930s literally had fellow citizens fighting in the streets. Most who supported communism regarded it as an international movement that would radically alter existing economic, political, and social structures around the globe. In the economically and politically unstable aftermath of World War I, communism tapped into workers' deep discontent about extreme inequities in the distribution of wealth. The call for a worldwide revolution that would eliminate private industries, businesses, and services particularly threatened noncommunist governments.

It is difficult to overstate the fear communism produced in the Western democracies, from leaders of government to ordinary men and women. Many believed that their property would be taken, families separated, and churches destroyed—that communism would rupture the very basis of society. In fact, communism was not as powerful as the claims made in communist propaganda, but in a period of social and economic upheaval, outsiders found it hard to gauge the movement's strength. Its international objectives seemed to threaten the sovereignty of nations and the value it placed on collectivization to threaten individual freedom.

Fascism—a form of government first developed in Italy, but with similarities to other right-wing movements—presented itself as an antidote to the communist view. Its attraction perhaps lay in its inherently simple message at a time of uncertainty: one's country had been great and could be great again if its leaders exercised the will to power and had the support of the people. Nationalism—an unquestioning loyalty to the culture, values, and traditions of a particular nation (as opposed to the theoretically borderless international community aimed for by communism)—lay at the root of fascism's philosophy.

Although fascism manifested itself in different ways in different countries, several common features stood out. Fascist movements were fueled by political instability and economic depression. They were centered on national pride and emphasized the virtues of the past. A cult of personality was built around a single leader, who had absolute authority. Fascist governments felt a sense of superiority over other peoples and depended on territorial expansion to increase resources, settle excess population, build new markets, and provide cheap labor from subject populations. Internally, there was an emphasis on strength through purification (for example, the purging of liberal, democratic or, in the case of Asia, Western values). War was considered an energizing force and domination a path to security and prosperity, necessitating expansion of the military. Leaders placed a high value on myth, pageantry, and propaganda to manipulate the public; those who opposed fascism—or even the leader's version of it—were silenced or eliminated.

At the beginning of the 1920s, communism seemed the most likely benefactor of the chaos created by World War I. By the 1930s, although the Soviet Union had built considerable strength, fascism seemed to dominate. These systems were not just confined to the Soviet Union on the one hand,

and Italy, Germany, and Japan on the other. Fascists formed paramilitary squads in France (the Croix de Feu and Cagoulards), Belgium (Rexists), Spain (Falange), Britain (Union of Fascists), Romania (Iron Guard), and Yugoslavia (Ustashi). Both communists and fascists—and every shade in between—thrived and struggled for power in many countries.

The Russian Revolution

Until the 1917 Bolshevik Revolution, communists did not govern any nation, let alone a major power. But Vladimir Lenin and his cadre of socialist revolutionaries, returning from exile with German assistance, appealed to workers and peasants, who had formed the bulk of Russia's World War I fighting force. Lenin promised adequate food, land redistribution, and an end to war. By November 1917, the Bolsheviks had assumed control of the government. Civil war broke out between the Bolsheviks, called Reds, and the White Russians, an unruly alliance including moderates, liberals, dissident communists (Mensheviks), and right-wing czarists.

In March 1918, the Bolsheviks negotiated a separate peace with Germany. Russia's former allies were alarmed because this settlement freed a large contingent of German soldiers to move to the Western Front. Russia also possessed arms that could fall into German hands. Britain, France, the United States, and Japan sent troops to support the White Russians. The western powers withdrew their troops by the end of 1919; Japanese forces remained until 1922. By that time, the Reds had triumphed in the civil war and established the Union of Soviet Socialist Republics (USSR), with the state and the Communist Party constituting a parallel governing structure. The Soviet Union, in embracing communism, had isolated itself from the world community and engendered mistrust and fear.

Communist Uprisings in Europe and Asia

Even before the Bolsheviks took power, communism was asserting its force in other countries. Communist munitions workers in Germany went on strike in 1916, as well as in 1917 and 1918. In Berlin, German communists (called Spartacists) revolted against the new German republic in January 1919, but the anticommunist German army violently suppressed the incipient revolution. The army command employed Free Corps—vigilante, paramilitary right-wing groups of war veterans, who were precursors of the Nazi

Joseph Stalin (right) and Vladimir Lenin were leaders of the new Soviet Union founded in 1922, the year this photograph was taken.

stormtroopers known as the SA (*Sturmabteilung*). The Spartacists also briefly established a First Bavarian Socialist Republic in Munich and soviets in several towns and in the demilitarized Ruhr in 1920. That same year, German troops entered the Ruhr, in violation of Versailles, to vanquish the Spartacists.

In 1919, Bela Kun instituted communist measures in Hungary, including nationalization of businesses and seizure of private property, which proved so unpopular that Kun's government lasted only 133 days. In 1920, Bolsheviks briefly set up the Polish Revolutionary Committee in the eastern part of the country. Some discontented soldiers formed soviets in Britain and refused to follow orders or extend their enlistments.

In postwar Japan, there were rice riots, strikes, and other labor disputes. In July 1922, a Japanese Communist Party was secretly formed. In response, the Diet (legislature) passed the 1925 Public Peace Maintenance Law, which banned any ideologies that advocated against the state or private property. Nonetheless, workers and farmers attempted to organize for better economic and political conditions into the 1930s.

As noted above, a Communist Party formed in July 1921 in China, with Mao Tse-tung as one of its founding members. Also in Asia, Ho Chi Minh, a founding member of the French Communist Party in 1920, established and trained a communist youth league in China (1924–1926), a precursor to the Indochinese Communist Party. In China and southeast Asia, communism would come to be a major force. But in Europe, outside the USSR, despite the demonstrations and rebellions following World War I, communism did not take hold except as a party incorporated into democratic governments.

Communism never took deep root in the United States either. The Communist Party USA formed in 1919, the same year that strikes and worker demonstrations alarmed Americans. In 1920, Attorney General A. Mitchell Palmer rounded up and deported suspected radicals in what became known as the "Red Scare." When no violent overthrow of the government took place, hysteria soon subsided. Nonetheless, the perceived—if not actual—threat of communism affected labor unions, whose membership fell drastically as company owners and workers worried about Soviet involvement in American affairs.

The Rise of Totalitarianism

The governments that rose to power in Italy, Germany, Japan, and the Soviet Union in the interwar years can be collectively described as *totalitarian*—in each country, the political authority strove for total control of the state. The USSR had a *communist* government, while the term *fascist* has been applied to the other three governments. But Italy, Japan, and Germany were not identical. In fact, the government of Nazi Germany more closely resembled that of the USSR, although the two espoused mutually antagonistic ideologies. Both countries experienced profound instability at the end of World War I, and both came under the rigid control of a single dictator—Adolf Hitler and Joseph Stalin respectively. In each, only one political party was allowed, and its organizational structure paralleled that of the government. Hitler and Stalin each had a base of support from a significant portion of the population who believed that a strong leader could guide them through difficult times to a better future—a belief fueled by continual propaganda. Each leader was the center of a cult of personality. Each ruthlessly eliminated political rivals and dissidents, using terror as a weapon to maintain his position.

Italy's Benito Mussolini, though a dictator and the object of a cult of personality, nonetheless had to consider the wishes of the king, the armed forces, industrialists, and the Catholic Church in devising his policies. In Japan, the emperor was regarded as a sacred figure, but the Meiji constitution required that the Diet consent to all laws. In practice, the emperor was hemmed in by numerous advisers, and government was influenced by their agendas. During the late 1920s and early 1930s, Japanese military factions supported by civilian ultranationalists gradually achieved the dominant voice in shaping government and national objectives.

The Dictators and Their Countries

ITALY

Benito Mussolini (1883–1945) worked as an agitator for the Italian Socialist Party, but when the party expelled him in 1914 for supporting Italy's entry into the war, he formed Fasci, or action groups, to promote his views. He served in the army and afterward edited the radical newspaper *Popolo d'Italia*. In 1919, he reorganized the Fasci, this time to attack Bolshevism. He identified himself as a guardian of law and order, stability, private property, and national pride, and won a following among the middle class and wealthy industrialists. Mussolini espoused a "doctrine of action," a dynamic relationship between a forceful leader and a continually excited, responsive populace, bound together by a vision of national glory.

Various Italian political factions joined Mussolini in forming the National Fascist Party (*Partito Nazionale Fascista*, or PNF). They shared a hatred of communism, a belief in violence, and disgust at the weaknesses of parliamentary government. The leaders of local PNF chapters and their squads, known as Blackshirts, had considerable power. On October 27, 1922, Blackshirts seized public places, intending to march on Rome to take over

After Italy's King Victor Emmanuel III made Benito Mussolini prime minister, members of Mussolini's Fascist Party marched in Rome, October 28, 1922.

the government. Mussolini did not take part in these demonstrations, but before the jubilant Fascists arrived in Rome, King Victor Emmanuel III asked him to become prime minister.

Italian Fascists proceeded to suppress trade unions, deny civil liberties, and censor opposition media, often relying on violence and terror. The party was reorganized in 1924, centralizing power in Rome. From 1925 on, Mussolini ruled as a dictator. In 1926, a Public Safety Law made the security of the state, rather than the liberty of the individual, the foremost goal of the Italian government. Mussolini instituted the corporate state: the workers and employers of each profession and industrial branch were included in a corporation to which they paid dues. In 1929, he successfully negotiated the *Lateran Accords*, in which the Vatican became a small sovereign state in return for recognition of Mussolini's government.

Leaders and civilians in other countries, including Britain and the United States, initially admired Mussolini for imposing order and strengthening the Italian state. Perceiving himself as a major player on the world stage, throughout the 1920s and 1930s Mussolini made, broke, and brokered alliances and agreements. He financed fascist movements in other European countries and sought to secure the Mediterranean for Italy and to expand into the Balkans and Africa as a way of building an empire. In 1935, Italians invaded Ethiopia. The war proved very popular in Italy, especially when the Italians claimed victory in 1936, but it put Mussolini at odds with the world community (see "War in the 1930s" later in this chapter).

THE SOVIET UNION

Born Josef Dzhugashvili, Joseph Stalin (1879–1953) took the name of Stalin (steel) and was a political radical who edited a Marxist newspaper before he was imprisoned, then exiled, by the czarist regime. He escaped to Western Europe and participated in leftist planning sessions and conventions, supporting Lenin and Bolshevism over other factions. Returning to Russia, he founded the Communist Party newspaper *Pravda* and in 1922 became secretary general of the Communist Party. After Lenin's death in 1924, Stalin—the man whom a colleague later referred to as a "ferocious savage"—discredited, expelled (from the party), or exiled his rivals to become the de facto sole leader of the Soviet Union.

Artfully employing his close relationship with Lenin, he had Lenin's body embalmed and enshrined as a symbol of the revolution; Stalin, too, attained cult status. On his fiftieth birthday, in 1929, villages and factories burned incense, and his portrait went up throughout the country. Throughout the 1930s, his supporters—especially members of the Communist Party, the rural poor, and urban workers—perceived him to be both stabilizing and dynamic.

In 1928, the Communist Party instituted its first "Five-Year Plan" to collectivize agriculture and aggressively develop industry. At the same time, Stalin engaged in mass purges of the Communist Party and sought to destroy opposition among the Soviet people. His targets included the *kulaks* (well-off peasants who resisted collectivization); more than 5 million people were killed in three years. The entire nation was being reshaped. A new calendar was instituted, with a five-day week that eliminated Saturdays and

Sundays and gave workers single rest days. Instead of religious holidays, there were five national public holidays celebrating aspects of the Revolution. Church buildings were destroyed and clergy persecuted, and literature deemed "anti-revolutionary" was removed from libraries. Schoolchildren were taught to praise Stalin and the communist system. Productive workers received better food and housing, but workers often were terrorized into doing their jobs.

Some 5 million people died in the Ukraine in 1932 (and 1.6 million in Kazakhstan) when collective farming failed to produce adequate crops. Widespread famine resulted, but not only did Stalin refuse to ask for outside aid, he exported grain to the West to disprove foreign rumors of Soviet food shortages. Yet modernization, however problematic, did move forward and economic growth exploded. From 1928 to 1932, the industrial labor force doubled and productivity of goods nearly doubled.

During this period, the government held show trials, where psychological torture and threats against a prisoner's family induced confessions to various anticommunist "crimes." To a remarkable extent, Stalin achieved complete control of the state. However, millions died in the USSR under Stalin's policy of eliminating anyone—political rivals, dissidents, foreign advisers, and those alleged to be bourgeois, lazy, or unenthusiastic—who stood in his way.

GERMANY

Adolf Hitler (1889–1945) was born in Austria, served in the German army during World War I, and was wounded just before the war ended with Germany's defeat. Appalled at what he felt was betrayal of the German nation by its civilian government, he became a fierce detractor of the Treaty of Versailles. He joined the German Workers Party, and soon after, at his behest, it was renamed the *National Socialist German Workers Party* (NSDAP, known as "Nazis"). In 1921, he assumed leadership of the group.

In 1923, Hitler led an attempted takeover of the Bavarian government in what became known as the "Beer Hall Putsch." (It originated in a Munich beer hall.) He spent less than a year in jail, where he wrote the first part of his autobiography and ideological tract, *Mein Kampf* (My Struggle). In 1925, he refounded the Nazi party, and after the onset of the Great Depression in 1929, it grew in popularity as unemployment increased.

On January 30, 1933, Hitler became Germany's chancellor. Political divisions and the failure to form viable coalitions during the Weimar period played a large role in bringing Germany's parliamentary republic to an end. Hitler quickly suppressed liberties. In February 1933, after a fire allegedly set by a Dutch communist (but probably set by the Nazis) burned down the Reichstag building (the seat of the legislature), the government passed an emergency decree "for protection of the people and the state." The decree made possible the seizure of communist buildings and presses. After an election in March in which the Nazis received more than 17 million votes (but still not a majority of votes), communists were not allowed to be seated in the Reichstag and trade unions were dissolved. On April 7, the first anti-Jewish ordinance removed all "non-Aryans" from the civil service, including one quarter of all the physicists in Germany, eleven of whom had won or would win a Nobel Prize. In May, "subversive" books were burned outside the Berlin Opera House. In July, the government declared the Nazis the only legal political party. Germany, which had been allowed to join the League of Nations in 1925, formally withdrew from the League in October.

Hitler also worked to neutralize the political power of Christian churches, which held Christ's authority above that of the state. Because he felt the Nazi SA Brownshirts had become too powerful, he ordered SA leaders imprisoned and killed on June 30, 1934, the "Night of the Long Knives." After the death of German President Hindenburg on August 2, 1934, the offices of president and chancellor were combined, and Hitler became the führer, the ultimate leader. Like Stalin, he achieved nearly complete control over the state.

Hitler attracted followers with his doctrine of *Lebensraum* (living space), a justification for expanding beyond Germany's territorial boundaries, considered necessary for the support of an ever increasing, dominant German population. Hitler also described Aryans, by whom he meant Germanic peoples, as a racial group. (He based his conclusions on the theories of Houston Stewart Chamberlain, an Englishman writing at the turn of the twentieth century.) Hitler's brand of nationalism called for racial purity and was rabidly anti-Semitic, regarding Jewish people as markedly inferior. He also considered other peoples inferior, including Slavs and Africans. (See Chapter 8.) He exploited the fear of communism and successfully made a scapegoat of German Jews to win acceptance of brutal acts of violence; and to carry out his militaristic ambitions, he cast war in terms of greatness and destiny.

By 1935, Germany was openly rearming, building tanks, heavy artillery, planes, and submarines in violation of the Treaty of Versailles. Hitler formally denounced the treaty on March 16, ordered a rearmament program, and reestablished mandatory military service. On September 15, Germany instituted the "Reich Citizenship Law" and the "Law for the Protection of

German citizens of Berchtesgaden crowd around Adolf Hitler (center, in car) as he arrives to give a speech, September 9, 1934, a month after assuming the title of "führer."

German Blood and German Honor." Together with several supplemental decrees and edicts, these became known as the "Nuremberg Laws" or "Nuremberg Decrees." They effectively stripped German Jews of their citizenship.

On March 6, 35,000 German troops entered the Rhineland, which had remained demilitarized since Versailles. No other country seriously challenged this treaty violation. In July, Germany drew closer to a union with Austria. Hitler was pushing the world closer to another large-scale war.

JAPAN

Japan emerged from World War I as the most cohesive of the major indigenous powers in the Asia-Pacific area—China and Russia were both torn by civil war. Industrialization of the economy and the prosperity of the mid-1920s strengthened the civilian government. When Hirohito became the emperor in 1926, however, he assumed an unusually active role for one of Japan's traditionally remote rulers, although he was more moderate than the military and rightist forces that hoped to control him. Hirohito became the central symbol of a revival by ultranationalist groups of the Shinto religion, a "State Shinto" that glorified the emperor and the military, emphasized traditional values such as self-sacrifice, and abhorred Western influences.

The Great Depression that hit Western countries in 1930 also affected Japan. Wage reduction and unemployment in industries such as textiles hurt urban workers, especially the unskilled. Communism again became attractive—a labor rally in Tokyo's Hibiya Park on May Day in 1930 drew large crowds. But, as in Europe, rightist groups responded to both the threat of communism and the economic crisis by extolling authoritarian government. Anti-Western policy seemed to offer solutions to economic problems and appeal to national pride. Japan resented its treatment by Western powers. They had refused to incorporate the principle of equality of all races in the Covenant of the League of Nations and limited the size of the Japanese navy in relation to those of Britain and the United States. Japan had also been insulted by the United States' 1924 Oriental Exclusion Act, which virtually barred the door to Japanese immigrants. Japan opposed Western concessions and extraterritorial rights in China, especially since the Japanese had long regarded China as an avenue to fulfilling their own imperial ambitions.

Components of the military were particularly upset by the government's diplomatic overtures toward the West and toward China. The early 1930s were marked by takeover plots and assassinations of more moderate politicians. Although branches of the service had differing objectives—the army to secure itself against Soviet initiatives and expansion in China, the navy to achieve dominance in the Pacific—in both services, the largest group of disaffected were young officers who came from rural communities and who believed that political parties were corrupt. They were supported, and sometimes financed, by rightist, intensely nationalistic political groups and press.

Japanese Expansion in China

On September 18, 1931, junior army officers in Japan's Kwantung Army, stationed in China since the army's formation in 1906, took action without approval from their commanders or the war minister in Tokyo, setting off an explosion on the South Manchurian Railway line. Blaming the incident on the Chinese, Japanese military units proceeded to attack the Chinese army,

In 1937, a Japanese soldier, his country's flag flying to his left, posts guard at the Great Wall of China after war breaks out between China and Japan.

citing the need to defend themselves from the alleged aggression. While the Japanese civilian government dealt with world opinion and struggled to formulate a policy based on events (signaling the extent to which they had ceded power to the military), the Kwantung Army moved further into Manchuria.

China itself was torn by fighting between Nationalists and communists. Chiang Kai-shek assumed the presidency, and a new constitution proclaimed a Nationalist Chinese government based in Nanking. Communist Party leader Mao Tse-tung, while educating peasants in communist doctrine, carried on guerilla warfare against Chiang's Kuomintang army. Taking advantage of this political instability, the Japanese army took control of southern Manchuria. Chiang's government requested mediation by the League of Nations; Japan refused to participate. The Chinese boycotted Japanese goods, and the Japanese responded by attacking Shanghai with 70,000 troops in early 1932.

That same year, Japan established the puppet state of Manchukuo, comprising the occupied area of Manchuria, and named Henry Puyi (the last Chinese emperor, who had abdicated in 1912) as nominal head. When the

League of Nations issued a report by the Lytton Commission in 1933, calling for Japan to stop aggression in China, Japan withdrew from the League. By the end of the year, it had taken control of China north of Peking and the Great Wall. In early 1937, the Chinese communist and Nationalist forces agreed to form a united front against Japan. But the Japanese continued to advance into China and, in 1937, would engage in all-out war.

Peace and Disarmament

The hard reality of the interwar years was that the League of Nations was ill-equipped to preserve peace. Rearmament went forward, and armed conflict erupted in Asia, Europe, and Africa. Yet most people—and, indeed, most politicians and governments—sincerely wanted to avoid another large-scale war. This quest for peace resulted in several international agreements regarding disarmament and the nonviolent settling of some disputes, both through the League of Nations and independent of it.

These agreements can perhaps best be understood not as attempts to secure international cooperation and amity, but as efforts toward collective security. More specifically, these were efforts by each signatory to increase its own security and to maintain a balance of power that ensured its own interests within its region and the world. Thus, treaties stated general principles, not binding obligations, or were compromises that eliminated any specific safeguard that one of the major powers disliked. Particular governments—whether socialist, moderate, conservative, or far right—often negotiated, only to have a different political faction assume power and refuse to ratify the terms. There were also rivalries between generally friendly countries, such as Britain and the United States, that disagreed over economic commitments.

The following major conferences took place during the interwar years:

WASHINGTON CONFERENCE. Representatives from the United States, Britain, France, Italy, and Japan met in 1921 and 1922 and agreed in the Five Power Treaty to limit the total tonnage of their aircraft carriers and capital ships according to the following ratio: United States, 5; Britain, 5; Japan, 3; France, 1.67; and Italy, 1.67. In other words, Japan agreed to keep its tonnage of carriers and ships at 60 percent of those of the United States and Britain.

1924 GENEVA PROTOCOL. League of Nations delegates drafted an agreement that would commit the signatories to compulsory arbitration.

The League Assembly accepted this Geneva Protocol for the Pacific Settlement of International Disputes on October 2, 1924. Some nations ratified it, but by the time it went before the British government, there was a newly elected Conservative leadership, which rejected it. This protocol never went into effect.

LOCARNO. In October 1925, several European powers meeting at Locarno, Switzerland, formulated a series of treaties that would confirm Germany's western boundaries according to the Treaty of Versailles. The Treaty of Mutual Guarantee was signed by representatives of France, Britain, Germany, Italy, and Belgium. Treaties were also signed between Germany and France and Germany and Belgium. Germany agreed to enter the League of Nations. Although Locarno was perceived at the time as a diplomatic victory

Adolf Hitler (left) and Benito Mussolini walk past saluting troops during Hitler's visit to Venice, Italy, June 14–16, 1934.

for peace, it did not satisfactorily resolve whether Germany would respect its borders with Czechoslovakia or Poland.

THE PACT OF PARIS (KELLOGG-BRIAND PACT). Fourteen countries including the United States, Italy, Germany, and Japan signed the Pact of Paris, or Kellogg-Briand Pact, on August 27, 1928. By 1930, some sixty other countries had signed. Article I called for each signatory to "condemn recourse to war for the solution of international controversies, and renounce it, as an instrument of national policy." The language in the Pact left rhetorical loopholes about the nature of aggression. Ultimately, the pact was ineffective, but it did advance the United States a step beyond its isolationist stance and acknowledged in a framework outside the League of Nations that countries should attempt to disavow war as a cornerstone of foreign policy.

LONDON NAVAL CONFERENCE TREATIES, 1930 AND 1936. Admiral Kato Kanji of the Imperial Japanese Navy sought to increase the Japanese percentage of capital ships in relation to the United States and Britain to 70 percent at the London Naval Conference of 1930. The United States and Japan reached the Reed-Matsudaira compromise that allowed Japan to possess tonnage equal to 69.75 percent of the American fleet. Kato opposed the compromise, but the Japanese cabinet, under Prime Minister Osachi Hamaguchi, nevertheless ratified the treaty. Appalled Japanese ultranationalists assassinated Hamaguchi in November 1930. The Japanese navy participated in disarmament negotiations again in 1934 and 1935, but withdrew in January 1936. Britain and the United States agreed to the Naval Arms Limitation Treaty on March 25, but Japan did not subscribe to it and, by the end of 1936, had rescinded the 1922 and 1930 treaties.

BI- AND MULTILATERAL AGREEMENTS. European and Asian countries signed hundreds of treaties of alliance, neutrality, and nonaggression and economic and trade-promoting pacts between 1920 and 1936, indicating the importance of national security to each country. What is even more striking—and indicative of mistrust and political maneuvering—is the number of times alliances were entered into and then revoked. Among the better known interwar agreements were the 1922 Treaty of Rapallo between the Soviet Union and Germany, ostensibly an economic pact, but with wider political implications, and the Little Entente formed by Czechoslovakia, Romania, and Yugoslavia, which signed a series of bilateral treaties in 1921 and 1922.

Interwar Economics and Depression

The factors that determined interwar economics and contributed to the worldwide depression of the 1930s had their roots in World War I. Shaping the economic landscape were the questions of how much in reparations Germany owed the Allies; how and whether the Allies would repay their debts to the United States; and how the United States would handle its new role as the leader in international finance (replacing Britain).

Reparations

The Treaty of Versailles made Germany responsible for paying reparations to the Allies and Associated Powers. In April 1921, a Reparations Commission composed of representatives of Allied victors declared that Germany must pay 132 billion gold marks, but this figure was revised downward to 50 billion gold marks at a second conference, and the amount continued to be lowered over the next decade.

This German woman lights her morning fire with marks—money that has become worthless during one of the periods of rampant inflation that undermined the German economy between 1920 and 1935.

Arguments flared, particularly between Britain and France, over whether Germany could afford to make the payments; how reparations would affect the German economy; and the effects of depression and inflation in Germany on the rest of Europe; how Germany could best become economically stable; and whether a productive Germany (free of overly burdensome reparations payments) would help stabilize the entire European economy or grow stronger and threaten security. The French government insisted that Germany pay the full amount on schedule; its most dramatic response to failure was the occupation of the Ruhr Valley industrial region in 1923. Britain in general would not back France's demands because Britain's leaders saw Germany's economic recovery as key to European stability and prosperity.

Debt

American economic concerns stemmed largely from some $10 billion in loans it had made to the Allies—an amount they were at first ill-prepared, and then reluctant, to repay. Britain and France maintained that their debts should be canceled, since they had fought in World War I longer and lost many more troops than had the United States. The Soviet Union would not pay Russia's czarist debt. The United States, however, was adamant that all debts be paid in full. Britain agreed to a payment plan in 1922 and France in 1926. The French linked debt repayment to reparations: the reparations paid by Germany would be used to pay the American debt. The British suggested that both reparations and debts be canceled. The United States disagreed with both. As long as it resolutely insisted on Allied debt repayment, the United States was involved in reparations.

The Dawes Plan (named for American Charles G. Dawes, who chaired the committee that developed it), presented in 1924, attempted to resolve these issues by stabilizing German currency, setting an annual reparations payment based on yearly productivity, and arranging a massive loan to put the German economy back on its feet. The plan recommended that France and Belgium evacuate the Ruhr, which they did. In sum, it restored investor confidence, so that British and American capital poured into Germany and Central Europe.

The Role of the United States in International Finance

After the wartime drain on Britain's finances, the United States became the main source of international finance. European countries, damaged by the war, increased their import of American goods, pumping income into the American economy. Instead of being a net international debtor, the United States was now a net international creditor in the private sector. It was positioned to influence financial matters worldwide. Yet as the United States became more politically isolationist, it failed to understand the relevance of the world economy to its own economic health.

American insistence on debt repayment forced the Allies to expend already strained European resources. Although the United States continued to loan to other countries after World War I, the amount was not enough to stimulate vulnerable and ailing economies. In fact, much of the amount lent by American bankers to Germany was paid to Britain and France as reparations; they, in turn, used it to pay their debts to the U.S. government. This economic situation could not spin on indefinitely. Moreover, many American banks and businesses considered overseas investment too risky and invested heavily in their own country. As the American economy expanded, other countries were denied access to U.S. markets by protective tariffs, such as the Fordney-McCumber Tariff, passed in 1922. Their economies were further weakened by not being able to sell to the United States.

The need to help European countries financially and to improve economic stability became crucial in 1929, when representatives of Britain, France, Germany, Italy, Belgium, and Japan devised what became known as the Young Plan. Germany's yearly reparations payment was reduced, and it had the right to postpone part of its annual payment for up to two years. The final document, approved in 1930, called for complete evacuation of the last French troops that guarded the Rhineland. Although the Nazis strenuously objected to paying any reparations, the German government finally accepted the Young Plan. Soon after, the Nazis leaped from 12 to 107 seats in the Reichstag elections.

The Great Depression

Beneath the relative prosperity of the mid-1920s lay long-standing economic weaknesses that erupted in the autumn of 1929 into what would come to be called the Great Depression—a period marked by trade and industrial stagnation, high unemployment, and bank failures that wiped out the savings of millions of people. Reparations and debt were two factors. National economies were also affected by the fact that World War I had disturbed prewar international patterns of trade that had made countries economically interdependent. In the postwar United States, disparities increased between the more robust industrial sector and agriculture, already depressed in the 1920s. Foreclosures plagued farmers who could not repay what they had borrowed to mechanize. In contrast, American industry had expanded before 1929, fueled by innovative technologies, assembly lines, and mass production. A rise in the income of industrial workers allowed them to buy consumer goods such as automobiles.

Yet as the 1920s ended, domestic demand for these goods slowed, while new agricultural and overseas markets failed to materialize. In Europe, Britain, and Japan as well, industrialization led to the overproduction of goods. Protectionist policies to insulate domestic manufacturers from competition particularly affected the ability of countries to export goods. In this, too, the United States played a part. The Hawley-Smoot Tariff, passed

In 1930, a year after the American stock market crash, an unemployed man sells apples in view of the U.S. Capitol, in Washington, D.C.

by an isolationist U.S. Congress in 1930, was even higher than the Fordney-McCumber Tariff. The combination of heavy domestic investment and high tariffs reflected an economic nationalism that had devastating effects on the international economy.

In the popular mind, the advent of the Great Depression is linked with the stock market crash of October 1929. However, less than 2.5 percent of Americans owned stock, and therefore the crash had little economic impact on most of the population. More pertinent was the crippling of international trade. Because other nations retaliated against American tariffs with their own high tariffs, the United States could not stimulate its economy by increasing trade abroad. The spreading economic nationalism and concurrent economic deadlock pushed the world further into depression. By the end of 1930, nearly 5 million people in Germany were unemployed. In 1932, the United States' national income was half of what it had been in 1929, and the number of unemployed reached 11 million, an estimated 20 to 25 percent of the working population.

Banking

In addition to the collapse of trade, bank failure (and the consequent loss of personal savings and business credit) was both a symptom and contributing cause of the Great Depression. The number of American banks that had failed reached 1,326 by the end of 1930. In Germany, the Weimar Republic government proposed a customs union with Austria in 1931 to alleviate economic problems. An alarmed French government, seeing this as a first step toward German annexation of Austria, began withdrawing French money from Austrian banks to forestall such a union. In May, the largest bank, the Kreditanstalt, failed, precipitating the collapse of the banking system not only in Austria, but in Germany and Hungary as well.

In June 1931, President Herbert Hoover proposed, and Congress eventually agreed to, a one-year moratorium on all intergovernmental debts and reparations. The moratorium was accepted by other countries. Intended to provide some relief for Germany, it was insufficient to repair either the German, or the international, economy. The next blow came in September 1931, when the British government took British currency off the gold standard. Rather than raising the domestic prices of British goods, it chose to endanger the exchange value of the pound and defaulted on the outstanding gold payments owed to other countries. This decision, together with the debt moratorium, brought international trade to a halt. With trade frozen, panicked international investors now withdrew their gold and money from banks.

Reparations and Debt Revisited

In January 1932, before the Hoover Moratorium had expired, Germany announced that it could not pay any more reparations. As much in response to the depression as to this claim, British, French, Belgian, Italian, Japanese, and German representatives drew up the Lausanne Convention in 1932, calling for an end to reparations after Germany had paid 3 billion marks. Britain and France agreed to ratify the convention only if the United States agreed to cancel their debts, which it did not. The Lausanne Convention was never ratified, Germany never again paid reparations (not even the final settlement), and France and Belgium never made another payment on their American debt. In 1933—the year that Hitler assumed power—Britain and Italy paid a small amount. In 1934, Finland became the only country to pay its debt in full. Thus, although the issues surrounding World War I debt and reparations were not adequately resolved, they did finally come to an end.

Economic Isolation and Autarky

On March 4, 1933, Franklin D. Roosevelt became president of the United States, inheriting a country mired in depression. He immediately faced the same decision the British had dealt with in 1931—whether to adhere to the gold standard or to devalue the dollar and raise prices to help American industry and business. In the spring of 1933, the United States effectively suspended the gold standard. When, in June, the World Economic Conference met under the auspices of the League of Nations, immediate stabilization of currencies became a central issue. Roosevelt would not agree to stabilize the American dollar. His wholly unexpected decision ended the possibility of an international solution to the Great Depression.

The American president was not alone in believing that economic problems should and could be solved on a national rather than on a global level. The American stance was economic isolationism from the rest of the world. Countries like Britain and France formed closed trading blocks within their empires. Germany, Italy, and Japan developed policies of autarky; they attempted to achieve economic self-sufficiency within their countries and not rely on trade. Autarky required colonies, or conquered territories, to sustain it. These countries looked to building their own empires as a source of raw materials and controlled markets. Japan pursued expansion in China and the western Pacific; Italy in North Africa; and Germany, as a first step, in eastern Europe. Increased arms production, aimed at war, provided work for the unemployed. For many people suffering through the Depression, jobs and visions of imperial glory had greater appeal than vague promises of cooperation and peace.

War in the 1930s

Italy in Ethiopia

By the mid-1930s, the soon-to-be Axis powers were contemplating or engaging in war in areas thought to be essential for economic colonization and political fulfillment. Since 1931, Japan had essentially been engaged in a simmering war in China; and in 1935, Italy invaded Ethiopia (Abyssinia). Mussolini saw Ethiopia as a relatively weak country with no strong ties to European powers that would come to its defense. (He was right.) Moreover, Ethiopians had defeated Italian troops at Adua in 1896, an event many Italians found humiliating. A tussle between Italian and Ethiopian troops in 1934, in Walwal, a disputed area bordering on Somaliland, sent Ethiopia for help to the League of Nations. But Italy stalled on any settlement, demanded an apology from Ethiopia, and continued to build up supplies and send troops to Africa.

The League of Nations and the major powers spent months ineffectually debating what to do. France and Britain, both with many interests in the Mediterranean and afraid of losing Italy as an ally while Germany's power continued to grow, came to a secret agreement in December (the Hoare-Laval Pact), proposing a settlement in which Ethiopia essentially made all the concessions. The agreement was leaked to the press, and public outrage ensued. The League applied mild economic sanctions against Italy, while the United States invoked its August 1935 Neutrality Act to avoid trading arms with either Ethiopia or Italy. On January 3, 1936, the Ethiopian emperor Haile Selassie made a passionate appeal to the League to increase sanctions, but by May 1936, the Italians had occupied Addis Ababa and Selassie was forced into exile. To defeat Ethiopian troops, the Italians used poison gas—an emotionally charged and ethically reprehensible option after the horrors it had caused in World War I. Yet, in July 1936, the League of Nations withdrew all sanctions. It was a damaging and dangerous admission of ineffectiveness in an increasingly hostile and aggressive world.

AMERICAN ISOLATIONISM AND NEUTRALITY IN THE 1930s

Isolationism was a consistent strain in American foreign policy. Many Americans called World War I "the European war"—reflecting the feeling that the United States had been unwittingly dragged or duped into participating in a conflict whose antagonisms and outcome had little to do with American needs, safety, or the preservation of democracy. As Europe remained mired in contention during the 1930s, isolationism grew more powerful. A Senate Special Committee Investigating the Munitions Industry, led by Gerald Nye, a fierce isolationist from North Dakota, criticized big business for its influence on foreign policy. It reinforced the isolationist, pacifist sentiments expressed in demonstrations and lobbying by groups such as the Women's International League for Peace and Freedom. A majority of the American public and the popular press were against involvement in another European war.

Several influential congressmen believed solving the economic problems of the Depression at home was the country's top priority. They viewed American involvement in international affairs as a dangerous distraction. Regarding Japanese aggression in China, the United States, though a friend of China's, continued to trade with Japan and did nothing more than declare that it would not recognize Japan's claim to Chinese territory. Congress further wanted to protect U.S. interests as a creditor nation. When Britain and France defaulted on war debt payments, Congress passed the Johnson Act in 1934, which banned financial credit to governments that had not met their monetary obligations to the United States.

Congress passed additional legislation designed to distance the United States from foreign wars. The First Neutrality Act in 1935 established a mandatory arms embargo against belligerents and restricted travel by U.S. citizens on the ships of belligerents. It gave President Roosevelt the power to define arms and to determine when to implement the embargo. The second Neutrality Act in 1936 extended the first law for fourteen months, but removed the president's discretionary options. Three additional neutrality acts followed.

In addition, even if it had wanted to militarily support an ally in war, the United States in the 1930s had no army or navy large enough for the task. Britain and France knew this, just as they knew that they would get no overt help in building up their own arms in trade or loans from the United States. Looked at in this light, the response of Britain and France to the growing crises in Europe, their failure to stop conflict in Ethiopia and China or to aid the Republicans in Spain, and their appeasement of Hitler in the coming years demonstrate the caution of countries that lacked the resources and support to build up arms and engage in another large war.

The Spanish Civil War

A Republican coalition, known as the Popular Front, won the Spanish elections in 1936, precipitating a civil war. In July, the Spanish military revolted and Generalissimo Francisco Franco assumed leadership of the opposing right-wing forces. Germany and Italy sent troops, military equipment, and advisers to support France. The Western democracies, which might have aided the Republicans, did not. France (governed, at the time, by a similar and sympathetic Popular Front) and Britain, fearful of escalation into a worldwide war, prohibited the shipment of arms to Spain. The United States broadened its neutrality laws to cover civil wars and therefore forbade the purchase of weapons by either side. The Soviet Union, however, backed the Republicans, supplying tanks, planes, technicians, and military advisers; but distance prevented it from sending much-needed troops.

The Spanish Civil War provoked strong antifascist emotions. Thousands of volunteers poured into Spain from Europe and the United States to aid the Republicans. Some 2,800 Americans took part. Before the war

A battalion of young shock troops marches down a street in Madrid early in the Spanish Civil War, which began in 1936.

ended in fascist victory, Germany, Italy, and the Soviet Union had the opportunity to test their weapons—and in the case of Germany and Italy, their troops—in combat. The world also had a preview of German military tactics. Spain became a microcosm of the world war to come. The Spanish Civil War also brought Hitler and Mussolini closer together. Italy, already estranged from Britain and France by its actions in Ethiopia, acknowledged its affinity to Germany. In October 1936, the two countries signed the Rome-Berlin Axis agreement, a profession of mutual interest. A month later, Japan and Germany signed the Anti-Comintern Pact, ostensibly as protection against the activities of the Communist International, but more importantly as an alliance based on the commonality of their territorial ambitions. Italy joined the pact in 1937.

Conclusion: Into the Future

In the summer of 1936, France and Germany together established a permanent memorial to all the World War I dead at Vimy Ridge in France, the site of a great battle. Thousands of Canadian war veterans crossed the ocean to attend a ceremony dedicating a special monument to their fallen comrades. War was still fresh in the minds of the people of Europe and Asia, and few wanted to repeat the devastation wrought on their own countries by World War I. Yet in Germany, Italy, and Japan, war was being glorified as the way to national triumph and redemption.

After the dedication, the Canadian veterans visited Britain, where Stanley Baldwin, the British prime minister, addres-

Cartoonist Willard Witmore Combes created this powerful depiction of a tank rolling into World War II combat over the graves of soldiers killed in the Great War of 1914–1918—supposedly the "war to end all wars."

sed them. "I am confident of this," Baldwin said. "If the dead could come back today there would be no war. They would never let the younger generation taste what they did. You all tasted the bitter cup of war. They drank it to the dregs. . . . If Europe and the world can find no other way of settling disputes than the way of war, even now when we are still finding and burying the bodies of those who fell twenty years ago—if they can find no other way, the world deserves to perish."

The world did not perish. Nor did it find another way.

PART II: A GLOBAL CONFLICT: SCOPE AND DEFINITIONS

This kind of war is a new kind of war. It is warfare in terms of every continent, every island, every sea, every air lane in the world.

—*U.S. President Franklin D. Roosevelt,*
fireside radio chat, February 23, 1942

All the peoples of the world are entered into the current war. Since the dawn of history there has been no war equal to this one in magnitude or in the maze of its international implications.

—*Japanese Premier Kuniashi Koiso,*
New Year's Address, January 1, 1945

Few places on Earth escaped the horrors of World War II. More than fifty nations declared war, and those that remained neutral or otherwise beyond the terrain of battle were affected nonetheless. In a world of 2.3 billion people, more than 100 million uniformed men and women went to war, several million more fought in partisan or resistance movements, hundreds of millions of others worked directly in the war effort, and anywhere from 50 to 65 million people perished before Japan, the last Axis power to surrender, submitted to the Allies in Tokyo Bay on a mild September day in 1945. This section describes the participants and the elements that made World War II a global conflict.

Alliances and Colonies

Alliances and mutual defense agreements quickly multiplied the number of combatants: Germany's invasion of Poland brought a declaration of war and armed response from Britain and France. The far-flung British Empire, as well as other colonial systems maintained by Belgium, France, Italy, Japan, the Netherlands, Portugal, and Spain meant that vast territories around the world were drawn into the conflict. Britain's entry into the war prompted the participation of four of its self-governing dominions—Australia, Canada, New Zealand, and South Africa—as well as its colonial African, Asian, and Indian forces. Italy's attack on British possessions in East Africa prompted a reply, and made Italian territory outside Italy fair game to British guns; likewise, Japan's attack on the American-held Hawaiian Islands drew the United States into battle and made every Japanese-occupied island in the Pacific or stronghold in Asia a potential Allied target (see Global Possessions Chart on pp. 50–53).

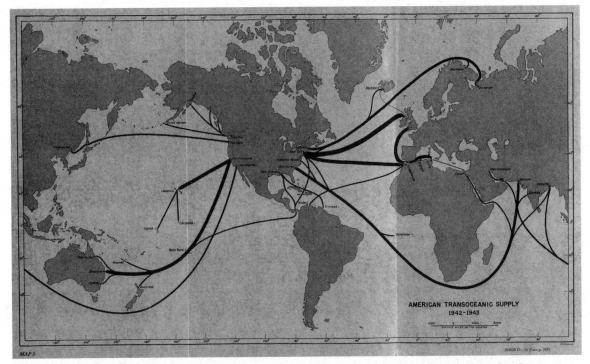

Major supply routes originating in the United States served every theater during the war. Ports in Australia, Great Britain, Hawaii, and North Africa, and very small entities such as New Caledonia and Espiritu Santo in the South Pacific, were developed as major American supply reservoirs to support the military campaigns getting under way in 1942.

Global Transport

The war also came to unlikely places through an emerging web of air and sea routes. Dramatic improvements in aircraft, ships, and communications, using technology unavailable or even unimaginable in World War I, allowed the Allies and the Axis to operate almost anywhere. Combatants used airstrips, bases, and refueling and supply centers on little-known islands and out-of-the-way territory to link major supply depots with war zones. Cargo loaded in Dorval, outside Montreal, Canada, destined for the Russian Front might first be flown to Nassau or perhaps Miami and then on to the Caribbean with stops in northern South America before reaching Natal, Brazil; from there, flights headed to destinations in Africa including Monrovia, Lagos, Khartoum, and Cairo before arriving in Iran, where Allied matériel was trucked into the Soviet Union. A ship departing the United States from New Orleans for Asia would pass through the Panama Canal into the Pacific, round southern Australia, then dock in Calcutta, from where supplies could be flown into China. At many cargo transit points, locals were hired to assist with the work, in some cases sparking economic boomlets. All the while, ship convoys and submarines battled each other at sea, forcing the creation of new supply routes, which, while safer from the enemy, exposed vessels to harsher weather and natural obstacles.

The Panama Canal was vital to the United States for quickly transiting American troops and cargo between the Pacific and Atlantic oceans. On October 27, 1945, the aircraft carrier USS Enterprise (with the USS Washington at left), a hardy veteran of the Pacific campaigns, passed through the canal en route to New York City for Fleet Review.

To span the wide-ranging war zones, combatants established isolated weather and radio stations in little-known Arctic and subarctic locales and on seldom-visited islands in the South Pacific and South Atlantic. The Germans waged unsuccessful intermittent warfare on Jan Mayen, a barren, wind-lashed frozen volcanic island north of Norway where the Allies operated a critical weather station. On Tristan da Cunha, located in the South Atlantic and called "the most remote inhabited island in the world," the British Royal Navy stationed a handful of servicemen to maintain radio communication with the African cape, aiding Allied aircraft and shipping with weather reports and forecasts.

Migrations and Refugees

As the war widened, the flow of refugees surged toward anyplace, no matter how distant, that might offer safe haven. Tens of millions of people took to the roads during the war years, as monumental tides of humanity flowed into unfamiliar territory, carrying the war with them. Thousands of European Jews fleeing the Nazis found refuge in China, Turkey, and various countries in the Americas; thousands more made their way to Palestine, and others massed elsewhere in the Middle East, poised to enter the Holy Land when

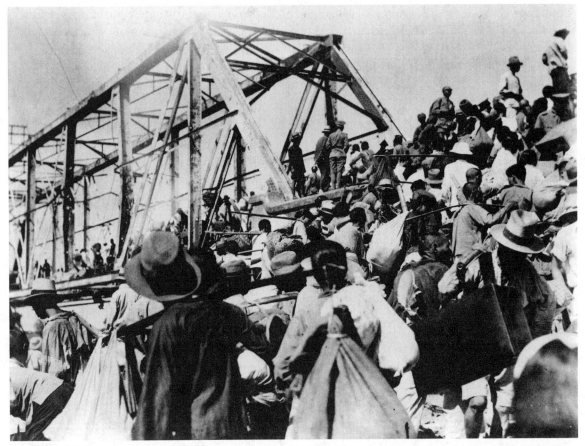

A mass of refugees reaches a bridge crossing in Chungking in one of many wartime migrations in China. Tens of millions set out on foot during the war to escape Japanese invaders.

the war ended. During the London Blitz, British schoolchildren were evacuated to Canada and Australia, and the latter took in thousands of refugees fleeing the Japanese. In the wake of Japanese occupation, about 12 million Chinese evacuated from the east to rural provinces in the primitive western regions—hauling the tools of industry with them and jolting the local populations. Germany and Russia expelled millions of people from their newly conquered territories, many of them bound for Soviet labor camps or near certain death in Nazi extermination camps. After Germany attacked the Soviet Union, Joseph Stalin evicted hundreds of thousands of Russians of German descent from their homes and moved them deep into the Soviet interior. Throughout the world, millions more fled their homes in anticipation of enemy occupation or, after an attack, when no home was left standing. In various locales, the good fortune to be bypassed by combat operations meant that local populations were then overwhelmed by the arrival of numerous, and usually destitute, refugees from other regions. In the United States, huge defense industries and the crush of military activity on the West Coast prompted a demographic shift. In the East, Washington, D.C., transformed almost overnight from a quiet, seasonal city into a bustling, overcrowded capital as new government workers and military personnel poured in.

Combatants

The Axis

Led by Germany, Italy, and Japan (the Berlin-Rome-Tokyo Axis), the Axis included Finland (allied separately with Germany), Bulgaria, Croatia, Hungary, Romania, and Slovakia. Before the war's end, Finland ended its German partnership and Bulgaria, Italy, and Romania withdrew from the alliance. After Italy surrendered to the Allies in September 1943, loyalties split; some Italians continued to fight for the Axis under Mussolini's German-backed puppet government, others supported the Allied cause.

The Allies

Led by Britain, the United States, and the Soviet Union, the Allies broadly comprised those in opposition to the fascist Axis, despite their own political differences. The first Allied association (Britain, France, and Poland) began in September 1939, following the German invasion of Poland, and other

A group of German infantrymen taken prisoner by a New Zealand unit are marched from a North African battlefield in 1942; an injured enemy soldier, however, gets a ride in the back of the carrier vehicle.

states later joined. On January 1, 1942, 26 nations issued the United Nations Declaration, a pledge of cooperation and commitment to defeat the Axis. The signatories were the United States of America, the United Kingdom of Great Britain and Northern Ireland, the Union of Soviet Socialist Republics, China, Australia, Belgium, Canada, Costa Rica, Cuba, Czechoslovakia, Dominican Republic, El Salvador, Greece, Guatemala, Haiti, Honduras, India, Luxembourg, Netherlands, New Zealand, Nicaragua, Norway, Panama, Poland, South Africa, and Yugoslavia. Later adherents, in order of signing, were Mexico, the Philippines, Ethiopia (1942); Iraq, Brazil, Bolivia, Iran, Colombia (1943); Liberia, France (1944); and Ecuador, Peru, Chile, Paraguay, Venezuela, Uruguay, Turkey, Egypt, Saudi Arabia, Lebanon, and Syria (1945). A number of countries under Axis occupation had Allied governments-in-exile, usually located in Cairo or London. In the case of France, under German occupation, the Vichy government, named for the city where it was based, accommodated Nazi rule. The opposition Free

French movement operated with the Allies and on its own as a military force under General Charles de Gaulle.

Neutral Nations

Neutrality had been a well-established concept in international warfare since the early nineteenth century. Under the accepted rules, a state that declared itself neutral showed no favoritism toward any of the warring states (such as opening its seaports to some but not to others). In return, belligerent states were to respect the sovereignty and territory of the neutral nation. By the early twentieth century, neutrality was codified in international law (including the 1856 Declaration of Paris, the 1907 Hague Conference, and the 1909 Declaration of London), and explicit rules were set down on the rights and obligations of neutral and belligerent nations.

The major neutrals during the war were Argentina (until March 1945), Ireland, Portugal, Spain, Sweden, Switzerland, and Turkey. Complete neutrality proved difficult to maintain; in Europe, neutral nations found it nearly impossible to remain totally impartial because of varying internal political sympathies, the threat of German invasion, and the monetary rewards that came from doing business with the Nazis. At the same time, some government officials and citizens of neutral nations showed their favoritism in other ways and exhibited tremendous courage and ingenuity assisting escaped or injured military personnel, harboring refugees, and saving lives during the Holocaust.

A new notion that evolved during the war was *nonbelligerency*, in which a declared neutral state favored a belligerent power (and perhaps that power's allies) while retaining the privileges of neutrality. This could include permitting or overlooking the covert use of its territory or facilities by a combatant. Over repeated Allied objections, several neutral nations engaged in particular trade and business practices with Germany that prolonged the Nazis' ability to wage war. It should be noted, however, that two of those objecting Allies, the Soviet Union and the United States, had done the very same thing, supplying aid to combatants even as they claimed neutrality early in the war: the USSR supplied Germany with raw materials from 1939 to 1941, and the United States provided Britain and France—even Japan—with aircraft and other war matériel. Scholars and legal experts in international law hold that nonbelligerency is not a legitimate status under the law, yet it was common during the war.

The change in approach to neutrality, which originally was to protect smaller sovereign nations and their self-sufficiency, signaled that World War II was a significantly different conflict from the trade wars of the nineteenth century. Instead, it was a massive, ideologically driven enterprise. As a 1997 U.S. State Department report on Nazi theft and its abetment by neutral nations observed,

> In the unique circumstances of World War II, neutrality collided with morality; too often being neutral provided a pretext for avoiding moral considerations. . . . It is painfully clear that Argentina, Portugal, Spain, Sweden, Switzerland, Turkey and other neutral countries were slow to recognize and acknowledge that this was not just another war. Most never did. Nazi Germany was a mortal threat to Western civilization itself, and had it been victorious, to the survival of even the neutral countries themselves.

The Geography of War

In World War II, the *theater of war* (generally defined as "the entire land, sea, and air area that is or may become involved directly in war operations") encompassed the entire globe. Within that vast expanse, there were several *theaters of operation*—specific areas in which military operations, or intensive support for military operations, were carried out. The Theaters of Operation Chart lists the nations in each theater. Within these regions, borders were often in flux and place names changed to reflect the prevailing military and political conditions. In China, the Japanese renamed Manchuria "Manchukuo." Germany annexed Austria, part of Czechoslovakia (the Sudetenland, Bohemia, and Moravia), western Poland, and Luxembourg, referring to this acquired territory as part of "Greater Germany." Perhaps the greatest geographic muddle occurred on the Eastern front, where for centuries German, Polish, Russian, Baltic, Ukrainian, Belorussian, Romanian, and Hungarian borders had moved and nations even disappeared from time to time until another event altered the map. As a Jewish Holocaust and World War II survivor from Ruthenia explained toward the end of the twentieth century: "I was born in the Austro-Hungarian Empire. As a youngster I lived in Czechoslovakia. Later I lived in Hungary. After the war I lived in the Soviet Union. Most recently I live in Ukraine. . . . I never moved from my town. It was the countries and the borders that changed. I stayed put."

The World at War: At a facility in India, workers clean and oil tank parts, April 1943; New Guinea natives—essential as guides and supply workers for Allied forces—pose with servicemen near a combat zone in March 1943.

THEATERS OF OPERATION

The Americas
Canada, United States of America, Latin American nations, the Caribbean

China-Burma-India (CBI)
Burma, Ceylon (Sri Lanka), China, India, Indochina, Korea, Malay, Manchuria (Manchukuo), Mongolia, Nepal, Thailand (Siam)

East Africa
British Somaliland, Eritrea, Ethiopia, Italian Somaliland, Madagascar

Europe
Western Europe: Austria (part of Greater Germany), Belgium, Britain, France, Germany, Greenland, Iceland, Ireland, Luxembourg, Holland (the Netherlands)

Eastern Europe: Bulgaria, Czechoslovakia, Estonia, Hungary, Latvia, Lithuania, Poland, Romania, the Soviet Union (Russia)

Scandinavia: Denmark, Finland, Norway

Mediterranean
Mediterranean Europe: Albania, Balearic Islands, Corsica, Cyprus, Dodecanese Islands, Gibraltar, Greece, Italy, Malta, Yugoslavia

North Africa: Algeria, Egypt, Libya, Morocco, Spanish Morocco, Spanish Sahara, Sudan (under Anglo-Egyptian condominium), Tunisia

Near and Middle Eastern
Aden (city), Afghanistan, Iran, Iraq, Kuwait, Lebanon, Oman, Palestine, Qatar, Saudi Arabia, Syria, Transjordan, Trucial Oman, Yemen

Pacific
Central Pacific: Bonin Islands, Caroline Islands, Gilbert Islands, Guam, Hawaiian Islands, Japan, Mariana Islands, Marshall Islands, Midway Island, Taiwan (Formosa), Volcano Islands, Wake Island

Southwest Pacific: Australia, Bismarck Archipelago, Brunei, Cook Islands, Dutch East Indies, Fiji, French Polynesia, Malaya, New Zealand, New Hebrides, North Borneo, Papua and New Guinea, the Philippines, Sarawak, Singapore, Solomon Islands, Western Samoa

WARTIME AFRICA AND LATIN AMERICA

Because the bulk of combat and carnage occurred in Asia, Europe, and on various Pacific islands, the wartime roles of Latin America and Africa (particularly sub-Saharan Africa) tend to be overlooked. The war affected both areas, and each had an impact on the war. In Africa, the Axis and Allies repeatedly clashed along the north coast of a continent that provided a bevy of troops, laborers, and natural resources to the war effort. Physically unscathed Latin America was also a tremendous source of vital materials as well as a haven for spies and, beginning in 1944, a refuge for Axis war criminals. In both these regions, wartime military and commercial contributions, political alliances, and nationalist movements would have lasting effects in the postwar era.

Africa

On the eve of the war, European colonial powers enjoyed their peak strength in Africa: Liberia

Members of the South African Pioneer Corps pose with a Boston Bomber (as American Douglas bombers were called in British Commonwealth air forces) and their mascot, Dolly, ca. 1942.

Warehouse workers in Casablanca, Morocco, stack a mountainous supply of Lend-Lease sugar sent from the United States, 1943.

and South Africa were the only fully independent nations, which meant that about 94 percent of the remaining population—nearly 170 million Africans—was under some form of European rule. (In Egypt, Britain retained certain rights and its soldiers remained there, while historically independent Ethiopia was under Italian occupation.) The war was a foreign endeavor foisted on Africa, whose geographic location, resources, and supply of human labor rendered it both a battleground and a sought-after territory. British control of North Africa was critical to maintaining dominance in the Mediterranean and access to the Suez Canal; Allied authority on the west coast, secured in 1942, was an asset in the Battle of the Atlantic and prevented the Germans from possibly using Dakar as a jumping-off point for Brazil's eastern bulge. The Takoradi Air Route, a series of well-spaced airstrips, spanned the continent from the Gold Coast in the west to Egypt in the northeast, enabling the Allies to support the Western Desert campaigns and to safely ferry Lend-Lease aircraft and other goods to the Soviet Union. The ports at Accra, Dakar, Lagos, and Monrovia, and later Dar es Salaam and Mombasa were also essential to the Allied effort in North Africa.

Many historians date Africa's role in World War II to 1935, referring to Italy's invasion of Ethiopia as the "first front of the Second World War." Early on, Africans were divided in their support for various belligerents, but by 1943— after Axis forces were driven out—nearly all of Africa was in the Allied camp. Although the heaviest fighting occurred in the north, there were also military campaigns in French West Africa, Somaliland, Ethiopia, and Madagascar. In addition, Africans fought in Europe, the Middle East, and the China-Burma-India Theater; and a group of *Africanistas,* recruited from Spain's colonies, served in the Spanish "Blue Division" that operated with Germany in the Soviet Union. In all, about 1 million Africans served in colonial forces as volunteers or conscripts.

Meanwhile, under terrible conditions, millions of laborers toiled for food and raw materials in fields, mines, jungles, or on plantations. Japanese conquest of the British and Dutch East Indies forced Britain to rely on its African holdings and the Belgian Congo for palm oil, rubber, sisal (a plant used for making rope), and tin. To improve production, Belgian officials increased forced labor among rural peasants from 60 to 120 days annually; elsewhere, people were conscripted for plantation labor, and even nomads had to sell their cattle for the war effort. However, Liberia (founded by former American slaves) received a major American boost to its infrastructure, and

U.S. manufacturers relied on it as the sole African source of natural latex rubber. In South Africa, a 60 percent increase in manufacturing jobs drew low-paid rural laborers to the cities and overcrowded shantytowns.

World War II left indelible marks on Africa. The Desert War caused extensive destruction in urban North Africa, especially in Tunisia, and Libya was left littered with land mines that killed or wounded thousands of civilians. Colonial wartime policies also took their toll on the landscape, as the constant requisition of food exhausted soil that was not left fallow. And in many places, the tribal chiefs who did the colonial governments' bidding fell into contempt, while the migration of so many rural people to the cities disrupted traditional African societies. The harsh wartime experience catalyzed the nascent "Africa for the Africans" cause, which would soon mature into a powerful liberation movement, as the irony in fighting against oppressive fascists in the service of oppressive colonial powers was not lost on anyone.

Latin America

When the European war began in 1939, Latin America was the greatest source of raw materials not under the sway of any combatant. In contrast to Africa, which was under European domination, Latin America was virtually unfettered, and all but a few areas (such as various Caribbean islands and the colonized Guianas) pursued their own interests. For Central American nations, that meant lining up squarely behind the United States and the Allies after the 1941 Japanese attack on Pearl Harbor, Hawaii. Costa Rica even declared war on Japan shortly before the United States did. Central American states wanted wartime protection and economic assistance; in return, the United States wanted hemispheric stability, security of the Panama Canal, and access to whatever resources might be needed in a world war. Each was able to accommodate the other, and by the end of 1941, Central America had cut its ties to Axis states. In Mexico, little popular support for the war, a respected local German community, and conflict with the United States over oil concessions kept the country from joining the Allies until mid-1942.

In South America, especially in the most industrially advanced nations—Argentina, Brazil, and Chile—immediate interests did not include ending relations with the Axis. Japanese immigration and exports to Latin America as a whole were on the rise, and Germany alone provided 16 percent of its imports. In Rio at the January 1942 pan-American meeting of foreign affairs ministers, Chile and Argentina refused to end relations with Axis nations, as each traded heavily with Germany and had influential German and Italian immigrant populations. Capitalizing on Latin American resentment of U.S. dominance, Axis commercial penetration of South America was purposeful, its military assistance discreet, and its espionage activities rampant. Germany and Italy supplied and sometimes trained military forces (as in Ecuador and Chile) and courted profascist generals ever poised to stage coups. Neutral Argentina viewed the war as an opportunity to increase its regional influence and become the leader of the Hispanic world. Others also bided their time as neutrals. Not until early 1945 did Chile, Ecuador, Paraguay, Peru,

Liberated Italians welcome Brazilian troops in Massarosa (near Pisa) in October 1944 as Allied forces pushed the Germans back up the Italian boot.

Uruguay, and Venezuela sign the United Nations Declaration. Argentina, embarrassed when the U.S. ambassador publicly documented its fascist activities and pro-German version of neutrality, finally declared war on Germany on March 27, 1945, just weeks before the Nazi surrender.

Meanwhile, President Roosevelt's "Good Neighbor Policy" of respectful bilateralism with his southern neighbors paid off in imperfect but effective Western Hemisphere solidarity. Even neutral but fascist Uruguay expelled the German battleship *Graf Spee* from the Montevideo harbor in 1939. Through the American Lend-Lease program, nations gained infrastructural improvements and workers found employment in the new wartime industries or those that were otherwise acquired, as when Guatemala expropriated Germany's extensive coffee holdings. Bolivia's tin was in much greater demand after Japan occupied competing Malaysia, as was Venezuela's oil. Nitrates, copper, tungsten, beef, coffee, cotton, and cacao were other exports the Allies needed and relied on, and in 1942 the United States purchased the entire Cuban sugar harvest. Cooperation extended further, as several states, including Costa Rica and Colombia, interned or deported suspected Nazis or allocated bases to U.S. forces. And the Americas as a whole supported the Act of Havana (1940), which committed all states to protect the hemisphere from outside attack.

Mexico and Brazil were the only two Latin American nations to send forces into battle. A Mexican air squadron saw six weeks' action in the Pacific, and Brazil committed 25,000 infantry to major combat in Italy, suffering nearly 2,500 casualties. Brazil also conducted joint patrols with the U.S. Navy and provided military bases vital to South Atlantic submarine defense and transatlantic air transport. On the open seas, German U-boats sank hundreds of ships (often owned by U.S. companies) flying the flags of various Latin American nations. Panama suffered the most among them, losing eighty-eight merchant marine ships and many crewmen. In the meantime, internal military conflict and political turmoil played out in the shadow of the world war. Ecuador and Peru went to war over a border dispute in July 1941, and successful revolts or military coups occurred in Bolivia, Guatemala, El Salvador, Panama, and Argentina, as repressive dictatorships or single-party rule cloaked in democratic trappings flourished throughout Latin America. Yet, on the whole, Latin America benefited economically from World War II, and despite some exceptions, the Americas maintained hemispheric solidarity given the varied circumstances of its nations.

Generally, the place names given throughout this book are those that were in use during the war; alternative names may be shown in parentheses. Westerners usually used "Russia" and "Soviet Union" or "Russians" and "Soviets" interchangeably, regarding ethnic Russians and the more than sixty recognized nationalities of the USSR as one and the same, even though "Russia" technically referred to the Russian Federation, by far the largest republic in the USSR. The United Kingdom (U.K.) was usually referred to as "Britain," "Great Britain," or "England," even though the U.K. comprises England, Scotland, Wales, and Northern Ireland. The name Britain is primarily used here.

COLONIES, PROTECTORATES, TERRITORIES, AND MANDATES

A *colony* is an area or country under the jurisdiction of another nation. That nation may settle its own citizens there as an expansion of the parent country, or it may use the indigenous people and resources solely for its own gain, with limited settlement. Historically, some colonies eventually were permitted to run their own internal affairs, and their people became nationals or citizens of the parent country. A *protectorate* is a sovereign entity that gives up part of its self-governance to a dominative state; usually this means retaining control (though often only minimal) over internal matters. Some areas became protectorates after being threatened by a superior power, others chose to exchange much of their sovereignty for military protection. Unlike colonies, protectorates do not become part of the dominative state. American possessions, called *territories*, have limited self-rule under the U.S. government and in some cases are groomed for eventual statehood. A *mandate* is an area overseen by a dominant power under the auspices of the League of Nations. (After World War I, the League made the colonies of defeated Germany mandates of other nations.) The state had obligations to the League and to the mandates themselves, such as guaranteeing certain rights, but otherwise the state was permitted to rule the area as it saw fit. Mandates are marked [M] in the Global Possessions Chart.

GLOBAL POSSESSIONS, WORLD WAR II ERA

Australia
Bismarck Archipelago (including the Admiralty Islands),[M] Papua and New Guinea,[M] the Solomon Islands,[M] and Nauru Islands[M] (shared with Britain and New Zealand).

Belgium
Belgian Congo (Zaire) and Ruanda-Urundi (Rwanda).[M]

Denmark
Greenland (colony) and Iceland (independent but united with Denmark under the Danish king).

GLOBAL POSSESSIONS, WORLD WAR II ERA (CONTINUED)

France

French Indochina: Cochin-China, Annam (Vietnam), Tonkin, Laos, Kwangchow.

French Middle East: Lebanon,[M] Syria.[M]

French North Africa: Algeria, Morocco, Tunisia.

French Equatorial, East and West Africa: Comoros Islands, French Cameroons,[M] French Equatorial Africa, French Somaliland (Djibouti), French West Africa, Madagascar, Reunion Island, Togoland.[M]

French Pacific: New Caledonia; *Polynesia:* Austral Islands (Tubuai), Marquesas Islands, Society Islands (including Tahiti), Tuamotu Archipelago.

French West Indies: French Guiana, Guadeloupe, Martinique, Saint Martin.

Holland (the Netherlands)
Surinam (Dutch Guiana).

Dutch East Indies: Java, Sumatra, Timor, Malay Archipelago islands.

Dutch West Indies (Netherlands Antilles): Aruba, Bonaire, Curaçao, Leeward Islands (Saba, Saint [Sint] Eustatius, Saint Martin [Sint Maarten]).

Italy
Albania, Aegean Isles (including Rhodes), Dodecanese Isles, Eritrea, Ethiopia (Abyssinia; it was occupied, rather than colonized, from 1936 to 1941), Italian Somaliland, Libya.

Japan

Asia: Korea, Manchuria (Manchukuo, a northern portion of China), Taiwan (Formosa).

Pacific: Caroline Islands,[M] Marshall Islands,[M] Mariana Islands[M] (including Saipan and Tinian, excluding Guam).

New Zealand
Held mandates or other control over the Cook Islands, Western Samoa, and smaller South Pacific entities.

Portugal

Africa: Angola, Cabinda, Mozambique, Portuguese Guinea (Guinea-Bissau), São Tomé and Príncipe.

Asia: East Timor, Macao (Macau).

(continued)

GLOBAL POSSESSIONS, WORLD WAR II ERA (CONTINUED)

Atlantic: The Azores, Cape Verde Islands, Madeira, and other island groups.

India: Goa, Daman and Diu.

Spain
Balearic Islands, Canary Islands, Spanish Guinea (Río Muni/Equatorial Guinea), Spanish Morocco, Spanish Sahara.

South Africa
South-West Africa[M] (Namibia).

United Kingdom (Britain)
Including Great Britain (England, Scotland, Wales) and Northern Ireland. Some areas in the British Empire retained authority over their internal affairs, with Britain overseeing defense and foreign policy. Sovereign dominions were Australia, Canada, Ireland (Irish Free State), New Zealand, and South Africa. From London to the Leeward Islands, the empire encompassed nearly 500 million people—about 20 percent of the world's population.

British Empire

British Africa: Basutoland (Lesotho), Bechuanaland (Botswana), British Cameroons,[M] British Somaliland (Somalia), British Togoland (Togo),[M] Gambia, Gold Coast (Ghana), Kenya, Nigeria, Northern Rhodesia (Zambia), Nyasaland (Malawi), the Seychelles, Sierra Leone, Southern Rhodesia (Zimbabwe), Swaziland, Tanganyika (Tanzania),[M] Uganda, Zanzibar. Sudan was under Anglo-Egyptian stewardship.

British Atlantic: Ascension Island, Falkland Islands, Newfoundland, St. Helena, South Georgia, South Sandwich Islands, Tristan da Cunha.

British Mediterranean: Cypress, Gibraltar, Malta.

British Middle East: Aden (free port city under British protection), Bahrain, Kuwait, Oman, Palestine,[M] Qatar, Transjordan (Jordan), Trucial Oman.

British Pacific: Ellice Islands (Tuvalu), Fiji, Gilbert Islands (Kiribati), Pitcairn Island, New Hebrides (Vanuatu), Tonga. Shared a mandate with Australia over Papua and New Guinea and with New Zealand over Western Samoa and Nauru.

British Southeast Asia, the Subcontinent and Indian Ocean: The Indian Empire, including India and other Indian territory (Bangladesh and Pakistan); Bhutan, British North Borneo,

GLOBAL POSSESSIONS, WORLD WAR II ERA (CONTINUED)

Burma (Myanmar), Brunei, Ceylon (Sri Lanka), Hong Kong, Malaya (Malaysia), Maldives, Mauritius, Sarawak, the Seychelles, Singapore.

British West Indies: Bahamas, Barbados, Bermuda, British Guiana (Guyana), British Honduras (Belize), Cayman Islands, Jamaica, Leeward Islands (Anguilla, Antigua, British Virgin Islands, Montserrat, St. Kitts and Nevis), Trinidad and Tobago, Turks and Caicos, Windward Islands (Dominica, Grenada, St. Lucia, St. Vincent).

United States of America

Pacific: Alaska and the Aleutian Islands, American Samoa, Guam, Hawaiian Islands, Midway Island, the Philippines, Wake Island.

Caribbean: Puerto Rico, U.S. Virgin Islands, Panama Canal Zone; the United States maintained financial control of Haiti and the Dominican Republic.

PRINCIPAL SOURCES AND FURTHER READING

Part I: Prelude

Bailey, Thomas A. *A Diplomatic History of the American People.* New York: Appleton, Century-Crofts, 1950.

Bessel, Richard, ed. *Fascist Italy and Nazi Germany.* New York: Cambridge University Press, 1996.

Brendon, Piers. *The Dark Valley: A Panorama of the 1930s.* New York: Knopf, 2000.

Crozier, Andrew. *The Causes of the Second World War.* Oxford: Blackwell Publishers, 1997.

Duggan, Christopher. *A Concise History of Italy.* Cambridge: Cambridge University Press, 1994.

Duss, Peter. *The Cambridge History of Japan.* Vol. 6. Cambridge: Cambridge University Press, 1988.

Elson, Robert, and eds. of Time-Life Books. *Prelude to War.* New York: Time-Life Books, 1976.

Gilbert, Martin. *History of the Twentieth Century.* New York: William Morrow, 2001.

Grossman, Mark. *Encyclopedia of the Interwar Years from 1919 to 1939.* New York: Facts on File, 2000.

Gupta, Madan Gopal. *International Relations since 1919* (Part One, 1919–1945). Allahabad, India: Chaitanya Publishing House, 1957.

Haines, Charles Grove, and Ross Hoffman. *The Origins and Background of the Second World War.* New York: Oxford University Press, 1947.

Iriye, Akira. *The Origins of World War II in Japan and the Pacific.* New York: Longman, 1987.

Kennedy, David M. *Freedom from Fear: The American People in Depression and War, 1929–1945.* New York: Oxford University Press, 1982.

_____. *Over Here: The First World War and American Society.* New York: Oxford University Press, 1982.

Kitchen, Martin. *The Cambridge Illustrated History of Germany.* Cambridge: Cambridge University Press, 1996.

McClain, James. *Japan: A Modern History.* New York: W.W. Norton, 2002.

Mack Smith, Dennis. *Mussolini's Roman Empire.* New York: Longman, 1976.

Newman, William J. *The Balance of Power in the Interwar Years, 1919–1939.* New York: Random House, 1968.

Overy, Richard. *The Dictators: Hitler's Germany and Stalin's Russia.* New York: W.W. Norton, 2004.

_____. *The Origins of the Second World War.* New York: Longman, 1998.

Palmer, Robert R., and Joel Colton. *A History of the Modern World.* New York: McGraw-Hill, 1995.

Treaty of Peace Between the Allied and Associated Powers and Germany. London: His Majesty's Stationery Office, 1923.

Part II: A Global Conflict

Humphreys, Robert A. *Latin America and the Second World War.* 2 Vols. London: Althone, 1981.

Kelshall, Gaylord T. M. *The U-Boat War in the Caribbean.* Annapolis: Naval Institute Press, 1994.

McKernan, Michael. *All In! Australia during the Second World War.* Melbourne, Vic.: Nelson, 1983.

Osborne, Richard E. *World War II in Colonial Africa: The Death Knell of Colonialism.* Indianapolis, IN: Riebel-Roque Publishing, 2001.

Packard, Jerrold M. *Neither Friend nor Foe: The European Neutrals in World War II.* New York: Scribner, 1992.

Ready, J. Lee. *World War Two: Nation by Nation.* London: Arms and Armour, 1995.

_____. *Forgotten Allies.* Vol. I, *The European Theater.* London: Arms and Armour, 1985.

_____. *Forgotten Allies.* Vol. II, *The Asian Theater.* London: Arms and Armour, 1985.

Rigge, Simon. *War in the Outposts.* Alexandria, VA: Time-Life Books, WWII Series, 1980.

Rout, Leslie B. Jr., and John F. Bratzel. *The Shadow War: German Espionage and United States Counterespionage in Latin America during World War II.* Frederick, MD: University Publications of America, 1986.

UNESCO. *Africa and the Second World War.* Reports and papers of the symposium organized by UNESCO at Benghazi, Libyan Arab Jamahiriya, November 10–13, 1980. Paris: UNESCO, 1985.

Wylie, Neville, ed. *European Neutrals and Non-Belligerents during the Second World War.* London: Cambridge University, 2002.

WARTIME POLITICS

In the Depression-ravaged United States of 1936, "Brother, Can You Spare a Dime" was a common street phrase as well as a popular song. Most Americans were turned inward: domestic problems seemed more than enough to handle. Yet, in a speech at Chautauqua, New York, on August 14, President Franklin Delano Roosevelt (FDR) reminded the nation of troubles stirring abroad:

> It is a bitter experience . . . for the whole company of Nations to witness not only the spirit but the letter of international agreements violated with impunity and without regard to the simple principles of honor. Permanent friendships between Nations, as between men, can be sustained only by scrupulous respect for the pledged word.

In March, German dictator Adolf Hitler, swearing "to yield to no force whatever in restoration of the honor of our people," had renounced the Treaty of Locarno and sent troops to reoccupy the Rhineland. Italian troops of Fascist dictator Benito Mussolini were then engaged in the brutal conquest of Abyssinia (Ethiopia). A fascist-nationalist military junta headed by Generalissimo Francisco Franco had started a vicious civil war in Spain to oust a duly elected left-wing government. And the increasing influence of the Japanese military—then firmly entrenched in China and seeking to expand Japan's power in Asia—had led that country to renounce painstakingly negotiated naval limitations treaties that prevented Japan from building a navy as great as those of Great Britain and the United States.

"We have sought steadfastly to assist international movements to prevent war," Roosevelt told his audience. "We shun political commitments which might entangle us in foreign wars. . . . Yet we must remember that so long as war exists on earth there will be some danger that even the Nation which most ardently desires peace may be drawn into war."

In 1939, after war erupted in Europe in September, political cartoonist Herbert Block ("Herblock") envisioned the threatening outcome of isolationist policies embraced by many politicians and civilians in the United States with international totalitarianism on the march. © the Herblock Foundation

Eleven months later, Japan ignited the full-scale conflict its government referred to as the "China Incident." Thereafter, in Europe, the politics of appeasement proved no match for the politics of aggression—as expressed, most brutally, by the armed forces Adolf Hitler unleashed on September 1, 1939. This chapter presents a broad overview of the complex and volatile political currents of World War II. (See also Chapter 4 for further information on the impact of politics on military performance and the military leadership qualities of the heads of major combatant nations.)

THE OPPOSING POLITICAL SPHERES

In simplest terms, World War II was a contest between a loose confederation of repressive totalitarian nations seeking territorial conquests (the Axis) and an alliance of nations seeking to defend and liberate their territories and preserve the freedom of their people (the Allies). Yet simple terms cannot accurately convey the volatile tangle of political motivations that lay behind every aspect of the war—and forged some unusual alliances. For example, Hitler, defender of the purity of the so-called Aryan race and its right to dominate all others, allied Germany with non-Aryan Japan; while the Allied nations defending democratic principles included (after a brief Russo-German alliance) the Soviet Union—whose government, under Stalin, bore much more striking similarities to the brutal Nazi regime than it did to any democratic body.

Within the more than sixty national groups that composed the Soviet Union (the largest, after the Russians, being Ukrainians, Uzbecks, Belorussians, and Kazakhs) were groups who resented Russian-Communist domination so strongly that they allied themselves with the German invaders. In the Far East, some nationalists seeking independence from British and French colonial rule supported Japan—until it became clear that the Japanese new order in East Asia would not allow them the independence they sought. In China, Chiang Kai-shek and his Nationalists increasingly frustrated their American allies by defending Nationalist prerogatives against the Communist Chinese more stoutly than they defended Chinese territory against the Japanese. Other warring countries—from Burma to Yugoslavia to France—were riven by bitter internal differences as they coped with Axis occupation. At the same time, nations that had proclaimed their neutrality were swayed, first in one direction and then another, by pressures from the Axis and the Allies, and by their own political imperatives. Even the close Anglo-American relationship that lay at the center of the Allied war effort was sometimes shaken by intense disagreement.

Within the United States, conflicts between isolationists and interventionists ceased with the Japanese attack on Pearl Harbor, but other political arguments continued. This was possible because, despite wartime strictures—and some terrible injustices—freedom of expression remained a right cherished by the people and effectively protected by law. People of the Axis nations did not enjoy such freedom. Their laws, their courts, and the far-reaching tentacles of political party organizations primarily protected the aims and territorial ambitions of the totalitarian governments that had plunged the world into war.

TIME LINE

War is itself a political act with primarily political objects.

—*Captain Dudley W. Knox,* A History of the United States Navy, *1936*

1937–1939: Conflict in Asia, A European War

1937

May 1: President Roosevelt signs the "permanent" Neutrality Act that essentially bans the U.S. government and American businesses from providing arms or financial assistance to belligerent nations. The legislation reflects the continuing determination of most American people to avoid entanglement in foreign wars.

July 7: An incident at the Marco Polo Bridge, near Peking, leads to clashes between Chinese and Japanese troops, with heavy casualties on both sides. The Chinese move more troops into the area; the Japanese (also being reinforced) demand, on July 26, that the Chinese withdraw their troops. Chinese rejection of this demand plunges the two countries, which have been jousting for six years, into a full-scale war. American sympathy rests overwhelmingly with the Chinese. *On July 8,* the *Report of the Palestine Royal Commission* (Peel Report) is published in Great Britain. It recommends ending the British mandate in Palestine (except for Jerusalem, Bethlehem, and a corridor to the sea) and dividing the area into Arab and Jewish states. This does not please Parliament, Jews, or Arabs. The question is to be reconsidered.

July 16: The German government inaugurates the new Buchenwald concentration camp, at first, imprisoning purely political prisoners. Later, Buchenwald will play its deadly part in the Holocaust (see Chapter 8).

August 30–September 15: As a large section of Shanghai continues to burn after the Chinese army loses the city to the Japanese, China's representative to the League of Nations, Dr. Wellington Koo, presents his country's case against the invading nation during meetings at the League headquarters in Geneva, Switzerland; he calls Japan's action "a case of aggression pure and simple," and a violation of the League's Covenant, which Japan signed. After a particularly eloquent speech on September 15, Koo receives the unusual tribute of sustained applause. But the League provides little in the way of concrete support beyond minimal financial assistance. Many League members fear that diverting too much attention and too many resources (particularly military forces) to the crisis in Asia will allow Hitler more room to maneuver in Europe.

September 9: In London, two newspapers, the *Times* and *Ethiopia News,* sponsor "Abyssinia and Justice," a conference to protest Italian rule in Abyssinia (Ethiopia). Mussolini's Fascist regime has been unable to suppress guerrilla warfare in this new Italian colony despite embarking on a bloody rampage in February (see Chapter 8).

September 28: Before an estimated 3 million people assembled at Berlin's Olympic City, Adolf Hitler and Benito Mussolini affirm the "fraternity" of their two fascist regimes. To date, the treaty violations, militarism, and expansionist policies of both leaders have remained essentially unopposed by other European governments, which are preoccupied with their own economic troubles and haunted by World War I.

October 5: Speaking in Chicago, President Roosevelt states that "the peace, the freedom and the security of 90 percent of the population of the world is being jeopardized by the remaining 10 percent" and advocates international action "to uphold laws and principles on which alone peace can rest secure." Reflecting the country's prevailing isolationism, public and political reaction is overwhelmingly negative—two congressmen even threaten to impeach the president. This reaction, Secretary of State Cordell Hull later writes, "undoubtedly emboldened the aggressor countries, and caused the democracies of Europe to wonder if we could ever be with them in more than words."

November 3–24: Representatives of the Nine Powers (the United States, Belgium, British Empire, China, France, Italy, Japan, the Netherlands, and Portugal) meet in Brussels to discuss the Sino-Japanese war. Although, in his October 5 speech, President Roosevelt had urged "a concerted effort to uphold laws and principles" to secure peace, the Americans bow to home-front isolationism at this conference and don't back those words with action; the last opportunity to end the Asian war by joint international action slips away.

November 5: Colonel Friedrich Hossbach takes minutes at a secret conference Hitler has called at the Reich Chancellery in Berlin. The führer speaks of Germany's need to acquire "greater living space than in the case of other peoples." Further, "Germany's problem could only be solved by means of force . . . it was while the rest of the world was still preparing its defenses that we were obliged to take the offensive." Hossbach's minutes (also known as the Hossbach Memorandum) will survive the war and be used as evidence during the Nuremberg war crimes trials.

December 11: Italy follows the example of Nazi Germany and withdraws from the League of Nations. The League has imposed (largely ineffective) sanctions on Italy for its war of conquest in Abyssinia, where Mussolini's forces violated the Hague Convention (see Chapter 8) and used poison gas.

1938

February 4: Hitler assumes the role of commander-in-chief of the German Army (see Chapter 4). He also names former SS (Schutzstaffel, Nazi Intelligence) colonel Joachim von Ribbentrop—a man with a deep and abiding dislike of Britain—as Germany's new foreign minister.

The main member of the United Nations alliance in Asia, China was beset by internal rivalries. The greatest contest was between the communists led by Mao Tse-tung (arms on his hips, in 1938) and the officially recognized Nationalist Chinese government under Chiang Kai-shek (at microphone, 1935). Chiang's preoccupation with smashing Mao's communists increasingly frustrated the U.S. government.

February 12: Though Germany was barred by World War I treaties from uniting with Austria, Austrian-born Hitler has been working steadily to achieve that forbidden *Anschluss*—assisted by Austrian Nazis whose terror tactics included the assassination of Austrian chancellor Engelbert Dollfuss in 1934. Today, Hitler summons Austria's chancellor Kurt von Schusschnigg to the führer's headquarters at Berchtesgaden, where the Austrian leader is subjected to a diatribe and an ultimatum, which he accepts under threat of German invasion. This *Berchtesgaden Agreement*—which greatly increases Nazi influence in Austria's government—is the beginning of the end of Austrian independence. On March 9, when Schusschnigg announces a plebiscite to be held March 13, to determine if a majority of Austrians favor union with Germany, Hitler objects; 200,000 German troops mass on the Austrian border. No other European power is able or willing to help Austria in the face of this imminent invasion. Even Italy, long regarded as an

Austrian protector, backs away in favor of Germany. To help assure that Mussolini will not interfere, on March 10 Hitler dispatches a letter to Il Duce filled with false accusations of an Austrian-Czechoslovakian plot against Germany. "Consider this step only as one of national self-defense," Hitler will write. "You too, Excellency, could not act differently if the fate of Italians were at stake."

February 20: In protest against Neville Chamberlain's appeasement policy toward the Germans, Anthony Eden resigns as British foreign secretary. He will be replaced by Lord Halifax, who came away from a November 1937 meeting with Hitler convinced that the Germans did not intend to make war. *Also this day:* In a three-hour speech to the German Reichstag, Hitler gives public notice that the fate of 7 million Austrians—and 3 million ethnic Germans living in the Sudetenland area of Czechoslovakia—is a matter of German concern: "To the interest of the German Reich belongs the protection of those German peoples who are not in a position to secure along our frontiers their political and spiritual freedom by their own efforts." On March 4, Czechoslovak Prime Minister Milan Hodza tells the Chamber of Deputies that, if attacked, Czechoslovakia will defend itself "to the very last."

March 13: Two days after Nazi Artur Seyss-Inquart replaces von Schusschnigg as Austrian chancellor, Hitler achieves the long-desired Anschluss and declares that Austria is now "Ostmark," a province of Germany. Austria's resources are now Germany's; Austria's army is incorporated into the German Wehrmacht (minus two-thirds of the officers, who are interned); and German territory now surrounds Czechoslovakia on three sides. German and Austrian Nazis quickly begin a campaign of repression and terror. Thirty thousand Jews are among the tens of thousands of Austrians—including Catholics, Social Democrats, Socialists, and Communists—who are arrested and sent to concentration camps. Some people commit suicide; others (including Sigmund Freud) become refugees.

March 14: During a debate in the House of Commons, Winston Churchill, a vigorous opponent of Neville Chamberlain's appeasement policies, cites the fate of Austria and urges the British government to take effective measures against Germany's increasing aggression.

March 22: Acting in direct opposition to the harsh stance advocated by Winston Churchill, the British cabinet and Prime Minister Neville Chamberlain agree to pressure the Czechoslovakian government to make concessions to the Sudeten Germans. "It is a disagreeable business," Foreign Minister Halifax writes to a friend, "which has to be done as pleasantly as possible."

March 26: Nine months into the Sino-Japanese war, which the Japanese high command had believed would be very short, the Japanese government passes the National Mobilization Bill, giving the government dictatorial powers over most areas of Japan's economic life.

April 10: The people of Greater Germany (Germany and Austria combined) vote in a plebiscite called by Hitler to approve the annexation of Austria. The German government will report that 99.08 percent of German voters and 99.75 percent of Austrian voters vote yes.

April 14: In one of his "Fireside Chat" radio addresses, President Roosevelt takes note of the burgeoning international crisis:

> Democracy has disappeared in several other great nations—not because the people of those nations disliked democracy, but because they had grown tired of unemployment and insecurity, of seeing their children hungry while they sat helpless in the face of government confusion and government weakness through lack of leadership in government. Finally, in desperation, they chose to sacrifice liberty in the hope of getting something to eat. We in America know that our own democratic institutions can be preserved and made to work. But in order to preserve them we need to act together, to meet the problems of the Nation boldly, and to prove that the practical operation of democratic government is equal to the task of protecting the security of the people.

April 16: In an effort to divide and weaken the Axis in Europe, the British government concludes the *Anglo-Italian Mediterranean Agreement*, which, among other provisions, recognizes Italy's annexation of Abyssinia. *Two days later,* Chamberlain will declare in a speech that he does not approve of dictatorships, but "There they are. You cannot remove them. We have to live with them."

April 18: The leftist Popular Front government of Leon Blum—which had introduced the forty-hour work week and collective bargaining and nationalized the French munitions industry—falls in France.

April 24: Konrad Henlein, leader of the Sudeten German Party (SDP)—which secretly receives substantial subsidies from the German government—announces eight demands, including complete autonomy for Sudetenland. This *Karlsbad Program* will be rejected by the beleaguered Eduard Benes, leader of the Czech government that is trying to deal not only with Germany's threatening presence on its borders, but also with the increasing demands of Czechoslovakia's many minorities.

May 3–9: Hitler makes a state visit to Rome, during which he establishes a personal rapport with Mussolini. The two dictators pledge "eternal friendship."

May 17: Motivated by Japanese aggression in China and Axis expansionism in Europe the U.S. Congress, although still determined to avoid war, passes the *Naval Expansion Act of 1938*. It authorizes a 23 percent increase in the number and the tonnage allowances of the navy's warships.

May 26: The 480,000-strong German-American Bund (whose members salute the Swastika flag) and suspect activities of the American Communist Party together inspire the creation of the House Committee to Investigate Un-American Activities (HUAC), chaired by Representative Martin Dies, Democrat from Texas. More than a bit overzealous, it will proceed, during its early hearings, to label 483 newspapers, 280 labor organizations, and 640 other organizations "Communistic"—including the Boy Scouts, the Catholic Association for International Peace, and the Camp Fire Girls.

June 23: As plans go forward to construct fortifications along Germany's western frontier to stymie any hostile French reaction to Hitler's planned invasion of Czechoslovakia, the Nazi government issues a decree making labor service on essential government projects compulsory. Factory owners along the Rhine River are required to transfer 10 percent of their work force to assist in constructing fortifications. *Two days later,* President Roosevelt signs the Fair Labor Standards Act, establishing minimum wages (25¢ per hour for the first year, raised to 30¢ for the next six years) and maximum working hours (forty-four per week the first year, forty-two the second, forty thereafter).

July 6: In this month when Italian dictator Mussolini declares, "Jews do not belong to the Italian race," a nine-day, thirty-three-nation conference on refugees convenes in Évian-les-Bains, France. Partially funded by the U.S. State Department, the conference will fail to adopt any effective measures to address the growing numbers of people seeking to escape the brutality and anti-Semitism of the Hitler regime. Fearful of an influx of aliens, most countries refuse to increase their immigration quotas. Some tighten restrictions. Only the Netherlands, Denmark, and the Dominican Republic agree to accept refugees without any restrictions. The conference does establish the *Intergovernmental Committee on Political Refugees* to negotiate for Jewish lives; but this unenthusiastically supported body will prove largely ineffective.

September 12: Provoked by a broadcast speech in which Hitler declares that the "oppression of the Sudeten Germans by the Czechs must end," some 6,000 Sudeten-German followers of Konrad Henlein, leader of the Sudeten German Home Front political party, surge through the streets of Karlsbad. Twenty-three people are killed and many Czech and Jewish homes are wrecked in rioting throughout the Sudetenland that continues into the next day. Czechoslovakia declares martial law. In the United States, popular CBS commentator H. V. Kaltenborn takes up temporary residence in the network's Studio Nine. For the next eighteen days, he will keep his American audience informed as the Czechoslovakian crisis reaches its climax. Meanwhile, Winston Churchill has written to a friend on September 11: "We seem to be very near the black choice between War and Shame. My feeling is that we shall choose Shame, and then have War thrown in a little later, on even more adverse terms than at present."

September 23–28: On September 23, heroic American aviator Charles A. Lindbergh, greatly impressed by his tours of Germany, writes to American ambassador to Britain Joseph P. Kennedy: "I am convinced that it is wiser to permit Germany eastward expansion than to throw England and France, unprepared, into a war at this time." Two days later, demonstrators march through London carrying signs that urge the government to "Stand by the Czechs" and "Stop Hitler." On September 26, President Roosevelt sends memoranda to the British, French, German, and Czechoslovakian governments recommending arbitration of the crisis. The next day, before going to Germany for a conference with Hitler, Neville Chamberlain speaks in the House of Commons, telling his countrymen, "However much we may sympathize with a small nation confronted by a big and powerful neighbor, we cannot . . . undertake to involve the whole British Empire in war simply on her account. If we have to fight it must be on larger issues than that."

September 27–28: A year after Chinese representative Wellington Koo's eloquent plea to the League of Nations, the League declares Japan an aggressor and invites its members to support China.

September 29: Following days of proposals and counterproposals, German führer Adolf Hitler, British prime minister Neville Chamberlain, French prime minister Edouard Daladier, and Italian dictator Benito Mussolini hold a twelve-hour meeting in Munich, Germany, during which they arrange the transfer of Czechoslovakian territory to Germany—while Czech officials wait in another room. Under threat of German military action, and with the knowledge that no other country will assist them, the Czech government is forced to accept the agreement. In the wake of this capitulation to Hitler, the United States will revise its preparedness program to deal with the growing threat from Germany across the Atlantic as well as the long-anticipated threat of Japan across the Pacific. (See Chapter 4.)

October 1: German troops begin a swift occupation of the Sudetenland, reducing Czech territory by more than a third—and bringing under German control manpower, resources, and many of Czechoslovakia's arms factories. Three days later, Poland occupies the Czech district of Teschen, in which some Poles have been living, and the important railway junction of Bohumin.

October 10: In a memo to his staff at the U.S. Federal Bureau of Investigation, J. Edgar Hoover stresses the importance of maintaining the "utmost degree of secrecy in order to avoid criticisms" as the FBI gathers information on "subversive activities," which include, among other things "the distribution of literature . . . opposed to the American way of life." This year, Hoover will inform President Roosevelt that the FBI has compiled a detailed index of 2,500 people classified as probable subversives. During the post-World War I Red Scare, Hoover had masterminded an even broader information-gathering effort on probable subversives. The nation's attorneys general and the U.S. Supreme Court will—with some notable exceptions (see sidebar "The Decision for Japanese American Interment," later in this chapter)—guard the civil liberties of individual Americans much more closely during World War II.

October 31: Orson Welles and his radio troupe panic American listeners with an intensely realistic production of "War of the Worlds" that convinces millions that Martians really *are* invading New Jersey. The resulting uproar convinces Hitler that his low estimate of American intelligence is justified.

November 4: Declaring the Nine-Power Treaty guaranteeing China's integrity obsolete, Japan announces a "New Order" in East Asia.

November 8: In U.S. congressional elections, the Democrats lose seven Senate seats and seventy seats in the House, but maintain a comfortable majority in both houses.

November 9–10: In the wake of the assassination in Paris of German diplomat Ernst von Rath by Jewish teenager Herschel Grynzpan—whose parents were among the thousands of Jews just expelled from Germany—Adolf Hitler approves a massive attack on the Jews of Greater Germany.

Nationwide dedication to supporting the war effort did not bring an end to U.S. partisan politics. In 1942, Republicans gained seats in both houses of Congress—resulting in greater resistance to Roosevelt's domestic and foreign policies. On July 4, 1943, the Washington, D.C., Evening Star *published this political cartoon by Clifford Berryman advocating better cooperation between Capitol Hill and the White House.*

NATIONAL LEGISLATIVE BODIES OF
MAJOR COMBATANT NATIONS

Germany	Federal parliament, comprising, under the Weimar Constitution, a lower house, the Reichstag, and an upper house, the Reichrat, representing the German states. With the Enabling Act of March 1933, the Reichstag ceded most of its legislative powers to the cabinet (to Hitler). The Reichrat was abolished in 1934, when the German states lost their sovereignty. Although it remained in existence throughout the war, the Reichstag was an all-Nazi body (no other parties were allowed in Germany) and simply served to ratify government action.
Great Britain	Parliament, comprising the House of Commons and the House of Lords—with most of the power residing in the former. The prime minister was responsible to Parliament and was leader of the House of Commons. Although many conventions of parliamentary democracy were suspended during the war (for example, the election scheduled for 1940 was postponed by parliamentary amendments), Parliament continued to be the principal governmental body throughout the war.
Italy	Parliament, comprising two bodies, the Senate (a largely honorific body of appointees) and the Chamber of Deputies (elected). Like the Reichstag in Germany, the Italian parliament had no independent power under the Fascists. Ministers reported directly to Mussolini—and all members of parliament were Fascists (the only political party permitted) or were approved by Fascist organizations.
Japan	Diet, comprising the House of Representatives (elected legislators primarily belonging to the Minseito and Seiyuka political parties) and the House of Peers (appointed or with a hereditary claim to office). The Diet functioned throughout the war, although its members were pressured to forsake political parties and toe the official lines as members of the cabinet-created *Imperial Rule Assistance Association* and later the *Imperial Rule Assistance Political Association*. Most legislators did; but at least two—the

NATIONAL LEGISLATIVE BODIES OF
MAJOR COMBATANT NATIONS (CONTINUED)

	conservative Seigo Nakano and the liberal Yukio Ozaki—braved harassment and prison to criticize the government's military policies.
United States of America	Congress, comprising the House of Representatives and the Senate. It holds constitutional responsibility for declaring war, which it exercised December 8, 1941. It also continued to exercise its other constitutionally mandated powers throughout the war, including the "Power to lay and collect taxes . . . and provide for the common Defense and general welfare of the United States . . . To raise and support Armies, to provide and maintain a Navy, To make Rules for the Government and Regulation of the land and Naval forces . . . [and] To make all Laws which shall be necessary and proper for" executing these powers.

Principal sources: William Bridgewater and Seymour Kurtz, eds. *The Columbia Encyclopedia*, New York: Columbia University Press, 1963; Frank J. Coppa, ed., *Dictionary of Modern Italian History*, Westport, CT: Greenwood Press, 1985; I. C. B. Dear and M. R. D. Foot, eds., *Oxford Companion to World War II*, Oxford: Oxford University Press, 2004; Marcel Baudot, *The Historical Encyclopedia of World War II*, New York: Greenwich House, 1984; Saburo Ienaga, *Japan's Last War*, Canberra: Australian National University Press, 1979; Constitution of the United States of America, Washington, D.C.: Government Printing Office.

During this *Kristallnact* (Night of Broken Glass), Nazis and their sympathizers rage through cities and towns wreaking havoc on Jewish shops, homes, and synagogues. A hundred Jews are murdered; more than 20,000 will be arrested and sent to concentration camps (see Chapter 8). Other countries react to this state-sponsored riot with revulsion. In America, former president Herbert Hoover, Democratic politician Al Smith, progressive Republican Alf Landon, and Secretary of the Interior Harold Ickes are among the public figures to denounce the violence on radio. The United States will recall its ambassador to Germany; Germany will reciprocate.

November 10: Turkey's president Kemal Atatürk, 57, dies after fifteen years in office during which he established a modern republic—in a strategic Near Eastern location. He is succeeded as president by Ismet Inönü, who has also been influential in building the republic.

November 14: The increasing importance of military air power—and the menacing strength of Germany's still-growing Luftwaffe—is reflected in President Roosevelt's determination, expressed at a White House meeting, to vastly expand the capability of the American aircraft industry. Roosevelt plans to provide aircraft to Britain and France even while building a 10,000-plane U.S. air force.

December 24: In Peru, delegates to the Eighth International Conference of American States issue the *Declaration of Lima,* in which they pledge to consult if the "peace, security, or territorial integrity" of any one of these North and South American states is threatened. The first tangible fruit of the Good Neighbor Policy that President Roosevelt proclaimed in 1933, it is a step toward his goal of hemispheric solidarity.

1939

January 2: *Time* magazine names Adolf Hitler its "Man of the Year" for 1938, the year the German dictator had become, in *Time*'s words, "the greatest threatening force the democratic, freedom-loving world faces today." Two days later, President Roosevelt will declare, in his State of the Union message, "There comes a time in the affairs of men when they must prepare to defend not their homes alone but the tenets of faith and humanity on which their churches, their governments and their very civilization are founded. The defense of religion, of democracy, and of good faith among nations is all the same fight. To save one we must now make up our minds to save all."

January 16: In their continuing campaign to remove British troops from Irish soil, the Irish Republican Army begins a campaign of terror bombing in England that will last until May 1940.

January 25: German foreign minister Joachim von Ribbentrop sends a circular titled "The Jewish Question, A Factor in Our Foreign Policy for 1938" to diplomatic and consular offices:

> It is not by chance that 1938, the year of our destiny, saw the realization of our plan for Greater Germany as well as a major step towards the solution of the Jewish problem. . . . The spread of Jewish influence and its corruption of our political, economic, and cultural life has perhaps done more to undermine the German people's will to prevail than all the hostility shown us by the Allied powers since the Great War. This disease in the body of our people had first to be eradicated before the Great German Reich could assemble its forces in 1938 to overcome the will of the world.

January 30: After declaring his intention to punish "world Jewry" for the devastating conflict that he, in fact, is about to begin, Hitler states, in a speech to the Reichstag, that Germany will require *Lebensraum* (living space) to provide for its people. Though he has in mind, primarily, expansion into the Soviet Union, there will be extensive military and diplomatic operations to prepare for this eastward move. Over the next two months, he will make a series of impossible demands on the government of what remains of Czechoslovakia. The Czech government will refuse these demands, and Hitler will refuse to sign the Munich pact, which is supposed to guarantee Czechoslovakian borders.

February 27: Japanese Foreign Minister Arita Hachirō announces to Japan's House of Peers that "Jewish residents in Japan are to be treated in the same manner as other foreign residents. . . . They never will be denied entry simply because of their race." There has been great debate, and more than a bit of intragovernmental confusion, about Japanese policy regarding Jewish refugees (Japan's Foreign Ministry formed a *Moslem and Jewish Problem Committee* early in 1938). Meanwhile, Japanese diplomats in Europe have been issuing an ever-growing number of transit visas to Jews for travel through Japan and China—often stretching the law to accommodate a refugee's desperate request. Very few Jews will find refuge in Japan; but some 21,000 will survive the war in Japanese-occupied Shanghai.

March 13–15: Summoning the Czech president, Dr. Emil Hacha, to Berlin, Hitler says that Prague will be reduced to "a heap of ruins" by aerial attack if the Czechoslovakian government does not accede to Hitler's demands—most particularly that the Czech heartland, Bohemia and Moravia, become a "Reich Protectorate." Even as this is being discussed, German troops move into the Czech town of Moravska-Ostrava, and by March 15, the German occupation of Bohemia and Moravia is a fact. This new possession brings Germany substantial gains—including the Skoda and Brünn armament complexes. The Munich pact guarantees of Czech territorial integrity not having been signed, neither France nor Britain attempts to negate this latest expression of Hitler's territorial ambitions. Yet the occupation does inspire a revival of the World War I-era Anglo-French alliance.

March 20: With a careful eye on Germany's expanding borders, the Romanian government agrees to reserve one half of Romania's considerable oil production for the Third Reich.

March 22: Under pressure, Lithuania cedes the small territory of Memel to the German Reich, as Germany continues exerting diplomatic pressures on Poland aimed at securing the Free City of Danzig. Poland continues to resist, stating that it will consider any unilateral action by Germany to secure the city an act of war.

March 31: As the Spanish Civil War comes to an end with the fall of Madrid to Franco's fascist-nationalist troops, Britain and France mark the end of their unsuccessful appeasement policy by promising to support Poland if that country is faced with "action which . . . the Polish Government . . . considered it vital to resist with the national forces." France, meanwhile, refuses Italian demands for control over some of its African territories but can do nothing about Japan's occupation of the Spratly Islands in the South China Sea, only seven hundred miles from Britain's key Asian outpost of Singapore. Japan will soon base submarines there.

April: The Hungarian government introduces a law that restricts the rights and benefits of Jewish Hungarians. Hungary also signs the *Anti-Comintern Pact,* joining Germany, Italy, and Japan in a vague general agreement to guard against the designs of international communism.

April 9: Seventy-five thousand people—including Chief Justice and Mrs. Charles Evans Hughes, Associate Justice Hugo Black, Secretary of the Treasury Henry Morgenthau, and Secretary of the Interior Harold Ickes—gather at the Lincoln Memorial in Washington to hear a concert by Marian Anderson. The monument was chosen for the concert after the Daughters of the American Revolution refused to allow the celebrated American singer to perform in Constitution Hall because she is an African American, an action that caused First Lady Eleanor Roosevelt to resign from the DAR in protest.

April 13: Six days after Italy's successful invasion of Albania, Italy's king, Victor Emmanuel III, declares the "personal union" of these two countries under his crown. Italy will establish an Albanian fascist government under Shefqet Verlaci, as the worried British and French governments extend assurances of assistance to Greece and Romania.

April 15: Both Hitler and Mussolini receive a communication from President Roosevelt seeking a pledge that Italy and Germany will not "attack or invade the territory" of thirty-one listed independent nations including Poland, Britain, France, the Baltic States, Russia, Denmark, the Netherlands, and Belgium. Mussolini dismisses the message as "a result of infantile paralysis" (poliomyelitis). Hitler, however, determines to answer it—after the German foreign office conducts a survey of many of the named nations to ascertain whether they felt threatened. Most declare (a few after some pressure is applied) that they do not. Then, on April 28, Hitler delivers a masterful two-hour-plus reply to the American president before a specially convened session of the Reichstag about which the attending American journalist William Shirer will say: "For sheer eloquence, craftiness, irony, sarcasm and hypocrisy, it reached a new level that he was never to approach again."

April 26: Worried about the relative weakness of its armed forces, the British government passes the Military Training Act, introducing conscription. (See also Chapter 4.)

May 8: Spain withdraws from the League of Nations.

May 22: Germany and Italy form the "Pact of Steel," confirming "the intimate ties of friendship and solidarity existing between Fascist Italy and National Socialist Germany."

May 27: The SS *St. Louis,* carrying 927 German-Jewish refugees arrives in the harbor of Havana, Cuba, on a voyage that began in Hamburg on May 13. Only twenty-two passengers are allowed to land, after which the ship is forced to leave. Appeals to the governments of Colombia, Paraguay, Argentina, Chile, and the United States are refused or go unanswered, and on June 6, the ship returns to Europe. Passengers are accepted in Britain, Belgium, France, and Holland; 254 of them will not survive the war. *As this occurs,* a vast effort is being undertaken in Europe to save German, Austrian, and Czech Jewish children from the Nazis. This *Kindertransporte* will eventually bring some 10,000 children to safety in the British Isles.

June 7–12: King George VI and Queen Elizabeth become the first British monarchs to visit the United States. In addition to Washington, D.C., they visit New York City, where they tour the

World's Fair. At a picnic at the Roosevelt family estate at Hyde Park, they become acquainted with what the king describes as "this delightful hot-dog sandwich."

June 14: After authorities in the British concession at Tientsin (Tianjin) refuse to surrender four Chinese that the Japanese have accused of "terrorism," the Japanese blockade the British and French concessions and announce that Britain must cease supporting the Nationalist Chinese regime and cooperate with Japan's campaign to establish a new order in East Asia.

June 29: By a close margin, the U.S. House of Representatives votes to retain the arms embargo in the Neutrality Act.

July 18: At a bitterly argumentative evening meeting at the White House with Senate leaders, FDR discovers he does not have the votes in the Senate to reverse the arms embargo in the Neutrality Act.

July 22: Enmeshed in his own nonviolent campaign to free India from British colonial rule, pacifist Mohandas Gandhi writes to Adolf Hitler: "You are today the one person who can prevent a war which may reduce humanity to a savage state. Listen to the appeal of one who has deliberately shunned the method of war not without inconsiderable success." He will receive no reply.

August 4: Some two weeks after the former Czechoslovakian president (1935–1938) Eduard Benes arrives in London to establish a Czech government-in-exile (July 18), the Polish government issues an ultimatum to the senate of the Free City of Danzig—whose presiding officer, Arthur Greiser, is a committed Nazi—to cease practices that reflect the city's desire to become part of Germany. Greiser's compliance with the Polish demands is much heralded in the Polish, British, and French press. Meanwhile, German troops begin massing on the Polish border.

August 7: Hermann Göring and his stepson, Thomas von Kantzow, meet seven British businessmen at a remote farmhouse in Schleswig-Holstein. The meeting—held with both Hitler's and British foreign secretary Halifax's approval—has been arranged by Göring's and von Kantzow's friend, Swedish businessman Birger Dahlerus, as a first step toward finding some way of keeping Britain and France out of the looming European conflict. The British businessmen tell Göring that Britain will stand by Poland, but the British government is willing to keep lines of communication open.

August 23: Stunning communists around the world, as well as Germany's Japanese allies, the Soviet Union signs a ten-year mutual nonaggression pact with fascist Germany, a heretofore devoted enemy of Bolshevism. Sought by Hitler chiefly to remove the threat of military action in the east while German forces are engaged in Poland and Western Europe, and by Stalin for complex political and strategic motives (including Russia's troubled relations with Japan), the pact is a general expression of nonaggressive intent. It is accompanied, however, by a secret protocol that defines the "spheres of influence" each signatory will control "in the event of territorial and political rearrangement" in the Baltic States, Poland, and southeastern Europe. Under a credit and trade agreement reached between the two governments August 19, the USSR will also supply Germany with food and raw materials—an obligation the Soviets will keep, even as Stalin begins receiving repeated warnings that Hitler plans to attack the Soviet Union.

August 25: The British sign a formal treaty of alliance with Poland, similar to a treaty already in place between Poland and France. Both these nations are now obligated to aid Poland if it is attacked. Yet neither Britain nor France has fully abandoned appeasement: despite the buildup of German troops on its border, Poland has been urged by its new allies to refrain from provoking Hitler by fully mobilizing its own armed forces, an inclination members of its own government share. Full mobilization will not be ordered until August 29, when Hitler's demand that a Polish representative go to Berlin is refused. In Germany, a plot to stage an ostensibly Polish provocation for war is set in motion. *Also August 25:* Canadian Prime Minister MacKenzie King warns Adolf Hitler that Canada will join England if that country goes to war with Germany. *And in Germany:* Hitler receives an unwelcome reply from a message he sent Mussolini that war with Poland was imminent. "If Germany attacks Poland and the conflict remains localized," Mussolini writes, "Italy will afford Germany every form of political and economic assistance which is requested of her. If Germany attacks Poland and the latter's allies open a counterattack against Germany, I inform you in advance that it will be opportune for me not to take the initiative in military operations in view of the present state of Italian war preparations. . . . At our meetings the war was envisaged for 1942." Hitler is overheard muttering about his "disloyal Axis partner."

September 1: War in Europe begins as German troops smash across Poland's borders. From the first day, exceptional brutality marks the German advance; three SS Death's Head regiments following behind the front-line troops have been ordered to "incarcerate or annihilate" every person who might pose a threat to Nazi rule. In the United States, President Roosevelt meets with his cabinet and reiterates his determination to provide support for the anti-Hitler nations by all possible means short of war. As of this day, the entire United States Army comprises less than 200,000 men; the German forces invading Poland number more than a million. *Also this day:* The U.S. State Department establishes a small Special Division "to handle special problems arising out of the disturbed conditions in Europe, such as aiding in the repatriation of American citizens, [and] the representation of the interests of other governments, . . ." Five ships will soon be dispatched to bring Americans home from Europe. Meanwhile, as tensions between the United States and Japan increase, the Special Division will grow increasingly concerned about the 30,000 Americans working and living in Asia.

September 3: As Britain and France declare war on Germany, a *Washington Post* headline trumpets: "BOTH SIDES AGREE NOT TO BOMB CIVILIANS." *Also this day:* A German submarine sinks the British passenger liner *Athenia*—killing 112 passengers, including 28 Americans. In a Fireside Chat this evening, President Roosevelt declares: "This nation will remain a neutral nation." But he adds, "I cannot ask that every American remain neutral in thought as well. . . . Even a neutral cannot be asked to close his mind or close his conscience."

September 5: After delaying for two days, so that materials previously ordered by Britain and France could clear U.S. ports, President Roosevelt issues two Neutrality Proclamations. The first is in accordance with international law. The second is required under the Johnson Act of 1934 (see Chapter 1) and the U.S. Neutrality Act of 1937, which includes a strict embargo on all "arms, ammunition, or implements of war," to all belligerent nations. Repealing this act becomes one of Roosevelt's highest priorities.

September 11: Three days after declaring a state of "Limited National Emergency," President Roosevelt begins to forge a friendship with Winston Churchill that will be a boon to wartime Allied relations when he sends a note after Churchill's appointment as First Lord of the Admiralty in Chamberlain's cabinet: "What I want you and the Prime Minister to know is that I shall at all times welcome it if you will keep me in touch personally with anything you want me to know about."

September 12: At its first meeting in Abbeville, France, the new *Anglo-French Supreme War Council* decides not to undertake large-scale military operations, as they need time to build up their armed forces.

September 21: Armand Calinescu, the prime minister of Romania, is assassinated by members of the profascist and German-trained Iron Guard—an organization Calinescu had been attempting to suppress.

September 26: In the wake of German-Soviet agreements and the USSR's occupation of Polish territory, France outlaws the Communist Party at home and in its colonies. In French Indochina, Vo Nguyen Giap and Ho Chi Minh are among the communists who will battle the French, the Japanese, and in decades to come, the Americans, in their quest for control of Vietnam. *Also this day:* After watching the bombing of Warsaw from a vantage point on the outskirts of the city, Hitler returns to Berlin, where he and Hermann Göring meet with Göring's friend Swedish businessman Birger Dahlerus. Dahlerus is then sent to meet Lord Halifax in London to see if there might be some way to reach an accommodation with the British. Nevertheless, that same night, Hitler orders his military commanders to prepare for *Operation (Case) Yellow,* an attack on western Europe. Its purpose, Hitler says, is "to destroy France and bring Britain to her knees."

September 29: The same day that the division of Poland is formalized with the *Soviet-German Boundary and Friendship Treaty,* the USSR signs a *Treaty of Mutual Assistance* with the Baltic country of Estonia, allowing the Soviets to occupy all Estonian naval bases. Within two weeks, similar treaties will be signed with Latvia and Lithuania. At the same time, the Soviet Union increases its pressure on traditionally neutral Finland to engage in joint security measures that would protect Russia's western flanks. But Finland refuses.

Members of the U.S. Office of Strategic Services "Deer Team," including Lt. René Défourneaux (standing, second from left), served in French Indochina with allies who would become postwar enemies: Ho Chi Minh (standing third from left) and Gen. Vo Nguyen Giap later led the North Vietnamese forces that opposed South Vietnamese and U.S. troops throughout the Vietnam War.

October 8: After annexing Poland's frontier regions to Germany and incorporating its western provinces into the Reich, Hitler appoints Nazi Party legal adviser Dr. Hans Frank to rule over the central section of the conquered country, to be known as the "General Government." He tells Frank to treat Poland "like a colony" and that the Poles are to become "slaves of the Greater German Empire."

October 18: The same day Hitler authorizes German U-boats to attack any passenger ship traveling in a convoy or without lights, President Roosevelt orders all U.S. ports and waters closed to belligerent submarines.

October 19: England, France, and Turkey sign a fifteen-year *Treaty of Mutual Assistance,* in which the Turks pledge to aid the Allies if war reaches the Mediterranean—as long as such aid will not bring them into conflict with the Soviet Union. Though this treaty will remain in effect, Turkey will also sign a *Treaty of Friendship and Non-aggression with Germany* on June 18, 1941.

October 21: Having been warned of the possibility of an atomic bomb (see Chapter 5), President Roosevelt establishes an advisory committee on uranium.

November 4: As Europe settles into the fitful period known as the *Phony War* (there was little ground combat and only limited air campaigns, though the Battle of the Atlantic continued; see Chapter 6), Congress amends the U.S. Neutrality Act to permit arms sales to belligerents—but only on a cash-and-carry basis. Neither the U.S. Treasury nor private American banks may extend credit to purchasers of war materials; they must be paid for in full before they leave American docks. The amended law also forbids American merchant vessels from traveling in a broad danger zone of Atlantic sea lanes to avoid an incident that might lead the United States into war.

November 8–9: A bomb explodes in the Munich beer hall where Hitler has been leading the celebration of the 1923 Beer Hall Putsch. Set by Johann George Elser, recently released from imprisonment at Dachau for being a communist sympathizer, the bomb kills seven people and injures more than sixty—but Hitler, who left the hall early, is not among them. He will view his escape as a sign "of Providence's intention to let me reach my goal."

November 30: Soviet air, land, and sea forces attack Finland. More than 60 people are killed when Helsinki is bombed, an act that outrages the Finns, adding steel to the stubborn resistance that will characterize their initially successful fight against numerically superior Soviet forces. In the United States, former president Herbert Hoover will organize a drive for Finnish relief, and Congress will grant Finland $10 million in credits reflecting the sympathy Finland's plight arouses in many countries around the world. Hitler, meanwhile, will view the difficulties Soviet forces are having in Finland as proof that German armies will have little trouble defeating the USSR when he turns them east.

December 12: The League of Nations expels the Soviet Union.

December 30: In his New Year message for the German people, Hitler declares, "The Jewish-capitalist world will not survive the Twentieth Century."

1940: Arsenal of Democracy

January: After the six-months' notice required by treaty stipulations, the United States abrogates a commercial treaty with Japan that has been in effect since 1911. This action will allow the future imposition of trade embargoes on materials vital to Japan, such as oil, in retaliation for Japan's continuing aggression in China, where the United States has certain rights and interests to protect. Japan's expansionist policies also endanger U.S. military bases and other holdings in the Pacific including the Philippine Islands, Wake Island, and Guam.

January 13: FBI agents arrest seventeen members of a bitterly anti-Semitic, pro-Nazi, and anti-Roosevelt organization called the "Christian Front" and charge them with planning, in the words of FBI director J. Edgar Hoover, to "knock off about a dozen congressmen" and "blow up the goddamed [New York City] police department." There is little hard evidence to support these charges, however. The jury that considers the case will refuse to convict the accused.

January 20: At a meeting of the Anglo-French Supreme War Council, the British and French Prime Ministers agree to send a military force to assist the Finns in their war with the Soviets, although it will take two or more months to organize the operation. The force will travel via Norway, where they are to take control of the port of Narvik through which Germany receives vital shipments of iron ore from Sweden. Eventually catching wind of this plan via intelligence, Hitler will add Norway and Denmark to the German list of conquests.

January 30: Soviet dictator Joseph Stalin authorizes secret negotiations in Sweden to help end the Russo-Finnish "Winter War." *Also this day:* The U.S. government sends out the first Social Security check—for $22.54—to Vermonter Ida May Fuller, a 66-year-old retired teacher and secretary.

February 2: Takao Saito, a member of Japan's Diet (legislature), courageously makes a final attempt to curtail the military's campaign to establish a "new order" in East Asia. Branding the conflict with China as "nothing but aggression cloaked in self-righteous language," he declares, "If we miss a chance for peace, the politicians of today will be unable to erase their crime even by their deaths."

February 9: President Roosevelt announces that he will send Undersecretary of State Sumner Welles on a "fact-finding" mission to Rome, Berlin, Paris, and London. The principal fact that the president wishes to find (though he does not state it publicly) is whether it might be possible for the United States to mediate a peace settlement, which would be far preferable to a peace imposed on Hitler's terms. Welles will come away from interviews with Mussolini and Hitler believing "that it was only too tragically plain that all decisions had already been made. The best that could be hoped for was delay, for what little that might be worth."

February 11: As Soviet numerical superiority begins to turn the tide in the war with Finland, Germany and the USSR sign a new economic treaty involving exchange of Soviet raw materials for German manufactured goods, adding to the resources on which Germany will be able to draw during the planned attack on the Low Countries and France.

March 13: The Soviet-Finnish war ends with a treaty accepted in Moscow by Finnish Prime Minister Risto Ryti ceding the USSR territory and the use of its naval base at the entrance to the Gulf of Finland. The settlement causes the Anglo-French War Council to cancel its plans to send an expedition to Scandinavia. One week later, however, after the appeasement-oriented Edouard Daladier is replaced as French prime minister by the more aggressive Paul Reynaud, the council decides to mine Norwegian waters. Allied forces will be in those waters when the German Scandinavian offensive begins.

March 22: Roosevelt signs *Executive Order 8381*, which asserts presidential control of the classification system of "all official military or naval books, pamphlets, documents, reports, maps, charts, plans, designs, models, drawings, photographs, contracts or specifications." The order also gives the president discretion to classify other "articles or equipment" as needed.

March 30: Japanese authorities establish a Chinese puppet government at the former Nationalist Chinese capital of Nanking (the Nationalists have been forced to retreat to a new capital at Chungking). The Japanese install former Nationalist and perpetual Chiang Kai-shek rival Wang Ching-wei as head of government—although all his actions will be dictated by Japanese "advisers."

April 9: Germany invades Denmark and Norway. This evening, after the capital, Oslo, falls, the head of Norway's fascist National Unity Party, Vidkun Quisling, announces that he is head of a new government—and directs all resistance to end. (It does not.) Six days later, the Germans will unceremoniously dump the universally unpopular Quisling from the post he assumed, temporarily replacing him with an Administrative Council of six (well-supervised) leading Norwegian citizens—including Paal Berg, president of the supreme court and later head of the Norwegian resistance. On April 24, Hitler will appoint loyal German Nazi Josef Terboven as Reich Commissar for Norway. Terboven will be the true ruler of Norway for the rest of the war—although Quisling will remain, even serving as premier from 1942. Quisling's last name, lower-cased, will become a synonym for traitor.

April 15: Senator Gerald P. Nye (Rep. N.D.) tells a meeting in Pennsylvania that the European war is not "worthy of the sacrifice of one American mule, much less one American son."

May 8: The Chamberlain government maintains a comfortable majority in the House of Commons although confidence in Chamberlain, ebbing since Britain's declaration of war, has plunged further over the continuing Allied debacle in Norway. Understanding this, Chamberlain seeks a successor. On May 9, he will summon both his foreign minister, Lord Halifax (a proponent of appeasement), and First Lord of the Admiralty Winston Churchill (long an opponent of appeasement) to a meeting.

May 10: Activating Hitler's long-planned *Operation (Case) Yellow*, German troops smash into the Low Countries and France. In Britain, Neville Chamberlain steps down as prime minister in favor of Winston Churchill, who quickly names himself minister of defense as well. On his first day in office, Churchill acts to protect Britain's transatlantic lifeline by sending troops to occupy the Danish dependency of Iceland. *Also this day:* President Roosevelt speaks at the Pan American Scientific Congress in Washington. After stating, "We are shocked and angered by the tragic news" from Europe, he notes, "In modern times it is a shorter distance from Europe to San Francisco, California, than it was for the ships and legions of Julius Caesar to move from Rome to Spain. . . . I am a pacifist, but I believe that by overwhelming majorities . . . you and I, in the long run if it be necessary, will act together to protect and defend by every means at our command our science, our culture, our American freedom and our civilization."

May 13: In Buckingham Palace, King George VI is awakened by a desperate phone call from Holland's Queen Wilhelmina, begging for British aircraft to help defend her country. The king passes the message along. Shortly thereafter, cautioned that she and her family might be taken hostage by the Germans, Wilhelmina, with Crown Princess Juliana and key government officials, boards the British destroyer *Hereward* and sails for England. *Meanwhile,* that afternoon, Churchill addresses the House of Commons. Declaring, "I have nothing to offer but blood, toil, tears and sweat," he describes what is to be his government's policy: "to wage war, by sea, land and air, with all our might and with all the strength that God can give us; to wage war against a monstrous tyranny, never surpassed in the dark, lamentable catalog of human crime."

May 14: Churchill receives a welcome message from Arthur Purvis, head of the Anglo-French purchasing mission in Washington. The Roosevelt administration will allow Britain to purchase 81 of 100 fighter planes then being built in America, and more than half the 324 planes already on order will be ready "within two to three months." This channeling of aircraft to Britain represents, Purvis notes, "real sacrifices by United States Services"—sacrifices about which the chiefs of U.S. armed forces are far from happy. Army Chief of Staff George C. Marshall, worried about having too few suitable aircraft for pilot training, will say, "I do not think we can afford to submit ourselves to the delay and consequences involved in accommodating the British Government."

May 15: Despairing French premier Paul Reynaud phones Churchill to declare, "We are beaten; we have lost the battle," though fighting will continue in France for another month. *That same day,* Churchill writes Roosevelt a brutally frank overview of the Anglo-French war situation and lists Britain's most desperate needs. Sixth among them: "I am looking to you to keep that Japanese dog quiet in the Pacific."

May 16: "These are ominous days," President Roosevelt states to a joint session of Congress. He then asks the legislature to authorize a tremendous increase in annual aircraft production: from the current level of 2,100 planes per year to 50,000. This "seemed at first like an utterly impossible goal," FDR adviser Edward R. Stettinius will later write, "but it caught the imagination of the Americans, who have always believed they could accomplish the impossible." In the same speech, the president notes "the treacherous use of the fifth column by which persons supposed to be peaceful visitors were actually a part of an enemy unit of occupation" in Europe. Wariness of similar subversion by visitors to the United States will blunt his support for the work of the refugee committee that First Lady Eleanor Roosevelt will soon chair. *At the same time,* U.S. Army maneuvers in Louisiana are going so poorly that *Time* magazine will report on May 27, "Against Europe's total war, the U.S. Army looked like a few nice boys with BB guns."

May 18: In a nationwide radio address, isolationist spokesman Charles Lindbergh accuses the Roosevelt administration of creating "a defense hysteria," and states that "there are powerful elements in America who desire us to take part" in the war—an evocation of the vested interests many Americans believed had pushed the country into World War I.

May 19: With Allied troops trapped in a pocket on the French coast, their backs to the sea, Churchill orders the British Admiralty to assemble "a large number of vessels" to engage in a rescue mission. The result will be "the miracle of Dunkirk" (see Chapter 6). *Also this day:* The *Non-Partisan Committee for Peace through Revision of the Neutrality Law,* formed after the outbreak of the European war in 1939 by American internationalists led by the Kansas newspaperman William

FIFTH-COLUMN FEARS

Fifth Column: a term coined in 1936 by General Emilio Mola during the Spanish Civil War when he boasted he had four columns of troops heading toward Madrid and a fifth column of sympathizers in the city itself.

In the years immediately preceding Pearl Harbor, the White House, Congress, the FBI, and the British all fueled public fear of subversive Axis activities in the United States. Stories of real Nazi spy rings, exaggerated in the media, also increased public apprehension about this danger. Fear peaked in 1940. Following the Wehrmacht's sweep through Norway, the Low Countries, and France, British newspapers carried stories about German spies disguised as priests, and postmen and German nationals in the Netherlands who helped invading parachutists. Later that summer, U.S. Colonel William J. Donovan (future head of the Office of Strategic Services) and journalist Edgar Mowrer asserted in a series of widely circulated articles, "It is conceivable that the United States possesses the finest Nazi-schooled fifth column in the world, one which, in case of war, could be our undoing."

FBI director J. Edgar Hoover also fueled American unease: between 1940 and 1942 (when Hollywood released seventy films dealing with fifth columnists), Hoover repeatedly averred that subversives had infiltrated every layer of American society. By 1943, however, after several successful FBI operations against saboteurs, he deemphasized the danger from the fifth column. (Oddly, though government and media feared Nazi intrigue, they had little concern over Italian or Japanese fifth columnists before Pearl Harbor.)

President Roosevelt also believed that Nazi fifth-column activities jeopardized American security. In a Fireside Chat on May 26, 1940, he told the American people:

Today's threat to our national security is not a matter of military weapons alone. We know of new methods of attack. The Trojan Horse. The Fifth Column that betrays a nation unprepared for treachery. Spies, saboteurs, and traitors are the actors in this new strategy. With all of this, we must and will deal vigorously.

Fifth-column fears contributed to the passage of the Alien Registration Act (see entry for June 29, 1940) and to the adoption of other measures—including the internment of Japanese Americans.

Allen White, is reorganized as the *Committee to Defend America by Aiding the Allies*. It will soon have more than six hundred local branches.

May 21: Sir Oswald Mosley, head of the British Union of Fascists, is imprisoned after saying, "I know I can save this country and that no one else can." Within a week, nearly four hundred other British fascists will also be incarcerated.

May 28: In Belgium, a cease-fire takes effect after King Leopold III, his armies shattered, surrenders unconditionally. In Paris, the Belgian government-in-exile repudiates the king's action as does the governor-general of the Belgian Congo, Pierre Ryckmans. Under his direction, the colony will increase war production of such vital resources as copper and uranium and recruit Congolese soldiers for service in Africa. *Also this day:* President Roosevelt announces the creation of the *National Defense Advisory Commission* (NDAC) to assist in coordinating civilian and military defense. The seven men he appoints to the commission represent two often warring elements: politically conservative businessmen and liberal supporters of Roosevelt's revolutionary Great-Depression-inspired New Deal program. *In Britain:* Foreign Minister Lord Halifax suggests accepting Mussolini's offer to mediate an Anglo-German settlement in a secret meeting of the war cabinet, prompting a thoroughly disgusted Churchill to tell the full cabinet: "Every man of you would rise up and tear me down from my place if I were for one moment to contemplate parley or surrender. If this long island history of ours is to end at last, let it end only when each one of us lies choking in his own blood upon the ground."

June 4: In a morale-lifting speech in the House of Commons, Churchill vows that England's people "will not flag or fail. . . . We shall defend our island, whatever the cost may be . . . until in God's good time, the new world, with all its power and might, steps forth to the rescue and the liberation of the old." *In the new world,* President Roosevelt agonizes over his chosen course of action—providing maximum possible aid to England—telling Secretary of the Interior Harold Ickes, "There is no use endangering ourselves unless we can achieve some results for the Allies."

June 6: After broadcasting to the Norwegian people the unhappy news that all military operations against the Germans had ceased, King Haakon VII, the royal family, and members of the government board the British cruiser *Devonshire,* pledging to "use all our strength, our life, and all we possess for Norway's cause" during their exile.

June 10: Moved by Germany's swift conquests, Mussolini declares war against Britain and France. Hitler mutters: "First they were too cowardly to take part. Now they are in a hurry so that they can share in the spoils." "The hand that held the dagger," Roosevelt says during a speech in Virginia, "has struck it into the back of its neighbor." Sending forth "our prayers and our hopes to those beyond the seas who are maintaining with magnificent valor their battle for freedom," the president also promises, in the same speech, to "extend to the opponents of force the material resources of this nation." *Time* magazine will report on June 17 that in this "fighting speech . . . the U.S. had taken sides . . . nothing remained now but to get on with the job."

June 12: As German forces come within twelve miles of the French capital, French officials protect Paris from bombardment by declaring it an open city. Evacuating the capital, the French government will relocate, first to Tours and then to Bordeaux, moving among throngs of civilians and military units that are clogging the roads, intermittently strafed by German aircraft. *Also this day:* Spain declares its neutrality.

June 14: German forces enter Paris. *Also this day:* President Roosevelt signs the *Eleven Percent Naval Expansion Act*.

June 16: After days of argument and agonizing—and the dispatch of a futile plea to President Roosevelt for a declaration of war or an open declaration of support—the French government determines that it is impossible to continue fighting, even from bases in France's North African colonies. French President Reynaud resigns and is succeeded by World War I hero Marshal Philippe Petain, who immediately seeks an armistice with the Germans. As negotiations begin, more than 160,000 Allied troops are evacuated from French ports to England. Among civilian evacuees are two scientists who carry with them the world's current supply of heavy water (deuterium oxide)—an element essential in the creation of a nuclear weapon.

June 18: On the same day that General Charles de Gaulle reaches Britain, determined to continue French resistance abroad, Soviet Foreign Minister Vyacheslav Molotov proffers to the German ambassador in Moscow, "the warmest congratulations of the Soviet Government on the splendid successes of the German Wehrmacht"—not realizing that the Wehrmacht's "spendid successes" mean that Hitler will now begin to plan in earnest the German invasion of the Soviet Union.

June 19: Watching events in Europe, the Japanese government announces its opposition to any change in the status quo of French Indochina and demands that Japan be allowed to establish a military mission there to make certain that the Haiphong-Yunnan railway sends no more supplies into China. General Georges Catroux (soon to join Charles de Gaulle's Free French forces) sees no way to stop them. Very soon, the new Vichy French government will send Vice-Admiral Jean Decoux to replace Catroux. When the Japanese make additional demands, Vichy will order him to negotiate rather than resist. This comports with Japanese plans to control Indochina through the existing French administration—while expropriating the region's rich resources.

June 20: Roosevelt announces a sweeping reorganization of his cabinet. Firing Secretary of War Henry Woodring, who opposes sending munitions to Britain, the president replaces him with conservative Republican Henry Stimson—a paragon of the Eastern Establishment who served as secretary of war under William Taft and secretary of state under Herbert Hoover. Roosevelt also appoints *Chicago Daily News* publisher Frank Knox as secretary of the navy. An unstinting critic of the New Deal, Knox was the Republican candidate for vice-president in 1936. Stimson and Knox have one valuable trait in common: they ardently oppose isolationism. Reflecting a general sentiment (some angry Republicans notwithstanding), *New York Herald Tribune* columnist Dorothy Thompson writes: "Not since that titanic conservative, Alexander Hamilton,

The national unity cabinet served through the war with very little change. Pictured along with other advisers are (clockwise from foreground): Harry L. Hopkins, presidential aide/advisory; Secretary of Labor Frances Perkins; Admiral William D. Leahy, chief of staff; Vice President Henry A. Wallace; Civil Defense director Fiorello H. LaGuardia; Federal Security Administrator Paul V. McNutt; Secretary of Commerce Jesse H. Jones; Secretary of the Interior Harold Ickes; Postmaster General Frank C. Walker; Secretary of War Henry L. Stimson; Secretary of State Cordell Hull; President Roosevelt; Secretary of the Treasury Henry Morgenthau, Jr.; Attorney General Francis Biddle; Secretary of the Navy Frank Knox; and Secretary of Agriculture Claude R. Wickard. Hull resigned because of health problems, and Knox died in 1944. Harry S. Truman became president in 1945.

handed the election of 1800 to his hated rival, the liberal Jefferson, to save and unite the nation in a time of crisis, has a political leader of America made a more magnanimous and whole-hearted gesture." *Also this day:* First Lady Eleanor Roosevelt meets with the newly formed *U.S. Committee for the Care of European Children,* of which she is honorary chair. Formed to coordinate refugee assistance organizations and resources, the committee will repeatedly meet resistance from Breckinridge Long, head of the State Department's Special War Problems Division—which includes the visa section. Wary of Fifth-Columnists, Long generally opposes the admission of refugees.

June 21: On the same day that Hitler presents surrender terms to a French delegation at a historic site outside Compiegne, France, Senator David I. Walsh (Dem. Mass.) opposes providing American armaments to Britain: "I do not want our forces deprived of one gun, or one bomb or one ship which can aid that American boy whom you and I may some day have to draft." *Also this*

First Lady Eleanor Roosevelt was nearly in perpetual motion, visiting factories, touring overseas bases, writing her "My Day" newspaper column, promoting civil rights for African Americans—and serving as FDR's eyes and ears. In February 1944, photographer Joseph A. Horne photographed her enjoying a performance by folk singer Pete Seeger at the opening of a servicemen's canteen in the nation's capital.

PROMINENT U.S. POLITICAL FIGURES

**President (1941–April 1945): Franklin Delano Roosevelt
(April 1945–August 1945): Harry S. Truman** (See Chapter 4.)

Bullitt, William C. (1891–1967)	In the early 1930s, Bullitt attempted to forge a positive U.S.–Soviet relationship. He seemed successful, but became disillusioned when, as ambassador to the USSR from 1933 to 1936, he realized that Stalin would not keep his earlier agreements. Roosevelt did not accept his warnings about Soviet imperialism. He served as ambassador to France from 1936 to 1941.
Byrnes, James F. (1879–1972)	Known as the "assistant president," Byrnes, a former Democratic senator, served as director of the Office of Economic Stabilization (1942) and, beginning in May 1943, the Office of War Mobilization. He was highly influential in shaping the wartime economy.
Dewey, Thomas E. (1902–1971)	Known as a "racket buster" who tamed organized crime and corruption as the district attorney of New York County, Dewey served as governor of New York from 1942 to 1954. He was the unsuccessful Republican nominee for president in 1944 (losing to Roosevelt) and 1948 (losing to Truman).
Harriman, W. Averell (1891–1986)	After a short stint at the War Department, Harriman became the administrator of the Lend-Lease program in Britain. He also handled Lend-Lease payments to the Soviet Union, where he served as American ambassador from 1943 to 1946.
Hastie, William H. (1904–1976)	Hastie was a law professor at Howard University and the first African American to serve as a federal judge; Roosevelt appointed him to a post in the Virgin Islands in 1937. He served as Secretary of War Henry Stimson's civilian aide from 1941 to 1943, resigning in protest of racial segregation in the military. He remained a civil rights advocate and activist attorney.
Hopkins, Harry (1890–1946)	An ardent New Dealer, Hopkins was Roosevelt's trusted adviser and an aide to the president at most Allied conferences. He briefly directed the Lend-Lease program. He developed good relationships with Churchill and Stalin, as well as American military leaders, serving at times as liaison between them and Roosevelt.

PROMINENT U.S. POLITICAL FIGURES (CONTINUED)

Nye, Gerald
(1892–1971)

North Dakota Republican Senator Nye was a leading isolationist opposing American entry into World War II. From 1934 to 1936, he chaired the Senate Munitions Committee ("Nye Committee"), which investigated the influence of American weapons manufacturers (who made a huge profit) on the decision to enter World War I. Nye was a leading force behind the passage of the Neutrality Acts in the 1930s.

Rayburn, Sam
(1882–1961)

A Texas Democrat, elected to Congress in 1912, who served until his death in 1961. He commenced his long service as a powerful speaker of the House of Representatives (or minority leader when the Democrats were not in power) in 1940. He was a vocal supporter of Roosevelt's New Deal, guiding much legislation through Congress, and also ensured that the legislature would provide adequate financial support for fighting the war.

Roosevelt, Eleanor
(1884–1962)

The First Lady was briefly the assistant director of the Office of Civilian Defense, but resigned because her actions opened FDR to political attacks. Instead, she was an advocate for women's participation in wartime work, integration of the armed forces, and the safety of refugees. Journalist Raymond Clapper wrote that she had "almost the importance of a cabinet minister without portfolio," in her influence on FDR.

Willkie, Wendell
(1892–1944)

Nominated by the Republicans, Willkie lost the presidential election to Roosevelt in 1940, but supported Roosevelt's internationalist policies and the Lend-Lease program. At the president's request, he was an effective goodwill ambassador to the Middle East, the Soviet Union, and China; and his resulting book, *One World* (1943), was a best seller.

Note: For cabinet members, see picture.

day: the Polish government-in-exile reaches London after being forced from its first refuge in Paris.

June 22: As the Franco-German Armistice is signed in the Forest of Compiégne, Roosevelt meets with his army and navy chiefs to discuss their assessments of a list of strategic assumptions he sent them on June 13. They disagree with him on several accounts—particularly doubting that Britain will survive and objecting to his decision to keep a major portion of the U.S. fleet at Pearl Harbor (see Chapter 4).

June 24: Anticipating a German invasion, the British government sends a shipment of gold bullion and securities, code-named *Fish,* to Canada for safekeeping.

June 24–28: The Republican National Convention nominates Wendell L. Willkie of Indiana as its candidate for the presidency.

June 25: In Britain, the government detains more than 10,000 Italians between the ages of 17 and 60 as "enemy aliens" along with about 50,000 Germans and Austrians—many of them Jewish refugees. Some 14,000 of those detained are placed in internment camps on the Isle of Man.

June 27: In the wake of King Carol II's refusal to cede the territories of Bessarabia and Bukovina to the USSR, Soviet troops invade Romania. Determined to maintain good relations with the Soviets for the present, Hitler counsels the Romanians to accede to the Soviet demands.

June 29: President Roosevelt signs the *Alien Registration Act* (Smith Act), requiring the registration and fingerprinting of all aliens living in the United States. The act also streamlines deportation procedures and forbids any person to "knowingly or willfully advocate, abet, advise, or teach the duty, necessity, desirability, or propriety of overthrowing or destroying any government in the United States by force or violence." In this time of pressing threats, the measure sailed through Congress, despite questions about the encroachment on civil liberties—although some legislators, among them Democrat Emmanuel Celler of Brooklyn, support the bill only "in fear of a worse one." During this first complete U.S. inventory of noncitizens, some 5 million aliens will register (among them, 600,000 Italians, 260,000 Germans, and 40,000 Japanese)—under circumstances particularly structured to make them feel at ease. (As Solicitor General Francis Biddle will note, they had all "seen Hitler register the Jews as a preliminary to stripping them of their rights.") Current and future attorneys general Frank Murphy, Robert H. Jackson, and Biddle—who remember the vigilantism and prosecutorial excesses of the World War I era—all oppose the bill. Throughout the war, there will be only two prosecutions under the Smith Act.

June 30: As Britain prepares for a German invasion—and despite memories of its horrific effects on the Western Front during World War I—the British Cabinet approves the use of poison gas against the invaders.

July 2: Congress passes an Export Control Act, giving the president power to halt or curtail the export of materials vital to U.S. defense. Under this act, President Roosevelt will embargo the sale of an increasing number of materials to Japan, contributing to the rise of tensions between the two nations.

July 15: The Democratic National Convention nominates Franklin D. Roosevelt for an unprecedented third presidential term. To help get Henry A. Wallace on the ballot as vice presidential candidate, Eleanor Roosevelt becomes the first wife of a nominee ever to address a national political convention. "This is no ordinary time," she tells the delegates. "No man who is a candidate or who is president can carry this situation alone. This responsibility is only carried by a united people who love their country and who will live for it . . . to the fullest of their ability." Wallace receives the required votes on the first ballot.

July 18: Facing the threat of invasion at home and not wishing to face another belligerent in its Far Eastern territories, the British accede to Japanese demands and close the Burma Road. China is thus deprived of its main supply line. Britain will reopen the road in October, but it will be closed again as war rages throughout the Far East in 1942.

July 19: President Roosevelt signs the *Two-Ocean Navy Expansion Act*, which authorizes a stunning 70 percent increase in U.S. naval strength.

July 22: As Japanese frustration over the military stalemate in China builds, and debate continues over the correct route for Japanese expansion, a new government, under Prime Minister Prince Fumimaro Konoye, assumes power in Japan.

July 26: Attempting to restrain Japanese expansionist policies, the United States embargoes shipments of high-octane aviation fuel and premium scrap iron and steel.

August 18: The Ogdensburg (New York) Agreement between the United States and Canada calls for the establishment of a Permanent Joint Board on Defense.

August 27: Congress authorizes a one-year call-up of the National Guard. *In Africa,* the Free French take control of Cameroon; they will take Brazzaville the next day.

September 3: President Roosevelt sends a message to Congress announcing the exchange arrangement whereby Britain will receive 50 "over-age" U.S. destroyers in return for giving the United States the right to lease naval and air bases in Newfoundland, on several Caribbean islands, and in British Guiana. Undertaken to provide aid to Britain while strengthening U.S. coastal defenses, the deal is suspiciously regarded by American isolationists. The next day, the newly formed *America First Committee* will issue its first public statement in which it declares that the president's policy of providing "aid short of war" to the Allies "weakens national defense at home and threatens to involve America in war abroad."

September 5: In the wake of Romania's territorial concessions to the USSR, which he opposed, General Ion Antonescu is appointed premier of Romania. He will force King Carol II to abdicate in favor of the king's 19-year-old son and quickly imposes dictatorial rule that will see the arrest of democratic leaders and the persecution of Jews by members of Romania's fascist Iron Guard.

September 16: Congress approves the Selective Training and Service Act, the first peacetime conscription in U.S. history. All men between the ages of 20 and 36 are required to register; within two years, the age requirement will be amended to include men between 18 and 65. By the end of 1942, there will be 43 million registrants. (See Chapter 3.)

September 27: In Berlin, Italy, Japan, and Germany strengthen the Axis alliance by signing the Tripartite Pact, a ten-year military and economic agreement. The United States government will quickly embargo *all* shipments of iron and steel to Japan. U.S. Ambassador Joseph Kennedy cables Washington from London: "Britain is doomed."

PROMINENT AXIS POLITICAL FIGURES

Germany
Head of State: Adolf Hitler (See Chapter 4.)

Bormann, Martin (1900–1945)	Chief of Staff to Deputy Führer Rudolf Hess (1933–1941), head of Nazi Party chancellery (1941–1943), head of the Volkssturm civil defense force (1944–1945). Six months after the Nazis came to power, Bormann was appointed by Hitler to be Hess's chief of staff. In April 1943, he became Hitler's personal secretary, and remained the führer's shadowy right-hand man until the end. After leaving the Berlin bunker where Hitler committed suicide, he was either killed or committed suicide on May 2, 1945. Because this fact was not known at the time, Bormann was sentenced to death in absentia at the Nuremberg war crimes trials in 1946.
Freisler, Rolande (1893–1945)	State Secretary in the Ministry of Justice (1934–1942), President of the People's Court (1942–1945). Served as a Nazi judge and presided over the trial of the co-conspirators in the July 1944 bomb plot against Hitler. Killed in Berlin during an American air raid on February 3, 1945.
Goebbels, Joseph (1897–1945)	Gauleiter of Berlin and Nazi propaganda chief (1930–1933), Reich Minister for Propaganda and National Enlightenment (1933–1945). The mastermind behind Hitler's public image, Goebbels introduced the phrase "Heil Hitler" and the title

PROMINENT AXIS POLITICAL FIGURES (CONTINUED)

"führer" into Nazi vocabulary and made their use mandatory. He understood radio's potential as a propaganda tool, drawing huge radio audiences for his speeches. In 1935, he introduced the world's first regular television service in Berlin. In 1944, after the assassination attempt against Hitler, he was appointed Reich Plenipotentiary for Total War. Loyal to the end, on May 1, 1945, the day after Hitler committed suicide, he and his wife killed their six children and then committed suicide.

Göring, Hermann (1893–1946)

Nazi Reichstag deputy (1928–1932), president of the Reichstag (1932), Reich commissioner for aviation (1933), Commander in Chief of the Luftwaffe (1935–1945), Special Commissioner for the Four Year Economic Plan (1936), Minister of Economic Affairs (1937–1945). A decorated fighter pilot in World War I, Göring was one of the first Nazis elected to the Reichstag. By the following year, he was second in command in Germany. In 1933, he established his own intelligence agency, the *Forschungsamt* (Research Office), within his Air Ministry to intercept communications, tap telephones, open mail, and decode telegrams. He created the first Nazi concentration camps and ordered Reinhard Heydrich to prepare for the "overall solution of the Jewish problem." In July 1940, after the Reich's lightning victories in western Europe, he was promoted to Reichsmarschall. After the Luftwaffe failed in the Battle of Britain and at Stalingrad, Hitler's faith in him waned. Addicted to morphine in the 1920s, he was a man of huge appetites—for gaudy uniforms, looted works of art, wealth, and power. In April 1945, when he suggested he assume power as Hitler was trapped in Berlin, the fürher fired him and had him placed under house arrest. Sentenced to death at Nuremberg, he committed suicide by swallowing a cyanide capsule on October 15, 1945, just before he was to be hanged.

Hess, Rudolf (1894–1987)

Member of Hitler's Cabinet Council (1933–1941) and Nazi party deputy. During World War I, he served in the same

(continued)

PROMINENT AXIS POLITICAL FIGURES (CONTINUED)

regiment as Hitler, where he was twice wounded. He joined the Nazi party in 1920. While sharing a cell with Hitler in Landsberg Prison after the Beer Hall Putsch, he wrote down *Mein Kampf* as Hitler dictated it to him. In 1941, without Hitler's knowledge or approval, he flew to Scotland to present a peace proposal to the British government. Jailed by the British, Hess was sentenced at Nuremberg to life imprisonment, which he served at Spandau prison in Berlin.

Heinrich Himmler
(1900–1945)

Head of the SS (1929–1945), Chief of the Gestapo, the secret state police (1934–1945), Minister of the Interior (1943–1945), Chief of the Home Army (1944–1945). As head of the SS (Nazi party protection squads), Himmler accumulated great power; his organization eventually became dominant in every aspect of state security and domestic policy. He established Dachau, one of the first Nazi concentration camps, in 1933, and after the invasion of Poland, he oversaw all racial matters as Reich Commissioner for the Strengthening of German Nationhood. As Minister of the Interior, he was responsible for the administration of the "Final Solution" and forced labor, and authorized SS doctors' medical experiments. Without Hitler's consent, he tried to negotiate Germany's surrender in April 1945. When that failed, he disguised himself and unsuccessfully attempted to elude the Allies. He killed himself on May 23, 1945, by taking potassium cyanide.

Ley, Robert
(1890–1945)

Reich Organization Leader (1932—1945). Destroyed the free trade unions when he founded the German Labor Front (DAF) in 1933. He later founded the successful *Kraft durch Freude* (KdF or Strength Through Joy) organization, which offered workers leisure activities that complied with Nazi principles. He hanged himself on October 25, 1945.

Ribbentrop, Joachim von
(1893–1946)

Plenipotentiary for Matters of Disarmament (1934), Ambassador Extraordinary of the German Reich on Special Mission (1935), Ambassador to Great Britain (1936–1938), Foreign

PROMINENT AXIS POLITICAL FIGURES (CONTINUED)

Minister (1938–1945). Awarded the Iron Cross for bravery during World War I, he was transferred to the intelligence division. His friend Himmler made him an honorary SS-Gruppenführer in 1936. In November 1936, he persuaded Japan to join the Anti-Comintern Pact, and in 1939 he negotiated the agreement with the Soviet Union to attack and divide Poland. He later directly supervised *Pers-z*, the Foreign Office's cryptanalytic and cryptographic service and started his own spy service (*Informationsstelle III*) and a new radio monitoring service that he was forced to share with Joseph Goebbels. For his role in encouraging Germany's allies to exterminate Jews, he was sentenced to death at Nuremberg and hanged on October 16, 1946.

Speer, Albert
(1905–1981)

Reich Minister of Armaments and Munitions (1942); Minister for Armaments and War Production (1943–1945). An architect, Speer joined the Nazi Party in 1932 and choreographed the spectacle of the 1934 Nuremberg rally. As Minister for Armaments and War Production, he oversaw Germany's war economy and armament production, tripling its output in three years. By 1945, Speer had grown disillusioned with Hitler and refused his orders to implement a "scorched earth" policy as German troops retreated. At Nuremberg, he was given a twenty-year sentence for using forced labor to meet industrial goals.

Italy
Monarch: King Victor Emmanuel III (See Chapter 4.)
Head of State: Benito Mussolini (See Chapters 1 and 4.)

Badoglio, Marshal Pietro
(1871–1956)

Formerly chief of the Italian general staff (see Chapter 4); became head of the government after Mussolini's ouster in 1943. He negotiated and signed the surrender to the Allies and declared war on Germany. After a year, he finally convinced the anti-Fascist parties to enter his government; he was forced to resign in June 1944.

Bonomi, Ivanoe
(1873–1951)

An anti-Fascist who retired after Mussolini consolidated his power, then resumed anti-Fascist activity in 1942. After Italy's surrender,

(continued)

PROMINENT AXIS POLITICAL FIGURES (CONTINUED)

he became president of the *Committee of National Liberation* (CLN), comprising all the anti-Fascist parties. In June 1944, after the Allies entered Rome, he headed a new cabinet and was instrumental in defusing revolutionary pressures that had built up during the war.

Ciano, Count Galeazzo (1903–1944)

Mussolini's son-in-law; a minor diplomat who became head of the Ministry of Press and Propaganda (1935), was a bomber pilot in the Abyssinian war, then was appointed foreign minister (1936–February 1943). He promoted Italian participation in the Spanish Civil War, the invasion of Albania, and the disastrous invasion of Greece (1940–1941); he kept a diary that reveals much about people, places, and events pertaining to the Italian/German Alliance. After being demoted to ambassador to the Holy See (1943), he fell in with anti-Mussolini conspirators and voted for Mussolini's ouster. He was captured by the Germans and executed, January 11, 1944.

Farinacci, Roberto (1892–1945)

A militant Fascist who participated in the March on Rome (see Chapter 1) and sought total Fascist-Party control over the state (unlike Mussolini, who tried to accommodate a number of powerful groups). He pressed for the alliance with Germany and favored harsh treatment of Italian Jews. After Mussolini's ouster, he was influential in the short-lived Italian Social Republic—Mussolini's Fascist regime in northern Italy (1943–1945), fostered by the Germans. He was executed by partisans in April 1945.

Grandi, Dino (1895–1988)

Fascist official who participated in the March on Rome, served on the Fascist Grand Council, and was ambassador to Britain (1932–1939). Becoming less militant, he was named minister of justice and president of the Chamber of Fasces and Corporations in 1939. He supported Mussolini's declaration of war, but began pressing for a new government after the debacle in Greece. At a Fascist Grand Council meeting in July 1943, he presented the resolution that resulted in Mussolini's ouster. He was sentenced to death *in absentia* by both Fascist and anti-Fascist tribunals, but was granted amnesty.

PROMINENT AXIS POLITICAL FIGURES (CONTINUED)

Japan
Monarch: Hirohito (See Chapter 4.)
Head of State: Prime Minister (See following entries.)

Higashikuni, Prince Naruhiko (1887–1990)	Headed the Home Defense Command (December 1941–April 1945), but opposed Tojo's extreme militarism, advocated his resignation, and supported making peace with the Allies. On August 17, 1945, he formed the first postwar cabinet, but resigned as prime minister in October.
Koiso, Kuniaki (1880–1950)	Former governor-general of Korea; succeeded Tojo as prime minister (July 1944–April 1945), opposing those who favored negotiating a peace. He resigned after his failure to also become war minister and died while serving a life sentence for war crimes.
Konoe, Fumimaro (1891–1945)	Former member of the House of Peers, Prince Konoe headed three cabinets between 1937 and 1941. Oversaw passage of the National Mobilization Bill (March 1938), entered the Tripartite Pact (September 1940) and worked towards greater national unity. Oversaw formation of the Imperial Rule Assistance Association to replace political parties (October 1940). He tried to avoid war with the United States before resigning in October 1941. In 1945, he advocated Tojo's resignation and negotiating with the United States. After arrest by the Allies, he committed suicide, December 1945.
Oshima, Hiroshi (1886–1975)	Military attaché to Berlin during the 1930s, Lieutenant General Oshima served twice as ambassador to Germany (1938–1939; 1941–1945). He negotiated on both the Anti-Comintern Pact and the Tripartite Pact. Pro-Nazi and friendly with Hitler, he unwittingly assisted the Allies when his communications with Japan regarding meetings with Hitler and German war strategy were tapped by Allied intelligence. Sentenced to life in prison for war crimes, he was paroled in 1955.

(continued)

PROMINENT AXIS POLITICAL FIGURES (CONTINUED)

Shigemitsu, Mamoru (1887–1957)	Ambassador to the USSR (1936–1938), Britain (1938–1941) and to Wang Ching-wei's collaborationist Chinese government (1942), before becoming foreign minister in Tojo's cabinet in April 1943. After Tojo's resignation in 1944, he served as foreign minister and minister for Greater East Asia in the Koiso cabinet. As the first postwar foreign minister, he attended the official surrender ceremonies on September 2, 1945. Sentenced to seven years for war crimes, he was released in 1950.
Togo, Shigenori (1882–1950)	Ambassador to Germany (1937–1938) and the USSR (1938–1940); became foreign minister under Tojo in October 1941. Continued trying to negotiate a settlement with the United States as Japan prepared for war. Resigned September 1942 after creation of the Greater East Asia Ministry, which marginalized the Foreign Ministry. Served in the House of Peers until April 1945, when he again became foreign minister. He supported negotiations with the Allies and opposed Japan fighting to the end. Sentenced to twenty years labor for war crimes, he died in prison in July 1950.
Tojo, Hideki (1884–1948)	An army general who was appointed Prime Minister in October 1941; during his term, he also served as army minister, foreign minister, home minister, army chief of staff, and director of the ministry of munitions—though never all at once. Although he enjoyed the most consolidated political power of any Japanese prime minister, he was never a true dictator. He urged the cabinet toward war with the United States and attempted to reorganize the Diet. He resigned in July 1944 in the wake of battlefield disasters and criticism from political opponents. He shot himself, August 1945, but recovered. Convicted of war crimes, he was hanged, December 22, 1948.

Vichy France

Marshal Henri-Philippe Pétain (1856–1951)	A World War I military hero, Pétain was appointed minister of state and vice-premier by Prime Minister Paul Reynaud as France faced imminent defeat in May 1940. Immediately after replacing Reynaud in June, Pétain deemed it hopeless to continue

PROMINENT AXIS POLITICAL FIGURES (CONTINUED)

After France fell in June 1940, the Germans ruled with an iron hand in the north, while allowing 84-year-old Marshal Henri Philippe Pétain (left) to set up an ostensibly independent government at Vichy in the south. Pétain's powerful vice-premier, Pierre Laval (center, in a wartime drawing by Edwin Marcus) initiated and avidly pursued the collaborationist policy under which Vichy operated. Meanwhile, Charles de Gaulle (right) emerged as the leader of the Free French resistance to the Axis and its Vichy collaborators.

fighting the Germans and negotiated for an armistice. As head of the French government at Vichy with near-dictatorial powers, he sought unsuccessfully to collaborate with Germany on an equal basis; supposedly independent, Vichy came increasingly under Germany's thumb. Remote and austere, Pétain was dissatisfied with his vice-premier, Pierre Laval, and made him resign, but was forced by the Germans to take him back. Although he resigned and fled from France after the Allied landings, Pétain returned of his own accord early in 1945 and was placed on trial for treason. (See also entry for July 23, 1945.)

Pierre Laval
(1883–1945)

Vichy Vice-Premier, Minister of Foreign Affairs, and Minister of State (July–December 1940); Vice Premier, Minister of State, Minister of the Interior, Minister of Foreign Affairs, and Minister of Information (April 1942–1944); President of the Milice (January 1943–1944). Laval, an oft-disliked right-wing politician

(continued)

PROMINENT AXIS POLITICAL FIGURES (CONTINUED)

known for cultivating closer relations with the Germans than any other minister, introduced the constitution that made Pétain dictator. Although he accepted an ideological partnership with fascist Germany, he offered only small concessions until pressured into handing over foreign Jews and making French labor service compulsory. After fleeing from France at the behest of the Germans, he was forced to return. Convicted of treason, he was executed by a French firing squad.

Admiral Jean François Darlan (1881–1942)

Commander of French Naval Forces (1939–July 1940); Minister of Marine (July 1940–April 1942); Vice-premier, Minister of Foreign Affairs, Minister of Information, and Minister of the Interior (February 1941–April 1942); Commander-in-Chief of French army (April–December 1942). A powerful Vichy figure and no friend of the British (particularly after they destroyed French vessels at Mers-el-Kébir; see Chapter 6), Darlan nevertheless issued orders that the remaining French fleet be scuttled should the Germans ever attempt to possess it—and this was done in 1942. Yet he also collaborated with the Germans. In May 1941, he initialed the Paris Protocols, by which Vichy gained certain concessions in return for ceding Germany military facilities in Syria, Tunisia, and French West Africa. (Although unratified, this agreement sparked the successful British-Free French Syrian campaign of June–July 1941.) Replaced as vice-premier by Laval in April 1942, Darlan remained in overall command of Vichy French forces. By happenstance, he was in Algiers at the time of the Allied North African landings and, after extensive negotiations, arranged a cease-fire. He subsequently agreed to work for the Allies, who appointed him high commissioner for French North Africa. But he served little more than a month before he was assassinated. (See also entry for December 24, 1942.)

Darnand, Joseph (1897–1945)

In 1940, as head of the Légion Français de Combattants, Darnand created a fascist military elite, the Service d'Ordre Légionnaire (SOL), which swore allegiance to Pétain and aided the

PROMINENT AXIS POLITICAL FIGURES (CONTINUED)

Germans. In January 1943, the SOL became the Milice Française, a 30,000-member Vichy paramilitary police force that swore an oath condemning democracy, bolshevism, and "Jewish leprosy." The Milice helped the Germans fight the French resistance forces and round up Jews for deportation and were noted for ruthlessness and brutality. As the Vichy regime began to collapse, it effectively became a Milice-run police state. The Allies brought Darnand to trial and executed him for war crimes.

Principal sources: Robert Aron, *The Vichy Regime: 1940–1944*, Boston: Beacon Press, 1969; Frank J. Coppa, ed., *Dictionary of Modern Italian History*, Westport, CT: Greenwood Press, 1985; James McClain, *Japan: A Modern History*, New York: W. W. Norton, 2002; Anthony Read, *The Devil's Disciples: Hitler's Inner Circle*, New York: W. W. Norton, 2004; Peter N. Stearns, ed., *The Encyclopedia of World History*, 6th ed., Boston: Houghton Mifflin, 2001; I. C. B. Dear and M. R. D. Foot, eds., *The Oxford Companion to World War II*, Oxford: Oxford University Press, 2001.

October 7: Japan protests the U.S. embargo of a growing number of items—from steel scraps to aviation fuel—as "an unfriendly act." *Also this day:* German troops move into Romania, ostensibly to train Romanian soldiers—but more importantly to protect the vitally important Ploesti oil fields.

October 12: In Japan, a coalition of extreme nationalist groups form the *Imperial Rule Association,* aspiring to build a mass party similar to Germany's Nazis. All Japanese are by now required to belong to neighborhood associations. These *tonarigumis* will be an effective means of social control throughout the war; their members are encouraged to report misdeeds to Japan's Thought Police and other authorities.

October 13: "It is wrong to help the British war effort with men or money: the only worthy effort is to resist all war with non-violent resistance." Under this slogan, the anticolonial Indian National Congress initiates a program of civil disobedience; the British will eventually jail some 14,000 Indian antiwar protesters.

October 23: After a nine-hour meeting at Hendaye, on the French-Spanish border, Hitler fails to persuade Francisco Franco to bring Spain into the war. Franco evades, dodges, and ducks the führer's arguments and territorial offers in a dull monotone that drives Hitler to moments of furious anger. "Rather than go through that again," he will later tell Mussolini, "I would prefer

Although considered divine by the Japanese people, Emperor Hirohito was severely constrained in his exercise of political power. The victorious Allies allowed him to remain as emperor although he was no longer to be considered divine. Late in 1945, photographer Tom Shafer was present as Hirohito addressed the formal opening of the Japanese Diet in Tokyo.

to have three or four teeth yanked out." *The next day,* he has better luck with the head of the Vichy-French government, Marshal Philippe Pétain, whom he convinces to state, in writing: "The Axis Powers and France have an identical interest in seeing the defeat of England accomplished as soon as possible. Consequently, the French Government will support, within the limits of its ability, the measures which the Axis Powers may take to this end." In return, Hitler promises France a fitting place in his "New Europe" and compensation—in British imperial holdings—for any territory France may be forced to cede.

November 5: Franklin Delano Roosevelt is elected for an unprecedented third term as president of the United States.

November 20: Hungary joins the Axis.

November 27: Four days after Romania joins the Axis, the country is wracked by riots after dictator Antonescu's Iron Guard execute sixty-four officials of the deposed king's government.

November 26: In Africa, Niger and Chad declare themselves in favor of the Free French.

November 30: Wang Ching-wei, head of the collaborationist Central Government of China, signs a treaty giving Japan effective control of China's mineral resources. *Also this day:* President Roosevelt announces a substantial increase in American financial aid to Nationalist Chinese leader Chiang Kai-shek.

December 9: On a postelection vacation in the Caribbean, President Roosevelt receives a painstakingly crafted letter from Winston Churchill outlining the challenges, including lack of finances, that Britain is facing as the only combatant nation standing against the Nazis. The letter will serve as the catalyst for development of the American Lend-Lease program.

December 17: In the United States, as the number of men objecting to the military draft for reasons of conscience increases, the first of 151 Civilian Public Service camps for conscientious objectors is established.

December 19: The day after signing the draft of *Barbarossa*—the plan for invading the Soviet Union—Hitler politely receives the credentials of the new Soviet Ambassador, V. G. Dekanozov.

December 29: In a Fireside Chat, President Roosevelt tells the nation, "We must be the great arsenal of democracy." Those standing against Hitler, the president says, "do not ask us to do their fighting. They ask us for the implements of war. . . . Emphatically we must get these weapons to them in sufficient volume and quickly enough, so that we and our children will be saved the agony and suffering of war which others have had to endure."

1941: A Second *World* War

January 6: In his annual address to Congress, President Roosevelt calls for a "swift and driving increase in our armament production" as part of a campaign to achieve a secure world founded on four essential freedoms: freedom of speech and expression; freedom of worship; freedom from want; and freedom from fear. In the same speech, the president initiates a debate on what will become the U.S. Lend-Lease program by noting that the Allied nations now at war are growing short of resources. "We cannot, and we will not, tell them they must surrender," the president says, "merely because of present inability to pay for the weapons which we know they must have."

February 6: As the Germans begin covertly transporting troops to the east in preparation for the invasion of the Soviet Union, and British and American military staffs begin very-low-profile talks in Washington (so as not to disturb remaining isolationists or jeopardize passage of the Lend-Lease bill), a new Japanese ambassador arrives in the United States. Kichisaburo Nomura declares: "There is no question whatsoever outstanding between the two countries which cannot be settled in an amicable and satisfactory manner through a timely display of statesmanship by the respective peoples of both sides."

March 1: A Special Senate *Committee to Investigate the National Defense Program* is created, with Senator Harry S. Truman as chairman. The Truman Committee proceeds to investigate and expose profiteering, mismanagement, the undue influence of international cartels, and other problems in American defense industries, and to enhance Truman's reputation for honesty.

March 11: President Roosevelt signs the *Lend-Lease Act,* hallmark legislation that will precipitate a flow of war matériel to war-pressed Allied nations unable to make immediate payment. Isolationists insert some restrictive language in the legislation including a clause that reads: "Nothing in this Act shall be construed to authorize or to permit the authorization of convoying vessels by naval vessels of the United States." Administration officials agreed to the language—while maintaining that the president had sufficient constitutional authority to order naval escorts for convoys on his own. The administration will establish an Office of Lend-Lease Administration that will be active throughout the war. Initially, Britain is the principal beneficiary of the new program, but the new act also allows the consideration of direct military aid to Chiang Kai-shek's Nationalist Chinese.

March 27: Yugoslavia's regent, Prince Paul, is deposed two days after finally signing the Axis Tripartite Pact and agreeing to let German troops through his country to reinforce the Italians who are bogged down in a disastrous campaign in Greece (see Chapter 6). Infuriated by new Prime Minister Dusan Simovic's opposition to German passage through his country, Hitler tells his military commanders to "smash Yugoslavia militarily, and as a State." His decision to invade Greece and Yugoslavia simultaneously is accompanied by a decision to postpone the invasion of the USSR until June 22.

April 6: The British enter Addis Ababa, Abyssinia—the first national capital liberated from the Axis.

April 10: Employing creative logic to comply with Selective Service restrictions on where U.S. draftees may serve, President Roosevelt declares the remote Danish colony of Greenland part of the Western Hemisphere and announces its occupation by American forces. Some two months later, he will employ similar logic to justify the occupation of another Danish territory—Iceland.

April 13: Soviet and Japanese authorities sign a *Pact of Neutrality* in Moscow.

April 23: Sixteen American conscientious objectors who have been jailed for their refusal to serve in the military or in Civilian Public Service camps refuse to eat or work after the warden stops them from supporting a national student strike for peace. Throughout the war, more than 6,000 objectors will be sent to prison, about 75 percent of them Jehovah's Witnesses. Others will include Nation of Islam leader Elijah Muhammad, jazz musician Sun Ra, members of the traditionally pacifist Hopi Indian nation, Puerto Ricans protesting their island's colonial status—and seventy-three Japanese-Americans who receive their draft notices while they and their families are imprisoned in internment camps.

May 1: U.S. Defense Savings Bonds and Stamps go on sale.

May 6: Consolidating his already supreme authority, Joseph Stalin replaces V. M. Molotov as chairman of the Council of People's Commissars (*Sovnarkom*), a post generally regarded as equivalent to prime minister of the Soviet Union. Molotov retains his position as minister and also assumes the duties of vice-chairman of *Sovnarkom.*

May 10: One year after the start of the German blitzkrieg through Western Europe, Germany's deputy führer, Rudolf Hess, stuns his fellow Nazis by expropriating a Messerschmitt 110 fighter plane and flying to Scotland, apparently to try to arrange a peace settlement with the British. Hitler reacts, his chief translator Dr. Paul Schmitt will report, "as though a bomb had struck the Berghof" and begins to mutter that Hess must have gone crazy. As the German government scrambles to create some plausible explanation to the public, Allied leaders respond with a mixture of confusion and suspicion. Somewhat muddled of mind, Hess will remain in Allied custody throughout the war, be sentenced to life imprisonment at the postwar Nuremberg trials, and will die while still in prison in 1987.

May 15: Richard Sorge, an accomplished and trusted Soviet spy, sends Stalin details about a coming German invasion of the USSR. Stalin will discount such reports as efforts to alienate the Soviet and German governments and force the USSR into the war.

May 27: President Roosevelt issues a *Proclamation of Unlimited National Emergency* due to the growing threat from the European war which is emphasized when the American merchant ship *Robin Moore* is sunk this month. The proclamation requires "that [America's] military, naval, air and civilian defenses be put on the basis of readiness to repel any and all acts or threats of aggression directed toward any part of the Western Hemisphere."

June 9: More than 2,000 soldiers with fixed bayonets end a strike at the North American Aviation plant in Inglewood, California, that threatens to shut down 25 percent of all fighter aircraft production. Labor's wartime fears include the prospect of rising prices coupled with stagnant wages, and the loss of hard-won union rights.

June 16: Two days after President Roosevelt freezes German and Italian assets in the United States, as well as the assets of all invaded and occupied European countries, the German and Italian U.S. consulates are ordered to close.

June 22: With the beginning of Operation Barbarossa—an invasion by some 3 million troops along a thousand-mile front that sets the Red Army reeling—Hitler abrogates his treaty with the Soviet Union (see Chapter 6). Communist organizations around the world, including in the United States, adjust their thinking from support of the Nazi-Soviet pact toward support of the Allies. The Japanese are almost as surprised as the Soviets by the German move. However, with the Soviets now fighting the Germans in the West, and the threat from Soviet Far Eastern armies removed by the *Pact of Neutrality* they recently signed with the USSR, the Japanese are now free to turn their attentions southward, toward the resource-rich European holdings in Asia.

June 25: A week after meeting with African American activist A. Philip Randolph, who is organizing a march on Washington to protest discrimination in defense industries and the military, President Roosevelt issues *Executive Order 8802* barring discrimination in the employment of workers in U.S. defense industries and government because of race, creed, color, or national origin. A *Fair Employment Practices Committee* is established, and the black community will soon embark on a "Double V" campaign: "Victory over our enemies at home and victory over our enemies on the battlefield abroad" (see Chapter 11).

July 9: President Roosevelt asks the secretaries of war and navy to prepare a comprehensive war program, based on specific assumptions about matériel needs and about adversaries and allies. The collapse of the Soviet Union is one of the assumptions that will be reflected in the "Victory Plan" submitted on September 1.

July 12: In Moscow, representatives from the United Kingdom and the Soviet Union sign an agreement stating "(1) The two Governments mutually undertake to render each other assistance and support of all kinds in the present war against Hitlerite Germany. (2) They further undertake that during this war they will neither negotiate nor conclude an armistice or treaty of peace except by mutual agreement." One week later, Winston Churchill will launch the *V for Victory campaign* during a midnight radio broadcast: "The V sign is the symbol of the unconquerable will of the occupied territories and a portent of the fate awaiting Nazi tyranny" (see Chapter 10).

July 26: Roosevelt orders a freeze on all Japanese assets in the United States—pending review and approval of Japanese export requests by a government committee. Overzealous enforcement by government officials while Roosevelt is out of the country meeting with Churchill turns what the president intended as a temporary increase of trade-sanction pressures on Japan into a total embargo from which the government will not be able to retreat, lest that be seen as a sign of weakness. All trade with Japan is cut off.

July 28–August 3: Presidential aide Harry Hopkins visits Moscow and talks with Stalin and his top aides—ascertaining their supply needs and assessing the Soviet Union's will to fight the German

PROMINENT (NON-U.S.) ALLIED POLITICAL FIGURES

Nationalist China

Chiang Kai-shek
(1887–1975) (See also
Chapters 1 and 4.)

By 1937, Chiang controlled the Nationalist government and armed forces, dominating a complex hierarchy of generals and civilian officials that was increasingly marked by corruption and inefficiency. After the uneasy alliance he had forged with the Chinese Communists crumbled early in 1941, Chiang was as concerned with subduing his Communist rivals for political power as he was with defeating the Japanese—a trait that gradually eroded his wartime relations with Nationalist China's closest ally, the United States. His reliance on U.S. aid was reflected in the inclusion of American civilians in his inner circle. They included personal adviser Owen Lattimore, sent to China by President Roosevelt, and U.S. ambassadors to China—first Clarence Gauss, then Patrick Hurley. These Americans sometimes disagreed over Chiang's value to the Allied war effort, as did his U.S. military advisers. Yet Chiang and his politically astute wife remained international symbols of resistance to the Axis, a fact that Chiang recognized and exploited. ("Wherever I go is the Government and the center of resistance," he told Australian journalist Rhodes Farmer in 1938. "I am the state.") Chiang was included in only one of the major Inter-Allied conferences, the late-1943 SEXTANT conference in Egypt.

Madame Chiang (Soong
May-ling) (1898–2003)

Member of a prominent Chinese family, Madame Chiang graduated from Wellesley College, married Chiang in 1927, and thereafter was thoroughly immersed in Nationalist Chinese politics. In the early 1930s, she served as a member of the Legislative Yuan (one of five yuan, or branches of the Nationalist government) and was secretary general of the Chinese Aeronautical Affairs Commission when the war with Japan started in 1937. Tough and adept at Machiavellian stratagems, Madame Chiang employed her charm, beauty, and fluency in both written and spoken English to

(continued)

PROMINENT (NON-U.S.) ALLIED POLITICAL FIGURES (CONTINUED)

	further Chiang's and China's cause throughout the war. In 1943, during a successful tour of the United States, she addressed a joint session of the U.S. Congress. Later that year, she served as her husband's interpreter during the Allied conference in Cairo.
T. V. Soong (Soong Tzu-wen) (1894–1971)	Eldest brother in a family that included Soong May-ling (Madame Chiang); Governor of the Central Bank of China and Minister of Finance (1928–1931, 1932–1933); Minister of Foreign Affairs (1942–1945); and President of the Executive Yuan (1945–1947). Soong was educated at Harvard, and during World War II negotiated loans from the United States to sustain China's war effort. In December 1941, he was appointed foreign minister by Chiang Kai-shek and lived in Washington, D.C., from 1942 to 1945. As Chiang's most trusted adviser, Soong was one of the most powerful and influential officials in the Nationalist government. After the war, he worked to save China's war-ravaged economy before the Chinese Communist Party came to power. In 1949, he moved to the United States.

Free France

de Gaulle, Charles (1890–1970)	A World War I veteran chiefly known during the interwar years as the author of controversial books on military theory, strategy, and armored warfare, in June 1940 de Gaulle had just been promoted to brigadier general when he was appointed undersecretary for national defense by his political mentor, Prime Minister Paul Reynaud. During his two-week tenure in that office, he impressed Winston Churchill, who endorsed de Gaulle as the leader of all free Frenchmen after the general escaped to Britain. Proud, aloof, bitterly opposed to Vichy, and not given to compromise, de Gaulle struggled with single-minded persistence for four years to win acceptance by all the major Allies, and by his fellow French citizens, as the Free French leader who would head the government of liberated France. The *French National Committee* he formed in September 1941 was a framework for a national government; the

PROMINENT (NON-U.S.) ALLIED POLITICAL FIGURES (CONTINUED)

Bureau Central de Renseignements et d'Action (BCRA), established January 1942, linked de Gaulle more closely with the resistance movements within France (see Chapter 9). In 1943, he agreed to share with General Henri Giraud leadership of the *French Committee for National Liberation* (FCNL), but, more politically adept than Giraud, he quickly emerged as its undisputed head. Eight days after the Allied landings, de Gaulle arrived in France to establish a provisional government at Bayeux. A month later, he visited the United States, where his warm reception denoted an end to years of frosty relations with the Americans. By fall, both the United States and Britain formally recognized de Gaulle's administration as the provisional government of France.

Giraud, Henri
(1879–1949)

Commander of French troops in North Africa (November 1942–April 1944); High Commissioner in French North Africa (December 1942–April 1944); cochairman (with de Gaulle) of the French Committee for National Liberation (June–November 1943). Much celebrated for his heroic escape from German captivity, Giraud was preferred over de Gaulle by the Americans as leader of the Free French. However, he had limited political acumen and gradually became less influential.

Pleven, René
(1901–1993)

Free French ambassador to the United States (May–October 1941); commissioner on economy and finances (September 1941–October 1942); commissioner on the colonies (September 1941–July 1942, October 1942–September 1944); vice president of the National Committee of the Free French (1943–1944); commissioner of foreign affairs (October 1942–February 1943); minister of colonies (September–November 1944); minister of finance (November 1944–January 1946). A mild-mannered businessman who was an early supporter of de Gaulle; as ambassador to the United States in 1941, he won several important concessions from the Department of State, despite the U.S. government's generally skeptical attitude toward de Gaulle.

(continued)

PROMINENT (NON-U.S.) ALLIED POLITICAL FIGURES (CONTINUED)

Great Britain
Monarch: King George VI
Head of State (1937–1940): Neville Chamberlain; (1940–1945):
Winston Churchill; (1945–1951): Clement Atlee (See Chapter 4.)

Bracken, Brenden (1901–1958)	Churchill's parliamentary private secretary from 1939 to 1941, Bracken then became Minister of Information, heading the propaganda ministry responsible for distributing information and news about the war. In this role, he was responsible for the day-to-day administration of the clandestine Political Warfare Executive, which was devoted to propaganda and subversion. (See Chapter 9.)
Attlee, Clement R. (1883–1967)	Before succeeding Conservative Party leader Winston Churchill as prime minister, Labour Party leader Attlee served in several capacities in the coalition government that oversaw the British war effort from 1940 to 1945: Lord Privy Seal (1940–1942), secretary of state for the dominions (1942–1943), and lord president of the council (1943–1945). As of February 1942, he was also designated deputy prime minister. Although general elections were suspended in Britain during the war, political differences still existed and had to be confronted. Attlee, whose outlook and temperament differed greatly from Churchill's, managed to steer a middle course between the tenets of the Labour Party and the requirements of maintaining an effective coalition—although he angered some of his more left-leaning Labour colleagues in doing so. In 1945, he attended the founding conference of the United Nations in San Francisco, then returned home, where his party won a majority of seats in the House of Commons in the July elections, making him the country's new prime minister.
Eden, Sir Anthony (1897–1977)	After Churchill became prime minister in May 1940, Eden was appointed secretary of state for war. He supported several generals who proved right in their judgments, although Churchill had been uncertain about them. In December, Eden became foreign secretary, assuming a seat in the war cabinet. He was with Churchill at nearly all major international conferences and was considered a likely successor if Churchill could not serve.

PROMINENT (NON-U.S.) ALLIED POLITICAL FIGURES (CONTINUED)

Halifax, Lord (1881–1959)	Initially a supporter of appeasement, Halifax was serving as foreign secretary when, in September 1938, he opposed compromise with Hitler. In May 1940, he refused Chamberlain and King George VI's requests to become prime minister. In December 1940, Churchill made him ambassador to the United States, a position he held until 1946. At the same time, he remained a member of the war cabinet.

Union of Soviet Socialist Republics
Head of State (1938–1953): Joseph Stalin (See Chapters 1 and 4.)

Beria, Lavrenti Pavlovich (1899–1953)	Made head of the People's Commissariat of International Affairs (NKVD) in 1938 and quickly purged the existing NKVD leadership; as deputy Soviet premier, oversaw the evacuation of defense industries to the east and conversion of peacetime industry to war production. He supervised internal security (including prisons and the Soviet Gulag), foreign intelligence and counterintelligence, and NKVD troops (see Chapter 4). He also deported thousands of non-Russians suspected of disloyalty and earned a reputation for ruthlessness.
Gromyko, Andrei Andreyevich (1909–1989)	A trained economist who switched to diplomacy in 1939, he became section head for the Americas in the People's Commissariat of Foreign Affairs; later that year, he became a counselor in the Soviet embassy in Washington. He was Soviet ambassador to the United States and Cuba (1943–1946). He helped organize the wartime Big Three conferences and attended the Dumbarton Oaks Conference (1944) and the 1945 San Francisco conference that established the United Nations (UN).
Litvinov, Maxim Maximovich (1876–1951)	Commissar for foreign affairs (1930–1939)—a period that saw the "Great Terror" of Stalin's purges; thus his efforts at diplomacy were generally rebuffed. Ambassador to the United States (1941–1943), after the German invasion; constantly urged the western Allies to open a second front. Recalled and made a

(continued)

PROMINENT (NON-U.S.) ALLIED POLITICAL FIGURES (CONTINUED)

	deputy commissar of foreign affairs, he advocated cooperation among the Allied powers after the war—but came to understand, and warned the West via journalist Richard C. Hottelet, that cooperation was not Stalin's wish.
Molotov, Vyacheslav Mikhailovich (1880–1986)	Named chairman of the Council of People's Commissars in 1930 (a near equivalent to prime minister) Molotov was also foreign minister (1939–1949). In May 1941, Stalin assumed the chair of the Council of People's Commissars, but Molotov remained as vice-chairman as well as deputy chairman of the State Defense Committee. Negotiated the alliance with the United States and Britain in 1942; headed the Soviet delegation to the San Francisco UN conference, 1945.

Principal sources: I. C. B. Dear and M. R. D. Foot, eds., *Oxford Companion to World War II*, Oxford: Oxford University Press, 2001; Jonathan Fenby, *Chiang Kai-Shek: China's Generalissimo and the Nation He Lost*, New York: Carroll & Graf, 2004; James R. Millar, ed., *Encyclopedia of Russian History*, New York: MacMillan Reference USA/Thompson-Gale, 2004.

invaders. He cables Roosevelt: "I feel ever so confident about this front. . . . There is unbounded determination." Others in the U.S. high command are not so optimistic about the Soviet Union's chances for survival—and their pessimism will soon be reinforced by further Red Army reverses. But the report from Hopkins helps Roosevelt persuade Congress to include the USSR in the Lend-Lease program.

August 9–12: President Roosevelt and Prime Minister Churchill meet at sea off Newfoundland. On August 14, they will announce the *Atlantic Charter,* in which they make known eight "common principles in the national policies of their respective countries on which they base their hopes for a better future of the world."

August 18: President Roosevelt signs an extension of the Selective Service Act, which extends draftees' tours of duty another eighteen months over the original twelve. The extension, which passed Congress by a single vote, still prohibits draftees from serving outside the Western Hemisphere.

August 28: Another wave of displaced persons is created by the *Decree of Banishment* issued today by Stalin's government, under which some 400,000 Volga Germans (descendants of Germans who emigrated to Russia in the mid-1700s) are stripped of Soviet citizenship and deported to

THE PRINCIPLES OF THE ATLANTIC CHARTER
(AS STATED IN THE CHARTER)

First, their countries seek no aggrandizement, territorial or other;

Second, they desire to see no territorial changes that do not accord with the freely expressed wishes of the peoples concerned;

Third, they respect the right of all peoples to choose the form of government under which they will live; and they wish to see sovereign rights and self-government restored to those who have been forcibly deprived of them;

Fourth, they will endeavor, with due respect for their existing obligations, to further the enjoyment by all States, great or small, victor or vanquished, of access, on equal terms to the trade and to the raw materials of the world which are needed for their economic prosperity;

Fifth, they desire to bring about the fullest collaboration between all nations in the economic field with the object of securing, for all, improved labor standards, economic advancement and social security;

Sixth, after the final destruction of the Nazi tyranny, they hope to see established a peace which will afford to all nations the means of dwelling in safety within their own boundaries, and which will afford assurance that all the men in all the lands may live out their lives in freedom from fear and want;

Seventh, such a peace should enable all men to traverse the high seas and oceans without hindrance;

Eighth, they believe that all of the nations of the world, for realistic as well as spiritual reasons must come to the abandonment of the use of force. Since no future peace can be maintained if land, sea or air armaments continue to be employed by nations which threaten, or may threaten, aggression outside of their frontiers, they believe, pending the establishment of a wider and permanent system of general security, that the disarmament of such nations is essential. They will likewise aid and encourage all other practicable measures which will lighten for peace-loving peoples the crushing burden of armaments.

Siberia and Kazakhstan. Stalin will also deport suspect national groups from the oil-rich Caucasus, a particular Nazi target.

September 6: Edging closer to war with the United States and its allies, Japanese government officials, meeting in Imperial Conference, decide that, if diplomacy does not reverse America's policy of restricting Japan's access to vital resources by early October, the "Southern Operation"—attacking British and American bases and securing the oil-rich Dutch East Indies—will be implemented. A week later, a Japanese military staff exercise will prove the feasibility of the proposed attack on Pearl Harbor. *As this occurs,* the U.S. State Department continues low-key efforts to bring Americans in Asia home. On September 23, Secretary of State Hull will write the chairman of the U.S. Maritime Commission, who has been diverting American shipping from Asian waters as war tensions build, to ask for continued U.S. passenger service in the Far East.

September 9: The Iranian government formally submits to the Allied occupation that began on August 25 and included the immediate deployment of troops to protect oil fields. Within a week, Shah Reza Pahlevi, who is openly partial to the Axis, will abdicate in favor of his son. The *Persian Corridor* will become a vital line of Lend-Lease supply to the Soviet Union.

September 11: As the battle to maintain the Allies' Atlantic-Ocean supply routes continues (Battle of the Atlantic, see Chapters 6 and 7), President Roosevelt stretches the truth of a complex U.S.-British-German sea encounter and tells the American people, "the German submarine fired first upon this American destroyer [USS *Greer*] without warning, and with deliberate design to sink her. These Nazi submarines and raiders are the rattlesnakes of the Atlantic." He orders the U.S. Navy to attack on sight German or Italian vessels discovered operating in American defensive waters.

September 24: Nine Allied governments-in-exile—those of Belgium, Free France, Czechoslovakia, Greece, Luxembourg, the Netherlands, Norway, Poland, and Yugoslavia—pledge to adhere to the principles of the Atlantic Charter.

September 28: An Anglo-American mission, headed by Lord Beaverbrook and Averell Harriman, arrives in Moscow to discuss Allied assistance to the Soviet Union. In October, President Roosevelt will convince Congress to include the Soviet Union in the Lend-Lease program, and enormous quantities of war supplies soon begin flowing toward Russia. Some of these supplies are diverted from Britain; some are sent *by* Britain. Should the Soviet Union fall, Germany will be able to draw on conquered Russian resources as well as its own to defeat England.

October 17: The German submarine U-568 attacks the United States destroyer *Kearney* off the coast of Iceland, killing eleven American sailors. On October 27, President Roosevelt will declare to the American public that "we do not propose to take this lying down." He does not seek a declaration of war; but he asks Congress for authorization to arm American merchant

ALLIED GOVERNMENTS-IN-EXILE

Country/Location	Principal Leaders/Organization
Belgium: London (1940–1945)	King Leopold III (commander in chief, armed forces); Prime Minister, Hubert Pierlot; Minister of Foreign Affairs, Paul-Henri Spaak; Finance Minister, Camille Gutt; Minister of Colonies, Albert de Vleechauwer; Defense Minister, Camille Gutt (1940–1942), Hubert Pierelot (1942–1945).
Czechoslovakia: London (1939, established); 1941–1945 (recognized)	President, Eduard Benes; Prime Minister, Jan Sramek, Zdenek Fierlinger; Foreign Minister, Jan Masaryk.
France: London (1940–1944)	President/commander in chief of armed forces, Charles de Gaulle; Foreign Minister/Commissioner, Maurice Dejean (1941–1942), René Massigil (1942–1944), Georges Bidault; Finance Minister, René Pleven (1941–1943), Pierre Mendès-France (1943–September 1944).
Greece: London and Cairo (1941–1944)	King George II; Prime Minister, Emmanouil Tsouderos.
Luxembourg: London (1940–1945)	Grand Duchess Charlotte.
Netherlands: London (1940–1945)	Queen Wilhelmina; Prime Minister, D. J. De Geer (1939–1940), P. J. Gerbrandy; Foreign Minister, Eelco Nicholas van Kleffens.
Norway: London (1940–1945)	King Haakon VII; Prime Minister, Johan Nygaardsvold (1940–1945).
Philippines: Washington, D.C. (1942–1945)	President, Manuel Quezon (d. 1944), Sergio Osmena. *Note:* President Roosevelt signed a bill that extended President Quezon's term in office until the Japanese were defeated.
Poland (A): Paris (1939–1940); London (1940–1945)	President, Wladyslaw Raczkiewicz; Prime Minister, Wladyslaw Sikorski (d. 1943), Stanislaw Mikolajczyk (1943–1944), Tomasz Arciszewski (1945).
Poland (B): USSR, Poland (1944–1945)	Soviet-backed rival of the London-based Polish government.
Yugoslavia: London (1941–1943); Cairo (1943–1945)	King Peter II; Prime Minister, Dusan Simovitch (1941–1942), Slobodan Jovanovic (1942–1943). *Note:* Concerned about problems within the existing government, Churchill facilitated a political collaboration between King Peter and resistance leader Josip Broz (Tito) that would ultimately allow Tito to assume control of Yugoslavia.

Principal sources: Martin Conway, ed., *Europe in Exile: European Exile Communities in Britain 1940–1945*, New York: Berghahn Books, 2001; I. C. B. Dear and M. R. D. Foot, eds., *Oxford Companion to World War II*, Oxford: Oxford University Press, 2004; Lucy Sayre, *Freedom in Exile: A Handbook of the Governments in Exile*, revised ed., Washington, D.C.: Office of the American Association of University Women, 1942.

vessels and allow them to enter combat zones, two measures forbidden by the U.S. Neutrality law. Congress will comply with the president's request by early November, soon after the destroyer USS *Reuben James* is torpedoed and sunk off Iceland on October 30, with a loss of 115 American lives.

November 5: In an Imperial Conference of Japanese officials attended by the emperor, aggressive Japanese general Hideki Tojo—Japan's new prime minister and minister of war—declares, "We must be prepared to go to war, with the time for military action tentatively set at December 1, while at the same time doing our best to solve the problem [of relations with the United States and the European colonial powers] by diplomacy." The Japanese foreign minister reports to the group that prospects for diplomatic success are "we most deeply regret, dim." *Also this day:* The Joint Board of the U.S. Army and Navy (see Chapter 4), reaffirming that the primary objective of the United States must be "the defeat of Germany," concludes that "[W]ar between the United States and Japan should be avoided."

November 18: The Japanese Diet approves a resolution of hostility directed against the United States.

November 20–30: In Washington, D.C., Japanese ambassador Kichisaburo Nomura and newly arrived special envoy Saburo Kurusu propose to U.S. Secretary of State Cordell Hull that, in return for Japanese withdrawal from Indochina and a pledge that Japan will make no further armed advances in Southeast Asia, the United States give Japan a free hand in China and relief from American trade restrictions. China, however, is becoming ever more important to the Allied war effort, tying down Japanese troops that might otherwise attack the Soviet Union. The U.S. response, delivered November 25, reiterates American insistence that Japan withdraw from China and stop its Southeast Asian incursions. *Also that day,* a Japanese task force departs the Kuril Islands, heading for Hawaii, *while, in Berlin,* representatives of Japan, Italy, and Germany renew the generally meaningless Anti-Comintern Pact with great pomp and ceremony. German foreign minister Joachim von Ribbentrop takes the opportunity to denounce Franklin Roosevelt as "the chief culprit of this war."

November 28: Meeting with Hitler in Berlin, Haj Amin al-Husseini, Mufti of Jerusalem, receives a sympathetic hearing but no formal declaration of support for the Arab cause in the ongoing Arab-Jewish conflict in Palestine. The Mufti will continue his efforts to win Hitler's support (in 1943 he will help organize a 20,000-man Muslim SS unit in Bosnia).

December 4: The *Chicago Tribune* prints an article revealing details of the American "Victory Plan" (see July 9, 1941)—including its assertion that the United States will not be able to field forces in strength until mid-1943. Secretary of War Stimson calls the source of the leak "wanting in loyalty and patriotism"; the German chargé in Washington radios a report on the article to Berlin.

December 6: Two days after introducing National Service for both men and women, Britain declares war on Finland, Hungary, and Romania—countries that have joined in Germany's attack on the Soviet Union.

December 7: The Japanese stage a surprise attack on the U.S. naval base at Pearl Harbor, Hawaii that devastates America's Pacific Fleet. Within a week, Congress will revise the Selective Service Act to require that draftees serve "for the duration of the war." *Also this day:* Hitler issues the *Nact und Nebel Erlass* ("Night and Fog Decree") a top secret directive authorizing the seizure without warrant or explanation, of any person in occupied countries "endangering German security." They are not to be executed immediately, but are to "vanish without trace" into the "night and fog" of a concentration camp within Germany. This will have a deterrent effect against subversive activities. German camp authorities, precise in their record keeping, will place the initials "NN" beside the names of Night and Fog prisoners who have been executed.

December 11: Three days after the United States formally declares war on Japan—and the day Germany and Italy declare war on the United States—the U.S. border is closed to all enemy aliens, and to all people of Japanese ancestry, even American citizens. Japanese aliens, as well as Germans and Italians who have been under surveillance as possible security risks, are detained.

December 18: Congress passes the *First War Powers Act,* which includes authorization for the president to censor international mail, cable, radio, and other means of cross-border communication. *The next day,* President Roosevelt issues *Executive Order 8985,* establishing the Office of Censorship. Headed by former Associated Press executive Byron Price, this office will oversee a successful, and largely voluntary program of newspaper, magazine, and radio censorship throughout the war (see Chapter 10). *At about this same time,* American unions pledge not to strike as long as fighting continues. With some notable exceptions, this pledge will be kept.

December 21: Japan concludes a ten-year treaty of alliance with Thailand. On January 25, 1942, Thailand will declare war on the United States and Great Britain.

1942: The Axis Ascendant

January 1: Twenty-six Allied countries issue a *Declaration by the United Nations,* a pledge to use their full resources against the Axis powers. A product of the Roosevelt–Churchill Washington meeting known as the *Arcadia Conference* (December 22, 1941–January 14, 1942), the declaration will be signed by an additional nineteen nations by March 1945.

Soviet dictator Joseph Stalin joined Roosevelt and Churchill at a major Allied strategy conference for the first time in 1943, at Teheran, Iran. Behind the "Big Three" are, from left to right: General "Hap" Arnold, commander, U.S. Army Air Force; unidentified British officer; Admiral Sir Andrew Cunningham; and Admiral William Leahy, chief of staff to Roosevelt.

MAJOR INTER-ALLIED CONFERENCES, 1941–1945

Name/Code Name/Location	*Principal Participants*	*Focus or Outcome*
Placentia Bay/RIVIERA Placentia Bay, Newfoundland August 9–12, 1941	Roosevelt, Churchill, political and military advisers	Although Churchill failed to bring Roosevelt into the war, they issued the joint Atlantic Charter (see box p. 109). Roosevelt also offered Churchill

MAJOR INTER-ALLIED CONFERENCES, 1941–1945 (CONTINUED)

Name/Code Name/Location	Principal Participants	Focus or Outcome
		economic aid through Lend-Lease assistance and protection of British shipping between Newfoundland and Iceland.
ARCADIA Washington, D.C. December 24, 1941– January 14, 1942	Roosevelt, Churchill, U.S. and British Chiefs of Staff (CCS)	The first strategic conference following Pearl Harbor, Arcadia established the combined Allied command (ABDA, or American-British-Dutch-Australian), and framed the United Nations Declaration (see January 1, 1942). Roosevelt and Churchill also discussed military options.
Post-Arcadia Washington, D.C., and London January 23, 1942– May 19, 1942	Combined Chiefs of Staff (CCS) (See Chapter 4.)	As CCS took steps to implement Arcadia decisions by hammering out logistics, deployment, and command assignments, debates continued on the viability of GYMNAST, the British-proposed invasion of North Africa, and SLEDGEHAMMER, an American plan for a landing on the Normandy coast of France.
SYMBOL Casablanca, Morocco January 14–23, 1943	Roosevelt, Churchill, CCS, Generals Alexander (U.K.), Eisenhower (U.S.), de Gaulle, and Giraud (France)	Roosevelt and Churchill facilitated a settlement between French resistance leaders de Gaulle and Giraud. The Allies agreed on a Combined Bomber Offensive against Germany and appointed Frederick Morgan as Chief of Staff to the Supreme Allied Commander (COSSAC), a first step in planning the invasion of France (OVERLORD). After the conference, Roosevelt announced that the Allies would require "unconditional surrender" by the Axis powers.
TRIDENT Washington, D.C. May 11–25, 1943	Roosevelt, Churchill, CCS, Generals Wavell, Wilson (U.K.); Chennault, Eisenhower, and Stilwell (U.S.)	The Allies agreed to pursue the "unconditional surrender" policy with regard to Italy, despite objections from Eisenhower and Wilson. They briefly discussed shipping deficits and the progress of the Battle of the

(continued)

MAJOR INTER-ALLIED CONFERENCES, 1941–1945 (CONTINUED)

Name/Code Name/Location	Principal Participants	Focus or Outcome
		Atlantic. Most significantly, they decided to delay the invasion of France until May 1944.
QUADRANT Quebec, Canada August 17–24, 1943	Roosevelt, Churchill, CCS	Plans for OVERLORD occupied much of the conference. The Allies formed the South-East Asia Command (SEAC) and agreed to pressure Spain to stop supplying Germany with tungsten and withdraw the Spanish Blue Division from the German-Soviet war. Churchill and Roosevelt signed the *Quebec Agreement*, mandating cooperative development of the atomic bomb and mutual consent before either party used nuclear weapons or helped another party produce nuclear weapons.
SEXTANT Cairo, Egypt November 23–26, and December 3–7, 1943	Churchill, Roosevelt, Chiang Kai-shek, President Ismet Inönü of Turkey; CCS	Part I of SEXTANT focused on operations in South-East Asia. Roosevelt, Churchill, and Chiang issued the *Cairo Declaration*, which affirmed their commitment to future action against Japan and stated that after the war, defeated Japan would lose all post-World War I territories. In Part II, they attempted unsuccessfully to persuade President Inönü to bring Turkey into the war against the Axis.
EUREKA Teheran, Persia (Iran) November 28–December 1, 1943	Churchill, Roosevelt, Stalin, CCS	The first Allied conference Stalin attended, EUREKA focused primarily on strategic coordination between the western Allies and the USSR. Stalin supported Churchill and Roosevelt's decision to delay OVERLORD, promised a simultaneous full-scale offensive on the Russian front and agreed to declare war on Japan after Germany's defeat. The Allies also discussed ways to bring Turkey into the war, the future of Poland and Finland, and the postwar division of Germany.

MAJOR INTER-ALLIED CONFERENCES, 1941–1945 (CONTINUED)

Name/Code Name/Location	Principal Participants	Focus or Outcome
OCTAGON Quebec, Canada September 12–16, 1944	Churchill, Roosevelt, CCS	Roosevelt accepted Churchill's offer of a British fleet to aid in the Pacific War. Discussing the postwar world, they agreed to divide defeated Germany into occupation zones and considered the Morgenthau Plan for Germany's de-industrialization. (See time line entry September 12–16, 1944.) Although the plan required no financial reparations of Germany, all industrial machinery would be dismantled and given to Allied nations. (Never adopted)
ARGONAUT, Part 1, aka CRICKET Island of Malta January 30–February 3, 1945	Roosevelt, Churchill, CCS, Anthony Eden (U.K.), Edward Stettinius (U.S.)	Basically a series of preliminary meetings for the later conference in Yalta that shared the same code name. Most discussions focused on Allied strategy in the final phase of the European war. Neither Churchill nor Roosevelt attended the entire conference, and over the five-day period they met with each other only twice.
ARGONAUT, Part 2, aka MAGNETO Yalta, Crimea February 4–11, 1945	Churchill, Roosevelt, Stalin, CCS	This was the first conference that focused on the postwar world. The Allies agreed on an *Allied Control Commission* to oversee defeated Germany. Germany and Austria, the countries and their capitals, would be divided into four occupation zones (British, American, French, and Soviet). Poland's boundaries would be extended westward into Germany, and the western Allies recognized Poland's Soviet-controlled communist government. The *Declaration on Liberated Europe* affirmed the Allies' commitment to free elections and democratic governments in the

(continued)

MAJOR INTER-ALLIED CONFERENCES, 1941–1945 (CONTINUED)

Name/Code Name/Location	Principal Participants	Focus or Outcome
		liberated nations. A secret agreement between Roosevelt and Stalin granted Soviet demands for certain Chinese territories in exchange for Soviet entrance into the war with Japan.
TERMINAL Potsdam, Germany July 17– August 2, 1945	Truman, Stalin, Churchill (replaced by Attlee after British elections), U.K. foreign minister Bevin, CCS	With victory in Europe achieved, discussions focused on surrender terms for Japan. The *Potsdam Declaration*, issued on July 26, with China's approval, affirmed the terms of the Cairo Declaration, but also required unconditional surrender, the removal of war leaders, the facilitation of democratic principles, and the protection of human rights. Japan's sovereignty was limited to its four main islands. Japan was to be occupied until these things had been achieved. There was discussion of Poland's postwar government and boundaries, and the *Council of Foreign Ministers*, which would determine boundaries of postwar Europe, was formed.

Principal sources: I. C. B. Dear and M. R. D. Foot, eds., *Oxford Companion to WWII*, Oxford: Oxford University Press, 2001; World War II, Conference documents at http://www.paperlessarchives.com/wwii_conferences.html; "Index of Operational and Code Names," http://www.army.mil/cmh-pg/reference/code.htm.

January 15–28: Three days after the establishment of a joint U.S.–Mexican defense commission, representatives of the United States join delegates from twenty other American republics for an Inter-American Conference in Rio de Janeiro to discuss defense of the Western Hemisphere. Of the countries represented, only Argentina and Chile do not subsequently sever relations with the Axis.

February 15: Singapore, Britain's vital outpost in the Far East, falls to the Japanese (see Chapter 7).

February 19: President Roosevelt signs *Executive Order 9066,* which will result in the removal of more than 100,000 Japanese Americans from the West Coast to guarded internment camps, as well as the loss of the internees' homes, businesses, and personal assets. (West Coast Japanese Canadians suffer similar treatment.) As this order goes into effect, the recently established Military Intelligence Language School (see "Combating Babel" in Chapter 4), with its primarily Japanese American students, is moved from San Francisco to Minnesota.

THE DECISION FOR JAPANESE AMERICAN INTERNMENT (See also Chapter 11.)

Even before the 1941 attack on Pearl Harbor, exclusionary laws in the United States were contributing to racism and animosity toward those of Asian heritage (see policy list in this sidebar). In the days after the Pearl Harbor attack, fears and rumors of Asian spies and sabotage abounded, leading to a heated debate regarding internment. At the time, Attorney General Francis Biddle wrote that he "was determined to avoid mass internment, and the persecution of aliens that had characterized the First World War." However, Biddle was up against a wave of public opinion and paranoia.

With his assistant James H. Rowe, and Edward J. Ennis, head of the Justice Department's Alien Enemy Control Unit, Biddle advocated a less sweeping detention program, but they were blasted with accusations and proposals recommending that the military assume control. The growing pressure finally pushed Biddle to agree that enemy aliens should be evacuated from sensitive areas of the West Coast. On February 19, 1942, President Roosevelt made this possible by signing Executive Order 9066. Within a month, the government established the *War Relocation Authority* (WRA), headed first by

U.S. EXCLUSIONARY POLICY

1790 Japanese immigrants ineligible for U.S. citizenship, which is limited to "free whites."

1882 Chinese Exclusion Act limits Chinese immigration and exacerbates resentment of "Orientals."

1908 A "Gentlemen's Agreement," between President Theodore Roosevelt and Japanese officials limits Japanese immigration.

1913 The California Alien Land Act makes it unlawful for those ineligible for citizenship to own or lease land. Other states pass similar laws; some remain in effect for decades.

1924 The Oriental Exclusion Act blocks anyone not eligible to become a citizen from immigrating to the United States.

Milton S. Eisenhower (brother of General Dwight Eisenhower), then, after Eisenhower resigned for reasons of conscience, by Dillon S. Meyer. A new *Office of the Alien Property Custodian* was given the auhority to seize or freeze property and assets held by the targeted enemy "aliens"—most of whom were citizens of the United States. Meanwhile, almost no Japanese or Japanese-Americans in Hawaii were ever interned; about one-third of the Hawaiian population was of Japanese ancestry, and thus, the economic effect would have been devastating, but the territory was also under martial law, so internment was deemed unnecessary.

In Canada, a similar program of internment was underway by 1942, with over 20,000 Japanese and Japanese-Canadians detained, around 75 percent of whom were Canadian citizens. Over 2,000 Latin Americans of Japanese heritage, mainly from Peru, were deported to the United States and interned in camps under a separate program intended to ensure the safety of the Panama Canal, the security of the entire Western Hemisphere, and, according to Army chief of staff General George Marshall, to provide "interned nationals . . . to be used in exchange for American Civilian nationals now interned."

German Americans, Italian Americans, and German and Italian U.S. residents escaped a similar fate and were not interned en masse, although some 4,000 individuals of German or Italian ancestry were detained in camps operated by the Department of Justice.

February 23: In Washington, D.C., U.S. Acting Secretary of State Sumner Welles and British Ambassador Viscount Halifax sign a *Preliminary Agreement between the United States and the United Kingdom,* that is the Master Lend-Lease Agreement.

March 12: The Allies cede the oil-rich Dutch East Indies to the Japanese.

April 8: U.S. Army chief of staff General George Marshall and presidential adviser Harry Hopkins meet with Churchill in London to urge mounting an Allied offensive in western Europe in spring 1943. It is essential, Roosevelt cables Churchill, "to draw off pressure on the Russians" by forcing Germany to divert divisions from the Eastern Front. Although Churchill seems to agree with the Americans, he will tell visiting Soviet Foreign Minister Vyacheslav Molotov on May 20 that the Allies are not yet ready to mount such an offensive.

May 7: The Japanese execute José Abad Santos, chief justice of the Philippines, who has refused to participate in a pro-Japanese government.

May 20: The U.S. War Department executes a contract with a business consortium comprising three companies, W. A. Bechtel, H. C. Price, and W. E. Callahan Construction, to begin what will become known as the Canol (Canadian Oil) project. Eventually costing $134 million and employing some 20,000 people, the project—which even President Roosevelt recognizes as "not commercially feasible"—is intended to develop the Norman Wells oil fields in Canada's

Northwest Territories. Fuel for the war effort is a major concern of all combatant nations. German "oil commandos" (experts who could get conquered European fields up and running again for the Reich) accompanied the first waves of troops invading Poland, France, and the Low Countries. Japan's thirst for oil has been partially sated by its appropriation of the Dutch East Indies. Though British troops are now protecting oil facilities in Iran and Iraq, Britain remains intensely vulnerable to German U-boats: 573 British-controlled oil tankers were sunk in the first year of the war alone. Most major combatants are developing synthetic oil programs (manufacture of fuel from coal and other materials), an area in which Germany has been a strong leader since well before the war.

June 13: *Executive Order 9182* establishes the U.S. Office of War Information to coordinate dissemination of war information (and propaganda) domestically and abroad and to gather foreign news. (See Chapter 10.)

July: U.S. Attorney General Francis Biddle announces the indictment of twenty-six American fascist leaders who will be prosecuted for undermining the morale of U.S. armed forces under both the Espionage Act of 1917 and the Smith Act of 1940 (Alien Registration Act). The charges are the result of political and public pressure and are based on minimal substantive evidence: the defendants, who are charged with conspiracy, have little in common, and there is no evidence that they were acting in collusion with the enemy. Nevertheless, the indictments and the widely reported "Great Sedition Trial" that will finally convene in April 1944 will curtail U.S. right-wing propaganda—although the trial quickly devolves into a circus. The defendants shout and wear Halloween masks, and the prosecution appeals more to emotions than fact. Biddle will be among many public figures to call the debacle "degrading" before it ends in a mistrial in November. In December 1945, the government will dismiss all indictments.

August 14: From a British prison in India (his incarceration August 9 caused widespread rioting), Mahatma Gandhi writes President Roosevelt: "I have suggested that if the Allies think it necessary they may keep their troops, at their own expense, in India, not for keeping internal order but for preventing Japanese aggression and defending China. So far as India is concerned, she must become free even as America and Great Britain are." He receives no reply. American troops in India are ordered to "exercise scrupulous care to avoid the slightest participation in India's internal political problems."

August 24: The United States and Mexico formally agree to recruit Mexican temporary workers for U.S. farms in every state except Texas, where Mexican authorities are concerned about discrimination. Some 200,000 Mexican *braceros* will work in the United States during the war.

August 25–26: The Swedish ship SS *Gripsholm* arrives in New York carrying 287 Allied officials, missionaries, correspondents, and teachers, who have been exchanged for Japanese diplomats. Among them is America's longtime ambassador to Japan, Joseph C. Grew, who will issue a statement describing the treatment that the ship's passengers had endured while interned in Japan, many "in solitary confinement in small, bitterly cold prison cells, inadequately clothed and inadequately fed and at times subjected to the most cruel and barbaric tortures." *Also this day,* Wendell Willkie, President Roosevelt's Republican opponent in the 1940 election, departs on a fifty-day round-the-world goodwill tour of U.S. allies to demonstrate that, domestic political debates notwithstanding, America is united in the fight against fascism. Undertaken at the president's request, the tour will result in the best-selling book *One World,* Willkie's influential argument for postwar international cooperation.

August 30: Under German occupation since May 1940 (its lawful government exiled to England), Luxembourg is formally annexed by Germany and military conscription is introduced. The resulting general strike ends after the Germans shoot some of the strikers.

October 21: The U.S. Congress passes the *Revenue Act of 1942,* a revolutionary measure that calls for nearly $7 billion in new individual income taxes (a near-doubling of federal taxes) and lowers the personal exemption drastically enough to bring some 13 million new taxpayers into the system. By the end of the war, taxes paid by individuals will total more than the amount paid by corporations—the beginning of a new trend in American tax history.

November 8–17: Vichy resistance to the Anglo-American Operation Torch landings in northwest Africa (see Chapter 7) collapses after General Eisenhower agrees to recognize Vichy Admiral Jean-François Darlan as high commissioner for French North Africa in return for a general cease-fire. As many in the United States vehemently protest this deal with a prominent collaborator, German troops begin to occupy Vichy-controlled France.

December 17: Allied governments issue a declaration condemning the "German Policy of Extermination of the Jewish Race." In Britain's House of Lords, Lord Samuel states: "This is not an occasion on which we are expressing sorrow and sympathy to sufferers from some terrible catastrophe due unavoidably to flood or earthquake, or some other convulsion of nature. These dreadful events are an outcome of quite deliberate, planned, conscious cruelty of human beings."

December 24: Vichy French Admiral Jean-François Darlan, recently appointed high commissioner of French North Africa, is assassinated by 20-year-old former French resistance member Ferdinand Bonnier de la Chapelle, apparently acting on his own. Bonnier will be executed for the crime.

1943: Turning Points

January 14–24: Churchill and Roosevelt meet in Casablanca, Morocco, to discuss war strategy (rivals for Free French leadership Henri Giraud and Charles de Gaulle are also present). Regarding the Pacific War, the "Big Two" declare, "There are many roads which lead right to Tokyo. We shall neglect none of them." At a postmeeting press conference, President Roosevelt also calls for the "unconditional surrender" of Germany, Italy, and Japan. (See also chart "Major Inter-Allied Conferences, 1941–1945," earlier in this chapter.)

January 30: Hitler appoints Ernst Kaltenbrunner head of the Reich Central Security Office (RSHA). Kaltenbrunner will enthusiastically take charge of the deportation of Jews to extermination camps with the help of his primary assistant, Adolf Eichmann.

February 16: Under constant pressure from Germany's Commissar-General for Labor Fritz Sauckel, the government of Vichy France introduces Compulsory Labor Service (STO), which requires that men born between 1920 and 1922, except for those in a few excluded categories, go to work in Germany. Sauckel's initial manpower goals for France will be met—nearly 300,000 workers go to Germany (others, slated to go, will run away, many to join the resistance). But, on August 6, collaborationist French Premier Pierre Laval will refuse Sauckel's demand for a half million additional workers (including, for the first time, women).

February 18: On a tour of the United States to reinforce support for her husband's Nationalist Chinese regime, Madame Chiang Kai-shek becomes the first woman and the first Chinese to address a joint session of Congress: "It is necessary for us not only to have ideals and to proclaim . . . them," she states, "it is necessary that we act to implement them." Charming, glamorous—and adjudged by President Roosevelt to be "hard as nails"—Mme. Chiang is a guest in the White House. Soon, she will meet in New York with *Look* magazine publisher Gardner Cowles, who backs Wendell Willkie for president, and will offer to reimburse him for whatever it takes to elect Willkie in 1944. She and Willkie developed a close friendship during his 1942 round-the-world tour.

March 13: Operation Flash, an attempt by anti-Nazi German Army officers to assassinate Hitler, fails when the detonator in the bomb that has been placed on the führer's plane proves to be defective. As Germany sustains terrible losses on the battlefield—and bombs fall on the German homeland—dissatisfaction with the Nazi regime, while muted, begins to grow. Among the manifestations of civilian discontent is an underground student group called the White Rose, whose leaders, young siblings Hans and Sophie Scholl, will be arrested, "tried," and decapitated this spring (see Chapter 9).

April 13: In Washington, President Roosevelt dedicates the Thomas Jefferson Memorial on the two hundredth anniversary of Jefferson's birth. The Declaration of Independence, temporarily removed from Fort Knox, is displayed for one week in this monument to its principal author.

May 12–25: At the Anglo-American Trident Conference in Washington, Churchill secures Roosevelt's agreement for American involvement in the Mediterranean beyond the planned invasion of Sicily. Churchill, in turn, agrees on a target date of May 1, 1944, for the invasion of France, which the United States considers of paramount importance.

June 14: As racial tensions in the United States are exacerbated by wartime conditions (race-related violence will explode this year in Detroit, Los Angeles, New York City, Mobile, Los Angeles, and Beaumont, Texas), James Farmer and George Houser found the *Congress of Racial Equality*. *Also this day,* informally celebrated as Flag Day in many American communities (National Flag

During a 1943 tour of the United States to increase sympathy and support for China, the tough, sophisticated, and politically adept Madame Chiang Kai-shek became the first Chinese to address a joint session of Congress. On the day of her address, she was photographed with Speaker of the House Sam Rayburn.

Day will be established in 1949), the U.S. Supreme Court reverses an earlier decision and rules, 6 to 3, in *West Virginia State Board of Education v. Barnette*, that under the Bill of Rights, schoolchildren cannot be compelled to salute the flag if the ceremony conflicts with their religious beliefs.

June 25: As U.S. polls show that John L. Lewis, head of the United Mine Workers of America, has become the most unpopular man in the country since leading coal miners out on a strike earlier in the year, Congress passes—over a presidential veto—the *Smith Connally War Labor Disputes Act*, giving the president broad powers to combat labor problems during the war.

July 5: Thailand acquires 74,770 square miles of territory and 2.9 million additional people when the Japanese government announces that it has approved the cession of portions of the Shan states in Burma and the four northernmost Malay states to the Thais. A reward for the cooperation of Thai leader Luang Plaek Phibunsongkhram ("Phibun"), this action will not reduce the strong undercurrent of pro-Allied sentiment in the country or impede the formation of an anti-Japanese resistance force.

July 14: In Krasnodar, Russia, the first war crimes trial of World War II begins. Evidence presented against the eleven German defendants accused of the mass murder of Soviet civilians is heard and seen by Allied journalists, who publish reports of these Nazi atrocities in the West. (Eight of the Germans will be sentenced to death and shot.)

July 25: Six days after a five-hundred-plane Allied air raid on Rome, and two days after crowds in Palermo, Sicily, greet American General George Patton by shouting "Down with Mussolini!" and "Long live America!," Italy's Fascist Grand Council and King Victor Emmanuel force dictator Benito Mussolini to resign, and he is placed under arrest. As Marshal Pietro Badoglio assumes the premiership, Italians in the field start to defect to the Allies. The new government soon begins secret negotiations with the Allies, while Hitler increases German strength in the Italian boot, anticipating Italian repudiation of the Axis.

August 1: Japan declares Burma independent. Ba Maw, former premier of the British protectorate of Burma (1937–1939), but later imprisoned by the British for sedition, becomes *Naingandaw Adipadi* ("head of state") of a government that is, essentially, a Japanese puppet.

August 11–25: Churchill, Roosevelt, and many advisers meet in the first of two Anglo-American war strategy conferences to be held in Quebec. A representative from China also attends the "Quadrant" conference, where one of the measures decided on is intensification of Allied military operations in the Far East.

August 29: A day after the Danish government refuses demands for greater cooperation presented by the Third Reich's representative in Denmark, the German army again moves into Copenhagen and the king is confined to his palace. As this is done, the Danes scuttle their fleet, leaving only a few small craft to be taken by the Germans.

September 3: On the same day a British force lands at Reggio, Italy, and British paratroops stage a diversion at Taranto, the Italians sign a secret armistice agreement guaranteeing that Italian troops won't go into action against the Allies. The Italian surrender—condemned by Berlin as cowardly and treacherous—will be officially announced September 8, one day before the main Allied landings in Italy. As German troops contest fiercely on the battlefield, the SS will begin deporting Italy's Jews to labor and death camps, something the Italian government has previously refused to do.

September 12: A small German commando force led by Captain Otto Skorzeny stages a spectacular raid, snatching recently deposed dictator Benito Mussolini from his confinement in an isolated mountain hotel. Flown to Hitler's headquarters in Germany, he will soon be returned to German-occupied northern Italy as self-proclaimed head of the "Italian Social Republic."

September 13: The Nationalist Chinese Central Executive Committee elects Chiang Kai-shek to a three-year term as president of the Chinese Republic. China's new president—who has been garnering the increasing contempt of the ranking U.S. officer in China, General Joseph Stilwell—retains his post of commander in chief of the Chinese Army.

October 2: In Japan, the draft is expanded to include college students, previously exempted from conscription that has applied to all other males at the age of 20 (within six months, minimum conscription age will be lowered to 18). The only exceptions to this new measure are students of science or medicine. Boys as young as 17 may volunteer for Japan's armed forces; before too long, 15-year-old volunteers will be accepted.

October 13: The Italian government of Pietro Badoglio declares war on Germany.

October 19–30: British Foreign Secretary Anthony Eden, U.S. Secretary of State Cordell Hull, and Soviet Foreign Minister V. M. Molotov, meeting in Moscow, agree (with China's adherence) to establish an international organization for peace and security and to set up a European Advisory Commission for long-range planning. Tensions arise over Poland, which will, within the next year, have *two* governments-in-exile: the one currently established in London and the Polish Committee for National Liberation (to be established July 22, 1944), based on Polish soil and backed by Moscow.

October 23: In Singapore, the provisional government of India just proclaimed by pro-Axis Indian dissident Subhas Chandra Bose declares war on Britain and the United States. Other pro-Japanese leaders will assemble in Tokyo within a few weeks, when Prime Minister Tojo hosts the "Greater East Asia Co-Prosperity Sphere Conference." "This is not the time to think with our minds," Burma's Ba Maw will state at the meeting, "this is the time to think with our blood, . . . I seem to hear the voice of Asia gathering her children together."

November 8: In Lebanon—proclaimed independent by its Free French governors in 1941, but still actually under French control—the Chamber of Deputies amends the constitution to unilaterally end the French Mandate. French authorities immediately arrest Lebanese leaders. The country's Christian and Muslim leaders unite in opposition to the French action; amid strikes and riots, international pressure is applied. The prisoners will be released November 22, which will thereafter be celebrated as Lebanon's Independence Day.

November 9: Representatives of 44 countries meeting in Atlantic City, New Jersey, establish the *United Nations Relief and Rehabilitation Administration* to prepare for reconstruction of Europe and the Far East.

November 22–26: Roosevelt, Churchill, and Chiang Kai-shek meet in Cairo, Egypt, to discuss war strategy in the Far East. "Japan shall be stripped of all the islands in the Pacific which she has seized or occupied since the beginning of the first World War," they will state in the Declaration issued December 1, "and . . . be expelled from all other territories which she has taken by violence and greed."

November 28–December 2: In Teheran, Roosevelt and Churchill hold their first face-to-face meeting with Stalin to discuss war strategy—including the opening of a second European front in France—and postwar plans. "No power on earth," they will state in the *Declaration of the Three Powers* December 1, "can prevent our destroying the German armies by land, their U Boats by sea, and their war plants from the air."

December 4–6: Returning to Cairo, Roosevelt and Churchill meet with Turkish President Ismet Inönü. Despite declarations of friendship from all parties, Inönü cannot be induced to bring neutral Turkey into the war. Turkish chromate continues to harden the steel that makes German weapons.

December 24: In a Christmas Eve broadcast, President Roosevelt tells the American people: "The war is now reaching the stage when we shall all have to look forward to large casualty lists—dead, wounded, and missing. War entails just that. There is no easy road to victory. And the end is not yet in sight."

1944: Allied Momentum

January 22: Responding to a critical government report and an urgent recommendation from Secretary of the Treasury Henry Morgenthau, President Roosevelt signs *Executive Order 9417,* establishing the War Refugee Board (WRB) "to take action for the immediate rescue from the Nazis of as many as possible of the persecuted minorities of Europe—racial, religious or political—all civilian victims of enemy savagery." Until the WRB is terminated, September 14, 1945, it will cooperate with Jewish organizations, diplomats from neutral countries, and European resistance groups in the rescue of an estimated 200,000 Jews and other Nazi victims.

January 26: Liberia declares war on Germany and Japan.

January 30–February 8: At the *Brazzaville Conference* in the French Congo, the Free French administration under Charles de Gaulle announces a series of major economic, social, and legal reforms in France's West African colonies in recognition of the colonies' wartime support. But the French do not consider this action a step toward colonial self-government.

March 19: A day after Hitler forces Hungary's regent, Admiral Miklos Horthy, to agree to new terms of "alliance"—including the deportation to Auschwitz of Hungary's 750,000 Jews—German troops enter Hungary.

April 20: With Soviet armies once again in control of the Crimea and Germany's fortunes elsewhere on the wane, Turkey announces that it is now "pro-Allied," rather than strictly neutral—but it is still a nonbelligerent nation.

May 28: As Allied bombers pound German installations and transport systems in France, in preparation for the coming invasion, Winston Churchill reads a report that the raids have caused 3,000 French civilian casualties in forty-eight hours. He writes Air Chief Marshal Tedder, Deputy Supreme Commander of the Allied Expeditionary Force: "You are piling up an awful load of hatred."

June 6: A massive Allied force commences *Operation Overlord,* troops landing on the beaches of Normandy, France, under withering fire (see Chapter 7). Three days later, Joseph Stalin, who has long pressed for such an operation, writes Churchill: "We all greet you and the valiant British and American armies and warmly wish you further successes. . . . Tomorrow . . . the first stage [of the Soviet summer offensive] will open . . . on The Leningrad front."

June 17: Cutting its ties with the Danish throne, the government of Iceland establishes the Icelandic Republic.

June 22: President Roosevelt signs the *Serviceman's Readjustment Act of 1944*—enacted by Congress after six months of debate and despite some continuing misgivings. This hallmark legislation, providing education, training, medical, and other benefits for war veterans, will become better known as the "GI Bill of Rights."

June 26–28: In Chicago, the Republican National Convention nominates Thomas E. Dewey for president of the United States. Chicago will host the Democratic convention as well, July 19–21. Nominating Franklin D. Roosevelt for a fourth term, the Democrats will also confirm Roosevelt's choice of a reluctant Harry S. Truman as the nominee for vice president.

July 1–22: At Bretton Woods, New Hampshire, delegates from forty-four Allied nations assemble for the *United Nations Monetary and Financial Conference,* where they propose creating an International Monetary Fund and an International Bank for Reconstruction and Development to alleviate anticipated postwar foreign-exchange problems, encourage world trade, and promote economic progress and political stability in the postwar world.

July 20: A bomb explodes inside Hitler's "Wolf's Lair" in Rastenberg, East Prussia, as the Nazi leader is bending over a table examining a map. Colonel Count Claus von Stauffenberg, the army conspirator who placed the explosive, is already on his way back to Berlin, where fellow conspirators are set to put "Operation Valkyrie," the military overthrow of the rest of the Nazi leadership, into effect. But Hitler has survived. He will exact a vicious revenge for this attempt on his life, executions continuing until Germany surrenders. Because so many military officers are found to be involved in the plot, Hitler will also place a Nazi political officer in every army company (see Chapter 9).

August 15: During his "Confidentially Yours" program on the U.S. Mutual radio network, newscaster Arthur Hale creates a fervor of apprehension in official circles when he states that the army will soon split the atom and create a weapon. This unintentional leak of most-secret information immediately puts the U.S. Office of Censorship under pressure from military authorities who want—Broadcast Division chief John Fetzer will later report—"to move in and install censors in every radio station in the country." This will not happen. But all recordings of Hale's broadcast will be destroyed.

August 21: The month-long *Dumbarton Oaks International Peace and Security Conference* opens in Washington, D.C. Delegates from the United States, Great Britain, China, and the Soviet Union will lay the groundwork for establishing a permanent international organization to be called the United Nations.

August 22: As Soviet troops cross the Romanian border, King Michael orders Marshal Ion Antonescu to come to an armistice with the Allies immediately. The king orders the dictator arrested when Antonescu refuses. An armistice is soon achieved.

September 5: The Soviet Union declares war on Bulgaria. *Three days later,* Bulgaria will accept the Soviets' terms for an armistice, which have been approved by the other Allied governments. *On September 12,* in Moscow, representatives of the Romanian government will sign an armistice agreement with the Allies. Thenceforward, Romanian forces will fight against the Axis.

September 12–16: Meeting in Quebec, Churchill and Roosevelt approve a plan proposed by U.S. Treasury Secretary Henry Morgenthau to convert postwar Germany into a pastoral country devoid of industries that might be used for making war. The *Morgenthau Plan* will horrify Secretary of State Cordell Hull and raise opposition among other Roosevelt and Churchill advisers. It will quickly be abandoned. Canadian Prime Minister W. L. Mackenzie King, also participating in the conference, becomes concerned about Roosevelt's physical appearance. "It seemed to me . . . that he had failed very much since I last saw him," he will note in his diary. The president, and those closest to him, are concealing a serious heart ailment from the public.

September 19: Finland signs an armistice with the Soviet Union. Under a secret agreement, Germany's 20th Mountain Army continues its withdrawal from northern Finland toward Norway without laying waste to Finnish territory. Finland's forces do not interfere until given an ultimatum by the Soviet Union September 30. At this time, there are some 200,000 German troops in northern Finland and adjoining areas.

October 1: With the War Department's approval, the Library of Congress once again displays the Declaration of Independence and the U.S. Constitution, recently retrieved from their wartime sanctuary at Fort Knox. The documents are guarded by U.S. Marines who have returned from combat duty.

October 15: Three hours after broadcasting a request for armistice terms from the Allies, Hungary's regent, Admiral Mikos Horthy, is deposed by the Germans. He is replaced by Ferenc Szalasi, head of the fascist Arrow Cross Party, who will cooperate fervently with the Nazis in all areas, including the deportation and murder of Hungarian Jews. With Hitler's supplies of vital war materials now severely restricted, the Nazi leader is determined to maintain control over Hungary, a prime supplier of oil, manganese, and bauxite.

November 7: President Franklin Delano Roosevelt becomes the only American president to win a fourth term in office.

1945: An Uneasy Peace

January 5: The Soviet government officially recognizes the Communist-controlled committee that has been established in Lublin as the Provisional Government of Poland, a position the British and Americans refuse to accept. They support a Polish government-in-exile in London that the Soviets do not recognize and have long been attempting to subvert. Tension is building around other points as well, including Soviet espionage in the West, which is more wide-ranging than either Roosevelt or Churchill is aware.

January 6: The Turkish government severs diplomatic relations with Japan.

January 20: On this day of his fourth inauguration, President Roosevelt asks Special Counsel to the President Samuel I. Rosenman to lead a mission to the United Kingdom, France, Belgium, and the Netherlands "to ascertain what the needs of these countries will be . . . to repair the destruction and devastation of the war and to build some of the economic foundations of peace." Rosenman's detailed report, *Civilian Supplies for the Liberated Areas of Northwest Europe*, will be delivered to President Truman at the end of April.

February 4–11: After a preliminary conference with the Combined Chiefs of Staff on Malta (where the British and the Americans differ over European strategy and the best way to deal with the Soviets), Roosevelt and Churchill meet with Stalin at Yalta, in the Crimea. The nascent United Nations Organization, Soviet entry into the war against Japan, and the treatment of defeated Germany are discussed—as is the fate of Eastern Europe. Stalin's promise, extracted under pressure, that free and open elections will be held in Poland will prove empty—as will other of his assurances. As the meeting proceeds, President Roosevelt's physical condition alarms some observers, among them Churchill's doctor, Lord Moran, who believes the president has only a short time to live: "But men shut their eyes when they do not want to see, and the Americans here cannot bring themselves to believe that he is finished."

February 8: Paraguay declares war on Germany and Japan.

February 11: Stopping in Egypt on his way back from Yalta, President Roosevelt meets briefly with kings Farouk of Egypt, Haile Selassie of Ethiopia, and Ibn Saud of Saudi Arabia. A presidential query to Ibn Saud about the possibility of letting more Jewish refugees into Palestine receives a sharply negative answer: Arabs, the Saudi declares, will take up arms to prevent it. The president is also concerned about oil, aware, as interior secretary Harold Ickes stated in a radio address nearly a year earlier, that the United States is "using up our oil reserves faster than we have been discovering new ones. . . . We don't have enough oil right now . . . [to] supply the military and essential industry with all that they require, and still have enough left for normal civilian consumption." American oilmen have been allowed in Saudi Arabia since the 1930s; the king prefers ties to businesses from the United States, which has no apparent Mideast colonial ambitions, over companies based in Great Britain. The two national leaders will emerge from this meeting favorably impressed with each other, and ties between the U.S. and Saudi governments will grow stronger.

February 23: Turkey declares war on Germany and Japan.

February 24: The same day Prime Minister Ahmed Pasha announces Egypt's declaration of war against the Axis powers, he is assassinated. He is succeeded by Nokrashy Pasha.

March 8: Having sent an emissary to Switzerland February 25 to open negotiations via the office of Strategic Services (OSS) intermediary Allen Dulles regarding surrender of German troops in Italy, SS General Karl Wolff releases an Italian resistance leader and an American agent to the Allies as a sign of his serious intent. These negotiations, code-named Operation Sunrise by the Allies, will continue until the Germans in Italy surrender on May 2.

March 28: Burmese patriot Aung San leads his small Burma National Army in a revolt against the Japanese, with whom, until recently, he has been allied—though he has long been growing restive. His countryman Thein Pe wrote of Aung San in 1944: "he is a true patriot although he sometimes loses sight of the broader issues, blinded by one-sided nationalism." Aung San's daughter, Aung San Suu Kyi, future recipient of the Nobel Peace Prize, will be born June 19 of this year.

April 12: President Franklin Delano Roosevelt dies at his "Little White House" retreat in Warm Springs, Georgia. Harry S. Truman becomes thirty-third president of the United States. He will tell reporters: "I felt like the moon and stars and all the planets had fallen on me." On duty on separate ships in the waters off Okinawa, Roosevelt's sons John and FDR Jr., confer via radio; they decide against going home, Franklin, Jr. saying: "Let's clean it up out here, first." *Also this day,* as Japan fortifies its home islands—creating booby traps and training suicide pilots and

President Roosevelt acknowledged the growing importance of strategically located and oil-rich Saudi Arabia to U.S. foreign policy on February 14, 1945, when he met with Saudi king Abdul Aziz bin Abdul Rahman al-Faisal al-Saud (King Ibn Saud) and his entourage aboard the cruiser USS Quincy north of the Suez Canal. This was a pivotal meeting in the development of a close relationship between the two nations.

divers—the government authorizes the organization of a Volunteer Army of men from ages 15 to 55 and women from 17 to 45 to combat the expected Allied invasion.

April 22: SS commander Heinrich Himmler, meeting with a Swedish representative, offers to surrender Germany's Rhine and Vistula armies, which he now commands—but only to the Western Allies, whom he hopes to divide from the Russians now bearing down on Berlin. His offer is refused. Himmler will commit suicide May 23, one day after his capture by the British.

April 24–June 26: Delegates of 50 nations meet in San Francisco to develop the charter of the United Nations Organization.

April 28: Benito Mussolini and his mistress, Clara Petacci, who were captured while attempting to escape from northern Italy to Switzerland, are executed by anti-fascist Italians who leave them hanging upside down on public display in Milan.

April 30: The day after his marriage to long-time mistress Eva Braun, Adolf Hitler and his wife commit suicide in the "Führerbunker" beneath the Reich chancellery in Berlin. As aides take their bodies outside to incinerate them, the Red Army continues its advance into the German capital. Fires burn, buildings are shattered by bombs and artillery; the city is largely in ruins. The thousand-year Reich Hitler proclaimed twelve years before is at an end, and the promise Hitler made that year—"Give me ten years' time and you will not recognize Germany anymore"—has come true with a bitter twist.

May 8: VE Day. As the Allies celebrate victory in Europe, nationalists and French forces clash in Algeria. More than one thousand Algerians and eighty-eight Frenchmen are killed. The French face other troubles in the Mediterranean region: in Syria tensions will explode into fighting. On May 29, the French will bombard Damascus. After British intervention, negotiations will begin that will result in removal of all French troops from Syria by April 17, 1946—celebrated thereafter in Syria as Evacuation Day.

May 10: Seven years after he was forced to flee Czechoslovakia, President Eduard Benes re-establishes his government in Prague. Among the first orders of business: arresting, trying, and executing those convicted of collaboration with the Nazis.

June 5: The *Allied Control Council* that is to oversee the occupation of Germany convenes, comprising representatives of each of the four Allies who are to administer a zone of occupation: the United States, Britain, the Soviet Union, and France.

June 22: In Tokyo, Emperor Hirohito, his Imperial Navy in tatters, his country smoldering from the effects of Allied incendiary raids, takes the extraordinary step of summoning the country's leaders to his palace and suggesting they approach the Soviet Union, a country with which Japan is not yet at war, as an intermediary for arranging a negotiated peace. Since the Japanese are not prepared to accept unconditional surrender, the peace feelers will come to nothing.

July 13: The director of the U.S. War Relocation Authority announces that all but one of the internment camps for Japanese Americans will be closed between October 15 and December 15.

July 17–August 2: Truman, Churchill, and Stalin gather for the Potsdam Conference, seventeen miles from Berlin, to discuss postwar arrangements in Europe and the continuing war in Asia—often without agreement. The *Potsdam Declaration*, issued during the conference, calls on Japan to surrender or face terrible consequences. Japan rejects the declaration.

July 23: "I sacrificed my prestige for the French people," the former Vichy leader Marshal Henri Philippe Pétain states in Paris as he goes on trial for treason. "If I treated with the enemy, it was to save you." This argument does not convince the court. Pétain's death sentence will later be commuted to life imprisonment.

July 26–28: In the midst of the Potsdam Conference, Britain holds elections, July 26, in which the Labor Party wins handily. Conservative party leader Winston Churchill submits his resignation, and Clement Attlee, the new prime minister, immediately replaces him at the conference. "All our enemies having surrendered unconditionally, or being about to do so," Churchill will write, "I was immediately dismissed by the British electorate from all further conduct of their affairs."

August 3: Czechoslovakia, which had been engulfed in Greater Germany under the pretext of rescuing Germans living in the country, expels Germans and Hungarians from its territories.

August 8: Two days after a U.S. Army Air Force B-29 drops an atomic bomb on Hiroshima, the Soviet Union declares war on Japan. Soviet troops pour into Manchuria.

August 10: One day after a second atomic bomb explodes over Nagasaki a message reaches Washington through Swiss diplomatic channels: "The Japanese Government are ready to accept the terms enumerated in the Joint Declaration which was issued at Potsdam on 26 July, 1945, . . . with the understanding that the said Declaration does not comprise any demand which prejudices the prerogatives of His Majesty as a sovereign ruler." On August 12, the Allies agree: the emperor will be allowed to remain, but will no longer be considered divine. Japan's future is, eventually, to be decided by "the freely expressed will of the Japanese people."

August 14–15: On this day that sees the final air raid against Japan, Japanese who wish to resist to the end attempt a coup d'etat. A thousand soldiers attack the Imperial Palace killing the commander of the Imperial Guards Division before loyal troops drive them away. After the revolt is quelled, the Japanese people hear their emperor's voice for the first time on the radio, as Hirohito officially proclaims Japan's surrender.

August 15: The Allies declare V-J Day, though fighting will continue between Japanese and Soviet forces in Manchuria through August 19.

THE A-BOMB DECISION

"We have discovered the most terrible bomb in the history of the world," President Truman wrote in his diary during the Potsdam conference, on receiving news that the atomic bomb had just been successfully tested. By then, tens of millions of people had been killed in the war, and military planners were projecting many thousands of Allied casualties during the invasion of the Japanese home islands, set to begin in November. Thus, when Japan rejected the Potsdam declaration, very few Allied leaders expressed reservations about using "the most terrible bomb" on Japanese population centers. However, in a "Memorandum of Conversation with General Marshall" dated May 29, 1945, Assistant Secretary of War John J. McCloy reported that U.S. Army Chief of Staff George C. Marshall had urged that day, before the bomb had even been tested, that the new weapon "might first be used against straight military objectives such as a large naval installation and then if no complete result was derived from the effect of that, he thought we ought to designate a number of large manufacturing areas from which the people would be warned to leave." The suggestion was rebuffed and Marshall did not reiterate it. At about that same time, a committee considering alternatives to immediate use of the bomb (such as a more detailed warning to the Japanese government and a demonstration explosion over the ocean) rejected them all as impracticable. On July 25, Truman reported to his diary, "This weapon is to be used against Japan between now and August 10th. . . . The Sec. of War, Mr. Stimson . . . and I are in accord. The target will be a purely military one and we will issue a warning statement asking the Japs to surrender and save lives. I'm sure they will not do that, but we will have given them the chance." In fact, Hiroshima, hit by a 12.5 kiloton bomb on August 6, and Nagasaki, on which a larger plutonium-based bomb was dropped on August 9, were not purely military targets. The blasts killed more than 100,000 people outright, most of them civilians. (Several American prisoners of war being held in Hiroshima also died in the August 6 blast—a fact that was not revealed to the American public for some time.) Many more died over the next several years from the effects of radiation poisoning—a phenomenon few people understood at the time. Use of the atomic bombs did result in Japan's surrender.

Since the 12.5 kiloton explosion over Hiroshima inaugurated the nuclear age, many nations have acquired nuclear weapons, and the power of atomic and hydrogen bombs has increased to the *mega*tons (a 12.5 megaton blast would be the equivalent of 12.5 *million* tons of TNT, or one thousand Hiroshima bombs). To date, no other nuclear weapon has been used in warfare. (See also Chapter 5 and Chapter 7.)

August 25: In China, American Special Services Captain John Birch is killed in a skirmish with Chinese Communist troops. He will become a symbol, considered by some "the first casualty in the Third World War between Communists and the ever shrinking Free World."

September 11: President Harry S. Truman approves a brief proposal written by Secretary of War Stimson and Secretary of the Navy Forrestal the previous day: "It is recommended that 'World War II' be the officially designated name for the present war." World War II has killed between 50 and 65 million people, devastated entire nations, and opened an era in which the destruction of the entire planet by nuclear conflict will become possible. Though the skies are free of bomber fleets, and huge armies no longer clash, the world remains unquiet: nationalist movements are gaining force, the first chill blasts of the Cold War are raising the specter of renewed world conflict, and the bitter aftermath of war crimes and the Holocaust will continue into the next century.

PRINCIPAL SOURCES AND FURTHER READING

Baudot, Marcel. *The Historical Encyclopedia of World War II.* New York: Greenwich House, 1984.

Brinkley, Alan. *The End of Reform: New Deal Liberalism in Recession and War.* New York: Alfred A. Knopf, 1995.

Bronson, Rachel. *Thicker than Oil: America's Uneasy Partnership with Saudi Arabia.* New York: Oxford University Press, 2006.

Carruth, Gorton, ed. *The Encyclopedia of American Facts and Dates.* 5th ed. New York: Crowell, 1970.

Corbett, P. Scott. *Quiet Passages: The Exchange of Civilians between the United States and Japan during the Second World War.* Kent, OH: Kent State University Press, 1987.

de Roussy de Sales, Raoul, ed. *Adolf Hitler: My New Order.* New York: Octagon Books, 1973.

Fenby, Jonathan. *Chiang Kai-shek: China's Generalissimo and the Nation He Lost.* New York: Carroll & Graff, 2004.

Fussell, Paul. *Wartime: Understanding and Behavior in the Second World War.* New York: Oxford University Press, 1989.

Gilbert, Sir Martin. *A History of the Twentieth Century.* Vol. 2. *1933–1951.* New York: William Morrow, 1998.

_____. *The Second World War: A Complete History.* New York: Henry Holt, 1989.

Goodwin, Doris Kearns. *No Ordinary Time: Franklin and Eleanor Roosevelt: The Home Front in World War II.* New York: Simon & Schuster, 1994.

Jefferys, Kevin. *The Churchill Coalition and Wartime Politics, 1940–1945.* Manchester, U.K.; New York: Manchester University Press, 1991.

Kennedy, David M. *Freedom from Fear: The American People in Depression and War, 1929–1945*. New York, Oxford: Oxford University Press, 1999.

Large, Stephen. *Showa Japan: Political, Economic and Social History, 1926–1989*. London: New York: Routledge, 1998.

Leitz. Christian. *Sympathy for the Devil: Neutral Europe and Nazi Germany in WWII*. New York: New York University Press, 2001.

MacDonnell, Francis. *Insidious Foes*. New York: Oxford University Press, 1995.

Maddox, Robert Franklin. *The War within World War II: The United States and International Cartels*. Westport, CT: Praeger, 2001.

Manchester, William. *The Glory and the Dream: A Narrative History of America, 1932–1972*. New York: Little Brown, 1974.

Maxxon, Yale Candee. *Control of Japanese Foreign Policy: A Study of Civil-Military Rivalry 1930–1945*. Berkeley, CA: University of California Press, 1957.

McClain, James. *Japan: A Modern History*. New York: W. W. Norton, 2002.

Millar, James R., ed. in chief. *Encyclopedia of Russian History*. New York: Thomson/Gale (Macmillan Reference), 2004.

Murray, Williamson and Allan R. Millett. *A War to Be Won: Fighting the Second World War*. Cambridge, MA: Belknap Press of Harvard University Press, 2000.

Ng, Wendy, *Japanese American Internment during World War II*. Westport, CT: Greenwood Press, 2002.

Overy, Richard. *The Dictators: Hitler's Germany, Stalin's Russia*. New York: W. W. Norton, 2004.

Read, Anthony. *The Devil's Disciples: Hitler's Inner Circle*. New York: W. W. Norton, 2003.

Sakamoto, Pamela Rotner. *Japanese Diplomats and Jewish Refugees: A World War II Dilemma*. Westport, CT: Praeger, 1998.

Shirer, William L. *The Rise and Fall of the Third Reich: A History of Nazi Germany*. New York: Simon & Schuster, 1981. Most recent edition 1990.

Shunsuke, Tsurumi. *An Intellectual History of Wartime Japan, 1931–1945*. London: KPI, 1986.

Smith, Denis Mack. *Mussolini's Roman Empire*. New York: Viking Press, 1976.

Stearns, Peter N., gen. ed. *The Encyclopedia of World History: Ancient, Medieval, and Modern, Chronologically Arranged*. 6th ed. Boston: Houghton Mifflin, 2001.

Stone, Geoffrey R. *Perilous Times: Free Speech in Wartime*. New York: W.W. Norton, 2004.

Time-Life Books. *Japan at War*. Alexandria, VA: Time-Life Books, 1980.

Toland, John. *The Rising Sun: The Decline and Fall of the Japanese Empire, 1936–1945*. Barnsley, South Yorkshire: Pen & Sword Military Classics, 2005.

Weinberg, Gerhard L. *Germany, Hitler, & World War II: Essays in Modern German and World History*. Cambridge: Cambridge University Press, 1995.

_____. *A World at Arms: A Global History of World War II*, 2nd ed. Cambridge: Cambridge University Press, 2005.

Willkie, Wendell. *One World*. New York: Simon & Schuster, 1943. Reissued 1966, by University of Illinois Press.

MOBILIZATION: THE RIFLE, THE WRENCH, AND THE RATIONING BOOK

"I tell you that Japanese planes were over this community. Death and destruction are likely to come to this city at any minute." That was the assessment in San Francisco of Lt. General John DeWitt, U.S. Fourth Army Commander, charged with defense of the Pacific Coast and western states. A day after the Japanese attacked the American naval base at Pearl Harbor in Hawaii, cities up and down the West Coast were ordered blacked out amid rumors of Japanese squadrons flying overhead. Harbors went on alert, soldiers patrolled bridges, and radio stations in the Bay Area went off the air lest enemy planes follow radio beams into the city. And DeWitt was irate that Alcatraz, the island-top federal prison in San Francisco Bay, had not gone dark at all. When the prison warden protested that he needed further federal authority to black out the facility, the general barked, "Who in hell do you think the Japs are at war with? The city of San Francisco? I represent the U.S. government, and I say turn out your god damn lights next time!"

The erroneous reports continued. On December 9, Southern California residents awoke to a large front-page banner headline in the *Los Angeles Times*: "ENEMY PLANES SIGHTED OVER CALIFORNIA COAST." In the early afternoon, word of air raids on New York City and hostile aircraft off the coast of Virginia sent the East Coast into a panic. Civilian plane spotters raced to their posts, servicemen manned antiaircraft guns, interceptor planes took to the skies as government officials grounded commercial flights, and the curious or the fearful created massive traffic jams complicated by orders to limit highway access to law enforcement and government vehicles. More than a million

Civil defense workers at the Potomac Electric Power Company building in Washington, D.C., demonstrate their responsibilities using three volunteer victims during an air raid drill.

schoolchildren were sent home or moved into school basements. The stock market dropped. Hours later, it was apparent that there was no enemy attack, and the false reports were traced to a misunderstood telephone call from a radio listener. Later, New York City officials noted that police and fire department sirens had failed to compel citizens to take immediate shelter; many had simply milled about outdoors, to the distress of Mayor Fiorello La Guardia, who, in his capacity as director of the Office of Civilian Defense (OCD), was touring the West Coast. In Seattle, where vigilantes out looking for Japanese parachutists smashed the windows of places that kept their lights on, La-Guardia told reporters, "Won't somebody catch hell about this when I get home? Here I go around the country telling people they must stay inside during air raid alarms. . . . Why won't you people realize that our whole coast, Atlantic, Gulf and Pacific, for 300 miles inland, is a target area?" Only the week before, La Guardia had met with the governors of six central states (seven others invited to meet did not attend) and discovered that the geographically buffered Midwest was even more lax. "We're situated in the middle of the nation," said Nebraska Governor Dwight Griswold, "and our citizens can't be sold on the idea that they're about to be bombed."

On December 10, thousands of Los Angeles residents mistook a tremendous electrical storm for a Japanese attack. The next day, Fourth Army headquarters claimed, "The main Japanese battle fleet is 164 miles off San Francisco. General alert of all units." Those living near the beach in Santa Cruz, Carmel, and Pebble Beach were briefly evacuated, and the army prepared to blow up the 6,000-foot long Summit railroad tunnel through the Santa Cruz mountains, opening the way into San Francisco. The alert proved to be a false alarm, and the tunnel was spared. "Had the Japs only known," said General Joseph Stilwell, III Corps Commander, "they could have landed anywhere on the coast, and after our hatful of ammunition was gone, they could have shot us like pigs in a pen." The following day the army command ordered a blackout from San Diego to Boulder City and Las Vegas, Nevada. In Hawaii, where martial law had been proclaimed, soldiers in Honolulu found themselves delivering babies of women unable to reach hospitals because of the blackouts.

Things were not much better in the nation's capital. On December 12, officials tested an air raid siren that supposedly had a three-mile range and learned it could not be heard beyond three blocks. When an official, much publicized, and highly anticipated air raid drill occurred December 21, half the city missed it, unable to hear weak air raid and fire sirens, as well as activated railroad and factory whistles. The *Washington Post*, in its front-page story headlined, "Raid-Alarm Test Works Well, Except for Sirens," reported an angry local official vowing that "every shortcut will be made to get some that really work." Police, firemen, air raid workers, and taxicab drivers, among others, received praise for their performance, and further, the *Post* noted somewhat incredulously, "Some of those who heard the alarm actually followed directions." On the other hand, "Police reported that as late as 11 A.M. people called in to ask when the air-raid practice would be held. That was an hour and a half after it was all over."

Throughout December on the jittery West Coast, car accidents increased dramatically in Los Angeles because of blackouts, overwhelming local ambulance service; meanwhile, new young sentries, shooting at car tires, accidentally killed or injured several passengers in vehicles unknow-ingly driven through checkpoints. Lightning strikes were mistaken for bomb strikes, a streetsweeper for a Japanese tank, whales for enemy sub-marines—and cattle were shot for not responding to "Who goes there?" On Christmas Day, it was reported that San Francisco would be getting louder air raid sirens "following numerous complaints that the noise they emitted during Saturday night's blackout was not alarming enough." But in Tacoma, Washington, after an air raid alarm test, callers complained that sirens had so many dogs in the city howling, they could not hear the all-clear signal. And at the National Guard Armory in Seattle, the alarm went off whenever some-one at the armory picked up the telephone. Except for torpedoes that Japa-nese submarines fired at several oil tankers and fishing boats off the California coast, every claim of enemy aircraft sightings, invasion forces and approaching battle fleets that December was false.

Clearly, the United States was not prepared for war. But that would change.

★   ★   ★

Mobilization—the preparation of governmental, military, industrial, and civilian entities to wage war and defend the homeland.

Introduction

Preparation for war was a massive undertaking that required converting from a peacetime to a wartime economy. It involved putting millions of peo-ple into uniform and training them as soldiers, sailors, and airmen; instruct-ing others for civilian war work, revising war plans and developing new ones; marshaling human expertise in science, engineering, medicine, design, and numerous other fields; and instituting measures (such as rationing and recy-cling) that would direct resources where they were needed most to build up and sustain the war effort. With many mobilization procedures already well under way in the 1930s, Japan and Germany prepared for a war of conquest; the Allies mobilized for self-preservation through homeland defense in re-sponse to Axis aggression. The Allies were also resolute that their efforts not only turn back the fascist threat, but destroy it. Among the major Allied combatants (Great Britain, the Soviet Union, and the United States as well as China), long-term mobilization efforts were especially effective because of the sharing of resources—including military bases—and the resulting standardization of procedures and matériel (particularly in munitions). For some nations, having mutual-assistance pacts was vital. (See also Chapter 2.) The United States also had a unique card to play: its massive Lend-Lease program (see "Lend-Lease" later in this chapter), intended to help keep the Allies armed, supplied, and capable of holding off the Axis until America joined the fight, should it come to that. Lend-Lease was so successful and crucial that it continued throughout the war.

Even so, no nation was completely ready for war when it came—including the aggressors. Japan, despite combat and occupation in parts of China since 1931, never resolved production obstacles and manpower shortages exacerbated by the intense rivalry between its army and navy. German industrial planners were expecting at least another year to develop the war economy when Adolf Hitler ordered the 1939 invasion of Poland. Neither Germany nor Japan yet had an organization to oversee economic mobilization between the military and civilian sectors. As for Italy, it had signed the May 1939 Pact of Steel alliance with Germany on the verbal understanding that it would need several years to modernize its industries and armed forces. Just over a year later, on learning from Mussolini that Italy would be invading France, Marshall Pietro Badoglio, chief of the armed forces general staff protested: "We have no arms, no tanks, no airplanes, not even shirts for our soldiers!"

Successful mobilization demanded competent management of food, labor, and matériel, a Herculean administrative and logistical task. Those doing the managing had to effectively allocate resources where they were needed most and could be most efficiently used. They also had to deal with competing corporate interests, intragovernmental rivalries, corruption, incompetence and other uncertainties, such as reliability in agricultural production (e.g., favorable weather, or the amount of arable land not being converted into military bases or manufacturing plants) and human labor (e.g., the availability of workers not already in the military who could be added to the workforce). Captains of industry, military leaders, and government officials hashed out how to set priorities for materials and manpower and how to supply firms and factories with what they needed to produce what the army and navy required. What happened—or did not happen—in the factory had a direct impact on the battlefield, including timing. Because of a shortage of one hundred-octane gasoline in 1942, for example, more American aircraft had been built than could fly, forcing a reduction in air operations. Thus, both the government and the military had to master the intricacies of industrial production and its timetables while industry had to come up with better designs and large-scale production methods to meet the military's voracious demands.

Nearly everyone with access to a newspaper in 1939 knew that the growing Axis threat meant war was likely, yet the rest of the world remained largely unprepared for war despite belated efforts to catch up. The War Resources Board—the first U.S. government agency expressly established to study and prepare for war mobilization—did not appear until August 1939. Particularly in totalitarian Germany and Japan, ongoing militarization was an established way of life, and the ideological need for military readiness had been relentlessly drummed into citizens' heads by way of incessant state propaganda, student organizations (such as Germany's *Hitler Youth*), and government-run labor and neighborhood associations. Conversely, in the democracies, streamlining disparate segments of society and ideas into a unified fighting machine presented a greater challenge. "When a democracy like our own is confronted with a national emergency, the government can operate only within the limits granted under the Constitution," observed *Washington Post* writer S. F. Perkins Jr., in 1938. A dictator, however, had fewer such obstacles to overcome in preparing for war.

Nevertheless, for all the combatant nations, managing such vast material resources resulted in a complex and bewildering matrix of government boards, commissions, committees, agencies, departments, ministries, and so on. The length to which a government could establish a cooperative, working relationship with business—whether by creating more state-owned and operated businesses, as the Soviets did, developing additional elite business cartels with close government ties, as the Japanese did, or forming public-private sector partnerships, as the Americans did—was a critical factor in successful mobilization. Inevitably, both government authority and the number of government employees needed to run the war increased dramatically. In Germany, the civil service found that its departments and functions were duplicated by the Nazi Party, bent on instilling its ideology in every facet of government, and the two entities continually stepped on each other. In Britain, the civil service grew from 375,000 employees to 670,000 during the war; in the United States, the federal government quadrupled in size, from 950,000 civilian employees in 1939 to 3.8 million in 1945.

Despite incessant Allied bombing and the loss of millions of workers to the Wehrmacht (the German armed forces), Germany managed to maintain high production levels. The Soviet Union, having transported more than 1,500 large industrial complexes and tens of thousands of smaller factories and workshops to the east (as well as building some 3,500 new factories) beyond the range of German aircraft, was second only to the United States in total aircraft production even as it battled Axis forces in its own front yard. Still, Soviet dictator Joseph Stalin, usually reluctant to credit others, observed more than once that American productivity made victory possible in both Europe and the Pacific. The United States staged a dramatic turnaround in enlarging its armed forces and producing weapons and equipment not only for itself but its allies. With the country spared from the bombing and destruction that ruined European and Japanese industrial might, military bases, inventory, housing, and morale, the American economy lumbered—then surged—forward, out of the Great Depression, and the nation's massive industrial effort would serve as a foundation for postwar prosperity.

Resources and Raw Materials

More mechanized, motorized, and modernized than any previous war, World War II ran on oil. The Allies and Axis also required rubber, coal, tin, iron ore, steel, wood, wool, industrial diamonds, and hundreds of other metals, natural resources, and raw materials. Oil was needed in many forms: refined gasoline, high-octane aviation fuel, petroleum lubricants, and much more. The need to have access to it sent Hitler into Romania with its productive oil fields, fueling the German drive into the Soviet Caucasus; drove the Japanese to attack the Dutch East Indies; spurred American defense of the Caribbean and southern Atlantic coast; and kept the British waist deep in the Middle East. Building a tank (which ran on gasoline) required steel, producing the steel required coal, digging the coal required steel, as did the vehicles used to service oil depots; those trucks or planes needed rubber tires, and Japan's corner on the world's rubber supply prompted greater production of synthetic rubbers, whose creation, in turn, demanded all manner of resources to construct and operate the manufacturing plants. Thus, the insatiable demand and consumption of raw materials during World War II affected every aspect of the conflict, from scheduling combat operations and selecting targets to political alliances and civilian morale.

Paying for War

How to finance the cost of raising armies and producing state-of-the-art weaponry and other goods was a critical part of mobilization planning.

INDUSTRIAL PRODUCTION OF KEY RESOURCES, BY COUNTRY, 1939–1945

(Millions of Metric Tons, Unless Otherwise Specified)

Resource by Year	U.K.	USA	USSR	Germany	Italy	Japan
Aluminum						
(in thousands)						
1939	25.0	—	—	239.4	—	—
1940	18.9	—	—	265.3	—	—
1941	22.7	—	—	315.6	—	—
1942	46.8	751.9	51.7	420.0	—	103.0
1943	55.7	1,251.7	62.3	432.0	—	141.0
1944	35.5	1,092.9	82.7	470.0	—	110.0
1945	31.9	1,026.7	86.3	—	—	7.0
Total	**283.0**	**4,123.2**	**236.5**	**2,142.3**	**—**	**361.0**
Coal						
1939	231.3	—	—	332.8	—	—
1940	224.3	—	—	364.8	4.4	—
1941	206.3	—	151.4	402.8	4.4	—
1942	204.9	528.5	75.5	407.8	4.8	61.3
1943	198.9	535.3	93.1	429.0	3.3	60.5
1944	192.7	562.0	121.5	432.8	—	51.7
1945	182.8	523.9	149.3	50.3	—	11.0
Total	**1,441.2**	**2,149.7**	**590.8**	**2,420.3**	**16.9**	**184.5**
Iron Ore						
1939	14.5	—	—	18.5	—	—
1940	17.7	—	—	29.5	1.2	—
1941	19.0	—	24.7	53.3	1.3	—
1942	19.9	107.6	9.7	50.6	1.1	7.4
1943	18.5	103.1	9.3	56.2	0.8	6.7
1944	15.5	96.0	11.7	32.6	—	6.0
1945	14.2	90.2	15.9	—	—	0.9
Total	**119.3**	**396.9**	**71.3**	**240.7**	**4.4**	**21.0**

INDUSTRIAL PRODUCTION OF KEY RESOURCES, BY COUNTRY, 1939–1945 (CONTINUED)

Resource by Year	U.K.	USA	USSR	Germany	Italy	Japan
Crude Oil						
1939	—	—	—	3.1	—	—
1940	11.9	—	—	4.8	0.01	—
1941	13.9	—	33.0	5.7	0.12	—
1942	11.2	183.9	22.0	6.6	0.01	1.8
1943	15.8	199.6	18.0	7.6	0.01	2.3
1944	21.4	222.5	18.2	5.6	—	1.0
1945	16.6	227.2	19.4	—	—	0.1
Total	**90.8**	**833.2**	**110.6**	**33.4**	**0.17**	**5.2**
Steel						
1939	13.2	—	—	23.7	—	—
1940	13.0	—	—	21.5	2.1	—
1941	12.3	—	17.9	28.2	2.1	—
1942	12.8	80.6	8.1	28.7	1.9	8.0
1943	13.3	82.2	8.5	30.6	1.7	8.8
1944	12.1	85.1	10.9	25.8	—	6.5
1945	11.8	86.6	12.3	1.4	—	0.8
Total	**88.5**	**334.5**	**57.7**	**159.9**	**7.8**	**24.1**

Source: John Ellis, *The World War II Databook*, London: BCA, under an arrangement with Arum Press, 2003.

Governments taxed citizens and businesses, sold war bonds, went into debt, printed more money (which China frequently did, resulting in rampant inflation), sought donations, especially in the form of gold and jewelry (in Italy, women turned in or were forced to give up their gold wedding rings, receiving steel rings from the government in return; in Chungking, schoolchildren solicited funds through the "Offer Gold to the State Movement"). In the historically unmatched case of Germany, the Nazi regime systematically stole from its victims on a monumental and astonishingly thorough scale.

TAXATION

Taxes, collected in various ways, were an obvious source of revenue in every country. In the Soviet Union, peasants, farm laborers, and others in agricultural industries made up about 60 percent of the population; the government took from them so much food as a form of tax that to feed themselves farmers had to work smaller private plots in addition to working on state farms. Food delivered to city markets also came with a high sales tax. Italians paid taxes on goods and consumption but had little trouble evading or simply ignoring newly imposed property taxes because assessment and collection were erratic. The government turned to state-owned banks for significant loans; the government's deficit grew by nearly 75 percent, from 29.4 billion lire in 1939–1940 to 109.8 billion in 1942–1943. In Japan, income tax was modest for those making a modest living (10 percent in 1942, 15 percent in 1944). But for those making just under $700 annually, then considered a princely sum, taxes could reach half of one's income. In Britain, the average middle class-household income was taxed at 29 percent in 1939 and 50 percent by the last year of the war. The government initiated an Excess Profits Tax (a tax on corporate profits that exceeded those during peacetime) that was first set at 60 percent, but in 1940, the year of the Blitz, reached 100 percent.

In Germany, about 18 to 20 percent of the typical factory worker's income was taken out in taxes and other government deductions, including mandatory dues for the German Labor Front and the People's Welfare Fund. Another 10 percent was taken out from October to March for Winter Relief, the Nazis' showcase charity for the poor. (Those who did not participate or donate as generously as expected were subject to harassment, public criticism, and physical beatings.) Between 1935 and 1938, the Reich paid war industries with special vouchers—kept off the open books by both the government and national bank—used solely for the purchase of armaments. This system amounted to merely printing more money. In early 1939, Germany's inability to cover the cost of its expanding military led the Nazi regime to implement a New Financial Plan: the government issued tax prepayment certificates for use as legal tender (except to pay wages and salaries), just like the regular currency, the Reichsmark. These certificates served as a mortgage on future taxes for current expenditures. The system was based on the belief, as Edwin James wrote in the *New York Times*, "that things are going to be so much better in the new and Greater Germany that things will arrange themselves. It is all a matter of faith in the Fuehrer." There may have been a shortage of government funds, but at the time, there was no shortage of confidence in Hitler.

In the United States, there were four major categories of taxes: on corporate income, individual income, employment, and alcohol and tobacco. Corporate income taxes rose several times during the war, and from 1942 to 1945 the government also collected an excess corporate profits tax. The average American citizen was soon taxed as well. In the prewar years, only about 10 percent of the wealthiest American households paid income tax; during the war, only the bottom 10 percent of households did not pay taxes—a shift from 4 million households taxed in 1939 to 43 million by 1945. The huge increase in taxpayers required a more efficient method of revenue collection, and in July 1943, the government required employers to withhold money for income taxes from workers' paychecks so that those funds would reach the Treasury Department regularly throughout the year, not in an annual lump sum. (The British would do the same under their PAYE plan—"Pay As You Earn.") The typical American taxpaying household, with a median income of about $2,000, paid a little more than 10 percent of its income in taxes, while the wealthiest households—those making more than $1 million, paid out about 90 percent. Still, U.S. income tax revenue—$147 billion—did not come close to covering the government's $350 billion war costs.

WAR BONDS
Government borrowing in the form of war bond sales was also essential. Soviet citizens purchased bonds to support the Red Army Fund and the Victory Fund, albeit not without government insistence at times. The British ran successful bond campaigns, and the German government stipulated that excess corporate dividends be invested in war bonds. Japan's *tonarigumi* (neighborhood associations, comprising ten to twelve families) also vigorously pushed workers to contribute another 20 percent of their income, in addition to taxes. But the bond program was most successful and enthusiastically supported in the United States. The bonds not only paid for a significant portion of war costs but also served to check inflation. As more Americans accepted high-paying jobs in the defense industry and as industry produced more war goods and fewer consumer products, the large surplus of individual income with less to spend it on made inflation—and the depression that would likely follow—a serious economic threat. By investing in war bonds (as well as paying income taxes), Americans could both support the war effort and divert excess income from the undersupplied marketplace, keeping inflation low.

Accompanied by the start of a four-year promotional blizzard backed by the War Advertising Council, the U.S. Treasury began selling *Victory Bonds* in May 1941 (President Franklin D. Roosevelt was the first to buy a Series E U.S. Savings Bond, the type most commonly purchased by individuals because it came in increments as low as $25; other bonds, for up to $10,000 were available to companies and commercial banks). The media donated hundreds of millions of dollars in free print, radio, and billboard advertising; and bond posters were ubiquitous. Beginning in 1942, buyers could participate in the Payroll Savings Plan, paying for their bond certificates through automatic paycheck deductions. The bonds yielded a return of 2.9 percent after ten years, but could be cashed in earlier. The War Finance Committee in the Department of the Treasury oversaw eight major bond campaigns featuring patriotic rallies with bands, auctions, and competitions. Six million volunteers (including entertainment and sports celebrities and even cartoon icons) sold $157 billion worth of war bonds. In one eighteen-hour marathon on September 21, 1943, broadcast nationwide on radio, singer Kate Smith—best known for introducing Irving Berlin's "God Bless America"—single-handedly raised $39 million in bond pledges. The campaigns surpassed their sales goals by more than $50 billion, as 85 million Americans invested in war bonds.

CRIMINAL ACTS

Theft, looting, and slave labor—all long-standing methods used to help cover war costs—reached unprecedented, staggering proportions in World War II. Both Japan and Germany officially sanctioned deliberate criminal activity and authorized extreme cruelty, but whatever corrupt or unjust methods of obtaining revenue other nations may have used, German activity was in a notorious class by itself. Besides a huge increase in sales and income tax initiated at the beginning of the war, outright and highly organized theft kept the Nazi war machine humming without requiring additional sacrifices on the home front before 1943. The Germans charged occupation fees in the countries it conquered; the French paid the Reich more than half of its revenue for occupation expenses, some 20 million marks a day. France also became the Nazis' most valuable source for food, raw materials, manufactured products (the Germans snatched more than 40 percent of France's industrial output), and a large forced-labor source. Germany took more than half of France's mineral ores, aluminum, steel, cement, wool, wood, and, of course, its champagne. German occupying forces in Greece sent massive quantities of food to its armies around Europe, largely contributing to the deaths from starvation of between 250,000 and 400,000 Greek civilians. In conquered countries, the Nazis stole state wealth (including gold reserves), art treasures, food supplies, and inhabitants' property, including furniture and livestock; they also forcibly sent some 5 million people to Germany to work in factories, on farms, in mines, and elsewhere as needed, for little or no pay and most often in horrendous conditions. Millions more were forced into labor outside Germany. Another despicable Nazi scheme was the meticulous, cataloged theft from millions of people held in concentration camps and systematically murdered in death camps. Train load after packed train load of cash, clothes, jewelry, children's toys and other goods seized from victims were sent to Berlin for German use and to fund the war effort. (See also Chapter 8.)

"We Will Not Accept a Hitler-Dominated World"

Until the attack on Pearl Harbor brought the United States into the war and American isolationism virtually evaporated, many Americans argued against increasing military spending while others, such as Democratic Senator Harry S. Truman of Missouri, pushed for more government action since the country "went rather hysterical on disarmament" after the first world war and unloaded all manner of equipment at bargain prices. Still, prewar isolationist sentiment helped shape national debate. On September 8, 1939, following the German invasion of Poland, Roosevelt cautiously declared a "limited national emergency" to strengthen national defense and safeguard American neutrality. On May 16, 1940, after Hitler's invasions of Scandinavia, Belgium, and France, Roosevelt called on Congress "not to take any action which would in any way hamper or delay the delivery of American-made planes to foreign [allied] nations." He urged production of 50,000 planes a year and a speedup in manufacture of trucks, artillery, tanks, and other items. He also requested an immediate appropriation of $896 million in military spending. Modest expansion and upgrades in the armed forces continued apace, but by the spring of 1941, with most of Europe under Nazi occupation (and in light of recent news from the War Department that labor strikes had cost companies with defense contracts 1.7 million man hours in lost production time since January 1, 1940), the president addressed a record radio audience on May 27, 1941.

Roosevelt described the threat Hitler posed: "[W]hat started as a European war has developed, as the Nazis always intended it should develop, into a war for world domination." He pledged a national policy to "actively resist wherever necessary, and with all our resources, every attempt by Hitler to extend his Nazi domination to the Western Hemisphere, or to threaten it," and to "give every possible assistance to Britain and to all who . . . are resisting Hitlerism or its equivalent with force of arms." He pointed out, "Your government has the right to expect of all citizens that they take part in the common work of our common defense" and "The future of all free enterprise—of capital and labor alike—is at stake." The president condemned both excess corporate profits and work stoppages that interfere "with the production of materials essential to the nation's security." He concluded, "I have tonight issued a proclamation that an unlimited national emergency exists and requires the strengthening of our defense to the extreme limit of our national power and authority. The nation will expect all individuals and all groups to play their full parts without stint, without selfishness, and without doubt that our democracy will triumphantly survive."

The Hotel Yucca, outside Capulin, New Mexico, advertises its new name in September 1939. Many German-sounding American business and street names were changed during the war.

Lend-Lease

What British Prime Minister Winston Churchill called "without question . . . the most unsordid act in the whole of recorded history" became U.S. law on March 11, 1941. The Lend-Lease Act (followed by a Lend-Lease Executive Order on October 28, 1941) provided for the procurement, manufacture, and transfer (by loan, lease, or sale) of defense items—most crucially, aircraft, tanks, ships, trucks, jeeps, munitions, and high-octane fuel—as well as food and services to countries whose defense was deemed crucial to the United States. Developed to assist Britain and countries in the British Empire, as well as China, the program was expanded in November 1941 to include the Soviet Union, which had been attacked by Germany in June; and eventually, it included most other Allied nations. Several Latin American countries, particularly Brazil, also received aid to shore up regional defenses. The following table shows the value of aid given to each country with a Lend-Lease agreement (or exiled governments and free military forces from occupied countries). A "reverse Lend-Lease program" of goods from Allies to American forces overseas was introduced in 1942.

LEND-LEASE AID FROM THE UNITED STATES TO ALLIED NATIONS, MARCH 1941–JULY 1946

Theater	Country	Amount ($)
The Americas	Bolivia	5,633,989.02
	Brazil	332,545,226.45
	Chile	21,817,478.16
	Colombia	7,809,732.58
	Costa Rica	155,022.73
	Cuba	5,739,133.33
	Dominican Republic	1,610,590.38
	Ecuador	7,063,079.96
	El Salvador	892,358.28

(continued)

LEND-LEASE AID FROM THE UNITED STATES TO ALLIED NATIONS, MARCH 1941–JULY 1946 (CONTINUED)

Theater	Country	Amount ($)
	Guatemala	1,819,403.19
	Haiti	1,449,096.40
	Honduras	372,358.11
	Mexico	36,287,010.67
	Nicaragua	872,841.73
	Panama	83,555.92
	Paraguay	1,933,302.00
	Peru	18,525,771.19
	Uruguay	7,148,610.13
	Venezuela	4,336,079.35
China-Burma-India	China	1,548,794,965.99
European	Belgium	148,394,457.76
	British Empire and Commonwealth*	31,267,240,530.63
	Czechoslovakia	413,398.78
	France (Free French and its possessions)	3,207,608,188.75
	Greece	75,475,880.30
	Iceland	4,795,027.90
	Netherlands (and its possessions)	230,127,717.63
	Norway	51,524,124.36
	Poland	16,934,163.60
	Soviet Union	11,260,343,603.02
	Yugoslavia	32,026,355.58
North African and Mid East	Egypt	1,019,169.14
	Ethiopia	5,151,163.25

LEND-LEASE AID FROM THE UNITED STATES TO ALLIED NATIONS, MARCH 1941–JULY 1946 (CONTINUED)

Theater	Country	Amount ($)
	Iran	4,797,092.50
	Iraq	4,144.14
	Liberia	6,408,240.13
	Saudi Arabia	17,417,878.70
	Turkey	26,640,031.50
	Total charges to Allies	48,361,210,768.24
	U.S. program costs	2,578,827,000.00
	Total cost/aid	**50,940,037,768.24**

Source: New York Times, October 20, 1946.

*Great Britain received the bulk of this Lend-Lease aid, but portions of it also went to its Commonwealth members and dominions, including Australia, Canada, India, New Zealand, and South Africa

Military Mobilization

All the major combatants built military forces with millions of uniformed troops—so many, once the war began, that industry had to catch up in producing weapons to arm them. Mobilization also meant upgrading and expanding housing and training facilities, mastering new weapons, devices, and maneuvers (such as combined land, sea, and air operations), building fortifications, and much more. Fledgling air forces and refurbishing navies competed with armies for more of the growing defense budgets. The consensus among European military experts in July 1939 was that the standing 600,000-man French army, which could mobilize up to 10 million men, was the finest in the world while the Germans had the best air force and the British the strongest navy. Within a year, the Nazis occupied France and were bombarding Britain. In October 1940, the United States, prompted by these recent developments, would hold its first peacetime draft, the initial step toward creating the largest military force in American history. (See also Chapter 4.)

Building and Mobilizing the Armed Forces

AXIS FORCES

JAPAN. The Imperial Japanese Army had maintained conscription since its inception in 1873, and Japan's forces in the 1930s were disciplined, well trained, battle-tested and fit—even more so after the government enacted new public health regulations in May 1937. Between 1937 and 1941, the army grew from seventeen divisions to thirty-one (not counting its colonial Korean, Formosan, and Kwantung [Manchuria] armies). After Japan attacked the United States, it drafted most men at age 20 who were not attending college; by 1944 the age of eligibility was lowered to 18 and exemptions were limited to students studying the sciences. Japan also formed auxiliary forces in Java and elsewhere to help with coastal defense in the East Indies, and later helped raise the Indian National Army and the Burma Independence Army, both of which would serve in the Burma campaign. Japan's large naval rearmament program—which began in the 1930s with violations of tonnage limits set at the 1922 arms conference—included additional aircraft carriers, two of the most powerful battleships ever built, improved cruisers, and an expanded submarine force.

GERMANY. On March 16, 1935, Hitler announced that the German army was raising thirty-six new divisions through conscription, giving him an army well beyond the 100,000-man limit permitted in the Treaty of Versailles, although secret rearmament plans had been well under way in Germany long before he came to power. Two months later, Hitler announced a program to develop the *Wehrmacht* ("power for defense"), a term encompassing the army, navy, and the newly created air force. Thanks to the draft, an enthusiastic recruitment campaign, and a large supply of former Hitler Youth members, military troop strength reached 4.5 million by 1939. To ensure that new troops knew what they would be fighting for, classes in Nazi ideology became part of basic training.

Although Hitler lavished attention on the army, in early 1939 Germany put into effect an eight-year program (Plan Z) to improve the navy, focusing on new battleships and a modern surface fleet. However, submarines proved to be Germany's greatest maritime asset, devastating Allied shipping and naval communication in the Atlantic. With the success of the U-boat program and the sudden starts and stops in aircraft carrier production in response to battlefield events and the needs of the army, Plan Z was subsequently tossed overboard, and the navy commissioned more than 1,100 new U-boats over the next several years. Work on the *Zeppelin*, the one aircraft carrier under construction after 1940, was abandoned and the unfinished ship scuttled two weeks before the war ended. Many factors, from labor shortages to transfer of raw materials to political infighting, prevented the development of a strong and balanced naval fleet.

In building and expanding the German *Luftwaffe* (air force), private industry, led by such firms as Folke Wulf, Junkers, and Messerschmitt, made pioneering advancements in aircraft design. German pilots honed their combat skills in the Condor Legion, which fought on the side of Generalissimo Francisco Franco's Nationalists in the Spanish Civil War. As of September 1939, the Luftwaffe had more than 3,600 high-quality aircraft manned by well trained, experienced crews. The Luftwaffe took delivery of nearly 120,000 planes during the war, though not necessarily the most suitable type for strategic bombing of enemy assets. By 1943, Allied bombing raids on industrial and military centers in Germany had prompted increased production of rapid fighters; as for the slow, inadequately armed German bombers (whose operational deficiencies became apparent during the Battle of Britain), the aircraft industry had no improved versions in the production pipeline until very late in the war. Resources were also redirected to the *Vergeltungswaffen*, the V1 and V2 unmanned weaponized rockets. About 30,000 were built, but only about a third had been used by war's end.

ITALY. Conscripted soldiers formed the bulk of the 1.6-million-man Italian army in 1940, and about 300,000 Blackshirts (Fascist militia) were also on duty at home and in the colonies. Attempts to strengthen the Italian army were hampered by pressing units into action before they—and Italian industry—were ready. Italy's radio-less tanks were among the worst in Europe, its transportation vehicles were desperately out of date, and soldiers were often sent out with obsolete or inadequate equipment. Italian units in the North African desert were not even supplied with proper compasses until late in the campaign. With the war going badly, plans to replace World War I-era artillery and other stock beginning in 1942 were not executed before the Italian surrender in 1943. Italy did, however, dramatically increase its naval personnel from 168,614 in June 1940 to 259,000 by August 1943, yet it lacked aircraft carriers, radar, spare parts, and frequently fuel. Meanwhile, the Italian merchant marine hardly had a chance to mobilize—

Mussolini did not order Italian ships in foreign ports to sea before he declared war on France on June 10, 1940. Thus 218 ships, about a third of the merchant marine fleet, were trapped in what suddenly became enemy ports. This huge loss was not made up in the course of the war. As for the *Regia Aeronautica* (Royal Air Force), its collective combat experience in Spain, Ethiopia, and Albania in the 1930s did not make up for its—and the aircraft industry's—failure to keep up with new technology. Among the major combatants, only Italy regularly continued to use bi-planes on the front line, and the air force, like the other service branches, suffered from inadequate industrial mobilization.

OTHER AXIS PARTNERS. Germany's other Axis partners also were not ready or modernized enough to follow Hitler into war given their lack of wealth and industrial infrastructure, as well as their large rural populations. Two years after participating in the invasion of Russia, Hungary still had only a third of the motorized vehicles it needed, and six of its ten Alpine battalions traveled on bicycles. Bulgaria's conscript soldiers were underequipped and untrained for modern warfare. And Romania left development and mobilization of its armed forces primarily to its Nazi mentor. Because of German largesse, the Romanian air force (956 aircraft) and modest navy (19 naval vessels) were robust compared with those of other eastern and southern European nations.

ALLIED FORCES

CHINA. Japan's principal victim in the 1930s, China fought back in a haphazard manner, given the political divisions in the country. Both the Chinese Communists and the Nationalists (the government that the United States recognized) had their own forces, which fought each other as well as Japan. It was often difficult for the Chinese to build and maintain regional armies when local troops found it necessary to change sides from time to time simply to survive. Nationalist General Chiang Kai-shek chaired the National Military Council, which controlled mobilization and military operations. During the war, the Nationalists drafted some 14 million men and eventually built up three hundred divisions, although they were undermanned, poorly trained, and ill-equipped. Despite U.S. assistance in 1942, the Chinese air force—decimated by Japan in 1938—remained insignificant. Communist regular forces, better trained but even more poorly equipped, grew in strength from a mere 92,000 in 1937 to 500,000 in 1940 to 910,000 by the spring of 1945. Instead of conscription, the Communists formed a system of part-time village militias and recruited men between the ages of 15 and 50 years, especially in rural areas, who were suitably trained before reaching the regular ranks.

GREAT BRITAIN. Meanwhile, Britain had approved a peacetime draft in April 1939, its first in three hundred years, to supplement its Regular Army and a Territorial Army. The latter produced what became the British Expeditionary Force, deployed to the Franco-Belgium border in September 1939. Regular army forces grew from 879,000 then to 2.9 million in 1945. Britain also benefited from its empire. (See also British forces charts in Chapter 4.) Its Commonwealth members, except for the Irish Free State, willingly mobilized for war in September 1939; and its African, Asian, and Indian colonial armies made tremendous contributions to the Allied war effort. Australia began conscription in July 1940 but used draftees for home defense, sending only volunteers overseas until February 1943, when the government yielded to U.S. pressure. Canada similarly limited draftees to home duty when conscription was approved in June 1940. With additional Allied forces needed, this policy changed in 1942, resulting in political crises that year and in 1944. In all, more than 533,000 Canadians enlisted and another half million were drafted. New Zealand was antimilitaristic, but the government, understanding the Japanese threat, planned its defense under Britain's imperial umbrella (the indigenous Maoris even raised an infantry battalion) and contributed financially toward a naval base in Singapore. South African and Indian forces both lacked modern equipment and transport; in addition, South Africa's segregated army was short of white recruits, and blacks were restricted to support service. Indian troops, initially hampered by a large number of uneducated volunteers speaking various languages, had become a formidable force by summer 1940, and India raised the largest volunteer army the world had ever seen, numbering 2.5 million.

Britannia still ruled the seas in 1939, and its three major fleets (Home, Mediterranean, and Eastern) comprised 332 ships and 60 submarines. More than 550 additional vessels were commissioned during the war, but shipping losses outpaced British shipyards. Not until 1944, with regular shipments of American Liberty Ships (quickly mass-produced using a standard design) could Britain make up for shortages in its merchant fleet. The government decided in February 1940 to begin arming merchant ships, and that summer to requisition all vessels. Some merchant ships, converted to accommodate aircraft, served as convoy escorts. The British Royal Navy also incorporated the ships from Axis-occupied nations (e.g., France, Holland, Norway, Poland), and despite very small navies, Australia, Canada, and New Zealand all contributed to the British Fleet. Canada began with only ten warships but grew to be the third largest Allied navy, with 365 ships. Most crucially, it escorted convoys in the Atlantic, but it also assisted in the Mediterranean and in the Normandy invasion. The Royal Indian Navy, charged with coastline defense, grew considerably as well—from 1,708 men to 30,478—and performed duties in the Mediterranean and Atlantic.

The British air force became unusually international in nature: men from all over the British Empire and occupied Europe (even Americans before the U.S. entry into the war) served in the Royal Air Force (RAF). Before the RAF's legendary defense of England in 1940, Canada became home to the British Empire Air Training Scheme, which eventually trained nearly 170,000 men, more than 75,000 as pilots. Canada, selected for its secure location and expansive territory, managed the program and covered more than half of the $607 million cost, with Britain, Australia, and New Zealand sharing the rest. Training a pilot took longer than producing a plane, so state-of-the-art aircraft had to wait for qualified pilots before they could go into action.

Soviet Union. On paper, the military might of the Soviet Union was colossal—including millions of troops—but the Red Army faced considerable disadvantages, including the murder and imprisonment of thousands of officers in the political purges of 1937–1938, resulting in a terrible loss of military and technical knowledge. (See also Chapter 4.) Although it was fairly quick to make necessary adjustments—such as noticeably improving winter combat wear following disastrous experiences with frostbite and disintegrating boots in its war with Finland (1939–1940), soldiers vastly outnumbered supplies after the huge military call-ups beginning in late June 1941. There were not enough weapons or ammunition to go around, and during training, one serviceman recalled, he and his comrades were only shown a Tokarev rifle and a Maksim machine gun; neither was demonstrated.

Having received substantial intelligence that Germany was preparing to invade, the Soviets started moving five armies, including troops from the Far East, to take up positions in the west; some 800,000 reservists were activated and another fifty-three divisions were deployed. About 4,000 top military personnel imprisoned in gulags, the harsh labor camps in the east, were gradually released and returned to active duty. The Russians were still deploying forces when Germany attacked, and commanders struggled westward against a wave of civilian evacuees surging east. At the time of the invasion, there were nearly 5.4 million uniformed soldiers (mostly young conscripts, though men up to age 36 were also drafted), and within ten days 5 million more were activated. However, the Soviets initially could not effectively maneuver and coordinate their forces. Hastily formed, partially armed, and completely untrained divisions of volunteers were thrown against the Nazi onslaught and annihilated. Since the USSR had a population of more than 170 million (nearly two and a half times larger than Germany's), new conscripts quickly took the place of those killed in action. In addition, 800,000 women also enlisted in the Red Army. Still, the Soviet leadership recognized that mobilizing ill-equipped militias was also harming war industries, which desperately needed workers, but that, above all, it was essential to buy time—despite devastating losses of lives and territory—so that the frantically mobilized war economy could produce the arsenal needed to win. In the meantime, the Soviets had an underutilized navy. Despite a massive undertaking begun in 1938, the navy had no aircraft carriers, and only a handful of ships had been constructed by the time Germany invaded. Fifty-four submarines were built during the war, comprising about a quarter of the underwater fleet. Air Reserve was created in the fall of 1941, and army and navy aircraft constituted the largest air force in Europe. The USSR also availed itself of an asset as did no other belligerent nation: it permitted women to fly in combat, and women entirely composed three air force regiments.

OTHER ALLIED PARTNERS. Poland, with a population that was half the size of Germany and largely rural, still boasted a 280,000-man army, a navy with nine modern vessels and a four-hundred-plane air force. When the Germans invaded, the Poles were in the process of producing an automatic rifle and were manufacturing improved antitank guns. They were building fifty tanks a year and taking delivery of more from France, and had ordered British and French aircraft. Despite considerable economic limitations, the Poles had made serious efforts to prepare for war, and they managed to hold out for more than a month. France was in the midst of a major rearmament program when the war began and was not as prepared or capable as outside observers believed. Half of its field guns were horse-drawn relics from World War I, suited for static, trench-style warfare; nor could slow-moving French aircraft or tanks resist the high-speed German blitzkrieg style of war. When the fighting started, France had produced only 27 percent of its planned new machine guns, cannon, and antiaircraft weapons. The air force had fewer than nine hundred modern or serviceable fighters and bombers along with antiquated French and British aircraft; the navy had several new battleships but, like Germany, no aircraft carriers. France mobilized nearly 5 million soldiers and had ninety-four divisions to defend itself and its colonies, with three divisions added in early 1940.

NEUTRAL STATES. For smaller nations, unpreparedness was not a matter of having fewer citizens for an army or a war industry, or insufficient natural resources; Switzerland demonstrated that its population was well trained and equipped. However, after seeing the horrors of World War I from the trenches or the sidelines, most European countries wanted to avoid another major conflict. Beginning in the mid-1930s, the smaller states concluded—too late—that the increasing fascist aggression meant rearmament was necessary. They did develop plans for evacuating, establishing governments-in-exile, and securing state treasuries. They also constructed a variety of expensive and labor-intensive fortifications. Realistically, however, nations such as Denmark or Luxembourg knew they could not hold off the German army for even a week. If their neutrality was violated, they expected Britain and France would somehow come to their rescue.

The United States Armed Forces

THE U.S. ARMY

In 1937, Czechoslovakia had about the same number of men in its armed forces as there were in the American military, yet the United States, with 132 million citizens, had a population nine times larger and seventy times as much continental territory to defend. Experts believed that the regular army (175,000 men in 1938) and the national guard (400,000) would need to expand to about 730,000 "all purpose" men during wartime, with another 270,000 in reserve. The War Department then created the enlisted reserve: 75,000 former servicemen who would be immediately available at any time during their four-year commitment. But as Germany swallowed up much of western Europe in the spring of 1940, the U.S. Army began a pivotal phase of reorganization, expansion, modernization, and mobilization. With ten undermanned Regular Army divisions and eighteen manned but under-trained National Guard divisions, Congress passed the Selective Service Act in September 1940. The army initially could not provide all of the hundreds of thousands of draftees with equipment or housing, and it was trying simultaneously to cope with other challenges: the cavalry was making the transition from literal horse power to motorized vehicles; military commanders were reconfiguring training programs for new combat forces (including

AMERICAN CONSCRIPTION

Just six weeks after Congress approved the Selective Service Act, an enormous effort that would transform the U.S. military and an entire generation was under way. All men aged 18–45 were required to register, but initially only those 21 to 31 years old would be eligible for the military draft (later, eligibility began at 18, and men up to age 65 had to register). On October 16, at 6,443 local draft boards nationwide, 16.3 million men registered and each received a draft number. Sixteen days later, a blindfolded Henry L. Stimson, secretary of war, joined by President Roosevelt, drew from a large glass bowl filled with nine thousand small capsules, each containing a single draft number. All men who held the number drawn had to report to their draft boards for questioning and a physical exam. Each board, comprising citizens appointed by that state's governor, determined every draftee's suitability for service and heard any appeals. These boards exercised great independence and wielded considerable control over a young man's fate. Men deemed fit for service were soon directed when to report for induction. About 5 million men were rejected, for reasons including poor vision or teeth, or poor general health, venereal disease, illiteracy, flat feet, and emotional instability. Boards could also grant deferments for economic, educational, religious, or family reasons; nearly 2 million farm workers received waivers, as did students in certain fields, such as the sciences. Gradually, with more men needed, deferments and exemptions became more difficult to obtain, and young fathers were eligible for the draft. All told, almost 50 million men registered and 10 million were drafted; relatively few, perhaps 170,000, apparently tried deception to avoid conscription. More than 35,000 conscientious objectors were assigned to noncombat military duty or to nonpaying public service jobs, including construction and hospital work. In 1940, the United States had 270,000 men in the army, 161,000 in the navy, and 28,000 marines; by late summer of 1941, the army had reached its goal of 1.5 million men and curtailed further enlistments while new base housing was constructed. Despite the crowds at some recruiting centers following Pearl Harbor, about two-thirds of those who served in the military were drafted.

armored, antiaircraft and antitank units, mountain troops, and paratroopers) in Arctic, desert, jungle, or mountain settings; and there was a need for improved officer instruction. In September, General Lesley McNair, commander of the Army Ground Forces, visited a division in training and reported that "they were simply at 'drill'—blind leading the blind." Inspections at training sites revealed deficiencies such as troops failing to monitor ammunition supplies or evacuate the wounded, as well as lapses in signal communications, inadequate use of antitank guns, and perhaps most disconcerting in highly mechanized warfare, a lack of understanding among commanders on employing motor vehicles to full advantage.

In August 1940, Roosevelt won a struggle over presidential authority when Congress approved a bill federalizing the normally state-controlled National Guard for a year of emergency service; within two weeks tens of thousands were mobilized for duty. About the same time, 14,000 of the 104,000-man Officer Reserve Corps went on active duty. In August and through the fall, large-scale maneuvers took place in the Carolinas, Louisiana, and Washington State. To gain additional officers, the War Department in December accelerated graduation at the U.S. Military Academy (West Point) and U.S. Naval Academy (Annapolis) by six months. In a February 16, 1942, General Headquarters directive, the army established the concept of a ten- to twelve-month training period to ready a division for combat, and nearly 4.5 million men would train for ground combat duty this way.

U.S. ARMY AIR FORCES

A component of the U.S. Army, the Army Air Corps in 1939 began frantically trying to catch up to the German Luftwaffe in numbers and technology. Congress authorized some $8 billion in spending from 1939 to 1941 for increased personnel and aircraft production, and aircraft manufacturers were alerted to expect massive new orders. In 1941, the air corps became the Army Air Forces (the U.S. Air Force, an independent service branch, was established in 1947) and was given temporary autonomy, which it battled to maintain. The USAAF soared from 150,000 men before the war to a peak of 2.4 million; its air fleet expanded from 4,000 planes to nearly 80,000 at its peak in July 1944, as American industry sought to meet—and then exceeded—Roosevelt's call for 50,000 new planes a year. At newly established air corps training centers, some still under construction, young pilots learned specialized types of flying and lessons drawn from Allied combat experience in Europe.

THE U.S. NAVY

For the first two years of the draft, conscripts were sent to the army; the navy (and marine corps) did not begin taking draftees until the end of 1942. However, the navy's long post-World War I stagnation ended when Congress appropriated $50 million in 1937 for new ships; $15 million in 1938 for new light surface craft; and $65 million in 1939 for new naval air bases as

A. L. Way (fourth from left) directs an industrial film at the Bethlehem-Fairfield Shipyard in Baltimore, Maryland, where Victory ships, such as the Madawaska, *were built. More than 500 Victory ships were produced for the U.S. Army Transport Service.*

well as $55 million to include dry-dock construction. In 1939, the navy had fifteen battleships along with five aircraft carriers, more than one hundred submarines, and its own aviation wing. Besides the U.S. Pacific Fleet, the navy had an Asiatic Fleet operating out of Manila and a small Atlantic Squadron (renamed the Atlantic Fleet in early 1941) on the East Coast. Four days after the European war began, the squadron's ships and aircraft served as a Neutrality Patrol, monitoring the Atlantic coastline throughout the Western Hemisphere. In 1940, the navy launched the USS *Washington*, its first battleship in twenty years; and the $300 million Vinson-Walsh Act reflected a fundamental shift to create a "two-ocean navy." As a result, shipyards expanded and new ones were built on both coasts. From July 1940 to August 1945, the navy obtained nearly 75,000 vessels, including more than 66,000 landing craft from which marines and soldiers would assault beaches throughout the Pacific, in North Africa and Italy, and at Normandy.

SERVICEWOMEN

Women were not drafted for military service; they were recruited. Inspired, in part, by the success and contributions of British military women, Representative Edith Nourse Rogers (R-Massachusetts) proposed legislation in March 1941 permitting women to enlist. At the time, Congress allowed them only in the Army Nurse Corps (established 1901) and the Navy Nurse Corps (1908). But after Pearl Harbor, and with the strong support of Secretary of War Stimson and General George Marshall, army chief of staff, most of Congress suddenly found servicewomen an excellent idea. Despite a declaration from Representative Hampton P. Fulman, D-South Carolina, that "This is the most ridiculous bill ever presented to Congress. Woman's place is in the home," the House approved Rogers' follow-up bill 249-86 in March 1942. It reflected a surge of support that had been building for the plan, also evidenced by stacks of mail in the congresswoman's office from women eager to serve. As one woman from Newark, New Jersey, wrote, "If there is any doubt of our ability, look at what women are doing in England and Russia." And a schoolteacher from Santa Fe, New Mexico, told the congresswoman, "I sincerely hope you can make the men see it our way."

The Women's Army Auxiliary Corps (later called Women's Army Corps, or WACs), which recruited heavily among college students, was soon followed by the Women's Naval Reserve (1942), known as the WAVES (Women Accepted for Volunteer Emergency Service); the Coast Guard

A major part of the American mobilization effort involved moving women into occupations formerly held by men or encouraging women to serve in the armed forces. This 1943 WAAC recruiting poster suggests that more men can be sent overseas—and returned home sooner—if women enlist in the military.

Women's Reserve (1942), known as SPARs (an acronym derived from the Coast Guard motto—*semper paratus*, meaning "always ready"), and the Marine Corps Women's Reserve (1943). A civilian branch, run by the army, called the WAFS (Women's Auxiliary Ferrying Squadron), comprised female pilots, as did its spin-off, the WASPs (Women Airforce Service Pilots). About 300,000 women served in the military during the war, taking on hundreds of scientific, technical, and administrative occupations, which released servicemen for combat duty. (See also Chapter 4.)

American Military Planning for War and Industry

To determine the military's manufacturing needs, army and navy planners developed possible scenarios that would then suggest the amount and type of resources that were required. In the mid-1930s, the War Plans Division had envisioned a scenario (code-named Rainbow 5—potential enemies were assigned different colors) of a coalition with Britain against Germany and Italy, while the Army War College studied scenarios pitting an Allied coalition against Japan or an enemy coalition against the United States. As late as January 1941, thanks to the United States' ocean buffer zones, its comparatively meager defense budgets, and its isolationist sentiment, many planners expected the army's primary duty would lie in defending the United States and perhaps other regions in the Western Hemisphere, and not waging war on a global scale. The major shift in thinking to worldwide operations manifested itself in the Victory Program. That September, Major Albert Wedemeyer of the War Plans Division, who worked closely with navy planners, issued the program report that became the foundation for planning American military operations and determining production needs. To accomplish the most critical objective—the total defeat of Germany—the United States would have to employ 8.7 million soldiers and double existing production and manufacturing plans at an estimated cost of $150 billion. The actual financial bill was more than twice as much. On the other hand, the United States fought with just 89 divisions, not the 215 that Wedemeyer estimated would be needed.

SUPPLY PLANNING

By 1937, the War Department had assigned 10,000 manufacturing plants to one or more of the military supply branches in case of mobilization, and most plants agreed to these voluntary assignments. In early 1938, Assistant Secretary of War Colonel Louis Johnson told the press, "We have enough of the ordinary supplies to take care of our soldiers for a period of six months. The same cannot be said, however, of . . . airplanes, anti-aircraft and long-range guns, gas masks and other more modern and essential accouterments." Shortly before the European war began, Roosevelt put the Army-Navy Munitions Board under his direct oversight. The board stockpiled key industrial resources, determined manufacturing capacity and, most significantly, awarded contracts for new products as World War I era supplies ran low or became obsolete. Despite its procurement powers, the Munitions Board could not order up a new calendar to give the military what it needed most—time. In December 1940, to keep the newly enlarged forces adequately supplied, Roosevelt named Robert P. Patterson, a former appellate judge and assistant secretary of war, to a specially created position as undersecretary of war in the War Department. Patterson's responsibilities were critical, wide-ranging, and gargantuan. He managed the army's production and procurement program, visited military bases (where he tried out machine guns and antiaircraft guns himself) and overseas battle areas, and simultaneously served on several other boards. As Roosevelt had witnessed, equipment was scarce. In an August 1940 inspection of army units in upstate New York, generals told FDR that some men drilled with drainpipes instead of trench mortars, while others substituted broomsticks for machine guns; and a procession past the presidential motorcade included trucks doubling as "tanks" and taxicabs impersonating the motor transport pool. A year later, the situation had improved considerably, but not entirely. In 1941, Charles Wilkinson was a 21-year-old second lieutenant and platoon leader assigned to the 76th Tank Battalion at Fort Lewis, Washington. "We began trying to set up a training program," he would later recall. "Trouble was, we had little or nothing to train with. We were a tank battalion without tanks. We actually made wooden frameworks to use as tanks, so we could practice."

CONSTRUCTION

Even before conscription, Roosevelt ordered $25 million in preparatory work for cantonments (temporary housing) for 400,000 soldiers. Improving military bases was urgent; the huge influx of personnel into limited training facilities and frequently obsolete installations drastically slowed down mobilization. Resources were also stretched to meet the construction demands for industrial production. To improve efficiency, Patterson and Secretary of War Stimson put the Army Corps of Engineers (COE) in charge of all army (and some industrial) construction, replacing the overextended Quartermasters Corps. The COE built barracks, factories, hospitals, and installations throughout the country. Before the war, the army had fewer than 20 mainland military air fields available, but by the end of 1943, the corps had built 345 bases, 116 sub-bases, and 322 auxiliary fields.

Simultaneously, the COE was involved in other major projects. A feared Japanese invasion of Alaska prompted construction of the 1,520-mile Alaska Highway (Alcan) to transport military goods to bases there. In brutal conditions, seven COE regiments plowed through uncharted territory and dense forests from Canada's Dawson Creek in British Columbia to Fairbanks, completing the road in just seven months (April–October 1942). With most of its engineers deployed to the South Pacific, the COE called on three regiments of black engineers to serve with four white regiments, an example of

THE PENTAGON: HOUSING FOR THE WAR DEPARTMENT

Groundbreaking for the Pentagon took place on September 11, 1941, and some departments moved in as early as April 1942. The sixteen-month, $83-million construction project operated around the clock with 12,000 workers in three eight-hour shifts. Workers dredged 380,000 tons of sand from the Potomac River for the building's reinforced concrete facade. On completion, the neoclassic facility measured 6.5 million square feet and had some 17.5 miles of corridors. It housed the secretary of war, the Joint Chiefs of Staff, and about 27,000 civilian and military employees.

how mobilization demands created opportunities for minorities. Meanwhile, to consolidate under one roof the War Department agencies that were scattered in offices around Washington, D.C., the COE helped design and construct the Pentagon, a mammoth five-sided, five-ringed, five-story building on reclaimed waste and swampland in Arlington, Virginia. The corps' deputy chief of construction, General Leslie R. Groves, also would oversee the Manhattan Project (the development of the atomic bomb), which entailed large construction programs in Oak Ridge, Tennessee; Hanford, Washington; and Los Alamos, New Mexico. (See Chapter 5.)

CONTINENTAL AND REGIONAL DEFENSE

Immediately after Pearl Harbor, the War Department scrambled to fortify the American garrison in Hawaii and mobilize Regular Army units from the Pacific Northwest to Southern California. Nearly a quarter-million troops were in place on the West Coast by the end of February 1942. In March, the Provost Marshall General began an Auxiliary Military Police program for security at all War Department posts and plants as well as significant civilian-owned and operated defense plants. By the summer of 1943, some 200,000 auxiliary military policemen were on the job, freeing up Regular Army soldiers for other duty. San Francisco, the major embarkation point to Pacific destinations and home to a massive shipbuilding industry, was the best-defended American city. Eight military bases were located near the harbor entrance alone, and the area was outfitted with antiaircraft batteries, underwater minefields, radar installations, and searchlights. Camouflaged fortifications built into manmade hillsides featured state-of-the-art elevated sixteen-inch rifled guns capable of hurling 21,000-pound projectiles twenty-five miles out to sea, and buildings were sandbagged to minimize any bomb-fragment damage. Los Angeles, San Pedro, Long Beach, and San Diego, with busy ports and naval installations, were also reinforced. New large-caliber gun batteries were rapidly built for installations on both coasts, and American and Canadian forces set up defenses at the Sault Sainte Marie Canal, between Lake Superior and Lake Huron. About 379,000 soldiers were assigned to continental defense by 1943, although only half were combat troops. In late 1942, as the Japanese and German threats to the mainland receded, troops were reassigned to other activities, such as training new servicemen and preparing for overseas duty.

Protecting industrial sites and utility services was also an immediate priority. On December 8, 1941, Secretary of the Interior Harold Ickes requested military assistance to guard critical facilities such as Boulder (now Hoover) Dam, which provided water and hydroelectric power to the Southwest and Southern California, including aircraft and shipbuilding industries and vast agricultural areas. The army assigned soldiers to guard numerous sites deemed susceptible to aerial attack or sabotage, including aircraft plants, naval shipyards, major telephone and communications buildings, harbors, reservoirs, and oil wells.

FROM THE HOME FRONT TO THE FRONT DESK TO THE FRONT LINES (AND BACK AGAIN)

Shortly after the United States entered the war, numerous hotels nationwide went from offering room service to providing military service. Bellboys enlisted, ballrooms became mess halls, and landscaped grounds turned into firing ranges; later, verandas were filled not with vacationers in swim suits and deck chairs but with wounded servicemen in bathrobes and wheelchairs. Not even the fast-moving Army Corps of Engineers could produce needed facilities quickly enough, thus rapid hotel conversions into mini bases, barracks, and hospitals were essential to mobilizing the war effort.

Through eminent domain, the U.S. military rented, bought and commandeered both modest and grand establishments for use as induction centers, auxiliary housing, training facilities, civil defense posts, and medical, convalescent and detainment centers. In Southern California, the Ojai Valley Inn, renamed Camp Oak, served an army battalionin training. Quonset huts and more than a hundred tents dotted the golf course—which was not completely restored to its pre-war appearance until 1999—and in 1944 the navy took over the inn for use as a recuperation facility. The huge Hotel del Coronado near San Diego housed naval personnel and wealthy displaced European nobility, and its formal landscaping was turned into a large victory garden. At La Valencia, in nearby La Jolla, spotters on duty around the clock in the domed tower watched for Japanese aircraft. In Pompano Beach, Florida, the U.S. Coast Guard housed a mounted beach patrol, which monitored German U-boat activity, at the Silver Thatch Inn and built adjacent tables, corrals and a paddock for its equine members. Over in St. Petersburg, the War Department leased the Vinoy Resort for use as an Army Air Corps Training Center, and the hotel's large kitchen facilities were well suited for courses in cooking regiment-size meals. Hospitals and convalescent facilities were established at Yosemite's Awahni Hotel (navy), the pink beachside Don CeSar Resort (army) in St. Petersburg, Florida, and the ornate Biltmore Hotel (army air forces) in Coral Gables,

Florida. As the war continued, hotels and resorts also served as rest and relaxation centers for military personnel on furlough after combat or other hazardous duty.

Early on, the State Department requested several hotels close to the public and house foreign diplomats, their families, and other professionals from Axis nations until they could be deported in return for American personnel overseas. (Expenses were paid for out of financial assets held in the United States by their respective governments.) The detainees, although under armed guard, were treated as guests, not prisoners, and were permitted to keep their belongings. The Greenbrier, in White Sulphur Springs, West Virginia, housed more than a thousand Germans as well as Italians, Bulgarians and Hungarians, including those sent to the United States from their diplomatic posts in Latin America. The resort was later renamed Ashford General Hospital and employed a mix of army personnel, Greenbrier staff, and prisoners-of-war from a nearby camp who worked in the laundry, kitchens, and post office. With a two-thousand-bed capacity, the hospital treated some twenty-five thousand servicemen during the war. (Afterward, the Greenbrier underwent an extensive renovation before reopening to the public in 1948.) In the spring of 1944, the U.S.-recognized government of the Philippines was located in a cottage at the Grove Park Inn in Asheville, North Carolina, where exiled president Manuel L. Quezon and his staff were in residence.

Like many hotels around the United States, the Greenbrier in White Sulphur Springs, West Virginia, was converted for military use in 1942. The U.S. Army renamed the resort Ashford General Hospital, and it served as a surgical and rehabilitation center. It also allowed servicemen to relax and dine in far more elegant surroundings than on typical army bases.

ALL-AMERICAN DEFENSE: MOBILIZING THE WESTERN HEMISPHERE

To focus on building up its own industrial might without fear of an Axis attack from Latin America, the United States sought to ensure security in much of the Western Hemisphere. In February 1942, the United States created the Caribbean Defense Command and the bases acquired from Britain on Bermuda, the Bahamas, Jamaica, Antigua, St. Lucia, and Trinidad were reinforced with new or improved air strips, docks, radio stations, and gun batteries. Mobilization efforts centered on protecting the Panama Canal, which allowed the U.S. Pacific Fleet to operate between the American coasts before an Atlantic Fleet was established, and troop strength in Panama increased from 13,000 in 1939 to more than 40,000 in 1942. In the spring of 1941, Roosevelt and the War Plans Division creatively extended the American conception of the Western Hemisphere further east, sending an army garrison to Greenland and later providing troops to Iceland. The following January, the Inter-American Joint Defense Board was created in Rio de Janeiro; the meetings there also produced plans to defend the hemisphere, including economic cooperation and industrial assistance for the Allied nations in combat. Brazil, Mexico, and Chile also contributed to naval coastal patrols and, with other nations, permitted construction of U.S. military bases and airfields in their territory and American use of their air space.

Civil Defense

How horrible, fantastic, incredible it is that we should be digging trenches and trying on gas masks here because of a quarrel in a far away country between people of whom we know nothing.

—*British Prime Minister Neville Chamberlain, September 27, 1938, on his nation's war mobilization efforts in response to the Czechoslovakian crisis.*

Civil defense—in the most uncivil of times—became an integral part of everyday life. It comprised civilian preparations for an air raid or invasion, procedures to follow during an attack, the rescues and cleanup afterward, and unwavering vigilance. German and British citizens were particularly well trained before the war and hardened veterans in wartime. Ordinary citizens, from the shell-shocked Soviet Union to the unscathed United States to burned-out Japan also learned to watch the skies for enemy aircraft, function in blackouts, respond quickly to air raid sirens, construct and use bomb shelters, conduct evacuation drills, don a gas mask correctly, and perform first aid. Civil defense further encompassed nonmilitary home guard units and such matters as looking out for saboteurs in the workplace and using discretion in discussing even seemingly innocuous topics. (See also Chapter 11.)

Civil Defense in Europe and Asia

Civil defense usually operated at every level—national, state or province, and local—right down to neighborhood blocks. In Germany, citizens were taught everything from first aid to firefighting to surviving an air raid; by the height of the Allied bombing campaign in 1944–1945, the Air Protection League's 13 million civilian volunteers had rescued thousands from the rubble. Civilians, Hitler Youth, and—in the last year—women assisted Luftwaffe artillery men in operating more than 20,000 antiaircraft batteries and in performing other combat-related jobs. In Britain, the Home Office oversaw civil defense, and by the height of the Blitz in the fall of 1940, the government had issued 2,854 new defense regulations. In the meantime, the Air Raids Precautions (ARP, later known as the Civil Defense Service), had dug trenches to shelter some half-million people. The Women's Voluntary Services drove ambulances, assisted victims of air raids, and ran street kitchens and canteens. In 1940, there were 127,000 full-time civil defense workers, but more than a million volunteers served as well, including about 28,000 Observer Corps members on the lookout for enemy aircraft. Australia created an ARP program similar to Britain's, and the Royal Automobile Club of Victoria put together a volunteer network to run messages.

In France, civil defense measures included fines for "negative or defeatist" remarks, and looters during an air raid could be sentenced to death. One of its more unusual civil defense committees was the Union Feminine Civique et Sociale, which taught women how to detect nearly odorless gasses without taking a life-threatening breath. The People's Commissariat of Defense in the Soviet Union oversaw local groups that were responsible for organizing and training citizens, aged 16 to 60, in their civil defense responsibilities. Sweden registered all citizens aged sixteen and older for assignments such as maintaining shelters or serving in field kitchens. Civil defense workers in Chungking, China, created bomb shelters and a tunnel system, and hung red paper lanterns from poles to warn of impending air raids. The city also relied on its town criers, equipped with sticks and gongs, to relay government orders, warnings, and precautions. After the April 1942 Doolittle raid over Japan (see p. 508), fire defense associations sponsored civil defense training, and neighborhood associations held surprise drills and taught members standard civil defense measures as well as aircraft identification and bucket brigade operations.

CIVILIAN MILITIA AND HOME GUARDS

In Britain, the Local Defense Volunteers, comprising men over conscription age (and so dubbed "Dad's Army") was formed in May 1940 and drew 1.4 million members by June. Later renamed the Home Guards, these men kept watch over coastlines, airfields, and factories; manned roadblocks, checkpoints, and antiaircraft batteries; and occasionally captured downed Luftwaffe aircrews. Soviet civilians were in the thick of resistance to the Wehrmacht, from sabotage to hand-to-hand combat. Nearly 2 million men and women of the sixty People's Militia divisions constructed and rebuilt defenses and relieved younger men for military service. Often lacking guns, they were told matter-of-factly, "You can find yourself weapons in the fight." Thousands of Moscow women were transported to the city outskirts to dig trenches and help with antitank measures. Militias in Stalingrad held on throughout the siege; those in Leningrad prevented a German occupation. Out of desperate need in September 1944, Hitler authorized a new German civil defense organization, the *Deutscher Volkssturm* (the German People's Storm). Males between the ages of sixteen and sixty were drafted for weekend military training (some women volunteered as auxiliaries), but within months of its creation this home guard was fighting veteran Soviet troops.

Civil Defense Planning in the United States

As early as 1935, the U.S. Army began planning how to incorporate civil defense procedures into continental defense particularly in developing an air raid warning system. Its civil defense branch released a series of pamphlets and manuals in 1941 and 1942 on implementing civil defense organization and surviving aerial attacks. It did not reach another of its goals—increasing the nation's supply of gas masks from 60,000 to 50 million. Only about 5 million had been produced when it became clear in 1943 that Japanese and German threats to the mainland were remote.

In May 1941, Roosevelt established the Office of Civilian Defense (OCD), which copied features from the British program, including the widespread involvement of women and a regional management system. Civilians ran the OCD but with military technical support; and FDR appointed Fiorello La Guardia, mayor of New York City, as director and, later, First

Lady Eleanor Roosevelt as his assistant. James Landis, dean of Harvard Law School, replaced the overstretched mayor in February 1942, and Mrs. Roosevelt resigned that month because of criticism that her friends had received positions in the agency, as well as Southern objections to her plan to racially integrate the OCD. The office issued blackout procedures, produced publications on safety and first aid, organized blood-plasma banks, encouraged fitness and nutrition (healthy citizens did not require as much in medical services or other aid), and developed a plan for hospitals during emergencies. Among its more controversial activities were "storytelling and community dancing," which Landis acknowledged as "nice things" that had a place, but no longer would there be a place for them in the OCD. The national agency oversaw nine regional offices that supervised and assisted state and local operations. More than 11,000 defense councils nationwide coordinated local activities and assigned volunteers. The Civil Air Patrol (CAP), fortuitously formed December 1, 1941, proved to be especially valuable. After Pearl Harbor, the government grounded all civilian pilots until their citizenship status as an American or as a national of an Allied nation was confirmed. The OCD and the army used the CAP flyers and their private aircraft for courier service, shore patrol, and surveillance over industrial sites. CAP flew more than 24 million miles monitoring coastlines, located 173 enemy submarines, and actually sank two. In 1943, Roosevelt made CAP an auxiliary of the Army Air Forces.

The government considered vigilance in the workplace and anywhere else people gathered an essential form of civil defense. Former FBI agent Blayney F. Matthews' 1941 book *The Specter of Sabotage* pointed out potential threats to the nation's defense industries, food and water supplies, public utilities, transportation networks, and other likely targets. The United States, as an open society, was especially vulnerable because, as Matthews wrote, "Our own air, rail and bus timetables, our tourist booklets and maps available at automobile clubs, hotels and filling stations—all contain facts of great interest to enemy agents. No country on the face of the earth has been so profligate in praising its own resources, both natural and industrial. Is it any wonder, then, that foreign governments have been able to arm their saboteurs with a vast fund of detailed information relative to the operation of our industrial units—information which will be invaluable to them when secret orders are released throughout the country to burn, bomb, murder and destroy!" Matthews urged employers to ask job applicants ninety-three questions covering patriotism, ethnic background and nationality, drinking

Lockheed's Vega Airplane Company in Burbank, California, lies camouflaged under a fake suburban neighborhood (top). In the company parking lot, beneath a canvas of artificial grass (bottom), employees gather to receive the highly coveted "E" pennant, the Army-Navy Production Award given to defense plants demonstrating excellent performance.

and gambling habits, debts, and membership in "any society organized to keep alive the traditions of a foreign country" or "antagonistic to the principles of our American form of government." About 2,400 defense plant workers were fired for suspected subversion or sabotage; 20 percent of them later won back their jobs.

A year before the United States entered the war, Kansas City's Art Institute offered the country's first classes in industrial camouflage, and other schools soon followed suit. In a short-lived blackout measure, steel mills in Gary, Indiana, were shrouded in thick smoke to hide their location from enemy planes. The gold dome of the Massachusetts state house in Boston was painted gray, so it would not stand out, and elsewhere other important secular structures were topped with church steeples. However, Congress did not pursue a proposal to paint gray Washington, D.C.'s grand white marble buildings and memorials. The most ambitious deceptions, which fooled even local pilots, were the fake suburban neighborhoods and small towns built of plywood and chicken wire atop aircraft factories on the West Coast. In April 1942, designers, technicians, and craftsmen from the major Hollywood film studios began shrouding the Douglas aircraft factory in Santa Monica under a green canopy. Small plywood houses, rubber cars, clotheslines, and artificial plants dotted the three-dimensional landscape. The work was completed in about six months, and similar false suburbs went up above Lockheed-Vega's aircraft factory in Burbank, California, and the Boeing plant in Seattle, Washington.

MONA LISA MOBILIZES FOR WAR: PROTECTING CULTURAL TREASURES

Art for art's sake and as a historical record and expression of civilization was threatened not just by bomb damage, fire, and looting, but by Germany's leaders, intent on destroying works they detested and stealing the rest for future sales, their own galleries and for the grand new museums the Reich was planning. Saving Europe's irreplaceable catalog of paintings, sculptures, illuminated manuscripts, jewels, tapestries, and objets d'art as well as literary, cartographic, and historical treasures from theft and destruction required foresight and ingenuity, and despite precautions, many masterpieces were lost in the war. (See also Chapter 8.) Europe's revered art— and the frequently inspiring architecture that contained it—flourished in a cultural landscape beyond capital cities and national museums, and a wealth of valuable objects and associated scholarship thrived in private homes and local galleries; in castles, cathedrals, and cloisters; and in specialized libraries and ancient archives.

As early as 1935, the British Museum completed plans to protect its collections in the event of war, and the British government used quarries and castles in Wales as main storage sites. It also designated unused subway tunnels and country estates for art storage (the British Museum's Elgin Marbles—sculpture from the Parthenon in Athens, Greece, were housed deep under London in the Aldwych tube station). By September 1939, most of the National Gallery's treasures were already moving into their distant new homes. London's Public Record Office delivered three hundred tons of documents (including the Great and Little Domesday books) to its safe storage facility, the disused women's wing of the old Shepton Mallet prison in Somerset. The Tate Gallery's larger items stayed in the museum's bomb-proof basement, where they survived several bomb blasts. In London's Trafalgar Square, workers had boarded up Nelson's Column, and a network of firewatchers kept an eye on historic sites. When a one-ton bomb embedded itself twenty-seven feet into the ground next to St. Paul's Cathedral on September 12, 1940, a Royal Engineers bomb squad spent three days extracting it before taking it away to be detonated.

Like the British, French curators ran prewar drills to practice quickly removing and packaging artworks. In 1937, they inventoried their holdings and scouted churches and chateaux as potential hiding places; the next year they were building customized packing cases for individual works. Where especially valuable stained-glass windows could not be re-moved, sandbags and other material were used to keep out bullets and debris. In August 1939, staff at the Louvre began packing its masterpieces—leading the list, Leonardo da Vinci's *Mona Lisa*—for transfer to Chambord, where other museums sent objects to be sorted and dispersed to safe houses. Major works found refuge in eleven northwestern châteaus; the *Mona Lisa* and other works moved several times, just out of reach of Nazi occupying forces, with stops at Louvigney and the abbey of Loc-Dieu.

Practically all of Italy was a museum of architectural and artistic riches. In 1940, Florence began evacuating its collections to villas and palazzos. In Naples, museum officials shipped the most valuable items to a Benedictine monastery, and other collections went to rural churches and country estates. Da Vinci's fresco, *The Last Supper,* on a refectory wall in a fifteenth-century convent in Milan, was carefully boarded up, which helped it to survive by inches the August 16, 1943, bombing that destroyed part of the building. Both the Germans and the Allies made greater efforts in Italy than anywhere else to safeguard cultural treasures when possible, but military commanders did not always share museum curators' definition of "when possible." In Florence, German forces spared the historic fourteenth-century Ponte Vecchio, the only city bridge they did not blow up during their retreat in August 1944. Earlier that year, the famed Benedictine monastery at Monte Cassino was destroyed in battle by Allied aircraft despite appeals that it be spared, but the occupying Germans did manage first to transfer some of its art treasures and library to the Vatican.

The Soviet Union did not begin moving its art until it was invaded, and only about half of its collections in the State Hermitage Museum in Leningrad (St. Petersburg) could be evacuated to safety in Siberia, where collections throughout Russia were also sent. About 1.2 million art objects made it to safety in two large trainloads. The rest was stored in cellars and bunkers, and 30 older but determined women replaced 650 security guards in protecting the treasures around the clock. As Germany later became increasingly vulnerable, the Reich ordered that gold bars and vast caches of art—its own and what it had stolen—be housed in Neuschwanstein, a castle in the Bavarian Alps. In Hungary, monarchists fearful of their German ally—and later of the Red Army—arranged to turn the royal regalia over to the U.S. government for safekeeping with America's gold bullion at Fort Knox, Kentucky.

Private collectors also took protective measures from bombing raids and armies. Some collections in Britain were housed in government-provided sanctuaries, with owners paying the expenses, and some French collectors were able to send their art with the Louvre convoys or ship items to New York. European Jews, whose collections the Nazis immediately targeted, often left artwork in the care of non-Jewish friends or deposited it in banks and warehouses under pseudonyms. Others smuggled treasures into Switzerland via diplomatic pouches or dispersed collections among various museums and caretakers, making them harder to recover after the war.

There were major efforts to save cultural resources in Asia and the Pacific as well. In 1937, the National Library of China sent nearly three thousand rare books to the Library of Congress for safekeeping. When Nanking came under attack, nineteen thousand cases packed with treasures previously moved from the Palace Museum in Peking (Beijing) were sent by rail, truck, and ship to hiding places in the provinces of Szechuan and Shensi. After Pearl Harbor, Australian officials made contingency plans, and the Tasmanian Museum and Royal Society in Hobart evacuated items to the mainland. There, librarians packed documents and books for emergency removal, which never became necessary, unlike in the Philippines, where the National Library could only save less than 5 percent of its collection before the Japanese swept through.

In the United States, Roosevelt created the Committee on Conservation of Cultural Resources, under the National Resources Planning Board in March 1941, charging it with "the protection of the nation's cultural heritage. . . ." Many museums and libraries, particularly on the East and West Coasts, evacuated their collections to the nation's interior or to underground vaults. In Washington, D.C., the National Archives placed its most valuable items—such as the Bill of Rights and the official copy of the Emancipation Proclamation—in the strongest areas of its bomb-shelter-like new building (built in 1935). Until October 1942, employees and air wardens operated a round-the-clock patrol of the building. The Smithsonian Institution's prized possessions, including the original "Star Spangled Banner," were evacuated to a Virginia storage facility. In early January 1942, the National Gallery of Art transferred its masterpieces to the Biltmore Mansion in Asheville, North Carolina.

In a mammoth effort, more than seven hundred staff members at the Library of Congress assessed 6 million items to determine what should be stored off site. After plans for a large bomb shelter nearby faltered, Library staff evaluated caverns, tobacco warehouses, universities, and other institutions looking for fireproof, well-ventilated storage space. After consulting with the War Department to make sure selected sites were unlikely enemy military objectives, Library staff evacuated 4,719 boxes (equivalent to more than eight miles of shelved items) of rare books, manuscripts, and maps (including L'Enfant's plan of Washington, D.C., some of George Washington's papers, and Thomas Jefferson's first inaugural address) to the University of Virginia, Washington and Lee University, and Denison University. Each site was under twenty-four-hour guard, and the Library provided instruments to regularly record atmospheric readings. The Library also made microfilm copies of its main, 8-million card catalog and stored them outside Washington, D.C.

The most valuable treasures at the Library were sent by train and truck—securely packed and under constant armed guard—to Fort Knox, Kentucky, in December 1941: the original Articles of Confederation; the Declaration of Independence; the Constitution; an original autograph copy of President Lincoln's second inaugural address; two autographed drafts of his Gettysburg Address; a Gutenberg Bible, in three volumes; and the Lincoln Cathedral copy of the Magna Carta (in the United States for the 1939 World's Fair in New York City, and being held for Britain during the war). Once out of danger and after conservation treatment, the last of the items was returned to Washington by September 1944.

Industry and War Production

Behind all combat organization and all modern strategy lies a nation's capacity to produce and provide the weapons of war. The present war has provided many examples of brave troops whose courage and determination were inadequate against an army with superior equipment.

—*Lieutenant Colonel John D. Millett, U.S. Army, 1945*

Raising troops went only so far in a nation's ability to wage and win a world war. For the armed forces to be effective, combatant nations had to convert to a war economy that, ideally, provided a constant stream of satisfactory matériel. No nation had every resource it would need, so the Axis and Allied countries set up trade agreements among themselves and with neutral nations to acquire coal, oil, tungsten, steel, milk, wool, and so on. The more numerous Allies, with vastly greater resources and inclination to cooperate, created an array of coordinating committees to manage the purchase, trade, and distribution of raw materials and finished products.

In a war economy, production of civilian consumer goods is strictly limited so that resources may be reserved for manufacturing war goods—everything from weapons and transport to uniforms and provisions. Even so, industry had to expand factories and build new plants, train workers in new skills, tap underused labor sources, and build the infrastructure (new housing, roads, utilities) needed to sustain a war economy. As American newspaper columnist Walter Lippmann wrote in December 1938: "Where we need to put our main emphasis and to invest most of our money is not in battleships but in shipyards that can build battleships, not in planes for next year but in a greatly enlarged airplane industry, not in more soldiers, sailors, and aviators but in the facilities for training soldiers, sailors, and aviators."

Conversion: From a Peace Economy to a War Economy

AXIS WAR ECONOMIES

JAPAN. Japan's invasion of Manchuria in 1931 led to militarization of the Japanese economy. The military budget soared from nearly 30 percent of all government expenditures in 1931 to more than 75 percent in 1938. Gradually the state exerted greater control over the economy, taking over rice production in 1936 and creating additional industry cartels in 1937; by the late 1930s, to end its dependence on oil from the United States and the Dutch East Indies, Japan had built new oil refineries, was experimenting in synthetic oils (even an effort to produce gasoline out of pine roots), and was stockpiling petroleum supplies. Japan's rapid expansion into chemical and heavy industries to meet its military needs in China was such that by 1939, Japan was settling in to a war economy.

The *zaibatsu* (family-dominated businesses, such as Mitsui and Mitsubishi) were central to the change and to Japan's highly centralized economic affairs. The zaibatsu comprised banking, manufacturing, mining, shipping, insurance and other key concerns, maintained close ties to government and military officials, and exerted indirect control over many smaller businesses. Their representatives were appointed to high government positions, allowing the zaibatsu to set policy for state agencies and the cartels. In 1941–1942, the government transformed the cartels into twenty-two control associations, each for a specific sector of industry and run by businessmen. The associations demanded industry standardization, forcing small businesses and nonmembers to follow their procedures. The government used the associations to allocate materials, labor, and capital to member firms, making them the major link between the military and business. As they came to influence the cabinet, associations battled for scarce resources and resisted reforms that might reduce their considerable profits. The overlap of the zai-batsu, the *gumbatsu* (a military-industrial coalition), the associations, and the government resulted in a stunningly complicated and poorly managed war economy.

Manchukuo, in occupied China, was to be the centerpiece of Japan's Greater East Asia Co-Prosperity Sphere and developed as a source for raw materials and a market for Japanese products while eliminating all uncooperative Chinese competition. Ultimately, Japan's overextended commitment to Manchukuo led to an unsustainable war economy: the more capital and effort that was invested there, the more important it was to maintain and save it, which could be done only by further expanding military operations, requiring ever more capital.

GERMANY. In 1932, the year before Hitler came to power, unemployment in Germany had reached 20 percent and 6 million citizens were out of work; the following year, that figure was cut in half, and by 1938 Germany had a labor shortage. This owed much to Hitler's huge public works projects (e.g., the autobahn), but also to his quietly rebuilding the German military and moving to a war economy. Dr. Hjalmar Schacht, twice president of the Reichs-bank (1923–1930 and 1933–1939) and minister of economics (1934–1937), developed *Wehrwirtschaft*, the planned military economy, essentially drafting capital, workers, and farmers into this system. The goals were to maintain self-sufficiency in the face of any League of Nations sanctions that might be imposed for violating the Treaty of Versailles, and to produce war matériel, not civilian consumables. Meanwhile, on May 1, 1933, Fritz Loeb, who had been studying economic mobilization since 1929, joined the newly resurrected German General Staff—whose existence did not become publicly known for another two years—and plunged into industrial mobilization to rebuild the military, including accelerated development of the Luftwaffe.

At the Nuremberg Party Congress on September 9, 1936, Hitler unveiled his Four Year Plan to ". . . make Germany wholly independent of other countries in those materials which German capacity, our chemistry, our machine industry, and our mining industry can produce at home." Because the military economy needed more than private industry could provide, it was necessary that the state control and finance firms to meet demand. In 1937, when the steel industry failed to increase production, the Reich established the Hermann Göring Works, granting it favored status in the allocation of labor and raw materials. (Initially an ironworks operation, it extended its activities outside Germany and later encompassed steel production, coal mining, oil refining, and armaments manufacturing, employing about 700,000 workers. It also acquired numerous businesses and other assets by confiscating Jewish-owned companies.) Meanwhile, the 1.4 million-man Todt Organization, a construction concern led by Fritz Todt, Hitler's chief architect and engineer, was reshaping the German landscape. It built the defensive West Wall (from Belgium to Switzerland) beginning in 1936, the Atlantic Wall (Netherlands to Spain) starting in 1942, and some 5,000 bunkers. Todt did so by mobilizing the Reich Labor Service, Wehrmacht construction battalions, autobahn workers, and later, slave laborers.

Hermann Göring, whose many titles as Hitler's second in command included Commander-in-Chief of the Luftwaffe and President of the Reichstag, took responsibility for the economy as the Plenipotentiary for the Four Year Plan. Entrusting the work to Göring was a mistake, given his complete lack of expertise in—or even passing acquaintance with—economics and agriculture. Göring himself wondered aloud: "How can I be expected to understand these complicated problems of economics?" Despite his later insistence on overseeing all aspects of the German economy and his success in building a huge personal business empire, he was at least refreshingly candid when he took on the job. "My department is not economics. . . . Neither am I an agriculturalist. Except for a few flowerpots on a balcony, I have never cultivated anything." Publicly good natured, Göring forged connections with Germany's top business leaders, eager to do business with the Reich, and encouraged firms to donate to the Nazi Party, but it was Fritz Loeb, as Göring's chief of staff, who prepared and took charge of the plan. To get needed materials, the Reich increased its exploitation of German resources, even though doing so was not always commercially profitable. It also relied heavily on developing and using synthetics, deriving oil from coal, and it made synthetic rubber for the army's tires.

Even after the 1939 invasion of Poland, Hitler did not fully mobilize and accelerate armament and civilian production. Stockpiles of raw materials, food, and other commodities were adequate for what appeared would be a short war, likely to end by late 1941. Following defeats at Stalingrad (February 1943) and in North Africa (May 1943), and with the Soviet Union and Britain still unconquered, Joseph Goebbels, minister of propaganda, responded to the lack of adequate planning by convincing Hitler to support a "Total War" plan. Goebbels launched it on February 18, 1943, at a major rally at Berlin's Sports Palace with a three-hour "Let the Storm Break

Loose!" speech, broadcast nationwide and to soldiers on the Eastern Front. It called for full mobilization and severe restrictions on consumption. Registration for mandatory labor was extended (ages 16 to 65 for men, 17 to 50 for women), with elderly men urged to work; children ten to fifteen years old were recruited for farmwork and scrap collection; older teenagers went into civil defense forces; and workplace lapses and offenses were punishable by jail terms or death. Theaters, movie houses, and beauty salons were to close, and those not in the defense industry had to find work there. (Just three weeks later, Goebbels changed his mind on closing salons after wives and mistresses of Nazi leaders complained. He noted in his diary on March 12, 1943: "Total War is still the principal theme of public discussion. . . . A number of specific questions are debated, especially that of beauty parlors for the ladies. These play a curiously important role, especially in the large cities. Perhaps one must not be too strict about them.") The next year, 1944, was Germany's most productive year industrially during the entire war.

ITALY. "While guns are roaring in many parts of the world, to harbor illusions would be folly, not to prepare, a crime," Italian premier Benito Mussolini told 25,000 assembled Italian troops in August 1938. "We do not delude ourselves, and we are preparing." In 1935, after Italy experienced mobilization problems in the Abyssinian campaign, the government created the General Commissariat for War Production under General Alfredo Dallolio, who had overseen industrial mobilization during World War I. His successor in August 1939, General Carlo Favagrossa, lacked his prestige in dealing with industrialists. Mussolini's inability to convince industrialists that the war would *not* be short prevented their full commitment to a war economy. Shortages and poor allocation of available resources (to public works projects at the expense of armaments), combined with the military high command's inappreciable grasp of the industrial needs for total war and Mussolini's chaotic governing style, further hampered efforts. Many industries never fully converted to wartime production. Italy also did not have many raw materials to work with; it finally got around to creating an electricity industry because it had no coal or oil. Germany provided 64 percent of Italy's coal imports in 1936 and oil from the Romanian oilfields it later controlled. Italian per capita income was far behind that of Germany and Britain (comparable in 1939 to the American level circa 1800). Throughout Mussolini's tenure, low wages, high unemployment, and industrial monopolies that did not foster innovation or research further hindered national development.

ALLIED WAR ECONOMIES

GREAT BRITAIN. Although British industry moved slowly before the war began, the nation spared nothing in its commitment to a war economy. Under the comprehensive Emergency Powers Act, passed in May 1940, Churchill converted civilians into defense workers and factories into war plants, in a highly centralized system. He established the Production Executive to oversee all ministries involved in war production, allocate raw materials and supplies, and coordinate industrial activities. Early on, steel was used primarily for building factory machinery; then it went into weaponry. Stringent wartime controls applied to nearly every aspect of life, dictating a citizen's occupation, housing, transportation, and even one's disposition ("Your Cheerfulness . . . Will Bring Us Victory" ran one government poster). Other nations in the British Empire followed in a similar, but less severe track: Australia established a Department of War Organization of Industry to coordinate commerce and the distribution of goods. New Zealand undertook large agricultural expansion to provide Britain with butter, cheese, and meat. Canada contributed 70 percent of its war production to the empire. Largely rural India moved toward industrialization and more government involvement in the economy, building hundreds of airstrips, supply depots, and upgraded ports. However, massive famines in 1942–1943, brought on by failed harvests and the Japanese occupation of neighboring Burma, disrupted economic progress and resulted in Allied decisions to limit relief efforts, lest those shipping and manpower needs detract from the war effort. (See also Chapter 11.)

CHINA. For China's Nationalist leader, Chiang Kai-shek, upgrading the army (with the help of German advisers) took priority over mobilizing the economy before the 1937 Japanese invasion. The National Resources Commission was established in 1935 to build up heavy industry, but it was initially underfunded and largely neglected. What little economic war planning there was primarily depended on the Allies, particularly American Lend-Lease aid. Although industrial output increased yearly during the war in Free China (even as Japan shipped huge amounts of resources to its home islands), there was no centralized direction of the war economy, and factory output was haphazard and often out of sync with the military's needs. Not until November 1944, with assistance from Donald Nelson (former head of the U.S. War Production Board) and his staff, did an economically devastated China finally establish a War Production Board. In just a matter of weeks, the board issued Ch$137 million in contracts for entrenching tools; surveyed mines to determine how best to increase production, and with American specialists built an experimental coke plant to increase fuel sources and save coal; and toured arsenals seeking to produce steel, trench mortars, land mines, and 300,000 bayonets. In areas under Communist Party control, the economy shaped up differently as leaders focused on developing agrarian reforms and labor collectives, and reducing land taxes.

SOVIET UNION. In the Soviet Union, the state owned many industries and easily confiscated privately owned factories; in addition, the country had ratcheted up war production in the late 1930s. Government officials were assigned to monitor factories and plants with defense contracts and prepare industrial mobilization plans. In June 1940, a year before the German attack, the seven-hour workday was extended to eight hours and factories were ordered to operate seven days a week. (Later in the war, exhausted workers put in twelve- to fifteen-hour days.) Nationwide, mobilization plans became obsolete when the German invasion and its occupation of the western third of the country sliced off almost half of the USSR's total industrial production and areas under cultivation. More than half of the Soviet Union's steel production and nearly two-thirds of its coal supply were in occupied territory, more than half its livestock was confiscated, and the Ukraine—the breadbasket of the Soviet Union—was also under German occupation. The Soviet destruction of industrial facilities and transportation elements (including rail tracks, bridges, and dams) that would be useful to the invaders also contributed to a devastating economic situation. However, as it happened, the large drop in production of consumer goods meant the Soviets could actually produce more war matériel at its remaining 3,000 state-owned industrial complexes. As chairman of the State Defense Committee, Stalin ran both the war and the economy, but with no comprehensive mobilization plan in place, efforts were cobbled together on an as-needed basis; in a positive light, this meant flexibility, which also had its advantages.

From July to December 1941, many Soviet businesses and factories were moved east, where citizens constructed wooden barracks, set up electrical and water supply systems, and evacuated workers reassembled their plants during the brutal Russian winter. The industrial revitalization was astounding: In 1942, the eastern industrial areas of the USSR produced about 75 percent of Soviet weaponry, and most of its iron and steel. Although overall production dropped during the war, war-related production increased, and nearly the entire population was part of the war economy.

THE U.S. WAR ECONOMY

To win a two-front war, U.S. planners estimated that 12 million trained servicemen and women would be required; they would need planes and ships; land, sea, and air weaponry; food, clothing, and other provisions; communications systems; medical staff and facilities; and unfettered oil supplies. Besides monumental production, American industries needed to manage resources and labor effectively. Through trial and error, with a flurry of executive orders that created a mural-sized organizational chart of federal agencies, Roosevelt set out to do that.

The president started with the 1939 Industrial Mobilization Plan (IMP), based on the national experience in World War I, with a War Resources Administration managing and coordinating all other agencies and setting priorities. However, the United States could no longer afford to wait for war to break out before activating mobilization plans; industry needed time to shift to war production, and the military needed time for training with new, more complex equipment. Roosevelt also had at his disposal the Council of National Defense, established in 1916, which comprised the secretaries of war, the navy, and the civilian cabinet secretaries of agriculture, commerce, the interior, and labor. Yet the president needed a larger pool of expertise to coordinate economic, industrial, and military needs. On May 25, 1940, he created the Office for Emergency Management, and three days later he appointed a National Defense Advisory Commission (NDAC) to assist in war planning. In June, the fall of France accelerated American mobilization planning. Even many isolationists agreed that the United States needed to be ready for combat. For the next eight months, NDAC, assisted by hundreds of volunteer business leaders and technical and scientific experts, put together staffs to plan for changes in industry and the economy.

Many of the NDAC's functions were taken over in January 1941 by the new, stronger Office of Production Management (OPM), which oversaw the federal procurement program and was jointly run by William S. Knudsen, former president of Chevrolet and General Motors, and labor union leader Sidney Hillman. The president's advisers kept pushing for a single mobilization czar to head up a top-level umbrella agency as envisioned in the IMP, but FDR was reluctant to remove himself from the picture. Over the next two years, he issued executive orders creating and consolidating more agencies to handle new responsibilities as the war progressed. Meanwhile, numerous "Dollar-a-Year-Men" (some of the nation's top corporate executives) provided free advice or volunteered as consultants and agency directors. During the war, thousands of prominent businessmen came to Washington to run government agencies.

In January 1942, Roosevelt created yet another major entity, the War Production Board (WPB), which was given greater authority than OPM. The director, Donald Nelson, a genial former Sears, Roebuck executive, wrote his own job description, which FDR issued as an Executive Order, giving him authority to requisition supplies and materials, determine their usage and allocation, prioritize production activities, require wartime conversion of essential plants and factories, and limit or prohibit production of hundreds of unnecessary commodities (such as waffle irons and beer cans). One of the first things Nelson did was order automotive plants converted into defense factories; it was accomplished by July. He also directly provided manufacturers with allocated materials instead of going through the Army-Navy Munitions Board first, and he established production timetables that realistically acknowledged proper industrial pacing. Called the mobilization czar in the press, Nelson preferred to converse and convince rather than confront. However, he stumbled in permitting the decreasingly influential

INCH BY INCH: FUELING AMERICA AND THE WAR EFFORT

Rivaling the Alcan Highway and the Pentagon, the $146 million Big Inch and Little Big Inch pipelines that ran from the rich oilfields of east Texas to the Northeast were among the greatest American construction and engineering achievements of the war. Harold Ickes, secretary of the interior, wanted an alternative to transporting oil east by tankers in the Atlantic Ocean, where German U-boats were feasting on Allied shipping. The pipelines also freed up truck and rail transportation for other uses.

The Big Inch pipe, twenty-four inches in diameter, made of 360,000 tons of seamless steel, and designed to carry crude and heating oils, was built from August 1942 to July 1943 and ran 1,250 miles from Longview, Texas, to Illinois, then east to Phoenixville, Pennsylvania, where it connected to smaller lines to refineries on the eastern seaboard. Along the way, twenty-six pumping stations kept the oil flowing and storage tanks accommodated some 5 million barrels of crude oil. In the spring of

Workers prepare to place a segment of the Big Inch pipeline in a trench as part of a massive effort to efficiently transport petroleum from Texas oil fields to refineries on the East Coast.

1943, work began on the twenty-inch Little Big Inch pipeline, which carried oil, gasoline, and kerosene from a refinery in Beaumont, Texas, along a parallel route ending in New Jersey; workers finished that job in less than a year as well, despite storms and serious flooding in May. Oil could flow through the Big Inch at a top rate of 300,000 barrels every twenty-four hours, taking at least two weeks to reach its destination. In its first full year of operation, the Little Big Inch pumped more than 65 million barrels of refined petroleum products east.

The oil industry and the federal Petroleum Administration for War engaged in other major projects including the costly—but unsuccessful—Canadian Oil, or Canol, pipeline project, which was hampered by oil spills. Large tankers were rapidly constructed and deployed, and more than 10,000 miles of new pipelines were built or existing lines rearranged to better meet delivery priorities. The government also ordered industry to reverse the flow direction of some pipelines by moving pumps to the opposite end of the line to accommodate oil deliveries overland rather than by sea tanker. A postwar Senate report noted that the Big Inch and Little Big Inch pipelines pumped through more than 350 million barrels of crude and refined oil during the course of the war and made a gross profit of $135 million by June 30, 1945.

Army-Navy Munitions Board to retain control of contract awards, which weakened unity among WPB members. Nevertheless, the WPB's more than one hundred field offices assisted businesses in navigating the government's procurement and production system to secure war contracts.

Meanwhile, to win the cooperation of corporate America before the war, FDR moved from offering a progressive tax structure for business to granting major concessions; firms happy with those concessions would then take on defense contracts. Many executives had hesitated to convert early to large-scale war production, an enormous financial investment amid uncertainty whether the nation would actually go to war. So in August 1940, the government established the Defense Plant Corporation (DPC), which financed a large share of American industrial expansion (including construction of the Big and Little Big Inch pipelines) and paid for worker training. The DPC distributed more than $9 billion to construct and equip new plants, factories, and mills. The government was eager to pay almost whatever it took to ensure fast and reliable production, and open-ended, cost-plus contracts provided critical incentives for companies to employ and train new workers, since the government would bear the costs. (Large firms also profited tremendously from additional incentives, including federal tax breaks, loans, and subsidies.) Government payment also gave companies the freedom to be creative in designs and plans and to maximize capacities. Secretary of War Stimson candidly noted in his diary, "If you are going to try to go to war, or to prepare for war, in a capitalist country, you have to let business make money out of the process or business won't work." Corporate profits nearly doubled, soaring from $6.4 billion in 1940 to $11 billion four years later.

In May 1943, FDR finally created the first government agency to have total oversight of all others in the war effort. The Office of War Mobilization (OWM), which grew out of, and superceded, the six-month-old Office of Economic Stabilization, brought together oversight of the two main components of economic mobilization: production and labor. James F. Byrnes, former U.S. Supreme Court justice and Democratic senator from South Carolina, assumed the lead role in what had been Nelson's production responsibilities as well as in manpower management. FDR had now gotten himself out of the daily grind of managing the home front. The OWM became the administrative center of managing the war economy, and the politically astute Byrnes came to be known as the "Assistant President." As industrial production peaked in 1943, the concern shifted from mobilization

RESOURCE MANAGEMENT—WHO IS IN CHARGE OF WHAT?

The matter of acquiring and producing rubber illustrates the confusing and labyrinthine situation American war planners faced in managing resources. Japanese conquests in Asia and the Dutch East Indies (major sources of the world's crude rubber supply) by February 1942 blocked further American acquisition of natural rubber. Even with the stingiest conservation measures (including tire rationing, recycling, materials substitution, and product redesigns), the United States expected to be out of rubber by late 1943. It was uncertain when, or even if, the newly planned synthetic-rubber industry would be capable of producing what was needed. Meanwhile, scarce materials needed for facilities construction and production had already been allocated for other manufacturing needs. The government agencies overseeing those endeavors, particularly petroleum and gasoline, clashed with the Rubber Administration. The battle between rubber and gasoline interests spilled over from numerous wartime agencies such as the National Resources Planning Board, the War Production Board, the Army-Navy Munitions Board, the Office of Defense Transportation, and the Office of Price Administration to include the secretaries of the army and the navy, the secretary of war, and the White House, before becoming the subject of congressional hearings.

Sales of new tires in the United States stopped on December 11, 1941, to conserve rubber for the war effort. The Boy Scouts collected 109 million pounds of rubber to be recycled at facilities such as this midwestern recovery plant, where millions of used tires fill a 100-plus-acre site.

to how to execute large military operations and maintain high levels of productivity using the available pool of American citizens.

Converting to a war economy inevitably created bottlenecks and confusion that not even the most thoughtful government committee or efficient firm could clear up quickly—it was physically impossible to produce everything the military ordered. It was, however, possible to produce a great deal of waste, an unfortunate by-product of conversion. Effort, money, and resources went for naught when factories retooled and changed from producing one commodity to another that was not yet needed, and some defense companies expanded far more than necessary. Ultimately, managing the war economy was a bipartisan operation: the Roosevelt administration was Democratic, but the civilian business leaders who headed up the new government agencies tended to be Republican. For the most part, the Democratic-controlled Congress cooperated with FDR. However, ideological clashes and policy differences between the administration's liberal New Dealers and the conservative business executives who managed the war economy, efforts to balance U.S. and other Allies' supply needs, labor disputes, debate over how and where to use black servicemen, when to begin demobilization and reconversion back to a regular economy, and army-navy rivalries created inevitable obstacles that could not always be overcome.

GOOD NEIGHBORS

Inter-American economic cooperation was extensive and directly contributed to the speed with which the United States could mobilize and maintain its war industries. As Nelson Rockefeller, coordinator of Inter-American affairs, told Congress in 1943, Latin American nations "were the most important and sometimes even the only source available for a large part of the [necessary] raw materials." Venezuela supplied the Allies with oil (it was the world's leading oil exporter); Mexico provided copper, lead, mercury, tungsten, zinc, rubber, and medicinal plants; Brazil exported strategic minerals such as quartz crystals and industrial diamonds, as well as bauxite, vegetable oils, coffee, cocoa and of course, Brazil nuts; Bolivia was the Allies' best source of tin, and also provided antimony, copper, rubber, and tungsten; Peru produced minerals and flax; and Uruguay and Paraguay helped keep Britain in beef. Canada also established several joint committees with the United States on materials coordination, economics, war production, and agriculture, and it provided crude oil as well as the uranium ore used to produce atomic bombs.

Labor

Having an adequate labor supply to maintain a war economy was a challenge to all combatant nations, even when they engaged in widespread use of forced and slave labor, as Axis countries regularly did. Residents of Japan, Korea, Formosa (Taiwan), and Manchukuo were subject to a Japanese labor draft, and more than 700,000 slave laborers—mostly Koreans, as well as Chinese—also toiled in Japanese industry. In Germany, factories and farms fell under government control and the Nazis made up for labor shortages by using prisoners of war (POWs) and foreign laborers. In the summer of 1944, the year German industry reached peak production, 7.8 million foreigners were toiling for Germany—nearly 6 million forced civilian laborers, a half-million foreign concentration camp inmates, and almost 2 million POWs—making up about a quarter of the German workforce. Unlike English households, which gave up about two-thirds of their servant staff for the war effort, most German households retained their employees—about 1.4 million of them nationwide—until the waning months of the war. In occupied France, under Nazi pressure, the Vichy government drafted hundreds of thousands to work in Germany and France beginning in February 1943.

In the wake of the Blitz, Britain's Essential Work Order required citizens to register with the government for assignment to defense work. Most women under 40 in Britain performed war work, from jobs in munitions factories to replacing 100,000 male railway workers. Bevin's Boys, named for Labor Minister Ernest Bevin, were young men drawn by lottery to work the undermanned coal industry. However, with an influx of Lend-Lease machine tools from the United States in 1941, British war industries flourished. On the other side of the world, Australia used more than 10,000 Axis POWs for farm work and other labor. War demands added more than a million new jobs in Canada. In South Africa, there were more employment opportunities for semiskilled black workers, and after Japan entered the war, segregation and "pass laws" were temporarily relaxed to encourage national unity. When fear abated, the pass laws went back into effect, triggering protests among black South Africans. In China, many farmers worked in factories and on construction projects to sustain the war effort for whichever side (Nationalist, communist, warlord, or Japan) controlled a particular area. In the Soviet Union, about 60 percent of the population did not fall under German occupation. They endured endless shuttling and labor conscription from the countryside to factories and military assignments, and from there back to rural areas to help with harvests or civil defense projects. Women, children, and even elderly men willingly joined the factory workforce, which added some 12 million new workers. More than a million German POWs a year (along with dissidents and other prisoners) were forced into labor in notoriously harsh conditions.

To help maintain a steady work flow in the United States, where there had been numerous labor strikes in 1941, Roosevelt established the National War Labor Board in January 1942 to encourage management-labor cooperation, arbitrate disputes, and prevent lockouts and strikes from delaying defense work. In June 1943, the Smith-Connally Act permitted the president to, among other things, assume control of privately owned plants doing war work and prohibit strikes that threatened to halt war production. Once the government assumed control, as it did with about four dozen privately owned defense firms, workers were not permitted to strike. Paul McNutt, former governor of Indiana, led the War Manpower Commission, which endeavored to solve labor crises. An October 1942 *Time* magazine piece described some of the issues that crossed McNutt's desk in the course of a single day: "Last week came a frantic telegram from Washington's big Yakima Valley apple growers (they needed 35,000 more pickers right away or they would lose their crop), came the problem of a

LABOR MOBILIZATION, 1939–1945

(Totals Given in Thousands)

Year	U.K.	USA	USSR	Germany	Japan
1939	18,480	45,738	—	39,400	—
1940	20,031	47,520	86,800	36,000	32,996
1941	21,134	50,350	72,900	36,100	—
1942	21,969	53,750	54,700	35,500	—
1943	22,205	54,470	57,100	36,600	—
1944	21,934	53,960	67,100	36,100	31,695
1945	21,506	52,820	75,700	—	—

Principal source: Mark Harrison, ed., *The Economics of World War II: Six Great Powers in International Comparison*, Cambridge: Cambridge University Press, 1998.

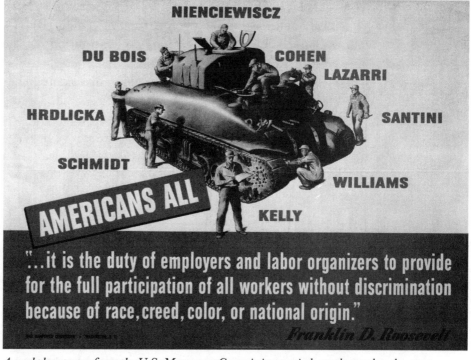

NIENCIEWISCZ

DU BOIS

COHEN

LAZARRI

HRDLICKA

SANTINI

SCHMIDT

WILLIAMS

AMERICANS ALL

KELLY

"...it is the duty of employers and labor organizers to provide for the full participation of all workers without discrimination because of race, creed, color, or national origin."

Franklin D. Roosevelt

A workplace poster from the U.S. Manpower Commission reminds employees that the country needs all Americans—no matter their ethnicity or background—to unite in the war effort. Defense industries offered many workers, especially African Americans, much higher wages than could be had during peacetime.

shipment of planes all ready to go to General [Douglas] MacArthur except for a single part (to come from a plant whose workers have been stolen by another factory), came an ugly message from one of McNutt's regional aides (a group of West Coast farmers, unable to get labor, threatened to plant no crops for next year)."

Wartime Production

AXIS NATIONS

When the war in the Pacific started souring for Japan in late 1942, its industry focused on shipbuilding and aircraft production. A year later, Prime Minister Hideki Tojo also headed the newly formed Ministry of Commerce and Industry, with exclusive authority to resolve supply and production problems by dictating production timetables and controlling contracts. Four ministers succeeded Tojo, but none succeeded as ministers. The army and navy had a deep-seated, crippling rivalry, which hampered not only military operations, but mobilization; one of the few things they agreed on was not to cooperate with the new ministry. The two services simply bypassed the control associations by forming their own. However, both services needed aircraft. Each service provided industry with so many airplane designs and variations that the efficiency of standardization was lost. Japan was producing only 10,000 planes a year when it was capable of five times that amount. The military, in its zeal, had also drafted 3 million skilled factory workers within the first two years of its war with the West, which impeded production.

In Germany, the outdated Four Year Plan supervised by Göring was supplemented by the Speer Plan, named for Albert Speer, Hitler's personal architect, who became his Minister of Armaments and Munitions in early 1942 (denying the Reichmarschall another department to mismanage). Speer got Göring to agree to establish a central planning board, which dictated labor allocation, fostered an atmosphere of industrial cooperation, and reduced military interference in industry. It operated within the framework of the Four Year Plan, to appease the Reichsmarschall, ever sensitive about visible signs of demotion and loss of prestige, but Speer actually oversaw his eponymous plan, and he was credited with almost single-handedly jump-starting the German war economy. Speer had the full support of industry leaders and direct access to Hitler, who backed him when military or political officials threatened to interfere. Under Speer, committees of specialists could openly discuss creative ideas and learn from mistakes, rather than cover them over. Technical experts, rather than their desk-bound, frequently politicized managers, were given substantial authority in project development and production. New committees consolidated and standardized production of items for tanks, fighter planes, or U-boats. Factories focused on producing one item, in large quantities, rather than multiple products (which had been an understandable approach, given Hitler's penchant for sudden changes in direction). Within six months, Speer increased total productivity an astonishing 59.6 percent. Despite repeated Allied bombings, production in 1944 was three times greater than in 1941, yet the workforce had grown only about 30 percent. Another element in German war production was SS Industries, an industrial operation run by the German secret police. The SS ran the Gestapo, and the concentration camp system, and its Economic and Administrative Main Office oversaw more than 40 businesses, comprising about 150 plants and factories.

ALLIED NATIONS

Britain's war production output increased dramatically, though it could not match the output of the United States, which had three times the population, much more land, and had not been repeatedly bombed. British production of warplanes quintupled from 3,000 in 1938 to 15,000 in 1940. Agriculture improved as well, although Britain relied heavily on its empire and the United States to keep its people adequately fed. To produce sufficient calories in the British diet, farmers were shifted from livestock to grain production, which soared more than 80 percent. Canada nearly doubled its manufacturing in six years, and 13 percent of its workforce was employed in the defense industry; Wartime Shipbuilding, Ltd., employed 126,000 Canadians, who produced more than four hundred Allied ships. South Africa's iron ore and coal were in great demand, and its industrial output nearly doubled as well; it built two huge explosives factories and provided armored cars, guns, ammunition, and other matériel; and some 13,000 Allied ships were repaired there. New Zealand also built more than

---

ALLIED TEAMWORK: THE COMBINED PLANNING BOARDS

More than two years before the 1944 Normandy invasion, the United States and Britain conceived a plan code named "Bolero" to build up Allied forces in England for an assault on Europe. At the same time, the two allies shared a common enemy in Japan. General Dwight D. Eisenhower, soon to become chief of the War Plans Division, strongly advocated a unified Allied military strategy in Asia and the Pacific as well as in Europe, pointing out, "We can't win by . . . giving our stuff in driblets all over the world with no theater getting enough." In January 1942, the two allies agreed to create not only a Combined Chiefs of Staff to spearhead joint military planning, but also nonmilitary planning boards on economic and industrial matters. The Combined Raw Materials Board would plan the development, increase, and use of such resources; and the Combined Shipping Adjustment Board would coordinate merchant shipping to improve efficiency and lower transportation costs. Five months later, the Combined Food Board and the Combined Production and Resources Board were established. The Food Board was responsible for ensuring relatively equitable distribution of available food resources; the other board pooled Allied resources and integrated production programs. It responded to British coal shortages in early 1943 by arranging to send used American strip-mining machinery to England; the greatly increased coal production also benefited the Supreme Headquarters Allied Expeditionary Force in northwest Europe. The boards worked with other nations as well, particularly as newly liberated countries required assistance with food supplies.

500 vessels, and India produced significant amounts of basic weaponry, machine and medical tools, and provisions.

The Soviets, working exceptionally long hours in factories open around the clock, and their overwhelming hatred of Germany fueling a work ethic that all the coal in the world could not, dramatically increased military production. It was either that or succumb to Hitler's avowed goal of their complete annihilation. More than 85,000 tanks and self-propelled field guns, greater in number and quality than Hitler ever expected, rolled from the factory into battle, and not a few of them all the way into Berlin. The Soviets also produced 12 million rifles, 800,000 field guns, and more than 100,000 aircraft. Meanwhile, key resources such as coal and steel decreased, foreign trade disappeared, and consumer goods virtually vanished.

THE UNITED STATES

INDUSTRIAL PRODUCTION. On Donald Nelson's orders, automobile production halted early in the war and auto plants converted into aircraft, tank, and bomb factories. Walter P. Reuther, head of the United Automobile Workers union, would later observe, "Like England's battles were won on the playing fields of Eton, America's were won on the assembly lines of Detroit." Ford's Willow Run plant, constructed outside Detroit in 1941, was the largest plane factory in the world, with 3.5 million square feet of space and, at its peak, more than 42,000 employees. Using the same assembly-line system Ford used for its cars, the plant built 8,685 aircraft in forty-three months, and once the system settled into place, a new plane rolled off the mile-long line every two hours. (A Douglas Aircraft factory in California eventually achieved a rate of producing one plane an hour.) The Packard Motor Company built engines for the Royal Air Force, Chrysler built bomber fuselages, and General Motors produced bomber parts and put together fighter planes. Meanwhile, indefatigable industrialist Henry J. Kaiser was crucial in driving the shipbuilding business. His revolutionary construction techniques (using prefabricated parts welded together, which required less employee training) accelerated ship production (by one third) and cut costs (by three-fourths), and his shipyards—including one in California that employed up to 100,000 workers—produced more than 1,490 ships, or 27 percent of all U.S. Maritime Commission construction. Civilian vessels were also refitted for military duty, such as the 1920s riverboat paddlewheelers the *Delta Queen* and *Delta King*, which were converted into military transport and troop barracks.

"Forty-one billion shells were made in World War II, and I made a few," said Helen Sudyk, who worked at the Chase Brass Company in Cleveland, Ohio. Americans also produced 15 million guns, more than 20 million helmets, and 165 million military coats. To generate such output, manufacturers increased the average workweek from thirty-eight hours to forty-three. Better training and machinery also contributed to increased production. In the steel industry, the number of workers remained steady but output increased; in 1940, workers produced 67 million tons of steel, but in 1944, the figure was 89 million tons. About 200,000 firms converted to war production, which jumped from 2 percent of the nation's total output in 1939 to 40 percent in 1943. Business conversions could be both practical and creative. In Los Angeles, the American Construction Company changed from building "The California Cottage" to the "American Bomb Shelter," which could later be turned into a swimming pool. Other manufacturing transformations were more puzzling. To avoid diverting aircraft makers from their main task, contracts for producing parts for a new fleet of Amercan gliders went to nearly 150 subcontractors, including the Heinz Pickle and Steinway Piano companies. (This problematic approach was soon reformed.) Some companies contributed to the war effort without changing their products by producing uniforms, personal supplies, and other items for the military. Coca-Cola opened sixty-four bottling plants overseas and produced more than 5 billion bottles and cans for the troops, and by 1945, the Hershey Company was producing weekly 24 million chocolate bars made to military specifications (including heat resistance and calories) for soldiers' rations.

Agricultural Production. More than 9 million farm workers, toiling on more than a billion acres of land, kept the nation fed and millions of British, Chinese, and Russians from starving. In October 1941, to coordinate food-related actions with other government agencies, Agriculture Secretary Claude Wickard created the Division of Labor in Rural Industries, which went through a dozen name changes before finally becoming the War Food Administration in April 1943. At the time, the United States produced enough for itself in fruits, vegetables, beef and poultry products, butter, milk, eggs, and cheese. However, it imported all its coffee, cocoa, and significant amounts of sugar, vegetable fats, and oils. When war in the Pacific stopped coconut oil imports, Americans compensated by nearly tripling production of homegrown flaxseed and almost doubling production of peanuts and soybeans.

PRODUCTION OF WEAPONS AND MILITARY VEHICLES BY COUNTRY, 1939–1945

(Figures in Units Unless Otherwise Specified)

	U.K.	USA	USSR	Germany	Italy	Japan
Aircraft (all types)						
1939	7,940	2,141	10,382	8,295	1,692	4,467
1940	15,049	6,086	10,565	10,826	2,142	4,768
1941	20,094	19,433	15,735	12,401	3,503	5,088
1942	23,672	47,836	25,436	15,409	2,818	8,861
1943	26,263	85,898	34,900	24,807	967	16,693
1944	26,461	96,318	40,300	40,593	—	28,180
1945	12,070	46,001	20,900	7,540	—	8,263
Total	**131,549**	**303,713**	**158,218**	**119,871**	**11,122**	**76,320**
Major naval vessels						
1939	57	—	—	15	40	21
1940	148	—	33	40	12	30
1941	236	544	62	196	41	49
1942	239	1,854	19	244	86	68
1943	224	2,654	13	270	148	122
1944	188	2,247	23	189	—	248
1945	64	1,513	11	0	—	51
Total	**1,156**	**8,812**	**161**	**954**	**327**	**589**
Production of merchant shipping (gross tons)						
1939	629,705	376,419	—	—	119,757	320,466
1940	842,910	528,697	—	—	35,299	293,612
1941	1,185,894	1,031,974	—	—	96,999	210,373
1942	1,270,714	5,479,766	—	—	153,656	260,059
1943	1,136,804	11,448,360	—	—	63,895	769,085
1944	919,357	9,288,156	—	—	—	1,699,203
1945	393,515	5,839,858	—	—	—	599,563
Total	**6,378,899**	**33,993,230**	**—**	**—**	**469,606**	**4,152,361**
Submarines						
1939	7	—	—	58	—	—
1940	15	—	—	68	2	—

PRODUCTION OF WEAPONS AND MILITARY VEHICLES
BY COUNTRY, 1939–1945 (CONTINUED)

	U.K.	USA	USSR	Germany	Italy	Japan
1941	20	2	—	129	7	—
1942	33	34	—	282	10	61
1943	39	55	—	207	9	37
1944	39	81	—	258	—	39
1945	14	31	—	139	—	30
Total	**167**	**203**	**52**	**1,141**	**28**	**167**
Tanks and SPGs						
(self-propelled guns)						
1939	969	—	2,950	247	40	—
1940	1,399	331	2,794	1,643	250	315
1941	4,841	4,052	6,590	3,790	595	595
1942	8,611	24,997	24,446	6,180	1,252	557
1943	7,476	29,497	24,089	12,063	336	558
1944	4,600	17,565	28,963	19,002	—	353
1945	—	11,968	15,419	3,932	—	137
Total	**27,896**	**88,410**	**105,251**	**46,857**	**2,473**	**2,515**
Rifles, carbines						
1939	18,000	—	—	451,000	—	83,000
1940	81,000	—	—	1,352,000	—	449,000
1941	79,000	38,000	1,567,000	1,359,000	—	729,000
1942	595,000	1,542,000	4,049,000	1,370,000	—	440,000
1943	910,000	5,683,000	3,436,000	2,275,000	—	634,000
1944	547,000	3,489,000	2,450,000	2,856,000	—	885,000
1945	227,000	1,578,000	637,000	665,000	—	349,000
Total	**2,457,000**	**12,330,000**	**12,139,000**	**10,328,000**	**—**	**3,570,000**
Machine guns						
1939	19,000	—	—	20,000	—	6,000
1940	102,000	—	—	59,000	—	21,000
1941	193,000	20,000	106,000	96,000	—	43,000
1942	284,000	662,000	356,000	117,000	—	71,000
1943	201,000	830,000	459,000	263,000	—	114,000
1944	125,000	799,000	439,000	509,000	—	156,000
1945	15,000	303,000	156,000	111,000	—	40,000
Total	**939,000**	**2,614,000**	**1,516,000**	**1,176,000**	**125,000**	**450,000**

(continued)

PRODUCTION OF WEAPONS AND MILITARY VEHICLES BY COUNTRY, 1939–1945 (CONTINUED)

	U.K.	USA	USSR	Germany	Italy	Japan
Artillery						
1939	538	—	17,348	1,214	—	—
1940	4,700	—	15,300	6,730	—	—
1941	16,700	—	42,300	11,200	—	2,250
1942	43,000	—	127,000	23,200	—	2,550
1943	38,000	—	130,000	46,100	—	3,600
1944	16,000	—	122,400	70,700	—	3,300
1945	5,939	—	62,000	—	—	1,650
Total	**124,877**	**257,390**	**516,648**	**159,144**	—	**13,350**
Mortars						
1939	1,300	—	—	1,400	—	500
1940	7,600	—	—	4,400	—	1,600
1941	21,700	400	42,300	4,200	—	1,100
1942	29,200	11,000	230,000	9,800	—	1,500
1943	17,100	25,800	69,400	23,000	—	1,700
1944	19,000	24,800	7,100	33,200	—	1,100
1945	5,000	40,100	3,000	2,800	—	300
Total	**100,900**	**102,100**	**351,800**	**78,800**	**17,000**	**7,800**

Principal sources: Robert Goralski, *World War II Almanac, 1931–1945: A Political and Military Record*, New York: Bonanza Books, 1984; John Ellis, *The World War II Databook: The Essential Facts and Figures for All the Combatants*, London: Aurum Press, 1993; Mark Harrison, ed., *The Economics of World War II: Six Great Powers in Internationaal Comparison*, Cambridge: Cambridge University Press, 1998.

To meet Lend-Lease program needs, the Department of Agriculture purchased farm produce at set prices, rather than at a fluctuating price based on supply and demand, so that farmers would not be punished financially for producing extra food. The "Ever Normal Granary," part of a 1938 price stabilization effort, proved essential during the war. The government sold animal feed and corn from the Granary (accumulated over time and sold at a price averaged out over many years) at prices low enough to encourage farmers to keep their livestock well fed and thus more productive. By paying farmers a guaranteed minimum and selling inexpensive feed, the agricultural industry produced a huge surplus for the United States. More than a million tons of food were shipped overseas in 1941 alone.

Although many farm workers left barns and fields for factories or the armed forces and major manufacturers of farm machinery converted to defense work, agricultural output did not diminish. In late 1942, the government put German and Italian POWs to work on farms and orchards and directed smaller manufacturing firms to continue serving the farm industry with new and improved equipment, such as field harvesters and mechanical cotton pickers, to increase efficiency. Other new developments, including agricultural chemicals and the recently introduced soybean crop, meant that fewer American farmers were producing 22 percent more food in 1945 than in 1940, and food grain production went up 50 percent.

Labor shortages meant every able-bodied American was needed in the war effort. At San Quentin Prison in California, 500 inmates prepare 8 million civilian ration books for distribution in June 1943. Nationwide, some prisoners were given early release by agreeing to serve in the armed forces.

Other Government Mobilization

Beyond building and supplying armies, there were other mobilization tasks for nations to tackle, involving people who had never seen so much as a blueprint or a ball bearing. Governments had to provide domestic security and drum up morale; set price controls, fight inflation, and ration goods (see Chapter 11). There was an urgent need to hire those with skills in foreign languages, mapmaking, medicine (including psychology and psychiatry), and other fields, and to expand training in those subjects. Scientific research and development was as essential to the war effort as fielding armies, and the enormous discoveries that came out of World War II had a tremendous impact on military strategy, operations, and survival. In addition, private organizations, with and without government encouragement, swung into action to provide assistance to servicemen and defense workers.

Domestic Security and Internment

Thanks to political policies and well-developed secret police, the Japanese, Germans, Italians, and Soviets had methods for dealing with suspicious foreigners and dissident citizens well in hand. In the democracies, the outbreak of war occasioned immediate mass arrests and internment of potential spies, saboteurs, and others who threatened the war effort. Three days after the war began, Britain established tribunals to determine the loyalty of its many foreign residents (mainly refugees, but there were some Nazis). In Canada, the mayor of Montreal, Camillien Houde, was arrested after encouraging French Canadians not to participate in a national registration for conscription, and 23,000 Japanese-Canadians, viewed as a security threat, were interned throughout the war. Australia interned its citizens of Japanese descent as well. South Africa imprisoned about 2,000 people, including those considered political threats, and Egypt held just under 1,000 Germans throughout the war, about 80 percent of them Nazis.

In the United States, the Federal Bureau of Investigation (FBI) nearly doubled in size from 7,400 employees at the end of 1941 to more than 13,000 in 1943. The FBI surveyed 978 defense plants and factories for security needs, tracked down draft dodgers and military deserters, investigated sabotage and espionage, increased intelligence collection and analysis capabilities, and expanded surveillance of German, Italian, and Japanese individuals and organizations. When the war began, about 5,000 German and Italian citizens were detained for a short time, and about 10,000 were temporarily removed from the West Coast. By the end of the day on December 7, 1941, hundreds of Japanese aliens under surveillance were brought into custody, and all of Hawaii, home to a large number of Japanese Americans, was soon under martial law. The fear that Japanese-Americans, mostly living on the West Coast, would serve as a fifth column for invading Japanese forces—a fear whose validity was greatly debated at the time—prompted Roosevelt to issue, on February 19, 1942, Executive Order 9066, which gave the secretary of war broad powers to send persons to military areas. The order did not specify Japanese-Americans by name, but only they were incarcerated as a group. A month later, the army began rounding up Japanese—two-thirds of them U.S. citizens—and on very short notice ordered them to settle their affairs and present themselves for evacuation to inland relocation centers. (See also Chapters 2 and 11.)

Long-term Mobilization: Population Enhancement Programs

In preparation for combat losses and to strengthen their populations, some nations had specific plans to increase their number of citizens for future armies and later wars. SS leader Heinrich Himmler's *Lebensborn* ("fountain of life") scheme was intended to keep Germany well supplied with strong, healthy Aryan youth fitting the Nazi ideal of a blond-haired, blue-eyed Master Race—which bore no physical resemblance to Hitler, Himmler, Goebbels, Göring, or most other top Nazis. Racially approved young women were encouraged to have children with SS officers, whose "pure" pedigree had already been researched. The marital status of either partner did not matter, only their genealogy did, and once the woman became pregnant, the SS saw to her every need and kept her identity secret. Himmler opened the first Lebensborn home in August 1936 at Steinhöring, near Munich. Nine comfortable, specially-built SS-run Lebensborn homes and a variety of renovated hotels and resort facilities quietly appeared around Germany. The mothers and children received excellent care and abundant food (Himmler, who had been a student of agriculture and a former chicken farmer, developed a protein-rich diet for the young residents), even when rationing became strict. The mother could raise the child if she wished, or a Nazi foster family would be found. About 10,000 Lebensborn children were born in Germany; more than 10,000 other Lebensborn children were born in occupied Europe, primarily in Norway, whose valued Nordic/Aryan population was to be incorporated into the German state. From 1940 to 1945, 400,000

German soldiers at any given time were stationed in Norway, and the SS eagerly promoted German-Norwegian liaisons. After the war, many of those offspring were severely mistreated by both the Norwegian government and the public, as they were living symbols of collaboration with the Nazis.

The Japanese had their own program to populate Japan's new territories, thus all contraception was banned (except condoms, which were produced for use by soldiers in government-sanctioned sex-slave camps). The government told women that reproducing was their patriotic duty, and it offered to pay for weddings to Japanese servicemen overseas and for advanced education of children from families with ten or more siblings. In the Soviet Union, the government offered cash grants to women after their third child. In July 1944, it began issuing medals to women with at least five children; those with ten or more were honored as "Heroine Mothers."

Mobilizing Research and Development

EUROPE AND ASIA

In matters of research and development, the Axis powers could not mobilize their scientific communities to the same extent as the Allies. Japan's intense army-navy rivalry created many obstacles, and military officials were leery about the country's Western-trained scientists. Germany and Italy lost many prominent scientists eager to escape fascism, including those who would be critical to the success of the Manhattan Project (the U.S. program that developed the atomic bomb), among them Enrico Fermi, Klaus Fuchs, Lise Meitner, Emilio Segre, and Leo Szilard. German science was still among the best in the world, and it was making progress in nuclear research under Werner Heisenberg. But Hitler relied for the most part on science that was already developed and did not give much encouragement to further nuclear research. Albert Speer, the German minister of armaments, noted after the war that even if Germany could have produced an atomic bomb by 1945, "It would have meant mobilizing all our technical and financial resources to that end. . . . It would have meant giving up all other projects, such as the development of the rocket weapons." Not until 1943, the year of Total War and full-scale mobilization in Germany, was a state research office created.

In Italy, which had a national research council, Mussolini was put off by expensive studies that could not produce immediate results. The Soviet Union invested heavily in scientific research, including nuclear fission, despite Stalin's fears that scientists and engineers might develop something he could not control or that might be useful to his rivals. In Britain, Churchill charged the Ministry of Defense early on with managing the nation's research, and its scientific endeavors flourished in well-funded government departments. Mathematician Alan Turing and his colleagues made phenomenal strides in cryptanalysis and computer development. The Committee for Scientific Survey of Air Defense provided the wherewithal for the creation and refinement of radar, one of the most significant technical accomplishments to come out of the war. In August 1940, as German attacks on Britain intensified, a team of scientists sailed for the United States to share with the Americans British military secrets. Among them was the newly invented cavity magnetron. Within six months, British and American planes were being equipped with this portable, life-saving radar technology. (See also Chapter 5.)

THE UNITED STATES

Five days after the French surrender in June 1940, Roosevelt established the National Defense Research Committee (later the Office of Scientific Research and Development, or OSRD). Vannevar Bush, an engineer at the Massachusetts Institute of Technology (MIT), was in charge of major policy issues and coordination with the military, other agencies, and industry. Rather than creating new government facilities, he relied on existing research programs in institutions of higher learning and private industry and on private experts to oversee scientific and engineering mobilization. The farsighted president of Tufts University, Dr. Leonard Carmichael, as head of the National Roster of Scientific and Specialized Personnel, assembled a punch-card index with data on some 200,000 scientists, translators, librarians, mathematicians, and other experts, that was a significant resource for the OSRD. During the war, the OSRD issued nearly 2,300 contracts worth about $5 billion for innovations and improvements in military technology. OSRD-sponsored achievements included radar improvement, the proximity fuze, research on the atomic bomb (until 1942, when it was transferred to the auspices of the army's Manhattan Project), design of the WEASEL, a versatile, multiweather vehicle; insecticides, such as DDT; and methods for producing mass amounts of penicillin.

Back in 1939, MIT ascertained the qualifications of alumni for vital roles in government and industry; it had renowned engineering programs and provided the nation with a large segment of the scientific expertise that would distinguish the American war effort. Its on-campus research focused on radar and gunfire accuracy. In December 1942, seventy-three colleges and universities organized the Engineering Colleges Research Association, headed by Raymond Woolrich, president of the University of Texas, to accelerate use of their expertise and laboratory space. Researchers carried out classified studies in plutonium and nuclear chemistry at the University of California, Berkeley, as part of the Manhattan Project. The thirty-ton Electronic Numerical Integrator and Computer (ENIAC), the first programmable computer in the United States, was developed at the University of Pennsylvania. It was built to calculate artillery projection tables, a task that specially recruited women performed during the war with pencil and paper, and was later used to calculate thermonuclear reactions. Completed in 1945 but not announced until February 1946, the ENIAC was hailed as one of the war's finest technical achievements.

Other university associations such as the American Defense Harvard Group formed to provide the government and military with useful expertise through lectures and seminars. A large number of academics also contributed to the intelligence field with the Office of Strategic Services. Through the National Inventors' Council, created in 1940, the public was encouraged to submit ideas, several of which were developed for wartime use, including a mirror signaling device for downed pilots and a mercury dry battery cell for walkie-talkies. In the same vein, the U.S. Patent Office directed promising patent proposals to the appropriate authorities.

The War Department asked Dr. Ancel Keys, cofounder of the Laboratory of Physiological Hygiene at the University of Minnesota, to develop rations for servicemen that could easily be carried and provide adequate calories for a soldier in combat. Keys's first rations contained hard biscuits, dry sausage, and chocolate. Later, the refined, 3,000-calorie K-Rations (named for the doctor, and distinct from the earlier C- and D-rations) contained concentrated or dehydrated breakfast, lunch, and dinner foods, including canned meat, eggs, cheese, biscuits, fruit bar, a bouillon packet, instant coffee and fruit drinks, cigarettes, and gum. The rations met the military's health and convenience requirements, but grew tiresome for the troops. As Alan Waterhouse, 25, of San Diego, a private in Company I, 10th Infantry, wrote to his mother from Germany on March 18, 1945, "I sure wish was home so I could set down to the table and have a good meal with lots of salad because it has been so long since I had one that I forgot just how it tastes." Dr. Keys also conducted a landmark study using consci-

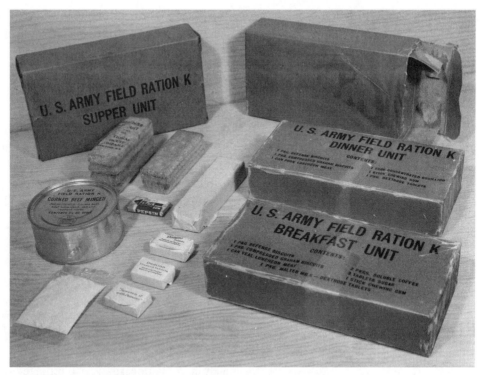

A complete set of military rations, seen here, was subject to testing at the U.S. Army quartermaster depot subsistence research laboratory in Chicago. The portable rations were packed to withstand temperatures ranging from 135 degrees Fahrenheit to 20 degrees below zero.

entious objector volunteers to measure the effects of starvation and rehabilitation diets.

In early 1942, the Smithsonian War Committee surveyed institution staff for suggested projects, and 10 percent of them were assigned to war-related work. Working outside the OSRD, Smithsonian Institution (SI) scientists mobilized to provide military forces with detailed biological, geographic, linguistic, and ethnological information; conduct research on tropical diseases, meteorology, and environmental effects on military fabrics; translate maps and documents; and respond to a daily stream of questions from various agencies. One of the most important SI contributions was a pocket-sized waterproof book, *Survival on Land and Sea,* that provided basic tips, such as identifying edible and poisonous plants and animals and how to prepare them. Nearly a million American servicemen had a copy by war's end. At the Library of Congress—by the mid-1930s the largest library in the world—staff handled government inquiries by telephone around the clock, prepared translations and abstracts of foreign language material, and developed bibliographies on everything from camouflage to synthetic rubber to labor strikes in war industries, as well as summaries of congressional hearings on war issues.

In the United States, more than 160 nonmilitary agencies came into existence as part of the war effort. Some were superseded by new agencies, others were disbanded when the war ended, and others were abolished but their functions absorbed into existing agencies and departments. The major agencies described in the following chart give only a glimpse of the depth and scope of government expansion during the war. (See also Chapter 2.)

MAJOR U.S. GOVERNMENT WAR AGENCIES

Army-Navy Munitions Board	June 22, 1922, established by the Joint Board of the Army and Navy. Moved under direct control of the president as commander-in-chief July 1, 1939. Coordinated military procurement of munitions and supplies; coordinated materials stockpiling, foreign purchases, machine tool allocation. Also reported to the War Production Board. Abolished July 26, 1947.
Office of Emergency Management	May 25, 1940, established by Executive Order. The office, within the executive office of the president, oversaw the national defense program and coordinated work among various government agencies. Within the OEM, FDR created by Executive Order in May 1941 the Office of Civilian Defense (OCD) to supervise a nationwide network of federal, state, and local civil defense activities, including air raid drills. The OEM was terminated November 3, 1943, and many functions dispersed to other agencies. The OCD closed June 4, 1945.
National Defense Research Committee	June 27, 1940, established by Executive Order. Responsible for scientific research on weaponry and other war-related devices; kept the president apprised of the latest scientific and medical developments related to defense. Compiled lists of scientists, laboratories, programs, and resources. Superseded by the Office of Scientific

MAJOR U.S. GOVERNMENT WAR AGENCIES

	Research and Development, created June 28, 1941. Abolished December 31, 1947.
Selective Service System	September 16, 1940, established by Congress. Administered conscription for military forces. Held eight separate draft registrations during the war. Oversaw local draft boards.
Office of Production Management	January 7, 1941, established by Executive Order. Replaced the War Resources Board. Regulated production and supply of war matériel and equipment and oversaw federal procurement program. Abolished November 3, 1945.
Office of Lend-Lease Administration	March 11, 1941, established by Congress, enhanced October 28, 1941, by Executive Order. Replaced the Interdepartmental Committee for Coordination of Foreign and Domestic Military Purchases (the President's Liaison Committee) established December 6, 1939, to represent the government in military or naval purchases and transactions conducted by foreign governments in the United States. Oversaw the production, lending, leasing, and selling of military equipment and goods exported to nations whose defense was deemed necessary to the United States and its interests. OLLA became part of the Foreign Economic Administration in 1943.
Office of Price Administration	April 11, 1941, by Executive Order. Charged with maintaining price stability, protecting consumer interests, setting maximum prices for commodities and maximum rents in defense areas. Administered the rationing program, overseeing local rationing boards and issuing billions of ration stamps. Abolished May 29, 1947.
Office of Coordinator of Inter-American Affairs	July 30, 1941, by Executive Order. Worked with nations in the Western Hemisphere to further defensive

(continued)

MAJOR U.S. GOVERNMENT WAR AGENCIES (CONTINUED)

	preparations, regional solidarity, economic cooperation, and commercial and cultural relations. Abolished April 10, 1946.
Office of Defense Transportation	December 18, 1941, by Executive Order. Created "to assure maximum utilization of the domestic transportation facilities of the nation," and manage seized transportation properties. Abolished July 1, 1949.
Office of Censorship	December 19, 1941, by Executive Order. Responsible for censoring communications between the United States and foreign countries by mail, cable, radio, and other means. Especially involved in the Safehaven program (to deny German transfer of goods for safekeeping in neutral countries). Abolished September 28, 1945.
National War Labor Board	January 12, 1942, by Executive Order. Developed procedures to settle management-labor disputes to prevent interruption of war production in key defense industries. Abolished December 31, 1945.
War Production Board	January 16, 1942, by Executive Order. Superseded the Supply Priorities Allocation Board and the Office of Production Management to function as the overall agency for war mobilization and federal procurement. Abolished November 3, 1945.
War Shipping Administration	February 7, 1942, by Executive Order. Acquired and operated nonmilitary and defense transportation ocean-going vessels, oversaw merchant marine crews' training, managed merchant marine shipping to war zones. Abolished September 1, 1946.
War Manpower Commission	April 18, 1942, by Executive Order. Responsible for recruiting labor for war industries, analyzing manpower usage for better efficiency, developing practices for improved worker efficiency. Abolished September 19, 1945.
Office of War Information	June 13, 1942, by Executive Order. Provided the media and the public news on the war effort, developed and

MAJOR U.S. GOVERNMENT WAR AGENCIES (CONTINUED)

	implemented programs to further the public's awareness and knowledge of the government's war policies, aims, and activities. Maintained a news bureau and photography unit. Abolished August 31, 1945.
Petroleum Administration for War	December 2, 1942, by Executive Order. Supervised domestic oil industry activities, including conservation to ensure adequate supply, research and development programs, and oil allocation and deliveries. Abolished May 8, 1946.
Office of Economic Stabilization	December 5, 1942, by Executive Order. Responsible for controlling inflation and minimizing economic dislocation related to the war and that could affect the war effort. Abolished September 20, 1945.
War Food Administration	March 26, 1943, by Executive Order. Formerly the Administration of Food Production and Distribution. Developed policies and procedures for the wartime production and distribution of food and oversaw war-related food activities in the Department of Agriculture. Abolished June 29, 1945.
Office of War Mobilization	May 27, 1943, by Executive Order. Superseded the Office of Production Management, exercised authority over all civilian war agencies, coordinated wartime economic planning. In October 1944 was renamed the Office of War Mobilization and Reconversion to include its responsibilities in postwar planning. Abolished December 12, 1946.
Foreign Economic Administration	September 25, 1943, by Executive Order. Controlled commercial imports and exports, performed economic analyses and consolidated oversight of federal activities associated with foreign economic affairs. Abolished September 27, 1945.

THE COMMITTEE OF COMMITTEES

Even before the United States entered the war, Americans formed relief organizations including Bundles for Britain (with a half-million members nationwide) and United China Relief. There were more than seven hundred private relief committees, many representing specific ethnic groups or nationalities (such as Greek War Relief and the National American-Denmark Association), that sent money, food, care packages, and more to meet the needs of those trapped by the war. The U.S. declaration of war spawned thousands of local organizations, with volunteers assisting foreign civilians and American servicemen. Roosevelt established the President's War Relief Control Board on July 25, 1942, to manage this overwhelming and sometimes tangled web of philanthropy. The volunteer board licensed, regulated, and coordinated most efforts except for those of the American Red Cross and organized religious groups. The board helped agencies vastly reduce their overhead, saving some $20 million in expenses that instead went directly to relief. The government also aided the National War Fund, created in 1942 by union leaders and the United Way, to finance other charitable relief agencies and the activities of the United Service Organization (USO). Responding to requests from post and field commanders, the USO provided a wide variety of live entertainment, often featuring leading celebrities, to U.S. military personnel around the world.

Mobilizing Morale

All combatant nations made efforts to raise morale and patriotic sentiment; it greased mobilization efforts as much as the fear of an impending invasion. The major Axis nations, however, specialized in generating morale to an extent unthinkable in the United States or Britain, in part through patriotic social organizations such as the Hitler Youth program in Germany and the National Spiritual Mobilization Central League in Japan, both of which sponsored activities and ideological indoctrination starting at an early age. Germany was also especially successful with its pervasive propaganda in the media, led by the fiery government minister of propaganda, Joseph Goebbels, as well as spectacular party rallies before hundreds of thousands. In addition, decrees issued in 1938 and 1939 called for the death penalty for anyone who refused, or encouraged others to refuse, military orders or who expressed "defeatism." The day war broke out in Europe, the Japanese government announced that the first day of each month would be Public Service for Asia Day, when sake sales were prohibited and everyone was to perform some duty for the war effort. A new clothing line—the basic "people's uniform"—went on sale in November 1940 to encourage social unity. It was unifying, but not especially attractive.

In the USSR, Soviet propaganda, the German invasion, and the atrocities the Nazis committed throughout the western areas they occupied were more than enough to mobilize and sustain national morale. In the United States, Arthur Upham Pope chaired the Committee for National Morale (formed in June 1940) to counter German propaganda, promote a clear understanding of war issues to the public, and study the mechanics of morale by consulting with leading anthropologists, psychologists, sociologists, and others. Citizens of the western Allies were also determined to destroy Fascist forces that threatened modern democratic civilizations. This was demonstrated by the millions who mobilized for war on military bases, in factories and government offices, and around kitchen tables stacked with civil defense literature, volunteer projects, and produce from the backyard victory garden. With morale up and mobilization under way, civilians and the armed forces would share the burden of achieving victory.

PRINCIPAL SOURCES AND FURTHER READING

Brinkley, David. *Washington Goes to War.* New York: Random House, Ballantine, 1988, 1989.

Cardozier, V. R. *The Mobilization of the United States in World War II: How the Government, Military, and Industry Prepared for War.* Jefferson, NC: McFarland 1995.

Eiler, Keith E. *Mobilizing America: Robert P. Patterson and the War Effort, 1940–1945.* Ithaca, London: Cornell University Press, 1997.

Goodwin, Doris Kearns. *No Ordinary Time: Franklin and Eleanor Roosevelt: The Home Front in World War II.* New York: Simon & Schuster, 1994.

Gropman, Alan L. *Mobilizing U.S. Industry in World War II: Myth and Reality.* Washington, D.C.: National Defense University, Institute for National Strategic Defense Studies, 1996.

Harrison, Mark, ed. *The Economics of World War II: Six Great Powers in International Comparison.* Cambridge: Cambridge University Press, 1998.

Jefferies, John W. *Wartime America.* The American Ways Series. Chicago: Ivan R. Dee, 1996.

Kennedy, David M. *Freedom from Fear: The American People in the Depression and War, 1929–1945.* New York: Oxford University Press, 1999.

Ohly, John H. *The U.S. Army in World War II: Industrialists in Olive Drab: The Emergency Operation of Private Industries during World War II.* Washington, D.C.: U.S. Army, Center of Military History, 1999.

Overy, Richard. *Göring.* London: Phoenix Press, 1984.

MILITARY LEADERSHIP AND ORGANIZATION

Everything is very simple in war, but the simplest thing is difficult. These difficulties accumulate and produce a friction which no man can imagine exactly who has not seen war.

—Karl von Clausewitz, On War, *1832*

Just over a century after the Prussian general Karl von Clausewitz wrote his classic treatise on military strategy, the world was engulfed in the most widespread and destructive conflict in history. As in all preceding wars, everything in World War II was very simple: attack and retreat, conquest and destruction, terror, survival, death. More than in any preceding war, the simplest things were difficult. This was true in all areas, from politics to manufacturing; it was particularly true of the military conduct of the war, where everything converged in the actual clash of arms.

Military operations often involved the coordination of regular air, land, and naval units, specialized detachments (such as commandos and deception units), and partisan or resistance groups—complex forces wielding more firepower than had ever been known before. Reflecting the global scope of the conflict, the armed forces of the opposing sides each comprised diverse peoples united in fighting the same enemies—but also divided by language, customs, prejudices, and political imperatives. Particularly among the Allies, top military leaders had to consider the differences within their alliance as well as the common objectives—along with the combat readiness of individual field forces and, often, political and other circumstances—in organizing, then planning the deployment and use of armed forces. Field commanders, meanwhile, had to determine the best ways to coordinate polyglot forces effectively in battle.

Throughout the war, military leaders also faced a stream of stunning technological developments as well as improvements in, and new uses of, previously existing technology. (See Chapter 5.) Not only were they obligated to make certain their armed forces were equipped with the best possible weapons and were trained and organized to use them to maximum effect; they also had to be prepared to defend against new enemy weapons and tactics. Flexibility, creativity, persistence, and resilience were premium qualities (not always in evidence, and not always rewarded) all along the military lines of authority—the *chain of command*.

These same qualities were required to keep frontline units adequately supplied with other essential war matériel, from fuel and replacement parts to food and good socks and boots for the infantry. When supplies weren't where they were needed when they were needed, people died and objectives were lost. Frontline fighters understood this full well. Those in rear echelons and on the home front often did not. "If quartermasters and civilian officials are left to take their own time over the organization of supplies," German field marshal Erwin Rommel said, "everything is bound to be very slow. . . . This can lead to frightful disasters when there is a man on the other side who carries out his plans with greater drive and thus greater speed."

The flow of supplies and other vital logistical duties were generally within the purview of armed forces quartermaster corps. World War II armies and navies also included hosts of other specialized units. Some, such as engineering, signal, and medical units, had long been part of military tables of organization, but in this total war they faced many novel and daunting challenges that required innovative methods and means. Other specialized detachments were newer, and their structure and placement within the armed forces evolved throughout the war. Aerial photography units proved their value to military intelligence and mapmaking. Rescue units—including a few American and German detachments equipped with a new type of aircraft, the helicopter—established systems for picking up drifting sailors and downed flyers. Special entertainment and morale units attempted to keep spirits high. And, within some armed forces (including those of the Soviets, Germans, and Chinese Communists and Nationalists), political indoctrination personnel were deployed to ensure that officers and enlisted men spoke and acted in accord with party ideology.

As the war continued and casualties mounted, structures and methods for training and integrating replacements were devised and revised. Provision also had to be made for thousands—ultimately millions—of prisoners. Within the U.S. Army, military prisoners were the responsibility of the Office of the Provost Marshal General, which also had other wide-ranging duties, from supervising military police to ensuring the security of homefront production facilities threatened by saboteurs or strikes. In all armed forces, military justice, military security, and military government organizations dealt not only with armed forces personnel but also, and in many ways, with civilians.

When Allied armed forces liberated or occupied new territory, civilians were generally assisted. With the major exception of the initial Soviet thrusts into Germany at the end of the war, the Allied military, as a norm, treated even hostile populations humanely. Axis forces often had very different instructions. In what quickly became a hallmark evil of World War II, Axis military units—regular troops as well as specialized killing squads—systematically, and as a part of their assigned duties, murdered unarmed civilians. In both Asia and Europe, such murders were sometimes committed in so-called retaliation for acts of resistance. In Europe, dominated by Nazi Germany, Axis forces more often committed mass murders because the civilian victims belonged to targeted ethnic or political groups. (See also Chapters 8 and 12.)

By the end of 1938, the territorial ambitions of the three major Axis nations had become apparent, and the leading members of what would become the United Nations (more commonly called "the Allies") were revising military contingency plans, trying to prepare as best they could, given prevailing pacifist sentiments, for the spread of the conflict then raging in China and the European war that Adolf Hitler seemed determined to provoke. British, French, and American military planners were not privy to Hitler's timetables, however, nor could they anticipate the attack strategy and timing of the Japanese high command. When World War II actually began, the United Nations were, initially, unable to counter the Axis onslaught. Unlike the Allies, the major Axis powers had been building, organizing, and planning the aggressive use of their armed forces for years.

BASIC WORLD WAR II MILITARY FORCE STRUCTURE

(From Smallest to Largest Units; U.S. Command Ranks Are Given)

Ground Forces	Description
Squad	A group, usually between 8 and 14 soldiers, organized from a platoon for special duties, generally led by a sergeant.
Platoon	Sometimes as small as 20 soldiers, but generally between 40 and 50, depending on the type of unit; some U.S. military police platoons had an authorized strength of 106 men. The smallest units in the U.S. Army and Marine Corps to be led by a commissioned officer, usually, in the army, by a 2nd lieutenant.
Company ("battery" in artillery units; sometimes "troop" in cavalry units)	Usually between 100 and 200 soldiers; in a few cases (e.g., a U.S. Army airborne division's signal company) more than 250 men. Grouped in 3 to 5 platoons and commanded by captains, companies were the smallest units to have mess, supply, and other support functions.
Battalion	Generally comprised 3 or 4 companies with an overall complement of 600 to 1,100 soldiers—although this often depended on a battalion's function (in the U.S. Army in 1943, an infantry battalion had 871 officers and men; an armored battalion 1,000, an airborne battalion 530). Usually commanded by lieutenant colonels, battalions were often components of regiments, but they could be attached to higher army formations or be independent.
Regiment	1,800 to more than 3,000 soldiers comprising two or more battalions, commanded by a colonel. The principal troop component of a division.
Brigade	Usually comprising two or more regiments and led by a brigadier general. Although the U.S. Army had long included brigades, a prewar reorganization changed an army division's structure from "square" or "rectangular" (the division infantry comprising two brigades, each with two regiments) to "triangular" (three infantry regiments). So with a few exceptions, brigades were not included in U.S. Army structure during the war. Other armed forces continued to use them.

BASIC WORLD WAR II MILITARY FORCE STRUCTURE (CONTINUED)

Ground Forces	Description
Division	The smallest unit in modern warfare combining all elements (infantry, artillery, engineers, plus service and supply units), it usually comprised two or more regiments or brigades and was led by a major general. There were various types (e.g., armored, infantry), and, within most armies, division size fluctuated (the average U.S. division comprised 15,514 soldiers in June 1941; in June 1943 it was 13,746; in January 1945, 14,037). There were sometimes great differences in the strength of divisions that opposed each other. In North Africa in 1942, the Italian *Ariete* armored division comprised 8,600 men and 189 tanks whereas a British armored division included 13,235 men and 280 tanks.
Corps	Usually led by a major general or a lieutenant general, on average included 50,000 soldiers comprising from three to six divisions, with headquarters troops (e.g., staff officers and support personnel). In the U.S. Army, the makeup of a corps varied with the tactical situation; in addition to divisions, there might be specialized (e.g., artillery engineer) companies, battalions, and regiments. The U.S. Marine Corps used amphibious corps.
Army	Comprising two or more corps and on average 100,000 men (see U.S. Armies in World War II chart in this chapter).
Army Group	"Front" in the USSR; averaged two or more armies with 500,000 men.

Navies	Description
Division	An administrative unit generally comprising four ships of the same type (e.g., battleships, submarines).
Squadron	Primarily indicates groups of destroyers or submarines, but there might be other types of squadrons. Generally composed of 2 or 3 divisions totaling from 8 to 12 vessels and under the command of a captain.
Flotilla	Spanish for "little fleet." Generally comprised 2 or more squadrons of small warships.

(continued)

BASIC WORLD WAR II MILITARY FORCE STRUCTURE (CONTINUED)

Navies	*Description*
Task Force/Task Groups/Task Units	Semipermanent tactical organizations devoted to specific types of operations. Commanded by a *flag officer* (an officer above the rank of captain, and thus entitled to display a flag of one or more stars indicating his rank).
Fleet	The largest naval formation, generally defined as "an organization of ships and aircraft under the command of a flag officer."
Combined Fleet	General designation for the entire operational strength of the Japanese Imperial Navy. Elements of the Combined Fleet were designated as fleets, task forces, strike forces, and special units as required through the war.

Air Forces	*Description*
Flight	Usually two or more aircraft (in the Soviet air force, this small unit was designated a "squadron").
Group	The basic organizational unit of the U.S. Army Air Force; also the largest tactical unit in the British Royal Air Force (large British "groups" were sometimes called "wings"), in which groups comprised from 9 to 24 squadrons.
Wing	The largest tactical unit in the U.S. Army Air Force (comprising from 2 to 4 groups each containing from 2 to 5 squadrons). Also the largest tactical unit in the German *Luftwaffe* (in which a wing, or *Geschwader*, comprised 3 groups, or *gruppen* of some 30 aircraft). The equivalent organizational unit was designated "aviation regiment" by the USSR, in which each regiment comprised either 4 or 5 squadrons.
Air Forces	In the USAAF, these were complex air units established to perform comprehensive combat missions (e.g., the strategic bombing campaign against Germany) and comprised various subordinate "commands" (e.g., a bomber command, a fighter command).

Principal sources: Norman Polmar and Thomas B. Allen, *World War II: The Encyclopedia of the War Years, 1941–1945*, New York: Random House, 1996; Murray Williamson and Allan R. Millet, appendix, *A War to Be Won*, Cambridge, MA: Belknap Press of Harvard University Press, 2000; Robert Leckie, *Warfare*, New York: Harper & Row, 1970.

THE AXIS

In 1936, the year Benito Mussolini made the first reference to a "Rome–Berlin Axis" in a speech, Italian forces triumphed in Abyssinia (Ethiopia), inspiring Mussolini's exultation to an audience in Rome on May 9, that "Italy has at last her Empire—a Fascist Empire." Yet Ethiopia was only the first step toward achieving Mussolini's imperial dreams. To fully realize his vision of Italian dominance over the entire Mediterranean world would require a strong ally, whose support could help counter Italy's many strategic weaknesses. Since first acquiring national authority in 1922, Mussolini had looked toward Germany, anticipating that country's resurgence from the consequences of its defeat in World War I.

In fact, the German officer corps had begun laying clandestine plans to rebuild their military even before unhappy German representatives signed the punitive Treaty of Versailles in 1919 (see Chapter 1). German rearmament came out into the open in 1935, two years after Adolf Hitler assumed power. Hitler, meanwhile, had followed Mussolini's assumption of power with interest, declaring "I have the keenest admiration for the great man who governs south of the Alps." Both dictators not only expected, they desired another war.

"War alone brings up to their highest tension all human energies," Mussolini asserted, "and puts the stamp of nobility upon the peoples who have the courage to meet it."

"Any alliance whose purpose is not the intention to wage war," Hitler wrote in *Mein Kampf*, "is senseless and useless."

As early as February 1933, almost immediately after assuming power, Hitler told a meeting of his generals that German military might, once properly restored, would be used "for the conquest and ruthless Germanization of new living space in the East." The fertile farmlands and rich oilfields of the Soviet Union were always Hitler's primary target. When German armed forces were ready (having secured western Europe), Hitler did not anticipate they would have much trouble overcoming what he regarded as the inferior and incompetently led Soviet armed forces. Still, he believed it would be helpful to have Italy (as well as Bulgaria, Hungary, and oil-rich Romania) guarding Germany's flanks and providing needed human and material resources. It would also be helpful for increasingly belligerent Japan to press the Soviet Union in Asia, so that significant Soviet forces would have

Italian dictator Benito Mussolini looks over Field Marshal Hermann Göring's shoulder as Göring confers with Hitler during a 1941 briefing. Although Hitler and Mussolini admired each other, the Italian-German alliance rapidly deteriorated under the multiple strains caused by differing objectives, German arrogance, and Italian battlefield reverses.

to remain in the Far East. And Japanese aggression would have other benefits: "The purpose of the cooperation based on the Three Power Pact must be to induce Japan to take action in the Far East as soon as possible," Hitler wrote in Directive No. 24, issued a few months before the June 1941 German invasion of Russia. "This will tie down strong English forces and will divert the main effort of the United States of America to the Pacific."

In 1936, while both Italy and Germany provided fighting men and matériel to Generalissimo Francisco Franco's fascist/nationalist forces in the Spanish Civil War and the Soviet Union dispatched aid to the opposing Spanish Popular Front, the most aggressive elements of Japan's military were solidifying their political control of their own country. At the same time, the Japanese were consolidating their position in Manchukuo (Manchuria) and preparing for further penetration into China. Russia had been Japan's chief rival in the area since well before the 1904–1905 Russo-Japanese war, when Japan surprised the European world by defeating the Czar's imperial forces. Transformed in the 1920s into the Soviet Union, the embodiment of the threatening communist ideology, this rival, with its considerable military strength, still posed a major threat to Japan's expansionist plans. In fact, Japanese forces on the Manchukuo/Mongolia border suffered a humiliating defeat in a full-scale, months-long battle with the Soviets in the summer of 1939 (see Chapter 6). Thus the USSR was a major factor in the development of Japanese military strategies. Britain and the United States, with their powerful navies, were other prime factors in Japanese calculations.

Like Hitler and Mussolini, fervent Japanese militarists bathed combat in a glorious light: "War is the father of creation and the mother of culture," a 1930s army pamphlet declared, "both in individuals and competing nations." On September 27, 1940, four months after Germany's swift conquest of western Europe, the governments of Japan, Germany, and Italy signed a ten-year, three-power pact that formalized the Axis alliance.

Axis Military Leaders and Their Armed Forces

Germany

After World War I, the kaiser—to whom the elite corps of German officers had sworn allegiance—was forced into exile, the Treaty of Versailles reduced Germany's army to a skeleton force of 100,000, and political discord and economic distress shook the country (see Chapter 1). As the corps of officers, now sworn to "protect the German nation and its lawful establishments," secretly rebuilt the German armed forces, some among them abandoned the traditional Prussian view that the military should be above politics. Among the rising political figures they believed they could use for their own ends was a former army corporal named Adolf Hitler. Reciprocally, as he gained influence, Hitler well understood that he could not achieve his aims of political power and military conquest without the support, expertise, and battlefield leadership of Germany's professional officer corps. Although his courtship of the army was not entirely successful, he did secure the allegiance of many officers. In 1933, when Hitler became chancellor, then-Colonel Walther Reichenau, assistant to Hitler's first minister of defense, Field Marshal Werner von Blomberg, declared, "Never were the armed forces more identical with the state than they are today."

The next year, Hitler backed the army, rather than the *Sturmabteilung* (the Nazi militia, with 4 million members) in a vicious power struggle.

When, shortly thereafter, the elderly President Paul von Hindenburg died, and Hitler added the powers of president to his authority as chancellor, becoming the führer, Blomberg had Reichenau instruct all armed forces units to abandon their oath to the German nation. Their allegiance, thereafter, was to be to one man: "I will render to Adolf Hitler, Leader of the German nation and people, Supreme Commander of the Armed Forces, unconditional obedience." Although many officers continued to disdain the Nazi ideology, the armed forces and führer were united in a quest to return Germany to a position of power from which it could forge a new order in Europe.

GERMAN ARMED FORCES AND THEIR TOP COMMANDERS

ADOLF HITLER: "DER FÜHRER" (THE LEADER) (1889–1945). A decorated veteran of the vicious bloodletting on World War I's Western Front ("the greatest and most unforgettable time of my earthly existence," he wrote in *Mein Kampf*), Adolf Hitler declared in 1936, as Germany's führer, that preparation for war must be the nation's primary focus and that Germany must build, as swiftly as possible, *the premier army in the world.*" Yet Hitler's faith in the corps of officers he had inherited, and whose support he continued to cultivate, was always far from absolute. "The generals are . . . trapped in their own professional expertise," he said in the early 1930s. "The creative genius is always an outsider. . . . I have the gift of reducing the problems to their essential core." The führer's regard for the professional military further ebbed as his own megalomania increased; plunged precipitously after dreams of quick victory over the Soviet Union deteriorated into a long nightmare of brutish combat; and was all but destroyed by the July 1944 attempt to assassinate him, a plot largely organized by army officers.

Hitler took action against some military professionals well before the German invasion of Poland. On November 5, 1937, he declared his intention to take the country to war, perhaps as early as 1938, should the proper opportunity occur. Blomberg, minister of war and commander in chief of the armed forces, and Colonel-General Baron Werner von Fritsch, commander in chief of the army, protested that the armed forces were not yet ready. Within three months, Hitler relieved both men of their commands because of scandals. (Blomberg's new wife was revealed as a former prostitute. Although the false accusation that Fritsch had engaged in homosexual acts was quickly proven to be the work of the Gestapo, he was still dismissed pending the outcome of a military court of honor.) On February 4, 1938, Hitler took advantage of the opportunity provided by these two dismissals to restructure the entire military high command. He abolished the ministry of war and established the *Oberkommando der Wehrmacht* (OKW, the armed forces high command), with himself as its supreme commander and the pliable Field Marshal Wilhelm Keitel as its chief. Sixteen senior generals were relieved of command (a number would return to serve during the war), and forty-four others suspected of insufficient enthusiasm were transferred. That August, another important change occurred when Colonel-General Ludwig Beck, anti-Nazi chief of the army general staff, resigned in protest over Hitler's plan to invade Czechoslovakia—a plan aborted, much to Hitler's regret, after a frenzy of international diplomacy. By the fall of 1938, the alliance between Hitler and the officer corps had shifted, finally and decisively, in the führer's favor.

In December 1941, with German forces bogged down before Moscow, Hitler accepted the resignation of Fritsch's successor as army commander in chief, Field Marshal Walther von Brauchitsch, and assumed direct command of the army himself. The following September, when German operations in the Caucasus were not going well, he replaced the chief of the army general staff, Colonel-General Franz Halder, with Colonel-General Kurt Zeitzler, angrily proclaiming a new direction in armed forces command when he told Halder, "We need National Socialist ardor now, not professional ability. I cannot expect this of an officer of the old school like you." Although Hitler supervised naval and air force operations much less closely, these services, too, were profoundly affected by the führer's decisions, reversals, and bouts of indecision, by his festering distrust of the officer corps, and his generally mercurial nature.

Armed with unrelenting faith in his own military judgment (which seemed nearly infallible to others, as well, during the conquests of 1939–1941), Hitler steadily pushed his armed forces into the jaws of disaster. Overburdened with multilevel command responsibilities he had insisted on assuming, he countered resistance to his battle plans with a combination of explosive anger and nearly overwhelming charm. "Hitler's acts of persuasion, his ferocious desire to win you over, were virtually limitless," army high command operations officer General Adolf Heusinger stated after the war. "I met with him six or seven hundred times at the daily conferences, and time and time again after I left the room I would allow myself an hour of relaxation . . . to forget every word he said, and only then could I arrive at a rational and realistic decision." But final decisions were

Hitler's, and at crucial points (such as the decision to invade the Soviet Union in 1941), they were based on miscalculations and false assumptions.

Traveling either by plane or on his special train, *Amerika,* Hitler shuttled between various field headquarters as the war intensified, spending less and less time on nonmilitary matters. Although he adamantly refused, until late in the war, to allow his armies to retreat and regroup to fight another day when battles were going badly (a policy that resulted in the senseless destruction of Axis fighting men and matériel), the führer, himself, increasingly retreated from reality as the Allies gained ground. Near the end, issuing commands from the underground bunker in Berlin where he was to commit suicide, Hitler was ordering the deployment of forces that no longer existed as effective fighting units.

Armed Forces High Command (*Oberkommando der Wehrmacht,* OKW)

Leader and Supreme Commander of the Wehrmacht: Adolf Hitler (1938–1945)

Chief of High Command: Field Marshal Wilhelm Keitel (1938–1945)

Chief of Operations Staff: Colonel-General Alfred Jodl (1938–1945)

Created to coordinate the activities of all German forces, the Oberkommando der Wehrmacht (OKW) fell far short of this objective, largely due to its supreme commander, Adolf Hitler. Comprising representatives of each of the three services, OKW was organized into main sections devoted to Operations, Communications, and Foreign and Counterintelligence. It also included a War Economy and Armaments Department that was headed, until 1943, by the ardently nationalist but anti-Nazi general Georg Richard Thomas, a fervent proponent of organized, coordinated preparation for total war. Thomas was also prescient: "The essential thing is to see that our armament is set for all eventualities," he declared in May 1939, "including [not only blitzkrieg campaigns but] a long war." His persistence in pressing this point led to his demotion to "adviser" in 1943, at which time Field Marshal Keitel, conceding that Thomas's judgments had been correct, reminded the officer, "Hitler has made clear that he has no use for men who seek continually to instruct him."

In late 1941, the OKW was assigned to direct army operations in all theaters of operations—*except* eastern Europe, where at least 60 percent of the

German army was deployed from June 1941 on. (The army high command, led by commander in chief Hitler after December 1941, directed operations in the East.) Yet, despite its responsibilities, its impressive structure, and its capable staff, the OKW did not truly coordinate the operations of all the armed services. If anything, interservice rivalries intensified as each service scrambled to secure increasingly scarce manpower and equipment. Each of the armed forces jealously cultivated and placated Hitler, the ultimate arbiter; and each tended to be tight-lipped about information (such as data on equipment and personnel) that the other services might use against it as they jockeyed for men, ordnance, and favor.

Nor did the OKW ever fulfill the role of an informed (and restraining) advisory body. It did conduct studies and made recommendations (many of which the temperamental führer ignored), but the OKW chiefly served as a funnel for Hitler's war directives and sounding-board for his views, which were rarely, if ever, disputed. As its deputy chief of operations, General Walter Warlimont, noted in his postwar memoir, *Inside Hitler's Headquarters* (1964), "The advice of the British Chiefs of Staff and the U.S. Joint Chiefs was a deciding factor in Allied strategy. At the comparable level in Germany there was nothing but a disastrous vacuum."

DAS HEER (ARMY)

Supreme Commander: Adolf Hitler (1934–1945)

Commander in Chief: Colonel-General Freiherr Werner von Fritsch (1934–1938); Field-Marshal Walter von Brauchitsch (1938–1941); Adolf Hitler (1941–1945)

General Staff (*Oberkommando das Heer, OKH*)

Chief of the General Staff: Colonel-General Ludwig Beck (1935–1938); Colonel-General Franz Halder (1938–1942); Colonel-General Kurt Zeitzler (1942–1944); Colonel-General Heinz Guderian (1944–1945); General of Infantry Hans Krebs (May 1945)

Force Size (at Peak): 6.5 million

Theaters of Operation: Europe (western Europe, Scandinavia, and the USSR); Mediterranean (including the Balkans and North Africa)

Casualties (September 1, 1939–January 31, 1945): 7,430,977 (includes 1,622,561 dead from enemy action; 160,237 dead from other causes; 4,145,863 wounded; 1,646,316 missing; and the Waffen SS, profiled later in this chapter)

Superbly trained, disciplined, and supported by the Luftwaffe, Germany's armored and motorized divisions formed the first-strike "fist" that stunned the rest of the world. Successful blitzkrieg tactics placed most of western Europe under German domination by mid-1940.

Unleashed on September 1, 1939, the German army awed the world for two years with stunning sweeps through Poland, Scandinavia, and western Europe. Led in the field by experienced and well-schooled commanders, das Heer had the formidably effective Panzer divisions as its first-strike "fist" and many supremely motivated "graduates" of the Hitler Youth in its ranks. It seemed invincible—until December 1941, when Army Group Center, on the Eastern Front, ground to a halt in front of Moscow. Thereafter, more than half of the German army fought and bled in the Soviet Union under a commander in chief who equated defeat in battle with treason and requests for strategic withdrawal with cowardice. German forces elsewhere, and Germany's Axis allies, increasingly suffered from the drain of resources on the Eastern Front. By the time an entire German army was lost at Stalingrad (December 1942–February 1943)—a stunning blow to army and home-front morale and to Hitler's grand plans—the war had changed irrevocably. As had been foreseen by General Georg R. Thomas, instead of engaging in relatively short and successful blitzkrieg campaigns that allowed them to exploit conquered territories, regroup, and plan before driving on, the Germans were mired in an unrelenting, many-front conflict against the powerful United Nations alliance, anchored by the abundant resources and massive industrial production of the United States.

By the end of 1942, das Heer was spread thin and getting thinner. Losses on the Eastern Front, alone, sometimes exceeded 150,000 men *a month*, and adequate replacements were increasingly difficult to secure; as early as September 1942, Army Groups A and B reported that they had received only 33,150 replacements for the 79,200 men they had lost that month. Since Hitler would not allow the consolidation of divisions, which would have resulted in fewer, but all at full fighting strength (he felt that the enemy would view a reduction in the number of divisions as a sign of weakness), divisional complements were reduced by more than 6,000 men. The ratio of "teeth to tail" (front line to support troops) also was steadily reduced, often with unhappy results, and infantry divisions were raided for trucks and other motorized equipment (replaced, if at all, by horses, mules, and bicycles) so that Panzer divisions could remain well equipped.

More replacements were found by expanding age limits for conscription in both directions: teenagers and men in their forties were sent to the front. So were some men previously considered unfit to serve, such as convicts and political dissidents. Before the Allied invasion of Normandy, units of the "Replacement Army" (the branch responsible for preparing new soldiers for combat) completed their training while on active duty as occupying forces in western Europe; the more experienced units they replaced were sent into combat. Clerks and other rear-echelon personnel with little combat experience were also sent to the front, where they were integrated into divisions as needed, one of many factors that adversely affected unit cohesion. Often, casualties more than offset all these measures. Morale suffered and desertions increased despite harsh punishment. By the end of September 1943, the army high command, distressed by the increasing demands on its weakened divisions, issued an uncharacteristically blunt assessment: "We are not fighting now for the political future and the New Order in Europe, we are fighting for our lives. We can no longer afford to deploy our divisions in the wrong place, we have no more divisions to spare."

Nevertheless, das Heer remained a remarkably well-disciplined and effective fighting force to the end of the war. Long military tradition, meticulous training and preparation before and early in the war, and the encouragement of excellent (though not overfriendly) rapport between officers and men contributed significantly to the army's resilience. Men at all levels were also prepared during training to assume responsibilities two ranks above their own. This helped front-line units to better weather their bitter losses.

WAFFEN SS   (See also Chapter 8.)

Supreme Commander: Adolf Hitler

Commander in Chief: Heinrich Himmler

Chief of Leadership Main Office: SS-Obergruppenführer Hans Jüttner

Chief of SS Central Bureau: SS-Obergruppenführer Gottlob Berger

Force Size (at Peak): 800,000

Theaters of Operation: Europe (all sections); Mediterranean (Balkans/ Southern Europe)

Casualties: Between 160,000 and 200,000

The military arm of Heinrich Himmler's "black corps," the much-feared SS (*Schutzstaffel*, or protection organization), the Waffen SS (named from the German word for weapon, *die waffe*) grew out of small SS "Political Readiness Squads"—that performed such functions as the assassination of Nazi militia leaders during the 1934 power struggle. That same year, Hitler authorized *Verfügungstruppe* (VT), armed formations within the SS, which the army was assured would be used only for "special internal political tasks." In fact, Himmler planned to build an ideologically pure and militarily effective force within his SS that might one day replace the army.

Shortly after a VT regiment staged a demonstration of its fighting prowess in May 1939, Hitler authorized formation of an SS field-combat division. Fighting in Poland three months later, the division both impressed and shocked army commanders with its reckless courage, appalling casualties, and what they considered subpar leadership. Hitler was more favorably impressed: the Waffen SS was officially born in October. Eventually, thirty-eight Waffen SS divisions were formed, twenty-five entirely or largely comprising *Volksdeutsch* (ethnic Germans living abroad) and foreign troops (including Scandinavians, Croats, Ukrainians, Hungarians, Italians, Slovenes, Belgians, Dutch, Spanish, and Arabs), usually under the command of German officers. As German fortunes waned, Waffen-SS "volunteers," foreign and otherwise, were increasingly secured with the assistance of bribery and intimidation.

Under army control in combat, but otherwise answerable only to the SS high command, Waffen SS units fought—generally well, often fanatically—in all the main German theaters of operation. Like other SS branches, the Waffen SS was steeped in war crimes—including the massacre of eighty-six unarmed U.S. prisoners of war near Malmédy, Belgium, on December 17, 1944.

KRIEGSMARINE (NAVY) (See also "Naval Vessels and Weaponry" in Chapter 5.)

Supreme Commander: Adolf Hitler

Commander in Chief: Grand Admiral Erich Raeder (1928–1943); Grand Admiral Karl Dönitz (1943–1945); General-Admiral Hans von Friedeburg (May 1945)

Supreme Headquarters (*Oberkommando der Marine, OKM*)

General Staff (*Seekriegsleitung, SKL*)

Force Size (at Peak): 810,000

Theaters of Operation: European (western and eastern, including the Black Sea); Mediterranean; American; German commerce raiders and some submarines operated around the globe

Casualties (September 1, 1939–January 31, 1945): 185,544 (includes 48,904 combat deaths; 11,125 deaths from other causes; 25,259 wounded; 100,256 missing); of 1,175 U-boats committed to battle throughout the war, more than 700 were lost from enemy action

Despite a twelvefold increase in spending between 1932 and 1939, the German navy remained almost wholly unprepared for war when Germany invaded Poland. Although, in his first meeting with Hitler in 1933, Navy commander in chief Erich Raeder had emphasized the long lead time and comprehensive planning that would be required to reconstitute the navy that had been eviscerated by the Versailles treaty, the Kriegsmarine never had a steady or adequate flow of required resources or the stable political environment necessary to complete any of the several naval construction plans submitted, then altered or abandoned, between 1934 and 1939. Moreover, most naval war plans assumed that the initial primary opponent would be the

French navy; Hitler repeatedly assured Kriegsmarine planners that a political accommodation would postpone any military confrontation with Britain until 1944 or 1945. Only after the Czechoslovakian crisis of 1938 did the navy begin to plan for the war it would actually fight, although it could not plan at the time for one later development: it was to wage war largely without the assistance of air power.

On January 27, 1939, at Raeder's insistence, Hitler directed that the navy be given top priority for resources used to construct ships. Air force commander in chief Herman Göring (acting in his capacity of commissioner of the Four Year Plan, an economic program for war preparation) supported this directive—but only after Raeder agreed not to develop a naval air arm. Yet despite Göring's assurances, the Luftwaffe never gave the navy adequate air support.

In September 1939, the navy's surface fleet included only two battleships, two pocket battleships, seven cruisers, twenty-one destroyers, twelve torpedo boats, and fifty-seven submarines (*unterseeboots*, or U-boats), only twenty-seven of which were fit for deployment in the Atlantic. One aircraft carrier, *Graf Zeppelin*, had been launched in December 1938, but was never finished; a second remained on the drawing boards. War plans were incomplete, and the naval high command was divided both doctrinally and physically (the submarine command was not located at Raeder's headquarters in Berlin). Raeder planned a surface-fleet offensive against Allied commerce, with U-boat support; Commander of Submarines Karl Dönitz believed that reliance on submarines could result in an even more devastating campaign against Allied shipping than during World War I, despite interwar improvements in antisubmarine-warfare technology.

Although the surface fleet had some early successes (see Chapters 6 and 7), other operations did not end well; heavy losses among the few capital ships and the unacceptable amounts of time and resources it would take to replace them conspired to reduce Hitler's support for Raeder and his surface navy. Dönitz replaced Raeder in January 1943 and quickly ordered "All work to be discontinued on battleships, heavy cruisers, light cruisers, aircraft carriers and troop transports, with the exception of ships appointed for training purposes."

Meanwhile, Germany's U-boat fleet finally reached the number Dönitz had been urging all along: 400, of which 222 were first-line vessels. Since the first days of the war, U-boats had steadily assaulted the Allies' vital maritime supply lines with near-devastating effect. But problems had plagued the undersea fleet, including defective torpedoes. (The U.S. Navy had even greater problems. See "Damn the Torpedoes" in Chapter 5.) With inadequate Luftwaffe reconnaissance, U-boats relied heavily on radio communication with headquarters for direction. This contributed to their heavy losses, since—with one major interruption—the Allies could "read" much of their coded radio traffic (see Chapter 9). German resources shrank and German scientists failed to develop enough suitable countermeasures to ever-improving Allied antisubmarine resources and technology. In May 1943, with 241 U-boats already lost in combat operations, along with many experienced commanders and crewmen, Dönitz recalled most of his submarines, essentially ceding the battle of the Atlantic to the Allies. He continued to deploy U-boats until the end of the war (losing a further 389 in combat) in an effort to divert as many Allied resources as possible from the campaign against the German homeland.

Closer to home, the navy's Security Force comprised some 100,000 men and 3,000 light vessels (including, from 1944, the remnants of the surface fleet). Dedicated to protect shipping, defend the coastline, and support land forces, this naval arm was also active in inland waters and the Black Sea. In the Baltic region, at the end of the war, it assisted in efforts to rescue German soldiers and civilians retreating from Soviet armies.

LUFTWAFFE (AIR FORCE)

Supreme Commander: Adolf Hitler

Reich Aviation Ministry (*Reichsluftfahrtministerium*)

Supreme Headquarters (*Oberkommando der Luftwaffe*) established 1944

Aviation Minister: Reichsminister Hermann Göring (1935–1945); General-Field Marshal Robert Ritter von Greim (April–May 1945)

Commander in Chief: Field Marshal Hermann Göring

Secretary of State for Air: General-Field Marshal Erhard Milch (1933–1944; handled all matters other than operations)

Chief of General Staff: General Hans-Jürgen Stumpff (June 1937–January 1939); General Hans Jeschonnek (1939–1943); General Günther Korten (1943–July 1944); General Werner Kreipe (August–October 1944); General Karl Koller (November 1944–May 1945)

Force Size (at Peak): 2 million: this included airmen and ground-support troops, antiaircraft artillery personnel, paratroopers (who generally

fought as ground troops after 1941); 21 Luftwaffe field divisions (under army authority after 1943), and the Herman Göring Panzer division
Casualties: 608,000 (including 294,728 killed and missing in both air and field units)

During the interwar years, the German military circumvented the Treaty of Versailles by producing military aircraft abroad and training future Luftwaffe airmen in civilian flight-training schools and friendly foreign countries, including Italy and the Soviet Union. On May 10, 1933, soon after coming to power, Hitler appointed his close Nazi-Party associate and former First World War air ace Herman Göring to head a new aviation ministry. Luftwaffe personnel, including former army and navy officers newly transferred to the air force, were secretly trained in army and navy schools.

In addition to the separate Luftwaffe, General Werner von Blomberg, Hitler's first defense minister, wanted the army and navy to retain their own air arms. Göring objected—and prevailed. His hands in many pots, he left most of the practical aspects of Luftwaffe development to his deputy since 1933, Erhard Milch, a director of Lufthansa airline after World War I and an early Nazi supporter who possessed abundant organizational skills. By 1935, when Göring announced the Luftwaffe's existence, the air force comprised 900 flying officers, 200 flak (antiaircraft artillery) officers, and about 17,000 enlisted men. Four years later, there were more than 15,000 officers and 370,000 men. However, this astonishingly rapid growth resulted in many critical problems, a number of which were never solved and were exacerbated under wartime conditions.

The Luftwaffe always suffered from procurement and supply difficulties springing from Germany's limited resources, the fluctuating economic situation, Hitler's ever-changing plans and demands, and its own administrative disorders. (Between July 1934 and 1939, the air force floated fourteen different aircraft procurement plans, some of them overlapping and contradictory.) Like the navy, the Luftwaffe did not begin planning until October 1938 for a war that would immediately include Great Britain as an enemy. Planners had revised early operational doctrine emphasizing strategic bombing; thus plans for the manufacture of long-range bombers were postponed (and never reactivated) in favor of shorter-range dive-bombers and fighters. This severely restricted bomber payloads and the time fighter escorts could stay in English air space during the battle of Britain in 1940. Later, when the Soviet Union proved to be a more stubborn opponent than anticipated, Germany lacked bombers of sufficient range to reach the war industries that the Soviets had moved to the east.

An unnecessarily complex Luftwaffe command structure created delays and confusion, only partially remedied when the *Oberkommando der Luftwaffe* was established in 1944. Göring's tendency to favor old cronies of dubious abilities also proved problematical. Ernst Udet, a man with no technical expertise or organizational ability, committed suicide in 1941 amid revelations about his falsification of production figures and general chaos in the aircraft development and manufacturing programs he was supposed to be controlling as head of the vital Luftwaffe Technical Office. (The public was told he died as the result of a plane crash.) Personal rivalries also affected the high command: Göring respected his deputy but resented what he viewed as Milch's encroachment on his authority—part of the reason for a steady reduction in Milch's authority. Milch, meanwhile, did not get along with General Hans Jeschonnek, who, as chief of the Luftwaffe general staff, was responsible for air force operations. Jeschonnek committed suicide in 1943, after both Hitler and Göring blamed him for catastrophes such as the July Allied firebombing of Hamburg. (The public was told that he died of a stomach ailment.)

By 1944, the Luftwaffe was critically short of fuel and losing an average of 1,755 pilots per month. Unlike the Allies, the Germans did not have the manpower resources to replace their heavy losses, nor was there time or fuel enough to adequately train the new pilots the Luftwaffe managed to secure. Continuously battered by the Allies, Luftwaffe airmen were also increasingly subjected to morale-destroying verbal assaults from members of the other German services, who accused them of lack of support, and from their own führer, who blamed Luftwaffe incompetence for the devastation that Allied bombs were wreaking on Germany.

On New Year's Day 1945, Göring ordered every available plane into the sky for a raid on Allied air bases in Belgium, Holland, and northern France in support of Hitler's last-ditch offensive through the Ardennes Forest in the West (Battle of the Bulge, December 1944–January 1945). More than three hundred Luftwaffe flyers, most of them inexperienced and ill-trained, were shot out of the sky—including a few who were downed by German antiaircraft gunners protecting V-2 launching sites, who had not been told of the raid. "The fighter arm received its death blow during the Ardennes offensive," German ace and Chief of Fighters Adolf Galland later wrote. The fighter arm was all the air force that the Germans had left.

VOLKSSTURM. The *Deutscher Volkssturm*, a last-ditch defense force comprising men and boys between the ages of 16 and 60, was established on September 25, 1944, as Allied troops pressed toward Germany's eastern and western borders, home-front morale was plummeting, and there was widespread fear of revolt by forced laborers and prisoners. Hitler placed it under Nazi Party control, dreaming of a large, ideologically committed militia that would help rouse the entire German population to a fanatical resistance that would stymie the Allied advance. However, fanaticism was beyond much of the war-weary population, the Party was ill-prepared to organize a militia, equipment was scarce and often of poor quality, and men called up for *Volkssturm* duty received minimal military training. Organized to defend the members' own localities (though some battalions were transferred where needed), the Volkssturm included formations of Hitler Youth—whose fanaticism at one location on the Western Front in 1945 was cited in a U.S. 4th Armored Division report as "one of the stumbling blocks in mopping up operations." A number of women also volunteered as informal Volkssturm auxiliary.

Initially, Volkssturm formations engaged primarily in support activities, such as laying mines, assisting in refugee evacuations, and picking up downed Allied flyers—thus releasing more regular troops for combat. By the end of January 1945, however, Volkssturm troops were increasingly being integrated into front-line army formations, with extremely uneven results. Where Party–Army cooperation was good and army officers were able (or inclined) to better arm and supply Volkssturm units and improve on their training—and where there were sufficient regular army troops to back them up—the militia battalions often held their own when facing the enemy. Unit cohesion (or lack of it), level of morale, and degrees of desperation were also factors in the militia's combat performance. On the Eastern Front, the estimated 650,000 Volkssturm troops, who knew the Soviets would show little mercy, often put up stout resistance (as at the "Fortress City" of Breslau, at Pyritz, Pomerania, and during the desperate defense of Berlin). In the West, an estimated 150,000 of the more than 1 million Volkssturm troops taken prisoner experienced extended combat, and, with some exceptions, their performance was generally poor. Further, although there was some reluctance to fall into the hands of the French, who had endured German occupation, there was comparatively little dread of falling into the hands of American and British forces, whose well-fed, well-clothed condition and apparently limitless resources also made it clear that Germany could not win the war.

MERCHANT MARINE. Operating under navy control from 1939 to 1942, and then under the authority of Karl Kaufmann, Reich Commissioner of Shipping, the German merchant marine lost 268 of its nearly 2,500 ships in the first eight months of the war. Only fifteen of these were sunk by enemy action. Two hundred took refuge in neutral ports; others were confiscated by the Allies or scuttled by their own crews. With the resources of occupied countries at its disposal, Germany did not depend on its merchant shipping to the same extent as Great Britain and other nations. Merchant vessels did move vital iron ore across the Baltic from Sweden and equally important Romanian oil along the Danube. They also served as troop transports and as "blockade runners," dodging Allied vessels and aircraft to bring in supplies. Some 3 million tons of German merchant shipping were sunk during the war, while only 176 new merchant vessels totaling 338,000 tons were constructed.

Italy

Benito Mussolini's vision of a "Fascist Empire" around the Mediterranean faced powerful opposition: Great Britain and France held strategically vital Mediterranean territories. (The British possessed both Gibraltar, which allowed them to control the only western passageway to and from the Mediterranean, and the Suez Canal, the only passageway at the eastern end.) Moreover, Mussolini's plans for achieving his empire were ill-defined and rested on the shakiest of foundations. Italy's alliance with resurgent Germany was a fundamental problem. This was always a double-edged sword: one edge provided reassuring strength at Italy's back; the other cast deep and threatening shadows over Italian plans to conquer and then rule the Mediterranean world *unmolested.*

Another major problem, as Germany's first chancellor, Otto von Bismarck, had observed decades earlier, was that Italy had a large territorial appetite, but "very poor teeth." In the realm of natural resources, Italy hardly had teeth at all and would be almost wholly dependent, throughout the war, on foreign sources, particularly Germany and Romania, for such vital war resources as coal and oil. Italy also suffered from a relative dearth of martial expertise; unlike its two major Axis partners, it was not a profoundly militaristic nation and could not draw on military tradition and experience to prepare its armies for conquest. Moreover, the human resources that were to comprise the nation's conquering armies were plagued by illiteracy and

The roster of major Axis commanders included (left to right, top to bottom): Row 1: Marshal Pietro Badoglio, Grand Admiral Karl Dönitz, Marshal Rodolfo Graziani, General Heinz Guderian; Row 2: Colonel-General Alfred Jodl, Field Marshal Wilhelm Keitel, Admiral Osami Nagano, Grand Admiral Erich Raeder; Row 3: Admiral Arturo Riccardi, Field Marshal Erwin Rommel, General Hideki Tojo, Admiral Isoroku Yamamoto.

semiliteracy and spoke in a range of dialects that made communication difficult and favored regional rather than national loyalty.

In addition, the Fascists never enjoyed the degree of political control over their country that the Nazis exerted in Germany and the militarists enjoyed in Japan. Mussolini could maintain power only by placating several powerful groups. Prominent among them were Italy's top military leaders, who pledged their loyalty not to the Fascist dictator but to the king. "The work of the Duce is mainly hampered by the fact that his power is limited by the Crown," Hitler noted in one of the rambling discourses later published in *Hitler's Table Talk*. "One cannot lead a nation when the army, for example, has sworn fealty to another who is not the effective head of the state. Just as a man cannot run a commercial firm if others hold a majority of the shares and thus have the power to cancel all his decisions."

ITALIAN ARMED FORCES AND THEIR TOP COMMANDERS

KING VICTOR EMMANUEL III (1869–1947). Although king of Italy since 1900—and therefore supreme commander of the armed forces—Victor Emmanuel III exercised only limited control over the Italian military throughout much of his reign. This was particularly true after Italy's Ethiopian victory of 1936 and Mussolini's subsequent decision to commit Italian units to the Spanish Civil War without consulting the monarch. On June 10, 1940, the day Italy entered World War II, the king formally (though perhaps half-heartedly) acknowledged Mussolini's predominance by issuing a royal proclamation (rather than a more legally forceful royal decree) that declared Mussolini to be commander of "the troops operating on all fronts." The troops still, however, pledged their loyalty to the king. Throughout the truncated Italian Fascist world war of 1940–1943, Victor Emmanuel remained in the background of military affairs, reasserting his authority only when Italy faced humiliating military disaster in 1943. Yet, when he did so, his conduct was far from exemplary. With two others who had helped achieve Mussolini's removal from power and Italy's armistice with the Allies, Marshal Pietro Badoglio and General Vittorio Ambrosio, he fled to the Allied camp, leaving Italy's armed forces without leadership or clear orders. Those forces were thus terribly vulnerable to the viciously punitive German reaction.

BENITO MUSSOLINI: "IL DUCE" (THE LEADER) (1883–1945). "He is a rabbit," Italian Communist Giacinto Serrati said of Benito Mussolini in 1919. "A phenomenal rabbit: he roars. People who see him and who do not know him mistake him for a lion." A considerable underestimation of Mussolini's political skills, Serrati's assessment proved to be very close to the mark regarding Il Duce's military leadership. Mussolini had even less military training and leadership experience than fellow World War I enlisted man Adolf Hitler. (Mussolini spent much time in the trenches but, unlike Hitler, did not participate in any major battles, and he rose only as high as squad leader.) Yet, in 1933 he dismissed the ministers of all three Italian armed services and assumed all those offices himself, holding them until he was removed from power in 1943. While the move may have helped Mussolini consolidate his own power (he oversaw the Fascist Militia, or "Blackshirts" as well), it also exacerbated existing weaknesses in Italy's military and was a major factor in the country's stunning inability to participate in a "total war."

Il Duce appointed the undersecretaries of the army, navy, and air force ministries as chiefs of staff of those services and had them report directly to him, rather than going through his primary military adviser, *the chief of general staff*. The chief of general staff was therefore deprived of information vital to the direction and coordination of the Italian armed forces—which were, at least theoretically, his primary functions. Mussolini was the only person in a position to remedy this administrative conundrum, but he failed to coordinate the actions and plans of the Italian services effectively. Each service thus developed plans based on its commanders' (generally outdated) assumptions, developed and ordered its own weapons, collected its own intelligence, and provided its own logistical support to field forces—all without proper interservice communication and coordination. Under this divide-and-control system, in which he was the only official who had a complete picture of Italy's military status, Il Duce never developed—or had top commanders develop—a clear overarching military strategy focused on conquering the Mediterranean world.

Mussolini had early determined to fight a "parallel war" in concert with Germany's larger endeavor, and supported by German expertise and matériel, but without an actual German military presence in the Mediterranean Theater. Such a presence would limit Italy's ability to establish and maintain exclusive control in the region. At the same time, he was determined to provide enough military assistance to Germany to secure a proper share of the massive spoils of war that the Wehrmacht's stunning early advances seemed to promise. "I need several thousand dead to be able to take my place at the peace table," Il Duce said to Chief of General Staff Pietro Badoglio as he led Italy into the war.

Struggling with these conflicting imperatives, Mussolini repeatedly overextended his forces—creating situations that resulted in heavy losses of men and matériel. After the Wehrmacht invaded the Soviet Union in 1941, he insisted on dispatching 60,000 men to fight alongside the Germans, even though Italy had no territorial ambitions on that front. In 1942, as German forces in the USSR bogged down, Mussolini sent an additional 160,000, this time at Hitler's request. Il Duce allowed this large force to remain in the East (where it was decimated when the Russians retook Stalingrad), even as Italian-German armies in North Africa, a major Italian objective, were caught between two Allied armies (see "Operation Torch" in Chapter 7).

Mussolini made other military decisions that proved disastrous to his wartime goals. Particularly damaging was his attempt to defuse growing home-front unrest by demobilizing 600,000 of the 1.2 million servicemen on the Italian mainland immediately before Italy's October 1940 invasion of Greece. The ensuing battlefield debacle provoked German invasions of Yugoslavia and Greece to rescue the Italians, to secure Yugoslavia's important mineral resources, and to ensure Axis control of Germany's southern flank during the forthcoming campaign against the USSR. These Balkan invasions, coupled with the Wehrmacht units sent in February 1941 to assist floundering Italian forces in North Africa, established the heavy German military presence in the Mediterranean Theater—and with it, the increased German control over Italy's destiny—that Mussolini had been determined to avoid.

COMANDO SUPREMO (SUPREME GENERAL STAFF; STATO MAGGIORE GENERALE, [STAMAGE])

Chief of General Staff: Marshal Pietro Badoglio (June–December 1940); Marshal Count Ugo Cavallero (December 1940–February 1943); General Vittorio Ambrosio (February–September 1943)

In theory, the central authority, under Mussolini, for the direction and coordination of the armed forces, the Comando Supremo was a largely ineffectual organization, initially comprising only the chief of general staff and a seven-officer secretariat (slightly augmented by the appointment of General Ubaldo Soddu as deputy chief in June 1940). During the first six months of Italy's war, not only did the undersecretaries/chiefs of staff of the individual services bypass Comando Supremo entirely, but even major field commanders reported directly to Mussolini, who often neglected to share the resulting information with the chief of general staff. By the end of the year, this muddled command structure and lack of interservice coordination had contributed to a series of military disasters. Unwilling to acknowledge his own culpability, Mussolini first replaced deputy head Soddu with General Alfredo Guzzoni, then sacked Badoglio and replaced him with Marshal Count Ugo Cavallero. A more capable and assertive commander, Cavallero began to expand, reform, and restructure Comando Supremo (the position of deputy chief was quickly abolished). However, his reforms were never enough, and the chief of general staff was still excluded from most of Mussolini's meetings with the navy and air force service chiefs and from his conversations with German military representatives in Rome. Cavallero also failed to establish a system for the development and procurement of war matériel that could reinforce or replace the *Commissariat for War Production*, which was run during the war—with numbing inefficiency—by General Carlo Favagrossa. Weapons procurement remained a Byzantine tangle of sometimes conflicting requests by each of the three services to the various industrial combines—which were essentially free to undertake war production as they saw fit. Meanwhile, traffic along the supply lines jealously maintained by each of the three services to their men in the field was often slowed to a trickle by interservice bickering over such matters as the assignment of space in supply vessels.

In January 1943, after the Allies had driven Italian forces out of Libya and Italy's Eighth Army was essentially destroyed near Stalingrad, Mussolini fired Cavallero. This action alarmed the Germans, who had come to rely on Cavallero's cooperative attitude. Indeed, General Vittorio Ambrosio did prove to be much less concerned with pleasing Italy's chief ally than with finding some way out of his country's harrowing predicament. As fighting raged in North Africa and the Allies poured resources into the Mediterranean region, Ambrosio sought a significant increase in direct military assistance from the Wehrmacht. However, turning the tide in the Mediterranean and strengthening the defense of western Europe would have required Germany to make a separate peace with the Soviets to free up German divisions and the Luftwaffe. Yet Hitler continued to spurn the timorous suggestions, from both Italian and Japanese sources, that he do so. (The Japanese favored a Russo-German peace because they believed that the Allies would then have to divert men and matériel from Asia to meet the increased Axis threat in the West.)

In April 1943, Axis forces in North Africa were finally defeated, and the Italian homeland was in immediate danger of Allied invasion. By then, the possible replacement of Mussolini had blossomed from scattered mutterings to active planning, and Chief of General Staff Ambrosio was among the planners.

REGIO ESCERCITO (ROYAL ARMY)

Supreme Commander and Minister of the Army: Benito Mussolini

Army Chief of Staff: Marshal Rodolfo Graziani (October 1939–February 1941); Lieutenant General Mario Roatta (March–December 1941); General Vittorio Ambrosio (January 1942–January 1943); General Ezio Rosi (February–June 1943); Lieutenant General Mario Roatta (June 1943–until taken prisoner by the Germans after Italy's capitulation to the Allies)

Force Size (at Peak): 3.7 million

Theaters of Operation: Mediterranean (including East and North Africa and the Balkans); European (France and the Soviet Union)

Casualties (vs. Allies): 200,000 known dead, unknown number of wounded, 600,000 prisoners taken by the Allies (an equal number of Italian soldiers were taken prisoner by Germany when Italy surrendered in 1943)

Although the army absorbed nearly two-thirds of Italy's military budget and grew to include more than 3 million men, the money was ill-used and the men were ill-served by top commanders who, with some exceptions, were hidebound, myopic, jealous of their own and their service's prerogatives, and strategically and tactically unimaginative. They presided over a bloated and entrenched army bureaucracy that absorbed far too much of the army budget considering its dearth of accomplishments.

Many in the army high command disregarded the need for flexibility, interservice coordination, and speed in this era of total war and, as one Italian staff officer noted, many also believed that "in battle, intuition and individual valor counted for more than training." After the Italian military disasters of 1940–1941 disproved that assumption, Chief of Staff Mario Roatta authorized a study that pinpointed deficiencies among junior officers that had resulted from the careless attitude toward preparation for combat. These included "insufficient capacity for command . . . inadequate knowledge of the mechanical side of weapons, limited knowledge of small-unit tactics, rudimentary knowledge of communications equipment and organization, insufficient knowledge of how to read topographic maps . . . , and . . . insufficient knowledge of field fortification." Special combat-training battalions were established for junior officers—but little real improvement occurred. Moreover, the 56,500 Italian army officers were assisted by just 41,200 noncommissioned officers and technical specialists—and the "noncoms" had little incentive to excel; unlike other armies, the Italian army had no provision for a "battlefield commission" (field promotion to officer). Army morale also suffered from top-command battle plans that often proved impractical under battlefront conditions, as well as from deficient medical services, inefficient mail delivery, and insufficient leave and rotation home. (German soldiers averaged a twelve-month tour of duty before rotation; Italian enlisted men in North Africa had to serve thirty-four months—nearly three years—before rotation.)

Despite the overwhelming problems, the men of the Regio Escercito often performed with amazing courage and resilience and displayed creativity born of a dearth of first-rate equipment. In September 1943, however, Italian forces were wholly unprepared for Italy's capitulation. When the king and others involved in deposing Mussolini decamped to the Allies without warning to their subcommanders and men in the field, hundreds of thousands of Italian soldiers became prisoners/slave laborers of the Germans—and thousands who resisted the Wehrmacht were murdered after they were captured and disarmed.

REGIA MARINA (ROYAL NAVY)

Supreme Commander and Minister of the Navy: Benito Mussolini

Chief of Staff: Admiral Domenico Cavagnari (1933–December 1940); Admiral Arturo Riccardi (December 1940–1943); Admiral Raffaele De Courten (March 1943 to armistice)

Force Size (1943): 259,000

Theaters of Operation: Mediterranean; European (chiefly submarines in the battle of the Atlantic and smaller operations on the Black Sea); Indian Ocean; three Italian auxiliary cruisers (raiders) operated around the world

Casualties: 36,141 (including 1,284 officers, 30,667 men, and 4,190 seamen; an estimated 15,000 of these men were killed)

Much smaller, better trained, and more competently led than the army, the Italian navy entered World War II with one of the largest submarine fleets in the world and a well-balanced surface fleet organized around battleships. On paper, it seemed an adequate, even formidable force capable of effective combat operations in the Mediterranean Sea. That this limited arena could be patrolled by land-based planes and the small planes carried by Italian cruisers and battleships was a principal factor in the interwar decision not to build aircraft carriers. Another contributing factor was the navy's loss of its own air arm in the 1920s, when the Fascists combined the army and navy air forces into a single, autonomous air force. (The no-carriers decision was reversed too late; conversion of the ocean liner *Roma*, renamed the *Aquila*, had just been completed when Italy surrendered to the Allies in 1943.)

The interwar model for the development of the Regia Marina was the French navy, which was also built around battleships, for France was the chief maritime force that the Italians anticipated facing in combat. (Problems with Britain, Italian leaders initially assumed, could be resolved diplomatically; then, in 1940, when Italy entered the war, it seemed certain that Britain would soon be forced to surrender or to seek an accommodation with the Axis.) The chaos of war, British stubbornness, the early capitulation of France, and America's entry into the conflict at the end of 1941—as well as the Italian army's battlefield reverses—swept the Regia Marina into a longer and more widespread contest than its commanders had anticipated and for which the navy was ill prepared. Insufficient resources (particularly fuel oil), Italy's poor industrial base (which produced, among other flawed items, notably inaccurate naval gun ammunition), and insufficient grasp, among top naval commanders, of the importance of such technologies as sonar and radar (the navy operated without either, except for prototypes), became increasing handicaps as the war lengthened and Axis fortunes waned.

All these factors contributed to the naval high command's caution—particularly in deploying capital ships. As a result, only one of Italy's seven battleships had been sunk by 1943. Yet, the navy lost twelve cruisers, thrity-seven destroyers, thirty-nine torpedo boats, and sixty-three submarines—losses that resource-strapped Italian shipbuilders could not make up. (Nor could the incorporation of a number of French and Yugoslav vessels into the Italian navy in 1942–1943; most were torpedo boats and destroyers, and they had little impact on Italy's naval war.)

The Regia Marina's principal success was in convoying men and supplies between southern Europe and North Africa—although even this harrowing effort, augmented by German and Italian air transport, was insufficient to sustain Axis forces there. A number of small special operations (particularly those of the elite "Tenth Light Flotilla") were also highly successful. Overall, however, the Regia Marina operated with ever-decreasing effectiveness.

Regia Aeronautica (Royal Air Force)

Supreme Commander and Minister of the Air Force: Benito Mussolini

Chief of Staff: General Giuseppe Valle (1933–1939); General Francesco Pricolo (1939–1941); General Rino Corso Fougier (1941–1943)

Force Size (1940): 101,400 men, of whom 6,340 were pilots; 3,296 aircraft of which 1,796 were combat-ready

Theaters of Operation: Mediterranean (including East and North Africa, the Balkans, and the Near East); Europe (including France and the Eastern Front)

Casualties: Casualty statistics unknown

Pioneers in aviation, Italians were the first to use planes for bombing raids (against the Turks in Libya in 1911), and they also blazed trails in night flying and aerial photo reconnaissance. Moreover, Italian aviator and military theorist Giulio Douhet (1869–1930) was an early and influential proponent of what was to become known as *strategic bombing* (aimed at destroying all an enemy's war assets, from heavy industry to civilian morale), which was employed to devastating effect during World War II. Attached to the army and navy during World War I, Italian air units were reorganized into a single autonomous service after Mussolini came to power in 1922.

As the newborn Regia Aeronautica became a potent propaganda instrument for Fascist Italy by means of celebrated intercontinental air "cruises" and successes in aerial competitions, Italian air squadrons were also gaining combat experience fighting against the Senussi rebels in Libya and in Italy's Abyssinia campaign. During the Spanish Civil War (1936–1939), Italian flyers supporting the fascist/nationalist forces briefly experimented with a new tactic, the *guerra de rapido corso*, a sort of aerial blitzkrieg. All these activities created the widespread impression that the Italian air arm was a fighting force to be feared. In fact, by 1939 it had already begun the steady decline that would continue until the armistice of 1943. In part, this was a result of losses of men and aircraft in Ethiopia and Spain. Yet these losses might not have been so damaging were it not for more corrosive, and less remediable problems.

Italy entered World War II with military planes that were nearing obsolescence. While Italians did develop a prototype prop-jet and other superior aircraft, the country did not possess the industrial base, cadres of skilled technicians, or sufficient material and administrative resources to develop, test, and produce adequate numbers of improved aircraft models quickly and efficiently. Thus, Italian factories continued to produce obsolescent craft—and even so, their production lagged far behind that of the other major combatants. (See also Chapter 3.)

Yet the air force did occasionally pack a powerful punch. After the Regio Aeronautica began employing torpedo bombers, Italian flyers tenaciously attacked and considerably damaged Allied convoys making the harrowing run to the besieged island of Malta (an important Allied air and submarine base). Generally, however, air force effectiveness suffered from the lack of interservice coordination; and as the Allied presence in the Mediterranean and attacks on the Italian mainland increased, Italian losses in pilots and planes could not be replaced. By the 1943 armistice, Regia Aeronautica was a mere shadow of the proud air arm that had so impressed the world in the interwar years.

FASCIST MILITIA ("BLACKSHIRTS"), CARABINIERI, AND FASCIST YOUTH. When Italy entered the war, the Fascist Militia (a paramilitary force that had helped bring Mussolini to power and keep him there) was organized into 177 "legions." Forty-five of those units, plus smaller detachments—more than 300,000 men, in all—served as reinforcements to the military, either on homeland defense or attached to overseas army divisions (sometimes in specialized roles, such as artillery or machine-gun units). In Libya, three divisions entirely comprised militia. Some of the battalions of Fascist youth formed during the war were also attached to front-line army units in North Africa in 1941–1943, as were some members of the *carabinieri*, a police force that predated the Fascists by more than a century. Carabinieri served chiefly as military police in North and East Africa, as well as Albania.

MERCHANT MARINE. Italy started the war with the fifth-largest merchant marine in the world (after those of Great Britain, the United States, Japan, and Norway). Despite its need to import resources and supply Axis forces in North Africa, largely unsuccessful attempts to warn the 218 Italian merchant vessels then in neutral or Allied ports began only two days before Mussolini declared war June 10, 1940. As a result, more than a third of Italy's merchant shipping was immediately confiscated by the Allies or interned by neutral powers. By 1943, another 1,800 vessels were lost—over 2.2 million tons of shipping. Meanwhile, Italian shipbuilders produced less than 400,000 tons of shipping, which was insufficiently augmented by French vessels seized after Germany occupied all of France in 1942 and by other captured shipping.

Japan

Effectively closed to the outside world for more than two centuries, the feudal nation of Japan was forced to reopen its doors to foreigners in 1854 by
the guns on American naval officer Matthew C. Perry's ships. Eighty years
later, the sovereign, industrialized Empire of Japan had become the most
powerful indigenous Asian nation. Its burgeoning army and increasingly
powerful navy were modern expressions of a centuries-old military tradition
tracing back to the elite caste of samurai warriors and their code of *Bushido*
("the way of the warrior"). They also benefited from skillful adaptation of
Western methods and technologies and the assistance of European (primarily French, British, and German) military and technical advisers. Yet Japanese appreciation of the West's contributions to its new international role
was greatly tempered by festering resentments over Western racial prejudice
and continuing Western exploitation of Far Eastern resources that Japanese
nationalists felt should more properly fall under their own control.

Beginning in the nineteenth century, the new Japan wrested control of
Korea from China and Imperial Russia, astonished the Western world by defeating Russia in the 1905–1906 Russo-Japanese War, took control, after
World War I, of Pacific islands formerly controlled by Germany, and established a firm presence on the Chinese mainland through war, diplomatic
agreements—and the occasional dirty trick. By 1931, Japan controlled all of
Manchuria (thereafter the puppet-state of Manchukuo); six years later, the
Japanese used a minor incident outside Peking as an excuse to ignite a full-
scale war to bring more of China's land and resources under their control.
With the examples of the European colonial powers before them, and continually in the shadow of the Soviet Union's powerful Far Eastern forces
(whose planes and submarines could easily strike the Japanese home islands),
Japan's leaders, with members of the military high command increasingly
prominent among them, moved toward their goal of creating, and dominating, a "New Order" in East Asia.

JAPANESE ARMED FORCES AND THEIR
TOP COMMANDERS

EMPEROR HIROHITO (B. 1901, EMPEROR FROM 1926 UNTIL HIS DEATH
IN 1989). Revered by his subjects as a living god whose "Imperial Will" was a
guiding force in all facets of Japanese life, Hirohito was, in theory, the
supreme commander of the Japanese armed forces. Yet his exercise of wide-

spread powers of command and military administration was severely circum-scribed by tradition and tacit understandings, and by provisions of the 1889 Meiji constitution delegating powers to others within the government and military. Tightly controlled by law and tradition (and by increasingly influential military officers who distrusted his preference for peaceful accommodation with the Western powers), Hirohito sat in traditional Imperial silence as members of the Liaison Conference outlined national and military policies, which he generally approved with a nod. These policies then became expressions of the Imperial Will. After reluctantly sanctioning war in this manner, Hirohito performed largely ceremonial duties during the war, fulfilling his role as the sovereign to whom his soldiers and sailors owed absolute obedience and loyalty unto death. In August 1945, however, he used his influence to help thwart plans for continued resistance despite the devastation that Allied firebombing, and two atomic bombs, had wrought on Japan.

SUPREME MILITARY COUNCIL (SUPREME WAR COUNCIL); BOARD OF FIELD MARSHALS AND FLEET ADMIRALS. Both groups were military advisers to the emperor with extremely limited influence

LIAISON CONFERENCE/IMPERIAL CONFERENCE; SUPREME COUNCIL FOR THE DIRECTION OF THE WAR. Established at about the same time as the World War II Imperial General Headquarters (IGH), this coordinative body included representatives from both the civilian and military branches of government—although the military became preeminent. In addition to the prime minister (for much of the war, General Hideki Tojo), it usually included the armed service ministers, the army and navy chiefs of staff and other representatives of IGH, the foreign minister, and sometimes the finance minister. The Liaison Conference was essentially the Japanese war cabinet. It was the principal forum in which opposing opinions were reconciled and policies were determined. As a matter of form, the emperor then sanctioned those policies during Imperial Conferences (*Gozen Kaigi*), after which the regular cabinet also endorsed them.

IMPERIAL GENERAL HEADQUARTERS (IGH). The first Japanese Imperial General Headquarters was set up in 1894, on the eve of a war with China, and was an instrument for establishing coordinated command and control during wartime. War with China was also the impetus for creating the World War II IGH, which was established in 1937. The later IGH had two main divisions, representing the Army (comprising the office of the Army Minister and the Army Section or army high command/general staff) and the Navy (comprising the office of the Navy Minister and the Navy Section or naval high command/general staff), as well as a separate office of the Inspector General of Military Training. The primary body directing Japanese forces, IGH failed in its central purpose of coordination principally because of intense and long-standing interservice rivalry. The army and navy each had its own operations, intelligence, and logistics systems, and each failed to consult and coordinate with the other—often guarding information as if the other service were as much an enemy as were the Allies. Compounding these problems, the high command generally emphasized tactics over long-term strategy and operations over the vital intelligence gathering and logistical functions required to support operations and maintain effective forces in the field. By the time IGH attempted to remedy its previous neglect of logistics—establishing a Ministry of Munitions in November 1943, for example, to coordinate the distribution of vital supplies, and that same month forming a Grand Escort Fleet to better protect Japan's dwindling merchant fleet—it was far too late.

Imperial Japanese Army (IJA)

Army Minister/Minister of War: Hajime Sugiyama (February 1937–June 1938); Seishiró Itagaki (June 1938–August 1939); Shunroku Hata (August 1939–July 1940); Hideki Tojo (July 1940–July 1944); Hajime Sugiyama (July 1944–April 1945); Korechika Anami (April 1945–August 1945); Naruhiko Higashikuni (August 1945)

Chief of IGH, Army Section (Army Chief of Staff): General Hajime Sugiyama (1940–1944); General Hideki Tojo (February–July 1944); General Yoshijiro Umezu (July 1944–September 1945)

Force Size (1945): 5.5 million

Theaters of Operation: China-Burma-India; Pacific; Americas (Aleutian Islands)

Casualties: 1,524,721 (includes 1,439,100 killed and missing, 85,620 wounded)

The IJA of the World War II era was the product of decades of tumultuous evolution from the peasant armies and samurai clans of feudal Japan to a modern, severely disciplined force with a centralized command structure. Its

As Japanese armies remained mired in the war with China, the war and the soldiers' experiences were glossed and celebrated in a 980-page volume, Seisen Gafu *("A Picture Album of the Holy War"), published in Tokyo, 1939, in both Japanese and English. Among the hundreds of images is this depiction of "Human Pontoons of the Yanagisawa Detachment (Yanghangchen)" by combat artist Gyosui Suzuki.*

harsh code of conduct abandoned the most chivalric tenets of the ancient code of Bushido, which called for humaneness and kindness (which had characterized the army's exemplary treatment of prisoners of war through World War I) as well as self-sacrifice and indifference to pain. Instead, the army emphasized hatred of the enemy, contempt for those willing to endure the dishonor of surrender, and victory by any means, as well as absolute loyalty to the emperor and blind obedience to the superior officers who expressed the emperor's will.

As the anticipated short war against China dragged on and Japan's war against the United States and the European colonial powers spread far across the Pacific, the IJA was increasingly crippled by problems, only some of them caused by its enemies. Many of its weapons were obsolete or inferior (see

Chapter 5). Because of neglect by the Japanese high command and assaults by the Allies, logistical support gradually deteriorated from poor to atrocious. There were shortages of food, drinking water, medicine, fuel, and motorized transport (the last partially offset by the widespread use of bicycles and horses). Rifle ammunition was poorly packed and often damaged by moisture, ants, and corrosion, resulting in many misfires. Army medical services, inferior in 1941, steadily deteriorated. Wounds, malnutrition, and tropical diseases took a heavy toll, particularly in garrisons cut off by the Allies' "island hopping" Pacific campaigns.

Emphasis, during training, on fighting with the "cold steel" of the bayonet translated in the field to an ever-increasing reliance on ill-advised frontal assaults—and in hopeless situations, the increasing use of the suicidal *Banzai* charge. (These were all-out massed attacks on the enemy regardless of the strength of his position—or the often inferior Japanese weaponry and depleted physical condition of IJA troops. The term was derived from the battle cry *Tenno heika banzai*, or "Long live the emperor.") Fear of dishonor (for soldiers and for their families), as well as fear of the brutish treatment Japanese propaganda led them to expect from the enemy, also caused many soldiers and Pacific-island civilians to choose suicide over surrender when a battle was lost. Toward the end of the war, Japan became the only World War II combatant to form and deploy units specifically dedicated to mounting suicide, or *kamikaze* attacks, using planes, piloted gliders with rocket boosters, small boats, and human torpedoes. (See also "The Divine Wind: Tokkotai and Kamikaze" in Chapter 7.) As with most other areas of combat, the army and navy each formed and directed its own suicide force. The army air force organized its *Banda*, or "Ten Thousand Petals," suicide unit in October 1944.

The Japanese army was also the only force actually to use poison gas in combat between 1937 and 1945. (The Italians had used gas during their 1935–1936 Ethiopian campaign; the Germans' ample wartime use of poison gas was directed against civilians in death camps. See also "Weapons of Terror, Desperation, and Mass Destruction" in Chapter 5.) The Japanese reserved the use of gas, as well as limited bacteriological warfare, for the China-Burma-India theater of operations, where they were targeted almost exclusively against the Chinese (although there was some use of poison-gas cylinders called *chibi-dan*, or "tich bombs," against British tanks in Burma). (See also "Japanese War Crimes—Unit 731" in Chapter 8.)

With so much area to hold, and so many casualties, the army absorbed more and more of Japan's male population, and training of these rushed replacements often suffered. The army grew from 24 divisions in 1937 to 51 in 1941; by the end of the war IJA had raised more than 170 divisions.

IMPERIAL JAPANESE NAVY (IJN)

Navy Minister: Yonai Mitsumasa (February 1937–August 1939); Yoshida Zengo (August 1939–September 1940); Admiral Oikawa Koshiro (September 1940–October 1941); Shigetaro Shimada (October 1941–July 1944); Nomura Naokuni (July 1944); Yonai Mitsumasa (July 1944–December 1945)

Chief of IGH, Navy Section (Navy Chief of Staff): Admiral Osami Nagano (1941–1944); Admiral Shigetaro Shimada (February–July 18, 1944; served again from later in July to an undetermined date); Admiral Soemu Toyoda (May–September 1945)

Force Size (at Peak): 1.7 million

Theaters of Operation: China-Burma-India; Pacific; Americas (Aleutian Islands and in American Pacific coastal waters)

Casualties: 424,000

The Imperial Japanese Navy (IJN) began the war as the third largest navy in the world, with 10 battleships, 18 heavy cruisers, 112 destroyers, and a formidable submarine force equipped with excellent "long-lance" torpedoes—all concentrated entirely in the Pacific (unlike the American and British fleets). Although many in the naval high command remained firmly devoted to battleships as the focal point of the fleet, the Japanese Combined Fleet also included ten aircraft carriers whose capabilities were amply demonstrated during the raid that six of them conducted against Pearl Harbor, Hawaii, on December 7, 1941. The planes that conducted that raid were among more than 3,000, nearly half of front-line quality, in the naval air arm. Their pilots were the most thoroughly trained naval aviators in the world; each had an average of eight hundred hours of flight time, more than triple the average for Allied flyers at the time.

Yet all these initial advantages quickly disintegrated under the weight of problems generated by Japan's confused industrial mobilization, intense interservice rivalries, the organization of and attitudes within the navy—and a series of costly defeats at the hands of the U.S. Navy from which IJN did not have the time or resources to recover. Some problems stemmed from the low regard for logistical support of operations that characterized both Japanese services. Furthermore, the naval high command placed much greater emphasis on destroying enemy warships than on sinking supply vessels or even troop transports, while the navy did little to hinder the progressive destruction of Japan's own vital merchantmen. It made only tepid, ill-organized efforts at convoy escort throughout the war. (The resulting toll on merchantmen made it necessary for IJN to divert some of its submarines to supply cut-off island garrisons.) In addition, it failed to develop adequate antisubmarine warfare doctrine and technology, in large part because such measures were widely considered to be too defensive—an example of the Japanese military's emphasis on attack over defense.

The stunning run of Japanese victories in the eighteen months after Pearl Harbor incited, within the navy high command, a phenomenon known as the "victory disease" (a belief that Japan's forces would continue to be invincible). This belief was shattered when one arm of the divided and overextended Combined Fleet suffered a near-devastating defeat at the battle of Midway (June 1942), with four carriers sunk and 70 percent of the carrier pilots casualties (30 percent of them killed). The loss of the carriers would never be made up, nor would the loss of so many of the fleet's best-trained pilots. To bring replacements more quickly into the ranks, the stringent and selective prewar pilot training program (which had graduated a mere one hundred pilots per year) was expanded and shortened. It was also conducted without the benefit of the experience of combat pilots, who were no longer rotated back to aid with instruction. As the Allies poured more resources into the Pacific and China-Burma-India theaters and more aircraft and pilots were lost, the naval air arm, which both shielded the Japanese Fleet and was its primary offensive weapon, was steadily reduced to ineffectiveness. At the end, the remnants of the fleet relied chiefly on a few mostly inexperienced pilots for defense and on kamikaze units for offense.

PEOPLE'S VOLUNTEER COMBAT CORPS. Established in June 1945, as Japan faced the prospect of an Allied invasion, this defense force of men and boys aged 15 to 60 and women aged 17 to 40 incorporated People's Volunteer Units established several months earlier. Under local control and armed with such primitive weapons as bamboo spears, this civilian militia was to support the 1.9 million troops then on the home islands—or, failing that, to be part of what Japanese propagandists called "The Glorious Death of One Hundred Million." After Japan surrendered, the militia was disbanded.

MERCHANT MARINE. A resource-poor island nation, Japan depended heavily on its merchant fleet (comprising some 6 million tons in 1939) to deliver needed supplies, such as food and fuel. Yet the government and armed forces took muddled, contradictory, and sometimes destructive measures to protect and enhance this fleet. The army and navy weakened the merchant fleet by requisitioning many of its vessels as troop transports. The navy failed to institute adequate escort operations to protect the remaining merchantmen and also bled the merchant marine of experienced officers and men. These measures helped make possible the fearful toll that Allied submarines, mines, and planes took on Japanese merchant shipping: In February 1944 alone, twenty-five oil tankers were sunk; that November, U.S. submarines sank 170 transports; by the end of the war, 90 percent of all Japanese cargo vessels over five hundred tons had been destroyed.

Vichy France

Under its armistice agreement with Germany, the collaborationist French government was limited to an army, within metropolitan France, of 100,000 men, including 4,000 officers. Its mission was restricted to keeping order within France; it was allowed few heavy weapons (and those were largely obsolete), no motor transport, and a limited supply of ammunition. Additional troops, including units of the French Foreign Legion, were stationed in Indochina and in other French colonial holdings. The powerful French fleet (the fourth largest in the world) was widely scattered when France capitulated. Ships that fell under Allied control eventually formed the nucleus of the Free French Navy. The armistice stipulation that the rest of the fleet be deactivated was abandoned after the British attacked French vessels moored in North Africa, fearing that the Germans would use them (see "Mers el Kébir" in Chapter 6). Thereafter, while nominally under Vichy French control, the navy was strictly supervised by the Germans and suffered with scarce supplies (sagging fuel supplies had to be augmented with peanut oil), poor maintenance due to German requisitioning requirements, and severely curtailed naval exercises and training. Elements of the fleet did, however, support Vichy forces fighting against the Allies (including Free French units) in North Africa and the Middle East (1941–1942) and at Madagascar (1942). In November 1942, however, after the Allied landings in North Africa, the French scuttled the seventy-five warships at Toulon to prevent their seizure by German troops advancing into the previously unoccupied portion of France.

Vichy French troops and the small French naval contingent in Indochina, meanwhile, defended national interests against the Siamese at the battle of Ko-chang (January 1941) but collaborated (often grudgingly) with the Japanese, who had occupied all of Indochina by mid-1941. Other Axis-affiliated French forces included the *Armée d'Afrique*, comprising more than 200,000 regulars and 16,000 irregular Moroccan *goums* (by 1943, it had switched allegiance to the Allies). The *Légion des volontaires français contre le bolchévisme* ("Legion of French Volunteers against Bolshevism," LVF), established in 1942, was decimated fighting on the Russian front; survivors formed the nucleus of the Waffen-SS Charlemagne Brigade in October 1944. Frenchmen in the Waffen SS fought in the Baltic region during the German retreat, and, in April 1945, took part in the final defense of Hitler's bunker. The *Phalange Africaine*, with three hundred Frenchmen and Tunisians, was formed in the winter of 1942–1943 to assist the German army in Tunisia.

AXIS MILITARY COORDINATION

The Axis military alliance, like its political alliance, was, from the beginning, riven with mutual suspicions, secrecy, and self-interest, despite some attempts at cooperation: On January 18, 1942, the three major countries signed an agreement dividing the world into "Zones of Operation." Japan was to operate "to the east of approximately 70 degrees east longitude up to the west coast of the American Continent"; Germany and Italy were to operate to the west of that line; operations by all parties were allowed in the Indian Ocean. Yet the agreement's call for "mutual liaison" went largely unanswered. When the German army's chief of operations, General Alfred Jodl, met with his Japanese counterparts on February 13, 1942, for example, he was under instructions not to allow the Japanese to participate in any German operations or to learn of German plans. The cooperation between Germany and Italy, meanwhile, was increasingly that of a senior partner dictating to a junior and troublesome associate. Yet various German and Italian representatives met often, if irregularly, and military cooperation (based largely on each country's separate military goals) continued until Italy's surrender in 1943.

The great distances between Europe and Asia, and the strengthening Allied blockades of water and air routes between the two regions, made mutual Italian-Japanese or German-Japanese military assistance much more difficult. Exchanges of goods between Germany and Japan via the Trans-Siberian Railroad were possible between the Russo-German nonaggression pact of August 1939 and Germany's June 1941 invasion of the USSR—both actions surprising the Japanese. However, under the terms of the nonaggression pact Japan signed with the Soviets in April 1941 (concluded without notifying the Germans), Japanese military officers and diplomats could continue traveling toward Germany via that railroad until 1943. A few blockade-running surface vessels and submarines also carried goods, people (such as Indian nationalist leader Subhas Chandra Bose), and technical information between Germany and Japan, and the two navies cooperated somewhat: German surface raiders were repaired and resupplied in Japan or in Japanese-held territories; the Germans were allowed to establish a few small naval outposts in Asia; and Germany gave Japan two U-boats. Essentially, however, the Axis leaders viewed their alliance as a propaganda tool and a means to further their individual military and political goals—not to implement an overall, mutually beneficial strategy to defeat the Allies.

THE ALLIES

In Washington, D.C., on January 1, 1942, three weeks after the Japanese attacks on the U.S. naval base at Pearl Harbor, Hawaii, and European holdings in Asia, twenty-six (of an eventual forty-seven) countries issued a "Declaration by the United Nations" pledging their "full resources" to the "common struggle against savage and brutal forces seeking to subjugate the world." Sorely pressed or retreating on all fronts, their battered armed forces too weak to strike back effectively, the Allies desperately needed time: to produce armaments, to build or rebuild their military strength, and to strengthen the complex web of military/political relationships constituting their multinational alliance.

Four nations—China, Great Britain, the Soviet Union, and the United States—were at the center of this Grand Alliance. Two of the "Big Four," the United States and Great Britain, together formed its head and heart. Since 1937, British and American war planners had gradually developed an especially close collaborative relationship, trying to prepare for an increasingly likely war. Yet the "special relationship" between their two nations was not only characterized by mutual regard and need; it was also marked by a mutual wariness that erupted at times into bitter argument. Many U.S. military commanders, still resenting what they regarded as British manipulation during World War I, were intensely wary of being maneuvered into actions that would protect Britain's endangered overseas empire rather than further

American interests. They were also determined not to surrender control of American forces to British command. Many of Great Britain's top commanders, meanwhile, having been impatient for the United States to become an active combatant, looked askance at combatant America's impatient insistence on landing Allied troops in northwestern France as early as the end of 1942—when most of the available ground forces would be British. They also resented American threats to focus on the war with Japan if such an early European invasion did not happen, despite an agreement between the two nations to concentrate on defeating Germany first. "Just because the Americans can't have a massacre in France this year," Winston Churchill grumped during this disagreement, "they want to sulk and bathe in the Pacific." In early 1943, mutual resentments had reached such a pass that U.S. general Dwight D. Eisenhower warned, in a letter to General Thomas T. Handy, that "one of the constant sources of danger to us in this war is the temptation to regard as our first enemy the partner that must work with us in defeating the real enemy." Overall, that temptation was resisted. Although the special, and complicated, U.S./U.K. relationship changed in many respects during the war, it remained strong.

One thread uniting the two countries was distrust of Joseph Stalin and the Soviet Union, incubator of international communism and purveyor of vast stores of supplies to Germany until the Wehrmacht had invaded Soviet lands. Yet, as Soviet forces held out, against expectations, most American and British commanders came to understand the crucial role the USSR was now playing in the Allied war effort. "It must be constantly reiterated that Russian armies are killing more Germans and destroying more Axis material than all the twenty-five united nations put together," President Roosevelt wrote in a memo on May 6, 1942. "To help Russia, therefore, is the primary consideration." Helping Russia (and keeping Stalin from making a separate peace with the Germans) remained a constant consideration in British and American war planning until late 1944.

Planning also had to take into account Allied military progress or setbacks in all theaters of war and the availability of troops, equipment, and adequate transport. Moreover, military leaders as disparate as the Yugoslavian communist/partisan leader Josip Broz (Tito) and Free French Brigadier General Charles de Gaulle made requests and exerted pressure for help. In the Pacific and China-Burma-India theaters, where Great Britain had imperial interests and the United States had commercial and security interests to protect, China was, for years, as important as the Soviet Union had become

American general Dwight D. ("Ike") Eisenhower, supreme commander, Allied Expeditionary Force, talks with British prime minister Winston Churchill as Chief of the Imperial General Staff General Sir Alan Brooke (left) and Eisenhower's deputy supreme commander, RAF general Sir Arthur Tedder (right), listen in. Ike used his military and diplomatic skills so effectively as supreme commander of the Allied Expeditionary Force in North Africa, 1942–1943, that he was chosen as supreme commander of the Allied force that liberated western Europe. Replying to praise that Churchill had accorded him in a letter to President Roosevelt six weeks before the German surrender, Eisenhower underlined the importance of the special Anglo-American relationship, stating that he was determined to sustain "among the forces of the United States and Great Britain those feelings of mutual respect and unification that have been the mainspring of effectiveness in this command."

to the course of the war in Europe—and for similar reasons. The long conflict in China was absorbing men and matériel that Japan could otherwise use to thwart Allied campaigns elsewhere in Asia. Yet the Nationalist Chinese government of Chiang Kai-shek was an increasingly disappointing Allied partner. Fiercely nationalistic and resentful of its Western allies, it was also deeply corrupt and militarily inept. Intermittent internal conflicts with Chinese Communists and warlords fed Chiang's persistent reluctance to commit Nationalist armed forces to all-out campaigns against the Japanese. Yet his government peppered Washington with demands for cash and equipment, threatening collapse or a separate peace should it not be forthcoming, and demanding that the money and equipment arrive with no strings attached. "Now let me get this straight," an exasperated General George C. Marshall said to Chinese delegates at the 1943 Allied conference in Cairo. "You are talking about your 'rights' in this matter. I thought these were *American* planes, and *American* personnel, and *American* matériel."

Even staunch supporters of Chiang became impatient. In mid-1944, as the Japanese were pushing Nationalist armies back during their largest campaign of the war (Operation Ichigo) a U.S. delegation including eight military observers visited Chinese Communist leader Mao Tse-tung at his headquarters—and were favorably impressed. (The communists were careful to cloak their own weaknesses from their visitors.) Yet U.S. support for Chiang did not cease. By 1944, Allied military as well as political planners were looking ahead to a postwar world fundamentally altered by eight years of brutal conflict. Bubbling with nationalist movements of every political stripe, that world would include huge, battle-hardened Soviet armed forces under the command of leaders hungry to get a firm hold on Eastern Europe and to increase communist influence in the Far East. However disappointing they had been as Allied combatants, Chiang Kai-shek and his Nationalist armed forces were viewed as valuable assets in this new, and potentially dangerous environment.

Allied Military Leaders and Their Armed Forces

China

In 1937, China was only beginning to emerge from decades of chaos that followed the fall of the Manchu dynasty in 1911. Chiang Kai-shek, a graduate of the Shimbu Gakkô military school in Japan, had emerged as the strongest political and military leader in the country—although provincial warlords still had their own armed forces, and the 16-year-old Chinese Communist Party

A column of Chinese soldiers at the central sector of the Salween Front, 1943.

(CCP) was building both political and military strength. In 1924, while serving as military aide to Chinese revolutionary leader Sun Yat-sen (1866–1925), Chiang, with Soviet aid, had founded the Whampoa Military Academy, creating the nucleus of the Nationalist Chinese Army. Distrusting the Soviets (although he continued to accept military assistance from them intermittently), he strengthened Nationalist armed forces throughout the 1920s and 1930s with assistance from other nations, including both pre-Nazi and Nazi Germany. German-trained divisions were among the strongest in the Nationalist army, and German advisers, including General Alexander von Falkenhausen (later, German military governor of occupied Belgium and northern France), assisted Chiang for more than a year after full-scale war with Japan started in July 1937. During that bloody eight-year conflict, two main Chinese armed forces fought the Japanese invaders, and only one was under Chiang's control.

Chinese Armed Forces, 1937–1945

KUOMINTANG (KMT), OR NATIONALIST ARMED FORCES	CHINESE COMMUNIST ARMED FORCES
Supreme commander and chairman of the national military council: Generalissimo Chiang Kai-shek (1925–1975)	*Supreme commander:* Mao Tse-tung, chairman of the Chinese Communist Party Central Committee, Military Affairs Committee
Chief of staff: Lieutenant General Joseph ("Vinegar Joe") Stilwell, USA (February 1942–October 1944); Lieutenant General Albert C. Wedemeyer, USA (October 1944–April 1946)	*Principal field generals:* Chu Te, P'eng Te-huai, Lin Piao, Ho Lung, Liu P-ch'eng
Special adviser: Madame Chiang Kai-shek (Soong May-ling), who also served as translator/interpreter and spokesperson for Generalissimo Chiang	*Principal liaison with Nationalists/ KMT:* Chou En-lai, premier communist diplomat and military/ political organizer
Force size (1941): 5.7 million (includes the tiny, mostly riverine Nationalist navy and a small Nationalist air force, largely destroyed in 1938, but partially rebuilt with U.S. assistance)	*Force size (1945):* Nearly 1 million regular army, supported/augmented by more than 2 million local and militia soldiers

Theaters of operation: China-Burma-India

Total Chinese casualties: These can only be estimated. Many official accounts put military casualties near 3.3 million, of whom more than 1.3 million were killed, while civilian casualties are estimated at 8.4 million.

Principal sources: I. C. B. Dear and M. R. D. Foot, eds., *Oxford Companion to WW II*, Oxford: Oxford University Press, 2001; Jonathan Fenby, *Chiang Kai-shek: China's Generalissimo and the Nation He Lost*, New York: Carroll & Graf, 2004; Donald W. Klein and Anne B. Clark, *Biographic Dictionary of Chinese Communism, 1921–1965*, Cambridge: Harvard University Press, 1971.

The corruption and poor military leadership that permeated the Chinese Nationalist high command rapidly eroded relations between Chiang and his first American chief of staff, the outspoken Lieutenant General Joseph Stilwell. It also exacerbated the problems of Chinese troops on the ground, including lack of equipment (despite Lend-Lease assistance) and desperately inadequate medical services. Yet Nationalist forces did not collapse. Nor did the communists, who operated without anything resembling the material assistance Chiang was receiving. The communists also suffered from generally poor resources in the area that was their stronghold. Both forces expropriated food and other supplies from civilians, but in general the communists treated the local populations with much greater consideration—a fact reflected in the rapid wartime growth of the Communist Party and its armed forces. Generally better disciplined than Nationalist forces, communist fighters proved particularly adept at guerrilla warfare against the Japanese.

In 1937, Chiang agreed to form a "United Front" against Japan with the communists, whose emerging leader, Mao Tse-tung, had been urging such a move for several years, as had Joseph Stalin. It proved little more than a nominal alliance. By January 1941, when Nationalist forces ambushed the communist New Fourth Army in Anhwei province, inflicting heavy casualties, the United Front, though still formally in effect, was essentially dead. In the midst of the war with Japan, Nationalist versus Communist clashes continued, presaging the full-scale civil war that would begin less than a year after the Japanese surrender.

Free French Forces (Forces Françaises Libres)

As France fell to the Germans in June 1940, some members of its shattered armed forces escaped from the Continent to Great Britain. With others stationed in France's African colonies and elsewhere abroad, they formed the first elements of the Free French Forces. Among the first to reach England was Charles de Gaulle, whose aggressive leadership of the French 4th Armored Division had recently brought him a promotion to brigadier general and an extremely brief stint as undersecretary for national defense. Although he was still little known outside France, he had impressed Winston Churchill, who declared the general "head of all free Frenchmen . . . who rally around you to support the Allied cause." Armed with this endorsement and other British support (including some Lend-Lease equipment Britain had received), de Gaulle organized ground, naval, and air units. By October 1942, Free French Forces were 35,000 strong and included two main ground forces: the 1st and 2nd Free French Brigades—later the 1st Free French Division—under the command of General Pierre Koenig; and *L Force* (also known as the "Leclerc Column" after its commander, Jacques Leclerc—the pseudonym adopted by Philippe de Hauteclocque). This later became the 2nd Free French Armored Division. Both forces fought alongside the British in North Africa and the Middle East. There were also small naval forces (primarily destroyers and smaller craft) and five air squadrons (two in Britain, one in the Mediterranean, one in Africa, and one that had recently begun operating under Soviet direction in the USSR as the Normandie-Niemen [Air] Regiment). Meanwhile, American agents secretly contacted General Henri Giraud, a French hero after his escape from German captivity to the relative safety of Vichy territory. The American government believed he, rather than de Gaulle, would be the best man to lead Vichy French forces then in North and West Africa back into the Allied fold after Anglo-American landings there (Operation Torch, November 1942). Giraud remained de Gaulle's rival for leadership until late in 1943.

A clandestine meeting between U.S. general Mark Clark and Giraud's representative at Cherchel, Algeria, one month before Torch, led to an American pledge "to furnish the French forces with arms and modern equipment." (Subsequently, the United States fully equipped and trained eight French divisions in North Africa, trained and partially equipped three more in France, provided matériel for nineteen air squadrons, and helped rehabilitate the French Navy.) After the success of Torch, Free French Forces expanded to some 300,000 men with the addition of units previously affiliated with Vichy. They participated in operations in Sicily and Italy; drove a German force out of Corsica (the first French *département* to be liberated); and were fully involved in liberating the rest of France. Leclerc's Second Armored Division was in the vanguard when the Allies marched into Paris.

Great Britain/United Kingdom

In December 1937, a secret report from a subcommittee of Britain's military chiefs of staff declared, "We cannot foresee the time when our defense forces will be strong enough to safeguard our trade, territory, and vital interests against Germany, Italy, and Japan at the same time" and called for "any political or international action that can be taken to reduce the number of potential enemies and to gain the support of potential allies."

Political/diplomatic efforts to reduce the number of potential enemies—what came to be known as the policy of *appeasement*—proved wholly unsuccessful. Less than two years later, Great Britain was at war, its survival depending on support from the United States and from British Dominions. It also depended, British war planners believed, on postponing full-out, frontal assaults on strong Axis armies as long as possible so British armed forces could be strengthened and better trained. Once the USSR was under attack and it was clear that the Soviets would not immediately collapse, the most optimistic British planners believed that the strain on Germany produced by war in the East, a sea blockade, and constant aerial bombing might lead to a German collapse before an invasion of France became necessary. Meanwhile, they proposed to American military leaders that the western Allies conduct more limited campaigns—particularly in North Africa, the Balkans, and elsewhere in the Mediterranean Theater. This strategy (which Winston Churchill called "closing the ring") would, they believed, increase the pressure on Germany, especially if it brought about an Italian collapse. At the same time, limited campaigns in the Pacific and ongoing combat in China would keep pressure on the Japanese, to whom the Allies would turn in force once Germany was defeated.

American military planners disagreed with the British emphasis on the Mediterranean and the degree of reliance the British placed on blockades and area bombing against Germany (see "Bombers" in Chapter 5). As such debates continued and compromises were reached, the balance of the military partnership shifted inexorably toward the United States. Britain, however, remained a crucially important partner. By 1944, the British home islands had become a giant "aircraft carrier" from which round-the-clock bombing raids were launched against Germany; it was also the staging area for the greatest amphibious assault in history.

BRITISH ARMED FORCES AND THEIR TOP COMMANDERS

KING GEORGE VI. As sovereign, the king was formally commander in chief of the armed forces. Under British custom, however, most powers related to this position are delegated to the prime minister. During the war, King George worked tirelessly to maintain the morale of the armed forces.

PRIME MINISTER. Responsible to Parliament and the king, the prime minister guided the military and political course of the nation. Britain had three wartime prime ministers.

Neville Chamberlain (1937–May 10, 1940). The architect of "appeasement" policies through which he hoped to avoid another major war, Chamberlain initially balked at increasing defense spending from its parsimonious interwar level. Then he favored increased rearmament under a "limited liability" strategy: British troops abroad would concentrate on defending the empire, particularly the vital Mediterranean area, with protection of the Continent relying on the "impregnable" Maginot Line and France's strong army, backed by the British navy and the Royal Air Force. Circumstances changed rapidly as war approached, and in September 1939, four British divisions crossed the English Channel to France. Shattered by the onset of war and his political support weakened by the Allied failure in Norway, Chamberlain stepped down on May 10, 1940, the day German armies began their blitzkrieg conquest of the Low Countries and France.

Winston S. Churchill (1940–1945). The embodiment and voice of Allied resistance to the Axis from May 1940 until the United States entered the war a year and a half later, Churchill was a graduate of Sandhurst Royal Military College (20th in a class of 130) and had accumulated a great deal of battlefield experience in sixty-five adventurous years. This included clashes in India, celebrated exploits during the Boer War, and service as an officer on the Western Front during World War I (after the 1915 Dardanelles campaign that he advocated as First Lord of the Admiralty became the disaster of Gallipoli). Once named prime minister, Churchill created for himself the additional office of *minister of defense*—appointing as his ministry chief of staff General Sir Hastings Ismay, who became his closest and most trusted military aide. The two met at least once every day with the chiefs of staff of all the military services (441 meetings in 1941 and 414 in 1944). This group ran Britain's military war, the chiefs of staff becoming adept at restraining their pugnacious prime minister's more impractical schemes. Many of Churchill's ideas were practical, however, and displayed an inventiveness born of desperation, military experience, and an ever-inquiring mind. In 1940, he suggested the formation of small "striking parties," which evolved into special forces such as commandos. He was an early and fervent proponent of paratroops and development of specialized landing craft. He designed (in 1917) a prototype of the floating "Mulberry" harbors the Allies used at

Normandy, and he advocated placing artillery along the English coast with sufficient range to fire across the English Channel.

Promising the British people nothing but "blood, sweat, toil, and tears," as he assumed wartime leadership, Churchill grimly told Soviet ambassador Ivan Maisky in July 1940 that his general strategy was simply "to last out the next three months." Yet his strategic vision was generally more optimistic and sweeping, rooted in his absolute determination that the Allies would prevail—and that the far-flung British Empire must remain intact and ready for post-war challenges. To achieve these ends, he maintained the best possible relations with his allies (while growing increasingly wary of Soviet intentions for the future); encouraged maximum support from the British Dominions; backed effective guerrilla organizations in occupied countries; incorporated thousands of nationals of occupied countries into the British armed forces; and advocated his closing-the-ring strategy favoring operations around the periphery of Europe. His emphasis on the Mediterranean remained a source of friction between Churchill and the Americans, who by late 1943 had taken command of the Allied effort. From their position of strength (and because of their eagerness to bring the Soviet Union into the war against Japan), the Americans became more willing to accommodate the Soviet Union during discussions of military strategy—and less willing to be swayed by Churchill's arguments. After one such argument was ignored at the November 28–December 1, 1943, Allied conference, Churchill wrote: "I realized at Teheran for the first time what a small nation we are. There I sat with the great Russian bear on one side of me with paws outstretched, and on the other side the great American buffalo, and between the two sat the poor little English donkey who was the only one, the only one of the three, who knew the right way home."

Clement Attlee (1945–1951). Effectively deputy prime minister from 1942, Attlee replaced Churchill in the middle of the Allied conference in Potsdam, Germany (July–August 1945) after the first British elections in a decade. His last major wartime duty occurred soon afterward, when he broadcast to the British people the news of Japan's surrender.

COMMITTEE OF IMPERIAL DEFENSE (CID). Established in 1904, this prewar committee (and temporary subcommittees) formulated strategy and studied defense requirements. The *minister for coordination of defense* reported to the cabinet. The CID was dissolved after a war cabinet was formed on September 1, 1939. The office of minister for coordination of defense was abolished in April 1940.

WAR CABINET. Based on the smaller body that replaced the full British Cabinet midway through World War I to increase government efficiency in directing Britain's war effort, the first War Cabinet of World War II was appointed by Neville Chamberlain in September 1939. It comprised nine members: Prime Minister, Lord Privy Seal, Chancellor of the Exchequer, Foreign Secretary, First Lord of the Admiralty, Secretary of State for Air, Minister for Coordination of Defense, Minister without Portfolio, and Secretary of State for War. Although Chamberlain, leader of the Conservative Party, had attempted to include members of the opposition Labour Party, most Labour leaders distrusted him, and they declined. But Winston Churchill, a rogue Conservative and critic of Chamberlain's earlier appeasement policy, accepted the prime minister's invitation to become First Lord of the Admiralty. When, eight months later, he succeeded Chamberlain as prime minister, Churchill formed a coalition government, including (in both the larger Cabinet and the War Cabinet) representatives of the Liberal and Labour parties—including Labour leader Clement Atlee. Churchill's War Cabinet was somewhat larger than Chamberlain's, and its membership fluctuated throughout the war. Attlee (Lord Privy Seal and also, from September 1943, Lord President of the Council), Foreign Minister Anthony Eden, Minister of Labour and National Service Ernest Bevin (a Labour politician), and Sir John Anderson (Lord President of the Council, 1940–1943, Chancellor of the Exchequer, 1943–1945) remained in the War Cabinet throughout the conflict.

CHIEFS OF STAFF COMMITTEE. Primarily comprising the chiefs of staff of the three military services, this committee met with Churchill and General Sir Hastings Ismay at least once a day and was also responsible to the full War Cabinet. Its subcommittees included the Joint (combined services) Intelligence Committee and the Joint Planning Staff. The latter was particularly prone to criticism from Churchill. However, its head, Sir John Kennedy, later wrote that Churchill's "taunts and exhortations, and his criticism of every detail of our work, kept us continuously on our toes."

BRITISH ARMY

Chief of the Imperial General Staff (CIGS): John Vereker, Field Marshal Lord Gort (1937–August 1939); Field Marshal Sir Edmund Ironside (September 1939–May 1940); Field Marshal Sir John Dill (May 1940–

December 1941); Field Marshal Sir Alan Brooke (December 1941–January 1946)

Army Council: Responsible for the conduct of army affairs, the council comprised the secretary of state for war, the CIGS, adjutant-general (personnel matters), quartermaster general (logistics), master general of ordnance, vice-chief of the Imperial General Staff (operations, plans, intelligence, and training), and the deputy chief of the Imperial General Staff (organization for war)

Force Size (at Peak): 3.1 million (including more than 200,000 women of the Auxiliary Territorial Service [ATS])

Theaters of Operation: Europe (western and Scandinavia); Mediterranean (including North and East Africa); China-Burma-India

Casualties: 569,501 (including 144,079 killed, 33,771 missing, 239,575 wounded, 152,076 prisoners of war)

After the huge losses of World War I—more than 2.3 million casualties, including more than 700,000 killed—no one in Britain wanted to face the prospect of another major war. Financial and civilian support for the army dwindled in the interwar years and remained low, despite the growing menace of German rearmament. "The nation does not believe an Army is necessary," British general Edmund Ironside wrote in August 1937, "and the Government, so democratic is it, will not make up the nation's mind for it." By January 1, 1938, the Regular Army included only 197,338 men. Of these, more than 90,000 were guarding the overseas empire (including 56,000 in India and Burma and nearly 22,000 in the Mediterranean area) with lighter, more mobile weaponry and equipment than would be needed in the coming war. Men of the home-based Territorial Army (TA), which was not obligated to serve overseas, received even fewer resources. The army remained third in priority among the armed services; its major functions were maintaining control of the empire and preparing a stout home-island antiaircraft defense against any attempt at a "knock-out" air assault by the increasingly strong German Luftwaffe. The Royal Navy and Royal Air Force would bear the major offensive burdens. This policy of "limited liability," with no major commitment of ground forces on the Continent, did not begin to change until April 1939, when the government authorized an expansion of the TA and instituted conscription. Thus, less than five months before Germany invaded Poland, the army was faced with the need to (1) significantly adjust its strategic and tactical plans, (2) incorporate tens of thousands of untrained men into the ranks, and (3) vastly expand and improve its weaponry. "What an unholy mess our politicians have made of the rebirth of the Army," Major General Henry R. Pownall wrote in his diary on April 30, "through short-sightedness, unwillingness to face facts and prejudice against the Army."

During the first two and a half years of war, the army contended with inadequate equipment, inexperienced officers, insufficiently trained men, and deeply flawed military doctrine that could not cope with the German blitzkrieg. "War has changed," General Sir Claude Auchinleck wrote to General Sir John Dill on May 30, 1940, as British and French troops were being evacuated from the Continent via the "Miracle of Dunkirk" (leaving masses of vital equipment and 40,000 prisoners behind). "We are in the same position as were Napoleon's adversaries when he started in on them with his new organization and tactics." Over the next two years, British and Dominion forces suffered other hard blows—among them, Hong Kong, Malaya, Burma (the longest withdrawal in British Army history), Crete, and, in June 1942, the fall of the long-embattled port garrison of Tobruk, Libya. Mean-

A British brigadier general commanding tank units conducts a briefing in Tobruk, Libya.

while, training gradually improved (with more battle drills using live ammunition); and commanders relearned and reapplied lessons on the necessity for cooperation among infantry, artillery, and armor—and between ground and air forces—that had been forgotten since World War I. Still, Britain's limited manpower reserves, the continuing need to pour resources into the production of warships and fighter planes, and British commanders' concern over maintaining the morale of their forces and avoiding the dreadful slaughters of 1914–1918 led Prime Minister Churchill to write, in a directive of March 1941, that it was "impossible for the Army, except in resisting invasion, to play a primary role in the defeat of the enemy. That task can only be done by the staying power of the Navy, and above all by the effect of Air predominance. Very valuable and important services may be rendered overseas by the Army in operations of a secondary order, and it is for these special operations that its organization and character should be adapted." After Dunkirk, in May–June 1940, the bulk of the army remained in Britain until the Normandy landings four years later.

By the end of 1942, the increasingly better trained and organized army at last had sufficient weapons and equipment. In contrast with its Soviet and American allies, however, Britain was by then reaching the end of its military manpower reserves—a principal reason that British commanders were relatively cautious in committing their men to battle. Though its contribution to defeating the Axis could not match those of the armies of its two more resource- and manpower-rich allies, the British army fought tenaciously and creatively for six long and wearing years.

ROYAL NAVY

Admiralty: This was the authority responsible for overall command of the navy, which was organized in two "commands" (North Atlantic and South Atlantic) and three "stations" (China [Singapore], American and West Indies, and East Indies). The head of the admiralty was the *First Lord of the Admiralty:* Sir Samual Hoare (1936–1937); Alfred Duff Cooper (1937–1938); Winston Churchill (1939–1940); A. V. Alexander (1940–1945); Brendan Bracken (1945); A. V. Alexander (1945–1946)

Admiralty Board: This body exercised operational control of the navy. It comprised a president or First Lord, the First Sea Lord/Chief of Naval Staff, and subordinate sea lords responsible for particular tasks (e.g., personnel and recruiting, the Fleet Air Arm)

First Sea Lord/Chief of Naval Staff: Admiral Ernle Chatfield, 1st Baron Chatfield (1933–1938); Admiral Sir Roger Backhouse (1938–1939); Admiral Sir Dudley Pound (1939–1943); Admiral Andrew Cunningham, 1st Baron Cunningham of Hyndhope (1943–1946)

Force Size (at Peak): 857,000 (including 74,000 Royal Marines and an equal number of Women's Royal Naval Service [WRNS])

Theaters of Operation: European; Mediterranean; Pacific; Americas

Casualties: 73,642 (including 50,758 killed, 820 missing, 14,663 wounded, and 7,401 prisoners; 102 WRNS were killed, and 22 wounded)

In mid-1939, Britain's most venerable service, the Royal Navy, was still the most powerful naval force in the world, capable of defending both the British Isles and the British Empire against any *one* of its three potential Axis enemies. By 1937, however, it had become clear that the navy could not counter a strong sea-power alliance. The navy, too, had suffered from budget and manpower cuts between 1919 and 1935, the year German rearmament came out into the open. During the next three years, naval expenditures increased from £68.8 million to £127.2 million. By September 3, 1939, more than a hundred vessels (including 7 battleships and battle cruisers and 6 aircraft carriers) were under construction. As first lord of the admiralty and then prime minister, Churchill oversaw a quadrupling of the navy between 1939 and June 1944. Manpower came from three naval reserve organizations, conscripts, and volunteers—from Britain, the Dominions, and occupied nations. Shipbuilding was augmented by U.S. Lend-Lease, purchase, and incorporation of ships from occupied nations (Poland, Norway, Holland, and France) that had eluded the Germans. This growth was punctuated, however, by costly disasters. In 1941 alone (the Royal Navy's worst war year), two battleships, two battle cruisers, two aircraft carriers, ten cruisers, twenty-three destroyers, twelve submarines—and thousands of seamen—were lost.

In 1939, the navy comprised a submarine fleet of sixty-one (an additional fifteen being built) and three main surface forces: The *Home Fleet* protected the British Isles, jousted with the German fleet in the Atlantic, blockaded Germany (though most goods reached Germany by land routes), and escorted convoys supplying Great Britain and the Soviet Union. The

Mediterranean Fleet (based at Alexandria, Egypt, and augmented from June 1940 to October 1943 by "Force H," a small fleet at Gibraltar, and "Force K," a Malta-based squadron), guarded the Suez canal, parried with the Italian navy, attacked Axis convoys to North Africa, and protected Allied Mediterranean convoys. On December 2, 1941, the ships of the "China Station" were redesignated the *Eastern Fleet*. It removed to British East Africa after strategically vital Singapore fell—and after the sinking of the battleship *Prince of Wales* and the battle cruiser *Repulse*, December 10, 1941. It then formed the basis of the Pacific Fleet, later Task Force 57, which augmented U.S. naval power in the war against Japan from March through August 1945. The largest, most powerful British fleet of the war, Task Force 57 participated in the battle for Okinawa and attacks against Formosa and Japan.

FLEET AIR ARM (FAA). The navy did not control its own air arm from 1918, when the Royal Naval Air Service was merged with the newborn Royal Air Force, until 1937, when the Fleet Air Arm was formed and given authority over all ship-based aircraft. The RAF controlled land-based aircraft operating over water and continued to train navy pilots. Beginning in July 1941, many navy pilots were also trained in the United States (first at Grosse Ile, Michigan, then at Pensacola, Florida). This training was conducted unobtrusively until Pearl Harbor (British trainees wore civilian clothing when off the base). By the end of 1944, 44 percent of FAA pilots were being trained under this *Towers Scheme* (after Admiral John H. Towers, chief of the Bureau of Aeronautics, USN). FAA began the war with only 500 trained aircrews and 232 front-line aircraft—of modest capability. Its role then was to slow down enemy ships by damaging them with torpedoes and machine-gun fire, so that the approaching fleet could finish them off. As the aircraft carrier proved to be more important than expected, the Royal Navy acquired more modern and capable carrier aircraft, primarily by purchase and Lend-Lease from the United States; by 1945, FAA had 1,336 front-line aircraft.

ROYAL MARINES (RM). The main duties of the RM were to man guns on naval vessels, establish and temporarily defend Naval and Fleet Air Arm bases (for which purpose the RM created two Mobile Naval Base Defense Organizations), and undertake coastal raids and amphibious operations. Marines also were gunners on board Defensively Armed Merchant Ships

(DEMS), manned the coastal artillery that fired across the English Channel at Axis-occupied Europe and the Maunsell Forts that defended the Thames Estuary (see "Fortifications" in Chapter 5), and helped run captured ports and manned antiaircraft batteries after the Normandy landings. Some marines were pilots in the Fleet Air Arm; many served as commandos, conducting reconnaissance, raids, and other special operations; and others made up all Royal Navy bands.

ROYAL AIR FORCE (RAF)

Air Council: This body determined policy and was headed by the *Secretary of State for Air:* Philip Cunliffe-Lister, 1st Viscount Swing (June 1935–May 1938); Sir Kingsley Wood (May 1938–April 1940); Sir Samuel Hoare (April–May 1940); Sir Archibald Sinclair (May 1940–May 1945)

Chief of the Air Staff (CAS): Air Chief Marshal Sir Cyril Newell (1937–1940); Sir Charles Portal (1940–1946)

Air Officer Commander in Chief of:

Bomber Command: Air Chief Marshal Sir Edgar Ludlow-Hewitt (September 1937–April 1940); Air Marshal Sir Charles Portal (April–October 1940); Air Marshal Sir Richard Peirse (October 1940–January 1942); Air Vice Marshal J. E. A. Baldwin (acting, January 1942); Air Chief Marshal Sir Arthur "Bomber" Harris (February 1942–September 1945)

Fighter Command: Air Chief Marshal Sir Hugh Dowding (July 1936–November 1940); Air Marshal Sir Sholto Douglas (November 1940–November 1942); Air Marshal Sir Trafford Leigh-Mallory (November 1942–November 1943); Air Marshal Sir Roderic Hill (November 1943–May 1945); Air Marshal Sir James Robb (May 1945–November 1947)

Coastal Command: Air Marshal Sir Frederick Bowhill (August 1937–June 1941); Air Chief Marshal Sir Philip Joubert de la Ferte (June 1941–February 1943); Air Marshal Sir John Slessor (February 1943–January 1944); Air Chief Marshal Sir William Sholto Douglas (January 1944–June 1945); Air Marshal Sir Leonard Slatter (June 1945–November 1948)

Force Size (at Peak): 1.2 million (including 180,000 members of the Women's Auxiliary Air Force [WAAF])

Casualties: 112,296 (including 69,606 killed; 6,736 missing, 22,839 wounded, 13,115 prisoners of war; 187 WAAF personnel were killed, 4 missing, and 420 wounded (no WAAFs became prisoners of war)

The full manpower complement of the RAF—the world's first independent (not controlled by army or navy) air force—was only 31,000 in 1933, down from 240,256 officers and men at the end of World War I. Yet as this small air force helped defend British interests in Turkey, Iraq, Palestine, Aden, China, and India during the interwar years, defense planners became increasingly nervous about the establishment and growth of the German Luftwaffe. In 1934, the year Hitler became führer, the Cabinet approved a plan for expanding the RAF (including improving and increasing its arsenal of fighters and bombers). Seven other plans (reflecting the outcome of political debates and changes in military strategy) had been approved by the end of 1938. Yet on the eve of war, the RAF still had significantly fewer men than the Luftwaffe and fewer combat aircraft. Meanwhile, in 1936, the RAF underwent a major reorganization, dividing into several different "Commands." Others were added later.

The 1.2 million men and women in the RAF at its wartime peak included individuals and units from the British Dominions (particularly Canada,

PRINCIPAL RAF COMMANDS, 1936–1945

RAF Command Name	Description
Army Cooperation Command (est. 1940; disbanded 1943)	Devised improved tactics for air tactical support of ground operations.
Balloon Command (est. 1938)	Coordinating with Fighter Command, controlled the "barrage balloons" defending vital ports, factories, invasion beaches, and ships (see "Balloons" in Chapter 5).
Bomber Command (est. 1936)	The principal offensive air arm, engaged in strategic—and the controversial "area"—bombing (see "Aircraft–Bombers" in Chapter 5); tactical support of ground operations; and limited support of the navy and Coastal Command in antishipping and antisubmarine warfare.

(continued)

PRINCIPAL RAF COMMANDS, 1936–1945 (CONTINUED)

RAF Command Name	Description
Coastal Command (est. 1936)	Comprised land-based aircraft and crews that protected coastal convoys and engaged in antisubmarine and antishipping warfare, long-range sea patrols, and air-sea rescue.
Fighter Command (est. 1936)	Famous as "the few" who won the aerial Battle of Britain, RAF fighters initially engaged primarily in air defense (assisted by the chain of radar stations under Fighter Command control); later, increasingly active as bomber escorts and in tactical support of ground operations in Europe, the Middle East, and China-Burma-India.
Maintenance Command (est. 1938)	Provided supply and engineering support; repair and maintenance; devised and administered an aircraft storage and distribution system.
Training Command (est. 1936)	Prepared air crews for front-line service; divided into Flying Training Command and Technical Training Command in 1940.
Ferry Command (est. 1941) subsumed under Transport Command (est. 1943)	Responsible for delivering aircraft bought from or loaned by the United States to the United Kingdom as well as other general ferrying duties; moved troops, stores, and equipment. At the end of the war, flew recovered POWs home.

Principal source: Ken Delve, *The Source Book of the RAF*, Shrewsbury, England: Airlife Publishing, 1994.

Australia, and South Africa) and from occupied countries, notably Poland and France. For three years, the RAF also included three *Eagle Squadrons* (71st, 121st, and 133rd), comprising 240 Americans who had joined up while the United States was still neutral (including 37 in the Royal Canadian Air Force). The Eagle squadrons compiled a proud combat record at a heavy cost in casualties. As the U.S. Army Air Force began operations in England, most men of the Eagle Squadrons transferred to the American air force. At a change of command ceremony in late September 1942, the Eagles became the Fourth Fighter Group of the USAAF. "We of Fighter Command deeply regret this parting," chief of Fighter Command Sholto Douglas said at the ceremony. "In . . . the past 18 months we have seen the stuff of which you are made. We could not ask for better companions with whom to see this fight through to a finish."

HOME GUARD. (See Chapters 3 and 11.)

MERCHANT MARINE. In 1939, the British government transformed the nation's merchant fleet, the largest in the world, into the "Merchant Navy," supervised by the Ministry of War Transport and controlled by the Admiralty. When the war began, this service controlled 18,710 vessels of over 1,600 gross tons. Eventually, merchant vessels from the British Dominions, Norway, Holland, and other occupied countries became part of this merchant fleet, as did vessels chartered or on Lend-Lease from the United States. Some Axis vessels caught in friendly ports were also confiscated. Yet there was a constant shipping shortage until the last year of the war. Ships were needed to import food, oil, and other vital supplies; to move troops and their supplies; and to provide material aid to the Soviet Union and other Allies. Voyages took longer because ships were rerouted to avoid areas of maximum danger: those bound for the Middle East and beyond detoured for a time around Africa rather than through the Mediterranean—sailing an additional 10,000 miles. Nevertheless, losses were heavy: by 1945, 4,700 British-flagged merchant vessels had been destroyed and 29,180 merchant seamen killed. Although volunteers for merchant crews were generally plentiful, Britain's underefficient shipbuilding industry could not replace all the lost vessels. By 1944, however, sufficient numbers of U.S.-manufactured and Lend-Lease-provided *Liberty ships* (mass-produced merchantmen) had done much to solve the shipping shortage. In 1945, there were 22,143 British-flagged merchantmen of more than 1,600 gross tons.

ARMED FORCES OF THE BRITISH COMMONWEALTH AND DOMINIONS

Country/Territory	Armed Forces		Theater(s) of Operation
Australia	Army Navy Air Force	727,500 48,100 216,900	Pacific, European, Mediterranean (North Africa, Balkans, Syria, Crete)
British Central Africa	Total	71,000	Mediterranean (North Africa), East Africa (including Madagascar), China-Burma-India
British East Africa	Total	100,000	East Africa, China-Burma-India
British West Africa	Total	169,000	East Africa, China-Burma-India
British West Indies (Caribbean colonies)	RAF	5,800	American, European; one army regiment, the 1st Caribbean, was stationed in Egypt
Canada	Army Navy Air Force	730,159 106,522 249,662	American, European, Mediterranean (North Africa, Sicily, Italy), China-Burma-India, Pacific (armed merchant cruisers, air transport squadrons)
Fiji	Total	8,513	Pacific, including the Solomon Islands (especially Guadalcanal and Bougainville) and New Guinea
India	Army* Navy	2.5 million 30,478	European, Mediterranean (Italy, Syria, Iraq, and North Africa), East Africa, China-Burma-India, Pacific (Malaya)
Mauritius	Numbers uncertain		Mediterranean (North Africa); the "Mauritius Regiment" served on Madagascar
New Zealand	Army Navy Air Force	157,000 7,000 55,000	European, Mediterranean (North Africa, Balkans, Crete, Italy), Pacific
Palestine	An estimated 30,000 Jews and 9,000 Palestinian Arabs in various U.K. forces		European, Mediterranean (Middle East, North Africa)

ARMED FORCES OF THE BRITISH COMMONWEALTH AND DOMINIONS (CONTINUED)

Country/Territory	Armed Forces		Theater(s) of Operation
South Africa	Army	255,000	Mediterranean (Mediterranean Europe [Balkans], North Africa), sub-Saharan Africa, Madagascar
	Navy	9,455	
	Air Force	44,569	
Sudan	Total	4,500	Mediterranean (Africa)
Transjordan	Numbers uncertain		Mediterranean (Middle and Near East)

Principal sources: I. C. B. Dear and M. R. D. Foot, eds., *Oxford Companion to World War II*, Oxford University Press, 2001; Robin Kay, comp., *Chronology: New Zealand in the War, 1939–1946*, Wellington, NZ: Historical Publications Branch, Department of Internal Affairs, 1968.

*The largest all-volunteer army in the world.

Outstanding commanders of the United States' two major allies, Great Britain and the Soviet Union, included (left to right, top to bottom), Row 1: Admiral Andrew Cunningham, Sir Arthur ("Bomber") Harris, Admiral Nikolai Gerasimovich Kuznetsov, Air Marshal Sir Trafford Leigh-Mallory, Field Marshal Sir Bernard Montgomery; Row 2: Marshal of the Royal Air Force Sir Charles Portal, Admiral of the Fleet Sir (Alfred) Dudley Pound, Marshal Semyon Timoshenko, Marshal Alexander M. Vasilevsky, Marshal Georgi Zhukov.

Union of Soviet Socialist Republics (USSR, Soviet Union)

Between 1922 and 1939, the Communist regime in the newly established Soviet Union dissolved the old Russian imperial armed forces and built new Red armed forces. Military spending surged and military manpower increased from 562,000 in 1931 to 4.2 million in 1940. This military buildup was an often bitter process of Communist-Party-controlled trial and error that left Soviet forces terribly vulnerable to the smashing efficiency of the Wehrmacht invasion in 1941. Although the Soviet military appeared powerful and well-equipped (possessing more tanks than all other nations combined and the largest submarine force in the world), it suffered from multiple near-crippling problems. These ranged from a dearth of practical necessities (barracks, spare parts, clothing, food, naval equipment) to unrealistic military doctrine, inadequate military training, and a stultifying system of dual military–political command. Before issuing orders, military officers had to have them approved by political commissars, most of whom were Party ideologues with no military training. (Commissars' command authority waxed and waned during the war.) Men in the ranks, meanwhile, were diverted from training by hours of political instruction by omnipresent lower-level political officers (*politruks*), whose many roles included propagandist, counselor, morale officer—and informer about unorthodox political beliefs. Moreover, between 1937 and 1940 more than 48,000 officers were purged from the army and navy (some executed, others imprisoned) and many were replaced by inexperienced men. (About 11,000 army officers were reinstated by 1940.) Even experienced surviving officers were cowed. As a 1991 Russian study reported, "Many commanders became afraid to display initiative and take reasonable risks."

Thus, it is not surprising that the performance of Soviet armed forces ranged from poor to dismal in Poland (1939) and Finland (1940)—while the USSR was supporting, and benefiting from the German war effort—and during the first months of the Soviet war against Germany. (Only the Far Eastern forces, under Georgi Zhukov, facing the Japanese, fared much better. See "Nomonhan Incident" in Chapter 6.) Nevertheless, although wracked by the loss of millions of men and most of its air power and armor in the initial German onslaught, the Soviet military hung on, slowly recovered, and began a bitterly contested offensive that gradually pushed the Germans back to Berlin. The vicious Eastern-Front conflict—in which some 10 million Soviet soldiers and sailors, and millions more civilians, died—anchored the Allied ground war against Germany.

SOVIET ARMED FORCES AND THEIR
TOP COMMANDERS

CHAIRMAN OF THE COUNCIL OF PEOPLE'S COMMISSARS/
ARMED FORCES SUPREME COMMANDER

JOSEPH STALIN (JOSEF VISSARIONOVICH DJUGASHVILI) (1879–1953). A ruthless dictator who had never been a soldier, Stalin had developed a keen appreciation for military matters during the Russian Civil War and worked with the Red Army during the 1920 Soviet incursion into Poland. He pushed the expansion of Soviet forces (reducing the manufacture of consumer goods in favor of tanks and airplanes)—but was a principal source of the problems that led to the Soviets' poor military performance from 1939 to 1942. Stalin's refusal to act on the overwhelming evidence of imminent German attack contributed to the crushing success of the initial German assault. His later refusal to countenance strategic withdrawals resulted in the destruction of entire Soviet armies.

Stalin seldom visited the front. Yet, after rallying the Soviet people and inspiring many in the military with a belated radio speech on July 3, 1941, he exercised tight control over the military conduct of the war (giving himself the rank of marshal in February 1943 and generalissimo of the Soviet Union in July 1945). Using trusted military and political representatives as his eyes and ears in the field, he called commanders back to Moscow for consultation (and sometimes punishment) and issued orders that were often brutal. Order No. 270, issued August 16, 1941, declared that any so-called malicious deserter—which meant, in effect, any soldier taken prisoner (and 3.3 million were captured in 1941 alone)—would be deemed a traitor, and the soldier's family could be imprisoned. (This order even imperiled the families of soldiers killed in battle but whose bodies were never found.) On July 28, 1942, as Soviet armies continued to lose ground, Stalin issued Order No. 227, "Not One Step Backward," prohibiting abandonment of a position and specifying that any officer who let his men retreat without explicit orders was to be charged with a capital offense. (It has been estimated that 158,000 Soviet soldiers were condemned to death during the war.)

Yet Stalin was also learning the limits of central control and the drawbacks of the dual political–military command system. By the end of 1942, he was giving much wider latitude to such trusted generals as Zhukov. By then, Soviet war production and an influx of Lend-Lease supplies were increasing the Red military's capabilities, while constant combat—and exposure to German brutality toward an enemy they regarded as subhuman—had provided much-needed experience. "I've seen the burned-out towns and villages, the corpses of women and children, the unhappy, plundered residents," a soldier named Misha Volkov wrote to his wife in February 1942, "but also I've seen the tears of joy when these people encountered us. . . . The spirit of these places has affected me and it has grown in all our soldiers." Victory at Stalingrad in February 1943 marked a turning point for the Red Army—and in the European war. Thereafter, the Soviet army acted in accordance with Stalin's 1940 declaration, "The Red Army is a modern army, and a modern army is an offensive army."

STATE DEFENSE COMMITTEE (GKO)
Chairman: Joseph Stalin (June 1941–1945)

Organized on June 30, 1941, eight days after the German invasion, GKO functioned as a powerful war cabinet. According to a 1988 report of the Lenin Political-Military Academy, its mission was to mobilize "all of the nation's strength and resources, employing them in concentrated fashion in the interests of achieving victory in war, centralizing the leadership of the state to a maximum, and concentrating all power in the hands of one all-powerful organ." In addition to its chairman, the committee initially included Commissar for Foreign Affairs V. M. Molotov (vice chairman); Marshal of the Soviet Union K. E. Voroshilov; L. E. Beria, head of the People's Commissariat of Internal Affairs (the shadowy and much-feared NKVD); and G. M. Malenkov, a prominent Communist Party figure and one of Stalin's trusted aides. N. A. Voznesensky, L. M. Kaganovich, and A. I. Mikoian were added to the committee roster in 1942, and N. A. Bulganin became a member in 1944. The committee supervised the work of all government and military organizations involved in the war effort, issuing directives that had the full force of law. Although it worked as a true committee, with each member developing his own area of expertise, Stalin made all the final decisions.

STAVKA OF THE SUPREME HIGH COMMAND (STAVKA VGK)
Chairman: S. K. Timoshenko (June–July 1941); Joseph Stalin (July 1941–1945)

Formed by the State Defense Committee as the "highest organ of strategic leadership for the Armed Forces," the Stavka VGK comprised army and navy officers as well as Commissar for Foreign Affairs Vyacheslav Molotov and Chairman Stalin (assisted by an "institute" of advisers, the counsel of armed forces commanders, and political and military representatives in the field). It directed all crucial aspects of military campaigns; supervised the navy, long-range bomber aviation, and all Red Army fronts (groups of armies); and organized and directed the Soviet partisan movement.

CENTRAL STAFF OF THE PARTISAN MOVEMENT (TsShPD). (See also Chapters 8 and 9.)
Chief of Staff: Lieutenant General P. K. Ponomarenko (March 1942–March 1943; May 1943–January 1944)

The State Defense Committee created the Central Staff of the Partisan Movement (March 30, 1942), under direct control of the Stavka, to communicate with, supply, train, and coordinate partisan groups, as well as facilitate their cooperation with regular armies. With central direction, the partisans became increasingly effective. Yet Stalin never trusted these comparatively difficult-to-control fighters. In 1943, he authorized the disbandment of the central staff, re-formed it in May of that year, and finally abolished it on January 13, 1944. Nevertheless, partisans continued their war against the Axis.

PEOPLE'S COMMISSARIAT OF DEFENSE (NKO)
People's Commissar of Defense: K. E. Voroshilov (1934–May 1940, replaced after the Red Army's poor performance in the war with Finland); S. K. Timoshenko (May 1940–July 1941); Joseph Stalin (July 1941–)

NKO was the focal point of Soviet armed forces command and control until late June 1941—assisted, and its decisions approved by, a political/military group, the *Military Council*. It acted through central directorates and a network of local commissariats and administrations (each of them subordinate to the district military council). After the creation of the Stavka, the NKO was placed under its direction.

NKVD FORCES (VOISKA NKVD). Part of the People's Commissariat of Internal Affairs (NKVD), the USSR's dreaded secret police, these security forces were organized early in 1941 to support the Red Army and maintain security in case of war. By 1944, they numbered well over half a million men. Their duties included protecting Soviet frontiers, important government personnel and strategic facilities such as transportation and communications hubs and industrial centers. They also convoyed prisoners (enemy troops and Soviet soldiers and civilians destined for the Soviet Gulag); guarded and administered prison camps; conducted reconnaissance and diversionary activities; prevented desertions; enforced army discipline; and assisted with army recruitment—chiefly by impressing reluctant civilians of liberated areas into the service. When needed, NKVD forces also participated in combat operations.

RED ARMY

Supreme Commander: Joseph Stalin

Deputy Supreme Commander: General G. K. Zhukov (1942)

Red Army General Staff (GshKA)

Chief of General Staff: General G. K. Zhukov (January–July 1941); Marshal of the Soviet Union B. M. Shaposhnikov (July 1941–May 1942); Colonel-General (later Army General, then Marshal of the Soviet Union) A. M. Vasilevsky (May 1942–February 1945); Army General A. I. Antonov (February 1945–1946)

Main Political Directorate of the Red Army (GlavPU)

Commander of the Red Army Air Force: General P. F. Zhigarev (April 1941–April 1942); General A Novikov (April 1942–1946)

Force Size (at Peak): 6.5 million

Casualties: Estimated deaths in all Soviet Forces, 10 million; the vast majority in the army

After the Red Army's poor performance against Finland (November 1939–March 1940), Stalin began to push for improvements in equipment, doctrine, and training. Yet few improvements had been made in the rapidly expanding army—which had been trained for battle on enemy soil, not defense against invasion—when the Wehrmacht smashed into the Soviet Union on June 22, 1941. Sheer courage—assisted by the mud of late October rains, the early arrival of a brutal winter, and the threat of execution by special security forces—allowed this army, bereft of nearly all its air cover and tank support, to save Moscow from German occupation. However, the Wehrmacht continued to advance elsewhere, and defeat on the battlefield battered morale. ("We wept as we retreated," one veteran later recalled.) Streams of ill-trained replacements further disrupted already tenuous Red Army unit cohesion, while civilians angrily resisted army units ordered to move them out of the line of march. (Soviet leaders eventually ruled that

Horribly mauled at the beginning of the German-Soviet war, the Red Army was transformed—in the midst of brutal combat—into a powerful force that smashed Germany's Eastern-Front armies. In April 1944, as the Soviets pushed the Wehrmacht out of Ukraine, Georgii Zel'ma photographed the 8th Guard of the Army of General Vasili Chuikov marching proudly through the streets of Odessa.

only the NKVD would deal with civilian evacuations.) With communications uncertain and leave almost unknown, millions of Soviet soldiers were desperately anxious about families suffering under a pitiless German occupation. Frictions also increased in this multiethnic army, with Russians insulting Ukrainians, or atheists and Christians objecting to Muslim prayers. Food was scarce, and soldiers were often assigned to help farmers plant or harvest crops. Stealing from civilians became commonplace and an army black market boomed, bootleg liquor being the chief barter currency.

Despite these problems, a better army began to emerge. Planes and tanks—newly manufactured in Soviet factories or acquired by Lend-Lease—began arriving on the front lines, as did other much-needed equipment such as radios and trucks. Commanders, given more leeway by Stalin, learned to better coordinate artillery, armor, infantry, and air support. To instill pride among men in the ranks, more awards were given for valor, laundresses were recruited to wash uniforms, and men were provided equipment to fix their boots. (U.S. Lend-Lease provided 15 million pairs of boots to the USSR. But, as it marched across the vast Eastern-Front distances, the Red Army was generally sockless; soldiers wrapped their feet in less-than-comfortable footcloths called *portyanki*.) With each battlefield victory, pride increased; with each mile of ground retaken, the thirst for vengeance on the Germans and their allies grew. As the Red Army pushed the Axis invaders off Soviet soil, their victory was sullied by atrocities: looting, burning, the murder of officials, the strafing of civilian refugees and, most common of all, rape. (See also Chapter 8.) Yet it was not for this, alone, that, before demobilization, soldiers were required to sign a pledge not to discuss anything but warm recollections of comaraderie when they returned home. Home was a country where information was strictly controlled. The stunning courage so often displayed by Soviet fighting men and women would be justly celebrated. But state-generated myths of the "Great Patriotic War" would long obscure the Soviet war's darker truths.

RED ARMY AIR FORCE (VOENNO-VOZDUSHNYE SILY, VVS). (See "Red Navy" for naval aviation.) In 1941, the Red Army air force (VVS) was the world's largest, with 20,662 aircraft, including 15,559 combat aircraft—although a large number were obsolete. Many of them, with their trained pilots and crews, were destroyed early in the German invasion. (Shortage of personnel prompted the Soviets to open air combat to women; see "Women in Military Service," later in this chapter.) As the Soviets established aircraft production centers out of range of the Luftwaffe (and received the first of some 14,000 Lend-Lease planes from the United States and Great Britain), war leaders repeatedly reorganized VVS, seeking the best structure to effectively support ground forces. Shock aviation groups gave way to air armies, comprising air regiments and air corps. Each of the seventeen air armies eventually organized averaged four to five hundred planes—although, later in the war, some could field up to one thousand. This was due to a surge in Soviet production; the USSR built approximately 100,000 planes including long-range bombers for attacks far behind enemy lines. However, because of the scale and constancy of combat on the Eastern Front, the VVS Long-Range Bomber Aviation component generally joined fighters, dive-bombers, and other aircraft in providing ground forces with tactical support. After

1943, the sheer size of the VVS helped overwhelm the increasingly hard-pressed Luftwaffe and turn the tide against the Axis.

RED NAVY (VOENNO-MORSKOI FLOT, VMF)

Supreme Commander: Joseph Stalin

People's Commissar of the Navy and Commander in Chief of the Navy: Admiral N. Kuznetsov (1939–1946)

Commander in Chief of Naval Aviation: General S. Zhavoronkov (1938–1946)

Facing the threat of growing militarism from Japan and Germany, Stalin approved expanding the long-neglected Red Navy and creating a "Big Ocean-Going Fleet." However, the plans proved too great a strain on Soviet shipbuilders. Meanwhile, Stalin's 1937–1940 purge cost the navy its commander in chief, at least two fleet commanders, many ship captains and base commanders, and hundreds of other officers who were often replaced by young and inexperienced (but politically reliable) men. Overall training and efficiency suffered accordingly.

The Red Navy had the largest submarine fleet in the world (between 212 and 230 boats), along with respectable complements of destroyers and numerous small craft (e.g., minesweepers and motor torpedo boats). It also included three battleships and about a dozen cruisers, but no aircraft carriers. The *Red Navy air force*, which in 1939 comprised seven hundred planes of all types, operated mostly from land bases and small seaplane tenders or flew off vessels (such as destroyers and icebreakers) modified to carry reconnaissance aircraft. Throughout the war, the Red Navy lagged well behind those of other major combatants in technological sophistication.

The Soviet navy failed to live up even to its limited potential. Its commanders were unwilling to risk their few capital ships and were not adept at coordinating air reconnaissance with surface and submarine operations. Its large submarine force sank fewer enemy vessels than did the naval air force—which was largely destroyed during the initial German invasion, but quickly rebuilt. Yet the navy performed many duties with varying degrees of success. Of particular note are its more than one hundred amphibious operations, conducted primarily in the Baltic and Black Sea areas and along inland waterways. Much smaller and more ad hoc (and often less successful) than the large-scale amphibious operations conducted by the U.S. Navy and Marine Corps in the Pacific Theater, these amphibious operations nevertheless provided valuable support to Red Army operations.

RED NAVY FLEETS AND FLOTILLAS

Name	Description
Baltic Fleet	Faced both German and Finnish forces as it defended Soviet bases, laid and swept mines, conducted small landing operations, performed limited convoy escort duty, and attacked enemy shipping. In 1945, submarines attached to this fleet were responsible for sinking two vessels, *Wilhelm Gustloff* and *Goya*, filled with thousands of German refugees—the two greatest losses of life in maritime history.
Black Sea Fleet	Conducted the largest Soviet amphibious operation, to relieve pressure on besieged Sevastopol. Submarines and surface vessels also supplied that city and evacuated the wounded. In general, it supported land operations.
Northern or Polar Fleet	Engaged in convoy escort duty (in Russian waters), minelaying, minesweeping, aerial attacks on enemy bases and vessels, and at least two amphibious operations (during the German offensive against Murmansk in 1941 and at Petsamo in 1944). This was the one area in which Soviet, British, and American naval personnel had extensive close contact.
Pacific Fleet	Until August 1945, when the USSR declared war on Japan, this fleet remained on guard (laying defensive minefields) and trained replacement submarine crews for other fleets. Against Japan, it conducted landings in Korea, Sakhalin Island, and the Kuril Islands.
Flotillas	Supported the Red Army along the Soviet Union's extensive inland waterways. The *Lake Ladoga Flotilla* helped supply besieged Leningrad; the *Volga River Flotilla* supported troops during the battle for Stalingrad; the *Danube River Flotilla* participated in successful operations against the Romanian navy and played an important role in the capture of Vienna; the *Amur River Flotilla* supported Red troops moving into Manchuria in August 1945.

United States of America (USA/US)

"As always, the Americans are neglecting their army in peacetime," German military attaché Friedrich von Boetticher reported to Berlin from Washington, D.C., in 1935. Yet he also noted, "In time of great political tension, the little recognized work of the Army in peacetime will move to the fore. In a surprisingly short time the United States will undergo a very strong mobilization on land and in the air. They will become a united nation, which on the basis of its riches in men and material is capable of all manner of deployments of great strength." Six years later, the Japanese attack on Pearl Harbor did unite the nation in striving to win a war that had been thrust upon it. During most of the interim, however, neglect of the military prevailed. Amid growing Axis aggression, American war planners struggled to anticipate the probable circumstances of American involvement in another major conflict, repeatedly revising old war plans—particularly plan "Orange," which posited a Pacific-Ocean war with Japan. After Germany occupied the Czech Sudetenland in 1938, however, U.S. war planners began to focus on the growing danger from across the Atlantic. At the end of that year, President Roosevelt warned that renewed German power presented the Americas with the first serious threat of hemispheric invasion—including a strike at the vital Panama Canal—since the early nineteenth century, particularly if German/Italian forces secured bases on Atlantic islands or in North Africa. Protecting the hemisphere's Atlantic approaches was therefore crucial ("If we lose in the Atlantic," U.S. Army chief of staff George C. Marshall said, "we lose everywhere"). After the Wehrmacht occupied the rest of Czechoslovakia in March 1939, war planners devised a new set of five war plans (the "Rainbow" plans). They laid out alternative strategies for U.S. involvement—with or without major allies—in a war fought across the Pacific and the Atlantic simultaneously. These strategies all required vastly expanding and improving U.S. armed forces.

All this sparked heated debates within the U.S. high command; more questions arose as the Wehrmacht pushed British troops off the Continent and, for a time, it was uncertain whether Britain would survive. As Secretary of War Henry Stimson later wrote, with most of the U. S. Navy guarding the Pacific, "One force remained between the Nazis and the Western Hemisphere—the British fleet." Even after Britain's survival was assured, German U-boats and sea raiders pushed the British Fleet to the limit, and U.S. military leaders debated how much of the United States' limited naval power could be transferred to the Atlantic. They also considered what resources could be expended on reinforcing America's Far Eastern and Pacific bases at the Philippines, Guam, and Wake Island; which weapons should be given top priority for manufacture and how they should be distributed among the services; and how much war material the United States could provide to its allies without endangering its own war effort.

Volatile wartime conditions continually produced new questions. Differences among the leaders of U.S. armed forces—like differences between the United States and Great Britain—were settled under the impetus of an absolute determination to smash the Axis. To that end, the United States increased its armed forces from hundreds of thousands to more than 16 million men and women and deployed them to every theater of war.

SEGREGATION IN THE ARMED FORCES (See also, Chapters 2 and 12.)

Dedicated to preserving the Four Freedoms that Commander in Chief Roosevelt declared, in a January 1941 speech, should prevail everywhere in the world (see Chapter 2), the U.S. armed forces also reflected the ongoing struggle for equality being waged on the home front by the nation's African Americans and other minorities. The interwar years had seen a resurgence of negative assumptions about black soldiers, although these had been repeatedly disproved in earlier conflicts. By June 1940, the U.S. Army included only about 4,000 black soldiers (1.5 percent of the total), and only five black officers—three of them chaplains. Most of the soldiers served in four all-black units established by Congress in the 1860s, and blacks were not allowed in the Army Air Corps. The navy included 4,007 African Americans (2.3 percent of the total). All were enlisted men, and all but six were steward's mates—what the black press dubbed "seagoing bellhops." The few in the Coast Guard were restricted to particular duties, and there were no black U.S. Marines. Pressure for equality in the armed forces came primarily from the black press and organizations such as the Committee for Negro Participation in the National Defense and the NAACP as well as from sympathetic whites—and it met with much resistance.

Partially because of this pressure, the Selective Service Act (September 1940) stipulated that, in selecting and training men, "there shall be no discrimination against any person on account of race or color." Within the armed services, however, segregation of black from white was not interpreted as discrimination. Nevertheless, separation of the races often resulted in blatant discrimination against African American servicemen in housing, transportation, recreational facilities, and even blood banks ("black" blood was maintained separately from "white" blood). Discrimination also prevailed in duty assignments. "Half a million

Negroes are now bearing arms in the service of their country," Dwight Macdonald of the March on Washington Movement wrote early in a 1943 pamphlet, *The War's Greatest Scandal: Jim Crow in Uniform.* "In return for their patriotism, the Negroes of America have been jim-crowed into segregated regiments and used largely as servants and laborers. . . . And so a doctrine of 'White Supremacy' which is simply Hitler's 'Nordic Supremacy' in Cracker lingo has become the official policy of the American armed forces." That year, festering resentments resulted in race riots at military reservations in Mississippi, Georgia, California, Texas, and Kentucky. In 1944, black seamen mutinied after a massive explosion of two ammunition ships at Port Chicago, California, killed 320 people, including 202 black sailors in labor battalions; on Guam, a riot resulted from tension between black seamen and white Marines. In 1945, members of a black Seabees (naval construction) battalion staged a hunger strike to protest discrimination.

Concern over racial tensions, political pressure, and wartime manpower requirements slowly led to some improvements. In the army, integrated training for officers—more economical and efficient than a dual training program—had been instituted successfully early in the war. (However, the number of black officer candidates remained small, and blacks were forbidden from outranking or commanding white officers serving in the same unit.) In 1944, two black infantry divisions activated during World War I (the 92nd and 93rd) were reactivated, and some components were sent into combat. Also that year, 2,500 of 5,500 volunteers from black service units were accepted and trained for combat duty in the European Theater, then organized into 53 platoons—

under white leadership. All were successfully integrated into elements of the First and Seventh Armies, and all saw action. After Germany surrendered, however, the army made clear to these men that integration was over.

The Navy initially resisted an increase in black enlistments, as did the Coast Guard—and Marine Corps commandant General Thomas Holcomb strenuously objected to inducting black Marines. Under pressure, all relented. By the end of the war, the navy included 164,942 black enlistees (5.37 percent of the total); 19,168 African Americans, or approximately 4 percent of total enlistment, had served in the Marine Corps; and some 5,000 had served in the Coast Guard.

The small size of the Coast Guard militated against strict segregation. Many black Coast Guardsmen were assigned to shore duty (such as beach patrol). Others served aboard vessels in various capacities, including as stewards and mess attendants (the rank initially held by future *Roots* author Alex Haley). Unlike Navy and Marine stewards, many in the Coast Guard also manned battle stations: one group, operating a gun aboard USS *Campbell,* won a citation for helping to destroy an enemy submarine. In November 1943, the Coast Guard successfully integrated USS *Sea Cloud,* a weather ship serving in the North Atlantic. In addition to both black and white seamen, the ship's complement included four black officers and some African American petty officers. This success did not lead to widespread integration.

Within the Marine Corps, black inductees were generally assigned to noncombat duties (many served as stewards). Yet nearly 8,000 black Marines—who had not been trained for combat—handled ammunition and hauled supplies

Finally getting their chance to prove themselves in battle, pilots of the 332nd Fighter Group—graduates of the flight-training program for African Americans at Tuskegee, Alabama—were deployed to Italy in January 1944 and became the first Italy-based fighter group to escort bombers on the 1,600-mile run to Berlin. In March 1945, Toni Frissell photographed the group's leader, Colonel Benjamin O. Davis Jr. (hands folded in lap) with his pilots at a briefing.

under heavy fire in such hotly contested Pacific Theater battle zones as Saipan.

About 40 percent of black navy personnel remained stewards or stewards' mates. Many others, including most who served in Seabees battalions, were restricted to duty as steve-

dores, although two all-black Seabees construction units served with distinction in the Pacific. Yet, again under pressure, in 1944 the navy began training the first of 60 black officers commissioned during the war. Also that year, it sent the newly commissioned destroyer escort USS *Mason* on patrol with 196 black enlisted men and 44 white officers and petty officers. This was a first (and successful) test of black sailors' seamanship—and of limited integration. Only five other patrol craft with similar arrangements were added to the fleet during the war. However, black seamen were assigned to fleet auxiliary (nonwarship) vessels, under guidelines stipulating that not more than 10 percent of the crew could be black. Meanwhile, black women were belatedly admitted to the WAVES, which WAVES director Captain Mildred H. McAfee had been recommending for two years. McAfee also successfully petitioned Secretary of the Navy James Forrestal for a ruling that black WAVES receive equal treatment.

Segregation also affected other people of color, as a result of rulings by local draft boards: some Choctaw Indians in Texas and Rappahannocks in Virginia were assigned to segregated units based on the darkness of the individuals' skin. In 1942 three Rappahannocks filed suit to serve in a nonsegregated unit. They lost their case, *Branham* v. *Langley et al.*—and were sentenced to six months in prison. Many Japanese Americans—whose families were often in internment camps—also served in special units. One of these, the 442nd Regimental Combat Team, became the most decorated American unit of its size in World War II.

U.S. ARMED FORCES AND THEIR TOP COMMANDERS

PRESIDENT/COMMANDER IN CHIEF. (See also Chapter 2.)

FRANKLIN DELANO ROOSEVELT (MARCH 1933–APRIL 1945). Franklin Roosevelt's closest involvement with the military before becoming commander in chief was as assistant secretary of the navy (March 1913–August 1920). In 1918, near the end of World War I, he toured the Western Front, visiting troops, witnessing an aerial dogfight and an artillery barrage, and observing the gruesome aftermath of combat. Denied a naval commission by President Wilson shortly thereafter, Roosevelt went on to battle polio, political opponents, and the effects of the Great Depression before becoming a "hands-on" commander in chief during the greatest conflict in history. As president, he maintained a dedication to peace that reflected the prevailing sentiment of the American people—until that sentiment sharply changed with the Japanese attack on Pearl Harbor in December 1941. However, after the German-engineered *Anschluss* (takeover of Austria) in 1938, he also took what measures he could to prepare the long-neglected U.S. armed forces for their increasingly probable involvement in a major war. By the end of 1940, Selective Service had been enacted and all the services were growing. Yet they were far from battle-ready, and Commander in Chief Roosevelt did not want the army "committed to any aggressive action," Army Chief of Staff George Marshall noted in January 1941, "until it was fully prepared to undertake it." Meanwhile, Roosevelt reorganized the top command so that the army and navy chiefs reported directly to him, rather than going through the armed service secretaries; coaxed increased military appropriations and other defense measures out of a reluctant Congress; and continued to cultivate a special relationship with Britain. Over the objections of his service chiefs (who also needed equipment), he maintained shipments of planes and other war material to Britain and other Allies while providing increased protection to convoys delivering those goods—still hoping that this method of fighting the Axis would keep the United States out of a shooting war.

After Pearl Harbor, Roosevelt worked closely with the newly organized Joint Chiefs of Staff (JCS), bombarding his top commanders with questions on everything from grand strategy and weapons systems to personnel assignments and outpost defenses. He listened carefully to their counsel, read their proposals closely, and gradually gave them wide latitude in prosecuting the war. Yet there was no question who was commander in chief. Roosevelt overruled his top commanders when broader considerations made that action seem necessary. In 1942, for instance, he chose North Africa for the first Allied offensive over the strenuous objections of General George Marshall. "My impression was that Roosevelt had no lack of respect for the training, judgment, and advice of his generals and his admirals on the special subjects that were within their technical competence," presidential adviser Robert H. Jackson observed. "But . . . as commander-in-chief he was more apt than most presidents to assert his personal authority over the military, naval, and air authorities." He also asserted his authority within the Grand Alliance. Determined that Washington be the center of Allied strategy formation, he insisted in 1941 that the U.S./U.K. Combined Chiefs of Staff Committee be headquartered there. After what presidential adviser Harry Hopkins described as "a hell of a row" with the British, the president got his way.

Roosevelt's personal war headquarters was the Map Room on the ground floor of the White House, inspired by a similar room in Winston Churchill's underground headquarters in London. Crammed with intelligence reports, plans, and presidential communications with other Allied leaders, the White House Map Room was off-limits to all but a few staff members and officials. When the president was away from this nerve center, he received regular briefings from his military aides. When he attended the several Allied military/political conferences held during the war (see chart of "Major Inter-Allied Conferences, 1941–1945" in Chapter 2), the Joint Chiefs of Staff were always with him. For years a tireless and inspiring leader—especially early in the war, when the Allies were on the defensive—Roosevelt's health began to fail under the multiple pressures of war and domestic politics. When he suddenly died in April 1945, victory was in sight, but only one of the three major Axis nations, Italy, had surrendered.

HARRY S. TRUMAN (APRIL 1945–JANUARY 1953). An experienced politician and a World War I veteran (he was an artillery officer in France), Truman faced the daunting challenge of replacing an iconic figure who had been commander in chief for twelve years. He was a relative unknown to many of his troops and did not inspire immediate confidence in some of his field commanders, such as the acerbic General George Patton (who said, "It seems very unfortunate that in order to secure political preference, people are made Vice President who are never intended, neither by Party nor by the Lord to be Presidents"). Most who knew Truman better had a much higher opinion of him. Reassuring the Allies that Roosevelt's war policies would continue, Truman announced in his first speech that the United States would continue to insist on unconditional surrender by Germany and Japan. Apprised of the existence of the atomic-bomb project (see Chapters 2 and 5), he did not interfere with the weapon's final development. His most controversial decision as wartime commander in chief was allowing its use against Japan.

> **Secretary of War:** Harry H. Woodring (September 1936–June 1940); Henry L. Stimson (July 1940–September 1945)
>
> **Secretary of the Navy:** Claude A. Swanson (March 1933–July 1939); Charles Edison (January–June, 1940); William Franklin (Frank) Knox (July 1940–April 1944); James V. Forrestal (May 1944–September 1947)

JOINT BOARD (JB). Established in 1903, the JB was an advisory body that considered all matters requiring coordination between the army and navy. It comprised six members: the Army Chief of Staff, the Chief of Naval Operations, their deputies, and the chiefs of the services' War Plans Divisions. The JB reported to the secretaries of war and the navy until 1939, when President Roosevelt made it a part of the newly created Executive

Office of the President. In February 1942, though not officially abolished, it was replaced by the Joint Chiefs of Staff. An important offshoot was the *Joint Planning Committee*, a working group that conducted research and made recommendations regarding joint Army-Navy actions.

JOINT CHIEFS OF STAFF (JCS). An ad hoc group created after Pearl Harbor as a parallel body to the British Chiefs of Staff Committee (together the two formed the *Combined Chiefs of Staff*), the JCS existed solely at the president's discretion. (The current Joint Chiefs of Staff was formally established under the National Security Act of 1947.) JCS members served as the chief military advisers to President Roosevelt, and JCS was the primary coordinating body within the U.S. military. With its auxiliary committees (including the Joint Planning Committee), it devised U.S. operational strategy. With the president, and reporting directly to him rather than through the armed forces secretaries, the JCS gradually took the lead in developing overall Allied strategy. In the process, it plunged into issues of foreign policy, previously the exclusive domain of the State Department and other civilian government agencies. (The closer military involvement in foreign policy was to continue after the war.) In contrast to the similar coordinating bodies of the Axis armed forces, and in marked similarity to the British Chiefs of Staff Committee, the JCS proved exceptionally effective in all its duties—despite multiple problems. These included sometimes bitter interservice disagreements over strategic decisions, allocation of resources, and other matters, and even more intense disagreements with the British on similar issues. Early in the war, the British high command, seemingly better prepared, prevailed in most such debates. Nowhere was this more evident than at the January 1943 Allied conference at Casablanca. There the British were accompanied by HMS *Bulolo*, which historian Stephen Ambrose described as a "floating file cabinet . . . complete with technical details on all possible aspects of any proposed operation." The Americans had no such backup. "We came, we listened, and we were conquered," conference participant Major General Albert C. Wedemeyer later wrote. In fact, the parties compromised; but the compromise—involving extensive commitments to the Mediterranean Theater—was far from General George Marshall's liking. By the time of the Allied conference at Cairo that fall, the JCS was much better prepared; and the Americans, with their seemingly inexhaustible supplies of men, resources, and ideas of how best to use them had become the senior partner in the Grand Alliance.

MEMBERS OF THE JOINT CHIEFS OF STAFF, 1942–1945

Name/Dates	Description
Lieutenant General Henry ("Hap") Arnold (1886–1950), commander, U.S. Army Air Force; on JCS 1942–1945	"My recognition of the growing importance of air power," President Roosevelt wrote in 1943, "is made obvious by the fact that the Commanding General of the Army Air Forces is a member of both the Joint and Combined Chiefs of Staff." Father of the postwar independent U.S. Air Force (est. 1947), Arnold brought tremendous drive and experience (the Wright brothers were his flying instructors) and a strong and persuasive voice to JCS deliberations. His presence on JCS marked the emergence of the AAF as a semiautonomous U.S. armed service.
Admiral Ernest J. King (1878–1956), chief of naval operations, commander in chief, U.S. Fleet; on JCS March 1942–1945	"He is the most even tempered man in the Navy," Admiral King's daughter once said. "He is always in a rage." Irascible and strong-minded, King could also be pragmatic and straightforward. (He had no love for the press, but held 15 candid wartime briefings with selected editors/reporters, relying on their discretion.) After King replaced Harold Stark as the navy chief on the JCS, the president developed profound respect for the admiral's judgment and characterized King as one of his "shrewdest" strategists.
Chairman: Admiral William D. Leahy (1875–1959); on JCS 1942–1945	A friend of the president since World War I and a former chief of naval operations, Leahy served as Roosevelt's own chief of staff as well as JCS chairman. Through the most difficult days of the war, Leahy saw the president almost daily. Well-organized and tactful, he was an excellent moderator among the strong JCS personalities and between JCS and the president.

(continued)

MEMBERS OF THE JOINT CHIEFS OF STAFF, 1942–1945 (CONTINUED)

Name/Dates	Description
General of the Army George C. Marshall (1880–1959), chief of staff, U.S. Army; on JCS 1942–1945	A man of utmost integrity, Marshall had superior judgment regarding the potential of subordinates and displayed both tact and forthright persistence as army chief of staff in achieving and maintaining a war-ready army. He demonstrated the same qualities in the sometimes heated debates within the JCS and between the U.S. high command and its Allies—in the process winning and holding the respect of everyone with whom he dealt. (Winston Churchill called him "the noblest Roman of them all.") Roosevelt may have chosen Dwight Eisenhower rather than Marshall to command the 1944 Allied landings in France because he did not want to break up the very effective JCS team; but it was also because, as he told Marshall, "I didn't feel I could sleep at ease with you out of Washington."
Admiral Harold R. Stark (1880–1972); chief of naval operations (August 1939–March 1942); on JCS February–March 1942	Characterized by naval historian Samuel Eliot Morison as "Gentle in manner and unobtrusive in personality," Stark could also be blunt. "If you attack us," he said to Japanese ambassador Kichisaburo Nomura, "we will break your empire before we are through with you." As prewar chief of naval operations, Stark prepared in 1940 the memo that came to be known as "Plan Dog." (A singularly important document in the formation of U.S. wartime strategy, it linked U.S. security to the balance of power in Europe and, particularly to the survival of Britain, advocating the "defeat Germany first" policy that the United States adopted.) Replaced by King on the JCS shortly after its formation, Stark assumed command of U.S. naval forces in Europe.

Principal sources: Eric Larrabee, *Commander in Chief: Franklin Delano Roosevelt, His Lieutenants, and Their War*, New York: Harper & Row, 1987; I. C. B. Dear and M. R. D. Foot, eds., *Oxford Companion to World War II*, Oxford: Oxford University Press, 2001.

UNITED STATES ARMY

Chief of Staff: General of the Army George C. Marshall (1939–1945)

Force Size (at Peak): 8.5 million

Theaters of Operation: American; European; Mediterranean; Pacific; China-Burma-India

Casualties: 936,259, including 307,764 dead and missing (includes both Army and Army Air Force)

"These days the entire nation is following operations on its war maps," Lieutenant General Lesley McNair, commander of Army Ground Forces, said in 1943. "It is to be noted that the front lines of these maps are simply where the infantryman is. It is true that he is supported magnificently by artillery and air, but this support is behind and above him. There is nothing in front of him but the enemy." That year, the U.S. Army, nearing its apex of 8.5 million men, was active in all major theaters of operation. Only three years earlier, it had numbered just 257,000 men and 14,000 officers—augmented by the 242,000 men and 15,000 officers of the National Guard and a reservoir of 104,228 trained officers in the Organized Reserve Corps. Its few divisions were understrength and insufficently trained and equipped. In September 1940, Congress passed the Selective Service Act, a major step in transforming this inadequate force—with breathtaking speed that generated multiple problems—into an army capable of waging a multifront war. Plagued by shortages in housing and equipment, the Army also suffered from failures within its administrative structure, which proved incapable of coping with the service's explosive growth. A *General Headquarters* (GHQ) established in July 1940 as the central control for army expansion was abolished in March 1942 during a reorganization that established three major army components: Ground Forces, Air Forces, and Service Forces. This restructuring considerably eased the process of expansion. Yet even as new troops were being inducted and trained, top commanders debated many questions. Among the most vexing was how many combat divisions would be needed. Initial estimates, made under the assumption that the USSR would be conquered or would make a separate peace with the Germans, placed the number at 213 (nearly 3.2 million front-line ground troops, backed up by support troops and a vast array of equipment). Yet the other armed services also had manpower needs, and fulfilling manpower requirements for home-front production was equally important. As Soviet armies continued to tie down 60 percent of the German army, estimates of the number of divisions required were gradually lowered. In May 1944, a combat-force strength of 90 divisions became the official target—a decision that came to be known as "the 90-division gamble." (In actuality, it was an 89-division gamble, once the 2nd Cavalry Division was deactivated in North Africa.) Although U.S. commanders suffered some tense moments during the German breakthrough in the Ardennes Forest (December 1944–January 1945), when all remaining combat-ready divisions were dispatched from the United States to Europe, 89 divisions proved to be adequate.

During the war, these combat divisions were organized and reorganized into various armies as noted in the United States Armies in World War II chart.

UNITED STATES ARMIES IN WORLD WAR II

Army Designation	Commanding Officers	Dates of Command
European Theater		
First Army	Lieutenant General George Grunert	October 1943–March 1944
	General Omar N. Bradley	March 1944–August 1944
	General Courtney Hodges	August 1944–May 1945
Third Army	Lieutenant General Courtney Hodges	February 1943–March 1944
	General George S. Patton	March 1944–May 1945
Fifth Army	Lieutenant General Mark W. Clark	January 1944–December 1944
	Lieutenant General Lucian K. Truscott	December 1944–May 1945
Seventh Army	Lieutenant General George S. Patton	July 1943–January 1944
	Lieutenant General Mark W. Clark	January 1944–February 28, 1944
	Lieutenant General Alexander M. Patch	March 1944–May 1945
Ninth Army	Lieutenant General William H. Simpson	May 1944–May 1945
Fifteenth Army	Major General Ray E. Porter	January 1945
	Lieutenant General Leonard T. Gerow	January–May 1945
Pacific Theater		
Sixth Army	General Walter E. Krueger	February 1943–September 1945
Eighth Army	Lieutenant General Robert L Eichelberger	September 1944–September 1945
Tenth Army	Lieutenant General Simon B. Buckner*	June 1944–June 1945
	General Joseph W. Stilwell	June–September 1945

Principal source: Norman Polmar and Thomas B. Allen, *World War II: The Encyclopedia of the War Years, 1941–1945*, New York: Random House, 1996.
* Killed in action, June 18, 1945.

UNITED STATES ARMY AIR FORCES (USAAF OR AAF; WAS U.S. ARMY AIR CORPS, 1926–JUNE 1941). (See also "Aircraft" in Chapter 5.)

Assistant Secretary of War for Air: Robert A. Lovett (1941–1945)

Commanding General, USAAF: Lieutenant General Henry "Hap" Arnold (1941–1946)

With war raging in China and the increasingly powerful Luftwaffe supporting German aggression in Europe, President Roosevelt convened a secret meeting at the White House on November 14, 1938, at which he called for a tenfold expansion of Army Air Corps strength to 20,000 planes—a wildly optimistic goal, given prevailing circumstances. Yet the meeting did mark the beginning of a stunning air force expansion that was supported not only by the president (a belated convert to air force capabilities) but also by Army chief of staff Marshall and, after 1941, by Robert A. Lovett, the extraordinarily effective assistant secretary of war for air. Lovett helped establish and maintain a superb relationship with civilian aircraft manufacturers and with scientists and engineers who developed new equipment as the AAF grew exponentially: the number of planes rose from 2,546 in 1939 to 72,726 in 1944; personnel increased from 20,126 in 1938 (11 percent of total army strength) to 2,372,293 in 1944 (31 percent). Businessmen also helped war planners establish uniform methods to evaluate the effectiveness of air operations more accurately. Meanwhile, the AAF developed new training programs to accommodate its exploding requirements for aircrews and support personnel. (From 1922 to 1940, the AAF had trained fewer than 2,900 pilots; from July 1941 to December 1942 it trained more than 29,000.) The growing air service also required several reorganizations to maintain maximum effectiveness—although AAF organization at all levels remained flexible and variable. The key AAF unit was the *group* (usually combining several *squadrons* and roughly analogous to a ground-force regiment; at peak there were more than two hundred AAF groups; see "Basic Force Structure" chart, earlier in this chapter). Broad functional *commands* were established to coordinate particular activities (e.g., training, air material). One of the AAF's most spectacular achievements was the development of its *Air Transport Command*, an unprecedented worldwide global transport system for both men and matériel that evolved, with the help of civilian airlines, to become a mainstay of Allied logistics—and a larger operation than all commercial U.S. airlines combined. The USAAF was active in all theaters of war, engaging in strategic

UNITED STATES ARMY AIR FORCES

Air Force Designation	Commanding Officers	Dates of Command
Europe		
Eighth Air Force	Major General Ira C. Eaker	February–December 1942
	Brigadier General Newton Longfellow	December 1942–July 1943
	Major General Frank L. Andrews	July 1943–January 1944
	Lieutenant General James H. Doolittle	January 1944–May 1945
Ninth Air Force	Brigadier General Junius W. Jones	September 1941–November 1942
	Lieutenant General Lewis H. Brereton	November 1942–August 1944
	Lieutenant General Hoyt S. Vandenberg	August 1944–May 1945
Twelfth Air Force	Major General James H. Doolittle	September 1942–March 1943
	Lieutenant General Carl Spaatz	March 1943–December 1943
	Lieutenant General John K. Cannon	December 1943–April 1945
	Major General B. W. Chidlaw	April 1945–May 1945
	Brigadier General Charles T. Myers	May 1945–August 1945
Fifteenth Air Force	Major General James H. Doolittle	November 1943–January 1944
	Major General Nathan F. Twining	January 1944–May 1945
Pacific		
Fifth Air Force	Major General Lewis H. Brereton	October 1941–February 1942
	Lieutenant General George H. Brett	February 1942–September 1942
	Lieutenant General George C. Kenney	September 1942–June 1944
	Lieutenant General Ennis C. Whithead	June 1944–September 1945
Seventh Air Force	Major General Frederick L. Martin	November 1940–December 1941
	Major General Clarence L. Tinker	December 1941–June 1942
	Brigadier General Howard C. Davidson	June 1942
	Major General Willis H. Hale	June 1942–April 1944
	Major General Robert W. Douglass	April 1944–June 1945
	Major General Thomas D. White	June 1945–October 1946
Eleventh Air Force	Lieutenant Colonel Everett S. Davis	January 1942
	Colonel Lionel H. Dunlap	February 1942–March 1942
	Major General William O. Butler	March 1942–September 1943
	Major General Davenport Johnson	September 1943–May 1945
	Brigadier General Isaiah Davies	May 1945–June 1945
	Major General John B. Brooks	June 1945–September 1945

UNITED STATES ARMY AIR FORCES (CONTINUED)

Air Force Designation	Commanding Officers	Dates of Command
Thirteenth Air Force	Major General Nathan F. Twining	January–July 1943
	Brigadier General Ray L. Owens	July 1943–January 1944
	Major General Hubert R. Harmon	January–June 1944
	Major General St. Clair Strett	June 1944–February 1945
	Major General Paul B. Wurtsmith	February 1945–September 1945
Twentieth Air Force	General H. H. Arnold	April 1944–July 1945
	Major General Curtis LeMay	July 1945
	Lieutenant General Nathan F. Twining	August–September 1945
China-Burma-India		
Tenth Air Force	Colonel Harry A. Halverson	February–March 1942
	Major General Lewis H. Brereton	March–June 1942
	Brigadier General Earl L. Naiden	June–August 1942
	Major General Clayton L. Bissel	August 1942–August 1943
	Major General Howard C. Davidson	August 1943–August 1945
	Major General A. F. Hegenberge	August–September 1945
Fourteenth Air Force (included the former American Volunteer Group, better known as the "Flying Tigers")*	Major General Claire L. Chennault	March 1943–August 1945
	Major General Charles B. Stone III	August–September 1945
Caribbean		
Sixth Air Force	Major General Davenport Johnson	September 1941–November 1942
	Major General Hubert R. Harmon	November 1942–November 1943
	Brigadier General Ralph H. Wooten	November 1943–May 1944
	Brigadier General Edgar P. Sorenson	May–September 1944
	Major General William O. Butler	September 1944–July 1945

Principal sources: Norman Polmar and Thomas B. Allen, *World War II: The Encyclopedia of the War Years, 1941–1945*, New York: Random House, 1996; Wesley Frank Craven and James Lea Cate, *The Army Air Forces in World War II*, Vol. 6, *Men and Planes*, Washington, D.C.: Office of Air Force History, U.S. Government Printing Office, 1983.

Note: The First, Second, Third, and Fourth Air Forces were based in the Zone of the Interior (continental U.S.), where they were responsible for homeland defense (the particular responsibility of the First and Fourth) and training airmen for deployment overseas (Second and Third).

*Included a composite wing comprising both U.S. and Chinese pilots.

THE PIONEERS OF "FORT ROACH"

In March 1942, USAAF commander General Hap Arnold gave film producer Jack Warner and Warner Brothers screenwriter Owen Crump military commissions and ordered them to organize the *First Motion Picture Unit* (FMPU) of the USAAF—the first time that a military unit was formed comprising only motion picture professionals. Based at "Fort Roach" (the Hal Roach Studios in Culver City, California), the FMPU eventually included some 1,110 studio personnel, directors, producers, screenwriters, and actors (including Captain Ronald Reagan)—all of whom had been through army basic training. Besides making more than four hundred films (the first, *Winning Your Wings*, is credited with drawing 150,000 new enlistments), the FMPU trained combat camera crews that routinely went on bombing missions—and suffered many casualties. FMPU personnel also secretly created a huge miniature of the main island of Japan, exactly to scale, then filmed the model as if from an airplane. The film was shown to B-29 crewmen to prepare them for their bombing campaigns.

bombing, fighter escort of bombers and tactical support of ground units, rescue, and reconnaissance, as well as worldwide air transport.

UNITED STATES ARMY GROUND FORCES (AGF)

Commanding General, AGF: Lieutenant General Lesley J. McNair (1940–1944)

Established in March 1942, the AGF was responsible, according to a 1942 War Department circular, for making "ground force units properly organized, trained and equipped for combat operations." With jurisdiction over all ground combat soldiers (in the infantry, cavalry, armor, and artillery) from induction until they embarked for fighting overseas, it became, in 1942–1943, the largest single command in the Army, as the United States prepared to field more than ten times the number of combat divisions it had before the war. (Each new division—comprising, on average, 15,000 men—was built from volunteers and draftees around an experienced "cadre" of 185 officers and 1,190 enlisted men; each division required a full year to be adequately prepared for combat.) In developing this largest single training organization in American history, McNair and his staff had to balance the growing need for specialized training, such as paratroops and armor, with the

A Gold-Star Family. The much-respected AGF commander, Lieutenant General Lesley McNair (standing left), with his wife, Clare Huster McNair (right), their only son, Colonel Douglas McNair, the colonel's wife, and their infant daughter, Bonny Clare McNair. A general who preferred the field over his desk in Washington, Lesley McNair was wounded while observing operations in North Africa in 1943. One year later, he was among those killed when American bombers dropped their loads too close to U.S. lines near Saint-Lô, France—the first three-star general in American history to be killed in combat. Answering one of many letters of condolence, Clare McNair wrote of her husband, "He never asked a soldier to do what he would not do." Twelve days after the general's death, his son was killed by Japanese gunfire on Guam.

continuing need to form complex and flexible fighting forces that could operate as a single integrated entity. The solution was *progressive* training: each individual learned the fundamentals of soldiering, then underwent small-unit training and combined arms training before finally practicing large-scale maneuvers involving armies and corps. Training had to be adapted to new weapons and tactics as well as lessons learned on the battlefield. (AGF observers were often at the front, taking notes.) McNair placed particular emphasis on effective leadership. "Your knowledge and personal example must inspire as well as teach your men," he told one graduating class of young officers. "I have seen too often in this emergency the two infallible signs of utter lack of leadership: reading from the book, and turning things over to the sergeant while the officer tries to look important." But, if the officer does his job: "The Army's peerless soldiers will follow you, believe in you, trust in you, need you, and fight for you."

United States Army Service Forces (ASF)

Commanding General, ASF: Lieutenant General Brehon Somervell (1942–1946)

Adopting the motto "The impossible we do at once; the miraculous may take a little longer," the ASF comprised many components that provided the massive administrative and logistical support needed by a huge army fighting a global war—while funneling massive amounts of Lend-Lease material to the Allies. Descriptions of major ASF support components are included in the U.S. Army Service Forces (ASF) chart.

UNITED STATES ARMY SERVICE FORCES (ASF)

Major Logistical-Support Components

Component	Description
Administrative Services	Included Personnel, the Fiscal Division, and the Adjutant General's Office, which kept records, issued casualty notifications to next of kin, and administered the Army Postal Service. Also the offices of the Provost Marshal General (included military police) and Judge Advocate General; and the Women's Army Auxiliary Corps (WAACs). Provided/supervised training in all ASF specialized areas noted on this chart.

UNITED STATES ARMY SERVICE FORCES (ASF) (CONTINUED)

Component	Description
Army Medical Department	At peak comprised 47,000 physicians, 15,000 dentists, 57,000 nurses, 2,171 veterinarians, and more than 600,000 technicians, aid men, and other specialists (such as the more than 2,600 dietitians and physical and occupational therapists of the Women's Medical Specialist Corps). Cared for a wartime total of 15 million patients in 1,200 separate hospital units around the world. Established "chains of evacuation" suited to each area of operation. Saved approximately 96 out of every 100 wounded who reached Army hospitals, and 994 of every 1,000 suffering from disease. Gradually developed an elaborate system of rehabilitation for patients with neuropsychiatric disorders ("combat fatigue"), which affected 18.7 percent of all U.S. Army patients evacuated to the United States in 1942–1945.
Chemical Warfare Service (CWS)	Comprising 69,791 military personnel and nearly 30,000 civilians, the CWS prepared to defend against and respond to poison gas attacks; conducted civilian defense training; and developed smoke-screen devices and incendiary weapons.
Corps of Chaplains	In addition to distributing more than 10 million religious books and documents, the Corps of Chaplains trained and deployed more than 8,000 chaplains of all faiths to assist Army servicemen and women with counseling and spiritual guidance. Like their counterparts (chaplains and morale officers) in the services of most major combatants, Army chaplains were on, not just behind the front lines.
Corps of Engineers	Expanding from a prewar force of 11,000 officers and men to just under 700,000, the Corps of Engineers constructed and maintained housing, hospital, and training facilities; constructed air bases and landing fields (241 in post-D-Day

(continued)

UNITED STATES ARMY SERVICE FORCES (ASF) (CONTINUED)

Component	Description
	Europe alone); constructed, repaired, or extended railroads and highways; reproduced and distributed maps; removed mines and other obstacles to Allied troop movements; constructed obstacles or destroyed structures to impede enemy movements; laid, disarmed, and recovered mines; constructed and maintained pipelines (including a 2,000-mile pipeline from the Indian Ocean to Kunming, China, that was the longest of its type in the world); supplied water for all troops; and rehabilitated public utilities.
Ordnance Department (OD)	Responsible for designing, developing, procuring, storing, issuing, and maintaining the guns, ammunition, and (from August 1942) certain transport vehicles (including tanks) used by the Army (and provided some supplies to the Navy, Marine Corps, and 43 Allied nations). Because vehicles required tires, OD also supervised the development of a U.S. synthetic rubber industry. OD maintenance/repair personnel operating near the front lines were sometimes swept into combat.
Quartermaster Corps (QM)	Expanding from a prewar force of 11,267 to a peak of 502,265 in 1944, the QM was responsible for feeding, clothing, and equipping the Army (and in the process developed new foods, materials, and packaging). QM troops near the front lines often engaged in combat. In addition to procuring and distributing millions of tons of supplies, QM trained war dogs (K-9 Corps) and provided more than 70 services, such as portable bakeries and laundries, salvage, shoe testing and repair, and lost-and-found depots. QM troops' most somber duties were to bury and record the burial places of the dead and maintain military cemeteries.
Signal Corps	Responsible for communication, the Signal Corps expanded from 6,543 officers and men to 531,105. Supplied the entire army with more than 100,000 signal items; established an

UNITED STATES ARMY SERVICE FORCES (ASF) (CONTINUED)

Component	Description
	800,000-mile global wartime radio and wire net; took still pictures and movies of front-line action in all theaters; made and distributed training films; distributed and trained projectionists for entertainment films supplied by Hollywood; trained and maintained carrier pigeons; assisted in the development of radio, radar, and other technologies; and photographed V-mail (letters transferred to film overseas, then printed out on lightweight photo paper for delivery at home).
Special Services	Originally named the Entertainment Branch, Special Services coordinated its activities with a similar unit in the Navy. It provided recreational equipment, showed films, held dances and bingo games, published games and quizzes, and distributed guides to help soldiers and sailors stage their own shows. It also coordinated with USO–Camp Show, Inc. to provide troops with live entertainment; established the Armed Forces Radio Service; and supported publications ranging from the weekly army-wide publication *Yank* to camp and unit newspapers.
Transportation Corps	Responsible for transporting Army men and matériel. Operated railroads at home and overseas. Also operated 1,706 oceangoing vessels and 12,466 smaller boats. Designed (and occasionally built) special railroad cars such as troop sleepers and hospital ward cars; procured, stored, and assigned all types of transportation equipment. Moved 324,891,000 short tons of freight and 33,678,000 passengers.

Principal sources: Unsung Heroes! Your Service Forces in Action, New York: William H. Wise, 1949; John D. Millet, *United States Army in World War II: The Organization and Role of the Army Service Forces*, Washington, DC: Office of the Chief of Military History, Department of the Army, 1954.

UNITED STATES NAVY. (See also "Naval Vessels and Weaponry" in Chapter 5.)

Chief of Naval Operations (CNO): Admiral Harold R. Stark (1939–March 1942)

Chief of Naval Operations/Commander in Chief U.S. Fleet (COMINCH): Admiral Ernest J. King (December 1941, COMINCH/March 1942, CNO)

Deputy Chief of Naval Operations (Air) (Position Created August 1943): Rear Admiral John S. McCain (August 1943–August 1944); Vice-Admiral Aubrey W. Fitch (August 1944–August 1945); Vice-Admiral Mark A. Mitscher (August 1945–January 1946)

Force Size (1945): 4,031,097 (including 484,000 Marines, 170,000 Coast Guard, and 93,000 WAVES)

Theaters of Operation: European, Pacific, Mediterranean, American, China-Burma-India

Casualties: 150,854 (includes Marines and Coast Guard; 65,133 combat deaths; 80,301 wounded; 5,495 POWs—1,369 of whom died in captivity)

In 1940, the Coast Guard and the Navy (including the Marines) together numbered 203,127—less than half the number on active duty at the end of World War I. That same year, the navy listed 1,099 vessels of all types, including 343 major warships (17 battleships, 7 aircraft carriers, 37 cruisers, 171 destroyers, and 111 submarines), and 1,709 aircraft. A number of the vessels and aircraft were nearing obsolescence. Although the navy had fared somewhat better than the army during the interwar cutbacks, it, too, had been pinched for resources. Various congressional appropriations—and President Roosevelt's direction of some general relief funds to naval construction—chiefly went to replace old vessels and planes. Little was done, however, to significantly reinforce and improve the navy until July 1940, when the Vinson-Walsh Act (the Two-Ocean Navy Act) authorized a whopping 70 percent naval expansion. This launched what Admiral Ernest J. King characterized as "the largest single building program ever undertaken by the United States or any other country." When the war ended just over five years later, the U.S. Navy listed 50,759 vessels (including 1,171 major warships) and 40,392 planes—a force more powerful than all other navies combined. Volunteers initially met the manpower needs for this vastly expanded force, but later the Navy accepted draftees. Both the Navy and Marines also drew officers from the *V-12 Navy College Training Program.* Begun in 1943 and eventually active at 131 American colleges and universities, it provided officer candidates (including some enlisted men recommended by their commanding officers) with academic and physical training. Most graduates then received further training at Navy or Marine facilities before being commissioned as ensigns or second lieutenants.

The expanding wartime navy was required to fight two types of war, as described by Admiral King in a 1946 report: "The war in Europe was primarily a ground and air war with naval support, while the war in the Pacific was primarily a naval war with ground and air support." Convoy escort across the Atlantic, coastal patrols (by both seacraft and aircraft, including Navy blimps), and the extended battle against German U-boats were all part of the Navy's European war. In cooperation with other Allies, the Navy also mounted large-scale amphibious operations in North Africa, Sicily, Italy, and France that were supported by naval gunfire, the effect of which was "so immense," General Erwin Rommel reported to Hitler after D-Day, "that no operation of any kind is possible in the area commanded by this rapid-fire [naval] artillery, by either infantry or tanks." Specially trained Navy teams ferried U.S. Army detachments across the Rhine River at several points during the heavily contested operations of March 1945, and the Navy also operated ports in England and liberated Europe, and at Bremen and Bremerhaven in American-occupied Germany.

In the Pacific Theater, supported by complex *fleet trains* (supply and repair vessels and facilities) that allowed warships to remain at sea for months, the Navy transported, landed, and supported Marine and army units in a series of amphibious operations. U.S. submarines made increasingly effective attacks on Japanese warships and wrought near-complete havoc on the merchant shipping that was Japan's lifeline (at high cost to American submariners: 3,406 killed, or 22 percent of the 16,000 men who made war patrols). Japan also lost control of the skies to U.S. land- and carrier-based Navy and Marine pilots flying top-of-the-line fighters and dive-bombers. The key to this naval success, Admiral King reported, was "a highly flexible and well balanced fleet, in which ships, planes, amphibious forces and service forces in due proportion were available for unified action whenever and wherever called upon."

UNITED STATES NAVY ORGANIZATION, 1941–1945

Fleet	*Description*
Major fleets	In 1941, there were three main fleets—the Asiatic, Atlantic, and Pacific. The Atlantic and Pacific existed throughout the war. The Asiatic Fleet was abolished on February 4, 1942, after its base of operations, the Philippine Islands, fell to the Japanese.
Numbered fleets	The United States established several numbered fleets during the war: In the Pacific, the *Third Fleet* shared naval forces with the *Fifth Fleet* (while the Third Fleet commander and his staff were ashore to plan future operations, another commander and his staff would take operational command, and its designation would change to Fifth Fleet); the III Marine Amphibious Corps was assigned to the Third Fleet, the V Marine Amphibious Corps to the Fifth Fleet.
	The *Fourth Fleet* was known as the U.S. South Atlantic Force.
	The *Seventh Fleet*, or "MacArthur's Navy," supported General Douglas MacArthur's operations in the Southwest Pacific.
	The *Eighth Fleet* was established in 1943 to support Mediterranean Theater amphibious operations.
	The *Tenth Fleet*, established May 20, 1943, was an administrative body or "fleet without ships" that coordinated antisubmarine warfare.
	The *Twelfth Fleet*, based in London, comprised U.S. Naval Forces in Europe.
Task Forces	In March 1941, the navy reorganized the Atlantic Fleet into ten task forces: TF1, Ocean Escort Force; TF2, Striking Force; TF3, Scouting Force; TF4, Support Force; TF5, Submarine Force; TF6, Naval Coastal Frontier Forces; TF7, Bermuda Force; TF8, Patrol Wings; TF9, Service Force; and TF10, First Marine Division (commanded by a brigadier general). In June 1941, the U.S. Pacific Fleet began organizing into task forces, establishing No. 1, Covering Force; No. 2, Reconnoitering and Raiding Force; and No. 3, Amphibious Force. More followed throughout the war, including some that were not composed exclusively of ships but were more complex entities devoted to particular activities. (Pacific Fleet, Task Force 4, for example, comprised the island bases in the 14th Naval District, organized for self-defense and for support of fleet units on advanced operations.)

Principal source: Julius A. Furer, *Administration of the Navy Department in World War II*, Washington, DC: U.S. Government Printing Office, 1959.

A band of 2,500 Navy men was the only American unit in China's armed forces. Led by Commander Milton E. Miles and Nationalist Chinese general and spymaster Tai Li, *Navy Group China*—or, the *Sino-American Cooperative Organization* (SACO, pronounced "socko")—manned weather stations, monitored the coast, and engaged in guerrilla warfare from 1943 through 1945.

Prominent U.S. military leaders included (left to right, top to bottom), Row 1: General Omar N. Bradley (Army), Lieutenant General Simon B. Buckner (Army), Lieutenant General Mark W. Clark (Army), Lieutenant General James H. Doolittle (USAAF), Major General Ira C. Eaker (USAAF); Row 2: Admiral William ("Bull") Halsey (USN), Colonel Oveta Culp Hobby (WAC), General Thomas Holcomb (USMC), General Douglas MacArthur (Army), Captain Mildred H. McAfee (USN); Row 3: Admiral John S. McCain, Sr. (USN), Fleet Admiral Chester W. Nimitz (USN), General George S. Patton (Army), Lieutenant General Brehon Somervell (Army), Lieutenant General Carl Spaatz (USAAF).

United States Marine Corps (USMC)

Commandant: General Thomas Holcomb (1936–1943); General Alexander Vandegrift (1944–1947)

Force Size (at Peak): 475,604

Theaters of Operation: Pacific, China-Burma-India (1945–1949); Iceland and Greenland (1941)

Casualties: 87,940 (19,733 dead, 68,207 wounded)

A separate service under the Department of the Navy, the venerable Marine Corps (established 1775) comprised 19,432 officers and men in 1939; in December 1941, it numbered 54,539; and by 1944, it included nearly half a million officers, men, and women of the Marine Corps Women's Reserve. Prewar Marine Corps leaders had developed U.S. amphibious warfare doctrine; during the war, Marines led the way in proving the doctrine's effectiveness in a host of bitterly contested operations from Guadalcanal through Saipan and Peleliu, to Iwo Jima and Okinawa. In these and other actions, Marines on the ground were supported by the 118,086 officers and men who constituted the four air wings of Marine Corps Aviation—often flying from hastily constructed or recently liberated airfields. Other Marines served aboard navy vessels or provided security at naval bases, both at home and overseas. In 1945, some Marines formed part of the U.S. force that occupied Japan. Others—including recent veterans of bloody Okinawa—were sent to China. There they disarmed defeated Japanese armies and helped maintain order in a war-ravaged country described by former Marine colonel Joseph A. Alexander as "a tinderbox of conflicting [Chinese] armed forces scraping against each other like giant tectonic plates." U.S. Marines remained in China until 1949.

United States Coast Guard

Commandant of the Coast Guard: Rear Admiral Russell R. Waesche (1936–1945)

Force Size (1944): 241,000 (includes 10,000 "SPARS," of the women's reserve)

Theaters of Operation: American, European, Pacific

Casualties: 1,918 dead, 640 in combat

The Coast Guard operated as part of the Navy between November 1941 and January 1946 (in peacetime it was under the Treasury Department). Manpower needs for the expanded wartime service (Coast Guard aviation, for example, tripled in size) were met by recruitment of volunteers, creation of the Coast Guard Reserve, and establishment of the Women's Reserve (SPARS) in 1942. In addition, some 50,000 volunteer officers and enlisted men of the Coast Guard's unique Temporary Reserve served without pay, generally as harbor pilots or on port or industrial security details. Using aircraft, boats, horse patrols, and sentry dogs, the Coast Guard kept watch on America's coasts and ports. Coast Guardsmen also improved navigation on inland waters—and conveyed landing craft to the seacoast from factories along the Mississippi River and the Great Lakes. They also piloted landing craft during amphibious operations in the Pacific, the Mediterranean, and the Atlantic and manned many other types of U.S. Navy ships as well as six hundred Coast Guard cutters, 3,000 small craft employed in escort service and harbor security duty, and more than two hundred U.S. Army cargo vessels. Coast Guardsmen excelled at search-and-rescue operations (during the 1944 Allied landing at Normandy, sixty Coast Guard patrol craft were assigned to rescue men from the water). The Coast Guard's roster of duties also included inspection of merchant vessels and safety instruction for merchant crews; survey and aerial mapping activity; cold-weather operations in Iceland and Greenland (where Coast Guard units helped locate German weather stations that were providing crucial information to U-boats); and air and seaborne antisubmarine patrols.

MERCHANT MARINE, THE UNITED STATES MARITIME SERVICE (USMS), AND THE NAVAL ARMED GUARD. A vital lifeline for the United States and its armed forces—as well as for primary Lend-Lease beneficiaries Great Britain and the Soviet Union—the U.S. Merchant Marine underwent a near-miraculous transformation from a prewar complement of 55,000 mariners manning a modest fleet that included many near-obsolescent ships to a service of more than 215,000 mariners and the world's largest merchant fleet. Under the guidance of the U.S. Maritime Commission (established in 1936), American shipbuilders constructed nearly 6,000 merchant vessels during the war. This was particularly remarkable given the simultaneous frenzy of warship construction. (See also Chapter 3.) The *U.S. Maritime Service (USMS)*, established in 1938, provided training for the tens of thousands of new merchant seamen and officers on topics such as navigation, engine operation and maintenance, and deck operations. (The USMS also trained members of the U.S. Army Transport Service who were to serve, along with 15,000 volunteer civilian seamen, aboard nearly 14,000 vessels—from troopships and tankers to tugs and patrol craft—that the army operated during the war.) In addition to enduring the rigors of convoy duty American merchant mariners braved enemy fire repeatedly bringing troops and equipment to and from invasion beaches from Guadalcanal to Normandy, Anzio to Okinawa; and they returned to those beaches time and again with more men and supplies to sustain operations. More than 9,000 merchant mariners were killed and 12,000 were wounded. In addition, more than 1,800 men of the *Naval Armed Guard* were killed, and many more were wounded as they manned the guns, operated the radios and radar equipment, and performed other protective services onboard 5,114 U.S. vessels and 1,122 foreign-owned merchant ships. The essential services rendered and bravery demonstrated by the 144,970 officers and men who served in the Naval Armed Guard during the war were little noted then and generally uncelebrated afterward.

ALLIED MILITARY COORDINATION (See Chapter 2 and "The Allies," earlier in this chapter.)

By any measure—but particularly in comparison with the Axis powers' tepid efforts at military cooperation—Allied military organizations were models of cooperative efficiency, despite frequent disagreements. Grand strategy flowed chiefly from a dozen major conferences of Allied political and military leaders (see chart of "Major Inter-Allied Conferences" in Chapter 2). All these meetings included the British and the Americans; Soviet leaders, whose armed forces were waging their own desperate war in relative isolation, attended three; representatives of the Free French were present at the Casablanca conference in January 1943; and a Chinese delegation led by Chiang Kai-shek attended the Cairo Conference later that year.

The *Combined Chiefs of Staff Committee (CCS)* implemented strategy decisions. Established in 1942 and headquartered in Washington, CCS comprised the U.S. Joint Chiefs of Staff (JCS) and the British *Joint Staff Mission*, which represented Britain's Chiefs of Staff Committee (COS) and kept in close touch with that body—at crucial times on an hourly basis. Chaired by JCS chairman Admiral William D. Leahy, the CCS met every week while in Washington, with additional meetings during the major Allied strategy conferences. It also oversaw a network of organizations: the Combined Staff Planners' Committee, the Combined Military Trans-

American and British chiefs of staff confer in the Anfa Hotel, Casablanca, Morocco, January 1943. To the left of the table, in the foreground, are U. S. Admiral Ernest King, General George C. Marshall, and USAAF commander Lieutenant General Henry ("Hap") Arnold (other officers are unidentified). To the right, from the foreground: Field Marshal Sir John Dill (head of the British Joint Staff Mission), Air Chief Marshal Sir Charles Portal, General Sir Alan Brooke, Admiral Sir Dudley Pound, Vice Admiral Lord Louis Mountbatten, and unidentified man.

portation Committee, the Combined Intelligence Committee, the Combined Munitions Assignment Board, the Combined Communications Board, the Combined Meteorological Committee, and the Combined Civil Affairs Committee.

In March 1942, during a Washington conference, President Roosevelt proposed to Prime Minister Churchill that, to simplify operations, the two major Allies divide the world into three areas, for each of which either the United States or Great Britain would assume primary command responsibility. This suggestion was refined in a study by General Dwight Eisenhower, then of the U.S. Army War Plans Division:

> *Pacific area* (including the Americas, China, Australia, New Zealand, and Japan, but excluding Sumatra and the Malay Peninsula)—U.S. responsibility;

Indian Ocean and Middle [and Near] East—British responsibility, but the United States would have access to bases in India and routes to China and would support the British with material aid;

Europe and the Atlantic—joint British-U.S. responsibility.

In general, this plan was adopted, but it was an elastic framework. For example, in Operation Torch, the November 1942 Allied invasion of North(west) Africa (an area of British responsibility), the bulk of the invading force was to be American. Thus the British asked for an American commander. General Eisenhower, who had recently been named commander of U.S. forces in the European theater, was chosen for the job in July. Commanding Torch, Eisenhower demonstrated the military and diplomatic skills that were to lead to his selection as Supreme Commander Allied Expeditionary Force before the 1944 Allied landings in France.

In May 1942, representatives of the United States and Britain signed the *Loper–Hotine Agreement* dividing responsibilities for making the millions of up-to-date maps that were essential to allied armed forces throughout the war.

WOMEN IN MILITARY SERVICE

This war, more than any other war in history, is a woman's war.

—*John G. Winant, U.S. ambassador in London*

Although women were traditionally regarded as insufficiently hardy and too precious a child-bearing resource to brave the hazards of military service, the scope of World War II led most major combatants to begin enlisting women, generally as volunteers. In December 1941, however, England became the first country to conscript women into military service with the passage of the National Service Act, which let the government draft single women between the ages of 20 and 30. Although most of the approximately 450,000 women in the British armed forces remained volunteers—chiefly in such all-female auxiliaries as the Auxiliary Territorial Services (ATS), the Women's Auxiliary Air Force (WAAF), and the Women's Royal Navy Service (WRNS)—some 125,000 women were conscripted between 1942 and 1945. No matter how close they came to falling bombs or enemy gunfire, Britain's uniformed women were barred by law from firing on the enemy. Even the ATS "gunner girls" who helped "man" home-front antiaircraft guns were not actually allowed to fire the guns. Similar restrictions applied to the all-female auxiliaries formed by the nations of the British Commonwealth.

At their greatest strength, U.S. women's auxiliaries constituted only 2 percent of the American military, or about 272,000 women. In 1942, women were organized into the Women's Army Auxiliary Corps (WAAC—which became Women's Army Corps, or WAC, in 1943), Women Appointed for Voluntary Emergency Service (WAVES), and Women's Coast Guard Reserve (SPARS). In 1943, the Marine Corps also established a women's auxiliary. Military women generally served in clerical roles, organized data for intelligence and codebreaking, operated communications equipment, were active in scientific fields, worked as translators and for the U.S. Army Mapping Service, and provided other behind-the-lines support. Women pilots ferried fighters and bombers from base to base within the United States, freeing more male pilots for combat duty. In August 1943, the

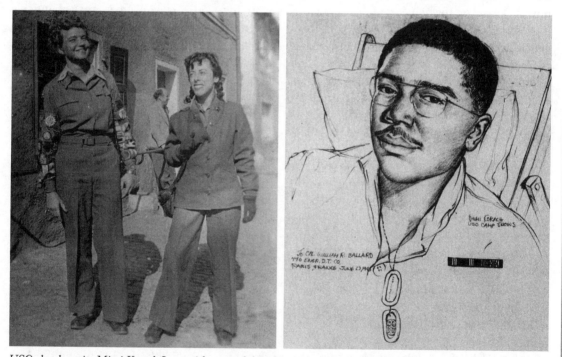

USO sketch artist Mimi Korach Lesser (above, with braids) poses with friend and fellow USO artist Ann (last name unknown) during their two-year tour of Europe (1944–1946) to sketch wounded soldiers, such as Corporal William R. Ballard (right). "It was a real challenge to sit by the bedside of a suffering soldier or sailor and try to coax a smile so that when the portrait was sent home, his mother or wife or girlfriend would be reassured," Lesser wrote. This was particularly true in a stateside hospital specializing in plastic surgery, where she was challenged by one GI, "with half his face disfigured," as to what she would do about him. "Posing him with his good side facing me I was able to sketch what his face would look like after rehabilitation. . . . Talk about success—this opened up a stream of eager brave, sad men. . . . Now they could . . . let relatives see that they would eventually be whole again."

Women's Auxiliary Ferrying Squadron (commanded by Nancy Harkness Love) and the Women's Flying Training Detachment (led by Jacqueline Cochran) were combined to form the Women's Airforce Service Pilots (WASPs). In addition to ferrying, WASP pilots towed targets for antiaircraft firing practice and tested experimental planes—always far from actual combat zones. The U.S. women who came closest to combat were those who served as armed forces nurses—some 59,000 in the Army Nurse Corps and 11,000 in the Navy Nurse Corps. Although nurses worked on the home front, others served in hospitals in the field and in mobile emergency units; some became prisoners of war, and more than two hundred were killed in the line of duty. Several U.S. nurses were decorated for valor under fire.

Other major combatants also established female auxiliaries, although Italy did so only late in the war. Japanese authorities refused to recruit women for any military auxiliary until the summer of 1945, when women aged 17 to 40 were included in the People's Patriotic Volunteer Corps, established to defend the home islands. Germany established volunteer female *Helferinnen* (literally "helpers" or "assistants") much earlier. Helferinnen became integrated into every branch of the military (more than 100,000 were in the Luftwaffe), serving as clerks, communications workers, drivers, translators, antiaircraft searchlight operators, and radar operators. Helferinnen did not have military status (their uniforms were adapted from Red Cross attire specifically to emphasize this fact), and they could not use weapons even in self-defense or to avoid capture. Thus, if captured, they could not claim the Geneva Convention protections accorded to military prisoners of war. As Germany began to suffer terrible battlefield reverses, there

was some discussion of allowing women to engage in combat, but this did not happen.

Women in Combat

Elsewhere, many women did see various types of combat, as members of partisan groups or semiregular forces (as in Yugoslavia) or in clandestine organizations such as Britain's Special Operations Executive (see Chapter 9). One major combatant employed women in their regular front-line armed forces: after the German invasion, Soviet women moved quickly from auxiliary to front-line duty, serving in all branches of military service and in both all-female and mixed-gender units. Female officers, on occasion, commanded forces largely comprising men. By 1943, about 800,000 women constituted about 8 percent of the Soviet regular armed forces.

Soviet women fought in the infantry, the artillery, and as crewmen in tanks. They also excelled as snipers: some 12,000 enemy kills were attributed to the more than 1,000 female graduates of the USSR's Central Sniper Training Center. (Many of these women were killed in sniper duels.) Marina Raskova, who was instrumental in getting Russian women into aerial warfare, was among the most celebrated of the Red Army's female fighter and bomber pilots. She took command of the first female air force in the world, Aviation Group 122, composed of three units, the 586th, the 125th, and the 46th (nicknamed the "night witches"). In September 1942, Soviet pilot Liliia Litviak became the first woman in history to down an enemy aircraft. Soviet women in all branches took pride in fighting just as well and as hard as men, and they gradually won the respect of the men they fought beside.

COMBATING BABEL: OVERCOMING LANGUAGE BARRIERS IN A GLOBAL WAR

Each [scene of military operations] presents its own specific language problems, which to the individual soldier are apt to prove of paramount importance, because even a smattering of the tongue of an ally or enemy may spell the difference between life and death.

—*Professor Mario A. Pei*, What Languages Are Our Soldiers up Against? *1944*

Few books on World War II focus on the mad scramble to recruit and train linguists for military duties that ranged from intelligence gathering to linguistic liaison among allied military forces—or within the armed forces of a single, polyglot nation. (Hundreds of thousands of conscripts from outlying Soviet states did not know one word of Russian.) Among the major combatants, the Japanese military seems to have relied most on Japanese-speaking locals whom they either hired or impressed into service as they advanced into new areas. Most other major combatants created military language training programs. The German army established interpreter companies in 1940, then organized the Armed Forces Interpreter Training Battalion in 1941. Other German services established similar programs. Recruiting students who trained in linguistics, these Wehrmacht schools concentrated on specialized skills, including map-reading and interrogation techniques.

Interrogation was also a principal duty of graduates of the U.S. Military Intelligence Service (MIS) Language School (MISLS), established in 1941 at the Presidio near San Fran-

cisco. Most MISLS students were Nisei (a person of Japanese descent, born and educated in the United States) or Kibei (Japanese Americans who received formal education in Japan). After West Coast Japanese Americans were forced into relocation camps, the MISLS was moved to Fort Snelling, Minnesota. The school trained more than 6,000 language specialists, including dozens (primarily Nisei) from the Women's Army Corps. These Army linguists also served as translators, interpreters, radio monitors, and propagandists. More than half the male graduates served in combat areas, most notably in the Pacific Theater. The Army Specialized Training Program (December 1942–February 1944), offered accelerated courses in more than thirty languages. The U.S. Navy's language training facility in Boulder, Colorado, was primarily devoted to teaching Japanese.

Most ordinary soldiers and sailors, however, continued to confront frustrating and sometimes dangerous language barriers on foreign terrain; troops in Europe were always clamoring for hard-to-find English-French dictionaries. And, as Ollie Stewart, war correspondent for the U.S. *Afro-American Newspapers,* noted, translation was sometimes required even among allies who spoke the same language: in one article he mentioned Rudolph Dunbar, a British musician and writer, whose "British accent is so British that half our guys can't follow his questions; and . . . our slang is so outlandish to him, that he can't dig the most of our jive."

PRINCIPAL SOURCES AND FURTHER READING

Craven, Wesley Frank and James Lea Cate, eds. *The Army Air Forces in World War II.* 7 Vols. Washington, D.C.: Office of Air Force History, U.S. Government Printing Office, 1983.

Deakin, F. W. *Brutal Friendship: Mussolini, Hitler and the Fall of Italian Fascism.* London: Phoenix Press, 2000.

Edgerton, Robert. *Warriors of the Rising Sun.* New York: Norton, 1997.

Erickson, John. *The Soviet High Command: A Military-Political History, 1918–1941,* 3rd ed. London: Frank Cass, 2001.

Fenby, Jonathan. *Chiang Kai-Shek: China's Generalissimo and the Nation He Lost.* New York: Carroll & Graf, 2004.

Furer, Julius A. *Administration of the Navy Department in World War II.* Washington, D.C.: U.S. Department of the Navy, Navy Historical Division, 1959.

Glantz, David M. *Colossus Reborn: The Red Army at War, 1941–1943.* Lawrence: University of Kansas Press, 2005.

Harries, Meirion and Susie Harries. *Soldiers of the Sun: The Rise and Fall of the Imperial Japanese Army, 1868–1945.* London: Heinemann, 1991.

Jackson, Robert H. *That Man: An Insider's Portrait of Franklin D. Roosevelt.* Oxford, New York: Oxford University Press, 2003.

Knox, MacGregor. *Hitler's Italian Allies: Royal Armed Forces, Fascist Regime, and the War of 1940–1943.* Cambridge: Cambridge University Press, 2000.

Larrabee, Eric. *Commander in Chief: Franklin Delano Roosevelt, His Lieutenants, and Their War.* New York: Harper & Row, 1987.

Macdonald, Dwight and Nancy Macdonald. *The War's Greatest Scandal: Jim Crow in Uniform.* New York: The March on Washington Movement, 1943.

MacGregor, Morris J. Jr. *Integration of the Armed Forces, 1940–1965.* Washington, D.C., Center of Military History, 1981.

Merridale, Catherine. *Ivan's War: Life and Death in the Red Army, 1939–1945.* Metropolitan Books/Henry Holt, 2006.

Morison, Samuel Eliot. *History of United States Naval Operations in World War II,* 15 Volumes. Boston: Little, Brown, 1962.

Office of the Chief of Military History, Department of the Army. *The United States Army in World War II,* 78 Vols.

Read, Anthony. *The Devil's Disciples: Hitler's Inner Circle.* New York: Norton, 2003.

Stoler, Mark A. *Allies and Adversaries: The Joint Chiefs of Staff, the Grand Alliance, and U.S. Strategy in WW II.* Chapel Hill: University of North Carolina Press, 2000.

Wheeler-Bennett, John. *The Nemisis of Power: The German Army in Politics, 1918–1945.* London: McMillan, 1964.

Wilt, Alan F. *War from the Top: German and British Military Decision Making during World War II.* Bloomington: University of Indiana Press, 1990.

Yelton, David K. *Hitler's Volkssturm: The Nazi Militia and the Fall of Germany, 1944–1945.* Lawrence: University of Kansas Press, 2002.

INSTRUMENTS OF WAR

At the turn of the twentieth century, U.S. troops dispatched by President Theodore Roosevelt and commanded by Brigadier General Arthur MacArthur battled insurgents in the Philippine Islands, a territory transferred from Spanish to U.S. possession after the 1898 Spanish-American War. The small but brutal "Philippine Insurrection," which Roosevelt declared finished in 1902, was fought before the invention of the airplane; even automobiles were primitive and rare. Like all other soldiers then, MacArthur's troops traveled largely by foot or by actual horse power. Their only air cover was tropical foliage and sky.

Forty-two years later, in 1944, Arthur MacArthur's son, General Douglas MacArthur, serving under Theodore Roosevelt's cousin, President Franklin D. Roosevelt, led the American forces that landed on the island of Leyte, beginning the final struggle to liberate the Philippines from Japan during World War II. This combined force was equipped with transport and weaponry the earlier MacArthur and Roosevelt could hardly have imagined. Many kinds of amphibious craft, jeeps, trucks, and tanks kept the ground forces moving. Lethal aircraft, some armed with rockets, zoomed through the skies at hundreds of miles per hour. Many of the planes took off from aircraft carriers, a type of ship introduced to warfare in 1918, then gradually developed into the most potent element in the American, British, and Japanese surface navies of the 1940s. Around the world, jet aircraft, long-range bombers, radar, sonar, and many other weapons and technological devices were supporting armed forces—until two blinding explosions over Hiroshima and Nagasaki, Japan, ended the war and announced, in terrifying fashion, the advent of the nuclear age.

The weapons-related technological achievements of the World War II era were derived from many earlier accomplishments. Of particular importance were the breakthroughs during World War I, which introduced air forces, tanks, poison gas, and effective submarine warfare—and took more than 10 million lives. Behind the lines, the "Great War," as it was called at the time, was marked by a new collaboration between government and the military, on the one hand, and civilian scientists and industrialists, on the other. Government bodies, such as Britain's Department of Scientific and Industrial Research (1915) and the U.S. National Advisory Committee for Aeronautics (1915) and National Research Council (1916), were maintained in the interwar years and provided bases for the vast mobilization of scientists and civilian engineers who would labor on World War II weapons and defenses. Yet even as new war clouds gathered in the 1930s, few people comprehended the scale of devastation a second world conflict would bring.

As armies, navies, and air forces began fighting, political and military leaders confronted difficult strategic, tactical, political, and ethical questions regarding their rapidly growing and increasingly powerful arsenals—often (especially in the war's early years) without much practical knowledge to guide them. Such questions continued to be argued throughout the war; the use of various weapons was repeatedly reexamined and adjusted in the light of changing circumstances. National, political, and ideological imperatives; the personal prejudices and rivalries of political and military leaders; the cooperation or non-cooperation of scientists, academics, and industrialists; the availability or lack of technicians and skilled laborers; procurement and analysis of technical intelligence regarding enemy weapons development and war production; the plenitude or dearth of natural resources; the effects of blockades and bombing; the mounting cost of the war, in lives and in fortune; desperation to keep the enemy at bay—all were among the vast tangle of factors affecting the development and use of weapons during World War II.

Aircraft

The Nazis and fascists have asked for it, and they are going to get it . . . we and the British and the Russians will hit them from the air heavily and relentlessly.

—*President Franklin D. Roosevelt,*
Report to Congress, January 7, 1943

In the 1920s and 1930s, few doubted that aircraft would play an important role in future combat, though how important a role, and exactly what it might be was debated, sometimes heatedly. Only countries with advanced industrial bases could afford to develop and maintain significant air forces. Thus airplane production increased primarily in Britain, the United States, France, Germany, Italy, and Japan, but the largest air force in Europe during the 1930s was that of the Soviet Union.

In the interwar years, biplanes began giving way to monoplanes (although some biplanes, such as Britain's "Swordfish," remained in service throughout World War II). More efficient engines and higher-octane fuel led to improved aircraft performance. Long-range bombers went on the drawing boards: the prototype of America's soon-to-be-legendary B-17 rolled off the production line in 1935. The design of this "Flying Fortress," like the designs of other effective combat aircraft, was continually modified during the war: there were seven main, and several experimental models of the B-17 alone.

Military doctrine for air power evolved much more slowly. Many fundamental questions were at issue in the 1930s, and throughout the war. Should air forces be employed *tactically* (supporting specific ground and naval military operations) or *strategically* (aimed at the destruction of enemy war resources, such as factories, transportation facilities, and oil refineries), or both? If bombing was adopted (there were some attempts, in the 1930s, to ban or limit air attacks), would "the bombers always get through" because of their altitude, armament, and formation flying, as was widely believed in the interwar years, thus arguing against the development of long-range fighter aircraft to escort and protect them; or would enemy antiaircraft measures create unforeseen problems? Could air power *alone* force an enemy to capitulate by destroying its means and will to fight on (thus avoiding the need to expend the lives of infantrymen in costly invasions of Europe and Japan)?

During the war, operational questions—such as how to maintain effective communication between ground forces and the aircraft supporting them, who should have direct control over air groups involved in complex combined operations, and how to ensure fast aircraft repair and resupply—also had to be addressed, with different answers emerging as circumstances changed. As new or improved types of aircraft were incorporated into frontline air forces (more powerful long-range bombers such as the B-29, long-range fighters, jet aircraft) unforeseen operational and tactical questions sometimes arose.

A general air strategy gradually emerged among the Allies—specifically within the United States/United Kingdom partnership. Encompassing air defense, strategic bombing, air-naval cooperation, and support for ground

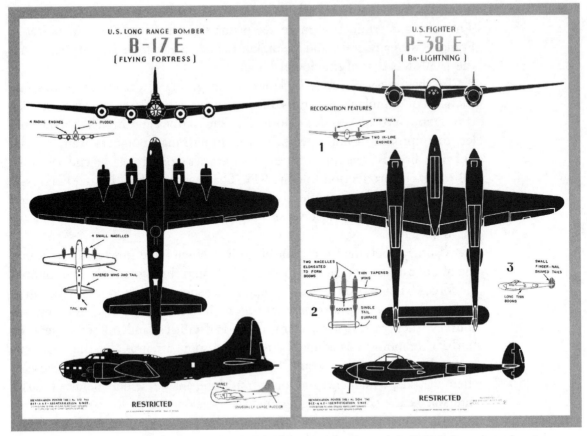

Two of the most powerful U.S. warplanes were the B-17 long-range bomber and the P-38 fighter, shown here in identification posters issued by the U.S. Army Adjutant General's Office in 1943.

troops, this strategy bested the more limited air strategy of the Axis powers that was dictated by shrinking resources and by Axis leaders' prejudices and miscalculations. Although Germany did attempt the strategic use of air power, the overall limited strategy of the individual Axis powers primarily emphasized tactical support for specific ground and naval operations.

Amphibious Aircraft ("Flying Boats" and Float Planes)

Within twenty years after the first hydroplane took off from and landed on the water of California's San Diego Bay in 1911, giant *flying boats* were serving commercial passengers and the military. America's famous Consolidated PBY Catalina (the "Cat") became a mainstay of Allied marine aviation in

World War II. The Cat and other long-range flying boats, such as the giant Boeing 314 "Clipper," requiring only sheltered coves as bases, were a primary means of personnel transport and communication in the Pacific Theater. In the Mediterranean, Allied flying boats evacuated personnel from Greece in 1941 and delivered vital supplies to besieged Allied soldiers in Tobruk. Germany's Blohm and Voss BV 222 Wikings, the largest wartime flying boats, transported reinforcements to North Africa. Allied and Axis forces worldwide assigned flying boats to air-sea rescue, reconnaissance, and antisubmarine patrols—at which Britain's depth-charge equipped Short Sunderlands were particularly lethal, as was the American Consolidated Coronado. The well-armored and armed Japanese "Emily" long-range reconnaissance craft was the fastest flying boat of the war.

Eleven combatant countries also employed smaller *float planes*, which landed entirely on special floats (flying boats landed on their fuselage, as well as on wing floats). More than 70 types flew during the war, including America's Grumman J2F Duck, Britain's amply insulted yet beloved three-seater biplane "the Walrus," Germany's Arado, and Japan's Aichi E13AI "Jake" (which flew reconnaissance over Pearl Harbor). Sometimes launched by catapults from battleships and cruisers, float planes were used for observation and artillery spotting, air-sea rescue, laying mines, and making torpedo attacks against shipping. Japan had one model of fighter float plane, the Kawanishi Shiden.

Balloons

Manned observation balloons were used for intelligence and artillery spotting in the American Civil War and in subsequent conflicts, but during World War I, they quickly became prime targets for the world's first air forces. Balloons used during World War II were generally unmanned, though some manned observation balloons may have been used along the USSR/Manchukuo (China) border. The Americans and British also used balloons with gondolas or attached cages for training paratroopers and men of the U.S. Navy's unique Fleet Airship Wings (see "Blimps" later in this chapter).

Huge, hydrogen-filled unmanned *barrage balloons*, attached to wire cables capable of snagging low-flying enemy planes, were familiar sights over the British mainland, both Allied and Axis ports in the Mediterranean theater, and ships off the Normandy Beachhead in June 1944. (One of the very few African American units to land on Omaha Beach June 6, 1944, was the

320th Antiaircraft Balloon Battalion.) Hundreds also protected U.S. coastal areas early in the war. The balloons' cables were connected to winches so that height and location could be changed. Problems with these relatively simple craft included accumulations of ice that sometimes brought them down and buildups of static electricity that could discharge toward earth, killing or injuring crewmen. While they protected ships from aircraft, they also marked the locations of vessels and made them more vulnerable to artillery fire.

The British also briefly experimented with incendiary *balloon bombs*, intended to set Germany's Black Forest ablaze via their cargo: explosive devices called "deckers" (a "sandwich" of phosphorous and gelatinized gasoline). These quickly proved ineffective. Between November 1944 and March 1945, the Japanese mounted a similar campaign, sending 9,300 incendiary-loaded balloons made of bonded mulberry paper aloft to 38,000 feet, where, aided by clever altitude-regulating mechanisms, they sailed the jet stream toward North America. Only about 285 reached the Americas—coming down from Mexico to Canada and Alaska. One of the bombs killed five children and an adult in Oregon—the only known World War II deaths from enemy attack on the U.S. mainland—but they caused very little other damage.

Hydrogen balloons also gathered meteorological information, crucial in planning military operations, from artillery barrages to invasions. Tracked by radar and *theodolite* (an instrument for measuring horizontal and vertical angles), each balloon carried a *radiosonde* that recorded data on wind speed and direction as well as the temperature, pressure, and humidity in the upper atmosphere. At a certain altitude, the balloon burst and the radiosonde, descending by parachute, was retrieved manually. By 1944, American scientists had developed a radiosonde that transmitted data to a ground receiver.

Blimps (Airships)

During World War I, German motor-driven airships traveling at less than sixty miles per hour dropped bombs on the British home islands. At altitudes beyond the reach of artillery and the era's primitive planes, these hydrogen-filled, rigid-framework zeppelins (named for their creator, Count Ferdinand von Zeppelin) did relatively little damage—but their attacks, and later raids by German "Gotha" airplanes, demonstrated the need for effective defense against air attacks far behind the battle lines.

Improved airplanes and antiaircraft artillery, as well as the invention of incendiary bullets (hydrogen is intensely flammable), soon neutralized airships as offensive weapons. But during World War II, one nation deployed nonrigid (without a solid frame), *helium*-filled airships, nicknamed "blimps," for support and defensive missions. With some 5,000 miles of American coast-line to protect, the U.S. Navy built a fleet of airships from the ten aging blimps available on December 7, 1941, to 168 airships in 1945. Except for thirty blimps reserved for training, all were patrol craft, deployed throughout the Western Hemisphere and in the Mediterranean and North Africa. At peak, the Navy reported, its airships patrolled about 3 million square miles.

First used primarily for observation, blimps were later assigned to photo-reconnaissance and search-and-rescue duty. They also helped in mine-spotting and mine-sweeping operations and in providing communication and other assistance to convoys. They proved particularly useful in antisub-marine patrols; moving slowly, they could spot submerged subs in clear waters, such as parts of the Mediterranean—and well-armed airships also attacked surfaced U-boats. On July 18, 1943, airship K-74 engaged in a gun battle with the surfaced German submarine U-134 in the Caribbean and became the only airship lost to enemy action. (All but one of its crew were rescued the next day.)

Bombers

> The ruthless bombing from the air of civilians in unfortified centers of population . . . has sickened the hearts of every civilized man and woman, and has profoundly shocked the conscience of humanity. . . . I am therefore addressing this urgent appeal to every Government which may be engaged in hostilities publicly to affirm its determination that its armed forces shall in no event, and under no circumstances, undertake the bombardment from the air of civilian populations or of unfortified cities, upon the understanding that these same rules of warfare will be scrupulously observed by all of their opponents. I request an immediate reply.
>
> —*President Franklin D. Roosevelt, appeal to Great Britain, France, Italy, Germany, and Poland, September 1, 1939*

President Roosevelt's earnest appeal, issued the day war engulfed Europe, reflected the widespread abhorrence of "terror bombing" that had characterized the interwar period. British Prime Minister Neville Chamberlain encouraged the Royal Air Force to concentrate on "legitimate military targets" as the war started; French General Maxime Weygand stated, about that same time, "There is something in these bombardments of defenseless people behind the front that smacks of cowardice which is repugnant to the soldier." Even Hitler declared his willingness to limit his attacks to military targets if the RAF would do the same. But as the war expanded and increased in intensity, these early intentions disappeared. In July 1940, as the Battle of Britain raged in England's skies, the new prime minister, Winston Churchill, whose nation was by then the lone European holdout against Germany, wrote Minister of Aircraft Production Lord Beaverbrook:

> We have no Continental army which can defeat the German military power . . . there is one thing that will bring . . . [Hitler] down, and that is an absolutely devastating exterminating attack by very heavy bombers from this country upon the Nazi homeland.

Nevertheless, the British intention in 1940 was to wreak havoc primarily on war resources by *precision bombing*—a bombing strategy U.S. war planners also favored. However, the technology necessary to effect true precision bombing was in its infancy; existing methods (such as Germany's pathfinding radio beams) were unreliable and extremely vulnerable to enemy interference. In August 1941, a British study, the Butt Report (named for its author, D. M. Butt), based on the analysis of photographs of RAF bomb damage inflicted on twenty-eight targets between June 2, and July 25, 1941, revealed that only 30 percent of the British bombs had fallen within five miles of their targets; only 10 percent achieved that proximity in the Ruhr, Germany's prime industrial area, where targets were obscured by smoke even in daylight. This became a major factor in Britain's increasing embrace of *area bombing*—the targeting of entire urban or industrial areas—even as technological developments improved the prospects for precision attacks. The United States remained firmly in favor of precision bombing. This caused significant friction between the two Allies once American bomber groups became active in the European Theater.

Friction eased when they developed a joint round-the-clock bombing campaign aimed at putting maximum strain on German defense resources as well as destroying Germany's capacity to make war: the USAAF undertook daylight bombing raids that aimed at precise targets (making American planes easier targets for German fighters and antiaircraft batteries); the RAF bombed at night. Growing numbers of Allied bombers hit aircraft and ball bearing factories, transportation lines, oil refineries and factories for the manufacture of synthetic oil and rubber, and other crucial targets. To protect these facilities, Germany began producing many more fighters than bombers, thus reducing its own ability to bomb Allied bases and other strategically important targets. (Japan's warplane production took a similar course.) Germany did deploy the world's first jet bomber, the Arado Ar-234 in 1944. But the jets were too few and too late to affect the war significantly.

Changing circumstances affected the debates over bombing strategies; meanwhile bombs devastated hundreds of cities in all major theaters of war. A few were swept by raging "firestorms," a rare phenomenon in which separate fires merged and intensified, generating flame-filled, hurricane-force winds that sucked oxygen even out of underground air-raid shelters. These unstoppable bomber-sparked incendiary storms killed hundreds of thousands of civilians, including more than 100,000 killed by a USAAF raid on Tokyo on the night of March 9, 1945. This raid resulted from a change in American air strategy to area bombing, a change that occurred largely because Allied war planners had determined that much of Japan's industry was widely dispersed in small shops and other facilities throughout the country's urban areas. With Japanese civilians mobilized into a volunteer army to defend the home islands, American leaders considered all Japanese to be military targets.

Three major types of bombers were employed during the war:

1. *Dive bombers and torpedo bombers.* Examples are the famous German Junkers 87 *Stuka*, Japan's Aichi D3A "Val," (the first Japanese plane to bomb American targets), America's Grumman TBF-1 "Avenger" and the formidable U.S. Curtiss SB2C "Helldiver" (known to many of its crews as "the Beast"). Capable of greater precision in dropping their bomb loads than the higher-altitude medium- and long-range bombers (the entire aircraft aimed at the target, and bombs or torpedoes were released right over it as the bomber pulled out of its dive), these smaller bombers were most often used for tactical bombing in support of naval and ground operations. They also engaged in air-to-air combat. Dive and torpedo bombers had limited range and relatively small bomb loads (the "Avenger" could fly 1,215 miles and carry 1,600 pounds of bombs). Early in the war, American torpedo bombers were often equipped with faulty torpedoes that strayed off course or

BOMB LOADS AND BOMBSIGHTS

Bombers dropped high-explosive, antipersonnel, armor-piercing, fragmentation, smoke, and other types of bombs, ranging in size from under ten pounds to over twenty thousand pounds. Factors determining what would be dropped on particular missions included the character of the target (factory, fortification, railroad trestle, dam, armored column, etc.) and level of concentration of ordnance achievable against the target. Notable special-purpose bombs include:

Atomic Bombs

See "Weapons of Terror, Desperation, and Mass Destruction," later in this chapter.

Bouncing/Dam-Buster Bombs

Developed by Briton Barnes Wallis, bouncing bombs were used primarily in what became the famous RAF 617 Squadron's "dambusters" raid of May 16, 1943, against the Mohne and Eder dams in Germany's industrial area, the Ruhr. Delivered by low-flying aircraft (many of which were lost), the cylindrical bombs spun over the water, exploding as they sank to the base of the dam wall.

Deep Penetration Bombs

Known as "Tall Boy" and "Grand Slam" or "Earthquake," these huge, powerful bombs were designed (also by Wallis) to penetrate the earth before they exploded and to bring down strong edifices (such as railroad tunnels) by their "earthquake" effect. When dropped from 20,000 feet, the 12,000-pound "Tall Boy" created an eighty-foot crater and could penetrate sixteen feet of concrete. In 1945, the 22,000-pound "Grand Slam" bombs proved effective against Germany's submarine pens at Bremen, which were protected by more than twenty feet of concrete.

Guided and Rocket-Assisted Bombs

See "Drones/Guided Weapons," later in this chapter.

Incendiaries

These were much used in both area and precision bombing. (Of the 153,000 tons of bombs the United States dropped on Japan, approximately 98,000 tons were firebombs.) Magnesium, phosphorous, and, later, napalm (jellied gasoline) were among the most potent ingredients—and their effects could be hideous. When phosphorous incendiary bombs exploded, molten phosphorous adhered to whatever it touched—and it could not be extinguished with water. Napalm incendiaries, such as America's six-pound M69, had much the same torturous effect.

One bomber could carry many "aimable cluster bombs," each of which contained thirty-eight M69s; upon crashing to earth, each M69 sent a jet of fiery, adhesive napalm up to one hundred feet long shooting out of its tail, coating everything—and everyone—in its path.

Photoflash Bombs

Designed only to provide illumination for nighttime aerial reconnaissance photography, these operated on a time fuze that caused flashpowder to ignite seconds after the bomb had been dropped. The powder "flashed" (burned intensely) for only about one-fifth of a second at a peak intensity of about 500 million candlepower, a level of brightness that made it dangerous to look at a photoflash bomb as it exploded.

Bombsights

Aircraft bombardiers zeroed in on their targets using these precision optical devices. The United States used two different bombsights during the war. The *Sperry bombsight*, invented by Elmer A. Sperry, was phased out in 1943. It was replaced in American planes by the more sensitive *Norden bombsight*, an improved version of a device first used in the 1930s (and rumored, inaccurately, to allow bombardiers to drop their ordnance precisely on targets that were only the size of pickle barrels). This device was one of America's most closely guarded wartime secrets.

bounced off their targets. Torpedo problems, not unique to U.S. forces, were gradually solved as the war progressed. (See "Naval Vessels and Weaponry—'Damn the Torpedoes,'" later in this chapter.)

2. *Medium bombers.* Examples are the American B-25 "Mitchell" (modified versions of which were used in the April 1942 Doolittle raid on Japan), Germany's Junkers Ju 88, and Britain's deHavilland "Mosquito" (which relied on its impressive speed rather than armament as its defense against fighters). Usually two-engine aircraft, the medium bombers had a shorter reach than heavy long-range planes and carried relatively modest bomb loads (Doolittle's B-25s had a range of 1,350 miles and could carry three thousand pounds of bombs). In addition to attacking land targets, medium-range bombers proved extremely effective against submarines and surface ships.

3. *Heavy/long-range bombers.* Examples are the American B-17 and the B-29 (the type of bomber that dropped the atomic bombs), Britain's Avro Lancaster, and Germany's Heinkel He177A-5. Dedicated to

long, generally strategic bombing missions, these aircraft usually were equipped with four engines (Germany's Heinkel had two), providing greater range and power to carry much heavier bomb loads. The B-17G—a 1943 version of the "Flying Fortress"—could fly 2,000 miles and carry 17,600 pounds of bombs; the B-29, deployed in 1944, had a range of 4,100 miles and carried a 20,000-pound bomb load. In Europe, the Allies' long-range bombers sustained extremely heavy losses to enemy fighters until long-range fighter-escort planes were put in service late in 1943. (Fighter escorts did nothing, of course, to ease concentrated fire from Axis antiaircraft guns.)

Drones and other Guided Weapons

See also "Weapons of Terror and Mass Destruction—V-weapons," later in this chapter.

The comparatively primitive guided weapons of World War II included *target drones*, such as the U.S. Navy's TD series, small aircraft piloted to particular locations, then flown by radio-control when used as targets for gunnery practice. The U.S. Navy's TDR *assault drones* were rudimentary guided missiles, used with limited success in the Pacific Theater in the fall of 1944. In the European Theater, also on a limited basis, the Allies used larger assault drones—essentially, stripped down B-17s and PBY aircraft packed with explosives; some were equipped with television cameras to give controllers a view of their progress. Flown by two men who bailed out at the edge of enemy territory, these large drones were then controlled by radio from another aircraft and put in a steep dive when over their targets. (Joseph Kennedy Jr., the older brother of future president John F. Kennedy, was killed, along with his copilot, on August 12, 1944, when the drone PBY aircraft they were piloting exploded prematurely.) Late in the war, Germany used a few similar drones: *Mistel* "Mistletoe" composite aircraft, comprising an old bomber packed with explosives and a piloted fighter craft attached to its topside. The fighter brought the drone near its destination, then released it, and the fighter pilot guided it by remote control onto the target.

Glider bombs also debuted in World War II. They were carried by aircraft then released to glide to their targets under radio guidance; some had rocket boosters to give them greater range. In August 1943, a German Henschel Hs293 became the first guided missile to sink a ship when it struck the British sloop *Egret*. That year German glide bombs also sank the Italian battleship *Roma* before it could be turned over to the Allies. The American AZON was successful in the Mediterranean and China-Burma-India theaters, where it proved most effective in destroying bridges used by Axis forces. The U.S. Navy's "Bat," which had built-in short-range radar that locked onto the target once it was close enough, went into operation in May 1945, primarily against Japanese shipping.

Ferret Aircraft

See "Technological Devices—Radar and Radio Countermeasures," later in this chapter.

Fighters and Fighter-Bombers

Bomber escort, tactical support for ground and sea operations, and air defense against enemy bombers were essential missions of the compact one-, two-, and (occasionally) three-crewman fighter aircraft of World War II; speed, maneuverability, firepower, and range were among their most important attributes. Armed primarily with machine guns, cannons, and later in the war, rockets (and, in the case of fighter-bombers, a limited bomb load), the fighters' primary function was to gain and maintain control of the sky. This epic, near-constant battle was fought primarily in the twisting confusion of tens of thousands of individual "dog fights" with enemy fighters. Fighters and fighter-bombers also strafed (raked with machine-gun fire) and bombed enemy troops, support bases, and antiaircraft installations and flew cover during rescue operations. After the Battle of Britain in 1940, and continuing into 1942, the British sent massed fighters—sometimes as many as three to five hundred at once—over the English Channel in less-than-successful operations dubbed "rhubarbs" or "circuses," trying to draw the Luftwaffe out to do battle. (By 1942, the objective was also to incite Germany to transfer aircraft to the west from the Eastern Front, thus providing some relief for the Soviet Union.)

Britain's "Spitfire" and "Hurricane"; America's P-38 and P-40 (flown by Claire Chennault's famed "Flying Tigers" in China); Germany's Messerschmitt 109 and Focke-Wulf 190; and Japan's Mitsubishi A6M "Zero" and Nakajima Ki-43 Hayabusa were initially among the war's most feared fighter aircraft. (The Zero's 1,930-mile range provided an unhappy surprise to Allied airmen flying more limited-range fighters early in the war. The American Curtiss P40B Warhawk deployed in 1941, for example, had a range of 940 miles.) In 1943, the Allies deployed their own long-range fighters, prominent among them America's P-51 "Mustang." This made life somewhat more secure for Allied bomber crews flying deep over enemy-controlled territory.

Faced with round-the-clock bombing and these new Allied long-range fighters, and with the Luftwaffe suffering severely from attrition, Hitler invested more of Germany's dwindling resources on completing new types of aircraft. In 1944, Germany deployed the Messerschmitt 163, a *rocket-powered fighter*, with limited success, as well as an effective German jet fighter, the Messerschmitt 262. More than one hundred of these jet fighters were eventually deployed—but too late to have much impact, especially after Allied fighters, having discovered the jets' relative slowness and vulnerability at takeoff and landing, staked out the air around Me 262 bases. Britain also deployed a jet fighter, the Gloster "Meteor," in 1944, using a small group to down several German V-1 rockets zooming in over England.

As radar and other guidance technologies improved, *night fighter* groups became increasingly effective operating under cover of darkness (much less costly than daylight raids). Initially, night fighter planes were adapted day fighters (such as Britain's Bristol Beaufighter, Germany's Me 110, and the U.S. P-38); later, specialized night fighter aircraft (such as the U.S. P-61 "Black Widow") were deployed. Night fighters generally employed airborne intercept (AI) radar, which added weight to a plane and usually required a radar operator. (Early in the war, some night fighters, such as Hurricanes and P-38s went up without radar on what were dubbed "cat's-eye" missions, relying on ground reports, searchlight illumination, and visual contact.) Throughout the war, AI radar increased in range and efficiency, each improvement by one side calling forth countermeasures from the other. Reflecting their special mission, many Allied night fighters, whose aircraft were often specially painted in dark colors, decorated their planes with night-flying-appropriate nose art and gave them names like "Black Magic," "Moonhappy," and "Midnight Belle."

By late in the war, significant numbers of the fighters of most major combatants had been modified to carry rockets under their wings, weapons that could be fired more accurately by fighters and dive-bombers than by ground-based rocket launchers (see "Artillery, Tanks, and Tank Destroyers," later in this chapter). The USSR used them first in 1942, but the Luftwaffe used them with particular success against Allied bombers in 1943. By 1945, the United States—which had become the foremost designer, producer, and exploiter of military aircraft rockets—had developed its largest wartime air-launched rocket, the "Tiny Tim" (10 feet long, 1,284 pounds, including a 590-pound bomb with a 150-pound explosive charge of TNT), which was used at Okinawa. From Normandy to Burma, air-launched rockets were especially effective against transport and escort ships and warships up to destroyer size. They were also successful against enemy airfields, radar stations and other smaller installations; parked planes and fuel dumps; and tanks, light guns, concrete pillboxes, and locomotives.

Gliders

Primarily a sport in the interwar years, "soaring" or "gliding," usually in one- or two-person unpowered aircraft, also provided excellent flight training for thousands of Hitler Youth, later recruited for the Luftwaffe. Field tests in the 1930s demonstrated that gliders also could deliver soldiers to specified zones behind or near enemy lines in combat-ready groups, unlike often widely scattered paratroopers dropped from planes. Thus, on May 10, 1940, Germany became the first nation to use gliders in combat during the blitzkrieg assault on western Europe. Most spectacularly, ten of these silent war birds carrying seventy-eight German troops—along with machine guns, grenades, and twenty-eight new and very potent hollow (or shaped) explosive charges—bypassed impregnable outer defenses and drifted down atop Belgium's formidable Fort Eben Emael. Surprise, disciplined action, and powerful ordnance soon overwhelmed the garrison despite its huge numerical superiority. Other nations, particularly Britain and the United States, soon developed their own glider programs. (Russia also used military gliders; Japan developed a few, but never used them in combat.)

The longtime leader in gliders, Germany created many models: the Messerschmitt Me 321 *Gigant*—at least four times the size of any British or American glider—could carry twenty-four tons, or two hundred fully equipped men. But it had only limited use, in part because its size required multiple towplanes. (Eventually, most were turned into six-engine Me 323 *Gigant* transport planes.) In May 1941, Germany used a fleet of its smaller gliders in history's first wholly airborne invasion, the successful assault on Crete, but at great cost, as gliders crashed on obstacles in the rough terrain and were torn apart by fearsome ground fire. Hitler was reluctant to risk severe losses in similar operations. While German gliders participated in small-scale actions after Crete, including the daring 1943 raid that plucked Mussolini from Allied hands, they were generally used to supply and evacuate troops—towplanes "snatching" the loaded gliders from the ground.

Britain and the United States developed a workable glider program very slowly, with some costly failures. One occurred on July 9, 1943, during the invasion of Sicily, when hundreds of Allied troops drowned after dozens of gliders were released prematurely over the sea. On the other hand, in the China-Burma-India Theater, gliders of USAAF Lieutenant Colonel Phil Cochran's First Air Commando Group were stunningly successful in transporting British general Orde Wingate's "Chindit" guerrilla fighters and vast amounts of equipment (along with the mules to carry it) behind Japanese lines, then helping to keep the Chindits and other Allied forces supplied, and evacuating the wounded and ill personnel (see Chapter 7). In Europe, among other important operations, thousands of towed gliders dropped Allied troops and supplies behind German lines on and after D-Day, and a glider drop of desperately needed fuel and artillery ammunition, as well as volunteer surgical teams, near Bastogne, helped Americans hold on during the December 1944–January 1945 Battle of the Bulge.

In Europe, Allied glider-borne troops encountered an effective German countermeasure: profusions of upright poles (about the thickness of telephone poles), dubbed "Rommel's asparagus," stuck in the ground across potential landing sites. Many British "Horsa" and "Hamilcar" gliders and American CG-4A "Wacos" came to grief on these poles. Other problems included difficulty in identifying landing zones, particularly in the dark, and occasional traffic jams as dozens of gliders landed in fields surrounded by hedges or trees.

Helicopters and Autogyros

Invented in the early 1920s, the *autogyro* was a precursor to the helicopter, with a motor either in front of or behind the pilot and an unpowered rotary wing above. These small aircraft require very little space for takeoff and can make vertical landings, but unlike helicopters, they cannot hover. During World War II, Germany provided a disassembled version (the Focke-Achgelis Fa 330 "Water Wagtail") to an unknown number of U-boats for observation purposes. Like barrage balloons over ships, however, these aircraft could give away a U-boat's location, so it is uncertain how often they were used. Britain used its autogyros primarily to assist in home-island radar calibration. Japan deployed about fifty, primarily for observation, though a few were equipped with depth charges for use against submarines. Russia's distinctive short-winged autogyro, the A-7, was armed with two movable machine guns for self-defense during reconnaissance missions.

America's own military focused on the possibilities of the helicopter (though the Navy was initially very skeptical), first successfully flown by the French in 1935. Germany developed and eventually deployed a few helicopters, chiefly for rescue, reconnaissance, and artillery spotting. But it was the American R-4 helicopter (designated HNS-1 by the Navy), developed by Igor Sikorsky and first delivered in late 1943, that was used most widely and successfully for rescue/evacuation, reconnaissance, and airborne observation—assisting, for example, in the 1944–1945 campaign to liberate the Philippine Islands. Perhaps the most remarkable wartime helicopter story is that of Lieutenant Carter Harmon, who flew his untried R-4 over a 6,000-foot-high mountain range and other rough terrain from India to Burma, where he rescued a pilot and three casualties from an area behind enemy lines that was inaccessible to other types of aircraft. Harman completed eighteen more helicopter rescues before his R-4 expired from tropical conditions and lack of replacement parts.

Missiles

See "Drones and other Guided Weapons" earlier in this chapter, and "Weapons of Terror, Desperation, and Mass Destruction—V-Weapons" later in this chapter.

Small Planes/Light Aircraft

Small unarmed, or lightly armed airplanes, such as the American Stinson L-5 "Sentinel" and Piper L-4 "Grasshopper," and Japan's Mitsubishi K3M, played several wartime roles chiefly in reconnaissance, liaison, coastal patrol, search-and-rescue operations, and pilot training. They were particularly valuable in observation and artillery spotting: "The little two-seater Piper Cub planes," wrote one American correspondent at Anzio, "are all over the beachhead like smoke over Pittsburgh." Some light planes, such as Britain's Westland Lysander, which could use very short runways, transported agents into and out of enemy territory, and a German light plane, a Fieseler Storch, spirited Mussolini away from his mountain prison in 1943 after glider-borne troops had secured his release.

Transport Aircraft

In the interwar years, Germany and the USSR pioneered in military air transport, especially to deploy paratroops. But during the war, Britain and the United States developed the most elaborate and effective air-support services—a vital supplement to beleaguered sea-convoys and land routes. American transport planes flew war matériel into all theaters of operation. (See "Global Transport" in Chapter 1 and "Gong over the Hump" in Chapter 7.) Eventually, hundreds of tons of supplies and thousands of passengers would travel these air routes every day.

Douglas C-47 "Skytrains" (called "Dakotas" by the British) and Curtiss C-46 "Commandos" were among the standard U.S. transport planes used in all theaters of war. America's Douglas C-54 "Skymasters"—also widely deployed—were so reliable that one was chosen to be President Roosevelt's personal transport (it was promptly dubbed "the Sacred Cow"). Britain also relied on the Armstrong Whitworth Albemarles and Avro York. Germany's transport aircraft included the Me 323 *Gigant* (the motorized version of their huge glider) and the Junkers Ju.52/3m; Japan used the Tachikawa Ki-54 and the Kawasaki Ki-56; Italy's ever-shrinking air forces included the Savoia Marchetti SM 82 transport.

Artillery, Tanks, and Tank Destroyers

Artillery

The bewildering maze of light, medium, heavy, and very-heavy guns, mortars, and howitzers used during World War II did not fundamentally differ from artillery used in World War I. But with greater range, velocity, accuracy, and mobility, artillery often proved devastating in offense and provided a frighteningly effective defensive shield—whether against ground, air, or naval assault. Smashing into advancing infantry units, reducing towns to rubble, shattering fortifications and armored columns, and shooting aircraft out of the skies, artillery inflicted more than half the battle casualties of World War II. It fell into four basic groups:

1. *Guns.* high-velocity fire, with a relatively flat trajectory
2. *Howitzers.* low-velocity fire, with a higher trajectory (thus moving over intervening obstacles)

Part of the formidable defenses of Corregidor, the fortified island in Manila Harbor, the Philippines, this big gun fell victim to the overwhelming force the Japanese sent against the Allied troops besieged on "the Rock" in 1942.

3. *Mortars.* firing at angles greater than forty-five degrees (dropping shells from a greater height onto targets shielded behind such cover as walls, trees, or rock formations)

4. *Rocket launchers.* constituted a unique kind of artillery (see also "Aircraft—Fighters and Fighter-Bombers," earlier in this chapter).

A special branch of the jet-propelled family, rockets are defined as "missiles propelled by the high speed, rearward expulsion of gases generated by the combustion of an internally carried fuel"; this eliminates *recoil*—no metal parts are pushed backward by the force of the shot. Although rockets had been used in combat intermittently since the thirteenth century, as with other technologies, the onset of World War II incited a spurt in the development of rocket weaponry (after decades of limited change).

Ground- (and ship-) based rocket launchers hurled multiple high-explosive, incendiary, or smoke shells from clustered barrels or racks, compensating in quantity for a relative lack of precision. On the Eastern Front of the European Theater, the USSR's *Katyusha* rocket launchers vied with Germany's much more sophisticated *Nebelwerfer* 41. In western Europe, the 18th Field Artillery Battalion of the U.S. First Army used 75 eight-tube "Xylophone" rocket launchers against attacking Germans during the Battle of the Bulge (December 1944–January 1945), at one point firing 1,800 rounds in eighteen minutes. In the Pacific, the U.S. Marines formed four Provisional Rocket Detachments, each with twelve one-ton trucks mounting three twelve-round automatic launchers, supplemented by lighter installations. They provided concentrated "saturation" or "drenching" rocket barrages against Japanese strongholds on Guam, Saipan, Tinian, Iwo Jima, and Okinawa. In addition to physical destruction, screaming, fiery, saturation rocket barrages tended to badly batter enemy morale.

Artillery could also be classified according to mobility. It could be:

Fixed. Installed to remain in one place, as in coastal batteries, bunkers, and other fortifications;

Mobile. Transportable from place to place via horse-drawn or motorized vehicles;

Self-propelled. Mounted on a wheeled chassis or, more usually, a chassis with treads (many models were mounted on tank chassis). These manned, self-propelled guns could go into action immediately, whereas it could take an hour to get horse- or motor-drawn artillery ready to fire. On difficult terrain, self-propelled artillery could keep up with tanks, where towed artillery could not. Germany, the United States, the United Kingdom, and the Soviet Union each developed a variety of self-propelled guns.

Some standard artillery pieces were primarily dedicated, or adapted, for use as *antiaircraft* weapons. The most effective light antiaircraft guns—used by Allied and Axis armies and navies against low-flying aircraft—were originally designed and manufactured by two neutral nations: Sweden (the Bofors 40 mm automatic gun) and Switzerland (the 20 mm Oerlikon cannon). Heavier antiaircraft guns, with greater power and higher reach, included the American 90 mm and Germany's famously adaptable 88 mm gun—originally designed as an antitank weapon (see "Tanks and Tank Destroyers," later in this chapter).

Front-line army units usually traveled with *field guns* (including guns, howitzers, and mortars; soldiers could carry some mortars, while most other field guns were mobile or self-propelled). *Heavy artillery* (larger guns and howitzers), usually under the control of larger land units such as corps or armies, could be called in to support forward units or mustered for offensives. When the two-hundred-or-more big guns of an American army corps were used in concert against a single target, GIs called the action a *serenade*. To achieve maximum effect, all the guns were sometimes fired to achieve *Time on Target* (TOT)—following calculations so that all two hundred shells exploded on target at the same time. As infantry advanced, artillery support might occur in the form of "walking," "creeping," or "rolling" barrages moving ahead of the troops.

Ranging from small to very large caliber (the diameter of the inside of an artillery-piece barrel, given in millimeters or inches), the artillery of World War II fired shells that varied in size, weight, and explosive power: the U.S. 75 mm (2.95-inch) M1 howitzer, with a maximum range of about two miles, fired shells weighing 14.1 pounds; Germany's gigantic but little-used 800 mm (31.5-inch) railroad guns, "Gustav" and "Dora," with a maximum range near thirty miles, fired shells weighing more than ten thousand pounds. Many artillery pieces were adapted to fire different types of shells, including smoke (to cover advancing or retreating forces), high-explosive, armor-piercing, and phosphorus (often used to make smoke but also able to cause terrible burns). The impact of artillery shells was, in turn, governed by the fuze (a shell might explode on impact, after impact, or at a predetermined height or distance—sometimes in midair over a target, for broader impact).

THE LADY AND THE SPIDERS

"I saw the spiders marching through the air," Robert Lowell wrote in his poem, "Mr. Edwards and the Spider." Published at the end of World War II, the poem contains subtle and most likely unintentional hints of a little-known (and sometimes disputed) chapter in the American war effort within its poetic imagery. Among America's earliest home-front animal recruits were hosts of menacing black widow spiders, whose silk (the material from which spiders spin their webs) was used to make crosshairs on tens of thousands of gun sights. Pliable and

In August 1943, Life *magazine ran a story featuring spider production shop director Armada Ruffner, shown here with one of her hardworking charges (name unknown). Spider silk was used for the crosshairs on gun sights as well as on implements like this surveyor's transit.*

Technical factors as well as battlefield conditions could affect use of artillery. On the Eastern Front, for example, Soviet armies, which depended heavily on their generally excellent artillery pieces, often massed their big guns to compensate for a lack of radios (used to communicate targeting information), insufficient meteorological information (winds and atmospheric conditions affected shell trajectories), and inadequate maps. Meanwhile the Germans adapted the design of their standard 105 mm howitzer—so that it could turn 360 degrees and fire at higher trajectories—after Soviet forces repeatedly surrounded Wermacht units in tree-filled terrain.

tougher than steel or platinum wire of the same diameter, spider silk has long been used in creating precision optics. Because so much silk was needed, U.S. experts chose the relatively large, hardy black widow as the best species to Spin for Victory. A major "recruitment" area was Fort Knox, Kentucky, where black widows were notorious nuisances to army trainees already amply discomfited by their drill sergeants. The U.S. Army Quartermaster Corps scooped up the offending spiders and transported them to the Quartermaster Corps Depot at Columbus, Ohio, where the director of the depot's spider web production shop, Armada (Ar-MADE-a) Ruffner, introduced the arachnids to a regimen of being "silked" every two days (for which the spiders were reportedly paid two flies per week).

Trained by a New Jersey spider expert, Ruffner was devoted to her atypical war work. She was never bitten, even though her overworked charges produced so much silk every week (between 100 and 180 feet of usable thread) that the average spider-draftee's life span was reduced from one year to four months. The main method Ruffner used to "silk" her spiders was to coax one onto a long stick, which she would lift higher and higher as the spider then dropped toward the ground on a silk "dragline." The silk thus procured would be wound onto a wire spindle. After fine brushes dipped in acetone cleaned the collected silk of dust particles, it was sent to the factories where gun sights were assembled. Lengths of silk then became part of the precision optical devices that allowed Allied gunners to home in more precisely on such enemy instruments of war as the feared German tanks that were named for big predator cats. As Robert Lowell noted in his poem,

"A very little thing, a little worm
Or hourglass-blazoned spider, it is said,
Can kill a tiger."

Tanks and Tank Destroyers

From ancient war chariots to thick-skinned elephants, to armored knights and horses, potent, mobile fighting power virtually impervious to harm has long been a quest of the world's armies. In the twentieth century, this culminated in the development of armored fighting vehicles (AFVs). Always protected by armor (though armor design and thickness can differ widely), generally tracked rather than wheeled, AFVs comprise a many-branched family, including self-propelled artillery and armored personnel carriers—and the lines between types can sometimes blur. The best-known type, and the most significant to armored warfare, is called the "tank"—but only because Britain's William Foster and Company Ltd., to maintain secrecy during World War I, declared that the armored vehicles it was manufacturing were mobile water cisterns (tanks).

The tank's successful debut in significant numbers, spearheading a temporary British breakthrough in long-stagnant trench lines at the November 1917 battle of Cambrai, France, was followed by two decades of uncertainty in most nations regarding how best to develop and use the new armored weapon with a rotating turret. Germany, however, quickly saw the potential of armored fighting vehicles. Despite prohibitions under the 1919 Treaty of Versailles, Germans engaged in clandestine technical research in Sweden and covertly built a few prototype tanks. They also established a secret aviation and armored training school (where the Soviets allowed them to use the mediocre Red Army tanks) five hundred miles east of Moscow in 1926, four years after Germany and the USSR reestablished relations. (Meanwhile, German military academies trained hundreds of Soviet officers—including Georgi Zhukov, who later commanded the Soviet forces that defeated German armor in World War II's greatest confrontation of tanks, the 1943 battle of Kursk.)

German officers, most notably future panzer leader Heinz Guderian, also learned much from British theorists Colonel J. F. C. Fuller and Captain Basil Liddell Hart, who advocated penetration in depth of enemy lines by armored units with aircraft support. In 1939 and 1940, Germany demonstrated its resounding leadership in armored-warfare doctrine when the Wehrmacht smashed into Poland, the Low Countries, and France with Panzer armored units spearheading breakthroughs deep into enemy territory. In France, the Wehrmacht destroyed or rendered ineffective the six-plus French armored divisions, which suffered, during their brief period of combat, from flawed tank-warfare doctrine and poor coordination and communication.

The British theorists also influenced some military thinkers in the United States and the Soviet Union—as did a 1927 military exercise, observed by Americans and Soviets, in which Britain's Experimental Mechanized Force (tanks, self-propelled guns, and various other motorized units) easily bested conventional forces. In the Soviet Union, which had only ninety-two obsolete tanks in 1927, a tremendous surge in tank production ensued, but no truly effective armored-warfare doctrine was developed, due largely to internal political conditions. In the United States, some officers, notably World War I tank commander Major George S. Patton and Major Dwight D. Eisenhower, envisioned less conservative roles for armored units

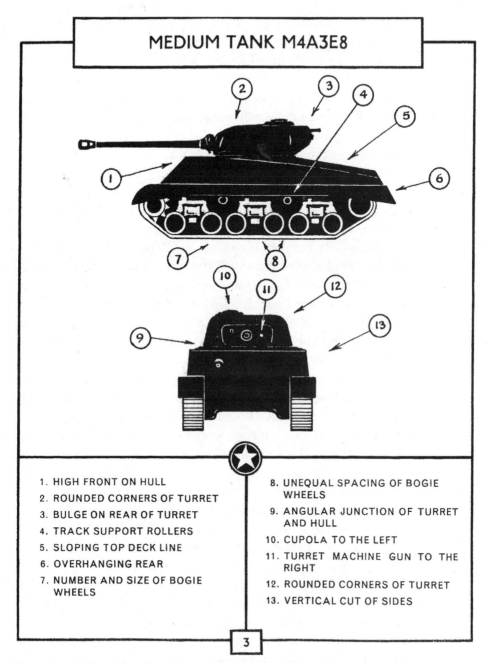

MEDIUM TANK M4A3E8

1. HIGH FRONT ON HULL
2. ROUNDED CORNERS OF TURRET
3. BULGE ON REAR OF TURRET
4. TRACK SUPPORT ROLLERS
5. SLOPING TOP DECK LINE
6. OVERHANGING REAR
7. NUMBER AND SIZE OF BOGIE WHEELS
8. UNEQUAL SPACING OF BOGIE WHEELS
9. ANGULAR JUNCTION OF TURRET AND HULL
10. CUPOLA TO THE LEFT
11. TURRET MACHINE GUN TO THE RIGHT
12. ROUNDED CORNERS OF TURRET
13. VERTICAL CUT OF SIDES

Most major combatants continued developing tanks throughout the war, sending new and improved models onto the battlefield. This chart identifying the characteristics of an American medium tank is among the illustrations in "Friend or Foe?" a pamphlet issued by the Armored Section, First U.S. Army, to help troops avoid unhappy encounters with enemy tanks—and help prevent "friendly fire" incidents against new American models.

than those prescribed by existing U.S. doctrine, in which the tank's primary mission was "to facilitate the uninterrupted advance of the rifleman." Short-lived American mechanized forces (formed in 1928 and again in 1930 and modeled on the British unit) demonstrated the benefits of mechanization and the use of tanks in broader missions. But more conservative theories prevailed until German Panzer divisions spearheaded Hitler's attacks on Poland and western Europe.

In 1940, as the Third Reich was swallowing Europe, the United States had 500 tanks in its arsenal, compared with 1,150 British, 2,000 Japanese, 3,000 French, and 3,200 German tanks (several hundred of them snatched from occupied Czechoslovakia). The Soviets had 24,000 tanks—of which more than 17,000 would be destroyed in the first months of the 1941 German invasion. By the end of the war, the United States alone had produced about 61,000 of the nearly 139,000 tanks manufactured by the Allied "Big Three" (U.S., U.K., USSR) and had organized sixteen armored divisions (each including tanks; armored infantry, artillery, reconnaissance units; engineer, medical, and ordnance battalions; and an armored signal company).

Tanks operated best in open terrain, such as the deserts of North Africa and the Russian steppes, but were effectively employed in all theaters of operation. Formidably armed, with machine guns augmenting their main weapon (the daunting 88 mm antitank/antiaircraft gun on Germany's Tiger II heavy tank; a 105 mm howitzer on one variant of the American M4 Sherman medium tank), tanks, with their crews of two to six men, were not only the anchors of independent armored-unit operations. They also engaged in toe-to-toe battles with enemy armor, served as self-propelled artillery (in general, tanks fired most accurately when not moving), and provided support for infantry assaults. (In turn, heavily armed infantry troops provided essential protection for tanks—whose crews had a very limited field of vision—against enemy attacks with mines, flamethrowers, and other disabling weaponry.)

Coordination between individual tanks and between armored ground units and other attack or defense elements—particularly covering air units—was also crucial. Good communication was required to maintain flexibility of movement, necessitated by the always-uncertain dynamics of battle. Initially, however, not all tanks were radio equipped (one theory being that only command tanks needed transceivers); many crews used hand-held flag signals and recognition and signal pennants. Command tanks proved far from immune to damage or destruction in battle, however; and tank-mounted pennants were often shredded by wind or enemy ordnance or proved difficult to "read" by men looking into the sun. Radios quickly became standard equipment in individual tanks (though in some cases—especially in the radio-poor Soviet Union—hand-flag signals were used throughout the war). (See also "Technological Devices—Radio," later in this chapter.)

Tanks were generally classified into three main groups according to weight and armament:

1. *Light.* These included the U.S. M3 (Stuart); the German Panzerkampf-wagen (PzKw) I and II; the British Mk. VI A; and the Japanese Type 95, generally regarded as the best Japanese tank (although, like the Italians, the Japanese lagged well behind the other major combatants in tank development and armored-warfare doctrine). Light tanks' relative speed, due in part to lighter armor, made them particularly suitable for scouting operations and strikes at vulnerable enemy positions.

2. *Medium.* These included the American M4 Sherman; Germany's out-standing PzKw IV; most of Britain's "Cruiser" tanks (models included the Covenanter, the Crusader, the Cromwell, and the Challenger); and the USSR's excellent T-34, much respected by the Germans. Maneu-verable, well-armored, and with good speed (the T-34 could manage thirty-three miles per hour), medium tanks were the mainstay of wartime tank operations.

3. *Heavy.* These included Germany's much-feared "Tiger," Britain's "Matilda" and "Churchill," and the U.S. M26 "Pershing" (introduced late in the war). Compensating in thickness of armor and firepower for less speed and maneuverability (Russia's fifty-seven-ton JS [Josef Stalin]–III had a top speed of twenty miles per hour), heavy tanks were most valuable for breakthrough operations.

Armored fighting vehicles were continually improved, redesigned, re-armored, and "up-gunned," propelled by the "gun/armor spiral": better armor on enemy tanks called for more powerful guns on one's own, which caused the enemy to develop better armor. Battlefield experience also re-sulted in the creation of special-purpose tanks, including:

Amphibious tanks. Examples are the German Schwimmpanzer III, de-veloped for "Operation Sealion," the canceled invasion of Great Britain, and used instead on the Eastern Front. Allied Sherman "Duplex Drive"

(DD) tanks, fitted with inflatable skirts, were developed primarily to help clear enemy emplacements and armor obstructing the first waves of infantry to hit invasion beaches.

Flamethrower tanks. Examples are the American Sherman Flamethrower, on which a flamethrower replaced the bow machine gun; and Britain's Churchill Crocodile.

Flail tanks and tanks equipped with other special devices. Flail tanks, such as the U.S. Sherman "Crab" and the U.S./U.K. Grant Scorpion III, were standard models with attached devices that churned up the ground ahead of them to detonate mines and clear a path through a minefield. A later U.S. mine-exploder tank was equipped with giant rollers. Some tanks had special attachments that allowed them to lay explosive charges against particularly hard-to-breach fortifications; after the tank backed away, an electric signal detonated the charges. Other tanks, with special bridge-decks attached to their tops, actually became bridges, driving into hard-to-cross ditches, for example, with other vehicles moving across the bridge-decks. After the Normandy landings, with the Allies facing countless hedgerows impassable even by tanks, American sergeant Curtis G. Culin invented the "hedgerow cutter"—a rakelike implement made of heavy angle iron salvaged from German underwater obstacles off the beaches. More than three hundred hedgerow cutters, produced in only forty-eight hours, were attached to tanks and played an important part in the advance that led to the Allied breakthrough at Saint-Lô.

Remote-controlled/radio-operated tanks. Developed and used by the Germans, at first for mine-clearing purposes, these small drone armored vehicles, which could be controlled by radio from just over a mile, were, later in the war, packed with explosives and used as remote-controlled bombs. By war's end, the German army included several battalions and independent companies equipped with mine-clearing and explosive-charge-carrying drone tanks; some were amphibious.

The fearsome firepower and mobility of tanks led to potent countermeasures. The term *tank destroyers* can be used to describe everything from self-propelled guns to individual soldiers wielding mines, bazookas, or grenades—and a great deal of courage. On the Eastern Front, the Soviet Union deployed several effective assault gun/tank destroyers, including the SU-85 and SU-100—85 mm and 100 mm high-velocity guns, respectively, mounted on a T-34 tank chassis. The larger ISU-152 assault howitzer, mounted on a Joseph

Stalin heavy-tank chassis, became known as the "Animal Killer," because it destroyed so many German Tiger and Elefant tanks. Germany's tank destroyers included the Nashorn (rhinoceros), an 88 mm gun mounted on a PzKpfw IV tank chassis, the heavier Jagdpanther, mounted on a Panther tank chassis, and the even more powerful Jagdtiger, which mounted a 128 mm gun and weighed more than seventy tons.

American-made tank destroyer weapons included the early-war M10 Gun Motor Carriage, a self-propelled assault gun mounted on a Sherman tank chassis; the fast (forty-five miles per hour) M18; and the M36, which mounted a formidable 90 mm antiaircraft gun. Speed, essential when pursuing tanks (and getting out of the range of their guns), was achieved by giving these tank-destroyer self-propelled guns lighter armor—which made them vulnerable to their targets' heavy guns.

Rockets, fired from aircraft or land-based launchers (sometimes mounted on opposing tanks and tank-destroyer assault guns), were effective against tanks, as were hand-held weapons that fired potent shaped charges. These included the American bazooka, the British PIAT, and the German Panzerfaust (officially, the Racketenpanzerbuchse—a weapon based on the bazooka). *Mines* were also a formidable threat to tanks—a fact that led to the development of the mine-clearing tanks, noted earlier. Often, minefields were laid to force tanks into an area that had been staked out by enemy antitank forces as a tank-killing ground.

Cameras

See Chapter 9.

Camouflage, Decoys, and Deception

See also Chapters 3 and 9.

At Anzio, Italy, as Allied tanks pulled out to prepare for a coming offensive, their place was taken by inflatable ersatz tanks that looked equally fierce—from a distance. On Iwo Jima, American forces surrounded a Japanese tank that had been drawing fire from U.S. guns—and found it was actually a tank-sculpture carved out of the island's volcanic ash. Such decoys and other deceptive devices (dubbed "spoofs" by the British) were used throughout the war—often by special spoofing units—in an ongoing campaign to divert, confuse, and generally beflummox the enemy.

U.S. forces, which had fallen behind in the spoofing-and-camouflage realm in the interwar years, began a fast game of catch-up in 1940. Americans developed new nongloss camouflage paints (more likely to fool cameras); tested colors to see which most effectively blended in various terrains; conducted intensive research on decoys and dummies; and tested nets to disguise field artillery and mechanisms for raising and lowering the nets quickly. Engineer Camouflage Battalions were formed to instruct and assist front-line units. Throughout the war, home-front experimentation and battlefield ingenuity were partners in developing camouflage for everything from foxholes to artillery bunkers, army camps to ships and military and industrial installations.

Camouflage was also important for the individual soldier. As American forces battled to hang onto Bataan in early 1942, men wearing their government-issued white T-shirts or using white towels or handkerchiefs were killed by snipers. While quartermasters back home worked to produce less targetable apparel and accouterments, Pacific Theater front-line units used the juice of berries or the tannin of tree bark to camouflage their clothing. Because of production bottlenecks, it was not until 1943 that ample supplies of olive-drab socks, underwear, handkerchiefs, and towels were available to Pacific Theater combat units.

In Europe during the bloody, cold—and very snowy—winter of 1944–1945, American forces were plagued by a shortage of white snow-camouflage capes and suits. Troops without them were perfect targets, their dark uniforms standing out against the snow-covered earth. Quartermasters instituted a crash program, buying as much white cloth as the French and Belgians could spare; in recently occupied German towns, military government personnel used loudspeakers to urge civilians to turn in white sheeting, issuing receipts that could be redeemed later for payment. Factories in Holland, Belgium, and Germany were commissioned to make capes and snowsuits, and U.S. Army units also pitched in: one Third Army salvage repair company turned out seven hundred capes in less than twenty-four hours. All these efforts yielded 300,000 camouflage suits. In the meantime, white paint was issued as fast as it could be secured to camouflage front-line vehicles and artillery.

Fortifications

See also Chapters 3 and 7.

Fearfully wounded by the bloodletting of World War I, the French constructed one of World War II's most elaborate—and, eventually, most ridiculed—fortified lines to keep German armies from invading their country again. Named for Minister of War André Maginot, the Maginot Line was a three-and-a-half- to six-mile-deep complex of pillboxes, fortified houses, sunken fortresses, and blockhouses, interconnected by 62 miles of tunnels and 280 miles of railroad. Its formidable defenses included minefields, 344 major artillery pieces in receded emplacements, machine guns, and grenade throwers. Political, financial, and logistical problems prevented the Line's extension completely across France—which is a principal reason the name "Maginot Line" is generally found in World War II literature quite close to the phrase "outflanked by the Germans."

The Wehrmacht circumvented the Line in the spring of 1940 by wheeling around its flank, a large part of the German column passing through the Ardennes Forest, generally regarded—before that event—as impassable to armored columns. The Germans only attacked one part of the Line directly: a specially trained assault group equipped with flamethrowers and supported

British troops march into a section of France's Maginot Line in December 1939. Although World War II was a mobile war, a number of such fixed, fortified lines challenged both Axis and Allied troops.

by artillery and air power overwhelmed a detached fort near Malmedy. Ironically, after France fell, the Maginot Line became an effective German fortification from which the Wehrmacht made a determined stand against George S. Patton's U.S. Third Army from September to mid-December 1944.

The dynamics of World War II—dominated by air forces, improved artillery, and mobile armored fighting vehicles—meant that field fortifications (such as pillboxes, trench lines, front-line bunkers, and the lowly but lifesaving foxhole) assumed prominence over more elaborate, fixed fortified defensive lines, such as the Maginot. But such lines did exist—the most elaborate built by the Germans during the war—and in some cases were extremely effective at disrupting even large-scale enemy assaults. Major fortified lines are described in the following chart.

MAJOR WORLD WAR II FORTIFIED LINES

Line	Description
Atlantic Wall	A veritable forest of German fortifications extending for over 1,600 miles (though not continuously) from the Netherlands to Spain. This was the foundation of Hitler's loudly proclaimed *Festung Europa* ("Fortress Europe").
Belgian fortresses; Polish and Russian fortified areas	Though neutral, Belgium began constructing a line of forts in the early 1930s as Germany was rearming; these proved no match for the 1940 blitzkrieg. The Wehrmacht had already easily breached a loose line of less-sophisticated Polish fortifications along the German-Polish border in September 1939. Nearly two years later, the Germans also had little trouble bypassing the so-called Stalin Line (a sporadic Soviet line of fortified areas)—except the fortress town of Brest Litovsk, where the Soviet garrison held out almost to the last man.
Czechoslovakian fortifications	Built in the 1930s, these incorporated many of the characteristics of the Maginot Line, such as underground passages connecting more than 200 heavy fortresses and blockhouses. They passed into German hands in 1938, without a shot being fired.

MAJOR WORLD WAR II FORTIFIED LINES (CONTINUED)

Line	Description
German defensive lines in Italy	These elaborate fortifications comprised two distinct systems: (1) The Reinhard, Hitler, and Gustav lines were south of Rome (the Gustav line was anchored by Monte Cassino); (2) farther north, the Gothic Line—a ten-mile-deep belt of minefields and deep bunkers, protected by antitank ditches, more than 2,000 machine-gun emplacements, and 120,000 yards of wire—extended two hundred miles from coast to coast along the Apennine Mountains.
Pomeranian Wall	Built in the mid-1930s in east Prussia, this seventy-five-mile-long German defensive line of tank traps and artillery emplacements was tenaciously defended against the Soviet army for weeks in 1945 before Soviet-led Polish troops overwhelmed it.
West Wall/Siegfried Line	Supposedly impregnable, this fortified line running four hundred miles from Switzerland to Holland, though never completed, was a formidable barrier. It included 14,000 bunkers and pillboxes fronted by scattered trenches, observation posts, minefields, barbed-wire entanglements, and fearsome "Dragon's Teeth"—continuous rows of concrete pyramids, several feet high, that effectively blocked tanks and other armored vehicles.
Kammhuber Line	These German air defenses can be regarded as a type of fortification. Established in 1940 by General Josef Kammhuber, first commander of the Luftwaffe's night fighter units, it comprised flak (antiaircraft weapons), radio beams, radar units, and searchlights, coordinated with night-fighter aircraft to counter Allied planes engaged in strategic bombing. (See also "Technological Devices," later in this chapter.)

Principal sources: Ian Hogg, *The History of Fortification: "The Great Defensive Lines,"* New York: St. Martin's Press, 1981; I. C. B. Dear and M. R. D. Foot, eds., *Oxford Companion to World War II*, New York: Oxford University Press, 2001.

Field fortifications, usually more temporary, ranged from improvised walls and foxholes (usually one- or two-man pits hastily dug by front-line infantrymen), to barriers raised from the rubble of besieged cities, such as Leningrad and Stalingrad, and the fortified gun emplacements and underground operations centers constructed in Hawaii in the weeks after Pearl Harbor, in anticipation of Japanese invasion.

Among British coastal fortifications built under the threat of invasion were the unique, specially designed concrete "Maunsell Forts" (after civil engineer G. A. Maunsell, who suggested them). Fully equipped with antiaircraft guns and radar, they were constructed in drydock, then floated to strategic locations in the Thames, Humber, and Mersey estuaries, their foundations then anchored on the bottom by a process of controlled sinking. These distinctive fortifications (in variations favored by either the Admiralty or the army) proved their worth against air and sea attacks. The British also established many coastal artillery emplacements and other shoreline defenses; some of their coastal guns could reach targets across the English Channel.

The United States began tentatively establishing its own coastal defenses in the late 1930s, expanding efforts under congressional authorization in September 1940. Defenses included laying submarine nets and minefields to protect several important areas (see the following section, "Mines and Booby Traps") and establishing bunkers, each housing coastal artillery, at some nineteen American harbors.

Japan's home defense installations proved increasingly inadequate, especially after the American concentrated bombing campaign against the home islands began late in 1944. Japanese field defenses in the China-Burma-India and Pacific Theaters, however, were elaborate and difficult to penetrate, obstructing Allied forces up to the last days of the war. When Americans landed on Iwo Jima, for example, they faced more than eight hundred pillboxes (small fortlike constructions with firing slits) carefully sited over a mere eight square miles of territory. The Japanese also made extremely effective use of terrain during the war, fortifying caves and often interconnecting defensive emplacements with deep tunnels. In 1945, an American war correspondent described a hidden field fortification on Okinawa:

In the face of a rocky hill was a narrow horizontal slit five feet long and eighteen inches high, with pine logs for header and low growing bushes for camouflage. At a distance of a hundred feet it could not be seen. We had to wriggle through on our bellies to reach the interior of the cave. There in a room about fifteen feet square was a Japanese antitank gun mounted on pneumatic-tired wheels. Piled high around three walls were cases of ammunition, . . . From that room a drift or tunnel ran 125 feet through the hill, opening on another side. At intervals along its length were other rooms in each of which large quantities of ammunition were stored. From the slit through which we entered the gun crew commanded the field of fire covering the broad, level plain across which American tanks had to advance to reach Kakazu Ridge.

Thus protected, Japanese troops could wait out bombardments, then use their weapons to devastating effect once Allied troops were in range. Overcoming these defenses was very slow, difficult, and costly. (One U.S. Tenth Army Ordnance officer estimated that, in the month following the first landings on April 1, 1945, American forces on Okinawa expended an average of 1.65 tons of ground ammunition to kill one defending Japanese soldier.) Eventually, the Americans on Okinawa developed successful anticave tactics: artillery fire against the entrances forced the Japanese back into their tunnels; infantry and tanks then closed in, sealing the caves with flamethrowers or explosives. In some places, dogs were used to sniff out enemy cave emplacements. U.S. interrogations of Japanese prisoners revealed a marked respect for American combat canines.

Mines and Booby Traps

I want mines to sink ships and mines to sink landing craft. I want some minefields designed so that our infantry can cross them but not enemy tanks. I want mines that detonate when a wire is tripped; mines that explode when a wire is cut; mines that can be remotely controlled and mines that will explode when a beam of light is interrupted. Some of them must be encased in a nonferrous metal, so that the enemy's mine detectors won't register them.

—*Field Marshal Erwin Rommel, to his chief engineer, General Wilhelm Meise, 1944, while preparing for the expected Allied landing in western Europe*

An ancient concept, mine warfare received a new and more terrible lease on death during World War II, when millions—perhaps hundreds of millions—of land mines were deployed. The U.S. Army alone procured 24,402,000, and estimates for the number of Soviet mines run as high as 200 million. Allied soldiers encountered German minefields, often planted in the tens or hundreds of thousands, nearly everywhere they marched—something for which American commanders were not, initially, prepared.

In June 1943, after a tour of North Africa, U.S. General Lesley J. McNair told *Life* magazine,

> The enemy's tremendous application of land mines makes them almost a new arm of combat. When our troops retreated from Kasserine Pass, they . . . planted all the mines they could, but didn't slow down the German advance appreciably. When the Germans were driven out of the Pass, they left in a hurry too. Somehow, though, they were able to leave mines all over the place. They slowed us down. So we are putting a lot more emphasis on mines now.

There were two basic types of land mines:

1. *Antitank* mines, such as Italian bar mines (shaped like a wooden slat) deployed in North Africa, the several models of Germany's plate-shaped Tellermine, and the U.S. M1A1. Usually pressure-activated and calibrated so that only a vehicle, not a person, would cause detonation, antitank mines could destroy jeep-sized vehicles and shatter the treads and undercarriages of tanks and other heavy armored fighting vehicles. Fields of such mines were laid both as defenses against armored attack and as offensive weapons; for example, to channel armored columns into range of tank destroyers or armor-killing artillery. Antitank mines were often interspersed with antipersonnel mines, which made lifting or deactivating them even more hazardous. Among other uses besides minefields, a retreating army certain it would not return to an area might scatter uncharted mines behind them to slow its pursuers. A favorite German trick was to bury mines too deep to be detected or triggered by passing traffic until deep enough ruts were eventually worn in the road. These wholly unexpected detonations had a major psychological impact in addition to the mines' explosive power, and even a few such mines could halt everything while an entire roadway was checked.

2. *Antipersonnel* mines contained smaller explosive charges than antitank mines and came in a wide variety of types and models—all devoted to killing or maiming the humans who triggered them. Allied soldiers were particularly wary of Germany's "S" mine, which British troops dubbed the "Bouncing Betty": when one was tripped, a small charge of black powder threw a grapeshot canister up to waist level, where it

exploded, sending a deadly hail of steel ball bearings in all directions. Also dreaded was the Germans' six-by-four-by-two-inch Schu mine, with one-half to two pounds of explosives; easily carried and very easily concealed under dirt, grass, or leaves, it was tripped by as little as five pounds of pressure and destroyed feet, ankles, and shin bones.

Both antitank and antipersonnel mines could be detonated by delayed-action fuzes and trip wires as well as pressure and other means. And antipersonnel mines could be anywhere, outdoors or indoors.

Improvised Mines and Booby Traps

In 1941 and early 1942, hard-pressed American forces in the Philippines had few actual antitank mines so they improvised substitutes: wooden boxes, each rigged with about five pounds of dynamite, a flashlight battery, and a detonator. Later in the war, as the Allies squeezed Japan's supply lines to a trickle, Japanese field units were forced to improvise many types of mines, including aerial bombs or naval artillery shells buried nose-up so passing Allied forces would trigger them, and makeshift mines (grenades surrounded by nails) placed inside scooped-out coconuts.

Variations on mines, unhappy explosive surprises generally called *booby traps*, were rife in all theaters of the war. The Germans were particularly adept at creating them, booby-trapping such items as field glasses, Luger pistols, wallets, pencils, chocolate bars, soap, windows, doors, furniture, toilets, demolished German equipment, and bodies. They also booby-trapped antitank mines, doubling their potential for exploding. Even in checked areas, front-line soldiers could never be certain of the roads they walked on, the houses they sheltered in, the apples that dangled enticingly in trees.

Land Mine Detection and Clearing

Detection, clearance, and disposal of so many mines and booby traps became a major challenge for all combatants. Engineers were generally assigned to the task when available. (In Russia, untrained—and thus presumably more expendable—infantrymen were sometimes given the job.) American engineers relied primarily on the most reliable method of minesweeping: a man carefully probing the ground with a bayonet held at a thirty-degree angle. To speed things up, there were also mechanical devices, including remote-controlled tanks and tanks equipped with special equipment (see "Tanks and Tank Destroyers,"

Medics attend to a U.S. combat engineer who triggered a mine during a sweep of a danger area (marked by white tape) in France, June 1944. In the foreground, another engineer continues probing for mines by hand—having set his metal detector on the ground beside him.

earlier in this chapter), as well as flexible line charges ("snakes") and bangalore torpedoes (pipes filled with explosives) that tanks pushed into minefields. Artillery and machine-gun fire (and occasionally animals herded into suspect areas) cleared paths through minefields by exploding mines. And metal detectors were used to locate mines so they could be lifted or exploded.

No method was guaranteed successful. American metal detectors were fragile and often stopped working when they got damp, their hum was audible to enemies, and their operators had to be standing up—an often hazardous posture for front-line soldiers. Metal detectors were also often baffled by soil with high metal content or by shell fragments and expended ammunition. And many mines had explosives encased in wood, plastic, or paper, not metal. Some methods of mine disposal created additional dangers. Clearing a path through a minefield by exploding mines could alert an enemy to one's approach and increase the sensitivity of nearby mines, making those "tender mines" prone to explode at the slightest jarring. Even supposedly deactivated mines could be dangerous, the explosive material within them made sensitive by age or wear and tear. In March 1943, in North Africa, all twelve men in one squad of the U.S. 109th Engineer Combat Battalion, transporting 450 deactivated mines by truck, were killed when the mines exploded.

Sea Mines

Sailors were not immune to mine warfare. Hundreds of thousands of sea mines infested waters from the Pacific Islands to the harbor at Murmansk, from the Danube River to approaches to the Mississippi. Britain alone deployed 263,000; the U.S. Navy deployed nearly 50,000. Among the most destructive of these sea mines were: *acoustic mines*, equipped with microphones that "listened" for ships; *magnetic mines* that exploded when their instrumentation detected a ship's magnetic field; and, perhaps most insidious, *pressure mines* that reacted to variations in water pressure caused by ships moving overhead.

Initially using recommissioned World War I mines and *minelayers* (boats equipped with special "tracks" off which mines were dropped in the water), the U.S. Navy and the army's seagoing Mineplanter Service laid defensive minefields from Casco Bay, Maine, New York Harbor, and Chesapeake Bay in the East, to Key West and Pensacola, Florida, Mobile Bay, Alabama, and Galveston, Texas, in the South. German U-boats later laid offensive mines in some of these same locations, leaving at least 338 mines in American coastal waters in 1942. The Japanese also laid mines in American waters: one damaged the U.S. Navy destroyer *Abner Read* near the Aleutian island of Kiska on August 18, 1943.

Axis and Allied mines laid by submarines, surface vessels, and aircraft sank or damaged thousands of merchant and combat vessels. The United States and Britain reported nearly 2,700 enemy ships lost due to minelaying; in the Pacific, where most Allied mines were laid by the United States, the Japanese lost one ship for every twenty-three of the more than 23,000 mines laid. Axis mines sank or severely damaged nearly six hundred British ships and nearly one hundred U.S. combat and merchant vessels.

Charting Land and Sea Minefields

All mines shared a lack of discrimination: it made no difference to them whether friend or foe tripped them. "Friendly" mines destroyed or damaged twenty-one Japanese ships and, in American waters, seventeen Allied vessels, and friendly land mines killed or maimed many soldiers. On the fiercely contested beachhead at Anzio, Italy, in early 1944, Allied infantry casualties rose significantly after U.S. Army engineers planted fields of defensive land mines in areas devoid of distinctive landmarks without making accurate records of their locations.

Careful charting of minefields and prompt dissemination of the information to friendly field units was essential to avoid such tragedies and to locate and remove active mines after combat had ended in a particular area. In 1942 and early 1943, U.S. Navy minelayers had many hair-raising experiences placing mines in the waters surrounding Guadalcanal and other eastern Solomon Islands. Well-informed about the mines' locations, Navy mine-sweepers were usually successful when they were dispatched to remove them. On land, American soldiers were generally required to learn mine warfare by being thrust into it (though training did improve during the war). The haphazard approach to charting and reporting minefields that resulted was in marked contrast to the meticulous charting practiced by mine-warfare-savvy German units. The official U.S. Army history of World War II reports, "A postwar engineer investigating board recommended the American imitation of the German system, at least in establishing a centralized theater-level mine information network."

Naval Vessels and Weaponry

The Atlantic and Pacific Oceans, the Mediterranean Sea, and many lesser waters were constant battlegrounds of the war, bitterly contested by the nations that had emerged as the major early twentieth-century naval powers: Britain, the United States, and Japan. Germany's surface navy, dismembered by the 1919 Treaty of Versailles and then rebuilt by the Nazis without operational aircraft carriers, did not prove to be a major World War II force. German submarines, on the other hand, were an enormous threat to Allied supply lines until mid-1943. The technologically challenged Italian navy (devoid of radar, sonar, and operational aircraft carriers) also suffered from a shortage of oil and the high command's reluctance to place its capital ships at risk. (See discussions of individual navies in Chapter 4.)

Submarines gradually became an important factor in naval warfare during World War I; by 1917, German *Unterseeboots* (U-boats) were sinking so many merchant ships carrying vital supplies that they threatened Britain's continuing ability to wage war—a role U-boats would again assume two decades later. The Allied response—a convoy system, organizing groups of merchant ships under armed naval escort—was so successful that the British instituted a similar system immediately upon the outbreak of World War II.

During the Great War, the Royal Navy also employed seaplane tenders that carried multiple aircraft (launched from the deck, they landed on and were retrieved from the sea); other vessels carried one or two reconnaissance aircraft. On July 18, 1918, seven British Sopwith Camels—wheeled airplanes rather than seaplanes—took off from the flight deck of HMS *Furious*, a converted cruiser, and successfully raided the German Zeppelin base at Tondern, Germany (now in Denmark)—thus launching the age of the aircraft carrier. (Remodeled several times, *Furious* continued its service with the Royal Navy through World War II.) The new era of naval air power developed rapidly during the interwar years. But an understanding of the pivotal role of aircraft carriers came more slowly. Despite Britain's successful carrier-based aircraft attack on Italian ships at Taranto (November 1, 1940), many American naval planners continued to believe that the battleship still ruled the waves and that carrier-based aircraft would engage primarily in reconnaissance, serving as the "eyes of the fleet"—until Japan's carrier-based air attack at Pearl Harbor devastated the U.S. Pacific Fleet.

Most serious American naval planners of the 1920s and 1930s envisioned a possible maritime conflict with Japan, so they studied amphibious warfare and the need to secure support bases for U.S. naval forces pushing across the Pacific toward Japan. The Americans closely studied the Allied disaster at Gallipoli in 1915, during which amphibious landings and other naval operations went terribly wrong, as they prepared the U.S. *Landing Operations Manual*, first published in 1934. Amphibious doctrine presented in the manual and in its 1938 revision, *Fleet Training Publication 167*, proved to be very sound when tested by World War II combat. Only two major adjustments had to be made: command of an amphibious operation did not remain with the admiral who was in command as U.S. forces approached their objective, but shifted to the Marine Corps or army commander on the ground once the landing force was established; and long-range naval fire proved to be inadequate support for troops on the ground, requiring even large ships to brave the consequences of close approach to fire most effectively.

To land those troops, the Allies developed many sorts of amphibious craft; and manufacturers—chiefly American—produced them in the tens of thousands. (See "Landing Craft and Amphibious Vessels" later in this section.) These smaller amphibious vessels joined the thousands of larger ships that significantly increased the strength of major Allied naval forces—particularly the American Navy—during the war (in sharp contrast to the precipitous ebb in Axis naval power).

Aircraft Carriers

Under the 1922 Five-Power Naval Limitation Treaty, the United States and Britain were restricted in aircraft carriers to a total of 135,000 tons and Japan to 81,000 tons, but each nation found ways to "stretch" or circumvent some of the treaty's restrictions. U.S. aircraft carriers included USS *Langley* (1919–1921), converted from a collier; *Lexington* and *Saratoga* (1928), built on battle cruiser hulls; *Ranger* (1934), the first American carrier not converted from another type of ship; and, between 1937 and 1941, the larger and much-improved *Yorktown, Enterprise, Wasp,* and *Hornet.*

The world's leaders in naval aviation, the British continued their own aircraft carrier development in the interwar years including a series of carriers so heavily armored that they carried fewer aircraft. The British also gave a boost to the Imperial Japanese Navy's naval aircraft and carrier development, even as the formal Anglo-Japanese Alliance, forged in 1902, was coming to an end. Responding to a Japanese request for technical assistance, the British sent a semiofficial mission, comprising some thirty ex-Royal Naval Air Service officers, to Japan (1921–1923), despite the Royal Navy's strong reservations. Japan's first naval aviators were trained in Europe and at the Glen Curtiss flight training schools in the United States. (Those trained at the latter included Chikuhei Nakajima, founder of Nakajima Aircraft, which produced some of Japan's best World War II combat aircraft.) This assistance, plus intense Japanese scrutiny of European and American carrier progress, greatly accelerated the development of Japan's naval air arm. The Japanese made their first landing on the carrier *Hosho* (converted from a tanker) in 1923, just a few months after the first American landing on USS *Langley.*

Like their American counterparts, Imperial Japanese Navy planners debated for years whether to produce smaller carriers, less vulnerable to attack, and how to use carrier forces most effectively. In 1936, Chief of Naval Aeronautics Admiral Isoroku Yamamoto, who later masterminded the attack on

Pearl Harbor, argued unsuccessfully for producing more carriers instead of battleships. Resources poured into battleship construction well into the war, including two huge "super-battleships," *Yamato* and *Musashi*, neither of which saw much action before Allied aircraft sank them in 1944. Due in part to a huge, secret naval building program, Japan did start the war slightly ahead of the United States in carrier strength, though somewhat behind the British (who, early on, lost three of their initial ten carriers). Lagging far behind in industrial capacity, however, the Japanese could not recover from the loss of four of their fleet carriers at the pivotal battle of Midway (June 3–6, 1942). Thereafter, they relied chiefly on smaller carriers, many of them converted from other types of vessels.

The United States, meanwhile, more than made up for its own early carrier losses by building carriers at an amazing pace, including many smaller *escort carriers* that proved extremely effective in antisubmarine warfare. By the end of the war, some 150 American-built carriers were in operation or well on their way to completion.

Carriers and their aircraft were the primary weapons when U.S. and Japanese fleets fought the battle of the Coral Sea on May 4–8, 1942—the first naval clash in history where the opposing warships never came within sight of each other. This encounter confirmed the end of the age of the battleship.

Battleships and Cruisers

Evolved from the ironclad warships of the U.S. Civil War era, battleships (sometimes called "battlewagons") were essentially large, armored naval artillery platforms, their big guns packing immense firepower. Cruisers (battle, heavy and light) were the combat vessels next in size and firepower to battleships, and were generally more lightly armored and faster. Heavy and light cruisers provided antiaircraft defense and fire support for carriers and convoys throughout the war.

Battleships were initially considered the major unit of a naval attack force, but aircraft carriers rapidly displaced these powerful gunships after they proved vulnerable to air attack. At Pearl Harbor, Japanese bombers sank or severely damaged all eight U.S. Pacific Fleet battlewagons birthed on "battleship row" the morning of December 7, 1941. (All except the USS *Arizona* and the USS *Oklahoma* were repaired.) Three days later, Japanese bombs and torpedoes sank the British battleship HMS *Prince of Wales* and battle cruiser HMS *Repulse* in the Far East.

Battleships, with their formidable array of big guns, proved particularly valuable in support of amphibious landings. And the USS *Missouri*, anchored in Tokyo Bay, was the site of the formal ceremonies marking Japan's surrender to the Allies.

Destroyers

Smaller than cruisers, fast, and armed with multiple guns (generally five-inch), depth charges, and torpedo tubes, destroyers—omnipresent workhorses of the war—protected convoys and fleets, engaged in aggressive antisubmarine warfare, laid down smoke screens, and provided antiaircraft cover.

Landing Craft/Amphibious Vessels

Approximately eighty types of amphibious naval craft were used during the war, primarily by American, British Commonwealth, and Japanese forces, and particularly in the Pacific and western European Theaters, but also in the Mediterranean. On the Eastern Front, German and Soviet forces made limited use of amphibious vehicles: The Germans used amphibious tanks and Volkswagen reconnaissance vehicles, as well as an amphibious tractor. In their amphibious operations, Soviet forces often relied on *bolinders*, non-self-propelling landing barges capable of carrying up to ten tanks or a battalion of troops each. The Japanese developed the Type A (*daihatsu*) and the smaller Type B (*shohatsu*) landing craft in the 1930s, as well as specialized carrier ships—the 8,000-ton *Shinso-maru* (1935) and the 9,000-ton *Akitsu-maru* (1941). (These inspired postwar American all-purpose amphibious carriers.) In the 1940s, Japan developed beaching craft comparable to the Allies Landing Ship Tanks, discussed later in this section.

Major types of U.S. and British amphibious craft were:

The DUKW. This was a six-wheeled, boat-shaped amphibious vehicle based on the U.S. Army's two-and-a-half-ton truck. Popularly called the "Duck," its name derived from factory specifications (D = model year 1942, U = amphibian, K = all-wheel drive, W = dual rear axles). It was used to ferry ammunition and supplies to landing areas; each DUKW could carry five thousand pounds of cargo, an artillery piece, or twenty-five men and their equipment. The United States produced 20,000

Tracked amphibious landing vehicles carry infantrymen of the U.S. Army's 81st Division ("the Wildcats") toward the beach of Angaur Island in the Palau island group in September 1944.

DUKWs, of which 2,000 went to Britain via Lend-Lease. They were first used during the invasion of Sicily, July 1943.

Landing craft. These self-propelled vessels were produced in a host of variations, capable of transporting various weights in equipment or from 25 to 250 fully equipped men. Some were equipped with rockets; some were armed to provide antiaircraft or artillery support for troops until artillery emplacements were operational. Many subtypes of landing craft were also produced: the *Landing Craft Mechanized* (LCM)— used to transport vehicles and troops—came in about a dozen varieties. The *Landing Craft Control* (LCC), with special navigational equipment, was designed to help keep landings on target (see "Technological

Devices–Radar," later in this chapter). America's leading pioneer in creating landing craft was Andrew J. Higgins, whose prewar shallow-draft "Eureka" boats were moved onto and off beaches. The *Landing Craft Vehicle Personnel* (LCVP) Higgins developed, popularly known as "Higgins Boats," were such important factors in wartime strategy that in 1964 Dwight D. Eisenhower called Higgins "the man who won the war for us."

Landing ships. These were larger vessels that carried personnel and vehicles and smaller boats to land them. Some served more specialized purposes: the *Landing Ship Headquarters*, or *LSH*, for example, was a seagoing corps and division command center until an HQ could be set up on land. Foremost among the Landing Ships was the *Landing Ship Tank* (LST). Designed by the British as part of a crash program after western Europe fell to the Nazis in 1940, and mass-produced in the United States, the LST was the largest ship that could land on and extract itself from a beach. Produced in three variations, LSTs could land up to seventy tanks via a bow hull opening.

Landing vehicle, tracked. These hardy assault vehicles were developed from the "Alligator" designed by Donald Roebling for errands of mercy in the Florida swamps. Produced in a variety of models starting in 1941, LVTs carried troops from ships, across such obstacles as coral reefs, and onto shore—often as other, armored and heavily armed, LVTs provided covering fire.

Merchant Vessels, Armed, and German Auxiliary Cruisers

Post–World War I British naval planners reckoned that the shipping tonnage restrictions of the Washington Naval Treaty would leave them short of some seventy-five cruisers should hopes be dashed and a major war come again. Throughout the 1930s, the British prepared to fill that cruiser gap, at least temporarily, by "stiffening" about fifty merchant vessels so that they could immediately be converted to armed merchant cruisers. (Stiffening involved adding armor and mountings for the pedestals of six-inch and four-inch guns; such mountings were concealed under teak planking on the tonier passenger liners.) As of September 3, 1939, these ships were converted and put into action with limited success, but in a number of cases with striking heroism on the part of their crews. On November 4, 1940, Britain's SS *Jervis Bay*, a converted Australian passenger liner captained by Irish World War I veteran Edward Stephen Fogarty Fegen, attempted to ram the German surface raider *Admiral Scheer*. Despite taking fierce fire, the cruiser managed to hold the Germans at bay long enough for all but five of the convoy vessels it was protecting to get away. *Jervis Bay*, itself, went down with a loss of 189 officers and men. Captain Fegen was posthumously awarded the Victoria Cross.

Admiral Scheer was one of the *German surface raiders* sent out to sink or capture shipping and disrupt Allied supply lines. Three "pocket" battleships (smaller battleships mounting eleven-inch guns) designed for such duty were joined by heavier German surface vessels including the heavy cruisers *Admiral Hipper* and *Prinz Eugen*, the battle cruisers *Scharnhorst* and *Gneisenau*, and the much-feared battleship *Bismarck*. German raiders sank or captured fifty-seven Allied vessels by June 1941. After the *Bismarck* was sunk in May, the raiders were sent to guard the Norwegian coastline against Allied invasion and to threaten merchantmen on the Allied Arctic convoy route.

Axis *auxiliary cruisers*, warships disguised as merchantmen, constituted a second surface-vessel threat to Allied shipping. Flying a variety of non-Axis flags to lure their prey closer, like privateers and commerce raiders of old, these cruisers bedeviled Allied shipping until early 1943. Though Japan had two in action and Italy three, Germany's nine active auxiliary cruisers (*Atlantis, Komet, Kormoran, Michel, Orion, Pinguin, Stier, Thor,* and *Widder*) did the most damage. Together, they sank 110 Allied merchant vessels and took 31 as prizes. *Pinguin* alone sank or captured 28 before being sunk May 8, 1941, and it laid many mines; *City of Rayville* struck one of them November 8, 1940, becoming the first American merchantman sunk in World War II.

In addition to cargo, the auxiliary cruisers sometimes reaped important intelligence with their prizes: in 1940 *Atlantis* captured copies of the Allied Merchant Navy Code; in 1942 *Thor* confiscated top secret correspondence from the captured Australian vessel *Nankin*. Allied navies and air forces, aided by Ultra intelligence, hunted down these vessels, sinking all but *Orion* and *Widder* by 1943.

The U.S. Navy and the Army Air Forces protected America's burgeoning merchant fleet with increasing effectiveness as the war went on. But America, too, armed many of its merchant vessels—chiefly with three- and four-inch guns and machine guns of various calibers—so they could defend themselves against Axis planes and surfaced submarines. Many of these guns were manned by the U.S. Naval Armed Guards, a unique element of the navy comprising more than 144,000 men who served alongside the nation's civilian merchant mariners.

Minelayers and Minesweepers

See "Mines and Booby Traps–Sea Mines," earlier in this chapter.

Submarines and Antisubmarine Weapons

Immediately after the Japanese attack on Pearl Harbor, December 7, 1941, American submarines were dispatched from Hawaii's largely undamaged submarine pens to begin unrestricted operations off Japan. (The immediate declaration of unrestricted submarine warfare against Japan was a sharp break with U.S. traditions and a marked contrast with the restrictions placed on British Royal Navy submariners in the early months of their war with Germany.) Arriving in early January 1942, *Plunger* and *Pollack* sank three Japanese freighters. On its way home, *Gudgeon* became the first U.S. Navy sub to sink an enemy combatant vessel, Japan's submarine *I-173*. The U.S. Navy's "silent service" would come to dominate the undersea struggle for control of the Pacific despite damaging technical problems through the first half of the war (see "'Damn the Torpedoes,'" later in this section).

In the battle of the Atlantic, which began two years earlier, Allied submarines, surface vessels, and woefully insufficient aircraft faced German U-boats and Italian subs, which often attacked in groups called "wolf packs." An equally intense naval battle was being waged for control of the Mediterranean, where so many British warships were sunk or badly damaged during the Allied withdrawal from Crete (May 1941) that the Royal Navy relied heavily on U-class (mid-size) submarines for both offense and defense—and occasionally for getting supplies through to the people of the besieged island of Malta. Both Italian and German subs also fought in the Mediterranean. In January 1942, the submarine war spread to the East Coast of the United States (there was some Japanese submarine activity off the West Coast as well) and, shortly thereafter, to the Gulf of Mexico, the Caribbean, and the east coast of South America as far as the "bulge" of Brazil. (See also Chapters 6 and 7.)

World War II submarines were generally larger, often had longer range, and had more sophisticated equipment than those employed during World War I (some of which were still in service). All subs used a gasoline or diesel engine when on the surface (where they could travel faster), and electric batteries when submerged (the greater their underwater speed, the faster they used up the battery power). Batteries could only be recharged, and air inside the vessel refreshed, while submarines were on the surface, where they were extremely vulnerable. Near the end of the war, Germany deployed a few *schnorkel* and Walter submarines that could recharge batteries without surfacing.

All the leading combatants entered the war with significant submarine fleets, the Soviet Union having the greatest number (160) followed by Italy (115), and the United States (113). Germany had only fifty-six operational U-boats in September 1939 and Great Britain had sixty-one, twelve of which were World War I veterans; Japan had about sixty. All these nations built subs throughout the war—Japan's building program barely keeping even with its losses, Germany's steadily falling behind. Of 1,175 U-boats committed to battle throughout the war, 781—along with 32,000 of Germany's 38,000 submariners—were lost. (See individual descriptions of naval organizations in Chapter 4.)

Submarines varied in size: smaller coastal-duty boats displaced about 260 tons when submerged; medium-size vessels displaced about 880 to 900 tons while submerged; and the largest submarines displaced between 1,000 and 6,500 tons—the latter being Japanese "carrier subs" that carried three float planes for reconnaissance and bombing missions. Operational ranges also varied widely, with the carrier subs having an operational range of 37,500 miles. The U.S. Navy's standard "Gato/Balao Class" submarines displaced just over 2,400 tons when submerged and had a range of just under 12,000 miles. Besides torpedoes, submarines were armed with deck guns and machine guns; some were equipped to lay mines. The U.S. submarines had crew complements ranging from thirty-two (in the World War I-era "O Class" subs) to ninety (in "Narwhal Class" subs).

A variety of very small submarines and other submersibles also were used:

Midget submarines. Japan, Italy, Britain, and Germany used midget subs, which were capable of sustained independent operation. Japan deployed five at Pearl Harbor. Italy's, with crews of two to four men, were assigned to coastal defense and to Black Sea operations. Italy also planned a midget-sub raid on New York Harbor, which was aborted after the British destroyer HMS *Active* sank the midget's transport submarine, the *Leonardo da Vinci*, May 25, 1943. The best of Germany's midget submarines was the *Seehund* class, or Type 127; Germany built 285 of these two-man, torpedo-armed subs. First deployed in December 1944, they sank nine ships, at a cost of 35 *Seehunds*. Britain's midget subs, the *X-craft* (produced in several models) were the most effective of this variety of undersea vessel. X-craft missions included damaging assaults on the German battleship *Tirpitz* and the Japanese cruiser *Takao*, reconnaissance of the Normandy landing beaches, and missions to sever Japanese telephone cable connections.

Submersibles. These were generally one-man vessels not capable of sustained independent operations. Usually designed and built quickly and therefore not elegant examples of submarine engineering, they included the British *Welman*, used in one operation in Norwegian coastal waters, and a four-man version, the *Welfreighter*, capable of carrying 2 tons of material. The latter ran supplies to Allied troops on the Malay Peninsula. Germany's *Neger/Marder* submersible was used at Anzio, Italy, and at Normandy; the *Molch* took part in the bitter 1944–1945 contest for the Schedlt Estuary; and the *Biber*-type submersibles were also deployed off Normandy and in the Scheldt Estuary as well as at Nijmegen, Holland. The German submersibles were risky to operate and not very effective, but the Allies devoted significant resources to defending against them. Japan's one-man submersible, the *Kaiten*, was deployed as a suicide weapon as the Allies closed in on the Japanese home islands. Two other, larger, suicide submersibles, the five-man *Koryu* and the two-man *Kairyu* types, were in production but not deployed before the war ended.

Human torpedoes. These were two-man submersibles with detachable warheads, which the crew affixed to their targets before swimming away in oxygen-equipped underwater suits or driving the main part of the torpedo away. Italy pioneered their development and achieved spectacular success with their *Maiale* human torpedoes when the *Regia Marina*'s Tenth Light Flotilla damaged the British battleships *Queen Elizabeth* and *Valiant*, moored at Alexandria, Egypt. They also used *Maiale* against Allied shipping at Gibraltar and Malta. The British used their own *Chariot* human torpedoes mainly in the Mediterranean, as well as against two Italian liners in the Far East in 1944.

Germany's *milchkuh* ("milk cow"), officially designated Type XIV, was unique. Displacing 1,932 tons when submerged and carrying a crew of fifty-two, these vessels supplied other U-boats with fuel (a milk cow could haul up to 203 tons of fuel, in addition to its own), as well as fresh food and other supplies. (Britain's nine *submarine depots* and the U.S. Navy's *submarine tenders*, all surface vessels, provided similar services to Allied submarines on station.) Particularly sought-after Allied targets, the milk cows were all lost; though schnorkel devices made it possible for them to recharge their own batteries while submerged, they still had to surface to transfer fuel. On occasion, Allied carrier-based planes arrived overhead during refueling and were able to sink both U-boats.

Allied and Axis submarines were often used for supply missions. In early 1942, U.S. subs delivered supplies to the battered forces on Bataan and Corregidor and left with gold, other valuables, and people—including the Philippine president Manuel Quezon and Vice President Sergio Osmeña. Later, Japanese submarines carried essentials to garrisons cut off by the Allied Pacific "island-hopping" campaigns. In all theaters, submarines were used to transport spies and, occasionally, as rescue vehicles. In the Pacific, U.S. subs formed a *Lifeguard League*, devoted to the rescue of downed Allied fliers, and saved more than five hundred. On April 1, 1944, for example, Commander S. D. Dealey of USS *Harder*, which sank more than twenty enemy vessels during the war (the boat's motto was "hit 'em *Harder*"), threaded the sub through shoals, bringing it as close as possible to Woleai Island in the western Carolines. Three *Harder* crewmen then went ashore, dodging sniper fire, to rescue a downed Navy fighter pilot. (Five months later, USS *Harder* and all seventy-nine of its crewmen went down near the Philippines—one of fifty-two U.S. submarines lost during World War II. Dealey was awarded the Medal of Honor, posthumously.)

"DAMN THE TORPEDOES": AMERICA'S SUBMARINE ORDNANCE PROBLEM

Also used by torpedo boats, and some destroyers, cruisers, battleships, and aircraft, torpedoes are most closely associated with submarines. During World War II, they were a sub's primary offensive weapons. Nicknamed "fish" (or "eels," by Germans), torpedoes were a form of minisubmarine, with mechanisms that automatically regulated depth and heading, and detonators/firing-pin assemblies that governed their explosion. A number of types and variations were developed during the war. Few were flawless in combat. Problems with magnetic detonators (designed to detonate a torpedo near the underwater hull of a ship) plagued the German, British, and American navies, and the Soviets reportedly suffered numerous problems with "duds" (torpedoes that failed to explode).

(continued)

No submarine service had as many torpedo problems for as long as the U.S. Navy. Its torpedoes suffered from unreliable depth control, premature explosions, or no explosions at all. Many of these problems resided in the detonators (both magnetic and impact), in part a result of insufficient testing due to tight prewar navy budgets. (Each torpedo cost about $10,000—a significant amount in the Depression era—so only torpedoes without warheads were used in prewar tests.) Once armed torpedoes were used in actual combat, a steady flow of increasingly bitter complaints indicated far too great a percentage of failures.

For nearly two years these complaints did not generate adequate corrective action by the Navy's Bureau of Ordnance (which exhibited a submariner-irritating tendency to blame boat commanders for torpedo malfunctions). Then, in July 1943, Lieutenant Commander Lawrence Daspit's sub *Tinosa*, having already stopped a large Japanese "whale factory" with two torpedoes fired at an awkward angle into its stern, fired nine carefully checked and aimed torpedoes, one at a time, at good range and from an optimum angle toward the ship. One after the other, the torpedoes hit the vessel; one after the other, they failed to explode. Very close to exploding, himself, Daspit took his boat's one remaining torpedo back to Pearl Harbor and *demanded* it be carefully tested. The testing revealed weak firing-pin assemblies, and the most widespread U.S. torpedo problem was finally corrected. Yet there were other torpedo mishaps.

In 1944, American submarines began using the Mark 18, a relatively slow-moving "wakeless" electric torpedo (with relatively slow maximum speed of 28 to 30 knots, it left no visible trail while en route to its target). The night of October 24, 1944, USS *Tang* (which had sunk a U.S. record of 31 enemy vessels) was on its fifth wartime patrol. Sighting a Japanese convoy bound for the Philippines, commanding officer Richard Hetherington O'Kane prepared to attack. After the torpedoes were carefully checked, O'Kane fired one that ran true toward its target. The second torpedo, however, curved sharply to the left, circling back around toward the *Tang*, which attempted to evade the rogue but was struck in the stern. The sub quickly went down, its compartments flooding, a Japanese depth-charge attack delaying escape attempts by the surviving crew. Thirteen men eventually reached the surface, but only eight, including Commander O'Kane, were picked up alive by the Japanese—some of whom began beating and kicking them. O'Kane, who, with his men, spent the rest of the war as a prisoner, discovered that the Japanese abusing his men were survivors from a convoy *Tang* had attacked the previous night. Later awarded the Medal of Honor, he said of this treatment, "When we realized that our clubbing and kickings were being administered by the burned, mutilated survivors of our handiwork, we found we could take it with less prejudice."

As a result of one faulty electric torpedo, seventy-eight *Tang* crewmen died. More than 60 percent of the torpedoes used by U.S. submarines in 1944 and 1945 were electrically propelled. Though there were some mishaps, most functioned properly.

ANTISUBMARINE WEAPONS

Some antisubmarine devices that were available as the war began were improved, during the war, and new devices were developed, adding to the considerable dangers submariners faced. Submarines, themselves, were effective antisubmarine weapons. Large surface vessels could also destroy surfaced or shallow-running submarines by gunfire or ramming. Smaller sub-chasers were especially useful against surfaced subs. As the British had done, unsuccessfully, during World War I, the United States briefly floated a number of so-called Q-ships (armed vessels disguised as merchantmen) to lure U-boats close enough to sink them. The results were not good. Aircraft of several types (including bombers, flying boats, and blimps) were extremely effective, dropping bombs, torpedoes, or special finned depth charges. Forests of concealed sea mines in coastal areas, estuaries, and sea lanes claimed a significant number of victims.

Depth charges, canisters of high explosives dropped from ships or aircraft, were the most common antisubmarine weapon, each containing two to three hundred pounds of explosive that could be set to explode at various depths. They were tumbled off a rack in the boat's stern or hurled seaward by a depth-charge thrower, usually in patterns. Most successful attacks involved multiple explosions very close to a submarine's hull, or a few detonations close to a damaged boat. But depth-charge attacks often failed to destroy their target. The shape a submarine was in, the skill of its commander, the persistence and skill of the attacker, and sheer dumb luck were all factors in whether a sub survived. Axis sub commanders faced longer odds in 1943 as the Allies introduced the "Hedgehog," a mortar that hurled a ring of depth charges 250 feet ahead of a ship, and a similar device called the "Mousetrap." The depth charges they delivered exploded only on contact. The British later introduced a three-barreled mortar, the "Squid," that hurled two-hundred-pound canisters of the powerful explosive Minol II set to explode at particular depths.

Radar, developed just before the war, and Sonar (called "ASDIC" by the British), were useful in detecting and tracking submarines—as they were useful to submarines in tracking their targets. (The Italians lacked radar. Japanese submarines were not equipped with it until late in the war. See "Technological Devices" later in this chapter.) From late 1942, sonobuoys—a combination of hydrophone (a sound-detecting device) and radio—were dropped near the suspected location of a submarine, and an aircraft would listen for telltale sounds via radio receiver. The United States also developed the Magnetic Airborne Detector (MAD), able to detect changes in magnetic fields produced by submarines to a depth of about five hundred feet. Aircraft often used MAD in conjunction with antisubmarine searchlights called Leigh lights. In December 1942, the Americans also introduced radar-guided "Fido" air-dropped torpedoes.

Torpedo Boats

Called by the British *Motor Torpedo Boats*, by the Americans *PT boats* (officially, "Patrol Craft Torpedo"), and by the Germans *Schnellboot* ("fast boat"), these small, speedy, shallow-draft vessels were used by most major combatants. Usually equipped with two on-deck torpedo tubes, antiaircraft guns, machine guns, and sometimes two depth charges, torpedo boats had a variety of wartime jobs, including reconnaissance, liaison, coastal patrol duties; swift, sharp attacks on enemy warships; and protection of amphibious landings with gunfire and smokescreens. (The Russians, suffering from a lack of good landing craft, used torpedo boats instead during some amphibious operations.) Torpedo boat crews rescued seamen and downed flyers and occasionally evacuated VIPs. When the United States entered the war, the operations of one PT-boat unit against the Japanese invading the Philippines raised American home-front morale while it bought some time for retreating American and Filipino forces. When General Douglas MacArthur was ordered to leave the islands, the unit's leader, Lieutenant Commander John D. Bulkeley, evacuated the general, his wife, and staff from Corregidor to Mindanao aboard his boat, PT 41, after which he returned to continue the fight. Awarded the Medal of Honor for his Philippines actions, Bulkeley later commanded PT boats guarding Allied ships off the Normandy beaches on D-Day and for weeks thereafter.

In addition to service in western Europe and throughout the Pacific Theater (where future president John F. Kennedy commanded PT 109), America's "Mosquito Fleet" of mostly wood-hulled PT boats (a few were aluminum) served in the Mediterranean and around the Aleutian Islands.

Small Arms

I don't know what a hero is. This business of the captain taking all the credit, ordering someone else and so forth—that's not it. The men who do the actual fighting, man the guns, they're the guys that really win the war.

—*John D. Bulkeley, retired U.S. naval officer and World War II Medal of Honor recipient, during an interview on CNN, 1995*

The catalog of small arms, manufactured and makeshift, used in combat from 1937 to 1945 is immense. In addition to knives and bayonets, used also for more mundane tasks such as cutting food and digging, there are the following basic categories.

Pistols

In the infantry, pistols were mostly an officer's weapon. (Many officers didn't wear pistols near the front, however, because an infantryman with a pistol but no rifle tended to stir the intense interest of enemy snipers.) They were more widely used within armored divisions and by commandos and other special forces who engaged in close battle. All the major wartime pistol models had been developed prewar, and there were no major innovations. (The United States clandestinely developed the single-shot, smooth-bore *Liberator pistol* for people in occupied countries, but these eccentric creations were distributed widely only in China.) The standard U.S. pistol, the .45-caliber M1911A1, was overall the best one in the war. The German Luger (Parabellum, Model 1908) was perhaps the most famous—and much sought after as souvenirs by GIs—but Germany's Walther Model 38 pistol was more reliable. The chief officially issued British pistol was a .38-caliber weapon, though many British soldiers preferred heavier ones such as the American .45 or the Walther Model 38s they "liberated" from the Germans. The two main Soviet pistols, the venerable Nagant revolver (dating back to 1895) and the more modern Tokarev automatic pistol, Model TT33, were not widely issued. Of Italy's wartime pistols the *Pistola automatica, M1934* (Beretta), neither powerful nor consistently accurate, was perhaps most widely used. Japan's less-than-first-class pistols included the automatic Type 94, nominated by World War II ordnance expert Ian V. Hogg as "a prominent contender for the title of worst military pistol ever issued"—clumsy to handle, susceptible to dirt, and easily fired by accident.

Rifles

The standard infantryman's weapon is the rifle. Armies generally began the war with World War I-era rifles—in the case of Japanese soldiers, rifle models dating back to the 1904–1905 Russo-Japanese War. In 1941, most U.S. troops still carried the 1903 Springfield bolt-action rifle; by 1945, all American infantrymen had been issued the Garand M1, the first semiautomatic rifle used as a standard combat weapon. Germany made the greatest innovation in design, issuing the *Sturmgewehr 44* (Machine Pistol 43) assault rifle midway through the war. It fired a lighter, less powerful bullet with a shorter range than most other rifles, and was therefore more controllable and more compact—and the lighter bullets meant each soldier could carry more ammunition. (Hitler favored longer-range rifles, but the new shorter-range rifle garnered such glowing reviews from Eastern-Front troops that he relented.) With the capacity for either single shots or full automatic fire, the Sturmgewehr 44 inspired a new class of postwar military rifle. Rifles used by other major combatants included the Lee-Enfield No. 4 and No. 5 rifles (Great Britain); the Carcano M1891 and the Mannlicher-Parravicino-Carcano Mod-

As the Wehrmacht and SS killing squads sweep viciously across Soviet soil in 1942, Russian workers—inspired by patriotic anti-Nazi slogans on the banner in the background—assemble small machine guns to help reequip the battered Red Army.

ello 91 (Italy); the Arisaka rifle, Meiji 38 (Japan); and the Mosin-Nagant Model 1891, and variations (USSR).

Submachine Guns

These short-range automatic weapons fired pistol ammunition. Developed in Germany at the end of World War I, they were very popular with American gangsters in the interwar years. The Spanish Civil War (1936–1939) demonstrated the ease and effectiveness with which largely amateur soldiers used submachine guns. Their high rate of fire also recommended their use by World War II airborne troops and special forces. The Soviets began mass-producing them in 1938; German troops (particularly in the Panzer divisions) were well supplied by 1939. The British considered the Finnish Suomi the best model available—but the Finns needed all they had for their desperate war with the Soviet Union, so the British bought Thompson submachine guns ("Tommy guns") from the United States until they could produce their own highly successful Sten gun. Most major combatants used many models—except Japan. The Japanese did develop two submachine guns, Type 100/40 and Type 100/44, but did not produce them in large numbers and issued relatively few. (Their only recorded use in combat was during a 1942 Japanese raid to capture Dutch oilfields in Java.)

Machine Guns

These guns directed deadly streams of fire against attacking forces. By World War II, Czechoslovakian and other weapons developers had designed a version that was lighter and thus easier for troops to use than the very heavy machine guns that repeatedly ripped apart attacking formations during the costly World War I stalemate at the Western Front. World War II infantry machine guns were either heavy (water-cooled, mounted on tripods) or light (air- or gas-cooled, mounted on bipods). The best light machine gun was Britain's Bren gun, based on a Czech design, manufactured in several variations, and used in all theaters. German armies used both light and heavy machine guns, and Germany's innovative General Purpose Machine Gun (GPMG) could be mounted on a bipod and used with a shoulder butt as a light machine gun, or mounted on a tripod and used with optical sight as a heavy weapon. When its barrel became overheated—a major problem with machine guns—it could be removed and replaced by a spare. America's

Browning Automatic Rifle (BAR) served as a light machine gun, and U.S. forces also used heavier Brownings, including the M1917A1, M1919A4, and M1919A6. Of the major combatants, Italy and Japan fielded the least effective machine guns—but their soldiers generally used these weapons very effectively.

Antitank Weapons (Hand-Held)

See "Tanks and Tank Destroyers," earlier in this chapter.

Flamethrowers

A primary weapon of war from ancient times, fire was one of the great destroyers during World War II (see "Aircraft—Bombs—Incendiary" and "Tanks and Tank Destroyers—Flamethrower Tanks," earlier in this chapter). Germans introduced the modern infantry weapon, the flamethrower, during World War I—and the horrified Allies quickly developed their own. Flamethrowers consist of a canister of thickened gasoline, usually carried on a soldier's back, and a hose and nozzle through which pressurized nitrogen propels the liquid, which ignites as it leaves the launcher. During World War II, flamethrowers were used most intensively, by both Americans and Japanese, in the Pacific Theater, primarily to flush enemies out of field fortifications such as foxholes, pillboxes, and caves. Soldiers operating these much-feared weapons were prime targets and were often specially protected by riflemen.

Hand Grenades and "Molotov Cocktails"

An old and simple idea (a portable explosive that one throws), the hand grenade concept exploded into a profusion of World War II types and models because there was no "perfect" grenade for all desired uses. Offensive grenades were lighter and thus easier to carry, with lighter fragments less likely to fly back and harm the attacker; defensive grenades were heavier and more destructive, with the thrower presumably tucked behind his field fortification. Some grenades made smoke for signaling; others made smoke for screens. Allied soldiers facing tanks or similar opposition often used "sticky bombs" (officially, British Grenade No. 74) comprising breakable containers of plastic explosives (with a handle for throwing) that would adhere to, rather than bounce off, targets. There were also more bizarre grenades, such as Britain's Grenade No. 67, a one-hundred-watt lightbulb filled with tear gas.

Manufactured in various shapes and sizes, probably in the hundreds of millions (the U.S. Army alone procured 87,320,000 during the war), grenades were used in all theaters for close-quarters combat.

"Molotov cocktails" (named for Vyacheslav Molotov, a ruthless supporter of Soviet dictator Joseph Stalin and People's Commissar of Foreign Affairs during World War II) were used by fighters who did not have manufactured grenades or other suitable weapons available. Introduced during the Spanish Civil War, they were hurled in profusion by vastly outnumbered Finnish soldiers during their 1939–1940 Winter War with the Soviet Union; Russians fighting Germans on the Eastern Front; Poles during the 1943 and 1944 Warsaw uprisings; and many others. Glass containers about three-quarters filled with gasoline or other flammable substances, with a rag stuffed in the top as a fuze, Molotov cocktails were effective against light armored vehicles, advancing soldiers—and enemy morale. In May 1940, as western Europe was falling to the Germans, British authorities, expecting an invasion, ordered the production of millions of Molotov cocktails (filled with a solution of phosphorus dissolved in benzine) for civilians to employ against German troops. A shortage of screw-top milk and beer bottles immediately developed as British manufacturers commandeered them to make an eventual 7 million Molotov cocktails. Distributed around the British Isles, the lethal cocktails were usually stored in crates in various local streams. Since the Germans never invaded, none were ever used. Many were never taken up from their hiding places, but floated away down streams and into rivers. Molotov cocktails continued to bob up around Britain for years after the war.

Technological Devices

See also Chapters 3 and 9.

Front-line instruments of the war incorporated or were supported by a burgeoning host of technological devices. Wartime pressures greatly accelerated developments in areas from nuclear physics to medical care, guidance systems to guns. Fighters often wished that a little more attention were also being paid to seemingly mundane items—certain kinds of packaging, for instance. After the war, U.S. Marine Corps veteran Eugene Sledge remembered lugging boxes of ammunition by hand "under enemy fire, in driving rain, and through knee-deep mud for hours on end" during the battle for Okinawa:

> All ammunition was heavy, of course, but some was easier to handle than others. We praised the manufacturers of hand-grenade and belted machine-gun ammunition boxes. The former were wooden with a nice

rope handle on each side; the latter were metal and had a collapsible handle on top. But we cursed the dolts who made the wooden cases our .30 caliber rifle ammo came in. Each box contained one thousand rounds of ammunition. It was heavy and had only a small notch cut into either end. This allowed only a fingertip grip by the two men usually needed to handle a single crate.

The science/technology war waged in the shadows of the shooting war was often as complicated and confused, in its own ways, as actual battlegrounds are in theirs. Major "fronts" of this behind-the-scenes warfare involved the following devices.

Encryption/Decryption Devices

See Chapter 9.

Proximity Fuzes (VT Fuzes)

A quest for increased protection of naval surface vessels against air attack was the chief stimulation for development of the *proximity fuze*—one of the most important and closely guarded Allied technological achievements of the war. Prewar studies had shown that a shell that burst near an attacking aircraft (within sixty or seventy feet) spread fragments over a much wider area (about 3,000 square feet) than if a direct hit was needed to stimulate a shell's explosion (such as when an attacking aircraft had gotten uncomfortably close to a vessel). Thus, military inventors all over the world had long been interested in creating a proximity fuze. The British developed a rudimentary version in the late 1930s to use with naval rocket weapons. But this early version—an electro-optical sensor that detected an aircraft's shadow—was useless at night, which was when the Germans most frequently attacked, so this early version was shelved.

British research came to the United States in 1940 via a technical mission headed by Sir Henry Tizard and became part of the information base used by the U.S. National Defense Research Committee's "Section T"—established that August as the American body initially in charge of proximity fuze development. Over the next three years, responsibility for the project occasionally shifted but work went steadily forward, in the face of a host of daunting technical challenges: the fuze needed to withstand powerful accelerating and centrifugal forces, to be safely storable and transportable, to operate in all weather conditions, and, inside a shell, to fit in a space the size of a half-pint milk bottle.

By spring 1942, Johns Hopkins University (which established an Applied Physics Laboratory in Silver Spring, Maryland, primarily to coordinate work on the fuze), 87 private companies, and 110 American plants were working on the "VT fuze." ("VT" supposedly stood for "variable time," a designation chosen to conceal the real operating principles of the device.) The fuze that eventually emerged was essentially a small, battery-powered, active (both sending and receiving) radar set. Signals from the fuze would be reflected off the target; when the signal the fuze received grew strong enough (meaning the target was about sixty feet away), the fuze detonated the shell.

On August 12, 1942, a planned three-day trial in Chesapeake Bay ended on the first day, after all three target-drone aircraft were destroyed. Five thousand proximity-fuzed shells were soon in the Pacific, where they were first used successfully by the cruiser USS *Helena* on January 5, 1943. By the end of 1943, almost 2 million fuzes had been delivered; by the end of 1944, more than 40,000 were being manufactured every day. At first proximity-fuzed shells were restricted to use by the U.S. and British navies, and they were to be fired only over water, lest the enemy retrieve and analyze a "dud" shell. But by the end of 1944—after pressing for them for a year—the two countries' armies began using them; the armies ended up using more prox-imity-fuzed shells than the navies.

Proximity fuzes helped save the day against German V-weapons. The V-1 rockets flew too fast and high for light antiaircraft guns and too fast and low for heavy guns to track and hit with conventional shells. With proximity-fuzed shells, hit rates skyrocketed. Proximity-fuzed shells also became a terri-ble boon to the Allies during the December 1944–January 1945 Battle of the Bulge, when counterattacking German troops threatened to overwhelm Al-lied defenders. "With [proximity-fuzed] shells exploding some feet above the ground and showering the area with a hail of high velocity fragments," Rear Admiral Julius Furer wrote in a postwar history, "the foxholes became almost valueless as a sanctuary for the [German] foot soldier."

Radar

In 1925, American scientists attempting to measure the height of the layer of ionized air that reflects radio waves back to earth sent brief pulses of radio energy heavenward and timed the ensuing "echo." This open experiment, widely understood to hold the potential for detecting incoming aircraft, led to the interwar development of *radar* (*ra*dio *d*etection *a*nd *r*anging) systems, primarily in Britain, Germany, the United States, France, the Netherlands, Japan, and the Soviet Union. Japan's radar development soon lagged, however, and interservice rivalries compromised the effectiveness of the radar net that it eventually deployed. The Soviet radar program fell behind between 1937 and 1942, due to internal political upheaval. Guglielmo Marconi initiated radar development in Italy in the mid-1930s, but Italy made no effective use of radar during the war.

By 1939, Britain had established a chain of protective radar emplacements (the "Chain Home" stations). To the later surprise of many in Britain's high command, Germany had similar installations, having benefited since 1934 from the work of Dr. Rudolf Kuhnold and his company, GEMA. (RAF photo reconnaissance in 1941 finally provided irrefutable evidence of German radar.) In 1940, two Englishmen, Professor J. T. Randall and Mr. A. H. Boot, developed the *cavity magnetron*, a powerful electronic vacuum valve that made possible *centimetric radar* (so named because its high frequency corresponded to a wavelength of ten centimeters) capable of plotting targets with far greater precision than existing radar systems. The 1940 Tizard mission to the United States shared details of this achievement with American scientists. The two countries then worked closely on radar research and development.

The United States had already developed a radar device to control the fire of antiaircraft artillery, SCR (Signal Corps Radio)-268 (a prototype was tested in 1937), as well as more powerful fixed-installation air-defense systems (prototypes tested in 1939). Lack of funds and reliance on America's two shielding oceans kept the pace of production slow—until the Battle of Britain and growing difficulties with Japan made the possibility of air attack on the American mainland seem much less remote. As the Tizard mission ended, the Massachusetts Institute of Technology established a Radiation Laboratory, which became a leader in wartime radar development. By 1943, dozens of radar sites operated by the Aircraft Warning Service (AWS) protected the U.S. coasts and borders.

The war saw a vast flowering of radars of various strengths, on a wide band of frequencies, for a host of special purposes, with Allied and Axis experts vying to keep ahead of, and outfox each other's creations. *Gun-laying* radar helped artillery find its targets. *Airborne Surface Vessel* (ASV) radar

On a hillside in Italy in 1944, a five-man crew operates one type of U.S. radar device, designated SCR-268. It was designed to control the fire of antiaircraft artillery.

helped planes locate objectives at sea, including surfaced submarines. *Aircraft Intercept (AI)* radars, such as Germany's *Lichtenstein* and Britain's *Mark VII*, helped night fighters detect enemy planes. AI radars were also developed to home in on the frequencies of enemy AI radar, and the American *SCR-720* AI radar (designated the *Mark X*) could penetrate the most troublesome type of radar interference: aluminum strips (see "Opening 'Window,'" later in this chapter). The British also developed aircraft *radar-warning-receivers*—dubbed "Boozer" and "Monica"—to alert plane crews that they were being hit by radar beams from ground or enemy AI radar. Ground *early warning radars* included Germany's GEMA-produced *Wasserman*, perhaps the finest of its type in the war, and the American *MEW* (Microwave Early Warning), a central feature of Hawaii's post-Pearl Harbor defenses and part of the American defenses on Iwo Jima. America's AN/TPS-10 *height-finding radar*, dubbed "Little Abner," also installed on Iwo Jima, was particularly useful in regions bothered by ground clutter (buildings or land formations that produced radar reflections). *Ground Controlled Interception* (GCI) systems, such as the German networks centered on *Freya* and *Wurtzburg* radars, fixed the positions of incoming bombers and also controlled "master searchlights." In Germany's Kammhuber air defense line, each master was keyed to several other searchlights; Allied aircraft caught in their glare could only attempt to dive, pick up speed, and flee the area.

By mid-1944, Allied radar developments, such as Britain's *H2S* and *Oboe* systems and the American *H2X*, were making it possible to bomb much more precisely. Radar pulses could even penetrate cloud cover (something that became so common the Allies gave it its own designation, BTO, for Bombing Through Overcast)—as long as enemy jamming did not disrupt the systems. At sea, naval radar and sonar systems were also constantly under development, increasingly crowding warships' Combat Information Centers (where all incoming intelligence was sifted) with screens and communications equipment. Project Cadillac (1942–1945), in which high-powered microwave radar aboard a modified bomber flying well below the horizon relayed radar pictures to a ship, steadily improved Allied air-sea coordination and early-warning capabilities. To aid amphibious landings, combat scientists of the U.S. Office of Scientific Research and Development (OSRD) designed the *Virtual PPI Reflectoscope* (VPR) to help assure that landing craft located their assigned beach positions even when heading in to poorly mapped areas at first light under difficult combat conditions. It was installed in special *Landing Craft Control* (LCC) vehicles and used successfully in Europe, with limited deployment in the Pacific late in the war. Radar also aided the two atomic bombs that ended the war: to ensure that they exploded at the proper height for maximum destruction, the bombs were equipped with one barometric fuze, two impact fuzes, and four radar fuzes.

Radio (Wireless)

See also Chapters 9 and 10.

Radar's underlying technology and a familiar communications medium in the late 1930s, radio is generally defined as "the wireless transmission and reception of electric impulses or signals by means of electromagnetic waves." Despite some use of radio during the Russo-Japanese War of 1904–1905 and World War I, *wire* transmission (cable, telegraph, telephone, teletype) was still the primary form of ground-force communication in 1939, complemented by signal flags, blinkers, and other hand devices.

Wire transmission and hand signals were also complemented by military radio, which had continued to develop during the interwar years. The British and German armies used radio communication to coordinate the elements in armored warfare exercises in the mid-1930s, and German General Heinz Guderian, in particular, advocated radio communication to facilitate the blitzkrieg tactics then being developed. The limited Soviet radio capability did not improve until well into the war (with a boost from Lend-Lease), and Italian and Japanese radio never achieved the quality of the other major combatants. In the United States, most military radios developed in the interwar years were designed for limited use by particular types of unit—including one, the SCR (Signal Corps Radio)-511 produced especially for horse cavalry. (Built around a guidon staff, one end of which was supposed to go in a stirrup, the SCR-511, dubbed the "Pogo Stick" by GIs, was used by American infantry, beach details, and boatmen in amphibious operations into 1944.) Until the outbreak of war, the U.S. Army viewed radio as only a backup to wire communication.

Germany's blitzkrieg tactics, Japan's fast advance through the Pacific in 1941–1942, strategies involving complex combined operations, and the global sweep and general mobility of the war brought about a boom in wireless development and a revolution in military radio usage. "Crash" production sometimes resulted in equipment malfunction, and the proliferation of new equipment—even when it worked perfectly—created many unforseen problems.

The complex world of World War II radio communications included devices operating on high frequencies (HF), very high frequencies (VHF), and (to a limited extent) ultra high frequencies (UHF). The more radio was used, the more frequencies became crowded. *Amplitude-modulated* (AM) was the standard type of military (and commercial) radio, but AM was extremely prone to interference from such things as storms and vehicle ignitions. *Frequency-modulated* (FM) radios, less subject to interference, were introduced to military communications by the U.S. Signal Corps as the war began, but not even all U.S. forces favored its adoption. American air forces did not use it, partly because that would have left American aircrews unable to communicate with their RAF allies, who used AM-VHF radios. Men on the ground, however, particularly in the U.S. Armored Forces, embraced FM immediately. An Army radioman, Technician Zens (first name unknown), provided an example of why this was so:

> One night, up in the Siegfried Line, when we needed more equipment than we had [FM radios], we got out an AM set. The loudspeaker crackled and roared with static. Twenty different stations came in at once with a noise like a platoon of tanks. I think we heard everybody in Europe on the AM receiver. I mean at the same time . . . English, French, Russian, German, . . . At least, we heard everybody except the station we were trying to reach.

AM/FM differences and equipment geared to different frequency ranges sometimes prevented combat units from communicating with friendly forces whose radio equipment was newer, older, or otherwise incompatible with their own. Until well into 1944, an American tank commander needing air support had to call his ground headquarters on his tank's FM radio, the headquarters would call up an Air Forces control center that had wire lines or AM radio, and the controllers would then direct planes to the target via VHF equipment compatible with Allied air forces' radios. Infantry units were often plagued with similar problems that could be extremely hazardous as well as irritating. Complaints up the chain of command not resulting in quick enough action, U.S. front-line soldiers improvised by creating the *Veep*, a jeep-mounted VHS radio for direct communication with air support. Officially adopted by the U.S. Signal Corps as AN/VRC-1, Veeps were subsequently ordered in the thousands for infantry units and joint assault signal companies.

In a similar instance of communication problems, many U.S. infantry units were equipped with short-range "walkie-talkies," FM radios carried on an infantryman's back. But their FM frequency range did not overlap (could not communicate with) the FM radios in tanks, so tank and infantry teams could not easily talk to each other. (This was partially remedied by attaching to the outside of tanks telephones that were connected to the armored vehicles' interior communications systems. But strolling up to a tank to use the phone during combat was often problematical.) Another common infantry radio, the hand-carried "handie-talkies," were AM transceivers that could not talk to FM walkie-talkies or tank radios. The pace of the war made it impossible to remedy all these incompatibility problems.

Nevertheless, front-line units relied heavily on handie-talkies and walkie-talkies. More powerful equipment included the American SCR-299, a very large mobile set, occupying a truck and a trailer, that put out three to four hundred watts of power compared with the handie-talkie's one-fourth watt, giving the SCR-299 a voice-transmission range up to one hundred miles. In North Africa, a Signal Corps battalion, using *sky waves* (radio waves transmitted up from an antenna and reflected off the ionosphere) established a direct radio-telegraph channel to Britain on this equipment. One set of a later version, the SCR-499—housed in a quarter-ton trailer that could be hauled by a jeep—arrived in Normandy on D-Day via glider and immediately went into service as a link between two airborne divisions and Britain. Allied and German technicians also developed wireless *radio relay* equipment, allowing radio messages to "hop" over mountains and move quickly over long distances. Naval forces, long reliant on wireless telegraphy, began much more extensive use of the radio telephone during the war, particularly for control of carrier-based aircraft and convoy-escort duties.

One drawback to radio was its vulnerability. Despite codes and other precautions, radio communications of all major combatants were regularly penetrated by the enemy and were rich sources of military intelligence. Radio was also used as a tool in some major deception operations of the war.

Radio Beams and Other Navigation Aids

In the 1930s, commercial aircraft navigated at night with the assistance of ground *radio beacons* that a plane's *radio direction finder* could lock onto. Most World War II aircraft were also equipped with direction finders; radio-assisted navigation helped bring bombers safely back to home base. Beacons were also used on the offensive: at the beginning of D-Day operations, Allied paratroop "pathfinders" (landing behind German lines in Normandy ahead of the main invasion force) set up "Eureka" radio beacons to guide troop transports equipped with "Rebecca" direction finders to their drop zones. (Three groups did hit their zones precisely, but cloud formations, enemy antiaircraft fire, and some pilot errors widely dispersed the other transports.) The United States, following British precedents, developed several specialized types of radio beacons, including a Blind Approach Beacon System (BABS) and one (AN/CPT-2) developed especially for rescue at sea. Other radio aids to navigation included the *radio altimeter*, actually a radar whose downward rays and upward reflections could give exact clearance above the ground or water below; various types of *radio compasses*; the British

GEE pulse-transmission system; and the American *Loran* (Long Range) and *Shoran* (Short Range) beacon-assisted navigation systems.

A "Battle of the Beams" became part of the Battle of Britain when Germany activated radio-beam guidance systems, designated *Knickebein* (usable by all Luftwaffe bombers) and *X-Gerät* and *Y-Gerät* (requiring specially equipped *pathfinder bombers* to guide the main force by dropping flares or other devices). A first (and ultimately unsuccessful) step toward achieving "precision bombing," these radio beams, transmitted from German stations in occupied Europe, proved extremely vulnerable to British jamming—once the British evaluated the exact frequency and configuration of each beam, then determined, manufactured, and distributed an effective method precisely geared to disrupting each particular type of beam. In the meantime, Luftwaffe pathfinders, following beams that the British weren't yet able to jam, were dropping incendiary markers to guide bombers to their targets, including Coventry, which endured a devastating ten-hour attack on November 14, 1940. Because beams could be adjusted and successful jamming was never guaranteed, the British also came up with a less technical method of befuddling pathfinder-led German bombers: facilities to create carefully planned and controlled decoy fires, code-named *Starfish*, were placed outside major target areas. The first Starfish was ignited during an attack on Bristol on December 2, 1940—and was promptly plastered with sixty-six high-explosive bombs that would otherwise have hit the city.

Radio and Radar Countermeasures (RCM)

All major combatants expended great effort on acquiring scientific intelligence about the latest in enemy radio and radar developments in order to develop ways to baffle them. (See also Chapter 9.) A particularly effective Allied method of finding enemy transmission sources was the use of *Ferret aircraft*. Precursors to postwar AWAC aircraft, these winged electronic laboratories were crammed with equipment to detect radar and radio signals and locate ground transmission stations. British Ferrets flew over Europe and the Mediterranean; American Ferrets shared Mediterranean duties and flew throughout the huge Pacific Theater, where by 1945, there were some fifteen U.S. B-24 Ferrets and a number of B-29s. A few were specially equipped to detect and destroy Japanese aircraft that carried radar.

Both sides developed hosts of jamming devices. In the European Theater, they proliferated after February 1942, when the Germans aimed jamming transmitters, sited in occupied Europe, at Britain's coastal radar stations, blinding them to the successful run by battle cruisers *Scharnhorst* and *Gneisenau* through the Straits of Dover to the safety of German ports. The British quickly responded by developing ground- and aircraft-based jamming equipment (code-named "Moonshine") that received pulses from German early-warning *Freya* radar, amplified them, and sent them right back, creating huge and confusing echoes on German radar screens. Airborne Moonshine echoes often drew German fighters to intercept phantom flights

OPENING "WINDOW"

The Germans and the Allies both experimented successfully with radar interference using metal strips; when bombers dropped them in bundles at regular intervals while approaching a target, the metal strips filled radar screens—both on the ground and most AI radar in planes—with blips indistinguishable from actual bombers. However, each side hesitated to use the stunningly effective measure until they could find some way to counteract it should the enemy use it on them. The success of a 1942 German experiment with metal strips (code-named *Düppel*) against their own radar horrified Reichsmarshal Göring, who ordered all written evidence destroyed and forbade any leaks. "It was thus extremely difficult to work out countermeasures," Luftwaffe General Wolfgang Martini later reported, "because we dared not experiment. . . . Had the wind blown when we dropped the metal strips, people would have picked them up, talked about them, and our secret would have been betrayed." The Allies' metal strips (code-named *Window*) were likewise effective against Allied radar—leading to postponement of its use so that the Axis could not discover it themselves (although they already had) and use it when defending against the Allied invasion of Sicily. Window was first used—with total success—during the late-July 1943 bombing raids on Hamburg that created a devastating firestorm. German aircraft began dropping *Düppel* shortly thereafter, using it in a September 1943 raid on North Africa and after the Anglo-American landings at Anzio, Italy. By February 1944, however, the Allies at Anzio had a new ground radar (SCR 584), which was not easily duped by *Düppel*.

Japanese bombers also used metal strips, code-named *Giman-shi*, developed by Lieutenant Commander Hajime Sudo, achieving modest success in confusing American gun-laying radar in May 1943, as the contest for the Solomon Islands was drawing to a close. Meanwhile, the Americans were developing a refinement of Window (code-named *Chaff*) and longer strips (code-named *Rope*).

of bombers while flights of real bombers hit the intended targets. The British also developed a radio jamming transmitter ("Jostle") capable of overpowering the enemy's command radio telephones with meaningless noise. The most powerful radio jammer was a U.S.-produced transmitter ("Tuba"), introduced in late 1944, that came in both fifteen- and fifty-kilowatt versions. Each jamming enterprise inspired reciprocal measures, including the creation of *antijamming* (AJ) devices. Two developed for U.S. aircraft were code-named "Mary" and "George." Of the two, George was the more intriguing: the workers who developed it at the Camp Evans Signal Laboratory at Ft. Monmouth, New Jersey, had no idea why the thing worked.

Sonar

See also "Submarines and Antisubmarine Weapons," earlier in this chapter.

This underwater sound-based detection system was also called "ASDIC" (an acronym for the Anglo-French Allied Submarine Detection Investigation Committee established in 1917). "SONAR," the American designation (which the British adopted in 1943) stood for *So*und, *Na*vigation, and *R*anging. The system emits pulses of sound that "bounce" off a submarine's hull and "echo" on a receiver in either another submarine or a surface vessel. Sonar indicated the distance and depth of a mass, but not with pinpoint accuracy, and it could be confounded by tempestuous weather (as was the case in the North Atlantic in the winter of 1942–1943, the height of the Allies' anti-U-boat campaign). By 1943, German U-boats were equipped with a sonar-confusing bubble-making device, further complicating detection. Sonar also sometimes detected "submarines" that were not submarines. In 1943, *Chicago Daily Times* war correspondent Keith Wheeler reported, "There are more whales than submarines in the Pacific, but whales and submarines produce the same reaction in a destroyer's sound detection gear. This is a terrible war for whales."

In 1943, the University of California War Research Division developed short-range FM sonar, which could detect sea mines a quarter of a mile away. Originally designated the QLA Small Object Detector, it proved its value in June 1945 when Hydeman's Hellcats, a nine-boat U.S. submarine wolf pack named for the operation's commander, Earl Twinning Hydeman, used it while penetrating the mine-bestrewn Sea of Japan. By the time eight of the nine boats returned from the operation, they had sunk Japanese submarine *I-122* and twenty-eight merchant ships.

Vehicles (Land)

Global and mobile, World War II required that tremendous resources be devoted to land transport for armed forces and their supplies. There are several categories for land vehicles.

Armored Vehicles

See also "Tanks and Tank Destroyers," earlier in this chapter.

This category includes vehicles that were designed for front-line use, such as armored personnel carriers and armored cars. Many vehicles such as tractors and bulldozers (vital mechanical workhorses of the war) were armored after they went into service in combat zones, to protect their drivers.

Cargo Carriers (Animal and Human)

The German Wehrmacht and the Red Army made perhaps the heaviest regular use of horses. For example, more than 700,000 horses pulled supply wagons and artillery in the 1941 invasion of the Soviet Union. The Red Army, meanwhile, deployed the most mounted cavalry, which could maneuver better than tracked vehicles in some parts of the vast country: on January 1, 1942, there were seven Soviet cavalry corps and eighty-two cavalry divisions. All other major combatants also relied to some extent on horses, mules, and donkeys to carry men and supplies in areas unfriendly to vehicles, such as the rugged interior and northern coastal regions of Sicily. In northern Italy Allied forces included nine Italian pack mule companies (260 mules each; 250 mules per day could supply one regiment with basic needs). Horses and mules were also used in many areas in the Pacific and China-Burma-India Theaters; in the latter, camels and elephants were also occasionally pressed into duty. U.S. forces used sled dogs for transport in Alaska and Greenland, and German medics harnessed both dogs and, in the far north, reindeer. When even animals could not do the job, humans did. U.S. Infantry "pack teams" carried supplies near the Futa Pass in Italy, and Allied stretcher bearers in that area carried victims of German mines down steep mountainsides to nearby roads. On Okinawa, torrential rains turned the ground to mud that engulfed trucks up to the vehicle frames. There were some air drops, but exhausted American marines often could replenish much-needed ammunition and other supplies only if they hauled them by hand where they were needed.

Cargo Carriers (Wheeled and Tracked)

The logistical backbone of all fighting forces, *trucks* came in a wide variety of sizes and types. U.S. forces initially relied on a standard two-and-a-half-ton 6 × 6 truck, but expanded their motor pools to include much larger varieties such as twelve-ton trucks that could tow forty-five-ton trailers crammed full of supplies. Trucks frequently offloaded from Landing Ship Tanks onto invasion beaches along with the men. They also served as troop carriers, ambulances, and carriers for rocket-launchers. On Pacific island beaches and in other difficult terrain, steel matting was often laid down to help get the trucks to firmer ground. The elements often made roads, trails, or countryside impassable to trucks, so other types of motorized cargo carriers were used, including tractors and bulldozers. The U.S. Army officially designated one small, but extremely hardy, tracked vehicle cargo carrier M29—but its many admirers called it the *Weasel*. Carrying a crew of two and a payload of approximately one thousand pounds, the Weasel came into its own carrying cargo in the Italian Apennines. Weasels were also deployed to other theaters, including the Southwest Pacific.

Jeeps and Other Small Vehicles

The American four-wheel-drive Jeeps deserve a category of their own. U.S. Army Chief of Staff General George C. Marshall called them the greatest American contribution to modern warfare, and General Dwight Eisenhower regarded them as one of three types of vehicles that won the war (the other two were the C-47 transport plane and landing craft). Sturdy, rugged, and almost indefatigable, Jeeps were the product of an interwar search for just such a hardy general-purpose vehicle. The Willys-Overland company's winning design started rolling off production lines in 1941; by the end of 1945, more than 650,000 had been manufactured, many for Lend-Lease distribution. (There are various explanations for the name "Jeep," ranging from the initials of "General Purpose"—GP—to an indefatigable character from the *Popeye* comic strip.) Jeeps went everywhere and did almost everything, inspiring the World War II term *jeepable*, meaning rough roads impassable except by Jeep. Jeeps could reach sixty-five miles per hour on a level road, climb a 60 percent grade, and, without special equipment, ford a stream eighteen inches deep while fully loaded. American forces depended on Jeeps especially for reconnaissance and liaison, but

The only general in the first amphibious wave to hit the Normandy beachhead in 1944, Theodore Roosevelt Jr. (1887–1944) provided leadership that saved many lives and earned him a Medal of Honor. Once established ashore, he traveled in a hardy jeep that he dubbed "Rough Rider" in honor of his father's celebrated role in the Spanish American War.

also for every imaginable jeepable duty—including laying communications wire, transporting wounded, and inspecting Allied overseas fuel pipelines. An amphibious Jeep, dubbed the *Seep*, was developed for the U.S. Marines (a development echoed by Germany's inferior jeeplike *Volkswagen* amphibious vehicle, the *Schwimmwagen*). Britain's Special Air Service (SAS) used Lend-Lease Jeeps—stripped of windshields and other expendable items, heavily armed with machine guns, and packed with water and other supplies—for hit-and-run raids in North Africa and Europe.

Armed forces used vast numbers of other small vehicles—specially manufactured for war use, purchased, and commandeered. Nonarmored automobiles of various makes were used as staff cars and for courier and other duties; motorcycles were used for reconnaissance, courier duty, and liaison. Some troops even traveled by bicycle.

Railroads (Locomotives, Rolling Stock)

See also "United States Army, Army Service Forces" in Chapter 4.

Vital for transporting armies and supplies, railroads were a major target and a major focus of rebuilding efforts after attackers took an area. Before the 1944 landings in Normandy, Allied bombers repeatedly attacked French rail lines, and they dropped 8,500 tons of bombs on railway targets in the first five days of the Normandy campaign, preventing supplies and reinforcements from reaching German units near the beachhead. As part of invasion preparations, 1,000 American locomotives and 20,000 railroad cars were stored around Britain—necessitating the construction of 270 miles of additional tracks. American and British equipment was subsequently transported to France to replace destroyed material. The first scheduled Allied railroad run in France was made between Cherbourg and Carentan on July 11, 1944—in this case using a combination of U.S./U.K. and salvaged French equipment.

American railroad stock went all over the world: locomotives and rail cars augmented captured equipment on the railroad from Casablanca to Tunis in North Africa, which played an important part in the buildup of men and supplies for the invasion of Sicily and southern Europe. Millions of long tons (2,240 pounds each) of Lend-Lease locomotives and other cargo were also shipped to the Soviet Union by northern-route convoys and by land via the Persian Corridor, through Iran. From early 1943, U.S. troops ran the southern sector of the Iranian State Railway.

A TERRIBLE QUEST: DEVELOPING THE A-BOMB

Among the thousands of people who fled the growing Nazi oppression in the early 1930s were German and Austrian physicists, including Albert Einstein, Lise Meitner, Klaus Fuchs, and Otto Frisch. Some of them fled to the United States, some to Britain, and a few to the Soviet Union. Within a few years, it was widely understood within the international scientific community that nuclear fission was theoretically possible and that splitting the atom could release tremendous energy. Many feared that the talented physicists still in Germany would develop a powerful nuclear-fission weapon.

On October 11, 1939, President Roosevelt received a letter, written by émigré physicists Eugene Wigner and Leo Szliard and signed by Albert Einstein, outlining this threat and suggesting that "some permanent contact [be] maintained" between the U.S. government and physicists working to achieve the chain reactions necessary to activate a nuclear weapon. Roosevelt immediately asked Lyman Briggs, director of the U.S. Bureau of Standards, to establish an Advisory Committee on Uranium (considered the most probable fissionable material). The committee met on October 21, participants including Wigner and Szliard, physicists Robert B. Roberts and Edward Teller, and U.S. Army and Navy representatives. Largely because the military participants had reservations about the feasibility and cost of nuclear weapons research, however, the committee fell into bureaucratic limbo.

In fact, nuclear fission had been achieved at Germany's Kaiser Wilhelm Institute for Chemistry on December 13, 1938. At a secret conference in Berlin on April 29, 1939, scientists discussed the possibility of nuclear weapons with representatives of the German War Office—who agreed to sponsor nuclear weapons research. Within the next year, British Intelligence learned of Germany's quest for *heavy water* (made with an isotope of hydrogen, called deuterium), which could moderate, or help sustain, a chain reaction, a necessary step in achieving a nuclear explosion. This discovery spurred the British to spirit existing supplies of heavy water out of Norway, the site of the only plant that manufactured the substance in quantity—and soon, a victim of Nazi invasion. Britain also intensified its own nuclear weapons program. German Jewish refugees Rudolph Peierls and Otto Frisch, working at the University of Birmingham, had already made some crucial discoveries—yet Britain's scientists still had no idea how a nuclear weapon would work.

In October 1940, at the behest of the director of the Japanese Imperial Army Air Force's research institute, researchers at Tokyo's Physical and Chemical Research Institute (Riken) also began studying fission aspects of elements; in April 1941, they were authorized to research and develop an atomic bomb. In the Soviet Union, where nuclear research was well established, a nuclear weapons program had just begun when Germany invaded the country on June 22, 1941. Laboratories, as well as major industries, were hurriedly moved eastward to safety, but nuclear weapons research was suspended until 1943, in favor of developing more immediate necessities. However, the Soviet Union proved adept at securing information on the nuclear weapons research of its Allies via its spy networks.

Major General Leslie R. Groves, head of the Manhattan Project, and the project's scientific director, J. Robert Oppenheimer, examine the remains of the tower from which a test atomic bomb was detonated near Alamogordo, New Mexico, July 16, 1945.

American entry into the war in December 1941 breathed new life into the U.S. nuclear weapons project. The Uranium Committee transmuted into the U.S. Army Corps of Engineers' "Manhattan Project," administered by no-nonsense General Leslie Groves. The brilliant theoretical physicist Robert Oppenheimer was named scientific director, and he and Groves assembled a stellar group of scientific minds, including Edward Teller, Hans Bethe, Richard Feynman, Robert R. Wilson, Victor Weisskopf—and German refugee-scientist Klaus Fuchs, a communist whose leftist idealism would lead him to disclose Manhattan Project information to the Soviet Union. After leading a group that achieved a sustained chain reaction at the University of Chicago in December 1942, Enrico Fermi joined Oppenheimer and the others at an isolated former ranch school at Los Alamos, New Mexico, thereafter the center of the intensely secret blitzkrieg development of what could be referred to only as "the gadget." Only the United States had adequate resources to explore all possible methods of creating a nuclear bomb. Americans constructed huge plants in Oak Ridge, Tennessee, and Hanford, Washington, for the manufacture of fission materials—activity shielded by censorship and artful cover stories.

In a little more than two years gadgets were created using both uranium 235 ("Thin Man," shortly displaced by the improved "Little Boy") and plutonium ("Fat Man"). In addition, the complex problem of a sufficiently safe and reliable method for detonating these as-yet-untried weapons had been solved in two ways: Little Boy would be detonated by what was called the "gun" method—a separated section of the fissionable material was fired into the main "critical mass." Fat Man would be detonated by implosion—squeezing the critical mass of fissionable material into a hollow core around which it was constructed.

Meanwhile, in the "Alsos Mission," Allied intelligence agents who had landed with combat units on the Normandy beaches in June 1944 raced to find and assess information on Germany's progress toward achieving a nuclear bomb. In late July, in Strasbourg, France, they discovered the private papers of German physicist Carl von Weizsäcker, from which they learned that the Third Reich had made serious missteps and fallen far behind. (Hitler was relying instead on the V-1 pilotless bombs that had begun dropping on Britain in June and the V-2 rockets that Germany would begin launching in September, as terror weapons.) Japan's nuclear weapons efforts had also fizzled. (The two Axis partners had apparently never consulted on atomic-bomb research.)

Work on the Manhattan Project did not slow. At 5:30 A.M. on July 16, 1945, a huge explosion equal to 12,500 tons of TNT brightened the sky over the desert near Alamogordo, New Mexico, with a flash that temporarily blinded people twenty miles away who were looking in its direction. As windows rattled nearly 200 miles away, an immense mushroom-shaped cloud formed, and the surface temperature at the detonation site became 10,000 times hotter than the surface of the sun. Code-named *Trinity,* this test explosion of a prototype Fat Man was a mind-numbing success. A new age in warfare, a new era in human history had begun. "A few people laughed, a few people cried, most people were silent," Robert Oppenheimer later wrote. "There floated through my mind a line from the *Bhagavad-Gita,* . . : 'I am become death: the destroyer of worlds.'" (See also "The A-Bomb Decision" in Chapter 2 and "Dropping the A-Bomb" in Chapter 7.)

Weapons of Terror, Desperation, and Mass Destruction

Biological and Chemical Weapons

By the time war erupted in Europe, forty-one countries had signed the 1925 Geneva Protocol for the Prohibition of the Use in War of Asphyxiating, Poisonous or Other Gases, and of Bacteriological Methods of Warfare. These signatories included all but two of the major World War II combatants: the United States (which signed in 1975) and Japan (1970). Japan, primarily via the infamous Unit 100 and Unit 731, was the only major combatant to wage a dedicated campaign of biological warfare (BW), as the U.S. Army defined it: "The intentional cultivation or production of pathogenic bacteria, fungi, viruses, rickettsia, and their toxic products, as well as certain chemical compounds, for the purpose of producing disease or death in men, animals, or crops." Conducted in China, Japan's BW operations included gruesome experimentation on human beings; the development of special bombs to spread diseases, and the use of cholera, dysentery, typhoid, plague, anthrax, and paratyphoid germs to infect Chinese forces in 1942. An unsuccessful attempt was also made to infect U.S. forces on Saipan with plague. (See also "War Crimes, Japan" in Chapter 8.) The only other known instance of BW involved guerrilla groups fighting the Germans in Poland and Russia. The guerrillas reportedly used typhoid bacilli, botulinum toxin, and typhus, dysentery, glanders, cholera, anthrax, and paratyphoid agents in attempts to infect German troops and Gestapo agents, killing a few hundred.

Because of interwar reports that both Japan and Germany were preparing to wage biological warfare, the United States, Britain, and Canada all engaged in secret biological warfare research, which they shared with one another. (As the war progressed, the Allies became particularly worried that unmanned German V-weapons would be used to infect Allied troops and people in the British Isles.) Ongoing research concentrated on defense against BW attacks, but also included preparations to retaliate. By 1941, Britain had established a program to produce infected cattle feed to be dropped into Germany; a small anthrax bomb was also developed. In the course of this research, the Scottish island of Gruinard was so contaminated by anthrax in 1942 (destroying its intended victims, a flock of sheep), that the island was not declared safe until April 24, 1990.

Anthrax was also among the subjects of BW research in the United States, where a special research center, Camp Detrick, was established near Frederick, Maryland, in 1943. (A greatly expanded facility redesigned as

Fort Detrick, it was, at the turn of the twenty-first century, the home of the United States Army Medical Research and Material Command.) Test sites were developed at Horn Island in Mississippi Sound (quickly restricted to very small BW experiments when it was belatedly discovered that prevailing winds blew toward the mainland) and Granite Peak, Utah (not far from Dugway Proving Ground, where incendiary devices and toxic gasses were tested). Extensive safety tests were run at a plant outside Terre Haute, Indiana, in preparation for possible production of lethal bacterial agents, including anthrax and botulin—something that never proved necessary. America's wartime BW research led to new vaccines against influenza as well as livestock and fowl diseases, and a new BW mask for U.S. troops that, fortunately, was never needed.

★　★　★

The effects of World War I chemical warfare were burned into the minds of World War II political and military leaders and other veterans who had witnessed them firsthand. This produced a profound reluctance to release poison gases again and an equal determination to be fully prepared to retaliate should the enemy employ chemical warfare. Winston Churchill authorized the use of poison gas against German troops, should they invade Britain. The United States sent toxic materials to various theaters of war so that American troops could immediately retaliate in the event of an Axis chemical attack—viewed as a not unlikely event. Germany had introduced gas to World War I battlefields, and Italy had used gas against Ethiopians in the campaign of 1935–1936. On June 5, 1942, President Roosevelt publicly threatened Japan with "retaliation in kind and in full measure" after receiving reports of Japanese use of "poisonous or noxious gases" in China. The United States was amply supplied to retaliate. The official U.S. Army history of the war reports that, from 1940 to the end of 1945, the United States produced 146,000 tons of noxious chemicals, a significant percentage of which was placed in artillery shells, mines, grenades and toxic-gas "candles" that were ready to use should gas warfare begin.

The United States and most other combatants manufactured phosgene, hydrogen cyanide, cyanogen chloride, tear gas (chloroacetophenone), lewisite (a blistering agent), and adamsite (a gas that causes vomiting) in quantity. Mustard gas, which attacks the respiratory system and raises agonizing blisters on skin, had been widely used in World War I and was the toxic agent produced in the greatest volume during World War II: the United States alone manufactured 174,610,000 pounds. American mustard gas caused battle casualties once—inadvertently: a supply on a merchant vessel in the harbor at Bari, Italy, was released on December 2, 1943, when German bombers hit the ship. The gas caused 617 casualties, 83 of whom died.

Germany, which employed poison gas chiefly to murder millions of unarmed civilians in death camps, also produced and stockpiled seventy-eight tons of poisonous chemicals for possible battlefield use. This supply included new *nerve gases: tabun* (developed in 1936 by Dr. Gerhard Schrader of I. G. Farbenindustrie), *sarin* (1938), and *soman* (1944). Although Allied intelligence had received hints about their existence, it was not confirmed until 1945, when chemical shells were captured and analyzed.

V-Weapons

Called *Vergeltunsgwaffen*, or retaliation weapons, by the Germans, the V-weapons were also intended to terrorize those they were used against, perhaps even coerce an armistice. Frightening as they were, they did not inspire much terror, just all-out efforts to knock them down. Defense efforts improved markedly when antiaircraft emplacements began using proximity-fuzed shells. V-weapons had their most profound impact on postwar rocket development. There were three major types of V-weapons (a fourth was planned but never developed):

V-1. Pilotless flying bombs that were ground-launched or air-launched from Heinkel 111 bombers, V-1s were powered by pulse-jet engines and carried 1,875 pounds of impact-fuzed high explosives. First tested in 1942 and mass-produced as of 1943, V-1s began crashing into Britain June 13, 1944. That fall, Belgian cities, primarily the vitally important port-city of Antwerp, came under V-1 fire as well. These attacks killed more than 6,000 people and injured more than 20,000.

V-2. Rockets fueled mainly by alcohol and liquid oxygen, with a secondary power system that used hydrogen peroxide and calcium permanganate to drive the fuel pumps, V-2s were first test-fired in 1942. They were first used offensively in September 1944, when a rocket killed three people and injured seventeen in southwest London. Ground-launched from concealable small concrete pads using easily transportable launching equipment, V-2s were difficult to destroy at their source. More than 900 were fired toward Antwerp in the last three months of 1944;

In March 1941, Hitler greeted celebrated German test pilot Hanna Reitsch, as Hermann Göring and others looked on. Two years later, Reitsch made daring test flights that helped solve structural problems plaguing the V-1 flying bomb. She was one of only two women to be awarded the Iron Cross during the war. (The other was dive-bomber test pilot Melitta Schiller, 1903–1945.)

between September 1944 and March 1945, just over a thousand V-2s fell on Britain.

V-3. Code-named *Hochdruckpumpe* (high-pressure pump) and *Fleisigges Leichen* (begonia) by the Germans, this long-range smooth-bore gun designed to fire fin-stabilized high-explosive shells was the least effective V-weapon. The Germans planned to fire ten shells every minute from two firing sites in France, each equipped with 25 V-3 barrels. But an Allied air raid destroyed one of the sites in November 1943, while the V-3s were still being developed. The finished weapon had nowhere near the required range, and the barrel tended to split when the weapon was fired. Plans to fire on Britain had to be abandoned, but modified V-3s bombarded Antwerp and Allied troops in Luxembourg in December 1944—without much effect. German forces destroyed the weapons as they retreated.

PROMINANT FIGURES IN WORLD WAR II WEAPONS DEVELOPMENT

Braun, Wernher von (1912–1977): German engineer who developed the prototype of the V-2 rocket. Named technical director of the German army's Ordnance Office, he saw the rocket project through to the first launching in 1944. He became an important figure in the postwar U.S. space program. (See also "Securing Axis Scientists" in Chapter 12.)

Bush, Vannevar (1890–1974): American scientist and electrical engineer, head of the Massachusetts Institute of Technology school of engineering (1932–1939) and the Carnegie Institution (1939). In 1940, President Roosevelt named him to head the National Defense Research Committee, created to supplement army and navy work on war materials development. In 1941, Bush became head of the Office of Scientific Research and Development, which mobilized and coordinated American scientific resources for the war effort.

Conant, James Bryant (1893–1978): American chemist and president of Harvard University (1933–1953). Headed a three-man U.S. scientific commission sent to Britain in 1941 to exchange information with British scientists, including data on atomic-weapons research. Also that year, he succeeded Vannevar Bush as head of the National Defense Research Committee.

Jones, R. V. (Reginald Victor) (1911–1997): British physicist, who concentrated initially on infrared technology. Attached to the intelligence service, Jones was assigned to investigate the German application of science to air warfare. He played a pivotal role in identifying and counteracting German weapons developments.

Lindemann, Frederick (Lord Cherwell) (1886–1957): British physicist, born in Baden Baden, Germany, who became wartime scientific adviser to Winston Churchill. Known as "the Prof," Lindemann strongly supported research into electronic warfare systems and countermeasures, improvements in conventional explosives, and the development of new weapons, including the proximity fuze and the atomic bomb.

Loomis, Alfred Lee (1887–1975): American lawyer, financier, and physicist. Head of the radar research division of the Office of Scientific Research and Development (he was one of the developers of the LORAN navigation aid), Loomis was also involved in nuclear research.

Tizard, Sir Henry (1885–1959): British chemist and scientific administrator. A pilot in World War I, Tizard was named to head the Scientific Survey of Air Defense (later Air Warfare) in 1934. He helped develop the radar defense system that played a key role in winning the Battle of Britain, and he encouraged the development of airborne radar. He headed the influential Tizard Committee that traveled to the United States in 1940, opening a new era of information exchange between U.S. and British scientists.

HABBAKUK AND "COMBATS"

Two names associated with World War II weapons history illustrate, in a somewhat eccentric fashion, the try-nearly-anything attitude that gripped nations locked in all-out war. Britain's Geoffrey Pike (1894–1948), described by a countryman as "not a scientist, but a man of a vivid and uncontrollable imagination, and a totally uninhibited tongue," was the inventor of "Pykrete," a mixture of ice and wood pulp that was stronger than conventional ice and much less inclined to melt. Pyke convinced British authorities that he could create a 2,000-foot-long Pykrete aircraft carrier displacing a stupendous 2 *million* tons and capable of carrying up to 150 aircraft. The giant manned iceberg, code-named "Habbakuk," was also to be equipped with a massive refrigeration unit to make absolutely certain the ship didn't become part of the sea on which it was intended to sail (very slowly). Habbakuk fascinated Lord Mountbatten, chief adviser of Britain's Combined Operations, and tickled the fancy of Winston Churchill. However, it got only as far as prototype development (a smaller Pykrete ship was successfully floated in a Canadian lake) before the need for a giant portable ice-airfield evaporated in the heat of Allied advances.

American dentist Lytle S. Adams was returning from a visit to bat-filled Carlsbad Caverns December 7, 1941, when he heard the Pearl Harbor bulletin on his car radio. It immediately occurred to Dr. Adams that bats, easily handled when hibernating and conveniently equipped with wings, might make excellent incendiary bombs. He drove back to Carlsbad, captured some bats, conducted some tests and sent a proposal to the White House—where the president approved it.

Adams assembled a team that identified the largest U.S. bat colony (at Ney Cave, Texas), whence bats were procured, while the Army Chemical Warfare Service and the National Defense Research Council developed incendiary devices weighing less than an ounce. These were attached to the loose skin on the chests of unfortunate test bats by means of a surgical clip and a piece of string. Bats were to be dropped from bombers in containers that opened in mid-air, after which the bats were *supposed* to fly into wooden Japanese buildings, gnaw through the string, and leave the bombs behind. However, . . .

The first bats tested were cooled too much when they were forced to hibernate (for transport and so the bombs could be attached) and did not wake up. The next batch, who made it as far as test aircraft releases, either flew away or did not fly at all, dropping like stones to the earth. A few did finally demonstrate they could do the intended job: escaping from a careless bat-wrangler, they set fire to (1) a U.S. Army aircraft hanger and (2) a U.S. Army general's car. Shortly thereafter, the project was transferred to the Navy, which assigned it to the Marine Corps, where it languished. No bat bombs were released over Japan.

Suicide Weapons

See "The Divine Wind: Tokkotai and Kamikaze" in Chapter 7.

PRINCIPAL SOURCES AND FURTHER READING

Bartlett, Merrill L., ed. *Assault from the Sea: Essays on the History of Amphibious Warfare.* Annapolis: Naval Institute Press, 1983.

Brophy, Leo P., Wyndham D. Miles, and Rexmond C. Cochrane. *The Chemical Warfare Service: From Laboratory to Field,* 1959. (*The United States Army in World War II* series. Washington, D.C.: Department of the Army, Office of the Chief of Military History).

Dod, Karl C. *The Corps of Engineers: The War against Japan,* 1966. (*The United States Army in World War II* series. Washington, D.C.: Department of the Army, Office of the Chief of Military History).

Furer, Admiral Julius Augustus. *Administration of the Navy Department in World War II.* Washington, D.C.: Department of the Navy, 1959.

Hogg, Ian. *The History of Fortification.* London: Orbis Publishing, 1981.

Jarrett, Philip. *Aircraft of the Second World War: The Development of the Warplane, 1939–1945.* London: Putnam Aeronautical Books, 1997.

Lott, Arnold S. *Most Dangerous Sea: A History of Mine Warfare and an Account of U.S. Navy Mine Warfare Operations in WWII and Korea.* Annapolis: U.S. Naval Institute, 1959.

Lowell, Robert. *Lord Weary's Castle.* New York: Harcourt, Brace and Company, 1946.

Mrazek, James E. *The Glider War.* London: Robert Hale. New York: St. Martin's Press, 1975.

Overy, Richard J. *The Air War, 1939–1945.* New York: Stein and Day, 1980.

Perrett, Bryan. *Tank Warfare.* London: Arms and Armor, Distributed in the United States by Sterling Publishing, 1990.

Piekalkiewicz, Janucz. *Tank War, 1939–1945,* trans. by Jan van Heurck. Poole, Dorset: Blandford Press; Harrisburg, PA: Historical Times; New York: Distributed in the U.S. by Sterling Publishing, 1986.

Potter, E. B. *Sea Power: A Naval History.* 2nd ed. Annapolis: Naval Institute Press, 1981.

Price, Alfred. *Instruments of Darkness: The History of Electronic Warfare.* London: Macdonald and Jane's, 1997.

Rhodes, Richard. *The Making of the Atom Bomb.* New York: Simon & Schuster, 1986.

Robbins, Guy. *The Aircraft Carrier Story, 1908–1945.* London: Cassell, 2001.

Ruppenthal, Roland G. *Logistical Support of the Armies,* 1995. (*The United States Army in World War II* series. Washington, D.C.: Department of the Army, Office of the Chief of Military History).

Stauffer, Alvin P. *Quartermaster Corps: Operations in the War against Japan,* 1956. (*The United States Army in World War II* series. Washington, D.C.: Department of the Army, Office of the Chief of Military History).

Thomson, Harry C. *The Ordnance Department: Procurement and Supply*, 1960. (*The United States Army in World War II* series. Washington, D.C.: Department of the Army, Office of the Chief of Military History).

Thompson, George Raynor and Dixie R. Harris. *The Signal Corps: The Outcome*, 1966. (*The United States Army in World War II* series. Washington, D.C.: Department of the Army, Office of the Chief of Military History).

Sledge, Eugene B. *With the Old Breed at Peleliu and Okinawa*. Annapolis: Naval Institute Press, 1990.

United States, Joint Board on Scientific Information Policy. *U.S. Rocket Ordnance Development and Use in World War II*. Washington, D.C.: 1946.

MILITARY OPERATIONS, 1937–1941

They dispersed their load a ton at a time. . . . Besides many fifty- and hundred-pound bombs, they dropped great torpedoes weighing a thousand. Guernica is a compact little town, and most of these hit buildings, tearing them to pieces. . . . The spirit of the people had been good, but now they panicked. An escort of Heinkel 51s, . . . were waiting for this moment. . . . As the terrified population streamed out of the town they dived low to drill them with their guns. . . .The terrified people lay face down in ditches, pressed their backs against tree trunks, coiled themselves in holes, shut their eyes and ran across sweet green open Meadow. Many were foolish, and fled back before the aerial tide into the village. It was then that the heavy bombing of Guernica began. It was then that Guernica was smudged out of that rich landscape, the province of Vizcaya, with a heavy fist.

—*G. L. Steer*, The Tree of Gernika *[sic], 1938*

April 26, 1937: As civil war raged in Spain, pitting the fascist/nationalist forces of General Francisco Franco against the Republican forces of a leftist political coalition, the British journalist George Steer recorded one of the first coordinated Axis aerial attacks on civilian targets. Supporting Franco, planes from the "Condor Legion" of Germany's Luftwaffe, accompanied by a few Italian aircraft, destroyed most of Guernica, a Basque town sheltering 7,000 citizens and 3,000 war refugees. In addition to explosives, the German and Italian bombers dropped incendiaries: "Tubes of two pounds, long as your forearm, glistening silver from their aluminium and elektron casing. . . . So, as the houses were broken to pieces over the people, sheathed fire descended from heaven to burn them up." The raid killed 1,654 people and wounded 889. It was a portent of much more terrible Axis assaults to come.

This antifascist poster, printed during the Spanish Civil War, decries the bombing of civilian targets. Text on the left reads, "We accuse the fascists of being murderers! Innocent women and children are falling." An arrow (right), above the words "Here are the victims," points to a suffering mother and child.

July 7, 1937: A company of one hundred Japanese soldiers, part of the army that had been occupying Manchuria (which the Japanese renamed Manchukuo) were in the midst of war games about ten miles southwest of Peking (Beijing), China. As they approached the Lukouchiao Bridge, an ancient stone edifice that foreigners called the Marco Polo Bridge because the legendary Venetian explorer had allegedly been there, they found two hundred Chinese soldiers working nearby. The Japanese troops detoured around them and proceeded with their maneuvers, until, at 10:30 P.M., the Japanese commander called them to a halt, dispatching messengers to notify outlying positions. Shortly after they left, the commander heard gunfire; summoning the bugler, he mustered his men—and discovered one messenger was missing. The officer notified his superiors and began a search, questioning the nearby Chinese. Then the messenger returned unharmed. The incident might have stopped there.

Instead, the Japanese insisted on investigating the gunfire that had led them to fear for the messenger's life. Proceeding to the nearby town of Wanping, they demanded to search it. They "called up reinforcements," New Zealand journalist James Bertram, who was on the scene, later reported, "and began to shell the town. The Chinese, flourishing their bigswords [sic] and making insulting remarks, manned the walls and were unusually full of fight." As tensions mounted, the high command in Tokyo debated whether to seize this opportunity to begin military action that would bring them more Chinese territory or reserve their strength for action against the Soviet Union's Far Eastern forces. They opted for immediate gain from what they believed would be a short China war and ordered that five more divisions be sent there. As the Japanese were reaching this decision, Nationalist Chinese leader Chiang Kai-shek declared in a speech on July 19: "The four Northeastern provinces have already been lost to us [occupied by the Japanese] for six years. Now the point of conflict—Lukouch'aio—has reached the very gates of Peiping [Peking]. If we allow Lukouch'aio to be occupied by force . . . the Hopei and Chahar provinces would share the fate of the four Northeastern Provinces. . . . We do not want war, but we may be forced to defend ourselves."

On July 26, the Japanese ordered all Chinese troops out of Peking. They bombed Wanping and occupied the city. Fighting spread to the town of Langfang, where ground clashes led the Japanese to call in a devastating aerial raid. In Tungchow (Dongzhou), Chinese militiamen massacred Japanese and Korean civilians after the Japanese garrison had left to join the fighting at Wanping. Then Japanese soldiers returned to Tungchow and slaughtered all the Chinese they could find. Peking fell; the Japanese occupied Tientsin. And so it started: the Japanese pressed ruthlessly forward; the Chinese began a slow, battle-punctuated retreat into the interior of their vast country.

As Japan's war against the Chinese dragged on and the Japanese prepared for aggression against other nations, in Europe the Luftwaffe used the tactics it had tested at Guernica to support German troops as they surged across Poland's borders, igniting a bitter conflict in the West. This chapter presents an outline of notable military operations that occurred from 1937 through 1941, as these two major conflicts merged into one. Descriptions of **major battlefield clashes** are highlighted in the narrative in chronological order. The *THEATER OF OPERATION* in which each major battle or campaign occurred is noted CAP/SMALL CAP in the text. (Theaters of operation are defined in Chapter 1.) Significant actions not described in the text are noted on the "Theaters of War" charts in this chapter.

1937–August 1939: Fire in the East

Combat crackled around the globe throughout 1937. In Abyssinia (*Ethiopia*), battlefield resistance to the Italians who had invaded in 1935 had been crushed the previous year, but guerrilla resistance was growing. In retaliation for an unsuccessful attempt early in the year to assassinate the military governor, General Rodolfo Graziani, Italian troops raged through the country, executing an estimated 30,000 Abyssinians (see Chapter 8). This bloody campaign strengthened, rather than quelled the resistance. By September, foreign embassies were reporting to their governments that the Italians had little control of the country except for the main cities. At the same time, Italy continued to invest military resources in Spain, as did Germany and the Soviet Union. The war leaders of each of these nations would draw different lessons from their Spanish experience, which they would apply in the wider conflict that was to come. Half a world away, Japanese troops clashed briefly in the spring with Soviet gunboats in northern Manchukuo (Manchuria)—one deadly episode in a long dispute over the ownership of islands in the Amur River, a waterway that marked the boundary between eastern Manchuria and the Soviet Union. The high commands of both sides restrained their field forces and settled the matter by negotiation. But Soviet-Japanese tensions remained high.

The fighting in China raged on. In August, Chiang Kai-shek lured the Japanese into battle at the port city of Shanghai, an urban stronghold in the heavily fortified triangle defined by the cities of Shanghai, Nanking, and Hang-chou (Hangzhou). This opened a second front some seven hundred miles to the southeast of the site of the Chinese defeats near Peking. Ordering his units to fight to the last man, Chiang removed himself to a town northwest of the embattled city. From there, he issued detailed battle orders without proper, up-to-date knowledge of the situation—something he would continue to do throughout the war. In the months-long battle for Shanghai, the Japanese repeatedly outflanked Chinese forces, wreaking havoc on soldiers and civilians alike, as reported by a Swedish observer, Gunnar Andersson, in his 1939 book *China Fights for the World:* "air-bombs, guns, trench-mortars, machine-guns and rifles, every means of destruction this powerfully mechanized enemy had at his disposal was let loose in a rain of explosives, fire and steel over this quarter of the city that had been tortured for months and was now doomed to destruction." On November 8, Chiang ordered Chinese troops to withdraw. Refugees and soldiers clogged the roads as the army set one section of the city ablaze to cover the retreat. The fire raced out of control, eventually covering five miles as it continued to burn for many days. In the nearly three months of bitter combat that preceded this fiery conclusion, it is estimated that between 180,000 and 300,000 Chinese soldiers, 70,000 Japanese, and an unknown number of civilians were lost. "What is it really worth, this wonderful machine of civilization," Andersson wrote, "if it has no inherent force to prevent a destruction like this?"

Shanghai was only the beginning. With the port city in their possession—and after a tentative peace initiative sponsored by Japanese vice-chief of staff Hayao Tada came to nothing due to expansionist pressure in Japan and Chiang Kai-shek's miscalculations—the Japanese moved on to the Nationalist Chinese capital of Nanking. On December 8, Chiang fled the capital with Madame Chiang and an Australian adviser, William Henry Donald, leaving General Shengzhi Tang and a far-from-battle-ready force of 22,500 to face the enemy. (Tang had selected these men, who were marked as members of the Nanking "Defense Corps" by yellow armbands, sending less-well-trained provincial militia away from the city.) Two days later, the Japanese started bombing and shelling the city. When their ground troops moved in, there was fierce, often hand-to-hand fighting in which the Chinese defenders suffered heavy casualties. By the time Chiang, from his distant refuge, ordered a withdrawal, the Chinese troops in Nanking were fighting in widely scattered units and could not stage an orderly retreat. After General Tang eluded the Japanese on the river and made his own escape on December 12, chaos ensued among the now leaderless Chinese. Exploding ammunition dumps, crashing bombs and artillery shells, and raging fires surrounded soldiers and civilians as they tried to escape the city via one narrow avenue, the Chungshan Gate, to reach the Yangtze River. Thousands died at the gate, thousands more who managed to get through it died as overloaded boats sank or were bombed. (As the Japanese approached the city, their planes also sank the American gunboat *Panay*—and raked the boat's surviving crewmen with machine gun fire as they swam from the wreckage. The Japanese later apologized.) Nanking fell the night of December 12–13—and the conquering Japanese embarked on an orgy of killing, looting, and raping that has since become infamous as the Rape of Nanking. Japanese troops perpetrated similar crimes, on a smaller scale, throughout the first months of their savage advance (see Chapter 8).

Early in 1938, at the walled town of Taierzhuang, the Chinese enjoyed a brief taste of victory. Falling back into the town, luring the Japanese after them, the Chinese managed to get behind the attacking force of 10,000 and cut them off. After fierce fighting, 2,000 Japanese were able to fight their way out, leaving 8,000 dead comrades behind. The Nationalist Chinese war zone commander, General Li Tsung-jen (Li Zongren) called the encounter "the first happy occasion since the war of resistance had started." There were few other "happy" occasions, as the Chinese were forced to yield town after town. Yet, along with strength and ruthlessness, the Japanese forces were demonstrating some exploitable vulnerabilities. "The Japanese infantry, we have found, are not very good at independent action," Chinese Communist army commander Chu Teh (Zhu De) noted in a conversation with journalist James Bertram. "They depend entirely on mechanical means of transport for communications and supply. . . . They cannot take advantage of the hill country, but must follow the easiest and most level route. When we fight the Japanese," Chu went on, "we try to avoid their strong points, and select their weak points for attack. So we always fight in the hills, not in open country. And we have the assistance of the people, whom we organize and train into partisan units, to harass the enemy lines of communication."

Chiang's Nationalist forces could not rely so heavily on the support of their civilian countrymen, whom they tended to exploit and abuse and whose welfare they sacrificed in favor of their own needs as well as the necessities of war. In June 1938, to delay the Japanese forces pursuing his army, Chiang ordered the dikes restraining the Yellow River destroyed—without first warning the millions of Chinese in the path of the huge flood that resulted. Towns, roads, villages, and fields disappeared under the surging waters. Thousands died; millions more escaped with their lives but lost their homes and possessions. This deliberately created catastrophe, which German propaganda minister Joseph Goebbels described as worse than the bombing of Guernica, deeply embittered many Chinese against Chiang's regime. The flood also fostered conditions that precipitated a devastating famine a few years later (see Chapter 11).

In July, far to the northeast, Japanese and Soviet forces clashed at strategically located Changkufeng Hill near Lake Khasan at the junction of northeast Korea, southeast Manchukuo, and the Soviet maritime province near Posyet Bay. What began as a minor incident triggered when a small detachment of Russian troops occupied the hill soon developed into major combat involving thousands of men, tanks, and two Soviet air brigades. After twelve days of intense combat, Japanese diplomats in Moscow succeeded in negotiating a cease-fire. The badly mauled Japanese withdrew from the area they had been defending, yielding it to Soviet troops. This costly encounter (there were an estimated 2,500 casualties on both sides) stiffened Soviet dictator Joseph Stalin's resolve to meet any further threats to the Soviet Union's Far Eastern borders with overwhelming force. Moreover, the simmering Far Eastern tensions made Stalin more receptive to an accommodation with potential enemies in the West. Japanese commanders, meanwhile, had learned little from the drubbing their units took at Changkufeng. This became obvious the following spring during a much larger and longer Japanese-Soviet battle that took place seven hundred miles to the west, on the border between Manchukuo and Outer Mongolia.

NOMONHAN INCIDENT (KHALKHIN GOL), MAY 11–SEPTEMBER 1939
CHINA-BURMA-INDIA

Primary Objectives: *Japanese:* to push the border of occupied Chinese Manchuria (Manchukuo) farther into an area claimed by Outer Mongolia and protected by Soviet troops; *Soviet:* defense of their eastern flank

Forces: *Japanese:* 30,000 elite troops of the Kwantung Army; *Soviet:* 57,000 Russian and Mongolian troops of the 57th Special Corps, 500 to 1,000 tanks throughout the incident

Commanders: *Japanese:* Lieutenant General Michitaro Komatsubara; *Soviet:* General Georgi Zhukov

Military Losses: *Japanese:* 8,630 killed, 8,766 wounded; *Soviet:* 9,284 total (killed and wounded)

Result: The Japanese suffered a costly and humiliating defeat that pointed out major faults in their equipment, tactics, logistics, and armor and anti-tank doctrines. Led by one of the USSR's best commanders, the Soviet Far Eastern forces demonstrated superior grasp of mechanized warfare and military proficiency. Their experience in combat was to prove useful when veterans of this encounter later faced invading Germans. "It was not accidental," General Zhukov later wrote, "that the units which had fought in Mongolia . . . when moved to the Moscow area in 1941, fought the German troops so well that no praise is too high for them."

Seeking to protect its borders, the Soviet Union concluded a mutual assistance pact with Outer Mongolia in 1936, under which Soviet forces entered Mongolia in 1938. Their presence so close to the Japanese in Manchukuo sparked what became the largest tank battle ever fought to that time. Occurring in the anxious months preceding the German invasion of Poland, this encounter raged, as the *New York Times* noted on July 20, 1939, "in a thoroughly out-of-the-way corner of the world where it cannot attract a great deal of attention." It began with a foray by a small detachment of Outer Mongolian cavalry troops into disputed borderland near the village of Nomonhan along the Halha River (in Russian: Khalkhin Gol). They were driven back by Manchukuoan cavalry operating under the auspices of Japan's Kwantung Army, which was responsible for border security in that area.

The Mongolians returned, and a Japanese army unit that was dispatched to reinforce the Manchukuoans was surrounded and destroyed by Mongolians and Soviet troops. As the Soviet buildup in the area continued, the Japanese dispatched a division to the area. Its attack, which began on July 1, was initially successful, driving the Soviets back, but by July 3, the Japanese advance had stalled. Without waiting for infantry support, the Soviet commander, Georgi Zhukov, threw a tank brigade and other motorized units against the Japanese. The Soviets succeeded in driving the Japanese back—at heavy cost: 120 of more than 180 Soviet tanks committed in the clash were destroyed by Japanese infantrymen hurling what would later become known as Molotov cocktails; several hundred Japanese troops were killed or wounded. Both sides brought up more guns. Heavy artillery duels punctuated the ensuing weeks until, on July 23, the Japanese launched a frontal assault that pushed the Soviets back at a cost of 5,000 Japanese casualties.

Both sides dug in and, over the next two weeks, fighting was limited to probes and battalion-strength assaults. Meanwhile, in complete secrecy, Zhukov built up his forces. On August 20, he launched a crushing weeks-long offensive that began with an attack by more than two hundred aircraft and included as many as five hundred Soviet tanks (some equipped with flamethrowers) and vicious hand-to-hand fighting. Despite individual acts of remarkable Japanese valor (one lieutenant charged a tank with only a sword), the Soviets routed the Japanese. But Zhukov's force did not pursue them into Manchukuo; when the Red Army reached what the Soviets claimed was the

Outer Mongolian border, Zhukov ordered his men to stop and dig in. Diplomatic negotiations resulted in an official cease-fire on September 16.

Under a general cloak of secrecy—the Japanese public were told little of the Nomonhan defeat—the high command of the Japanese Imperial Army conducted studies to determine its cause. Although some officers were brutally frank about the poor quality of Japan's own tanks and the ineffectiveness of antitank tactics, the army of this industrially limited nation could do little to rectify some of these problems, as a Japanese war ministry section chief, Hideo Iwakuro, reported in early October: "Although we can fabricate equipment that resembles that of the Russians, we cannot be expected to exceed a capacity of 80 percent or so. The only method of making up for the missing 20 percent is to draw upon spiritual strength." A reliance on massed manpower evincing the spiritual strength needed for sometimes suicidal frontal assaults would remain a Japanese Imperial Army hallmark throughout the war. Meanwhile, the growing Soviet strength in the Far East—and the recently disclosed German–Soviet nonaggression pact, which removed Germany as an ally against the Communist giant to the north—contributed to the Japanese high command's decision two years later, to pursue a course of aggression into the resource-rich south instead of moving against the Soviets (with whom, by then, they had forged a nonaggression pact of their own).

★   ★   ★

As the Japanese dealt with the aftereffects of Nomonhan, victory continued to elude their armies in China proper, although they were making some progress. In October 1938, they took Canton, the last major deepwater port in southern China through which Chiang Kai-shek's Nationalist forces could receive supplies. Another temporary Nationalist capital city, Wuhan, fell later that year. By 1939, Chiang had settled in the southwest at Chungking, at the junction of the Yangtze and Jialing rivers and only some five hundred miles from the Burmese border. Perched on cliffs and so often shrouded in mists and fog that the inhabitants said "when the sun shines, even the dogs bark in fear," this was to remain the Nationalist capital for the rest of the war. Yet even this far in the interior, Chungking proved to be within the reach of the enemy. On a clear day in early May 1939, Japanese navy planes suddenly appeared and started dropping bombs. It was the first of many raids against a city that had no effective antiaircraft defense. Explosions tore buildings to pieces. People were incinerated as fires raged through the streets. "Chungking has become one vast cemetery," a French missionary wrote. The May

Smoke rises above buildings in the Chinese city of Chungking, heavily bombed by Japanese planes in 1939. Thousands of people lost their homes or their lives in the attacks.

strikes alone took an estimated 6,000 to 8,000 lives—and raids continued. Between May and September 1939, Chungking became the most heavily bombed city in history. It would surrender that dubious honor to many other cities in turn, after Adolf Hitler sent his armies across Germany's border with Poland to begin the European war that, in less than two years, would merge with the conflict in Asia.

September 1939– December 1940: Fire in the West

By the summer of 1939, Germany had gained control of Austria and Czecho-slovakia (and Czech weapons and armaments factories) without resorting to war. In a diplomatic coup that astonished the world, Hitler had also engi-neered a pact with the Soviet Union that freed him of the fear of a Soviet at-tack as he implemented his plan to move against Poland (just as it freed Stalin of the fear of a German attack from the west while the Japanese threatened Soviet armies in the Far East). A secret addendum to that agree-ment guaranteed Polish territory to the complicitous Soviets.

In April, Hitler ordered the General Staff to begin planning for an invasion, and in a May 23 meeting with senior military commanders, he told them plainly that war with Poland was inevitable. According to Rudolf Schmundt, Hitler's adjutant, who kept a record of the meeting, the führer pointed out that with "minor exceptions German national unification has been achieved [Austria and the Czech Sudetenland had been brought into the Reich]. Further successes cannot be achieved without bloodshed. . . . Poland sees danger in a German victory over the west and will try and deprive us of our victory. There is therefore no question of sparing Poland, and the decision remains to attack Poland at the first suitable opportunity. . . . There will be war." In Directive No. 1 for the Conduct of the War, issued on August 31, Hitler ordered the invasion to begin at 4:45 A.M., September 1, and outlined the steps to be taken should Britain and France come to Poland's defense. Not only would the invasion by the regular German army be utterly devastating, but the specialized SS units that followed the Wehrmacht were instructed to ravage the population. These units, the *Einsatzgruppen*, systematically committed atrocities and mass murder of civilians—primarily intellectuals and prominent citizens, and other "undesirables." (See also Chapter 8.)

THE INVASION OF POLAND:
GERMAN INVASION (CASE WHITE)—SEPTEMBER 1–28, 1939;
RUSSIAN INVASION—SEPTEMBER 17–28, 1939
EUROPEAN THEATER (WESTERN EUROPE)

Primary Objectives: *German:* to conquer and destroy Poland, acquire a vital port city, Danzig, and the Polish corridor and other territory lost in the Treaty of Versailles; *Polish:* to hold out at least until Allied assistance arrived; *Soviet:* to acquire additional territory; claimed the invasion was to ensure the interests and safety of local ethnic Ukrainians and Russians

Forces: *German:* 5 armies comprising 75 divisions (54 of them front-line), 1,500 aircraft; *Polish:* 30 infantry divisions, 11 cavalry brigades, 2 mechanized brigades, 313 combat aircraft; *Soviet:* 2 armies

Commanders: *German:* General Fedor von Bock (North Army Group), General Gerd von Rundstedt (South Army Group); *Polish:* Marshal Edward Smigly-Rydz (Polish Army); *Soviet:* General M.P. Kowalow (Byelorussian Front), General Semyon Timoshenko (Ukrainian Front)

Military Losses: *German:* 14,000; *Polish:* 60,000; *Soviet:* 737 (some historians dispute the Soviet figure and estimate losses at 5,000 or more)

Civilian Deaths: 25,000 Poles

Other: Germany captured 694,000 Polish soldiers; the Soviets captured 217,000. About 90,000 Polish troops escaped many later served with the Allies

Result: Poland was defeated and divided between Germany and the Soviet Union. Germany took Danzig and the western portion of the country for German settlement; it used the central section (referred to as the "General Government") for extermination and slave camps. The campaign affirmed the value of blitzkrieg and the panzer units; it gave Hitler reason to believe he was a military genius, a notion that would have horrific consequences for his generals and soldiers. The USSR gained eastern Poland, a buffer zone Stalin wanted against possible German aggression. The incursion into Poland also allowed the Soviets to easily place troops in the neighboring Baltic States, as permitted in the secret protocol of the German-Soviet pact. This, in turn, facilitated the Soviet annexation of Estonia, Latvia, and Lithuania in 1940.

On the last August evening in 1939, eight Germans dressed as Polish soldiers staged a fake raid on a German radio station in a bizarre attempt to show the world that Poland had initiated armed hostilities. In another odd episode, early the next morning an antique German battleship, ostensibly on a goodwill mission, opened fire on a small Polish garrison on the Westerplatte peninsula, near Danzig (Gdansk). The salvos from the training vessel-turned-retrofitted battleship *Schleswig Holstein* were immediately followed elsewhere by Luftwaffe air strikes, and columns of panzer units, with more than 1,500 tanks, burst across the western borders. Blitzkrieg—and the undeclared war on Poland—had begun. Most of the army—about 1.5 million men—took part in the assault; the remaining forces in Germany were positioned toward the west should Britain or France somehow launch an attack before Poland surrendered. The Poles eventually sent a million men into battle, but when the invasion came, two-thirds of the Polish army was still mobilizing and unable to fully respond to the attack.

According to plan, the North Army Group, comprising the Third and Fourth Armies, swept down from East Prussia and Pomerania while the South Army Group, consisting of the Eighth, Tenth and Fourteenth Armies, moved in from Silesia and Slovakia in the south, taking advantage of the area's flat landscape. Both army groups zeroed in on Warsaw, in the geographic heart of Poland. In the northwest, forces in the German Fourth

German troops invaded Poland on September 1, 1939, causing Britain and France to declare war on Germany two days later. This British newspaper seller, outside Whitehall in London on September 7, holds a stack of special edition newspapers confirming that the war is official.

Army in Pomerania drove toward Danzig, while others sped through the southern end of the Polish corridor, cutting it off from the rest of Poland by September 3, then linking up with the Third Army. In the south, the Eighth and Tenth Armies pushed forward to Warsaw while the Fourteenth Army diverged to take Cracow and move east toward the Bug River. On the first day of battle, the Luftwaffe bombed more than two dozen cities, launched five raids on the capital alone, and wiped out most of the Polish air force, thus gaining immediate air superiority. Amid the rapid accumulation of losses, shell-shocked Polish forces had a few modest successes and fought back gallantly with what they had, including horse cavalry. (Contrary to postwar myth, however, the horse cavalry was not in the habit of charging German panzers.) At Westerplatte, the small but determined Polish force repelled continued German assaults. Out past the peninsula, additional German warships waited, preventing an escape by sea. Finally, after withstanding waves of infantry attacks, aerial bombing, and continual shelling from the *Schleswig Holstein*, the garrison, out of ammunition, surrendered on September 7. During the battle, they killed hundreds of German soldiers and lost fifteen of their own.

Within a week of the German invasion, the large city of Cracow fell. Still staggering from German blows, Poland was blindsided again as the Red Army charged across its virtually undefended eastern frontiers. The Russian invasion on September 17 met little resistance and was in keeping with the month-old secret German-Soviet agreement to conquer and share the spoils of a divided Poland. The Soviets, who had not declared war, easily reached the Bug River and established themselves in Galicia, Poland's oil-rich southeast corner, adjacent to the Carpathian Mountains near the Hungarian and Romanian borders. The eastern third of Poland quickly fell under Soviet occupation. Meanwhile, Polish forces, overwhelmed at every turn, pulled back to defend their nearly starving capital, Warsaw, which had been without gas, electricity, and water for a week. Hitler escalated the bombing, claiming the city was a military fortress (it clearly was not to the numerous eyewitnesses who were there), and most of Warsaw was rubble when it surrendered on the 27th.

In the meantime, Britain and France, honoring their commitment to Polish defense (see Chapters 2 and 3), declared war on Germany on September 3. The next day, Britain's Royal Air Force (RAF) struck German naval bases at Wilhelmshaven and Brunsbuttel, doing little damage but signaling a modest willingness to act. At the same time, advance units of the British Expeditionary Force arrived in France, and shortly after that, French troops crossed into the Saarland, on Germany's western frontier, engaging in minor skirmishes that came to nothing. In response to these rather unimpressive moves, the German Tenth Army departed Poland on October 3 to take up positions on Germany's Western Front, where thirty-five divisions, some of which had also operated in Poland, were already in place along the line of fortifications known as the West Wall. Militarily, there was little the Allies could do for Poland immediately. They had scant enthusiasm for another ground war in western Europe and feared the Wehrmacht's advertised strength. The British commenced a Leaflet War and instituted a naval blockade in the North Sea that dramatically decreased German imports. Germany responded with its own blockade against Britain, and both sides began laying underwater mines. Beyond that, continued indecision about exactly what else to do fostered a six-month virtual standstill among belligerents referred to as the "Phony War" (described later in this chapter).

The quick conquest of the country was not the only key objective as the panzers punctured Polish lines, and in their wake, the German infantry fanned out over the countryside. The destruction of Poland, Polish culture, and Polish Jews was intrinsic to the military campaign. Both regular army and SS units, which arrived with specially prepared lists of targets, torched entire thatched-roof villages, burned or blew up synagogues, shot fleeing residents, rounded up the intelligentsia, and killed unarmed Polish prisoners of war. (Within eight weeks, they destroyed more than five hundred villages and towns.) SS units lined civilians up against walls, over pits, or in forests in mass executions. Meanwhile, the Russian conquerors were nearly as merciless as their Nazi counterparts; like the SS units that operated in the wake of the Wehrmacht, the Soviet secret police (the NKVD) followed the Red Army, arresting and murdering thousands of Polish servicemen and civilians. (See also Chapter 8.)

By the third week of September, SS units began herding rural Jews to the major cities to join those already living there in cramped, vile ghettos, the first step in a tortuous process that would annihilate 90 percent of Poland's Jewish population. (It was also a process that the Nazis used repeatedly in central and eastern European territory.) On the 28th, Poland was officially divided between Germany and the Soviet Union. Hitler set aside the central part of the country for other purposes, and this area would become the heart of the Holocaust, where the Nazis built and operated a web of concentration camps, as well as all of their extermination camps. The rapid conquest of Poland demonstrated to the world the might of the

THE BIRTH OF BLITZKRIEG

Blitzkrieg (lightning war) made its terrifying debut as a new style of combat on the morning of September 1, 1939, as German forces surged into Poland, surrounding Warsaw, its capital, sixteen days later. Unlike the trench warfare, rigid front lines, and large armies facing each other from fixed fortifications that characterized World War I, in World War II, military planners embraced multiple, moving front lines and mobile, mechanized units. As early as the 1920s, strategists both inside and outside Germany had proposed using blitzkrieg-like tactics, but Hitler, having the technology, the well-trained professional forces, the motive, and the opportunity to employ it, was the first to do so. General Heinz Guderian, a radio-specialist in World War I, recognized the expanded role radio communication must play in future military operations. He pushed the manufacture of mechanized armored units and the outlawed panzers his strategy would require. (Panzer, short for *panzerkampfwagen,* refers to armored combat vehicles, such as tanks. See Chapter 5.) Influenced by such leading military theorists as Britain's J. F. C. Fuller and even the less well-known Charles de Gaulle, who was emerging as a French authority on armored warfare, Guderian laid out the concept that would become blitzkrieg in his 1937 book *Achtung-Panzer!* His intent (including a hoped-for job promotion) was to secure greater emphasis on and investment in panzer units among the German high command. By 1939, Germany had outfitted all its tanks with radio receivers, essential for executing coordinated attacks. Within two years Guderian was a master of blitzkrieg not only on paper but in prac-

tice, successfully leading forces into Poland and later against France, the Soviet Union, and Allied forces in Belgium's Ardennes Forest.

Blitzkrieg was designed to so stun and disorient the enemy that it was unable to mount a response. Reliable two-way radio communication in the field and technologically advanced aircraft and armored units now made it possible to launch well-coordinated, fast-paced, mobile military operations that could quickly change course if needed. Blitzkrieg combined surprise air and land assaults. Heavy aerial attacks focused on communication lines and transportation networks (airfields and grounded aircraft were the top priority so as to obtain immediate air superiority). Massed tanks simultaneously charged forward making deep incisions into enemy lines followed by reconnaissance, anti-tank, artillery, engineer, and signal units as well as armored personnel vehicles. There was virtually no halting or slowing down as invading forces raced to their destinations; in the meantime, trailing infantrymen began to fan out, widening the incision and attacking enemy units the tanks had cleared away or bypassed. In concert with this, covert agents established behind enemy lines before the attack or paratroopers dropped in (as was done in German blitzkriegs after the Polish campaign) pounced on critical locations—such as enemy command posts, bridgeheads, key street intersections, and radio stations—and linked up with the tank and other armored units speeding to the same target. As these forces secured their objectives and then pushed further into enemy territory, additional units, relying on information radioed from constant air and field reconnaissance, attacked weakened areas along the fluid battle lines while the opposition was still scrambling to respond to the initial thrusts.

The hot-tempered Guderian, popular with his men but repeatedly at odds with the top military leadership over the value of panzer units (many officials favored the infantry) made a believer out of Adolf Hitler. Five days after the German invasion of Poland, Guderian joined Hitler on a tour of battle sites in the north, to Grudziadz, along the Vistula River. Surveying the destruction, Hitler was shocked to learn that it was the panzers, rather than the Luftwaffe, that had inflicted such damage. Still, as much as Hitler valued Guderian, an ardent Nazi, the führer twice dismissed him (December 1941 and March 1945) over disagreements in strategy.

Despite their tremendous success in combat, the panzer units remained a small segment of the Wehrmacht, in part because of stiff competition for resources needed to build U-boats, aircraft, and rockets. (Germany produced nearly 20,000 tanks during the war but about 100,000 more aircraft.) Blitzkrieg was exceptionally effective in Europe, where smaller states had shorter distances for an invading force to travel. But the method, initially successful in the Soviet Union, would ultimately fail there. Sprinting panzer divisions were not cut out for the marathon that expansive Russian geography demanded or the harsh winters and deep spring mud. But the undeniable effectiveness of blitzkrieg in the right situations with the proper conditions influenced others, including the Americans, who adapted and modified it for their own use during the war. However, unlike the Germans, who never built a fleet of heavy or long-range bombers, the United States and Britain also relied heavily—and effectively—on the strategic use of air power.

Wehrmacht and confirmed Hitler's pattern of cruelty and duplicity. It put the Western powers sufficiently on notice, as events in Austria and Czechoslovakia had not, that European civilization was truly in peril. "Take a look around Warsaw," Hitler told news reporters during his October 5 visit to the shattered capital. "That is how I can deal with any European city."

The Battle of the Atlantic Begins (September 1939–December 1940)

The Battle of the Atlantic was an epic, multiyear struggle—and a war of attrition. British survival, and, ultimately, the defeat of Nazi Germany required Allied control of shipping lanes and sea routes that linked North America and Europe; German survival hinged on preventing the Atlantic from becoming a busy freeway for Allied supplies and war matériel. Britain depended on food and raw material imports, and the Allies had to transport massive amounts of cargo and personnel there (and later to the Soviet Union and continental Europe) to withstand—and then overcome—the Nazi onslaught. Thus, breaking Britain was a fundamental German objective. "The defeat of England is essential to final victory," wrote Hitler in Directive No. 9, issued November 29, 1939. "The most effective way of ensuring this is to cripple the English economy by attacking it at decisive points." As Churchill later put it, "The Battle of the Atlantic was the dominating factor all through the war. Never for one moment could we forget that everything happening elsewhere, on land, at sea, or in the air, depended ultimately on its outcome." Admiral of the Fleet Sir Dudley P. R. Pound, First Sea Lord and Chief of Naval Staff, would put it more succinctly in March 1942: "If we lose the war at sea, we lose the war."

German efforts in the Atlantic aimed at disrupting Allied communication and destroying shipping that would sustain Britain and facilitate military operations against the Reich. Among its many other benefits to Hitler, the Nazi occupation of Denmark, Norway, Belgium, Holland, and France in 1940 gave Germany a long coastline of ports from which to conduct naval operations. The French ports, in particular, offered more convenient safe havens for the German U-boats previously stationed at bases in the Baltic region. Germany's Todt Organization built massive, enclosed bomb-proof U-boat pens on the French Atlantic coast, and German submarines operating out of Brest, Lorient, and Bordeaux sank an increasing amount of Allied shipping. In addition to the U-boat scourge, ferocious storms (with waves approaching one hundred feet high) and frequently tumultuous weather conditions in the Atlantic imperiled Allied convoys. The battle also marked the decline of the battleship, which would later be the case as well in the Pacific War. (See also Chapter 5.) Ultimately, the failure of the German surface navy's campaign against Allied shipping and the shortage of U-boats in 1940 meant the irrevocable loss of a major opportunity to defeat Britain when it was especially vulnerable. Competing demands on German industry and resources only increased as the war dragged on longer than Hitler had anticipated, and he could not—or was too distracted to—provide his navy with the means to execute the strategy laid out in Directive No. 9. The Allies would sustain huge losses to the U-boats for the next several years, but to the dismay of Admiral Karl Dönitz, U-boat commander in chief, Hitler and his military leadership's recognition of the U-boats' importance came too late.

WOLF PACKS AND CONVOYS

Under Admiral Dönitz's centralized wolf pack strategy, derived from German submarine experience in World War I and first employed in early 1940, German U-boats operated in groups of as many as twenty that preyed on Allied shipping. In the wolf-pack system, which the Americans adopted a few years later for use in the Pacific War, when a U-boat spotted an Allied convoy of ships, it radioed the position to headquarters, which then told other U-boats in the area where and when to rendezvous. Once assembled, the U-boats struck. Before British ships began using radar, U-boats attacked above surface and at night, banking on the darkness to keep their conning towers obscured and achieving a high kill rate (see "Allied and Neutral Shipping Losses" chart in this chapter).

The transatlantic convoys that were Britain's lifeline and that kept the Allies supplied throughout the war were absolutely essential in defeating the Axis. Even before the United States entered the war, the use of U.S. Navy escort vessels in convoys increased, to protect Lend-Lease shipments. In the convoy system, also used during World War I, warships escorted a group of merchant or commercial ships to its destination. There was considerable debate early on in the British admiralty over whether

Allied warships that guarded supply vessels against German U-boat attacks in the Atlantic Ocean significantly reduced the number of merchantmen losses. In this photograph, officers watch for enemy submarines from the bridge of a destroyer.

to use warships to escort convoys or to pursue the U-boats. Eventually, the latter method was dropped when it was found to be quite inefficient, but trial and error continued as the Allies sought the best way to secure the convoys. Air raids over U-boat pens in France did little damage, and maintaining constantly patrolled sea lanes, already difficult, became more so as the convoy routes increased in length, from North America to the Soviet Union and points throughout the Pacific Ocean. The best defense against the Axis was a combination of air patrols operating from both ends of the sea route, a large number of escort ships, and, in the North Atlantic, using routes well to the north of traditional shipping lanes. The importance of escort ships became particularly apparent in late 1942, when Allied escort ships were transferred to the Mediterranean to support Operation Torch (the landings in North Africa). U-boat success soared, and the Allies were not able to put a stop to it until the escort ships returned to convoy duty in the spring of 1943.

EYEWITNESS ACCOUNT—CONVOY DUTY: LIFE ABOARD A DESTROYER ESCORT

Albert Green, a 19-year-old sonarman from New Jersey, was assigned to the 200-man USS *Enright*, a new destroyer escort, in September 1943. He spent fifteen months aboard the ship on convoy duty, escorting cargo and troopships from New York to the United Kingdom. Green's job entailed submarine detection, but his crew's success in destroying U-boats remained uncertain since "the Germans had a lot of tricks—they would send oil slicks to the surface and pretend they had been damaged or sunk and then they would sneak away." In addition to the U-boat threat, the convoy ships endured tremendous storms in the frigid North Atlantic; "Everyone on the ship got seasick at one time or another. . . . There were so many times when it was so rough that they couldn't cook. So we'd eat . . . boiled potatoes, or a hot dog, or peanut butter sandwiches." In April 1944, poor weather wreaked havoc on the *Enright*:

> We were coming back to New York with some ships. . . . We had a target on our radar. . . . Well, it was very, very foggy, we couldn't see ten feet in front of us. And I worked on the bridge and we were in general quarters and all of a sudden I saw this—what looked like the Empire State building just coming on us. A big tanker. . . . And the executive officer, if he hadn't taken over, we'd have been sliced in two. . . . He said, 'Hard right rudder!' . . . so instead of getting cut in half we got a 65-foot hole in a ship that's 300 feet long . . . and one man . . . he was at a gun mount, he was knocked overboard by the impact, and we had our depth charges set because we thought it might be a submarine, and the depth charges started to go off under the ship. So he was obviously killed by the explosions of the depth charges.

In December 1944, Green left the *Enright*. "I got on a real destroyer then, which was like being in the Taj Mahal after [being on a] destroyer escort."

From 1939 through 1944, the Allies lost nearly 5,000 ships filled with crewmen, cargo, and troops primarily to the Axis, but also because of accidents, bad weather, and other causes. The following chart shows the dominance of German U-boats and Japanese submarines in sinking Allied shipping, reaching peak efficiency in 1942. Successful attacks by aircraft rose dramatically early in the war before tapering off. In 1943, the Allies, while still losing a great deal of shipping, cut their losses in half with improved convoy protection measures, better technology, and the changing fortunes of Germany and Japan. Neither country could maintain the quality of its navies because of key personnel losses, limited resources for ongoing naval construction, and more pressing needs elsewhere as the Allies steadily gained strength on all fronts.

WORLDWIDE ALLIED AND NEUTRAL SHIPPING LOSSES TO AXIS FORCES

September 1939–May 1944

Cause	Shipping Tonnage	Number of Ships	Percentage of Ships Lost
Aircraft			
1939	2,949	10	5
1940	580,074	192	18
1941	1,017,422	371	29
1942	700,020	146	9
1943	424,411	76	13
1944	68,481	11	12
Total	**2,793,357**	**806**	—
Merchant Raiders			
1939	—	—	—
1940	366,644	54	5
1941	226,527	44	3
1942	194,625	30	2
1943	41,848	5	1
1944	—	—	—
Total	**829,644**	**133**	—

(continued)

WORLDWIDE ALLIED AND NEUTRAL SHIPPING
LOSSES TO AXIS FORCES (CONTINUED)

Cause	Shipping Tonnage	Number of Ships	Percentage of Ships Lost
Mines			
1939	262,542	78	35
1940	509,889	201	18
1941	230,842	111	9
1942	104,588	51	3
1943	108,658	37	6
1944	14,352	2	2
Total	**1,230,871**	**480**	—
Submarines			
1939	421,156	114	52
1940	2,186,158	471	44
1941	2,171,754	432	33
1942	6,266,215	1,160	70
1943	2,586,905	463	77
1944	414,718	67	73
Total	**14,046,906**	**2,707**	—
Torpedo Boats			
1939	—	—	—
1940	47,985	23	2
1941	58,854	29	2
1942	71,156	23	1
1943	15,138	6	1
1944	8,973	7	8
Total	**202,106**	**88**	—
Warships			
1939	61,337	15	7
1940	96,986	17	2
1941	201,823	40	3
1942	130,461	31	2
1943	—	—	—
1944	7,840	1	1
Total	**498,447**	**104**	—

WORLDWIDE ALLIED AND NEUTRAL SHIPPING
LOSSES TO AXIS FORCES (CONTINUED)

Cause	Shipping Tonnage	Number of Ships	Percentage of Ships Lost
Unknown and Miscellaneous			
1939	7,253	4	2
1940	203,905	101	10
1941	421,336	272	21
1942	323,632	223	13
1943	43,177	10	2
1944	755	4	4
Total	**1,000,058**	**614**	—
Total (All Causes)			
1939	755,237	221	—
1940	3,991,641	1,059	—
1941	4,328,558	1,299	—
1942	7,790,967	1,664	—
1943	3,220,137	597	—
1944	515,119	92	—
Total (All Causes, All Years)	**20,601,659**	**4,932**	—

Because of rounding, some yearly totals do not add up to 100 percent for ships lost by cause. *Principal sources:* S. W. Roskill, *The War at Sea: 1939–1945*, vols. 1–3, London: H. M. Stationery Office, 1954, 1956, 1961; the Library of Congress.

The Phony War, October 1939–April 1940,
EUROPEAN THEATER (WESTERN EUROPE)

Between the final surrender of Polish forces in early October and Germany's spring offensive in the West, there was little activity on the Western Front, the continental region that comprised the Low Countries (the Netherlands, Belgium, Luxembourg), northern France, and western Germany. The Phony War (also called *Sitzkrieg*—the sit-down war—a pun on blitzkrieg) was a time of strategic planning mixed with indecision, mobilization, and minor operations. Beginning September 4, the day after the Allies declared war,

RAF bombers dropped 6 million leaflets over Germany entitled "Warning! A Message from Great Britain." The first leaflet raid over Berlin, on October 1, began a shower of more than 3 million leaflets with the heading "These Are Your Leaders" that described the hypocrisy of top German officials and gave the particulars of their personal wealth that had been stashed outside the country. The usefulness of the Leaflet War was widely debated (and ridiculed) in Great Britain, but the British cabinet believed it a potent psychological strategy following reports that the Nazis were scooping up copies to keep them out of citizens' hands. Ultimately, the British dropped more than 60 million leaflets, in the process giving RAF crews much-needed operational experience. German bombers did not strike British soil until November 13, when a raid on the Shetland Islands did minor damage to an unoccupied house and left a few craters in the ground. Because prying the Germans out of Poland did not appear at all feasible, Britain and France began to greatly expand their forces in anticipation of a war they now calculated would last several years. In the meantime, Hitler clashed with his generals over Germany's next move. The führer was anxious to establish bases in northern France and the Low Countries, figuring these actions would prompt Britain to accept a peace settlement; once the meddlesome West was subdued and no longer an obstacle to German expansion, Hitler could then safely turn to the east and focus on his primary goal: conquest of the Soviet Union. He felt compelled to act before Germany's food and fuel supplies dwindled, but neither the weather nor his military leadership cooperated. Despite the Wehrmacht's decisive performance in Poland, the generals argued for more time to train and make improvements before the next strike. Nor did it help that in January 1940 a German aircraft crash-landed outside Mechelen-sur-Meuse and the Allies recovered a courier's copy of Luftwaffe plans for an imminent attack through Belgium, forcing Hitler to revise his attack routes and wait for better weather. Thus, an uneasy quiet hung over most of Europe until the spring.

In Scandinavia, meanwhile, a bloody war that had been raging between Finland and the Soviet Union since November was coming to an end.

THE WINTER WAR (FINNISH-SOVIET WAR), NOVEMBER 1939–MARCH 1940
EUROPEAN THEATER (SCANDINAVIA)

> **Primary Objectives:** *Soviet:* to gain the Karelian Isthmus as a buffer for Leningrad; *Finnish:* to defend their homeland

Forces: *Soviet:* began with 26 divisions; *Finnish:* 9 divisions

Commanders: *Soviet:* Marshal Kliment Voroshilov, later replaced by General Semyon K. Timoshenko; *Finnish:* Marshal Carl Mannerheim

Military Losses: *Soviet:* 200,000 of 1.2 million total troops; *Finnish:* 25,000

Result: USSR captured the Karelian Isthmus and additional territory, more than a tenth of Finnish land. About 400,000 Finnish refugees were required to resettle quickly elsewhere in Finland after the Soviets acquired their land. Hitler saw the Soviets' poor performance as proof that he could conquer the USSR. Russian military officials began trying to improve their armed forces.

Unable to persuade the resolute Finns to give up territory that Stalin deemed vital to Russian defense, the Soviet dictator, fresh from his conquest of eastern Poland, ordered the invasion of Finland, and on November 30 the Red Army launched a three-pronged attack, accompanied by air raids, on the Karelian Isthmus. The goal was to acquire the military bases there and maintain an extended defensive barrier between mainland Finland and Leningrad (St. Petersburg). The Russians also attacked central Finland and its northernmost tip, and were stunned to find themselves stymied. They had expected to achieve their objective in less than two weeks; they did not expect the hardy Finns, initially outnumbered four to one (later eight to one; in some battlefields fifty to one), to wage such a spirited or well-fought defense. Despite the Red Army's experience living and training in harsh climates, Soviet forces—initially 465,000 men—were completely unprepared for the paralyzing conditions of a Finnish winter. Ill-equipped and poorly outfitted for snowbound warfare, with only a few hours of light each day, the Red Army bogged down before the fortifications of the Mannerheim Line on the Karelian Isthmus, which separates the Gulf of Finland from Lake Ladoga. The Finns were not perfectly equipped either, but they were highly trained and motivated. Ski troops camouflaged in white darted in and out of forests and expertly handled the difficult terrain to outflank and isolate enemy units. As it happened, many Russian troops froze to death before the Finns moved in for the kill. In late December 1939, at Suomussalmi, the Finns utterly destroyed two Soviet divisions in a battle that shocked the world.

But even with the advantage of fighting on familiar territory, the ineptitude of Red Army leadership during the campaign, and several astonishing battle victories, the Finns could not match Soviet numbers in personnel, tanks, planes, or ammunition. Soviet bombing of Helsinki at the beginning of the war had inspired Finnish resilience and only made the Russian task more difficult; eventually the Soviets expanded their air raids to civilian targets throughout southwestern Finland, even striking health resorts and recreational areas to terrorize and wear out citizens. On February 11, the Red Army finally broke through the Mannerheim Line. Finnish resistance, the heavy toll inflicted on the Russians, and perhaps Stalin's desire to have his armies available for other endeavors, prompted the Soviets to negotiate an end to the fighting in March. Finland ceded the territory Stalin had demanded, but the rest of the country remained free of Soviet occupation. Russian miscues and outright operational disasters (what Marshal Carl Mannerheim, head of Finnish forces, likened to "a performance by a badly directed orchestra") convinced Hitler that the Red Army, though large, would quickly fall to the Wehrmacht, and to Stalin's extreme embarrassment, international opinion was inclined to agree. This conclusion, though, would have painful consequences for Hitler and his army.

★　　★　　★

While the Finns were startling the Soviets and inspiring admiration in the West, in the East, the Chinese continued to resist the Imperial Japanese Army.

Catastrophe at Changsha and Chiang's Winter Offensive, November 1939–April 1940

Japan's "short war" in China had continued for more than two years, yet the Japanese remained confident, in fact, *over*confident of victory. As September turned to October, they marched on the city of Changsha in Hunan province without their heavy equipment and vehicles and were beaten back by Chinese Nationalist forces that attacked their vulnerable flanks. Yet this proved to be almost as much a defeat as a victory for the Nationalists. Notified that the Japanese were nearing the city, the defenders of Changsha had prematurely ignited firetraps they had created as last-ditch defenses. Leaping out of control, the fires licked into the city, raging for several days; thousands of people died. (After courts-martial ordered by Chiang Kai-shek, the commander of the garrison, one other general, and the city police chief were executed.)

On November 19, Chiang committed half of his armies to a Winter Offensive; in a surge of optimism, he spoke of possibly retaking the former capital of Nanking. Yet his armies were in no condition to mount a successful campaign. Weak from battlefield losses and woefully ill-equipped, they nevertheless staged more than 2,000 attacks between mid-December and the end of January 1940, temporarily regaining some territory. By April, however, the Winter Offensive had ended in failure—and that failure marked a turning point in the Nationalists' war. It reduced Chiang's authority over local warlords and the detested communists with whom he had forged a tenuous alliance against the invader. It also reinforced the belief, within high Nationalist circles, that their forces could not win what now would obviously be a long war unless the United States became a combatant and brought its power to bear in Asia. Financial and other aid was already flowing to China from the still-neutral United States.

The Americans were also doing everything in their power, short of going to war, to support the European Allies, for it was all but certain that Germany would not maintain the relative quiet of the "Phony War."

OPERATION WESERÜBUNG, APRIL 9–JUNE 9, 1940
EUROPEAN THEATER (SCANDINAVIA)

Primary Objectives: *German:* secure Germany's northern flank before attacking Western Europe; prevent the Allies from using Scandinavia as a staging area for military operations; secure sea routes (particularly to safeguard shipments of Swedish iron ore) as well as naval and air bases for future attacks on the West; *Norwegian:* resist the German assault with British and French assistance

Forces: *German* (in Norway): 7 army divisions; 23 warships and 28 U-boats; 335 fighters and bombers plus support aircraft; **Allied**—*Danish:* 2 divisions (only partially mobilized); *Norwegian:* 6 divisions; 9 warships, 9 submarines; *British:* 4 brigades; 42 warships, 17 submarines; *French:* 3 brigades; 13 warships; *Free Polish:* 1 brigade, 3 warships

Commanders: *German:* General Nikolaus von Falkenhorst, Maj. General Eduard Dietl, Vice Admiral Gunther Lutgens (in Norway); *Danish (neutral):* General William Wain Prior; **Allied**—*Norwegian:* General Kristian Laake, later replaced by Colonel Otto Ruge; *British:* Admiral Sir Charles Forbes, Vice Admiral W. J. Whitworth, Maj. General Adrian Carton de Wiart, Maj. General Bernard Paget, Maj. General Pierse Mackesy

Military Losses: *German:* 3,700; **Allied**—*British:* 4,400; *Norwegian:* 1,335; *French* and *Free Polish* combined: 530; *Danish:* 13

Result: German conquest and occupation of Denmark and Norway; Germany controlled access to the Baltic Sea, but its naval surface fleet suffered severe damage that would not be remedied.

The Phony War ended the morning of April 9, 1940, as the Danes awoke to find 40,000 German troops crossing the border and occupying Copenhagen. Danish soldiers dressed in ceremonial uniforms on duty outside Amalienborg Castle shot at approaching German forces until their commanding officer demanded a cease-fire on the king's orders. Minor resistance ended under the threat of air attacks, and the Germans captured Denmark that day with fewer than two dozen casualties. Conquering Denmark was one thing; controlling it was another. In time, 130,000 German soldiers maintained the occupation.

Meanwhile, further north in Norway, the Germans mounted their only major combined air-and-sea operation of the war, and their first military operation using paratroopers. German aircraft bombed key installations near Oslo and dropped paratroopers into the capital, Narvik in the north, and Trondheim, on the central coast; these forces quickly gained control of airfields to ensure that the Luftwaffe ruled the skies before the Norwegians and the Allies could respond. The Kriegsmarine sailed into the major fjords, seizing harbors and offloading infantrymen at Oslo and around the coast at Kristiansand, Stavenger, Bergen, Trondheim and Narvik. While Denmark had immediately crumbled before the Wehrmacht, a stunned Norway rose up to defend itself. Its greatest success was against German warships that pressed into the Oslo fjord: Norwegian heavy artillery and torpedoes sank the heavy cruiser *Blücher*, killing more than a thousand men, and damaged another cruiser and a pocket battleship. But the invasion was so efficient that by late in the day, the royal family and Norwegian government had fled the capital, fascist collaborator Vidkun Quisling (whose name would become synonymous with traitor) installed himself as premier, and the country was in German hands. (See also "April 9, 1940" in Chapter 2.)

Norwegian forces continued to resist, attacking German troops where possible. From April 10 to 13, in the course of two battles off Narvik, the British Royal Navy sank ten German destroyers, and shortly afterward, ill-equipped British and French forces arrived at Namsos and Andalsnes, on either side of Trondheim, to reinforce the Norwegians. The Germans, with air support and superior armored units, drove the outnumbered Allies out of central Norway by early May. On April 15, British, French, and Polish troops came ashore near Narvik, taking the town as German forces fell back. But ultimately, the Allied experience in Scandinavia that spring was a smorgasbord of disasters. Wind, snow, lack of air support, and the Luftwaffe hampered their efforts, and as German units along the coast linked up and secured their objectives, the Allies retreated and evacuated, until the last of them began to leave Narvik on June 7 to help bolster the defense of France. Two days later, the Norwegian High Command ordered its forces, depleted of ammunition and fuel, to give up the fight.

With the conquest of western Scandinavia, Germany now controlled Atlantic access to the Baltic Sea. But the loss of three cruisers, ten destroyers, four U-boats, and many auxiliary vessels, as well as damage to additional ships during the campaign was a severe blow to the Kriegsmarine, and one from which it never recovered. Most of its surface fleet had been destroyed and would not be replaced, as naval construction shifted to producing more U-boats. Britain's Royal Navy, which lost a dozen warships, including an aircraft carrier, had a vastly larger and superior fleet and better sustained its losses. But British naval leaders discovered during the campaign that their service, the best navy in the world, could not gain the upper hand if the enemy controlled the skies. From now on, sufficient air power at sea was essential. Most of the Norwegian fleet remained intact and escaped to serve with the Allies.

In the long run, Norway's value to Germany was not worth the investment made; hundreds of thousands of soldiers remained on occupation duty there throughout the war when they were needed elsewhere, and soon-to-be-occupied France provided iron ore (supplementing shipments from Sweden) as well as U-boat bases that were more convenient for Germany than those in Norway.

Taking Aim in the West

Even before Germany's conquest of Poland was complete, Hitler informed his top military officials of his plans to overrun the Low Countries (Belgium, Luxembourg, and the Netherlands), from which his forces could outflank French defensive fortifications along the German border, and then invade France. Successful execution of *Fall Gelb* ("Case Yellow") would force Britain to negotiate a settlement, Hitler reasoned, but if not, the Wehrmacht could launch an invasion of the British Isles from occupied Western Europe. However, bouts of poor weather, losing the element of surprise in the courier crash-landing incident (see "The Phony War," earlier in this chapter), the decision to capture Scandinavia first, and disagreements with his generals on scheduling pushed the operation's start date to May 1940. Meanwhile, additional French forces reinforced the Maginot Line and deployed along the Italian border. Fearful of antagonizing Hitler, even as German forces gathered on the Western Front, Belgium and the Netherlands did not mobilize for war.

The British Expeditionary Force (BEF) had begun arriving in France in September 1939 in anticipation of possible German action, and by May 1940, thirteen divisions (comprising 394,165 men) of varying quality and experience, were in the country. Throughout the Phony War, as the Manstein Plan (named for one of its creators, General Erich von Manstein) took shape, the *Oberkommando das Heer* (OKH, the army high command) revised its scheme to invade Belgium and Holland, which would draw British and French forces to the rescue. In the plan's new twist, the main thrust of the attack would actually occur through the Ardennes Forest, around the western end of France's Maginot Line. The French assumed the Ardennes and its poor roads would be especially difficult for tanks to navigate, so they installed few defenses in the area. The Germans planned to emerge from the Ardennes and cross the Meuse River as quickly as possible, lest the Allies counterattack and pin them within the dense confines of the forest. Once across the river, the Germans would head for the Channel Coast, trapping the large Allied force in Belgium and Holland. If all went well, other panzer units, after bursting through the forest, would proceed around the northwest terminal of the Maginot Line, moving swiftly on the flat French frontier, bound for Paris and other points south. Under General Maurice Gamelin, commander in chief of French forces, Allied plans called for the French Seventh Army, positioned outside of Dunkirk, France, to move through Belgium toward Bred, Holland, to assist the Dutch should the Germans attack. Those forces would establish a line that reached from Fortress Holland (the country's most defended sector) to Antwerp, where the BEF and French First Army would take up defensive positions along the River Dyle, which runs from Antwerp to the French-Belgian border. Here the Allies could defend Brussels, block the anticipated German route into France, and keep the fighting off French soil. In northeastern France, thirty French divisions were positioned behind the Maginot Line. The British provided some aircraft to supplement the French air force, but kept its best planes—the Spitfires—behind should they be needed at home.

THE WESTERN OFFENSIVE—FALL GELB (CASE YELLOW), INVASION OF THE LOW COUNTRIES AND FRANCE, MAY 10–JUNE 22, 1940

EUROPEAN THEATER (WESTERN EUROPE)

Primary Objectives: *German:* to conquer northwestern Europe and France; knock out and destroy Allied armies to force Britain to withdraw from the war, thus securing Germany's back before the planned invasion of the USSR; *Belgian, French*, and *Dutch:* to resist the German onslaught long enough to mount effective counterattacks; *British:* to assist in the defense of western Europe

Forces: *German:* 136 divisions, including 10 panzer divisions, 3.3 million men; 2,445 available tanks; 2,500 aircraft open attack (1,520 additional aircraft on hand); **Allied**—149 total divisions, 2.8 million troops (*French:* 106 divisions; *Belgian:* 20; *British:* 13; *Dutch:* 10); 3,383 total available tanks (all but 320 were French); 3,099 total available aircraft (*French:* 1,368; *Belgian:* 250; *British:* 456 on the Continent, 850 at home; *Dutch:* 175)

Commanders: *German:* General Gerd von Rundstedt, General Fedor von Bock, General Wilhelm von Leeb, General Erwin Rommel, General Heinz Guderian; **Allied**—*Belgian:* King Leopold, C-in-C of armed forces; *French:* General Maurice Gamelin, C-in-C of French forces, later replaced by General Maxime Weygand; *British:* General John Vereker (Lord Gort), commander of the British Expeditionary Force; *Dutch:* Henri Winkelman, C-in-C of Dutch armed forces

Military Losses: *German:* 29,640; **Allied**—*French:* 90,000+; *Belgian:* 6,100; *British:* 70,000 killed, wounded, and captured; *Dutch:* 7,000 dead and wounded

Other: 1.9 million French troops captured or missing

Result: German forces occupied northwestern Europe (France agreed to end all resistance, not to interfere in Germany's actions with Britain, to neutralize its naval fleet, and to provide reparations for damage done by French forces); the validity of German blitzkrieg warfare was confirmed; Hitler could now begin planning an attack on Britain if it did not accept a settlement; General Charles de Gaulle recruited free French to continue the fight. Luxembourg was incorporated into the German Reich in 1942.

At three A.M., May 10, the German Western Offensive began.

THE NETHERLANDS

Almost immediately, the Wehrmacht rendered useless the Dutch plan to barricade themselves behind Fortress Holland, in the northwest section of the country (including Amsterdam, The Hague, and Rotterdam), and open dikes and canals to inhibit the invading army with floodwaters. For one thing, German troops came prepared with rubber boats. More importantly, the Luftwaffe carried two airborne divisions over the Dutch waterways and dropped them on key locations, where, blitzkrieg style, they secured bridges and railroad stations and linked up several days later with the oncoming panzers and the three columns of the Eighteenth Army. The Luftwaffe took out about half of the small Dutch air force's 125 planes before they could even get into the air. But Dutch forces in Maastricht blew up bridges before German commandos reached them, holding off the Wehrmacht's advance for twenty-four hours, and at The Hague, the paratroop mission went awry. German transport aircraft came under heavy fire, just-won airfields were lost again, and a plan to kidnap Queen Wilhelmina foundered. After three days of fierce resistance that surprised the Germans, an angry and annoyed Hitler ordered the Luftwaffe to attack Rotterdam, Europe's busiest port, not for strategic purposes but to terrorize the population, even as Dutch officials were preparing to surrender. The resistance collapsed as German planes wiped out the downtown area, killing more than eight hundred civilians. The queen, departing The Hague and hoping to establish herself elsewhere in Holland even as the situation worsened, finally sailed aboard a British destroyer into an active exile in London. With the Dutch surrender on May 15, the Eighteenth Army turned south toward Antwerp, Belgium.

LUXEMBOURG

Shortly before German forces flicked aside Luxembourg's eighty-seven-man ceremonial military force, which suffered a few injuries, Grand Duchess Charlotte and her government escaped, eventually reaching London. About 40,000 of their fellow citizens were also on the move, crossing the frontier to seek refuge in France. Meanwhile, Luxembourg's 1,300-man police and volunteer force manned roadblocks near the German border, not to stop the invaders—that was impossible—but rather to officially inform them that they were violating Luxembourg's neutrality. Within a few hours, the duchy was under German control.

BELGIUM

With impressive speed and finesse, the Wehrmacht overcame Belgium's three major obstacles: Fort Eben-Emael, the heavily defended Albert Canal, and the dense Ardennes Forest. Tow planes departed from Germany and once over the Belgian border, they released gliders each carrying about ten combat engineers of the Koch Storm Detachment. Beginning around 9 A.M., ten

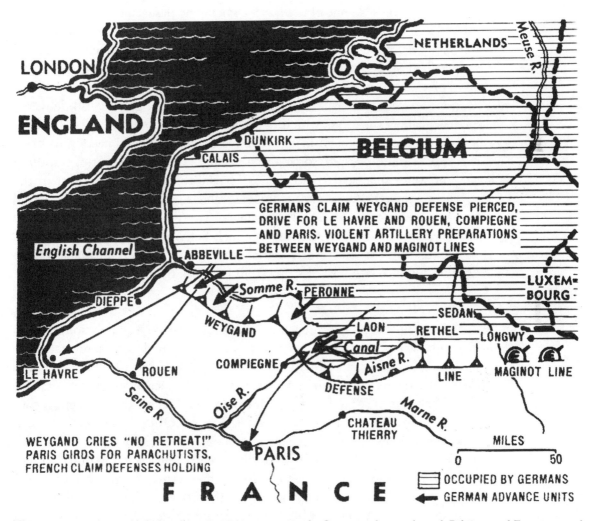

This newspaper map, published on June 7, 1940, represents the German advance through Belgium and France toward Paris. The French military claimed at the time that few German troops were breaking through their Weygand defensive line.

gliders landed atop the largely underground fort and others came to a stop at its walls. Within minutes, these forces, which had trained for six months on a replica of the fort, used new extremely potent hollow charges of varying sizes to blow up concrete pillboxes, gun casemates, and the guns themselves by spiking the huge artillery gun barrels with the devices (see also "Gliders" in Chapter 5). Low-flying Stuka bombers prevented Belgian defenders from arising to load, aim, and fire their huge guns as the engineers ran about setting their charges. At one of the fort's cement cupolas, armed with two colossal 120 mm guns that could fire in any direction from a rotating turret, the Belgians were reduced to using small arms fire against the attackers who had so quickly destroyed the heavy weaponry. The next day, the seemingly invincible fort and its thousand-man force surrendered, opening the way to the Meuse River and the Albert Canal. In the meantime, gliders also delivered engineers along the canal, which ran west-northwest to Antwerp from Eben-Emael, to secure the major bridges the German army would need in its drive through Belgium. Despite some glitches, the first glider combat operation of the war was a spectacular success. As for the thick Ardennes Forest in the southeast, thought to be almost impenetrable to tanks, the panzers plowed through it in just two days. They swept westward and nine days later, those tanks were in sight of the English Channel. Belgium surrendered May 28, as thousands of its troops joined British and French soldiers in retreating to Dunkirk, France (see box, "Escape from Dunkirk").

FRANCE

Like a building imploding, from the top floor to the foundation, the Allied collapse quickly rippled from north to south. Dutch forces, retreating to Fortress Holland, exposed Belgian positions at the Albert Canal, which the German panzers easily circumvented. With the nearly immediate fall of Fort-Eban Emael (May 11), the path toward the Meuse River was clear; successfully crossing it was the key to the Western Offensive, since it opened the door to France. The Germans crossed the river (May 12–14), but with heavy casualties, and it was a watershed event: the last opportunity to halt German domination of Europe was lost. The German army made excellent time over the flat northern terrain, the Luftwaffe having just established air superiority. The Allies still had not determined the main point of attack (a classic effect of blitzkrieg) as the invaders drove forward from multiple directions, nor were they sure whether the English Channel or Paris was the primary German objective.

After sweeping across northern France, the Wehrmacht lurched across the last miles to the Channel and, at Hitler's command, halted on May 24, outside Dunkirk. There they forfeited an opportunity to capture the bulk of the retreating Allied forces and perhaps end the European war. After the Allies successfully evacuated from Dunkirk, the Germans turned south and

ESCAPE FROM DUNKIRK

Surprised by their rapid success against the Allies, particularly the French army—thought to be the finest in the world—the German High Command ordered its Channel Coast-bound armies to halt on May 24. This decision, approved by Hitler, would be studiously analyzed and debated after the war. Why was the order given, when the Germans might have pushed the Allies into the sea and destroyed or captured hundreds of thousands of troops? The British position has been that an effective British Expeditionary Force (BEF) counterattack at Arras caused the Germans to halt; German historians have cited the army's need to rest and tend to their tanks. The Ultra intelligence derived from deciphered German codes (see Chapter 9) had tipped off the British to the halt order, allowing them time to plan and begin evacuating troops from the French port of Dunkirk, the only escape route available, on May 26. That day, the Germans started moving again. French units near Dunkirk, unaware of British plans, intended to make a stand there, and found themselves battling oncoming Germans at Lille and Cassel as the British departed, resulting in considerable tension among the Allies. Getting the troops across the English Channel became an even greater imperative as the Luftwaffe attacked the port, battling both the weather and the overstretched RAF overhead.

British civilians played a remarkable role in the nine-day evacuation (Operation Dynamo), which ballooned from the original notion of rescuing perhaps as many as 45,000 men from the main BEF to saving more than 300,000 Allied soldiers. Beginning on the fourth evening, civilian owned and manned craft joined with the Royal Navy to form a motley armada of some nine hundred vessels, including warships, yachts, ferryboats, and fishing boats, to pick up troops waiting on the beach. The successful, though initially chaotic, evacuation process—a rightfully celebrated feat in British history—has tended to obscure a critical factor in its success, the heroic French and Belgian defense at Lille that kept the Germans at bay and bought the Allies time. On June 3, the last of the men got off the beach, leaving behind massive amounts of equipment, including tanks, heavy guns, field equipment, and some 38,000 vehicles. Dunkirk smoldered in ruins. All told, 338,226 British, French, and Belgian men were rescued in what became known as the *Miracle of Dunkirk*. These Allied forces would be back to fight another day.

overran the fragile defenses on the Weygand Line (June 5), which was more of a concept than an actual line since French tanks were spread out so thinly. Overwhelmed, French troops retreated, joining tens of thousands of evacuating civilians who clogged the roads and hampered attempts to counterattack. As German planes strafed evacuees, the Luftwaffe also attacked Paris. By the time German forces entered the city on June 14, the French capital had been declared an open city (unresistant and thus not subject to attack), two-thirds of the local population had fled, and the government had escaped to Bordeaux. In northeastern France, German forces assaulted one part of the Maginot Line from Saarbrücken and went over the line toward Colmar, while the panzers made an end run around its western flank, pinning the

After the relatively quick fall of France to the Germans—long believed to be impossible—German soldiers sit atop tanks in the occupied city of Metz while civilians walk by, 1940.

French against their own stone monument to security. By the time the French surrendered on June 22, the battlefront was some 350 miles south of the Franco-Belgian border, below the soon-to-be-infamous resort town of Vichy. There, French collaborators established a government that ultimately answered to Germany.

The fall of France dispelled long-standing beliefs held not only by the French: that massive fortifications, such as Eban-Emael and the Maginot Line (which alone gobbled up 20 percent of the French annual defense budget) were invincible; that the Ardennes was impermeable; that the French military was unbeatable; and that air power could not be decisive. Nor had the Allies coordinated their efforts well, either before the war, when Belgium declined to participate in military maneuvers with the British and French, or after the war had begun. The German army, even with its success, identified what it needed for future military operations: improved traffic management; foot soldiers keeping up with the panzers; the need for ongoing vehicle maintenance; and quick redeployment to take advantage of success.

Enter Italy: War Spreads to the Mediterranean

Italy's Fascist dictator Benito Mussolini seized the opportunity presented by Germany's stunning advances in western Europe to enter a war he believed would be relatively easy and short, and would allow him to claim territories bordering the Mediterranean that he coveted for his "new Fascist Empire." Abandoning the caution that had earlier irritated Hitler, he took Italy into the war on June 10, 1940. The following day, Italian aircraft attacked French bases in Tunisia and Corsica as well as British installations on the strategically located island of Malta. (Mussolini was greatly offended when, in retaliation, the British bombed Milan and Turin that night and a French naval squadron bombarded Genoa shortly thereafter—without much interference from Italy's wholly inadequate defenses.)

At the same time, the Italians began a campaign against the British island fortress of Malta that would last for three years.

The Siege of Malta, Part I: June 11, 1940–December 1941

At five minutes before 7 A.M. on the morning of June 11, 1940, the Maltese people were awakened by the first of thousands of air-raid warnings that would sear through their lives for more than three punishing years. Located in the central Mediterranean, 58 miles south of Sicily and 180 miles from the nearest point of the North African mainland, the island of Malta was a strategically crucial British holding. Although Winston Churchill was to call the island an "unsinkable aircraft carrier," that first morning the only aircraft it carried were three near-obsolete Gloster Gladiator aircraft— "Faith," "Hope," and "Charity." Manned by volunteer pilots, the Gladiators rose that day and for eleven days thereafter to defend the island against Italian air force raiders while Britain prepared to send whatever reinforcements it could muster, including more planes for defense—and offense. Under an increasing barrage of nearly nonstop air raids during the first half of a three-year siege, Malta and its dauntless inhabitants proved, beyond the shadow of a doubt, the island's vital importance to Allied success in the Mediterranean. Warplanes based on the island struck at the Italian mainland and pummeled convoys bound from Italy to supply and reinforce Axis forces in North Africa: there were 122 bomber sorties between June 30 and July 13, 1941, alone. By the fall of that year, German Afrika Korps commander General Erwin Rommel complained that over 60 percent of the supplies slated for his desert fighters had not gotten through. Submarines based and resupplied at Malta were doing a great part of that damage. Malta also became a transit depot for equipment and an Allied center for information distribution and intelligence gathering. Small wonder that Rommel dubbed the island the "scorpion of the sea."

Yet the scorpion, itself, was continually stung. Air raids intensified after the Luftwaffe arrived in the Mediterranean early in 1941. On January 16, German and Italian aircraft swarmed over the island in the largest raid it had endured to that time. The merciless pounding drove civilians to live in caves and the island's defenders to carve subsurface bunkers and aircraft repair facilities. Supplies were lost when convoys trying to reach the island were attacked. Food was strictly rationed, medicine became scarce, and the steady rain of bombs continued throughout a nerve-racking 1941. On December 2, Hitler issued his Directive No. 38, which reinforced the Luftwaffe presence in the Mediterranean, "To secure mastery of the air and sea in the area between Southern Italy and North Africa . . . and, in particular, to keep Malta in subjection." The year 1942 was destined to become much worse for the people of Britain's "island fortress."

★   ★   ★

On June 17, 1940, France had asked Germany for terms of surrender, and Mussolini had ordered a cease-fire against France at that time. He reversed his decision almost immediately, sending inadequately prepared Italian troops into the French Alps on June 21. The Italian propaganda machine made much of this effort, but in truth, the Italians did not do well. At the cost of 631 lives (as opposed to 37 French soldiers killed), they snared only thirteen small villages before the armistice was officially signed. Yet Mussolini had established an Italian presence on French soil and thus had a legitimate claim to the French territories he coveted. The only remaining enemy was Britain, and on June 26, Mussolini offered Hitler Italian assistance with the projected invasion of the British Isles—an offer Hitler politely refused. (Later, when the Battle of Britain was going badly, the führer reversed that decision and asked for help from the Italian air force.) Meanwhile in East Africa, Italy's Amedeo II of Savoia-Aosta, Duke of Aosta, and now Viceroy of Ethiopia, was eager for action against British installations in Sudan and British Somaliland. Il Duce was also looking toward North Africa, where more than 200,000 Italian troops, based in Libya, seemed more than adequate to deal with the mere 36,000 British troops guarding the United Kingdom's interests in Egypt (including the vitally important Suez Canal). Another 27,500 British soldiers were stationed in Palestine, but they were fully occupied, Mussolini reasoned, keeping order between Arabs and Jews in that perpetually smoldering region. Therefore, he ordered General Rodolfo Graziani, army chief of staff and his North African commander, to prepare for battle—although action could not commence until it was clear whether the governors of France's North African colonies would declare for Vichy or continue to fight against the Axis.

The British, too, were wondering. With their backs against the wall, and their own naval fleets stretched to the limit, they were deeply concerned that the French Mediterranean Fleet might be turned against Britain. This concern led to a wrenching naval engagement.

MERS-EL-KÉBIR, ALGERIA, JULY 3, 1940
MEDITERRANEAN THEATER (NORTH AFRICA)

Primary Objectives: *British:* to neutralize the French Mediterranean fleet after France signed an armistice with Germany on June 25, so the vessels would not fall under German control and be used against the British; *French:* to defend their fleet and their prerogative to determine its use

Forces: *British:* Force H from Gibraltar under the command of Vice Admiral Sir James Somerville (2 battleships, 1 battle cruiser, 1 aircraft carrier, 2 cruisers, 11 destroyers); *French:* a squadron under the command of Admiral Marcel Gensoul (2 battleships, 2 battle cruisers, 11 destroyers, 5 submarines)

Military Losses: *French:* 1,297 killed; *British:* none killed, only a few wounded

Result: Although Vichy still maintained control of some naval vessels (including those that would help fend off the Anglo-Free French assault on Dakar), the British action did significant damage.

After the French rejected an ultimatum to disarm or scuttle their ships, Great Britain's Force H attacked and, in fifteen minutes, damaged the battleships, a battle cruiser, and a destroyer, killing nearly 1,300 French sailors. (In a related action, July 8, torpedo planes from a British aircraft carrier severely damaged the French battleship *Richelieu* at Dakar, French West Africa. Meanwhile, French Admiral René Godfroy, in command of French vessels moored at the British base at Alexandria, Egypt, had reluctantly agreed to disarm his ships on July 4.) The attack at Mers-el-Kébir, with its heavy casualties, was a bitter blow to the French people, who resented the British attack for decades after the war. The British, too, found it repugnant: Winston Churchill described it as "a hateful decision, the most unnatural and painful in which I have ever been concerned." Yet he also believed it was necessary. It may, in fact, have reduced the danger the British faced from Axis-controlled French ships in the Mediterranean Sea, especially had they operated in tandem with the Italian navy. At the time, Italy's navy was larger in number, more maneuverable, and faster than Britain's Mediterranean naval forces, which were divided between Alexandria, at the east end of the Mediterranean, and Gibraltar in the west. Perhaps as important, the action helped prove British resolve to the Americans. In fact, Churchill later cited this action as "the turning point in our fortunes," for "it made the world realise that we were in earnest in our intentions to carry on." Yet, as naval historian E. B. Potter has observed, it also "stiffened Vichy French resistance to the British and Free French in North Africa and Syria."

★   ★   ★

One week after this bitter clash between former allies, the Germans began an aerial campaign that would severely test the mettle of the Royal Air Force and British civilians.

A Great Battle above the Earth

Four days before France officially surrendered to Germany, Winston Churchill, who had just recently replaced Neville Chamberlain as Britain's prime minister, saw clearly what was to come next: "I expect that the battle of Britain is about to begin." It was. The British refusal to negotiate an end to hostilities compelled Hitler to plan an invasion (Operation Sea Lion) and eliminate Britain's ability to interfere with German policy and military pursuits. But Britain's commitment to the fight, its resilience, and its high morale under a near-constant onslaught of tremendous bombing surprised Germany, which had expected to wrap up its Western Campaign that summer.

THE BATTLE OF BRITAIN, JULY 10, 1940–JUNE 1941
EUROPEAN THEATER (WESTERN EUROPE)

The first phase of the battle began July 10. The *Blitz*, the most intense and sustained period of Luftwaffe bombing over Britain, lasted from September through November 1940. Raids continued until June 1941, when the Luftwaffe moved east for operations in the USSR.

> **Primary Objectives:** *German:* to destroy the RAF, its ground facilities, and aircraft manufacturing capability; cut off British trade by bombing ports and sinking shipping; demoralize the British in a heavy bombing campaign prior to invading; *British:* to prevent German command of the skies
>
> **Forces:** *German:* 2,800 aircraft; *British:* 700 aircraft when the battle began (continuing aircraft production reinforced strength and helped replace losses)
>
> **Commanders:** *German:* Reichsmarshal Hermann Göring, Field Marshal Albert Kesselring, Field Marshal Hugo Sperrle, and General Hans-Juergen Stumpff; *British:* Air Chief Marshal Sir Hugh Dowding, Air Vice Marshal Sir Trafford Leigh-Mallory, Air Vice Marshal Sir Quintin Brand, Air Vice Marshal Richard Saul
>
> **Military Losses:** *German:* 3,363 airmen, August 1940–March 1941; *British:* 544 airmen, July 10–October 31, 1940
>
> **Civilian Deaths:** 23,000 British, July–December 1940
>
> **Other:** 120,000 British civilians wounded through June 1941; the Luftwaffe lost 1,733 aircraft; the RAF lost 915

Result: This first major Allied victory over the Axis was vital for morale. It prevented a German invasion and occupation of the British Isles—it was in Britain that the Allies would train and assemble their forces for the 1944 invasion of Europe (D-Day).

The Battle of Britain differed significantly from any previous major battle in that it was fought almost entirely in the air. The remnants of the German navy's surface fleet were no match for the three dozen British destroyers patrolling the English Channel and the southern coastline, and no German tanks or columns of foot soldiers rumbled through Britain. Instead, the fate of the island nation rested in the hands of its Royal Air Force and the 30,000 members of the volunteer Observer Corps who watched the skies for enemy planes. In a burst of optimism enthusiastically supported by Reichsmarshal Hermann Göring, and based on assumptions rather than concrete evidence, German military planners expected the Luftwaffe to wipe out most of the RAF within a week and whatever remained of it and Britain's aircraft industry in about a month. Once Germany held air superiority over the United Kingdom, the invasion could commence, before poor autumn weather set in. In occupied France, thirteen army divisions and the haphazard fleet of barges and tugboats that would spearhead the invasion assembled on the Channel Coast to prepare for landings in Kent and Sussex.

German aircraft, departing from bases in northwestern France, began their attacks on Britain July 10, 1940; RAF bases and seaports in southern England were the primary land targets. The frequency and intensity of German raids picked up in August, as the Luftwaffe attempted to lure British planes out over the English Channel, where the faster Messerschmitt fighters could destroy the RAF's Spitfires and Hurricanes and avoid ground fire. Meanwhile, the slow Stuka dive-bombers, highly effective working in concert with army ground forces in blitzkrieg operations, were too vulnerable to RAF fighters and were soon withdrawn from the battle. Both sides suffered heavy losses in aircraft and experienced, but greatly fatigued, pilots that September; nearly one in four German pilots was lost, and 28 percent of British pilots perished. On September 7, the Battle of Britain entered its deadliest period, the Blitz (September–November). Three hundred bombers and six hundred fighters descended over London, striking the docks (the primary target) and nearby residences, and British forces braced for an imminent invasion. No invasion occurred, but a second stage of the battle began.

Although German aircraft attacked Great Britain as early as July 10, 1940, the period known as the Blitz *began on September 7, with British cities the main target. This photograph shows British firemen near a bombed building in the Ludgate Hill neighborhood of London.*

The Germans shifted their focus from eliminating the RAF to bombing cities nationwide, and they switched from daylight to night missions. Several factors contributed to these changes: the need to reduce the number of Luftwaffe planes shot down, the hopeful expectation that Britain could be blasted into submission and civilian morale quickly destroyed, and the demand for revenge as the RAF's attacks on German targets were producing ever greater civilian casualties. The Germans also introduced London to UXBs (delayed action time bombs) which brought city life to a halt as buildings were evacuated and streets closed during the hours-long process it took to defuse and remove the bombs. September 15, a date later acknowledged as Battle of Britain Day, marked a decisive moment: Germany needed to deliver a knockout punch if the planned invasion was to occur before the weather turned. In a massive attack over southeastern England, the Luftwaffe flew nearly a thousand sorties that day, losing fifty-six aircraft to the RAF's twenty-three. Two days later, when Hitler called off Operation Sea Lion, it was apparent that the Luftwaffe had lost the battle for the air, yet the air raids continued. The Luftwaffe subjected London to a pounding that let up for only two 24-hour periods over three months.

On October 15, 440 German bombers dropped 70,000 incendiary bombs on London, creating large-scale fires and the need for new emergency response measures. (See also "Civil Defense" in Chapters 3 and 11.) The scope of destruction expanded on the night of November 14–15, when the Luftwaffe attacked Coventry in response to a November 8 RAF raid on Munich. A tourist destination renowned for its medieval architecture and the legend of Lady Godiva, downtown Coventry had no military value in itself, but the aircraft factories outside the city center area were vital. For the first time, German advance planes (called "pathfinders") dropped parachute flares and incendiary bombs over selected targets as a guide for the large wave of bombers with high explosives and incendiaries that followed (the RAF would later adopt this method as well). During the ten-hour raid, under a full moon, the Germans hit 27 major factories, destroyed 80 percent of the city center, and killed 568 civilians. Dozens of British cities, including Birmingham, Liverpool, Manchester, Sheffield, and Southampton, received similar treatment. The Coventry raid sparked vigorous calls for revenge, which came in the form of comparable British air raids on German cities.

Despite the widespread damage Germany inflicted, Britain gave as good as it got: the Luftwaffe lost planes by a margin of more than 2 to 1 early in the battle, a pace that rapidly depleted the German air fleet. Ultimately, the Luftwaffe could not secure air superiority. Britain had several other important advantages as well: its use of Ultra intelligence, radar, and its Observer Corps, outfitted with telephones for instant communication with Fighter Command, gave the RAF crucial extra minutes to get into the air and precise coordinates to meet the oncoming German planes and prevent them from reaching their targets. Tangling with British fighters, in and of itself lethal, also weighed heavily on German pilots lest they use up fuel before reaching their targets and have little left for the flight back across the Channel. The Germans were hampered with poor intelligence and even worse analysis; they believed British radar facilities were underground rather than above and removed radar towers from their target lists; they never understood how Fighter Command and its defensive system operated; they underestimated the rate of British aircraft production; and they assumed the Luftwaffe had destroyed more enemy planes than it had. Air Marshal Hugh Dowding kept one-third of his fighters stationed at well-defended bases in the south to protect all of Britain, and the remaining two-thirds were held out of reach in the north and used as needed. The RAF also parked its planes in E-pens (a series of outdoor earth-covered brick berms and bays shaped like the letter E), rather than lining them up wingtip-to-wingtip for easy maintenance, a common practice. The E-pens protected nearby aircraft from being destroyed or damaged if a bomb struck a parked plane.

The raids became less frequent in the spring of 1941, as the Luftwaffe was needed for operations in the Balkans, the Mediterranean, and elsewhere. Yet the worst air strike on London occurred May 10–11, 1941, when 1,436 people were killed in a raid that also damaged the House of Commons and Westminster Abbey. In June, much of the Luftwaffe moved east for the invasion of the Soviet Union. Although attacks on Britain would continue into 1945—the Observer Corps could never rest—the essential issue had been determined: weary as they were, the British would not break.

★　★　★

As German air raids over Britain increased in August 1940, communist leader Mao Tse-tung launched an offensive in China that led to a change in official Japanese policy.

Mao's Hundred Regiments Offensive, August–December 1940, and New Japanese Orders for Warfare in China

The Chinese Communist forces of Mao Tse-tung, the Eighth Route Army in the north and the New Fourth Army in the coastal region north of Shanghai, were gaining strength. This led to increasing agitation by the most fervently anticommunist of Chiang Kai-shek's Nationalist generals to advocate smashing the Red Chinese Army. The communists' increasing strength seemed to threaten the Nationalists far more than it did the Japanese, for, as the Nationalist party secretary general remarked, the Red Army "has not actually participated in any great battles." Small-group guerrilla warfare against the Japanese had become the communist hallmark. Yet, at least in part to offset the growing Nationalist criticism, in August 1940 the communists embarked on what they called the "Hundred Regiments Offensive" (although many of the participating units were smaller than regiments). Some 400,000 Red Chinese troops, operating across a wide front in north China, mounted frontal assaults on Japanese positions, catching their enemy by surprise. Initially, these attacks resulted in major damage to railroads, roads, mines, industry, and some of the fortified blockhouses the Japanese used to keep the communists penned in the north. But the Japanese quickly recovered and regrouped, and by late fall, the communist offensive was petering out. Its main achievements had been widespread publicity about the Red Army's increasing aggressiveness—and a new respect within the Japanese high command for a threat they had taken somewhat lightly before. It had also become clear to Tokyo that achieving victory in China by the end of 1940 would not be possible. Thus, early in 1941 the Japanese general staff promulgated "Outline Measures for a Protracted War in China." This new policy called for "requisitioning all materials needed for the survival of the army and acquiring from China the full amount of materials needed for Japan's mobilization, especially mineral resources." Although most Japanese forces had not, to that time, been shy about taking what they required from the Chinese in their path, this new official directive meant that the Chinese would face even greater torment at the hands of the invader in the years ahead.

At the same time, the Japanese were turning their attention to other territories whose resources could feed their burgeoning war machine. Among the first to draw their attention was French Indochina, whose military governors were loyal to the Vichy collaborationist government. The French in Indochina were soon to yield to Japanese demands. Elsewhere on the globe, some French fighters who rejected Vichy had begun to rally around a relatively unknown figure whose leadership in battle in May 1940 had brought him a promotion to brigadier general.

Italy's "Parallel War"

While Charles de Gaulle and his British Allies were failing at Dakar, Benito Mussolini was beset by disappointments, his own miscalculations, and distrust

GENERAL CHARLES DE GAULLE'S FIRST MILITARY VENTURES, SEPTEMBER 1940–DECEMBER 1941

After France surrendered to Germany, Brigadier General Charles de Gaulle fled to Britain, where he was quickly recognized by the British government as the leader of all Free French forces (although the Americans and many free Frenchmen continued to resist his leadership). By September 1940, he had mobilized a limited number of Free French forces and, with British units leading the way, embarked on his first military offensive, *Operation Menace,* to secure the Vichy-held port of Dakar, in French West Africa. The operation took place September 23–25, 1940, and involved 4,200 British troops and a naval force under Vice Admiral J. H. D. Cunningham comprising two battleships, one aircraft carrier, three heavy cruisers, and six destroyers; de Gaulle led 2,700 Free French troops.

De Gaulle apparently assumed that his presence and that of Free French forces would be enough to convince Vichy forces to transfer their loyalties on the spot. However, Vichy forces in Dakar (French West African governor Pierre Boisson had at his disposal one battleship, two cruisers, two destroyers, and three submarines) refused the ultimatum to hand over their ships and opened fire with coastal artillery and the fifteen-inch guns of the repaired battleship *Richelieu,* damaging two British destroyers and a cruiser. The British returned fire, sinking a Vichy submarine and destroyer. De Gaulle tried to land Free French forces at Rufisque, east of Dakar, but was driven back, Vichy forces having been alerted earlier to the invasion attempt. After a Vichy submarine damaged a battleship, the

British decided to abandon the operation, Churchill telling Roosevelt that it "would have tied us to an undue commitment, when you think of what we have on our hands already." This relatively small military disaster (called the "Great Dakar F_____ up" by British troops who took part in it) did little to enhance de Gaulle's reputation with his British and American Allies. A year later, the Americans were to have another, more immediate reason to regard the imperious French general with a jaundiced eye.

A Conquest in North America

The French citizens on Saint-Pierre and Miquelon, two small islands off Newfoundland, had asked to join the Free French rather than submit to Vichy rule after the June 1940 armistice with Germany. The United States, which maintained diplomatic relations with Vichy until late 1942, had signed an agreement with the Vichy government to maintain the status quo of French holdings in the Western Hemisphere. However, a radio station on Saint-Pierre worried the Allies; the British and Canadians feared that Vichy might use the strong signal to alert U-boats to merchant convoys crossing the North Atlantic. Taking matters into his own hands, General de Gaulle ordered four French cruisers under Free French command to occupy the colony, which they did on Christmas Eve, 1941. No shots were fired, and residents held a plebiscite; an overwhelming majority favored Free French citizenship. The British and Canadians were relieved; the Americans were angry. In de Gaulle's memoirs, he said that he had decided to take the action when he heard that Canadian troops would be sent to secure the radio station. Seeing this as "foreign intervention" on French soil, he wrote, "no hesitation seemed permissible." He called the American attitude "strange" and "troubling," believing "that this small operation, carried out so happily, would have been ratified by the American government." In the end, de Gaulle admitted, "I had provoked it in order to stir up the bottom of things, as one throws a stone into a pond." In fact, he had stirred ire within the American government that would contribute to the U.S. refusal to officially recognize his leadership of all Free French forces, and of liberated France, until October 1944.

of his German ally's actions as he pursued a parallel war—one fought with German support, but without the intrusion of German forces in the Mediterranean region. Frustrated by German opposition to his long-cherished plans to attack Yugoslavia, he was also annoyed by Germany's less-than-forthcoming reports on the air campaign against Britain and the progress of Germany's plan to invade the British Isles. However, in late August, when the Germans requested assistance in the Battle of Britain, Mussolini sent some two hundred Italian fighters and bombers to bases in Belgium that he could have used to better effect in the Mediterranean. At the same time, he was upset by overstated reports that the Germans were attempting to negotiate a settlement with the British without Italian participation and before Italy had taken Egypt and secured for itself the Suez Canal. This would not do: as Italian chief of general staff Pietro Badoglio wrote in his orders to General Roldolfo Graziani in late August, calling for movement in North Africa, "if there is an agreement between the Germans and the English, we will be out of any discussions if we do not have at least one battle against the English."

At the same time, naval encounters with the British were proving much less than satisfactory. On July 9, 1940, the Italian fleet, under orders from the high command to proceed with caution, suffered an embarrassing failure when it attacked an inferior British naval force off the southern Italian region of Calabria. Although the greater speed of the Italian ships allowed them to escape, they had been wounded by fire from the British battleship

Warspite. Nor were the Italians helped by their own air force, whose planes, manned by poorly trained crews, bombed both British and Italian ships indiscriminately. "Never again did they [the Italian fleet] willingly face up to the fire of British battleships," the commander of the British naval force, Admiral Andrew Cunningham, later wrote, "though on several subsequent occasions they were in a position to give battle with great preponderance in force."

Later that month, Italian forces under Amadeo (the viceroy of Ethiopia) enjoyed greater success when they moved into British Somaliland, although they moved too slowly to prevent the much smaller British force from reaching the coast and escaping. Moreover, that campaign, plagued by heavy Italian casualties, pointed up a crucial weakness in many young field officers that the high command never successfully countered (see Chapter 4). "As long as it is a question of risking one's skin," theater chief of staff General Claudio Trezzani reported to General Pietro Badoglio, "[the junior leaders] are admirable; when, instead, they have to open their eyes, think, decide in cold blood, they are hopeless. In terms of reconnaissance, security, movement to contact, preparatory fire, coordinated movement and so on, they are practically illiterate." Farther north, General Graziani, though not eager for battle, reluctantly ordered his forces to advance toward British-held Sidi Barrāni in Egypt—a movement slightly delayed when one brigade, whose commander had neglected to take his local Arab guides with him, got lost in the desert. After the brigade was put back on course, a slow advance succeeded in pushing the outnumbered British from Sidi Barrāni on September 16. Graziani ordered his troops to halt and dig in, despite Mussolini's exhortations to push on.

In October, German troops moved into Romania to secure the oil fields at Ploesti that were of great importance to both Germany and Italy. Although Mussolini had been aware that Hitler was contemplating such a move, he became livid when it actually took place without his being informed in advance and without Italian participation. Mussolini, too, had been considering a move of which Hitler was vaguely aware and which Il Duce knew the führer was not eager to have happen at this time. In secrecy and denying his intentions when German officials asked, Mussolini issued orders for the Italian invasion of Greece. "Hitler always faces me with *faits accomplis*," he railed to his son-in-law (and Italy's foreign minister), Count Galeazzo Ciano. "This time I will pay him back in his own coin. He will discover from the newspapers that I have occupied Greece. In this way the equilibrium will be reestablished."

ITALIAN CAMPAIGN IN GREECE, OCTOBER 28, 1940–DECEMBER 1940
MEDITERRANEAN THEATER (MEDITERRANEAN EUROPE)

Primary Objectives: *Italian:* to expand Italy's control in the Mediterranean and the Balkans and to provide a means of support for the slated North African campaign; *Greek:* first, to defend the country; then to push the Italians back through Albania and into the sea

Forces: *Italian:* initially, 150,000; *Greek:* 220,000; *British:* during the first phase of fighting in Greece and Albania, British military support was limited to a small RAF contingent with a few support troops because the Greek government was still hoping for a settlement via Germany

Commanders: *Italian:* General Sebastiano Visconti Prasca, followed by General Ubaldo Soddu, then General Ugo Cavallero; *Greek:* General Alexander Papagos

Military Losses: (October 1940–April 1941): *Italian:* 38,380; *Greek:* 13,408 killed; 42,485 wounded

Result: Italy's anticipated "easy" victory over the Greeks became a desperate fight against superior forces that threatened to deprive Italy of Albania, which had been under Italian control since May 1939.

Germany's refusal to countenance his cherished plans for an attack on Yugoslavia, the Wehrmacht's move into Romania, and General Graziani's stubborn refusal to push forward in North Africa combined to spur Mussolini into ordering the chief of general staff, General Pietro Badoglio, on October 13, 1940, to prepare the army to attack Greece—a neutral country, but one the Italians charged with having un-neutral ties to Britain. (In April 1939, the British government had guaranteed Greek independence.) The invasion was to be launched from Italian-controlled Albania less than two weeks later (the original date of October 26 was later pushed back to October 28). The high command scrambled to prepare, under a major handicap of Mussolini's own making. After Mussolini canceled the attack on Yugoslavia in September, he had ordered demobilization of some 600,000 of the 1.1 million soldiers in Italy, principally to work in agriculture. (Il Duce's intention to wage a war without creating hardships at home had already been damaged by the introduction of rationing, and civilian unrest was growing. See also Chapter 11.) The demobilization totally disrupted army organization, and Mussolini refused to order a total remobilization until November 23—when the Greek campaign was well on its way to disaster. Il Duce had also been so certain that the Bulgarians would join in his Greek adventure that he waited until ten days before the invasion to issue a formal invitation to King Boris to participate. To his annoyance, the king declined. Thus, when it became obvious that Bulgaria's armies were not going to move against them, the Greeks were free to move units from the Bulgarian border toward Albania, meeting the invaders with far greater numbers of supremely motivated troops than the Italians had anticipated. Other difficulties resulted from long-existing flaws in Italy's military organization. Throughout the mobilization stages and during the campaign, logistical support ranged from poor to appalling. Transport vessels were scarce, and Albanian port space was so limited that bottlenecks inevitably occurred. Understrength units went into the field without proper equipment; many lacked heavy artillery, trucks, and the horses and mules that were crucial to the movement of supplies in difficult terrain. As had been the case in Italy's campaign in British Somaliland, many junior officers, lacking sufficient training in battlefield tactics, proved incapable of leading their units effectively under fire.

Nevertheless, a three-pronged attack went forward as scheduled, Mussolini anticipating an easy victory against the Greeks, whom the Italians rated as very poor soldiers. Slogging into Greece under torrential rains, the Italians made some progress along the coast but quickly bogged down in the center and on the left. The Greeks opposing them were better trained and better disciplined, and they had much better fire support from their artillery. Yet, initially, Mussolini and the high command were not aware of the disaster that was rapidly building. Confusing reports came back from the field: General Visconti Prasca pleaded for reinforcements, but he also declared that the operation was proceeding "at an accelerated rhythm." By November 8, however, it wasn't proceeding at all: Greek resistance had halted the Italian advance. By November 14, shortly after a British attack on the Italian fleet at Taranto removed the possibility of significant support from the navy, the Greeks had begun a counteroffensive that pushed the disorganized Italians back into Albania.

Both the Germans and the British had been observing events in Greece with alarm. Responding to pleas from Greek Prime Minister Metaxas, the British promised to help. However, their obligations in North Africa (and

Metaxas's desire not to provoke the Germans into interfering) restricted their assistance, at first, to landing a few ground units on Crete and sending a small force of RAF fighters and light bombers to the Greek mainland. For his part, Hitler had no objection to Italian subjugation of Greece, but the timing of this military action was extremely inconvenient: the Balkan crisis was stirring trouble on Germany's southern flank even as Hitler was preparing a directive for his military commanders (issued December 18) for planning the invasion of the Soviet Union in the spring. Worse, the Italians were showing no signs of achieving Mussolini's promised rapid victory either in Greece or North Africa, where Graziani's still-immobile forces were doing nothing to damage the British. There was also the danger—enhanced by the presence of RAF planes in Greece and British troops on Crete—that the Greeks might sever all ties with Germany and join the Allies. Allied bases in Greece would threaten Hitler's Russian offensive as well as the Romanian oilfields. (On November 6, as the small RAF contingent arrived in Greece, Hitler had asked the Bulgarian government to set up an air raid system along the Bulgarian-Greek border, and the Bulgarians immediately complied.) Hitler, therefore, began making tentative plans to intercede and prevent an Italian fiasco even before he received Mussolini's first limited appeals for help (a request for German transport aircraft) in mid-November. At that time, the Greeks were steadily pushing the Italians ever deeper into Albania. Gradually, however, Italian resistance stiffened.

In mid-December, the bad situation in Albania was compounded by another Italian battlefield debacle. A British counteroffensive in North Africa—that Graziani had failed to anticipate, although there had been ample evidence of British preparation—smashed through several Italian divisions and pushed on toward Libya (see "Western Desert Campaign," later in this chapter). By December 19, Mussolini was asking for direct military assistance in both of his major campaigns. Hitler had already issued a directive (December 13) to prepare for military operations in Greece, but he informed Mussolini that the Italians would have to hold on their own until spring. The North Africa situation, however, called for more immediate action. The führer soon issued orders that established a panzer force under General Erwin Rommel in North Africa by February. Although Hitler would maintain the fiction that the Italians were in command in the Mediterranean Theater, Mussolini's parallel war was over. The Germans were in control.

BRITISH RAID ON TARANTO (OPERATION JUDGMENT)
NOVEMBER 11–12, 1940
MEDITERRANEAN THEATER (MEDITERRANEAN EUROPE)

Primary Objectives: *British:* to damage or destroy as much of the Italian fleet as possible as it sat at anchor; *Italian:* to defend the fleet

Forces: *British:* Alexandria-based fleet comprising 4 cruisers, 4 destroyers, 1 aircraft carrier with torpedo bombers aboard; *Italian:* 6 battleships, 3 cruisers, 4 destroyers moored at Taranto, Italy

Commanders: *British:* Admiral Andrew B. Cunningham; *Italian:* Admiral Domenico Cavagnari

Military Losses: *British:* 2 planes, 4 airmen to antiaircraft fire; *Italian:* 2 battleships sunk, 1 damaged; 1 cruiser and 1 destroyer damaged; fuel tanks destroyed

Result: The damage inflicted on ships and supplies (including vital fuel tanks) tipped the balance of sea power toward the British in the central Mediterranean. The Italian navy abandoned its base at Taranto and moved the fleet up to Naples.

On the night of November 11–12, 1940, Admiral Cunningham launched an attack that had been under preparation since August and was based on a plan first suggested in 1938. Twelve Swordfish biplanes from the carrier *Illustrious* approached the poorly defended Italian fleet base at Taranto (near the top of the heel of the Italian boot): four aircraft, fitted with bombs, peeled off to create a diversion; two planes dropped flares to illuminate targets; and planes equipped with torpedoes attacked the six battleships moored below, the pride of the Italian fleet. One plane went down; two battleships were hit. An hour later, a second wave of nine Swordfish attacked. The raid put the *Littorio* and the *Duilo* out of action for months and a third battleship, *Cavour*, never again went to sea. At one stroke, the British had severely damaged Italian naval strength in the central Mediterranean. "A black day for the Italian Navy," a German naval staff diarist wrote upon hearing the news. "The English success must be spoken of as the greatest naval victory of the war. . . . The smartly executed attack of British torpedo aircraft . . . presents the Italian leadership with a bitter final accounting for the minimal activity displayed up to now by the weapon that at the beginning of the war was considered their sharpest: the fleet!" Japanese Admiral Isoroku Yamamoto also

THEATERS OF WAR, SEPTEMBER 1939–DECEMBER 1940

Europe	*Mediterranean/North Africa*

1939

September 1: Germany invades Poland.*

September: British Expeditionary Force units begin arriving in France; last of troops arrive in April 1940.

September 17: The USSR invades Poland.*

September 28: Poland surrenders.

November 30: The USSR invades Finland.*

1940

March 12: Finland surrenders to USSR.

April 9: Germany invades Denmark and Norway.*

May 10: Germany invades the Low Countries and France.* British marines land on Iceland—a Danish dependency—to protect Allied North Atlantic supply lines.

May 26–June 4: Under heavy German fire, Allied forces evacuate from the European continent at Dunkirk, France.*

June 21: Italy attacks France.*

June 22: France surrenders to Germany; all of Western Europe (except Portugal and fascist Spain) is under German control.

June 28: Soviet forces occupy Besserabia and northern Bukovino, Romania.

June 30: German troops, unopposed, occupy Britain's Channel Islands.

July 10: Germany begins air war over England (the Battle of Britain).*

August 1–7: Soviet forces occupy Estonia, Latvia, and Lithuania.

September 7: The Blitz begins, a period of intense German air raids over London and other populated areas.*

1939

April 7: Italy invades Albania.

June 11: Italian planes attack French bases in North Africa and the British island fortress of Malta.*

1940

July 3: British navy attacks the French fleet at Mers-el-Kébir, North Africa.*

August 4: Italy opens its East Africa campaign, invading British Somaliland and capturing Berbera, the capital, 15 days later. British forces evacuate Aug 20.*

September 13: Italian forces in Libya attack British forces in Egypt.

Sepember 23–25: Operation Menace—Free French and British forces unsuccessfully attack Dakar, French West Africa.*

October 12–November 11: Gabon Campaign—Free French forces invade Gabon, a French African colony, via French Cameroons and the Middle Congo. Vichy French forces from Dakar and Toulon are defeated defending Gabon.

October 28: Italian forces, based in Albania, invade Greece.*

November 11–12: British carrier-based planes attack the Italian naval base at Taranto.*

December 9: British forces in Egypt begin counteroffensive against Italians.*

Other Military Activity

November 1939: The "Phony War,"* a lull in military operations as nations prepare for future conflict.

Spring/Summer 1940: In the Caribbean, British and French troops land at Aruba and Curaçao to prevent German sabotage of local oil refineries; British naval forces blockade the French West Indies

The Atlantic	*China-Burma-India (CBI)*
1939	**1939**

The Atlantic

1939

Autumn: The Battle of the Atlantic begins.*

September 3: The German submarine U-30 sinks an unarmed passenger ship, the *Athenia*, en route from Britain to Canada.

September 17: U-29 sinks the aircraft carrier *Courageous*, the first British warship lost in the war.

October 13: U-47 penetrates the British fleet base at Scapa Flow and sinks the battleship *Royal Oak*.

December 13–17, 1939: The British navy traps the *Graf Spee*, a German pocket battleship that had sunk nine Allied vessels, off the River Plate on the coast of Uruguay. The damaged ship retreats to Montevideo Harbor, and, unable to escape, is scuttled.

1940

February 16: British board the German supply ship *Altmark* in Norwegian waters, freeing 299 captured Royal Navy sailors. Falsely believing that Norway abetted the British, Hitler accelerates plans to invade the country.

March–April: In Operation Berlin, the German warships *Scharnhorst* and *Gneisenau* sink 22 Allied ships.

Spring: Operation Rheinubung begins. This German surface-navy campaign against Allied merchant shipping involves the huge, new battleship *Bismarck*.

May 9: British navy seizes U-110 off the coast of Greenland, capturing a prized German Enigma coding device and code books, a major intelligence coup.

China-Burma-India (CBI)

1939

October 6: Chinese Nationalists claim a huge victory outside the Hunan provincial capital of Changsha–but at great expense to its armies, and to the city, where overzealous Chinese defenders caused a major catastrophe.* Japanese forces retreat.

November 19: Chiang Kai-shek's Nationalist Chinese forces begin a major winter offensive.*

1940

May: Japan renews operations in China's Hupei province to gain further control over the Yangtze River.

June 10: Japanese forces on the Yangtze River attack Ichang and move toward Chungking.

August: British forces withdraw from Shanghai and northern China for use elsewhere; Japan takes military control of Indochina's Tonkin region.

August–December: Mao Tse-tung's Chinese Communist forces begin the "Hundred Regiments Offensive."*

now under Vichy control. Other naval blockades go into effect elsewhere in August, as Germany imposes blockade of Britain and Italy activates one on British Mediterranean and North African ports.

* See text for further discussion.

took special note of the British victory. Just over a year later, he would dispatch Japanese carriers to Hawaii, where their planes would do even greater damage to American warships moored at Pearl Harbor.

1941: The World's Wars Become a World War

On January 21, 1941, Prime Minister Fumimaro Konoye addressed the 76th session of the Imperial Diet. After tendering "heartfelt gratitude" to the forces engaged in China, he declared:

> Japan is now confronted with an emergency unparalleled in her long history. The present world situation makes it urgent that she should . . . take appropriate measures centering on the establishment of a new order in Great East Asia and placing emphasis on the settlement of the China Affair.

For two-and-a-half years, Japan had been bleeding in China; for two-and-a-half years, Japan had been making China bleed. Not long before the prime minister's speech, the Imperial Army had launched what became known as the "Three Alls Campaign" (kill all, burn all, destroy all), aimed primarily at the Communist main base area in Yenan, in retaliation for the communist Hundred Regiments Offensive. Before it ended, millions of Chinese would die, millions more become refugees, and the campaign would severely test China's Communist Party and its armed forces. Communist forces were also under attack from another quarter. In December 1940, Chiang Kai-shek had given Mao's 100,000-strong New Fourth Army a deadline of December 31 to pull back north of the Yangtze River. (Tensions between communists and local Nationalist forces had sparked fighting that autumn in an engagement that the communists won.) The generalissimo also ordered Nationalist forces to move up and keep careful watch to make certain that the New Fourth Army complied. However, the officers at the scene were led to understand that their purpose was to "mop up the bandits." As the communists began to pull out on January 4, the Nationalists followed. Some fired on the communists, and similar harassment continued. Then, on January 12, the Nationalists unleashed an intense artillery and bombing attack that lasted for two days, until Mao and Chiang secured a cease-fire. Between 2,000 and 10,000 communist soldiers were killed. With this battle, the Nationalist/communist "united front" was effectively ended, although diplomatic channels between the two factions remained open throughout the war.

Joseph Stalin was among those pressing the two sides to work together to defeat Japan. Yet that April, the USSR concluded a neutrality pact with the

Japanese. This was not pleasing news to Adolf Hitler, who would have preferred that Japan remain a threat to the Soviet rear as his own forces crossed the USSR's western borders. He also would have preferred a more militarily competent ally in the Mediterranean Theater. For Germany's southern flank was now vulnerable—a matter that would have to be dealt with before the Wehrmacht's thrust to the East.

Mussolini, meanwhile, was learning of further reverses—this time in East Africa. A British campaign that had begun tentatively with an attack in November 1940 was launched in full force on January 19, 1941. The British swept into the Italian colony of Eritrea, where they encountered stiff resistance from Italian forces led by General Luigi Frusci. But the Italians were forced back by the end of March. By that time, there was better news from North Africa, where Axis forces were beginning to retake the ground that the British had secured just a few months earlier.

WESTERN DESERT CAMPAIGN, PART I: JANUARY–DECEMBER 1941
MEDITERRANEAN THEATER (NORTH AFRICA)

Primary Objectives: *German:* to bolster Italian troops, then on the run in Libya, push toward Suez, with the possible further objective of linking with German troops heading south from a conquered Soviet Union and to tie up British forces while the Wehrmacht consolidated its victories in Yugoslavia, Greece, and Crete; *Italian:* to secure more territory for the Fascist empire (and to recover its status as a full partner with Germany); *British:* to defend Egypt, especially the vital Suez Canal

Forces: *German:* Deutsche Afrika Korps (5th Light Division), 15th Panzer Division, and the 90th Light Division (comprising 4 infantry battalions); *Italian:* Tenth Army, 1st Libyan Division, 2nd Libyan Division, 4th Militia Division "3 Gennaio"; *British:* 7th Armored Division, 7th Royal Tank Division, 4th Indian Division, the garrison at Marsa Matruth

Commanders: *German:* Major General Erwin Rommel; *Italian:* Marshal Rodolfo Graziani; *British:* Field Marshal Sir Archibald Wavell, Commander in Chief Middle East (to June 1941), General Sir Claude Auchinleck (June 1941–August 1942)

Military Losses (Entire African Campaign): *German:* 18,594 killed, 3,400 missing; *Italian:* 13,748 killed, 8,821 missing; *British Commonwealth:* 35,476 combat deaths

Result: In a near-continuous seesaw campaign, British gains against the Italians were reversed; Axis forces secured air bases from which Malta and other Allied Mediterranean assets could be attacked and put the Allied-occupied port city of Tobruk under siege. Unsuccessful counterattacks led the British to create a Western Desert Air Force and adopt new methods to increase air-ground coordination. The British Eighth Army, formed in September, forced Rommel to give ground by the end of the year.

In December 1940, as the Italians were attempting to hold on against the Greeks in Albania, the British Western Desert Force—comprising British, Indian, Australian, New Zealand, French, and Polish units led by Lieutenant General Sir Richard O'Connor—attacked isolated sections of the much stronger Italian Tenth Army under Marshal Rodolfo Graziani. O'Connor quickly retook Sidi Barrāni, Egypt. On January 5, 1941, Italy's Libyan stronghold of Bardia fell—netting the British an intact water plant and port facilities, 40,000 prisoners, and so much war matériel that British foreign secretary Anthony Eden quipped to Winston Churchill that never had "so much been surrendered by so many to so few." By January 21, the British force, spearheaded by Australians, had overcome an uncoordinated Italian defense and taken the vitally important Libyan port city of Tobruk. Along with that prize came an additional 25,000 Italian prisoners, 258 artillery pieces, and 87 tanks. The British defeated the balance of Graziani's retreating force (absent Graziani, who had flown to Tripoli, leaving General Giuseppe Tellera in command) February 5–7, 1941, at Beda Fomm, where they took an additional 25,000 Italian prisoners. This sweep, constituting the first victory on land that the British had achieved in the war, briefly relieved pressure on the Suez Canal.

Five days after the Beda Fomm victory, Major General Erwin Rommel arrived in North Africa and assumed command of what was designated the Afrika Korps. Theoretically subordinate to the Italian *Comando Supremo*, and definitely subordinate to the German *Oberkommado der Wehrmacht*, Rommel proceeded to ignore the cautions of both bodies that his forces maintain a chiefly defensive posture. On March 24, he captured El Agheila from the British; on April 1, he took Mersa Brega. British commanders—whose forces were weakened by transfers of men and equipment to Greece and Crete—had not expected Rommel to move before May and were wholly unprepared. Amid a confusion of orders and counterorders as British forces retreated toward Egypt, the two main front-line commanders, O'Connor

Italian General Italo Garibaldi (left), the governor of Libya, and General Erwin Rommel, the German commander in North Africa, review Axis troops on April 13, 1941.

and Lieutenant General Philip Neame, were taken prisoner by Rommel's swift and mobile armored troops. In April, the Germans reached Tobruk, then occupied by two stubbornly resistant Australian brigades under Major General Sir Leslie Morshead. Placing the city under siege, Rommel moved on to Sollum at the Libyan-Egyptian border. Yet he could not push farther into Egypt while Tobruk remained in British hands. The Tobruk siege ultimately lasted 242 days, as an Inshore Squadron of small ships moved tons of supplies daily to keep the Australian defenders' garrison going.

Meanwhile, Churchill sent every bit of hardware he could spare—chiefly tanks and fighters—to North Africa. The prime minister was aware, via decrypted messages snared from Ultra intelligence (see Chapter 9) that the German high command was trying to restrain Rommel. This inspired him to press General Wavell to attack. Two subsequent British assaults, code-named Brevity (May 15) and Battleaxe (June 15) failed because of poor planning, lax radio security, and Rommel's innovative use of 88 mm antiaircraft guns as antitank weapons. After the second failure, Claude Auchinleck replaced Archibald Wavell as Commander in Chief Middle East. (At the same time, most of the Australian troops were withdrawn from Tobruk and replaced with British and Polish troops.) The British formed a new Eighth Army, under the command of Lieutenant General Sir Alan Cunningham. In October, they also established the Western Desert Air Force, at the behest of Air Marshal Sir Arthur Tedder, Commander in Chief of Middle East Air Forces. The techniques this new air unit established to improve air-ground cooperation in North Africa would later be adopted by the United States.

On November 9, the Malta-based Force K (2 cruisers, 2 destroyers) attacked an Italian supply convoy en route to Libya, sinking all seven freighters and one escorting destroyer, with no loss to the British fleet. November 18, after intercepted Enigma messages indicated that Rommel's forces were weakened by Hitler's focus on the Eastern Front, the British and Commonwealth forces began Operation Crusader—a month-long series of armored clashes that took a heavy toll on both sides. Rommel and his force (which had been renamed Panzer Group Afrika in July) initially outmaneuvered and outgunned the British. But the British soon gained the advantage after Rommel divided his forces to stage a raid into Egypt. With his supply lines stretched too thin and his resources depleted, Rommel was forced to withdraw across the Libyan province of Cyrenaica. By mid-December, he was back in El Agheila, where he had begun his offensive in March.

★   ★   ★

In February 1941, just as Rommel was arriving in North Africa, the British government decided to increase its assistance to the beleaguered Greeks. However, their resources in the area were limited. Men and matériel would have to be transferred from North Africa, a fact that would weaken British efforts in both areas. (By April 5, Rommel's advances in the Western Desert Campaign had prevented the British from transferring more than eighty usable aircraft to Greece—no match for the Luftwaffe force that would be arrayed against them.) German plans for action in the Balkans, meanwhile, were proceeding apace. Both sides were drawing their military plans while also engaging in frenzied, often sub rosa negotiations through which they were attempting to secure greater cooperation from Turkey and various Balkan states. As Germany built up armed forces in Romania and began moving them into Bulgaria, Hitler also kept a weather eye on the Soviet Union (from which he wanted no trouble before he attacked it). He and his diplomats continually assured the Soviet government that German action in the Balkans was directed against the British and constituted no threat to Soviet interests in the region. Greece, meanwhile, kept making

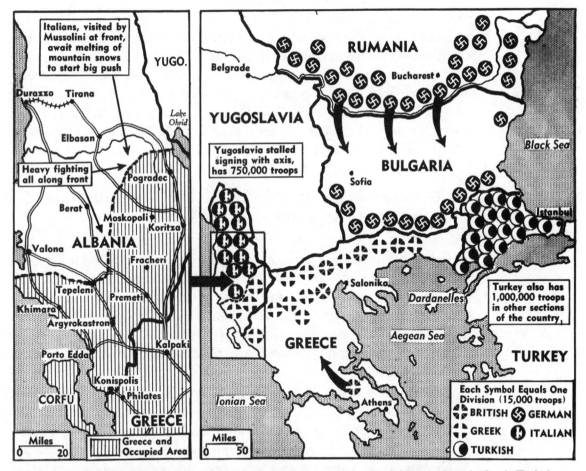

These newspaper maps, published on March 14, 1941, show the competing array of forces—British, Greek, Turkish (neutral), German, and Italian—vying for power in the Balkans, as Germany prepares to go to the aid of Italian forces that have been forced back into Albania (shown left) during their attempted invasion of Greece.

desperate attempts to prevent German interference, reassuring the Germans that they had requested assistance from the British solely to fight the Italians.

Both Germany and Britain (with some help from the United States) put particular pressure on Yugoslavia, whose delicate position with regard to the European powers was complicated by ethnic rivalries within its own borders. On March 25, 1941, the Yugoslav government yielded to German pressure, joined the Axis Tripartite Alliance, and agreed to let German troops cross its territory—despite growing opposition among the Yugoslav people to closer association with the Germans. Two days later, a coup d'etat toppled the government. The new leadership, headed by air force general Dusan Simovic, was determined to stay out of the coming German-Greek conflict, but went to great lengths to assure the Germans that it was friendly. Hitler, who harbored a long-standing antipathy toward the Yugoslav nation, ignored these assurances and added Yugoslavia as a target of invasion. Yugoslavia's armed forces were hardly prepared to meet what was about to be sent against them. The Greeks and their British allies had at least planned and were braced for the attack, although some Australian units had not reached the defensive lines by the Palm Sunday morning that it began.

THE GERMAN INVASION OF GREECE AND YUGOSLAVIA (BALKAN CAMPAIGN, OPERATION MARITA), APRIL 6–MAY 3, 1941
MEDITERRANEAN THEATER (MEDITERRANEAN EUROPE)

Primary Objectives: *German:* to protect its southern flanks prior to the invasion of the Soviet Union, push the British away from southern Europe, secure access to Balkan natural resources, and support its Italian allies; *British:* to secure Greece from Axis control, after which they would establish bases from which to attack Axis assets and perhaps defeat Italy and thus weaken Hitler; *Greek:* to resist occupation by Italian and German forces

Forces: *German:* 1st Panzer Group, XL and XIV Panzer Corps, XVIII and XXX Infantry Corps, 16th Panzer Division, supported by the Luftwaffe's VIII Air Corps and the Hungarian Third Army; *Italian:* Second, Ninth, and Eleventh armies; *Greek:* First and Second armies; *British and Commonwealth:* I Australian Corps, 6th Australian Division, 2nd New Zealand Division, 1st Tank Brigade of the 2nd British Armored Division, a total expeditionary force of 53,051 men

Commanders: *German:* Field Marshal Siegmund List; *Italian:* General Ugo Cavellero; *Greek:* General Alexander Papagos; *British:* Field Marshal Sir Henry Maitland Wilson

Military Losses: *German:* 1,000 killed, 4,000 wounded; *Italian:* 13,755; *Greek:* 15,700 dead or missing; *British Commonwealth:* 11,840 dead or captured

Result: The Germans crushed Yugoslavia, conquered Greece, and shored up their Italian allies, while establishing the military presence in the Mediterranean area that Mussolini had tried to avoid.

A few hours before German forces moved against Greece, the German minister in Athens presented a note to Greek prime minister Alexandros Koryzis

In April 1941, German Panzer units move southward through Greece despite heavy spring rains and muddy roads. Germany justified the attack by citing Greek cooperation with Great Britain.

ALLIED INVASIONS AND OCCUPATIONS IN THE MIDDLE EAST

The Middle East was valuable to both the Axis and Allied powers for its resources and its geographic position. With Vichy France in control of Syria (a French colonial state) and a fervent anti-British movement in Iraq, the Germans saw the area's potential as an avenue through which forces descending from a presumably conquered Soviet Union could meet Axis North African forces (perhaps supported from Japanese bases on the island of Madagascar; see "The Fight for Madagascar" in Chapter 7) to crush the British and gain control of the Mediterranean and Africa. Tensions in the area increased when, on April 2, 1941, an anti-British general, Rashid Ali, overthrew the Iraqi government and Hitler ordered arms sent from Vichy-held Syria to Baghdad to support Ali. In response, a British brigade landed at the Persian Gulf port city of Basra, repelled an attack by 9,000 Iraqis, and moved toward Baghdad. Because the Axis command could not spare more arms or air support, the overmatched Ali fled to Iran on May 28. Two days later, the mayor of Baghdad signed an armistice with the British, who retained nominal control of Iraq. In early June, perhaps as a harbinger of tensions that would rock the Middle East for decades thereafter, a mob of Ali loyalists rampaged through the Jewish quarter of Baghdad, looting shops and homes and killing 150 Jews. Meanwhile, the Vichy government began to use its small naval force against the British. After some skirmishes in the Mediterranean, British troops landed at Haifa, Palestine, and British and Free French forces advanced on Syria and Lebanon (the Syrian Campaign, June–July 1941). There, as at Dakar, Free French troops were among those battling Vichy French forces until the Vichy French high commissioner, General Henri-Fernand Dentz, was forced to request an armistice (July 14).

On August 25, British and Soviet troops entered oil-rich Iran, which had maintained strong ties to Germany. The Allies advanced quickly against weak Iranian resistance, and the country's ruler, Shah Reza Pahlavi, abdicated in favor of his son. Under the new shah, Mohammed Reza Pahlavi, the Iranian government quickly severed diplomatic relations with both Germany and Italy (and, in spring of 1942, with Japan). The Iranian government entered into a Tri-Partite Treaty of Alliance with Britain and the Soviet Union (its assurances to Iran subsequently affirmed by the United States as well). Thereafter, Iran became a major conduit for Lend-Lease supplies to the USSR.

On November 28, 1941, the Mufti of Jerusalem, Haj Amin el-Husseini, visited Hitler in Berlin to pledge the support of "the Arab world," which he said "was firmly convinced of a German victory . . . because Allah could never grant victory to an unjust cause." Hitler reassured the Mufti that his "uncompromising war on the Jews" extended to the Middle East and included "stiff opposition to the Jewish homeland in Palestine." Hitler pledged to free the Arab world from the yoke of British rule.

that attempted to justify the action by blaming Greece for its cooperation with Britain. No such niceties preceded the German attack on Yugoslavia. Determined to destroy Yugoslavia as a nation, Hitler ordered the Luftwaffe to demolish the capital city of Belgrade (this operation was code-named Retribution), and his orders stood, even after the Yugoslav government declared Belgrade an open city on April 4. Two days later, Luftwaffe attacks ravaged the city and killed 17,000 civilians—the largest number killed in one day since the war began. At the same time, German troops, with close Luftwaffe support, slashed into southern Yugoslavia and northern Greece from Bulgaria as other Luftwaffe units bombed the ports of Salonica and Piraeus. The Germans' progress into Greece was impeded at several points by the strength of Greek fortifications and such stubborn defense that one German division commander said, sarcastically, "It seems the Greeks are prepared to fight to the last man for England's sake." Yet neither the Yugoslavs nor the Greek/British armies could hold. They were steadily forced back—the Greeks in Albania forced to abandon their hard-won gains.

On April 8, the Greek commander of the region near Salonica surrendered his 70,000 soldiers; three days later, Italian troops once again invaded Greece from Albania. The Yugoslav government surrendered on April 17 with 6,000 officers and 335,000 troops taken prisoner. Despite stiff resistance from New Zealander, Australian, British and Polish troops, the Greek situation was hopeless. Prime Minister Koryzis committed suicide, and on April 23, the Greek Army surrendered. The next day, the British began evacuating troops from several beaches near Athens and Peloponnesus, completing the action (Operation Demon) on April 29, with 50,732 British and Greek troops safely transported to Crete and Alexandria. Greece suffered under Axis occupation until 1944, its citizens enduring starvation and brutal partisan and internecine warfare (see Chapter 8).

★   ★   ★

As the Allies were preparing for the Syrian Campaign (see box, opposite), German forces began an operation to crush the Allies on Crete, where many of the British and Greek troops that had been evacuated from Greece had retreated and dug in. The British had hoped to hold the island as a base from which to mount aerial attacks on the Romanian oil fields and other Axis assets. However, the battered force that now prepared for the German assault (the British high command had been alerted by Ultra intelligence intercepts) was poorly equipped and had not had time to be forged into a cohesive and

DEATH OF THE BISMARCK

Germany's brand-new, fully loaded battleship, the *Bismarck*, which had taken two-and-a-half years to build and another year to test, finally set out on its first mission on May 18, 1941. Six days later, the British battle cruiser *Hood* and the battleship *Prince of Wales* fired on the *Bismarck* and the heavy cruiser *Prinz Eugen* in the Denmark Strait, southeast of Iceland, as the German warships prepared to take part in attacks on Allied convoys (Operation Rheinubung). The two German ships directed their guns on the *Hood*, which lost all but three sailors of its 1,500-man crew and sank within minutes after its magazines exploded. The *Prince of Wales* retreated and the *Bismarck*, leaking oil, limped toward Brest, France, but before it could reach port, it was struck again by British aircraft. In a 1,750-mile pursuit, the Royal Navy, after correcting a navigational error that sent them in the wrong direction, tracked the battleship down. They were helped considerably when the *Bismarck* broke radio silence and by the fact that the wounded warship was still leaving a telltale oil slick in its wake. Torpedo-laden Swordfish aircraft from the carrier *Ark Royal* swooped down shortly before nightfall on May 26, as the battleship neared the French coast; a successful hit jammed the Bismarck's rudders in the midst of a turning maneuver. The next morning, the British battleships *King George V* and *Rodney*, joined by smaller warships, moved in for the kill. Two thousand *Bismarck* crewmen were lost; only 110 were rescued. The destruction of the *Bismarck* significantly altered the style of war in the Atlantic. Hitler was so concerned about losing another expensive capital ship that when the *Tirpitz*, the *Bismarck's* sister ship, was launched, it was based in occupied Norway, targeting convoys bound for the Soviet Union. Out in the open Atlantic, however, the German navy would rely on its U-boats.

coordinated fighting force. The Germans faced obstacles, too. They had underestimated the size of the force they would be fighting, and the British Navy and Royal Air Force would prevent reinforcements from reaching Crete from the nearby island of Milos.

German Invasion of Crete (Operation "Merkur"/Mercury), May 20–May 29, 1941
Mediterranean Theater

Primary Objectives: *German:* to occupy this strategically important gateway to Palestine and Egypt and prevent the British from using Crete as a base from which to strike Romanian oil fields and other valuable Axis assets; *British/Commonwealth:* to hold the island as a base from which to strike at Axis assets in the Balkans and support Allied Mediterranean operations

Forces: *German:* 23,000 (16,000 airborne, 7,000 seaborne); *Commonwealth (British, New Zealander, Australian):* 32,000; *Greek:* 10,000

Commanders: *German:* General Kurt Student; *Allied:* Lieutenant General Sir Bernard Freyberg

Military Losses: *German:* more than 7,000 killed, more than 3,000 wounded; *British/Commonwealth:* 4,007 killed (2,265 seamen, 1,742 ground troops), 2,000 wounded (approximately), 12,000 taken prisoner as well as 3 cruisers, 6 destroyers, 1 aircraft carrier lost; 3 battleships, 6 cruisers, and 7 destroyers damaged. The RAF lost 46 planes

Result: German victory, although at such exorbitant loss of human life and matériel that Hitler forbade any future large-scale paratroop operations. Britain lost ground in the Mediterranean.

On Crete, the British held Máleme airfield near the west end of the island, a fueling port at Suda Bay and two other airfields, at Heraklion and Retimo. Most of the troops defending the island were evacuees from Greece, including 10,000 Greek troops. German airfields on the Greek mainland, sixty miles northwest of Crete, and an Italian base on the Dodecanese island of Scarpanto, forty-five miles east, left the Allies vulnerable to attack. Axis planes began intensive bombing on May 15 and five days later dropped invasion parachute troops, who took Máleme field by May 21. The only advantage the British had was in sea defense; cruisers bombarded Scarpanto's airfield and kept Italian forces out of the initial conflict. A cruiser force also sank a number of German landing craft, killing thousands of troops the same day Máleme fell. Yet this setback at sea did not prevent the Germans from landing troops at the Máleme airfield, augmenting the initial force of 7,000 with another 7,000. Meanwhile, Axis planes continually battered British land and sea forces. (Prince Philip of Greece, future consort of Queen Elizabeth II, on board the battleship *Valiant*, and his uncle, Captain Lord Louis Mountbatten, whose destroyer, the *Kelly*, was sunk, were among the Allied naval forces enduring the German onslaught.) Their position on Crete untenable, on May 27 the British began evacuating troops. Some managed to withdraw unhampered, but the men who had been defending the Retimo airfield were forced to surrender. The Luftwaffe also pounded the Royal Navy as it attempted to evacuate men at Sphakia, across the island to the southeast of Máleme airfield. On May 30, the Navy was forced to end the operation, leaving 5,000 men behind. (Most were captured; many of those who were not joined the Cretan resistance, which continued throughout the three years that Germans occupied the island.) Although the British sustained severe losses during the battle for Crete, the Germans did as well. In fact, German losses were so heavy that Hitler never again allowed a major airborne operation against Allied-held territory.

★   ★   ★

After nearly two years of steady conquest, the Axis held sway over fifteen European countries and an area that stretched from the Arctic Circle to the Mediterranean. Now, with the Balkans under Axis control and the British who had escaped from Greece and Crete retreating toward North Africa, Hitler was free to implement the plan that had always been at the center of his strategy for achieving a new world order.

HITLER TURNS EAST: THE GERMAN INVASION OF RUSSIA (OPERATION BARBAROSSA), JUNE 22–DECEMBER 1941
EUROPEAN THEATER (EASTERN EUROPE)

Primary Objectives: *German:* to gain control of the Soviet Union's vast natural and agricultural resources and obtain lebensraum (living space) for the German people; to destroy the Soviet armed forces and defeat Bolshevism; *Soviet:* to defend their homeland

Forces: *German:* 180 divisions (air, armored, infantry) with 3 million troops; *Soviet:* initially 158 divisions with 300 more reserve divisions ready within six months, a total of approximately 4.5 million troops

Commanders: *German:* Army Group North, Field Marshal Wilhelm Ritter von Leeb; Army Group Center, Field Marshal Fedor von Bock; Army Group South, Field Marshal Gerd von Rundstedt; *Soviet:* Marshal Semyon Timoshenko, commander of the Western Front; Marshal Georgi Zhukov

Military Losses: *German:* an estimated 918,000 killed, wounded and missing; *Soviet:* 4.4 million killed, wounded, or missing

Result: Stunningly successful in the early weeks of this three-pronged campaign, the German Army Group Center was halted in front of Moscow by winter and a Red Army counteroffensive. The Germans had not achieved the quick victory Hitler and many of his top commanders had anticipated, and their campaign to subdue the USSR would continue.

Previously, German troops had subdued countries swiftly through superior force, relentless firepower, and unflinching cruelty to civilians. However, the Soviet Union was a nation of 192 million people and vast land area with a potential battlefront 1,800 miles long (though the initial front covered approximately 1,000 miles). Moving into this vast land, the Wehrmacht was divided into three distinct groups—North, Center, and South—backed by 5 Luftwaffe divisions with 3,200 planes, and 20 armored divisions with 8,000 tanks. Army Group North moved through the Baltic region (Lithuania, Latvia, Estonia) toward Leningrad; Army Group Center struck toward Moscow; and Army Group South moved through the Ukraine to Kiev. The initial thrust was accompanied by intensive bombing of Kovno, Minsk, Rovno, Odessa, Sevastopol and the Libava naval base on the Baltic Sea. By noon on June 22, 1941, nearly a quarter of the Soviet air combat fleet (of 15,559 planes) had been destroyed; within three weeks, 2,585 Soviet tanks were destroyed and 287,704 Soviet troops taken prisoner. Goebbels read Hitler's war proclamation over national radio: "German people! At this moment a march is taking place that, for its extent, compares with the greatest the world has ever seen. I have decided again today to place the fate and future of the Reich and our people in the hands of our soldiers." As if to add exclamation points, Italy and Romania declared war on the Soviet Union on June 22; Finland, which had lost an unprovoked war with the Soviet Union the previous year, on June 26; Hungary on June 27 and Albania on June 28.

The Wehrmacht struck hard, cutting supply and communication lines and trapping hundreds of thousands of Red Army soldiers. Civilians and prisoners of war were shot by the thousands, to some misgivings within the German Army command—misgivings not taken further than tentative complaints to superior officers. Before the campaign began, Hitler had issued the order that political commissars and partisans "be taken aside and shot," and on July 16, the German high command issued an order that supported the brute tactics the Wehrmacht was to use throughout the German-Soviet war: "The necessary rapid pacification of the country can be attained only if every threat on the part of the hostile civil population is ruthlessly taken care of. All pity and softness are evidence of weakness and constitute a danger." Jews were also summarily "liquidated" wherever they were found. In some areas, the local populations did the killings themselves. In Kovno, Lithuanians killed 2,500 Jews even before the Germans entered the city; German soldiers were told not to interfere in such "political questions." Such a massive scale of carnage and conquest continued for much of the summer of 1941, as the German forces—despite British intercepts of Nazi Enigma messages, Allied raw

The United States War Department created this map featuring the German plan of attack on the Soviet Union. The German invasion began on June 22, 1941, with rapid thrusts into the country that trapped hundreds of thousands of Red Army troops behind German lines.

material and armaments being sent to Stalin, and their own intermittent supply problems—inexorably moved on Leningrad, beginning what was to be a terrible siege. By the end of the year, farther south, they were approaching the gates of Moscow. As they moved forward, the Germans took ever more waves of prisoners (Bock alone took 850,000 POWs as he advanced to Smolensk by August 7; and 3 million total were taken by October). Prisoners were routinely starved and shot—in August–October 1941, 18,000 Russian

POWs were executed at Sachsenhausen concentration camp alone. The killing of Jews accelerated. (See also Chapter 8.)

Rundstedt's Army Group South progressed more slowly, meeting unexpectedly stiff resistance at Kiev in Ukraine and Kerch and Sevastopol in the Crimea. Coupled with halts necessitated by logistical problems, this delay proved decisive, as Bock was required to postpone any assault on Moscow for two months. By the time forces from the south joined him, Bock was still twenty-five miles from the Soviet capital. Hitler's contradictory orders caused further delays, as Soviet troops at Kiev and Leningrad held the German advance at bay for two crucial weeks, almost guaranteeing a winter campaign for which the Germans were not prepared—the first ominous snowflakes fell on September 12. As Hitler funneled Leningrad divisions to Kiev and Moscow, the Soviets began a massive infusion of food and armaments by air to Leningrad, which had been on the verge of collapse. Leningrad continued to resist, although the city was now ringed by German troops and artillery. Kiev, which the Red Army held at Stalin's insistence while the German noose tightened around them, fell September 19. The Germans captured more than 600,000 Soviet soldiers—a terrible disaster among many disasters for the Soviets.

The Germans launched Operation Typhoon, a massive assault on Moscow, on October 2; the goal, to conquer the city before winter fully arrived. Yet, even as the campaign began, weather conditions (snowfall followed by rain) created a thick, glutinous mud through which German tanks could not move, whereas the Soviet T-34 tanks, with wider treads, could. The Soviets mined more than seventy bridges in the Moscow area, to be detonated if the Germans approached them. Stalin ordered government buildings evacuated and the equipment of five hundred factories moved from Moscow eastward to the Urals. With German troops sixty-five miles away, Stalin declared a "state of siege" on October 19. Nearly 500,000 Russian men and women began digging what would be 5,000 miles of trenches and antitank ditches around Moscow, and the city's defenders strung 185 miles of barbed wire.

By mid-November, the Russian winter had arrived in full force. German soldiers, most of whom were still clothed in summer uniforms, suffered frostbite; those who fell asleep on sentry duty were found frozen to death the next morning. Even so, Hitler continued to anticipate imminent victory. Meanwhile, the Soviets brought in specially trained Siberian ski battalions, and partisan bands multiplied and increased their attacks. The Soviet defense on Moscow's perimeter stiffened and, on December 5, three separate

Soviet armies along a 500-mile front from Kalinin to Yelets launched a massive counteroffensive in a blinding blizzard twenty-five and thirty degrees below zero celcius, catching the German troops off guard. But Soviet progress was slow: on December 7 (the day of the Japanese attack on Pearl Harbor), Marshal Zhukov ordered the Red Army to avoid frontal attacks—to outflank the enemy and attack the German rear, to infiltrate Wehrmacht positions. Fighting continued as blizzards raged on and snow rose to waist-high levels, and slowly Germany's Army Group Center was pushed away from Moscow to new defensive lines. By the end of December, both the German and Soviet armies had lost many men and were suffering from lack of food, fuel, and ammunition. Stalin was convinced his troops could break Army Group Center; Hitler had ordered Army Group Center to stand fast where it was. So the situation remained at the end of the year. The Red Army had saved Moscow; in the south, the Soviets had retaken the Crimean port city of Kerch; and in the north, an unbowed Leningrad was enduring the deprivations and artillery bombardment from the surrounding German forces that would continue for nine hundred terrible days.

On December 19, Hitler, furious at these Eastern-Front setbacks, relieved army commander in chief Field Marshal Walther von Brauchitsch and placed himself in direct command in the East. Bogged down in the Soviet Union, with Britain stubbornly unsubdued in the west, Hitler nevertheless broadened Germany's conflict on December 11, when, in support of his Japanese ally, he declared war on the United States of America.

MILITARY OPERATIONS VERSUS CIVILIANS

Military operations were far more devastating to civilian populations in World War II than in World War I, in part because military operations occurred over much wider areas and the means of destruction were more powerful, more varied, and had greater range. Perhaps even more significant is that the hesitation to use those means on nonmilitary targets eventually all but disappeared. As a result, many—but not all—of the accepted rules of war vanished (see "The Rules of War" in Chapter 8).

In World War I, the ratio of soldiers killed per civilian was ten to one. For World War II, the estimates of civilians killed vary (numbers from China and the Soviet Union have been the most difficult to gauge), but many leading scholars estimate at least twice as many civilians died as the number of soldiers killed.

Whether civilian areas were intentionally targeted in an effort to terrorize the population and poison morale or were hit because of inevitable accidents and errors mattered little to those affected—they were victims of war either way. On October 18, 1939, Hitler formally authorized attacks on British naval vessels and passenger ships sailing in convoys. Admiral Karl Dönitz, then commander in chief of German U-boats, issued the order: "Rescue no one and take no one on board . . . we must be hard in this war." On the ground, the massive entrenched armies of World War I had given way to mobile military forces working on multiple, fluid fronts over vast miles of territory and using artillery and field guns that could strike from miles away. Irregular forces, partisans, and guerrillas employed tactics, such as street fighting and door-to-door combat, that pulled civilians into the conflict to a far greater degree. Not surprisingly, the growing disregard for noncombatants extended to unarmed prisoners of war. (See also Chapter 8.)

Initially, the Allies attempted to avoid damaging nonmilitary sites as much as possible (Hitler, disingenuously, as the Poles discovered, had agreed to do the same), in keeping with the League of Nations unanimous resolution of September 30, 1938: "The intentional bombing of civilian populations is illegal; Objectives aimed at from the air must be legitimate military objectives and must be identifiable; Any attack on legitimate military objectives must be carried out in such a way that civilian populations in the neighborhood are not bombed through negligence." The Soviets met President Franklin D. Roosevelt's request for an explanation of Russian air attacks on Finnish civilians in 1939 with a denial that such activity even occurred, all evidence to the contrary. Britain's RAF pilots, on their first air raid mission of the war, were specifically directed not to threaten civilian areas when they attacked the

German naval base at Wilhelmshaven on September 4, 1939; but on May 11, 1940, a British night raid on Mönchengladbach, outside Düsseldorf, marked the RAF's first significant attack on a populated area.

The shift from attempts at "precision bombing," which aimed at particular war-related targets, to "area bombing," which blanketed cities and nonmilitary areas to weaken civilian morale, greatly increased civilian casualties. (Night bombing, which the Luftwaffe began in large waves over Britain in September 1940, was considerably less accurate than daylight attacks and also led to greater civilian casualties. See also "Aircraft-Bombers" in Chapter 5.) In the course of the war, the Luftwaffe attacked at least 20 British cities more than 50 times, killing 60,000 British civilians, destroying 456,000 homes, and damaging another 4 million houses. British Air Marshall Arthur Harris, with Prime Minister Churchill's approval, initiated area bombing against Germany in February 1942, a strategy that lasted until March 1945, not only because precision bombing was difficult and ineffective, but also, as Churchill clinically phrased it, to "de-house" German workers. More than a half million German civilians perished in the air war, and 1.5 million houses were damaged or destroyed. Both the Axis and the Allies employed area bombing, and early 1945, when General Curtis LeMay became the new head of the 21st Bomber Command, marked the beginning of American area bombing using incendiaries on Japan. LeMay's B-29s, flying at night to avoid Japanese fighter planes, and at lower altitudes to conserve fuel and carry a maximum payload, incinerated major industrial cities and killed some 300,000 civilians, leaving more than 8 million homeless.

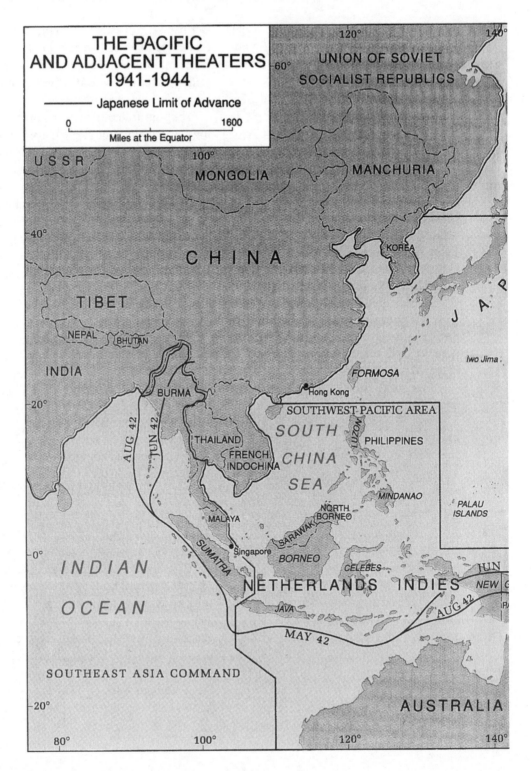

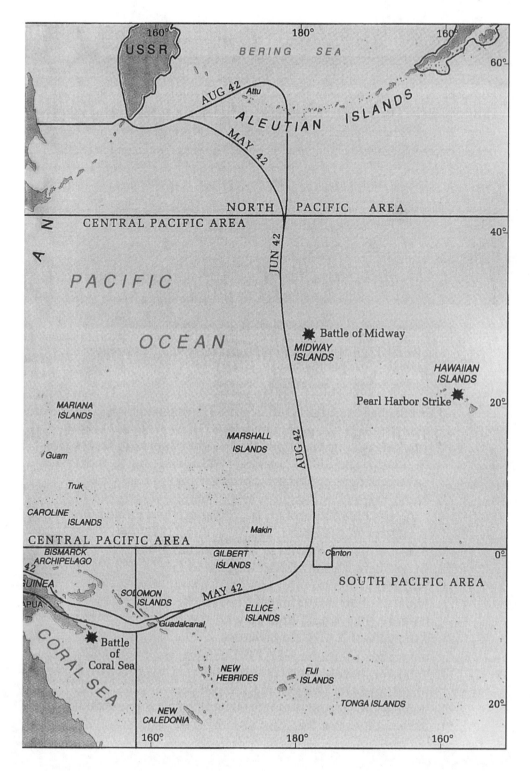

A New Theater Opens: War in the Pacific

Late 1941 marked the beginning of the Pacific War, an extension of the war Japan had been waging in Asia. In July, Japanese forces arrived in southern Indochina, their presence in the area constituting a potential threat to the Philippines, a former American territory and home of the small U.S. Asiatic fleet. Responding to these military moves, the U.S. government froze Japanese assets in America and implemented further trade embargoes; Japan viewed this as justifying its expansionist policies, since it would need to obtain oil and other resources it could no longer buy from the Americans. The idea to attack Pearl Harbor grew out of earlier Japanese plans for defeating the U.S. Navy. For years Japanese planners envisioned, if the need arose, attacking the Philippines to draw the main U.S. naval forces to the rescue; they expected it might take the Americans months to prepare a task force and respond. Japanese submarines would then trail the American warships, and as the fleet neared the Philippines, the subs and surface ships of the Imperial navy would surround and attack. Thus, destruction of American naval might had long been the key to Japanese war plans. Admiral Isoroku Yamamoto, commander in chief of the Japanese Combined Fleet, developed a plan to destroy the bulk of American naval power in one risky shot, a surprise attack on the military installations at Pearl Harbor, Hawaii. In Yamamoto's estimation, the attack, if completely successful, would render the United States incapable of interfering with or preventing Japanese domination of southeast Asia and the western Pacific for up to two years. As it happened, the Japanese had good reason to believe the December 7, 1941, attack was a success—the Americans were caught by surprise, six battleships were sunk, army and navy aircraft were easily destroyed on the ground, few American planes got into the air, and Pearl Harbor was left in flames. Although the attack lasted only two hours, it immediately began a three-and-a-half-year war that Japan could not—and would not—win. In that sense, the attack was a failure.

ATTACK ON PEARL HARBOR, DECEMBER 7, 1941
PACIFIC THEATER

Primary Objectives: *Japanese:* knock out American naval power to prevent U.S. interference in its Pacific expansion

Forces: *Japanese:* naval strike force comprising 33 ships, including 6 aircraft carriers; *American:* 86 warships in harbor

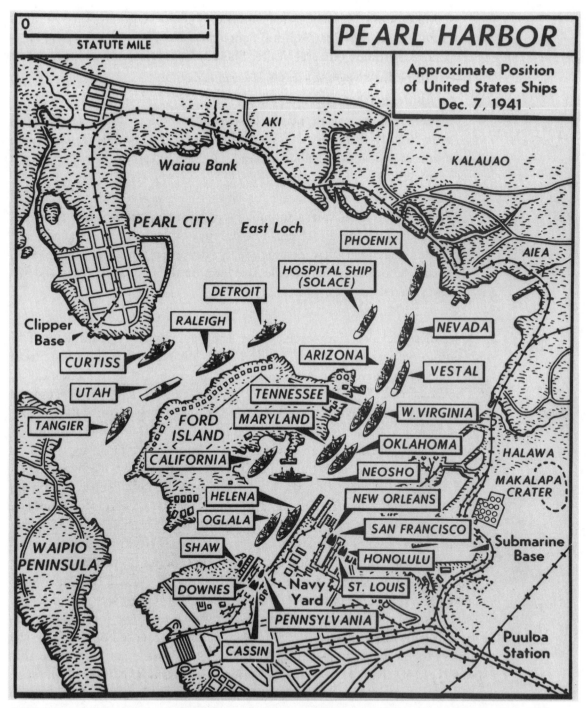

A U.S. Navy map shows the location of American facilities and ships at Pearl Harbor, the headquarters of the U.S. Pacific Command, just before the Japanese attack on December 7, 1941.

Commanders: *Japanese:* Vice Admiral Chuichi Nagumo; Vice Admiral Gunichi Mikawa; Rear Admiral Sentaro Omori; *American:* Admiral Husband E. Kimmel; General Walter Short

Military Losses: *Japanese:* 64; *American:* 2,343

Civilian Deaths: *American:* 60

Other: 188 American planes destroyed on the ground; 18 warships sunk/heavily damaged; 29 Japanese planes, 6 submarines (five of them miniatures) lost. Minisub commander Ensign Sakamaki became the first Japanese POW in U.S. custody

Result: A short-term success for Japan that greatly weakened the U.S. Pacific Fleet. The American public was galvanized for war and the isolationist movement dissolved. The United States, Britain, Canada, the Netherlands, and New Zealand declared war on Japan on December 8; Japan's fellow Axis members declared war on the United States in the following days.

A Japanese naval strike force, under the command of Admiral Chuichi Nagumo, left its base at the Kurile Islands on November 26, 1941, for a destination so secret that most of the officers on board were unaware of it. The next day, U.S. military commanders were put on alert, not because the Americans knew that Nagumo was on the move—they did not—but because political dealings with Japan had reached such a low ebb that immediate armed conflict was a very real possibility. Where Japan would strike could only be guessed at, but the Philippines seemed most likely to American officials. Pearl Harbor, the headquarters of the U.S. Pacific Command on Oahu Island, appeared to be a greater candidate for acts of sabotage. Thus, the defensive preparations carried out there were not effective for an aerial attack. Planes were parked in clusters so they could easily be guarded (but also easily bombed); locked ammunition supplies prevented tampering (but delayed American forces from returning fire until the guns were loaded); and no underwater netting to hinder torpedoes was placed in the harbor since it was thought that the water was too shallow for a torpedo attack. Meanwhile, American reconnaissance planes focused on scouring the waters to the southwest of Hawaii for signs of hostile activity, since that was the direction of the nearest Japanese-held islands. Nagumo, however, had taken a northern route toward Hawaii and maintained strict radio

A Japanese pilot photographed the destruction he and his comrades were wreaking December 7, 1941, with one of the Japanese bombers in the foreground.

silence; no one outside the strike force, not even his superiors in Japan, knew exactly where he was. The ships remained undetected 230 miles north of Oahu, and on December 7, at 6 A.M., the first of two main waves of aircraft took off from the carrier flight decks. They reached their destination at about 7:55 A.M. Sunday morning, when few American servicemen were on duty—or even awake.

American radar picked up the 189 Japanese planes, but they were thought to be either planes returning from the carrier USS *Enterprise* or an expected arrival from California. Once over Oahu, the Japanese dive bombers descended on Hickam and Wheeler Fields and Ford Island, bombing and strafing hundreds of aircraft. Fighters, bombers, and torpedo planes homed in on Ford Island and Battleship Row, where seven battleships lay at anchor. The Japanese had adapted their torpedoes for shallow water runs and scored numerous direct hits. Within minutes, ships were in flames as bombs and torpedoes hit their targets and near misses violently rocked vessels against each other. At 8:40 A.M., a second wave of 171 planes attacked the harbor and the stunned Americans—many of them dazed and wounded—readily returned

---

EYEWITNESS ACCOUNT: ATTACK ON PEARL HARBOR

Lee E. Metcalfe, a newly commissioned second lieutenant in the Army Air Corps, was assigned to a B-18 bomber squadron at Hickam Field and had been in Hawaii only a month when Pearl Harbor was attacked. That morning, while standing on a balcony at the Bachelor Officers Quarters, he witnessed the attack on the airfield:

> I looked up and saw planes diving on the end of the Hickam runway, then I saw smoke coming up from the runway where the planes had been diving. I thought the navy flyers were certainly making their practice look realistic. Then one of the planes pulled out of the dive and made a steep climb close to where I was standing and I could see a Japanese pilot and the red ball painted on the wings. Then I saw flames coming from the hanger area. . . . I left the building and headed for the flight line. . . . Bodies and pieces of bodies lay all around where the bombs had hit.

Metcalfe made his way toward a hanger when

> I saw a formation of aircraft coming in from the ocean over the end of the flight line. I made the decision to cross the runway toward the trees that bordered the field. I had just crossed the runway and started across the taxi strip which had B-18s lined up, wing tip to wing tip, when a Japanese fighter plane started strafing the planes. I stood and watched as B-18 after B-18 caught fire after being hit. I saw someone in a B-18 moving the nose turret and firing at the fighter plane. As the fighter approached, a burst from its guns hit the B-18 turret and it exploded. The fighter kept firing and swung slightly towards me with the bullets hitting the ramp and coming straight toward where I was lying under the wing of a B-18. Just before the fighter plane reached me it stopped firing, pulled up, made a turn, dove down and started strafing the B-18s that were lined up on an intersecting taxi strip.

fire. A smaller dive bomber raid occurred at 9:15 A.M., and by 10 A.M. the last Japanese plane turned back toward its carrier.

It was a nearly textbook-perfect attack, but it was not without errors or, for the Americans, a bit of good luck. Five miniature Japanese submarines, launched from five of the sixteen submarines lurking outside Pearl Harbor, were to sink any warships the aircraft missed. Only two minisubs got into the harbor, and all five sank or were captured. The Pacific fleet's three aircraft carriers (the *Enterprise*, *Lexington*, and *Saratoga*) were away at sea and spared. The most critical Japanese error was the failure to destroy Pearl Harbor's repair facilities, submarine pens, and huge fuel supplies. Had those been destroyed, the U.S. Navy would have been forced to rely on its mainland bases in California and Washington state, 2,400 miles away, until Pearl Harbor was rebuilt, while the Japanese could freely secure their objectives in the Pacific. But Nagumo opted not to order an additional attack that morning, figuring American opposition would only strengthen and that major damage had already been achieved.

The physical damage done was extensive but not insurmountable—of the battleships, the *Arizona* exploded when a second bomb struck and detonated a powder magazine; the ship split in two, the forecastle decks gave way, and the forward turrets and conning tower plunged into the hull. The *Arizona* was lost and 1,177 of its crewmen killed, many still in their bunks. The capsized *Oklahoma* was also lost. The *Maryland*, struck by two bombs, and the *Tennessee*, hit by two duds, reached the West Coast for repairs in late December and were back in service in early 1942. The *Nevada*, which managed to escape the harbor during the attack and took five bombs and a torpedo, and the *California*, sunk and later raised, returned to the fleet in 1943. The torpedoed *West Virginia*, also sunk and raised, was again at sea in 1944.

Japan violently pulled the United States into war, and its subsequent attacks on British and Dutch holdings in the Far East that December forged a large opposing Allied coalition. These actions also prompted Germany and its Axis partners to declare war on the United States, a significant error in judgment on Hitler's part. Until then, the United States had been at least nominally neutral in Europe (Lend-Lease activity notwithstanding); now its untapped industrial might that would wear down the Japanese would also be brought to bear on Germany, already trapped in a much longer conflict in the Soviet Union than Hitler had anticipated. As 1941 closed, the scope of the war had opened worldwide.

THEATERS OF WAR, 1941

Europe	*Mediterranean/North Africa*
April 6: Germany invades Yugoslavia and Greece. Yugoslavia surrenders April 17; Greece surrenders April 23. Germany, Italy, Hungary, and Bulgaria all share in the spoils from this victory. Yugoslavs and Greeks continue to wage guerrilla warfare against the occupiers but divide into partisan camps.* (See also Chapter 8.)	**January:** German Luftwaffe intensifies its air attacks over Malta.*
	January: In North Africa, the British capture Tobruk January 22, as the Western Desert Campaign continues.*
May 27: As the battle of the Atlantic continues, British ships sink the German battleship Bismarck.*	**January:** Free French forces in French Equatorial Africa (Chad) launch attack on Italians in Libya to protect the Allied Takoradi air route from the Gold Coast to the Sudan.
June: Battle of Britain* winds down as the Luftwaffe concentrates in eastern Europe.	**January 19–May:** East African Campaign continues—British and Dominion forces battle Italians and their colonial conscripts. Italy's forces surrender at Amba Alagi, Ethiopia May 16.
June 22: Operation Barbarossa—More than 3 million German and Axis troops invade the Soviet Union.* Finland enters the conflict in what is called "The Continuation War" to win back territory lost to the Soviets in the Winter War.	**February 12:** German Afrika Korps lands in Libya.
	March 6: German planes begin dropping mines at the Suez Canal.
September 8: The German 900-day siege of Leningrad begins.	**March 28:** The British navy defeats the Italian fleet at the Battle of Cape Matapan, near southern Greece.
October 2: Operation Typhoon—German forces advance on Moscow.	**March:** Free French forces capture Kufra, Libya.
November 24: German siege of Sevastopol begins.	**April 10:** Germans begin siege of the Libyan port city of Tobruk.*
	May 20: The battle for Crete begins.*
December 5: The Battle of Moscow*—the Soviets commence a major counterattack (the Winter Campaign) against German forces outside the city.	**June 8:** British, Indian, Jewish units from Palestine and Free French forces begin a campaign against Vichy French and French colonial forces in Syria and Lebanon, an area where German aircraft are based. Vichy forces surrender on July 14.
	December 17: Off the coast of Libya, an Italian fleet exchanges fire with British warships in the first battle of Syrte.

Other Military Activity

Battle of the Atlantic continues. The United States enlarges the range of its air and sea "neutrality" patrols off the Eastern Seaboard; Britain and the United States divide the Atlantic: the British patrol the eastern zone, the Americans the western.

April: British forces enter Iraq to enforce a treaty granting Britain rights to oil fields; Germans can offer Iraqis only limited assistance as the Wehrmacht prepares for action on Crete.

July: In the first paratroop combat assault in the Western Hemisphere, Peru invades Ecuador following a border dispute regarding Ecuador's lack of access to the Amazon and the Rio Maranon. Peru's victory confirms its territorial claims.

The Pacific	*China-Burma-India (CBI)*

November 26: Japan's Pearl Harbor Attack Force departs from the Kuril Islands for Hawaii. Submarines stationed at the Marshall Islands also leave for Pearl Harbor.

December 7: Japanese forces attack the U.S. naval base at Pearl Harbor, Honolulu, and army airfields, drawing the United States into the war,* and bomb or shell the Pacific islands Guam, Midway, and Wake. Japanese troops land on Malaya.

December 8: Japanese warplanes strike Hong Kong, the Philippines, and Singapore.

December 10: Guam, a strategically located U.S. Pacific territory with a small, ill-armed garrison of U.S. Marines and Navy personnel, surrenders to the Japanese.

December 20: Japanese forces attack Dutch Borneo, Celebes, and the Moluccas in the Dutch East Indies.

December 22: Battle of the Philippines—The main Japanese invasion force lands at Lingayen Gulf, following smaller landings of advance units. Allied forces depart Luzon for Bataan.

December 23: Japanese troops capture Wake Island, an American outpost between Hawaii and the Philippines, defeating greatly outnumbered U.S. forces after 11 days.

December 25: Hong Kong surrenders to Japan.

December 26: To protect the capital city from further attacks, the Philippine government declares Manila an open city. Japanese bombing continues.

January: In northern China, the Japanese begin their "Three Alls" campaign ("kill all, burn all, destroy all") aimed primarily at Communist forces.*

July 21: Japan begins a military buildup in Indochina that will continue throughout the year.

September 6–October 8: Second Battle of Changsha—Chinese forces are again victorious and inflict heavy casualties on the Japanese.

December 8: Malayan Campaign begins—Japan invades southern Thailand and northern Malaya to prepare an approach to Singapore (a British colony).

December 10: Japanese warplanes sink the British battleship *Prince of Wales* and a cruiser off the southwestern coast of Malaya. Meanwhile, the small, Japanese-trained Burma Independence Army marches into Burma from Thailand to help remove the British and close the Burma Road. Japan plans to hold Burma as a buffer for its Malayan campaign and as a future launching pad into India.

December 20: Planes of the American Volunteer Group (Claire Chennault's "Flying Tigers") first go into combat in the skies over Kunming, China.

August 25: Britain and the USSR invade Iran, which refused to evict its German industrial advisers. Iran surrenders three days later.*

October 31: German U-boat U552 sinks a destroyer, the USS *Reuben James*, the first American warship sunk by hostile fire in the war.

December: Japanese submarines begin attacking American shipping, primarily oil tankers, off the California coast.

* See text for further discussion.

PRINCIPAL SOURCES AND FURTHER READING

Andersson, J. Gunnar. *China Fights for the World*. London: K. Paul, Trench, Trubner, 1939.

Bradford, Ernle. *Siege: Malta, 1940–1943*. London: Hamish Hamilton, 1985.

Calvocoressi, Peter, Guy Wint, and John Pritchard. *The Penguin History of the Second World War*. London: Penguin Books, 1999.

Coox, Alvin D. *Nomonhan: Japan against Russia, 1939*. 2 vols. Stanford, CA: Stanford University Press, 1985.

Erickson, John. *The Road to Stalingrad (Stalin's War with Germany)*. Vol. 1. New Haven, London: Yale University Press, 1999.

Fenby, Jonathan. *Generalissimo: Chiang Kai-shek and the China He Lost*. London: Free Press, 2003.

Gilbert, Martin. *The Second World War: A Complete History*. New York: Henry Holt, 1989.

Goralski, Robert. *World War II Almanac, 1931–1945*. New York: Bonanza Books, 1981.

Harries, Meirion, and Susie Harries. *Soldiers of the Sun: The Rise and Fall of the Imperial Japanese Army*. New York: Random House, 1991.

Keegan, John. *The Second World War*. New York: Viking, 1989.

Knox, MacGregor. *Mussolini Unleashed, 1939–1941: Politics and Strategy in Fascist Italy's Last War*. Cambridge: Cambridge University Press, 1982.

Murray, Williamson, and Allan R. Millet. *A War to Be Won: Fighting the Second World War*. Cambridge: Belknap Press, of Harvard University Press, 2000.

Prange, Gordon W., with Donald M. Goldstein and Katherine V. Dillon. *At Dawn We Slept: The Untold Story of Pearl Harbor*. New York: Penguin Books, 2001. Originally published in 1981.

Price, Alfred. *Battle of Britain Day, 15 September 1940*. London: Greenhill Books, 1990; Mechanicsburg, PA: Stackpole Books, 1999.

Spector, Ronald H. *Eagle against the Sun: The American War with Japan*. New York: Free Press/MacMillan, 1985.

Steer, G. L. *The Tree of Gernika*. London: Hodder and Stoughton, 1938.

Weinberg, Gerhard. *A World at Arms: A Global History of World War II*. Cambridge: Cambridge University Press, 2005.

7

MILITARY OPERATIONS, 1942–1945

In the *izba*, surrounded by his staff, stands Khasin, with his bulging dark eyes, crooked nose and cheeks blue from recent shaving. . . . He is explaining to me about the recent raid carried out by the tank brigade. . . . I was told back at the front headquarters that Khasin's family had all been killed in Kerch by Germans carrying out a mass execution of civilians. Purely by chance, Khasin saw photographs of the dead people in a ditch and recognized his wife and children. I was thinking, what does he feel when he leads his tanks into the fighting?

Vasily Grossman, correspondent for the Red Star, *USSR, 1942*

In December 1941, the Red Army had stopped the Germans in front of Moscow; but from Leningrad in the north to the Crimea in the south, the Wehrmacht was pushing the Soviets hard. In November, the Germans of Army Group South had taken the Crimean port city of Kerch, on the peninsula between the Sea of Azov and the Black Sea, only to be forced out by the Soviets at the end of December. In the spring of 1942, as the Germans began their big push into the Caucasus, the Soviets lost Kerch again after bloody fighting that took more than 100,000 Soviet lives. Some three thousand soldiers, nurses, and civilians from Kerch, trapped on the peninsula, then took refuge in a nearby maze of caves and tunnels. The Germans hurled explosives into the caves, they released gas in the tunnels. Very few Soviets escaped; over agonizing months, most died from German attacks or starvation. They never tried to surrender; they had learned the character of their enemy.

In 1942, the Allies were on the defensive on all fronts. As the Americans built up and trained their armed forces, they pushed the production of war matériel. American Lend-Lease supplies began reaching the Soviet Union, and with American aid, the battered British continued to hold out at home and at sea. In February, American general Joseph Stilwell arrived in China to head the United States military mission, oversee Lend-Lease in the region, and serve as Nationalist leader Chiang Kai-shek's chief of staff. Soon American commanders began contemplating their first offensive action in the Pacific Theater against the Japanese juggernaut.

This chapter presents an outline of notable military operations that occurred from 1942 through 1945, as the Allies moved from defense to offense to finally defeating the Axis. Descriptions of **major battlefield clashes** are highlighted in the narrative in chronological order. The THEATER OF OPERATION in which each major battle or campaign occurred is noted in CAP/SMALL CAP in the text. (Theaters of operation are defined in Chapter 1.) Significant actions not described in the text are noted on the four "Theaters of War" charts in this chapter.

1942: The Allies Against the Ropes

"This war will give us much trouble in the future," Admiral Isoroku Yamamoto wrote to a fellow admiral early in 1942. "The fact that we have had a small success at Pearl Harbor is nothing." The devastating Japanese surprise attack on the American fleet in Hawaii and the equally successful strikes on European holdings in Asia that followed seemed far from nothing to the Allies, who watched in frustration as the emperor's troops swept forward through even the most difficult terrain. Most Japanese officers also watched—with an arrogant pride. "On an average our troops had fought two battles, repaired four or five bridges, and advanced twenty kilometers every day," Masanobu Tsuji of the Taiwan Army Research Section boasted. What could stop them? On January 2, they entered the Philippine Islands capital of Manila, after a brutal bombing campaign that had continued even after the government had declared Manila an "open city" to preserve it from just such an aerial assault. Forced to retreat, General Douglas MacArthur, the Allied commander, established defensive lines on the Bataan Peninsula and at Corregidor, a fortified island about two miles off the peninsula, at the entrance to Manila Bay.

THE SIEGE OF BATAAN AND CORREGIDOR, JANUARY–MAY 5, 1942
PACIFIC THEATER

> **Primary Objectives:** *Allied:* to defend the islands and repel the Japanese as long as possible; *Japanese:* to take American military installations, eradicate American and Filipino resistance, and eliminate the Philippines as a threat

Forces: *On Bataan:* 67,500 Filipino troops, 12,500 American—with 26,000 civilians, versus between 23,000 and 40,000 Japanese troops; *On Corregidor:* 11,000 Allied (American and Filipino) troops versus two Japanese battalions reinforced by artillery and tanks and supported by aircraft

Commanders: *Allied:* Lieutenant General Douglas MacArthur, Lieutenant General Jonathan Wainright, Major General Edward King; *Japanese:* Lieutenant General Masaharu Homma

Military Losses: *Allied:* 22,000 killed and wounded, more than 50,000 prisoners; *Japanese:* estimated 8,000 to 9,000 killed and wounded

Result: The Japanese gradually overwhelmed the defending Allied forces. A few Allied soldiers escaped into the hills to continue guerrilla warfare; most became prisoners of war. The loss of the Philippines was a bitter blow to American morale.

Despite breaking through MacArthur's first defensive line on Bataan on January 6, the Japanese offensive stalled as the Allies took advantage of favorable terrain. Yet Japanese victory here was inevitable: the Allied soldiers were low on supplies, particularly food and vital medicine (more and more soldiers were succumbing to malaria). They also knew they would not be resupplied or reinforced. "We're the battling bastards of Bataan," they sang, "No mama, no papa, no Uncle Sam / No aunts, no uncles, no nephews, no nieces / No rifles, no planes, or artillery pieces / And nobody gives a damn."

Morale plunged further after President Roosevelt ordered MacArthur to leave the Philippines, a difficult journey that began on March 11. (The general established his command in Australia, after pledging to those he left behind, "I shall return.") The American and Filipino soldiers on Bataan, now led in the field by Major General Edward King, serving under Lieutenant General Jonathan Wainwright, held against an attack on April 3, then counterattacked unsuccessfully. The Japanese, meanwhile, had managed to land some men behind the Allied lines. Finally, with no hope of mounting further effective resistance, King ignored MacArthur's order to General Wainwright not to surrender and capitulated on April 9. Two thousand of his soldiers made their way to Corregidor; the others embarked on what would become known as the *Bataan Death March.* Those who survived endured nearly three years of privation and abuse as Japanese prisoners of war. (See also Chapter 8.)

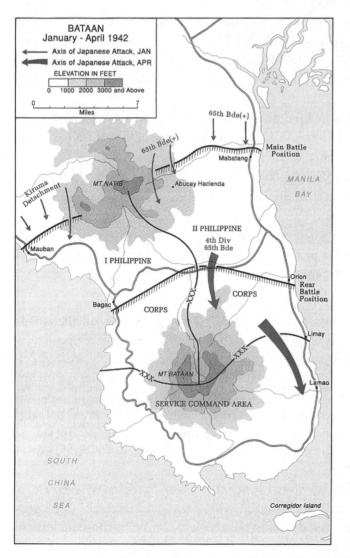

BATAAN
January - April 1942
→ Axis of Japanese Attack, JAN
➡ Axis of Japanese Attack, APR
ELEVATION IN FEET
0 1000 2000 3000 and Above
0 ———— 7
Miles

Corregidor was laced with tunnels that protected the wounded and served as air raid shelters; they were stocked with enough provisions for 10,000 people to endure a six-month siege. As the Japanese campaign to take the fortress began, about 13,000 people were crammed into the tunnels, while some defenders manned the island's big guns. Physical and psychological casualties abounded under a mind-numbing artillery and aerial bombing barrage that pounded the island so unmercifully that most of the defensive emplacements were destroyed and the island's topography was altered. On the night of May 5, the Japanese established a beachhead and then pushed forward to the tunnels. "Everyone is bawling like a baby," an army telegrapher signaled home. "They are piling dead and wounded in our tunnel. . . . The jig is up." There followed, on May 6, a message from General Wainwright to President Roosevelt: "With broken heart and head bowed in sadness but not in shame, I report to your excellency that today I must arrange terms for the surrender of the fortified islands of Manila Bay. . . . With profound regret and with continued pride in my gallant troops I go to meet the Japanese Commander. Good-bye, Mr. President." (Released from captivity in 1945, an emaciated Wainwright was flown to Japan to witness the surrender ceremonies before he returned home—to be awarded the Medal of Honor.)

★   ★   ★

As they pushed through to victory in the Philippines, the Japanese were also advancing in Malaya, where, on January 11, the Imperial Army took Kuala

Lumpur after a spectacular campaign that forced British troops to retreat down the Malay Peninsula toward Singapore—their unwieldy military columns mingling with thousands of Malay and Chinese refugees on congested roads in brutal heat. They were retreating to a prime Japanese target. Singapore, Japanese officer Masanobu Tsuji wrote, was "Britain's . . . eastern gate for the defense of India and the northern gate for the defense of Australia." At the southern tip of the peninsula and connected to the mainland by a causeway, the diamond-shaped island was thirteen miles long and

As the Japanese swept southward in early 1942, driving the Allies out of the Philippine Islands and capturing scores of prisoners of war at the siege of Bataan and Corregidor (top), British forces were retreating down the Malayan Peninsula. Anticipating the imminent Japanese invasion, British women and children were evacuated from Singapore (bottom).

twenty-seven across at its widest point. Most of its defenses were located in the south, facing seaward. Defenses in the north, facing the mainland and the Japanese—and defending three of the island's four airfields and a number of ammunition dumps—were sparse. The British commander, General Arthur Percival, initially refused to improve them lest the effort further demoralize Singapore's already frightened civilian population. Moreover, most of the troops defending the island were either battered from their recent retreat down the Malay Peninsula or new and insufficiently trained; all were inadequately armed. Nevertheless, Winston Churchill insisted that Singapore be held to the last man. This proved to be beyond Percival's capacities.

THE FALL OF SINGAPORE, JANUARY 31–FEBRUARY 15, 1942
CHINA-BURMA-INDIA

> **Primary Objectives:** *British:* to hold this vital base at all costs; *Japanese:* to take the base and push the British out of Malaya
>
> **Forces:** *British:* approximately 70,000 fighting troops (British, Indian, Australian, Malayan volunteers) plus 15,000 nonmilitary defenders; *Japanese:* 35,000 troops, well supported by aircraft
>
> **Commanders:** *British:* Lieutenant General Arthur Percival; *Japanese:* General Tomoyuki Yamashita
>
> **Military Losses:** *British and Commonwealth:* (entire Malay campaign), 138,708, including 62,000 prisoners taken at Singapore; *Japanese:* 1,714 killed, 3,378 wounded
>
> **Result:** A triumph for the Japanese; for the British, what Churchill termed "the worst disaster and largest capitulation in British history."

As the Japanese prepared on the mainland to assault the island (under the watchful eyes of General Yamashita, headquartered in a large glassed observation tower atop the palace of the Sultan of Johore), General Percival hastily established a badly flawed defensive line near the beaches in the north: jungle growth blocked lines of fire, there was poor communication between strong points, and no troops were held in reserve to plug breaches the Japanese might make in the line. Furthermore, Percival had not anticipated the point of the Japanese attack, which occurred on the night of February 8–9. Well supported by aircraft and tanks, Yamashita's troops quickly overwhelmed the defenders, and the British fell back toward Singapore City. With little food and almost no drinking water, the city quickly deteriorated into chaos as terrified civilians, looters, and drunken deserters moved through the fearful detritus of aerial attacks. Judging that further attempts at defense would be futile, Percival surrendered unconditionally on February 15. The Japanese were surprised at the relatively easy victory, and they regarded the surrendered troops with disdain. Their contempt bred atrocities, including the slaughter of the medical staff and all the sick and wounded in the Alexandra Hospital. The Japanese forced many of the surviving soldiers to become slave laborers on military projects, a war crime under both the Hague and Geneva conventions. (See also Chapter 8.)

★   ★   ★

The capture of the Malayan Peninsula and Singapore was among the Japanese Army's greatest wartime achievements. The loss of Singapore was among Britain's worst Far Eastern defeats—but it was not an isolated blow. As Singapore fell, the Japanese were also pushing the British Army out of Burma.

The Burma Campaign, Part I: 1942, Defeat and Retreat

The British dominion of Burma was a vital conduit of supplies to China, which were transported from the port of Rangoon to the rail terminus of Lashio, then over the 717-mile Burma Road to Chungking. Small Japanese units began crossing the Thailand-Burma border in mid-December 1941; a month later, two divisions under Lieutenant General Iida Shojiro, well supported by aircraft, moved swiftly into the country, taking Rangoon on March 8, Lashio on April 29, and the port of Akyab on May 4.

The Japanese success prompted a massive Allied retreat—the British (after March, under the command of Sir William Slim) fighting their way back to India in the longest retreat (about 900 miles) in the history of the British Army. At the same time, General Joseph W. ("Vinegar Joe") Stilwell, Chiang Kai-shek's American chief of staff and the U.S. military commander in the theater, was also leading a retreat. He had entered Burma in March as titular commander of two understrength Chinese armies dispatched to help the British. (The Chinese were also receiving orders from Chiang Kai-shek, though the generalissimo was much too far away to appreciate the battle situation and had no wish to risk units he would prefer to have kept at home.) When the campaign failed, Stilwell led a hardy band of refugees across the mountains to India—an act for which he was thereafter criticized, since he remained out of touch with Chiang and U.S. authorities. After his 140-mile, 20-day trek through the Burmese jungle to New Delhi, Stilwell told reporters, "I claim we took a hell of a beating. We got run out of Burma and it's humiliating as hell . . . we ought to find out what caused it, go back, and retake it." The evacuees reached India just as monsoon season set in; thus, all plans for counteroffensives were shelved until the winter. Japan now had control of all of Burma except for the remotest northern regions, where Kachin tribesmen and other guerrillas would prove a deadly presence against the Japanese occupation for the next three years. (See also Chapter 9.)

The Burma Campaign was to be the longest waged by the British during the war—it would continue until August 1945. Meanwhile, in December 1942, work began on the 478-mile Ledo road, planned as another land supply line for Chinese forces. The road was to run across treacherous mountain terrain from Ledo, India, through northern Burma, to connect with the existing Burma Road into China. One of the war's most stunning engineering achievements—accomplished by American engineers and troops, with Indian, Nepali, Sri Lankan, and Chinese laborers—the Ledo Road would not be completed until 1945. Meanwhile, the Allies would have to find another route for supplying the Chinese, even as they continued their desperate battle to keep sea lanes open to Britain.

The Battle of the Atlantic Continues: January–December, 1942

Wolf packs of German U-boats continued to roam the Atlantic attacking Allied convoys—their efforts augmented by mines and occasional sorties by the Luftwaffe. In January 1942, U-boats sank 62 Allied ships; 44 others were sunk by mines or aircraft, resulting in a loss of more than 400,000 tons for the month. Losses continued to mount during the year. With the United States now an official combatant, German submarine commander Admiral Karl Dönitz sent U-boats into American waters off Bermuda, in the Caribbean and the Gulf of Mexico, and along the Atlantic seaboard. There, most merchant ships, carrying tin and bauxite for U.S. armaments or fuel from the Dutch oil refineries in Aruba, sailed alone and were easy prey. Ships were not the U-boats' only targets: In the spring, U-boat Group *Neuland* began Operation *Westindien* in the Caribbean, during which some of the subs conducted daring raids into the harbors at Trinidad, St. Lucia, and Aruba—site of an oil refinery. By the end of 1942, U-boats had sunk 337 Allied ships in the Caribbean alone. On May 12, 1942, a U-boat sank the oil tanker *Virginia* while it was in the mouth of the Mississippi River. In June, U-boats sank 121 ships in the Gulf. Further south, anti-German riots erupted in Rio de Janeiro after U-boats sank five

Brazilian freighters off Bahia in a twenty-four-hour period. Within a week, Brazil declared war on Germany and Italy (see Part II of Chapter 1).

Despite the growing losses, the United States was extremely slow to institute blackout policies on its eastern seaboard. German U-boats involved in Operation *Paukenschlag* ("Drumbeat" or "Drumroll"), which started in January, could easily target ships silhouetted against the glowing coastal lights. On February 28, a U-boat torpedoed the navy destroyer *Jacob Jones* within sight of the New Jersey coast; only 11 of 136 sailors survived. Another U-boat fatally damaged the oil tanker SS *Gulfamerica* on April 10, off Jacksonville Beach, Florida—within easy sight of thousands of tourists. On June 15, tourists were horrified witnesses to another successful U-boat attack on two freighters off Virginia Beach. The same month, U-boats mined the waters off Boston Harbor, Delaware Bay, and Chesapeake Bay, part of a widespread minelaying campaign. On September 5, after sinking two oil tankers at Bell Island, Newfoundland, German submariners staged a torpedo attack on the pier; this was the only land area attacked directly by the Germans in North America during the war. By then, the United States had established more effective eastern-seaboard defenses. Rear Admiral Adolphus ("Dolly") Andrews, appointed commander of the U.S. Eastern Sea Frontier in March, developed a "Bucket Brigade" system of escorting ships from port to port.

By July, Admiral Dönitz had moved his U-boats back to the convoy routes in the North Atlantic, basing his fleet in an area around Greenland and Iceland out of range of most Allied aircraft. During this intense U-boat offensive, Allied shipping was in constant peril. American merchant shipping suffered a heavy blow when the Germans attacked Arctic Convoy PQ17, en route from Iceland to deliver desperately needed food, fuel, and armaments to the Soviet Union. Scattered and with little in the way of protection (their escort had departed to meet a German naval force rumored to be in the area), the ships were under nearly continuous assault—by U-boats and aircraft—for more than a week (July 1–10), with only machine guns and a few heavier weapons to defend themselves. More than three-fourths of the American merchantmen in this convoy were lost in the icy northern waters. Late in the year, U-boat assaults tapered off due to a ferocious winter. But the wolf packs would be on the prowl again by spring 1943.

★ ★ ★

On January 15, the Allies established the ABDA (American-British-Dutch-Australian) Command to meet the threat of the Japanese southward drive into the Dutch East Indies (now Indonesia), but from the beginning

SUB ASSAULTS ON THE AMERICAN WEST COAST

Unlike the Germans, the Japanese Navy did not mount organized campaigns against Allied merchantmen. (See also Chapters 4 and 5.) Yet Japanese subs ranging the Pacific did sink some merchant vessels, and a few staged daring attacks on coastal targets. On February 23, 1942, submarine I-17, under the command of Nishino Kozo, staged the first foreign attack on the U.S. mainland since the War of 1812 when it surfaced and fired on an oil refinery near Santa Barbara, California. The shells went wide of their mark, damaging only rigging and pumping equipment. On June 20, submarine I-26, having participated in the Japanese invasion of Kiska, in the Aleutian Islands, turned its attentions to Canada, where it lobbed some shells at the lighthouse on Estevan Point, British Columbia. The shelling did little damage, but it moved the Canadians to shut down the lights on all their outer coastal stations, and this hampered shipping for the rest of the war. (I-26 later caused the deaths of all five Sullivan brothers when it sank the USS *Juneau* during the campaign for Guadalcanal; see "Operation Watchtower and the Battle for Guadalcanal" later in this chapter.) The next day, submarine I-25 surfaced and fired on Fort Stevens, Oregon, slightly damaging a baseball field. While on a subsequent war patrol, it launched, on September 9, a single-engine plane piloted by Warrant Officer Nobuo Fujita and carrying two 168-pound incendiary bombs. Fujita dropped the bombs in the woods above Brookings, Oregon, intending to start a forest fire. Three weeks later, he made another run. His bombs were the only four to fall from an enemy aircraft onto any of the 48 states in the war. Though minor, these attacks contributed to the atmosphere that made possible the internment of West Coast Japanese-Americans and Japanese-Canadians. (See also Chapters 2 and 11.)

ABDA suffered from differences in materials, language, signals and tactical documents, and lack of command and coordination. Meanwhile, Japanese forward momentum continued: they took the port at Rabaul, New Britain, on January 23; landed on Java, the largest of the Dutch East Indies, on February 2; and took Ambon, the second largest naval base there on February 4. Early Allied attempts to strike back had little impact beyond the psychological. On February 1, two U.S. task forces formed around the aircraft carriers *Yorktown* and *Enterprise* made surprise raids on Japanese bases in the Marshall and Gilbert Islands, giving a boost to U.S. Navy morale. However, on February 4, another Allied naval force, led by Dutch Rear Admiral Karel Doorman, was forced to retreat from a Japanese landing force in Borneo's Makassar Straits. Three weeks later, the Japanese shattered this same Allied fleet at the Battle of the Java Sea.

BATTLE OF THE JAVA SEA, BETWEEN JAVA AND BORNEO, FEBRUARY 27, 1942
PACIFIC THEATER

> **Primary Objectives:** *Allied:* to prevent the Japanese from taking the Dutch East Indies (of which Java, with its naval base at Surabaya, was a part); *Japanese:* to continue troop landings on Java and consolidate the occupation of the island chain comprising the Dutch East Indies (now Indonesia)
>
> **Forces:** *Allied:* 2 heavy cruisers, 3 light cruisers, 9 destroyers; *Japanese:* 2 heavy cruisers, 2 light cruisers, 14 destroyers
>
> **Commanders:** *Allied:* Rear Admiral Karel W. F. M. Doorman; *Japanese:* Rear Admiral Takagi Takeo
>
> **Military Losses:** *Allied:* 5 cruisers, 5 destroyers sunk; 2,300 sailors killed, including Doorman; *Japanese:* 4 troop transports sunk
>
> **Result:** An overwhelming victory for the Japanese. On March 1, the ABDA Command was officially dissolved.

On February 27, Dutch Rear Admiral Karel Doorman, head of the ABDA Command force, sortied his fleet to intercept a large Japanese convoy approaching Java and Surabaya. In the fight that followed, the Allies, suffering from poor communication and a lack of air cover and training time as a unit, were outgunned by the Japanese forces. One of ABDA's two heavy cruisers, the British *Exeter*, was hit and withdrew to Surabaya as the Japanese continued their attacks. Then the Japanese mounted a devastating torpedo attack that sank both Dutch light cruisers in a matter of minutes, killing Admiral Doorman. The remaining two Allied cruisers, the Australian *Perth* and U.S. *Houston*, fled toward Batavia, on the north coast of Java.

The next night the *Perth* and *Houston* sank two Japanese ships of a separate fleet and damaged three others before being sunk themselves. On March 1, the damaged *Exeter* and two destroyers trying to withdraw to Ceylon were trapped and sunk by Japanese vessels. The only surviving Allied ships were four American destroyers that had left the battle early and managed to slip past the Japanese through the Bali Straits and escape to Australia.

★　　★　　★

On March 9, Allied land forces on Java surrendered. The Japanese had now reached the line the United States had determined to hold. Admiral Ernest J.

King, U.S. naval commander in chief, deemed it essential to hold Hawaii and keep open a line of communications with Australia. Meanwhile, he had been developing an idea for a daring operation that, if successful, would bolster American morale while damaging morale in Japan.

The Doolittle Raid: The Americans' First Strike at Japanese Cities, April 18, 1942

U.S. naval officers devised a daring plan for the first bombing raid on Japan, and they chose USAAF Lieutenant Colonel James H. ("Jimmy") Doolittle, a veteran stunt and military pilot, to lead it. The plan required pilots to take off in B-25 bombers from an aircraft carrier (which normally did not launch such large aircraft and would not be able to land them after the mission), bomb the Japanese cities of Kobe, Nagoya, Yokosuka, Yokohama, and Toyko, and land farther west in China. After special training, Doolittle and his all-volunteer group and sixteen specially modified B-25s were loaded onto USS *Hornet* on April 1. *Hornet* then sailed to join Admiral William ("Bull") Halsey's Task Force 16. On April 18, the *Hornet* sighted a Japanese boat, which navy pilots quickly sank. Yet, fearing it might have had time to radio Japan, Halsey decided to launch the bombers immediately—some 800 miles from Japan rather than the planned 400. The pilots, who had trained for short take-offs but had never actually taken off from a flight deck, scrambled to their planes. One of them, Captain Ted W. Lawson, described the scene in his 1943 book *Thirty Seconds over Tokyo*:

> It was good enough flying weather, but the sea was tremendous. The *Hornet* bit into the rough-house waves, dipping and rising until the flat deck was a crazy see-saw. Some of the waves actually were breaking over the deck. . . . [Doolittle took off first] We watched him like hawks, wondering what the wind would do to him, and whether he could get off in that little run toward the bow. If he couldn't, we couldn't. Doolittle picked up more speed and held to his line, and, just as the *Hornet* lifted itself up on the top of a wave and cut through it at full speed, Doolittle's plane took off. . . . The engines of three other ships were warming up, and the thump and hiss of the turbulent sea made additional noise. But loud and clear above those sounds I could hear the hoarse cheers of every Navy man on the ship.

Loaded with two 500-pound high-explosive and two incendiary bombs each, the planes completed their mission, doing little physical damage, but shaking civilian confidence and enraging the Japanese high command (which moved

After dropping their bombs on the Japanese capital, most of Major General James Doolittle's Tokyo Raiders landed in China. Above, some of the survivors assemble for a photograph outside the mountain shelters where they hid from Japanese search parties. The map (below), showing major Japanese and coastal Chinese cities, was included in Thirty Seconds over Tokyo, *Captain Ted W. Lawson's account of the Doolittle raid.*

up the planned attack on Midway, see "Battle of Midway" later in this chapter). Flying on fumes after the raid, fifteen of the planes crash-landed in China and one landed at a Soviet air base north of Vladivostok. Seventy-two of the eighty crew members survived: of eight picked up by Japanese patrols, three were eventually executed, one died in prison, and four were released after the war. The Japanese also punished those who helped, or were suspected of helping, the American flyers. In May, the high command dispatched 53 battalions to destroy airfields and execute Chinese in the provinces where the planes landed. Over the following four months of terror, as many as 250,000 Chinese people were killed.

✻ ✻ ✻

As the units in China were engaged in the post-Doolittle-raid reign of terror, a Japanese fleet moved toward Papua, an Australian colony comprising the southeastern quarter of the island of New Guinea. In January, the Japanese had established bases in northeastern New Guinea, an Australian mandate, forcing the Australian units there to retreat into the mountains. If the Japanese also took Port Moresby, in the south, they could launch bombers to attack Australia, less than 400 miles away. Allied intelligence had caught wind of the Japanese movements, however, and Allied command formed Task Force 17 to stop the Japanese. In early May, Allied and Japanese forces clashed in the Coral Sea.

Battle of the Coral Sea, May 4–8, 1942
Pacific Theater

Primary Objectives: *Allied:* to prevent the Japanese from reaching Port Moresby, on the southeast coast of New Guinea; *Japanese:* to attack and take Port Moresby and Tulagi in the nearby Solomon Islands to expand bases to the east and protect the home islands from future air raids

Forces: *Allied (U.S., Australian):* Task Force 17, comprising 2 aircraft carrier groups (formed around USS *Yorktown* and USS *Lexington*), plus a combined force of 3 cruisers and 2 destroyers; *Japanese:* 2 large aircraft carriers (*Zuikaku* and *Shokaku*), 1 small aircraft carrier (*Shoho*), 6 cruisers, 7 destroyers

Commanders: *Allied:* Rear Admiral Frank Jack Fletcher (task force commander), Rear Admiral Aubrey Fitch (*Lexington* group), Rear Admiral John Crace, RN (combined cruiser-destroyer force); *Japanese:* Vice Admiral Inouye Shigeyoshi (operational commander), Vice Admiral Takagi Takeo (main carrier striking force)

Military Losses: *Allied:* 1 aircraft carrier, 1 destroyer, 1 oil tanker sunk, 543 killed; *Japanese:* 1 small aircraft carrier, 1 destroyer, one fleet carrier badly damaged, 1,074 killed

Result: Considered a tactical victory, but a strategic failure for the Japanese. The Allied fleet prevented the Japanese from taking Port Moresby and prevented two Japanese carriers from joining the battle at Midway.

On May 3, the Japanese landed unopposed on Tulagi, an island in the Solomons twenty miles north of Guadalcanal. The next day planes from the U.S. carrier *Yorktown* attacked Tulagi. The occupying force remained on the island but the vessels supporting the invasion retreated to Rabaul, New Britain. One day later, the Japanese carrier strike force and the Allied task force hunted each other. After contact was made on the morning of May 7, the Battle of Coral Sea began with an attack by aircraft from the *Yorktown* and *Lexington* that sank the Japanese small carrier *Shoho*; but the fiercest fighting took place May 8, as planes from both sides crisscrossed the 200 miles separating their fleets. The U.S. carrier *Lexington*, damaged by a dive-bomber torpedo attack, had to be scuttled when pierced fuel lines ignited and exploded. The Japanese heavy carrier *Shokaku* survived the battle—but was so severely damaged that it was not available a month later for the Battle of Midway. (Zuikaku was not at Midway because it had lost too many aircraft.) The loss of the *Lexington* made this a tactical victory for the Japanese; but it was a strategic victory for the Allies, who had forestalled Japan's Port Moresby operation. The Battle of the Coral Sea was the first naval battle in history where the two groups of ships were never in visual contact.

★   ★   ★

Thwarted in this seaward attempt at Port Moresby, the Japanese also missed the opportunity to establish a naval base at a strategic location off the east coast of Africa by preventive British action.

The Fight for Madagascar, May 5–November 5, 1942

In March, British intelligence learned that the Germans were urging Japan to occupy Madagascar, a French colony (in the Indian Ocean off the southeast coast of Africa) that had declared loyalty to the Vichy government after the British attack on the French Fleet at Mers-el-Kébir (see Chapter 6). Fearing the Axis would use the island as a base for attacks on British convoys, British chiefs of staff decided to capture Diégo-Suarez, the site of a large French naval base, at the north end of the island. The operation, code-named Ironclad, was the first Allied invasion, and Britain's first major amphibious operation, of the war.

On May 5, a strong naval force under Rear Admiral Neville Syfret landed a ground force comprising troops from Britain, British East Africa, and South Africa, led by Major General Robert Sturges. The Allies met stiff resistance but, following a diversionary night attack by Royal Marines on Antsirane on May 6, and with strong naval and air support, overcame the French, who retreated south the next day. The British had planned to go no further than Diégo-Suarez. However, the presence of at least one Japanese submarine in the area (a British battleship was damaged in an attack after the landings), the South African government's insistence that the island's other ports also be captured, and the Vichy governor's adamant refusal to surrender necessitated further action to secure the whole island. The campaign began on September 10 and concluded with an armistice on November 5 that gave the Free French control of the island.

★　★　★

One reason the Germans had been urging the Japanese to take Madagascar may have been a grand German plan to sweep into the Middle East, via Turkey, once the Wehrmacht had conquered the Soviet Union, and smash the British between that force and the Axis army in North Africa, while the Japanese in Madagascar covered their southern flank. But the Soviets, though severely battered, still refused to be conquered. Thus, Hitler—now in direct command of his Eastern-Front armies—planned a new offensive, code-named Blue, to begin as soon as the ground had hardened after the spring thaw.

The German Eastern-Front Offensive, "Operation Blue," from Kerch to Stalingrad, May 8–September 12, 1942

As winter turned into spring in the Soviet Union, the Wehrmacht's Army Group North was proceeding with its pitiless siege of Leningrad as the Russians within the city starved; Army Group Center now held its position after being forced 175 miles west of Moscow during the Soviets' counteroffensive;

and Army Group South was dug in behind Rostov-on-Don, the gateway to the Caucasus Mountains and Russia's rich oilfields. Stalin believed that the next major German offensive would be in the center—a renewed push toward Moscow. Hitler, however, declared in Führer Directive No. 41, issued on April 5, 1942, that, "all available forces will be concentrated on the *main operations in the Southern sector* [italics in the original text], with the aim of destroying the enemy before the Don, in order to secure the Caucasian oilfields."

On May 8, the Wehrmacht ripped into the Kerch peninsula in the Crimea with such force that the battle was over within a week. Only the port city of Sevastopol managed to hold out—until early July. As the Germans besieged that city, a Russian counterattack near Kharkov failed by late May. These actions were only a prelude to Operation Blue, which officially began June 28. Within a few days the Russian troops in the southern sector were falling back in confusion as German armored columns roared across the grassy steppes.

Acting under Hitler's Führer Directive No. 45 (July 23), Generalfeldmarschall Wilhelm List's Army Group A quickly swept south across the River Don and to the foothills of the Caucasus Mountains, where German soldiers raised the Nazi flag on Mount Elbrus, the highest peak in Europe, on August 21. As the Soviet forces fell back, they sabotaged the oil fields, leaving nothing of value for the oncoming German troops. List stood within seventy miles of the Caspian Sea, but when stiff Russian resistance in the mountains and logistical problems slowed his momentum, Hitler dismissed him and took command himself in early September. By that time, the Sixth Army under General Friedrich Paulus was outside of the major river port and railroad center of Stalingrad. Both arms of the Germans' southern offensive were poised to accomplish the goals Hitler had set for them. Yet they were at the end of very long supply lines, and another winter was fast approaching.

Meanwhile, the Red Army was not only facing an implacable invader, it was also dealing with morale problems within the ranks. On July 27, Stalin issued Order No. 227: "Panic-makers and cowards must be liquidated on the spot. Not one step backward without orders from higher headquarters. Commanders, commissars, and political workers who abandon a position without an order from higher headquarters are traitors to the Fatherland." For months Stalin had moved troops and materials into Stalingrad, appointed vigorous new commanders, and had his forces create multiple lines of defense. He made it clear that Order No. 227 was to be followed in Stalingrad most of all.

★ ★ ★

Stalin's western Allies, meanwhile, had informed the Communist dictator that they were not yet able to ease the pressure on the Soviets by staging a ground offensive in Europe that would draw German troops from the East. However, the Allies were proceeding with an aerial assault on Axis assets in Europe—a campaign that would steadily increase in destructive power.

The Strategic Bombing Campaign in Western Europe: 1942

Unlike the Axis, whose air forces engaged primarily in *tactical* operations (supporting ground and naval units in achieving particular military objectives), the Allies mounted concentrated *strategic* bombing campaigns (aimed at destroying such enemy assets as heavy industry, as well as civilian morale). In February, Air Chief Marshal Arthur Harris assumed control of the Royal Air Force Bomber Command and immediately stepped up aerial assaults on German cities and industrial areas. Harris's appointment coincided with two new developments: an influx of heavy four-engine bombers capable of carrying large bomb loads greater distances; and the introduction of *Gee*, a navigational tool that improved the ability of bombers to hit their targets at night. (Within six months, the Germans developed countermeasures for Gee—an example of the ongoing technological warfare waged behind the front lines; see Chapter 5.) Harris launched destructive raids on the German cities of Lübeck and Rostock—to which an enraged Hitler responded, from April to June, with the so-called Baedecker raids (named after a famous series of travel guidebooks) on the scenic English cities of Bath, Canterbury, Exeter, Norwich, and York. Undeterred, on May 30–31 Harris staged the first thousand-bomber raid, giving Cologne a terrible battering. People all over occupied Europe rejoiced at this raid, which essentially put all Germans on notice that, as Churchill told Roosevelt, "There is plenty more to come." Yet the Cologne bombing would be the only time in 1942 that Bomber Command could muster that much firepower at once.

As American forces arrived in Britain, U.S. commanders made it clear that, unlike the British nighttime area bombing (targeting entire areas), they envisioned a large daytime bombing force that would conduct precision attacks on key facilities—the electrical grid, transportation networks, aircraft factories, ball-bearing plants, and oil installations. (The technology necessary to hit targets with precision was, however, still being developed; see "Aircraft–Bombers" in Chapter 5.) The American air force made its first strategic bombing sortie to the Continent in August 1942 when B-17s, escorted by British fighters, attacked railroad yards in Rouen. Less than three months later, however, much of the U.S. Eighth Air Force's bomber command was diverted to the Mediterranean to support a new Allied offensive in North Africa—an area that had been the scene of heavy fighting throughout the year.

Western Desert Campaign, Part II: January–June 1942: Bitter Days for the Allies

As the newly formed Allied Combined Chiefs of Staff debated what, if any, offensives Anglo-American ground troops could mount on the European Continent proper in 1942, the seasaw battles across North Africa continued. With the Luftwaffe and the Italian air force focusing their attentions on Malta, Rommel's supply situation eased. In early January he received new tanks and fuel, and by January 21, his mixed German-Italian force was on the attack, within a week retaking Benghazi, about one hundred miles to the northwest of El Agheila (at the eastern edge of the Libyan province of Cyrenaica, where they had withdrawn the previous December). There they paused until May 26, when Rommel led them against the new British line some 200 miles to the west. The Gazala Line comprised a series of strongpoints stretching from Gazala to Bir Hakeim, and it lay only about forty miles east of the vital port city of Tobruk.

Combining a frontal assault with a right-hook strike against the most southerly strongpoint, Rommel ran into a heavier Allied force than he had anticipated, new American-manufactured Grant tanks, and unexpectedly tenacious resistance by Lieutenant General Marie Pierre Koenig's 1st Free French Brigade in the south at Bir Hakeim. After three days of hard-fought armored warfare, Rommel withdrew to reorganize his forces and his supply lines. He was not immediately pursued by the British, whose commander, Lieutenant General Neil Ritchie, initially believed the battle was over. Belated attempts to crush Rommel were not successful. When, on June 10, Rommel's men finally pushed the French out of Bir Hakeim, the Gazala Line was no longer a tenable defensive line. The British withdrew, leaving the way to Tobruk open. The swift fall of the long-besieged port city on

June 21 was a bitter blow to British morale. In Washington for a meeting, Churchill learned of Tobruk's fall from President Roosevelt, who asked him what America could do to help. "Give us as many Sherman tanks as you can spare, and ship them to the Middle East as quickly as possible," Churchill replied. Within three days, 100 tanks and an equal number of self-propelled guns were on their way. Yet transport took time, and on June 26–27, after Rommel's forces hit them again at the Egyptian port town of Mersa Matruh, the British had to withdraw once more—to El Alamein, only sixty miles from their Mediterranean Fleet base at Alexandria.

★   ★   ★

While Rommel's forces were closing in on Tobruk, Japanese and American fleets met in a battle that proved to be a turning point in the Pacific War.

BATTLE OF MIDWAY, JUNE 3–6, 1942
PACIFIC THEATER

Primary Objectives: *American:* to protect Midway and Hawaii and destroy the Japanese fleet; *Japanese:* to invade and take Midway Island (depriving the Americans of a forward submarine base), while simultaneously staging a (partly diversionary) attack on the Aleutian Islands—thus forcing the U.S. fleet into a decisive sea battle. In Japanese hands, Midway could also be a base for a campaign to push the Americans out of Hawaii.

Forces: *American:* 2 carrier forces with 3 carriers (*Enterprise, Hornet, Yorktown*), 8 cruisers, 15 destroyers, 230 aircraft; *Japanese:* a carrier fleet comprising 4 carriers (*Akagi, Hiryu, Kaga, Soryu*), 2 battleships, 3 cruisers, 12 destoyers, 270 aircraft; a battle fleet comprising 7 battleships, 1 light carrier, 3 cruisers, 13 destroyers; the Midway Assault Group comprising 1 carrier, 2 battleships, 10 cruisers, 21 destroyers; the Aleutian Assault Group comprising 2 light carriers, 5 cruisers, 13 destroyers, 15 submarines

Commanders: *American:* Fleet Admiral Chester W. Nimitz (commander in chief, Pacific Fleet), Vice Admiral Frank Jack Fletcher (tactical command, until his flagship, *Yorktown*, was sunk), Admiral Raymond A. Spruance (commander Task Force 16, built around *Enterprise* and *Hornet*, and assumed tactical command from Fletcher); *Japanese:* Admiral Isoroku Yamamoto (commander of the Combined Fleet), Vice Admiral Chuichi Nagumo (carrier strike force)

Military Losses: *American:* 1 aircraft carrier, 1 destroyer sunk, 307 killed; *Japanese:* 4 aircraft carriers, 1 cruiser sunk, 250 planes shot down, 3,000 killed

Result: A pivotal victory for U.S. naval forces and the first American battle victory of the war, boosting U.S. morale. Japan lost four of its six first-line fleet carriers, as well as over 300 airplanes and many well-trained pilots, mechanics, and crewmen. This defeat caused the Japanese to delay an offensive in New Guinea and postpone plans to advance on New Caledonia, Fiji, and Samoa.

In early May, Allied cryptanalytic units were reading about 90 percent of ordinary Japanese cryptograms using the naval code, JN-25b. Thus, Nimitz knew that the Japanese planned to attack Midway in early June. The admiral quickly sent 3 carriers—including the *Yorktown*, its damage from the Battle of the Coral Sea hastily repaired—more than 200 airplanes, and an escort including 7 heavy cruisers to the waters near Midway before Japanese submarines could get in place to intercept them. By May 25, Nimitz also knew Japan's move on the Aleutian Islands was chiefly diversionary and that the main Japanese strike, at Midway, would occur on June 4. Even so, the Americans were at a serious disadvantage; Yamamoto was prepared to use the entire might of his navy to achieve a decisive victory.

On June 3, American land-based bombers spotted and attacked the Japanese invasion force, doing little damage. At dawn the next day, Nagumo launched his initial attack: 108 aircraft bombed and heavily damaged the U.S. base on Midway. Advised that a second bombing wave would be necessary, Nagumo ordered his reserve torpedo-bombers rearmed; the work was in progress when a scout plane discovered the American naval force. Nagumo decided to wait for his first strike force to return from Midway before launching the reserves. This was the situation when low-flying torpedo-bombers from *Enterprise*, *Hornet*, and *Yorktown* staged their initial attack. It was a disaster: the Japanese combat air patrol, flying the much faster Zero fighters, quickly destroyed all but 6 of 41 U.S. torpedo-bombers, and none of the attacking planes had scored hits. However, the U.S. planes had prevented the Japanese from launching more fighters and had drawn the combat air patrol to lower altitudes.

The Japanese carriers were still rearming their own attack aircraft. Their decks were filled with planes, bombs, and torpedoes when high-flying American SBD Dauntless dive-bombers from *Enterprise* attacked *Soryu* and

A Japanese dive-bomber plunges toward the ocean after being hit by antiair-craft fire from a navy carrier.

Akagi, and planes from *Yorktown* attacked the *Kaga*. Within minutes, all three targets were so badly damaged the Japanese had to scuttle them. Counterattacking, dive-bombers from the surviving Japanese fleet carrier, *Hiryu*, badly damaged the *Yorktown*. After more damage was done by a second strike, Fletcher ordered his men to abandon ship. (A Japanese submarine finished *Yorktown* on June 7.) The strikes on *Yorktown* were *Hiryu*'s last actions before planes from the *Enterprise* left

the carrier ablaze. The night of June 4–5, the Japanese suffered another disaster: while trying to evade an American submarine, the cruiser *Mogami* rammed the cruiser *Mikuma*. Attacking the damaged ships June 5 and 6, U.S. planes sank *Mikuma* and further damaged *Mogami*. By that time, the Americans had dealt the Imperial Japanese Navy its first major defeat—and a blow from which it would never recover. Yet, as the surviving ships moved away, they left behind a ground force successfully established on a chain of islands that might be used as stepping stones toward the coast of North America.

Aleutian Islands Campaign Begins, June 5–7, 1942

The Americans and the Japanese each feared that the other would someday use the Aleutian Islands, stretching from North America far into the Pacific Ocean, as a base for hostile action. Yet, the Japanese occupation of two of the westernmost Aleutians was chiefly diversionary—part of the plan to draw the U.S. Pacific Fleet north and divide it, to help assure Japanese victory at the Battle of Midway. Advised by intelligence, Admiral Nimitz kept the most powerful elements of the fleet near Midway—but he also dispatched Task Force 8, under Rear Admiral Robert Theobald, to the stormy, mist-shrouded Aleutian waters. Theobald believed that the Japanese were actually heading toward Alaska (the Japanese did stage a diversionary air attack on the eastern Aleutian island of Unalaska). However, Vice Admiral Hosogaya Boshiro's task force was aiming for Kiska and Attu, where they landed unopposed on June 5 and 7— and remained for three days before the Americans realized they were on the two islands. For the rest of the year, U.S. ships and planes harassed the Japanese from new air bases constructed on Adak and Amchitka islands. But the Americans were not yet ready to launch an invasion to drive the Japanese out.

★   ★   ★

The Japanese digging in on Kiska and Attu were at the end of a long supply line that their battered navy would find difficult to maintain. Across the world in North Africa, Erwin Rommel was also facing supply problems as he prepared to move forward in Egypt: Allied planes that had recently arrived on the island of Malta were hitting the convoys carrying supplies for the Afrika Korps. Despite shortages of fuel and equipment, Rommel, the "Desert Fox"—looking toward Alexandria and the crucially important Suez Canal—attacked the British at El Alamein.

FGHTING NEAR EL ALAMEIN, JULY 1–SEPTEMBER 4, 1942
MEDITERRANEAN THEATER (NORTH AFRICA)

Primary Objectives: *Allied:* to hold Axis forces and prevent them from conquering Egypt and capturing the Suez Canal; *Axis:* to break through British lines or keep them retreating toward Alexandria and Cairo

Forces: *Allied:* 150,000 British and Commonwealth troops of the Eighth Army in 3 army corps, 7 infantry, and 3 armored divisions 1,114 tanks; 1,500 planes; *Axis:* 40,000 Germans (including 2 Afrika Korps panzer divisions), 56,000 Italian infantry and armored troops, 585 tanks (panzers and Italian) of the Panzer Army Africa, 500 aircraft

Commanders: *Allied:* General Sir Claude Auchinleck; *Axis:* Field Marshal Erwin Rommel

Result: Despite two months of attacks and counterattacks, neither side really could claim a victory, though the Allied forces kept the Axis from advancing on Alexandria.

On July 1, Rommel's forces attacked the El Alamein line, but Allied units kept them from breaking through. Counterattacking the next day, the British swept around Rommel from the south, keeping him from Alexandria and making his unfavorable situation worse. By July 3, the Panzer Army Africa was low on ammunition and reduced to 36 tanks. This four-day encounter is often referred to as the First Battle of El Alamein, but the fighting did not end when Rommel's men failed to break through.

A week later, armed with information from Ultra intelligence intercepts, Auchinleck altered his strategy and attacked Italian units under Rommel's command. By July 17, Rommel was writing his wife, "The enemy is using his superiority, especially in infantry, to destroy the Italian formations one by one, and the German formations are much too weak to stand alone. It's enough to make one weep." Through the rest of July, both sides attacked and counterattacked in battles marred by confusion, dwindling supplies, and poor coordination between infantry and armor units. In August, as the combatants paused to regroup, Churchill appointed General Sir Harold Alexander to replace Auchinleck as Commander in Chief, Middle East. That same month, after Sir William Gott was killed on his way to assume command of the British Eighth Army, Churchill appointed Lieutenant General Bernard Montgomery to replace him. Montgomery's arrival in North Africa on August 15 marked the beginning of a new chapter in the Western Desert Campaign. He instilled fresh spirit in his British and Commonwealth troops as he prepared them for new encounters with a determined enemy.

Again assisted by Ultra intelligence, the British were able to sink Axis ships carrying tank and aircraft fuel at the end of the month. Yet Rommel still decided to hit the El Alamein line again on August 30, telling a colleague that it was "the most serious [decision] I have taken in my life. Either the Army in Russia succeeds in getting through to Grozny, and we in Africa manage to reach the Suez Canal or—." His body language made clear that the "or" was German defeat. In a week of furious fighting at Alam Halfa, in front of the El Alamein line, Axis troops again failed to break through the stout resistance of British, New Zealand, Australian, South African, and Indian troops. With next to no fuel, Rommel began to withdraw as Allied aircraft pounded his retreating columns. Montgomery had achieved his first North African victory.

★ ★ ★

During the following two months, Montgomery carefully planned his next moves, while Rommel returned to Germany on sick leave, lamenting his low fuel supplies and the generally dismal state of his logistics. Meanwhile, the Allies had opened a new—and harrowing—route to funnel supplies into China.

Going over "The Hump," July 1942–1945

After the Japanese severed the southern end of the Burma Road in April, the India-China Wing of the U.S. Air Transport Command opened an air-supply route between India and China. Dubbed "the Hump," this route required pilots to fly from bases in India and—flying at their maximum altitude and using oxygen masks—thread through 15,000-foot-high mountain ridges in the wind-swept Himalayas to reach Kunming, China. Beset by ice, terrible weather, and enemy planes, they soon began calling the treacherous route the "Aluminum Trail" because of all the planes that crashed along the way. During the first month, U.S. pilots delivered 82 tons of supplies via the Hump; in December they delivered 1,000 tons. Yet this was far from enough to satisfy the needs of Allied forces in the China-Burma-India Theater. More people and planes were put into the effort, and monthly tallies steadily rose—as did the number of plane crashes (in January 1945, alone, there were 23). By the end of the war, the 22,000 servicemen and 47,000 civilians of the India-China Wing had delivered 650,000 tons of supplies to China.

★　★　★

As the first U.S. planes were braving the Hump, farther south, in the Pacific Theater, Allied troops under General Douglas MacArthur were planning to go on the offensive in what would be a three-year New Guinea Campaign. Responding to high-command orders to remove Japanese troops that had landed, in March, at Lae and Salamaua on the northeast coast of the island, MacArthur ordered his small Allied force to move from the southeastern coast, across the Owen Stanley Mountains via the treacherous jungle path called the Kokoda Trail, to the northeastern coast, below the Japanese. Before they could do this, however, Japanese units under Major General Horii Tomitaro landed on the northeastern coast (July 12) precisely where the Allies were headed. The Japanese quickly moved inland, pushing an Australian battalion and a Papuan regiment before them, while Japanese reinforcements landed to secure the beachhead. Tomitaro's troops faced limited opposition; only a few Australian reinforcements joined their colleagues in the terrible contest on the Kokoda Trail. MacArthur had turned his attention to preparing for a Japanese landing at Milne Bay on the extreme southeastern tip of the island. When the landing occurred, the night of August 25–26, Australian troops and air units assisted by American engineers prevented the invaders from holding their beachhead. By September 4, the Japanese had withdrawn from Milne Bay.

By that time, in the nearby Solomon Islands, U.S. Marines were waging the first entirely American ground offensive of the Pacific War.

OPERATION WATCHTOWER AND THE BATTLE FOR GUADALCANAL, AUGUST 7, 1942–FEBRUARY 1943
PACIFIC THEATER

Primary Objectives: *American:* to prevent the Japanese from advancing southward toward Australia and severing communication lines between Australia and the USA and to capture a partially built Japanese airfield before it became operational; *Japanese:* to hold their bases in the Solomons

Forces: *American:* initially, 19,000 marines—10,000+ on Guadalcanal, eventually more than 50,000 on Guadalcanal; *Japanese:* initially 8,400 troops on Guadalcanal—eventually more than 30,000

Commanders: *American:* Vice Admiral Robert L. Ghormley (C in C, South Pacific Area) replaced on October 18, 1942 by Vice Admiral William F. Halsey; Rear Admiral Thomas Kinkaid, Vice Admiral Frank J. Fletcher (air support from three-carrier task force), Rear Admiral Richmond K. Turner (amphibious force), and Major General Alexander A. Vandegrift (1st Marine Division) until December 8, 1942, then Major General Alexander M. Patch (XIV Corps including 2nd Marine Division); *Japanese:* Vice Admiral Mikawa Gunichi, Admiral Kondo Nobutake, Admiral Tanaka Raizo, Lieutenant General Hyakutake Haruyoshi (Seventeenth Army)

Military Losses: *American:* 7,100 killed and missing; *Japanese:* over 22,000 troops killed (including more than 9,000 to disease or starvation) during the entire Guadalcanal campaign

Result: After six months of fierce fighting, the Americans pushed the Japanese off Guadalcanal, stopping Japan's southward advance and keeping access to Australia open.

The first major U.S. ground offensive of the war, Operation Watchtower, began on August 7, when U.S. Marines landed on several Japanese-held islands in the Solomon chain, including Guadalcanal, Tulagi, Florida, Gavutu, and Tanambogo. Though they met fierce resistance on some of the other islands, the landing on Guadalcanal initially went very smoothly. The Americans quickly captured the small airfield the Japanese were building and

Above, photographer Sergeant John A. Bushemi and correspondent Sergeant Mack Morris of the U.S. Army's weekly magazine, Yank, take a break on New Georgia in the Solomon Islands in 1943. On February 19, 1944, Bushemi was killed by a mortar shell as he photographed the American landing on the island of Eniwetok. In his photo (below), a machine gunner looks for enemy targets on New Georgia.

named it Henderson Field (in honor of Major Lofton R. Henderson, a Marine pilot killed at Midway). This was just the first act in a long battle in which the island, itself, would prove to be almost as difficult an adversary as the Japanese (see box).

As a prelude to the months of hard fighting that would follow the Americans' "soft" landing, the Japanese dealt an American naval force screening the Guadalcanal operations a bitter defeat at the battle of Savo Sound on the night of August 8–9. Seven cruisers and one destroyer commanded by Vice Admiral Gunichi demonstrated the Japanese navy's marked superiority at night attacks by slipping past guarding destroyers to sink four U.S. cruisers and a destroyer, damage a cruiser, and kill or wound nearly 2,000 Allied seamen. Admiral Fletcher had already withdrawn his carriers (due to lack of fuel and fear they would be lost if they remained in close support of island operations). After Savo Sound, Admiral Turner pulled the other ships back, leaving the Marines on Guadalcanal without air support and low on critical supplies. Augmenting what they had with captured material—and with a small supply drop on August 15—they repaired the airstrip in time for its use by more than 30 Marine Corps planes that arrived on August 20. On the same day, the Japanese, who had been reinforced on August 18, precipitated the Battle of Tenaru River (actually fought on the River Ilu) and lost 900 of their troops.

GUADALCANAL: THE ISLAND AS ENEMY

A teenage U.S. Marine during the war, historian William Manchester provided a vivid description of Guadalcanal in his 1980 memoir *Goodbye Darkness*:

Except for occasional patches of shoulder-high kunai grass, the blades of which could lay a man's hand open as quickly as a scalpel, the tropical forest swathed the island. . . . It looked solid enough to walk on. In reality the ground—if you could find it—lay a hundred feet below the cloying beauty of the treetops, the cathedrals of banyan, ipils, and eucalyptus. In between were thick, steamy, matted, almost impenetrable screens of cassia, liana vines, and twisted creepers, masked here and there by mangrove swamps and clumps of bamboo. . . . The forest [emitted] faint whiffs of foul breath, a vile stench of rotting undergrowth and stink lilies. [Soldiers were warned of] serpents, crocodiles, centipedes, land crabs, scorpions, lizards, tree leeches, cockatoos that screamed like the leader of a banzai charge, wasps as long as your finger and spiders as large as your fist, and mosquitoes, mosquitoes, mosquitoes, all carriers of malaria.

Meanwhile, a group of fast destroyers, dubbed the "Tokyo Express," began shelling the island nightly (when U.S. planes could not operate as effectively) to cover a buildup of infantry and supplies. September 12–14, the 3,000-strong Kawaguchi Brigade and survivors of the Tenaru River battle launched, and Marines repulsed, a series of major attacks at *Bloody Ridge* near Henderson Field. In two intense days, 1,500 Japanese and 40 Americans were killed.

October 11–12, the Americans, assisted by radar, had their first success fighting a night engagement against the Japanese in the confused action of the Battle of Cape Esperance (both navies fired on their own ships). The Americans lost one destroyer, but damaged the Japanese flagship *Aoba* (fleet leader Rear Admiral Aritomo Goto was killed) and sank one cruiser and one destroyer. Two nights later, the Japanese battleships *Kongo* and *Haruna* pounded Henderson field for ninety minutes, destroying fifty planes—one-half the U.S. complement. The next day, a Japanese convoy unloaded more troops bringing the total on the island to 22,000, versus the Americans' 23,000. Immediately before the U.S. Navy fended off a large Japanese naval force at the Battle of the Santa Cruz Islands (October 26–27), during which the American carrier USS *Hornet* was lost, the Japanese launched a third counterattack, a land assault known as the Battle of Henderson Field (October 24–26). The crucially important airfield remained in American hands.

With additional reinforcements, by early November Japanese troops outnumbered Americans on Guadalcanal. The situation had become so precarious that Admiral William Halsey rushed 6,000 additional troops to the island and Roosevelt interceded to ensure additional cruisers, destroyers, and submarines were sent to the South Pacific. This buildup led directly into a series of engagements, November 11–15, collectively known as the Naval Battle of Guadalcanal, in which both Americans and Japanese suffered heavy losses. During the first of these engagements—a confused melee the night of November 11–12, the Americans sank four Japanese ships and the Japanese sank six U.S. vessels. One was the cruiser USS *Juneau*, on which all five sons of Mr. and Mrs. Thomas F. Sullivan of Waterloo, Iowa, were serving. George, 29, Francis, 26, Joseph 23, Madison, 22, and Albert, 20, all died either in the initial attack or in the sea afterward. Further naval encounters damaged both sides, but unlike the Americans, the Japanese knew they had little hope of replacing the vessels they were losing. Although they continued their attempts to reinforce their Guadalcanal garrison, after a naval engagement at Tassafaronga Point, November 30, the Japanese realized they could not afford the naval losses required to hold the island.

On land, the advantage shifted decidedly in favor of the Americans. In December, Major General Alexander M. Patch assumed command of a force that, by January, stood at more than 50,000 infantrymen and Marines. Though the Japanese fought bravely, at the end of the month, they were ordered to withdraw. In daring night operations in early February, more than 10,000 troops—including General Haruyoshi—were ferried safely off the island to waiting destroyers.

★   ★   ★

On another island—this one in the Mediterranean—both military forces and civilians were desperately holding on through a determined Axis campaign to destroy them.

The Siege of Malta, Part II: Some Relief by Operation Pedestal, August 10–15, 1942

After Field Marshal Albert Kesselring arrived in Sicily as Commander in Chief South in December 1941, the Luftwaffe concentrated its attentions on Malta, and Axis supply problems in North Africa dramatically decreased. Mussolini strongly backed an invasion of the island, but by spring, Hitler had decided against it. Yet that provided little relief to the Maltese. Subjected to unrelenting air attacks, they were also nearly cut off from much-needed supplies that could be brought in only by ship. Axis air and U-boat attacks decimated a convoy attempting to reach the island from Alexandria, Egypt, in June (Operation Vigorous). In August, the Allies tried again with Operation Pedestal (August 10–15), when a convoy of 14 freighters, under heavy escort, sailed toward Malta from Gibralter. It, too, came under fierce attack—more than half the freighters were sunk. But the 42,000 tons of food and fuel the surviving ships delivered, all carefully rationed, allowed the long-suffering Maltese to survive. Meanwhile, Malta's striking power was gradually reinforced: aircraft were flown in from May through December, many of them long-range torpedo planes. By November these planes, Allied submarines, and mines had pushed Axis shipping losses to an all-time high of 77 percent. By that time, the Allies had retaken airfields in Libya from which Axis planes had sortied to strike Malta, and another convoy (Operation Stonehenge) had arrived from Alexandria—barely in time. The Maltese only had fuel for a week and less than a two-week supply of food left. By the end of the year, although the island remained an Axis target, the worst of the siege of Malta was over. (See also Chapter 6.)

★   ★   ★

At the same time the surviving ships of Operation Pedestal were bringing relief to the Maltese, the Allies were staging a disastrous hit-and-run assault on the coast of France. Mounted to test coastal defenses and amphibious landing tactics, to demonstrate to the people of occupied Europe that they had not been forgotten—and to respond to Joseph Stalin's continuing insistence that his Allies open a second front in western Europe—the commando raid on Dieppe (Operation Jubilee), August 19, 1942, was ill-omened from the start. By the time it was over, more than 1,000 of the 6,000 participating commandos were dead, another 2,000 were prisoners, and the RAF had lost more than a hundred planes. Whether these heavy losses were worth the major lesson the Allies learned from the venture—that heavy bombardment must precede any major landing—is still being debated.

Moreover, the raid did nothing to remove Soviet pressure for action, for the Soviets were hard-pressed themselves. Units of the German Sixth Army under Field Marshal Friedrich Paulus were preparing to take Stalingrad on the Volga River—a gateway to Asia, and a city that Stalin was determined to hold. Pouring reinforcements into the sector, the Soviet dictator also shifted Marshal Georgii Zhukov from Moscow to the Stalingrad front and put General Vasili Chuikov in charge of the city's defenses. In mid-September, the battle was joined.

BATTLE OF STALINGRAD, SEPTEMBER 12, 1942–FEBRUARY 1943
EUROPEAN THEATER (EAST)

Primary Objectives: *Soviet:* to maintain control of a strategic city; *Axis:* to capture Stalingrad and thus gain control of an important rail terminus on a major river and control valuable industrial resources

Forces: *Soviet:* 3 fronts (army groups) comprising 1.7 million troops; *Axis:* German Sixth Army, German 4th Panzer Army, Romanian Third and Fourth Armies, Hungarian Second Army, Italian Eighth Army

Commanders: *Soviet:* Marshal Georgi Zhukov, General Vasili Chuikov; *Axis:* Field Marshal Freidrich Paulus

Military Losses: *Soviet:* 478,741 killed, 650,878 wounded, 40,000 civilians killed; *Axis:* more than 200,000 Germans, an estimated 173,000

Romanians, 105,000 Italians, 146,000 Hungarians, and 5,000 Croats were killed in the entire Stalingrad campaign; only 5,000 of the 90,000 Germans taken prisoner at the end of the battle survived the forced march to Siberia and Soviet captivity

Result: A German defeat that marked a turning point in the European Theater and the entire war; Allied armies everywhere now had ample evidence that the German war machine could be beaten. The Soviet Union emerged as a major military power.

The first phase of the battle began in September with thousands of Luftwaffe bombing runs to "soften up" Soviet defenses. By September 22, the Germans penetrated into the central city initiating four months of vicious house-to-house and hand-to-hand combat (punctuated by artillery duels and major offensives surrounding the city). Chuikov had mined many of the buildings and laced the city with sniper posts.

With his troops bogged down in Stalingrad's rubble, struggling against an enemy that held on to bits and pieces of buildings as if they were precious stones, an angry Hitler replaced General Franz Halder as Chief of the Army General Staff with General Kurt Zeitzler. Meanwhile, between September 25 and October 5, a total of 160,000 fresh Soviet troops crossed the Volga into the city. On November 19–20, the Soviets hurled six armies at the Axis forces; they smashed through two Romanian armies and, by November 23,

---

EYEWITNESS ACCOUNT: FIGHTING AT STALINGRAD

Soviet *Red Star* correspondent Vasily Grossman arrived in Stalingrad soon after the battle began; among those he interviewed was 19-year-old sniper Anatoly Ivanovich Chekhov:

When I first got the rifle, I couldn't bring myself to kill a living being: one German was standing there for about four minutes, talking, and I let him go. When I killed my first one, he fell at once. Another one ran out and stooped over the killed one, and I knocked him down, too. . . . I felt scared: I'd killed a person! Then I remembered our people and started killing them without mercy. . . . I've become a beast of a man: . . . I've killed forty men, . . . Sometimes . . . in the evening, I look around and my heart sings, I would love to spend half an hour in a city which is alive. I come out and think: the Volga is flowing so quietly, how come such terrible things are happening here?

completely encircled the Wehrmacht troops that were encircling the city. The Sixth Army was now in a trap, and winter was nearly upon them. Compounding their difficulties, Luftwaffe commander Hermann Göring was unable to keep his promise that the Luftwaffe would fly in all the supplies the Sixth Army required. Weather and maintenance problems intruded, as did the need to send additional men and planes to North Africa, where Axis forces were caught between two Allied forces after the Anglo-American Torch landings November 8 (see "Operation Torch" later in this chapter.)

Hitler refused Paulus's request to attempt a breakout and instead scraped together a new force, Army Group Don that comprised armored units along with the remains of the two nearly destroyed Romanian armies—and directed its commander, Field Marshal Erich von Manstein, to break the Soviet encirclement. While von Manstein dispatched a relief force (Operation Winter Storm), Zhukov launched an operation (Little Saturn) to push Army Group

Two German sailors hunker down in a bunker outside the occupied city of Novgorad, 120 miles southeast of Leningrad in January 1943 (left). Captured German officers await their fate in the hands of the Red Army. More than twenty German generals were among the 90,000 German troops captured after their defeat at Stalingrad (right).

Don away from Stalingrad. During this confusions of offensives, the Germans failed to relieve Paulus and the Soviets smashed another Axis army, the Italian Eighth. In January, Paulus lost his last airfield and with it any chance of receiving even meager supplies. Moreover, his troops were now divided into two small pockets within Stalingrad and had no hope of relief. On January 31 (the day Hitler promoted him to Field Marshal), Paulus surrendered—an act that his führer contemptuously described as less than "what a weakling of a woman can do." Hitler ordered the troops in the other Stalingrad pocket to fight to the last man; but two days later, they, too, capitulated.

A terrible blow to the Germans and their Axis partners, and a grand boost to the Soviets, the Red Army's victory at Stalingrad also erased prevailing doubts among British and American war planners that the Soviet Union would survive. Future Allied strategic planning could assume that the Soviets would continue to keep significant German forces tied down in the East.

★   ★   ★

In mid-October, as Paulus's cornered army was dodging snipers in the Stalingrad trap, Axis forces near El Alamein in North Africa were facing a new Allied challenge. General Bernard Montgomery, now in command of the British Eighth Army, had more tanks and significantly more artillery and aircraft than the Axis units facing his forces possessed. Montgomery also had the advantage of Ultra intelligence regarding German strength, logistics, and troop positions. Yet Axis forces were not without advantages. Before Field Marshal Rommel left for Germany on sick leave, he had strengthened his defenses, which now included five-mile-deep arrays of carefully placed antitank guns as well as more than half a million antitank mines interspersed with smaller antipersonnel devices—lethal fields the Germans dubbed the "Garden of Death." These defenses would slow Allied progress as Montgomery began his campaign to push the Axis out of Egypt.

SECOND BATTLE OF EL ALAMEIN, OCTOBER 23–NOVEMBER 4, 1942
MEDITERRANEAN THEATER (NORTH AFRICA)

Primary Objectives: *Allied:* to break the enemy line and push Axis forces out of Egypt; *Axis:* to hold their line so that they might eventually move forward to take Alexandria and the Suez Canal

Forces: *Allied:* 195,000 men (including troops from Australia, New Zealand, South Africa), 1,030 tanks (including new U.S. Sherman tanks), 2,182 artillery pieces, 530 fighter planes, 200 bombers; *Axis:* 50,000 Germans, 54,000 Italians, 496 tanks, 500 artillery pieces, 350 aircraft

Commanders: *Allied:* Field Marshal Bernard Law Montgomery; *Axis:* General Georg Stumme (died October 23); Field Marshal Erwin Rommel (returned to Egypt October 25)

Military Losses: *Allied:* 23,500 dead or wounded; *Axis:* 59,000 killed, wounded, or captured (34,000 German, 25,000 Italian)

Result: An Allied victory, and one of the pivotal battles of the war. After second El Alamein and the November Torch landings (see "Operation Torch" later in this chapter) the Axis was on the defensive in North Africa.

The British began their attack at 9:40 P.M. on October 23 with a 1,000-gun artillery barrage along the forty-mile front. Montgomery's troops advanced with four infantry divisions working to clear paths through the minefields for the armored divisions. After Stumme, the acting German commander, died of a heart attack in this first onslaught, Rommel returned to duty, arriving in North Africa on October 25. Shortly thereafter, the Germans launched fierce counterattacks. The Allies responded with heavy air attacks and artillery bombardments—but after two days of fierce combat, they still had not broken through the German lines. Finally, on November 2, in a push code-named Operation Supercharge, Montgomery's troops succeeded. By the end of the day, Rommel had only 35 German and 20 Italian tanks able to fight while Montgomery had two armored divisions in reserve.

When Rommel radioed Hitler that he was planning to withdraw 40 miles to the west, the führer responded: "It would not be the first time in history that the stronger will has triumphed over the enemy's strong battalions. You can show your troops no other way than that which leads to victory or to death." General Ritter von Thoma, the Afrika Korps commander, said, "Hitler's order is a piece of unparalleled madness." On November 4, as Rommel ordered his troops to withdraw, Thoma surrendered personally to Montgomery. Rommel later wrote, "From that time on, we had continually to circumvent orders from the Führer or Duce in order to save the army from destruction."

On November 10, after Rommel and the battered remnants of his army had fallen back through Sidi Barrani, Winston Churchill told guests at a

London event: "This is not the end. It is not even the beginning of the end, but it is perhaps the end of the beginning." Three days later, British forces retook Tobruk.

*   *   *

As Rommel staged a masterly withdrawal westward, into Libya and toward Tunisia, British and American ships arrived off the northwest African coast to begin the first major Anglo-American offensive of the war.

The North African Campaign Begins: The Anglo-American Landings in Northwest Africa

Roosevelt, who had promised Stalin the western Allies would begin an invasion in 1942, directed his military advisers to reach an agreement with the British for an offensive that could take place before the end of the year. In July (over the strenuous objections of U.S. Army Chief of Staff George C. Marshall, among others), the Allies agreed to mount Operation Torch, a landing in North Africa that Roosevelt keenly supported. At this stage in the war, a North Africa landing had a much greater chance for success than an amphibious assault on western Europe. Winning North Africa would also give the Allies bases that could be used to support operations against Axis forces in Italy, Greece, or mainland Europe and bomb Mediterranean shipping and targets in southern Europe.

Under an agreement reached by Roosevelt, Churchill, and the Combined Chiefs of Staff, the Mediterranean region was primarily a British responsibility. (See "Allied Military Coordination" in Chapter 4.) However, since most invasion troops were to be American, the British asked for an American commander. The American high command's choice, Lieutenant General Dwight D. Eisenhower, expended great effort to create a well-coordinated Anglo-American command.

The troops the Allies would be facing in northwestern Africa were primarily Vichy French. The United States still had diplomatic relations with Vichy and wished to find an accommodation that would not only prevent strong Vichy resistance to the landings but would also encourage the French in North Africa to join the Allies. Therefore, as Montgomery was preparing to strike at El Alamein, General Mark Clark held secret meetings in Algeria with Major General Charles Mast, a representative of French hero General Henri Giraud, (see Chapter 4). Just before the landings, Robert Murphy, President Roosevelt's personal representative in North Africa, advised General Alphonse Juin, the commander of Vichy French forces there, that the operation was about to begin. Negotiations with the French continued during Torch with results that included a cease-fire agreement between the Allies and Vichy North African authorities two days after the initial landings, disruption of Vichy-U.S. diplomatic relations, and the German occupation of Vichy territory, including Tunisia, toward which Rommel was then retreating. All this was of little immediate moment to the American troops involved in Torch, most of whom were assaulting an enemy beachhead for the first time.

OPERATION TORCH (CASABLANCA, ORAN, ALGIERS), NOVEMBER 8–11, 1942
MEDITERRANEAN THEATER (NORTH AFRICA)

Primary Objectives: *Allied:* to (eventually) gain control of North Africa from the Atlantic to the Red Sea, relieve pressure on the Soviet Union by placing greater strain on the Axis, and build up a force in Morocco in case the Spanish or Germans tried to take Gibraltar; *Axis:* to keep the Allies from gaining a foothold in northwest Africa

Forces: *Allied:* 670 vessels (300 warships, including escort and aircraft carriers; 370 merchant ships and transports), about 65,000 men involved in the actual landing; *Axis:* about 120,000 Vichy French troops

Commanders: *Allied:* Lieutenant General Dwight D. Eisenhower (supreme commander), Major General Mark Clark (deputy supreme commander), Brigadier General James Doolittle (western air commander), Lieutenant General Kenneth Anderson, Admiral Sir Andrew B. Cunningham (naval commander, expeditionary force), Air Marshal William Welsh (eastern air commander), Major General George Patton (western invasion force), Major General Lloyd Fredendall (central invasion force), Major General Charles Ryder (eastern invasion force); *Axis:* Admiral Jean François Darlan (commander in chief, Vichy French forces), General Alphonse Juin (commander, Vichy land forces in North Africa)

Military Losses: *Allied:* 556 Americans killed, 837 wounded; 330 total British casualties; *Axis:* 700 Vichy French killed and approximately 1,400 wounded

Result: A swift and dramatic Allied victory. Within seventy-six hours of the first landings, Allied troops were in undisputed control of 1,300 miles of the African coast, from Safi, Morocco, to Algiers.

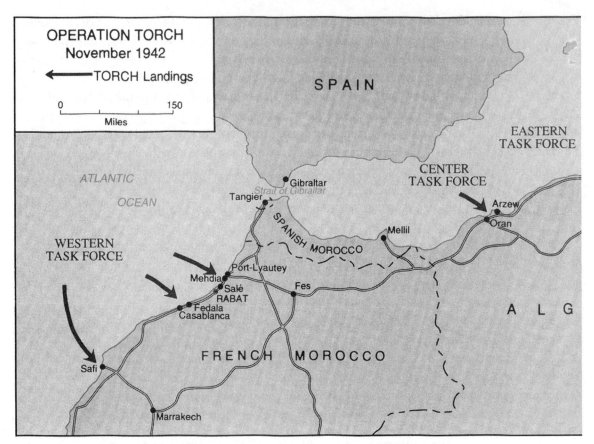

Keeping Roosevelt's promise to Stalin to begin an invasion in 1942 (though not in western Europe, as Stalin insisted), Allied forces under Supreme Commander Lieutenant General Dwight D. Eisenhower landed in North Africa on November 8, catching Axis forces off guard and forcing Hitler to move troops from the Eastern Front to Tunisia.

On November 8, American and British forces mounted the largest amphibious invasion force in the history of warfare to date when they landed at Casablanca in Morocco and Algiers and Oran in Algeria. The landings were a complete surprise to the Axis; Hitler had anticipated landings to augment Montgomery's forces much farther east, or an invasion of Sicily. Allied troops were divided into three forces: Eastern Task Force met little resistance at Algiers and occupied the city that day. In Oran, the Central Task Force came up against strong resistance from French forces but beat it back in two days. The heaviest fighting took place around Casablanca as the French battled Patton's Western Task Force. French naval units, including the unfinished battleship *Jean Bart*, unsuccessfully opposed Allied vessels, including the battleship USS *Massachusetts*.

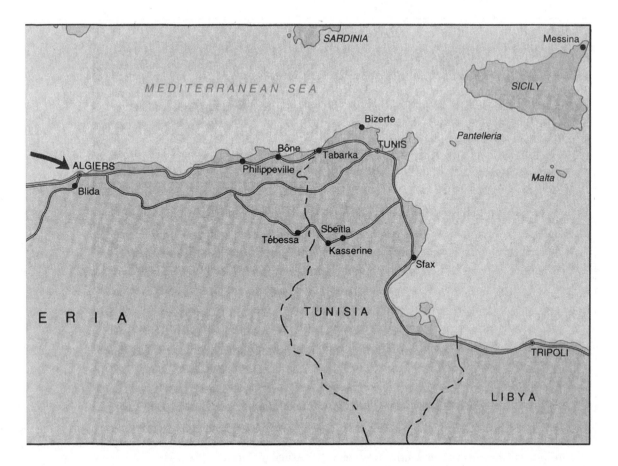

The fighting ended on November 11 after Vichy commander in chief Admiral Jean François Darlan (who happened to be in Algiers during the invasion) met with the Americans and agreed to an armistice. The Vichy government immediately denounced the agreement and repudiated Darlan, hoping to placate the Germans. (Eisenhower, meanwhile, stirred up a home-front hornets' nest by appointing Admiral Darlan—a Vichy official and thus a Nazi collaborator—high commissioner for French North Africa. The appointment did not last long; an anti-Nazi French monarchrist assassinated Darlan on Christmas Eve.)

The Allied success in Torch forced Hitler to transfer desperately needed German aircraft from the Russian front to Tunisia, where German troops seized control from the Vichy authorities. At the same time, other

THEATERS OF WAR, 1942

Europe	*Mediterranean/North Africa*
March 28: British commandos stage a successful raid on St. Nazaire, France	**January–April:** Luftwaffe carries out regular, intensive bombing raids on Malta
March 28–29: British bombers destroy 80 percent of the medieval city Lubeck, a Baltic port	**January 28:** Axis forces, led by Rommel, win tank battle and retake Benghazi, a month after the British had taken the city
April: Luftwaffe retaliates with Baedeker raids on British cities	**June:** Rommel's forces push to within seventy miles of the Nile River*
May 30–31: 1,000-bomber RAF raid levels Cologne	**June 21:** Port city Tobruk falls to German forces
June 12: U.S. planes bomb Ploesti oil fields in Romania	**July 1:** First Battle of El Alamein begins, stopping Rommel's momentum*
July: Germany's Ruhr region systematically bombed	**August 10–15:** In Operation Pedestal, Allies bring desperately needed supplies to Malta*
July 3–4: The Black Sea port Sevastopol falls to the Germans	**August 31:** Axis advance slowed at Battle of Alam el Halfa
August 19: Allies stage a disastrous raid on Dieppe, on the French coast*	**October 23:** Second Battle of El Alamein results in decisive, tide-turning victory for the Allies*
August 20: German forces cross the River Don and take aim at Stalingrad, which is relentlessly bombed by air and artillery	**November 4:** Allied force, under Montgomery, breaks through at El Alamein; Rommel retreats from Egypt
September 12: The Battle for Stalingrad begins, tying up the German Army. Goebbels will note in his diary, "We are in danger of bleeding to death in the East"*	**November 8:** Allies land at Morocco and Algeria, part of Operation Torch*
November: Germans occupy southern France and Tunisia*	**November 13:** Montgomery captures Tobruk, squeezing Rommel between two large advancing Allied forces*
	November 20: Montgomery captures Benghazi
	November 27: Vichy French forces scuttle their fleet at Toulon to keep the ships out of German or Allied hands*
	December: Luftwaffe suspends bombings of Malta after sustaining huge plane losses
	December 25: Effort to save the German Sixth Army trapped in Stalingrad fails*

The Pacific	China-Burma-India
January–April: Japanese push U.S. and Filipino forces onto the Bataan Peninsula	**February–May:** Japanese push Allied forces in Southeast Asia to the border of India
January 11: Kuala Lumpur falls to the Japanese; British in full retreat in Malaya	**February 8:** Rangoon falls to the Japanese
January 23: Rabaul, New Britain, and Kieta on Bougainville fall to the Japanese	**April:** Japanese bomb Ceylon and make incursions into the Indian Ocean
January 24–27: Battle of Macassar Strait off Borneo	**April:** Lashio falls to the Japanese, who then close the Burma Road
February 15: British surrender at Singapore*	**May 1–3:** Mandalay falls to the Japanese
February 19: Japanese airplanes sink 17 ships in the harbor at Port Darwin, Australia	**May 24:** U.S. General Joseph Stilwell arrives in New Delhi, India, after a long retreat
February 27–March 1: Battle of the Java Sea*	**August:** Gandhi announces campaign of civil disobedience against British in India
March 10: Allied forces on Java surrender to the Japanese	**October 23:** In Burma, Allies begin the first Arakan campaign
March 11: FDR orders General MacArthur to leave the Philippines	
April 18: Lieutenant Colonel Doolittle leads bombing raid over four Japanese cities*	
May 6: U.S. forces at Corregidor surrender*	
May 7–8: Battle of the Coral Sea*	
June 4: Battles at Midway and Aleutians*	
June 5: Japanese occupy Attu, in the Aleutians	
July 22: Japanese land on the northern coast of New Guinea	
August 1942–February 1943: Allies conduct the Guadalcanal campaign*	
September 21: The Allies open an offensive in New Guinea	
October 11–12: U.S. defeats the Japanese fleet at the Battle of Cape Esperance, keeping supply lines open to Guadalcanal	

* See text for further discussion.

Wehrmacht units occupied the portion of France that had previously been under the nominal control of General Petain's government at Vichy. As the Germans moved into Vichy, Admiral de Laborde, commander in chief of the French navy, ordered his men to scuttle the vessels moored at Toulon: 77 ships, half the tonnage of the French navy, were rendered useless to the Germans.

1943: The Tide Begins to Turn

In 1943, the tide of war began to turn in favor of the Allies in nearly every theater of war. In the China-Burma-India Theater, the Burma campaign blazed on and planes continued to fly across "the Hump" to supply China. Work also went forward on the Ledo Road—under the auspices of the Americans, with local command assigned to Major General Lewis A. Pick (inspiring wags to dub the epic endeavor "Pick's Pike"). Meanwhile, the Red Army delivered some powerful blows to the Wehrmacht, which was increasingly strained by severe losses in men and equipment and overextended supply lines. Axis forces were also under pressure in North Africa. In the Italian-held Fezzan Desert in Libya, the Free French took two strongpoints, Murzouk and Mizda, in January, then went on to Tripoli. There they became part of Montgomery's British Eighth Army, then in hot pursuit of Rommel's army, which was retreating toward Tunisia.

The North African Campaign Continues and the Siege of Malta Ends: January–May, 1943

In North Africa, Allied forces were converging on the German-Italian armies from two directions. The British, under Montgomery, pressed forward from the east, taking the Libyan port city of Tripoli on January 23 and pushing Rommel's forces into southern Tunisia. Another German force under General Jürgen von Arnim had seized control of the central and northern parts of that Vichy French protectorate after the Allied Torch landings, described earlier. In the meantime, British and American forces, were moving east from Algeria into Tunisia, aiming to capture the ports of Birzerte and Tunis and to prevent Rommel from linking up with von Arnim.

Allied concern centered on the mountain passes that were crucial avenues for linking the German forces. In late December and early January, Free French forces were battered when they clashed with the Germans in the mountains near Ousseltia. Then, on January 30, the 10th and 21st Panzer divisions, under von Arnim, overwhelmed the French holding the Faid Pass and the next day drove off an American column. This caused minor dissension in the Allied ranks: the French accused the Americans of insufficient support, and arguments over the most effective deployment of American armor weakened an Allied attack on Maknassy on January 31.

Meanwhile, Rommel's columns continued northwestward. (Behind them, Axis units strengthened the Mareth Line—prewar French fortifications in the south—to delay Montgomery's Eighth Army, which would cross into Tunisia on February 12.) On February 14, during an intense sandstorm, von Arnim's forces attacked the Allies at Sidi bou Zid, where, well-supported by aircraft and with the advantage of seasoned troops, they quickly forced the Americans to fall back, attempting to destroy matériel and supplies as they retreated, and scrambling to bring up reinforcements. The Germans pushed on, occupying Sbeitla, twenty-five miles beyond Sidi Bou Zid, on the 17th. At the same time, they were picking up important information on their enemy's intentions by eavesdropping on uncoded U.S. communications as American forces took up a new defensive position at Kasserine Pass.

BATTLE OF KASSERINE PASS, TUNISIA, FEBRUARY 19–22, 1943
MEDITERRANEAN THEATER (NORTH AFRICA)

> **Primary Objectives:** *Allied:* to hold this pass and prevent further progress by Rommel's forces; *Axis:* to defeat Allied attempts to divide German forces; Rommel also wished to push toward Tebessa, Algeria, to unhinge the Allied line and capture supplies
>
> **Forces:** *Allied:* 30,000 Americans, more than 200 tanks; *Axis:* 74,000 Germans, 26,000 Italians, 280 tanks
>
> **Commanders:** *Allied:* Major General Lloyd R. Fredendall; *Axis:* Field Marshal Erwin Rommel
>
> **Military Losses (estimated):** *Allied:* more than 6,000 Americans killed, wounded, or missing; *Axis:* more than 1,500 German and Italian troops killed, wounded, missing, or prisoners
>
> **Result:** Rommel's armored thrusts were successful, and he broke through the American positions, dealing a blow to American morale. Yet the battle did not deter the Allies' Tunisia offensive.

The Kasserine Pass, running for two miles between 4,000-foot-high mountains in the Western Dorsal Range, was in the area defended by the U.S. II Corps, under Major General Fredendall, who had established his headquarters more than seventy miles away in Tébessa. Units of his main fighting force, the 1st Armored Division, were too widely scattered to mount a strong defense. The inadequate hodgepodge of battalions that held the Kasserine Pass included engineers whose principal experience was road building rather than combat. Yet Fredendall had directed the commander at the scene, Colonel Robert Stark, to "pull a Stonewall Jackson" (stand fast under fire). Rommel's forces attacked on February 19, and the Allied troops initially held them off despite their thin ranks and relative inexperience. Overnight, however, Rommel received reinforcements and, on February 20, his troops smashed through the pass, inflicting heavy casualties.

Although Rommel wanted to head north toward Tébessa, where he believed a strike would break open the Allies' Tunisian front, von Arnim disagreed. German Field Marshal Albert Kesselring, operating from Italy, eventually ordered Rommel to move north toward Le Kef—an Allied strong point. The Axis failure to move quickly and decisively provided the Allies time to regroup, and it deprived Rommel's offensive of momentum. Also threatened by Montgomery's approaching forces, the Desert Fox ordered a withdrawal. His troops streamed back through Kasserine Pass on February 23, having laid a deadly carpet of more than 43,000 land mines behind them. These held up the Allied pursuit. (A British officer reported that Allied "vehicles were blowing up on the minefields in all directions." See also "Mines and Booby Traps" in Chapter 5.)

★   ★   ★

After the Kasserine battle, General Eisenhower replaced General Fredendall with longtime armored-warfare proponent General George Patton. This was to be a temporary assignment: Patton was slated to command the Allied invasion of Sicily. In the meantime, he was to improve sagging American morale—and straighten out the tangled II Corps command structure, firing any commander whose ability he doubted. Patton went about his job with a vengeance, alienating many. Yet morale improved.

Meanwhile, Rommel had turned east to deal with the British Eighth Army at the Mareth Line. Joining his rearguard forces that included the Italian-German army of Marshal Giovanni Messe, he launched a frontal assault on March 6. But the British, apprised of Rommel's intent by Ultra intelligence, had dug in around Medenine and repulsed the initial, and later attacks. Rommel's forces fell back to their position on the Mareth line; on March 9, the ailing Rommel returned to Germany, leaving North Africa for good; von Arnim assumed command. On March 20–21, the British attacked the Mareth Line, with limited success; but they pushed on, trying to envelop and destroy von Arnim's force. However, by March 27, von Arnim had extricated his surviving troops from the trap and withdrawn deeper into Tunisia.

Shortly thereafter, Montgomery's army and the Allied forces advancing from the west linked up. They squeezed the German-Italian forces back to Tunis and Bizerte, taking those cities, and more than 200,000 prisoners, on May 12. (Eventually many of these, and other prisoners taken in North Africa, would be sent to prisoner-of-war camps in the United States. See Chapter 11, p. 899.) Allied victory in North Africa effectively ended Italy's plans for a new empire in Africa, and it ended the siege of Malta (which by then had earned the courageous Maltese a British decoration, the George Cross). The campaign also gave American soldiers combat experience and taught them and their commanders lessons that would prove invaluable as they moved on to Sicily and Italy.

★   ★   ★

As the North African campaign was nearing its conclusion, Americans in the Pacific Theater struck hard, and successfully, at the Japanese.

BATTLE OF THE BISMARCK SEA, MARCH 2–4, 1943
PACIFIC THEATER

Primary Objectives: *Allied:* to prevent Japanese reinforcements from reaching the New Guinea garrison; *Japanese:* to reinforce the garrison

Forces: *Allied:* aircraft including U.S. Army B-17 and B-25 bombers, Australian Beaufighters, motor torpedo boats; *Japanese:* 8 troop transports, 8 destroyers

Commanders: *Allied:* Lieutenant General George C. Kenney; *Japanese:* Rear Admiral Kimura Masatomi

Military Losses: *Allied:* 5 planes shot down; *Japanese:* 4 destroyers, all transports sunk, more than 3,600 men of the 51st Division killed

Result: Without any assistance from naval forces, Allied air forces sank all Japanese transports and half the destroyers, preventing the convoy from reaching New Guinea; Allied air power was now established in the Southwest Pacific.

On February 28, 1943, Admiral Masatomi's sixteen-ship Japanese convoy sailed from Rabaul, New Britain, under orders to resupply and reinforce the

Japanese fighting on New Guinea. Allied intelligence had detected the plan early enough to rehearse two new attack techniques, originally suggested by Major Paul Gunn and Jack Fox from North American Aviation and implemented by Lieutenant General George C. Kenney, commander of the 5th Air Force in the Pacific. Allied pilots—flying planes with extra machine guns to give them more strafing power—would employ *skip-bombing:* planes flying very low delivered time-delayed bombs by "skipping" them into the sides of the ships, as if skipping stones across water.

After scout planes located the convoy on March 2, the Allies began their attack, sinking one transport ship. Two Japanese destroyers managed to rescue 850–950 Japanese in the water and deliver them to Lae, New Guinea, returning to the convoy just before the second Allied attack on the morning of March 3. While the convoy's air cover sought the usual American heavy, high-flying B-17 bombers, Kenney's squadrons came in almost at masthead level, sinking the rest of the transports and four destroyers. The other destroyers rescued as many men as possible and escaped back to Rabaul. Over the following days, the Allies sent PT boats to kill survivors, to keep the Japanese, notorious for never surrendering, from living to fight another day. For the first time in the war, airplanes had, without help from naval forces, destroyed an enemy fleet.

★　　★　　★

While this two-day sea battle was raging, Allied forces were making what progress they could in the jungles of Burma.

The Burma Campaign, Part II: 1943

Guerrilla warfare was the Allied hallmark in Burma throughout the year. In February, British brigadier general Orde Wingate's Long Range Penetration groups (called the "Chindits" after the winged stone lions that guard Buddhist temples) launched Operation Longcloth behind Japanese lines. Supported by airborne supply drops, they succeeded in cutting some Japanese railway lines, fighting their way through more than a thousand miles of difficult terrain; only 2,182 of the 3,000-man force made it back to India. Of limited strategic value, this incursion into Japanese territory by the mixed force of British, Burmese, and Gurkhas (fierce fighters from Nepal) inspired a surge in British morale, demonstrated that the Allies could operate as well as the Japanese in the jungle—and helped spark the creation of a similar

A U.S. soldier instructs Burmese Kachin tribesmen, members of a British- and American-taught guerrilla force known as the Kachin Rangers. *They specialized in guerrilla activities, sabotaging Japanese airfields, railroads, bridges, and communication lines. General Orde Wingate and other officers of his* Chindit *irregulars await a night supply drop at an airfield in Burma. Composed of British regulars and colonial units, Chindits conducted guerrilla warfare deep behind Japanese lines.*

American group that would subsequently operate in Burma (see "The Burma Campaign, Part III," later in this chapter).

American "underground warriors" were already in the area, however. Detachment 101 of the U.S. Office of Strategic Services (OSS, see Chapter 9), had arrived in the theater in June 1942. Responsible to the Allied theater commander, General Stilwell, and under the direct command of Major Carl Eifler, the detachment recruited fighters among Anglo-Burmese soldiers and

Burmese refugees in India, trained them at an old British tea plantation in Assam, and sent them behind Japanese lines to wreak as much havoc as possible—and to contact other prospective guerrillas, particularly the formidable Kachin tribesmen. India was also a training ground for three Nationalist Chinese divisions, as Stilwell prepared for a Burma offensive. Delays and command disagreements (U.S. Army Air Forces general Claire Chennault favored an aerial campaign against the Japanese, while British support for a Burma incursion waxed and waned) eventually postponed this operation until the following year.

As the Allied commanders debated, the Japanese reorganized their forces in Burma and attempted to secure greater loyalty among the Burmese. In August, they proclaimed Burma's independence—under Japanese supervision—and the Japanese-trained and equipped Burmese Defense Army, led by nationalist leader Aung San, was renamed the Burma National Army.

Meanwhile, American devotion to creating a ground route for transporting supplies into China was reflected in progress on the Ledo Road, although not as much as planned. The Americans aimed to reach the northern Burmese city of Shingbwiyang by June; but the difficult terrain, rain, illness, and supply shortages caused repeated delays. On the other side of the world, however, there was good news in the continuing battle to secure the Allied supply lines across the Atlantic.

A Turning Point in the Battle of the Atlantic—Threats to the Americas Recede

At the January Casablanca conference, Allied leaders determined to step up attacks on German U-boats by synchronizing American, British, and Canadian antisubmarine units. The effort started slowly—and was hampered by a "hole" in Allied intelligence, which was temporarily unable to penetrate the main U-boat Enigma cipher (see Chapter 9). In what for the Allies was the terrible month of March, U-boats located all North Atlantic convoys, attacked half of them, and sank 108 ships. Yet, U-boat losses steadily mounted—and Allied sinkings decreased—as the Germans, whose U-boat Enigma ciphers had again been penetrated by the Allies, faced more compact and faster Allied escort carriers, new convoy patterns, and more comprehensive Allied air cover. The subs also suffered the effects of new Allied gadgets, including depth-charge salvo launchers ("Hedgehogs"), improved sonar, and microwave radar. (See also Chapter 5.) Finally, at the end of May, Admiral

Dönitz, having lost 100 submarines over the past five months, withdrew his boats from the Atlantic.

Now on the offensive, Allied submarines and aircraft stepped up attacks on German convoys and warships in the North Atlantic. On September 23, British midget submarines damaged the battleship *Tirpitz* off Norway. On October 4, Allied aircraft struck a German convoy off Narvik, Norway, sinking 40,000 tons of shipping. In the Americas, meanwhile, the Vichy government lost control of French Guiana in March, and by July, the Vichy high commissioner for the French West Indies had resigned and been replaced by a Free French representative. That same month, German U-boats mounted a final campaign in American waters, but the U.S. Navy effectively ended it by September. By the end of the year, the Germans had lost the battle of the Atlantic; the few U-boats still prowling the ocean were effectively pursued by Allied coastal aircraft and antisubmarine groups through the rest of the war.

In the Pacific, meanwhile, American forces prepared to push the Japanese out of the Aleutian Islands.

Americans Regain the Aleutians, May–August 1943

The Japanese invasion force that had landed on the Aleutian Islands of Attu and Kiska in June 1942, in connection with the Battle of Midway, had endured nine months of harassment by American naval and air forces—including planes flown from airstrips the Americans had specially constructed on two other Aleutian Islands, Adak and Amchitka. In March 1943, the Americans assembled a force of sufficient strength to assault the Japanese-occupied islands. On March 26, an American fleet of two cruisers and four destroyers attacked a Japanese convoy comprising two fast merchant ships, four cruisers, and four destroyers off the Komandorski Islands, which lie between the Aleutians and the Kamchatka Peninsula. A unique encounter in the Pacific naval war, with no participation by aircraft carriers, the battle did not result in a loss of ships by either side. However, the Americans did prevent the Japanese from reinforcing their small Aleutian garrisons—2,630 soldiers on Attu and more than 5,000 troops and civilians on Kiska.

On May 11, 11,000 troops of the 7th U.S. Infantry Division, supported by aircraft from an escort carrier and battleship artillery fire, landed on Attu, where they met stiff resistance from Colonel Yamazaki Yasuyo's troops. Badly supported and outnumbered, the Japanese fell back to high ground, from which, on May 29, they launched one of the biggest banzai charges of the war. Hitting hard, they overran two command posts and a medical station before the Americans halted their advance, inflicting grievous casualties. After a final attack on May 30, most of the surviving Japanese committed suicide; the Americans took only 28 prisoners.

The next American objective was Kiska. On August 15, after a two-week bombing campaign, 34,000 U.S. troops landed on the island. But the Japanese had evacuated Kiska at the end of July under the cover of fog—and while U.S. ships were refueling after a nighttime "battle" that actually wasn't a battle at all. The Americans fired at radar "pips" they believed were enemy vessels; in the daylight, however, the signals were revealed to be echoes returned from mountains more than one hundred miles away.

★   ★   ★

While the Americans were securing the Aleutians, the Red Army was preparing to face German troops in the greatest confrontation of armored forces the world had yet seen.

A Massive Clash of Armor

Fighting the Wehrmacht, the Red Army had created a salient (a bulge into German-held territory) near the middle of the vast Eastern Front, near Kursk, an important railroad junction. To destroy the salient and the Soviet armies within it—and to repair prestige badly battered by the defeat at Stalingrad—Hitler ordered planning to commence for Operation Citadel. From mid-March to July, relative calm prevailed in the area as both sides regrouped and rearmed. (Both President Roosevelt and Stalin's own intelligence organizations had informed the Soviet dictator that an offensive was imminent; see Chapter 9.) Throughout June, civilians and partisans helped Red Army detachments place tens of thousands of mines and booby traps in the Kursk salient, where, in early July, 2 million men and more than 6,000 tanks collided in one of the largest land battles in history.

THE BATTLE OF KURSK (OPERATION CITADEL), JULY 5–17, 1943
EUROPEAN THEATER (EAST)

> **Primary Objectives:** *Soviet:* to repel the attack, destroy as much German armor as possible and counterattack; *German:* to straighten out the line and push back the Russians' salient, to trap and destroy nearly one-fifth of the Red Army

Forces: *Soviet:* 1.3 million men, 3,600 tanks, 20,000 artillery pieces, 2,400 aircraft; *German:* 50 divisions, 900,000 men, 2,700 tanks and assault guns, 10,000 artillery pieces, 1,800 aircraft

Commanders: *Soviet:* Marshal Georgi Zhukov; General Konstantin Rokossovsky (Central Front); General Nikolai Vatutin (Voronezh Front); General I. S. Konev (Steppe Front); *German:* Field Marshal Gunther von Kluge (Army Group Center); Field Marshal Erich von Manstein (Army Group South)

Military Losses: *Soviet:* 177,847 dead, wounded, or captured, more than 400 tanks, 459 aircraft; *German:* 79,278 dead, wounded, or captured, 320 tanks, 200 aircraft

Result: The Germans failed to take Kursk; instead of pushing the Soviets back, they were forced to withdraw—beginning their long retreat from Soviet soil.

The Wehrmacht began Operation Citadel on July 5, aiming for a classic double envelopment, a familiar German strategy: General Walther Model's Ninth Army, part of Army Group Center, attacked toward Kursk from the north; Colonel General Hermann Hoth's 4th Panzer army, part of Army Group South, moved up from the south. Ferocious artillery barrages and tactical bombing runs and aerial dogfights by both supporting air forces preceded the

---

EYEWITNESS ACCOUNT: THE FIGHTING AT KURSK

One of the German infantrymen supporting the armor at Kursk was a soldier named Senneberg (first name unknown) whose account was quoted in *Servants of Evil* (2001):

First came a dreadful barrage. I knew in advance what it was going to be like, because my father, who had been injured at Verdun in the First World War, described it to me. He . . . said that he had had to jump into shell holes. . . . You saw on the left or the right of you that there was a new shell crater, so you jumped into that one and then the next one. . . . And that's what we did, too. The barrage ended after three hours and the fighting began. But our offensive collapsed, . . . Further and further we retreated. Fortunately we were protected by a German tank named Ferdinand, the biggest and heaviest tank that I had ever seen. It was so big that the ground was practically shaking when it was three kilometres away. Not even the Russians had one like it. But then there was this thunderstorm. . . . The ground went soggy and that was the end of Ferdinand.

clash of ground forces—and continued throughout the battle. Soviet partisans operating behind German lines made disjointed efforts to disrupt the Wehrmacht's avenues of supply and communication, but the Germans smashed their way forward, pinching in the sides of the salient and threatening to cut off and destroy a Soviet tank army. Zhukov countered by rushing in reinforcements. The ensuing clash of armor, July 12, involving some 1,800 tanks, was the largest tank battle of the war. At the end of the day, bodies and the shells of crushed and broken tanks littered the smoking, shell-hole-pocked

After driving the Wehrmacht out of Kursk and Kharkov, the Red Army continued their push westward. By October 1943, they retook Kiev, which the Germans had held since 1941, and erased the possibility of a German victory on the Eastern Front.

battlefield. Both sides had been terribly battered, but the Soviets had held the Germans. The next day, Hitler called off Citadel and withdrew panzer units to reinforce troops facing the Allied assault on Sicily that had begun four days earlier. The German operation was over, but the Soviet campaign to crush the Germans was not. The Red Army nipped at the retreating Wehrmacht's heels. On August 23, the Soviets retook Kharkov; by October they were poised to retake Kiev, where the Germans had taken 600,000 Soviet soldiers prisoner in 1941. The failure of Operation Citadel marked the beginning of the end for the Germans on the Eastern Front.

Hitler's transfer of men and machines in the midst of the desperate fighting around Kursk was another sign of the growing strain that fighting a multifront war was placing on German resources. It also reflected his concern over the progress the Allies were making toward southern Europe.

Moving toward Italy

After achieving victory in North Africa, Allied leaders selected Sicily, a large island off the southern coast of Italy, as the next major target. Although this would not be the full-scale assault on western Europe that Stalin wanted, the western Allies believed it would take some pressure off the Eastern Front. Sicily was also a possible launching point for an invasion of mainland Europe. Blocking Allied progress toward Sicily were two small islands that lay in the strait between Tunisia and Sicily: Pantelleria and Lampedusa. Pantelleria, the larger of the two islands, contained an Axis air base and was heavily defended. The Allies subjected it to aerial and naval bombardment during the week preceding a ground assault on June 11, when its defending troops surrendered without a fight. On June 12, the Allies secured Lampedusa. At the same time, a deception operation, Mincemeat (see "Deception—Decoys and Dummies" in Chapter 9) convinced Axis intelligence that the ultimate Allied goals were Sardinia and Greece, rather than Sicily and Italy. In July, the operation against Axis forces in Sicily began.

ALLIED INVASION OF SICILY (OPERATION HUSKY), JULY 9–AUGUST 17, 1943
MEDITERRANEAN THEATER

> **Primary Objectives:** *Allied:* to capture Sicily, draw German attention away from the Russian front, further secure supply routes and ensure safety of Allied shipping in the Mediterranean, put pressure on Italy to

surrender; *Axis:* to defend Sicily, keep the Allies from reaching southern Europe

Forces: *Allied:* about 180,000 men, 2,000 landing craft (including new LSIs, or landing ship infantry), 580 ships, including 6 battleships, 2 aircraft carriers, 6 cruisers, 24 destroyers; *Axis:* about 350,000 German and Italian defenders

Commanders: *Allied:* General Dwight D. Eisenhower (Supreme Commander), General Sir Harold Alexander (ground forces), Admiral Andrew B. Cunningham (naval forces), Air Chief Marshal Sir Arthur Tedder (air forces); *Axis:* General Hans Hube, General Alfredo Guzzoni

Military Losses: *Allied:* 7,500 Americans killed or wounded, 11,500 British killed or wounded; *Axis:* 12,000 Germans killed or captured, 145,000 Italians killed or captured (more than 100,000 were captured; many Italians no longer had their hearts in the fight)

Result: The Allies secured Sicily, although many Axis troops escaped across the Messina Strait to Italy; a cadre headed by King Victor Emmanuel III dismissed Mussolini and replaced him with Field Marshal Pietro Badoglio; the Allies decided to invade the Italian mainland; German forces prepared for a fight to hold on to Italy.

Operation Husky was one of the largest landing operations of World War II, comparable in scale to Operation Overlord (D-Day) in the European Theater and Okinawa in the Pacific. On the evening of July 9, the attack commenced with paratroopers and glider landings, during which strong winds and inexperience claimed hundreds of Allied lives, as many gliders missed their targets and landed in the sea. Early the next morning, under the gloom of foul weather, General Alexander's Fifteenth Army Group, inaugurating the new American DUKW amphibious vehicles, made landings on the southeastern part of the island. General Patton's U.S. Seventh Army came ashore along the Gulf of Gela, while General Montgomery's British and Canadian Eighth Army disembarked south of Syracuse. The British quickly took Syracuse, but the Americans faced worse weather and stiffer resistance—overcome with the help of naval gunfire. Another tragic incident occurred on the night of July 11, when Allied shore and ship guns mistook American C47 transport planes for German bombers and shot down 23 planes—killing at least 81 paratroopers (16 others were missing) and wounding 132.

Above, as the Allied invasion of Sicily (Operation Husky) began, Allied air and naval forces pounded Axis ships in the Sicilian harbors. After furiously battling Allied troops for a month, on August 11 German Field Marshall Albert Kesselring ordered Axis forces to evacuate the island. Below, in Karl Kae Knecht's February 1943 cartoon entitled "The Acme of Italian Sunsets," Axis leaders in Italy, Sicily, Sardinia, and Tunisia are stunned at Allied victories in Africa.

After a delay while his men protected Montgomery's left flank, Patton led his troops north toward Palermo, which on July 22, became the first major European city the Allies liberated. American forces also cut the island in half, but they failed to trap significant Axis forces, most of which had already withdrawn northeast toward the port of Messina. Patton and Montgomery raced toward that port, vying to see who could get there first. Patton won by a matter of hours, arriving August 17—just after 40,000 German and 62,000 Italian troops, with their supplies and equipment, had escaped to the Italian mainland, where they added to the menace the Allies would face when they advanced on their next major Mediterranean objective.

★   ★   ★

Allied aircraft based in North Africa and Sicily pounded targets in Italy, helping to prepare for a ground assault. At the same time, to the northwest, the vapor trails created by huge flights of Allied bombers and smoke from dogfights between escorting and attacking fighters webbed across the skies, a testament to the growing ferocity of the Allied Combined Bomber Offensive (launched in January, reinvigorated by a new directive in June). The round-the-clock offensive—the British bombing by night and the Americans by day—cost the Allies many planes and airmen, while wreaking fearful destruction below. The most terrible raid of this year for the Germans was the operation to destroy the major port and industrial center of Hamburg, a series of raids the Allies code-named Gomorrah. (See box opposite.)

The war's first firestorm raged through Hamburg as the Wehrmacht was falling back from its defeat at Kursk, Axis troops were losing the battle for Sicily, and Italian leaders deposed Mussolini. The war was turning in the Allies' favor, and they pursued their advantage. The Combined Bomber Offensive did not relent. The biggest attack to that time on extremely well-defended Berlin occurred on August 23. British Air Chief Marshal Sir Arthur Harris hoped to reduce the industrial power of the capital and score a devastating strike against German morale. Similar RAF raids followed, including two in November that killed 3,000 and damaged government buildings, among them the Chancellery and propaganda minister Joseph Goebbels' official residence. Many Berliners, including hundreds of thousands of children, were evacuated from the city.

As the raids on German cities increased, a group of Allied planes assembled for another raid on the oil fields and refineries near Ploesti, Romania,

HAMBURG—THE FIRST FIRESTORM

Hamburg endured more than 180 bombing attacks during the war, but it was hit hardest between July 24 and August 3, 1943, when the RAF and the American Eighth Air force, flying more than 3,000 sorties in a series of six attacks, dropped nearly 9,000 tons of explosive and incendiary bombs on the city. The campaign began with nighttime RAF strategic bombing attacks on July 24, using a new device—bundles of metallic strips code-named Window—that filled German radar screens with blips and concealed the true position of the approaching Allied planes (see "Opening Window" in Chapter 5). The Germans had no effective countermeasures. Day and night, the Allies pounded the city so relentlessly and effectively that the Germans thereafter referred to that terrible ten days as "the catastrophe." The heart of the catastrophe was the raid on the night of July 27.

Incendiary bombs that poured out of RAF bombers that hot, dry night ignited separate fires that quickly roared together, greedily devouring everything flammable and creating a savage firestorm before which local firefighters were helpless. An estimated 45,000 people were killed that night; nearly 1 million were left homeless. Survivors remembered a city where "Women and children were so charred as to be unrecognizable. Their brains had tumbled from their burst temples and their insides from the soft parts under the ribs. . . . The smallest children lay like fried eels on the pavement." Yet, despite the incredible damage, horrific casualties, and additional raids, Hamburg recovered. Meanwhile, the raid prompted a change in German air defense tactics that placed greater reliance on night fighters. Hamburg was the first, but would not be the only, German city to suffer through a firestorm. (See also Chapter 11.)

source of as much as 60 percent of Germany's oil. The American B-24 bombers that took off from Benghazi, Libya, on August 1, 1943, embarked on the longest journey from base to target (1,350 miles) undertaken to that time. On the first in a series of raids mounted under the code name Tidal Wave, the bomber crews also tested new, low-flying tactics. Under the command of Brigadier General Uzal G. Ent of the Ninth Air Force, the planes approached at altitudes under 500 feet—but the Germans, who had been reading the Ninth Air Force codes, were ready. Moreover, confusion resulting from the loss of two of the mission's best navigators before the bombers even reached their targets was compounded as smoke from bomb-damaged refineries filled the air. The raiders damaged 40 percent of the refineries, but at a heavy cost:

54 of the original 178 bombers were lost; more than 500 crewmen were killed, wounded, or captured. (Some damaged aircraft landed in neutral Turkey, and their crews were interned.) The U.S. government awarded five Medals of Honor to participants in this raid—three posthumously—the most awarded for any air attack during World War II.

The Germans and Romanians quickly repaired the damage and improved their defenses; among other measures, they added "smoke pots" to create heavy smoke screens during future raids. Many occurred: by the time the Soviet Army reached Ploesti in August 1944, a series of raids launched by the U.S. Fifteenth Air Force that April had reduced the output of Ploesti refineries by 80 to 90 percent.

★　　★　　★

Just over a month after the August raid on Ploesti, the new Italian government of Pietro Badoglio signed an armistice with the Allies. General Eisenhower announced the news on September 8—only hours before the Allied invasion of Italy and in time, it was hoped, to soften Italian resistance. However, the Germans, who had anticipated Italy's capitulation, had already reinforced their Italian garrison. After the armistice, they disarmed any Italian troops whose loyalty was suspect—shooting thousands who resisted and transporting hundreds of thousands to prison camps or to be used as slave labor. At the same time, the Wehrmacht dug in and prepared to hold Italy—and prevent an Allied breakthrough toward Germany.

ALLIED INVASION NEAR SALERNO, ITALY (OPERATION AVALANCHE), SEPTEMBER 3–16, 1943
MEDITERRANEAN THEATER (EUROPE)

> **Primary Objectives:** *Allied:* to secure a beachhead, then advance north to Naples and Rome; *Axis:* to prevent the Allies from achieving their objective and, ideally, to oust them from the European mainland
>
> **Forces:** *Allied:* Anglo-American Fifth Army (part of Fifteenth Army Group), comprising U.S. VI Corps and British X Corps, plus U.S. Rangers and British Commandos supported by British Naval Forces H and V (more than 600 vessels); British Eighth Army; *Axis:* Wehrmacht Army Group C, comprising some 10 divisions (including Italian units that remained loyal to the Axis)

Commanders: *Allied:* U.S. Navy Vice Admiral H. Kent Hewitt in overall operational command, General Sir Harold Alexander (Fifteenth Army Group), Lieutenant General Mark Clark (Fifth Army ground invasion force: VI Corps under Major General Ernest Dawley and X Corps under Lieutenant General Richard McCreery), Field Marshal Bernard Montgomery (Eighth Army); *Axis:* Field Marshal Albert Kesselring (commander in chief), General Heinrich von Vietinghoff (Tenth Army, charged with defense of southern Italy), Lieutenant General Hans Hube (Salerno defense)

Military Losses (September 9–16): *Allied:* 1,084 Americans killed, 3,263 wounded, 1,875 missing; 7,398 British and Commonwealth troops killed, wounded, or missing; *Axis:* 3,472 Germans killed, wounded, or missing

Result: The Allies gained a foothold in Italy, but German resistance remained strong—the Wehrmacht formed several defensive lines across Italy to prevent the Allies from moving north.

Avalanche began with small landings on September 3, when troops of Montgomery's British Eighth Army crossed the Straits of Messina from Sicily and landed at Reggio at the "toe" of the Italian boot (Operation Baytown), while British paratroopers created a diversion at Taranto on the Italian heel (Operation Slapstick). The main invasion commenced in the dark morning hours of September 9, when Allied troops under Clark landed at four points along thirty miles of rugged coast near Salerno—the northernmost point covered by air support from bases in Sicily. German troops kept the Allies from moving inland as Kesselring sent reinforcements (under von Vietinghoff) toward Salerno.

Montgomery, meanwhile, annoyed at being relegated to a supportive role, made his way slowly northward, delayed more by terrain, German-destroyed bridges, and his own pique than by actual German resistance. At Salerno, Clark's forces still could not advance, reinforcements had not arrived due to a shortage of landing craft, and their naval support was taking a beating from German glider bombs (see Chapter 5). Then, on September 12, the reinforced Germans began a counteroffensive that forced the Allied troops back toward the water. Clark's men held on—with the help of naval and air support and the timely arrival of reinforcements September 13 and 14: battalions from the 82nd Airborne Division, British armored infantry, and paratroopers

In an Army artist's depiction, Allied troops wade ashore at Salerno amid enemy machine gun and shell fire. In the distance, a landing craft erupts in flames after a hit from an enemy shell.

dropped (inaccurately, with a resulting 30 percent casualties) to the north. Two days later, Montgomery's forces linked up with Clark. Realizing that the Allies now had the upper hand, Kesselring ordered his troops to withdraw to defensive positions. The Allies had gained a foothold in Europe.

★　　★　　★

As they secured Salerno, the Allies also extended their control of the surrounding area by capturing Sardinia, from which the Germans had withdrawn their troops—sending them north to the island of Corsica, a prewar French possession that Charles de Gaulle was determined the French should retake. The first French forces landed on the island September 12. Others soon followed, with Free French and British naval support; and these regular troops were soon joined by local Maquis resistance fighters. Italian resistance crumbled, and on September 15, Hitler ordered the 40,000 troops in the German garrison to withdraw to the mainland, an operation completed

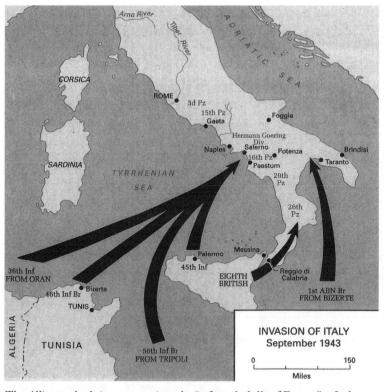

The Allies made their move against the "soft underbelly of Europe"—Italy—in Operation Avalanche, but their plans to capture Salerno and move quickly north toward Naples and its airfields were significantly slowed by stiff German resistance.

by October 4. Meanwhile, the British, who, unlike the Americans, placed great stock in securing the Dodecanese Islands in the Aegean Sea, staged landings there (Operation Accolade) shortly after the Italian surrender. Under-strength and insufficiently supported, the British troops suffered a costly defeat; the Germans forced them to withdraw by mid-November.

Meanwhile, the campaign on the Italian mainland was proving to be a grueling, muddy slog hindered by difficult mountainous terrain, wide rivers, and destroyed bridges and tunnels. The Germans had established several fortified positions that spanned Italy on lines south of Rome. Dubbed "The Winter Line" by the Allies, who were held there for months, these defenses included the Gustav Line—based along the Garigliano, Rapido, and Sangro rivers and grounded in the Apennine mountains and Monte Cassino—which would prove especially difficult to breach.

In late September, as the Fifth Army approached Naples, Neopolitans suffered many casualties as they staged an anti-German revolt that continued until October 1, when American troops arrived. The retreating Germans had demolished much of the city; but Allied engineers quickly restored the port. Meanwhile, Montgomery's troops took the major airfield at Foggia near the Adriatic Sea, giving the Allies an air base for tactical support—and from which to mount long-range bomber sorties against Germany.

So glittering did the prize of Rome seem to the Allied command that Eisenhower ordered a continued two-pronged advance. By mid-October, the Fifth Army had reached the rain-swollen Volturno River, which the troops crossed against heavy German opposition, proceeding slowly toward the Garigliano River. The Eighth Army, meanwhile, was also encountering intense combat as they crossed the Trigno River and reached the rising Sangro River in early November. Stymied by the Gustav Line and the onset of a harsh winter, the Allies decided to stage a relief operation, an amphibious landing north of the Gustav Line, at Anzio, in January. This would force the Germans to split their defense and give Allied forces a chance to break through. This plan did not work as anticipated; it would be more than five difficult months before the Allies were able to travel the one hundred miles from their positions in front of the Gustav Line to Rome.

★   ★   ★

In the Pacific, meanwhile, troops and naval units under MacArthur and Halsey continued operations in New Guinea and the Solomon Islands, aim-

ISLAND HOPPING IN THE PACIFIC

Island hopping involved the use of coordinated land, sea, and air attacks, as the Allies bypassed Japanese strongholds to focus on selected targets, leaving isolated Japanese troops under the constant, and often-realized, threat of Allied aerial attack. Practical application of this method of advancement—developed without prewar rehearsals and under combat conditions—did not proceed without flaws or disagreements. It required close cooperation among Allied armed forces and their various services—and among strong-willed American commanders. Yet, despite bumpy beginnings, island hopping proved extremely successful. In August 1943, the Allies elected to bypass rather than assault the strong Japanese air and naval base at Rabaul after heavy preassault air attacks only moved the Japanese to construct tunnels and caves. Thereafter,

Allied planes pounded Rabaul unremittingly. This caused the Japanese to withdraw all their major air and naval units to the atoll of Truk, in the Caroline Islands (leaving thousands of army troops, naval personnel, and civilian workers behind). The Allies then subjected Truk to heavy air attacks, destroying many aircraft and tons of Japanese shipping, before the U.S. Joint Chiefs of Staff decided to bypass that island as well. The Japanese cut off by island hopping were sometimes supplied by submarines—diverting those vessels from attacking Allied warships. But supplies were not guaranteed. As food and medical supplies dwindled, casualties from sickness and starvation increased. In a few of these isolated outposts, the Japanese resorted to cannibalism. (See "Cannibalism in the Pacific" in Chapter 8.)

ing toward the Philippines, while planners of the U.S. Joint Chiefs of Staff prepared for a second line of offensives, under Nimitz, that would proceed through the constellation of tiny islands that lay in the Central Pacific—including the Gilberts, the Marshals, the Carolines, and the Marianas.

Before pressing forward in June, MacArthur reorganized his forces into two main bodies: Alamo Force, composed mainly of Americans, and the New Guinea Force, comprising Australians. Units in New Guinea moved up the coast to the northwest, campaigning against Lieutenant General Hatazo Adachi's Eighteenth Army, which included the 6th Air Division—a major Allied objective being to isolate the important Japanese base at Rabaul on the nearby island of New Britain. As the New Guinea operations proceeded, troops under Halsey staged landings on New Georgia and the nearby islands of Rendova and Vangunu, which they secured after more than a month of hard fighting. Halsey then bypassed the island of Kolombangara, isolating the Japanese garrison there, and made a successful assault on the island of Vella Lavella—around which fighting continued until early October. This "island hopping" technique would become a hallmark of the Allied Pacific campaign (see box opposite).

On October 27, 6,000 New Zealand troops landed at the Treasury Islands and set up radar stations, while 700 U.S. Marines landed at Choiseul, to distract the Japanese from their real target, which lay a short distance to the north of these two operations: Bougainville, the largest of the Solomon Islands.

THE BOUGAINVILLE CAMPAIGN, SOLOMON ISLANDS, NOVEMBER 1, 1943–AUGUST 15, 1945
PACIFIC THEATER

Primary Objectives: *Allied:* to clear the Japanese garrison from the island and to further isolate the Japanese base at Rabaul; *Japanese:* to hold the island and protect Rabaul

Forces: *Allied:* an initial assault force of 14,000 U.S. Marines, building, by March 1944, to 60,000 infantrymen of the U.S. Army XIV Corps, replaced by 1 division and 2 brigades of the Australian II Corps in December 1944; *Japanese:* 37,500 troops of the Seventeenth Army, 20,000 naval personnel

Commanders: *Allied:* Lieutenant General Alexander A. Vandergrift, USMC (November 1–9), Major General Roy S. Geiger, USMC

(November 9–December, 1943), Major General Oscar W. Griswold, U.S. Army (December 1943–December 1944), Lieutenant General Sir Stanley Savige (Australia, December 1944–August 1945), Major General George Kenney, USAAF (air support), Admiral William Halsey (South Pacific area commander); *Japanese:* Lieutenant General Hyakutake Haruyoshi, Admiral Sentaro Omori (Eighth Fleet), Vice Admiral Takeo Kurita

Military Losses: *Allied:* 423 Americans killed, 1,418 wounded, 516 Australians killed, 1,572 wounded; *Japanese:* 18,000 dead (8,500 in combat, 9,800 from disease), 23,571 surrendered

Result: The Allies contained and severely damaged, but did not destroy, the Japanese garrison—the remnants of which surrendered only after Japan's capitulation in 1945.

On November 1, 1943, an American force of four light cruisers and eight destroyers entered Empress Augusta Bay on the western side of Bougainville

Wounded American soldiers, their hands crossed on their chests to indicate "patient suffering," lie on stretchers made out of poles lashed together as they wait to be treated and evacuated from New Guinea.

and successfully landed 14,000 troops and 6,200 tons of supplies by nightfall. The following day, the Japanese responded with a Rabaul-based air and naval assault under Omori. Tactical missteps cost his Eighth Fleet a cruiser, a destroyer, and 25 planes, while two American cruisers, *Birmingham* and *Denver*, were damaged and had to withdraw from action. With thirty-six square miles of the island secured, the Americans began to construct airfields for island air support—and to strike at Rabaul.

Meanwhile, Kurita led a task force to Rabaul, New Britain, just to the north of Bougainville, threatening the Americans' position on the island. Halsey countered by deploying two carrier groups within range of Japanese aircraft to mount an assault on the enemy fleet. After their planes severely damaged Kurita's forces, Kurita withdrew to Truk. By the end of the year, Rabaul had been bypassed and Allied command of the air had effectively neutralized it as a base for offensive action. On Bougainville, troops of the U.S. Army XIV Corps under Griswold replaced the Marines. Then on March 8, 1944, Haruyoshi sent 15,000 of his men against several points on the American perimeter. The attacks were repulsed, with heavy Japanese casualties. A period of relative calm ensued until Savige's Australian II Corps replaced the Americans in December. Launching an offensive in early 1945, the Australians captured Pearl Ridge at the center of the island and restricted the Japanese to an ever-smaller area—despite fierce resistance and several counterattacks. Haruyoshi's surviving men finally surrendered after Japan capitulated in August.

★   ★   ★

While the Marines were establishing their Bougainville beachhead in November 1943, Admiral Nimitz began his Central Pacific campaign with Operation Galvanic, amphibious landings by American troops on the Gilbert Islands, where the major targets were Makin and Tarawa.

LANDING AT MAKIN AND TARAWA ATOLLS IN THE GILBERT ISLANDS (OPERATION GALVANIC), NOVEMBER 19–23, 1943
PACIFIC THEATER

Primary Objectives: *American:* to launch a campaign that would close in on Japan via the Central Pacific; *Japanese:* to hold the Gilberts and prevent Allied progress toward Japan

Forces: *American:* Fifth Fleet (8 aircraft carriers, 7 battleships, 10 cruisers, 34 destroyers, 700 aircraft), 2nd Marine Division and 27th Infantry Division (nearly 6,500 troops sent to Makin, 18,000 to Tarawa); *Japanese:* around 4,500 Japanese troops on the Tarawa atoll's main island of Betio, smaller garrisons on other Tarawa islands; 500 on Makin

Commanders: *American:* Vice Admiral Raymond A. Spruance (commander, Central Pacific Force); MAKIN; *American:* Admiral Richmond Kelly Turner (Task Force 54/Fifth Amphibious Force), Major General Holland M. Smith, USMC (V Amphibious Corps); Major General Ralph C. Smith (27th Infantry Division); *Japanese:* Navy Junior Grade Lieutenant Seizo Ishikawa, TARAWA; *American:* Major General Holland M. Smith, USMC (V Amphibious Corps); Major General Julian C. Smith, USMC (2nd Marine Division); *Japanese:* Rear Admiral Shibasaki Keiji

Military Losses: *American:* off Makin, carrier *Liscombe Bay* sunk by torpedo with more than 640 crewmen killed; off Tarawa, light carrier *Independence* torpedoed with around 60 casualties; more than 60 killed and 150 wounded on Makin; more than 1,000 killed and 2,000 wounded on Tarawa; *Japanese:* about 5,000 killed—most fought rather than surrender; only 17 Japanese taken alive on Tarawa; around 125 Korean laborers also captured there

Result: Allies gained control of the Gilbert Islands, but learned how ferocious Japanese fighting could slow the capture of even small islands; the Americans reconsidered their equipment and tactics for future amphibious operations; subsequent improvements included better armored transport vessels (some with guns) and increased naval artillery and air support.

After heavy naval and air bombardments, U.S. forces approached the Makin and Tarawa atolls on the morning of November 20. Troops from the 27th Infantry Division landed at Butaritari (the largest island of Makin), while elements of the 2nd Marine Division, under Colonel David M. Shoup, approached the small island of Betio in the Tarawa atoll. On Makin, Allied troops faced limited, but fierce opposition. By November 23, with relatively few casualties, they declared, "Makin Taken."

Tarawa was another matter. Little affected by the bombardment that preceded the landing (and alerted them to it), the 4,500 Japanese on Betio were well dug in and took full advantage of the opportunities presented by

EYEWITNESS ACCOUNT: TARAWA

Corporal Robert Johnsmiller, 21, from Detroit, Michigan, was in the third wave of U.S. Marines to land on Red Beach, Tarawa, November 20, 1943. After climbing over a log wall where other marines lay dead and wounded,

We crawled on our bellies through the sand because to stand up meant a quick death. A Japanese hand grenade landed next to me. Alerted by my buddy to "roll," I quickly moved my body as it went off. I had sustained an injury and was bleeding [he would lose an eye], but I ignored the pain and continued on. I decided to crawl in the direction the grenade came from. I soon came upon a trench. As I inched forward I was able to peer over the edge and locked my eyes on a Japanese soldier looking up at me from below. I instantly pulled back and motioned to others my discovery. We swiftly dispatched grenades into the emplacement and silenced the threat.

the Americans' problem-plagued landing. A New Zealand officer who had lived in the Gilberts for years had warned that the troop transports (Higgins boats) would not clear the coral reef surrounding the atoll, but Allied planners reckoned they would at high tide. During the landing, however, the tide was low, and although the first assault wave, transported by amphibious tractors (amphtracs) was able to clear the reef, the following Higgins boats could not. Marines were forced to wade ashore through chest-high water under heavy Japanese gunfire (14 coastal guns, 100 machine gun nests). Waterlogged weapons misfired or broke, the heat and stench were oppressive, many officers were killed, and the men who made it to the beach were pinned down. More and more Marines waded ashore under fire. Eventually the weight of numbers made it possible for them to push inland—their every step contested by Japanese who preferred death to surrender. The night of November 22 was repeatedly shattered by screams of "Banzai" as the Japanese hurled themselves at American lines. By noon the next day, the United States had possession of Tarawa—at a cost of more than 1,000 dead and thousands more wounded. The human cost of securing that obscure atoll—revealed in news stories illustrated by carefully filtered photographs and newsreel footage of the dead—profoundly shocked the American public.

THEATERS OF WAR, 1943

Europe	*The Mediterranean*
January: Allies launch Combined Bomber Offensive against Axis targets, including Berlin*	**January:** Free French take Murzouk, Mizda, and Tripoli in Libya
January 5: Russians take Morozovsk, German air base vital to holding Stalingrad	**January 30:** Germans capture Faid Pass in Tunisia*
January 10: Last offensive at Stalingrad begins*	**February 19–22:** Battle of Kasserine Pass in Tunisia; Allies retake the pass February 25*
January 11: Red Army moves into the Caucasus	**March 17:** U.S. II Corps begins an advance in Tunisia
February 2: German resistance at Stalingrad ends	**March 26:** Allies breach Mareth Line (Tunisia)
February 8: Soviets retake Kursk	**April 8:** Allied attack begins on Fondouk line (Tunisia)
February 27–28: Norwegian commandoes destroy German heavy water tanks in Vemork, Norway	**May:** Allies take Tunis and Bizerte (Tunisia)
March 9–13: In a brilliant offensive, the Germans retake Kharkov, recently lost to the Red Army	**May 12:** General von Arnim surrenders North African Axis forces*
April 19: Jewish armed revolt in the Warsaw ghetto	**May:** Siege of Malta ends
May 16–17: RAF bombers attack the Ruhr, damaging two dams	**May:** Operation Mincemeat draws Axis attention away from the Allied landings in Sicily
June 22: U.S. bombers begin major daytime attacks on the Ruhr	**June 11 and 12:** Allies secure islands of Pantelleria and Lampedusa*
July 5–17: The Battle of Kursk*	**July 10:** Invasion of Sicily begins
July 27–28: Allied firebombing of Hamburg*	**July 22:** Sicily's strategic port, Palermo, falls to Allies*
August 1: Libyan-based U.S. bombers attack Ploesti oilfields in Romania*	**August 1:** Germans take over Crete from Italians
August 23: Red Army retakes Kharkov	**August 17:** Allies secure Sicily
August 26: Russians begin campaign in eastern Ukraine	**September 9:** Allies land on European mainland at Salerno, Italy*
September 11: Partisans in Yugoslavia secure the port Split	**September 10:** German troops occupy Rome
September 23: British midget submarines damage German battleship *Tirpitz* off Norway	**September 10:** British land on the Aegean Dodecanese Islands in an ultimately doomed operation
September 25: Russians move into Smolensk and Roslavl	**September 18:** Allies control Sardinia
October 4: Allied aircraft attack a German convoy off Narvik, sinking 40,000 tons of shipping	**October 1:** Allies enter Naples, Italy; Allies occupy key Italian airfield at Foggia
November 16: U.S. bombers attack heavy water facilities in Norway	**October 4:** Allies occupy Corsica
December 25–29: In the Battle of the North Cape, German battleship *Scharnhorst* sunk	**October 8:** Guerrilla warfare in Greece presages a civil war
	December: Allies continue to press the German Winter Line south of Rome
	December 28: Allies capture Ortona in Italy

Other

April 29: In one day, German submarine *U-515* sinks five ships off the coast of west Africa

May: Allies triumph in the North Atlantic, with heavy losses for German U-boats in a German-coined "Black May"

The Pacific	*China-Burma-India*
January 2: Japanese defeated at Buna, Papua New Guinea	**February 18:** British Chindits move behind Japanese lines in Burma and cut the Mandalay–Myitkyina rail line
January 10: Last Allied offensive begins in Guadalcanal	**March 8:** Japanese advance over the Yangtze River in China, but are turned back five days later
January 12: U.S. lands on Aleutian Island Amchitka	**March 18:** British troops fighting in Burma forced back; Chindits withdraw to India
February 9: U.S. controls Guadalcanal	**April 5:** Japanese attack British on Burma's Mayu peninsula
March 2–4: Battle of the Bismarck Sea*	**May 12:** In Burma, first Allied campaign in the Arakan area is unsuccessful
March 26: Battle of the Komandorski Islands prevents Japanese from reinforcing Aleutian Island Attu	**May 18:** Heading for Chungking, Japanese advance along the Yangtze River
May 2: Japanese flying from New Guinea bomb Darwin, Australia	**May 29:** Japanese offensive in China stopped in the Ichang area
May 11: U.S. lands on Attu in the Aleutians; U.S. controls island by May 30	**August:** Work by U.S. Army Engineers on the Ledo Road (intended to connect Burma and China) is slowly progressing
June 30: Operation Cartwheel launched against SW Pacific islands	**August 23:** Japanese attack Chungking by air
July 28: Japanese secretly leave Aleutian Island Kiska*	**October 3:** Japanese attack in a large offensive across central China
August 15: Allies land at (an abandoned) Kiska	**November 2:** Chinese strike at the Japanese along Burma's Tarung River
August: U.S. landings in the Solomons: Vella Lavella (15), New Georgia Island (25), Arundel Island (27)	**November 25:** U.S. aircraft operating from China assail Formosa; Allies attack Rangoon by air
August 27: U.S. lands in the Ellice Islands on Nukufetau	**November 25:** Japanese take over Changteh in China's Hunan Province
September 1: U.S. controls Baker Island; conducts air assault on Marcus Island	**December 18:** Japanese bomb Kunming (China)
September 16: Allies occupy Lae, New Guinea	**December 29:** Chinese troops press toward Burma's Tarung River
September 28: Japanese begin withdrawal from Kolombangara in the Solomons	
October 5: After a U.S. air raid on Wake Island, the Japanese execute 98 POWs	
October 27: Allied landings in the Treasury Islands	
November 1: Battle of Bougainville begins*	
November 12: Japanese remove aircraft from Rabaul	
November 20: Allies land in the Gilbert Islands, on the atolls of Makin and Tarawa*	
November 25: U.S. defeats Japan in the Battle of Cape St. George, New Ireland	
December 15: U.S. lands on New Britain	

September 11: Off the coast of South Carolina, a German submarine leaves mines that never result in any damage

September 26: U.S. Navy uses Natal, Brazil, as a base for operations

* See text for further discussion.

1944: Toward Tokyo and Berlin

In February 1944, U.S. Army Chief of Staff George C. Marshall spoke at an American Legion dinner at the Mayflower Hotel in Washington of the progress the Allies had made in "the gathering of our great reserves in preparation for a series of tremendous blows against the enemy all over the world. . . . The energy and spirit of the assaults will determine the duration of the war." Allied armies were still a long way from Berlin and Tokyo. They were much closer to Rome, but experienced and determined German armies stood between the Allies and victory in Italy.

The Italian Campaign Continues: January–October 1944

The new year opened with a change in command in the Mediterranean Theater: U.S. general Dwight D. Eisenhower left to oversee planning for the summer invasion of Normandy and was replaced as supreme commander by British field marshal Sir Henry Maitland Wilson. As one result, the influence of American strategists in the theater was overshadowed by that of the British—and Winston Churchill was eager to break the stalemate at the Gustav Line and get Allied armies moving toward Rome. This led to a fresh plan. First, the main elements of General Mark Clark's Fifth Army (comprising the British X Corps, the French Expeditionary Force, and the U.S. II Corps) were to push across the Rapido and Garigliano Rivers; at the same time, across the Italian boot, the British Eighth Army was to cross the Sangro River and take Pescara—tying down German troops that might otherwise be sent to the west. Once the Fifth Army achieved its objectives, it was to link up with troops from a third—and crucial—operation (from which the cross-river assaults would have diverted German attention): an amphibious landing at Anzio on Italy's west coast behind the main German defensive line and less than forty miles from Rome.

Elements of the Fifth Army launched operations at Cassino and on the Garigliano River January 12, and made some progress. Five days later, the U.S. II Corps began its attempt to cross the Rapido River; by January 20, they were approaching disaster. Failure to take the heights overlooking the river had left the Americans under constant, brutal enemy fire, yet Clark ordered the crossing to go forward as planned. Artillery and mortar rounds and machine-gun fire raked the troops as they struggled to cross through mist and icy weather, some gaining a toehold on the far shore. German fire wrecked boats and bridges; units were decimated. Men wandered in confusion through a lethal landscape covered with smoke and laced with land mines—some exhibiting extraordinary courage by holding fast and rallying the men around them. After two attempts to secure the far bank, Clark ordered II Corps to withdraw. Many Allied troops were either killed, wounded, or taken prisoner—while the Germans were relatively unscathed. Outrage over this costly assault led to a postwar congressional investigation. Yet the operation did divert German attention and resources from the landing at Anzio, which began as the Rapido River operation disintegrated into failure.

OPERATION SHINGLE: ALLIED LANDING AT ANZIO, ITALY, JANUARY 22–MAY 25, 1944
MEDITERRANEAN THEATER (MEDITERRANEAN EUROPE)

Primary Objectives: *Allied:* to break the stalemate caused by the German resistance at the Gustav Line and proceed to take Rome; *German:* to hold the Gustav Line and keep the Allies from advancing

Forces: *Allied:* VI Corps of the Allied Fifth Army and additional units—an initial landing force of 36,000, increased to more than 60,000 by early February and more than 90,000 by May; an Allied invasion fleet comprising more than 375 ships and landing craft of all sizes from six nations; close air support from approximately 2,600 Allied aircraft; *German:* German Fourteenth Army, comprising, at peak, more than 130,000 men

Commanders: *Allied:* General Sir Harold Alexander (Fifteenth Army Group); Major General John P. Lucas (invasion force, January 22–February 22); Major General Lucian K. Truscott (invasion force, February 23–May 25); *German:* Field Marshal Albert Kesselring (commander in chief, Army Group C), General Eberhard von Mackensen (Fourteenth Army)

Military Losses: *Allied:* 4,400 killed, 18,000 wounded, 6,800 prisoners or missing; *German:* 5,500 killed, 17,500 wounded, 4,500 captured

Result: Four-month stalemate, with heavy casualties on both sides; Allies failed to take pressure off the Gustav Line and did not accelerate progress toward Rome, although the operation tied up more than 100,000 Wehrmacht troops.

The Allied invasion force sailed from Naples undetected and met only slight resistance landing on a fifteen-mile front January 22. With little opposition, the Allies secured the towns of Anzio and Nettuno intact, and by the end of the day, put 36,000 men ashore. Within a few days, units had pushed several miles inland. Yet they progressed no farther. Although Lucas boasted of achieving "what is certainly one of the most complete surprises in history," he failed to exploit this advantage with a fast advance. As he consolidated the beachhead, organized logistical support, and awaited reinforcements, Kesselring organized the Fourteenth Army out of every unit he could spare (without weakening the Gustav Line), and Hitler transferred men from Yugoslavia, France, and Germany. By February 1, 70,000 Germans ringed 62,000 Allied troops—and more Axis troops were on the way.

From an unsuccessful attempt to break out on January 30 through March 4, the Allies fought bitterly just to hold their position, weathering two large and bloody German counteroffensives in February. A frustrated Churchill said of Anzio: "I had hoped that we were hurling a wildcat onto the shore, but all we got was a stranded whale." Yet the Germans were frus-

---

EYEWITNESS ACCOUNT: AN ARMY NURSE AT ANZIO

Lieutenant Deloris Buckley of Spring Valley, Wisconsin, 95th Evacuation Hospital, 5th Army, endured an air raid the moment she stepped off her landing craft at Anzio. Later she lived through a not-uncommon incident, when a German aircraft pursued by a British Spitfire jettisoned its bombs,

January 27 [1944] There had been severe shelling the night before and we got some really mangled patients. . . . I was putting a postoperative dressing on an abdominal case when I heard the sound of a plane that was quite low. I figured it was a friendly craft so I paid no further attention to it. I turned to Sergeant Smith, a truly wonderful guy who assisted me in the surgery. I said, "Smitty, will you hand me . . ." I never finished the sentence. There was a mighty roar. . . . My whole body went numb. . . . I saw Smitty clutch at his desk and then sink to the floor. . . . I saw blood spurting through a pair of holes in my thigh. A piece of shrapnel had entered through one side and gone clean through it. In Fern [Wingerd]'s tent, the slaughter was worse. . . . [Lieutenant] Gert Morrow lay on the floor, unconscious and bleeding to death. [First lieutenant] Blanche Sigman, our charge nurse, a woman we all adored, was killed outright. One of the majors had an arm blown off. . . . Captain Henry Luce was struck in the liver but he kept working and taking care of the others until he collapsed. . . . In all, the single blast killed and wounded 28 doctors, nurses, and patients. I lay in an ambulance alongside Smitty. . . . "What about a cigarette?" he asked. I got one out, lit it and handed it over to him. He drew two deep puffs and then it fell from his fingers. Smitty was dead.

trated, too. After their second counteroffensive failed in early March, they made no more tries to break the Allied line. Three months of relative quiet ensued—punctuated by artillery fire, occasional raids, overhead dogfights between German and Allied aircraft, and the explosion of land mines as the Germans settled in to contain the beachhead and harass the Allies. The Anzio–Nettuno area became a complex web of trenches, foxholes, and shell holes—the Allies caught within it were sustained by 1,500 tons of supplies sent from Naples every day. The Germans braced for an anticipated spring Allied offensive, while VI Corps, now under the command of General Lucian Truscott, reorganized and regrouped. Some troops were transferred to Britain to join the force being assembled to invade France; replacements arrived. At last, in early May, Clark gave Truscott orders to organize a breakout, to be coordinated with renewed Allied assaults on the Gustav Line. On May 23, Truscott's men broke through; on May 25, the two Allied forces that had been stuck for so long at the Gustav Line and at Anzio linked up and moved toward Rome.

★   ★   ★

Before the Allied breakout at Anzio, Field Marshal Sir Harold Alexander ordered elements of Eighth Army to reinforce Fifth Army and help jump-start the stalled advance against the Gustav Line. At the time, the Fifth Army objective was to capture Cassino, a town along the Rapido River resting in the shadow of Monte Cassino—a formidable defensive outpost overlooking the Liri Valley, gateway to Rome. The Allies made several costly attempts to take Monte Casino. The first, between January 12 and February 12 (as II Corps was being battered at the Rapido River) made some progress. During the second unsuccessful attempt, which began February 15, the Allies ignited a controversy that lasted for years by destroying an ancient monastery (see box on p. 570).

General Bernard Freyberg's New Zealanders, with the 4th Indian Division, made another attempt to take Monte Cassino in March, this time preceded by aerial bombardment and artillery barrages that left much of the town of Cassino in ruins. (Through an error, the bombers did not hit the new German positions in the monastery ruins.) Finally, May 11 to 18, during Alexander's broader offensive, Operation Diadem, the XIII Corps of the British Eighth Army took the town, while the Polish II Corps, commanded by General Wladyslaw Anders, faced Monastery Hill. The German paratroopers occupying the hill repulsed the Poles' first furious assault, virtually destroying two of Anders' battalions. The Poles made better progress in a second attempt—but they were still far

MONTE CASSINO

Dating from the year 529, the Benedictine monastery that loomed 1,700 feet above the town of Cassino was filled with church treasures and such irreplaceable items as ancient Latin manuscripts of works by Ovid, Virgil, Cicero, and Seneca. The monastery was also well-placed to assist in the German defense, for instance by sheltering artillery spotters. Lieutenant General Sir Bernard Freyberg, commander of the New Zealand Corps undertaking the offensive, asked that the monastery be destroyed by aerial bombing to remove that threat. Over the objections of American general Mark Clark, Field Marshal Alexander sided with Freyberg. A prebombardment leaflet drop advised civilians (10 monks, 800 refugees) to clear the area, but most were still there when Allied bombers dropped nearly 600 tons of bombs on February 15. Many civilians were killed, and the monastery was reduced to a mass of rubble—in which the Germans quickly took up defensive positions. Despite Freyberg's suspicions, they had not done so before. German authorities had assured the Vatican that their troops would respect the sanctity of the monastery; the Germans even helped evacuate its treasures (see Chapter 3). Now, concealed in the ruins, German troops were better prepared to repel the Allied assault.

from achieving their objective when, exhausted, they held where they were. By then, Allied action all along the Gustav Line had forced Kesselring to order a withdrawal, and Anders' men secured Monastery Hill on May 18.

Alexander directed VI Corps, now freed from Anzio and linked up with the rest of Clark's Fifth Army, to head inland and encircle the withdrawing German Tenth Army. However, Clark was eager to enter Rome before the British Eighth Army did. Allowing many Germans to escape, Clark led the Fifth Army into Rome June 4, an achievement eclipsed by the Normandy landings two days later.

The Germans, meanwhile, were regrouping north of Rome at another formidable defensive position, the Gothic Line (renamed the Green Line by Hitler, and known to the Allies as the Pisa-Rimini Line). Although slowed by a reorganization of forces (six divisions were withdrawn from Italy to prepare for landings in the south of France), Allied troops, aided by increased Italian partisan activity, pressed slowly forward—Montgomery's replacement, General Oliver Leese and his British Eighth Army on the right, Clark's Fifth Army on the left. Eighth Army breached the right of the Gothic Line by September 3, but then bogged down under autumn rains. Thereafter, Allied planes attacked German supply lines, creating an acute fuel shortage for Kesselring's forces, as both sides prepared for an Allied offensive in the spring.

★ ★ ★

The slow German retreat up the boot of Italy was matched by Wehrmacht reverses all along the Eastern Front.

The Soviet Advance, January–December, 1944

In January 1944, the Soviets launched a massive offensive in bitterly cold weather that finally succeeded in breaking the 900-day siege of Leningrad, a city that Hitler had been determined to destroy. By the time the Red Army broke through, more than 600,000 people inside Leningrad had died from the slow agony of starvation. (See also Chapters 8 and 11.)

All along the Eastern Front, the Red Army reclaimed Soviet territory: most of Ukraine in April, the Crimean bastion of Sevastopol in May. In January, they crossed into eastern Poland; in June, they crossed the border with Finland, whose troops had supported the Wehrmacht in the north, winning an armistice in September. (The Finns then initiated the Arctic War, a campaign to drive German troops out of their country.) In August, after reequipping and reinforcing at a rate the Germans could no longer match, the Red Army began a summer offensive into Romania; in September, they were in Bulgaria and on the Hungarian Plain. In Poland, they were closing in on Warsaw. Within the city, the Germans were contending with an uprising, part of a general revolt by the Polish Home Army, a resistance force loyal to the non-communist London-based Polish government-in-exile. The Red Army paused—for both military and political reasons—as the Poles fought the Germans for sixty-three days.

A SECOND WARSAW UPRISING

The 1943 Jewish uprising against the Germans had been restricted to the Warsaw Ghetto (see Chapter 9). The Warsaw uprising of 1944 raged throughout the city. More than 37,000 poorly equipped fighters of the anticommunist Polish Home Army, commanded by General Antoni Chrusciel, surprised the Germans with their initial attack on August 1 and, despite heavy losses, took much of the city, raising the Polish flag there for the first time in five years. On August 20, however, SS commander Heinrich Himmler dispatched 21,300 troops to bolster the German garrison, and the Home Army was soon in desperate straits—as were all Poles, insurgents or not, that the Germans encountered. Acting on Himmler's orders, the Germans massacred more than 40,000 people in a five-day period—and the killing was just beginning. Appeals to the Allies did not result in assistance. On August 14, the British referred the matter to the Soviets; on August 22, with his forces outside Warsaw confronting a German army, Stalin declined to become involved in "the Warsaw adventure." British and American representatives then pressed the Soviets to allow RAF and USAAF planes to use airfields in Soviet territory to refuel and reach Warsaw. The Soviets refused, relenting only on one occasion in mid-September—but by then the insurgents had been squeezed into such a small part of the city that most of the supplies fell into German hands.

Short of food, medicine, and ammunition; under constant bombardment that restricted their movements to underground passages; with all hope of help from outside finally extinguished, the remnants of the Home Army insurgents surrendered October 1. During the uprising more than 15,000 insurgents and an estimated 250,000 Polish civilians perished, while the Germans suffered an estimated 17,000 casualties. In retaliation for their losses and the Poles' resistance, the Germans systematically destroyed more than 80 percent of Warsaw before the Soviets took the city on January 17, 1945.

Throughout the Soviet advance, Allied bombers continued to shatter Axis assets in western Europe.

Allied Aerial Bombing Campaign in Europe: January–December, 1944

British and American air forces had been collaborating on air offensives throughout 1943, after the creation of the Combined Bomber Offensive (CBO) at the Casablanca Conference in January. Late in the year, however, after suffering extremely heavy losses in their daylight air attacks, particularly over Schweinfurt, the United States suspended attacks on targets deep in Germany and reevaluated its air strategy. The RAF continued attacks without the help of the Americans, pointedly starting the year by bombing Berlin on January 2. On February 19, 800 British bombers hit Leipzig in a nighttime raid, and U.S. bombers—back in the air and now under the protection of long-range P-51 fighters—followed up with a daytime raid the next day, killing 969 civilians, and displacing another 50,000.

On February 20, the Allies embarked on what came to be known as Big Week, an intensive six-day offensive (RAF at night, U.S. 8th and 15th air forces during the day), dropping nearly 20,000 tons of bombs on factories and other facilities involved in German aircraft production. Dogfights between Allied P-51s and Luftwaffe fighters did more lasting damage than the

Above, a bombardier in his domain. Air superiority was crucial to Allied victory. Waves of Allied bombers destroyed or disrupted Axis communication, transportation, and fuel supplies—and aimed, with only partial success, at destroying enemy morale. Below, Hamburg was one of the hardest-hit German cities; this rubble attests to the devastating Allied firebombing of the city in July 1943 that claimed tens of thousands of lives.

bombs, for although the Germans began repairs to aircraft production facilities relatively quickly, they could not as easily replace the experienced pilots lost during this Allied offensive. The British and Americans did not emerge unscathed: both lost approximately 6 percent of their planes.

British Air Chief Marshal Sir Arthur "Bomber" Harris remained determined to bomb German cities, particularly Berlin. These attacks displaced many civilians, but German morale did not crumble (see Chapter 11). In April, Allied air forces were placed under the command of General Eisenhower, who deployed them to help prepare for the D-Day landings by bombing key communications, industrial, and transportation targets. On May 12, Lieutenant General Carl Spaatz, head of the United States Strategic Air Forces in Europe (USSTAF), began concentrated attacks against Germany's synthetic oil plants, destroying more than a third of their production capacity the first day. By the fall of 1944, as the western Allies were moving rapidly toward Germany, fuel shortages increasingly restricted German military operations. Meanwhile, in June, American bombers began taking off from Italy for raids into Silesia, Hungary, and Romania before flying to Soviet bases for refueling.

A vital part of the Allied strategy against Germany, the Combined Bomber Offensive was a costly endeavor: the British lost 57,000 airmen (killed or missing), and 64,000 American airmen were killed. Many others were taken prisoner after their planes crash-landed on Axis territory. The cost to German civilians was much heavier: an estimated 700,000 died as a result of Allied strategic bombing.

★　　★　　★

As the Allies struck at the German Reich, their forces in the Far East were making slow progress across the Pacific toward Japan. In the Central Pacific, the next Allied goal was the Marshall Islands, a group of 32 separate atolls northwest of the recently secured Gilbert Islands. The first target was Kwajalein Atoll, the world's largest, comprising 91 inlets; in this amphibious operation, code-named Flintlock, troops would land only on the Kwajalein island (assigned to the army's 7th Infantry Division) and the linked islands of Roi and Namur (4th Marine Division). To avoid a repeat of the carnage at Tarawa, aircraft stationed on new bases in the Gilberts, carrier-based navy planes, and naval artillery bombarded the objectives in January. Just prior to the landings, "frogmen" from newly formed Underwater Demolition Teams scouted for hidden obstacles and marked landing craft lanes, and the troops hit the beach with potent firepower, including many automatic weapons and flamethrowers. The Marines met light resistance on Roi and somewhat heavier opposition on Namur, while the army had to fight briskly for four days before securing Kwajalein—even though almost half the 8,600-man Japanese garrison on the three islands had perished in the preassault bombardments. Most others died in the fighting; the Americans took only 265 prisoners, all but 100 of whom were Korean laborers. American casualties included 372 killed and 1,582 wounded.

On February 15, an 8,000-man invasion force (22nd Marine Regiment, elements of the army's 27th Division, and other units) embarked from Kwajalein, heading for Eniwetok Atoll, 326 miles away. Operations against the islands of Engebi (site of an airfield) commenced on the morning of February 17 and concluded the next day. Eniwetok Island was the site of hard fighting before it was secured on February 21. A day later, Marines secured the last objective, Parry Island. The operation, though smooth, had involved bitter combat that killed 195 Americans and wounded more than 500. Only 64 men of the Japanese force of 3,500 survived to be taken prisoner.

The same day that the Eniwetok operations commenced, U.S. carrier-based planes began bombing the Japanese naval base at Truk, in the Caroline Islands. Aware that the base would be an American target, the Japanese had sent most of their warships elsewhere. However, a substantial garrison with aircraft, a few warships, and various support vessels remained. Two days of air attacks destroyed or damaged most of the planes and sank 27 vessels (including 3 warships), while a task force under Admiral Spruance circumnavigated the atoll and destroyed three more Japanese ships that were attempting to escape. These assaults—and further air strikes—obviated the need for an assault on Truk; the Allies hopped over it and continued to move forward. (See "Island Hopping in the Pacific" earlier in this chapter.) Meanwhile MacArthur's forces were striking north from New Guinea to the Admiralty Islands and Emirau in the Bismarcks, both of which were taken by March 20. At the same time, the fighting on New Guinea continued: pushing west along the coast, MacArthur's forces would land at Hollandia April 22, the offshore island of Wadke May 17, and the island of Biak, just outside Geelvink Bay, on May 27.

At the same time, far to the northwest, Allied forces had begun to move back into Burma.

The Burma Campaign, Part III: 1944

In January, the Allies launched a three-pronged campaign into Burma. The first phase involved an advance by British, Indian, and West African troops of the 15th India Corps, under the command of Lieutenant General Sir Philip Christison (part of General Sir William Slim's Fourteenth Army) southward into Arakan (an area along the Burmese west coast) to take Akyab, on the Bay of Bengal. Christison's force fought their way slowly toward the objective, which they were poised to take by the end of the year.

The second phase involved Galahad, a U.S. volunteer force of about 3,000 American-trained Chinese soldiers and U.S. infantrymen that would become known as Merrill's Mauraders, after its commander, Brigadier General Frank D. Merrill. (The unit's official designation was 5307 Composite Unit, provisional.) Operating under the direction of General Joseph Stilwell, the U.S. theater commander, Merrill's irregulars were to cooperate with Nationalist Chinese troops to take the Hukawng Valley in the north and then proceed southward to take the town of Myitkyina, terminus of the rail line from Rangoon and Mandalay and site of the only hard-

---

INTO INDIA

On March 6, some 80,000 men of Lieutenant General Renya Mutaguchi's Fifteenth Army crossed the Chindwin River and invaded India. Their primary objective: to prevent Slim's Fourteenth Army from striking into Burma by destroying the British supply base at Imphal. (A lesser objective—stimulating an Indian revolt against the British colonial regime—was reflected in the presence of the collaborationist Indian National Army.) Pushing through difficult terrain into an area thick with Allied units, Mutaguchi knew success depended on surprise, speed—and capturing supplies to sustain it. Initially, he was successful. Slim—who had expected a Japanese offensive, but misjudged where it would strike—had to pull his men back to Imphal, where they were reinforced by two divisions flown in from Arakan. By mid-April, the Japanese had surrounded both Imphal and Kohima, a town commanding Imphal's supply lines. Cut off and besieged for two months, the British survived with the help of the RAF's Third Tactical Air Force, which landed supplies and reinforcements and removed casualties. Mutaguchi had no such assistance. Unable to breach the Allied lines at Imphal and Kohima, he tried and failed to secure supplies by taking Dimapur, then withdrew across the Chindwin as the monsoon season set in. Yet the battle was not over. Slim's army was in hot pursuit, their presence turning an orderly Japanese retreat into a rout. The Imphal offensive cost the Japanese 53,000 casualties (30,000 killed), all Fifteenth Army's tanks and other heavy weapons, and 17,000 pack animals. The Japanese Army in Burma never recovered from this disaster.

surfaced air strip in northern Burma. Orde Wingate's Chindit irregulars—now 20,000 strong—were to support this operation, which would allow the completion of the Ledo Road. The Chinese and the Mauraders held the Hukawng Valley by March, with the Chindits operating against Japanese communications slightly to their south. (That month, Wingate was killed in a plane crash; his men remained in the field.) By May, these combined forces had taken the Myitkyina airfield (which immediately became a conduit for moving supplies into China), although the Japanese held on to the town until August.

The third phase of the offensive involved a push by the 17th and 20th Indian Divisions of Slim's 4th Corps into north central Burma (Assam).

To meet this triple threat, the Japanese formed two new armies: the 28th in Arakan and the 33rd in northern Burma. Meanwhile, in the northwest, General Renya Mutaguchi's Japanese Fifteenth Army embarked on an ambitious offensive: a push toward Imphal, India. (See box opposite.)

★   ★   ★

As Mutaguchi's army was on the road to disaster at Imphal, the Japanese Imperial Army was pushing Allied Forces back in China.

The Ichi-Go Campaign (Operation Number One), April–December 1944

Launched in April, with the ultimate goal of forcing China out of the war, the campaign had several interim objectives: strengthening Japan's position in China, controlling major transportation routes, such as the Beijing-Hankow Railway, improving communication lines—and destroying the airbases from which Major General Claire Chennault's Fourteenth Air Force launched air strikes. Opposed primarily by Chinese Nationalist ground troops, the Japanese pushed forward month after month in a broad sweep, occupying Henan, Guangxi, Hunan, and Guizhou provinces. Their progress frustrated U.S. theater commander General Joseph Stilwell. Intelligence reports noted that the Japanese moved "virtually at will. The Chinese have shown only slight evidence of either plan or capability." In some cases, Chinese troops would disappear rather than fight; occasionally, villagers angered by their treatment under the Nationalists welcomed the Japanese. Chiang, meanwhile, assuming the Allies would eventually defeat Japan, remained consumed by the threat posed to the Nationalists by the Chinese Communists.

This exacerbated his already contentious relationship with Stilwell—who also had a contentious relationship with Chennault. These feuds led to Stilwell's replacement, in October 1944, by Lieutenant General Albert C. Wedemeyer. By that time, the Japanese had captured all but three of the Allied air bases in southeast China. Yet, by the end of the year, as conditions grew worse for them in the Pacific, their drive faltered. Although the Japanese would attempt to renew the offensive early in 1945, Ichi-Go was essentially over in December, after an unsuccessful attempt to take Guiyang, the capital of Guizhou province.

★   ★   ★

While the Chinese Nationalists were retreating before the Japanese in China, the western Allies were preparing to send a great invasion force across the English Channel to the Normandy coast. The preparations did not proceed without incident; but even a costly attack on an invasion rehearsal by German vessels did not slow Allied momentum.

DISASTER AT SLAPTON SANDS

On the night of April 28, nine German E-boats (torpedo boats) on routine patrol out of Cherbourg, France, investigated heavy radio traffic near Slapton Sands in southern England. They came upon an American convoy of eight ships transporting quartermaster, engineer, and chemical troops—part of an immense invasion rehearsal (although the Germans did not know this). Firing their torpedoes, the E-boats sank two U.S. Landing Ship Tanks (LST) and damaged another, killing 749 American soldiers and sailors. Allied authorities could not allow the event to be reported if they were to maintain the security of the invasion plan. The dead were buried in secret—after all identities had been checked to make certain that all ten officers on the two destroyed ships who had been involved in planning the invasion were accounted for. (They had all drowned.) The wounded were placed under quarantine and threatened with court-martial if they discussed what happened. (General Eisenhower issued a press release telling of the tragedy in July, after the need for secrecy ended. But other war news, and the passage of time, obscured the event for many years.) The deadliest American training incident of the war, the *Great Slapton Sands Disaster* was an ominous precursor to a huge Allied gamble that would decide the course of the war in Europe.

Operation Overlord, the Allied Invasion of Northwest Europe

Expecting an Allied invasion of western Europe, the Germans had a half-million men spread out along the French coast attempting to finish fortifying what Hitler called his "Atlantic Wall." The defenses at Calais, just thirty miles from England and believed to be the main Allied landing site, were strong, but those at Normandy to the south were not. Field Marshal Rommel ordered an elaborate series of underwater and above ground obstacles placed there.

The German commanders differed on the best method of defense: Field Marshal von Rundstedt wanted a flexible response capability, stationing his men outside of Paris, from which they could quickly move to strike Allied forces wherever they landed. Rommel favored battling on the beaches to prevent the Allies from gaining even a toehold on the Continent. Hitler split the difference, pleasing neither man; Rommel received three panzer divisions and three others went to Rundstedt, who could use them only on Hitler's orders.

Meanwhile, under cover of secrecy that included elaborate efforts to fool the Germans about the invasion's location and timing (see Chapter 9), the Allies had assembled an invasion force of some 150,000 American, British, and Canadian troops, as well as several thousand from other Allied nations, including France, Belgium, Holland, Poland, and Norway. Less than 15 percent of these men had ever seen combat. Selecting an invasion date with favorable moonlight and tidal conditions, Allied commanders chose a sixty-mile swath of Normandy coastline between Le Havre and Cherbourg as the invasion site. They divided this into five beaches, code-named *Sword, Juno, Gold, Omaha,* and *Utah*. British forces would attack Sword and Gold, the Canadians were assigned Juno, and Omaha and Utah went to the Americans. Poor weather that had caused Eisenhower to postpone the invasion by one day improved a little, but certainly not enough for the Germans to anticipate that the Allies would attempt a landing in such unfavorable conditions. Thus, on June 5, Rundstedt was comfortably settled at his headquarters in St. Germain, and Rommel was in Ulm celebrating his wife's birthday.

In Britain, Eisenhower was bidding godspeed to Allied paratroopers, who would be the first Allied troops to land on French soil. Two years of planning and the efforts of some 3 million people were about to come to fruition.

D-DAY, THE AMPHIBIOUS ASSAULT ON NORMANDY, FRANCE (OPERATION NEPTUNE), JUNE 6, 1944
EUROPEAN THEATER (WEST)

Primary Objectives: *Allied:* to establish a beachhead in western Europe, from which forces would then move east toward Germany, relieve pressure on the Soviets at the Eastern Front and, by pushing inland across France, trap the Wehrmacht between two forces; *German:* to prevent the Allies from securing a foothold in western Europe

Forces: *Allied:* 45 divisions (approx. 156,000 troops), including 73,000 Americans (23,250 at Utah, 34,250 at Omaha; 15,500 airborne troops); 83,115 British/Canadian (24,970 at Gold, 21,400 at Juno, 28,845 at Sword; 7,900 airborne troops); 11,590 aircraft supported the landings, flying 14,674 sorties on D-Day; more than 6,400 ships and landing craft; *German:* 70,000 troops in landing zones; 25 coastal divisions, 16 infantry and parachute divisions; 10 armored and mechanized divisions; 7 reserve divisions; 319 aircraft; 4 destroyers and 39 U-boats

Commanders: *Allied:* Supreme Commander General Dwight D. Eisenhower (U.S.); Allied ground troops under General Bernard Montgomery (Britain); U.S. First Army under General Omar Bradley, British Second Army under General Miles Dempsey; *German:* Field Marshal Gerd von Rundstedt, commander in chief in the West; Army Group B (Seventh and Fifteenth Armies) under Field Marshal Erwin Rommel

Military Losses: *Allied:* 2,500 dead, 7,500 wounded or missing—lighter than the Allies had estimated (25,000) at all but Omaha Beach (where there were about 2,000 casualties); 127 aircraft lost. U.S.—1,465 dead, 3,184 wounded, 1,928 missing, 26 captured; U.S. airborne troops accounted for 2,499 casualties, including 238 killed; British casualties—2,500–3,000; Canadian—946; *German:* 4,000–9,000 killed

Result: At day's end, more than 150,000 Allied men were on French soil; advance forces had pushed five or more miles inland (except at Omaha Beach). Allies had total air superiority. Within a week, the Germans had rushed 700 more planes and additional panzer divisions to the area, while the Allies had landed 326,547 troops, 54,186 vehicles and 104,428 tons of supplies. By July 1, more than a million Allied troops had come ashore.

Transport planes and gliders dropped the first paratroopers behind German lines in France shortly after midnight; the British 6th Airborne Division landed easily and troops quickly moved to secure positions on the Orne River, leading to Caen. On the right flank, above Utah beach, things went badly for the American 82nd and 101st Airborne Divisions. Some paratroopers landed and drowned in the Vire River valley marshes, which the Germans intentionally flooded; others wound up miles from their target areas; many spent days on their own wandering the countryside before finding their way to American units.

The confusion among the Americans on the western flank was shared by the German defenders, who were sending sketchy reports to headquarters of parachute landings and skirmishes. By jamming the radar stations in Normandy and manipulating those in the Pas de Calais region, the Allies led German commanders to believe there was a swarm of aircraft crossing the Channel; as a result, the Luftwaffe raced to meet the imaginary enemy aircraft at Calais. Even when the invasion fleet opened fire on the Normandy beaches at dawn, German commanders believed it was a decoy or covering action for the real attack. Rundstedt thought so, too, but at 4 A.M. he ordered two of his reserve panzer divisions to head toward Caen; these remained under Hitler's direct control and could not be moved without his permission. The führer, who usually slept late, was not informed of the invasion until 2 P.M.; only then were the panzers ordered to move. The 21st Panzer Division, near Caen, was the only armored unit close enough to go into action that day.

About eight to ten miles from shore, the first wave of assault forces descended from the transport ships into the small landing craft bobbing in cold, choppy water. Nearing shore, some craft struck mines or were hit by shells; other vessels were swamped, capsized, or inadvertently unloaded men into water over their heads. Weighed down by their equipment and packs, many drowned. A soldier in the first wave, 19-year-old Sgt. John Slaughter, Company D, 116th Infantry, 29th Division, later remembered: "people were screaming, hollering, you know, drowning, some hit, bleeding . . . they were hanging all over me trying to stay afloat . . . and they were pulling me under . . . it was terrible."

On the right flank, U.S. forces landed at 6:30 A.M. at Utah Beach, about a thousand yards off course, but they were aided immeasurably by the 101st Airborne, which had eliminated many German artillery positions. The landings on the left flank, beginning at 7 A.M., went relatively smoothly. At Sword and Juno, the British and Canadians moved rapidly across the beach, their "Swimming Sherman" tanks providing strong covering fire, and German

THE FINAL OVERLORD PLAN

Drop Zones
D-Day Phase Line

ELEVATION IN METERS

0   50   100   200 and Above

0   15

Miles

The Allied invasion routes at Normandy appear straightforward on paper, but to gain a foothold on shore landing forces had to overcome submerged gates, mines, and metal-pronged hedgehogs (girders and rails welded together) that ripped open landing craft. On shore, the invaders encountered barbed wire, antitank ditches, minefields, and withering gunfire from machine gun nests and bunkers in the bluffs above. Beyond that lay large German gun emplacements and trench works. At Omaha Beach, medics tend to the fallen.

resistance flagged. On Gold, the tanks were late getting ashore, but the British 50th Division overcame strong initial resistance and was moving off the beach by late morning.

The horror that was unfolding at what came to be known as "Bloody Omaha" with the struggle to get ashore only worsened: the Americans faced the crack German 352nd Infantry; landing craft foundered on sand bars, presenting German gunners with easy targets; Allied naval firepower occasionally hit forces on the beach; some of the immobile wounded lying on the sand drowned as the tide came in; tanks released too soon from cargo vessels wallowed in the surf and could not provide covering fire for troops on the beach. Only about a third of the men in the initial assault even got to the shore. The early morning naval bombardment, hindered by cloud cover, had overshot most of the German gun positions, leaving assault forces exposed to withering crossfire as they ran toward the stone seawall. Members of the 2nd Ranger Battalion scaling the nearby one-hundred-foot-high cliff at Pointe du Hoc suffered heavy casualties, only to discover on reaching the battery that the deadly 155mm cannons they had been sent to destroy had been removed from their casemate. The Rangers continued to their next objective. Meanwhile, the 1st Battalion of the 116th Infantry was shredded

---

EYEWITNESS ACCOUNT: D-DAY ON OMAHA BEACH

PFC Jesse Beazley, 21, of Nicholasville, Kentucky, was a rifleman in the 38th regiment, 2nd infantry division, who landed on Omaha Beach on D-Day:

I made it in to the beach . . . and most of that then to me is a nightmare. [S]oldiers . . . were begging for help and crying for help. I seen them with their face half blowed off and some of them with their intestines hanging out, and they'd just look at you with a pitiful look because you couldn't do nothing for them. Another thing I seen there was, those battleships firing over our head and everything, they would make big craters in the ground, deep. I saw a cow, a French cow, blew right up in a tree. . . . I was completely separated from anybody that I knew, but I fought there that day until night come, and I got in a German foxhole. . . . There was mortar shells coming in on us, artillery shells coming in on us, machine gun fire, everything imaginable, right on you. You could see the tracer bullets coming right at you. But I laid there in my foxhole with my bayonet on the end of my gun and put it in between my legs and let it stick up in the air in case they jumped in on me they would hit the bayonet. That's all I knew to do.

by sniper and machine-gun fire—"more or less sacrificed," surviving rifle-man Harold Baumgarten later said, "to achieve the landing." As a result, some of the other battalions that followed the 116th moved off Omaha Beach virtually untouched.

The Germans rushed reinforcements to Normandy, but kept the Pas de Calais fully manned. (The Allies' great deception operation, code-named Fortitude, led the Germans to believe for many weeks more that the main invasion was yet to come.) Allied aircraft severely damaged Rundstedt's much-delayed central reserve force as it moved toward Normandy, and naval artillery pounded German defenses. As more men came ashore, *beachmasters* organized traffic flow and the wounded were evacuated. By day's end, the 6th Airborne had hooked up with the British 3rd Division as planned, al-though they were unable to capture Caen. The British 50th Division reached the outskirts of Bayeux, and the Canadians came closest to securing assigned Allied objectives as they drew within view of Caen and Bayeaux.

CODE TALKERS

Some Allied units that landed on Utah Beach June 6 had secret weapons: men who spoke a com-plex and unfamiliar language that flummoxed Germans attempting to eavesdrop on Allied com-munications. Fourteen men of the Comanche Nation, members of the U.S. Army 4th Signal Corps, served as code talkers throughout the campaign to liberate Europe from *posah-tai-vo* ("crazy white man," aka Adolf Hitler). Men of the Choctaw, Creek, Menominee, Chippewa, and Hopi Nations also served as army code talkers—building on the pioneering efforts of more than a dozen Choctaw code talkers in World War I. The best known code talkers of World War II were the 400 Navajo U.S. Marines who participated in every Marine assault in the Pacific cam-paign. The idea for a code based on Navajo came from a civil engineer, Philip Johnston, who grew up on a Navajo reservation and knew that the Navajo language was little-known and ex-tremely complex. In the code devised from Navajo, words from nature represented military terms: airplanes, for example, were referred to as "chicken hawk" (dive bomber), "swallow" (tor-pedo plane), "owl" (observation plane), "hummingbird" (fighter plane), "buzzard" (bomber), "crow" (patrol plane), and "eagle" (transport). If the code talkers needed to spell something out that had no corresponding code term, there were code words that represented letters: "ant" for "a," "bear" for "b," and so on. The Navajo especially distinguished themselves at Iwo Jima, where they successfully and accurately conveyed over 800 crucial messages.

The Americans on Omaha had reached the coast road, while the U.S. 4th Division joined up with paratroopers around Sainte-Mère-Eglise. At Utah Beach, young naval officer Tracy Sugarman, who had spent the day taking men ashore, finally reached the landing site himself. "Jesus," he said, "we made it through D-Day."

★   ★   ★

While the Allies secured the Normandy beachhead and prepared to push inland, U.S. Marines were preparing to make another amphibious landing, part of the Central Pacific campaign. They were on the doorstep to the Marianas, a chain of islands that contained several key U.S. objectives: Saipan, Guam, and Tinian. Holding these islands would disrupt Japanese supply lines, give the U.S. Navy bases to support the anticipated offensive in the Philippines, and provide the Allies with airfields close enough to bomb Japan's home islands. Saipan would be the first target.

BATTLE OF SAIPAN (OPERATION FORAGER), JUNE 15–JULY 9, 1944
PACIFIC THEATER

Primary Objectives: *American:* to take Aslito airfield to provide a base for long-range B-29 bombers, and to secure Saipan in preparation for the upcoming battle to capture the Philippines; *Japanese:* to keep the United States from gaining a foothold within the Pacific inner defensive circle

Forces: *American:* initial landing force comprised 2nd and 4th Marine Divisions, reserve troops from 27th Infantry Division; *Japanese:* about 30,000 troops (43rd Division, 47th Brigade, two infantry battalions, naval infantry brigade)

Commanders: *American:* Admiral Raymond Spruance, commander of the Fifth Fleet, in overall operational command; Rear Admiral Richmond Kelly Turner in charge of the Saipan landing; Marine Major General Holland Smith commanding the 2nd and 4th Marine Divisions and ground commander of the assault; Major General Ralph C. Smith commanding the 27th Infantry Division; *Japanese:* Naval Fourth Fleet and Japanese 31st Army, headquartered on Saipan, under Vice Admiral Chuichi Nagumo and Lieutenant General Hideyoshi Obata respectively (Obata was away and did not participate in Saipan's defense); ground command on Saipan under Lieutenant General Saito Yoshitsugu

*Above, U.S. Marines duck and dodge their way around burning buildings on Saipan, June 1944.
Below, in September 1944, Chaplain Rufus W. Oakley holds services on Peleliu, just a few
hundred yards away from—and within range of—Japanese positions. Peleliu was yet another
island where the Japanese dug in and staunchly defended every inch of ground, causing thousands
of American casualties and extending the campaign there to months instead of the days that U.S.
military commanders initially expected.*

Military Losses: *American:* more than 3,100 killed, 13,400 wounded, or missing; *Japanese:* at least 27,000 killed

Result: The United States secured Saipan, was positioned to capture Guam and Tinian, and would soon be in a position to make air strikes on Japan. Heavy losses of Japanese troops on Saipan and in the Battle of the Philippine Sea led to the dissolution of the Tojo cabinet in July 1944.

Only fourteen miles long and a few miles wide, Saipan possessed many natural fortifications, such as rocky cliffs, mountains, and caves. The 8,000 U.S. Marines of the 2nd and 4th divisions who hit the southern beaches on June 15 quickly discovered that the preassault bombardment had not significantly weakened these formidable defenses. Within a few days, they had taken a prime objective, Aslito airfield—but at a high price: some 2,000 American casualties on the first day alone. This spurred Holland Smith to commit the 27th Infantry Division (held in reserve) to the battle June 16–17. Assisted by naval gunfire, the three divisions moved north (the 2nd moving along the west coast, the 4th up the east coast, and the 27th driving up the center), making slow progress against the tenacious enemy. On June 17, the Japanese mounted their largest tank operation outside China. Sending more than 100 tanks against the Americans, they slowed the U.S. advance.

As Saipan devolved into a battle of attrition, the Japanese launched Operation A-Go to reinforce troops in the Marianas and destroy U.S. naval power in the area. The operation drew American vessels and aircraft away from supporting the Marines on Saipan to meet this new threat.

BATTLE OF THE PHILIPPINE SEA (OPERATION A-GO), JUNE 19–21, 1944
PACIFIC THEATER

Primary Objectives: *American:* to stand between Japanese reinforcements and American troops landed on Saipan; *Japanese:* to relieve ground forces on Saipan, under attack from U.S. Marine and Army landing forces; to draw U.S. naval power out into a vulnerable position and destroy it

Forces: *American:* 15 aircraft carriers (7 heavy, 8 light), 956 planes, 7 battleships, 21 cruisers, 69 destroyers, 100,000 crewmen; *Japanese:* 9 aircraft carriers (5 heavy, 4 light), 473 planes, 5 battleships, 13 cruisers, 28 destroyers, 40,000 crewmen

Commanders: *American:* Admiral Raymond Spruance commanding the Fifth Fleet, Vice Admiral Marc Mitscher commanding Task Force 58,

Fifth Fleet's main fighting force; *Japanese:* Admiral Soemu Toyoda commander in chief of naval operations, Vice Admiral Jisaburo Ozawa commanding the First Mobile Fleet

Military Losses: *American:* 130 planes destroyed (most from crash-landing after running out of fuel); *Japanese:* 3 aircraft carriers sunk, 438 planes destroyed, 445 aviators killed

Result: A devastating defeat for the Japanese Navy; forced to retreat, the Japanese could not reinforce Saipan.

"The fate of the Empire depends on this one battle," Toyoda stated as he ordered A-Go to begin. "Everyone must give all he has." Ozawa's First Mobile Fleet then sailed from the Philippines, initiating what would become the largest carrier battle of the war. Ozawa planned to send a small detachment of ships ahead to draw the American Fifth Fleet into a position vulnerable to preliminary attacks by land-based planes and submarines that would, he calculated, destroy at least a third of the U.S. fleet before his main attack. Then his carrier-based aircraft would pounce on the Americans, land to rearm and refuel on Guam and Tinian, and hit the U.S. fleet again on the way back. No part of this plan was successful. American intelligence and submarine reports had conveyed the essentials of A-Go to Spruance; in preliminary engagements, the Americans sank 17 of the 25 Japanese submarines and plastered the Japanese bases on Guam and Tinian. Thereafter, the Americans determined the location of Ozawa's fleet by using "Huff-Duff" direction-finding equipment that zeroed in on Japanese radio signals and, on June 19, detected the attack formations of Japanese aircraft with radar. Experienced U.S. pilots shot nearly 300 Japanese planes out of the skies over the ocean and the island of Guam in what became known as "the Great Marianas Turkey Shoot." American submarines also struck a hard blow, sinking the Japanese carriers *Shokaku* and *Taiho* (Ozawa's flagship; the admiral transferred to another vessel).

The next afternoon, U.S. planes sighted Ozawa's main force—at the very edge of the range of American aircraft. Admiral Mitscher decided to launch a strike—although this would mean that pilots would be extremely low on fuel as they returned to their carriers in darkness. More than 200 took off on a raid that sank the carrier *Hiyu* (as well as two oilers) and damaged three other carriers and several other ships. Left with only 35 planes, Ozawa retreated as Mitscher concentrated on retrieving his aircraft—ordering all lights turned on to guide them, despite the danger of submarine attack.

Twenty planes had been lost in the fighting; 80 more crash-landed on their carriers or were ditched in the sea on returning. Rescue operations for the ditched pilots delayed the fleet's pursuit of Ozawa, and on June 21, the Fifth Fleet returned to the Marianas.

★   ★   ★

Back on Saipan, the 27th Infantry Division had run into trouble on what the Americans would soon be calling Purple Heart Ridge, a densely wooded escarpment near Mount Tapotchau. Frustrated by the division's lack of progress, the ground commander, Marine general Holland Smith, relieved the U.S. Army division commander, Ralph Smith—an action that did little for interservice amity. With the aid of well-placed naval gunfire, slow progress resumed against fierce resistance. On the night of July 6–7, the Japanese staged the largest banzai charge of the war; some 3,000 soldiers hurled themselves against the Americans, briefly overrunning some positions before the stunned U.S. troops reestablished their lines. That charge was the last organized Japanese resistance, but it was not the end of the anguish of Saipan. On July 9, the day the fighting ended, surviving Japanese soldiers and hundreds of civilians—men, women, and children—killed themselves, even as some horrified Americans tried to stop them. Japanese soldiers forced some civilians to their deaths; many died voluntarily, terrified of victorious Americans whom they had been taught to regard as barbarians. Entire families jumped from two cliffs at the north of the island. More than 20,000 civilians died on Saipan.

★   ★   ★

The capture of Saipan secured an airbase for the new B-29 Superfortress bombers to make daily raids over Tokyo and other Japanese cities. Similarly bloody but successful landings soon took place on Guam (July 21) and Tinian (July 24). The latter, just over 1,000 air miles from Japan's home island of Honshu, became the busiest airport in the world after Navy SeaBees built six runways on the tiny island. In August 1945, two special aircraft would take off from its runways, each carrying one atomic bomb. But in July 1944, the race to complete the bomb continued, Allied authorities fearing that the Germans would create the terrible weapon first. They would soon learn, from members of the *Alsos mission* who were moving forward with Allied troops in France, that the Germans were far behind the Allies in A-bomb development (see Chapter 5). Meanwhile, most of the Allied forces in France had more immediate concerns.

After D-Day: The Normandy Campaign Continues, while Operation Dragoon Begins, June 26–September 1944

Moving off the beaches, with more troops landing behind them, Allied units pushed their way inland. The Americans captured the major port town of Cherbourg on the Cotentin Peninsula, northwest of Utah Beach, on June 26, with the help of British and Canadian forces that held down German panzer divisions sent to relieve the city. By the end of the month, the entire Cotentin region had surrendered. Victory at Cherbourg ended Hitler's hope that the Allies might be pushed back across the English Channel, and Runstedt and Rommel asked to withdraw their forces from the area. But Hitler refused to allow retreat. In July, he replaced Runstedt with Field Marshal Gunther von Kluge—while Rommel was recuperating from wounds received when the RAF strafed his car. British planes were busy pounding newly reinforced Caen, a regional communications center and gateway to flat, open ground toward Paris. Caen fell to British and Canadian armored forces (which lost more than 200 tanks) on July 20 (the day Hitler was injured in an assassination attempt at his Rastenburg headquarters). At the same time, the Americans were engaged in a brutal battle for Saint-Lô, fought in treacherous *bocage* country. (Its steep wooded hills, small fields, and ancient hedgerows formed a foliage barrier that stymied even tanks—until GIs improvised; see "Tanks and Tank Destroyers" in Chapter 5.) The U.S. 29th and 35th divisions lost more than 2,000 men in the effort, including 136 killed by bombs dropped short of enemy lines by American aircraft; German losses were greater, and Saint-Lô was completely destroyed. Bradley's First Army took Avranches, at the base of the Cotentin, on July 30, opening the way toward Brittany, and the Allies prepared to break out of Normandy. On August 1, General George Patton returned to action from "leading" the nonexistent First U.S. Army Group in England (an element of the Allies' deception operation); he assumed command of the very real Third Army in France.

Under Patton, the Third Army swiftly advanced toward the Loire River. Within two weeks, it held a line that ran along the Loire from St. Nazaire to Angers. Then Patton turned northeast and, closing with Bradley's First Army, nearly surrounded the bulk of the retreating German Army. By August 13, the Germans' only escape lay in a fifteen-mile gap between Falaise and Argentan to the east. This bottleneck, the Falaise Pocket, became a massive killing field, with casualties so heavy that, as General Eisenhower witnessed later, it was literally possible to walk for hundreds of yards stepping on nothing but dead and decaying flesh. Perhaps 115,000 Germans managed to escape before the Allies closed the gap on August 20—but they left behind 10,000 dead and 50,000 prisoners.

Meanwhile news of Allied progress had sparked an uprising in Paris, where the German garrison under General Dietrich von Choltitz comprised 20,000 troops—including some Waffen SS armored units. On August 10, railroad workers struck; on August 15, the police. Sporadic street fighting began on August 19; Parisians built barricades in the streets or took to the rooftops and sniped at every German that crossed their sights. As the resistance gained force, Swedish diplomat Raoul Nordling convinced Choltitz not to destroy the city by following Hitler's orders to defend it stone by stone. On August 23, after a BBC news report that the Parisians were liberating their own city, Eisenhower and Patton released Lieutenant General Philippe Leclerc's 2nd French Armored Division from the Third Army to officially free the French capital. By the next evening, the first elements of the division were rumbling through Paris streets and, on August 25, joy reigned supreme as Choltitz signed an instrument of surrender. After four dark years of occupation, Paris could reclaim the title "City of Light." Allied troops were pushing the Germans off French soil in the north—and the south, where the Allies had just staged another amphibious landing.

This new operation, code-named Operation Dragoon (changed from its earlier designation, "Anvil") began on August 15 and involved 887 Allied warships, 1,370 landing craft, and some 2,000 planes. After a preassault bombardment, American, Canadian, British, and Free French troops of the U.S. Seventh Army landed on the French Riviera between Cannes and Hyères, supported on each flank by commandos and paratroops. The landing went smoothly; only three German divisions faced the invasion beach, and Allied aircraft outnumbered the Luftwaffe 10 to 1. Hitler had designated the important ports of Toulon and Marseilles fortresses that must be defended, and there was brisk fighting, but by August 28, the garrisons of both cities had surrendered to the Free French. Meanwhile, General Lucian Truscott's VI Corps (3 U.S. divisions), which had comprised the first assault wave, pushed northward into the Rhone Valley, pursuing the retreating Germans while sending armored units around to trap them. Held up by stiff resistance from the 11th Panzer Division that allowed much of the

German's Nineteenth Army to escape, the Americans overcame it and moved forward, taking Lyon on September 3. By September 15, the Seventh Army had linked up with Patton's Third Army and became part of Eisenhower's European Theater command.

★　★　★

Farther north, Allies in the European Theater faced a formidable German fortification, the Siegfried Line or West Wall (see "Fortifications" in Chapter 5). To outflank that line, Field Marshal Bernard Montgomery, forsaking his normal cautious approach to campaigning, proposed an ambitious operation.

OPERATION MARKET-GARDEN, SEPTEMBER 17–25, 1944
EUROPEAN THEATER (WEST)

Primary Objectives: *Allied:* to secure a bridge over the Rhine River so that troops could enter the Ruhr region; *German:* to defend the bridge and stop the Allied advance

Forces: *American:* 101st and 82nd Airborne Divisions; *Britain:* XXX Corps and 1st Airborne Division; *Polish:* 1st Parachute Brigade; *Germany:* Army Groups B, 1st Parachute Army, and remnants of 9th and 10th SS Panzer Divisions and other divisions

Commanders: *Allied:* Field Marshal Bernard Montgomery, Lietenant General Frederick Browning, Major General Roy Urquhart, Lieutenant General Brian Horrocks (Britain); General Maxwell Taylor, Major General James M. Gavin (U.S.); Major General Stanislaw Sosabowski (Poland); *German:* Field Marshal Walther Model, General Kurt Student, SS Gruppenführer Wilhelm Bittrich, Lieutenant General Kurt Chill

Military Losses: *Allied:* 17,200 casualties, including more than 6,000 prisoners of war; *German:* 2,500 killed, 7,500 wounded or missing

Result: A bitter defeat for the Allies, although the operation created a salient that proved useful in later operations.

Montgomery sought to secure a bridge over the lower Rhine at Arnhem, Holland, so that Allied forces could cross into the Ruhr. Eisenhower approved the plan, but, from the start, the operation was plagued by errors and miscalculations. Montgomery ignored intelligence reports that SS panzer divisions were in the area; the British Airborne Division was dropped six miles from its objective—and discovered that its radios did not work; the Germans retrieved a copy of the Allies' operational order from the pilot of a downed American glider (who should not have been carrying it); and reinforcements were delayed by bad weather and the unexpected strength of German resistance.

Yet Market-Garden began auspiciously enough on September 17. In the Market phase of the operation, troops from the U.S. 101st and 82nd Airborne Divisions and the British 1st Airborne Division landed near Eindhoven, Nijmegen, and Arnhem respectively, to form a protective corridor for the British XXX Corps advancing northeast from the Meuse-Escaut Canal in Belgium (the advance was designated Garden). By September 18, the American divisions had taken bridges over two canals and the Maas River, but the 82nd was not able to secure the railroad and road bridges over the Waal River until the XXX Corps reached them on September 20. The XXX Corps was then supposed to move on to Arnhem—but the German 9th and

Allied aircraft fly over Arnhem and Nijmegen, Holland, September 17, 1944. Despite the Allies' preparatory bombing attacks on German positions and the deployment of thousands of paratroopers, the Germans defeated this initial attempt to secure the area.

10th SS Panzer Divisions, refitting in the area, had rallied their forces and significantly slowed the progress of the corps.

At the same time, the Germans' Army Group B and First Parachute Army, stationed near Arnhem, had been putting up a spirited defense against the British airborne division (which had arrived at its objective despite its ill-placed landing), pushing most of the division into a pocket at Oosterbeek. Only one British battalion got through to take the north end of the Arnhem road bridge (the railroad bridge had been destroyed), and they held there until the Germans finally overwhelmed them and retook the bridge September 21—thus allowing the Germans to bring up more troops and artillery to block XXX Corps' progress toward the city. The Polish 1st Parachute Brigade, meant to support the British, did not land until September 22, having been delayed by bad weather and German resistance. With the situation around Arnhem deteriorating rapidly, on September 25, the British pulled as many paratroopers as possible back across the Rhine from the Oosterbeek pocket; but the Germans took more than 6,000 prisoners—more than half of them wounded. The Germans had successfully repulsed the first Allied attempt to breach the Rhine.

★　★　★

Operation Market-Garden was not the only Allied setback in Europe as 1944 came to a close. Even as Montgomery's operation was ending in failure, American troops were entering the deadly precincts of the land mine- and pillbox-laced woods not far from Aachen, Germany.

Battle of Huertgen Forest, near Aachen, Germany, September–December, 1944
European Theater (West)

Primary Objectives: *Allied:* to sweep the thick forest near the Belgian-German border clear of Germans; *German:* to defend their border

Forces: *Allied:* U.S. First and Ninth Armies, various infantry divisions; 120,000 troops used during the three-month campaign; *German:* Seventh Army, 9th and 116th Panzer divisions and various infantry divisions

Commanders: *American:* Lieutenant General Courtney Hodges; *German:* Field Marshal Walther Model

Military Losses: *Allied:* 33,000 killed, wounded, or captured; *German:* more than 30,000 killed or wounded

Result: The forest was eventually taken at an extreme, and unforeseen, cost in life, but the Germans delayed the First Army's progress enough to assist preparations for Germany's last counteroffensive in the Ardennes (Battle of the Bulge).

To protect the flank of the U.S. VII Corps as the Allies advanced toward Germany, in September, the U.S. First Army plunged into the fifty-square-mile morass of Huertgen Forest, just inside the Reich. The operation was inadvisable from the start: the defending Germans considered the area vital to their defense and were determined to hold; moreover, they could destroy dams on the Roer River to the south and the east and flood out any Allied advance in the north. But there was no advance through the forest: First Army quickly bogged down in the trackless, muddy terrain, creased by deep ridges and crowned by dense growths of towering evergreens, limiting visibility as well as maneuver. Worse, a portion of the Germans' Siegfried Line (West Wall)—two ranges of thoroughly camouflaged, interconnected pillboxes with overlapping fields of fire—lurked half-submerged in the forbidding landscape. Mines and booby traps lay hidden in the ground and trees, and shrapnel and shards of tree bark rained down after artillery shells burst high in the trees. Defying tanks and even jeeps, the impenetrable forest also neutralized American artillery and air superiority. This surreal, dark, disorienting environment, where incessant snow and rain added to the miseries, devastated the attackers psychologically, resulting in a spike in desertions, breakdowns, and self-inflicted wounds. Yet, for more than three months commanders at headquarters in Spa, Belgium, continued to send division after division into these impossible conditions. All took heavy casualties, with little else to show for their efforts. Of 120,000 U.S. troops who went into the woods, 33,000 were killed, wounded, or captured.

★　★　★

October was not a good month for many American soldiers in Europe. The First Army was caught in the Huertgen Forest, and Patton's Third Army was forced to relinquish its initial foothold on the fortress city of Metz. (They persisted, taking Metz in late November.) Meanwhile, October operations in the Pacific Theater included General Douglas MacArthur's long-awaited campaign to fulfill his promise to return to the Philippines, from which he had been forced to retreat in 1942. The major objectives lay on the largest island, Luzon. However, it was first necessary to secure the islands of Leyte and Mindero, south of Luzon. Landings on Leyte, which was initially defended by a 20,000-man Japanese garrison, began October 20, when U.S. troops secured their beachheads, started off-loading supplies, and began heading inland. Progress was such that MacArthur—along with Sergio Osmeña, successor to the late President Quezon—waded to shore through knee-deep water to announce triumphantly, "People of the Philippines, I have returned. By the grace of Almighty God, our forces stand again on Philippine soil." (He was later to reenact his arrival for cameramen.) Over the next several weeks, however, Japanese resistance on the island stiffened as the area commander sent reinforcements from Luzon. Fearing the loss of their connection to southern Asia and its valuable resources, the Japanese high command also rushed to implement a defense plan, Operation Sho-Go. Neither the Japanese, nor the Americans (who were kept in the dark due to a change in Japanese naval codes) knew that they would soon be involved in the greatest naval battle in history, a series of engagements fought over an area of more than 100,000 square miles.

BATTLE OF LEYTE GULF, OCTOBER 23–26, 1944
PACIFIC THEATER

Primary Objectives: *American:* to support the Leyte landings, secure the Philippines, and destroy the remnants of Japanese naval power (if possible); *Japanese:* to defend the Philippines at all costs, disrupt the U.S. landings on Leyte, and preserve Japan's supply lines

Forces: *American:* Third Fleet: 8 aircraft carriers, 8 light carriers, 1,000 planes, 6 battleships, 15 cruisers, 60 destroyers; Seventh Fleet: 6 battleships, 9 cruisers, 51 destroyers, 18 escort carriers, numerous PT boats, 400 planes, 29 submarines, 140,000 crew; *Japanese:* Northern (or "Decoy") Force: 4 aircraft carriers, 116 planes, 2 battleships, 3 cruisers, 8 destroyers; Center (or "A") Force: 5 battleships, 12 cruisers, 15 destroyers; Southern (or "C") Force: 2 battleships, 1 cruiser, 4 destroyers; Second Attack Force: 3 cruisers, 4 destroyers; about 300 planes on Luzon, 14 submarines, 43,000 crew

Commanders: *American:* Admiral William F. Halsey, commanding Third Fleet under Admiral Chester W. Nimitz, Central Pacific commander; Vice Admiral Thomas C. Kinkaid, commanding Seventh Fleet under General Douglas MacArthur, Southwest Pacific commander; *Japanese:* Admiral Soemu Toyoda, commander in chief; Vice Admiral

Jisaburo Ozawa, commanding Northern Force; Admiral Takeo Kurita, commanding Center Force; Vice Admiral Shoji Nishimura, commanding Southern Force; Vice Admiral Kiyohide Shima, commanding Second Attack Force

Military Losses: *American:* 3 carriers, 3 destroyers, more than 200 planes, more than 2,000 crew killed; *Japanese:* 4 carriers, 3 battleships, 10 cruisers, 11 destroyers, 1 submarine, more than 500 planes, more than 10,000 crew killed.

Result: This battle marked the end of Japanese naval power and destroyed what was left of Japan's naval air power; the Japanese introduced kamikaze missions; the U.S. Leyte landings were left undisturbed, allowing the Americans to continue fighting for control of the Philippines.

Japan's strategy called for Ozawa's force to approach from the north, acting as a decoy to draw Halsey's Third Fleet away from the Leyte landings. The main Japanese attack force, sailing from Brunei (on northwest Borneo) in the south, was broken into two groups—Center Force, under Kurita, and Southern Force under Nishimura—and would close on Leyte in a pincer movement. Kurita's force, with greater strength and two of the most powerful battleships ever built, the *Musashi* and *Yamato*, would come through the San Bernardino Strait to Leyte's north, while Nishimura would approach from the south through the Surigao Strait. A supporting attack force sailing from the north under Shima would travel directly behind Nishimura.

On October 23, however, U.S. submarines detected Kurita off the northern coast of Palawan and sank two of his cruisers. Admiral Halsey, the U.S. Third Fleet commander, learned of the approaching vessels, and on October 24, as the Japanese ships crossed the Sibuyan Sea heading for the San Bernardino Strait, they came under attack by U.S. aircraft from Task Force 38, under Vice Admiral Marc Mitscher. Kurita lost one superbattleship, the *Musashi* (along with more than 1,000 crew), while the Americans suffered the loss of their carrier *Princeton*. After sustaining more damage, Kurita retreated; Halsey incorrectly believed the force would not return.

By the early morning of October 25, Nishimura's Southern Force had reached the Surigao Strait, but they did not achieve surprise either and found Kinkaid's Seventh Fleet waiting for them. Only one Japanese destroyer was able to escape, retreating back through the strait just as Shima's Second Attack Force was arriving. This force withdrew. As Kinkaid was preparing for battle at the Surigao Strait, Halsey dispatched Third Fleet north to intercept Ozawa's decoy force, leaving Seventh Fleet to defend Leyte—just as the Japanese had hoped and planned. Kurita's Center Force, meanwhile, had turned around undetected and was making its way through the San Bernardino Strait. Both the Japanese and the Americans were sur-

---

THE DIVINE WIND: TOKKOTAI AND KAMIKAZE

As the attrition rate of Japanese aircraft and pilots increased with every new American offensive in the Pacific, Japan could not keep pace with American war production, or train new pilots quickly enough to replace those war-hardened veterans who had been killed. To stave off the Allied advance, Vice Admiral Onishi Takajiro recommended a weapon in late 1944 that would buy Japan some time to reequip and retrain. Inspired by the Bushido code, which saw glory in dying for the emperor, he devised the aerial equivalent of the infantry's banzai charge—*kamikaze,* or "Divine Wind," a term dating back to 1291 when a huge storm annihilated a Mongol armada bent on the conquest of Japan. Onishi told his pilots, who were to crash their planes into Allied ships, "Nothing but the sacrifice of our young men's lives to stab at the enemy carriers can annihilate the enemy fleet and put us back on the road to victory." On October 21, 1944, the Australian cruiser *Australia* sustained what appeared to be a kamikaze hit, and by October 25, after the U.S. landings on Leyte in the Philippines, the first coordinated Kamikaze attack force took off. One plane hit and sank the carrier *Saint-Lô,* while others damaged the *Suwanee, Santee, Kitkun Bay, Kalinin Bay,* and *White Plains.* Later in the war, kamikaze attacks were organized en masse; these *kikusui,* "floating chrysanthemums," could comprise hundreds of planes and inflict tremendous damage.

The kamikaze were just one facet of the Special Attack Forces or "Tokkotai," that the Japanese had experimented with throughout the war. Early on, members of the tokkotai had a chance of survival, but later, many attacks became true suicide missions. The Japanese developed or adapted a number of suicide attack vehicles, including planes, boats, gliders, midget submarines, and even manned torpedoes. Many of these were little more than piloted bombs steered through the air or sea by a young soldier who would commit the ultimate sacrifice. At first, there were more than enough tokkotai volunteers; their number decreased as the war wore on, although enough still succumbed to the pressure to serve.

Despite the men's dedication, tokkotai operations were often inefficient and unsuccessful. Kamikaze attacks enjoyed perhaps the most success; they were very demoralizing for the Allies, especially since there was little, at first, to stop them. For fear of a negative effect on morale, the Allied public was told nothing of kamikaze attacks until April 13, 1945. By war's end, the U.S. Navy estimated that there had been 2,600 kamikaze sorties against 474 U.S. ships. When Japan surrendered, there were still 7,700 planes on the home islands, many of them set aside for suicide attacks during the anticipated Allied invasion.

prised when Kurita ran into 16 small escort carriers of the Seventh Fleet (under the command of Rear Admiral Clifton A. F. Sprague) off the coast of Samar, an island to the north of Leyte. In the first action that saw the use of kamikaze plane attacks, the U.S. force lost two escort carriers and three other ships, with many others damaged. Then Kurita—having heard about the defeat of the Japanese in the Surigao Strait and misjudging American naval strength in the area—suddenly broke off the attack.

Also that morning, Halsey's Third Fleet began attacking Ozawa's decoy group off Luzon's Cape Engaño. Ozawa lost all four carriers and one destroyer, but Halsey was soon obliged to send help back to Seventh Fleet, now under attack by Kurita's force. This move prevented the total annihilation of Japan's naval force, since both Kurita and Ozawa were able to withdraw with minimal further damage. However, Japan's plan for the defense of the Philippines had failed; the U.S. Third and Seventh Fleets had successfully defended the landing force on Leyte.

Slogging along muddy trails in rain forests, into swamps and through mountainous terrain stoutly defended by Japanese units, MacArthur's troops on Leyte defeated the last organized resistance, on the west coast, by December 31. (Mop-up of stragglers continued until May 1945.) They had killed or wounded an estimated 49,000 Japanese troops, against 15,584 American casualties, 3,504 of them killed. Leyte proved to be the decisive battle for the Philippines; but much hard fighting lay ahead in the campaign for Luzon. To prepare for the assault on that island, MacArthur still needed to secure Mindoro, an island northwest of Leyte and just south of Luzon; American troops began landing there December 15.

★　★　★

The next day, in the European Theater, Hitler caught the Allies offguard when, against the advice of his generals, he launched a last-ditch offensive through the Ardennes.

THE ARDENNES CAMPAIGN (BATTLE OF THE BULGE; OPERATION HERBSTNEBEL, OR AUTUMN FOG), DECEMBER 16, 1944–JANUARY 1945
EUROPEAN THEATER (WEST)

Primary Objectives: *Allied:* to defend the Ardennes and push back the German advance; *German:* to divide American forces in the Ardennes and push on to take Antwerp

Forces: *Allied:* U.S. First Army (part of Twelfth Army Group), U.S. Third Army; British XXX Corps; *German:* Army Group B, including the 5th and 6th SS Panzer Armies and the Seventh Army

Commanders: *Allied:* General Omar Bradley (Twelfth Army Group), Lieutenant General Courtney Hodges (First Army), Lieutenant General George Patton (Third Army), Field Marshal Bernard Montgomery; *German:* Field Marshal Gerd von Rundstedt (overall command), Field Marshal Walther Model (Army Group B), Oberstgruppenführer Sepp Dietrich (6th SS Panzer Army), General Hasso von Manteuffel (5th Panzer Army), General Erich Brandenberger (Seventh Army)

Military Losses: *Allied:* (U.S.) 10,296 killed, 47,493 wounded, 23,218 missing or prisoners; (UK/Canada): 1,462 killed, wounded, or missing; *German:* 103,900 killed, wounded, or missing

Result: After setbacks and hard fighting, the Allies straightened the bulge, defeating Germany's last major offensive.

Calculating that winter weather would keep Allied planes on the ground, Hitler sent Model's Army Group B—including English-speaking soldiers specially trained to cause confusion behind enemy lines—into the Ardennes Forest in Belgium. There, they were to break through the American lines (thus dividing Allied forces), then advance northwest and retake the port of Antwerp. The führer believed that success would drive a wedge between the United States and Britain, making one or both more likely to negotiate a settlement; he could then concentrate his forces against the Russians in the east.

The Allied front across the Ardennes was lightly guarded by only about 80,000 U.S. troops, part of Bradley's Twelfth Army Group, many of them new recruits or still recovering from the grueling battle in the Huertgen Forest (see battle description earlier in this chapter). Although the Americans had received some intelligence reports of German activity east of the Ardennes, they were taken by complete surprise when, on December 16, Dietrich's Sixth SS Panzer Army, von Manteuffel's Fifth Panzer Army, and Brandenburger's Seventh Army made a three-pronged attack against several vulnerable divisions of Hodges' First Army. The Germans faced, from north to south, the 4th Division and part of the 9th Armored Division, the 28th and the 106th divisions—but in many places, resistance was far from organized. Small, tenacious groups of Americans, including normally noncombat-

EYEWITNESS ACCOUNT: THE BATTLE OF THE BULGE

Harold Smith, 30, was a sergeant in Company G, 101st Infantry, 26th Division of the U.S. Army. At Monstchuman Cross, he remembered that the

> Germans were giving our outfit a battle for our lives. I was then ordered to take my platoon and join the right flank of the 328th regiment. Upon arriving at the position I could readily surmise that this was going to be the worst [battle], especially if the Germans had schnapps in their canteens instead of water. . . . With this added encouragement, the Germans were charging us with fierce hand-to-hand attacks. . . . We fought with rifle butts, bayonets and anything we could get our hands on. Our platoon didn't even have time to dig a foxhole.

ant soldiers like cooks and military police, used rifles, grenades, small arms—and desperate hand-to-hand fighting—to hold off the enemy among the trees and thorny hedgerows in freezing, snowy weather.

While the Americans resisted Dietrich's troops as best they could, British Field Marshal Bernard Montgomery sent his XXX Corps to assist. They kept the Germans from taking the town of St. Vith until December 21 and ultimately halted Dietrich's advance; but Standartenführer (Colonel) Joachim Peiper's SS panzer unit was able to take Malmédy on December 17. (There his troops massacred 86 unarmed American prisoners. See also "German War Crimes" in Chapter 8.)

By December 18, the Fifth Panzer Army and the Seventh Army had advanced fifteen miles in the center of the American lines, while the north and south flanks held—creating the bulge that gave the operation its American nickname. However, a pocket of American troops remained in Bastogne, on the central path of the German advance. Although the 106th and the 28th Divisions had collapsed as the Germans plowed through, taking 8,000 American prisoners, remnants reinforced by the 101st and 82nd Airborne Divisions and the 10th Armored Division continued to hold out. In the meantime, Patton was ordering his Third Army to "drive like hell," batter the Germans, and relieve the Americans under siege in the bulge. On December 22, Supreme Commander Eisenhower exhorted his besieged soldiers "to destroy the enemy on the ground, in the air, everywhere to destroy him."

THEATERS OF WAR, 1944

Europe	*Mediterranean/North Africa*
January: Soviet Army goes on the offensive in Baltic and around Leningrad	**January 22:** Allied forces land at Anzio, Italy*
January 20: Red Army takes Novgorod	**February:** Allies bomb Monte Cassino abbey*
January 27: The 900-day siege of Leningrad ends.	**May:** U.S. Fifth Army finally succeeds in breaking out of the Anzio beachhead
March 6: U.S. planes drop 2,000 tons of bombs on Berlin	**June 4:** Allied troops enter Rome
March 20: Red Army enters Romania	**August–September:** Germans retreat northward in Italy and begin consolidating behind what will be the winter defensive (Gothic) line
April 10: Red Army takes Odessa, pushes on to soon retake Crimea	**September 29:** Soviet forces enter Yugoslavia
April: Intense Allied bombings of German cities and factories	**October 3:** British troops land in Greece
June 6: D-Day,* the Allied invasion of western Europe	**October 10:** British, Greeks retake Corinth; they take Athens four days later
June 13: First "buzz bombs" (V-1s) hit London	**December:** Civil war erupts in Greece
June 26: U.S. forces take Cherbourg	
July 3: Red Army captures Minsk	
July 9: British, Canadian troops take Caen	
July 11: Red Army enters Latvia and, two days later, takes Vilna, Lithuania	
July 17: In France, Rommel is wounded by Allied air attack	
July 20: Hitler assassination plot fails	
July 23: Red Army takes Lublin, Poland; four days later, Russians take Lvov, pressing on to the outskirts of Warsaw in another four days	
August: Anti-German revolt in Slovakia; Soviets train Czechoslovakian partisans and organize Czech Army units	
August: U.S. forces advance on Brittany, taking Rennes, Dinan, and Mortain; turning east, they join the French, Canadians and British at Falaise, encircling German 7th Army and 5th Panzer Army; after German forces surrender, Allies enter jubilant Paris	
August 18: Field Marshal Gunther von Kluge commits suicide, after writing Hitler that the war in the west is lost	
September: Allies retake most of France and seal buzz-bomb sites in Belgium and Holland; Allies push into Luxembourg and the German frontier	
September–December: Battle of Huertgen Forest*	
September 8: Germans launch first V-2 rocket	
September 14: U.S. troops take Aachen, first large German city to fall	
September 17: Allies begin Operation Market-Garden*	
October 11: Red Army enters eastern Germany	
December 16: Battle of the Bulge begins*	

The Pacific	*China-Burma-India*
February 6: Allies take Kwajalein, in the Marshall Islands	**January:** Indian troops resume Burma campaign, taking Maungdaw
February 10: U.S. and Australian troops take Huon Peninsula in New Guinea; New Britain is now under Allied control	**March 22:** Japanese enter India from Burma and move toward Imphal*
February 17–21: U.S. forces land on, and take Eniwetok, Marshall Islands	**March 24:** British commando leader Orde Wingate is killed in a plane crash in Burma
May 19–31: U.S. destroyer escort *England* sinks six Japanese submarines in twelve days, a record for one ship in the war*	**April 18:** Indian and British troops push Japanese back from Manipur, India
June 14: U.S. Marine and Army forces begin Iwo Jima campaign*	**May 11:** Japanese troops in China take Peiping-Hankow railroad line
June 15: U.S. forces land at Saipan*	**June 30:** U.S. forces abandon air base at Hengyang in face of Japanese offensive
June 19–20: Battle of Philippine Sea*	**August 11:** Japanese troops retreat from India
August 10: Japanese resistance on Guam ends	**September 17:** U.S. forces abandon air base at Kweilin
September: U.S. forces land at Peleliu, Morotai, Ulithi (in the Carolines), and close in on the Philippines	**October 28:** General Stilwell recalled by Roosevelt after he clashes with Chiang Kai-shek in China
October 7–14: U.S. carriers enter Japanese waters, attacking Ryukyus and Formosa	**November 26:** U.S. forces abandon air base at Yungning
October 23: In the Philippines, Allies begin Leyte campaign*	**December 18:** Japanese start retreat from Burma
November 5: U.S. planes bomb Singapore	
November 21: U.S. submarine sinks Japanese battleship *Kongo*	
November 27: U.S. submarine sinks new Japanese aircraft carrier *Shinano*	
November 24: U.S. bombers make first run on Tokyo from Saipan in the Marianas	
December 15: U.S. troops land on Mindoro in the Philippines	
December 19: U.S. submarine sinks new Japanese aircraft carrier *Unryu*	

* See text for further discussion.

That same day, Major General Anthony McAuliffe, whose troops were surrounded in Bastogne, answered a German demand for surrender with one syllable: "Nuts!"—which puzzled the Germans until someone explained that the general meant "Go to Hell." McAuliffe's 101st did not surrender, and on December 26, an element of Patton's Third Army, the 4th Armored Division, arrived and broke the siege of Bastogne.

On December 23, the weather cleared and American planes began bombarding German troops and supply lines; the battle then turned in favor of the Allies. On December 19, Eisenhower had given Montgomery command of Allied forces north of the bulge, while Bradley retained control of those to the south. Tank units from Patton's Third Army were redeployed to attack on a line between Bastogne and St. Hubert on December 30. Through early January, Allied forces pounded the Germans, pushing them back toward the Siegfried Line (West Wall). On January 16, 1945, U.S. troops from the First and Third Armies finally met at Houffalize, at the center of the bulge. By the end of January, surviving German troops—their depleted ranks reinforced by Hitler Youth and older men rushed into the lines—had been driven back to their starting point. Although Operation Autumn Fog had delayed the Allied advance into Germany by several weeks, this delay was purchased at too great a cost: In losing his gamble to sever the Allied lines, Hitler had eviscerated one of his last remaining forces. At the same time, U.S. forces had once again proven their mettle, in what Winston Churchill said should "be regarded as an ever famous American victory."

1945: Allied Victory and an Uneasy Peace

While the Germans still had Americans surrounded in Bastogne, German general Heinz Guderian tried to convince Hitler to break off the Autumn Fog offensive and turn his attention to the crisis situation in the east. Along a front that now stretched from tiny Memel on the Baltic, through German territory in East Prussia, across Poland and eastern Czechoslovakia, to a point on the Danube north of Budapest and on to the shore of the Adriatic, some 6 million Soviet soldiers (and, near the Adriatic, Josip Tito's Yugoslav National Liberation Army), were preparing offensives against the hard-pressed and increasingly ill-supplied Wehrmacht. Moreover, one German force of some 200,000 (which Hitler had refused to allow to retreat) was surrounded at Courland (Latvia), with its back to the Baltic. Another was surrounded in Budapest. Hitler dismissed Guderian's cautions—with one exception, already on his mind. On January 1, the Germans launched an attack on the Soviets outside Budapest, trying to relieve the Axis garrison. Neither the German attack nor the city's entrenched defenders prevented the Soviets from penetrating the eastern edge of Budapest by January 8.

Farther north, Soviet troops opened the gates of a complex of camps near Oswiecim (Auschwitz), Poland, on January 27. The Germans had evacuated all but about 7,000 prisoners—but the purpose of that death factory was chillingly clear. (See also Chapter 8.) At the same time, in the west, Allied ground forces were moving forward again, and Allied bombers continued to pound Germany from the air. On the night of February 13–14, they attacked the ancient and heretofore untouched city of Dresden, precipitating another terrible firestorm that killed an estimated 25,000 to 35,000 people.

Still, the increasingly delusional führer refused to believe that the Reich's days were numbered. Insisting that field commanders submit all plans and significant decisions to him for approval before they acted (thus slowing action and dampening initiative), he placed his faith in two last-ditch weapons that would prove ineffective: V-weapons (see Chapter 5) and the Volkssturm militia (see Chapter 4).

In the Far East, Germany's last major ally was equally hard pressed. In Burma, the Japanese continued to retreat before Allied offensives—even as Allied engineers and their multinational force of workers connected the Ledo Road with the Burma Road. Supplies again flowed via ground convoy from India to China. (The highway was soon renamed the Stilwell Road, after the American general who had championed it for so long.) Meanwhile, American forces were making progress in the Philippines. The landings on Mindoro, south of the main island of Luzon, had gone smoothly against about 1,000 poorly organized Japanese troops. Flying from airbases quickly built there by military engineers, U.S. aircraft pounded kamikaze air bases on Luzon, struck at Japanese shipping, and prepared to support the Luzon invasion, which commenced with amphibious landings on January 9.

THE BATTLE FOR LUZON, PHILIPPINE ISLANDS, JANUARY 9–JULY 4, 1945
PACIFIC THEATER

Primary Objectives: *American:* to drive the Japanese from the Philippines, secure the capital city, Manila, and the bastion of Corregidor; *Japanese:* to hold Luzon as long as possible

Forces: *American:* throughout the campaign, 10 divisions and 5 independent regiments (making this the largest campaign in the Pacific war); *Japanese:* 260,000 soldiers, divided into three groups: *Shobu Group,* in the north (152,000); *Kembu Group,* middle of the island, east coast, occupying Clark Field, Bataan, and Corregidor (30,000); and *Shimbu Group,* south including the mountains east of Manila, where they controlled the area's water supply (80,000)

Commanders: *American:* General Douglas MacArthur (overall command); Lieutenant General Walter Krueger (Sixth Army), Lieutenant General Robert L. Eichelberger (Eighth Army); *Japanese:* General Tomoyuki Yamashita (overall command, headquartered with Shobu Group); Major General Rikichi Tsukada (Kembu Group); General Shizuo Yokoyama (Shimbu Group). Rear Admiral Sanji Iwabachi (naval commander, Manila area; commander of Manila Naval Defense Force, 16,000 sailors fighting on land)

Military Losses: *American:* battle casualties, 10,380 killed, 36,550 wounded; noncombat casualties, 260 dead (primarily from disease), 93,140 sick and injured; *Japanese:* between 192,000 and 205,500 killed, 9,050 surrendered August 1945

Result: A difficult six-month campaign brought all strategically or economically important areas of Luzon under Allied control, a victory that dealt a severe blow to the Japanese—who did not admit defeat.

A key to this difficult campaign was Yamashita's decision to divide his forces into three groups, each based in a remote geographic region, to conduct a war of attrition. Therefore, the Americans landing on January 9 met minimal opposition until they fanned out toward their objectives. Lieutenant General Oscar W. Griswold's XIV Corps met determined resistance from Kembu Group near Clark Field, the former U.S. Army airbase, and did not secure the field until the end of the month.

MacArthur, meanwhile, chafed at the slow progress that the 37th Division of Krueger's Sixth Army was making toward the capital, criticizing Krueger on January 30 for "the noticeable lack of drive and aggressive initiative." Shortly thereafter, when the 1st Cavalry Division arrived on the island, MacArthur told its commander, "Go to Manila, go around the Nips, bounce off the Nips, but go to Manila." A 1st Cavalry mechanized column set out for the capital as MacArthur organized an amphibious landing of elements of Eichelberger's Eighth Army below the city (Operation Mike VI). Now three separate columns of Americans were approaching Manila. All three slammed into hard resistance as they reached the city outskirts. The fight to wrest the Philippine capital from the Manila Naval Defense Force would last until March 4 and leave much of the city in ruins. An estimated 100,000 civilians died during the battle, a number of them victims of Japanese atrocities (see "Japanese War Crimes" in Chapter 8).

The Philippine capital commanded Manila Bay, but that logistically crucial harbor could not be used until the Bataan Peninsula, flanking it on the northwest, and the fortress of Corregidor, at its mouth, were in Allied hands. Between January 29 and February 15, nearly 35,000 Americans (assisted by Filipino guerrillas) cleared Bataan of its 4,000 well-dug-in and difficult-to-find Japanese defenders. On February 16, paratroopers landed on the highest point on Corregidor, an island that was only five miles square. As they floated down, surprising the defenders, U.S. infantrymen stormed ashore from landing craft. After ten days of fierce fighting, Corregidor was back in American hands by February 26.

Yamashita and the 152,000-man Shobu Group still remained to be dealt with in the north, while most of the Shimbu Group was spread out east and south of Manila, including the far reaches of the Bicol Peninsula, the southernmost portion of Luzon. The campaign to subdue the Shimbu Group—involving brutal, foot-by-foot combat through mountains thick with Japanese strongholds and hidden machine-gun emplacements, and an amphibious landing on the Bicol Peninsula—was concluded by the end of May. The campaign against Yamashita's main force lasted until Japan surrendered on August 15. Nevertheless, Luzon was effectively under Allied control by early summer—at a staggering cost to both sides.

★   ★   ★

While the battle for Manila was still raging in the Philippines, Allied forces in the Central Pacific, moving inexorably toward Japan, set their sights on an island largely composed of volcanic pumice, unfriendly terrain for the Americans who were about to attempt an assault. The Japanese had worked hard to make it unfriendlier, digging 13,000 yards of tunnels, creating gun emplacements protected by fifty feet of earth overhead, and scattering defenders in some 5,000 caves and camouflaged pillboxes. Preassault bombardments denuded the island, but hardly touched these formidable defenses.

The Battle for Iwo Jima, February 19–March 16, 1945
Pacific Theater

> **Primary Objectives:** *American:* to acquire another air base closer to Japan and deprive Japan of a radar facility; *Japanese:* to prevent the Allies from securing another base so close to the home islands
>
> **Forces:** *American:* 7 battleships, 5 cruisers, 11 escort carriers, 500 landing transports, V Amphibious Corps, including the 3rd, 4th, 5th Marine divisions (30,000 initial force, eventually 110,000); *Japanese:* 22,000
>
> **Commanders:** *American:* Lieutenant General Holland M. Smith commanding Fleet Marine Forces, Pacific; Major General Harry Schmidt, commanding V Amphibious Corps; *Japanese:* Lieutenant General Tadamichi Kuribayashi
>
> **Military Losses:** *American:* 6,821 dead, 20,000 wounded; *Japanese:* 18,000 dead, only 216 prisoners taken alive
>
> **Result:** After a month of brutal fighting, U.S. troops secured the island.

Ten-mile-square Iwo Jima, 660 miles south of Tokyo and 625 miles north of the Marianas, was the site of two airstrips that the United States could use as a safe haven and repair depot for planes damaged in aerial warfare. The Americans also wished to destroy a radar facility that warned the Japanese of incoming American bombers. U.S. aircraft started bombing "Iwo" in the summer of 1944 (to little effect); that June, General Tadamichi Kuribayashi arrived to oversee the island's defense. Abandoning traditional military doctrine, Kuribayashi forbade his 22,000-man force from making banzai attacks, reduced the force stationed near the beaches, and concentrated artillery strength on the commanding heights of 556-ft Mt. Suribachi, from where the big guns could send a lethal rain of shells into the expected invaders.

On February 19, the first wave of some 10,000 men of the 3rd, 4th and 5th Marine Divisions landed and started struggling across terraces of volcanic ash, breathing air heavy with sulfur. They moved without opposition—for fifteen deceptive minutes. Then, as more Marines followed, all hell broke loose. Day after day, shells smashed into the Marines on the beachhead, incoming landing craft, and boats that attempted to transport the wounded to hospital ships. Taking heavy casualties (560 killed by the end of the first day), the Marines battled on, dealing with pillboxes and snipers—and blasting, or incinerating with flamethrowers, Japanese firing at them

General MacArthur returned to the Philippines, as he had promised, and led the salutes at a flag-raising ceremony on Corregidor in February 1945. Soon after, on Iwo Jima, photographer Joe Rosenthal captured the war's most famous image as six Americans raised the Stars and Stripes over Mount Suribachi. Three of the six, Private Rene Gagnon, Pharmacy Mate Second Class John Bradley, and Private Ira Hayes, seen here at Times Square, New York City, on May 11, survived the battle and participated in a war bonds tour that featured reenactments of the flag raising.

from fortified caves. By February 23, Americans were atop Mt. Suribachi—where photographer Joe Rosenthal snapped a picture of five Marines of the 28th Regiment, 5th Division, and one navy corpsman raising a large U.S. flag that became the most vivid American image of World War II. (Three of the men—Franklin Sousley, Harlon Block, and Michael Strank—died on Iwo Jima. Ira Hayes, John Bradley [USN], and Rene Gagnon survived to be celebrated as heroes.)

Although Marines were on the heights, bitter fighting continued; Iwo Jima was not secured until March 16. Twenty-seven Medals of Honor were awarded to 22 Marines and 5 sailors for heroism during the contest for this bleak, volcanic rock. Thirteen of the medals were awarded posthumously. On Iwo, observed Admiral Chester Nimitz, "uncommon valor was a common virtue."

★   ★   ★

The Allies were now winning the war against Japan on the ground and at sea (where U.S. submarines had all but destroyed Japanese merchant shipping). By 1945, the Allies also controlled the air—although not without some Japanese opposition. Japan's defenses, however, were not the major problem American bombers faced in fulfilling their mission to destroy Japanese war resources.

The Strategic Bombing Campaign against Japan

Bombers of the U.S. Army Air Force began hitting Japanese industrial and military facilities in Thailand and the Japanese home islands in the summer of 1944, flying in daylight and at high altitudes. The initial phase, designated Operation Matterhorn, involved bombers flying out of bases in China. It quickly ran into problems, including the Japanese Ichi-Go offensive, which overran many of the bombers' forward bases (see "The Ichi-Go Campaign" earlier in this chapter). Heavy headwinds at high altitudes made it necessary to carry more fuel and lighter bomb loads; but even with more fuel, winds and other atmospheric conditions led to more aircrew casualties from ditching in the ocean on the way back than from Japanese air defenses. Moreover, the high-altitude bombing of picked targets was not very accurate. Finally, the frustrated USAAF commander, Hap Arnold, called in a new operational commander for the XXI Bomber Command of the 20th Air Force. General Curtis LeMay arrived in the Pacific Theater in January 1945, as operations were transferred to the Marianas, and gradually evolved a new bombing strategy based on his experience in the European Theater. His B-29s would fly at night and at lower altitudes, and they would be loaded primarily with incendiary bombs. Since much Japanese industry was scattered throughout Japanese urban areas, entire cities were targeted.

The first major raid employing this technique was on Tokyo the night of March 9–10; 334 low-flying bombers, crisscrossing the city at 5,000 and 10,000 feet, dropped 1,665 tons of incendiary bombs. Separate wind-driven conflagrations merged into a horrible firestorm that incinerated much of the city and claimed more than 100,000 lives. During the final months of the war, incendiary raids continued, especially targeting 60 to 70 industrial cities and associated military installations. In April, tactics shifted to include daylight raids (escorted by P-51 Mustang and P-47 Thunderbolt fighters) and mixed bomb loads. Throughout these latter months, the Japanese defenses included night-fighter aircraft (see Chapter 5), which the United States countered with night fighters of its own. American bombers with these conventional loads continued to reach their targets, even after the two atomic bombs destroyed Hiroshima and Nagasaki (see p. 620).

★   ★   ★

In early March, as LeMay's bombers were crisscrossing the skies over Tokyo, eight Allied armies in Europe (American, British, Canadian, and Free French) had reached the banks of the Rhine River, the last great natural barrier standing in the way of a drive into the heart of Germany.

The Allies Cross the Rhine

The Rhine River had not been crossed by an enemy force since the time of Napoleon, and as the Germans retreated east across the rain-swollen river, they tried to maintain that record by detonating all the bridges. The Allies would have to stage amphibious assaults to clear the far bank, while combat engineers constructed bridges for the main columns—except in one lucky instance. On March 7, the U.S. 9th Armored Division (part of General Omar N. Bradley's Twelfth Army Group), found the Ludendorff railroad bridge in Remagen intact. American troops rushed 8,000 men across within twenty-four hours and quickly established a bridgehead on the other side. Elsewhere, Third Army commander General George Patton was so eager to reach the far bank that, during the night of March 22–23, he surprised the

Just weeks before the Allies crossed the Rhine River and entered the German heartland, photographer Toni Frissell came upon these exhausted U.S. soldiers resting in the ruins of a building on the Siegfried Line, the almost four-hundred-mile-long defensive line built by the Germans on the Western Front.

Germans by sending his 5th Infantry Division across the river without air or artillery support; they established a bridgehead at Oppenheim, near Mainz. Within a few days, additional crossings were made by elements of the Third Army, the U.S. Seventh Army, the British Second Army, and the Free French First Army.

Farther north, nearly 1 million troops under Field Marshal Montgomery looked across the Rhine toward Germany's industrial heartland, the Ruhr. Operation Plunder was to be the second-largest operation (after Overlord) that the British undertook during the war. The operation commenced on the night of March 23, with heavy air and artillery bombardment prior to amphibious crossings. On the 24th, the Allies launched a supporting airborne operation, code-named Varsity. (They calculated that the Germans would expect an airborne assault *in advance* of any amphibious attempts and hoped to achieve greater surprise with a later air drop.) More than 21,000 men from the British 6th Airborne Division and the U.S. 17th Airborne Division participated in the drops near Wesel. Within one day, the paratroopers had secured most of their objectives and captured more than 3,500 German prisoners, decimating the defending German 84th Division. More than 700 Allied airborne troops were killed and more than 1,200 were wounded—a higher casualty rate than that suffered by the troops engaged in the amphibious assault. By early April, seven Allied armies had crossed the Rhine, and Eisenhower's troops were ready to push through the Ruhr and on toward Berlin.

★   ★   ★

While the Allies were driving into the German heartland, American troops and the U.S. Navy—assisted by a powerful British naval task force—prepared for an assault on Okinawa, in the Ryukyu Islands, just south of Japan. The battle for the island began on April 1, both April Fool's Day and Easter Sunday (its Allied military designation was "L Day").

THE BATTLE FOR OKINAWA (OPERATION ICEBERG), APRIL 1–JUNE 22, 1945
PACIFIC THEATER

Primary Objectives: *American:* to capture the island of Okinawa as a base from which to launch an invasion of Japan; *Japanese:* to defend the island as long as possible and delay the U.S. attack on Japan.

Forces: *American:* Tenth Army, including the army's XXIV Corps and Marines' III Amphibious Corps; U.S. Navy's Fifth Fleet—with more than 1,000 ships (an estimated 200,000 U.S. servicemen participated in the battle); *British:* Royal Navy Pacific Fleet; *Japanese:* 32nd Japanese Army, including 24th and 62nd divisions, 44th Independent Mixed Brigade (some 77,000 troops), plus the 20,000-man Okinawan militia

Commanders: *American:* Lieutenant General Simon B. Buckner, ground force commander; Major General John Hodges, commanding U.S. Army XXIV Corps; Major General Roy S. Geiger, commanding U.S. Marine Corps III Amphibious Corps; Admiral Raymond Spruance, commanding Central Pacific Forces; *British:* Vice Admiral Sir Bernard Rawlings; *Japanese:* Lieutenant General Mitsuru Ushijima, Admiral Soemu Toyoda

Military Losses: *Allied:* 12,513 killed (including famed war correspondent Ernie Pyle), 31,807 wounded; 763 aircraft, 36 warships and landing craft; *Japanese:* of the 77,000-man island garrison, only 7,400 were taken prisoner (69,600 killed). In addition, thousands of Okinawan militia and civilians were killed—or killed themselves—during the battle.

Result: The Allies secured the island, at terrible cost to both sides.

Okinawa, the largest of the Ryukyu Islands, was some 350 miles southwest of Japan and had been a Japanese prefecture since 1879. Its population included ethnic Japanese and native Okinawans—many of whom participated in the island's defense. The United States had long targeted the island as a staging area from which to attack Japan itself and mounted the most complex operation of the Pacific War to take it. To resist this massive assault, General

TENTH ARMY INVASION PLAN
1 April 1945

Axis of Attack
Airfield

ELEVATION IN METERS
0   100   200   300 and Above

0   10

Miles

Ushijima concentrated his forces in the south, with a smaller number of troops on the Motobu Peninsula further north. As on Iwo Jima, the Japanese were firmly entrenched in a densely packed area of caves, tunnels, and fortifications from which the invaders would have to dig them out.

On April 1, 1945, soldiers from the 96th and 7th army divisions and Marines from the 1st and 6th divisions landed on the west side of the island, above Ushijima's southern stronghold, meeting little resistance. They secured two air bases. The Marines subdued the northern part of the island, including the Motobu Peninsula, by April 20. However, progress in the south was infinitesimal. Through April and May the army divisions, joined later by the Marines, attacked the first line of defense across the Uraseo-Mura escarpment, then the Shuri Line—Ushijima's defensive line reaching from Naha in the west to Yonabaru in the east, with Shuri Castle in the middle, where Ushijima had his underground headquarters.

Offshore, the supporting naval forces were fighting off a fierce onslaught of kamikaze attacks (see "The Divine Wind: Tokkotai and Kamikaze" earlier in this chapter); Okinawa would cost the navy more casualties than it had sustained over the preceding two years of the Pacific War. Meanwhile, farther away, U.S. aircraft prevented naval reinforcements from reaching Okinawa by sinking the huge Japanese battleship *Yamato* and all but a few vessels of its attendant task force at the Battle of the East China Sea, April 7. (Departing with only enough fuel for a one-way journey, *Yamato* was meant to fight and then be run aground on Okinawa so its guns could be used as stationary artillery.)

Near Naha, Okinawa, tired marines share their trench and a camouflaged poncho with a local boy. Elsewhere on the island, soldiers in the 27th Mechanized Cavalry Reconnaissance Group prepare to toss grenades into enemy caves, May 1945.

On the island, tropical rains had created a deep, glutinous mud that stopped even most tracked vehicles. This added one more dimension to the misery of American troops as they fought their way up each hill through a lethal rain of machine-gun fire and mortar shells, to meet, as they reached each crest, artillery and small-arms fire from the other side. Taking heavy casualties, but bolstered by reinforcements, they kept moving forward, wearing down the Japanese. Ushijima's counterattack behind American lines on the night of May 3–4 failed, and his forces were pushed to the southern tip of the island. There they continued their fierce resistance against the 6th Marine Division's equally fierce assault at Sugar Loaf Hill, May 13–17, during which the Marines suffered 2,000 casualties in the often hand-to-hand fighting. Combat continued for another month, U.S. troops often resorting to "cave flushing" (using flamethrowers to force those who would not surrender out into the open); some Japanese suffocated before they could leave the caves. Finally, on June 22, four days after shellfire killed U.S. ground

EYEWITNESS ACCOUNT: A STORM OF STEEL ON OKINAWA

A 22-year-old U.S. Marine on Okinawa, Eugene ("Sledgehammer") Sledge survived the war to write a classic memoir, *With the Old Breed at Peleliu and Okinawa*. In it, he describes this instance of trial-by-enemy-fire that the Marines met after moving from the relative security of northern Okinawa to reinforce the army in the south:

> As we raced across an open field, Japanese shells of all types whizzed, screamed, and roared around us with increasing frequency. . . . Rocks and dirt clattered down after each erupting shell blew open a crater. . . . Marines were running and crawling into position as soldiers streamed past us, trying desperately to get out alive. The yells for corpsmen and stretcher bearers began to be heard. . . . Japanese rifle and machine-gun fire increased into a constant rattle. Bullets snapped and popped overhead. . . . It was an appalling chaos. I was terribly afraid. Fear was obvious on the faces of my comrades, too, as we raced to the low slope and began to dig in rapidly. It was such a jolt to leave the quiet, beautiful countryside that morning and plunge into a thunderous, deadly storm of steel that afternoon. Going onto the beach to assault Peleliu and attacking across the airfield there, we had braced ourselves for the blows that fell. But the shock and shells of 1 May at Okinawa, after the reprieve of a pleasant April, caught us off balance.

commander General Simon B. Buckner Jr., and the day Japanese commander Ushijima committed suicide, the Americans declared Okinawa secure. They took 7,400 Japanese soldiers prisoner—an unprecedented number to that date in the Pacific War. But, as on Saipan, thousands of troops and civilians committed suicide rather than surrender.

The ferocity of Japanese resistance on Okinawa convinced many Americans that to subdue the Japanese home islands would be nothing short of a bloodbath for both sides. Nevertheless, planning continued for the invasion of Japan.

★   ★   ★

April 1, the day American boots hit Okinawa's beaches, Soviet dictator Joseph Stalin, increasingly concerned about the progress the British and Americans were making east of the Rhine River, asked his commanders, "Well, now, who is going to take Berlin, will we or the Allies?" Four days later, he replied disingenuously to a message from General Eisenhower by stating, "Berlin has lost its former strategic importance. The Soviet High

Command therefore plans to allot secondary forces in the direction of Berlin." In fact, he had set April 16 as the starting date for a major Soviet campaign to capture the city that—as capital of the German state of Prussia and capital of Imperial and Nazi Germany—had for generations been a potent symbol of German militarism.

The Battle for Berlin April 16–May 8, 1945

By January 16, when Hitler returned to Berlin for the last time, 1,350,000 Russians, under the command of Marshals Georgi Zhukov and Ivan Konev, were sweeping west across Poland and East Prussia. Farther south, the Red Army was also advancing: between January 17 and April 13, Warsaw (January 17), Budapest (February 13), and Vienna (April 13) would all be in Soviet hands.

With British and American air forces bombing Berlin day and night, Hitler was forced to move to his underground bunker beneath a Reich chancellory garden, making a last, defiant, radio address on January 30. A few days later, Zhukov's 1st Belorussian Front and Konev's 1st Ukrainian Front had advanced to the Oder River, where Stalin ordered them to pause—just thirty-five miles east of Berlin. They regrouped their forces for the final push toward the city.

Meanwhile, the western Allies kept moving forward—but, on March 28, the day he communicated with Stalin, Eisenhower ordered American forces not to race toward Berlin. Despite Churchill's request that the western Allies "shake hands with the Russians as far to the east as possible," Eisenhower ordered Allied troops to stop at the River Elbe, 50 miles west of Berlin and what would become the agreed-to demarcation line between Soviet and British, French, and American territories in a divided postwar Germany. Berlin became a purely Soviet objective, while Eisenhower's decision became, and remains, a subject of analysis and debate.

At 5:00 A.M. the morning of April 16 (the day the Allies ended their strategic bombing campaign against Germany), Soviet forces launched one of the most powerful artillery barrages in history, firing more than a million shells against German positions west of the Oder. Three Russian fronts (army groups) with over 2.5 million troops, 6,250 armored vehicles, and 7,500 aircraft attacked the 320,000-strong Army Group Vistula (comprising the German Ninth Army and Third Panzer armies). Attacking straight west against the Seelow Heights, Zukhov's forces encountered stiff resistance,

As victorious Soviet troops raised their flag over the Reichstag on April 30, Hitler and Eva Braun married and committed suicide in his bunker, leaving only children, older men, and the remnants of shattered German units to defend the burning ruins of Berlin. The Red Army had little mercy on defenders or civilians.

while Konev's troops, attacking from the south, made greater progress and reached Jüterbog and the German Army's largest ammunition depot in a few days. After several days of fierce fighting, Stalin ordered Zukhov to shift his troops to the north, where they linked up with Marshal Konstantin Rokossovsky's 2nd Belorussian Front and Konev's forces on April 25. The Soviets had encircled Berlin.

On April 20, when members of Hitler's command came to his bunker to wish him a happy birthday, he gave them permission to leave Berlin before all the roads were closed. But Hitler had also ordered that Berlin be defended "to the last man and the last shot." Men and boys of the Volkssturm and the Hitler Youth joined police and foreign SS units in the streets, where they commenced a house-by-house defense against the overwhelmingly superior Soviet forces. While Hitler clung to the hope that Lieutenant General Walther Wenck's Twelfth Army in the west or General Theodor Busse's Ninth Army to the southeast would rescue the city, on April 29, Lieutenant General Karl Weidling, commander of Berlin

THE END IN ITALY

As winter turned to spring, ground action began again in Italy, while Allied air attacks on German positions continued, against little resistance. Simultaneously, an estimated 50,000 Italian partisans—equipped by Allied air drops and matériel taken from their enemies—attacked German troops from all sides. Communist partisans also used this opportunity to take revenge on political enemies, including fascist Blackshirts. Partisan uprisings in Genoa, Milan, and Turin liberated those cities and took thousands of German prisoners. The British Eighth Army and the U.S. Fifth Army broke through the German defense line in mid-April and linked up at Finale nell'Emilia by April 25. In the meantime, Allied troops pressed into the Po Valley, taking Bologna and other villages in fierce fighting. (The U.S. 442nd Regimental Combat Team, comprising 8,400 Japanese-Americans, was instrumental in the overall offensive.) Allied troops were instructed to hold German divisions down and keep them from withdrawing to Germany as the allies steadily liberated one city after another, including Padua, Venice, and Milan. The Germans were on the run and began surrendering in huge numbers. Meanwhile, Hitler's chief ally, Benito Mussolini, attempting to escape disguised as a German soldier, was apprehended when partisans stopped his truck convoy near Dongo. The next day, both he and his mistress, Clara (Claretta) Petacci, were shot and their bodies hung upside down in Milan. The 20-month offensive in Italy came to an end.

defenses, announced that German ammunition would run out the next day. On April 30, as the Soviets stormed the Reichstag, Hitler married his longtime mistress Eva Braun, and shortly thereafter the two of them committed suicide. Two days later, Weidling surrendered Berlin, a city now reduced to rubble. As special NKVD troops entered the Kaiser Wilhelm Institute and secured three tons of uranium oxide for Soviet atomic-weapons research, victorious Soviet troops further ravaged the city with countless atrocities—including looting, murder, and rape (see "Soviet War Crimes" in Chapter 8). As this continued, on May 5, emissaries from the new German head of state, Admiral Karl Dönitz, arrived at Eisenhower's forward headquarters to negotiate terms of surrender.

★   ★   ★

Victory in Europe made it possible for the United States to begin transferring troops from the European to the Pacific Theater, as the war effort

V-E, VICTORY IN EUROPE

The Germans who came to negotiate peace terms with Eisenhower on May 5 hoped for either a separate surrender to the western Allies or a phased surrender that would allow time for them to pull as many German units as possible away from the Eastern Front and Soviet authorities. In line with Allied policy, Eisenhower demanded unconditional surrender on all fronts. German representatives signed the surrender on May 7, whereupon Prime Minister Churchill and the new U.S. president, Harry S. Truman, declared that May 8 would be celebrated as "V-E Day." The Soviets, however, demanded a separate signing on territory they occupied. Thus, the Germans surrendered a second time near midnight on May 8. Thenceforward, May 9 was the USSR's V-E Day.

now concentrated on the defeat of Japan. In May 1945, most Allied military authorities believed this would require a full-scale invasion of the Japanese home islands, which hard combat experience had taught them would take a long time and cost hundreds of thousands of Allied lives. A few scientists, military officers, and civilian officials, however, were aware of a new and terrible weapon, and the test on July 16 that had proven it was ready for use.

Dropping the A-Bomb

On the morning of August 6, 1945, a B-29 Superfortress from the U.S. 509th Composite Group, Twentieth Air Force, took off from a Tinian airfield, heading for Japan's largest home island, Honshu. The cargo was a uranium-based atomic bomb measuring nearly ten feet long and weighing around 8,000 pounds. Nicknamed "Little Boy," it held the power of approximately 12,500 tons of TNT explosives. Hiroshima had been chosen as the primary target from a list that included Kokura, Niigata, Kyoto, and Nagasaki—all cities relatively untouched by conventional bombing. Followed by two observation planes, the B-29, named *Enola Gay* after the mother of its pilot and commanding officer, Colonel Paul Tibbets, delivered the first atomic bomb by parachute at 8:15 A.M.; upon its explosion, an area of four to five square miles directly below the blast disappeared. The tail gunner in the *Enola Gay*, George Caron, later wrote:

> The giant purple mushroom . . . had already risen to a height of 45,000 feet, three miles above our altitude, and was still boiling upward like something terribly alive. It was a frightening sight, and even though we were several miles away, it gave the appearance of something that was about to engulf us. Even more fearsome was the sight on the ground below. At the base of the cloud, fires were springing up everywhere amid a turbulent mass of smoke that had the appearance of bubbling hot tar. . . . The city we had seen so clearly in the sunlight a few minutes before was now an ugly smudge. It had completely disappeared under this awful blanket of smoke and fire.

Below, temperatures on the ground reached thousands of degrees and shock waves were felt for miles; about fifteen minutes later a radioactive rain began falling. More than 70,000 people died immediately from the explosion; more than 60 percent of the city was completely destroyed; only 10 percent was undamaged. Three days later, another B-29, *Bockscar*, commanded by Major Charles Sweeny, took off from Tinian carrying an even larger plutonium-based atomic bomb nicknamed "Fat Man." Under strict orders for a visual drop only and frustrated by cloud and smoke cover over their primary target, Kokura, the plane diverted to its secondary target of Nagasaki. A break in cloud cover there allowed bombardier Kermit Beahan a visual drop at 11:02 A.M., after which *Bockscar*, dangerously low on fuel, set course for Okinawa rather than returning to more distant Tinian. Less than a minute passed before the bomb detonated, creating another giant mushroom cloud. Waves of heat, fire, and radiation destroyed between one-quarter and one-third of the city, and left only about one-third intact. Again, more than 70,000 people were killed—many were vaporized, leaving only eerie shadows imprinted on nearby surfaces. The many thousands of wounded, and others exposed to the bomb's radiation, would later suffer from the ravages of radiation sickness.

The war in Asia did not end on August 9, but the two atomic bombs confirmed, to most—though not all—Japanese leaders, that it would be futile to continue fighting.

★   ★   ★

THEATERS OF WAR, 1945

Europe	*Mediterranean/North Africa*
January: Soviet forces push toward Berlin from the east	**January 11:** Greek rebels declare truce with the British
January 17: Soviets take Warsaw	**February 23:** Turkey declares war on Axis
January 19: Red Army takes Krakow	**February 24:** Egypt declares war on Axis
January 27: Soviet troops liberate Auschwitz	**April 22:** Allied troops take Bologna, Italy
January 30: Soviet submarine sinks German liner with 10,000 civilians and wounded soldiers on board in the Baltic; most passengers drown	**April 27:** Allied troops take Genoa, Verona and advance through the Po River Valley
February 13: Budapest falls to Soviet troops	**April 28:** Partisans capture Mussolini after he tries to flee in disguise
March 17: Remagen bridge collapses, killing 28 U.S. Army engineers	**April 29:** German forces in Italy surrender
March 23: U.S. troops cross the Rhine; German defenses are disintegrating as Allied front presses toward Berlin	**April 30:** Tito's Partisans enter Trieste
March 27: Last V-2 rocket falls on London	**May 8:** French troops clash with nationalists in Algeria: more than 1,000 Algerians and 88 Frenchmen are killed; in Syria, tensions explode into fighting
April 9: Red Army takes Vienna	**May 29:** French forces bomb Damascus in the face of Syrian colonial uprising; negotiations begin after British intervention, which will result in the removal of French troops from Syria by April 1, 1946—celebrated thereafter in Syria as Evacuation Day
April 10: U.S. troops liberate Buchenwald	
April 18: Allied troops take Magdeburg and Leipzig	
April 20: Nuremberg falls: the city, once the scene of Hitler's prewar rallies, would soon become one of the postwar sites for war crimes trials of Nazi leaders	
April 25: U.S. and Soviet troops join forces at the Elbe River; Berlin is encircled	
April 29: Dachau is turned over to U.S. troops; (see Chapter 8)	
April 30: Hitler commits suicide	
May 7: German Chief of Operations Staff Alfred Jodl signs terms of unconditional surrender at Eisehhower's headquarters in Rheims	
May 8: V-E Day	
May 9: German Field Marshal Wilhelm Keitel signs terms of unconditional surrender at Zhukov's headquarters in Berlin	
May 9: Soviets take Prague	
May 22: Gestapo chief Himmler is caught trying to leave the country in disguise; he commits suicide the next day	

The Pacific	*China-Burma-India*
January: Japanese step up kamikaze attacks as U.S. forces led by MacArthur land on Luzon*	**January 28:** Burma Road reopened by Allies
February 3: Nearing Manila, U.S. troops liberate a POW camp	**March 28:** Burmese patriot Aung San leads his Burmese National Army in revolt against the Japanese
February 16–17: The first large-scale U.S. Navy air attack on Japan is launched from a carrier fleet; 500 Japanese planes are destroyed	**April 11:** British fleet in the Indian Ocean opens fire on Sabang, Sumatra
February 19: U.S. Marines land on Iwo Jima*	**May 2:** British forces land near Rangoon
April 1: Battle of Okinawa begins*	**August 19:** Soviet-Japanese fighting in Manchuria ends
April 7: In the Battle of the East China Sea, U.S. aircraft sink the battleship *Yamato* and most of its task force	**September 9:** Japanese authorities in China sign surrender terms
April 18: Ernie Pyle, beloved American journalist, is killed on Okinawa	**September 12:** British authorities receive the formal surrender of Japanese forces within the Southeast Asia Command
May 1: Australian troops land on Borneo	
June 27: Kamikaze hits U.S. aircraft carrier *Bunker Hill*, killing 400 crew members	
July 5: General MacArthur calls liberation of the Philippines complete, although fighting continues	
July 10: 1,000 U.S. planes bomb Tokyo	
July 23: Osaka, Kure, Nagoya, bombed	
August 2: 6,000 tons of bombs dropped on Japanese cities	
August 3: Blockade of Japanese islands is in place; invasion of Honshu anticipated	
August 6: Atomic bomb explodes over Hiroshima*	
August 8: Soviet Union declares war on Japan and goes on the offensive in Manchuria	
August 9: Atomic bomb explodes over Nagasaki*	
August 10: Soviet forces invade Korea	
August 14: Emperor Hirohito accepts U.S. terms of unconditional surrender, breaking deadlock of Tokyo War Council	
August 28–September 2: U.S. occupation forces, begin to arrive in Japan; they begin liberation of POWs	
September 2: Surrender ceremony is held on board the U.S. battleship *Missouri*, anchored in Tokyo Bay; V-J Day is declared	

* See text for further discussion.

August 9, the day *Bockscar* dropped the second A-bomb, Joseph Stalin fulfilled the commitment he had made at the February Allied conference at Yalta; the Soviet Union entered the war against Japan. The Soviet Far Eastern forces, doubled in strength since the German surrender in May, then numbered more than a million troops, 5,000 armored vehicles, an equal number of aircraft and more than 26,000 artillery pieces. During the short Japanese-Soviet war, the Red Army and Navy swept into Manchuria and Korea and seized the Kuril Islands and the southern part of the island of Sakhalin. Depleted Japanese forces were unable to effectively resist; in Manchuria, alone, more than 80,000 Japanese were killed versus some 8,000 Soviet deaths. Yet fighting between the two forces continued—in some cases, even after Emperor Hirohito announced the Japanese surrender on August 14. Thereafter, the Soviets transported some 500,000 Japanese prisoners to Siberia. Many remained there for several years; many others never returned to Japan.

V-J, VICTORY OVER JAPAN

Faced with a terrible new weapon and a new enemy, Japanese authorities decided they must surrender, against the violent objections of some who wished to resist to the end. On August 14, the day of the last Allied bombing sortie against Japan, the Japanese heard their emperor's voice on the radio for the first time. Never using the word "surrender," he told his "good and loyal subjects" . . . "We have ordered our Government to communicate to the Governments of the United States, Great Britain, China, and the Soviet Union that our Empire accepts the provisions of their joint declaration." That declaration, made at the Allied conference at Potsdam, required Japan's unconditional surrender. The Allies thus declared August 15 V-J Day—a designation also given to September 2, the date of the formal surrender ceremonies on USS *Missouri* in Tokyo Bay. (See also Chapter 12.) (Japanese forces in China signed surrender terms September 9, and British authorities received the formal surrender of Japanese forces within the South East Asia Command September 12. It took many weeks to inform all Japanese garrisons that the war was over.)

One unit of U.S. Marines who had survived the fighting on Okinawa and remained to occupy the islands heard of the August 14 surrender as soon as it happened. After the war, one among them, Eugene Sledge, remembered their reaction:

We received the news with quiet disbelief coupled with an indescribable sense of relief. We thought the Japanese would never surrender. Many refused to believe it. Sitting in stunned silence, we remembered our dead. So many dead. So many maimed. So many bright futures consigned to the ashes of the past. So many dreams lost in the madness that had engulfed us. Except for a few widely scattered shouts of joy, the survivors of the abyss sat hollow-eyed and silent, trying to comprehend a world without war.

On Memorial Day, 1943, two women decorate a soldier's grave in one of the African American sections of Arlington National Cemetery. Of the more than 50 million people killed during the war, 405,000 were Americans.

Principal Sources and Further Reading

Atkinson. Rick. *An Army at Dawn: The War in North Africa, 1942–1943.* New York: Henry Holt, 2002.

Beevor, Antony, ed., Luba Vinogradova, trans. *A Writer at War: Vasily Grossman with the Red Army, 1941–1945.* New York: Pantheon Books, 2005.

Borodziej, Wlodzimierz, Barbara Harshav, trans. *The Warsaw Uprising of 1944.* Madison, WI: University of Wisconsin Press, 2006.

Calvocoressi, Peter, Guy Wint, and R. John Pritchard. *Total War: The Causes and Courses of the Second World War.* Rev. 2nd ed. New York: Pantheon Books, 1989.

Carruthers, Bob. *Servants of Evil.* London: Andre Deutsch, 2001.

Center for Military History. *Anzio* (pamphlet in "The U.S. Army Campaigns of World War II" series). CMH Publication 72-19.

_____. *India Burma* ("The U.S. Army Campaigns of World War II"). CMH Publication 72-5.

_____. *Leyte 1944–1945* ("The U.S. Army Campaigns of World War II"). CMH publication 72–27.

_____. *Luzon 1944* ("The U.S. Army Campaigns of World War II"). CMH Publication 72-28.

_____. *Normandy* ("The U.S. Army Campaigns of World War II"). CMH Publication 72-18.

_____. *Po Valley* ("The U.S. Army Campaigns of World War II"). CMH Publication 72-33.

_____. *Rome-Arno 1944* ("The U.S. Army Campaigns of World War II"). CMH Publication 72-20.

Chant, Christopher. *The Encyclopedia of Codenames of World War II.* London: Routledge & Kegan Paul, 1986.

Chiechanowski, Jan M. *The Warsaw Rising of 1944.* New York: Cambridge University Press, 1974.

Dear, Ian, and M. R. D. Foot, eds. *The Oxford Companion to the Second World War.* Oxford: Oxford University Press, 1995.

Dunnigan, James, F., and Albert A. Nofi. *The Pacific War Encyclopedia.* New York: Facts on File, 1998.

Erickson, John. *The Road to Berlin.* Boulder, CO: Westview Press, 1983.

Fussell, Paul. *The Boys' Crusade: The American Infantry in Northwestern Europe, 1944–1945.* New York: The Modern Library, 2003.

Gilbert, Sir Martin. *The Second World War: A Complete History.* New York: Henry Holt, 1989.

Goralski, Robert. *World War II Almanac, 1931–1945: A Political and Military Record.* New York: Putnam, 1981.

Harries, Merion, and Susie Harries. *Soldiers of the Sun: The Rise and Fall of the Imperial Japanese Army.* New York: Random House, 1991.

Hoyt, Edwin P. *The Kamikazes.* New York: Arbor House, 1983.

Icks, Robert J. *Famous Tank Battles.* Garden City, NY: Doubleday, 1972.

Keegan, John. *The Second World War.* New York: Penguin Books, 2005.

Kennedy, David M. *Freedom from Fear: The American People in Depression and War, 1929–1945.* Oxford: Oxford University Press, 1999.

Lawson, Ted W. *Thirty Seconds over Tokyo,* edited by Robert Considine. New York: Random House, 1943.

Manchester, William. *Goodbye Darkness: A Memoir of the Pacific War.* Boston: Little, Brown, 1980.

Miller, Donald. *The Story of World War II.* New York: Simon & Schuster, 2001.

Murray, Williamson and Allan R. Millett. *A War to Be Won: Fighting the Second World War.* Cambridge, MA: Belknap Press of Harvard University Press, 2000.

Ohnuki-Tierney, Emiko. *Kamikaze, Cherry Blossoms, and Nationalisms: The Militarization of Aesthetics in Japanese History.* Chicago: University of Chicago Press, 2002.

Parrish, Thomas, ed. *The Simon and Schuster Encyclopedia of World War II.* New York: Simon & Schuster, 1978.

Paul, Doris A. *The Navajo Code Talkers.* Philadelphia: Dorrance, 1973.

Pemsel, Helmut. *A History of War at Sea.* Annapolis, MD: Naval Institute Press, 1989.

Polmar, Norman, and Thomas B. Allen. *World War II: The Encyclopedia of the War Years, 1941–1945.* New York: Random House, 1996.

Potter, E. B., ed. *The United States and World Sea Power.* New York: Prentice Hall, 1955.

Sledge, E. B. *With the Old Breed at Peleliu and Okinawa.* Annapolis, MD: Naval Institute Press, 1996.

Snyder, Louis Leo. *Historical Guide to World War II.* Westport, CT: Greenwood Press, 1982.

Spector, Ronald H. *Eagle against the Sun.* New York: Free Press, 1985.

Thompson, Robert Smith. *Empires on the Pacific: World War II and the Struggle for the Mastery of Asia.* New York: Basic Books, 2001.

Trevor-Roper, H. R., ed. *Hitler's War Directives 1939–1945.* London: Pan Books, 1966.

Tuchman, Barbara Wertheim. *Stilwell and the American Experience in China, 1911–1945.* New York: Grove Press, 2001.

Tucker, Spencer C. *Encyclopedia of World War II: A Political, Social, and Military History.* Santa Barbara: ABC-CLIO, 2005.

Wilson, Dick. *When Tigers Fight: The Story of the Sino-Japanese War, 1937–1945.* New York: Viking Press, 1982.

Young, Peter. *World Almanac of World War II.* New York: World Almanac, 1981.

8

WAR CRIMES AND THE HOLOCAUST

The Rules of War

The right of belligerents to adopt means of injuring the enemy is not unlimited. It is especially forbidden: to employ poison or poisoned weapons; to kill or wound treacherously individuals belonging to the hostile nation or army; to kill or wound an enemy who, having laid down his arms, or having no longer means of defense, has surrendered at discretion; . . . to employ arms, projectiles, or material calculated to cause unnecessary suffering; . . . to destroy or seize the enemy's property, unless such destruction or seizure be imperatively demanded by the necessities of war.

—Hague Convention on the Laws and Customs of War on Land, 1907

The end product of decades of international meetings and discussions that sought, in the words of one declaration, to fix "the technical limits at which the necessities of war ought to yield to the requirements of humanity," the Hague land-war convention comprises rules of warfare that were generally accepted by World War II belligerents. Additional international agreements addressed other aspects of war:

Naval Warfare

General rules for maritime warfare were first issued under the Geneva Convention of 1856, with changes promulgated at the Hague in 1899. Between 1907 and 1930, many nations subscribed to other naval agreements, including those in the "Conventions Regarding Maritime Warfare" chart on page 630.

Aerial Warfare

No similar agreements existed regarding aerial warfare. After the first air forces were formed during World War I, debates raged over the most

CONVENTIONS REGARDING MARITIME WARFARE, 1907–1936

Bombardment by Naval Forces in Time of War. The Hague, October 1907. Ratified by Austria-Hungary, Belgium, China, France, Germany, Japan, the Russian Federation, the United Kingdom, and the United States

Prohibits bombarding undefended ports, towns, villages, and dwellings—excepting military facilities. Care to be taken to spare "sacred edifices, buildings used for artistic, scientific, or charitable purposes, historic monuments, hospitals." If possible, warning must be given before the bombardment. Places taken by storm must not be pillaged.

Adaptation to Maritime Warfare of the Principles of the Geneva Convention. The Hague, October 1907. Ratified by 33 nations, including Austria-Hungary, Belgium, France, Germany, Japan, Russian Federation, Spain, Sweden, Switzerland, and the United States

Pertained principally to protections for hospital ships; care and treatment of the shipwrecked and wounded; the rights of prisoners taken as a result of naval warfare.

Laying of Automatic Submarine Contact Mines. The Hague, October 1907. 27 signatories including China, France, Germany, Japan, the United Kingdom, and the United States

Comprising 13 articles establishing rules for laying sea mines, the types of mines permitted, and procedures for recovering mines at the cessation of hostilities.

Treaty for the Limitation and Reduction of Naval Armaments. London, April 1930 (Treaty of London) was not ratified by all signatories and *expired in 1936*; and a *Procès-verbal* relating to the Rules of Submarine Warfare set forth in Part IV of the Treaty of London, November 1936. 39 signatories, including all those that signed the 1930 treaty (including the United States, Britain, Italy, and Japan), plus 11 subsequent adherents, among them Germany and the USSR

Article 22 of the 1930 treaty pertained to rules of submarine warfare. It declared that submarines must follow the same international law as surface vessels. Further, except under specified circumstances, "a warship, whether surface vessel or submarine, may not sink or render incapable of navigation a merchant vessel without having first placed passengers, crew and ship's papers in a place of safety." The 1936 Procès-verbal extended the life of this understanding.

Principal source: International Committee of the Red Cross Web pages on "International Humanitarian Law—Treaties and Documents," http://www.cicr.org/ihl.nsf.

effective uses of military aircraft and what restrictions should be placed on aerial bombing (see "Aircraft" in Chapter 5). In 1921, the Italian aviator Giulio Douhet published *The Command of the Air*, an influential treatise that advocated breaking the enemy's economy and morale by extensive bombing of what, by World War II, became known as the "home front." "How could a country go on living and working," Douhet wrote, "oppressed by the nightmare of imminent destruction and death?" During the interwar years, military planners of future Allied and Axis nations closely studied Douhet's brutal proposed strategy; but it was not reflected in the tentative "Rules of Air Warfare" that were drafted at the Hague between December 1922 and February 1923. Comprising 62 articles, this agreement dealt mainly with identification marks for aircraft, the rights of neutral nations, prisoners of war, and properly marking nonmilitary edifices (such as hospitals, churches,

In Canton, China, a woman searches for her 7-year-old child in the rubble left after Japanese aerial bombing (left). A Japanese-language leaflet distributed by the U.S. Army Forces Psychological Warfare Branch, warns Japanese people of an impending air attack: "Civilians! Evacuate at once!" It also informs the Japanese public that their military leaders are "powerless to protect you. . . . It is your responsibility to overthrow the military government now and save what is left of your beautiful country."

and historic monuments) to protect them from aerial bombardment. Article XVIII allowed "The use of tracer, incendiary, or explosive projectiles," while articles XXII–XXV placed restrictions on how these airborne weapons could be used: "Aerial bombardment for the purpose of terrorizing the civilian population, of destroying or damaging private property not of a military character, or of injuring non-combatants is prohibited"; "Aerial bombardment is legitimate only when directed at a military objective"; "The bombardment of cities, towns, villages, dwellings, or buildings not in the immediate neighborhood of the operations of land forces is prohibited." Although its basic principles were generally accepted in the 1920s and 1930s, this agreement was never formally adopted by any nation.

Throughout the total war that engulfed the world between 1937 and 1945, civilians and nonmilitary objectives were targets of air attacks:

EYEWITNESS ACCOUNT: STRATEGIC BOMBING

A teenage pacifist when the war started, renowned physicist and author Freeman Dyson watched Germany swallow Europe and witnessed the Luftwaffe's bombing of his native British Isles. Joining the RAF Bomber Command at age 19 in 1943, he was assigned to Operational Research. In his 1984 book *Weapons and Hope*, Dyson characterized his wartime duties as "writing memoranda and calculating how to murder people efficiently."

[1943–1944] The [German] defenses made it impossible for us to bomb accurately. We stopped trying to hit precise military objectives. Burning down cities was all we could do, and so we did that. Even in killing the civilian population we were inefficient. The Germans had killed one person for every ton of bombs that they dropped on England. To kill a German, we dropped on the average three tons.

[August 1945] I was all set to fly to Okinawa. We had defeated the Germans, but Mr. Churchill had . . . persuaded President Truman to let him join in the bombing of Japan with a fleet of three hundred bombers which he called Tiger Force. . . . I found this continuing slaughter of defenseless Japanese even more sickening than the slaughter of well-defended Germans. But still I did not quit. By that time I had been at war so long that I could hardly remember peace. No living poet had words to describe that emptiness of the soul which allowed me to go on killing without hatred and without remorse. . . . I was sitting at home, eating a quiet breakfast with my mother, when the morning paper arrived with the news of Hiroshima. I understood at once what it meant. "Thank God for that," I said. I knew that Tiger Force would not fly, and I would never have to kill anybody again.

Guernica and Shanghai in 1937; Warsaw, Rotterdam, and Coventry in 1939–1940; Hamburg in 1943, Dresden in February, and Tokyo in March 1945 were only a few of the places devastated as the air war steadily escalated. Five months after the Tokyo raid, American planes dropped atomic bombs on Hiroshima and Nagasaki.

United States ambassador to Japan Joseph Grew called the 1937 Japanese bombing of Shanghai "one of the most horrible episodes in modern times." Allied nations also roundly condemned the German bombing of Rotterdam and the firebombing of the cathedral city of Coventry. The Germans excoriated the Allied firebombing of ancient and beautiful Dresden, which killed an estimated 25,000 to 35,000 people, as "terror bombing"—and some Nazi officials proposed using the attacks on the city as a reason for abandoning adherence to the Geneva Conventions in western Europe. Whether, once the war turned in the Allies' favor, Allied commanders should have decided that the necessities of war could yield to the requirements of humanity in the case of strategic bombing campaigns and the use of nuclear weapons is still debated. Even during the war—and even as awareness of unprecedented Axis savagery became more widespread—some people in Allied nations struggled with this difficult question. (See Eyewitness Account, opposite.)

The Geneva Conventions

In 1929, two additional agreements governing the conduct of belligerents in wartime were adopted by forty nations: (1) the Geneva Convention for the Amelioration of the Condition of the Wounded and the Sick of Armies in the Field (also known as the Geneva Red Cross Convention), and (2) the Geneva Convention Relative to the Treatment of Prisoners of War. The POW convention covered virtually every aspect of prisoner life—although its provisions did not pertain to merchant mariners or to resistance forces caught in acts of spying, sabotage, or guerrilla warfare. In many areas, the Geneva POW convention echoed or expanded on rules established under the Hague land-warfare convention of 1907. The chart on pages 634–635 lists the major provisions of these agreements.

All the Allied powers of World War II, except the Soviet Union, ratified the Geneva conventions and abided by them. Both Italy and Germany ratified them, as well. However, during the war both those nations adhered to the conventions selectively, with German violations against certain groups of POWs being particularly egregious. Although Japan signed the accords, the Japanese government never ratified them.

MAJOR PROVISIONS GOVERNING THE TREATMENT
OF PRISONERS OF WAR

Hague Convention, 1907 (56 Articles)	*Geneva Convention, 1929 (143 Articles)*
(Art. 4) . . . Prisoners of war . . . must be humanely treated. (Art. 9) Every prisoner of war is bound to give, if he is questioned on the subject, his true name and rank, and if he infringes this rule, he is liable to have the advantages given to prisoners of his class curtailed.	(Art. 5–6) If questioned, prisoners are bound to give their name and rank or their regimental number. Coercion, threats, or other forms of maltreatment may not be used by the detaining power to secure information concerning the condition of the detainee's nation or army.
(Art. 5) Prisoners of war may be interned in a town, fortress, camp, or other place, and bound not to go beyond certain fixed limits, but they cannot be confined except as an indispensable measure of safety and only while the circumstances which necessitate the measure continue to exist.	(Art. 9) Prisoners of war may be interned in a town, fortress, or . . . in enclosed camps; they may not be confined or imprisoned except as an indispensable measure of safety or sanitation, and only while the circumstances which necessitate the measure continue to exist. . . . No prisoner may, . . . be sent into a region where he might be exposed to the fire of the combat zone, nor used to give protection from bombardment to certain points or certain regions by his presence.
(Art. 6) The State may utilize the labor of prisoners of war according to their rank and aptitude, officers excepted. The tasks shall not be excessive and shall have no connection with the operations of the war. . . . The wages of the prisoners shall go towards improving their position, and the balance shall be paid them on their release, after deducting the cost of their maintenance.	(Art. 27–34) The detaining Power may use able-bodied prisoners of war for labor, as long as the work befits the prisoner's personal rank and aptitude. . . . The detaining power is responsible for the care and monetary compensation due to prisoners of war in their employ. . . . Labor furnished by prisoners of war shall have no direct relation with war operations. . . . It is forbidden to use prisoners of war at unhealthful or dangerous work.
(Art. 8) Prisoners of war shall be subject to the laws, regulations, and orders in force in the army of the State in whose power they are. Any act of insubordination justifies the adoption towards them of such measures of severity as may be considered necessary. . . .	(Art. 45–59) Prisoners of war shall be subject to the laws, regulations and orders in force in the armies of the detaining Power. . . . Any corporal punishment, any imprisonment in quarters without daylight and, in general, any form of cruelty, is forbidden. Collective

MAJOR PROVISIONS GOVERNING THE TREATMENT OF PRISONERS OF WAR (CONTINUED)

Hague Convention, 1907 (56 Articles)	*Geneva Convention, 1929 (143 Articles)*
(Art. 18) Prisoners of war shall enjoy complete liberty in the exercise of their religion . . . on the sole condition that they comply with the measures of order and police issued by the military authorities.	punishment for individual acts is also forbidden. . . . Arrest is the most severe disciplinary punishment which may be imposed on a prisoner of war. The duration of a single punishment may not exceed thirty days. . . . In no case may prisoners of war be transferred to penitentiary establishments.

Geneva Convention Only

(Art. 60–67) At the opening of a judicial proceeding directed against a prisoner of war, the detaining Power shall advise the representative of the protecting Power thereof . . . before the date set for the opening of the trial. . . . No prisoner of war may be sentenced without having had an opportunity to defend himself. No prisoner may be obliged to admit himself guilty. . . . The prisoner of war shall be entitled to assistance by a qualified counsel of his choice and, if necessary have recourse to the services of a competent interpreter. . . . In default of a choice by the prisoner, the protecting Power may obtain a counsel for him.

Source: Text of Hague and Geneva conventions at the Yale University "Avalon Project" Web site for the Laws of War, http://www.yale.edu/lawweb/avalon/lawofwar/lawwar.htm.

The war that ignited in Asia in 1937 and, by 1941, had engulfed the world, burned with a fury, and on a scale unprecedented in human history. In this terrible conflagration—fueled by nationalism and ideological fervor, racial hatred and anticolonial aspirations, the thirst for conquest and the rage for revenge—the rules of war were often ignored. Many of those accused of violating them most egregiously were brought before the bar of justice and tried for war crimes.

War Crimes

War crimes are generally defined as violations of the established rules of war. In the August 1945 "Constitution of the International Military Tribunal," under which Axis war criminals were tried, war crimes were defined more specifically in Article 6c as:

昨日の敵は今日の友

昭和四年七月二十七日ジュネーブに於て俘虜取扱に關し廿九ヶ國代表により調印を見たる國際條約には次の箇條がある。

一、俘虜はつねに人道的待遇をうくべきものなり。

一、食糧は留守部隊のものに等しかるべき事。

一、各收容所には被收容者用病室の設置あるを要す。

18-J-1

PSYCHOLOGICAL WARFARE BRANCH
U.S. ARMY FORCES, PACIFIC AREA
APO 500

LEAFLET: "Yesterday we were enemies, today we are friends."

LANGUAGE: Japanese

DESIGNATION: 18-J-1

TARGET: Japanese troops

REMARKS: Suitable for Jap
Induce surrender
of prisoners

TEXT:

Articles approved by the International Convention on treatment of prisoners of war, which was signed by 29 nations at Geneva on July 27, 1929, contain the following:

1. Prisoners of war shall be treated humanely.

2. The food ration of prisoners of war shall be equivalent to that of the depot troops.

3. Each camp shall possess an infirmary for the prisoners of war.

The line under the illustration reads: "A scene during the rest period." (Eyes have been covered to protect their families in Japan.)

This leaflet, released by the U.S. Army Forces Psychological Warfare Branch, encourages Japanese soldiers to surrender by showing Japanese troops being well-treated by Americans. The leaflet also outlines aspects of the Geneva Convention, a document with which many Japanese were unfamiliar.

violations of the laws or customs of war. Such violations shall include, but not be limited to, murder, ill-treatment or deportation to slave labor or for any other purpose of civilian population of or in occupied territory, murder or ill-treatment of prisoners of war or persons on the seas, killing of hostages, plunder of public or private property, wanton destruction of cities, towns or villages, or devastation not justified by military necessity.

The scope and horror of German and Japanese atrocities throughout World War II placed them in a dark realm of their own. Categorized as *crimes against humanity* (a term first coined in 1915 to describe Turkish massacres of Armenians), these crimes—and the responsibility for them—were defined in the "Constitution of the International Military Tribunal" (Article 6c) and the January 1946 "Charter of the International Military Tribunal for the Far East" (Article 5c) as follows:

CRIMES AGAINST HUMANITY: namely, murder, extermination, enslavement, deportation, and other inhumane acts committed against any civilian population, before or during the war; or persecutions on political, racial or religious grounds in execution of or in connection with any crime within the jurisdiction of the Tribunal, whether or not in violation of the domestic law of the country where perpetrated. Leaders, organizers, instigators and accomplices participating in the formulation or execution of a common plan or conspiracy to commit any of the foregoing crimes are responsible for all acts performed by any persons in execution of such plan.

These definitions provided the bases for trying German and Japanese military officers and civilian officials, including members of secret police organizations (see box, "Confronting Internal Dissent" on p. 638). But no World War II combatant was innocent of violating the rules of war.

The Allies

"I have never heard or read of this kind of fighting," Major General Alexander A. Vandegrift of the U.S. Marine Corps wrote of the fighting on Guadalcanal. "These people refuse to surrender. The wounded will wait till men come up to examine them, and blow themselves and the other fellow to death with a hand grenade." Guadalcanal inaugurated the Allies' Pacific Theater offensive—and introduced American fighting men to combat of soul-shaking viciousness. In the jungles of Burma, at Singapore, in China, and elsewhere in Asia, Allied fighters were also confronting Japanese brutality in combat

CONFRONTING INTERNAL DISSENT

In April 1934, Hermann Göring relinquished authority over the Gestapo (Geheimes Staatspolizei) to Heinrich Himmler, a fervent Nazi whom historian William L. Shirer described as "a mild-mannered but sadistic former chicken farmer." Under the umbrella of Himmler's ever-expanding empire of SS (*Schutzstaffel*) protection organizations, the Gestapo grew to include 43,000 staff members, plus a network of 160,000 agents and informants that operated throughout German-occupied areas. Like secret police of other Axis powers (and the Soviet NKVD), the Gestapo conducted intelligence and counterintelligence; arrested, tortured, and sometimes murdered social undesirables and enemies of the state; and generally employed terror tactics to stamp out dissent and maintain iron Nazi control—without any legal constraints. Dr. Werner Best, one of Himmler's chief Gestapo deputies, declared: "As long as the police carries out the will of the leadership, it is acting legally." (See the "Chart of Axis Intelligence Organizations" in Chapter 9, for further information on secret police.)

The western democracies were also concerned with wartime dissent and subversion. At the same time, they struggled—with fluctuating success (see "Fifth Column Fears" and "The Decision for Japanese-American Internment" in Chapter 2)—to uphold the democratic principles for which their people were fighting. On December 15, 1941, acting U.S. Attorney General Francis Biddle, speaking on the 152nd anniversary of the Bill of Rights, reminded his audience, "Every man . . . who cares about freedom must fight [to protect it] for the *other* man with whom he disagrees."

and in their treatment of prisoners of war. In the midst of this bitter violence, Allied soldiers sometimes turned their backs on the rules of war: they pried gold teeth out of the mouths of captured enemies, shot prisoners, and mutilated the bodies of dead enemies. In marked contrast with the Japanese, this behavior was not sanctioned by most Allied commanders. As early as September 1942, after a month of fighting on Guadalcanal, the commander in chief of the U.S. Pacific Fleet was moved to order that "No part of the enemy's body may be used as a souvenir. Unit Commanders will take stern disciplinary action."

In the European theater, intense combat also eroded respect for the rules of war. Two cases involving Americans occurred in July 1943, after a sharp struggle for the airfield at Biscari, Sicily, near the Gulf of Gela. In the first case, Sergeant Horace T. West of the 180th Infantry Regiment, 45th Infantry Division, in charge of a detail of nine men who had custody of more than forty German and Italian prisoners, separated six of the prisoners from the rest, then killed all the others with his Thompson submachine gun. None of his men tried to stop him. Court-martialed that September for violating the 92nd Article of War ("Any person subject to military law who commits murder or rape shall suffer death or imprisonment for life, as a court-martial may direct . . ."), Sergeant West claimed, as mitigating circumstances, prolonged combat, lack of sleep, and stress resulting from witnessing the murder of two GIs who had been captured by the enemy. He was convicted and sentenced to life imprisonment.

In the second incident, forty Italian prisoners surrendered under a flag of truce to another sergeant of the 180th regiment, whose captain, John C. Compton, ordered all the prisoners shot. This order was carried out by a firing squad. Because the men on the squad believed they were carrying out a lawful order, only Captain Compton was charged with violating the 92nd Article of War. In his defense, Compton cited an address the commanding general, George C. Patton, had given to the officers of the 45th Division, which Compton claimed to remember nearly verbatim. In his testimony, the captain asserted that the general's speech had included the following statements: "When we meet the enemy, we will kill him. We will show him no mercy. He has killed thousands of your comrades, and he must die."

Compton then stated: "I ordered them shot because I thought it came directly under the General's instructions. Right or wrong, a three star general's advice, who has had combat experience, is good enough for me and I took him at his word." The captain was acquitted. (The disparity between the outcomes of these two cases, inquiries from Sergeant West's family, and the wish to avoid publicity led to a reduction in Sergeant West's sentence. On November 23, 1944, General Joseph McNarney, deputy commander of the Mediterranean theater, restored West to duty at the reduced rank of private.)

Despite the multiple pressures of combat, most western Allies generally adhered to the rules of war. Many American servicemen were appalled by incidents such as the Biscari massacres. Lieutenant Colonel William E. King, chaplain of the 45th Division, reported to the board of inquiry that, as news of those murders circulated, several men approached him and stated:

> they would not care to go on fighting if such brutal treatment [as] . . . the shooting down of prisoners who were being escorted to the rear was to continue . . . they had come into the war to fight against that sort of thing, and they felt ashamed of their countrymen who were doing these very things.

In the Balkans and the Soviet Union, the war assumed distinctive shades of chaos and brutality. There, Allied fighters, whose experiences in both peace and war were often very different from those of their western Allied counterparts, were less likely to protest their own army's violations of the rules of war, which were often ordered or approved by their commanders. In all areas, partisans, guerrillas, and other irregular fighters had a much more tenuous relationship with the rules of war than did members of recognized armed forces.

Partisan War Crimes in the Balkans

No laws specifically governed guerrilla warfare, although under the Hague Convention only partisans who followed the rules of war earned official belligerent status. However, mindful of the military importance of organized resistance, the Allies rarely withdrew support in response to partisan atrocities.

In Yugoslavia, throughout the war, Josip Tito's partisans and the Serbian nationalist Chetniks battled each other and slaughtered their ethnic rivals. Chetniks murdered thousands of Croatians and Muslims in retaliation for massacres of Serbs. One subordinate assured his general of the "extermination" of an entire Muslim population. Another reported an operation in which his men destroyed 7 villages, killed 900 Croatians, and burned several Catholic clergymen alive.

Tito's partisans viewed Croatians and local German and Hungarian communities as collaborators, and treated them brutally, killing thousands in so-called reprisals. Revenge and reprisal also sparked the murder of an estimated 6,000 to 15,000 Italians in the *Foibe Massacres* that occurred after the Italian Fascist regime capitulated in 1943 and again in 1945, when Yugoslav authorities took control of the country's traditionally multiethnic northwestern borderland. (A *foiba* is a deep sinkhole. The bodies of many victims were tossed into such holes or into mining pits.) After victory, partisans slaughtered thousands of Croatians, Slovenes, and Chetniks. (Croatia, affiliated with the Axis, compiled its own record of vicious war crimes between 1941 and 1945, as noted later in this chapter.)

In Axis-occupied Greece, the ELAS resistance group (*Ethnikos Laikos Apeleftherotikos Stratos*, the Greek People's Liberation Army)—which was associated with the Communist Party but included many fighters of no particular political persuasion—emerged as the most powerful guerrilla organization. Prominent among the noncommunist guerrilla groups that fought ELAS as well as the Axis, EDES (*Ethnikos Dimokratikos Ellinikos Syndesmos*, the National Republican Greek League) was headed by Napoleon Zervas, a political chameleon who cultivated the British (via the Special Operations Executive personnel who were in Greece from 1942) and the Americans (via Office of Strategic Service operatives). As the Greeks became increasingly polarized, right against left, the government, with German support, established right-wing Security Battalions that targeted ELAS and its sympathizers. The bloody fighting among all these groups led to crossed allegiances and appalling abuses by all parties, including torture and summary executions. Anticommunist vigilante squads and undisciplined Security Battalions roamed the countryside burning, looting, and arresting suspected communist sympathizers. In March 1944, at the town of Ayia Anna, members of a Security Battalion burned a factory and the library while they "recruited" men for their ranks. Three days later, ELAS fighters entered the town, shot men the Security Battalion had left behind and burned down their families' houses. Other right-wing paramilitary organizations, often in collusion with Germans, perpetrated massacres. In September 1944, a Greek unit under the command of Colonel George Poulos, who was assisted by a Greek-speaking German sergeant named Fritz Schubert, beat and shot to death seventy-five people of the town of Giannitsa. As German officers from the local garrison stood by taking pictures, the anticommunist Greeks looted the victims' bodies and burned many houses. Poulos and his men swept through many other towns in the region, burning, pillaging, and raping.

By mid-1944, Greece had emerged as one of the first battlegrounds in what would shortly become known as the "Cold War." (The British were worried about losing their influence in the Eastern Mediterranean to the Soviet Union.) After the Germans had retreated and British troops confronted the factional warfare that was raging in the streets of Athens, RAF planes strafed suspected ELAS positions in the city (causing noncombatant casualties), and British troops battled ELAS snipers. When the British rounded up and interned between 8,000 and 15,000 suspected left-wing sympathizers, ELAS responded by executing hundreds of what they termed "reactionary" families. ELAS also took thousands of hostages, whom they forced to march northward into the mountains. An American OSS operative reported coming across one of these sad processions:

> [They] presented a terrifying sight with their great numbers, holding blankets over their heads, their lack of clothing and shoes. Upon

approaching they would make wild gestures of being hungry, cold, of demanding salvation. Their voices, sobs and staring eyes were an accusation to all civilization.

Thousands of these hostages died, either from exposure to the cold or from ELAS bullets. ELAS's strength was soon broken, but bitter right-versus-left fighting continued, devolving into an ugly civil war.

Soviet War Crimes

For four agonizing years, the Soviet people were victims of horrific Axis war crimes and crimes against humanity. Especially near the end of the war, Soviet armed forces—operating under direct orders from the Soviet high command or with the encouragement of the political officers that traveled with them—were also responsible for rampant violations of the rules of war.

Although the Soviet government never signed the Geneva Conventions, regulations issued by the Council of People's Commissars (Sovnarkom) in 1941 included provisions outlawing cruel and humiliating treatment of prisoners and the use of violence to extract information and guaranteeing medical treatment, the right to habitable living conditions, and contact with the outside world. However, the general provisions gave great discretionary powers to the NKVD—the state security organization that, during the war, was responsible for guarding prisoners of war as well as domestic political prisoners. This loophole permitted the notorious treatment individuals often received under Soviet guardianship.

THE GULAG

Following their conquest of eastern Poland in 1939, the Soviets deported 1.5 million people, including children, to the Arctic and Asiatic regions of the Soviet Union, forcing those who survived the journey into lives of hard labor in the gulag (a system of forced labor camps run by the NKVD). Prisoners, who were often beaten, toiled in construction, industry, mining, and forestry under grueling and dangerous conditions. The inhospitable weather, combined with inadequate shelter, food, and medical facilities resulted in a devastating mortality rate. Prisoners were kept on a starvation diet and rations were issued on a quota basis; the more a prisoner produced, the more food he or she received, while decreases in production meant less to eat. Germany's invasion of the Soviet Union only exacerbated conditions;

whereas 8.7 percent of the camp population died in 1941, the percentage more than doubled in 1942 and 1943.

THE MASSACRE AT KATYN

In addition to the Polish civilians they deported, the Soviets took some 200,000 Polish troops prisoner in 1939. These prisoners were scattered throughout more than two dozen POW camps. About fifteen thousand officers, most of whom were staunchly anticommunist, were concentrated in three principal facilities: Kozelsk, Starobielsk and Ostashkov; only 448 of them were heard from again.

In April 1943, Germans announced the discovery of mass graves in Katyn forest near Smolensk and the Kozelsk camp. All 4,400 bodies had their hands tied behind them and gunshot wounds to the back of their heads; some had also been beaten and stabbed with bayonets. The Germans were quick to accuse the Soviets, and the Nazi propaganda machine exploited this opportunity to drive a wedge between the USSR and the other western Allies, particularly the Polish government-in-exile. Both the Polish and German governments asked the Red Cross to investigate. On inspecting the site and the last written records pertaining to the officers, it was determined that the murders took place in 1940 while the area was under Soviet control. Yet the Soviets continued to insist that the Nazis murdered the officers during the 1941 German

Remains of victims of the Katyn Massacre; thousands of bodies were discovered in mass graves in 1943.

Personal effects of those who died in the Katyn Massacre.

invasion of the USSR. During the postwar Nuremberg Trials, this was the only charge that the Nazi officials steadfastly denied. In 1990, the government of the newly established Russian Federation officially admitted that the NKVD was responsible for the Katyn murders.

REPRISALS AND RETRIBUTION: THE RED ARMY IN GERMANY

As the tide of war turned, and the Soviets began taking Axis territory, Soviet soldiers, encouraged by their leaders, were primed to seek vengeance against the enemy—civilians as well as soldiers. Reports of Soviet atrocities began to surface in Hungary after the fall of Budapest and escalated as the Red Army moved into East Prussia and Berlin. In addition to looting (everything from factory equipment to radios, rare books to bicycles), the Red Army set fires, strafed fleeing Germans, and murdered officials and members of Hitler Youth. Most particularly and incessantly, they raped German women. Commanding officers orchestrated these assaults, insisting that the gangs of men under their authority take part in the acts. Women were gang-raped in public, in their homes and in front of their families; victims or those who protested were killed. The bodies of slain victims were sometimes mutilated. Estimates of the number of raped women range from 95,000 to 130,000 in Berlin alone, to 2 million during the entire westward campaign.

In April 1945, Stalin and Marshal Georgi Zhukov finally intervened and ordered a return to military discipline, primarily because the rampage was adversely affecting the Red Army's reputation and the discipline and health of the troops. Rape was once again punishable by death. However, prison terms were more common, and even the typical five-year sentences were often reduced or deferred until the end of the war.

The Axis

In 1935, an overwhelming force of 25 Italian divisions equipped with modern arms and aircraft invaded Abyssinia (Ethiopia), a country with few modern arms and no aircraft. Throughout the campaign—which was, in part, retribution for a smashing defeat the Abyssinians had dealt Italy in 1896 at the battle of Adowa—Mussolini bombarded his commanders with orders that detail Italian war crimes.

> June 1936: "To finish off rebels as in case at Ancober use [poison] gas." One month later, "initiate and systematically conduct policy of terror and extermination against rebels and populations. . . . Without the law of ten eyes for one we cannot heal this wound in good time." February 1937: "Agreed that male population of Goggetti over 18 years of age is to be shot and village destroyed." And, in a separate order that same month: "All civilians and [Coptic] clerics in any way suspect are to be shot without delay."

Planes equipped with special sprayers showered mustard gas on Abyssinian civilians and fighters; Italians arrested and shot intellectuals, sometimes after mock trials, sometimes out of hand. Viciousness increased after a February 1937 attempt to assassinate Italian viceroy Rudolfo Graziani. Troops ran wild through the streets of towns and villages, looting, destroying homes, and killing; but the murder and destruction did not stop when the troops were reined in. Official reports indicate that there were as many as 200 executions a day. After weapons were found in a renowned monastery, the Italians summarily executed its entire population of 400 monks and deacons. In all, it is estimated that 30,000 people were killed in this orgy of violence—most of them in no way connected to the attempt on Graziani's life.

Mussolini did not shy away from brutality elsewhere. After many anti-Fascist Italians were captured in 1939 toward the end of the Spanish Civil War, Il Duce ordered them shot, telling his son-in-law, Count Galeazzo Ciano, "Dead men tell no tales." Two years later, with Italian occupation forces in the

Balkans, Ciano noted in his diary one of many Mussolini grumbles about his officers: "[Il Duce] says he likes only one general, I forget his name, who, in Albania, said to his soldiers, 'I have heard that you are good family men. That's very well at home, but not here. Here, you will never go too far in being thieves, murderers, and rapers [sic]." Italians were also guilty of mistreating captured colonial troops. A white South African officer captured in North Africa reported, "S.A. natives, Free French, Mauritians, and Indians singled out for bad treatment"; they were hit with "rifle butts, whips and sticks by Italian officers and men. Several [were] shot. Men who tried to escape manacled together or [sic] hands and feet." In violation of the Geneva Convention, the Italians and their German allies also forced non-European prisoners in North Africa to unload munitions ships. (In one case, this backfired: a black South African lance corporal, Job Masego, made a makeshift bomb out of cordite from old cartridges and, with the help of five other POWs, sank a German freighter in Tobruk harbor. Masego subsequently escaped.)

Other Axis partners in the Balkans also ignored the rules of war.

During the 1941 invasion of Yugoslavia, the Hungarian Arrow Cross fascist militia attacked and murdered Serb and Jewish civilians. In January 1942, Hungarian leaders ordered the murder of 3,309 Serbs, Jews, and antifascist Magyars in retaliation for the deaths of seventeen Hungarian soldiers. In 1940–1941, Hungarians murdered more than 900 Romanians in Transylvania, and many more were beaten or tortured. County Salaj suffered the two worst massacres—263 dead or wounded in Traznea, and 155 murdered in Ip. The Hungarians desecrated and destroyed Romanian churches, gave Hungarian Jews and Roma to the German SS, and even established their own concentration camps.

The Bulgarian occupation of Macedonia after the 1941 Axis Balkan Campaign quickly became brutal, as many people were murdered in reprisals for partisan attacks. In 1943 at the Macedonian capital Skopje, Bulgarian forces executed 228 civilians in retaliation for 32 dead and 26 wounded Bulgarian soldiers. Bulgarian officials also permitted the SS to deport 12,000 Jews from Macedonia and Thrace to extermination camps.

After the German/Italian conquest of Yugoslavia in 1941, Croatia was established as a separate Axis-affiliated territory. Soon thereafter, the ruling fascist Ustasha regime embarked on a genocidal campaign against the Serbs, ordering the murder of all who did not flee to Serbia or convert to Roman Catholicism. The Ustasha murdered Yugoslavians of all ethnic backgrounds. In response to Tito's invasion of Bosnia, they captured 21,362 "partisans," mostly young, old, or wounded, and executed 558. The Ustasha also collaborated with Germany in the deportation of Jews and murdered Jews and Roma (gypsies) in Croatia. Only 1 percent of the Roma population in Croatia survived the war. (See also "The Holocaust," later in this chapter.)

The fascist government formed by the Nazis in Serbia under Milan Nedic lacked the commitment to genocide displayed by the rulers of neighboring Croatia. However, Serbians, too, aided the Nazis in the deportation and murder of Jews and Roma and in reprisals against Tito's Yugoslavian Partisans and the Chetniks (Serbian nationalists). When Axis forces entered Belgrade in 1941, Serb police assisted German soldiers in the murder of 4,750 civilians.

Romanians committed war crimes primarily in occupied areas. Gheorghe Alexianu governed occupied Transnistria (an area of Ukraine) with immense cruelty, feeding the Romanian army through unrestrained pillaging and exacting harsh reprisals against civilians. In Odessa, a partisan bomb hit the army's headquarters in October 1941, killing 128 soldiers and civilians. On the orders of leader Ion Antonescu, Romanians hanged 417 hostages in retaliation. Although Romania refused to exile its Jews, they murdered or deported at least 110,000 Jews in satellite territories. Yet some war crimes occurred on Romanian land: on the return of northern Transylvania to Romania in 1944, Romanian soldiers murdered Hungarians in retaliation for atrocities Hungarians committed when the region was under their control.

Japanese War Crimes

In contrast to their exemplary behavior in the Russo-Japanese War and World War I, Japanese soldiers earned a reputation for extraordinarily cruel treatment of both prisoners of war and civilians in World War II.

CRIMES AGAINST CIVILIANS

Long before Japan embarked on full-scale war with China, the Japanese government had encouraged its people to consider themselves superior to other Asians. Racism even permeated the classroom; author Kansuke Naka recalled teachers urging schoolchildren to chant such phrases as "brave Japanese, cowardly Chinks." These sentiments contributed to the Japanese armed forces' particularly cruel treatment of Chinese civilians—even women and children—during the war. One of the most glaring atrocities during Japan's long war against China has become known as the *Rape of Nanking*.

The Japanese entered Nanking on December 13, 1937, and, over a period of days, the city descended into chaos; Japanese soldiers looted, murdered, and raped, with few official attempts at restraint, for at least six weeks. Historians estimate that tens of thousands of women and young girls were raped; afterward, many were killed and mutilated. Chinese soldiers and those suspected of being soldiers were shot or bayoneted en masse. Survivors recall people burned alive, beheadings, and other such horrors. The number of dead is still contested; estimates range from 10,000 to 300,000.

Since Nanking was China's capital, many foreigners—journalists, diplomats, businessmen, missionaries—were present when the Japanese occupied the city. A group of them, led by John Rabe, a German Nazi, established a safety zone to shelter civilians. Although the Japanese did occasionally enter the zone, remove Chinese civilians, and commit atrocities, they generally respected this haven, which is credited with saving thousands of lives. The journals and letters of those remaining in Nanking portray chilling events; on Christmas Eve, the American director of the Nanking Refugee Committee wrote:

> Complete anarchy has reigned for ten days—it has been a hell on earth. . . . While thousands of disarmed soldiers who had sought sanctuary with you, together with many hundreds of civilians, are taken out before your eyes to be shot or used for bayonet practice and you have to listen to the sound of the guns that are killing them; and while a thousand women kneel before you crying hysterically, begging you to save them from the beasts who are preying on them; to stand by and do nothing while your flag is taken down and insulted not once but a dozen times, and your own home is being looted; and then to watch the city you have come to love . . . deliberately and systematically burned by fire—this is a hell I had never before envisaged.

"The only consolation is that it can't be worse," surgeon Robert Wilson wrote six days later. "They can't kill as many people as there aren't any more to kill."

The Rape of Nanking was not an isolated incident; the Japanese ravaged other large Chinese cities. In smaller villages, entire populations were sometimes killed, often in retaliation for real or imagined assistance to Chinese troops. Shozo Tominaga, a Japanese infantry platoon leader who was sent to China in 1941 remembers: "Massacres of civilians were routine. They cooperated with the enemy, sheltered them in their houses, gave them information. We viewed them as the enemy."

In other Japanese-occupied areas, such as Korea, local men were forced into service in Japan's military or as guards at POW camps. Local police forces were obligated to help the Japanese find enough "volunteers" for duty.

Civilians throughout Japan's sphere of influence were enlisted or lured into labor details, where they were given meager food supplies and medical attention and were often worked to death. Native laborers toiled alongside POWs on many projects, including the 260-mile Burma–Thailand Railway. Constructed between 1943 and 1944, this project alone cost the lives of about 90,000 Asian laborers and 12,000 Allied POWs.

As in China, the Japanese retaliated against civilians for acts of guerrilla warfare in island nations. Cities were sacked, with behavior reminiscent of the Nanking Massacre; in February and March 1945, as Allied forces closed in on Manila, the Japanese looted and destroyed much of the city, subjecting its estimated 700,000 residents to rape and torture, and killing about 100,000. It has been estimated that indigenous prisoners of the Japanese throughout the Pacific died at a rate approaching 50 percent. Additionally, according to the United Nations' Working Group for Asia and The Far East, the combination of famine and forced labor in the Dutch East Indies (Indonesia) led to the deaths of an estimated 4 million people during the Japanese occupation.

COMFORT WOMEN

Although the first military "comfort station" appeared as early as 1931, such facilities became prevalent after the Rape of Nanking, for Japanese authorities hoped to reduce mass rape of civilians (not to protect civilians, but to reduce incidence of venereal disease among soldiers and to encourage civilians to accept Japanese occupation). Throughout the Pacific, the Japanese set up brothels for use by soldiers. Some of the comfort women who worked in them had signed legal agreements, but most were tricked with offers of factory work, threatened, or physically forced into service. Their recruitment took place on military orders, mostly by collaborating civilians or by the Kempeitai, Japan's military police. The women were moved, frequently far from their home countries, using military transports controlled by the head of Army supplies, and they were treated as if they were matériel; to conceal the movement of the women, some Japanese documents even listed them as "canteen supplies."

Estimates for the number of women exploited ranges from 80,000 to 200,000; an estimated 80 percent of these were Korean; the remaining 20 percent comprised Chinese, Indonesian, Vietnamese, Javanese, Formosan, Filipino, Malayan, and a few captured European women. Although much documentation about the program was destroyed after the war, some records were recovered. Combined with testimony from surviving comfort women and memoirs by Japanese military men, they help create a brutal picture of

Korean "comfort women," are shown here with American troops in Okinawa, 1945, after the island came under U.S. control and the women's "service" was terminated.

life in the comfort stations. Whether operated by the military or by private owners, most of these facilities were for military personnel only—although some allowed civilians. The stations followed regimented military guidelines regarding frequent medical examinations. Soldiers were required to use condoms, which the Japanese government supplied to the comfort stations and to soldiers in the field. As captive labor, comfort women were given quotas of soldiers and officers to serve (some as many as 30 to 40 men a day), and they were constantly at high risk for contracting disease. Many who survived were unable to bear children, and most survivors were physically and emotionally scarred for the rest of their lives.

MISTREATMENT OF ALLIED POWS

The Japanese held an estimated 193,000 Allied POWs in hundreds of camps—many more prisoners than the Japanese had been prepared to feed and house. In 1942, Prime Minister and Minister of War Hideki Tojo ordered the use of POWs for labor relating to the war effort. Prisoners were frequently denied adequate medical treatment and supplies, kept in unsanitary and inadequate conditions, subjected to starvation rations, beatings, and torture, and fell ill with such diseases as beriberi, malaria, and dysentery. They were often overworked, in some cases to death. Allied POWs suffered an overall death rate of 27 percent at the hands of the Japanese; under Germans and Italians, the Allied POW death rate—excluding Soviet military prisoners—was around 4 percent. On average, POWs in the Pacific endured captivity more than three times longer than POWs in Europe.

Captured noncombatants, such as European civilians and nurses, were also interned; many female prisoners endured relentless pressure from their Japanese captors to become prostitutes. Others were not even lucky enough to be detained: in the Banka Island Massacre off the coast of Sumatra, 22 Australian nurses who had survived the sinking of their vessel attempted to surrender to Japanese troops, along with about 20 British soldiers marooned on the same island. After the Japanese bayoneted and shot the men, they drove the women, whose Red Cross flag and armbands were clearly visible, into the ocean and strafed them with machine gun fire. Only one nurse, Vivian Bullwinkel, survived. She was injured but later swam back to shore, where she managed to surrender to different Japanese authorities.

DEATH MARCHES

The Japanese frequently moved masses of prisoners on foot. Whether marches were intended simply to move prisoners or to dispose of them is still debated, but historians have unearthed orders for some marches indicating that any prisoner that could not continue should be killed. For many Allied troops, facing inadequate food and water supplies, harsh weather conditions, and the random violence of individual Japanese soldiers, the marches were a death sentence.

After the surrender of the Philippines in early 1942, troops under the command of Lieutenant General Masahura Homma took an estimated 70,000–80,000 American and Filipino soldiers and Filipino civilians prisoners on the peninsula of Bataan. Many historians believe that the Japanese grossly underestimated the numbers of POWs (at about 25,000–30,000), and that this fact contributed to the disaster that followed. During the infamous Bataan Death March, the Japanese transferred these prisoners from Mariveles to Camp O'Donnell, sixty-five miles away. Some POWs traveled the whole way in vehicles, but most were forced to walk, enduring countless physical and psychological tortures. The Japanese denied medical attention

Artwork by Ben Steele (1946) depicted life of prisoners of war under the Japanese (inset). Steele survived the Bataan Death March and later labored on the Tyabas Road in the Philippines, shown here. Determined that a record of these events should survive, he risked his life to make and hide pencil sketches of his experiences during the war. The photo shows Allied troops beginning the "Bataan Death March" in 1942, a trek that many will never finish.

to prisoners who were starving and afflicted with disease after months of fighting. There was little food or water. Men died from dehydration, exposure to the sun and high temperatures, or from sheer exhaustion. They soiled themselves as they walked, as it was deadly to leave the line of the march for any reason. Prisoners were bayoneted, shot, beheaded, beaten, and buried alive for not keeping up, not obeying (sometimes incomprehensible) orders, or for no reason at all. Those in the rear traveled a road littered with the bodies of their dead comrades. An estimated 54,000 POWs managed to reach Camp O'Donnell; around 20,000 died on the march; a very few escaped. More men died in the weeks after the POWs reached their destination. By war's end, only around 7,500 of the original marchers remained.

In Sandakan, Borneo, about 2,400 British and Australian prisoners had worked under extremely harsh conditions—some for three years—to build a military airstrip for the Japanese. They were forced to evacuate the area as the Allies approached early in 1945. POWs too sick to make the journey were murdered or left behind with no supplies. Those who could not continue the 160-mile march toward Ranau were beaten or killed. The 2002 book *Horror in the East* includes this recollection by Toyoshige Karashima, a Taiwanese camp guard:

> We were told that if they fell over, we shouldn't leave them. We had to get rid of them. It was maybe three or five days into the march and there'd been very heavy rain the night before, so the prisoners were gathered up and we dealt with them. . . . The prisoners were put in a kind of valley and so we shot them from above. If they'd had weapons it would have been different—but it made me think, because I have a conscience. But we were told that we had to follow orders, and if we didn't then we would be killed.

The march covered such difficult terrain and the parties were so undersupplied that even some Japanese soldiers did not survive. The POWs that made it to Ranau continued to be worked until they died or became useless, then they were killed. There were only six survivors of the Sandakan march by the end of the war.

HELL SHIPS

While some POWs were enduring death marches and prison camps, others were loaded aboard ships and taken to Japan or occupied territory. Between 1942 and 1945, transport vessels moved more than 50,000 Allied prisoners of war. The ships bore no sign of holding POWs, and unsuspecting Allied forces sometimes attacked them. Depending on the season, the prisoners either sweltered or froze, food and water was grossly inadequate, and disease was rampant. The air in the ships' holds was close and foul and filled with the cries of the sick, starving, crazed, and dying. U.S. Army Air Corps Technical Sergeant Henry Peterson, who survived a voyage aboard the *Totori Maru* in 1942, described the terrible conditions:

> About 2,000 Americans were crammed into the lower deck. There was not enough room for all to lie down at once so some sat, some lay flat and some stood up. We were to trade places doing this for the next forty days and nights. A few men at a time were allowed to go topside once a day for ten minutes to go to the toilet and also to get one canteen of water. A quart a day didn't go far in the tropical heat. Our food for the first two weeks consisted of a cup of fish soup and crackers contaminated with soap. This gave all of us diarrhea, so we could not wait our turn to go topside to the toilet. Soon we were all sitting in excrement. Within a few days, we were afflicted with another curse—body lice, which we were to have for the next three years. . . . During the trip north, several dozen men died and were buried at sea. All we could do was wait and endure the heat and stench.

Survivors reported seeing prisoners who were so thirsty they drank their own urine or blood (from slashed wrists) or murdered others to drink their blood; those who attempted to escape the holds were killed by Japanese guards—who could inflict deadly violence at any time. Surviving prisoners told of guards firing at random into the holds and Japanese strafing prisoners struggling to swim after their ship had fallen victim to an Allied attack. More than 22,000 POWs who boarded the Japanese Hell Ships never made it off alive—a death rate of at least 35 percent.

CHEMICAL/BIOLOGICAL WARFARE AND MEDICAL EXPERIMENTATION

A cluster of buildings in the village of Pingfang, just outside of Harbin, Manchuria, housed the central facilities of the "Epidemic Prevention and Water Supply Unit of the Kwantung Army." This was actually the now infamous Unit 731, the largest and most active of several Japanese units in China and in Singapore that were devoted to chemical/biological warfare and medical experimentation. Under the command of General Shiro Ishii (and later, Masaji Kitano), workers at the compound bred germs (particularly plague) to be used as weapons; they also bred carrier rats and fleas. Workers also conducted extensive research to discover the best way to distribute infected fleas, notably in airdrops of contaminated clothing and food. The airdrops were not always accurate, and in at least one case, Japanese soldiers were inadvertently affected, resulting in over 1,500 deaths. Chemical/biological warfare units also examined a variety of foods as possible distribution methods; civilians—often children—who ate the chocolates and hot buns that mysteriously appeared in neighboring villages often became sick and died. Poison gas was also tested over China, and wells were deliberately contaminated with bacteria. In some cases, locals were told they were being "inoculated" when they were actually being injected with diseases such as cholera. Scholars estimate that as many as 748,000 people were killed as the result of bacterial and chemical attacks by the Japanese during the war.

Besides research on and production of diseases, Unit 731 conducted horrific experiments on humans, murdering and maiming mostly Chinese and Manchurian victims detained from the surrounding areas, as well as laborers and prisoners of war from Korea, Russia, the United States, and Europe. The Japanese experimenters regarded these unfortunates as materials; they called them *maruta*, meaning "timber" or "logs." Unit 731 used prisoners to study the effects of diseases, malnutrition, and contaminated food, various chemicals, extreme temperatures (particularly cold), pressure, centrifugal force, shrapnel, X-rays, and other stressors. Prisoners who were infected with disease were sometimes vivisected (at times without anesthetic) or dissected, so that the effects of and progression of the disease could be observed. More bizarre experiments involved blood transfusions, limb removal and reattachment, and electrocution. Estimates of those killed by Unit 731 through such experiments commonly range in the thousands, and the indirect effects of this deadly and secret group were devastating and wide-ranging.

Prisoners were also subjected to medical tortures outside the special experimentation units. Dr. Ken Yuasa, a young Japanese military doctor, although he was not attached to any such unit, did participate in seven vivisection experiments, which were used for medical "training"—a practice Yuasa claims was ordered twice annually for every division by the Japanese army command. Vivisection was preferred to give doctors experience in operations they would perform in the field on living soldiers. Yuasa recalled a case where blindfolded Chinese were shot several times in the stomach, and the doctors had to remove the bullets: "Could we remove them while they were still alive? That was how they measured the success or failure of the operation."

CANNIBALISM IN THE PACIFIC

Japanese troops were among the most poorly supplied soldiers in World War II, especially near the end of the war, when they, as well as their prisoners, often faced the threat of starvation. Unwilling to disgrace themselves through surrender, some Japanese soldiers resorted to cannibalism to stay alive. Ample evidence, including Japanese memoirs, proves that victims of cannibalism included POWs and Allied soldiers on the battlefield, local civilians, and even other Japanese soldiers. Some bodies were scavenged after they had perished from illness or in the line of fire, while, more rarely, others were killed specifically to provide food. Allied troops reported seeing mutilated bodies of the dead, with substantial flesh removed. The book *Hidden Horrors: Japanese War Crimes in World War II* includes this graphic account of incidents in New Guinea by former POW Hatam Ali, a member of the British Dominion forces:

> Due to Allied attacks and activity, the Japs ran out of rations. We prisoners were made to eat grass and leaves and due to starvation we even ate snakes, frogs, and other insects. At this stage the Japanese started selecting prisoners and everyday 1 prisoner was taken out and killed and eaten by the Japanese. I personally saw this happen and about 100 prisoners were eaten at this place by the Japanese. . . . Those selected were taken to a hut where flesh was cut from their bodies while they were still alive and they were then thrown into a ditch alive where they later died. When flesh was being cut from those selected terrible cries and shrieks came from them and also from the ditch where they were later thrown.

This is an extreme example; in most known cases, victims were killed before being dismembered. Despite a prevailing notion that cannibalism was perpetrated by individual soldiers driven to it by desperation, in some instances, groups of Japanese, still operating under a command structure, resorted to a more organized cannibalism. Even enforcement of official Japanese military regulations that classified cannibalism as a serious war crime softened as the war lagged on and desperation increased; by late 1944, Major General Aozu (first name unknown) issued a secret order implying permission to cannibalize enemy soldiers. The ultimate responsibility for this resort to cannibalism can be said to rest with the Japanese high command, which failed to support soldiers adequately.

German War Crimes

Fueled by Nazi ideology that declared Germans and other so-called Aryans superior and members of other ethnic and political groups subhuman, German officials and their armed forces compiled an appalling record of crimes against humanity beginning well before the war. German war crimes began the moment the Wehrmacht crossed the Polish border in 1939 and continued until the German surrender in 1945. Many of these crimes were perpetrated under orders from top political and military officials.

The "Commando Order," or *Kommandobefehl*, issued by Hitler on October 18, 1942, stated that "all men operating against German troops in so-called Commando raids in Europe or in Africa, are to be annihilated to the last man. This is to be carried out whether they be soldiers in uniform, or saboteurs, with or without arms; and whether fighting or seeking to escape." Hitler claimed that this order was in response to the killing of five bound German prisoners during a British commando raid on the German-occupied British Channel Island of Sark. Executions based on this order were carried out until the end of the war; some German commanders, however, including Field Marshal Erwin Rommel, chose to ignore it.

The "Commissar Order," or *Kommissarbefehl*, also directly from Hitler, was issued in March 1941 to Wehrmacht commanders and to troops just prior to the German invasion of the Soviet Union. "The war against Russia cannot be fought in knightly fashion," Hitler stated. "The struggle is one of ideologies and racial differences, and will have to be waged with unprecedented, unmerciful and unrelenting hardness." All captured Russian political officials and leaders, including the commissars who provided political instruction to Red Army soldiers, were to be summarily executed. The order was officially abolished in May 1942 after indiscriminate murders of "suspect" people by German soldiers began to adversely affect military discipline. Instead, German commanders were instructed to deliver captured commissars into the hands of Reich security forces for execution. Yet, as historian Omer Bartov notes in his 1991 book *Hitler's Army*, "having been instructed to shoot certain categories of POWs and civilians, not only did the troops go on with the killing even after the orders were changed, they also took to indiscriminate shooting without regard for the particular categories singled out by their superiors."

German soldiers burn a Serbian village near Kosovska Mitrovica during the Wehrmacht's campaign in the Balkans, ca. 1941.

The *Bullet Decree*, issued March 4 1944, required that POWs who had escaped and been recaptured be sent to the Gestapo for execution—with the exception of British and American prisoners. (The fate of recaptured Britons and Americans was to be determined on an individual basis by the German high command's chief of POWs.) German authorities informed the International Committee of the Red Cross that executed prisoners had escaped and had not been recaptured. Under this decree SS personnel at the Mauthausen concentration camp in Austria starved, gassed, shot, or tortured to death 5,040 POWs, including 4,300 Russians.

In Poland and, particularly, the Soviet Union, the Wehrmacht issued many orders that comported with Nazi ideology and flouted the rules of war. In 1941, official orders stated that all prisoners captured on antipartisan campaigns (these people might or might not be partisans or partisan sympathizers) should be briefly interrogated and then killed. Those who seemed to have important information would be sent to the Wehrmacht's Army Secret Police or to SD (Nazi Party Security Service) commandos; these prisoners were also killed after thorough interrogations. There were standing orders to shoot all civilians out after curfew, and others were hanged for offenses such as "feeding a Russian soldier" and "wandering about." In September 1941, Field Marshal Wilhelm Keitel, chief of the Oberkommando der Wehrmacht, supported such measures by stating: "It should be taken into account that in the countries concerned individual human life is widely felt to be worth nothing, so a deterrent can only be achieved through unaccustomed severity."

The Nazi government and members of the Wehrmacht high command also organized, and maintained throughout the war, a program of systematic looting that is unique in the annals of warfare.

THEFT AND PLUNDER OF ARTWORKS AND OTHER VALUABLES

The Nazis had methodically stolen from German Jews throughout the 1930s. Under the Eleventh Decree of the Reich Citizenship Law, companies holding Jewish assets—bank accounts, stock portfolios, insurance policies—were required to report them to the state for the purpose of blocking Jewish accounts, charging additional taxes, and eventually confiscating the funds. In the occupied territories, when Jews were arrested and deported, the Nazis laid claim to their "abandoned" property, and their home furnishings were frequently used to replace items Nazi Party members had lost in Allied attacks. As of October 3, 1942, 40,000 tons of confiscated furniture had been sent to Germany. An August 8, 1944, German report on plundered goods in the West detailed the number of Jewish homes confiscated (71,619), the number of railcars needed to haul household furnishings to Germany (26,984) and the number of boxes needed for various stolen goods, such as coat hangers (120) and toys (99). Meanwhile, Jews in concentration and extermination camps were robbed of their few remaining possessions, such as their gold dental fillings and wedding rings. Melted down, the gold was transformed into gold bars marked with the Reichsbank insignia and deposited in the Swiss National Bank. The Swiss then converted the gold into Swiss Francs for the Nazis, who used it to purchase raw materials—such as wolfram and chromium—that were vital to the German war effort. Neutral Portugal was only too happy to sell its wolfram for dirty Swiss Francs, even though, as its prime minister, António de Oliveira Salazar, observed, by cutting off sales to Germany it "would reduce her power of endurance and the war would accordingly be shortened." The Nazis also seized gold bullion from state treasuries and foreign central banks; the Swiss knew early on that German deposits were stolen since Germany's gold reserves had been quite small before the war. (In 1945, Allied soldiers found 337 metric tons of Nazi looted gold, then worth $500 million.) In the meantime, the Nazis confiscated communal property, including churches, synagogues, and schools, without compensation, and the loss for owners was more than financial: communal property by its very nature held people together, and breaking those bonds made it more difficult for a community to challenge German authority. Virtually all of Poland was plundered not only for its treasures, but in an effort to wipe out the Poles' cultural heritage, identity, and resistance.

Fine art was especially vulnerable during the war, to both bombs and passionate art collectors Hitler and Göring. The Nazis craved art for its associations with genius, beauty, and power; politically, they wanted the public to connect these celebrated works to the Reich and to German culture. On November 19, 1940, Hitler ordered that confiscated art in the occupied territories be sent to Germany and put at his disposal, and five German castles and a cloister were designated as storage centers. He had elaborate postwar plans for plundered art: the greatest treasures would be displayed in a spectacular new complex in Linz, Austria, his hometown; new and established German museums would also share in the bounty, and a new museum on "extinct peoples" would feature Jewish artifacts.

Throughout Europe, the Nazis helped themselves to paintings, sculpture, objets d'art, jewels, books, tapestries, and more, stealing from churches, libraries, universities, museums, galleries, and private homes.

Several government agencies organized this extensive program of theft. For example, the Kunstschutz, an art protection office attached to the Wehrmacht, located and identified important works for safeguarding or shipment to Berlin. The Sonderauftrag Linz acquired pieces for Hitler's masterworks museum, the Ahnenerbe (Ancestral Heritage) unit of the SS collected and secured archaeological material, and the Einsatzstab Reichsleiter Rosenberg (ERR), the best known thieving operation, rummaged through archives and libraries collecting items for the Hohe Schule, a future Nazi research institute specializing in enemy and inferior cultures. The ERR later expanded its mission to include Jewish and Masonic property and then art in general.

THEFT OF FOOD AND RESULTING STARVATION

Throughout the war, the Germans confiscated so much food from occupied territories that hundreds of thousands of civilians starved to death. One of the worst cases occurred in Greece. German businessmen in uniform pounced on the country soon after it surrendered in 1941, staking so many claims on resources needed by the German war machine that they ignited a "turf war" with their Italian allies. Meanwhile, Wehrmacht quartermasters requisitioned food for the occupying troops; other food was taken and shipped back to Germany. This started a chain reaction of inflation and hoarding that further restricted food supplies, particularly to the poorer sections of Greek cities. After a 1941 harvest that was 15 to 30 percent lower than in the previous year, things quickly worsened—and food supplies remained terribly tight throughout the occupation. A subsequent study by the Red Cross estimated that between 250,000 and 400,000 people died of starvation while Greece was under Axis control.

German crimes against civilians in the Soviet Union also caused starvation. Both via official requisitions and plain theft by roving soldiers, the Wehrmacht lived off the land with a vengeance, depriving already hard-pressed villages of crops and livestock. "The land was exploited to the utmost," a German 12th Infantry report stated in the winter of 1941–1942. "Thereby a situation of general lack of food supplies for the civilian population arose, which in some cases caused starving Russian civilians to turn to German units and ask for relief or beg to be shot." The Germans took boots, winter clothing, and sledges, so civilians had to walk great distances without proper clothing in search of food. They also refused to allow provisions for civilians classified as having "no value for the corps [the army] and the economy," turning those so designated out of their homes without provisions. (These were mostly children and women deemed incapable of working for the Reich.) Russian parents sent to the Reich as forced labor had to abandon their children, who were forced to fend for themselves. In setting up defensive lines and before withdrawing in the face of Red Army advances from 1943 on, the Germans destroyed villages, poisoned wells, confiscated or slaughtered livestock, and destroyed agricultural machinery.

Soviet civilians caught in the two-and-a-half-year siege of Leningrad suffered a multitude of harms, most especially starvation. Food rations were cut and cut again. Dogs, rats, and cats disappeared from the city. People ate wallpaper paste, sawdust, anything that might be digestible. "In the worst part of the siege," one survivor remembered, "Leningrad was in the power of the cannibals. God alone knows what terrible scenes went on behind the walls of the apartments." Gangs roamed the streets, preying on lone pedestrians; others stole body parts from corpses. More than 640,000 people inside the city had starved to death by the time the siege was lifted.

In Holland, during the winter of 1944–1945, the Germans responded to a Dutch railway strike undertaken at the urging of the British (who had just mounted the unsuccessful Operation Market-Garden; see "Operation Market-Garden" in Chapter 7) by blocking traffic on the canals so that food could not reach the people of the industrial west from the agricultural east. In some parts of the nation, people were reduced to eating tulip bulbs. During what is remembered as the "Hunger Winter," more than 15,000 people starved to death. (See also Chapter 11.)

MISTREATMENT OF PRISONERS OF WAR

Long before the Bullet Decree, the Germans were ignoring the Geneva Convention—when it came to prisoners with low positions on the German racial scale, such as Russians, Poles, other Slavic peoples, people of color (particularly black troops from France's African colonies), and Jewish POWs from all Allied nations. POWs from so-called Aryan nations that held many German prisoners, including the United States and Britain, fared far better than those from nations such as France, Belgium, and the Netherlands, which had no German POWs, in large part because the Nazis wished to spare their own compatriots from Allied reprisals. These Allied POWs still faced danger from their own armies because of Germany's human shield policy; in defiance of the 1929 Geneva Convention, the Germans placed some Allied POW camps in residential areas, including Frankfurt am Main, to discourage Allied bombing.

The Soviets endured particularly brutal treatment: of 5.7 million Soviet soldiers who became German POWs, only 2.4 million, or 40 percent, survived. It has been estimated that as many as 600,000 Soviet prisoners were shot outright. Others died on forced marches or as the result of orders to supply them "only with the most essential provisions" and "feed them with the most primitive means." Many of those who survived became slave laborers. Some suffered worse fates, such as becoming the subjects for medical or gassing experiments.

Medical care for most Soviet POWs was nearly nonexistent or actually contributed to the Soviet death toll. As early as August 1941, dysentery, typhus, and then tuberculosis began to sweep through Soviet POW camps. Many of the prisoners lacked the strength to withstand these diseases. By April 1945, some camps were losing 100 prisoners each day to disease. The effect of the epidemics was exacerbated by the German practice of quarantining the prisoners, allowing the disease to take its course, and then sending in other POWs to haul away the corpses.

MASSACRES

On June 10, 1940, 400 to 500 black African troops serving in the French army in western Europe were forced to surrender near Lyon after they ran out of ammunition. The German commander on the scene ordered the men, including the wounded, executed; those who attempted to escape were picked off by marksmen. In this case, the men's skin color seems to have been the primary reason for their murders. In other cases, military and political prisoners were slaughtered when keeping them in custody presented too great an inconvenience. British troops were victims of Nazi massacres at Le Paradis and Wormhout, France, in May 1940, when Waffen SS troops of the Totenkopf (Death's Head) division and the Leibstandarte Adolf Hitler Regiment murdered 182 unarmed prisoners from the Royal Norfolk and Warwickshire regiments. Four years later (December 17, 1944), at Malmédy, Belgium, other Waffen SS troops murdered eighty-six U.S. prisoners taken during the Battle of the Bulge. The following spring, soldiers of the U.S. 102nd Infantry Division followed an escaped Russian prisoner to the ruins of a large barn outside Gardelengen, Germany, and made the gruesome discovery of more than a thousand charred bodies of Russian and other political and military prisoners that SS troops had locked in before setting the barn ablaze. Prisoners who attempted to escape the conflagration by desperately digging their way out under the barn's old walls were shot.

Throughout the war, groups of civilians or soldiers were murdered in acts of so-called reprisal for everything from the assassination of German soldiers by resistance fighters to suspected support of partisan groups. Particularly in the Balkans and the Soviet Union—but also in France and Czechoslovakia—antipartisan campaigns became the excuse for much indiscriminate killing.

One massive German program of human exploitation and annihilation was so odious and unrelenting that it forms a separate and appalling chapter in the history of human crime.

The Holocaust

This is not the Second World War; this is the Great Racial War. The meaning of this war, and the reason we are fighting out there, is to decide whether the German and Aryan will prevail or if the Jew will rule the world.

—*Reichsmarshal Hermann Göring, 1942*

The Holocaust was the Nazi persecution and methodical destruction of European Jewry—the extermination of Jewish people and the effort to eliminate all traces of Jewish culture. Nazi policy initially emphasized emigration—ridding Germany of its Jewish citizens and confiscating their property. Gradually the policy developed into one of slave labor and genocide aimed at Jews throughout the European continent. To Hitler, history was a competition

During the war, Jews used the Hebrew word *sho'ah* and the Yiddish word *churban*, both meaning "destruction," to describe the Nazis' relentless persecution of the Jewish people. The English term *holocaust*, meaning "burnt offering," was first used to refer to annihilation of the Jews during the war but it did not come into common usage until the 1960s. The Holocaust, as capitalized, has come to refer specifically to the Nazi war on the Jews and conveys both destruction and genocide. Raphael Lemkin, a Polish Jew, coined the term *genocide* for use in his 1944 book *Axis Rule in Occupied Europe* to describe the deliberate, large-scale destruction of a specific national group based on race, ethnicity, or cultural identity.

among the races and various ethnic groups for living space and resources, thus annihilating or enslaving "inferior" groups and moving into their territory was all part of a natural process and, he believed, Germany's destiny. On the eve of the war, about 9 million Jews lived in Europe, a third of them in Poland. In a few years' time, Germans and their collaborators succeeded in wiping out 6 million Jews—1.5 million of them children—and more than 10,000 Jewish communities, some of which had existed for nearly two thousand years. For the Nazis, the war on the Jews was just as much of a war as those they waged on the Eastern and Western Fronts against the Allies, for it demanded tremendous planning, resources, effort, and commitment to carry out a program that was as massive as it was evil. Even as the Wehrmacht was collapsing at Stalingrad and in desperate need of relief in January 1943, SS-Reichsfuhrer Heinrich Himmler insisted, "I must have more trains" to take ever more Jews to their deaths. Nothing was to impede the Nazi process of extermination.

The Nazis defined themselves as Aryans—what they deemed as ethnically pure Germans who, like their Nordic kinsmen (such as Britons, Norwegians, Swedes, Danes, and the Dutch), formed a Master Race. Africans, Asians, Indians, Slavs, and others existed only to serve Aryans, but Jews posed the greatest threat. (Germany's alliance with Japan forced Hitler to maneuver around the obvious problem, which he neatly solved by declaring the Japanese "honorary Aryans.") Although Jews and the much smaller Gypsy (Roma) population were eventually designated for extinction, millions of other "undesirables" also perished during the Holocaust. The Nazis enslaved and murdered through overwork, deprivation, and execution Slavs (primarily Poles, Serbs, Belorussians, and Ukrainians) as well as other Europeans. Not even fellow Aryans were safe in the Third Reich if they weakened a robust German society: the Nazis incarcerated, sterilized, or killed mentally and physically handicapped Germans (considered genetically flawed and "useless mouths to feed") and arrested homosexual men (who were not likely to help breed the next generation of Germans). Communists and political dissidents, intellectuals, trade unionists, clergymen, and others who opposed the Nazi agenda were also persecuted. Some 10 million non-Jews died not in battles or bombings but directly at the hands of the Nazis, who exploited foreign labor and resources to support the war effort. Erich Koch, Reichskommissar for the Ukraine, declared in September 1941: "Our task is to suck from the Ukraine all the goods we can get hold of, without consideration of the feelings or the property of the Ukrainians. . . . I am expecting . . . the utmost severity toward the population."

History is bloodstained with massacres and genocidal actions; in the twentieth century alone, Stalinist Russia was responsible for the deaths of some 20 million people through government purges and manmade famines, and perhaps twice as many Chinese perished under Mao Tse-tung in similar circumstances. Yet the Holocaust remains historically unique. The Jews were specifically culled from the greater general population for the purpose of eliminating an entire ethnic group. Simply being Jewish—to even *exist*— became a capital offense. Unlike the Ottoman Turks' Armenian genocide (1915–1916), the Cambodian genocide (1975), or the Rwandan genocide (1994), the German assault on the Jews went beyond national borders, affecting all of Europe. The Nazis also applied technology and modern administrative methods to their pursuit as no other genocidal force had. They did not rely on wanton or haphazard murder sprees, but established protocols and methods to minimize revolts, facilitate theft, and improve efficiency. The quest for more productive killing methods and less psychological stress on the murderers prompted the Nazis to scientifically test and develop various techniques for human extermination.

Professional business practices were as much a part of the Holocaust as the Nazi sadists that preyed on defenseless victims. The Nazis required and issued continual reports on deportation statistics, death tolls by cause, and management of concentration camps. Operating stark camp facilities, shaving inmates' heads, issuing them prison numbers, and other practices were specifically designed to dehumanize victims, while exploiting labor from them at minimal cost through careful calculation of meager food rations. At peak efficiency in the extermination camps, the Nazis killed 3,000 or more people an hour in gas chambers and then destroyed bodies in customized crematoria. The victims' belongings were systematically processed for storage and dispersal. Such an expansive effort depended on the active participation, the utter indifference, or the fearfulness of vast numbers of seemingly ordinary people *who were neither government officials nor military personnel*. The Nazis also outsourced extermination work to Ukrainians, Lithuanians, Latvians, Estonians, Croatians, Romanians, and other collaborators. The Holocaust further warrants distinction because the Nazis, despite dealing with such large numbers of people, subjected their victims to a carefully calibrated depth of degradation and humiliation planned in advance that preceded a horrible death. Perhaps most excruciating of all, the Nazis mastered the art of turning victims into agents of their own destruction by forcing Jewish leaders to facilitate deportations and enslaved Jews to escort others to their deaths, all the while using funds stolen from the Jews to finance their annihilation.

TIME LINE

The Nazi War on Jews

Unless otherwise noted, the following events occurred in Germany.

1933

March 22: Dachau, Germany's first concentration camp, opens. Most inmates are non-Jewish political prisoners.

April 1: Hitler orders a one-day boycott of Jewish-owned businesses. Ongoing unofficial boycotts follow.

April 7: All Jews in the civil service (with a few exceptions) are dismissed.

May 10: Book burnings of works by Jewish and anti-Nazi authors occur throughout Germany.

July: Issue #34 of Julius Streicher's *Der Stürmer* (circ. 80,000), a Nazi weekly newspaper, demands, "The Jewish people must be exterminated from the face of the earth." The paper's circulation reaches nearly a half million in 1935.

July 12: German-Jewish relief agency bank accounts are frozen.

1934

January 7: Non-Aryans are prohibited from adopting Aryan children.

January 24: Jews are barred from the German Labor Front union.

May 17: Jews are denied national health insurance.

December: Hans Frank, Bavarian Minister of Justice, is named Reich Commissar for the Coordination of Justice in the States for the Reformation of Law. He crafts German law to fit Nazi ideology.

1935

May 21: Jews may no longer serve in the military.

August 17: Freemason lodges are ordered dissolved. The Nazis view Freemasonry as a liberal, Jewish-controlled threat to the state.

September 15: The **Nuremberg Laws** deprive Jews of their citizenship and provide a legal basis for later anti-Semitic state action. The laws define Jewishness based on ancestry, not religious practice, and prohibit marriage and sexual relations between Aryans and Jews. Additional laws reduce Jews to legal nonentities.

1936

March 7: Jews are barred from voting.

Summer: Prior to hosting the summer Olympic Games in Berlin, the government clears out Gypsies, the homeless, and common criminals and transfers them to temporary camps, forerunners to the elaborate concentration camp system that follows.

August 1: To minimize international controversy, the government temporarily suspends anti-Jewish laws during the Olympics.

October 13: The Ministry of Justice establishes special courts to hear cases resulting from the Nuremberg Laws.

1937

January: Jews are not permitted to work in various professions and are denied tax breaks given to Aryans. The Gestapo orders Jewish youth groups to disband.

April 9: B'nai B'rith lodges are seized.

November 8: The Ministry of Propaganda sponsors a traveling exhibition of derisive images, *The Eternal Jew.*

1938

March 13: Germany annexes Austria and applies its anti-Jewish laws there. The first deportation to Dachau of Austrian Jews begins within days.

April 24: All Jews are required to register their property with the state.

June 25: Jewish doctors are prohibited from treating non-Jewish patients.

July 6: Jewish-owned businesses are ordered to close by the end of the year.

July 8: The Great Synagogue of Munich is demolished.

August 17: German Jews with "Aryan" first names are ordered to change them to Jewish names (Israel for men and Sara for women).

September 27: Jews are prohibited from practicing law.

October 5: All Jewish passports are stamped with a large letter J.

October 18: Hitler declares 15,000 Polish Jews living in Germany as "stateless"; they are held in poor conditions at the Polish-German border until Poland accepts them.

November 6: In Paris, Hershel Grynszpan, 17, whose parents are among the "stateless" Polish Jews, shoots German diplomat Ernst vom Rath, who dies three days later.

November 9–10: Using vom Rath's murder as a pretext, the Nazis launch a coordinated attack on Jewish property across Germany, destroying some 400 synagogues and thousands of businesses; nearly 100 Jews are killed and more than 20,000 are arrested. The pogrom becomes known as **Kristallnacht**—Night of Broken Glass—a reference to the shattered storefront windows of Jewish-owned businesses. Jews are required to clean up the damage and are charged 1 billion Reichsmarks to cover the cost of insurance claims. More than 100,000 German Jews emigrate soon after.

1939

January 1: Jews are not permitted to work with non-Jews.

January 24: On Göring's order, SS-Obergruppenführer Reinhard Heydrich hastens emigration of Jews from Germany.

September 1: Jews are given an 8 P.M. curfew.

September 27: The Reich Security Main Office (RSHA), part of the SS, is established. It will oversee the concentration and death camp system.

October 8: In Piotrkow, the Germans set up the first Jewish ghetto in Poland.

October 12: Deportation of Austrian and Czech Jews to Poland begins.

December 1: In occupied Poland, Jews are required to wear a Star of David badge.

1940

April 27: Heinrich Himmler, head of the SS, orders construction of Auschwitz in Poland, the largest Nazi concentration and extermination camp.

September 17: Under Nazi ideologist Alfred Rosenberg, the Einsatzstab Rosenberg is established to confiscate Jewish and European cultural treasures.

October 22: In France, Jewish deportations begin from Alsace-Lorraine and the Rhineland.

1941

July 2–3: SS Einsatzgruppen massacres begin in the Soviet Union as 7,000 Jews are shot in Lvov. Similar scenes are repeated almost daily throughout the summer; ghettos are established in Minsk, Bialystok, and elsewhere.

July 31: Göring asks Heydrich to prepare a plan to exterminate all Jews in German-occupied territory.

September 1: In Germany, Jews over the age of six are required to wear a yellow badge, shaped like the Star of David. This form of identification is soon used throughout Nazi-occupied territory, except in Denmark, where the Nazis decline to stir up further public opposition.

September 3: Nazis use poison gas (Zyklon B) for the first time at Auschwitz, killing Russian POWs.

October: Jews are no longer permitted to emigrate from Germany or German-occupied territory.

October 6: The first mass deportations of Jews in Greater Germany to eastern camps begin.

December 8: At the Chelmno extermination camp in Poland, the Nazis begin killing Jews with poison gas.

1942

January 20: At the Wannsee Conference in Berlin, Heydrich presents the "Final Solution" to top government officials whose agencies will assist the SS in carrying it out. Attendees discuss how best to accomplish the task.

Spring: Mass deportations of Jews begin throughout occupied Europe to extermination camps in Poland.

December 31: By year's end, the Einsatzgruppen, operating in the USSR, have murdered 1.3 million Jews.

1943

April 19: In Poland, the Warsaw Ghetto Uprising begins as Jews resist deportation. It is finally crushed May 16.

May: Most Greek Jews are deported to Auschwitz.

June 11: Jews from all remaining ghettos in German-occupied territory are ordered deported.

October 18: The first transport of Italian Jews is sent to Auschwitz.

1944

May 15: In Hungary, deportation of Jews to Poland begins and the extermination system reaches peak efficiency.

June: Death marches begin as Nazis transfer prisoners from eastern concentration camps to the German interior prior to the arrival of the Red Army.

1945

January 18: The SS evacuates Auschwitz; the Red Army liberates the camp on January 27.

April: American and British forces liberate concentration camps throughout western and central Germany.

May 7: Germany surrenders to the Allies.

ANTI-SEMITISM

The Nazis sowed their ideology over a heavily-ploughed, anti-Semitic landscape. Anti-Semitism—hatred of, or prejudice against, Jews—was present in the pagan world, and as Christianity spread throughout the Roman Empire, anti-Semitism traveled with it. Christian discrimination and violence against Jews grew out of a belief that the Jewish people were collectively guilty for the crucifixion of Jesus Christ. For centuries, Christians falsely accused Jews of ritually murdering Gentile children (a claim revived in Nazi Germany), and Christian warriors murdered thousands of Jews en route to Jerusalem, stealing their gold to help fund the First and Second Crusades (the Nazis used Jewish wealth to finance the Holocaust). In 1215, the Roman Catholic Church's Fourth Lateran Council decreed that Jews wear special insignia lest Christians unwittingly have sex with them (such insignia, in the form of a yellow Star of David, would appear in Germany in 1941). The council also decreed that Jews not be appointed to public office "Since it is absurd that a blasphemer of Christ exercise authority over Christians" (the Nazis banned Jews from the civil service in 1933). During the Protestant Reformation, Christian anti-Semitism was left unreformed. As Martin Luther wrote in his book *On the Jews and Their Lies* (1543), "We are at fault for not slaying them," and he recommended that Christians "set fire to their synagogues and schools, and to bury and cover with dirt whatever will not burn" in addition to razing their homes, confiscating their prayer books and money, and prohibiting rabbis from teaching on pain of death. (The Nazis eagerly quoted Luther's pronouncements in their own propaganda and followed his suggestions.)

Anti-Semitism held cultural, economic and racial components as well. Historically, Jews were relegated to specific neighborhoods and professions, notably banking, accounting, and merchandising. Jews were then accused of overcharging Christians, which fed anti-Jewish sentiment. Frequent *pogroms* (government-backed organized violence against Jewish communities), particularly in Eastern Europe, occurred from medieval times into the twentieth century. The notorious *Protocols of the Elders of Zion*, a Russian-produced series of fictional documents first published in 1903 as "proof" of a Jewish conspiracy for world domination, was reprinted often and used to justify attacks against Jews. In Western Europe and the United States, Jews assimilated more easily than in the East, but even where there was legal equality for Jews, anti-Semitism remained. Sectarian organizations routinely published scurrilous articles on Jews, and beginning in

1920, automobile magnate Henry Ford, whom Hitler greatly admired, published a four-volume book series, *The International Jew: The World's Foremost Problem*, that was distributed worldwide. A long history of anti-Semitism helped make it possible for the Nazis' campaign to find a large, receptive audience.

GERMAN JEWS AND THE MASTER RACE

As of 1933, Jewish communities had existed in Germany for more than 1,600 years, and about 554,000 of the country's 65 million citizens were Jewish, *less than 1 percent of the population*. Well assimilated, nearly all regarded themselves as Germans who were Jewish rather than as Jews living in Germany. Despite their small numbers, Jews represented a large percentage of the cultural, scientific, intellectual, professional, and artistic elite in a nation pummeled by economic depression and national humiliation after World War I. Their success, in a nation accustomed to anti-Semitic sentiment, made them visible targets for embittered non-Jewish Germans. Hitler believed Jews were the driving force behind communism, and in *Mein Kampf* (*My Struggle*, published in 1925) he wrote, "No one need be surprised if among our people the personification of the devil as the symbol of all evil assumes the living shape of the Jew." Once in power, he began a campaign of intimidation fueled by incessant propaganda: The Nazis claimed Jews controlled international finance in their quest for world domination. They also blamed Jews for Germany's defeat in World War I and its subsequent economic woes. And they warned, in both coolly "scientific" tones and heated political hyperbole, of the social threat these "racially inferior" people posed to the purity of Aryan blood. From there, it was a short leap to regard the Jew as subhuman.

The Nazis' obsession with race extended well beyond anti-Semitism. The eugenics movement, which sought to improve the quality and health of humanity through the selection—or elimination—of certain physical and mental traits, had a profound influence on Western nations, including the United States. Nazi doctors took the movement even further: they sterilized about 300,000 Germans (including "asocials," criminals, and some 500 healthy black German children) and murdered another 200,000 in their T4 Euthanasia Program. (See also Chapter 11.) Scientists measured and analyzed the physical differences among ethnic groups (e.g., skull formation, nose and ear size, facial features, eye color, body type) to assess racial health and value, and they developed extensive racial classifications. *Racial hygiene*,

Above, Reichsmarschall Hermann Göring, left, SS Reichsführer Heinrich Himmler, center, and SS General Reinhard Heydrich, in 1938. (After the war, this photograph was found in one of Göring's personal photo albums.) Göring ordered the coolly calculating Heydrich to implement the Final Solution, which the SS ruthlessly carried out. Below, SS soldiers march Jews in Warsaw to the Umschlagplatz *for deportation during the 1943 ghetto uprising.*

as the Germans called eugenics, determined who was racially fit and had a place in Hitler's new world order.

In their persecution of the Jews, the Nazis made no distinction between religious and secular or those who had converted to Christianity. A full Jew was anyone with three Jewish grandparents; a first-class *Mischlinge* ("hybrid") had two Jewish grandparents and was thus a half-Jew; a second-class Mischlinge had one Jewish grandparent and was a quarter-Jew, or was an Aryan married to a Jew. Under Nazi policy, first-class Mischlinge were to be treated as full Jews but second-class Mischlinge could assimilate into

THE MATTER OF THE MISCHLINGE

Partial Jews were both an ideological and administrative problem for the Reich. Even Hitler was not certain how to deal with Mischlinge (he secretly worried that he might be one himself, given his father's uncertain parentage), and he devoted considerable time to reviewing Mischlinge applications for racial exemptions. Göring personally petitioned the führer that important Mischlinge in science, industry, and the military be declared honorary Aryans or given the *Genehmigung* (an exemption) from racial discrimination. Admiral Erich Raeder, the navy's commander in chief, also interceded on behalf of selected Jews and Mischlinge, who after the war credited him with saving their lives. Other high-ranking Nazi officials requested help for particular Mischlinge out of friendship, respect, or for financial gain. Goebbels and Himmler were especially disturbed that racial policies and laws were not consistently enforced, and Himmler complained that while everyone said they favored getting rid of the Jews, they each seemed to know "a decent Jew" worthy of protection.

Confusion reigned in the Wehrmacht, which drafted half-Jews, then discharged those men when their ancestry became known. Perhaps as many as 150,000 German men of Jewish descent served in the Wehrmacht, many going undiscovered. It was generally assumed that after the war Hitler would pronounce quarter-Jews *deutschblütig* ("of German blood"), thus it was not worth the disruption to root them out of the service or society at large. In the meantime, Hitler declared deutschblütig thousands of Mischlinge men—many posthumously—who had distinguished themselves in the Wehrmacht. As of late 1941, Nazi leadership was still unsure whether to include half-Jews in their extermination program. Eventually, it was decided that half-Jews and *Jüdischversippte* (Aryans married to Jews) were destined for forced labor and deportation. Such erratic policies only affirmed the quackery and senselessness of Nazi racial "science."

JEWISH IMMIGRANTS FROM GERMANY, 1933–1938

United States	102,222
Argentina	63,500
Great Britain	52,000
Palestine	33,399
France	30,000
Holland	30,000
South Africa	26,100
China (Shanghai)	20,000
Chile	14,000
Belgium	12,000
Portugal	10,000
Brazil	8,000
Switzerland	7,000
Bolivia	7,000
Yugoslavia	7,000
Canada	6,000
Italy	5,000
Australia	3,500
Sweden	3,200
Spain	3,000
Hungary	3,000
Uruguay	2,200
Norway	2,000
Denmark	2,000
Philippines	700
Venezuela	600
Japan	300
TOTAL	453,721

Data from Martin Gilbert, *Never Again: A History of the Holocaust*, 2000.

German society. Aside from Jews, Gypsies were the only other ethnic group specifically targeted for extermination. In Europe, they numbered about 800,000 and were primarily nomadic; like the Jews they, too, historically suffered from persecution. The Nazis murdered about a third of the Gypsy population, but settled Gypsies living in Scandinavia, Bulgaria, and Greece were not deported.

Germany's prohibitive restrictions on Jews were meant to eliminate their presence in national life and to prompt Jewish emigration. Especially effective was the process of "Aryanization" (*Arisierung*)—the underhanded acquisition of Jewish-owned businesses by ethnic Germans, particularly Nazi Party members. Beginning in 1933, the Nazis called for boycotts of Jewish-owned stores and threatened those who patronized Jewish businesses; in time, owners lost customers, went into bankruptcy, and were forced to sell, receiving only a small portion of the actual market value. Following the Kristallnacht pogrom in 1938, the Nazis made confiscation of Jewish property legal. By then, the number of Jewish-owned shops and retail stores had decreased by more than 80 percent; about a quarter million Jews had emigrated by 1938, though it meant leaving behind nearly all their financial assets and property—even their furniture. The exodus included internationally renowned scientists, doctors, scholars, artists, writers, musicians, and filmmakers as well as ordinary people. Emigration, however, became ever more difficult, requiring increasingly scarce visas, bribing Nazi officials for the proper paperwork, and preparing complicated travel arrangements. Making matters worse, in the midst of the Great Depression, no country wanted immigrants who would compete with its own citizens for work, and no government wanted to accept foreigners arriving with little or no money. Anti-Semitic sentiments also kept many nations from taking in more Jews (see chart on page 674).

Destruction of the Jews

Nazi policy toward the Jews evolved from emigration to extermination as a way to solve the "Jewish Problem," but complicating the matter was the German conquest of Europe, which increased by millions the Jewish population under Reich control. Thus, emigration was no longer a solution to the Jewish Problem. The next major step was to establish Jewish ghettos in occupied territory and construct work camps to which Jews were deported for slave labor. In the meantime, the SS unleashed its Einsatzgruppen (mobile killing squads) to massacre Jewish civilians and political opponents in Eastern Europe. But when Hitler failed to win his anticipated quick victory over the USSR in the fall of 1941 and thus secure Russia's subarctic regions for Jewish deportation, the Nazis sent Jews to an area in central Poland they called the "General Government." There, in camps specifically built for mass murder, they would attempt to completely exterminate European Jewry. The Nazis called it *Endlösung*—the "Final Solution."

The Reich Security Main Office (RSHA), a branch of the SS, took charge of the Final Solution. Under Reichsführer Himmler, SS Lieutenant General Heydrich organized the massive undertaking. After Heydrich's assassination, Ernst Kaltenbrunner took his place. With astounding precision and attention to detail, SS Lieutenant Colonel Adolf Eichmann, head of the RSHA's subsection IVB4, ran the massive deportation program that uprooted Jews from their homes and sent millions to the camps. To capture, process, and deport Jews, the SS had the assistance of local informers, police forces, and government agencies in both Germany and the occupied territories. The *Deutsche Reichsbahn* (DR), the German state railway, was essential to the system, transporting some 3 million victims to the camps. Especially useful were the automated Hollerith punch-card machines and tabulators that IBM's German subsidiary, Dehomag, leased, programmed, and maintained for the SS throughout the war. Information taken from census data and required Jewish registrations was recorded on the cards, which were then sorted by machine to identify local Jews, prepare deportation lists, track and manage available rail stock to the concentration and extermination camps, allocate skilled slave labor to various projects, and keep tabs on individual victims until their deaths.

EINSATZGRUPPEN

The Einsatzgruppen were active in annexed Austria and Czechoslovakia in 1938 and in Poland in 1939, but the most infamous units, comprising about 3,000 men, operated in the Soviet Union with orders to "liquidate" Jews and political commissars. In the East, large Jewish communities lived outside the general population, making it easier for the SS to identify, round up, and kill Jews on the spot. During a typical "special action," men, women, and children were gathered and then separated by sex, ordered to undress, and forced to stand at the edge of a ravine or a pit. Gunmen shot their victims, who tumbled onto the corpses below, and the next group was brought forward. Working steadily, the Einsatzgruppen could wipe out entire towns in a day or so; 33,771 Jews were shot at Babi Yar, outside Kiev,

An Einsatzgruppen squad, assisted by civilians, forces Jewish women to disrobe before their execution (left). At right, SS men shoot Russian peasants over a large ditch that served as a mass grave. This photograph belonged to a captured German soldier who served in a killing squad attached to the Sixteenth Army.

September 29–30, 1941. These scenes were regularly repeated as the German army advanced further into the Soviet Union, and soldiers in the Wehrmacht frequently participated in these crimes. German businessmen, regular soldiers, local civilians, and others reported seeing Jews digging their own graves, the massacres, or the aftermath, but in Western Europe, where Jews were well integrated in the general population, such mass killings could not be conducted openly. Instead, the intended victims were deported to camps.

GHETTOS

The Nazis established more than 400 Jewish ghettos in Poland, the occupied portions of the Soviet Union, Yugoslavia, Hungary, and elsewhere, housing Jews transported from as far away as Belgium and Greece. The ghettos served as assembly areas for those later deported to concentration and extermination camps; in the meantime, ghetto residents who could work labored for German industry. Sealed off from the rest of the city, Jews had little access to food or news of the outside world. Epidemics were frequent and starvation was rampant, leading to vicious crime sprees as residents turned on each other to save themselves and their families. To maintain order, German authorities required that a local Jewish Council (*Judenrat*) implement their orders and manage the community. The councils saw to children's education and organized medical and social services, but they were also ordered to select fellow Jews for deportation, allot scarce food supplies, and organize forced labor teams. If Nazi orders were not followed, council members or their families faced deportation or execution. The Nazis used Jewish police, under the same threats, to locate Jews in hiding and round up a quota of victims for deportation or execution. Not surprisingly, policemen and Judenrat members usually chose to protect themselves and their loved ones at the expense of others, which added to the already devastating environment. The Nazis' cruelly effective methodology reached its apex when Judenrat members, after doing the Germans' bidding, were themselves finally deported to the camps.

DEPORTATION

The Nazis methodically purged the ghettos in what were called *aktions* by rounding up residents and deporting them "to the East" in overcrowded trains according to carefully established schedules. (By cramming as many people as possible into freight cars, causing greater suffering, the SS received a reduced group fare from the Deutsche Reichsbahn. The SS paid the fares with Jewish funds.) Since ghettos were not set up in Western Europe, Jews were deported to transit camps, such as Drancy in France or Westerbork in Holland, where they were briefly held until they could be transported east to a concentration camp or extermination center. In the spring of 1942, large-scale deportations originating from all over occupied Europe were under way to the extermination centers in Poland.

On the journey to the camps, generally in tightly packed cattle or freight cars, there was usually no room for anyone to sit, nothing to eat or drink, and the nonstop trip could last many days; in some cases, few or none survived. Ben-Zvi Gedalia, a Jew from Bratislava imprisoned at Auschwitz-Birkenau, later testified about his experience unloading bodies from an overcrowded transport from Bedzin:

> When the SS opened the doors, people literally poured out onto the ground because the wagons were so packed. Only those who had been trampled or suffocated were still inside the wagons, either dead or half dead . . . we got into the wagons to disentangle the bodies. It was hard work because they were snarled up. . . . Sometimes when we pulled a leg or an arm, the skin tore because of the heat. . . . It took several hours to empty one wagon.

THE CONCENTRATION CAMPS

More than 17 million people—Jews and non-Jews alike—are known to have gone through the camp system as forced laborers, inmates, or those designated for extermination. Over time, the system comprised hundreds of facilities throughout Europe, with various purposes, although after the war *concentration camp* was used as a general term for all Nazi camps. At extermination camps, victims were murdered within hours of their arrival. In labor camps, prisoners worked on site or at nearby factories for the German war effort. Subcamps, attached to one of seventeen main camps (see chart of camps later in this chapter), varied in size, with as few as twenty prisoners to as many as several thousand. In some cases, these camps existed only until a work project was completed, and workers were sent elsewhere. Concentration camp prisoners subsisted on meager rations, such as a bowl of

NAZI PRISONER IDENTIFICATION

Inmates were issued striped uniforms bearing an individual identification number (at Auschwitz, numbers were also tattooed on a prisoner's left arm) and a colored badge that indicated one's status. Badges were shaped as inverted triangles; Jewish prisoners wore yellow badges shaped like the Star of David. Marked badges identified potential escapees, repeat offenders, military servicemen serving labor sentences, and "race defilers" (Aryans convicted of miscegenation). In the camp hierarchy, German criminals usually ranked highest, Jews the lowest. Prisoner badge colors and classifications:

Red	Political prisoner
Green	Criminal
Blue	Foreign forced laborer
Purple	Jehovah's Witness, other religious sectarian
Pink	Homosexual (males)
Black	Asocial (including vagrants, the mentally ill, prostitutes, and sometimes Gypsy prisoners)
Brown	Gypsy (Roma)
Yellow	Jew

thin turnip soup and a slice of bread a day, and they were subject to regular beatings and humiliation. Daily roll call could last several hours, with ill-clad inmates required to stand still even in extreme weather; those who could not were shot. Frequent and severe punishments included putting prisoners' arms behind their backs and then hanging them by the wrists for hours at a time; forcing people to swim or bathe in sewage; placing several prisoners at once in cramped "stand up" cells, in which one could neither sit nor lie down, for days or weeks at a time. Water tortures, floggings, rolling victims over stones, and setting vicious dogs on prisoners were routine. Women were vulnerable to frequent rape and forced abortions. In such a vile, desperate setting, *kapos* (prisoners granted privileges, such as larger food rations in exchange for maintaining order in barracks) were often cruel as part of their own survival strategy and to win the favor of SS guards. In several camps, most notably at Auschwitz and Dachau, Nazi doctors performed grotesque and lethal medical experiments on prisoners, including children. Thousands died after being subjected to tests involving chemical injections, hypothermia, air pressure, bone removal, sterilization and castration, dissection, contagious diseases, and resistance to pain.

EXTERMINATION CAMPS

As early as 1939, Himmler was exploring ways to dispose of the growing number of corpses in the concentration camps; later, he looked for more

FORCED AND SLAVE LABOR

Most of the millions who labored against their will for the Nazis were not Jewish. Ethnic Poles, the first group brought to Germany, received lower wages than German workers, put in longer hours, and were barred from interacting with Germans. When more German men were needed on the Eastern Front, the Nazis kidnapped, impressed, and arrested foreign civilians in occupied territory to fill the subsequent war industry labor shortages. Most were from the USSR (2.1 million) and Poland (1.6 million), and hundreds of thousands were from Belgium, France, Italy, Holland, and Bohemia-Moravia. Fritz Sauckel, Plenipotentiary General for Labor Mobilization, admitted after the war, "Of the five million foreign workers who came to Germany, less than 200,000 came voluntarily." (Twelve million additional workers are estimated to have slaved for the Reich in occupied territory outside Greater Germany.) While Western Europeans were treated similarly to German workers, Easterners were dealt with harshly. "The conditions were terrible," said Elsa Iwanowa who was abducted from Rostov, Russia, at 16 and forced to work at the Ford factory in Cologne. "It was very cold; they did not pay us at all and scarcely fed us. The only reason we survived was that we were young and fit." In the occupied territories, if laborers did not die of overwork, abuse, disease, and starvation, they could be executed for failing to meet production quotas or for the sadistic pleasure of the invaders and their collaborators. After the German defeat at Stalingrad in January 1943, the SS attempted to improve working conditions to generate greater productivity, but toward the end of the war, disease-ridden workers lived on smaller rations in ramshackle housing that had become increasingly indistinguishable from concentration camps.

Other major labor sources were Russian POWs, German Mischlinge, kidnapped or orphaned Slavic youth, and Jews. (Some 350 U.S. soldiers thought to be Jewish that were captured in the Battle of the Bulge were separated from the other American POWs and suffered as slave laborers at Berga, a subcamp of Buchenwald. When they were liberated April 5, 1945, more than 20 percent of their number had perished and the rest were brutalized, emaciated victims.) These laborers were not paid but typically worked twelve- to sixteen-hour days. At some labor camps, inmates survived an average of only thirty days. Men typically toiled in war industry plants, performed hard manual labor on farms, in mines and quarries, and built roads, fortifications, and underground factories meant to be impervious to Allied bombs. Women did factory and farmwork but also made German uniforms, cleaned up air raid debris in nearby cities, and at extermination camps, sorted the clothing and valuables of the dead.

In late 1942, the SS began to send out camp inmates as labor to private companies. Many prominent German firms used forced and slave labor, including I. G. Farben, a large conglomerate which had some 350,000 slave workers and produced Zyklon B, used in many camp gas chambers; Bayer, a pharmaceutical company that was part of I. G. Farben; Krupp, known for its high-quality steel and munitions; Seimens, an electronics firm; Kodak, a film and camera manufacturer; and vehicle manufacturers Daimler-Chrysler, BMW, Volkswagen, and Porsche. American-owned firms and their subsidiaries in Germany also benefited from slave labor; these included General Motors and the Ford Motor Company, known as Ford Werke, which during the war had a German-dominated board of directors and went into trusteeship. Ford was never nationalized by the Reich, which wanted to maintain access to the company's American sales staff. (In the United States, Ford produced aircraft and was a major contributor to the Allied cause.) By 1943, half of Ford's European workforce was forced and slave labor.

efficient and less bloody methods of extermination that were out of public view and not as psychologically taxing to the SS. Thus, gassing victims— as was done at the T4 euthanasia sites (see Chapter 11)—and cremating their remains came into practice. There were six designated extermination camps, all located in Poland: Belzec, Chelmno, Sobibor, and Treblinka; and two others, Auschwitz and Majdanek, that were also concentration camps with large inmate workforces. There, in a process called *selektion* that occurred as soon as Jews arrived, camp officials instantly decided who should go directly to the gas chambers and who should be put to work. (Gas chambers also existed at many other camps to kill prisoners after they could no longer work.) At Chelmno, the Nazis first employed gas vans— sealed vehicles that could hold up to sixty persons who died when carbon monoxide was piped in. During a visit to the camp, Eichmann witnessed the process:

> I couldn't even look at it. . . . The screaming and shrieking. . . . And then I saw the most breathtaking sight I have ever seen in my life. The van was making for an open pit. The doors were flung open and corpses were cast out as if they were some animals—some beasts. They were hurled into the ditch. I also saw how the teeth were being extracted [the Nazis removed victims' gold fillings]. . . . I had to leave because it was too much, as much as I could stand.

Gas chambers were used instead of vans at other camps, but early on they frequently malfunctioned. During those instances Jews were then crammed and locked into freight cars with quicklime covering the floor. The cars were moved to nearby fields and abandoned. Over the next several days, the victims suffocated, died of thirst or, coming in contact with the flesh-eating lime used both to contain the spread of disease and facilitate decomposition, essentially burned to death.

The extermination sites were chosen for their proximity to railroad lines and wooded locations in sparsely populated areas. The camps housed no prisoners except the Jews (called *Sonderkommandos*) forced to guide victims to the gas chambers, sort their belongings, and dispose of the corpses. Trains usually arrived at night; in the course of a few hours, victims were sent to a "reception area," ordered to undress and surrender their valuables, then taken down a narrow, covered pathway—called "the Road to Heaven" by the guards—to the gas chambers, which were deceptively labeled as showers. The aim was to keep victims calm, unsuspecting, and still believing that after delousing and bathing, they would be sent to work camps. As rumors spread about what really occurred, the guards struggled more with people who resisted their fate. When the gas chamber was filled to capacity and the doors sealed, diesel engines pumped in carbon monoxide and within thirty

---

HEINRICH HIMMLER ON THE FINAL SOLUTION

In a speech before SS leaders in Poznan, Poland, on October 6, 1943, SS Reichsführer Himmler commended them for their fortitude in carrying out the Final Solution, the difficulty of which other Nazis did not seem to appreciate:

I also want to talk to you quite frankly about a very grave matter. Among ourselves it should be mentioned quite frankly, and we will never speak of it publicly. . . . I am referring to the clearing out of the Jews, the extermination of the Jewish race. It's one of those things it is easy to talk about. 'The Jewish race is being exterminated,' says a Party member. 'That's quite clear, it's in our program—elimination of the Jews—and we're doing it, we're exterminating them.' . . . Not one of all those who talk this way has witnessed it. . . . Most of *you* must know what it means when a hundred corpses are lying side by side, or five hundred, or a thousand. To have stuck it out and at the same time, apart from exceptions caused by human weakness, to have remained decent fellows, that is what has made us tough. That is a page of glory in our history which has never been written and must never be written. . . . All in all, we can say that we have fulfilled this most difficult duty for the love of our people. And our spirit, our soul, our character has not suffered injury from it.

minutes, all were dead. (Other camps, such as Auschwitz-Birkenau, used Zyklon B, an inexpensive cyanide gas that had initially been used to kill lice on prisoner clothing. Each gas chamber there could hold up to 2,000 people.) Once the chamber was aired out, the Sonderkommandos removed the victims' soiled corpses. The bodies were then crudely searched for hidden valuables and buried or burned in the crematoria and in large outdoor pits. In some camps, victims suspected of swallowing valuables were marked with chalk, and after being gassed their bodies were carved open and the contents of their stomachs removed. Jewels, primarily diamonds, were the most common items retrieved.

Aside from the extermination centers, other notorious mass murder sites under Nazi supervision or approval operated outside Poland. Transnistria, a Ukrainian area Hitler turned over to Romania in 1941, comprised camps and ghettos; hundreds of thousands were murdered or starved to death here. At Jasenovac, a series of camps in Croatia, the ultranationalist, right-wing Ustasha murdered Serbs, Jews, Gypsies, Muslims, and political opponents not by gassing, but with hand tools or the infamous *graviso* or *srbosjek* (literally, "Serb cutter")—a long, curved knife attached to a partial glove and designed for rapid, easy killing. The Ustasha, the most vicious German ally and puppet government in Europe, murdered more than a million people.

NAZI EXTERMINATION CAMPS AND MAJOR CONCENTRATION CAMPS

The SS ran the concentration camp system and designated seventeen sites, including the extermination centers, as major camps. These camps oversaw hundreds of other concentration and labor camps.

Auschwitz

Concentration and Extermination Camp; Outside Oswiecim, Poland; June 1940–January 1945; Three main camps, 39 subcamps; 1.2–1.5 million deaths; Liberated by Red Army

The largest concentration and extermination camp, Auschwitz became the most prominent representation of the Holocaust. Those selected for labor entered the camp through its notorious iron gates marked *Arbeit Macht Frei* (Freedom through work). At nearby Birkenau (Auschwitz II) up to 6,000 people were gassed daily. Auschwitz III (Buna), was added for slave laborers working at the I.G. Farben chemical plants. On January 18, 1945, most prisoners began a death march to Germany. About 7,000 barely living victims were liberated on January 27.

(continued)

NAZI EXTERMINATION CAMPS AND MAJOR CONCENTRATION CAMPS (CONTINUED)

Belzec

Extermination Camp; Belzec, Poland; February 1942–December 1942; 600,000 deaths

Belzec was the first camp with permanent gas chambers. Nearly all victims were Polish Jews; volunteer Ukrainian POWs served as guards. In 1943–1944 Sonderkommandos destroyed and cremated the corpses in mass graves. The camp was planted over to disguise its former use.

Bergen-Belsen

Concentration Camp; Outside Celle, near Bergen, Germany; April 1943–April 1945; 50,000 deaths (non-POW), Liberated by British Army

Bergen-Belsen held political prisoners and Jews the Nazis offered in repatriation deals for Germans held by the Allies (few Jews were actually released). In February 1945, a typhus epidemic broke out; among its victims was fifteen-year-old diarist Anne Frank. At war's end, the camp was overcrowded with 60,000 prisoners, many of them evacuated from camps in the east. Well-known film footage was shot here of British troops bulldozing corpses to prevent the further spread of disease.

Buchenwald

Concentration Camp; Outside Weimar, Germany; July 1937–April 1945; 130 subcamps; 57,000 deaths; Liberated by U.S. Army

Buchenwald first held political prisoners and criminals; Jews arrived in 1938. The camp also held a large population of orphaned children. Extensive medical experiments were performed on prisoners, and the camp sold shrunken heads and the tattooed skin of prisoners. Inmates worked in on-site and nearby armament factories; they had a well-organized underground and a higher survival rate than average until 1944. Just prior to the arrival of U.S. troops, the inmates revolted to slow down evacuation of prisoners.

Chelmno

Extermination Camp; Chelmno (northwest of Lodz), Poland; December 1941–January 1945; 320,000 deaths; Red Army occupation January 1945

SS Major Christian Wirth, who gained expertise in gassing in the T4 Program, introduced the practice here. Chelmno was the first Nazi camp solely used for extermination by gassing. Victims were Polish Jews; 5,000 Gypsies and 1,000 Soviet and Polish POWs were also murdered here, and gas vans were used for the killings. In September 1944, mass graves in the woods were exhumed and the bodies cremated in Aktion 1005 (see "Aktion 1005" on p. 691).

Dachau

Concentration Camp; Dachau (outside Munich), Germany; March 1933–April 1945; 30+ large subcamps; 32,000 known deaths (figure thought to be considerably higher). Liberated by U.S. Army

The first Nazi concentration camp, Dachau opened to incarcerate political prisoners. Its brutal practices under camp Kommandant Theodor Eicke served as a model for all Nazi concentration camps, and Dachau was a training facility for SS camp guards. Dachau also had the largest population of

NAZI EXTERMINATION CAMPS AND MAJOR CONCENTRATION CAMPS (CONTINUED)

clergy (almost 3,000), nearly all of them Catholic priests; more than a third perished. Inmates worked in local armaments factories. Medical experiments were conducted on prisoners in 1941 and 1942.

Dora-Nordhausen

Concentration Camp; Outside Nordhausen, Germany; August 1943–April 1945; 30+ subcamps; 30,000 deaths; Liberated by U.S. Army

(Also known as Dora-Mittelbau.) Prisoners dug tunnels and supplied labor for a sodium sulfate mine and an underground factory in the Harz Mountains. About 100 men died daily constructing the factory, the highest mortality rate at the time in a German camp. Prisoners produced Germany's V-1 and V-2 rockets. Hundreds of prisoners were executed for sabotaging missile production. Most prisoners were marched to Bergen-Belsen in March 1945.

Flossenbürg

Flossenbürg, Germany; May 1938–May 1945; 100 subcamps; 30,000 deaths; Liberated by U.S. Army

The small isolated mountain camp was originally designed for "asocials" and criminals; later, political prisoners, Resistance members, and Soviet POWs arrived. Almost half of the inmate deaths occurred in the last 14 months of the war. Prisoners included top Abwehr officials Wilhelm Canaris and Hans Oster and church leader Dietrich Bonhoeffer, who were all executed here April 9, 1945.

Gross-Rosen

Near Stiegau (Strzegom), Poland; Summer 1940–February 1945; 97 subcamps; 40,000 deaths; Liberated by Red Army

Prisoners worked in a granite quarry and arms factories. Most prisoners were Poles and Hungarians, and Night and Fog victims (those who quietly disappeared in Nazi custody, their fates unknown to their families) were typically sent here. The camp also had the most active euthanasia program in the system. Prisoner evacuation began in December 1944.

Majdanek

Concentration and Extermination Camp; Lublin, Poland; Operated September 1941–July 1944; 360,000 deaths; Liberated by Red Army

Originally built as a POW camp, beginning in August 1942 it also operated as an extermination camp; seven gas chambers and two crematoriums were added. Of those that perished, about 40 percent were executed or died in the gas chambers. Soviet and Polish officials issued a report in October 1944 on Nazi war crimes here. Six SS men went on trial; four were convicted and executed.

Mauthausen

Concentration Camp; Mauthausen, Austria; August 1938–May 1945; 60+ subcamps; 119,000 deaths; Liberated by U.S. Army

(continued)

NAZI EXTERMINATION CAMPS AND MAJOR CONCENTRATION CAMPS (CONTINUED)

The main camp in Austria, it had a fortresslike appearance. Most inmates were political prisoners, criminals, and "asocials." Jews and Spaniards serving in the French Army and Foreign Legion were also sent here. The camp had a very high mortality rate; as punishment or for Nazi sport, men had to carry stones and climb the infamous 186 Steps until they died or were shot. Prisoners were also pushed off a quarry precipice known as the Parachute Drop.

Natzweiler/Struthof

Near Strasbourg, France; May 1941–September 1944; 50 subcamps; 17,000 deaths; Occupied by Free French forces, November 1944

A small, mountain camp, Natzweiler held many resistance fighters sentenced to hard labor. Prisoners worked in granite quarries and dug tunnels for underground factories. A small gas chamber was constructed in 1943, and a bath house was built next to the crematorium so that the heat generated in burning bodies also provided hot showers for SS men. University of Strasbourg medical professors and students visited frequently to observe experiments and obtain cadavers.

Neuengamme

Neuengamme, near Hamburg, Germany; December 1938–April 1945; 60 subcamps; 55,000 deaths; Liberated by British Army

In June 1940, the camp took in Belgian, Dutch, French, and Norwegian political prisoners. (Of the 13,000 French prisoners here, only 600 survived.) In early 1945, Scandinavian prisoners received Swedish Red Cross assistance and early release; according to a Nazi official, other prisoners did not since the defeated Germans wanted "to save the best of the remaining people of Western Europe."

Ravensbrück

Concentration Camp; Outside Ravensbrück, Germany; May 1939–April 1945; 40+ subcamps; 92,000 deaths; Liberated by Red Army

The only major concentration camp for women (women and men were separated in other camps), the camp had 150 female SS personnel and trained women for SS work elsewhere. Inmates worked in factories and did manual outdoor labor. Most were Russians, Poles, or other Slavs; about 15 percent were Jewish. Medical experiments were conducted here and a gas chamber was built in fall 1944. The infamous, whip-wielding SS guard Irma Grese had two tours of duty here.

Sachsenhausen

Concentration Camp; Oranienburg, Germany; July 1936–April 1945; 60+ subcamps; 45,000 deaths; Liberated by Red Army

Sachsenhausen held 50,000 prisoners (five times its capacity) at war's end. It was publicly visible and prisoners worked in local businesses. Inmates included prominent Germans, and it was regarded as an "easy camp" by Nazi standards. Jews were housed separately. Doctors conducted medical experiments on prisoners and supplied universities with cadavers. Under Operation Bernhard, 142 inmates forged British banknotes in a Nazi plan to disrupt the British economy.

NAZI EXTERMINATION CAMPS AND MAJOR CONCENTRATION CAMPS (CONTINUED)

Sobibor

Extermination Camp; Northeast of Lublin, Poland; March 1942–November 1943; 250,000 deaths

About two dozen SS soldiers and more than 100 Ukrainians staffed the small, compact camp. Most victims were gassed within hours of reaching Sobibor. In December 1942, the SS began cremating the remains of those in mass graves. A prisoners' revolt, led by POWs on October 14, 1943, prompted the camp's closure. Sobibor was demolished and planted over.

Stutthof

Near Danzig, Poland; September 1939–May 1945; 150 subcamps; 65,000 deaths; Liberated by the Red Army

Originally a civilian prison, it became a concentration camp in January 1942. Typhus epidemics struck in late 1942 and again in 1944. The camp had a small gas chamber, but most deaths occurred from starvation or pneumonia, especially during the harsh winters. Inmates made a 10-day death march in late 1944.

Theresienstadt

Transit and Concentration Camp; Terezin, Protectorate of Bohemia and Moravia (Czechoslovakia); November 1941–May 1945; 33,000 deaths; Liberated by the Red Army

A walled town used to detain prominent, wealthy, or older Jews and as a transit center. The Nazis allowed the International Red Cross to visit it in 1944 as an example of its camp system after first eliminating overcrowding by deporting Jews and beautifying the landscape. The Nazis gave the Red Cross control of Theresienstadt May 3, 1945; five days later the Red Army liberated it.

Treblinka

Extermination Camp; Malkinia, Poland; June 1942–November 1943; 870,000 deaths

Established for the extermination of Polish Jews, although more than 100,000 Russians and other Slavs were killed here. Carbon monoxide was used in the three gas chambers; in October 1942 ten more gas chambers were built. Corpses in mass graves were cremated in the spring of 1943; later, the Nazis destroyed the buildings and converted the area into farmland.

SURVIVAL

Well before emigration was no longer a possibility, Jews struggled to find other ways to evade arrest and deportation, including passing oneself off as a Gentile and marriage to a Christian (a limited form of protection that did not last). Others hid in churches, monasteries, and in the attics, cellars, and barns of Gentile friends or willing rescuers. The family of Anne Frank, a young Dutch German teenager who achieved posthumous international fame when her wartime diary was published in 1947, successfully hid for two-and-a-half years in an office annex in Amsterdam until they were betrayed and sent to concentration camps. Foster families and orphanages took in Jewish children, changing their names and raising them as Christians to deflect suspicion. Private and religious rescue organizations helped smuggle Jews into neutral nations or paid ransoms to free Jewish prisoners. Then there was the unique case of Solomon Perel, an orphaned German Jewish teenager who posed as an ethnic German and was adopted by an army unit on the Eastern Front before spending the rest of the war hiding in plain sight as a member of Hitler Youth. To survive in the ghettos, Jews smuggled in food, constructed bunkers and shelters, amassed weapons and supplies, and staged revolts; for most, these actions only prolonged their lives a short time. During the Warsaw Ghetto Uprising (the largest such uprising, which began April 19, 1943), Jews used hand grenades, incendiary bottles and pistols against German tanks, machine guns, and artillery. Many who escaped the ghettos went underground, joining resistance and parti-

Jewish prisoners at Auschwitz-Birkenau unload goods stolen from Hungarian Jews deported to the camp in May 1944. The warehouse and sorting areas, where looted items were organized for distribution throughout the Reich, was called "Canada" by prisoners, who regarded it as a place of wealth and relative comfort. Those fortunate enough to work there—mostly women— supplemented their meager rations with food found in other victims' belongings. Since they were generally spared beatings, these workers were more likely than other inmates to survive the camp's brutal conditions.

san groups. Underground organizations operated in the concentration camps, and prisoner rebellions contributed to the closure of the Treblinka and Sobibor extermination camps and the successful escape and survival of a handful of prisoners. (See also "Jewish Resistance" in Chapter 9.)

RESCUERS

Protecting Jews from Nazi persecution or performing any other humanitarian act toward them could result in arrest and execution. Thus, even Gentiles sympathetic to the Jewish plight chose not to help; some, however, did risk their lives to save others. (Yad Vashem, the Jewish Holocaust memorial in Israel, officially recognizes as "Righteous Among the Nations" more than 21,000 non-Jewish rescuers from more than 40 countries.) Swedish diplomat Raoul Wallenberg (1912–1947?) saved as many as 100,000 Hungarian Jews from deportation in 1944 by providing them with "protective passports" and safe houses and hiring hundreds of Jews to assist in his operation. Arrested by the Soviets in early 1945 and accused of being a German spy, Wallenberg disappeared into a Russian prison and was never seen publicly again. Sempo Sugihara (1900–1986), Japanese counsel in Lithuania, granted thousands of transit visas (many were forged) to Jews, who then found refuge in Australia, China, the Caribbean, Palestine, and the United States. Sugihara acted against the orders of his government, which was allied with Germany, and in so doing saved lives but lost his career in the Foreign Service after the war for disobedience. Aristides de Sousa Mendes (1885–1954), a Portuguese diplomat stationed in Bordeaux, France, acted similarly when he issued about 10,000 transit visas to Jews and others escaping Europe via Portugal. Sousa Mendes also lost his job and died destitute. Selahattin Ulkumen (1914–2003), Turkey's counsel-general on the German-occupied island of Rhodes, saved 42 Jews from deportation to Auschwitz in 1944 by convincing the Gestapo that they were all Turkish citizens (most of them were not). For this and his other actions to assist Jews, German aircraft attacked the Turkish consulate, mortally wounding Ulkumen's wife. He was interned in Greece until the war ended.

Among the best-known rescuers is Oskar Schindler (1908–1974), a German businessman and Nazi Party member who employed Jews in his factories, treated them well, and protected them from deportation. By pulling strings with his SS and party contacts Schindler saved some 1,100 Jewish lives. In Holland, Corrie ten Boom (1892–1983), a Christian evangelical, hid Jews in her Haarlem home—which the Gestapo searched—above the family watch and clock business. The ten Booms saved the lives of about 800 Jews and protected many in the Dutch resistance. Corrie ten Boom was later arrested and imprisoned at Ravensbrück, while several family members perished in Nazi custody. Monsignor Angelo Roncalli (1881–1963), who later became Pope John XXIII, saved thousands of Jews in his capacity as an apostolic delegate to Greece and Turkey and papal nuncio to France. In 1944, he issued baptismal certificates to Hungarian Jews, which prevented their deportation. Hundreds of Jews owed their lives to the efforts of Anton Schmid, an Austrian sergeant in the German army, who was stationed near Vilna, Lithuania. Schmid smuggled food into the ghetto, won the release of Jews from prison, and worked closely with the Jewish underground, which occasionally met at his home. He was arrested in January 1942 and executed in April.

Meanwhile, Jewish and non-Jewish organizations throughout Europe assisted Jews under extremely dangerous conditions. The Relief Committee for the War Stricken Population, formed in September 1939 and based in Geneva, helped Jews find haven in Palestine, Bolivia, Japan, and China. It worked with foreign consuls and representatives of the International Red Cross, the Vatican, the Quakers, and the Protestant Church Council in Switzerland to send relief packages to ghettos and camps and to report Nazi atrocities to foreign governments. In occupied Holland, the Dutch underground provided food and sanctuary to Jews in hiding after deportations began in mid-1942. About 4,000 Jewish children who were taken in by Dutch Gentiles survived the war. In France, the Society for the Rescue of Jewish Children, organized in March 1942, saved some 5,000 youngsters from the Nazis, and another 10,000 were saved by local rescue groups. Britain's Kindertransport program provided refuge for more than 9,000 German, Austrian, and Czech children, most of whom later lost their parents during the war. In a spectacular Danish rescue operation in October 1943, civilians secretly ferried more than 7,000 Jews from occupied Denmark to neutral Sweden by fishing boats and other available craft. More than 95 percent of Danish Jews survived the war. The Jewish community in Palestine ran small rescue voyages through its Jewish Agency; from 1939 to 1944, nearly 19,000 Jews and 9,000 children reached Palestine, and another 15,000 children were sent to safety in western Europe.

The American Jewish Joint Distribution Committee (JDC, or "The Joint") was American Jewry's overseas relief organization. It provided more financial and humanitarian aid to European Jews than the combined efforts of the Allied governments, and it contributed most of the funding for the War Refugee Board (see "The U.S. Treasury Department versus

JEWISH DEATH TOLL BY COUNTRY

Nation	Jewish Population (Prewar)	Jewish Deaths
Albania	400	200
Austria	181,778	65,000
Belgium	90,000	24,400
Bulgaria	48,565	0
Czechoslovakia	356,830	277,000
Denmark	5,577	77
Finland	2,000	11
France	300,000	83,000
Germany	554,000	160,000
Greece	77,000	65,000
Holland	139,687	106,000
Hungary	473,000	305,000
Italy	48,000	8,000
Luxembourg	3,500	1,945
Norway	1,728	728
Poland	3,225,000	3,000,000
Romania	796,000	364,632
Soviet Union	1,300,000	1,000,000
Estonia	4,566	1,000
Latvia	93,479	80,000
Lithuania	153,743	135,000
Yugoslavia	70,000	60,000
Other areas		
Danzig	1,600	1,000
Libya	30,000	567
Mediterranean Islands	2,192	2,080
Memel	9,000	8,000
Macedonia and Thrace	12,900	11,343
Total	Approx. 9,000,000	5,700,000 to 6,000,000+*

Data from Martin Gilbert, *Never Again: A History of the Holocaust*, London: Collins, 2000; Bohdan Wytwycky, *The Other Holocaust: Many Circles of Hell*, 1980.

*Actual death toll is most likely 6 million or more, to account for Jews whose identities were not recorded but who perished in German custody.

the U.S. State Department" later in this chapter). Another American organization, the Emergency Rescue Committee, sent Varian Fry to France, where he created the American Relief Center and helped rescue about 2,000 people. He and Martha and Waitstill Sharp of the Unitarian Service Committee are the three Americans Yad Vashem named "Righteous Among the Nations."

AKTION 1005

As Germany lost ground in the Soviet Union and the Allies announced their intention to prosecute war criminals, the Nazis implemented *Aktion 1005* to cover up their atrocities in the East. In autumn 1942, Paul Blobel, a former commander in the Einsatzgruppen, was ordered, as he later put it, to "eliminate traces of the mass graves which had resulted from the executions carried out by the Einsatzgruppen." After the war, Rudolf Hoess, the head of Auschwitz, acknowledged that he had received an order "that all the mass graves were to be dug up and the bodies were to be incinerated. The ashes were to be dispersed so that in the future it would be impossible to establish how many people had been burnt."

From mid-1942 until late 1944, the Nazis used Jews and Soviet POWs to dig up and burn the corpses. Hoess's own prisoners at Auschwitz, he explained, "provided a constant supply of Jews for Kommando 1005" and they were shot

OTHER NAZI VICTIMS DURING THE HOLOCAUST

Non-Jewish Death Toll

The following are noncombat death estimates of non-Jews at the hands of the Nazis and their collaborators. The figures do not include American, British, or Italian POWs that were massacred or died in non-POW concentration camps. The total figure, which may never be known, is likely between 9 and 11 million victims.

Russian POWs	3,300,000
Poles	3,000,000
Ukrainians	3,000,000
Belorussians	At least 1,400,000
Serbs	Up to 1,000,000
Gypsies (Roma and Sinti)	232,000
German T4 Patients (see Chapter 11)	200,000
German Political Prisoners	32,000
German Homosexual Men	10,000
Spaniards	9,500
German Blacks	2,000
Jehovah's Witnesses	At least 1,650

Data from Martin Gilbert, *Never Again: A History of the Holocaust*, London: Collins, 2000; United States Holocaust Memorial Museum; Michael Berenbaum, ed. *A Mosaic of Victims: Non Jews Persecuted and Murdered by the Nazis*, New York: New York University Press, 1990.

when the work was completed. *The Black Book* (compiled by Soviet authors Vasily Grossman and Illya Ehrenburg during the war and later banned by Stalin) described prisoner efforts to destroy evidence of the 1941 massacre at Babi Yar in August and September 1943:

> When the prisoners stripped off the upper layer of earth, they saw tens of thousands of bodies. . . . Since the bodies had been lying in the ground for a long time, they had fused together and had to be separated with poles. From 4 A.M. till late at night Vladimir Davydov and his comrades labored in Babi Yar. . . . Thousands of bodies were heaped on stacks of firewood and soaked with petrol. Enormous fires burned day and night. . . . The Germans forced the prisoners to grind up the remaining bones with large rollers, mix them with sand, and scatter them in the surrounding areas. During this terrible labor, Himmler . . . came to inspect the quality of the

work. On September 28, 1943, when the destruction of evidence was almost completed, the Germans ordered the prisoners to heat up the ovens again. The prisoners realized that they themselves were to be murdered. The Germans wanted to kill and then burn up the last living witnesses.

Twelve of the 300 prisoners managed to escape; the rest did not survive. Ultimately, Aktion 1005 failed; there were too many bodies and too many crimes to hide with too little time and not enough available fuel. Nor was there time to dismantle the camps or destroy all the meticulous records of the SS. As it was, endless evidence of Nazi atrocities—living or dead, on paper or in architecture—was thickly strewn all over Europe.

LIBERATION

In the waning weeks of the war, Allied forces came upon huge streams of refugees including death march prisoners, and the concentration camps from which they had come. The Red Army had liberated the first major camp, Majdanek, in July 1944 and Auschwitz in January 1945. But in March and April, the SS was rapidly abandoning the camps, after first removing foodstuffs and poisoning water supplies. The liberators, most of them battle-hardened veterans, were shocked, sickened, and appalled by what they found—they were also incredibly angry. Before them were dazed and nearly lifeless skeletal beings, so wracked with hunger, disease, and savage treatment that they would die in large numbers shortly after gaining their freedom, their health irrecoverable. They could no longer properly digest food, and those who eagerly ate up soldiers' provisions died as a result. (It took several months to gradually move the survivors back on to normal diets.) Patrick Gordon Walker, a BBC commentator, reported from Bergen-Belsen that "The first night of liberty, many hundreds of people died of joy." *Time* magazine correspondent Sidney Olson, reporting from Dachau, wrote that "Each of these pitiful, happy, starved, hysterical men wanted to tell us his home country, his home city, and ask us news and beg for cigarets. The eyes of these men defy my powers of description. They are the eyes of men who have lived in a super-hell of horrors for many years, and are now driven half-crazy by the liberation they have prayed so hopelessly for." Those inmates strong enough to function escorted Allied troops through the camps while others sought revenge on their tormentors. Healthy, well-fed SS guards attempting to blend into the population by wearing prison uniforms were easily identified, if they were not killed outright by the prisoners. Other SS men committed suicide.

On liberating Dachau in April 1945, U.S. forces encountered one gruesome scene after another, including piles of emaciated corpses next to the camp's crematorium (top). Outraged American soldiers responded by executing approximately 60 SS camp guards lined up along a wall (bottom), and some survivors joined soldiers in killing guards found elsewhere. The army investigated the case but let the matter drop, a decision that few Americans would have argued against.

General Eisenhower ordered army crews to film the tragic scenes in color realizing that Nazis would try to deny their crimes, and he arranged for members of the British Parliament, the U.S. Congress, officials from neutral nations, and the media to see the camps for themselves. The British and Russians also documented the camps on film. Allied officials marched German civilians, who claimed ignorance of the conditions, through the camps filled with corpses, and nearby residents were forced to assist with burying the dead (see "What the Germans Knew," later in this chapter). Unlike Allied

EYEWITNESS ACCOUNT: PRIVATE FIRST CLASS HAROLD PORTER AT DACHAU

Private First Class Harold Porter, 22, from Ypsilanti, Michigan, was assigned to the U.S. Army's 116th Evacuation Hospital and stationed at Dachau. He described the indescribable in his first of many letters from Dachau beginning May 7, written on stationery emblazoned with the Waffen SS Standortkommandantur Dachau letterhead:

Dear Mother and Father. . . . It is difficult to know how to begin. By this time I have recovered from my first emotional shock and am able to write without seeming like a hysterical gibbering idiot. Yet I know you will hesitate to believe me no matter how objective and factual I try to be. I even find myself trying to deny what I am looking at with my own eyes. Certainly, what I have seen in the past few days will affect my personality for the rest of my life. . . . [Marc Coyle, a friend] took me to the crematory. Dead SS troops were scattered around the grounds, but when we reached the furnace house we came upon a huge stack of corpses piled up like kindling, all nude so that their clothes wouldn't be wasted by the burning. There were furnaces for burning six bodies at once, and on each side of these was a room twenty-feet square crammed to the ceiling with more bodies—one big stinking rotten mess.

May 11, 1945

This camp is notorious not because it is one of the worst managed, but because of the type of prisoners here—or originally here. Not too many are prisoners of war but quite a portion are German political prisoners. Many are Jews, but not the majority. . . . There are Hungarians, Czechs, Austrians, Greeks, Poles, Russians, Frenchmen, Yugoslavians, Danes, Italians, Belgians, Dutch, Germans, and until recently, British and Americans. More than half are civilians. A surprising number speak English, a few French, and nearly all understand German. Some have been here as long as seven years; others as little as two weeks. For some this is their fourteenth concentration camp. This is one of the better camps say those who have seen others. . . .Ten thousand Americans are supposed to have been here, but when we came too close they were pulled out to Munich in hope that their presence there would prevent us from bombing and shelling the city. It didn't. The most amazing thing to me is that other camps could be worse. But the prisoners stress that this is a "concentration" camp, and that the extermination camps are, by far, worse in every respect.

military personnel, German civilians were not permitted to wear gloves in handling the dead, and several hundred contracted typhus and later died. American soldier John O' Reilly, of Spokane, Washington, a technician third class with the Third Army, wrote his mother on April 16, 1945, telling of his visit to the recently liberated Ohrdruf labor camp (a subcamp of Buchenwald): "Enclosed find a [newspaper] clipping about a concentration camp. I went to the place myself the other day and it is everything the clipping says it is. Terrible. I cannot hope to describe it. I trust to God that we shall not be easy in any respect on the Germans. They deserve the worst we can give them."

What the World Knew about the Holocaust

[The Germans plan to] wage this war until the Jews have been wiped off the face of the earth. . . . The Germans have, in fact, transformed Poland into one vast center for murdering Jews.

—*The United Nations' Inter-Allied Information
Committee public announcement, December 20, 1942*

Anyone paying attention to the news in the 1930s was aware of the harsh treatment the Jews received in Germany. But on November 24, 1942, the world at large learned of Nazi efforts to exterminate European Jewry when the Allies provided the media with chilling details, right down to the names of secretive extermination camps: Belzec, Sobibor, and Treblinka. The next day the *Washington Post* ran a front page story on local traffic fatalities, which had reached 99 for the year. Tucked away on page six, two brief Associated Press articles reported the systematic deaths of 2 million European Jews. As they had since the 1930s, major American newspapers continued to run stories on Nazi crimes, using the terms "annihilation" and "extermination," but the articles were seldom treated prominently.

HOW THE ALLIES LEARNED OF THE HOLOCAUST

British intelligence first knew of Einsatzgruppen massacres in the East in the summer of 1941 through the interception of German police reports coming out of the Soviet Union. They learned of the September massacre at Babi Yar later in the fall; Churchill had this in mind when he said in a November 14, 1941, broadcast, "None has suffered more cruelly than the Jew the unspeakable evils wrought upon the bodies and spirits of men by Hitler and his vile regime." On January 7, 1942, Soviet Foreign Minister

Vyacheslav Molotov informed ambassadors in Moscow of widespread German atrocities in western Russia, but neither the British nor the Soviets yet realized that the killings were part of an organized, systematic campaign of extermination. Nor did Bertrand Jacobson, the chief representative of the American Jewish Joint Distribution Committee's Budapest office, who gave a March 13, 1942, press conference in New York City describing the Nazis' persecution, deportation, and murder of Jews in the Balkans.

A variety of independent and consistent reports on the Holocaust reached the Allies throughout 1942. As early as January, the British were learning of Nazi atrocities from German POWs held in bugged facilities. Jacob Grojanowski, a Sonderkommando and the first person to escape from Chelmno, described the camp and gassing process to leaders in the Warsaw Ghetto, and his account reached London in June. The Polish government-in-exile's ministry of information compiled hundreds of reports and affidavits in *The Black Book of Poland*, published in New York, documenting Nazi crimes against Jews and the Catholic and Protestant churches. In August, Dr. Gerhart Riegner, a World Jewish Congress (WJC) representative in Switzerland cabled the first report to reach the West describing a plan to wipe out the Jewish population following deportation to the East. Later in the fall, the Vatican intelligence service confirmed to American officials additional Nazi atrocities. In November, Jan Karski of the Polish Underground briefed top British officials on the conditions he had witnessed when smuggled into the Warsaw Ghetto and at a camp where he was disguised as a Ukrainian guard. Other sources included Dr. Rudolf Bucher, a member of a privately sponsored Swiss medical mission to the Eastern Front, as well as diplomats and clergy. As the Allies soon confirmed, the pattern and purpose of the Einsatzgruppen massacres, the ghettos, and deportations began to fit into a much larger and more elaborate concept than they could have imagined.

As the killings continued unabated in autumn 1943, *Time* magazine reported in a cover story on Himmler that he "and his trained Gestapo animals have organized a program of extermination without parallel," stating that the Germans had killed about 10 million civilians. On April 7, 1944, Slovakian Jews Rudolf Vrba and Alfred Wetzler escaped from Auschwitz and wrote what became known as the *Auschwitz Protocols*, a document that contained their testimony, a specific warning to Hungarian Jews, maps of the camp, select names of staff, guards, and prisoners, and additional eyewitness accounts from three other escapees. There was also a plea to the Allies to bomb the camp and the rail lines leading to it. The report was translated into more languages as it passed through a network of diplomats, church officials, and rescue groups. The Swiss press printed excerpts in June, and Riegner cabled the gist of the report to American, British, and Czechoslovakian officials. Pope Pius XII and other world leaders responded by calling on the Hungarian government to halt the deportations to Auschwitz, and they ceased temporarily. The War Refugee Board publicly released sections of the Protocols on November 26, 1944, "in the firm conviction that they should be read and understood by all Americans."

Although the Allies knew a great deal about the Holocaust, the Nazis knew something else: since the Allies had done little to assist threatened Jews before the war, they would not go out of their way to rescue them during the war. What the Allied governments did—and did not—do would be a source of intense debate into the twenty-first century.

THE ALLIED RESPONSE

For most of those fleeing the Nazis, the United States was the first-choice destination, offering geographic safety and constitutional protection of life and liberty. Nobody expected any help from the Soviets, fighting for their own survival on the Eastern Front, and overstretched Britain made only some small gestures. To the persecuted Jews, then, of the major Allies, only the United States was in a position to be of much help. After the Kristallnacht pogrom in November 1938, President Roosevelt harshly condemned the German government and ordered the U.S. ambassador in Berlin to return home. FDR also permitted some 15,000 foreign Jews (mostly German) visiting on tourist visas to remain indefinitely. But plans to settle immigrants in Alaska or Denver, Colorado, went unrealized. The prevailing view among Americans was that the "Jewish Problem" was a European problem, and that the United States had already done more to help than any other country.

On December 17, 1942, the Allies issued a declaration that officially denounced Germany's "bestial policy of cold-blooded extermination" and reaffirmed their "solemn resolution to ensure that those responsible for those crimes shall not escape retribution." In the United States, the Congress of Industrial Organization and the American Federation of Laborers issued condemnations and a group called Loyal Americans of German Descent that included baseball great George Herman "Babe" Ruth released a declaration calling for Germans "to overthrow a regime which is the infamy of German

THE U.S. TREASURY DEPARTMENT VERSUS THE U.S. STATE DEPARTMENT

Contrary to federal government policy, some U.S. State Department officials blocked efforts to assist endangered Jews. Breckinridge Long, an assistant secretary in charge of immigration and visas wrote in a June 26, 1940, memorandum, "We can delay and effectively stop for a temporary period of indefinite length the number of immigrants into the United States . . . by simply advising our consuls to put every obstacle in the way and to require additional evidence and to resort to various administrative devices which would postpone . . . the granting of the visas."

In a bluntly titled document, "Report to the Secretary on the Acquiescence of this Government in the Murder of the Jews," U.S. Treasury Department lawyer Josiah DuBois wrote "I am convinced . . . that certain officials in our State Department, . . . have been guilty not only of gross procrastination and willful failure to act, but even of willful attempts to prevent action from being taken to rescue Jews from Hitler." The Treasury staff charged that State staff "surreptitiously" asked its legation in Bern, Switzerland, not to use diplomatic channels to forward reports on the Nazi extermination plan, making it more difficult for American Jewish organizations to learn the facts. The Treasury also presented evidence of foot dragging even after the State Department "received confirmation and shocking evidence that the extermination was being rapidly and effectively carried out."

DuBois pointed out, "While the State Department has been . . . 'exploring' the whole refugee problem, without distinguishing between those who are in imminent danger of death and those who are not, hundreds of thousands of Jews have been allowed to perish." Further, State officials "have tried to cover their guilt by . . . concealment and misrepresentation; . . . [and the] giving of false information and misleading explanations for their failures to act."

An outraged Treasury Secretary Henry Morgenthau shared the report and his concerns with President Roosevelt in January 1944. He was especially upset that from April until December 1943, State had held up a World Jewish Congress operation to rescue Jews in France and Romania and that the Treasury Department had caught Long trying to cover up these actions. Morganthau concluded, "The matter of rescuing Jews from extermination is a trust too great to remain in the hands of men who are indifferent, callous, and perhaps even hostile. Only a fervent will to accomplish, backed by persistent and untiring efforts can succeed where time is so precious." Roosevelt immediately established the War Refugee Board and agreed to Morgenthau's suggestion that Treasury, rather than State Department, staff lead the board. Despite its small budget and late start, the board was the most successful Allied agency to assist Jews and was credited with saving some 200,000 lives.

history." Its message was broadcast by the Office of War Information to American forces and to Axis nations. However, at this point, the Allies were still in no position to respond militarily. American and British forces would not land in Italy for another eight months or in France for another eighteen. The extermination camps, for the time being, were also beyond the range of Allied bombers.

Just as the Warsaw Ghetto Uprising began, on April 19, 1943, Britain and the United States, responding to pressure for action, convened a refugee conference in Bermuda, to which Jewish groups submitted a variety of rescue plans and proposals. No high-ranking government officials attended, nor were the Soviets involved, and nothing was accomplished. Both Roosevelt and Churchill believed that the best way to save the most Jews was "Rescue Through Victory" by defeating Germany. For this reason, FDR and U.S. Army officials did not bomb Auschwitz or other Nazi camps, as some requested, since it did not contribute to Allied military strategy. Many American Jews and Jewish organizations also agreed with this approach. Nonetheless, in November 1943, both the House and the Senate introduced resolutions asking Roosevelt to establish a commission to help rescue European Jews. At the same time, the Treasury Department was piecing together the State Department's role in hindering rescue efforts (see "The U.S. Treasury Department versus the U.S. State Department" on p. 699). Meanwhile, in March 1944, in Britain, Churchill also made an end run around British immigration restrictions by permitting the thousands of Jews who made it to Istanbul, Turkey, to continue on to Palestine.

THE JEWISH RESPONSE

The worldwide Jewish population was divided on what should and could be done. In the United States, the non-Zionist American Jewish Committee supported diplomatic methods and concerned itself more on settling Jews after the war. The pro-Zionist American Jewish Congress, led by Rabbi Stephen Wise, was more visibly active, staging rallies and boycotting German goods, but it, too, opposed increasing immigration quotas out of concern that it would cause an anti-Semitic backlash. The American Jewish Conference, an umbrella group established in 1943, promoted creation of a Palestinian Commonwealth over rescue efforts.

Beginning in late 1939, American Jews, on their own or through the American Jewish Joint Distribution Committee, sent care packages and funds to those in occupied Poland until Germany declared war on the

United States in December 1941. In March 1943, the Joint Emergency Committee for European Jewish Affairs submitted a rescue plan for the Bermuda conference and Rabbi Wise, a committee cochairman, noted that since the public revelations of the extermination program, "Six months have elapsed . . . and no action has as yet been taken. In the meantime it is reported that thousands of Jews continue to be murdered daily." Then on July 20, 1943, a five-day Emergency Conference to Save the Jewish People of Europe kicked off in New York City, led by Peter Bergson, a Zionist and strong advocate for rescue. Bergson attracted Jews and Gentiles of widely differing political persuasions, including former U.S. president Herbert Hoover, newspaper magnate William Randolph Hearst, and Harold Ickes, U.S. secretary of the interior. The group's efforts led to the introduction of a congressional resolution urging a government rescue agency, which, combined with Secretary Morgenthau's Treasury Report, moved FDR to form the War Refugee Board.

THE CHRISTIAN CHURCHES' RESPONSE

In Germany, both Protestants and Catholics accepted Nazism in the early 1930s as a bulwark against the Soviets' atheist and communist ideology. But Nazi interference in religious practice, education, and its support of a new movement (Positive Christianity, which adopted only those religious ideas that were acceptable to Nazism) caused many to reconsider their allegiance to the regime. (See also Chapter 11.) Some German Protestant churches removed historically Jewish prayers from their services, others opposed the Nazi regime but not its anti-Semitic laws, and a few made Jewish rescue part of their mission. Dietrich Bonhoeffer and Martin Niemoller (a decorated World War I U-boat veteran) cofounded the anti-Nazi Confessing Church, then spent years in concentration camps.

The Vatican learned the true nature of Nazi violence against the Jews early on when its priests and diplomats reported deportations from Austria and killings in Slovakia. In a 1942 Christmas Eve radio broadcast, Pope Pius XII condemned the ongoing racially motivated murders, but he did not refer to the Nazis or the Jews specifically. The pope did not speak out about the deportation of Italian Jews in October 1943, but some were given sanctuary at the Vatican and at Pius's summer residence. When Jews were forced to turn over gold to the Nazis as ransom for their lives, the Vatican assured Jewish leaders it would back their payments if needed. In the meantime, Secretary of State Cardinal Maglione instructed Vatican envoys in Nazi-occupied territory and Axis nations to pressure officials against deportation. Through these channels, the Vatican also supplied aid to some endangered Jewish communities.

Christian churches elsewhere exhibited everything from antagonism to ambivalence to activism, and older clergy tended to have greater anti-Semitic sentiment than younger men. The Dutch, French, Hungarian, and Swiss Reformed (Calvinist) Churches were especially active in Jewish rescue efforts, and Lutheran churches in Scandinavia actively opposed Jewish persecution. Both Catholic and Protestant officials spoke up for Jews who had converted to Christianity or who were married to Christians; however, Christian leaders worldwide, and especially those in Germany, did not officially challenge Nazi policy.

WHAT THE GERMANS KNEW

At the war's end, German civilians expressed shock when they saw what had occurred in the concentration camps. "We did not know" became a familiar national mantra, and although civilians were truly horrified by what they *saw*, Allied soldiers wondered how the locals could not *know* that terrible things happened there. After all, Germans knew that the Jews had disappeared; thousands had moved into houses taken from Jews and many more were driving their cars or wearing their clothes and jewelry. They had also known of the concentration camps since the early 1930s, and the term "Going up the chimney," a reference to death that invoked the image of the crematoriums' smokestacks, entered the language long before the war ended. For the most part, awareness depended on where one lived and worked. Those working in factories and war industries that used forced labor saw how victims were treated; railway employees saw human cargo; soldiers witnessed massacres in the East; and with camps scattered all over Germany, stories of what went on were prevalent. Patrons of a ski lodge near Natzweiler, a camp at the French-German border near Strasbourg, occasionally saw naked inmates lined up to enter the gas chamber, and the victims' screams could be heard while guests dined in the restaurant. After the war, a former inmate at Neuengamme testified that local civilians witnessed daily the suffering of "A long column of one thousand inmates . . . jogging along the road [to and from work]. The SS men . . . let their bloodhounds loose on the half-dying inmates in order to spur them on. . . . Nothing but a long mournful column, day after day. . . . On the left and right side of them, were the German people."

The British Second Army liberated Bergen-Belsen in April 1945 and forced SS guards—such as these well-fed SS women—and local civilians to bury the dead. Allied officials ordered German citizens to view the atrocities in the camps, in part to prevent the population from later denying what had occurred.

In a May 15, 1945, letter, Harold Porter wrote from Dachau:

German civilians are being used to help clean up this mess—the mountain of rotting corpses. They can hardly believe their eyes—exhibit every sign of genuine surprise, shock, and guilt—even to the extent of vomiting and fainting. I've talked with a French prisoner who was permitted to travel from camp to camp with an SS guard. He told of how the civilians on the trains recognized his striped uniform, exhibited genuine pity for him and even offered him cigarettes. He is sure that not one in a hundred of the German civilians has the faintest idea of what actually goes on in a concentration camp. Yet, I wonder.

PRINCIPAL SOURCES AND FURTHER READING

Bartov, Omer. *Hitler's Army: Soldiers, Nazis, and War in the Third Reich.* New York: Oxford University Press, 1991.

Berenbaum, Michael, ed. *A Mosaic of Victims: Non-Jews Persecuted and Murdered by the Nazis.* New York: New York University Press, 1990.

_____. *Witness to the Holocaust.* New York: HarperCollins, 1997.

Breitman, Richard. *The Architect of Genocide: Himmler and the Final Solution.* New York: Alfred A. Knopf, 1991.

_____. *Official Secrets: What the Nazis Planned, What the British and Americans Knew.* New York: Hill and Wang, 1998.

Ciano, Galeazzo. *The Ciano Diaries, 1939–1943,* edited by Hugh Gibson. New York: Howard Fertig, 1973.

Cook, Haruko Taya and Theodore F. Cook. *Japan at War: An Oral History.* New York: The New Press, 1992.

Dower, John W. *War without Mercy: Race and Power in the Pacific War.* New York: Pantheon Books, 1986.

Dyson, Freeman. *Weapons and Hope.* New York: Harper & Row, 1984.

Feig, Konnilyn G. *Hitler's Death Camps: The Sanity of Madness.* New York, London: Holmes & Meier, 1979.

Gilbert, Martin. *The Holocaust: The Jewish Tragedy.* London: Collins, 1986.

Harries, Meirion, and Susie Harries. *Soldiers of the Sun: The Rise and Fall of the Imperial Japanese Army.* New York: Random House, 1991.

Keith, Howard, ed. *True Stories of the Korean Comfort Women.* London, New York: Cassell, 1995.

Klee, Ernst, ed., et al. *The Good Old Days: The Holocaust as Seen by Its Perpetrators and Bystanders.* New York: Free Press, Macmillan, 1988.

Knox, MacGregor. *Mussolini Unleashed 1939–1941: Politics and Strategy in Fascist Italy's Last War.* Cambridge: Cambridge University Press, 1982.

Mazower, Mark. *Inside Hitler's Greece: The Experience of Occupation, 1941–1944.* New Haven, London: Yale University Press, 1993.

Merridale, Catherine. *Ivan's War: Life and Death in the Red Army, 1939–1945.* New York: Henry Holt, 2006.

Nicholas, Lynn H. *The Rape of Europa: The Fate of Europe's Treasures in the Third Reich and Second World War.* New York: Random House, 1994.

Perel, Solomon. *Europa, Europa.* New York: Wiley Books, 1999.

Rees, Laurence. *Horror in the East: Japan and the Atrocities of World War II.* Cambridge, MA: Da Capo Press, 2002.

Rozett, Robert, and Shmuel Spector, eds. *Encyclopedia of the Holocaust.* Yad Vashem, New York: Facts on File, 2000.

Russell, Edward Frederick Langley. *The Knights of Bushido: A Short History of Japanese War Crimes.* New York: Dutton, 1958.

Shelton, Dinah L., ed. *Encyclopedia of Genocide and Crimes against Humanity.* Detroit: Thomson-Gale, 2005.

Stetz, Margaret, and Bonnie B. C. Oh, ed. *Legacies of the Comfort Women of World War II.* Armonk, New York: M. E. Sharpe, 2001.

Tanaka, Tashiyuki. *Hidden Horrors: Japanese War Crimes in World War II.* Boulder, CO: Westview Press, 1996.

Vance, Jonathan F., ed. *Encyclopedia of Prisoners of War and Internment.* Santa Barbara: ABC-CLIO, 2000.

Veterans History Project, Library of Congress. Richard Henry Peterson papers.

Waterford, Van. *Prisoners of the Japanese in World War II.* Jefferson, NC: McFarland, 1994.

Weingartner, James J. "Massacre at Biscari: Patton and an American War Crime." *Historian*, Vol. LII, No. 1, November 1989, pp. 24–39.

Wiesel, Elie. *Night.* New York: Hill and Wang, 2005.

Williams, Peter, and David Wallace. *Unit 731: Japan's Secret Biological Warfare in World War II.* New York: Free Press, 1989.

9

THE UNDERGROUND WAR

COVERT OPERATIONS AND RESISTANCE

While the clash of uniformed forces took place on battlefields, covert war went on behind the scenes, through the airwaves and, often literally, underground. Thousands of men and women working in military and state intelligence agencies and partisan and covert resistance groups fought this hidden war to support their nations' or alliances' military and political objectives while eroding or destroying the enemy's capacity to meet its similar objectives.

Great Britain and the United States understood that intelligence could be a significant instrument of war and put much more money and people into intelligence agencies and activities than did the Axis countries. Allied intelligence, although flawed at times, was consistently better prepared to engage in sabotage and deception, estimate troop strength, and forecast enemy intentions. The Allies' superiority, especially in code breaking, led to crucial intelligence successes that greatly contributed to their overall victory.

Germany's and Japan's quick early victories contributed to their tendency to underrate the significance of intelligence, while the Axis powers' deeply held convictions of superiority caused them to consistently underestimate their enemies, despite what their intelligence showed. Later, political and military commanders discarded reliable information because they could not believe they might lose the war. These failures in the realm of intelligence were major contributing factors to the Axis defeat.

Underground Warriors: Intelligence Organizations

World War II was rife with secrets: classified plans for military, deception, and psychological warfare operations; clandestine codes and meetings; secrets about knowing the enemy's secrets.

The covert organizations that combatants assigned to protect their own—and ferret out the enemy's—secrets were also generally classified "secret."

British regulations, for example, specified that written communications about the Special Operations Executive and "MI" organizations (see "Allied Secret Service Organizations—Military" chart in this chapter) must be marked SECRET, and telephone conversations in which they were mentioned had to be scrambled (made incomprehensible to would-be interceptors—although since scrambling was in its infancy during World War II, this did not guarantee secrecy).

Each intelligence organization had a mandate to focus on particular aspects of intelligence work (e.g., psychological warfare, intelligence gathering, sabotage, or deception). Each had its own methods of operation and ways of relating to the work of other intelligence groups that were on its own side: rivalries were common, communication often imperfect. Axis intelligence agencies generally had more limited resources than their Allied counterparts. Moreover, these were not organized to cooperate well with each other, in part because Hitler and Mussolini believed their own roles were strengthened by the rivalries they encouraged between agencies. The Japanese situation was just as flawed: intelligence units in the field were assembled quickly, inadequately staffed, and largely ignored by military commanders. The main Allied and Axis intelligence organizations established and dismantled sub-organizations, as needed, and some organizations broke off from established groups to perform particular duties. The roster of wartime intelligence organizations described in the following chart constituted the central coordinating forces of the underground war.

SECRET SERVICE AND INTELLIGENCE ORGANIZATIONS

Allied Secret Service Organizations

Civilian

United States

Coordinator of Information (COI), which became Office of Strategic Services (OSS), headed by Colonel William J. Donovan (later Major General)

On July 11, 1941, President Roosevelt signed the order creating the COI to collect and analyze all information related to national security. On June 13, 1942, the COI became the OSS, with a focus only on overseas intelligence work. Donovan established OSS goals: infiltrate the enemy to collect intelligence; deploy sabotage and subversion; and coordinate operations with resistance groups, guerrillas,

SECRET SERVICE AND INTELLIGENCE
ORGANIZATIONS (CONTINUED)

and commandos. The OSS reported directly to the president and often worked closely with the British Special Operations Executive (SOE).

Federal Bureau of Investigation (FBI); J. Edgar Hoover, Director

To placate Hoover over the creation of the OSS and focus Donovan's energies on enemies overseas, Roosevelt mandated that the FBI collect all domestic (Western Hemisphere) intelligence. The FBI's war effort was mainly weeding out saboteurs and enemy agents on U.S. and Latin American soil. In June 1941, the FBI arrested 33 German spies, a death blow to Axis espionage in the United States.

Britain

Special Operations Executive (SOE), aka "Baker Street Irregulars" (main HQ at 64 Baker St., London); Charles Hambro (1942–1943), General Colin Gubbins (1943–1945), Directors

Created in July 1940, the SOE was mandated by Churchill for sabotage, spying, and aiding resistance movements in Axis occupied countries. It focused on Europe (with notable successes in Norway and France) but also worked in Algeria, Palestine, and Southeast Asia. The SOE was dissolved in 1946 and its job subsumed by MI-6 (see p. 710).

Government Code and Cipher School (GC&CS), headed by Leo Marks

Under the SOE umbrella, teams of civilians and experts in cryptanalysis gathered in 1939 at Bletchley Park, fifty miles northwest of London, to intercept and decrypt foreign transmissions. Though they focused primarily on the German Enigma codes and ciphers, they also analyzed diplomatic codes and ciphers from 25 other countries.

Political Warfare Executive (PWE), reported to the Foreign Office. Cover name: Political Intelligence Department (PID)

Splintered from the SOE in August 1941, the PWE's goal was to undercut Axis morale and buoy the spirits of citizens in countries under Axis occupation. Reporting to the Foreign Office, the PWE designed and distributed propaganda by radio, postcards, leaflets, and other printed matter. At the end of the war, the PWE reeducated Axis POWs.

Soviet Union

NKVD (Narodnyi Kommissariat Vnutrennikh Del); Lavrenty Pavlovich Beria, Director

This internal intelligence service oversaw all police activity within the borders of the Soviet Union. The functional equivalent of Nazi Germany's Gestapo and SS, the NKVD also had a vast intelligence network abroad that carried out purges in Poland and the Baltic states, mass deportations to Siberia, and executions of suspected spies, draft dodgers, and deserters.

Free France

Bureau Central de Renseignements et D'action (BCRA)

Established by London-based Charles de Gaulle, the BCRA worked with the resistance, the OSS, and the SOE to support activities against the German occupation force and Vichy Milice and to reestablish a free French government after the war.

(continued)

SECRET SERVICE AND INTELLIGENCE ORGANIZATIONS (CONTINUED)

Military

United States

Signal Intelligence Service (SIS), U.S. Army Signal Corps; became U.S. Army Signal Security Agency (SSA) in 1943, led by Lieutenant Colonel William Friedman

Based in Arlington Hall Station, Virginia, the SIS coordinated the army's code-breaking efforts. Its greatest success was breaking the Japanese Purple (diplomatic) code in September 1940, but its most secret success was intercepting Soviet diplomatic communications beginning in 1943 (an operation code-named Venona).

Office of Naval Intelligence (ONI), headed by Rear Admiral Theodore S. Wilkinson (October 1941–July 1942)

Responsible for decoding, translating, and evaluating intercepted Japanese government messages as part of Operation Magic, predating the war. After Pearl Harbor, the ONI's work was largely subsumed by other intelligence efforts.

MIS-X (Military Intelligence Service—Escape and Evasion Section)

Based at Fort Hunt, Virginia, MIS-X maintained covert contact with the 95,532 American POWs in Europe to coordinate training in "E&E" (escape and evasion). All traces of the MIS-X were destroyed within days after the war's end. (See also "Escape and Evasion" box in this chapter.)

MIS-Y (Military Intelligence Service)

A secret agency based at Fort Hunt, it interrogated Axis POWs for vital intelligence. It was disbanded at the war's end.

Counter Intelligence Corps (CIC) under the direction of the chief intelligence officer (or G-2) assigned to each general officer's staff in the U.S. Army's service commands

Fears that the Axis would infiltrate the United States led the army to expand its counterintelligence function and create the CIC in early 1942. As its functions overlapped those of other intelligence agencies, the CIC was phased out by 1944, though it was reinstated and reinvigorated after the war.

Britain

MI-5 (Military Intelligence, Section V), also known as the Security Service, led by Brigadier A.W.A. Harker (May 1940–April 1941) and later by David Petrie

This domestic intelligence service sought out enemy spies on British soil, intercepted Axis communications, and spread misinformation to the enemy.

MI-6 (Military Intelligence, Section VI), also known as British Secret Intelligence Service; Colonel Stewart G. Menzies, Director

After its agents were duped by the Abwehr in the 1939 Venlo incident (see "Resistance within the Axis," later in this chapter), MI-6 was overshadowed by the SOE. Its most important war role was operating the secure wireless system that carried Ultra intercepts of Axis Enigma transmissions broken by the

SECRET SERVICE AND INTELLIGENCE
ORGANIZATIONS (CONTINUED)

GC&CS. MI-6 also ran intelligence-gathering operations in occupied Europe, the Middle East, and the Pacific under the cover name "Interservice Liaison Department" (ISLD).

MI-9 (Military Intelligence, Section IX); the staff, led by Colonel Norman Crockatt, included escaped POWs Johnny Evans and Airey Neave

This organization provided the lifeline to Allied POWs, aided resistance efforts in occupied Europe, and rescued escaped POWs and Allied troops caught behind enemy lines. The British Army Aid Group (BAAG) led by Colonel Lindsay Ride and based in Hong Kong, then Chungking, was one of the most successful MI-9 units. BAAG assisted POWs who escaped from Japanese camps, gathered intelligence, recruited Chinese coast watchers, smuggled raw materials, and disrupted Hong Kong shipyards.

Soviet Union

Glavnoe Razvedyvatel'noe Upravlenie (GRU) or Chief Intelligence Directorate

Lenin established this military intelligence organization in 1918. During the war, the GRU conducted covert operations like the Tokyo Spy Ring led by Richard Sorge and the Switzerland-based Die Rote Drei spy ring led by Hungarian mapmaker Alexander Radolfi. (See "Notable Spies and Spy Rings" in this chapter.)

Australia

Allied Intelligence Bureau (AIB), codirected by Colonel G. C. Roberts, Director of Intelligence of the Australian Army, and Major General Charles A. Willoughby, General Douglas MacArthur's chief intelligence officer

Based in Brisbane, this collaborative effort of American, British, Dutch, New Zealand, Filipino, and Australian staff, augmented by native contacts in New Guinea, the Solomon Islands, and Borneo, mounted sabotage efforts behind enemy lines, conducted espionage in Japanese-held areas, served as coast watchers, and created/disseminated propaganda.

Axis Intelligence Organizations
Civilian

Germany

Schutzstaffel (SS) (literally "Protection Squads"), led by Reichsführer SS Heinrich Himmler

This secret police agency oversaw all internal security. What started with a few hundred agents in 1922 as Hitler's political police grew under Himmler (after 1929) into a 240,000-member security detail covering nearly every aspect of life in Germany, including guarding concentration camps. Though the SS was ostensibly a civilian police organization, it had a brutal military wing, the Waffen SS (see Chapter 4). The SS also euthanized the mentally ill, sterilized undesirables, and gathered intelligence behind German army lines. By early 1944, Himmler had folded the Abwehr's duties (see following Military chart) under his SS tent and began overseeing armed forces intelligence gathering.

(continued)

SECRET SERVICE AND INTELLIGENCE
ORGANIZATIONS (CONTINUED)

Reichssicherheitshauptampt (RSHA) included Sicherheitsdienst (SD) and Gestapo, or Geheime Staatspolizei (secret state police), headed by Heinrich Mueller

Created in 1939 to bring order to the massive intelligence bureaucracy that grew out of SS, the SD and the Gestapo were given equal status under the RSHA. The SD, or security service, was originally the informer network strictly for the Nazi Party, but when folded into the RSHA, as "Amt III," this intelligence service was mandated to "combat ideological enemies within the state."

Italy

Opera Vigilanza Repressione Antifascista (OVRA)

Mussolini's secret police, equivalent to the Gestapo, were assigned to halt any anti-Fascist activity or sentiment. Up to 50,000 OVRA agents infiltrated every aspect of domestic life in Italy.

Japan

Tokubetsu Koto Keisatus, or "Tokko" ("Special Higher Police")

Established in 1901, this was a civilian counterpart to the army's Kempeitai; it investigated internal cultural and patriotic lapses. The Thought Section of the Criminal Affairs Bureau, or Thought Police, was added in 1927, leading to the formation of Tonarigumi ("Neighborhood Associations"), that scrutinized activities in every building and block and monitored all phone calls. Tokko could arrest people for "dangerous thoughts."

Black Dragon Society, led by Mitsuru Toyama

An ultranationalist secret society with links to the criminal underworld (yakuza), it served in China and infiltrated the west coast of the United States.

TO

Code name for a global spy network made up of fishing fleets, diplomats, and prostitutes—and augmented with professional spies. The TO took photos and served as a fifth column as far away as the Middle East, North Africa, and Mexico, and infiltrated internment camps in the United States.

Vichy France

Milice (or "Militia"), the Vichy French equivalent of the Gestapo, headed by Joseph Darnand

A paramilitary organization of 250,000 created in 1943 to fight "terrorism" (the Resistance) in Vichy France, the Milice used summary execution and torture and was more feared by French residents than the Gestapo or the SS. The Milice also rounded up Jews and Resistance members for deportation to concentration camps.

Military

Germany

Abwehr, German Military Intelligence, led by Admiral Wilhelm Canaris

This worldwide espionage network had spy rings in the United States, Soviet Union, Latin America, and throughout Europe. It mainly gathered information on Allied troop buildups, airfields, and

SECRET SERVICE AND INTELLIGENCE
ORGANIZATIONS (CONTINUED)

armaments, but also spied on diplomats. Canaris kept the Abwehr independent of the SS; thus, it became a safe haven for anti-Hitler plotters. After the failed July 1944 plot to assassinate Hitler, the Abwehr was purged of its leadership and subsumed by the civilian RSHA.

Japan

Kempeitai (or Kempei Tai), "Law Soldier Regiment," or military police

Under the direction of the Army Ministry, the Kempeitai had the full support of Hideki Tojo who had, from 1935 to 1937, commanded the Kwantung Army's Kempeitai in Manchuria. Though a military organization, Kempeitai also had jurisdiction over civilians during the war. It had units in all countries or territories under Japanese occupation. As the de facto police force, it could arrest civilians and military staff. It oversaw travel permits, labor recruiting, counterintelligence, rationing, psy-ops, and propaganda, and ran POW camps. The U.S. Army estimated there were 36,000 Kempeitai, not counting native "auxiliaries" (often criminals or sociopaths), and 75,000 in all.

Tokeitai, or Tokei Tai, Imperial Japanese Navy's military police service

Attached to navy units and bases, Tokeitai provided security, sought traitors or defectors, and arrested "suspicious" non-naval persons. It also served as the colonial police in areas patrolled by the navy.

THE SPECIAL RELATIONSHIP IN SECRET: THE OSS AND THE SOE

The close connection between the COI/OSS and SOE grew out of the friendship between William Stephenson (aka "Intrepid"), Prime Minister Churchill's secret envoy to President Roosevelt, and William J. Donovan, Roosevelt's close adviser, who later headed the OSS. With Stephenson's help, Donovan set up a direct line between Churchill and Roosevelt for intelligence matters, a clandestine arrangement kept even from Secretary of State Cordell Hull and his British counterpart, Anthony Eden.

Donovan met many times with Stephenson, who was chief of the clandestine, New York-based British Security Coordination (BSC) in Manhattan, and traveled to England with him to learn firsthand how the British intelligence system worked. While a guest at Donovan's home, Ian Fleming, an assistant to British spymaster Admiral John Godfrey who worked closely with Stephenson (and would later create James Bond), helped Donovan draw up a template for what would become the OSS. Once the OSS was established, many American agents were trained in sabotage and subversion techniques at SOE facilities in England or its Camp X, a 275-acre farm in Ontario, Canada. The two agencies also shared innovations in gadgetry and explosives from their research and development departments. In March 1942, inspired by the SOE example, Donovan set up an OSS training camp at Area B in the Catoctin Mountains of Maryland.

The OSS/SOE bond was firm by mid-1941 when Donovan and Colin Gubbins, the SOE director, determined each agency's areas of responsibility. The SOE would handle India and most of Europe, while the COI/OSS would cover North Africa, Finland, Bulgaria, Romania, and China. Donovan set up OSS offices in London, Cairo, Lisbon, and Chungking and sent agents to Iran, French Equatorial Africa, Belgian Congo, Turkish Kurdistan, the Caucasus, Nigeria, Liberia, South Africa, Sweden, Spain, Syria, Turkey, and Afghanistan. He sent Count Ilya Tolstoy (grandson of *War and Peace* author Leo Tolstoy) across Tibet to find an overland supply route from India to China, in hopes of facilitating OSS/SOE activities in Asia. American and British agents combined operations and split duties in what were code-named Jedburgh teams. These three-man teams dropped behind enemy lines to coordinate resistance efforts in France, Greece, and Asia.

Among the first major collaborative SOE/OSS efforts was Operation Torch, the joint Anglo-American invasion of North Africa in November 1942 planned by Churchill and Roosevelt. SOE and OSS teams worked together to get arms to French resistance forces in Casablanca; guarded docks; sabotaged Axis air defenses, roads, and rails; and provided guides for the invasion forces. Despite some blunders, the SOE/OSS effort was a success, as was the invasion, and proved the effectiveness of the OSS to the U.S. military establishment, which until then had been skeptical of Donovan. By December 1942, the OSS was given elbow room by the Joint Chiefs of Staff. The special relationship between the OSS and the SOE remained intact until the end of the war, when the former eventually became the CIA and the latter was subsumed by the MI-6.

ESCAPE AND EVASION (E&E)

After 50,000 British soldiers were captured during the evacuation at Dunkirk, the British government established MI-9 to assist them. Headed by Brigadier General Norman Crockatt and staffed by the British Army, Navy, and Air Force, MI-9 created "E&E" (escape and evasion) codes and supplied to RAF flyers kits that contained compasses, waterproof maps, matches, dry food, money, and forged travel and work permits. Downed airmen thus stood a chance of making their way west toward England or to neutral Switzerland, Spain, or Portugal. One of the most popular escape routes was the "Pat Line," named for "Patrick O'Leary," the SOE undercover name for Belgian doctor Albert-Marie Guerisse, who blazed it. The Pat Line, stretching from the Dutch frontier through occupied and Vichy France, Spain, Portugal, and back to England, carried 600 Allied fugitives to safety. MI-9 also used, with their tacit approval, humanitarian agencies other than the Red Cross to give POWs E&E matériel hidden in such items as bars of

Covert U.S. agency MIS-X shipped decks of playing cards containing hidden escape maps to prisoners in German POW camps. The cards were placed in parcels indicating they were from charities in the United States. To retrieve the maps, prisoners soaked the cards to dissolve the glue and peeled apart the layers.

soap, chess sets, and shaving kits. MI-9's success at helping POWs escape inspired the U.S. military command to create MIS-X in October 1942. To facilitate escapes, MIS-X maintained covert radio and letter-code communication with the 95,532 American POWs in Europe. In all, 737 Americans escaped and returned to duty. All American troops carried an E&E kit containing a mirror, fish hook and line, knife, iodine, bandages, gold coins, halzone tablets to purify water, concealed button compass, maps and a thin, serrated wire known as a gigili saw.

Coded messages included in mail from POW camps were decoded by MIS-X cryptanalysts who, pretending to be wives or girlfriends, sent encoded responses. They also sent "their" POWs standard care packages from families and citizens groups that contained concealed radios, saws, razors, maps, foreign currency, film, developer, and compasses. Among the unique items MIS-X created were baseballs that housed radios and cigarette packs containing crystal radio receivers. MIS-X and MI-9 supplies and guides, however, did not work in the Pacific Theater, where western agents and POWs were unable to blend easily into the Asian population, and the jungle presented countless dangers and diseases the POWs in Europe did not face. The MI-9 British Army Aid Group (BAAG) provided what assistance it could to POWs in the camps and debriefed the few who managed to escape. Meanwhile, the United States created a subsidiary within MIS-X, called Air Ground Aid Service (AGAS), to set up outposts to help escapees or downed flyers between India and China. These efforts were aided, and subsumed, by the Allied Intelligence Bureau (AIB).

Methods of Underground Warfare

Underground Warfare Method 1: Gathering Intelligence

Beginning in World War II, a combatant's ability to gather and process military intelligence depended less on traditional methods—espionage and clandestine operations—and more on sophisticated technology such as electronic eavesdropping and communications intelligence. The key avenues for gathering information, as discussed in this section, were signals intelligence, photo reconnaissance, research and analysis, and human intelligence or spies. Each method provided unique information, but a clear picture of enemy strength and intention only emerged when intelligence from several sources was combined.

The Enigma machine was the primary cryptosystem used by German armed forces units (such as regiments or divisions). About the size of a portable typewriter, Enigma had a typewriter-style keyboard; a set of three, four, or five rotating disks called rotors *arranged adjacently along a spindle; and a stepping mechanism to turn one or more of the rotors with each key press. The rotors continually moved, so each key press would result in a different encrypted character.*

GATHERING INTELLIGENCE— "SIGINT"

The most useful sources of information about an enemy were the enemy's own military, commercial, diplomatic, and private messages and communications systems. Most of the major combatants worked to improve their signals intelligence (sigint) capabilities and develop or enhance their cryptography and cryptanalysis techniques. Throughout the war sigint provided the most important data at the tactical level. Acquisition of sigint was generally a six-step process.

SIGINT STEP 1: ESTABLISH PRIORITIES FOR TARGETING COMMUNICATIONS. In the 1940s, Axis and Allied nations had thousands of radio terminals on hundreds of radio networks around the world. These networks used hundreds of cryptographic systems varying from simple hand ciphers to complex book codes and such intricate devices as the German Enigma and the Japanese Purple machines. Additionally, neutral and Axis-friendly countries, as well as the Vatican, had in the aggregate hundreds of military, diplomatic, and commercial communications networks, so each country collecting sigint had to decide which communications to intercept, decipher, and report.

Initially, top U.S. priorities included German, Japanese, and Italian military traffic followed by Axis military attaché communications.

Diplomatic traffic between Axis capital cities was the third priority; the fourth was nonmilitary German intelligence and security radio networks; lowest priority was assigned to diplomatic messages sent by minor Axis and neutral countries. Changes on the battlefield and agreements among the Allies required the United States to reassess these priorities many times.

SIGINT STEP 2: INTERCEPTING MESSAGE TRAFFIC. To intercept the large numbers of messages that cryptanalysts needed as a basis for successfully cracking a code, intelligence agencies targeted two major types of communications media: cable (or wire) and radio.

Cable Intercepts. During the war, nations imposed restrictions on telegram and cable traffic. Censors often reviewed all personal, commercial, and diplomatic wire traffic, and foreign diplomats were required to submit a copy of each message they sent, even in its encrypted form, to a government censorship office in the country in which they were stationed. Even though all messages flowing through a country's terminals could be accessible to cryptologists, gathering sigint by monitoring cable traffic was a method with many limitations. Before the United States entered the war, only cables sent via a U.S. terminal connected to an overseas terminal (e.g., in London) were available to American cryptologists. Messages that were not routed through the United States were inaccessible. In occupied Europe, Nazi military and occupation authorities communicated through cable telephone or telegram systems where available, thus denying the Allies access to these communications except through dangerous and unreliable covert operations. Germany also expanded, repaired, and improved the European cable network in occupied Europe to support their operations. In four years, the German Army nearly doubled the size of the European cable trunk network to 6,900 miles, which further limited the Allies' ability to intercept messages.

Radio Intercepts. Diplomatic, naval, and air force messages transmitted by long-range, high frequency (HF) radio yielded far greater sigint than cable transmissions. Yet monitoring and intercepting radio transmissions was complicated by the thousands of radio terminals broadcasting around the world, interference from atmospheric conditions (e.g., sunspots, weather), geographic obstacles (e.g., mountains, heavily forested or jungle terrain), and the distance between transmitters and monitoring stations. The Allies built over 130 monitoring stations during the war, yet no combatant ever had enough stations to monitor all enemy radio transmissions. (According to one estimate, a Japanese area army command could send up to 1,400 messages each day.)

SIGINT STEP 3: ANALYZING THE INTERCEPT. To securely transmit intercepts from outlying intercept stations back to central processing centers, the Allies used high-level cipher machines like the British TypeX or the American SIGABA, which Axis cryptologists considered unbreakable. American traffic or signal centers in Washington, D.C., San Francisco, and Seattle relayed intercepted traffic from overseas stations via cable to U.S. Signals Intelligence Service (SIS) headquarters. Intercepts from British Commonwealth states destined for the SIS were routed through London, which passed them on to the British Security Coordination (BSC) in New York City. The BSC also relayed Canadian intercepts from Ottawa, Canada. Traffic analysts at the central processing centers analyzed each message for clues to its intended recipient or its content—they studied the intercept's station call signs, level of urgency, serial number, number of recipients and relays, and looked for tips about the cryptographic system.

SIGINT STEP 4: DECRYPTING MESSAGES. Allied code breakers had to contend with almost 500 codes and ciphers from Axis and neutral countries. British cryptanalysts worked against more than 100 German cryptographic systems. France used more than 100 systems for its armed forces, diplomatic, and colonial communications, while Switzerland had over ten manual systems and a simplified version of Enigma just for its diplomatic messages. The Vatican had nine diplomatic systems available for its apostolic delegates.

To decrypt messages in a timely fashion, cryptanalytic teams worked for months on a single system. Teams of Allied code breakers spent four and five years respectively working on the German diplomatic systems Floradora and GEE, and they never broke the German Gestapo Enigma (TGD) during the war. The codes of smaller countries, which had fewer resources to train staff or courier updated codebooks to distant offices, were generally easier to solve.

High-level cryptographic systems—Enigma, Purple, and Axis and neutral diplomatic messages—were processed at Great Britain's Government

Cipher—a system for encoding individual letters or pairs of letters in a message

Code—a system of letters, numbers, or symbols used to represent letters, numbers, or words

Key—instructions that control the encryption and decryption of a cipher back to original plaintext

Cryptanalysis—methods used to recover information from ciphers or codes without knowing the key

Cryptography—developing codes and ciphers

Cryptology—the study of enciphering and deciphering messages in secret codes or ciphers

From *Eavesdropping on Hell,* NSA, 2005.

Code and Cipher School (GC&CS), the U.S. Navy's cryptologic organization (OP-20-G), or the U.S. SIS headquarters (see "Allied Signals Intelligence," later in this chapter). Allied tactical field intercept units monitored, decrypted, and translated low-level encrypted or plaintext enemy messages before sending them to their commands, and communications between Axis units division-size or smaller were decrypted and translated at a large intercept site or at intermediate processing centers located in such places as Hawaii, Egypt, Ceylon, and Australia.

Little statistical information exists about the overall success of Allied code breakers, and there is no quantitative data about how many messages may have been missed altogether. The Allies had the most success against their main targets, such as German U-boat Enigma traffic, yet rarely were Allied cryptologists able to read enemy messages before the intended recipients read them.

SIGINT STEP 5: TRANSLATING TEXT INTO NATIVE LANGUAGE. After a message was decrypted, a linguist would translate the text into the interceptor's language—in itself a problematic process. The Axis, other Allied, and neutral countries targeted by the major Allied powers used over three dozen languages, and Allied linguists had to become proficient in a language and learn or develop specialized glossaries for military, nautical, and aerial jargon and equipment references. For example, in March 1943, the SIS received over 114,000 intercepts of Japanese army, weather, and diplomatic messages but could produce only 4,500 translations because it lacked enough translators. (See "Combating Babel" in Chapter 4.)

The Death of Admiral Yamamoto. In April 1943, U.S. cryptographers deciphered a message encoded in JN-25, the Japanese naval code, detailing Admiral Isoroku Yamamoto's itinerary for the next five days. U.S. Secretary of the Navy Frank Knox ordered that Yamamoto be shot down. On April 18, 16 P-38s flew 400 miles from Guadalcanal to Bougainville in the Solomon Islands at wave-top height to avoid radar. The mission was timed to the second: as the U.S. pilots approached the island, two Japanese bombers and six fighter escorts appeared. The Americans quickly shot down three fighters and the two bombers and killed Yamamoto. To maintain secrecy about the U.S. ability to read JN-25, the Army Air Force pilots who carried out the mission were told that Allied coast watchers had provided the information about Yamamoto's flight.

SIGINT STEP 6: DISSEMINATING THE INTELLIGENCE. In 1941, Great Britain formed Special Liaison Units (SLUs) to disseminate Ultra (high-level intelligence, discussed later in this chapter) that they received by enciphered radio or cable transmissions or via courier, to oversees commands in the Middle East. (To conceal and protect their sigint activities, the British frequently used cover stories when they distributed information. To hide the fact that they were reading Enigma messages, they used the cover name "Boniface" to suggest that the information came from a German agent controlled by MI-6.) SLUs were eventually present at every British armed forces command. As early as mid-1941, Churchill was receiving a daily summary of important Ultra material from the head of MI-6, Stewart Menzies.

In the United States the SIS initially produced and disseminated communications intelligence to other agencies. In 1942, the War Department formed the Special Branch to pass on intelligence the SIS had analyzed, and in 1944 the department's Military Intelligence Service took over analyzing and disseminating communications intelligence. Roosevelt's aides would brief him at least once daily on the highlights from the various summaries.

The American version of the SLU, the Special Security Officer (SSO) became the main method of Ultra distribution to major U.S. commands in late 1943. These officers received intelligence messages sent from the War Department, carried the intelligence to their designated recipients, briefed them, and then returned to their duty stations with the messages—which never left their custody.

In Germany, the messages deciphered by Pers z (pronounced "pers-zed"), the cryptanalytic and cryptographic service of the German Foreign Office, went to the state secretary and Foreign Minister Joachim von Ribbentrop's office. Messages for the führer were marked with a green "F," although Ribbentrop refused to pass along much bad news to Hitler. General Cesare Ame, Head of the Servizio Informazione Militare (SIM), the Italian Army's intelligence organization, published a daily bulletin that went to Mussolini, the king, and the chief of the general staff. Diplomatic messages went to the Foreign Minister, Count Galeazzo Ciano.

ALLIED SIGNALS INTELLIGENCE

United States, Britain, and Commonwealth Countries. Each major combatant had at least one organization that oversaw acquisition and decryption of enemy codes and ciphers. The primary Allied organizations were the U.S.

SIS at Arlington Hall, Virginia, the U.S. Navy's OP-20-G in Washington, D.C., and Britain's Government Code and Cipher School (GC&CS) at Bletchley Park. The SIS, later reorganized and redesignated numerous times, eventually became the Signal Security Agency (SSA).

American radio intercept personnel assigned to the SIS, the OP-20-G, the Coast Guard, the Office of Strategic Services, and the Federal Communication Commission manned over seventy-five intercept sites. In Britain, the Radio Security Service, the General Post Office, and units of the armed forces known as the "YService" were the major radio intercept organizations.

British Commonwealth nations contributed to sigint work by establishing radio monitoring stations, and personnel from New Zealand, Canada, and Australia served in cryptanalytic centers, particularly in the Pacific Theater. In May 1941, the Canadians hired American Herbert Yardley to set up a small cryptanalytic service, called the Examination Unit, in Ottawa. In 1942, the Examination Unit began passing intercepts and decrypts of Vichy French diplomatic traffic to the SIS. That spring, the SIS sent a small party of cryptanalytic personnel to Australia to establish a sigint capability within General Douglas MacArthur's Southwest Pacific command. American and Australian sigint personnel formed the "Central Bureau," which attacked Japanese army communications.

Canada's Examination Unit also conducted intercept operations, and Commonwealth and military personnel from Australia, New Zealand, and India were organized into units known as Special Wireless Groups to perform intercept services. The Commonwealth manned over sixty stations located in the British Isles, Australia, Ceylon (Sri Lanka), Egypt, Palestine, Malta, Iraq, Kenya, and India.

Combining Intelligence Resources. Although the United States had sought to coordinate intelligence activities with Britain since the fall of France, the Americans had little to offer in trade until they broke the Japanese Purple code in September 1940. By that time, Britain had made good use of information provided by Polish cryptographers in 1939 on Germany's main cipher system, which used the Enigma machine. By May 1940, the British were routinely reading one German air force key. (In 1941 they could read the German naval key and by 1942, the German army key.) In late 1940, a delegation from the U.S. Army and Navy traveled to Britain to meet with their counterparts at the GC&CS. In addition to Purple, the Americans offered the British other Japanese codes and ciphers, the German diplomatic code (DESAB3), the Italian diplomatic systems "X" and "TR," a Mexican diplomatic code and three diplomatic ciphers, and the work the U.S. Navy had accomplished on the Japanese Naval code, JN-25B.

In exchange, the British provided information on German, Italian, Japanese, and Russian cryptographic systems, a new Mexican cipher, a Brazilian codebook, partial Chilean and Argentine codes, and descriptions of German, Italian, and Russian meteorological codes. The British had been working on Russian traffic since 1918, and though they could not read Soviet diplomatic traffic, by 1941 they were reading Russian military, naval, and meteorological systems. In contrast, the Americans paid little attention to Russian sigint until early 1943 when they established a Russian section at Arlington Hall.

Britain and the U.S. finally signed the BRUSA (Britain-United States of America) Agreement in June 1943, which outlined how they would collaborate on intelligence work. The two Allies formally agreed to exchange finished intelligence, although they would not exchange "raw" (undecrypted) intercepts, except for U-boat messages. Under the agreement, the United States took responsibility for Japanese communications, while the British oversaw German and Italian military and security forces communications. The GC&CS remained the principal Allied cryptologic agency for the Axis ground and air forces in Europe. In the Pacific Theater, the American Army and Naval cryptologic organizations supervised Allied intercept and code-breaking operations. British stations in Ceylon and India had American contingents, and Canadian, Australian, and New Zealand personnel served at various Pacific and Asian sites with the Americans and British.

MAGIC AND ULTRA: THE ACES UP ALLIED SLEEVES

In February 1938, the Japanese Foreign Office began using a new diplomatic cryptographic machine (97-shiki O-bun In-ji-ki) in its embassies to send encoded diplomatic messages. The United States code-named this machine "Purple."

Throughout the war, the Japanese believed Purple was unbreakable, but after twenty months of intense work based on information gleaned from studying other Japanese codes, an SIS team led by Frank Rowlett broke it in September 1940. Rowlett's team soon constructed a machine to duplicate Purple cryptographically. They eventually created six more machines including two for Britain, the first of which was sent to England in January 1941.

Since Purple was a diplomatic code, it did not carry details about Japanese military planning or operations, but it yielded valuable information. For example, the Japanese ambassador in Berlin, Baron Hiroshi Oshima, studied German military developments and deployments and sent lengthy radiogram reports to Tokyo via Purple-enciphered messages that included details about German Atlantic Wall fortifications and information from private conversations with Hitler. In time, the Allies were reading every message Oshima sent via Purple to Tokyo. "Magic" was the code name given to this intelligence derived from Japanese diplomatic intercepts.

Other Japanese Ciphers

The Japanese Navy's operational code, called "JN-25" by U.S. Navy cryptographers, turned out to be a good source of Japanese strategic information. Although British and Dutch units in the Pacific could read some JN-25 messages before Pearl Harbor, the Japanese changed the code shortly before the attack. Within a few months, U.S. cryptographers broke into the new code enough to gather information that aided U.S. Naval success in the battles of the Coral Sea and Midway. The Japanese revised the code again after Midway and not until the end of 1942 were the Allies, with the help of additional code breakers and captured Japanese codebooks, able to read JN-25 again. The Allies did not fully break the Japanese Army code until they captured codebooks in New Guinea in January 1944.

Ultra

Ultra was the name the British used for intelligence they derived from decrypting German communications. The term eventually became the standard designation in both Britain and the United States for all intelligence from high-

level cryptanalytic sources and is most often associated with the intelligence obtained from the German Enigma machine.

In 1919, Dutchman Hugo Alexander Koch invented a "Geheinschrijfmachine" ("secret writing machine") that a German, Arthur Scherbius, further developed and marketed. Scherbius built the device, which he called "Enigma," to secure communications for commercial businesses but, in the late 1920s, the German military began using the machine. Even before World War II, the Poles, the French, and the British were all working to break military messages sent via Enigma. In 1938, Polish mathematician Marian Rejewski, working with Henryk Zygalski and Jerzy Rozycki, designed a cryptological device known as *bomba kryptologiczna*, which helped them find the keys needed for decryption. By September 1939, they could read some German army and air force messages. When forced to flee Poland, they passed on what they had learned about Enigma to the British.

Drawing from the Polish research, British mathematician Alan Turing designed a new electromechanical device, the British *Bombe*, that could break any Enigma-enciphered message provided the British knew the Enigma's hardware and could accurately guess a plaintext "crib" of about twenty letters.

The first Bombe, based on Turing's original design and built under the direction of Harold "Doc" Keen, arrived at Bletchley Park in March 1940. The second Bombe, equipped with an important enhancement developed by Gordon Welchman, was installed in August. From then on, British cryptographers could break messages enciphered on the relatively simple Enigma system used by the Luftwaffe.

The U-boat traffic, of great importance to the Allies, was enciphered on a far more secure

BOMBE

In 1942, the U.S. Navy asked engineers at the National Cash Register Company (NCR) to redesign the British bombe, *a device that could break messages enciphered on the three-rotor Enigma. Within a year, the new bombes, which worked against the four-rotor Enigma, were built and shipped to Washington, D.C., where navy WAVES (Women Accepted for Volunteer Emergency Service) operated them 24 hours a day, 7 days a week.*

Enigma system. In February 1942, the Germans introduced an Enigma with four rotors, instead of the usual three, along with new codebooks. For the next 10 months, the Allies suffered a virtual blackout of U-boat Enigma traffic and, as a result, shipping losses in the Atlantic and Mediterranean greatly increased. In late March, the Allies repenetrated the U-boat cipher, and this helped turn the tide in the Battle of the Atlantic by May. In the summer of 1943, the U.S. Navy and the British brought the first four-rotor Bombes into action and, by the end of the year, these new Bombes, coupled with information from captured German codebooks, made U-boat Enigma traffic much more vulnerable to the Allies.

At the height of operations, the Allies, including the Soviets, who had also cracked the German Enigma code in 1942, were reading over 2,000 daily Enigma intercepts from the German military. These decrypted messages, when appropriately used, were of great value in formulating Allied strategy and tactics. By 1945, the Allies could decrypt almost all German Enigma traffic within a day or two, yet until the war ended, the Germans remained confident that Enigma was secure.

Other German Systems

Later in the war the Germans began to use several stream cipher teleprinter systems for their most important traffic, which the British codenamed "Fish." Germany used several systems, principally the Lorenz SZ 40/42 (initially codenamed "Tunny") and the *Geheimfernschreiber* (code-named "Sturgeon"), which the British thoroughly penetrated.

726 ★ The Library of Congress World War II Companion

SWEDISH SIGNALS INTELLIGENCE

Although almost all neutral countries maintained cryptologic bureaus, Swedish cryptanalysts deserve a special mention. In 1936, Sweden set up a cryptologic bureau that grew from 22 to 1,000 cryptanalysts during the war. Sweden's greatest achievement was Dr. Arne Beurling's solution of the German Siemens machine, called Geheimschreiber ("secret writer") by the German Foreign Office. German messages between Norway and Berlin traveled over Swedish wires, allowing the Swedish cryptanalytic bureau to easily intercept them and give them to Beurling, one of the finest wartime cryptanalysts. He solved the cipher within two weeks and, as a result, twice when German troops planned to move toward the Swedish border, Sweden was quickly able to send its army to meet them. In spring 1941, the Swedes passed decrypted information about a coming German attack on the Soviet Union to the British ambassador to the Soviet Union. The ambassador, Sir Stafford Cripps, passed the information on to the Soviets, who did not act on it.

Soviet Union. The enciphered codes that the Red Army relied on in World War II could be read if an enemy could intercept enough traffic. During the 1939–1940 war with Finland, Swedish code breakers, including mathematician and cryptanalyst Dr. Arne Beurling, read Soviet messages and passed them on to Finland. As a result, Finland was able to repulse several Russian attacks and sound air raid alerts before Soviet bombers even took off to bomb Helsinki. For diplomatic messages, the Soviet Foreign Office used a completely secure but somewhat slow and tedious encryption method known as the one-time pad system that protected its messages from the Axis, Allies, and neutral intelligence services. The Germans were able to intercept tactical information from Russia but never solved its strategic cryptosystems.

China. From 1938 to 1940, Chiang Kai-shek paid American Herbert Yardley to decrypt Japanese Army messages, and though he spent most of his time teaching the Chinese the general principles of code breaking, Yardley also seems to have had some success deciphering the Japanese codes. In early 1942, in response to a U.S. request for copies of Japanese cryptographic materials, China sent 19 exhibits that included several Imperial Army codes.

In 1943, as U.S. relations with China became strained over disagreements about American military and financial pledges, the SIS established a

Chinese section. That March the British gave the Americans a report on Chinese diplomatic systems, and by the end of June, U.S. code breakers were reading two Nationalist Chinese systems, INVINCIBLE and WIN. China wrongly believed that its communications would be made more secure by using a number of cryptologic systems simultaneously. The United States solved eight more Chinese systems by March 1944 and another four by June 1945, including the system used by the foreign minister and military attachés. While the SIS did not attempt to read messages from the Chinese communists under Mao Tse-tung during the war, communist military operations were occasionally discussed in intercepted Japanese traffic.

AXIS SIGNALS INTELLIGENCE

Germany. Pers z (pronounced "pers-zed") was the German Foreign Office cryptanalytic and cryptographic service. Foreign Minister Joachim von Ribbentrop, who sought to limit access to his own coded telegrams, eventually directly supervised the office. Pers z staff grew from 30 in 1933 to 300 staff members in the cryptanalytic branch alone in 1943, including mathematicians, linguistic cryptanalysts, clerks, and support staff. Pers z eventually had experts in the language of almost every country large enough to have a diplomatic corp. Because the growing number of German intelligence organizations had to vie for skilled cryptanalysts by the late 1930s, Pers z stretched national policy to get qualified personnel—Ottfried Deubner was part Jewish but was made an honorary Aryan and allowed to join Pers z because his father had solved Russian cryptograms for Germany in World War I.

The high commands of the German army, navy, and air force each included a cryptanalytic agency, as did the Oberkommando der Wehrmacht (OKW), the armed forces high command. Oddly, the military intelligence agency, Abwehr, did not have its own code breakers and was forced to rely on the cryptanalytic agencies in the individual branches of the military.

The Luftwaffe's Radio Reconnaissance Service comprised more than 10,000 people. Its air intelligence regiment intercepted, solved, and evaluated radio traffic of Allied light and heavy bombers, fighters, transports, and air staffs in Western Europe. The 800-man staff of the Luftwaffe's center for basic cryptanalysis and traffic analysis also studied new enemy radars and radio navigation systems to find ways to deceive or jam them. One of the service's greatest successes came on August 1, 1943, when it intercepted and quickly deciphered an Allied message saying a large formation of four-engine aircraft was airborne from Libya. By the time the 178 Liberators roared over the oil fields at Ploesti, Romania, the German antiaircraft defenses were ready and downed almost one-third of the planes. (See also Chapter 7.)

Grand Admiral Karl Dönitz, commander of the German navy, built a small but successful cryptanalytic agency called the "B-Dienst" (Observation Service). By the start of World War II, B-Dienst had solved the most secret British naval codes and ciphers enabling the German navy to avoid the British Home Fleet, conduct surprise attacks on British warships, and locate and attack British submarines in 1940.

To solidify their hold on key intelligence and to get useful information about their rivals within the Nazi regime, a few German military leaders also established their own cryptanalytic offices. Hermann Göring was first off the mark when he set up an eight-man unit, the Forschungsamt (Research Office), within his Air Ministry in 1933 to intercept communications; unit staff tapped telephones, opened mail, and solved encoded telegrams.

After March 1942, Heinrich Himmler had Walter Schellenberg, an official in the SS intelligence service, establish a department within the Reich Central Security Office (RSHA) to research secret communications including microdots, invisible inks, and cryptography and cryptanalysis. In mid-1944, Wilhelm Hottl, an Austrian staff member of the RSHA, began purchasing information from the small but effective Hungarian communications intelligence unit that eventually read some American and British messages, as well as secret radiograms from embassies in Moscow.

Despite a lack of manpower and problems posed by competition among their own cryptanalytic organizations, German cryptanalysts had a number of important successes. German army intercept personnel had monitored Yugoslav messages since January 1940, and German forces that invaded Yugoslavia in 1941 were aided by intelligence gleaned from the broken military cryptosystem as they rapidly overran the country. In 1941, Pers z cracked the Japanese TSU diplomatic code, which the Japanese embassy in the Soviet Union relied on, giving the Germans information about Soviet war production and army activities. In late 1942, army cryptanalysts also solved messages sent on the American M-209, a portable, mechanical cipher machine used by the U.S. military.

By the war's end, German cryptanalysts were able to read at least some secret communications from 34 countries, including all the major combatants, Western Europe, countries in Central and South America, and much of the Middle East.

Italy. The Italian Army's intelligence organization, Servizio Informazione Militare (SIM), had a large, well-organized cryptologic group, Sezione 5, headed by General Vittorio Gamba, a noted linguist said to know 25 languages. Sezione 5 produced codes and ciphers for the army and higher level enciphered codes for the navy. Typically, SIM intercepted 8,000 radio messages a month, studied 6,000, and translated 3,500 to plain-text. Foreign Minister Count Galeazzo Ciano noted that Sezione 5 cryptanalysts routinely read British, Romanian, and neutral Turkey's diplomatic traffic. For more than two years, Italy learned about Allied war plans and programs from messages they intercepted from Turkey.

In January 1935, Admiral Wilhelm Canaris, a conservative and nationalist, was appointed head of the German military intelligence and counterintelligence organization, the Abwehr. After building the organization into a worldwide espionage network, and growing disillusioned with Hitler and pessimistic about Germany's prospects for victory, he worked covertly to undermine Nazi policy and, on occasion, save Jews from certain death. When the SS found his diaries in April 1945, he was executed, just weeks before the end of the war.

Italian cryptanalysts had several other important successes. After World War I they had solved Yugoslavia's military ciphers and exploited these in April 1941 during the German-led Axis invasion of Yugoslavia. As the Yugoslav Army was pushing the Italian Army south from Yugoslavia into Albania, SIM personnel wrote telegrams addressed to two Yugoslav divisional headquarters ordering them to suspend military action and withdraw their troops. The Italians enciphered the telegrams using Yugoslavia's army cipher, added the signature of Yugoslavia's new president General Dusan Simovic, and passed the messages. The next day, the two Yugoslav division commands gave orders to withdraw northward, allowing the Italian troops to advance.

In 1942, code breakers working for the Italian naval intelligence organization, Servizio Informazione Segreto, penetrated the British naval ciphers in the Mediterranean. But Italy's greatest cryptologic achievement, and one of the preeminent Axis sigint successes in the war, occurred in 1941 when SIM agents in Rome broke into a safe holding documents related to the United States' Black Code, used by U.S. military attachés and ambassadors worldwide.

After photographing the Black Code and its superencipherment tables, they replaced the documents and passed the code on to the Abwehr chief, Wilhelm Canaris.

The Axis was soon able to read much of the traffic from U.S. military attachés all over the world. In one case, the American military attaché in Cairo, Colonel Bonner Frank Fellers, used the Black Code to radio detailed messages to Washington about the activities of British forces. Axis intelligence forwarded this information to General Erwin Rommel, head of the German Afrika Korps, often just a few hours after Fellers had sent them. As Rommel continued to outwit them in North Africa in 1942, the British, who had previously broken the Black Code, began monitoring messages sent by Fellers. After reading his lengthy reports for ten days, the British notified U.S. authorities about the leak, and Fellers was recalled to Washington. The new American military attaché sent to Cairo used the M-138 strip cipher, which the Axis could not solve.

KEY CODES AND CIPHER MACHINES

Term	Used by	Description
Coral	U.S.A.	U.S. code name for the Imperial Japanese Navy cipher machines used by naval diplomatic attachés.
Enigma	Germany	Cipher machine by German engineer Arthur Scherbius.
Fish	Britain	The name the British gave to messages sent through the German Geheimschreiber; also the name used by British and American cryptologists for Sturgeon and Tunny machines.
Floradora	Allies	Also known as the Keyword System—Allied term for one of the most important German diplomatic systems.
Gee	U.S.A.	U.S. name for German OTP system.
Geheimschreiber ("secret writer")	Germany	German diplomatic cipher machine used by the Foreign Office and produced from the Siemens machine.
Impero	Italy	First high-grade Italian diplomatic cipher read by the SIS in the summer of 1941.
Jade	U.S.A.	U.S. code name for a machine used tactically by the Imperial Japanese Navy from late 1942 into 1944.
JN-25	U.S.A.	U.S. designation for the code used by the Japanese Fleet.

KEY CODES AND CIPHER MACHINES (CONTINUED)

Term	Used by	Description
Lorenz	Germany	The Lorenz "Schlusselzusatz 40/42 (SZ-40/42)" machine, used for high-level communications, was the best-known German telecipher machine.
Magic	U.S.A.	U.S. code name for intelligence derived from the cryptanalysis of Purple.
M-209	U.S.A.	Military designation for the American hand-operated, completely mechanical, man-portable cipher machine designed by Swedish cryptographer Boris Hagelin.
OTP	Germany	German system used for high grade diplomatic traffic.
Purple	U.S.A.	U.S. designation for a diplomatic cryptographic machine used by the Japanese Foreign Office for diplomatic communications.
SG-41	Germany	A purely mechanical device, with an internal organization along the lines of the M-209 but larger, with a real keyboard. Used by the Abwehr after 1944. Also called Schluesselgeraet 1941 and Cipher Device 1941.
SIGABA	U.S. Army	Called the ECM (Electric Cipher Machine) by the U.S. Navy, the only machine system used during World War II that was completely unbroken by an enemy.
Sturgeon	Britain	British code name for the German telecipher machine used for high-level communications, the Siemens & Halske "T-52" series. T-52 equipment was capable of producing high-speed teleprinter transmissions; it used cable rather than radio to transmit its messages.
Tunny	Britain	British designation for a German Army machine that could be used out of the back of a truck as well as at a fixed site. The British built the Colossus computer to decrypt Tunny messages.
Ultra	Britain, later the U.S.A.	Originally used by the British for intelligence resulting from decryption of German communications; eventually became the standard designation for all intelligence from high-level cryptanalytic sources.
Venona	U.S.A.	Code name for SIS efforts to crack Soviet diplomatic codes beginning in February 1943.
97-shiki O-bun In-ji-ki	Japan	The Japanese name for the diplomatic cryptographic machine the Americans called Purple. Japan adapted it from the German Enigma machine and called it "the machine" or "J."

Japan. The Japanese cryptanalytic group Tokumu Han ("Special Section") was founded in 1925 within the Department of the Navy's General Staff. By the end of the war it employed several thousand men and about 30 Nisei girls (born outside Japan to Japanese couples), who eavesdropped on American radio and telephone conversations. Meanwhile, the Japanese Army intercepted over 250 diplomatic and 800 military messages a day.

Overall, Japanese cryptanalysts had limited success against American codes and ciphers. Only in one attack in the Marshall Islands were the Japanese able to decrypt a message and warn a garrison to defend itself. Although they could read BAMS, the Allied merchant ship code (Germany had given them a copy of a captured BAMS codebook), they rarely attacked merchant ships (see "Imperial Japanese Navy" in Chapter 4). Army cryptanalysts in Manila had some success against the codes used by American and Filipino guerrillas in early 1943, allowing them to raid guerrilla posts. But when new ciphers were smuggled in to guerrillas on supply submarines, the Japanese Army's cryptanalytic success in the Philippines ended.

Japanese cryptographers were no more successful than their cryptanalysts. The Japanese used dozens, if not hundreds, of codes throughout the war and had continual problems getting updated codes and codebooks out to thousands of ships and islands scattered across 20 million square miles in the Pacific.

GATHERING INTELLIGENCE— PHOTORECONNAISSANCE

The nation with the best photo reconnaissance will win the next war.

—*Chief of the German General Staff*
Werner von Fritsch, 1938

No other source of intelligence was as readily accepted and trusted by military leaders as photographic intelligence, thus every major combatant had at least one organization that provided photoreconnaissance. Military commands used photography to select bombing targets, determine bombing accuracy and assess damage, analyze equipment capability, pinpoint defense positions, create maps, and get a better understanding of a potential battle site. Yet each nation had a different view of the role of photoreconnaissance, and their success in using it as an intelligence tool varied as widely as their programs.

Photographs were especially valuable when used to confirm intelligence received through other sources, such as agents or electronic surveillance. They worked particularly well alongside cryptanalysis. An intercepted radio message could let a combatant know what the enemy *intended* to do, but photographs showed the current status of the enemy's troops and equipment. By combining the two types of intelligence, combatants could get a clearer picture of an enemy's strength and intentions.

Most intelligence photos were taken from aircraft, yet each combatant also derived information from ground photos collected overtly and covertly through agents and embassies and through such readily available sources as newspapers, travel books, postcards, tourist photos, reports, and public relations photos. Many of these photos were not particularly useful on their own but could yield valuable information when combined with other sources.

Aerial photoreconnaissance was first conducted in the skies over northern France during World War I. The photos taken by early aircraft soon became so important to the combatants that they began building specialized planes designed to prevent enemy reconnaissance aircraft from entering their airspace as well as photographic equipment that could withstand the cold temperatures at high altitudes. In these early days, photographs were taken primarily for mapping, though some work in elementary photo interpretation (PI) was being done. By frequently photographing the same places, photo reconnaissance specialists began developing one of the key intelligence uses of photographs—change detection. Photographs were particularly effective when compared with previous photographs to identify changes in landscape or buildings.

Between the wars, military organizations developed innovations that would help aerial photography regardless of the mission. These included vibration-free vertically stabilized mounts, distortion-free wide-angle camera lenses, and cameras with multiple lenses to cover more ground on a single flight line.

ALLIED PHOTO RECONNAISSANCE. By 1939, World War I Royal Navy Air Service pilot F. Sidney ("Sid") Cotton had developed a warm, high-altitude flying suit, flown French-sponsored covert photoreconnaissance sorties against Germany, mounted three standard cameras into a three-fan configuration to cover a wide area when photographing, painted aircraft a pale duck-egg green so they would blend into the sky better, and routed hot air over the cameras to keep the film, mechanisms, and lenses from freezing at high altitudes. During World War II, Cotton's group, the Photographic Reconnaissance Unit (PRU), used Spitfire aircraft stripped of unnecessary weight and carrying extra fuel tanks to extend their range. The PRU became the model for Allied air reconnaissance.

AERIAL PHOTOGRAPHY IN THE UNITED STATES. The United States entered the war in the same way it ended World War I—unable to collect and exploit aerial photography for intelligence purposes. The army used aerial photography for mapmaking or to confirm a report from a visual observation, while the navy had no air photoreconnaissance capability at all. In mid-1941, after attending photo interpretation (PI) training at Medmenham, England, the home of British PI, U.S. Army Captain Harvey C. Brown set up a PI school at Harrisburg, Pennsylvania, to complement the training that troops received at the photography school at Denver's Lowry Field.

When American forces arrived in North Africa in late 1942, Allied reconnaissance capability expanded greatly. American Colonel Elliott Roosevelt, son of the president, created the Allied Northwest African Photographic Reconnaissance Wing, which included a joint Central Interpretation Unit. In this theater, both British and U.S. forces focused on tactical intelligence (supporting specific military operations) and contributed to the substantial photomapping tasks at hand.

When General Carl Spaatz took command of all army air forces in Britain in January 1944, he asked that Elliott Roosevelt be assigned as his chief photoreconnaissance deputy. Roosevelt headed the new U.S. 8th Reconnaissance Wing (Provisional), later the 325th Reconnaissance Wing, and a modest photo interpretation center at High Wycomb. The 325th Photo Wing took over 3 million exposures in 4,251 combat sorties, providing two priceless gifts—significant strategic intelligence for the bomber offensive against Germany and a model for future photoreconnaissance.

PROBLEMS IN THE PACIFIC. Allied photoreconnaissance in the Pacific differed greatly from that in Europe, in part because the British did not have an established reconnaissance program there and also because the Allies were fighting very different wars on the islands and in the China-Burma-India Theater.

The United States had no photo intelligence capability in the Pacific when the war began. Occasionally a flight crew took photos to confirm

Combatants used aerial reconnaissance photos to select targets and to assess the accuracy of an attack and the amount of damage inflicted. These photos of Marienburg, Germany, taken before and after an attack, show the results of an Allied bombing raid.

combat action, and photomapping units worked temporarily where they were needed, but none of the available aircraft could mount a camera—all cameras had to be hand-held. The only available photo labs on prewar military bases were used to develop pictures of dignitaries or ceremonies, and there was not one qualified American photo interpreter in the entire theater. Moreover, lack of accurate maps remained a problem: Americans discovered, as they began planning to retake Guam, that despite having had bases there since 1899, they did not have a single reliable map of the island.

In 1941, Lieutenant Commander Robert S. Quackenbush Jr., senior photographic officer in the U.S. Navy Bureau of Aeronautics, and a group of navy and U. S. Marine Corps officers went to Britain to view the activities at Medmenham. Quackenbush applied what he learned there to create a program that eventually became the Naval Photographic Group, consisting of aerial squadrons and an interpretation squadron. Photographic Squadron 1 was commissioned on October 1, 1942.

The U.S. Army's first photoreconnaissance unit in the Pacific became active in North Australia in April 1942. Without up-to-date maps, photos, or planes to take them, U.S. photo interpretation teams culled *National Geographic* magazines and other material from local libraries in New Zealand for information the marines could use to plan their landing on Guadalcanal. Toward the end of the year, U.S. service branches had combined their disparate resources—the navy's photographers, lab people, and PIs; the marines' mobile photo lab; and the army's planes—to establish photo reconnaissance capabilities. By the middle of 1943, the Allies had reconnaissance groups in New Guinea and India and, within a year, the U.S. Army and U.S. Navy each had enough resources to form their own centralized imagery collection and exploitation organization.

Throughout the war, imagery exploitation took place in Hawaii under the Joint Intelligence Center Pacific Ocean Area (JICPOA) where the information from photos, signals intelligence, and human source collection was merged. By 1944, ninety photo interpreters were working at JICPOA producing detailed reports, making photomosaics and models for upcoming operations, and disseminating the photos. At peak, over 2 million sheets of text and 100,000 prints left JICPOA every week.

AXIS PHOTORECONNAISSANCE
Germany. After World War I, Germany was ahead of everyone in understanding the value of aerial photography as an intelligence source. As soon as they began rebuilding the Luftwaffe in the mid-1930s, the Germans made

aerial photo collection a top priority for the air force. To proactively photograph key areas of Europe without arousing suspicion, Colonel Theodor Rowehl led a team that photographed from planes while claiming to prepare for a major route expansion by Deutsche Lufthansa airline. Rowehl's team shot covert large-scale photos in 1938 and 1939 as they explored air routes in Britain, the continental coast of the English Channel and the North Sea, and the Baltic Coast into Leningrad. By 1940, there was little the German military did not know about their opponents' installations or orders of battle.

After the war began, Rowehl attempted to develop high-speed, high-altitude aircraft, but the large cameras he had been using were difficult to fit into these high-performance planes. Eventually, Rowehl had excellent results from multiengined aircraft and developed several long-range high-flyers that he used over Great Britain.

Japan. The Japanese used photos from hand-held cameras during the Pearl Harbor attack to estimate the damage, photographed Lingayen Gulf beaches before they invaded Luzon in the Philippines, and shot mapping and strike-documentation photos in China. But after summer 1942, Japan rarely used aerial photography for anything other than mapping. The Japanese used photo intelligence only for tactical needs and had few photo collection units, no system in place to disseminate photos beyond the unit that requested the reconnaissance, and no program to improve either equipment or personnel skills. Nor did they ever develop a robust photo interpretation capability—by the end of the war only 18 army and 30 navy officers had been trained as photo interpreters. The few available PIs were attached, one or two at a time, to air groups at the division or lower level; they focused on airfield interpretation and did not coordinate with other units or maintain a central file of the imagery collected. Neither the army nor the navy had air units that specialized in photoreconnaissance. By the time the Japanese realized the value of intelligence derived from aerial photography, it was too late. They had lost aerial superiority.

GATHERING INTELLIGENCE—RESEARCH AND ANALYSIS

Intelligence agents, particularly those stationed in foreign lands, routinely scoured all available sources for information about enemy military operations or commercial production. They read newspapers, trade journals, scientific and academic papers, and magazines; listened to radio broadcasts; watched movies; studied recent maps; talked with ships' crews from friendly and neutral nations and noted the cargo arriving or departing; and met with cooperative diplomats and politicians. All this research was used by their agencies to get a clearer picture of enemy position and intent.

The United States made a unique and important contribution to intelligence work during the war—inventing *strategic intelligence analysis.* In late 1941 when the OSS set up its Research and Analysis Branch (R&A), headed by Harvard historian William Langer, it hired 900 scholars, mostly historians, economists, political scientists, geographers, psychologists, anthropologists, and diplomats, to collate and evaluate specific available information about the enemy. The R&A team analyzed ways to break enemy morale, use psychological warfare effectively, and exploit internal conditions in Germany to the Allies' advantage (e.g., inflation, fear of bombing raids, disruption of civilian life). They calculated how many tons of bombs the military would need to destroy a bridge so it could not be used for several weeks and analyzed specific German industries and plants to select targets whose loss would have the greatest, quickest, and longest-lasting impact on military operations.

Analysis by the R&A's Enemy Objectives Unit, a team of economists based at the American embassy in London, convinced Allied commanders that oil production was a vulnerable point in the German war effort. After American bombers attacked Germany's synthetic fuel plants and oil production facilities in May 1944, Ultra intelligence immediately confirmed the alarm throughout the German high command as the Germans made defending oil facilities their new top priority. Further attacks on oil production eventually grounded much of the Luftwaffe and immobilized thousands of German trucks and tanks.

Despite such successes, internal bickering and lack of coordination within U.S. intelligence agencies had a profound effect on R&A's usefulness. The R&A was forbidden to see army or navy signals intelligence data, and no group ever assembled all the intelligence being collected by the various agencies. Still, as the OSS was being dissolved at the end of the war, the R&A was the one unit that the competing U.S. agencies agreed to save; it was transferred to the Department of State.

GATHERING INTELLIGENCE—SPIES/HUMAN INTELLIGENCE

Although intelligence agencies now had the technology to listen in on enemy messages, decipher their codes, and wiretap the phones of suspected subversives, all major combatants still employed human spies.

By the late 1930s, German and Japanese agents had fanned out across the globe. Nests of spies found homes in Latin America, Spain, and Switzerland. Portuguese East Africa was home to German spies working in South Africa, and Japanese intelligence agents spent years living in the Philippine Islands, along the border between Manchuria (Manchukuo) and the Soviet Union, and throughout southeast Asia. These agents established relationships with local political and business leaders, familiarized themselves with military and commercial conditions, and continually reviewed available materials for

Spies (Left to right, top row): Many women, including Virginia Hall and Violette Szabo, who worked for the Special Operations Executive (SOE), and American entertainer Josephine Baker, who aided French intelligence, spent the war years as spies, collecting and transmitting enemy information and helping resistance fighters. Resistance Leaders: Resistance groups in occupied France, Indochina, and Yugoslavia, led by (left to right) Henri Frenay, Ho Chi Minh, and Josip Broz (Tito), used sabotage, underground newspapers, and open violent confrontation to battle their Axis oppressors.

new information. Their activities prompted the British and later the Americans to send counterintelligence agents to infiltrate these countries.

All major combatants spied on their allies and neutral nations as well as their enemies. The Soviet Union's greatest intelligence successes, in terms of the value of the information it received, which included research into the atomic bomb, were against its allies—Great Britain and the United States—rather than the Axis.

Many of the first agents selected for undercover work had two key attributes: knowledge of a foreign language and familiarity with a target nation. The British SOE routinely recruited young people who had fled continental Europe after the Nazis swept through, and in America, the OSS initially recruited well-educated young people who spoke foreign languages and had traveled abroad. Most nations also recruited women as covert agents. Women had a long history of obtaining national secrets by seducing or providing sexual favors to their targets, but during World War II, women also worked as couriers, undercover agents, radio operators, and cryptographers for intelligence agencies.

Good covert agents underwent months of specialized, intensive training. At the Nakano School, the Japanese institution that trained men for intelligence work, students were taught to grasp the basis for the enemy's thoughts and actions. They attended classes in ideology, propaganda, foreign studies (particularly the United States, China, and the Soviet Union), foreign languages, covert actions, secret weapons, codes, subversion, as well as safe-cracking, photographing documents, and disguises. The training at Nakano was similar to OSS/SOE training at Camp X in Oshawa, Ontario, administered by the British Security Coordination (BSC).

INFILTRATING THE AMERICAS. German Abwehr agents, called V-men (Vertrauensmann or confidential agents), first arrived in Latin America in May 1939 to keep on eye on British shipping and supply movements. As the United States increased its support to Britain, and German leaders realized the war would last much longer than originally anticipated, Central and South America suddenly took on a more important role. Here was the "soft underbelly" of the United States from which German agents could smuggle vital minerals back to the fatherland while spies relayed information about U.S. and British shipping and American war production and weaponry. Furthermore, in 1939, German engineers discovered that east-west transmissions were jeopardized by sunspots, atmospheric pressures, and geomagnetic problems. As south-north transmissions (e.g., South America to Germany) were less troublesome, Latin America became the broadcasting and reception center for the Reich's clandestine radio communications.

All V-men sent to Latin America received training in using secret inks, special codes, radio transmissions, and the microdot system. The microdot, invented by Dr. Rudolf Zapp, allowed a photographed page to be reduced to the size of a dot, which could appear in a letter as the dot over an i or a period at the end of a sentence. Dots could also be hidden under a stamp or under the flap of an envelope. By late 1940, the British discovered the German microdots and began scrutinizing letters between Latin America and Europe.

Once in Latin America, Abwehr agents received little support from the home organization; they were to recruit and train additional men on their own. Because of the distance and hazards of communications, these recruiters relied on army, navy, or air force attachés stationed in each country to provide funds, equipment, and instructions. The RSHA also sent SD agents to Latin America, but the potential advantage of having more agents in a foreign country was offset by the distrust, territorial disputes, and duplication of effort between the Abwehr and the RSHA.

American Interests in Latin America. In the late 1930s, President Roosevelt became aware of the buildup of German agents in Latin America and sought a series of covert agreements with willing nations in the region. In 1939, the first of these arrangements led Colombia—and later Ecuador, Bolivia, and Chile—to stop German-controlled airlines from operating in western South America. Pan American, a U.S. airline, conveniently stepped in and took over the air routes.

In June 1940, Roosevelt gave the FBI responsibility for intelligence work in the Western Hemisphere. (This was the first time a U.S. president authorized an undercover intelligence organization to operate outside the United States in peacetime.) FBI Director J. Edgar Hoover then created a Special Intelligence Service that used the services of U.S. businesses operating in Latin American countries to monitor Axis operations. By October, Hoover's agents were active in Mexico, Cuba, Argentina, Colombia, Brazil, Venezuela, and Chile.

The U.S. Federal Communications Commission (FCC) created the Radio Intelligence Division (RID) on July 1, 1940, and within two years had constructed twelve interception stations for clandestine transmissions coming from or going to Latin America. With the help of the ciphers provided by

William Sebold (see "Notable Spies," later in this chapter), by June 1941, RID was intercepting and the FBI Technical Laboratory was decoding almost all clandestine Abwehr communications between Latin America and Germany.

Their strategic locations and natural resources made the Abwehr, SD, and Special Intelligence Service particularly interested in the events in Mexico, Brazil, Chile, and Argentina.

When Mexican president Lazaro Cardenas confiscated most of the Anglo-American petroleum holdings in his country in March 1938, U.S. and British companies boycotted Mexican petroleum. Germany seized this opportunity to secure a much-needed commodity and purchased over 1.3 million tons by September 1939. The Germans hoped this increase in trade would encourage Mexico to allow Abwehr agents to operate in the country. In November 1941, however, the United States and Mexico reached an agreement calling for a joint defense board, air base rights, and intelligence cooperation. In December 1941, after the Japanese attack on Pearl Harbor and the German and Italian declarations of war on the United States and Britain, Mexico broke diplomatic ties with the Axis. On June 1, 1942, Mexico declared war on Germany, Italy, and Japan. (See also Part II of Chapter 1.)

Both Germany and the United States saw Brazil as a strategic ally, and Brazilian president Getulio Vargas willingly sold his friendship to each country. After securing U.S. Lend-Lease agreements in October 1941 and March 1942, Brazil allowed the FCC–RID (Federal Communications Commission–Radio Intelligence Division) to establish a U.S.-controlled radio monitoring unit on Brazilian soil and agreed to arrest over 80 Axis spies. German U-boats responded with attacks in Brazilian coastal waters, leading Vargas to announce in August that a "state of belligerency" existed between the Third Reich and Brazil.

After Germany lost bases for clandestine radio transmissions in Mexico and Brazil, Abwehr messages from as far away as Shanghai were mailed or cabled to Chile (which had a small but influential German community); from Chile, they were passed on to Germany. Meanwhile, in September 1941, the United States secretly promised Chile $50 million in arms aid in exchange for naval cooperation and increased surveillance of Axis espionage groups. Though Chile finally severed diplomatic relations with the Axis in January 1943, it provided only minimal help to U.S. counterintelligence operatives and thus received only $7 million of the promised Lend-Lease weaponry.

After 1942, one of the most important and active German intelligence networks, Bolivar, was established in Argentina; eventually, it transmitted from nine sites, broadcasting over 1,000 messages from its main site alone from July 1943 to February 1944. In January 1944, Argentina created the Coordinación Federal, an agency designed to suppress and prevent foreign intelligence activities. Within two days, a wave of SIS/Argentina, MI-6, and U.S. military attachés and agents were arrested. The last Anglo-American agents were not released from jail until May 1945.

NOTABLE SPIES AND SPY RINGS

Allied Spies and Spy Rings

Josephine Baker (1906–1975). From September 1939 to May 1940, expatriate African-American entertainer Josephine Baker passed information she overheard from powerful friends to Jacques Abty, a spy working for the French military. She later smuggled secret information written in invisible ink on her sheet music to her contact in Portugal and wrote down everything she heard when she hobnobbed with Nazi officials in Spain. For her efforts, Baker received the Legion of Honor, France's highest decoration, and became the first American woman to be buried on French soil with military honors.

Juan Pujol Garcia (code-named "Garbo") (1912–1988). As part of the "Double Cross" system, this British double agent sent 400 secret letters and 2,000 secret radio messages, all fake, to the Abwehr. His fabrications, especially as part of the ruse that the Allied D-Day invasion would not occur at Normandy, were vital contributions to Allied victory. (See p. 760.) As evidence of his success as a double agent, in 1944, he earned both a German Iron Cross and a British MBE for his work.

Virginia Hall (nicknamed "The Limping Lady") (1906–1982). An American fluent in French, Italian, and German, Hall was recruited by Britain's Special Operations Executive (SOE) in London. After completing SOE training in weaponry, communications, and security, in August 1941 she was sent to Vichy, France. Under cover as a stringer for the *New York Post*, she set up operations in Lyon, established agent networks, and coordinated the activities of the underground. When the Germans seized all of France in November 1942, Hall escaped to Spain by crossing the Pyrenees mountains on foot, which was no easy task as she had lost one leg in a hunting accident in 1933.

After she switched to the OSS, Hall and OSS agent Peter Harratt were dropped from a British boat in Brittany in March 1944. Traveling in disguise, Hall eluded the Gestapo while training three battalions of resistance agents in sabotage operations, maintaining radio contact between OSS headquarters and the resistance, and arranging supply drops from Britain. In September 1945, OSS head General William Donovan personally awarded Hall a Distinguished Service Cross—the only one awarded to a civilian woman in the war.

Dusko Popov (code-named Tricycle) (1912–1981). Popov was born into a wealthy Yugoslavian family and recruited by the Abwehr in 1940. He immediately offered his services to the British and throughout the war gave the Germans military intelligence vetted by MI-5. Viewed by Germany as an important and reliable agent, Popov built a network in the United States known as the Yugoslav Ring, which sent false information to Berlin and supplied vital intelligence to the Allies on German rocketry, strategy, and security. After the war, he was granted British citizenship. A renowned playboy, Popov was said be the inspiration for Ian Fleming's James Bond.

Rote Drei (Red Three). German Rudolf Roessler, the most important agent in the Soviet spy ring known as Rote Drei, emigrated from Germany to Switzerland in 1934 to escape the Nazis. In early 1939, as the Swiss General Staff was setting up intelligence services to collect and monitor information from Germany, Roessler met up with an old friend, Dr. Xavier Schneiper, who was working for Swiss intelligence. By July, Roessler was providing information to the Swiss about the political and military situation in Germany, Hitler's future plans, and the date of the attack on Poland.

Roessler's information turned out to be startlingly accurate, and by 1941, it was being shared with Dr. Christian Schneider, a journalist working at the same publishing house as Roessler, and his friend Rachel Dubendorfer, a German communist. Soon Dubendorfer gave another German communist, Paul Boettcher, the information, and Schneider, Roessler, and Boettcher agreed to collaborate.

From this point on, Roessler, operating under his cover name "Lucie," turned in information that made its way to Hungarian geographer Alexander Radolfi (aka Rado, cover name "Dora") who ran a Soviet military intelligence (GRU) network in Switzerland. Since 1939, Rado had been using a powerful short-wave transmitter to send messages to Moscow. Rado eventually expanded his network to three transmitters and several other agents, including British citizen Alexander Foote (cover name "Jim"), who sent more than 6,000 messages to Moscow after March 1941.

In spring 1943, Roessler gave Moscow accurate information about German preparations for the Battle of Kursk (see "Battle of Kursk" in Chapter 7), allowing the Soviets to concentrate massive forces, assign their best units, and create a maze of trenches, minefields, and underground bunkers in the area. Roessler updated his information as Germany delayed the attack several times. Roessler's daily information about the state of Germany's military and weapons systems was so accurate that Moscow suspected he might be a planted German agent. Though he would frequently know about decisions made by the Wehrmacht supreme command a few hours after they were made, Roessler refused to identify his sources.

The Germans, who were monitoring the group's messages, had been closing in on the spy ring since early 1942. Using direction-finding equipment, they realized the group had three transmitters in western Switzerland and named the group "Rote Drei" (The Red Three). Swiss intelligence arrested the first members of the group in late 1943; Roessler was finally arrested in May 1944 and spent 111 days in jail before being released. Although Rado managed to elude the Swiss agents and slip out of the country, Rote Drei was permanently broken up. Rudolf Roessler lived out his days in Switzerland and went to his grave without ever revealing his sources.

Rote Kapelle (Red Orchestra). Recruited by the Russians, Leopold Trepper, a Polish-born Palestinian exiled in France in the 1920s, became a Soviet secret police (NKVD) agent and, in 1939, established the Red Orchestra spy network in Europe. He eventually organized underground operations in Germany, France, Holland, and Switzerland.

The Trepper group reported on German troop strength, air attacks, aircraft production, and fuel shipments. In France, it worked with the underground French Communist Party and managed to tap the phone lines of the Abwehr in Paris.

The Gestapo formed the "Red Orchestra Special Detachment" (Sonderkommando Rote Kapelle) to destroy Trepper's group. In early 1942, after the Abwehr triangulated the radio transmissions of agent Johann Wenzel in Belgium, Wenzel informed on the leaders of the network. The Germans raided the Red Orchestra's headquarters in France in November 1942. Some agents broke under torture, and the Germans were able to liquidate the network in Europe by spring 1943. Most agents were executed. Trepper was arrested but managed to escape and remained in hiding until Paris was liberated; he later made his way to the Soviet Union.

The name "Rote Kapelle" or "Red Orchestra" came from German counterintelligence's practice of referring to spies' radio transmitters as "music boxes" and calling their agents "musicians."

Jan Smutek. In 1940, Smutek, a Czechoslovakian, stole plans from a Gestapo officer on a train, shipped them secretly to London, and slipped into Germany after killing two Germans who had come to arrest him. He was captured but killed his guards and got away, eventually reaching London, where he helped to plan and facilitate acts of sabotage and subversion by the Czech resistance.

Richard Sorge (NKVD code-named "Ramsay") (1895–1944). Sorge, a journalist, worked in Germany and Japan while spying for the Soviet Union before and during World War II. While working as the editor of a German news service in Shanghai in 1930, he met Hotsumi Ozaki, a Japanese journalist, who later became his informant. Sorge supplied the Soviets with information about the Anti-Comintern Pact and the German-Japanese Pact, and warned of the Pearl Harbor attack. He also informed the Soviet command of the exact launch date of Operation Barbarossa (the German invasion of the Soviet Union), that Japan did not intend to attack the Soviet Union during the battle of Moscow, and that Japan did plan to invade from the east as soon as the German Army captured any city on the Volga River. The Japanese secret service arrested Ozaki on October 14, 1941, and picked up Sorge four days later. Sorge and Ozaki were both hanged on November 7, 1944.

William Sebold (code-named "Tramp") (1899–1956). A U.S. citizen of German ancestry, Sebold was coerced by the Abwehr during a trip to Germany in 1939 and reluctantly agreed to become an agent. On returning home, Sebold told his tale to the FBI, who used him to set up a false operation in New York City. For sixteen months, German agents who came by Sebold's Manhattan office with war plans, weapon designs, and other information were filmed on hidden cameras. The operation eventually led to the arrest of 33 German agents. Sebold also helped the FBI-SIS break some of the Abwehr rings in Latin America by giving the FBI Technical Laboratory their cipher.

Violette Szabo (code-named "Louise") (1921–1945). Szabo, the daughter of an English mother and French father, worked for the SOE, which parachuted her into France in April 1944 to reorganize a resistance network the Germans had smashed. She led the network in sabotaging bridges, and her reports about factories producing German war materials helped the SOE establish bombing targets. Captured by German soldiers in June 1944, Szabo was interrogated, tortured, and sent to Ravensbrück concentration camp, where she was executed in February 1945.

Amy Elizabeth Thorpe (code-named "Cynthia") (1910–1963). The American Thorpe married a British diplomat and was living in Warsaw in 1938 when she was recruited by British intelligence. In one of her first assignments, she seduced the Polish Foreign Minister Joseph Beck to gain information about the office. Back in the United States, she obtained the Italian naval cryptosystem through an old friend, an admiral and naval attaché at Italy's embassy in Washington, D.C. In 1942, while the mistress of the Vichy French press attaché, she gained access to cables, letters, files, and accounts of embassy activities and personalities. In March 1942, she and the attaché had Vichy codebooks secretly photographed and passed them on to the British. The Vichy ciphers were extremely useful when the Allies landed in French-held North Africa in late 1942.

Nancy Wake-Fiocca (code-named Andreé, called the "White Mouse," by the Gestapo) (1912–). Wake, an Australian national, became the Allies' most decorated servicewoman of World War II. Living in France when it fell to the Nazis, she became a courier for the French Resistance. When her network was betrayed in December 1943, she escaped to Britain and joined the SOE. Left behind, her husband was captured and later tortured to death by the Nazis. In April 1944, Wake parachuted back into France and became a liaison between London and the local maquis (short for *maquisards*, or partisan group). She coordinated resistance activities before D-Day and led attacks on German installations and a Gestapo headquarters. Her 7,000 maquisards fought 22,000 SS soldiers causing 1,400 casualties.

Axis Spies

Elyesa Bazna (code-named Cicero) (1904–1970). Albanian Bazna began spying for the German SD in 1942, when he worked as valet to the British ambassador to Turkey, Sir Hughe Knatchbull-Huggessen. After photographing fifty-six secret British documents the ambassador kept in a locked dispatch box and selling them to the Germans for £20,000, he became a paid German agent. Both Hitler and his foreign minister, Joachim Von Ribbentrop, came to value the Cicero documents, which

Bazna continued to supply through early 1944. Once the British Embassy put in a new alarm system, he found it increasingly difficult to carry out his spying activities and, by February 1945, Turkey declared war on Germany and Bazna's spying career ended.

Albrecht Gustav Engels (code-named Alfredo). Engels was born in Germany and emigrated to Brazil in the 1920s. As chief engineer with German General Electric he had connections in business, military, and political circles and traveled frequently to Brazil's major industrial and

---

COUNTERINTELLIGENCE

While many spies were patriotic and dedicated to their nation's ultimate victory, the allegiance of others, particularly within the Axis, shifted as their circumstances changed or opportunities arose. One of the most successful counterintelligence operations during the war was the British Double Cross System that apprehended undercover Axis agents and "turned" them to work for the Allies.

Early in the war both the Abwehr and the SD sent undercover agents to Great Britain. A number of these agents, who arrived via parachute drops, submarines, or by traveling through neutral countries while impersonating refugees, were captured and given a choice by the MI-5— they could be hanged as spies or agree to work for the British. "Due to a combination of counter-espionage work prior to the war and signals intelligence during it, MI-5 was in a position to monitor and pick up German agents as they were 'dropped' into Britain," said J.C. Masterman, chairman of the Double Cross Committee, also known as the Twenty Committee because the Roman numerals XX formed a double cross.

The Double Cross System was originally developed to counter espionage, but over time, MI-5 realized its potential to spread strategic deceptive information. Double agents communicated a mix of real and inaccurate information, all carefully screened by the British, to their contacts in Germany through wireless telegraphy, letters written in secret ink, microphotography, and occasionally direct contact.

By 1942, most of the German spies in Britain were working as double agents, and by the last few years of the war, the British believed there were no "honest" German spies in Britain. When the British set up Operation Fortitude to weave the elaborate deception that the Allied army would invade Norway and Pas-de-Calais rather than Normandy on D-Day, the Germans were relying heavily on reports from Double Cross spies such as Juan Pujol Garcia (code-named Garbo). (See "D-Day Deceptions," p. 760.)

commercial centers. Enlisted by the Abwehr in 1939, he initially sent reports about U.S. industrial and military production and news of U.S. trade with Brazil. By 1940, he was in the center of the Abwehr's South American network, receiving reports from agents throughout the United States and Latin America about Allied ship movements, cargoes, armaments, and crew size, and forwarding the information to Berlin. Engels was arrested in Brazil in 1942 and sentenced to thirty years in prison.

Takeo Yoshikawa (code-named Tadashi Morimura) (1914–1993). A Japanese spy in Hawaii during World War II, Yoshikawa graduated top of his class at the Imperial Japanese Naval Academy. After an illness forced him to retire from the Navy, he was offered a job in Naval Intelligence and became an expert on the American Navy. While in encryption school, he intercepted a radio transmission from Australia that seventeen troopships were leaving Freetown, Sierra Leone, bound for England. The Japanese passed the information on to Nazi Germany, which attacked the ships.

In 1941 Yoshikawa received a diplomatic passport and went to Honolulu, where he rented planes to observe U.S. installations from the air. He learned which ships were in port, how heavily they were loaded, who their officers were, and what supplies were on board and sent coded messages to Tokyo every night. For a time, he posed as a Filipino and washed dishes in the American Naval Officers' Mess to listen for more information. In fall 1941, Yoshikawa passed information to Admiral Yamamoto about the ships, planes, and personnel at Pearl Harbor. On the morning of the attack, he was arrested by the FBI and later sent to an Arizona camp for Japanese Americans. He was eventually sent back to Japan in a diplomatic prisoner exchange.

LIVING BEHIND THE LINES

William Donovan, head of the U.S. Office of Strategic Services (OSS)—formerly the Coordinator of Information (COI)—had never imagined that his agency would become involved in espionage, but in September 1941 the undercover intelligence branches of the Office of Naval Intelligence (ONI) and the War Department's Intelligence Division (G-2) were placed under the OSS, along with unvouchered funds from the president's emergency fund. With this money, which was not audited in detail and could be dispensed and approved as he saw fit, Donovan had the ability to engage in clandestine operations.

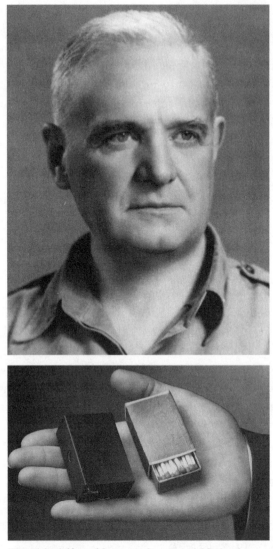

The U.S. Office of Strategic Services (OSS) head William "Wild Bill" Donovan created a Research and Development Branch within the OSS and reached out to some American businesses to develop specialty equipment for his agents. The tiny "M.B." (matchbox) camera (above) was built by the Eastman Kodak Company for the OSS and underground forces.

The year 1942 was a turning point for the OSS—its Special Operations branch began planning guerrilla operations and sabotage in Europe and Asia and placing saboteurs, guerrillas, commandos, and agents behind enemy lines. Small OSS "Operational Groups" of specially trained army soldiers fought in France, Italy, Greece, Yugoslavia, Burma, Malaya, and China, usually with partisan formations. The Secret Intelligence Branch was created to open field stations, train case officers, run agent operations, and process reports in Washington.

Because few businesses were willing to devote the time and resources to developing the specialized equipment required by undercover operatives, the OSS set up its own Research & Development Branch (R&D). The experts working in these labs developed silenced pistols, tiny cameras, wiretap devices, portable radios, and electronic beacons for agents in the field. A Maritime Unit developed specialized boats, explosives, underwater breathing gear, waterproof watches and compasses, and other equipment. The R&D staff also fabricated the papers—German and Japanese-issued ration cards, work passes, identification cards, and currency—that agents needed to live behind enemy lines and saw that each agent wore clothing sewn as if it were made in the local area where the agent would be living. The agent's eyeglasses, dental work, toothbrush, razor, briefcase, traveling bag, and shoes had to be accurate and look authentic.

Underground Warfare Method 2: Sabotage and Subversion

THE ALLIES

When the U.S. government created the Office of Strategic Services (OSS), the presidential order referred only to overseas intelligence gathering and "supplementary activities," the latter phrase a catchall for underground warfare, including psychological operations (psyops), deception, sabotage, and subversion. Churchill was not so secretive when the British created the Special Operations Executive (SOE), calling for the agency to "set Europe ablaze" through sabotage, subversion, spying, and facilitation of resistance movements in countries occupied by Axis powers. The two organizations, working both separately and together, engaged in acts of sabotage and subversion and encouraged and assisted the many indigenous groups and individuals who were resisting the Axis throughout the European and Pacific Theaters.

BELGIUM. Within a year of its occupation, Belgium was a hotbed of sabotage. Among other activities, resisters derailed trains; tossed grenades at Nazi headquarters; torched wheat- and corn-filled silos; hid nickel and copper coins rather than, as per Nazi orders, turn them in to be melted for military hardware; left lights on at night to attract Allied bombs; dynamited coal mines; and burned a metal plant.

CZECHOSLOVAKIA. Because German was a second language to most Czechs, some infiltrated and subverted the Nazi occupation leadership, even becoming fake Gestapo agents. Czechs also sabotaged trains with a rubber compound that clogged engine valves. The most famous act of sabotage occurred on May 27, 1942, when Czech army sergeants Jan Kubis and Josef Gabcik, having been trained and parachuted into the country by the SOE, ambushed and mortally wounded the "Butcher of Prague," Reinhard Heydrich, Chief of the SD. Kubis and Gabcik were arrested and executed, their severed heads kept as trophies at the Gestapo's Prague headquarters. There were other reprisals for Heydrich's assassination, including the destruction of the town of Lidice—the murder of its men and the deportation of its women and children.

DENMARK. Although the Nazis initially considered Denmark a "model protectorate," after the March 1943 mock elections the Danish resistance stepped up acts of sabotage on rail lines, shipyards, and ammunition caches, and subverted Nazi rule with labor strikes and riots. After Werner Best, the Nazi plenipotentiary, declared martial law on August 24, 1943, saboteurs blew up the Forum, a huge exhibition hall where the Nazis planned to house their troops. When the Gestapo tried to round up the 8,000 Danish Jews for deportation, resistance forces evacuated 7,200 of them to safety in Sweden. By the war's end, the resistance had carried out 2,160 operations against rail lines, 785 against German-run factories, 431 against German depots, and 167 against shipyards.

FRANCE. The first acts of resistance were by individuals, often unknown to each other. These acts included withholding letters to Germans or their collaborators, changing road signs to misdirect the occupiers, and posting widespread anti-Nazi or patriotic graffiti. Peasants hoarded guns and hid them in caves and cellars for use by resistance fighters in covert operations of sabotage and subversion. These early resisters created more irritation than actual damage but were following a basic rule of psychological warfare by letting the Germans know they were surrounded by hostile, elusive, and immeasurable forces. The complexities of French resistance moved SOE to establish six separate units in the country and in French North Africa.

HOLLAND. Working with the SOE, the De Geuzen resistance group's most successful collaborative act of sabotage came on July 16–17, 1941, when the RAF bombed Rotterdam harbor as it was filled with German cargo ships.

NORWAY. The SOE worked with the Milorg, an underground army, on numerous acts of sabotage and subversion, including the coordinated destruction of 100 German ships in harbors all over Norway in January 1942. Their most successful sabotage was of the Norsk Hydro works (see "Actually Underground" later in this chapter). Another sabotage, on February 20, 1944, sent a ferry carrying the remaining supplies of heavy water (required for the creation of nuclear weapons) to the bottom of Lake Tinnsjo. The Gestapo killed 336 resisters of the Home Front organization while 2,000 others died in custody and 40,000 were put in prison.

POLAND. The Nazi atrocities committed under Nazi governor of occupied Poland's General Government, Hans Frank, and Robert Ley, head of the Nazi German Labor Front, were among the worst in the war. Thus, the resistance struggle was a fight to the death; reprisals against saboteurs were severe and merciless. After Germany attacked the Soviet Union in June 1941, the Polish resistance went into high gear. Guerrilla activity by the 250,000-strong Armie Krajowie (AK) included sabotage of transplanted German industries and rail shipments and attacks on Gestapo officials. Resistance stiffened into direct combat clashes with the Wehrmacht and Nazi police, as well. The AK and other resistance groups, including the anti-Communist Narodowe Sily Zbrojne (NZS), killed as many as 1,000 Germans a month by early 1944 (compared with 300 per month in 1942).

SOVIET UNION. Partisans in the Soviet Union employed a "scorched-earth" policy toward the Germans that included blowing up bridges, rail lines, telephone and telegraph poles, and enemy ammunition dumps. In 1943, partisans caused 3,200 rail accidents, destroyed 260 bridges, and killed 36,000 Germans in Ukraine alone.

YUGOSLAVIA. The political situation was complicated by years of enmity among various factions in Yugoslavia, a collage of cultures, languages, and religions since 1918. The SOE and OSS collaborated with both the Chetniks (Serbian anticommunists) and the Partisans (Communists) (see "Major Guerrilla/Resistance Groups" chart, later in this chapter), and resistance groups that also fought each other. Acts of sabotage and subversion against the Axis occupation were widespread and often vicious, though similar acts of what were later called "ethnic cleansing" occurred among the Yugoslavian resistance.

THE AXIS

Axis organizations such as the Abwehr and the Kempeitai (see "Axis Intelligence Organizations" chart in this chapter) also engaged in acts of sabotage and subversion. One entire wing of the Abwehr (Division II, headed by Colonel Erwin von Lahousen-Vivremont) was devoted to sabotage and was partly responsible for facilitating Hitler's swift takeovers of Czechoslovakia and Poland and the success of the initial phase of the invasion of the Soviet Union. However, once Germany and Japan overran and occupied huge swaths of Europe and Asia, the nature of the conflict shifted. The need for German sabotage and subversion decreased while sabotage and subversion became the most effective tool at the disposal of those living under Axis control.

Underground Warfare Method 3: Deception

Since the time the Greek Army was said to have deceived and conquered the Trojans with a wooden horse, armies have used deceptive techniques to defeat their enemies. Over time, this art of tricking the enemy into doing or not doing something to weaken his position and aid the deceivers has grown to include camouflage, dummies and decoys, and disinformation campaigns using false radio broadcasts, leaflets and propaganda, and rumors circulated specifically to mislead.

Through a variety of techniques, combatants attempted to camouflage troops and equipment so they could not be seen from the air. The Soviet airplane (above) and the Japanese plane under attack on Boeroe Island (below) are both camouflaged, more or less successfully, by netting, branches, and hay.

CAMOUFLAGE

Camouflage is one of the oldest forms of deception, but after the advent of the airplane in World War I, it became an art form. To defend against enemy attacks, each combatant had to consider what things looked like from the air. For the first time, cities, factories, and airfields well behind the front lines were at risk. During World War II, combatants used camouflage in increasingly sophisticated ways. In Britain, more than 600 airfields were camouflaged with paint and artificial hedges. The Germans covered parts of Berlin's Tiergarten and Unter den Linden with huge camouflage nets and disguised the central business district in Hamburg so it looked like the terrain in the countryside. Both sides drained lakes and covered curves in rivers with netting to disguise landmarks so they could not be used as navigational aids by incoming aircraft and hid antiaircraft guns under fake barns, farmhouses, and haystacks. All major combatants trained their troops to conceal themselves, and camouflage uniforms were standard issue. Military organizations routinely painted armaments and buildings to match the climate and terrain or covered them with netting, branches, or hay. (See "Civil Defense" in Chapter 3 and "Camouflage, Decoys, and Deception" in Chapter 5.)

DECOYS AND DUMMIES

While decoys and dummies were widely used by both sides, the British took this deceptive technique to new levels. During the Battle of Britain, they created hundreds of fake docks, factories, shipyards, and supply depots to draw thousands of tons of enemy bombs. Their decoy airfields, lit at night, were so effective they actually drew more Luftwaffe bombs than the real RAF air bases. The British also successfully used fake gun batteries along the English coast and wood and canvas decoy tanks in the North African desert to exaggerate their defensive and offensive might. Since plopping a decoy tank in the desert sand would hardly create an accurate illusion from the air, the British developed a device that could be pulled behind a truck to leave what looked like tank tracks in the ground leading up to a decoy. By 1944, the British and U.S. militaries had lightweight, portable inflatable dummies for all weapons systems.

The RAF dropped another British invention, dummy paratroopers, over occupied Europe. From below, the two-foot-tall devices, which popped like gunfire when they hit the ground, looked like an invading force as they floated down against the sky.

Sonic subterfuge was also employed by special units, such as the U.S. 23rd Headquarters Special Troops and similar Soviet units. Moving very close to the front lines at night in trucks equipped with loud speakers, these units would play amplified recordings of approaching tanks or other sounds calculated to keep the enemy off balance.

To initiate and orchestrate deception in North Africa, the British established the "A-force" and hired famous illusionist and magician Jasper Maskelyne to devise and construct elaborate decoys and deceptions. Working with his team, nicknamed the "Magic Gang," Major Maskelyne used oil drums, canvas, pipes, cables, paint, and the remains of bombed railway cars to create four full-scale dummy submarines that were floated on railroad ties. The Luftwaffe later attacked and sank one of these decoys, a tribute to its success.

For one of his more elaborate hoaxes, in the summer of 1941 Maskelyne disguised the harbor at Alexandria, a city of 1 million Egyptians and a major British port that was the target of nightly Luftwaffe raids. Using photos of

Alexandria's harbor at night, the Magic Gang set up a similar light pattern at Maryut Bay, one mile down the coast. Two hundred army engineers and craftsman created canvas ship structures and lit them, placed lanterns in the sand and mud, constructed dozens of small buildings out of plywood, and packed them with explosives. They also trucked rubble throughout the real Alexandria and covered it with tarpaulins, painted bomb craters on plywood, and made thousands of papier-mâché bricks. They even moved antiaircraft guns down the beach to meet the attacking planes from the fake city.

OPERATION MINCEMEAT AND THE MAN WHO NEVER WAS

On April 30, 1943, a Spanish fisherman pulled the body of British Major William Martin from the sea off Huelva, Spain. The major, dressed as a Royal Marine, had a briefcase attached to his wrist containing personal papers and a letter detailing an impending Allied invasion of Greece. Spanish authorities notified the Abwehr who were active in the area and, after examining the corpse and papers, the Abwehr passed the information back to Berlin. Believing the documents to be authentic, the German High Command moved quickly to fortify the Greek coast, leaving the actual Allied target, Sicily, in a more vulnerable position for the invasion, which commenced on July 9 (see "Operation Husky" in Chapter 7).

This deception operation, code-named Mincemeat, was conceived by naval intelligence officer Lieutenant Commander Ewen Montagu, a member of the British Double Cross Committee (see "Counterintelligence," earlier in this chapter). Using the corpse of a 34-year-old man who had recently died of pneumonia, Montagu created a false military identity and packed his briefcase with personal items—letters from his bank manager and his father, overdue bills, a military I.D. card, theater tickets, money, love letters—along with the fake invasion letter. The body was then packed in dry ice and taken by submarine to Spain where "Martin" was dropped into the sea near the Spanish port of Huelva.

While the Abwehr was inspecting and photographing the body and papers, Britain demanded that Spain return Martin and his briefcase, which it eventually did. Martin was buried in Huelva with full military honors, and *The Times* included his name in the casualty lists. In London, a detailed examination proved the letters had been opened, read, and carefully resealed. Within days of Martin's appearance on the Spanish coast, British cryptanalysts intercepted Enigma messages from German High Command telling an Admiral in Greece to reinforce his defenses. Hitler also sent a Panzer division to Greece from France and a group of motor torpedo boats from Sicily to the Aegean Sea.

When word came that a German bomber force was approaching, Alexandria was blacked out and Maskelyne lit the lights at Maryut Bay. As the Luftwaffe dropped its bombs on the phony harbor, Maskelyne set off the explosives planted in the fake buildings. As soon as the bombers left, the Royal Engineers put out the fires and replaced destroyed buildings, lights, and shrubs with more decoys. Hundreds of crew members scrambled to uncover the rubble and painted bomb craters they had planted throughout Alexandria so German reconnaissance planes would believe the city had been hit. For the next eight nights, Luftwaffe bombers returned and attacked Maryut and each day the British replaced the destruction at Maryut and created wreckage in Alexandria.

DISINFORMATION

Information designed to create confusion and break an enemy's morale—disinformation—is at the heart of deception. All major combatants used various disinformation techniques from dropping leaflets, to airing radio broadcasts designed to simulate an enemy's own station, to planting false information with agents. The British created a German "newspaper for the troops" that presented itself as a newspaper from Berlin and dropped it on Germany every day at 6:00 A.M. Their "Radio Deutschland" station was disguised as a German resistance group broadcasting out of Germany. (For more information on disinformation, see Chapter 10.)

On the Eastern Front, the Soviet Union made "maskirovka"—measures to mislead the enemy about their military objectives, strategy, operations, or readiness—a key component of its tactical and strategic planning. The Soviets moved troops and equipment by night or used smoke screens to hide real and staged troop movements, placed decoys and diversionary forces to indicate troop buildups where there actually were none, and spread misinformation via radio channels they knew the Germans monitored and through false stories to the local population. In time, they mastered techniques to deceive the Germans about where they planned to attack next, forcing the Reich to leave troops in unnecessary positions, and then surprised the Germans by the location and scope of numerous attacks. In the summer of 1945, as they prepared to enter the war against Japan, the Soviets secretly transported an entire front (an army group, this one comprising a total of 700,000 men) from Europe to eastern Asia. As a result of such operations, the Germans, as well as the Japanese in Manchuria, continually underestimated the size of the Soviet forces.

Above, Allies use inflatable armaments, including inflatable rubber Sherman tanks, as part of their large pre-D-Day deception, Operation Fortitude. Below, U.S. forces use a smoke screen to hide paratroopers landing on New Guinea.

ACTUALLY UNDERGROUND

Few places on the earth went untouched by World War II; a few places under the earth played a role in the war as well.

Allied Bunkers

Churchill and his staff sought safety underground by moving the Cabinet War Rooms to chambers beneath the Cabinet Office. Churchill's retreat within this subterranean haven was a tiny cubbyhole with a lavatory-type latch that indicated "Vacant" or "Engaged" where the prime minister would retreat to telephone Roosevelt in Washington. In November 1942, Eisenhower had his own underground command post on Gibraltar, the headquarters of the British Mediterranean Command. From there, he oversaw the successful Allied invasion of North Africa.

Nazi Bunkers

A multi-leveled complex of rooms fifty feet below the garden of the Chancellery in Berlin formed the underground command bunker that Hitler used at the end of the war. The first level contained 12 rooms for servants and the kitchen. The next level down was the Führerbunker, an 18-room complex with offices and living quarters for Hitler and his mistress (and, near the end, his wife), Eva Braun; they committed suicide here on April 30, 1945. There were other underground bunkers in Berlin for Nazi officials. Martin Bormann and his staff resided in a bunker below the Party Chancellery while Goebbels and his staff initially took shelter in the Propaganda Ministry's cellars.

Subterranean Atomic Research

The main source of "heavy water" (water made with an isotope of hydrogen called deuterium and used in nuclear fission) was the Norsk Hydro-Electric plant in Norway, a country occupied by the Germans. Norsk Hydro was housed on a nearly impenetrable fjord with a series of tunnels and cellars leading to the main installation. In 1943, in a strikingly brave act of sabotage, Norwegian commandos trained by British intelligence halted the plant's production with a few well-placed grenades. Under orders from General Leslie Groves, the head of the Manhattan Project, which was developing the U.S. atomic bomb, American planes dropped 1,300 tons of high explosive and incendiary bombs there on March 15, 1945, slowing the Nazis' progress toward building their own nuclear weapon. In Germany, an atomic research facility was housed in an alleged bombproof wine cellar at Oranienburg, just north of Berlin. A thorium ore processing plant above the facility, the former Auer Factory, manufactured uranium metals for use in Germany's A-bomb research.

Underground Factories in Germany

In 1944, the Nazis constructed, with foreign (i.e., slave) labor, a vast subterranean work camp at Wansleben am See, seventy-five miles from Buchenwald. The SS had 300 workers from the concentration camps dig several underground chambers and lowered equipment into the chasm. Here in three around-the-clock shifts, Polish, French, and Russian laborers made weapons for the Nazi war effort. The SS also used these tunnels to hide stolen art and German artifacts, rare books, and the letters of Johann Goethe.

Maltese Caves

Situated near Italian shipping lanes in the Mediterranean, Malta was in the middle of the action and the target of regular bombing raids by Axis warplanes. (See material on "The Siege of Malta" in Chapters 6 and 7.) Its ancient geological features, consisting of numerous coastal caves and underground chambers, made it ideal for hiding war-related activities from the Axis powers. The archaeologically important Ghar Dalam Cave was used as a deep air raid shelter and an underground fuel storage depot.

Army Living Spaces

The safest haven for American troops and civilians in the Philippines was on "the Rock," the fort on Corregidor Island at the mouth of Manila Harbor. Running through the middle of the Rock was Malinta Tunnel, completed in 1934, a man-made passage through the bottom of 390-foot Malinta Hill. A trolley line wound around the outside of the hill on hairpin turns,

carrying passengers from "Topside" to "Bottomside." These trolley lines were later extended inside the tunnel. With an 800-foot-long main corridor, the tunnel resembled a giant anthill lit by blue mercury vapor lights. At various levels along its tall ceilings were assorted departments, including the hospital and General Douglas MacArthur's headquarters. After the Japanese bombing attack on Corregidor on December 29, 1941, MacArthur moved his USAFFE (United States Army Forces–Far East) headquarters from the Topside Barracks to Lateral Three in the Malinta Tunnel. Manuel Quezon's second inauguration as president of the Philippine Commonwealth occurred inside Malinta Tunnel on December 30, 1941, while bombs and artillery shells fell outside.

American troops found it virtually impossible to dig foxholes or conceal themselves below ground in the powdery volcanic ash while under enemy fire on islands such as Iwo Jima and Okinawa, but the Japanese facing them had, over time, created a virtual city of tunnels, caves, and pillboxes below the ground, complete with ventilator shafts and escape routes. As *Time* magazine noted, "All the explosives in the world could hardly have reached them." They could hold out for months but could be killed by cave-in, grenade, or flamethrower. (See also "Fortifications" in Chapter 5.)

D-DAY DECEPTIONS

The most elaborate, successful, and crucial Allied deception of World War II, code-named Fortitude South, deceived the Germans into believing the Normandy invasion was but a precursor to the main Allied invasion, which would take place six weeks later on the Pas de

Calais, two hundred miles to the east. Using all the deception techniques the Allies had honed over the previous years, including dummy aircraft, landing craft, and troops; false radio broadcasts; misdirection; stories planted with double agents; and the creation of a fake army group, the Allies created the illusion of a large invasion force stationed in southeast England. When coupled with the camouflaged and hidden invasion force to the west, the simulated signals traffic between illusionary divisions, the Allied bombing of Pas de Calais beaches, and the tight security clamped on the press and diplomats, the plan convinced the Germans to keep thousands of men stationed in the wrong place for weeks even after the Allies had landed in Normandy. (See also "Operation Overlord" in Chapter 7.)

A strikingly successful part of the plan involved the First United States Army Group (FUSAG) supposedly located in southeast England poised to invade the Pas de Calais. Details about the activities and strength of this wholly fictional army group and the name of its commander, General George Patton, were leaked to the Germans through double agents and radio transmissions that were so convincing that the Germans believed until three weeks after D-Day that the Allies still had 30 divisions stationed in southeast England.

Fake signals intelligence and information from double agents persuaded the Luftwaffe to carry out minimum photo reconnaissance in the weeks leading up to D-Day. The dummy landing craft and airplanes and fake lighting actually had little to do with the overall deception.

Meanwhile, the other component of this pre-D-Day deception, Fortitude North, based in Scotland, also used fake armies and radio broadcasts, double agents, and physical deception to lead the Germans to believe that the Allies were going to invade Norway. This, too, was successful: the Germans left several extra divisions in Norway to guard against this fake invasion.

Resistance Movements, Partisans, and Underground Political Organizations

Early in the war, journalist Curt Riess wrote about Europe, "Never has it happened before that a whole continent went underground." Though at first the world was stunned by the swiftness with which Hitler, Mussolini, and the Japanese military achieved their "New Order," citizens in each of the conquered countries resisted the occupation almost from the outset. In most countries, resistance began slowly, with spontaneous acts of disrespect or noncompliance. As forces grew more organized and communication lines opened among them, as well as with exiled governments and intelligence services like the SOE, the resistance became a formidable threat to Axis rule. Resistance groups staged violent confrontations, sniper attacks, and labor strikes; sabotaged train lines, bridges, and factories;

produced underground newspapers and pirate radio broadcasts; and concealed goods that would aid the occupiers. At grave risk to themselves, their families, and neighbors, these often unknown, unnamed resistance fighters (anonymity and pseudonyms assured secrecy) had a huge impact on the war's outcome.

The diverse ethnic and political makeups of some resistance groups complicated the main priority of defeating and expelling Axis forces. Some movements were organized mainly to defeat the Axis, but those in Bulgaria, Romania, Poland, Greece, Belgium, France, and China also sought to change the prewar status quo and were fraught with internecine politics and ideological squabbles.

MAJOR GUERRILLA/RESISTANCE GROUPS

European Theater

Belgium

Armée Secrète (AS)

The AS grew out of the Belgian Legion, formed in 1940, and by 1944 membership topped 45,000. It sabotaged the infrastructure in occupied Belgium and gathered intelligence on German troop movement for exile groups and the SOE.

Czechoslovakia

Czech National Committee, the government-in-exile, headed by President Eduard Benes. Jan Masaryk led its resistance from London

Czech patriots went underground, exhorted by exiled leaders in London via the BBC. By spring 1942, 15 underground Czech radio transmitters sent out news, one (Nazdar) audible from England. Sabotage and defiance were widespread. Of the Czechs, Himmler said, "We are dealing with a nation of 10 million traitors and saboteurs."

France

Conseil National de la Resistance (CNR), or the National Council of the Resistance, led by Jean Moulin under orders from Charles de Gaulle; after Moulin's death in July 1943, CNR was led by Georges Bidault

The resistance to Nazi occupation in France was large but widespread and not organized into one unit. The CNR was the attempt at an "umbrella" organization, under which the disparate groups could focus on the German occupiers and the Vichy collaborators. Given the passionate disagreements existing between resistance groups—many wanting to change the status quo in France after the war—it is a tribute to Moulin's leadership that he was able to organize the CNR at all. Trained by

MAJOR GUERRILLA/RESISTANCE GROUPS (CONTINUED)

In late August 1944, with Allied forces still more than fifty miles outside Paris, communist and Gaullist resistance fighters in the city rose up, capturing a police station, building barricades, and attacking Germans with small arms and homemade bombs.

the SOE, he gathered leaders from the *Armée Secrète, Comité d'Action Socialiste, Francs-Tireur, Front National,* and *Libération* under the CNR and held its first official meeting on May 27, 1943. He was arrested soon after by the Gestapo and tortured so severely he died of his injuries.

Combat, formed and led by Henri Frenay

Combat comprised soldiers and intellectuals (including the philosophers Albert Camus and Jean-Paul Sartre) who engaged in sabotage. The group also published a widely distributed and influential resistance newspaper that ran information to counter Nazi propaganda and mobilize clandestine activities.

Défense de la France

A group of Sorbonne students who produced an underground newspaper that survived throughout the occupation. The group also engaged in spying, set up escape routes for fugitives, and produced false identification documents for resistance members.

Front National (FN or National Front), led by Pierre Villon; Francs-Tireurs et Partisans (Français) (FTP)

The FN was founded by the French Communist Party in May 1942 with the FTP as its military wing.

(continued)

MAJOR GUERRILLA/RESISTANCE GROUPS (CONTINUED)

Greece

Ethnikon Apeleftherotikon Metopon (EAM) with its military, the *Ethnikos Laikos Apeleftherotikon Stratos* (ELAS), led by the fanatical Athanasios Klaras (aka Aris Velouchiotis) and the more moderate Colonel Stephanos Saraphis

With Axis occupation troops from Italy, Germany, and Bulgaria in disarray, conditions were ripe for underground activity in Greece. But rival Greek resistance groups rarely found common ground and often fought each other. By the end of the war, the EAM, a communist-led coalition of six parties, was dominant. After liberation, EAM's Allied backing was rescinded and shifted to George Papandreou's republican government, an act that added fuel to an already smoldering civil war.

Ethnikos Dimkratikas Ellinikos Syndesmas (EDES) led by Colonel Napoleon Zervas

A conservative nationalist faction that engaged in guerrilla attacks and sabotage, with British advice and backing, against the Axis, ELAS, and the Chams (pro-Axis Albanian refugees).

Holland

De Geuzen (The Beggars), led by "Colonel Verdun" (a pseudonym)

The leading Dutch resistance group, de Geuzen, engaged in sabotage, strikes, and destruction of supplies, and worked with British intelligence to help coordinate RAF bombings.

Norway

Home Front, with a military wing, *Militar Organisaasjonen* (Milorg) led by Colonel Otto Ruge, named commander in chief of Norway's army by exiled King Haakon VII

The Home Front included a civil section to raise public morale through publications and radio broadcasts. The Milorg comprised about 45,000 troops and worked closely with the SOE.

"Nortraship"

The name given to the merchant fleet of 1,000 ships and 25,000 seamen in the service of the Norwegian government-in-exile.

Poland

Armie Krajowie (AK); Home Army

Headquartered in Warsaw, Poland's Home Army had 250,000 troops that fought the Nazi occupiers and, after the war, the Soviets.

Soviet Union

Partisans

On July 3, 1941, Stalin challenged his people to "foment guerrilla warfare everywhere." Partisans, with the intermittent backing of the Soviet government, relentlessly attacked invading Germans, burned crops, and removed food, transports, fuel, and livestock to keep the matériel from falling into German

MAJOR GUERRILLA/RESISTANCE GROUPS (CONTINUED)

hands. Partisans often worked in small units behind German lines to create havoc. (See also "USSR" in Chapter 4.)

Ukrainian Insurgent Army (UPA)

The UPA attacked German troops, fought for Ukraine independence after the war, and battled Polish insurgents seeking to reclaim land taken by the Soviets. In the Ukrainian-Polish war within World War II, 32,000 Poles were killed and 200,000 forced out of the territory.

Yugoslavia

Chetniks, led by Colonel Draja Mihailovich

The first Yugoslavian resistance group to take on German and Italian occupation troops. Mainly Serbs, the Chetniks were nationalist, royalist, and anticommunist; after Allied support went to the Partisans, they collaborated with the Nazis.

Partisans, led by Josip Broz (Tito)

The Partisan slogan was "Death to Fascism, Liberty to the People." Their ruthlessness in fighting Axis troops prompted the Allies to shift their support from the Chetniks to the Partisans. Both the OSS and the British assisted them. Partisans also fought Chetniks and the Ustashi (an extreme ring-wing Croatian group allied with the Axis that killed thousands of Serbs, Jews, and Gypsies; see Chapter 8) for control of Yugoslavia. After the war, Tito became president of Yugoslavia.

Pacific Theater

Burma

Kachin Rangers, led by Zhing Htaw Naw and trained by OSS Detachment 101

Kachin tribal people were fierce warriors based in the thick forests and precipitous river valleys in northern Burma. Trained by the OSS to operate radio transmitters, the Kachins helped Allies like "Merrill's Marauders" destroy Japanese airfields, rail lines, bridges, and communications, as well as rescue downed airmen. The Kachins helped the OSS drive the Japanese out of northern Burma, earning a citation in 1946 from then Army Chief of Staff Dwight Eisenhower: "Alternating frontal attacks with guerrilla tactics, the Kachin Rangers remained in constant contact with the enemy . . . and persistently cut him down and demoralized him . . . leading to complete victory against an overwhelmingly superior force."

Indochina

Viet Minh, led by Ho Chi Minh

Communist, anti-Japanese guerrillas based in the north who ultimately wanted an end to French colonial rule. After the collapse of the French, the Viet Minh were the only pro-Allied movement of any consequence in the country. OSS agents supplied Ho and trained Viet Minh troops, but the United States backed away at French behest after the war.

(continued)

MAJOR GUERRILLA/RESISTANCE GROUPS (CONTINUED)

Kachin natives in Burma, trained and equipped by the Americans and British, worked as scouts, raiders, guides, and resistance fighters against the Japanese.

Siam

Free Thai Army, students trained by OSS Detachment 404

The Japanese considered Siam, with its pro-Axis prime minister, "friendly," meeting only passive resistance to occupation. Siamese students in the United States who formed the FTA were trained by the OSS in Ceylon. The FTA agents went into Siam and contacted the anti-Japanese underground, including army and government officials; they subsequently produced intelligence that covered all aspects of political, military, economic, and social affairs.

The Philippines

People's Anti-Japanese Army (*Hukbo ng Bayan Laban Sa Hapon*) also called Hukbalahaps, or "Huks," led by Luis Taruc; and President Quezon's own guerrillas

Guerrilla organizations in the Philippines included bands of stranded U.S. and Filipino soldiers who operated in northern Luzon and President Quezon's own guerrillas in southern Luzon. The Marxist-leaning Huks, who operated chiefly in central Luzon, were the largest group. They established radio contact with MacArthur in Australia and supplied the Allies with valuable intelligence. U.S. submarines supplied the guerrillas with radios and commando support.

SPECIAL EDITIONS—THE UNDERGROUND PRESS

Most occupied countries in Europe used underground publications to maintain national morale and facilitate resistance work, even though creating, distributing, owning, or reading these publications warranted severe punishment from the Gestapo or Milice (French secret police). In France, Henri Frenay founded one of the first resistance publications (*Les Petites Ailes de France*). Regular themes of the French underground press were German war losses and exploitation of local resources; instructions for conducting successful sabotage; methods of

Resistance newspapers like the long-lived French paper Combat *disseminated news in occupied countries about German defeats and Allied bombings and gave readers information about how to commit acts of sabotage and hide material from the Nazis. In London, the Polish government-in-exile published pamphlets featuring photos smuggled out of occupied Poland to alert the West to the horrors taking place under the Nazis. The pamphlets, published as early as 1941, warned readers that the Germans were determined to annihilate the Polish nation and it was time to "Stop Them Now."*

hiding matériel from the Nazis; work stoppages and slowdowns; and Allied bombing successes. In Belgium, underground papers such as *La Libre Belgique* were vital, as the Nazis had seized *Le Soir*, Brussels' biggest daily newspaper, and used it as a propaganda organ. Two days after the Nazis invaded Holland on May 15, 1940, the first underground newspaper, *Action de la Gueux*, began printing; by 1941, Holland had 120 underground papers. In Denmark, 538 underground papers published a total of 24 million copies by 1945. Even bitterly ravaged Poland had 60 underground papers by December 1939, most printed on hand-cranked presses.

NOTABLE RESISTANCE LEADERS

The anonymity of many in the underground makes it difficult to document all acts and campaigns undertaken. Pseudonyms, too, make identities hard to trace. "Colonel Verdun," for example, is still the only name by which most people know the head of de Geuzen in Holland; most of the French leaders had aliases and constantly changed them. In many cases, acts of bravery by ordinary people were noted only by their last name—in Prague's Skoda works, a vat of molten lead was overturned on 22 members of a German army commission, killing 14; the resistance perpetrator was a crane worker named Vacek, who died from a fall in the plant. Several prominent resistance leaders whose contributions are known are listed below.

Lucie Aubrac (1912–2007). A schoolteacher in Lyon, France. Though pregnant in 1943, she planned and took part in commando raids to free comrades, including her husband, from notorious Gestapo officer Klaus Barbie's prison in Lyon and worked with the maquis (short for *maquis-ards*, or partisans) to sabotage rail lines in southern France.

Georges Begue (1911–1993). The first British SOE agent dropped in France (May 5, 1941). Under the cover name George Noble, he set up radio communications, served as the contact person for other agents parachuted into Vichy France, and helped facilitate the work of 400 SOE agents sent to serve as sabotage and arms instructors to resistance fighters and radio operators. Begue escaped arrest and made his way back to England via Spain, serving as Signals Officer for the SOE.

Claire Chevrillon (1907–). Under the code name Christiane Clouet, the Parisian Chevrillon joined the resistance when members of her Jewish family were imprisoned and deported. She served mainly as a liaison between the Free French government in London and resistance operatives in Paris who were loyal to Charles de Gaulle. Arrested in 1943, she spent four months in Fresnes prison near Paris.

Ho Chi Minh (1890–1969). Vietnamese communist leader whose Viet Minh provided the only serious resistance to the Japanese occupation of Indochina during the war. He fought for an end to Japanese occupation and freedom from French colonial rule.

Victor de Laveleye (1894–1945). Brussels lawyer and member of the Belgian Parliament who went into exile in London, where he worked with the resistance. In a BBC broadcast to Belgium on January 14, 1941, he urged resistance fighters to scrawl "V" all over the country. As a result, "V" became resistance shorthand: "victoire" for the Walloons (French-speaking Belgians) and "vrijheid" for those who spoke Flemish.

Jean Moulin (1899–1943). Representative of the French Committee for National Liberation (CFLN), known as *Max* in the field and *Rex* to the SOE, who united France's fragmented resistance movements between 1941 and 1943. In June 1943, Moulin was captured by the Gestapo and tortured by the notorious Klaus Barbie. Refusing to yield any information, Moulin died from his injuries in July while being transported to Germany.

Major Carl Szokoll (1915–2004). Infantry officer who served as the German Resistance Circle's contact person and coconspirator in Austria. After the failed July 20, 1944, attack on Hitler (see p. 771), he was charged with seizing power in Vienna and arresting SS and Nazi officials—which he had done, not knowing the coup had failed. Somehow he avoided punishment. Toward the end of the year, he worked with the O5, the largest Austrian resistance group, to liberate Vienna with as little bloodshed as possible when Allied troops approached.

NEUTRAL NATIONS

Through shrewd diplomacy and self-protective mobilization, some major nations—Switzerland, Spain, Portugal, Sweden, Ireland, Turkey, and Argentina—remained neutral throughout the war and thus escaped the ravages of combat. Yet neutral nations often did lean toward one side or the other; they traded with both Axis and Allied nations and served as rendezvous points for intelligence agencies working through diplomatic or military attaché fronts. They were also magnets for displaced people, POWs, and refugees. Switzerland was headquarters of the lifesaving International Red Cross. As did Spain and Sweden, Switzerland also served as a "protecting power" throughout the war. (A protecting power is a neutral state that protects the interests of one or more belligerent nations and performs such functions as inspecting POW camps.) Portugal, Switzerland, and Spain provided safe havens for people involved in resistance movements, as well as bases for Axis and Allied spies. Lisbon was an escape route, via regular flights, to New York and London. Sweden, whose economy boomed with Axis trade (it supplied Germany with much iron ore) was also the site of meetings between German and British representatives hoping to negotiate terms early in the war. Moreover, Sweden sheltered 200,000 displaced Europeans, and its government spent $150 million to help them once they were on Swedish soil. Many POW exchanges were also transacted through Sweden.

Resistance within the Axis

GERMANY

The fear engendered by Hitler's burgeoning police state, which had informers at every level of society—provincial (Gau), district (Kreis), precinct (Bezirk), and block—makes it hard to gauge the actual extent of resistance in Germany. After the Venlo incident of November 9, 1939, in which British agents were deceived, captured, and interrogated by Gestapo agents who had lured them to a meeting by claiming to be anti-Hitler resistance fighters, Germans claiming to be anti-Nazi were treated with skepticism by the Allies. Nonetheless, a resistance movement existed. Clergyman, philosopher, and author Dietrich Bonhoeffer was one of its pivotal figures. Two days after Hitler became chancellor in 1933, Bonhoeffer made a national radio address in which he called Hitler a "misleader" and stated that, by making an idol of himself, the führer "mocks God." That same year, he supported fellow anti-Nazi pastor Martin Niemoller when Niemoller founded the Pastors Emergency League. He also helped Niemoller establish a new Confessing Church that remained free of Nazi influences for a time. In August 1937, the Himmler Decree prohibited the training of Confessing ministers and, in September, the Gestapo closed down Bonhoeffer's seminary at Finkenwalde and forbade him to speak in public or publish. Two months later, when the Gestapo arrested 27 of his seminarians, the movement went underground. Between February 1941 and July 1942, Bonhoeffer traveled widely outside Germany, visiting Switzerland, the United States, and Sweden to get support for the resistance and its plan to overthrow or kill Hitler. On April 5, 1943, he was arrested. He was hanged at Flossenbürg concentration camp on April 9, 1945.

An organization known as the Weisse Rose (White Rose) also resisted the Nazis. This group of Munich University students led by siblings Sophie and Hans Scholl wrote, printed, and distributed anti-Nazi pamphlets between June 1942 and February 1943, when it was ruthlessly smashed by the Nazis. The six main White Rose members were arrested and guillotined; others were imprisoned.

The greatest internal threat to Hitler came from the senior military officers who belonged to the same loosely organized group of anti-Nazis (including aristocrats, diplomats, and clergymen) as did Bonhoeffer; the Gestapo dubbed the group the *Schwarze Kapelle*, or "Black Orchestra." Prominent among the military members of the group were Ludwig Beck, former chief of the army general staff; Abwehr (military intelligence) chief Admiral Wilhelm Canaris; and Colonel Hans Oster, who was Canaris's assistant. Canaris, along with Bonhoeffer's brother-in-law, Hans von Dohnanyi, a lawyer in a key post in the Ministry of Justice who developed a record of Nazi criminal offenses, and General Erwin Lahousen, an Abwehr officer, participated in planning a March 13, 1944, attempt on Hitler's life. "Operation Flash" was actually carried out by Major General Henning von Tresckow, chief of staff of the Eastern-Front Army Group Center, and his subordinate, Fabian von Schlabrendorff—with the unwitting assistance of a staff officer, Colonel

TARGET HITLER—A FINAL ATTEMPT TO KILL THE FÜHRER

Early on July 20, 1944, German Colonel Claus von Stauffenberg flew from Berlin to Wolfschanze (Wolf's Lair, Hitler's retreat) where he was to attend Hitler's daily situation briefing. He carried a briefcase containing two bombs wired to a delay fuse. Once at Wolfschanze, Stauffenberg retired to a lounge and attempted to activate both two-pound bombs while his aide, Lieutenant Werner von Haeften, assisted and watched the door. Because they were interrupted, Stauffenberg could only activate one of the bombs before going into the briefing room. After asking to be seated near Hitler because he had lost some of his hearing in combat, Stauffenberg placed the briefcase under the table in front of him and left the meeting "to make a phone call." Instead, he and Haeften went to an awaiting car. A minute later, at 12:50 P.M., the bomb detonated and Stauffenberg, thinking he had killed Hitler, contacted his fellow conspirators and gave them the code word "Valkyrie," which indicated that the führer was dead and they could proceed with their anti-Nazi coup.

Though three people at the meeting died from their injuries and most had their eardrums damaged, Hitler survived with cuts and bruises. The conspirators, not realizing this, continued with their plot. Led by Stauffenberg and Friedrich Fromm, they appointed a new commander in chief of the Home Army (General Hoepner), had Gestapo leaders arrested in Paris and prepared to execute them, and occupied some radio stations. By 6:30 that evening, however, radio stations under Nazi control announced the failed attempt on Hitler's life and by midnight, the coup collapsed. Most of the plotters were quickly rounded up; four leaders (Stauffenberg, Haeften, Mertz von Quirnheim, and Olbricht) were immediately arrested and shot. Fromm was arrested and later shot. Hundreds of other people were detained, and a "People's Court" tried and convicted 200 people, who were executed soon after sentencing. The first few dozen executions were filmed so Hitler could watch them.

Heinz Brandt. The operation began when Brandt carried a package, supposedly containing two gift bottles of brandy but actually containing bombs, onto the führer's plane. But the bombs failed to detonate in flight as planned. (They were later recovered by one of the conspirators.) Another attempt, set for March 21, was foiled by a last-minute change in Hitler's schedule. The third attempt on Hitler's life (see box on p. 771) came closest to achieving its goal.

ITALY

From the beginning of Mussolini's reign in the 1920s, socialists and communists resisted his Fascist regime and were arrested and murdered by the thousands. A core of 150,000 anti-fascist émigrés assisted much of the opposition by funding resistance efforts. Acts of sabotage included explosions in munitions plants, arson at granaries, destruction of irrigation systems, derailment of trains, work slowdowns, strikes, and the hiding of grain, milk, and butter. During World War II, as Italy came increasingly under German influence, SS chief Heinrich Himmler may have had more power in Italy than Mussolini. Many of the most repressive measures imposed on Italians were enacted by the Nazi officials who had infiltrated every level of Italian government. Although Il Duce had his own secret police, OVRA (see "Secret Service and Intelligence Organizations" chart, p. 708), he had to contend with an Italian underground comprising socialists (sometimes called the Matteotti group after the leader, who was murdered by Mussolini in 1924), communists, and Giustizia e Libertà, a liberal group led by Count Carlo Sforza. All three groups united in October 1941 under the name "Italian Union for Action and Freedom," releasing a manifesto that demanded, "Mussolini's betrayal of his country must cease. We address our appeal to the liberal, democratic, Catholic, and other religious groups . . . to those who no longer want to share the terrible responsibility for the present policy of the Fascist government, to those betrayed by Fascist propaganda." After Il Duce's overthrow on July 25, 1943, and the capitulation of the Italian Royal Army on September 8, partisan resistance to the Germans and to Mussolini's new Italian Social Republic in the north grew. In 1944, as Allied forces began advancing in Italy, many partisan groups operated throughout northern Italy.

On April 27, 1945, Italian communist partisans captured Mussolini and his mistress, Clara (Claretta) Petacci, trying to escape to Switzerland and executed them the next day, later hanging their corpses, and those of five fellow Fascists, upside down at a gas station in the Piazzale Loreto in Milan.

JAPAN

In Japan, the emperor was venerated as a living god, and education inculcated conformity into the civilian population. Moreover, by the late 1930s, fervently nationalistic military officers were in control of the government. Thus, there was little resistance to government policies. The Ministry of Home Affairs, the Thought Police, and the Tonarigumi (neighborhood associations) carefully watched for disobedience to official command. (See chart, p. 708.)

Even among the privileged, resistance was weak. An effort by a group of nobles and politicians led by Prince Fumimaro Konoe to oust General Hideki Tojo's cabinet in mid-1943, and an attempt by retired General Kanji Ishiwara to replace Tojo as prime minister failed, and the general held onto power until the fall of Saipan in July 1944.

THE ISSUE OF COLLABORATION

Collaboration, in the context of war, has come to mean "working with the enemy," usually in a treasonable way. Yet the term was not always pejorative. The term collaboration was first used after a meeting between Adolf Hitler and Marshal Henri Philippe Pétain on October 24, 1940, four months after France had capitulated to the Germans. Assuming that Germany would win the war, and seeking to maintain the sovereignty of France, Pétain declared that "collaboration had been envisaged between our two countries" and that he accepted it "in principle."

Initially collaboration was a political arrangement between two countries—an occupying power and the occupied country trying to preserve some independence—but the term expanded to include the acts of individuals. A number of collaborators, particularly in Eastern Europe, were Volksdeutsche, people of German descent who lived outside the Reich. Nationals of occupied countries also volunteered to help the Nazis out of self-interest or belief in Nazi ideology. In most of occupied western Europe, many ordinary people were willing to try to work with the German occupiers if only to maintain order. In Asia, where Japan invaded and overran a number of territories colonized by Western nations, the indigenous populations initially believed helping the Japanese was a way to gain freedom from Western imperialism. But Japan's imperialism proved equally onerous.

Collaboration took many forms:

Political (Ideological). Vidkun Quisling, founder of the Norwegian Fascist National Union Party, became Norway's minister-president in 1942 and proceeded to nazify the

(continued)

country. The term "quisling" became synonymous with the term "traitor"; Quisling was tried for treason and executed after the war. In Greece, the Axis appointed a collaborationist regime initially under General Georgios Tsolakoglou. As anti-Axis resistance increased, this politically conservative regime set up Security Battalions, chiefly to fight communist insurgents. In the east, Chinese politician Wang Ching-wei became president of the Reformed government of the Republic of China, sponsored by the Japanese Central China Expeditionary Army. Though Wang originally intended to form an independent government, his role evolved into that of a pure collaborator who eventually bowed to the Japanese pressure and declared war on the Allies in January 1943.

Economic. Many industrialists in occupied countries insisted they collaborated with the Axis to preserve jobs and keep their workers from being deported to Germany. Large and medium-size companies negotiated contracts with the Nazis, and some entrepreneurs and businesspeople amassed fortunes by trading with the Germans on the black market. Among the economic collaborators in France, Louis Renault offered the Germans a tank factory, which was nationalized by the French as retribution after the war. In Indochina, Japan signed agreements with the French governor-general Admiral Jean Decoux, who was accountable to the Vichy government, to exploit the rice, rubber, coal, and heavy metal ores of Vietnam, Laos, and Cambodia.

Military. In 1943, the Japanese forged an alliance with the violently anti-British Indian nationalist Subhas Chandra Bose, who had fled India and taken refuge in Germany in 1941. Traveling back to Asia to operate under Japanese auspices, Bose established a Provisional government of Free India in Singapore and declared war on Britain and the United States. His small Indian National Army took part in the abortive Japanese invasion of India in 1944 (see "Into India," in Chapter 7). In Burma, Malaya, and elsewhere, people who sought freedom from European colonialism formed small units that served under the Japanese—at least temporarily. But the Japanese relied very little on indigenous people for military might compared with the Germans. Many people from occupied nations (from Norway to Ukraine) formed part of the Wehrmacht or the Waffen SS, took oaths to Hitler, and fought in German uniforms against the Allies. (See also "Germany" in Chapter 4.) Even in the General Government region of Poland, Polish "Blue Police" and Jewish police in the Nazi-created ghettos served under German command.

Resistance groups in occupied countries not only attacked their Axis occupiers, but also the individuals and organizations who collaborated with them. Many collaborators were tried and executed after the war; some women who fraternized with the occupiers had their heads shaved or suffered other indignities.

Jewish Resistance

Until well into 1942, when stories began to trickle out of concentration camps about the horrors taking place, many Jews, as well as the general population, still believed the Germans were deporting people to labor camps or resettlement areas (See also "The Holocaust" in Chapter 8). As Jews living in the occupied countries or the ghettos in eastern Europe came to understand that the camps meant certain death, increasing numbers joined partisan groups, created resistance organizations, or took part in armed uprisings.

But there were many barriers to Jewish resistance, including anti-Semitism in the local communities; in some cases, anti-Semitic farmers in eastern Europe would turn away Jewish partisans looking for food, clothing, or shelter. Jewish partisans were often unable to obtain arms. The Jewish tradition of close-knit family life militated against attempting to escape from a ghetto or concentration camp and leaving family behind. Partisan organizations were also selective about who they accepted into their ranks, preferring strong, skilled, healthy fighters, not children, the elderly, or the sick. Moreover, the Germans enforced a policy of collective responsibility, so anyone who resisted or attempted to escape or helped escapees would be harming their family, friends, neighbors, and acquaintances. Thus, for many Jews, passive resistance to the Nazis was their best option.

As country after country fell to Germany, Jews throughout Europe participated in passive, or spiritual, resistance by conducting Hebrew classes, praying, singing Jewish songs, studying the Bible, wearing payis (earlocks) and beards publicly, carrying on a Jewish artistic and cultural life, escaping from ghettos, and keeping diaries and records.

Active Resistance

While some Jews held out hope that they could survive the war by keeping a low profile and complying with the Nazis, others fully realized the scope of Nazi evil. For them, active resistance was the only option. Beginning in 1943, Jews fought in the ghettos, in concentration camps, and clandestinely in partisan groups and other fighting organizations.

UPRISINGS IN GHETTOS

Between 1941 and 1943, underground resistance organizations sprouted in the major Jewish ghettos throughout Eastern Europe. Initially these groups, based primarily on youth organizations, had to overcome ideological differences between communists, right-wing Zionists, and Bundists (members of a Jewish secular socialist political party). In their earliest phase, they concentrated on military training, communicating with resistance groups outside the ghetto, obtaining weapons, and making small, unsuccessful attempts at armed resistance. Members broke out of the ghettos to join partisan groups in the forests, sabotaged German factories, and attacked Germans. By 1943, uprisings and revolts broke out in Jewish ghettos including Warsaw, Bialystok, and Lachwa. These revolts usually led to certain death for the fighters, but thousands of Jews escaped the ghettos and fought with partisan groups.

UPRISINGS IN CONCENTRATION CAMPS

Almost all the uprisings in concentration camps were the work of Soviet prisoners of war and Jews. Three of the most notable uprisings occurred at the Treblinka, Sobibor, and Auschwitz extermination camps.

TREBLINKA. On August 2, 1943, members of the ZOB (Jewish Fighters Organization), led by survivors of the Warsaw ghetto uprising, attacked, killed, and wounded at least sixty SS men and Ukrainian guards and destroyed parts of the death camp, including the armory and the guardroom. Of the approximately 1,000 prisoners in Treblinka One and Two, about 500 broke out of the camps, but most were killed in the following days by German troops, Polish fascists, and right-wing units of the Polish Home Army.

SOBIBOR. On October 14, 1943, an organized group of 350 rebels, a mix of Red Army men and Polish Jews led by Jewish Soviet officer Aleksandr Pechersky, attacked and killed at least ten SS officers and killed or wounded thirty-eight Ukrainian guards. One hundred and fifty rebels were killed, but the surviving rebels and other inmates—more than three hundred prisoners in all—escaped, including Pechersky, who then joined a Soviet partisan unit. Himmler saw this revolt as a defeat of his security system and ordered Sobibor torn down and its gas chambers blown up.

AUSCHWITZ. On October 6, 1944, members of the Sonderkommando, prisoners assigned to burn and bury the bodies and clean the gas chambers, revolted and attacked the SS with makeshift weapons including stones, axes, hammers, work tools, and homemade grenades and bombs. They blew up a crematorium, killed SS troops, and broke out of the camp. Within a short time, the Germans captured and killed almost all the escapees; the revolt ultimately discouraged further mass uprisings in other camps.

Jewish Resistance Organizations

From Bulgaria to Italy to the Soviet Union to France, Jews organized clandestine organizations to help refugees; forge identity and work papers; and provide food, money, and other aid to Jews in need. While some of these groups did not immediately take up arms against the Germans, others were formed specifically as fighting units.

POLAND

The ZZW (Jewish Fighting Union) was founded in Warsaw in late 1939 by former Polish officers, members of right-wing Jewish-Polish parties, and right-wing Zionists (revisionists). The ZZW maintained communications with the Polish resistance group Armie Krajowa (AK), which helped them obtain weapons and ammunition and organize escapes from the ghetto.

The ZOB was formed in the Warsaw ghetto on July 28, 1942, and later merged with several Zionist youth groups and communist organizations. Although they tried to establish ties with and obtain arms from Polish resistance groups like the AK, they were largely unsuccessful, in part because of their leftist ties. Despite these limitations, ZOB shot and seriously wounded the head of the Jewish police force in Warsaw and executed Nazi collaborators.

When the Nazis began a round of deportations from the ghetto in January 1943, ZOB and ZZW fighters fought back with hand grenades, Molotov cocktails, revolvers, stones, and acid. Then, on Passover, April 19, 1943, as the Germans again entered the ghetto to begin what would be the final round of deportations, they were met with fierce armed resistance from fighters hiding on roofs and balconies and attacking from open windows. The ZZW alone had about four hundred well-armed fighters grouped in eleven units. For weeks, the battle raged in the ghetto as the ZOB and ZZW, aided by the AK and other Polish resistance groups, used guerrilla tactics against 3,000 German troops and their tanks, armored vehicles, and artillery. On May 8, ZOB leader Mordechaj Anielewicz and his command committed suicide in their bunker as the German troops closed in on them.

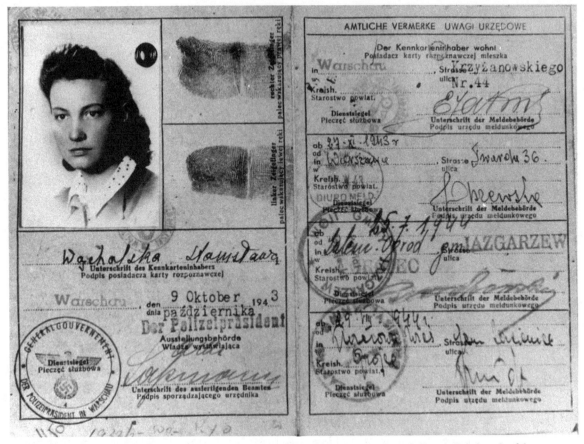

While working on the "Aryan" side of Warsaw as a courier for the Jewish underground, Feigele Peltel used a false identification card issued in the name of Stanislawa Wachalska. Peltel obtained arms for the resistance, found hiding places for Jewish women and children, and smuggled weapons, documents, and illegal correspondence in and out of the ghetto.

Eight days later, German General Stroop declared the operation over—the ghetto was destroyed and Warsaw's Great Synagogue was razed.

FRANCE

There were numerous Jewish rescue and resistance organizations in France such as EIF, the Jewish scouts, and Service Andre that provided services for the needy and only became militarized in the final phases of the war.

Solidarité-UJRE (Jewish Union for Resistance and Mutual Assistance) ran soup kitchens and published newspapers in Yiddish and French to spread the news of mass arrests and deportations among Jews and non-Jews. They also published *Notre parole* (Our Word) in French for Jews, the anti-racist publications *J'accuse* (I Accuse) and *Lumières* (Lights) for the general population, and *Combat medical* (Medical Combat) for physicians.

In August 1942, Solidarité formed the Second FTP-MOI-Yiddish detachment. These mostly young Jewish communists obtained weapons through their own means and attacked German soldiers. Under FTP command (see resistance groups chart, p. 762), they carried out many attacks against isolated elements of the Wehrmacht; restaurants, hotels, and cinemas frequented by German troops; and military vehicles and garages. While these attacks led to massive reprisals by the Germans, the partisans believed the reprisals were necessary to arouse more hatred of the Germans among the French people.

On June 15, 1940, shortly after the Germans entered Paris, members of the FSJF (Federation of French Jewish Organizations) met and agreed to reactivate the medical dispensary and soup kitchen programs they had provided to immigrant Jews in France for years. This group, headed by David Rapoport and known as Rue Amelot, also resolved not to submit to any German orders that would interfere with their programs. By August, other Jewish relief organizations, the OSE (Children's Rescue Network) and the ORT (Society for Manual Work), joined Rue Amelot to pursue this social mission. Unlike some of the population at large, these immigrant Jews, many having fled oppressive regimes in eastern Europe, had few illusions that collaborating with a dictatorship would guarantee them safety.

In every country they conquered, the Germans dissolved all Jewish associations, charities, and organizations, and transferred their assets to a Judenrat (Jewish council). In France, the Germans delegated this job to the Vichy government, which created the UGIF (General Union of French Jews). For over two years, Rapoport and Rue Amelot managed to maintain a level of independence from UGIF. Money funneled from JOINT (American Jewish Joint Distribution Committee) through the American Quaker organizations, who were widely active in western Europe, funded 50 to 60 percent of Rue Amelot's operations.

As laws were passed requiring Jews to register and authorizing them to be detained, the Jewish aid organizations operated more clandestinely. They monitored and helped Jews held in detainee camps in France by supplying food parcels and blankets and delivering mail. Jews who avoided being arrested relied on Rue Amelot and other relief organizations for money, false identity papers, ration cards, maps with escape routes, and lodging. By January 1942, Rapoport was hiding Jewish children with Christian families who were paid to care for them. He also hired Henry Bulawko, leader of a socialist Zionist party, to lead their efforts to falsify identity papers. Rapoport was finally arrested on June 1, 1943, and deported to his death at Auschwitz.

Unlike other Jewish resistance organizations, the AJ (Armée Juive) created in 1941 by two groups of militant Zionists, did not focus on social work or cultural activities—it was a political and military organization devoted to forming a Jewish state in Palestine. The irregular AJ corps in Lyon were the first to obtain arms, which they purchased from Italian soldiers and used against Gestapo agents who were hunting down Jews. From April to June 1943, the AJ Corps in Nice assassinated two Russian auxiliaries of the Gestapo and some informers. They also trained fighters and helped them get to Spain so they could make their way to Palestine and join the Jewish Brigade, and they later bombed a nightclub and antique shop that were headquarters for anti-Jewish activities.

PARTISAN ORGANIZATIONS

There were no independent Jewish partisan groups during the war. The Jews who did join partisan groups in occupied countries operated either in all-Jewish units of a larger organization or in non-Jewish units. While the estimates of the number of Jews who participated in partisan units vary widely from 20,000 to 100,000, it is clear that there were Jewish partisans in all regions of conflict. In eastern Europe, there were an estimated 850 Jewish partisans in the forests of Lithuania, and 1,500 participated in the Slovak National Uprising in Slovakia. They also joined units in Yugoslavia, Greece, and Bulgaria where, unlike other parts of Eastern Europe, they were treated as equals.

The occupied areas of the Soviet Union had the largest number of Jewish partisans. Many of the Soviet Jewish partisans were local doctors, teachers, administrators, and clerks. Since the Soviet Central Partisan Command would not approve separate Jewish partisan units, the Jewish groups that formed were merged into the all-partisan central command. This requirement arose, in part, from the Central Staff's fears that anti-Semitic farmers living near the partisan bases would refuse to supply food, clothing, or shelter to Jewish groups. For example, the Kruk Detachment, which fought in the western Ukraine, had over 200 Jewish fighters but was led by a Ukrainian, Nikolai Konishchuk, as it was safer to have non-Jews head the units. All of his assistant commanders were Jewish. The Soviet partisan organization eventually grew into such a formidable force that the Germans were required to devote 10 percent of their forces on the Eastern Front to combating these groups.

PRINCIPAL SOURCES AND FURTHER READING

Ainsztein, Reuben. *Jewish Resistance in Nazi-Occupied Eastern Europe*. London: Elek Books, 1974.

American Association for Jewish Education. *The Jewish Catastrophe in Europe*. New York, 1968.

Bonhoeffer, Dietrich. *Letters and Papers from Prison*, edited by Eberhard Bethge. New York: Macmillan, 1972.

Cruickshank, Charles. *Deception in World War II*. Oxford: Oxford University Press, 1979.

Dobbs, Michael. *Saboteurs: The Nazi Raid on America*. New York: Knopf, 2004.

Dunlop, Richard. *Donovan: America's Master Spy*. Chicago: Rand McNally, 1982.

_____. *Behind Japanese Lines: With the OSS in Burma*. Chicago: Rand McNally, 1979.

Frenay, Henri. *The Night Will End: Memoirs of a Revolutionary*. New York: McGraw-Hill, 1976.

Hoffmann, Peter. *German Resistance to Hitler*. Cambridge, MA: Harvard University Press, 1988.

Hymoff, Edward. *The OSS in World War II*. New York: Ballantine, 1972.

Kahn, David. *The Codebreakers*. New York: Macmillan, 1967.

_____. *Hitler's Spies*. New York: Macmillan, 1978.

Macksey, Kenneth. *The Partisans of Europe in the Second World War*. New York: Stein and Day, 1975.

Ophuls, Marcel. *The Sorrow and the Pity*. Documentary film, 1969.

Rhodes, Anthony. *Propaganda: The Art of Persuasion: World War II*. New York: Chelsea House, 1976.

Riess, Curt. *Underground Europe*. New York: Dial Press, 1942.

Rout, Leslie B., Jr., and John Bratzel. *The Shadow War*. Frederick, MD: University Publications of America, 1986.

Shoemaker, Lloyd R. *The Escape Factory: The Story of the MIS-X, the Super-Secret U.S. Agency Behind World War II's Greatest Escapes*. New York: St. Martin's Press, 1990.

Stanley, Roy M., III. *World War II Photo Intelligence*. New York: Charles Scribner's Sons, 1981.

Stevenson, William. *A Man Called Intrepid: The Secret War*. New York: Harcourt Brace Jovanovich, 1976.

10

THE MEDIA WAR

PROPAGANDA, CENSORSHIP, INFORMATION, AND ENTERTAINMENT

World War II in Europe began with an act of propaganda. On September 1, 1939, German newspapers ran front-page stories announcing that "Polish volunteers and Upper Silesian rebels" had attacked a German transmitter at Gleiwitz. Despite German claims that Poles were responsible, historians believe that the attackers were members of the German Security Service dressed in Polish uniforms. These men announced over the Gleiwitz transmitter that Poles had taken over the station. In "retaliation," Germany invaded Poland to "protect" itself against such acts of "terrorism."

By 1940, the German Ministry of People's Enlightenment and Propaganda (RMVP) considered that September 1, the day that Germany attacked Poland, was not the start of the war. Instead, they claimed it was September 3, the day that Britain and France declared war on Germany. In 1941, the RMVP reminded the press that "the second anniversary of the outbreak is not to be noticed until 3 September. 1 September was merely the day when the police operation against Poland began. To be sure, it is no occasion for festivity but justice can be done in weighty articles to the basic problems involved." In other words, facts could be shaped and altered to suit the German government's interests and used as a weapon to discredit the enemy and win public support. "The victor will not be asked afterwards whether he told the truth," Hitler commented on the subterfuge for invading Poland.

Wars are not fought with guns alone; they are also fought with information. The technological advances in transport, photography, radio, and film enabled larger quantities of information to be gathered, transmitted, interpreted, and disseminated during World War II than in any previous war. Information could be treated objectively or subjectively—it might be news, it might provide instruction or be conveyed through entertainment, or it might be propaganda. In every country, the relationships continually evolved between government policies, military successes and failures, and overall war and postwar goals on the one hand, and news reporting, propaganda strategies, and censorship on the other. Moreover, these relationships depended on the audiences at which information was aimed: civilians on the home front, civilians on the enemy's home front, one's own troops, enemy troops, civilians in occupied countries, or the governments of nations that remained neutral.

THE NEW ORDER

In 1942, American cartoonist Saul Steinberg published this cartoon of the precariously balanced Axis alliance led by Hitler, including leaders Mussolini, Hirohito, and Henri Petain of Vichy France.

Of the major combatants, the totalitarian nations—Germany, Japan, Italy, and the Soviet Union—sought total control of the news in their own nations and in those they occupied, although they did not always achieve it. By the time they entered the war, each of these countries had its propaganda organizations, censorship mechanisms, news distribution systems, and control of media and the arts largely in place. In China, both the Nationalists and communists attempted to control information in a way that conformed to their respective points of view. Democratic Great Britain and the United States, on the other hand, engaged in only partial control and urged that media be guided by voluntary restrictions.

Propaganda was the subject of debate in the prewar United States because during World War I the country's propaganda agency, the Committee on Public Information (CPI), had aggressively exaggerated both the enemy's evil nature and the eager heroism of the troops, who were depicted as relentlessly positive. George Creel, head of the CPI, had seen himself in a battle "for the minds of men, for the conquest of their convictions [so that] the gospel of Americanism might be carried to every corner of the globe." A staggering amount of material was produced for the World War I-era American media, including 6,000 press releases, some 750,000 prepared speeches, and more than 1,400 graphic designs for posters, advertisements, and buttons.

DEFINITIONS OF PROPAGANDA

Propaganda is visual, written, or verbal material designed to persuade and influence a given audience about an idea, cause, or ideology. Use of the word dates back to 1622, when Pope Gregory XV organized the Congregation for the Propagation of the Faith to develop methods for Catholic missionaries to win adherents in foreign countries. Propaganda is propagated—disseminated or spread—through graphic, oral, or written media. The word now has negative connotations, but for four centuries it merely referred to concepts, arguments, facts, or doctrines that needed to be communicated to a large audience. Not all information distributed by the government during a war is propaganda (there can be factual accounts of events or policies), but even factual information can be selectively presented or slanted to persuade or enhance a particular point of view.

British and American propagandists during World War II distinguished between what they called white and black propaganda. *White propaganda* indicates the correct source of its contents. It tends to be factual, although facts can be modified or omitted. *Black propaganda* is deliberately meant to deceive its intended audience. The term is generally used to describe propaganda composed of lies—"Black propaganda is essentially calumny and provocation, the age-old crafts of tyrant and conspirator, spread with twentieth-century technology," said Edmond Taylor, who designed the program followed by the American Office of Strategic Services (OSS) Morale Operations Branch. But strictly defined, black propaganda is propaganda that purports to come from an authoritative source in an enemy or occupied country when it is actually written in or broadcast from the country producing the propaganda.

Psychological warfare is the use of propaganda as a tool in military operations against enemy troops or civilians. Propaganda is a "military weapon in this day and age . . . an extension of a military concept . . . the idea of a super barrage to precede the artillery barrage—the barrage of ideas," declared John McCloy, U.S. assistant secretary of war. Propaganda used in such a way is often, but not always, deceitful or subversive.

Subversive warfare is the use of propaganda and sabotage to confuse and demoralize an enemy's troops and/or civilians so that they give up fighting. (See also "Sabotage and Subversion" in Chapter 9.)

"Within the life of the generation now in control of affairs, persuasion has become a self-conscious art and a regular organ of popular government" commented Walter Lippmann in his 1922 book *Public Opinion*. Lippmann described the communiques issued by the World War I French command, skewed because they emphasized the high number of German deaths without considering the Allied losses. "We have learned to call this propaganda," wrote Lippmann. "A group of men, who can prevent independent access to the event, arrange the news of it to suit their purpose. That the purpose was in this case patriotic does not affect the argument at all. They used their powers to make the Allied publics see affairs as they desired them to be seen."

Lippmann, who also distinguished between news and truth, expressed the distrust that many Americans developed toward information sources during World War I. Since many of those sources prior to U.S. entry in that war were Allied, particularly British, Americans could claim—and a significant number did in the 1930s—that they had been manipulated into joining in combat. In its October 10, 1939, issue, *Look* magazine ran an article with examples of misleading World War I propaganda. "War hysteria is spread by propaganda—a polite name for vicious lies which goad men to kill and be killed," stated the article's introduction. "Without these lies no modern war could be waged or even begun." The article featured images, including "a maniacal [German] arsonist" destroying a church and a "7 year-old boy shot for aiming his toy gun at the Germans." It also pointed out that Germans had been falsely accused of mutilating Belgian babies. Since the United States was strongly isolationist in 1939, the *Look* article reinforced the view that the country was once again being manipulated into a European war by exaggerated or deceitful propaganda. Later in World War II, skepticism about past propaganda efforts led many Americans to discount the first reports about the Holocaust, which were generally viewed as anti-German propaganda (not fact), just as the mutilated baby stories had been.

Propaganda and Censorship Organizations and Agendas

Each of the major combatants in World War II had organizations responsible for propaganda, censorship, and the distribution of information. Far from bringing about consensus on handling the media, the proliferation of civilian and military propaganda agencies and sources during the war made it virtually impossible to completely organize and control information. Interdepartmental bickering within a country and squabbles between the agencies of allied countries seems to have been the norm.

Perhaps because of the number and variety of organizations disseminating propaganda, it saturated the senses of those who lived in the major combatant and occupied countries. Posters with "support the war" or antienemy messages blanketed the walls of government and public institutions, flags flew, loudspeakers blared patriotic slogans, commercial advertisements featured war imagery, newsreels preceded film showings, radio voices encouraged and cajoled listeners to take part in the war effort, cartoons caricatured enemy leaders, and leaflets encouraging surrender dropped from airplanes over enemy territory. Even the clothes that people wore reflected war aims, battles, and victory. Some Japanese kimonos worked airplanes and bombs into their designs; in the United States, scarves bore the words "Remember Pearl Harbor" and "Freedom shall not perish from this earth."

In general, World War II propaganda from every country reiterated the same themes: the importance of patriotism, the necessity of sacrifice, and the imperative to become a soldier or, for those who could not, to otherwise serve in a war-related job. Domestic populations and troops were warned never to speak idly or give away vital information. Propaganda also emphasized the need for popular financial support through bond sales and fund-raising campaigns. Not just a response to a particular war, propaganda reflected each government's deeper political and ideological goals and values.

Propaganda and Censorship Organizations

Germany
Ministry of People's Enlightenment and Propaganda (RMVP)
Reich Chamber of Culture (RKK)

Italy
Ministry of Popular Culture

Japan
Government Information Bureau

Britain
Ministry of Information (MoI)
Special Operations Executive (SOE)
Political Warfare Executive (PWE)

Soviet Union
Agitation and Propaganda Department (Agitprop)
Main Administration for Literary and Publishing Affairs (Glavlit)
Soviet Information Bureau (Sovinformburo)

United States
Office of War Information (OWI)
Office of Strategic Services (OSS)
OSS Morale Operations Branch (OSS-MO)
Office of Censorship

Axis Countries

GERMANY

Before a shot was fired in World War II, the Nazis had formulated strong views on propaganda and taken control of the media. Germans thought highly of Allied propaganda from World War I, and attributed Germany's defeat to a lack of will on the home front exacerbated by effective enemy propaganda. This assessment disregarded the impact of Germany's declining resources, the failure of a last-ditch offensive in 1918, and the role of the military high command in requesting the armistice. The Nazis instead asserted that Germany had been "stabbed in the back" by its civilian government, whose lack of resolve stemmed at least in part from enemy propaganda. Partly from this skewed interpretation of events, the Germans concluded that propaganda was a powerful tool for winning a war.

Adolf Hitler stated his view of propaganda in his political manifesto, *Mein Kampf*: "[Its] function . . . does not lie in the scientific training of the individual, but in calling the masses' attention to certain facts, processes, necessities, etc., whose significance is thus for the first time placed within their field of vision. The whole art [of propaganda] consists in doing this so skillfully that everyone will be convinced that the fact is real." *Mein Kampf* was itself a kind of propaganda, illuminating an attitude and techniques that would affect not only Germany's, but the other major combatants' propaganda efforts during the war.

The "certain facts" mentioned by Hitler were those that reinforced the National Socialist worldview, in which Hitler was paramount, the German race superior, and conquest of other countries desirable and inevitable. German propaganda was violently anti-Semitic and anticommunist, and stressed the weaknesses of democracy. It also stressed Germany's military might and the speed with which it could occupy any place it chose, a threat partially aimed at keeping neutral countries from siding with the Allies.

Two months after Hitler became Germany's chancellor in 1933, he signed a decree establishing the Ministry of People's Enlightenment and Propaganda (*Reichsministerium fur Volksaufklarung und Propaganda*, or RMVP). Joseph Goebbels, the Nazi's premier propagandist, directed this ministry. He had served as the Nazi gauleiter (regional political leader) of Berlin since 1926 and was elected to the Reichstag in 1928, under the Weimar Republic. Goebbels worked assiduously against the Weimar government and for Nazi control. He believed that propaganda was the necessary link between the people and the government, and that it guided them toward a complete commitment to the goals of the state.

Goebbels was enormously skilled at manipulating facts and information to fit the Nazi view. "Neither the amount of news communicated matters

Joseph Goebbels, Reich Minister for Public Enlightenment and Propaganda, speaks during a book burning in Berlin, May 10, 1933. Courtesy of National Archives and Records.

nor the speed with which this is done," he said of the newspapers the state controlled. "The only thing which does matter is making German readers absorb a particular viewpoint. No announcement should be published as it stands. Make-up, headline or comment or all three should be designed to arouse in the reader the particular reaction at which, in conformity with government policy, the editor is aiming." He attributed the Nazis' success in gaining supporters to the use of "clever psychology and a pronounced ability to sense the thinking processes of the broad masses of the population."

Goebbels staffed the RMVP mainly with young, educated, and dedicated Nazis. Its departments included administration, propaganda coordination, radio broadcasting, press, foreign press (not established until 1934), film, theater, and music, fine arts, and folk culture. The RMVP formulated policy in each of these areas. Its role was to centralize control of the media and to provide content reinforcing Nazi precepts. It was funded by the sale of radio licenses, the number of which rose steadily as people bought more and more radios. Regional RMVP offices operated throughout Germany.

The RMVP's propaganda coordination department had the responsibility for disseminating "an active government propaganda that aims at winning people over," as Goebbels put it. "It is not enough to reconcile people more or less to our regime . . . we would rather work on people until they are addicted to us." This division managed media campaigns that disparaged communism, Jews, religion, or any other entity considered dangerous to the state. Other main functions included organizing state celebrations and addressing questions having to do with race, ideologies, or the Treaty of Versailles (see "Part I: Prelude" in Chapter 1) .

Goebbels was also the president of the Reich Chamber of Culture (*Reichskulturkammer*, or RKK), an organization structurally parallel to the RMVP that was enjoined with "furthering German culture and regulating economic and social aspects of cultural affairs." Seven chambers—presiding over literature, theater, music, radio, film, fine arts, and the press—were responsible for registering practitioners in each field and issuing work permits, without which a writer, artist, or journalist could not be employed. Permits were denied to dissidents, communists, and those of Jewish ancestry. By regulating the workforce, the RKK effectively controlled German culture. There was no need for a separate office of censorship, since "undesirable" artists were not allowed to work, and those who were approved practiced strict self-censorship to maintain their standing. (Proposals and scripts for films, however, were subject to censorship by the film department of the

RMVP.) Each of the seven chambers had a president, but Goebbels was involved in setting policy for all of them.

The Division for Defense Propaganda, under control of the Wehrmacht, was responsible for military censorship. It sent propaganda units to the front lines, from which they submitted reports on battlefield events. It also issued a daily press briefing, compiled from news sent in by the three armed services that was acceptable for publication. The propaganda division grew to be almost as large as a division of fighting men (13,000 to 17,000) by the end of the war.

ITALY

Italian propaganda, like Germany's, was intensely nationalistic, with the goal of creating exemplary Fascist citizens. "The whole country had to become a great school for perpetual political education which would make the Italians into complete fascists . . . changing their habits, their way of life, their mentality, their character and, finally, their physical makeup. . . . Creating a new kind of man who was tough, strong, strong-willed, a fighter, a latter-day legionary of Caesar for whom nothing was impossible," as Mussolini put it. Italian propaganda glorified militarism, spreading the idea that Italy could again assume control over the Mediterranean and reclaim the stature it had enjoyed in the days of the Roman Empire.

Italy's Fascist propaganda and censorship organization developed gradually. By 1929, there were press offices to distribute and censor domestic and foreign news and a propaganda service staffed by members of the Fascist Party. In August 1933, inspired by the Nazis' all-encompassing RMVP, the Press Office and Propaganda Service reorganized. Galeazzo Ciano, Mussolini's son-in-law, assumed control, setting up seven regional offices to better collect and distribute information. The following year, this organization was elevated to become the Undersecretariat for Press and Propaganda, with added responsibility for a film bureau, a bureau of tourism, a commission for radio regulation, and an inspectorate of the theater. In June 1935, the Undersecretariat became the Ministry of Press and Propaganda. The press bureaus gained greater authority to suppress newspapers, and the radio and film sections controlled programs and documentaries for foreign countries. There was also a section devoted specifically to generating anticommunist propaganda. In May 1937, the Ministry was again reorganized and expanded, and was renamed the Ministry of Popular Culture. Alessandro Pavolini directed the Ministry of Popular Culture through most of the time that Italy participated in World War II.

JAPAN

The Japanese used the term "thought war," rather than propaganda, to describe the techniques for persuading various groups to adopt a political and social viewpoint. Thought war, in fact, went deeper than persuasion—it was an attack against free and individual thought and an indoctrination into a controlled way of life that stressed conformity and uniformity of opinion. "Any public opinion which is not worthy of the prosecution of the war [World War II], must be strictly controlled," Major-General Yahazi, Chief of the Army Press Section of Imperial Headquarters quoted Tojo as saying in March 1943. "If our nation should by any chance lose this war it will be because public opinion has become divided."

Japanese propaganda placed loyalty to the emperor at the apex of its values. It lashed out against democracy and European and American imperialism in Asia and promised protection and an improved living standard to those in other countries that came within the Greater East Asian Co-Prosperity Sphere—a name that was itself misleading and propagandistic, since Japan intended to fully dominate and control the populations of the countries it occupied.

Although Japan did not have as fully organized a system as that of the Nazis, a unified policy determined the flow of information and propaganda from a network of agencies. The Government Information Bureau (*Naikaku Joho-bu*), also called the Cabinet Information Board, officially formed in December 1941 to centralize the dispensing of information. It was headed by Eiji Amau, a career diplomat who served as information director until Tojo's government fell in 1944.

Most government departments distributed their propaganda through this bureau, but information was also disseminated by the Foreign Office, the Ministry for Greater East Asiatic Affairs, the War Office and Admiralty, and the Ministries of Home Affairs, Education, and Communications. While civilians led some agencies, the army had ultimate control over the release of propaganda and information. The Government Information Office shared responsibility for press oversight with the Home Affairs and Foreign Offices, and for censorship with the Foreign Office and Ministry of Communications. With the Communications Ministry, it also distributed news and films to occupied areas and controlled the Overseas Services of the Japanese Broadcasting Company.

The Ministry of Greater East Asiatic Affairs, formed in 1942, which provided for the civilian administration of territories occupied by the Japanese army and navy, carried out propaganda efforts to persuade captive populations to adopt Japanese culture and values and acquire knowledge of the Japanese language. Four bureaus were responsible, respectively, for general policy planning, Manchurian affairs, Chinese affairs, and Southern affairs, including Thailand and French Indochina (Vietnam, Laos, and Cambodia). Nominally independent occupied areas, including Nanking (China), Thailand, Burma, and the Philippines, had their own national propaganda ministries under Japanese control.

Both the War Office and the Admiralty also had their own independent press and information bureaus to issue bulletins, periodicals, and books, and to provide information to the press and radio. In addition, the army and navy each had a press section at Imperial General Headquarters in Tokyo. Articles, lectures, or broadcasts by military officials expressed the official policies of a militaristic dictatorship. The armed services also chose their own war correspondents, who worked side by side with correspondents from the government-controlled Domei News Agency and large newspapers.

In December 1942, all Japanese writers, including fiction writers, as well as historians, philosophers, and scientists, became members in a new National Service Publicists' Association (aka Patriotic Association of Publicists). Members gave public lectures to boost morale. "The object of the association is the fostering of public opinion in favor of the prosecution of the war. . . . Today we publicists do not, in fact, stand in the front lines. However, the essence of war has many of the characteristics of a thought war. . . . We must emphasize that we fight through with the same determination as those soldiers at the front. . . . We are establishing world-wide knowledge of Japan and the Japanese Way," explained one committee member at the first meeting of the association.

Allied Countries

BRITAIN

In 1936, before war broke out, the British government planned to establish a Ministry of Information (MoI) to consolidate the functions of disseminating and censoring news in case of war. MoI included five divisions: administration, news (as distinct from propaganda), censorship, publicity (to promote the government view), and intelligence collecting. During the war, divisions handling film and broadcasting were added. This model was based on the centralized German propaganda/censorship/news organization, which, in an odd twist, had been based on the British Ministry of Information that had operated during World War I. After short tenures by others, Brendan Bracken headed the ministry.

In 1941, Prime Minister Winston Churchill signed a document stating that MoI had "the creative function of providing a steady flow of facts and opinions calculated to further the policy of the Government in the prosecution of the war." However, government departments, including the Foreign Office, which had historically held daily press conferences, often chose to give out their own information. They were encouraged to coordinate with the MoI—smaller newspapers and the Foreign Press Association preferred receiving news briefs from a central source—but they frequently failed to channel their announcements and information through the ministry.

Britain's propaganda was antifascist (although a small group of Britons had supported fascism before the outbreak of the war) and stressed the urgency of defending against takeover by Germany. However, it also reassured the public that in the long run, Britain would win. "The immense staying-power of democracy is the first guarantee of Allied triumph," declared an MoI leaflet in 1939.

In the first two years of the war, Britain was careful about the amount of propaganda it directed toward the United States, aware of the American isolationist charge that propaganda had pushed the United States into World War I. The British government fed the Roosevelt administration and other sympathizers information that they could use to convince Americans to intervene on the side of the Allies. In general, the British propaganda stance was that war with Germany was serious enough to require help from friends, but not hopeless enough that there was no chance of ultimate victory. Britain's propaganda also had defense of the British Empire as a theme, with the corollary that the Empire not only would be preserved, but that it should be preserved as the model of a humane and well-run world order, despite colonial agitation for independence.

THE SOVIET UNION

In the Soviet Union, the development of organizations to disseminate propaganda and to censor information dated back to the Russian civil war (1917–1922). Russian revolutionaries drew a distinction between what they called "agitation" and "propaganda," although both were practiced and often overlapped. Lenin explained in 1902 in *What Is to Be Done?* "the propagandist operates chiefly by means of the *printed* word; the agitator by means of the *spoken* word."

In 1920, the Central Committee of the Communist Party formed Agitprop—the Agitation and Propaganda Department—to transmit Bolshevist doctrine and values through the mass media. A series of propaganda centers, or *agitpunkty*, located near railway junctions or populous rural settlements, disseminated a continual stream of propaganda to regional communities, while Agitprop staff traveled throughout the country on special trains that contained books, printing presses, and broadcast and film equipment spreading the revolutionary message and reinforcing through words and images the cult of personality that was building around Lenin.

The Soviet Union's consistent propaganda message from its founding was the promotion of communism. First Lenin, then Stalin, were elevated as cult figures who embodied the hope of the masses. During the time of the Soviet-German Non-Aggression Pact (August 1939–June 1941), the Soviet Union railed against British and American capitalism and imperialism without criticizing Germany. After Germany invaded the Soviet Union June 22, 1941, Soviet propaganda virulently attacked Hitler and the Germans. It called for revenge and urged all Soviet citizens to fight for the motherland. At the same time, the USSR, now allied with the United States and Britain, toned down its criticism of capitalism, just as Britain and the United States about-faced on their anticommunist stance and promoted goodwill toward the Soviets and Stalin.

The Soviet Union censored any idea or expression considered "antirevolutionary" or "bourgeois." In 1922, the government organized the Main Administration for Literary and Publishing Affairs, known as Glavlit. Even after the name changed to the Main Administration for Safeguarding State Secrets in the Press, the acronym Glavlit continued to be used. In 1923, the Main Administration for Repertory (Glavrepertkom) was formed to censor theater performances. Censors read, "corrected," and returned every manuscript submitted, as well as censoring works written before the Russian Revolution. By 1939, they had taken 16,453 books and films out of circulation.

Like Germany's fascist government, the communist government in the Soviet Union also focused on organizing practitioners of various media into groups with established standards for work and rigidly controlled output, partly by making it difficult for dissidents to publish, perform, compose, and create. The All-Union Soviet Film Trust, the Union of Soviet Writers, and the Union of Soviet Artists (formed in 1930), the Union of Soviet Composers (1933), and the Union of Soviet Architects and of Journalists (1934) were all submerged into an All Union Committee of the Arts in 1936. Stalin's purges of the late 1930s helped to keep membership down, as artists, writers, and other creative intellectuals were killed or exiled.

Two days after the German invasion drew the Soviets into World War II, a newly formed Soviet Information Bureau (Sovinformburo) became the sole regular source of war information. Its basic job was to issue statements from Stalin's supreme wartime headquarters, the Stavka VGK. The government severely censored news of military defeats and civilian suffering but magnified Soviet victories. Sovinformburo incorrectly reported the loss of German soldiers killed and wounded as 10 million in June 1942, for example, while stating that Soviet losses were (comparatively) lighter, at 4.5 million troops. It issued no news of the deaths from starvation while the siege of Leningrad was taking place, although an estimated 1 million people in the city and the surrounding area perished of hunger.

Sovinformburo's many departments included those responsible for military news, counterpropaganda, international affairs, and literature. The bureau generated stories of Soviet heroism against German troops for placement in international publications. It also developed leaflets calling on German soldiers to surrender, which it disseminated behind German lines. Another function was directing the work of special interest organizations against the Nazis, including the Jewish Anti-Fascist Committee and groups comprising women or young people.

UNITED STATES

In the late 1930s, interventionist groups who supported American involvement in World War II had begun to track propaganda, convinced that a fifth column of Nazi supporters was planning sabotage within the country (see also "Fifth Column Fears" in Chapter 2). The threat was never as great as it was believed to be, but the belief was strong enough to fuel counterpropaganda efforts, including creation of the Office of Civil Defense, the Bureau of Facts and Figures, the Foreign Information Service (FIS) and the office of the Coordinator of Information (COI), headed by William Donovan. The COI collected, analyzed, and kept the government abreast of intelligence information, as well as disseminating propaganda overseas. Finally, in October, President Franklin Roosevelt created, within the Office of Emergency Management, the Office of Facts and Figures (OFF). Its job was to provide information to the media and to coordinate radio broadcasts. It lasted until July 1942, when it fell victim to the squabbles about the nature, uses, and methods of propaganda that divided government opinion.

For those who believed in Roosevelt's New Deal, World War II was a propaganda opportunity to highlight their vision of a new world order based on the liberal democratic model. Winning the war was a prelude to establishing international egalitarian democracy. For other Americans, winning the war by defeating fascist governments was a sufficient goal. They opposed propaganda that supported an international caretaker role for the U.S. government or the spread of the New Deal in the United States.

By the end of 1941, some twenty-six organizations dealt with propaganda, intelligence, or information in the United States. Roosevelt reduced duplication of effort and effectively reorganized the conflicting members of the COI and FIS by creating two new organizations in 1942, the Office of War Information (OWI) and the Office of Strategic Services (OSS). Former CBS radio commentator Elmer Davis directed the OWI, which was staffed by civilians, many of them journalists, broadcasters, and other media people hired to create white propaganda. The COI's Donovan now headed the OSS.

The OWI had two branches, one overseas run by Robert Sherwood, who had directed the FIS, and one domestic, headed by Gardner Cowles Jr. OWI's mission was to "formulate and carry out, through the use of press, radio, motion picture, and other facilities, information programs designed to facilitate the development of an informed and intelligent understanding, at home and abroad, of the status and progress of the war effort and of the war policies, activities, and aims of the government," according to Cowles. He further stated, in direct opposition to totalitarian governments, that "intelligent, informed, and honest criticism of government programs and policies is an indispensable part of the service of a free press to a free people in war."

The OWI's domestic branch coordinated and disseminated information to federal, state, and local agencies and acted as a liaison with other Allied information agencies. It also had responsibility for reviewing and approving radio programs and films. The overseas branch, based in New York and London, eventually grew to include thirty-six outposts in twenty-five countries. Its Radio Program Bureau controlled the Voice of America, and it produced most publications, leaflets, films and images distributed in Europe. The overseas OWI coordinated activities with the British clandestine Political

Warfare Executive (PWE). (See "Black Propaganda—Allied Countries" later in this chapter.)

While the Office of War Information was a civilian organization, the Office of Strategic Services (OSS) was under the control of the military's top coordinating body, the Joint Chiefs of Staff. A JCS directive explained that the OSS would engage in psychological warfare—"the integrated use of all means, moral and physical—other than those of recognized military actions—which tend to destroy the will of the enemy to achieve victory and to damage his political and economic capacity to do so; which tend to deprive the enemy of the support, assistance, or sympathy of his allies or associates or neutrals . . . or which tend to maintain, increase, or acquire the support, assistance, and sympathy of neutrals."

The Joint Chiefs of Staff enjoined the OSS to "collect and analyze . . . strategic information" and to "plan and operate . . . special services" that included the gathering of information by spying, making contact with resistance members in occupied countries, sabotage, subversive activities, [and] economic warfare. (See also Chapter 9.) A critical task was developing black propaganda.

CHINA

China was divided chiefly between Chiang Kai-shek's Nationalists and those loyal to Mao Tse-tung's Communist Party during World War II. Even when they allied in the United Front in 1937 to fight the Japanese, each side promulgated propaganda on behalf of the political system it supported. At the same time, both sides called for the population to be loyal to China and to support the war. Both also directed propaganda campaigns abroad. Chiang Kai-shek and his Nationalist government were particularly eager to maintain—and increase—political and military support from the other Allied nations, especially the United States.

When the United Front formed, Guo Muruo of the Communist Party became head of war propaganda under the Military Affairs Commission, which included both Nationalist and communist members. Without many resources (e.g., the Chinese made no films between 1937 and 1945) and with a large population of refugees and poor communication between rural and urban parts of the country to deal with, the commission relied on teams of artists and writers assigned to both communist and Nationalist troops to generate propaganda. They produced books, brochures, and posters, organized exhibitions, and gave theatrical performances conveying information about the war and the need to support it.

After the United Front effectively broke apart in 1940, the Nationalists limited funding for propaganda, but the communists continued to support cultural and propaganda efforts. The Lu Xun Academy of Arts and Literature, founded in October 1938 in communist-controlled Shaanxi Province, worked to develop a relationship between writers, artists, musicians, and theatrical professionals and the rural population. In 1943, Mao Tse-tung pronounced: "What we demand . . . is a unity of politics and art, a unity of content and form, a unity of revolutionary political content and the highest artistic form possible."

Censorship Issues

"Society has hit upon but three basic methods of controlling publication. One is the method of rigid government compulsion, with a censor always at the editor's elbow. One is a compromise procedure, under which enforcement is largely voluntary, but with a strictly worded statute hovering in the background. The third is a system of self-discipline under the leadership of the government, but with no statutory sanction and no penalty," declared Byron Price, director of the U.S. Office of Censorship. The totalitarian countries practiced the first method of censorship, Britain the second, and the United States the third.

Censorship went hand in hand with the dissemination of news or propaganda: it was used to control the flow of information. The most efficient way to censor the news was not to release it in the first place. The military in every country had the ultimate say on what news should be restricted, but propaganda and information agencies also shaped the decisions. Journalists tended to complain about restrictions more than the public did. The *New York Journal American*, for example, charged that the U.S. government would not issue "unpleasant 'facts and figures.' . . . Their 'information' is treacle for children." Australian journalists were chagrined when British censors banned their cables criticizing the British government. The censors believed that such information could create disunity between the Allies or jeopardize diplomatic negotiations.

Governments used censorship to winnow out information that would distract from its goals or suggest internal discord among civilians or soldiers. Just as propaganda aimed at constructing a morale-building image emphasizing a unified population achieving victory, censorship eliminated any words or photographs that could mar that image. In the United States, photographs depicting racial tension or violence, or conflict

U.S. OFFICE OF CENSORSHIP

Created by Executive Order No. 8985 on December 19, 1941, the United States Office of Censorship was responsible for censoring all international communications during the war and formulating a plan for voluntary censorship of domestic media so that no information useful to the enemy would be revealed. Newsman Byron Price, the executive director of the Associated Press, led the organization. Mail and cables had been subject to censorship since the passage of the First War Powers Act on December 18, 1941. Army officers examined letters and printed matter coming from or going abroad. Naval reserve officers handled cables, telegrams, radiograms, and telephone calls. These operations were placed under the Office of Censorship's control on March 15, 1942.

The Office of Censorship issued two compact publications, the *Code of Wartime Practices for American Broadcasters* and the *Code of Wartime Practices for the American Press,* in January 1942. These called for voluntary censorship of factual stories; the codes did not apply to opinions. Nor did they apply to journalists in combat zones, where the armed forces were responsible for censorship. Price was vigilant in keeping information that might endanger American security from reaching the public, while honoring the constitutional right to free speech. He encouraged the press, which respected his credentials as a journalist, to exercise self-censorship and common sense in reporting honestly, without exposing secrets. The codes were refined and updated several times during the war to reflect changing needs. After the *Chicago Tribune* published a story that revealed specifics about the Japanese fleet at the battle of Midway, which might have revealed to the Japanese that their code had been broken, a censorship code revision included a ban on writing about the movement of enemy ships in their own waters. Price received a special Pulitzer Prize in 1944 for his sensible and effective development of censorship codes.

Volunteer editors and publishers worked with smaller newspapers in their areas to explain the code. Newspapers and radio stations themselves decided whether to submit a story to the censors before publication or broadcast. Within a year of operation, 112 daily newspapers, and magazines, books, corporate reports, and almanacs were being submitted. Censors also generally monitored the media for compliance. The office quietly sent a letter to the editor of any periodical in which it found violations. Only once did it publicly announce the name of a newspaper, the *Philadelphia Daily News,* which had printed on June 6, 1942, that Soviet ambassador V.M. Molotov was in the United States on "a secret mission of vast importance." The infraction was relatively minor; the story served as an example to other newspapers. In nearly all cases, failure to comply with the codes was inadvertent.

The attorney general was also involved with censorship in the United States. At the request of Franklin Roosevelt, Francis Biddle explored the possibility of shutting down several profascist, antigovernment publications. The post office revoked the second-class mail permit of *Social Justice,* published by the reactionary and anti-Semitic Father Charles Coughlin, invoking Section 3, Title 1 of the Espionage Act on obstructing the war effort. The *Herold,* a German-language weekly, and the anti-Semitic and antiadministration periodicals *X-Ray* and *Publicity* also had their mail permits revoked. Since publications that were barred from the post office could not be transported in any other way, according to the terms of the Trading with the Enemy Act, they went out of circulation. Biddle brought charges against the *Chicago Tribune* for its story on Japanese ship movements at Midway, but the navy failed to provide evidence that a vital secret had been revealed and the grand jury did not indict the newspaper.

One writer was tried and sentenced under the 1917 Sedition Act: William Dudley Pelley, a novelist, journalist, and admirer of Hitler, who organized the profascist Silver Legion of America and its paramilitary arm, the Silver Shirts. He was rabidly anti-Semitic and enraged by the Roosevelt administration. After the United States entered the war, Pelley disbanded his group, but continued to excoriate Roosevelt in his journal, *The Galilean.* In April 1942, a month after Pelley claimed that the Japanese had devastated the U.S. Navy at Pearl Harbor, and that the American economy was bankrupt,

the U.S. government indicted him for "making false statements with the intent to interfere with the operation or success of the military or naval forces of the United States or to promote the success of its enemies." Although the degree of damage at Pearl Harbor was, in fact, greater than the government initially admitted to the public, Pelley was sentenced to fifteen years in prison. He was paroled in 1952, on the condition that he not be involved again in political activity.

Pelley's case was unique. Other journalists delayed releasing stories that contained information useful to the enemy. William L. Laurence (a reporter for the *New York Times* who was allowed special access to scientists) and columnist Drew Pearson knew about the creation of the atomic bomb but did not publish their stories until after the bomb was dropped on Hiroshima. Laurence won a 1946 Pulitzer Prize for his coverage, which included an eyewitness account of the bombing of Nagasaki.

On August 15, 1945, the day after the Japanese government ordered its troops to stop fighting, Price requested and received permission from President Harry Truman to close down his agency.

between American troops and civilians or military personnel from Allied countries were not distributed to the press. The Office of Censorship did not allow images of the racial riots on domestic military bases to be published. The office, through its postal censors, also prohibited the entry of photographs or films focusing on "labor, class, or other disturbances" into the United States.

A key question for censors involved photographs that showed the bodies of soldiers killed in combat. The Soviet Union released photographs of war dead, believing these would rally the population to defend itself. Germany showed brutal film footage of its military taking over other countries to intimidate neutral and Allied countries. For nearly two years, however, the

U.S. government released no photos of badly wounded or dead soldiers, thinking that bloody, grisly images would horrify the public and intensify the call for negotiated settlements, particularly with Germany.

Censorship could also be used to regulate cultural norms and language as well as news and political attitudes. The totalitarian countries, particularly, wanted to project an image that was wholesome and positive. There were to be no "coarse expressions [or] swearwords" in writing or performances, according to a 1935 directive in the Soviet Union. Mussolini expected that "newspapers must strive . . . to tell everyone the things it is useful for them to know, to turn to advantage whatsoever things are born healthy, good, beautiful and heroic, and to ignore the rest, burying it in the darkness of absolute indifference." In Nazi Germany, artists creating new works were told not to use "unnatural" colors or to portray misery and ugliness. Those who broke the rules could not exhibit; the Gestapo visited artists' studios and homes and if they were noncompliant they were prohibited from buying materials and supplies—the ultimate censorship, since they were forbidden the basic materials needed to create their visions.

Black Propaganda

Both Allied and Axis countries conducted so-called black propaganda campaigns. William Donovan, the head of the U.S. Office of Strategic Services (OSS), said that propaganda provided "the initial arrow of penetration" into an enemy country, the key to undermining its spirit and unity. Black propagandists spread false information and rumors through newspapers, radio transmissions, and whispering campaigns; scripted and produced fake radio broadcasts; and distributed misleading printed matter, including leaflets, postcards, books, and periodicals. Their role fell somewhere between that of white propagandists, who built morale in home and allied countries, and military groups that conducted sabotage and subversive activities against the enemy.

Axis Countries

The German Foreign Office (*Auswartiges Amt*, or AA) had control over propaganda directed at foreign countries, although the RMVP was charged with actually carrying out the campaigns. Goebbels chafed under this arrangement and asserted his own authority as often as possible, but the basic system stayed in place throughout the war. The Division for Defense

Propaganda, under the Wehrmacht, was responsible for propaganda to enemy troops. Its tasks included producing and distributing *Signal*, a magazine published in twenty languages, that portrayed Germany's strength to those who fought against the country.

In May 1940, German propagandists began a typical black radio campaign: Clandestine German stations aimed at France and masquerading as French operations, including Radio Humanite, Poste du Reveil de la France, and Voix de la Paix, were mobilized to spread panic among French civilians before the Germans advanced into their country. These stations propagated several rumors that victorious Germans would confiscate all deposits in local banks and that the French government was on the verge of leaving Paris. German propaganda also roused French sentiment against the British. The Germans distributed leaflets and postcards to French troops suggesting that British soldiers were romancing the wives they had left behind. These tactics were considered successful in damaging French morale.

The Italian government also used radio to discredit the British. It aimed Arabic-language programs at the Middle East that appealed to Arab anti-Semitism, charging that the British gave preference to Jews over Arabs. The Italians distributed free radios to Arabic café and shop owners, having first locked them to Italian frequencies. During the war, Italian propagandists operated the black radio station Voice of the Arab Nation; and Radio Himalaya, broadcast out of Italy, presented itself as a station based in northern India that was also critical of the British imperial role.

The government-controlled Broadcasting Corporation of Japan (BCJ), which broadcast domestically, also transmitted programs in twenty-two languages to enemy and occupied countries. Radio Jakarta (Batavia) was aimed at Australia; its programs included the English-language *Australian Home News*, with commentary on Allied news reports and prisoner-of-war broadcasts. These gave the names of prisoners held by the Japanese, an incentive for Australians to listen. Another Japanese clandestine station, the Indian Independence League Station, broadcast programs in several Indian languages from Singapore, including listings of the names of Indian prisoners of war.

Allied Countries

In July 1940, the British established the Special Operations Executive (SOE), an organization that Winston Churchill directed to "set Europe ablaze" through sabotage and other forms of "irregular warfare." Special Operations 1 (SO1) was the propaganda arm of SOE. From August 1941 onward, SO1 provided staffing for the newly formed Political Warfare Executive (PWE), which developed black propaganda for overseas broadcasts and aided in publishing underground newspapers in occupied countries.

The PWE also prepared and dropped leaflets over Germany and Axis-occupied countries. Britain, together with the United States, dropped 9.6 million leaflets over Italy with reminders of Allied might and appeals for surrender. Between D-Day and September 1944, the Allies dropped more than 250 million leaflets by air to civilians in occupied Europe. Britain produced the daily newspaper *Nachrichten fur die Truppe*, supposedly originating in Germany, but dropped by American planes to German troops. *Nachrichten* subtly distorted news and was sprinkled with lies aimed at undermining morale. The station Soldatensender Calais, purported to be from Germany,

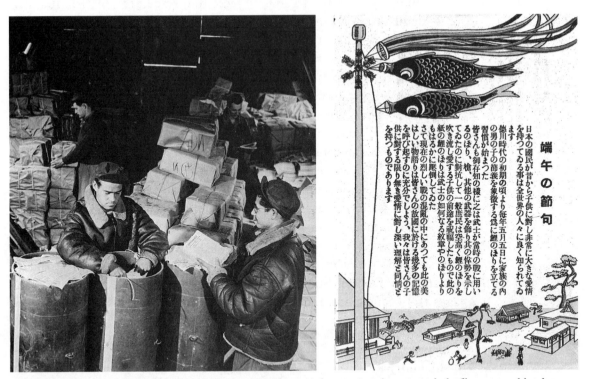

American soldiers pack leaflets for dispersal in enemy and occupied countries. A propaganda leaflet prepared by the Psychological Warfare Branch of the U.S. Army for Japanese troops plays on "the Japanese . . . love of their children," reminding them that the interests of children—"your treasure," the future—are being sacrificed for the war effort.

transmitted from Britain to German troops, and included popular contemporary music as well as news to attract listeners.

Soviet radio propaganda tended to be blunt, powerful, and brutal. Even clandestine radio stations generally acknowledged openly that they were pro-Soviet. The broadcasters were often leftist refugees purporting to transmit from their home countries when they were actually in the USSR. Italian communists living in the Soviet Union operated Radio Milano Liberta, which began broadcasting in 1937. Other stations, including Kossuth Radio (Hungary), Radio Free Yugoslavia, and Radio Espana Independiente (Spain), broadcast in support of communism in their respective countries. The Soviets produced the Voix Chretienne, aimed at listeners in occupied France. The Soviets also used a technique called "ghost" broadcasting to break into German official programs by transmitting on the German frequencies. They could then make rude replies to the German commentary on the air.

In the United States, William Donovan organized an office of Morale Operations (MO) within the Office of Strategic Services. The specific function of MO was "to incite and spread dissension, confusion and disorder" through black propaganda. OSS MO was immediately controversial: critics accused it of emulating Nazi tactics; supporters thought its practices provided a powerful and necessary weapon against totalitarian methods that already had damaged Allied morale. OSS MO operated throughout the war, sometimes in cooperation with international propaganda efforts made by the U.S. Office of War Information (OWI).

Examples of American black propaganda included the dropping of 10 million leaflets to Italian and German soldiers in North Africa. Italian soldiers, thought to be particularly vulnerable to desertion, were promised "safe conduct and a comfortable internment." OSS MO in the Far East operated primarily in the China-Burma-India Theater because General Douglas MacArthur did not want nonmilitary intelligence organizations working in the Pacific Theater. Short of resources and plagued by transportation problems, OSS MO Asia finally put two clandestine radio stations on the air in April 1945: Voice of the People, aimed at Japan, and Charlie Station, broadcast to Japanese-occupied Canton in China, supposedly from a guerrilla group. In Burma, an American-Chinese Task Force operating under the U.S. OWI distributed vegetable seed packets labeled, "Wherever the Japanese go, they bring destruction. Wherever the Allies come, the fields spring up green."

VOICES OF RADIO PROPAGANDA

Several radio broadcasters became well-known for their black propaganda programs, usually a mix of entertaining music and blatant blandishments to join the other side. These included the American Mildred Gillars, known as "Axis Sally," who spoke to Allied troops on behalf of Germany. "Lord Haw Haw" also broadcast from Germany to British listeners. A British journalist coined this nickname for a radio announcer using an exaggerated upper-class accent, now thought to be Norman Baillie-Stewart. William Joyce, a British fascist (born in the United States) who wrote scripts and broadcast for the Nazis, more famously claimed the name.

The eminent American poet Ezra Pound made radio broadcasts for the Italian Fascists. In 1940, he began writing scripts that were read by other Radio Rome broadcasters. From January 1941 through July 1943, when the Fascist government fell, he read the text himself. Pound was virulently anti-Semitic and against Franklin Roosevelt: "What you can do is to understand just how the President is an imbecile," he typically broadcast on February 18, 1943. "I mean that, learn JUST how, in what way he is a dumb cluck, a goof, a two fisted double-time liar."

Several women broadcast on the "Zero Hour" radio program from Japan, although they were given the single nickname "Tokyo Rose" by American troops. They included Filpinos, an Australian, and some Japanese Americans, among them Iva Toguri Ikoku, who was tried for treason, served in prison, and was later pardoned. John Flack, an American marine, remembered in a 2002 interview hearing Tokyo Rose on Okinawa. "We could hear her saying that the 1st Marine Division, all are dead, . . . by the thousands laying on the beach. . . . The Japanese control the beach. . . . Now, we couldn't see a [Japanese soldier]. . . . We got Tokyo Rose quite a bit and we looked forward to hearing from her because she had up-to-date music; Glenn Miller and things like that. And people say . . . she should be executed because it endangered our morale. It never bothered us a bit. We knew what we were, which is Marines."

Although Tokyo Rose was the only Japanese broadcaster widely known in the United States, other English speaking broadcasters included Stewart Tashiro and Charles Yoshii, who were American-educated. John Holland, a particularly persuasive Axis commentator, was an Australian who lived in Shanghai.

Sefton Delmer, a journalist for the *London Daily Express,* became the director of Britain's black propaganda broadcasts to Germany in 1941. His clandestine station, Gustav Siegfried Eins, purported to be an unofficial station run by members of the German military. The main broadcaster was known as "Der Chef" (The Chief), a noncommissioned officer who never attacked Hitler, only other leaders of the Nazi Party, whom he accused of war profiteering. "If it should be a question of choosing between Göring or Himmler, then, by God . . . let us have 30,000 hundred-weight of Hermann, rather than one milligram of this scheming political out-house flower, of this anemic inflated windbag, Heinrich Himmler," Der Chef said in one broadcast. The intention was to turn German servicemen against the Nazi leadership and pit the leaders against each other.

Propaganda Techniques

Allied and Axis countries used similar techniques to devise and convey propaganda to general audiences. These included limiting the sources issuing information, having prestigious leaders, soldiers, or celebrities present the intended message, and simplifying complex facts. "Be as faithful to the truth as necessary," recommended Goebbels, "but omit and expand it as you think right in relation to your public." Choices also had to be made about the use of hyperbolic versus understated language that gave the appearance of objectivity. The minutes of a meeting between the British Broadcasting Corporation (BBC) and the British Foreign Office suggested that "the root of the matter lay in skillful and subtle presentation of news in such a way that the propaganda content did not reveal itself."

Governments had to comment on the past and predict the future in ways that were favorable to a country's image but not so overly optimistic that they bred distrust. When battles and events were unfavorable, they applied what later came to be called "spin"—a positive take on the facts. "Politicians [need to be] adept at demonstrating that their action has succeeded in spite of appearances to the contrary," wrote Michael Balfour of Britain's MoI, "or else that its failure is in no way due to its character."

Propaganda sometimes appealed to specific ethnic audiences for their support. In the United States, OWI distributed two posters for the Second War Loan Drive. One showed a white soldier, the other, produced for the black press, showed an African American soldier. OWI supported the All-American Newsreel Company, formed by black businessmen, which made wartime newsreels for black audiences; almost no African Americans had appeared in the newsreels made by white companies. In 1944, the War Loan drive featured separate posters for Greek, Czechoslovak, and Polish Americans, ethnic groups whose home countries were occupied by Germany. In the Soviet Union, films were targeted toward Ukrainians, Armenians, Georgians and other Soviet national groups.

Each country developed a propaganda strategy for dealing with losses. In Britain, Winston Churchill's words were particularly successful in conveying that a situation was serious, but never hopeless, and that gritty persistence would eventually win the day. The Axis countries, on the other hand, generally hid losses from the public. Axis propagandists not only feared that the knowledge of losses would lower morale, but that it would contradict previous pronouncements of easy victory.

Propaganda was also spread through slogans and symbols. In Allied countries, the letter "V," the first letter of the English and French words for

Posters were ubiquitous in World War II—visual symbols of patriotism that combined the attractiveness of art with the persuasiveness of advertising. They were inexpensive to produce, easy to display, and quickly conveyed their messages. Some showed how each person could help to win the war. Others emphasized the brutality of the enemy or the power and heroism of one's own troops. The German poster (top left) shows a German soldier striking down a Russian dragon with a Soviet star on its head. The Russian poster (top right), created by Aleksei Kokorkin in 1945, depicts the Allied flags, supported by bayonets, stuck in a dead wolf with the Nazi swastika on its forehead. In the Italian poster (bottom left), an American "gangster pilot," wearing a flag for a scarf, stands over the body of a dead Italian child. United States Marines raise the flag at Iwo Jima (bottom right) in an American fund-raising poster created by C.C. Beall in 1945.

victory, became a morale-boosting symbol. Winston Churchill raised his fingers in a V. The Flemish word for freedom—*vrijheid*—also began with a V. In 1941, the BBC's Belgian Service suggested to the audience that they display the letter in any way they could think of. People used the Morse code signal for V—dot dot dot dash—and the similar rhythm of a short passage in Beethoven's Fifth Symphony—to indicate ultimate victory. African Americans used the "Double V" sign calling for victory against the Axis abroad and victory against segregation at home.

Many wartime slogans reflected the need for discretion about information that could aid the enemy. The main German slogan was "The Enemy Is Listening" (*Feind Hort Mit*); Goebbels rejected "Battle Is Bravery, Talk Is Treachery" (*Kampf ist Tat, Reden Verrat*) so that the public would not associate "talk" with propaganda. Japanese slogans included *Hakko Ichiu*, roughly translated as "the eight corners of the world under one roof," a statement of international brotherhood, and *Kodo*, "the way of the emperor," which also implied Japanese domination of the Asiatic world.

British propagandists used "Careless Talk Costs Lives" on posters. An ill-fated campaign tried the slogan "Be Like Dad—Keep Mum," which met objections for its antifeminist connotation. "Loose Lips Sink Ships" was used generically in the United States to caution silence; "Loose Lips Might Sink Ships" appeared on posters. Other American posters referred to careless talk— "Americans Suffer When Careless Talk Kills," "A Careless Word . . . A Needless Sinking," and "Wanted! For Murder: Her Careless Talk Costs Lives."

The Media   Journalism

AXIS COUNTRIES

In 1933, after the Nazis suppressed Communist and Social Democratic newspapers, the Eher Verlag, a Nazi Party publishing house, proceeded to buy out newspapers that were Catholic, democratic, or focused on entertainment. In 1934, it claimed ownership of Ullstein, a major Jewish publishing company. By 1939, it had quietly gained control of some two-thirds of the nation's newspapers; the papers kept their old names, giving no indication that ownership had changed. An Editors Law, enacted in October 1933, also facilitated government control of newspapers. Editors bore the responsibility for any content that violated RMVP rules. The Deutsches Nachrichtenburo (DNB) was the official German news agency, dispensing news to both the domestic and foreign press. Newspapers were frequently told not to alter DNB stories, but to print them verbatim.

Benito Mussolini, who had edited both the socialist newspaper *Avanti!* and the Fascist newspaper *Il Popolo d'Italia*, declared, "In a totalitarian regime . . . the press is an element of this regime, a force which is at its service. In a unitary regime the press cannot stand outside this unity . . . Italian journalism is free because it serves only one cause and one regime . . . within the parameters of the laws . . . it can exercise, and does exercise, its functions of control, criticism and projection."

Although newspapers in Italy were privately owned, the Press Office encouraged pro-Fascist businesspeople to buy up opposition newspapers, thus increasing the number of Fascist periodicals. For example, Fascist industrialists bought *Il Secolo*, which had criticized Mussolini's government before it changed ownership. The Fascist Party also provided funds to start its own newspapers, including *Impero*, *Nuovo Paese*, and *Corriere Italiano*, and maintained a fund to support proFascist periodicals. From the late 1920s onward, the Italian Press Office issued press directives (*ordini alla stampa*) banning topics considered unsuitable for print, not only political and military news, but also what the government considered unpleasant or unwholesome, such as stories on crimes and violence. The Press Office also subsidized politically compatible newspapers, journals, and journalists. The official, state-controlled Stefani News Agency distributed stories to the press. Despite this, Mussolini's government never completely controlled Italian journalism.

The wartime Japanese government consolidated the ownership of hundreds of newspapers and brought the press under tight controls. Newspapers were regulated by the Home Office and subject to the Police Censorship Bureau, which could forbid publication and force newspapers to close. Several laws governed what could be printed, beginning with the Peace Preservation Law of 1925, designed to crack down on the expression of communist ideology. The 1935 Press Law included provisions for maintaining tight control of military secrets, and in the same year the government enacted a Control of Seditious Literature Law. Further laws curtailing freedom of the press included a Military Secrets and Protection Law in 1937; a 1939 Military Resources Protection Law that banned writing about industrial and military resources and production; a State Secrets Defense Act in 1941, forbidding the disclosure of "political, economic and diplomatic information harmful to Japan" to anyone outside the country; and a Restrictions on Communications Order, also in 1941. Newspapers that violated these laws were fined or their staff imprisoned; they therefore employed "jail editors" whose role was to serve prison time while actual reporters and editors continued publishing. Jail editors were particularly common in occupied China.

The dispensing of news was controlled by the Domei News Agency, established in 1936 as a public company in which the Japanese government owned a majority of the shares. Domei was responsible for compiling and disseminating both domestic and foreign news. Before the war, Japan's major newspapers had their own independent correspondents, but they were forced to rely increasingly on Domei for information. Domei could ensure acquiescence to government restrictions by threatening to withhold information from editors and reporters. Foreign newspapers reporting on Japan also depended on Domei. All press leaving Japan, as well as coming from overseas, had to be approved by the Ministry of Communications.

Through Domei, the government controlled the flow of news. It also controlled the paper supply and, by withholding paper, could effectively shut down the voice of the press. (As the war continued, all Japanese newspapers were affected by shortages. Publishers discontinued all but morning editions and reduced the size to an average of four to six pages.) In 1941, newspapers were declared to be public utilities and were organized into a Newspaper League that included all owners and editors. The following year, the government merged the largest remaining papers. Commentators on news and politics continued to write for the combined periodicals, including several with military rank: Rear-Admiral Gumpei Sekine, Admiral Ryozo Nakamura and Rear-Admiral Tanetsugu Sosa.

ALLIED COUNTRIES

Press censorship in Britain, although under the Ministry of Information's umbrella, was voluntary. Francis Williams, the controller of news and censorship, held daily conferences with the press. But government departments did indicate what topics should be avoided in a series of D Notices (issued since 1911), limiting subject matter for security reasons. After publication, a writer or editor could be prosecuted if an article violated Defense Regulation 3, which prohibited publication of information useful to the enemy. Defense Regulation 2D banned the publication of "matter calculated to foment opposition in the prosecution of the war." Under this regulation, the MoI prohibited exportation of communist and fascist newspapers in 1940 and forbade publication of the *Daily Worker* and the *Week* from January 1941 until the summer of 1942.

Churchill generally distinguished between stories that threatened the country and those that annoyed the government. Yet in 1940, the prime minister chastised a director of the *Daily Mail* for "a spirit of hatred and malice against the Government. . . . One would have thought that in these hard times some hatred might be kept for the enemy." Criticisms of the government were feared to weaken morale.

Several news agencies operated in Britain, including Reuters, Exchange Telegraph, Britanova, and British Official Wireless. Unlike those in the Axis countries, they were not controlled by the government.

Two government agencies controlled the output of news and information in the Soviet Union: Tass distributed news within the USSR and Novosti provided news to other countries. Tass was also responsible for compiling a daily review of foreign newspapers, books, and other publications for the Communist Central Committee. Since the reviews were not secret, they were classified as "white TASS" documentation. The press and radio were allowed to view these compilations. Reporters who worked for Tass outside the Soviet Union compiled monthly "Letters of Tass Correspondents" containing summaries of news and political commentary.

Izvestia and *Pravda* were the two main Soviet newspapers, the former published by the Presidium of the Supreme Soviet and the latter by the Central Committee of the Communist Party. More than a thousand noted writers served as war correspondents; 417 were killed at the front. Novelist Ilya Ehrenburg, a Jewish Russian expatriate who supported revolution against the czar as a young man and returned to live in the Soviet Union in 1941, was the country's most prominent journalist. He published more than 300 articles, many calling for brutal revenge against the Germans, in *Pravda*, *Izvestia*, and *Krasnaya Zvezda* (*Red Star*), the military's daily newspaper. Other frontline

Soviet printers set type for the Red Army's frontline newspaper within earshot of a battle, July 19, 1942.

journalists included novelist Vasily Grossman, who reported on major battles (including Stalingrad) for *Krasnaya Zvezda*; poet and playwright Konstantin Simonov, who wrote for *Boevoe Znamya* (*Battle Flag*); and satirist Evgeny Petrov, who was killed in action.

Regarded as "an instrument of democracy," as Scripps-Howard Newspapers editor and publisher John Sorrells said in 1943, the American press generally accepted Sorrells's statement: "In peace time, the sole responsibility of the newspaper is to inform. . . . In war time, a great part of the responsibility is not to inform, but to suppress, to guard, to screen information of the most interesting sort" that might be of help to the enemy. The U.S. press successfully practiced voluntary censorship during the war (see "U.S. Office of Censorship" earlier in this chapter).

Two major news agencies operated in the United States: the United Press and the Associated Press. Hundreds of American newspapers ran UP and AP stories as well as those written by their own reporters and correspondents. Magazines like *Look* and Henry Luce's *Life*—with national circulations that reached millions of readers—also played a large role in conveying information and shaping public perception about the war. By 1943, since Americans had grown impatient with the length of the war and less committed to the war effort, the OWI suggested that not publicizing images of wounded and dead soldiers encouraged the public to believe that "some get hurt and ride smiling in aerial ambulances, but that none of them get badly shot or spill any blood." In May 1943, *Newsweek* showed photographs of wounded troops in the Pacific, released as part of the effort, as *Newsweek* stated, "to harden home-front morale . . . [by] letting civilians see photographically what warfare does to men who fight." The first photographs of U.S. war dead appeared in *Life* magazine that September. After other photographs of the dead were widely distributed on posters as well as in periodicals, the public bought more war bonds and industrial laborers hesitated to strike or not show up for work.

American photojournalists, like print journalists, were accredited to work in war zones. Carl Mydans and W. Eugene Smith worked for *Life* in the Pacific. Margaret Bourke-White, also with *Life*, was the first woman during World War II to be accredited as a correspondent. She was in the Soviet Union when Germany attacked and took the first American photos of this front, including the shelling of Moscow. In 1943, she became the first woman to accompany an American bombing mission. Lee Miller, who had been a model, published war photographs in *Vogue*. Both women photographed Nazi

The bodies of three dead American soldiers killed in a Japanese ambush lie on Buna Beach, February 1, 1943. Life *published this photo in September of that year. It was the first image of slain U.S. soldiers to be printed in an American periodical. Courtesy of Getty Images.*

concentration camps after these were liberated. Fashion and society photographer Toni Frissell documented the American Red Cross, the Women's Auxiliary Army Corps, and the African American pilots of the 332nd fighter group, the Tuskegee Airmen. Joe Rosenthal of the Associated Press captured the well-known image of troops raising the American flag on Iwo Jima. Thayer Souole and David Duncan were noted Marine Corps photographers. Robert Capa (born Andre Friedman in Budapest) photographed the Allied landing on D-Day. "I am a gambler," he commented. "I decided to go in with Company E in the first wave."

U.S. WAR CORRESPONDENTS

"To report this war adequately, correspondents must go into the field and take their chances," wrote *New York Times* correspondent Harold Denny in the July 13, 1943, issue of *Look*. "So we see them patrolling in trucks or staff cars, often far to the rear of the enemy, and getting into the midst of tank battles in thin-skinned vehicles. We see them on war vessels under withering attack by hostile aircraft and naval forces. We see them flying in bombers to the heart of enemy territory, and dropping with parachute troops behind enemy positions." When Denny published this story, 12 American war correspondents had been killed, 60 wounded, 28 captured, and 3 were missing. By the end of the war, 37 American correspondents had died.

U.S. correspondents were accredited by the War Department. "The correspondent is in the Army, but not of it," Denny explained in *Look*. "He wears an officer's uniform, but has no authority. A civilian, he is forbidden to carry arms, yet he is subject to military law and can be court-martialed for disobedience."

(In contrast, German war correspondents were not civilians, but part of Propaganda Kompanie [PK] units commanded by the German military.) If captured, war correspondents could be held as prisoners of war with the rank of captain.

Despite Denny's description of their activities, most war correspondents were not daily in the midst of battle. Both American and foreign (Allied and neutral) correspondents were assigned to U.S. press camps. "Correspondents here [in France after D-Day] really live like communists. Six or eight are parked in a pyramidal tent," wrote Ollie Stewart for the *Afro-American* newspaper. "We've got cots for a while (hoo-ray) and hope to keep them." Correspondents were accompanied by an officer who conducted them to various sites. They could interview troops and officers, but they received much information from designated public information officers. Paul Fussell, who was an army lieutenant in World War II and has written on the public relations role of war journalism, had another view of correspondents and their writing. "Those attentive to the maintenance of home-front morale became skilled at optimistic prose," he wrote in his 1989 book *Wartime*. Using euphemistic and soothing words smoothed over the brutality of combat, the horror of mangled American bodies and mass graves. Either the writer, the editor back home, or both could shape the message of the story, distorting the soldier's experience and treating devastating losses as heroic.

Correspondents' stories, photographs, and film footage also had to be submitted to military censors before they were dispatched. Each theater commander formulated the censorship rules in his combat zone, so the rules varied. The navy, under Chief of Naval Operations

Photographers and correspondents played a critical role in reporting information on the war to the American public. From left to right, top: Therese Bonney, Margaret Bourke-White, Robert Capa, Toni Frissel; middle: Stanley Johnson, Lee Miller, Edward R. Murrow, Carl Mydans; bottom: Ernie Pyle, Quentin Reynolds, Joseph Rosenthal, Eugene Smith.

Ernest King, called for greater censorship than did the army. In the army, Southwest Pacific theater commander General Douglas MacArthur, who preferred stories that highlighted his own role, was more restrictive than the European theater commander, General Dwight D. Eisenhower, who claimed it was "a matter of policy [that] accredited war correspondents should be accorded the greatest possible latitude in the gathering of legitimate news." Overall, relations between U.S. correspondents and the U.S. military were good, as the military understood the value of public relations to maintain public support. Nonetheless, the armed services were more restrictive than the correspondents about what was acceptable.

Among the print journalists who served as war correspondents were Quentin Reynolds for *Collier's,* Stanley Johnston for the *Chicago Tribune,* Bill Walton for *Time,* Ken Dixon and Don Whitehead for the Associated Press, Homer Bigart for the *New York Herald Tribune,* and William Laurence of the *New York Times.* Novelist John Steinbeck wrote for the *New York Herald Tribune:* "What the correspondent really saw was dust and the nasty burst of shells, low bushes and slit trenches. . . . He lay on his stomach, if he had any sense, and watched ants crawling among the little sticks on the sand dune."

Perhaps the best known correspondent was Ernie Pyle, a syndicated columnist for the Scripps-Howard newspaper chain whose writing captured—and mythologized—the experience of the ordinary soldier. Pyle traveled with the 9th Infantry Division for nine days in Nor-

mandy, in July 1944. "The men . . . weren't heroic figures. . . . You think of attackers as being savage and bold. These men were hesitant and cautious. . . . There was a confused excitement and a grim anxiety on their faces. . . . They weren't warriors. They were American boys who by mere chance of fate had wound up with guns in their hands sneaking up a death-laden street in a strange and shattered city in a faraway country in a driving rain. . . . They were good boys. . . . And even though they aren't warriors born to the kill, they win their battles. That's the point." After covering Europe, Pyle joined American soldiers in the Pacific. He was killed by the machine-gun fire of Japanese troops on the island of Ie Shima on April 18, 1945.

One hundred twenty-seven women were also accredited as U.S. correspondents during World War II. Martha Gellhorn, who reported for *Collier's,* covered the Spanish Civil War, as well as the war in China, Italy, and France. She wrote of a hospital for the wounded in Italy: "It smelled of many things, of men and dampness and old blankets and ether and pain. . . . War, which is such a large and incomprehensible and impersonal affair, becomes very personal indeed inside a hospital, for at last it is reduced to its basic matériel, the human body." Other female correspondents included Helen Camp, Ruth Cowan, and Flora Lewis for the Associated Press, Janet Flanner for the *New Yorker,* Marguerite Higgins for the *New York Herald Tribune,* Shelley Mydans for *Time-Life,* Sigrid Schultz for the *Chicago Tribune,* and Ann Stringer for the United Press.

Radio Broadcasting

By the time World War II began, governments had already used radio for two decades as an instrument of foreign politics. The Soviet Union broadcast calls for worldwide proletariat revolution in the 1920s and exploited events such as the British general strike to appeal to laborers in that country. During the 1921–1925 French occupation of Germany's prime industrial region, the Ruhr, the French and Germans each broadcast propaganda to the other country, as did Germany and Poland over the contested possession of Upper Silesia. Dramatically effective as a vehicle for inspiring and unifying its audience, radio could broadcast live major speeches and events.

World War II combatants broadcast domestically, as well as to enemy, occupied, and neutral countries. Radio was the principal propaganda organ in these countries, reaching a wider audience than print or film. Jamming programs—broadcasting a loud noise or static over the same frequency as an enemy broadcast—disrupted but failed to halt radio propaganda. "[In] the psychological attack against the moral and spiritual defenses of a nation . . . the most powerful weapon is radio," William Donovan, head of the American OSS, believed.

AXIS COUNTRIES

Germany's RMVP radio department assumed responsibility for the already existing Reich Radio Company (Reichsrundfunkgesellschaft or RRG), which included nine regional companies. Hermann Göring, then Prussian Minister of the Interior, wanted to maintain regional control, but Hitler authorized control by the RMVP.

The Nazis made available inexpensive Volksempfanger VE 3031 (people's receiver) radios to all Germans; more than 6 million sets were manufactured in 1934. By 1939, there were radios in more than 70 percent of German homes, and, since the VE 3031 had a limited range, they did not pick up foreign broadcasts. People were encouraged to listen together in groups to facilitate what Eugen Hadamovsky, head of the Reich Chamber of Radio, called "the organically developed spirituality of the community." Radio wardens, drawn from the Nazi party, organized local Stunden der Nation (National Moments) to focus attention on important radio broadcasts. Loudspeakers and sirens alerted people to stop what they were doing and tune in to hear, for example, a speech by Hitler or Goebbels. Six thousand loudspeakers on columns were erected in public places for special broadcasts.

Stations played the *Badenweiler*, Hitler's favorite march, before he spoke; he annually gave a speech on Heroes' Day, when Wagner's *Meistersinger* overture was also played. Goebbels gave the annual speech in honor of Hitler's birthday. Hitler was not a brilliant speaker when recorded in a studio, so it was his speeches at public gatherings that were broadcast.

Early German radio programming emphasized politics and Nazi doctrine, but by 1942, Goebbels allowed 70 percent of a broadcast to be light music to keep his audience engaged. As the war progressed, radio wardens not only were responsible for promoting community listening, but they also reported fellow Germans who were caught listening to foreign shortwave broadcasts.

Italy established a state radio system, Ente Italiano Audizioni Radiofoniche (EIAR) in 1927. Programs were political in content and many focused on Mussolini as a leader and exemplar. In 1929, Giornale radio (Radio News) made its debut, with six daily broadcasts covering national and international news, always from a Fascist Party perspective. In the 1930s, the Ente Radio Rurale was launched in rural areas, where the government gave radios to elementary schools. Run by the Fascist Party, programming included the *Ora dell'agricoltore* (*Farmer's Hour*) of advice. In 1939, the Ministry for Popular Culture assumed control of the broadcasts and soon absorbed them into the EIAR. National programs included *Dieci minuti del lavoratore* (*Ten Minutes with the Worker*), *Universita radiofonica italiana* (*Italian Radio University*), and *Cronache dello sport* (*Chronicles of Sport*). Propaganda peppered the broadcasts, but it was as much cultural as political until the war began. Italians could also listen to the Vatican Radio station as an alternate source of information.

Japan's first radio station began transmitting in Tokyo in 1925. In 1934, all Japanese radio stations merged into a public corporation, the Broadcasting Corporation of Japan (Nippon Hosokyoki), which was controlled by the Ministry of Communications and the Government Information Bureau. The BCJ became a part of the Domei News Agency (see "Journalism" earlier in this chapter). Supporting itself by charging owners of radio sets a monthly fee, the BCJ broadcast only to the Japanese mainland. Occupied countries had their own stations run by propaganda organizations ultimately under the command of the military.

In 1933, the Japanese government banned ownership of shortwave radios. As countries came under Japanese occupation, shortwave owners were required to turn in their sets to be converted into medium-wave receivers. The goal was to make it impossible to hear transmissions from overseas. Domei provided the news for domestic programs. These were broadcast from Tokyo and six other Japanese cities. Programs were also relayed from Formosa, Nanking, and other parts of the Asian Co-Prosperity Sphere. After December 1941, a cultural accord between Germany and Japan included an exchange of radio programming: a Japanese audience could hear about the heroism of the German military, and vice versa. Western classical music and opera, including *The Marriage of Figaro* and *Tannhäuser*, were broadcast on Japanese radio. There were also readings of works on Western imperialism (including *A History of American and British Aggression in Asia* by Okawa Shumei) and on Japanese history, as well as lectures on cultural subjects.

In occupied countries, the Japanese repaired transmitters destroyed by the Allies. Some radio broadcasts were in Japanese, with the intent of teaching the language to local populations, but most broadcasts were in local languages. In the Dutch East Indies, the Japanese first erected "singing trees," also called "singing towers"—loudspeakers suspended from poles outdoors, which broadcast to neighborhoods and communities. Singing trees were also erected at schools to familiarize children with the Japanese language.

RULER OF THE AIRWAVES: THE BBC

The most important British propaganda channel during World War II was the British Broadcasting Corporation (BBC) radio. Even in neutral countries, it enjoyed a substantial audience, and in occupied and enemy countries, it was by far the most reliable source of Allied news and propaganda.

Formed in 1922, the BBC was a quasi-governmental organization. Although it operated as an independent corporation, its governors were appointed by the British government. During the war, the Ministry of Information supervised its home broadcasts and those to Allied countries, and the Political Warfare Executive organized the broadcasts to enemy and occupied countries. Although they generally agreed with official British policy, BBC reporters and presenters sometimes veered from the strict government line.

The BBC Foreign Service (the Home Service broadcast domestically) first began broadcasting in Arabic, followed by a Latin American Service, both in 1938. By September 1939, the European Service was broadcasting twelve hours a day in sixteen languages. After the fall of Western Europe, several Allied governments-in-exile in London requested transmitting time from the BBC. The first of these services, Radio Oranje, began on July 28, 1940, with Queen Wilhelmina of the Netherlands giving the opening message.

Allied Countries

Regular radio broadcasts began in the Soviet Union in 1924, and in 1940, there were 90 radio stations operating. By then, the government had licensed 7 million radios. Glavlit censored radio broadcasts as it did written publications. Before the Soviet Union entered World War II, the large majority of programs played music; the remainder featured readings of classic literature, drama, and education in communist doctrine and politics.

After the war started, all news bulletins and information for radio, as well as the press, were issued through the Sovinformburo. Yuri Levitan gave daily broadcasts citing military activities, military and civilian bravery, and relevant international events. Stalin addressed the country on radio at various times.

During the alliance with Germany, Soviet overseas radio had ceased to attack fascism and concentrated on criticizing British and American imperialism. From mid-1941, however, Soviet broadcasts to domestic audiences and to Germany railed against Nazi leaders, most vehemently attacking Hitler (Britain and the United States did not, believing that the German people were very attached to him). Soviet radio stations also sponsored broadcasts by exiled communist groups, including the Union of Polish Patriots, the Hungarian National Independence Front, the National Committee of Germany (a group of German communist emigrants), and the League of German Officers (primarily disgruntled officers who had been captured at Stalingrad). The Jewish Antifascist Committee was a homegrown official Soviet organization that targeted propaganda to Jewish populations in neutral countries.

By the end of the 1930s, Americans owned some 60 million radios bringing news with unprecedented speed and directness into their homes, such as the live transmission of the speeches of British prime minister Neville Chamberlain and President Franklin Roosevelt after the British declared war on Germany. The home-front audience relied on the broadcasts of foreign correspondents, particularly Edward R. Murrow, who led the CBS radio team that also included William Shirer, Howard K. Smith, Charles Collingwood, and Eric Sevareid. NBC's radio broadcasts featured Francis McCall, Wright Bryan, David Anderson, Tom Traynor, and W.W. Chaplin.

Murrow broadcast live from London every evening; listeners could hear the bombs falling in the background as he spoke from rooftops during the Blitz. Some journalists, like Walter Winchell, whose program ran on Sunday nights, railed against the Nazis even before the United States entered the war, but for the most part, radio stations were concerned not to offend the large U.S. isolationist population by seeming to be anything other than neutral. After Pearl Harbor, their stance changed. In a legendary broadcast of Franklin Roosevelt's speech to Congress declaring war, the president memorably declared, "Yesterday, December 7, 1941—a date which will live in infamy." Roosevelt was an extremely effective radio speaker. Beginning in 1933, he gave twenty-eight Fireside Chats in prime time—thirteen of them in wartime—explaining events and policy to the public and encouraging morale.

In addition to war news, American radio's war-related programming included *The Man Behind the Gun*, which depicted battles, and *Stage Door Canteen*, a variety show for U.S. troops. On Wednesday afternoons, interviewer Mary Margaret McBride focused on the home-front experience. Special children's programs, broadcast in the late afternoons, included *Don Winslow of the Navy* and *Hop Harrigan*, both pilots who bombed the enemy. Even entertainment shows like *Fibber McGee and Molly*, the *Abbott and Costello Show*, and the *Kraft Music Hall* pitched the sale of war bonds.

In 1942, the Armed Forces Radio Service began delivering programs on transcription discs or by shortwave radio to American troops overseas. The shows featured popular and classical music, comedy, sports, news, and serials—AFRS produced some; most were commercial programs with advertising deleted. By 1945, 83,000 disks were shipped overseas per month.

Operated by the Office of War Information and aimed at enemy civilians, the Voice of America broadcast its first program to Germany on February 26, 1942. Programs usually lasted fifteen minutes and were transmitted from New York. By 1945, Germans could hear more than four and two-thirds hours of broadcasting each week. Programming emphasized news and accounts from the front, with some commentary and music. In the spring of 1944, OWI also opened the American Broadcasting Station in Europe (ABSIE), transmitting from England eight hours each day in the weeks leading up to D-Day. Broadcasts reported "the plain facts of the war, forcefully brought to the eyes and ears [that] would in the long run be more corrosive to Nazi morale than any amount of agitational propaganda," according to OWI records.

The Office of Censorship provided guidelines to the radio industry in the *Code of Wartime Practices for American Broadcasters* (see "U.S. Office of Censorship" earlier in this chapter). Items to be censored included the type and movements of troops and ships, damage from enemy action, the location of bases and fortifications, details about industrial production, rumors, unconfirmed reports or information from enemy propaganda, and data about the weather. The code added a note for "special events reporters covering sports events [who] are cautioned especially against the mention of weather conditions in describing contests, announcing their schedules, suspensions, or cancellations."

Film

Leon Trotsky, one of the leaders of the Bolshevik Revolution, could have been speaking for the propaganda organizations of all countries during World War II when he called film, "This weapon, which cries out to be used . . . [It] is the best instrument for propaganda . . . a propaganda which is accessible to everyone, cuts into the memory and may be made a possible source of revenue."

AXIS COUNTRIES

Both Hitler and Goebbels believed in the importance of film as propaganda, but Goebbels also understood that film should "keep our people happy because that is of strategic importance too." In June 1933, six months after Hitler came to power, the Nazi's formed a film chamber to organize film industry workers and to establish a bank (*Kreditbank*) to fund approved film projects. In February 1934, a Reich Cinema Law (*Reichslichtpielgesetz*, or RLG) declared that a film could be banned because of its treatment of politics or race. The RLG required that film scripts be submitted for approval. A film that passed all censorship hurdles was granted a censorship card for each print with an embossed stamp of the German eagle. Few films that had been made before Hitler came to power passed the censors, and the number of foreign films shown drastically declined.

Goebbels thought films not only should be unobjectionable, but should embody the values of National Socialism. Films were awarded marks for distinction (*Pradikate*); without one, a film could not be shown; with one, producers gained tax breaks. There were eleven categories, including "politically and artistically especially valuable," "culturally valuable," "Film of the Nation," and "valuable for youth." (The last category did not carry tax breaks but it increased distribution.)

After World War II began, German films dominated the European film market. To gain greater control over production—and profits—the

German filmmaker Leni Riefenstahl looks through a camera while shooting the spectacular rally organized by the Nazi party at Nuremberg, 1934. Her film, Triumph of the Will, *appeared a year later.*

government nationalized the film industry in January 1942 by creating a massive holding company, Ufa-Film GmbH, referred to as Ufi. Thereafter, all newsreels, shown regularly before features in theaters, were laden with images of heroism and victory. When the Soviet Union turned the tide on the Eastern Front and began advancing toward Germany, newsreels stressed atrocities by Soviet troops. After 1943, the German public no longer believed the newsreels' propaganda. Audiences began waiting outside theaters until the feature film began. Goebbels then issued an order barring access to theaters once the newsreels had begun.

Between 1933 and 1945, Germany produced some 1,100 German films, but only about one-sixth of these were directly propagandistic. Half of the feature films were comedies or love stories, and there were a significant number of crime dramas and musicals. Only 96 films were commissioned by the state, but these were generously financed and publicized. Among them were Leni Riefenstahl's *Triumph of the Will* in 1935, about the Nazi Party rally in Nuremberg the year before, and her *Olympia*, an artistic document of the 1936 Olympic Games in Berlin. *Die Rothschilds*, *Jud Suss*, and *Der ewige Jude* were anti-Semitic propaganda pieces. An early film, *Hans Westmar* (1933), was a largely fictionalized account of Horst Wessel, a young Nazi who wrote the Nazi party song and was murdered by a communist gang.

In 1945, as Germany was being pressed on all sides by approaching Allied armies, Goebbels produced *Kolberg*, a film celebrating the heroism of the besieged Prussian city during the Napoleonic Wars. By refusing to surrender, the city achieved victory over the French. *Kolberg* cost 8.5 million marks; 187,000 troops and 4,000 sailors were relieved from active duty to participate in making the film.

In Italy, feature filmmakers came under less control than did the press or radio broadcasters or the film industry in other totalitarian countries. Films were only censored if they dealt with political issues or were negative about Fascism or Italian society. Even American films passed the censors. Nor did the government utilize the medium to make feature propaganda films. The main organization to convey the Fascist view was the Istituto

Nazionale dell'Unione Cinematografica Educativa (LUCE), formed in 1924 to produce newsreels, documentaries on policy, and long films on Italy's involvement in such events as the Ethiopian War and the Spanish Civil War. Theaters were required to show the LUCE newsreels as part of their programs.

In Japan, where film production reached a peak in 1937 (at 2,500 films, more than 1,000 of which were newsreels), the number of feature films declined during the war, while the production of newsreels increased. In April 1939, a Motion Picture Law increased government control of all aspects of filmmaking and viewing, requiring all showings to include at least one educational or cultural film approved by the Ministry of Education.

Private production companies were consolidated into two conglomerates, the Shochiku company, which produced the majority of films in Japan, and the Toho company. The Japan Motion Picture Company (Nippon Eigasha) produced most of the newsreels aimed at a domestic audience, and newsreels in Japanese, Chinese, Tagalog, Thai, Malay, French, and English for the populations of occupied countries. The three largest Japanese newspaper groups also produced newsreels. American and British films were banned, but Axis films were shown—Germany's *Baptism of Fire* and *Victory in the West* were particularly admired. The Japanese produced their own war epics, including *Victory of the East*, commissioned by the Admiralty and featuring the naval battles near Hawaii and Malaya; *The Last Days of the British Empire*, commissioned by the War Office; and *God's Troops in the Sky*, about the Japanese Air Force. Actors recreated the events portrayed, but the films also incorporated newsreel footage and photographs.

The Japanese made an effort to show films to their troops and to rural populations in occupied countries, using mobile theaters that operated in the open air or out of small buildings or tents. The film subjects included Japanese cities, sports, and the bravery and skill of the armed forces at the front.

ALLIED COUNTRIES

Britain's Ministry of Information included a separate film division, but the commercial film industry remained independent of the government. The MoI considerably influenced production, however, since its approval meant access to supplies and financing and exemption from military service for those working on films. The British government also took over several studios during the war, including Pinewood, which was used as a food storage facility. From 1939 to 1945, the MoI was involved in the production of 1,887 films and approved 3,200 newsreels and 380 feature films. These included *In Which We Serve* (1942) and *Henry V* (1945), the Shakespeare play that recorded a historic victory for Britain against overwhelming odds. In 1942, Humphrey Jennings' *Fires Were Started*, a combination of documentary and dramatization, portrayed a London fire service unit over twenty-four hours during the Blitz. The Crown Film Unit was responsible for making documentaries for the government, enlisting the help of professional directors such as Jennings and Harry Watt, who filmed *Squadron 922*, *Target for Tonight*, and a fictional movie, *Nine Men*. The Crown Film Unit also produced short information films for the public. Theater owners allowed five minutes at each showing for these films or similar information "shorts" made by the film industry at MoI's request.

In the Soviet Union, where the cinema was nationalized in 1919, film was expected to convey communist values and be ideologically sound. The number of films produced each year declined, from about 120 in the 1920s to 35 in the 1930s to 25 per year during the war. Most foreign films were banned, and many films produced before 1935 could not be shown. One film that Stalin did approve—he even suggested its name change, from *Cinderella* to *The Radiant Path*—told the story of a maid who went to work in a textile factory, exposed an arsonist threatening production, and became a deputy in the Supreme Soviet (legislature).

After the Soviet Union entered the war, more than 250 Soviet cameramen at the front filmed 120 documentaries and newsreels. Early in the war, these were edited and released to the Allies, to show that the USSR would not be defeated. Among the first documentaries, made in 1941, were *All Efforts for the Smashing of the Enemy* and *In the Defense of Our Moscow*. Feature films such as *The Defense of Tsaritsyn* focused on the bravery of the Bolshevik Army during the Russian civil war. Others celebrated the bravery of Soviet troops in the contemporary war, among them *The German Soldiers' Defeat at Moscow*, *She Defends the Motherland*, and *Stalingrad*. Novels, including V.L. Vasilevskaya's *Raduga*, about the resistance against German occupation, were also made into films. The first part of famed director Sergei Eisenstein's *Ivan the Terrible* appeared in 1945.

In the United States, Hollywood was quicker than the government to produce antifascist films, including *Confessions of a Nazi Spy* (1939) and Charlie Chaplin's *The Great Dictator* (1940). Isolationist senator Gerald Nye accused American filmmakers of turning out films "designed to drug the reason of the American people, set aflame their emotions, turn their hatred into a blaze, fill them with fear that Hitler will come over here and capture them." He and fellow isolationist senator Bennett Champ headed a Senate Subcommittee that investigated whether the film industry was deliberately campaigning for the United States to enter World War II. After the Japanese bombed Pearl Harbor, the government's concern shifted to encouraging the production of films that would aid the war effort.

The Office of War Information's Motion Picture Board (disbanded in 1943) had no authority to censor commercial films, but it did provide a manual for guiding Hollywood. The guidelines asked filmmakers to distinguish between German, Japanese, and Italian people (who might be good or unwitting) and their leaders. The Soviet Union, as an ally, was to be portrayed in a positive light. The United States was always to appear favorably, a bastion of democracy in which class and race did not matter. In general, the film industry complied. Studios submitted screenplays on a voluntary basis, which the MPB read and commented on. The Office of Censorship actually had more control over Hollywood than did the MPB because the censors could prohibit an American film from being distributed overseas. Since studios depended on access to the British and Latin American markets, which produced one third of their income in 1944–1945, they complied with the Office of Censorship guidelines.

Among the best-known American wartime films depicting combat were *Bataan*; *Thirty Seconds over Tokyo*, about the April 1942 Jimmy Doolittle bombing raid on Tokyo; *The Purple Heart*, about some of Doolittle's flyers, captured and made to stand trial by the Japanese; *The Fighting Sullivans*, about five brothers serving on the same ship who were all killed in the same naval battle; *Wing and a Prayer*; *Guadalcanal Diary*; *Sahara*, about the Allies' fight against the Germans in North Africa; *Gung Ho*, about Marines taking Makin Island; *Flying Tigers*, about combat over China; *Wake Island*; and *The Story of G.I. Joe*, based on war correspondent Ernie Pyle's dispatches from the front. *Since You Went Away* depicted popular images of the home front: after a man leaves for war, his wife takes a job as a welder and his daughter goes to work as a nurse instead of beginning college. Dad comes home in time for Christmas.

Hollywood filmmakers, including Frank Capra, John Huston, William Wyler, William Wegman, George Cukor, and John Ford, worked with the Army Pictorial Service to make training films for troops. Some 1,300 films were produced from 1942 to 1944 in a studio lot in Queens, New York.

(Hollywood took over film production at the end of 1944.) Titles ranged from *Kill or Be Killed* to *Sex Hygiene* to *Hasty Sign Making*. Perhaps the best known was the series *Why We Fight*, seven short films directed by Capra and Anatole Litvak: *Prelude to War, The Nazis Strike, Divide and Conquer, Battle of Britain, Battle of Russia, Battle of China*, and *War Comes to America*. (See also "The Pioneers of Fort Roach" in Chapter 4.)

Art

The styles and themes of painting, sculpture, drawing, architecture, and other visual arts during World War II, as well as the policies and professional organizations affecting artists, often reflected the political goals of the government of each combatant nation. Each viewed art as it did other media—as a potential tool to reinforce nationalism, shape national culture, and imbue the citizen with certain values. Germany, Japan, and the Soviet Union imposed greater control on artists and subject matter than did Britain or the United States, while Italy organized its artists and yet allowed experimentation.

AXIS COUNTRIES

The German and Japanese governments rejected the avant-garde trends of the first third of the 20th century as provocative, disruptive, iconoclastic, and individualistic, rather than supportive of the traditions that they assumed held communities together and encouraged subservience to the state. After Japanese prime minister Fumimaro Konoe instituted rule by imperial decree in the spring of 1938, authorities cracked down on politically dissident artists; those associated with the surrealist movement were suspected of being communist and were put under police surveillance. In the early 1940s, the Government Information Bureau regulated artists as it did practitioners of other media.

In Germany, the Nazi Party equated avant-garde art with decadence. Expressionist and abstract paintings, drawings, and sculpture drew particular ire. Goebbels chose Hans Schweitzer, a cartoonist, to be the Reich Plenipotentiary for Artistic Formulation. Schweitzer closed the Berlin National Gallery's modern wing and, with three other commissioners, removed more than 16,000 modern works of art from other German galleries and museums. Their creators included Max Ernst and Kathe Kollwitz, as well as Pablo Picasso, Henri Matisse, and Vincent Van Gogh.

Selbst das wurde einmal ernst genommen und hoch bezahlt!

Die Titel heißen: „Der Gott der Flieger", „Am Strand", „Merzbild" und „Familienbild".
Die „Künstler" heißen: Molzahn, Metzinger und Schwitters.

Page 23 from the catalog for the "Exhibition of Degenerate Art." (See p. 830.) Arranged by Joseph Goebbels in 1937, the exhibition presented the German public with examples of painting and sculpture that violated Nazi values. The first sentence on this page reads, "Even this was once taken seriously and highly paid." The works shown here were by Johannes Molzahn, Jean Metzinger, and Kurt Schwitters.

In late 1936, Goebbels also banned art criticism. Only "commentary on the arts," reports that described basic features of a painting or sculpture, were allowed. These reports could also indicate how closely a work of art expressed National Socialist values. Acceptable articles on art were published in *Die Kunst im Dritten Reich* (*Art in the Third Reich*), a periodical under the control of Alfred Rosenberg, who set up Nazi party cultural organizations parallel to, and in competition with, the state organization of Goebbels.

In 1937, the House of German Art, a newly built museum in Munich, housed an exhibition of 900 works of art that the Nazi Party, and Hitler himself, considered admirable. Hitler felt that art must "confirm the sound instinct of the people" and a work was unacceptable if it "cannot rely on the joyous, heartfelt assent of the broad and healthy mass of the people." At the same time that the House of German Art exhibit opened, Goebbels arranged an "Exhibition of Degenerate Art" to display pieces by artists such as Marc Chagall and Wassily Kandinsky that were examples of what Hitler characterized as "artistic lunacy" and "artistic pollution." The "degenerate" exhibit ran for four months and was far more popular with the public than the exhibit of sanctioned art. It continued to tour other parts of Germany to demonstrate that modern art was "the monstrous offspring of insanity, impudence, ineptitude and sheer degeneracy," as described by Adolf Ziegler, head of the Reich Chamber of Visual Artists.

Although Italy was a totalitarian state, Mussolini proved more open to artistic experimentation than his Axis counterparts. "I declare that it is far from my idea to encourage anything like an art of the State," he said at the opening of an exhibit of seven twentieth-century painters in 1923. "Art belongs to the domain of the individual. The State has only one duty: not to undermine art, to provide humane conditions for artists, and to encourage them from the artistic and national point of view."

Italian Fascism had also been associated with the radical art movement called futurism. Its founder, Filippo Tomasso Marinetti, published the Futurist Manifesto in 1909, declaring that futurist art turned its back on the past to embrace the vibrant aspects of modern life, including technology and violence. Marinetti knew Mussolini; and the futurists, who did not separate politics from art, supported the Fascist Party's ascendance to power. In the 1930s, several futurists initiated the Aeropittura (aeropainting) school of art. One of them, Gherardo Dottori, painted a portrait of Mussolini's head surrounded by airplanes. A more traditional group, the Novecento artists, also worked in Fascist Italy, reinterpreting the style of Roman and Renaissance work, a goal the Italian Fascists agreed with.

A significant step in controlling Italian art came in 1938 when the government, drawing closer to Germany, promulgated laws against Italy's Jewish population. The work of Jewish artists could no longer be exhibited. In 1939, Roberto Farinacci, an antimodernist member of the Fascist grand council, established the Cremona Prize and exhibit, limiting subject matter to scenes and portraits such as Italians listening to Mussolini speak on the radio or members of the youth Fascist movement. Nonetheless, many artists found the Italian Fascist political philosophy too restrictive as a guide to what they could create. They were neither pro- nor anti-Fascist; they believed that propaganda and simplification should not determine art.

Japanese artists were also active in recording the war experience and creating propaganda. In 1939, Japan's Army Information Section founded an Army Art Association, hiring artists to paint large canvasses with patriotic themes in support of the war. About 300 artists who served in the military were stationed at the front. Their work was used to illustrate books, journals, and postcards. The New Cartoonists Association of Japan, founded in 1940, organized cartoon artists and published the monthly magazine *Manga*. Hidezo Kondo, *Manga*'s editor, was noted for his caricatures of enemy politicians. Japan's popular prewar comic strip "Little Fuku" (*Fuku-Chan*), drawn by Ryuichi Yokoyama, changed its title to the martial "Advance, Little Fuku!" in 1940, as Japanese troops were beginning a fourth year of full-scale warfare in China. Cartoonists created propaganda leaflets, decrying Western colonialism, aimed at people living in other Asian countries, and other leaflets for Allied soldiers suggesting that their wives and girlfriends would not be faithful.

ALLIED COUNTRIES

In Britain, Kenneth Clark, director of the National Gallery, whose paintings had been evacuated to the countryside to protect them from bombings, persuaded the Ministry of Information to organize the War Artists Advisory Committee (see Chapter 3). The committee commissioned artists to document home-front experiences and action at the front. More than 300 artists participated, including Henry Moore, Paul Nash, Anthony Gross, Edward Bawden, and Edward Ardizzone. Nash created a stark landscape of downed German planes in his famous oil painting *Totes Meer* (*Dead Sea*), painted in 1940–1941. Moore rendered a series of moving drawings of Londoners taking shelter from the Blitz in the city's Underground stations. The artwork was exhibited in London and throughout Britain during the war.

The Soviet government also distrusted avant-garde art, but it equally dismissed cultural traditions dating back to the time of the czars. In the Soviet Union, socialist realism was the prescribed mode of artistic expression, a style intended to depict the reality of progress and optimism under socialism, although in fact it depicted a highly idealized version of Soviet life. The government objected to formalist art, which emphasized the aesthetic form or structure of a work, not its content. As in Nazi Germany, art's purpose was to promote the state's values and reflect society, not showcase the artist's creative vision.

A 1939 "Industry of Socialism" exhibit displayed some 2,000 paintings and 700 sculptures by Soviet artists in a series of rooms with themes like "The USSR has become Metallic" and "Life has got better, life has got jollier," as Stalin had said. Among the paintings shown were Grigorii Shegal's *Leader, Teacher, Friend*, a portrait of Stalin, and Fedor Modorov's *Comrade Mikoyan at the Astrakhan Fish Processing Plant*. These were typical of the subject matter the state supported.

During the war, many Soviet artists were also recruited to produce poster images. This highly dramatic art included works by Iraklii Toidze ("The Motherland Calls!" and "Stalin Is Leading Us to Victory") and Aleksei Kokorekin ("Death to the Fascist Reptile!").

In the United States, artists were free to paint, sculpt, and draw what they wished, but many became involved in the war effort and tailored their work accordingly. John Steuart Curry, a recognized painter of midwestern scenes, created posters to sell war bonds with images entitled "The Farm Is a Battleground" and "Our Good Earth." Norman Rockwell, a renowned illustrator for the *Saturday Evening Post*, created images of the "Four Freedoms" defined in a Franklin Roosevelt speech: freedom from fear, freedom from want, freedom to worship, freedom of speech. Roosevelt had described these freedoms as universally applicable, expressing his aspirations for a transformed world order. Rockwell's paintings quite literally interpreted them as specifically American, in a manner that harkened back to prewar isolationist sentiments. These paintings toured the United States under the auspices of the Office of War Information during a 1943 war bond campaign. They were also made into posters captioned "OURS . . . to fight for."

Shortly after Pearl Harbor was attacked, more than thirty artists' organizations founded the Artists for Victory association, which organized exhibits of patriotic art; its members also participated in propaganda efforts. The U.S. War Department formed an Art Advisory Committee, chaired by artist George Biddle, that commissioned artists to record their impressions of the war for the government. The committee selected twenty-three artists already in uniform and nineteen civilian artists to form "war-artist" units with two to five men in each. These units served at the front under the command of the chief of engineers. Biddle, a social realist painter, worked in the North African and Italian campaigns; his works included *German Prisoner on Monte Casino* and *War Orphans, Italy.* When Congress cut funding for war artists in 1943, magazines like *Life, Collier's,* and *Fortune* continued to support them. Additional support came from Abbott Laboratories, a health care company, which spent more than $1 million to send artists to battlefields to record medical aspects of the war.

In China, where artists were also mobilized, the cartoonist Feng Zikai created images of the war with Japan, including the brutal takeover of Nanking (see "Japanese War Crimes" in Chapter 8). During the three-year anti-Japanese alliance between the communist and Nationalist Chinese factions, the United Front's National Salvation Cartoon Association created graphic propaganda under the direction of the Military Affairs Commission, including posters and images in newspapers. Its journal, *National Salvation Cartoons*, featured caricatures calling for Chinese resistance.

Graphic art from any combatant country had the power to convey, on an emotional level, what words sometimes could not. Several of Soviet artist Dementi Shmarinov's troubling and evocative drawings of the German treatment of Russian civilians appeared in *Life* magazine's June 14, 1943, issue with only a brief commentary: "War of a kind unknown to the U.S. and Britain has so far destroyed about 10,000,000 civilians of Soviet Russia and taken another 3,000,000 civilians into slavery. Probably 3,000,000 families have been wiped off the map, after such anguish as to make them glad to die. A whole generation of children in occupied Russia have been conditioned by seeing their parents killed, tortured, violated and led away. Of this war we know nothing."

Books

AXIS COUNTRIES

Germany is perhaps less known for books it produced during World War II than the books it burned.

In 1933, works by what Goebbels called "undesirable and pernicious authors—socialists, Jews, the independent-minded and avant garde"—went up in smoke in a ceremonial "Burning of the Books," in Berlin and four other cities. "The age of extreme intellectualism is over," Goebbels declared in a simultaneous radio broadcast. "The past is lying in flames."

Many German writers went into exile or were forbidden to publish if they remained. Only members of the Reich Chamber of Literature could publish, and the work of the members of this strictly vetted group generally incorporated National Socialist values. Accounts of contemporary or historical heroes were popular. Ernst Junger authored war novels, and Hans F. Blunck political mysteries. Gerhard Schumann, a member of the Nazi militia, the Sturmabteilung (SA) since 1931, won Germany's National Book Prize in 1936 for a collection that included a poem honoring sixteen Nazi "martyrs" who died during the Munich Putsch in 1923. In 1938, Schumann became the head of the Chamber of Literature's writing section, and the following year, his play *Entscheidung* (*Decision*) was performed before enthusiastic audiences. It told the story of two World War I veterans and friends, one who turns to communism, the other to National Socialism. The communist eventually embraces Naziism, as his Nazi friend is dying.

Several Italian writers worked in exile, including the novelists Ignazio Silone and Carlo Levi, who was arrested twice for his anti-Fascist activism. Jewish novelist Natalia Ginzburg lived in forced exile in a small Italian village from 1940 to 1943. The prominent novelist Alberto Moravia remained in Italy. The former Fascist Elio Vittorini published *Conversazione in Sicilia* in 1941, which portrayed the harshness of life on the island of Sicily. He was imprisoned the following year. Vittorini and Cesare Pavese translated works by William Faulkner, John Steinbeck, Herman Melville, Gertrude Stein, and other Americans, introducing their work to Italy. These works were critical, problematic, and differed distinctly from the spirit of Fascism, yet they were not banned by Italian censors.

In Japan, the Ministry of Education was responsible for censoring books and pamphlets, but the police also had censorship powers under the Seditious Literature Bill. Publishers submitted proofs to the ministry before the books were printed; if they were not banned within five days, the manuscript could be printed. Censorship increased over the course of the war, limiting the publication of works if they were not war-related, even if they were neutral about politics. In 1943, the first chapters of Tanizaki Junichiro's novel *The Makioka Sisters* appeared in a magazine; it was subsequently banned because it dealt with middle-class life before the war.

Japan also promoted books that reinforced the government's values and promoted the Japanese-dominated pan-Asianism of the Greater East Asia Co-

Prosperity Sphere. Acceptable writers had to belong to the Japanese Literary Society, which organized conferences and meetings on the correct goals of literature. Writers from occupied countries were included in the society's activities by the end of 1942. In November, the Greater East Asia Literary Conference, which included representatives from Manchukuo, China, and Mongolia, declared "its resolve to repudiate Anglo-American imperialism and to help cultivate the new spirit of righteousness in the Greater East Asia Sphere." The society issued an updated version of the widely read *Poems by One Hundred Poets*, called *Patriotic Poems by One Hundred Poets*. It also sponsored "literary patriotic rallies." An announcement for one in April 1943 stated, "its main subjects are the study of ten literature books on the extermination of America and Britain and the change of ideology in patriotic literature."

When the Japanese went to war with China in July 1937, most Japanese writers, whatever their politics, supported the government. That fall, well-known writers were sent to the front to cover battles, including Ashihei Hino, who recorded the war in *Wheat and Soldiers*, *Earth and Soldiers*, and *Flowers and Soldiers*. As the Japanese occupied other countries in the 1940s writers were again dispatched to record and reflect on events and be ambassadors of Japanese culture. In Japan, much war-related, patriotic literature took the form of poetry, as in Yonejiro Noguchi's "Slaughter Them, the English and Americans Are our Enemies."

Translation of Japanese books, particularly those about history, into the languages of occupied countries formed a significant part of literary output. In addition to distributing these translations, the Japanese government and military established Japanese libraries in Burma, the Philippines, and other countries. Forty Japanese picture books were distributed to children in Sumatra in 1943 to encourage them to assimilate the conqueror's culture.

ALLIED COUNTRIES

Some of the finest poetry in Britain's history was produced during the war, including T.S. Eliot's *Four Quartets* and Dylan Thomas's "A Refusal to Mourn the Death, by Fire, of a Child in London." Several poets served in the armed forces, among them Sidney Keyes, killed in North Africa just before his twenty-first birthday, and Keith Douglas, killed in Normandy in 1944. "I am the man who groped for words and found / An arrow in my hand," wrote Keyes in "War Poet." "Now in my dial of glass appears / the soldier who is going to die. . . . How easy it is to make a ghost," Douglas wrote in "How to Kill." Popular fiction writers included Graham Greene

(*The Power and the Glory*), Arthur Koestler (*Darkness at Noon*), and George Orwell (*Animal Farm*).

Penguin New Writing, a periodical in book form that had begun publication in 1936, became enormously popular with civilians and soldiers during the war; it published both traditional and new work. Penguin Books, also established in the 1930s, published inexpensive paperbacks, some for entertainment and some literary, that were widely read. The pieces in *Horizon*, a more sophisticated literary journal, had a pan-European outlook and an international roster of contributors, and strove to keep before its readers examples of the civilized culture they were fighting to maintain. Books and literary magazines continued to be published in Britain despite bombings, paper shortages, and other disruptions.

In the Soviet Union, socialist realism was also the mode for literature. Maxim Gorky, honorary chairman of the Union of Soviet Writers, stated that writing should depict "the heroic present" and be both optimistic and dignified. It should not portray need or negative emotions such as fear, greed, or conflict or exalt the individual imagination or originality of the writer. Model novels included Nikilai Ostrovsky's *How the Steel Was Tempered* and Fyodor Gladkov's *Cement*. Stalin also supported the publication of classical Russian writers, including Chekhov and Tolstoy. During the siege of Leningrad, some 500,000 copies of *War and Peace* were given to the city's inhabitants to boost their determination. Poets read their own work to factory workers and soldiers.

The war reduced tension between the government and writers concerned with intellectual freedom because both now had a common purpose, defeating Germany. Poetry, including Alexei Surkov's "We Swear Victory" and Lebedlev-Kumach's "Holy War" (set to music, it became the Soviet Union's battle hymn) expressed patriotism, resolution, and hatred of the German enemy. The playwright Konstantin Siminov (his *The Russian People* was performed at the front) wrote the poem "Kill Him," expressing the desire for revenge, while Olga Berggolt's "February Diary" captured the resistance to German troops during the siege of Leningrad. One of the most memorable and popular poems was Alexander Tvardovsky's "Vasilii Terkin," about an ordinary Soviet citizen's cleverness at survival. Well-known wartime fiction included V.S. Grossman's short story collection *The Immortal People* (1942) and Ilya Ehrenburg's novel *The Fall of Paris* (which won the Stalin Prize in 1942). Simonov's *Dni I Nochi* (*Days and Nights*), published in 1944, described the heroic efforts of a Soviet battalion that defended three wrecked apartment buildings in Stalingrad for seventy days.

In the United States, nonfiction outsold fiction during the war. Popular works included Richard Tregaskis's *Guadalcanal Diary*, William Shirer's *Berlin Diary*, Joseph E. Davies's *Mission to Moscow*, and John Hersey's *Into the Valley*. Cartoonist Bill Mauldin's collection of drawings and writings (*Up Front*) and Marion Hargrove's tales of boot camp, *See Here, Private Hargrove*, offered humorous views of the ordinary soldier's life.

As in Britain, paperbacks became increasingly popular in the United States—they were a boon with wartime paper rationing. Pocket Books sold its first ten titles in 1939. In addition to classic literature, mysteries, and poetry, Pocket Book Editions offered anthologies of short contemporary pieces, including *The Pocket Book of the War* (1941) and *I Saw It Happen: Eye-Witness Accounts of the War* (1942), which noted, "In order to cooperate with the government's war effort, this book has been made in strict conformity with WPB regulations restricting the use of certain materials." Millions of copies of Armed Services Editions, low-cost paperbacks of British and American

Cartoonist Bill Mauldin sits in his office in Rome, ca. 1945. Mauldin's cartoon of his well-known character Willie, here recognizing the face of an enemy soldier (the original caption read, "Didn't we meet at Cassino?"), was drawn between 1943 and 1945 and refers to the battle of Monte Cassino in Northern Italy.

classics, mysteries, westerns, and popular literature, as well as war-related works, were distributed only to troops overseas, so as not to compete with commercial products in the domestic market. These were funded by the Council on Books in Wartime, a private organization made up of librarians, publishers, and booksellers.

After war broke out with the Japanese in China in 1937, both Chinese communist and Nationalist writers dedicated themselves to *k'ang-chan*, a "war of resistance." In March 1938, the All-China Resistance Association of Writers and Artists was formed. Teams of writers tried to build troop morale and reported from the front. So-called literary reporters, usually young people from rural China, many of them students, also reported on writing activities in their areas. Literature written during the war focused on the lives and issues of the rural worker, a trend championed by Chinese communists during the 1930s. Writers were, in fact, moving closer to the rural population as they relocated inland, ahead of the Japanese occupation; Wuhan, Canton, and China's wartime capital, Chungking, became new centers of literature. However, after the United Front dissolved in 1940, Chiang Kai-shek's government persecuted communist writers. In February 1945, a group of authors and intellectuals issued a manifesto in newspapers calling for an end to suppression and censorship, but the government's response was to imprison or kill several of the group's leaders.

Two of China's popular wartime poets were Tsang K'o-chia, who spent five years at the front, and T'ien Chien. Their work employed direct language, popular idioms, slogans, and descriptions of rural life. "This Asian / Soil / Is dyed in / Anger and / Shame. 'O tillers of my fatherland! / . . . Drive away the imperialist / Armies," wrote T'ien Chien in a characteristic poem.

On May 2, 1942, at the Yenan Forum, Mao Tse-tung summarized the goals of Chinese communist literature: "The purpose of our meeting today is precisely to ensure that literature and art fit well into the whole revolutionary machine as a component part, that they operate as powerful weapons for uniting and educating the people and for attacking and destroying the enemy, and that they help the people fight the enemy with one heart and one mind."

Theater

AXIS COUNTRIES

Theaters were used as venues for propaganda and to reinforce cultural values. In 1934, the Nazi government passed a Theater Law, stating, "The arts are for the National Socialist State, a public exercise; they are not only aesthetic but also moral in nature and the public interest demands not only police supervision but also guidance." Jewish, left wing, and avant-garde playwrights, directors, stage designers, and other professionals were banned from work in the theater. After the war started in 1939, work by playwrights from enemy countries could not be performed. However, because Shakespeare was considered a classic or universal writer, rather than an Englishman, his plays continued to be produced. Hamlet became a Nordic Aryan and Germans noted that he had been a student at Germany's Wittenberg University. *The Merchant of Venice*, which reinforced Nazi stereotypes of Jewish people, was also popular.

German theaters sent proposed programs to be reviewed by the RMVP. After 1937, plays could not depict Hitler or other Nazi leaders, nor could actors wear uniforms of the military, political police, or Nazi militia on stage. Contemporary playwrights were encouraged to address historical themes. Strength through Joy (KdF), an organization that shaped the leisure time of German laborers by providing low-cost access to works of high culture, supported production of plays by German literary icons such as Goethe, Lessing, and Schiller.

In Italy, where the Fascists intended to integrate nation, history, and culture, theatrical performances and opera were often spectacular productions in which the individual played a small part, just as, in politics and society, the Fascist citizen was subsumed in the grandeur of the state. Public events such as rallies and parades were themselves theatrical. Mussolini believed that theater must be produced for all the people and embody Fascist ideas and values. This limited both the themes of drama—these tended to be based on mythology, the Bible, or the glories of the Roman Empire—and its expression, which was expected to be foursquare on the side of discipline, patriotism, and loyalty to the regime.

The Japanese government also used theater as a vehicle for propaganda. The Takarasuka Revue, an all-female theater company founded in 1913, which was known for its spectacular and colorful musicals, dramatized the importance of Japan's role in bringing together the Greater East Asian Co-Prosperity Sphere in order to purge Western influences and expel colonial powers. The wartime Japanese government also supported the classical, all-male Kabuki theater and the traditional Noh theater, indigenous art forms that lent themselves to patriotic themes. In one of the many anti-Western *kyogen* (farces) written and performed during the war, angry bees forced American and English imperialists into the sea. Plays were submitted to censors before they were performed, just as manuscripts were reviewed before publication. Japan had been developing a Western-style theater in the 1930s, where left-wing plays stressing social and political reform were common. Such plays were increasingly suppressed beginning in 1937, but the New Cooperative Troupe and the New Tsukiji Troupe kept working until the government ordered them to close in 1940 and arrested their leaders for propagating communism.

ALLIED COUNTRIES

Soviet and British theaters suffered early in the war because they lay in the path of battle. In 1941, for example, the Moscow Art Theater moved to Saratov, in the Volga River valley, and the Moscow Little Theater, the oldest theater in Russia, to the Urals. Theater companies and performers from the Ukraine and Belarus also relocated further east. By the end of 1942, forty-four theater and concert companies were operating in the Soviet interior and the Moscow theater groups were able to return. Most of Britain's theaters were damaged by bombs and many were forced to close. Blackouts also affected business and the draft limited the number of performers available, although actors who agreed to entertain the military in traveling shows might not be called to military service.

In the United States, removed from civilian bombing, theater provided entertainment or drama that had little to do with the war. *The Glass Menagerie* by Tennessee Williams and Rodgers and Hammerstein's *Oklahoma!* were perhaps the most memorable works from the period. Two war-related musicals, however, did capture the public imagination. Irving Berlin's *This Is the Army*, which opened in 1942, had an all-male cast, with 300 soldiers in the chorus. *On the Town* (1944), choreographed by Jerome Robbins, with music by Leonard Bernstein, followed the adventures of three sailors on shore leave in New York City.

Theater was the most popular art in wartime China, fueled by the communists. Soon after war began, the All-China Resistance Association of Writers and Artists sent ten acting troupes (each with thirty members) into the countryside to educate and entertain rural workers. By 1939, an estimated 130,000 Chinese were giving theatrical performances with participation from enthusiastic audiences. Actors performed impromptu one-act plays in places where people gathered, such as markets. Drama allowed communist authors to criticize the Nationalist government without directly violating censorship rules. Popular plays included *Foggy Chungking* (*Wu Ch'ung-ch'ing*) by Sung Chih-ti, about war profiteering; *Sheng-kuan t'u* by Ch'en Pai-ch'en,

MUSIC: WARTIME NOTES

Politics and propaganda affected music, as they did the other arts during World War II. Racial laws in Germany and Italy forced Jewish composers, conductors, and musicians to lose their jobs. In 1938, Goebbels organized the Exhibition of Degenerate Music (similar to the exhibit on visual art) to provide Germans with examples of music they should not listen to, primarily modern compositions (deemed "Jewish") and jazz (considered the music of blacks). While Italy looked more favorably on avant-garde music than did Germany, Italian Fascists also disapproved of jazz; and in Japan, a 1943 list of banned musical works put together by the Government Information Bureau included some 1,000 American and British pieces, largely jazz and swing. The Axis governments considered jazz decadent—not healthy or uplifting.

Although the Axis governments considered jazz decadent, it flourished in the United States. Big bands, led by stars like Duke Ellington, Benny Goodman, Harry James, Tommy Dorsey, and Kay Kyser performed throughout the country. Glenn Miller's Air Force Band entertained the troops for more than two years before Miller went missing after his small plane went down somewhere between England and Paris. Singer Jane Froman's plane also crashed while she was on a USO tour, but she survived severe injuries and eventually gave 95 shows throughout Europe.

ROYAL ALBERT HALL
(Manager   C. S. TAYLOR)

Saturday, January 27th, 1945, at 2.30
BEETHOVEN CONCERT

JAY POMEROY presents
(Under the auspices of the London Music, Art and Drama Society, Ltd.)

MYRA HESS
WITH THE
LONDON SYMPHONY ORCHESTRA
(Leader   -   GEORGE STRATTON)

Conductor:

GEORGE WELDON

STEINWAY PIANOFORTE

IBBS & TILLETT,
124, Wigmore Street, W.1.   Programme 6d.

Dame Myra Hess, here playing the piano, inspired and played in a series of concerts performed at the Royal Albert Hall during and after the Blitz. This program is from a performance by Hess and the London Symphony Orchestra given on January 27, 1945.

Major combatants on both sides encouraged patriotic music. Horst Wessel, a young Nazi killed by communists, wrote "Raise High the Flag," an SA marching song that became the alternate German national anthem. In the Soviet Union, Dmitri Shostakovich composed the *Seventh (Leningrad) Symphony* while the city was under siege; the music became a symbol of Soviet resistance to the Germans. To raise morale in Britain, pianist Myra Hess suggested a series of lunchtime performances, since the blackout made it difficult for people to attend in the evening. A total of 1,698 concerts, many featuring Hess, were held at the National Gallery of Art from 1939 to 1946.

which explored government corruption, and *Metamorphosis (Shui-pien)*, by Ts'ao Yu, about the dreadful state of a military hospital. In Shanghai, where the Japanese occupiers practiced strict censorship, comedies, romances, and historical dramas were written and performed. Yang Chiang, a woman and one of the most prominent playwrights, produced comedies including *As You Desire (Ch'eng-hsin ju-I)* and *Truth into Jest (Nung-chen ch'eng-chia)*.

Propaganda, Truth, and Influence

Was propaganda effective in influencing people's thinking? Those who propagated it thought it was; but as with anything subjective, it is, perhaps, impossible to measure the extent of its effectiveness. The Research Branch of the United States War Department's Information and Education Division issued a report in 1949 that considered the impact of its propaganda programs on American soldiers. One of its conclusions was that "the 'Why We Fight' [film series] had marked effects on the men's knowledge of factual material . . . [but] had only a very few effects on opinion"; the report did credit "Previous indoctrination as civilians" for those opinions. Attitudes built over a lifetime are easier to reinforce than to change, yet war creates a need for justification and persuasion.

In every medium, both Allied and Axis countries used propaganda to make each government's case for why it was engaged in war, why it was right, how it was succeeding and why it would ultimately win. Their political and social philosophies differed, but their goals were remarkably similar. "Each side sought to convince its own people, neutrals and the enemy not only that it would win because it was the stronger but also that its victory would be in the general interest because the principles by which it was motivated were more likely to bring peace and plenty," wrote Michael Balfour, who served as Assistant Director of Intelligence in Britain's PWE from 1942 to 1945. "Each side set out to establish its own credibility and to destroy that of the enemy."

But British and American officials and propagandists nonetheless debated their responsibilities toward the public. There is "a war between truthful methods supported by freedom of discussion . . . and the sinister kind of propaganda . . . supported by falsehood and terrorism," believed Henry Stimson, U.S. secretary of war. How much factual information could be withheld and still present a reasonably true view of events? Was British Prime Minister Winston Churchill right when he said, referring to the impending invasion on D-Day, that truth is "so precious that in war-time she should always be surrounded by a body-guard of lies"? In general, the democracies agreed with OWI's domestic director Gardner Cowles, Jr. on the balancing of truth and propaganda: "We try to allow the freest possible scope and exchange of information, comment, opinion and understanding. *But we aren't neutral.* We use facts, we employ the 'strategy of truth,' for a purpose—to help win the war."

Significantly, the public in both Allied and Axis countries tended to believe reports based in fact, rather than ideology or implausible optimism. People understood the need for some military censorship, but they also wanted the truth. They distrusted news and information that was too slanted and, particularly, that did not mesh with the reality they saw around them or the accounts that came back from troops at the front. They preferred a point of view that Balfour felt characterized the British, who "showed a greater willingness to face up to reality [than Germany], a greater desire to be objective and a greater ability to understand other people's point of view." A reporter for the *Stuttgarter NS Kurier* confirmed this when he wrote in May 1944, "There is one way in which the British . . . are ahead of us. They know that news can be a weapon and are experts in its strategy." Too much untruthful "good news" could induce complacency or boredom, as well as disbelief. Ultimately, if the public stopped trusting reports—as they did in Germany and Italy—people stopped reading the newspapers or listening to radio broadcasts and turned to other sources, particularly BBC radio programs, which were deemed to have more accurate information.

PRINCIPAL SOURCES AND FURTHER READING

Arnold, W. Vincent. *The Illusion of Victory: Fascist Propaganda and the Second World War.* New York: Peter Lang, 1998.

Balfour, Michael. *Propaganda in War, 1939–1945: Organisations, Policies and Publics in Britain and Germany.* London: Routledge and Kegan Paul, 1979.

Barber, John, and Mark Harrison. *The Soviet Home Front, 1941–1945: A Social and Economic History of the USSR in World War II.* London: Longman, 1991.

Broekmeyer, Marius. *Stalin, the Russians, and Their War.* Madison: University of Wisconsin Press, 1999.

Cole, Robert. *Britain and the War of Words in Neutral Europe, 1939–45: The Art of the Possible.* New York: St. Martin's Press, 1990.

DeMendelssohn, Peter. *Japan's Political Warfare.* Reprint of 1944 edition. New York: Arno Press, 1972.

Fairbank, John K., and Albert Feuerwerker, eds. *The Cambridge History of China.* Vol. 13. *Republican China 1912–1949*, part 2. Cambridge: Cambridge University Press, 1986.

Fussell, Paul. *Wartime: Understanding and Behavior in the Second World War.* New York: Oxford University Press, 1989.

Fyne, Robert. *The Hollywood Propaganda of World War II.* Metuchen, NJ: Scarecrow Press, 1994.

Goebbels, Joseph. *The Goebbels Diaries, 1939–1941*, edited and translated by Fred Taylor. London: Hamish Hamilton, 1982.

Laurie, Clayton D. *The Propaganda Warriors: America's Crusade Against Nazi Germany.* Lawrence: Kansas University Press, 1996.

McCloskey, Barbara. *Artists of World War II.* Westport, CT: Greenwood Press, 2005.

McLaughlin, Greg. *The War Correspondent.* London: Pluto Press, 2002.

Overy, Richard. *The Dictators: Hitler's Germany and Stalin's Russia.* New York: W.W. Norton, 2004.

Pyle, Ernie. *Ernie's War: The Best of Ernie Pyle's World War II Dispatches*, edited by David Nichols. New York: Random House, 1986.

Read, Anthony. *The Devil's Disciples: Hitler's Inner Circle.* New York: W.W. Norton, 2004.

Roeder, George H., Jr. *The Censored War: American Visual Experience during World War II.* New Haven: Yale University Press, 1993.

Schutz, W. W., and B. DeSevin. *German Home Front.* London: Victor Gollancz, 1943.

Soley, Lawrence. *Radio Warfare: OSS and CIA Subversive Propaganda.* New York: Praeger, 1989.

Sorel, Nancy Caldwell. *The Women Who Wrote the War.* New York: Arcade Publishing, 1999.

Stouffer, Samuel, et al. *The American Soldier: Adjustment during Army Life.* Vol. 1. Princeton, NJ: Princeton University Press, 1949.

Sweeney, Michael. *Secrets of Victory: The Office of Censorship and the American Press and Radio in World War II.* Chapel Hill: University of North Carolina Press, 2001.

Thompson, Doug. *State Control in Fascist Italy: Culture and Conformity, 1925–43.* New York: Manchester University Press, 1991.

Welch, David. *The Third Reich: Politics and Propaganda.* London: Routledge, 1993.

WAR ON THE HOME FRONT

The American people . . . are fighting this war wholeheartedly—with less flag-waving and fanfare than we had in World War I, but with more unanimity and with a clearer purpose," wrote Selden Menefee in 1943. Menefee had been commissioned by the Office of Public Opinion Research at Princeton University to travel 15,000 miles throughout the United States to record his observations of the American home front. In Virginia he met "a sixteen-year-old boy . . . who quit high school to work as a riveter's helper in a sheet metal shop . . . for 70 cents an hour seven days a week." Near Natchez, Mississippi, he passed "a tiny plantation cabin . . . with five service stars in the window"—one for each of its sons in the military. In Vermont, he spoke with "a teller in the local bank . . . who works four hours every night running a machine in one of three small factories," in the same town where four hundred women had volunteered for the Red Cross, "turning out surgical dressings, . . . and . . . making kit bags for soldiers and clothing for bombed out British families." Menefee also visited "the first Iowa county to oversubscribe its $817,200 war bond quota in 1942," and watched "a boisterous and excited carload of WACS on their way from Texas to Des Moines to be inducted."

Enlistments and bond drives, victory gardens and scrap collections, factories working at peak production, volunteers at a soldiers' canteen—these convey the spirit of energy and cooperation, the positive outlook and spunky, can-do attitude that is popularly associated with the American home front of World War II. The United States had preserved its constitutional structure through years of economic hardship during the Great Depression. In 1940, columnist Dorothy Thompson could write, "Here we are, and our basic institutions are still intact, our people relatively prosperous." After the country entered the war in December 1941, the revving up of the economy brought previously unimaginable prosperity to the average American. (See also Chapter 3.)

Nevertheless, some Americans faced the same biases and inequities as they did before the war. Although job opportunities for women, African Americans, Latinos, and American Indians increased, these groups still contended with stereotyping, discrimination, and racial violence. Many Japanese Americans were interned in camps in 1942. Large industries grew, while small businesses struggled, and strikes underlined the conflicts between management and labor.

The United States was not a perfectly unified society during the war, but on the other hand, its civilians did not experience the disruptions, hardships, and enormous loss of life of European and Asian countries. The other major combatant and occupied nations endured bombings, evacuations, imprisonment, hunger, disease, and destruction of homes, land, and property. "Materially, it seems to me we have been hardly touched by war here at home," wrote correspondent Ernie Pyle in his November 6, 1943, column. "Our little annoying restrictions and shortages are so puny compared to those of other countries. We are still so rich and so well fed and so plentiful."

What the citizens of countries other than the United States experienced was "total war," made possible by twentieth-century technology, in which the civilian was a fully mobilized war worker for his own country and a legitimate target for enemy forces. The twentieth-century homeland became another front—distinct from the traditional battlefront where enemy soldiers fought, but vulnerable to attack nonetheless. The Italian military theorist Giulio Douhet, whose work was influential in Europe and the United States, articulated the ways in which wide-ranging air power would change the conduct of war, including its impact on civilians. In his monograph *The Probable Aspects of the War of the Future*, published in 1928, he stated, "War is war. Either one wages war or one doesn't; but when one does, one must do it without gloves and without frills on either side. . . . Any distinction between belligerents and non-belligerents is no longer admissible to-day . . . nowadays the offensive may reach anyone." He further argued, "The woman loading shells in a factory, the farmer growing wheat, the scientist experimenting in his laboratory" should be treated just as "the soldier carrying his gun." Total war turned the home front into another battlefront, where civilians—and their morale—as well as property and industry, could be destroyed.

In 1941, months after the German Blitz against British cities had started, Louis Sigaud, an American army officer, commented on Douhet's theories: "If men wish really to be civilized they should abolish war itself. If they cannot succeed in doing so, [Douhet] does not see how civilization can be restricted effectively to a limited choice of more or less elegant methods to kill, destroy, and damage. To conquer an enemy nation, it is essential to inflict upon it a terrific sum total of damage. When this is understood clearly, it becomes obvious that there can be no significant or useful distinction between illegitimate and legitimate, humane and inhuman, and civilized and savage."

If civilians were vulnerable to offensive attacks deliberately directed toward them on the home front, by the same token, they were also responsible for making every effort to win the war defensively by working where they were needed and sacrificing in their domestic lives. Douhet also noted: "All citizens must be interested in the aspects of the war of the future, because all of them will have to fight in it . . . because it demands all the material and moral resources of a nation, it cannot be limited to a certain section of the nation, nor to a special class or number of its citizens. All forces and materials, tangible and intangible, have to be marshaled for the prosecution of war; and all citizens must become deeply interested in it, discussing and understanding it, in order to prepare themselves for the ordeal if it should come."

German theorists advocated this concept of total war—"total mobilization"—in writings of the early 1930s. Propaganda Minister Joseph Goebbels was a proponent. When civilian morale dropped in 1943 with the failure to win key victories in the Soviet Union, he rallied the people with a speech on February 18: "The danger before which we stand is gigantic. Gigantic, therefore, must be the efforts with which we meet it. . . . Are you ready to stand with the Führer as the phalanx of the homeland behind the fighting Wehrmacht? . . . are you determined to follow the Führer through thick and thin in the struggle for victory and to accept even the harshest personal sacrifices? . . . The mightiest ally in the world—the people themselves—has shown that they stand behind us in our determined fight for victory, regardless of the costs."

A banner above Goebbels's head as he spoke read *"Totaler Krieg—Kurzester Krieg"* (Total War—Shortest War). The same idea—that concentrated, massive destruction would so terrify a population that its government might settle or surrender, risking fewer losses overall than a protracted war of attrition— lay behind Hitler's civilian bombing strategy as well as Allied bombing of cities in Germany and Japan. But Hitler never acquiesced to total mobilization of the German people; for example, women were never used to their full potential, nor were they in Italy and Japan. Nevertheless, the countries fighting World War II generally put significant numbers of their civilians to work and also accepted that it was necessary to harm enemy civilians. These premises profoundly affected the home fronts of Europe and Asia, where war permeated every aspect of civilian existence. It regulated many people's employment, wages, and hours, and it also exposed them on a daily basis to the loss of food, shelter, comfort, and life.

The exception was the United States, where, as columnist Hugh Sidey, an Iowa teenager in the 1940s, wrote: "There was a sense of exhilaration during the war that brought people together. There was no real hardship and there was no fear, like people on the West Coast [had about Japanese bombs]. Nobody was going to get to Iowa. There was no deprivation, despite the rationing. So we didn't have enough stamps for meat—my uncle butchered a cow. There was no problem except for those families that lost sons. Even there . . . was a sense of pride, in some way."

Morale

The morale of a people in wartime has less to do with a continually optimistic outlook than with a belief in the necessity of the war and the willingness to accept extraordinary measures and circumstances to achieve victory. Morale reflects determination rather than a superficial patriotism that can be swayed by hardships or losses. Civilians in comfortable settings who feel no threat to themselves can have a low interest in war, while the morale of those being bombed can be high.

Allies

In 1942, Arthur Upham Pope, head of the United States' Committee for National Morale (founded in 1940 to teach the American public about war-related issues) defined morale in a distinctively American way: "Morale is the spine in your back, the lift to your chin, the song on your lips, the grit in your craw. Morale is the spirit that makes you say defiantly 'Is *that* so?' when you are told you aren't man enough to do something—and makes you do it!"

The violent act that drew the United States into World War II—the Japanese attack at Pearl Harbor—had a pronounced impact on the mood of the American people and the degree of support they gave to the war effort. Before Pearl Harbor, sentiment had been split. Those with an internationalist outlook—among them President Franklin Roosevelt—thought that support of the antifascist cause should include military aid and possibly military intervention. A strong isolationist element, however, resisted any involvement in what was seen as a foreign war.

Civilians in every combatant country were called on to give scrap metal, fats, and other needed materials for war production. Here, a boy contributes to a rubber salvage pile in Washington, D.C., June 1942.

However, after Pearl Harbor, "the American people were almost unanimous in their demand for an offensive war—a war carried to their enemies," Archibald MacLeish, then Librarian of Congress, noted in July 1942. Pope elaborated on the Japanese "mistake": "They got the American back up. . . . They made us mad clear through, and, most important of all, they helped make us *one*. . . . Our anger and our determination are terrible weapons, but it is the feeling of brotherhood that will make them effective."

Morale in the United States was generally strong, but in 1943, American civilians were beginning to tire of the length of the war and to be less supportive of bond and scrap drives. In May, censors allowed *Newsweek* to show the first photographs of wounded American soldiers to stiffen public resolve. *Life* ran the first photos of dead Americans in September. (See also "Journalism" in Chapter 10.) The war challenged the spirit of Americans with family and friends in the military in a particular way. They were subject to the same anxious waiting—and potential loss—as their counterparts on other home fronts. To help them feel pride, the government encouraged displaying a blue star on homes for every inhabitant who was in the service, a custom begun in World War I. If a soldier was wounded, the blue star was covered with a silver one; for a death, the star was covered with gold. The American Gold Star Mothers, a support organization founded in 1928, still operates today.

When Britain declared war on Germany for invading Poland in September 1939, the government instituted a mass evacuation to the countryside to protect civilians. The evacuees soon returned to urban centers during the "Phony War"—a period without major land combat or aerial bombing of cities that lasted until spring 1940. The expectation of military action against the homeland, while nothing significant happened, caused uncertainty. At the same time, because price controls had not yet been put into place, prices were increasing more than workers' income, causing dissatisfaction. The winter of 1939–1940 proved the hardest on morale; civilians expressed an anxious discontent. One sign of this was the large number of people who left their volunteer civil defense positions in the ARP (air raid precautions) and the Home Guard.

In the Luftwaffe's great air offensive, the Battle of Britain (July 1940–June 1941), and especially during the period of intense bombing of urban areas known as the Blitz (September–November 1940), many British civilians were killed and much property battered, but the public rallied to defend themselves and their country. "The blitz was a terrible experience for millions, yes," wrote Tom Harrisson, one of the organizers of the wartime social survey, Mass-Observation. "But it was not terrible enough to disrupt the basic decency, loyalty . . . morality and optimism of the vast majority. It was supposed to destroy 'mass morale.' Whatever it did destroy, it failed over any period of more than days appreciably to diminish the human will, or at least the capacity to endure."

Reports on morale prepared by Britain's Ministry of Information showed declines after Axis victories, for example, when British forces were forced to withdrew from Crete in 1941, and, in 1942, with the Allied loss of Singapore and Tobruk. After the Normandy invasion in 1944, Britons believed that the Allies would soon win the war; thus, morale was strong even when the Germans started using their "terror weapons," the V-1 and V-2 rockets.

For many civilians in the Soviet Union, the battlefront and the home front were one. Civilian casualties likely made up more than half of Soviet deaths, including people bombed or killed by ground forces as they stood in the path of war. Nationalist groups in the western part of the USSR, including Ukrainians, Estonians, Latvians, and Lithuanians, initially welcomed the German invasion in 1941, believing it would liberate them from Soviet rule. However, the Germans instituted a bloody and brutal occupation that solidified resistance against Germany. Even during the siege of Leningrad (1941), where a million people in the city and outskirts died of starvation, there was no breakdown of order or public clamoring for surrender.

The will of the majority of the Soviet people focused on saving "Mother Russia"—the country—not the government or communism. Stalin recognized the importance of boosting this nationalism in his speeches and propaganda. He praised the once-disparaged army (still reeling from his purge of political unreliables) as liberators of the people and forged a concordat with the dismantled Russian Orthodox church (see "Religion" later in this chapter). Nonetheless, the government continued to keep close and restrictive tabs on the population and at several key points in the war was willing to sacrifice civilians, rather than appear defeated, particularly in Leningrad and Stalingrad.

On March 12, 1939, the Chinese Nationalist government of Chiang Kaishek instituted a National Spiritual Mobilization movement to unite the civilian population in support of the war. People were asked to pledge to uphold a Citizens Pact with what amounted to rules rather than affirmations: "Not to disobey laws and orders of the government" and "Not to participate in traitorous organizations" were two of the pledges. The campaign roused little enthusiasm among the Chinese people, and as the war progressed, the Nationalists increasingly used force and imprisonment to protect their rule.

Rampant inflation, high taxes, shortages of food and goods, repression of dissent, media censorship, and persecution of intellectuals contributed to popular disaffection. One 1944 editorial, censored before it could be published in a newspaper in west China, stated, "Government officials are corrupt and laws are abused by them; the people's livelihood becomes daily more grievous and desperate. With the nation in hardship and the people in poverty, a small corrupt element is growing increasingly richer. . . . This rotten phenomenon, together with many other reactionary political factors, has lowered both the people's and the soldiers' morale nearly to the vanishing point." By the end of the war, resentment was directed toward the Nationalist government as much as to the Japanese, a factor in the civil war between Nationalists and communists that followed.

Axis

All the Axis governments made extraordinary efforts in the 1930s to shape unified citizenries instilled with unquestioning patriotism, trained to be physically fit, and convinced of the value of imperial expansion and military victory. Thus, they were expected not only to win in combat, but, as civilians, to support war even when it involved sacrifice. A constant barrage of propaganda, carefully orchestrated rallies, and repressive policing systems ensured that there would be little outward disagreement. Yet public commitment was never as universal as these governments wished, and morale depended more on personal safety and well-being, access to food and consumer goods, and success or losses on the battlefield than on propaganda or ideology. "Neither sweeping rubbish nor salvaging pillows has anything to do with Nazi sentiments," wrote German civilian Ruth Andreas-Friedrich in her diary. "Everyone, however, remembers that one cannot live in the cold. Before the evening comes and the air-raid sirens start howling, one has to have a hiding place where he can stretch out his limbs."

Memories of World War I led even the German population, which had a strong allegiance to Hitler, to feel anxiety, then resignation, as the war progressed. At first, quick and seemingly easy victories such as those in Poland, France, and Scandinavia buoyed spirits. But early conquests also led Germans to hope that the war would end quickly, rather than expand to dangerous proportions. When Germany failed to secure a rapid victory in the Soviet Union, "*The general mood* of a broad public spectrum . . . continues to deteriorate," stated a report by the Security Service (SD) on July 15, 1941. "Even if confidence in victory and trust in the leadership and military still exists, citizens are depressed, embittered, and angered by the severity of the Eastern struggle, the criminal conduct of the Red Army, the evident losses appearing in casualty reports, and . . . provisioning difficulties."

Not surprisingly, approval, apathy, and resistance fluctuated with victories and defeats, with increases and decreases in rationing and bombing raids, with the hope for prosperity and peace and the reality of continual, total war. The incendiary bombing of Cologne on May 30, 1942, marked a new stage in the experience on the German home front. This attack left 45,000 people without homes. From 1942 through 1945, as the Allies bombed some seventy-two cities, German civilians felt shocked that the invincibility the Nazis had promised had been breached. Yet, like the British who endured German bombs and rockets, Germans buckled down to the tasks of survival without excessive complaint. As the Soviet Army advanced through eastern Germany, the population's fear increased.

After Mussolini committed Italy to war in 1940, Italian attacks on France (June) and Greece (October) were unsuccessful—no swift and early victories boosted public morale. On the contrary, Allied bombing of Italian cities (although relatively light), blackouts, restrictions on automobile use, and escalating prices chilled enthusiasm. By late 1941, when the rationing of food and clothing began, Italians had grown weary of the war and cynical about the Fascist government, but not yet ready to oppose it in great numbers.

By summer 1943, when the Allies landed in Sicily, opposition had become more outspoken. That July, Mussolini was deposed, and a new Italian government surrendered to the Allies in September. This armistice prompted Germany, angry and betrayed, to occupy Italian cities and displace Italian troops with its own. Germany turned the Italian home front into a German front line, forcing the Allies and Italian partisans to struggle inch by inch to regain territory. Civilians suffered more violence and deprivation than they had during the first years of the war, but many also displayed a determined resistance to German occupation.

The bombing of Pearl Harbor not only shocked Americans, it surprised Japanese citizens. War with the United States and Britain created some concern, since Japan was already expending resources in its war with China. Yet few Japanese vocally expressed any doubt that their country was pursuing the right course or that it would be victorious. Japan's government-mandated network of neighborhood associations (*tonarigumi*), each composed of only ten to twelve households, fostered community as it stifled individualism. Tonarigumi were key organizational units; they collected taxes, were responsible for civil defense, and distributed rations. But families also kept an eye on each other and reported dissent or divergent opinions to the police (which operated under the Home Ministry); those who failed to cooperate with the war effort could be imprisoned.

However, most Japanese people seemed to accept the war and the domestic sacrifices it entailed as inevitable. "Because men were continually going off to the front, we were sent to help their families—planting rice, weeding the paddies, harvesting rice, growing barley," recalled Tetsuko Tanaka, then a high school student. "I carried charcoal down from the mountains. I'd had no farm experience before. It was very strenuous, physical labor, but I never thought of it as hardship. We patched soldiers' uniforms, sewed on new buttons, repaired torn seams. . . . Nobody complained about it. We were part of a divine country centered on the Emperor. The whole Japanese race was fighting a war."

Japan's early victories against the Western powers that had long dominated Asia boosted morale and fanned national pride. When the tide turned in favor of the Allies, Japanese civilians remained resolute. The American bombing campaign against Japanese cities that began early in 1945 aroused public anger. Although military strategists expected strikes against civilians would lower morale and prompt an outcry for armistice, mounting civilian losses provoked hatred of the enemy and a determination not to give in. This was true not only in Japan, but in Britain, the Soviet Union, and Germany, and in Italy during the German occupation.

Labor

The biggest issue regarding labor was common to Allied and Axis countries: since so many men were required for the armed forces, who would work in the war industries? In addition, how many workers could a country manage to devote to consumer industries? How much should labor be regulated? The use of women in the workforce was another controversial option, particularly in Germany and Japan, although all the major combatants believed the primary role of women was as homemakers (see "The Role of Women" later in this chapter).

Allies

In the United States, 10 million additional people joined the work force to compensate for those who became part of the military and to aid in war production. They were rewarded by increased wages: the average person who made $24 per week in 1939, was making $45 per week six years later. Most laborers also worked extended hours; real wages rose an estimated average of 50 percent. With the Depression fading and the growth of war-related industries, Americans had choices about where they worked, and even unskilled workers were in demand.

In 1941, as laborers sought higher wages and better working conditions, 2.4 million workers were involved in some 4,300 work stoppages. A National Defense Mediation Board, organized in March, lacked the power to compel workers back to their jobs. After the United States entered the war that December, the National War Labor Board (NWLB) was organized to mediate disagreements, a no-strike pledge governed management-labor relationships, and the number of strikes decreased dramatically. The NWLB settled some 20,000 wage disputes from 1942 to 1945 and approved 415,000 wage agreements. Union membership increased from 10.5 million in 1941 to 14.75 million in 1945.

However, in 1943, as Allied prospects improved and the urgency to produce war materials waned—and as prices rose faster than wages—some 2 million Americans struck in response to wage controls and freezes. These were mainly wildcat strikes, since union leaders did not want to anger the government or the public. Nonetheless, some 3,800 strikes cost 13.5 million lost worker-days. The coal industry witnessed the largest strikes in 1943, because miners endured especially poor working conditions and low wages. Almost a half-million men, under the leadership of John L. Lewis, struck four different times in the course of the year. The government took over the mines each time, but finally negotiated a contract with Lewis that the miners accepted.

The coal miners' strikes were a principal impetus for promulgation of the Smith-Connally Act, passed by Congress in June 1943. The act ordered that a thirty-day notice prior to strikes be given, succeeded by a thirty-day cooling off period and NWLB oversight of union voting. The act also permitted the president to assume control of privately owned plants doing war work when strikes and lockouts threatened to halt production. Once the government assumed control, as it did with about four dozen privately owned defense firms, workers were not permitted to strike.

Although the United States did not have labor conscription or strict worker controls, the War Manpower Commission, created in April 1942, established labor-management committees, facilitated employee distribution to different industries, urged the army and navy to consult with local draft boards on area labor shortages before taking up new conscripts, and endeavored to solve labor crises. During the war, labor shortages in some areas were so acute that 90 percent of new hires were not replacing former workers but filling new jobs, which exacerbated corporate competition for workers. In some plants, turnover was nearly constant. In Portland, Oregon, Henry Kaiser offered such high-paying jobs in his shipyards that a downtown department store was pleading for job applicants in large newspaper advertisements. In Wyoming, a desperate employer ran an ad stating, "If you can drive a nail, you can qualify as a carpenter."

Mexican Americans (more than 1.5 million lived in the United States) took industrial jobs in shipbuilding and airplane production, particularly on the West Coast. Although the war created these opportunities, employment and living arrangements also raised tensions with Anglo society. Gangs of young Mexicans who wore zoot suits (a long, full coat over pants flared at the knee and tight at the ankles, and a flat felt hat) were subject to police harassment and sometimes also attacked Anglos in the armed forces. In Los Angeles in June 1943, a "zoot suit riot" broke out when, with police looking on, sailors who said they had been assaulted beat Mexican Americans.

Nonetheless, Mexicans and Caribbean Islanders who had been sent home during the Great Depression returned to the United States, many taking jobs on farms as the workers there joined the military or went into factory work. Under the Bracero Program, the United States and Mexico agreed to a temporary guest worker program, in which more than 200,000 Mexicans came to the United States for jobs. In addition to farmwork, especially at harvest times, these laborers found employment in railroad construction and maintenance work.

Much of Britain's population, too, was relieved at the extent of work available after 1940 as more than 1 million had been unemployed when the war began. (By 1944, only 54,000 were registered with the government as

AFRICAN AMERICANS ON THE HOME FRONT

"Democracy must wage a two-front battle—a battle on far flung foreign fields against Hitler, and a battle on the home front against Hitlerism," declared Adam Clayton Powell Jr. in *Common Sense* in April 1942. "How can white Americans expect to have a tolerant world after this war when there is racial prejudice within the ranks of those who are fighting?" Most African Americans agreed and bent their efforts not only to winning victory against fascism abroad, but victory against segregation and racial discrimination in the United States. This "Double V" campaign, promoted especially by the *Pittsburgh Courier,* a black newspaper, enabled African Americans to demonstrate their patriotism and their determination for change at home.

Black Americans enthusiastically conducted war bond campaigns in their schools, churches, and communities and, although many of them had little income, purchased bonds. They volunteered through the United Service Organization (USO), the Red Cross, and other groups to support American troops. Nearly 1 million African Americans had served in the armed forces by 1945; nearly 500,000 were sent overseas. Black units—some of which, including the 332nd Fighter Group and the 761st Tank Battalion, received the Presidential Unit Citation—fought in Europe and the Pacific.

The armed forces remained segregated throughout World War II; they began the process of desegregation by order of President Harry Truman in 1948. (See also "Segregation in the Armed Forces" in Chapter 4.) Most black servicemen were shunted into noncombat jobs; for example, several hundred who had been poorly trained for handling ammunition were assigned as stevedores at Port Chicago, California, loading explosives onto ships. On July 17, 1944, some bombs exploded, killing 202 black sailors and 118 white sailors. When detailed to another ammunition depot, 328 black sailors refused to go. Most relented, but 50 who continued to strike were imprisoned for mutiny. (Most were released in 1946.)

The Port Chicago incident highlighted racial problems and tensions in the military, fodder for the Double V campaign. But Double V proponents also focused on the home front, on job discrimination in war industries and discrimination in training opportunities under the government's Vocational Education National Defense (VEND) Training Program. Although African Americans left the South in large numbers (more than a half million during the war) to seek employment in midwestern and western cities, they faced hiring practices like this one at North American Aviation, which had factories in California, Texas, and Kansas: "We will receive applications from both white and Negro workers. However, the Negroes will be considered only as janitors and in other similar capacities. . . . While we are in complete sympathy with the Negro, it is against the company policy to employ them as mechanics or aircraft workers."

To combat these practices, labor and civil rights leader A. Philip Randolph organized the March on Washington Movement (MOWM) in response to a woman's suggestion at a civil rights meeting in 1941 Chicago: "We ought to throw 50,000 Negroes around the White House, bring them from all over the country . . . and keep them there until we can get some action." Randolph and NAACP president Walter White told President Franklin Roosevelt that 100,000 people would march if there were no order

Jewal Mazique, an employee of the Library of Congress, urges members of a church congregation to participate in the war effort, 1942.

prohibiting discrimination. On June 24, 1941, Roosevelt issued Executive Order 8802, which prohibited discrimination in defense industries, training, and the federal government. He also created the Fair Employment Practices Committee (FEPC) to enforce the ban.

The FEPC, with a small budget and no power to punish offending employers, often failed to enforce Roosevelt's order. Black Americans, especially black women, continued to get less skilled jobs. However, the sheer need for war workers of any kind swelled the numbers and provided an entry into semiskilled and skilled labor for African Americans. In 1942, African Americans held only 3 percent of the jobs in war industries; by 1945, this had increased to more than 8 percent. The number of African American federal employees increased from 60,000 to 200,000.

Many white Americans resisted these changes. There were "hate strikes" by white workers—work stoppages of a few hours or days protesting the employment of blacks. The influx of population to cities resulted in housing shortages that pushed African Americans into ghettos. In 1943, two hundred forty-two violent racial confrontations took place in forty-seven cities. The most prominent occurred in Detroit in June, where riots killed nine whites and twenty-four blacks, and in Harlem in August, where six people were killed and hundreds injured or arrested. Nonetheless, a significant number of African Americans had migrated out of the South and gained a foothold in the American economy that would affect their prospects—and their outlook—after the war ended.

unemployed.) There was government control of labor: the Ministry of Labor and National Service (MLNS) could modify salaries and prohibit strikes starting in July 1940. Nonetheless, the number of work stoppages rose with each year of the war, reaching a peak in 1944 of 2,194 stoppages (3,696,000 worker-days lost). Most of the stoppages arose from disputes about wages. A labor draft that was instituted in 1941 at first registered men up to the age of 41, quickly extended the age to 46, then to ages 18 to 51. The first women registered for the labor draft were 20 and 21; by the end of 1941, the age limit had been raised to 30; and later, women between 18 and 50 were subject to the labor draft. Most labor draftees voluntarily worked where they were needed. About 1 million men and 88,000 women received compulsory orders to work in specific jobs over the course of the war.

The Minister of Labor, Ernest Bevin, issued an Essential Work Order (EWO) in March 1941. All work was deemed "essential"—employers could not fire workers and workers could not leave a job without permission from a Ministry of Labor national service officer. Bevin had been a union official; he ensured that workers bound by the EWO had decent wages. Where disagreements and work stoppages arose, he usually could persuade workers to cooperate with management, especially as salaries generally rose during the war. To allay a critical shortage of coal in 1943, he developed a system for drafting workers, who became known as "Bevin boys." Draftees were chosen by lot to avoid favoring any class or group of men; the scheme was nonetheless very unpopular, and the coal industry remained problematic. Bevin did not prosecute strikers in any industry and he generally improved working conditions. In a climate not unfavorable to labor, union membership increased from six and a quarter to nearly 8 million over the course of the war.

Soviet workers did not suffer from high unemployment when their country entered the war and adequately filled most jobs. The German invasion precipitated a labor crisis, however, when millions were suddenly withdrawn from the workforce into the military, which had already lost millions of men in the initial German advances. This created a severe labor shortage just as the Soviets required even more workers to produce war matériel. The government began labor conscription on June 22, 1941, drafting men between 18 and 45 and women between 18 and 40 years of age who did not already have jobs. The draft was extended in February 1942 to include men aged 16 to 55 and women aged 16 to 45, later raised to age 50. More women entered the workforce, the government drew workers from rural villages, and students and the elderly of both sexes volunteered without hesitation to fill jobs. Thus, the majority of workers were young, inexperienced, and/or women. In some factories, more than half the workers were under 25. In 1944, an estimated 712,000 workers were 14 or 15 years of age.

Soviet civilians already lived in a society rife with government restrictions. People were limited in their ability to move from one job to another and work hours were regulated. By 1942, workers were expected to work some fifty-five hours per week, and they could be punished for arriving late or not coming to work at all. Those working in war industries were subject to military-style regulations as early as December 1941. Yet military and civilian employers and agencies remained disorganized, competing with each other for the shrinking labor pool. It took until 1943 to place enough workers in jobs that were not directly war related, but supported life at a basic level by producing food, fuel, clothing, and housing, a situation more severe in hitherto undeveloped sections of the eastern Soviet Union where whole factories and communities of workers were evacuated.

In China, it was not uncommon, as areas changed hands among the Japanese, their puppet warlords, the Nationalists, and the communists, for workers to labor for any and all during the war. To bring in Allied supplies against

Chinese workers labor in a factory in this photograph from an exhibition demonstrating Nationalist (Kuomintang) wartime activity, ca. 1937–1943.

the Japanese, Chinese laborers built airfields, military bases, and thousands of miles of railroads and highway in the northwest and southwest, often in miserable conditions. The best known construction project was the 478-mile Ledo Road, begun in December 1942. It wound through jungles and mountains from India across Burma to Kunming, China. Nepali, Sri Lankan, and Chinese laborers toiled under the supervision of American engineers, removing ton after ton of dirt, vegetation, and debris by hand as well as by machine while beset by water leeches, mosquitoes, landslides, and monsoons.

Axis

Even before 1939, the German government had a system for controlling wages and placing workers where they were most needed in the workforce, but competition and lack of coordination between the military and the Economic Ministry made it function inefficiently. In the first weeks of September 1939, the government drafted 500,000 Germans for industrial work to fill in where they were most needed. But drafting workers (1.4 million were called on in 1940) did not solve the problem, especially since Hitler felt they should not be moved to locations away from their families. In December 1939, the government formulated a War Economy Decree proposing to cap wages, eliminate bonuses and holidays, and tax luxuries. Workers responded by staying away from their jobs; consequently, productivity dropped. The decree proposals were scrapped, even though the number of men entering the military continued to create labor shortages. Germany indirectly limited its labor pool by freezing wages, removing the incentive to relocate for a better-paying job. Yet wage freezes were an important tool in controlling inflation. Real wages rose from 1939 through 1941, then declined through 1943 at the same time that there were fewer commodities available for people to buy.

By September 1941, mining needed 50,000 additional workers and the metal industries more than 300,000. To fill these and other gaps, foreign workers were first recruited, then forced to labor on the German home front. In 1944 there were 5.7 million civilian workers from other countries, most of them forced labor, and 1.9 million prisoners of war toiled in German agricultural and industrial jobs. Most foreign Slavic workers (e.g., Poles and Russians), considered inferior by the Nazis, lived in deplorable conditions and were treated so badly that some starved to death. They were assigned the most unpopular jobs, protecting German citizens from engaging in them so as not to weaken home front morale. German workers were now part of a new hierarchy in which they supervised foreign workers, thus raising their own status while reinforcing the Nazi ideology of racial superiority.

Although there were no strikes, as there were in the United States and Britain, some German workers frequently missed workdays, or became *Bummelanten* (slackers). By 1944, the number of workers arrested for breach of discipline had increased to about 20,000 per month, a 52 percent increase over the number in 1941. Offenders were generally fined and sometimes jailed. They could be sent to Work Reeducation Camps, but those were usually used for foreign workers. Most offenses were committed by men too young to be drafted or by female workers.

Despite Fascist labor controls in Italy, much of the Italian workforce in Turin and Milan went on strike in March and April 1943. In effect, these strikes were political protests against the government and involvement in the war; the Communist Party, which had sustained an underground presence in Italy, was among the leaders. These strikes were a factor in persuading those Fascist politicians and businessmen who had become disillusioned with Mussolini to arrange for his downfall in July.

After Italy defected to the Allies, hundreds of thousands of captured Italian soldiers were sent to Germany as forced laborers; Italian civilians were also impressed. In early 1944, the Germans commandeered 1 million Italian workers, though even this fell short of the Reich's requirements. Italians working for factories in German-occupied Italy also helped fulfill Germany's war production needs. At risk of being deported, more Italians stayed away from their jobs and many joined the resistance, disrupting both the German and Italian economies.

A 1944 strike by Italian workers in northern Italy was the largest strike to occur in any of the countries that the Nazis occupied. Some 300,000 workers in the province of Milan joined strikers from Turin, Genoa, Bologna, and Florence to call for an end to war and cessation of labor that benefited Germany. The strike failed to achieve these goals and some 2,000 labor leaders were deported to Germany, but the protest raised the morale of partisan resisters and of many Italian civilians.

In November 1941, Japanese men (between 16 and 40) and young women (unmarried, between 16 and 25) had to register with the government for nonmilitary war work, but only men were actually employed. With 3 million men removed from the Japanese workforce to military duties from 1940 to 1944—and the duplication of effort resulting from competition in economic planning by government and military agencies—Japan faced a labor crisis comparable to that of the other major combatants. Skilled workers were particularly in demand at aircraft, ship-building, and weapons factories. In 1944, men who were 12 to 59 years old had to register. The shortage was also made up by employing men over 60 who volunteered, prisoners of war, contract Korean and Chinese laborers, and impressed laborers from the countries Japan occupied. As in the other Axis countries, employing women was a last resort.

The Japanese government capped wages, making it difficult for workers to pay for commodities on the black market. Workers were coerced into buying war bonds, and were also subject to income tax, and additional surtaxes if they earned an annual salary of more than 3,000 yen. Absenteeism was as high as 25 percent, particularly after the Allied bombing of Japanese cities began. Some left temporarily to engage in seasonal agricultural work.

Agriculture

Allies

American agriculture passed from depression into an unheard of prosperity during the war years. As employment increased in industry and business and Americans experienced greater financial security—and as the United States supported the Allies through the Lend-Lease and Food for Freedom programs—the demand for agricultural commodities grew. In the United States, unlike the other major combatants, people were eating more food, not less, as the war progressed, despite rationing. Civilian spending on food products increased from $14 billion to $24 billion between 1940 and 1944. The government played a role in agriculture's newfound prosperity. In 1942, at the urging of the farm lobby, Congress set ceilings on farm prices that were proportionately higher than those on industrial prices. To keep consumer food prices from rising, the government subsidized agriculture by buying at these high prices and selling to retailers at a loss. While the country's overall inflation rate during the war was 28 percent, farm prices rose nearly 50 percent in the same period. Farm income increased more than 100 percent.

Although the number of farmworkers decreased during the war—more than 6 million rural residents joined the armed forces or sought jobs in war industries, 3 million of them from the South—agricultural output increased by 17 percent as a result of new technology, use of fertilizers, and disease control. The war also continued a twentieth-century trend in American farming: a decline in the number of small family farms (as well as fewer tenant farmers and sharecroppers) and the growth of huge agribusinesses.

During the war, Americans were encouraged to grow Victory gardens, an idea developed by Claude Wickard, the secretary of agriculture, and energetically embraced by the American people. In 1943, there were an estimated 20.5 million gardens, planted in backyards, but also in public places like the zoo in Portland, Oregon, and Copley Square in Boston. Some 33 percent of vegetables eaten by Americans in 1943 came from Victory gardens, but their value lay more in morale and community building than in feeding a hungry population.

During the Depression, British agriculture had suffered a decline and most food was imported. Once the war began, food shipping was further limited, not only by Germany's campaign to blockade the British Isles (see "The Battle of the Atlantic" in Chapters 6 and 7) but because raw materials other than food that had to be imported occupied space in the ships that made it past the cordon of German U-boats. Imports continued to decline. German attacks resulted in the loss of 700,000 tons of food in 1940, and again in 1941, and 500,000 tons in 1942. To compensate, Britain made a heroic effort to increase agricultural production at home. Fifty percent more land was used for farming, and with the help of technology and fertilizers (and government grants and subsidies), production increased by 36 percent from 1938–1939 to 1941–1942, and by 91 percent the following year. Thus, with careful rationing, British civilians had enough to eat.

With many farm laborers in the armed services, some 70,000 schoolboys, in 1943 alone, helped with planting and harvesting. Holiday labor camps allowed older students and factory and civil service workers (who earned extra vacation time by volunteering) to spend a week or two assisting on farms. Italian prisoners of war were also put to work on farms. But the largest program was the Women's Land Army. Nearly 20,000 young women were voluntarily working on farms and in other rural occupations by the autumn of 1941. After that, women farmworkers were also conscripted; by 1945, some 80,000 were at work. Reginald Smith, the Minster of Agriculture, also urged civilians to Dig for Victory. By 1943, there were 1.4 million small garden plots.

In the first two years the Soviets were at war, agricultural production fell—in 1942, it was 40 percent below the amount it had been before the war began. The Germans occupied the USSR's richest farmland in the west and south and took the food that was grown there. Men were needed in the army

In this photograph taken by the U.S. Office for Emergency Management, victory gardeners proudly display the vegetables they grew, ca. 1942–1943 (top). In Great Britain during the same period, members of the Women's Land Army harvest beets (bottom).

rather than the agricultural workforce, and fewer horses and tractors were available to speed the work. Not only did overall output fall, but output per agricultural worker fell as well. At the same time, the government needed a higher percentage of crops and livestock to feed the growing armed forces, leaving less for civilians.

Government policy toward collective farmers—those who worked communally rather than on individually owned plots of land—was generally demanding, but uneven. Before the war, the government decided the amount each farm should be producing and took its percentage of food based on that estimate rather than on actual output. During the war, it appropriated even greater amounts of foodstuffs. Farmers saw some relaxation of the rules that governed collective farms, as farming families were allowed to make more management decisions than they had in peacetime and were also given space for allotments on collectivized land. However, farmers did not have guaranteed food rations as people in the cities did. Their main diet consisted of potatoes and milk.

An estimated 85 percent of the Chinese population labored as farmers, but when Japan invaded China in 1937, many of the male workers were drafted into the military. The Chinese Nationalist, communist, and Japanese armies also commandeered produce as well as carts and draft animals, further reducing food supplies and production capabilities. The Japanese banned the planting of sorghum, a major source of food for peasants, because the tall crops provided protective covering for Chinese guerrilla forces. Military forces appropriated crops and livestock. The war so decimated rural northern China that in many places crop yields in 1949 were still below that of crops harvested in the 1930s.

Axis

In Germany, the government formed the Reichnahrstand (farmers' league) to facilitate control of both markets and prices. The Nazis sought to stabilize the ownership of land through inheritance laws. Farms smaller than three hundred acres became "inheritance farms"—the owners and their eldest sons could not leave and were obliged to grow what the government demanded. The government also tried, without complete success, to control the mobility of agricultural workers, and issued credit to farmers who were in debt. Success in each of these programs varied. In general, wealthier farmers had more advantages, including more aid for debt reduction. Less prosperous farmers tended to be anti-Nazi, although they did not express their discontent too openly.

Although Hitler extolled the virtues of rural life, an increasing number of agricultural workers moved to urban areas. German agriculture experienced a significant labor shortage during the war. To compensate, boys between the ages of 14 and 18 and women between the ages of 17 and 25 were drafted for one-year periods to work in agriculture. Food shortages were also made up with imports from occupied countries—more came from western Europe than eastern Europe or the Soviet Union, where there were continuous battles. Thus, German civilians had more food available to them than did the people of many of the countries from which Germany's food came. German-occupied countries sometimes suffered such severe food shortages because of German confiscation that famine ensued. (See also Chapter 8.) As in the Soviet Union, farmers did not come under food rationing schemes. Although restricted in the amount of food they could keep, they often ate better than their urban counterparts.

Although Mussolini initially believed that Fascism would take root in the cities, he emphasized agricultural development as part of his plan to recast Italy. But the population of rural laborers dropped 16.6 percent from 1921 to 1936, as people in the countryside moved to cities and towns.

In the 1920s, concerned with a large deficit in the country's balance of payments, Mussolini also strove for self-sufficiency in the food supply. His widely publicized "Battle of the Grain" urged farmers to give up producing export products, including grapes, olives, and citrus fruits, and to raise grain instead. By 1939, Italian farms were supplying 75 percent of the grains needed to feed the population (with a concurrent loss of export income). However, especially in the south, where much of the land and climate were unsuitable for growing wheat, the plan made farmers dangerously dependent on a single crop. Mussolini's other major agricultural initiative involved reclaiming and improving uncultivated land. His agricultural programs generally increased the power of large landowners, created a class of tenant farmers rather than owners, and only marginally benefited the landless poor. Nor were most Italian agricultural workers excited about farming in the colonies of Libya, Eritrea, and Ethiopia.

Italy entered the war in a weak position agriculturally, and in the early 1940s, production dropped by 60 percent. Farm land, vineyards and orchards were heavily damaged by bombing and, from 1943 on, battles on the home front. In addition, many farmers secretly kept part of their produce for themselves or to sell at a good profit on the black market. Many peasants were better off financially than they had been before the war, but food shortages plagued Italian civilians, especially in the cities.

In Japan, as in the other major combatant nations, the agricultural labor supply dropped while the military's need for food increased. (The Japanese military also took food from occupied countries, sometimes causing famine. Japanese confiscations of rice spurred a 1944–1945 famine in Vietnam that took 2 million lives.) Since vegetables and fruits required more labor than other plants, production of vegetables alone dropped by 81 percent. Military rather than commercial use of vessels and later the Allied sea blockade made

FAMINE AND STARVATION

Chinese civilians faced famine several times during the war, exacerbated by the chaos of mass migrations and commandeering or theft of food by military forces and bandits. In 1937, 30 million people in Sichuan, Shaanxi, and Henan provinces suffered from a famine that caused the desperate population to eat mud, ants, and tree roots. In 1943, drought in Henan province contributed to a famine that *Time* magazine writer Theodore White estimated claimed 2 million lives. (Other estimates put the toll at 5 million deaths.) White reported that "half the villages were deserted; some simply abandoned, others already looted. . . . One saw, as one traveled, people . . . stripping bark from all the elms . . . because you could grind the bark and eat it." This famine was made worse because Chinese officers enforced a grain tax of some 30 to 50 percent of their crops on peasants to feed the armed forces, which warehoused food even though civilians were starving. It also reflected the long-term effects of destroying the dikes on the Yellow River to stop a Japanese advance in 1938; this caused massive floods and adversely affected the irrigation system of a large part of the country. Over 4,000 villages were washed away at the time. Meanwhile, in

nearby India, which fielded the largest all-volunteer army of any Allied nation during the war, a 1943 famine in Bengal killed an estimated 1.5 to 3 million people.

European countries also experienced starvation. In Axis-occupied Greece in the winter of 1941–1942, hundreds of thousands died when Athens and other Greek cities and provincial towns suffered from a lack of food compounded by high inflation, unemployment, and hoarding that stemmed from fear of confiscation by occupying forces. "Ex-clerks, workers, chauffeurs and cashiers, whose jobs have been scrapped, have become porters and try to earn their miserable daily bread carrying bags and shopping on carts or on their backs," a British Foreign Office memo reported.

The Nazi government cut off food supply lines to the northern part of the Netherlands it still controlled in the winter of 1944–1945 in retaliation for a railroad strike. The government went so far as to take bicycles and cars away from civilians so they could not travel to obtain food. Floods compounded the suffering—the pumps that held back the sea could not run because of an electrical power shortage. (See also "German War Crimes" in Chapter 8.)

it harder to import food, including staples—rice (20 percent was imported) from Korea and Taiwan, and soy beans from Manchukuo. The amount of cultivated land decreased by 8.5 percent when the government took it over for air bases and war factories.

Like farmers in the Soviet Union, those in Japan lacked tractors and horses, appropriated by the military, as well as fertilizer (used in explosives). In 1943, the government set quotas for rice, wheat, barley, and potatoes, sometimes requisitioning a farmer's entire crop. This led, as it did in other combatant countries, to farmers hiding some of their harvest for themselves or to sell on the black market. Labor shortages continued to be a problem; in the fall of 1944, 2 million schoolchildren were supplementing agricultural labor, and women and the elderly were performing the bulk of agricultural work.

The Role of Women

Allies

Total war brought more women of all major combatants into jobs that supported the war economy. The U.S. government, through the efforts of the War Manpower Commission and the Office of War Information, ran promotional campaigns to recruit women to fill labor shortages. "Rosie the Riveter" was a positive image of a woman who worked outside the home, developing her strength and abilities and serving her country at the same time. Such images were necessary to overcome, for the duration of the war, traditional imperatives that consigned women to the domestic sphere as mothers and housewives, or to such acceptable jobs as teaching and nursing. Newspapers and radio programs featured stories about the importance of adding women to the workforce. The Office of War Information (OWI) requested magazines to show workingwomen on the front covers of their September 1943 issues (the same month *Life* magazine published the first pictures of U.S. war dead; see "Journalism" in Chapter 10). OWI also pondered how to sell unappealing but necessary jobs. "A laundry, even with the most modern plant and equipment is still a pretty unpleasant place to work," read one OWI program plan. "These jobs will have to be glorified as a patriotic war service if American women are to be persuaded to take them and stick to them. Their importance to a nation engaged in total war must be convincingly presented."

In fact, American women, though willing to do volunteer work for the war effort, did not flock in huge numbers to fill industrial and other jobs usually held by men. Many women, especially married women, preferred not to be employed for wages. Among the other major combatants, the United States was ahead of Germany and Japan in the percentage of women working in war industries and other wartime employment, but well behind Britain and the Soviet Union. Some 70 to 75 percent of American women stayed at home over the span of the war years, while more than 70 percent of Soviet and British women worked outside the home.

Twelve million of the nearly 19 million American women who worked for wages during the war held jobs in 1940. Of the remaining 6 million women who answered the call of the spirited propaganda campaigns, 3 million were young, single, and newly graduated from school—women who were likely to be joining the workforce anyway. Therefore, only an estimated 2.7 to 3.5 million women went to work outside the home primarily because of the war. Some 2 million American women worked in the defense industries—about 25 percent of these in aircraft factories and some 225,000 in shipbuilding. Only 4.4 percent of women held skilled jobs such as riveting; the others did work that required little training.

By 1944, married women outnumbered single women in the workforce, but most of the married women were over 35 and did not have small children; the number of workingwomen with children younger than six remained under 15 percent, ranging from 9 percent in 1940 to 12 percent in 1944. To assist workingwomen, the government built 3,100 day-care centers, but only 130,000 children attended—about 25 percent of capacity. Nevertheless, pundits and the press blamed working mothers for the increase of latchkey kids, promiscuity in young women, and delinquency in young men, without considering the disruptions to family life caused by relocation, the growth of urban centers, hasty marriages, fathers away in the service, and the general excitement engendered by the war. What individual workingwomen did gain during World War II, in the United States and elsewhere, was a more confident sense of their abilities and choices and more latitude in deciding how to spend their lives.

Although many British women had already been working in textile mills and aircraft and light industry when the war began, the British government found it necessary to draft women between ages 20 and 30 in December 1941—it was the first labor draft of women ever in a western European country. Nineteen-year-old women were added to the draft in early 1942. Although the general attitude prevailed that women should focus on their homes and families, most people also realized the measure was necessary. By 1943, almost every woman under 40 was working, including 90 percent of single women and 80 percent of married women. (This included jobs in the armed forces.)

Women replaced men in transportation (as railroad porters and conductors, bus conductors, and on canal boats). Three hundred thousand women had jobs in the explosives and chemical industries and 1.5 million in engi-

South African women, in Great Britain to join the "First Aid and Nursing Yeomanry," learn stunt riding to build balance and confidence in training to serve as dispatch riders, November 1942 (top). American women working as locomotive engine cleaners walk along the tracks in the Long Island, New York, railroad yards (bottom).

neering and metal. Women accounted for 48 percent of civil service workers between 1939 and 1945. Younger women worked in agriculture, civil defense, hospitals, and as ambulance drivers, while older women assumed places in shops, textile mills, and offices. Women with families or the wives of servicemen could be classified as "immobile" so they could work near home, but many Scottish, Welsh, and women from northern Britain were relocated to factories in the midlands, where labor was most in demand. In July 1943, to free up young women for aircraft work, the labor draft was extended to women 51 years of age. Conservatives who opposed this as unseemly labeled it the "Grannies' Call Up," but Parliament passed the regulation.

In the Soviet Union, "Men to the front, women to the factories," was an accepted imperative, not surprising since women already comprised 40 percent of the workforce in 1940. This rose to 52 percent in 1942 and 53 percent by 1944. (All women between ages 18 and 40, working or not, were subject to a labor draft in 1941; in 1942, this was extended to include women 16 to 45 years old, and later 50 years old.) Women had already made up a large percentage of workers in light industry. During the war, the figure reached 80 to 90 percent. But after 1941, they were also operating turbines and climbing down coal shafts, making up more than 25 percent of the workers in the coal industry. Near the front line, where men were in even greater demand as soldiers, women formed a majority of workers in engineering factories. In Leningrad, women comprised 84 percent of the industrial workforce in February 1943.

Soviet women received training to perform industrial jobs, just as all young workers did, but while they took on more skilled jobs in factories, they did not rise in management or administrative positions. They also remained largely responsible for domestic chores and child rearing. "The women manufactured grenades, sewed soldiers' uniforms, made fur coats and felt boots, were woodcutters and carpenters," recorded a resident of Shadrinsk, a town in the Soviet hinterland. A laborer in the Shadrinsk factory, which produced detonators, explained in May 1943: "We worked twelve hours a day and eighteen hours on Sunday. . . . The little children were at the workbenches, which were too high for them, so they piled two or three crates on top of one another in front of the workbench, climbed up, and set to work just like the adults."

Soviet women also joined fighting units at the front, as combat pilots, infantry, tank drivers, and snipers. (See also "Women in Military Service" in Chapter 4.)

Axis

Hitler opposed women working outside the home—they were meant to breed Aryan children—and middle- and upper-class German women seemed to agree. Although women were technically subject to a labor draft as early as 1938, those who already worked were the only ones affected, when the government moved them to where they were most needed. In fact, between May 31, 1939, and May 31, 1941, the number of women in the German labor force dropped by 287,500. However, women still labored in agriculture and in family businesses, and some worked in industry. Employed women resented the leisure of unemployed women. Sensing a morale problem, and with Germany in the throes of a labor shortage, on February 13, 1941, Propaganda Minister Goebbels approved an order that childless women ages 14 to 40 must report to labor exchanges. "The psychological side to compulsory female labor . . . matters," recorded *Kreigspropaganda*, "since it is ideal for lifting significantly the working spirit of women who have already been laboring in German armaments factories for months or years." Still, over the next two years very few women reported for work, and the government did nothing to enforce conscription.

Faced with heavy battlefield losses in 1943 (the year the German Sixth Army was smashed at Stalingrad), the government insisted that women between ages 17 and 45 register at their local labor office. By the end of June, a little more than 3 million women had registered; six months later, only half a million of the newly registered women were employed. Levels of absenteeism for women were high, largely because they were still taking care of homes and families.

German women had another advantage over those in other countries. Since male forced or contract foreign labor performed most industrial work, they were able to step into higher paying administrative and office jobs. Most women were paid less than men for doing the same jobs, but the maximum time they were allowed to work was lower than that for men. Since women—and families—were still thought to need support, a Mother's Protection Law provided 32,000 day-care centers by 1944, serving some 1.2 million children.

Mussolini, like Hitler, believed that women should be mothers, not workers, producing the next generation of fighting men. In addition, during the economically depressed 1930s, with about 1 million men out of work, employers were unlikely to consider a woman for a job. But to meet wartime needs, the government decreed in June 1940 that women could replace men removed from the workforce to serve in the armed forces. Female workers filled the post offices, drove streetcars, and labored in factories. In 1942, with shortages of workers increasing, Mussolini reminded women, "Your duty is resistance on the home front." Women subsequently provided more than half the labor in some factories. As in other countries, war work increased their confidence and independence—and generated much-needed income for families—without overturning traditional notions of women's place in society.

Although unmarried Japanese women between 16 and 25 years of age registered for work in 1941, there was a deep cultural resistance to women working outside the home. The National Spiritual Mobilization program in 1937 called on women to be mothers and to nurture others in their communities as a mother would. Women collected stitches for one-thousand-stitch-belts. "People hoped they would prevent a man from getting hit by bullets," remembered Hiroyo Arakawa, who operated a bakery with her husband. Women were the center of families, and "the weakening of the family system would be the weakening of the nation," Tojo proclaimed in October 1943, despite severe workforce shortages that women could help to fill. Four months later, women ages 12 to 39 registered for work, but again, they were rarely drafted.

Still, from 1940 to 1944, 1.4 million women also joined the Japanese workforce, of their own volition or out of economic necessity when the men in their families were in the military. "It didn't seem to happen all at once," recalled Arakawa, "but soon you'd notice: 'The man of that house is gone,' or 'He's been taken away for labor.' Many shops and businesses . . . were left in the hands of women." In 1944, women represented 42 percent of the civilian labor force. Many unmarried women and female students participated in volunteer corps. In fact, by the end of 1943, despite societal values, social pressure from other civilians came to bear on unmarried women who were not working and therefore were perceived as unpatriotic.

Doing Without and Making Do: Rationing and Salvaging

Governments used rationing to control inflation and to shrink the disparity between what was available to the wealthy and to the poor. Belief that everyone was sacrificing for the war effort helped to sustain morale. "It is obviously fair that where there is not enough of any essential commodity to meet all civilian demands, those who can afford to pay more for the commodity should not be privileged over others who cannot," President Roosevelt told

Congress in April 1942. "I am confident that as to many basic necessities . . . rationing will not be necessary," he added. "But where any important article becomes scarce, rationing is the democratic, equitable solution."

Rationing did not guarantee that food and other commodities would actually be available. Shortages plagued both Allied and Axis countries in Europe and Asia. The need to supply the military first, disruptions from bombing and fighting on the home front, difficulties in transport, and the vulnerability of merchant ships to enemy action reduced the amount of available food and resources.

Allies

In April 1941, Roosevelt created the Office of Price Administration (OPA) to control inflation and discourage hoarding. A year later, the OPA froze prices for about 60 percent of the country's food items. Price regulation was not the same as rationing; the former capped costs, the latter determined the distribution of supplies. Both tools were used to stabilize the home-front economy. Moreover, although food production was high during the war, the needs of the military and the Lend-Lease program somewhat limited the amount available to civilians.

Tires were the first commodity rationed in the United States, shortly after Pearl Harbor, to compensate for the rubber once supplied by Asian countries that were now under Japanese control. Beginning in May 1942, sugar, then coffee, gasoline, butter, meat, and canned goods were rationed, as much to conserve shipping space for war matériel as to allocate scarce goods. Some 5,500 countywide ration boards staffed by more than 30,000 volunteers issued ration books to every American adult and child; the books contained coupons or stamps used to obtain items. To provide greater choice, the OPA also later instituted a point system. Each month a person was allocated sixty red points for meat and fifty blue points for processed foods; each item had a point value varying with availability. Families could buy readily obtainable items for fewer points or could save points to buy harder-to-obtain items over time.

Gasoline rationing was accomplished by issuing stickers that car owners affixed to their windshields. "A" stickers for "Sunday drivers" allowed an allotment of four gallons a week. "B" through "D" stickers permitted allotments based on how far a motorist traveled to work. "E" stickers went to those for whom driving was essential, such as law enforcement and emergency workers.

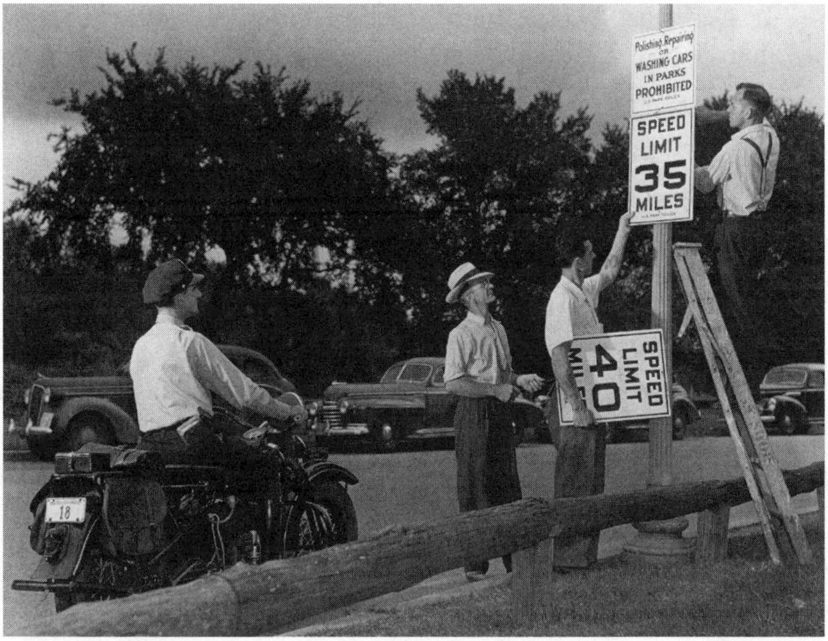

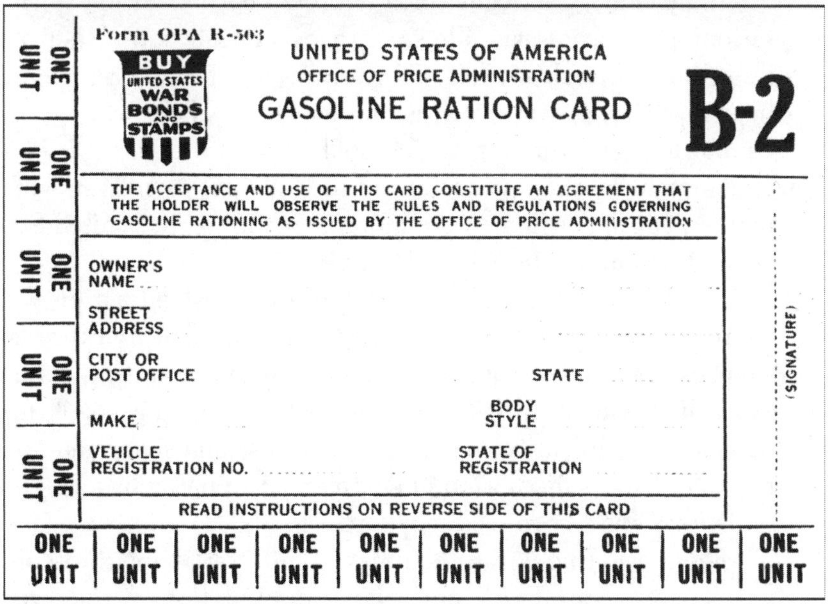
Form OPA R-503

BUY UNITED STATES WAR BONDS AND STAMPS

UNITED STATES OF AMERICA
OFFICE OF PRICE ADMINISTRATION
GASOLINE RATION CARD

B-2

THE ACCEPTANCE AND USE OF THIS CARD CONSTITUTE AN AGREEMENT THAT THE HOLDER WILL OBSERVE THE RULES AND REGULATIONS GOVERNING GASOLINE RATIONING AS ISSUED BY THE OFFICE OF PRICE ADMINISTRATION

OWNER'S NAME

STREET ADDRESS

CITY OR POST OFFICE STATE

MAKE BODY STYLE

VEHICLE REGISTRATION NO. STATE OF REGISTRATION

(SIGNATURE)

READ INSTRUCTIONS ON REVERSE SIDE OF THIS CARD

ONE UNIT | ONE UNIT | ONE UNIT | ONE UNIT | ONE UNIT | ONE UNIT | ONE UNIT | ONE UNIT | ONE UNIT | ONE UNIT | ONE UNIT | ONE UNIT | ONE UNIT | ONE UNIT | ONE UNIT

Most Americans accepted wartime restrictions. In Washington, D.C., workers replace the forty miles per hour legal speed sign with one that reads "35 mph" to conserve gasoline, September 1942. The gasoline ration card shown here was issued to a driver whose vehicle was classified as B2 because it was needed for work.

In December 1942, Congress declared a speed limit of thirty-five miles per hour to conserve gasoline. When national gas rationing went into effect, driving for pleasure was prohibited.

Shoes were officially rationed; clothes were not, but fabrics like silk and wool were devoted to the needs of the military, so civilians had less available to buy and were urged to mend and recycle clothing—for example, a child's outfit might be constructed from pieces of used adult clothing. Two-piece bathing suits, which saved on cloth, came into vogue.

The need for rubber, metal, paper, and even fats and grease (to make glycerin for high explosives) led to scrap drives. Americans collected thousands of tons of cardboard boxes, newsprint, car and bicycle tires, aluminum pots, tinfoil, and tin cans. Children were among the most enthusiastic scavengers. "I remember jumping on the tin cans to flatten them and . . . peeling the foil off my dad's cigarette packs to roll up into a ball to donate to the war effort," wrote Gerard Quinn, who was a child during the war. Civilians also contributed furs (to line merchant marine vests) and nylon and silk stockings (fashioned into powder bags for the navy).

In general, Americans collected scrap with a willing spirit and accepted rationing as necessary. Those with extra cash could also obtain rationed items on the black market. Consumers bought an estimated 20 percent of beef that way, as well as tires and gasoline—there was a brisk business in counterfeit gas coupons, which sold for up to 50¢ each. Nylon stockings could fetch the then princely sum of $5.00 per pair. Even without the black market, consumer items were more plentiful in the United States than they were in Britain or the Soviet Union.

Unlike the United States, Britain was an island nation with limited resources. "You know that our country is dependent to a very large extent on supplies of food from overseas," explained a government leaflet. "More than 20 million tons are brought into our ports from all parts of the world." This included 70 percent of the country's cheese and sugar and 50 percent of its meat. The war's disruption of commercial shipping had a significant impact on Britain's ability to feed its people.

Food rationing began in January 1940, starting with bacon, butter, margarine, and sugar. Two months later, meats followed; they were rationed by price. A person could buy a larger amount of a cheap cut than of an expensive cut. Tea was soon added, then cheese, sweets, and eggs (in the shell, not powdered). In 1941, the weekly milk allowance was approximately two to two-and-a-half pints per person. However, pregnant and nursing mothers and children under five were allowed one pint a day. In fact, overall nutrition among the poor actually improved during the war as people had access to more milk and ate more vegetables and fewer sweets. Canteens for miners and factory workers, and school programs for children, provided one good, ration-free meal per day. A point system allowed people to buy canned fish, meats, fruits and other foods and grains that were not rationed; the number of points required to buy, for example, a can of condensed milk, varied according to availability at a specific time.

Starting in June 1941, clothing was also rationed in Britain, partly to allow textile workers to work in war-related industries. Sixty-six coupons were allotted the first year, falling to sixty the next. In 1945, only forty-one clothing coupons per person were allowed. A man's suit used up a minimum of twenty-six coupons; three dozen cloth diapers, the amount needed for most babies, used up thirty-six coupons. Strict rules governed those clothes still produced: jackets could only be single-breasted, pants no more than nineteen inches wide with no double cuffs. Socks had to be shorter than nine and a half inches.

Gasoline rationing began three weeks after Britain declared war on Germany in 1939. Lighting of shop windows at night was prohibited, one of several measures taken to conserve power, as well as make cities harder to locate as bombing targets. Between 1942 and 1944, the use of coal in private homes fell by 25 percent. Britain's Control of Paper Order, issued in February 1940, allotted publishers 60 percent of their 1939 paper supply.

As in the United States, scrap drives were common. "Very few of us can be heroines on the battle-front, but we can all have the tiny thrill of thinking as we hear the news of an epic battle in the air, 'Perhaps it was my saucepan that made a part of that Hurricane,'" Lady Reading, head of the Women's Voluntary Service, broadcast to the nation on July 10, 1940. The Ministry of Supply collected 56 million old books during one paper drive, all but 6 million of which were sent to pulp mills.

The Soviet Union began a gradual system of rationing in July 1941, beginning in the prime German targets of Moscow and Leningrad. Items rationed included bread, grain products, butter, margarine and vegetable oil, meat, fish, sugar, and sweets. In August, some two hundred additional towns in central Russia and the Urals were required to initiate rationing of bread, sugar, and sweets. Three months later, those three items were rationed in all urban areas, while meat, fish, grain products and fat rationing began in forty-three additional cities. Food for the rural population was not rationed;

but, as noted under "Agriculture" earlier in this chapter, the government confiscated a percentage of farm produce. Farmers and others in the country were expected to fend for themselves.

Because German forces occupied some of the most fertile arable land in the USSR, the Soviets had to cope with a decrease in grain production. By 1943, 62 million people had to turn to the government for (sometimes inadequate) rations of bread; the figure rose to 81 million in 1945. Those living in German-occupied territory suffered particularly. Much of their land was ravaged by combat, and German authorities took foodstuffs for their armed forces and to ship back to Germany without considering the needs of the Soviet people in occupied regions. In rural areas, peasants were only allowed to keep ten kilos of grain a month, what amounted to two-thirds of a pound of bread per day, 60 percent of what they had been allowed by the Soviet government.

In unoccupied cities, only those able-bodied civilians who worked received rations. Cards were distributed in factories and schools and could only be redeemed at stores and workplace dining rooms where people were registered. Those who worked in heavy industries received higher rations than those who performed lighter manual tasks. Office workers received even less, as did children and the elderly. The government rewarded those who excelled at work or donated blood with higher rations. Shortages were so great, however, that often civilians did not receive even minimum rations.

To supplement rations, city dwellers cultivated all available spare land. Rural peasants, who did not receive rations, were allowed to farm their own plots and to sell excess produce to urbanites once they had supplied what the state demanded. As inflation rose, currency lost its value. People traded clothes and jewelry for food. They also traded bread, although it was illegal to use bread rations to obtain other food items. Owning a milk cow could mean the difference between life and death. People were sometimes forced to eat nettles, grass, and acorns. By 1944, after Russian troops had reclaimed Belorussia, the Ukraine, and the Caucasus the amount of food available to civilians increased.

Axis

Rationing began in Germany on August 28, 1939, four days before the country invaded Poland. Civilians received color-coded cards for milk and cheese, bread, meat, sugar, grains, eggs, and fruit. Rations were based on age and employment: distribution to most adults (64.5 percent of the entire population) amounted to 2,570 calories per day. Workers in heavy industry received more and those in very heavy industry the most. Children's rations were less, although for those between the ages of 6 and 14, they came close to the average adult's. After November 1939, additional rations were prescribed for those who worked longer days or at night.

When the government could not provide the full ration, morale declined. In March 1942, a Security Service (SD) report stated, "The announcement of the 'deep cuts' in food supplies has had a really 'devastating' effect on a large section of the population to a degree which is virtually unparalleled by any other incident during the war." Rations increased again in the fall. The German government made every effort to keep the amount of food rations constant, preferring to decrease quality with extenders and additives. However, as the war dragged on, production and distribution were

EUTHANASIA IN GERMANY

One odius means of conserving resources that derived from Nazi racial policies was the Nazi euthanasia program that Hitler authorized in September 1939. Named T4 for its headquarters at No. 4 Tiergartenstrasse in Berlin, it was devoted to eliminating mentally ill Germans through "mercy killings," at first by lethal injection. Between January 1940 and August 1941, 70,273 people were killed under this program, which included "mentally defective" children, insane adults, the physically disabled, and those with incurable diseases. A typical letter to a deceased patient's family read: "We regret to inform you that your _____ , who had been transferred for awhile to our institution, died here unexpectedly on _____ as a result of influenza accompanied by pneumonia. . . . All our medical efforts were unfortunately in vain. He passed away gently and without pain. With his severe, incurable illness, death was a release for him."

Victims were later gassed in what appeared to be shower rooms, forerunners to the gas chambers used to murder Jewish people. (T4 staff were prominent employees at the extermination camps.) When the first reports of the euthanasia program reached the public in 1940, Germans were shocked. The president of Bamberg's Appeals Court wrote in January 1941, "The elimination of [the] incurable mentally ill has now filtered down here and caused bitter indignation. . . . One can hear that for the time being it may only affect insane asylums, but that later, the incurably ill will also be eliminated in hospitals, after which it would only be a small step to render politically undesirable healthy people harmless." Some of the strongest protests came from the Catholic Church.

Public opposition to euthanasia prompted the government to publicly announce its discontinuation, but instead the program expanded when it was secretly moved to the concentration camps. In all, T4 killed some 200,000 Germans.

adversely affected. So many mills were destroyed that, in February 1945, civilians began receiving grain rather than flour, with instructions on how to process it in coffee grinders.

Clothing was also rationed in Germany, beginning in November 1939. Each civilian received a clothing card annually, with points to use for purchases. Children up to age seventeen received extra points because they were still growing. To wash clothes, families received half a pound of soap powder each month, but only two ounces of bath soap in the same period. One tube of shaving cream had to last four months. Suggestions for substitutes included the liquid from stewed pine needles for bath soap and from ivy leaves for cleaning clothes.

Although Italy was not at war in the autumn of 1939, civilians could not buy meat for two days every week. A year later, with the country then a combatant, pasta was rationed. Sugar was also rationed; peasants, who were not used to cooking with sugar, sold their rations to urban evacuees. In 1941, the government reduced the pasta ration, required civilians to register with specific butchers, and began rationing bread at 200 grams per person each day. In March 1942, this dropped to 150 grams, with potatoes or rice flour mixed in with the wheat. Cheeses made with fats, olive oil, and eggs were in short supply. By then, an estimated 10 million Italians, although not starving, were going hungry. In the winter of 1942–1943, food rations provided an adult about 1,000 calories a day. A black market thrived—wheat flour and pasta sold for eight to ten times, and meat eight times, the price set by the government—but this benefited the rich, not the poor.

Other shortages also plagued the Italians. Soap and coffee were scarce, and shoes became impossible to buy. To conserve fabric, those under age sixteen had to wear shorts rather than pants. Northern Italians suffered fuel shortages in 1942–1943. Gasoline was rationed, but it became impossible to get even the rationed amount. The government requisitioned private automobiles in 1942. Taxis could only be used in emergencies. Most people traveled by bicycle.

As in Italy, civilians in Japan generally did not starve, but malnutrition became prevalent as the war progressed and shortages of consumer goods were legion. To help stabilize and control the distribution of food and other necessities, the government began rationing matches, charcoal, and sugar in 1940. Individual cities began rationing some goods in 1940 and distribution amounts and methods varied locally throughout the war. In most places, people received tickets or stamps they could trade in for foods. They received rationed goods through their tonarigumi (neighborhood associations).

By early 1942, rice was rationed throughout the country; some locales also rationed dairy and wheat products, bean paste, and noodles. Distribution of fish and vegetables was also managed locally. By 1943, the national fish supply had decreased by half because fishing boats did not have sufficient gasoline, and there were meat and dairy shortages. Still, in April 1944, the average number of calories civilians consumed was a little over 1,900, nearly double that in Italy. Then, in 1945, Allied bombing and ship blockades dramatically affected the food supply. The national government distributed pumpkin seeds and sweet potato seedlings so that civilians could grow their own food, and acorns were used to make flour. People ate the herb mugwort, chickweed, thistle, and pumpkin, as well as ground potato stems, mulberry leaves, and the residue from soybeans.

Clothing in Japan was also rationed. Each year, a city dweller received one hundred points and rural dwellers eighty points. Overcoats and men's suits each cost fifty points, a shirt twelve points. In 1944, the clothing ration was halved. "Anything with a sense of elegance at all was forbidden under the prohibition regulations, even a single line of gold-embroidered thread in a kimono," recalled dressmaker Ayako Koshino. "Kimono sleeves had to be cut short. Your haori, the cloak you wear over a kimono, had to be shortened, too. They were supposed to look more gallant that way." Wooden clogs and shoes made of sharkskin replaced leather shoes. On a more basic level, by the winter of 1944–1945, fuel was so scarce that library books were burned for heat.

Civil Defense, Air Raids, and Bomb Shelters

Allies

"Living in San Francisco during the war, we were concerned that the Japanese might attack us. . . . We were asked to memorize the silhouette of American and Japanese planes so we could report if we ever saw a Japanese one," explained Gerard Quinn, who was seven years old when the United States entered World War II. Americans did not know that the mainland United States would not be attacked (except for some Japanese shelling of California and Oregon and small bombs carried by balloons that landed on the West Coast). They felt the same fear experienced by civilians of other nations; civil defense became part of Americans' lives. "Our first summer in Maine the neighbors asked us if we would be willing to go on the watch as airplane spotters," Lois Raymond remembered. "We said, 'Sure.' It was right up at the head of the hill in an old chickenhouse which had been cleaned up. We would go up there with a cribbage board, a lantern, a book or two, and a pot of coffee. Every fifteen minutes we would go out and look, but we never heard a thing. It was just as well, because the telephones hadn't been put in."

An estimated 10 to 11 million civilians, including teenagers, were involved in civil defense activities, supervising mock air raid and gas attack drills, serving as air raid wardens, block captains, and plane spotters, and learning first aid. The War Department instructed specially selected civilians to deal with aerial attacks on civilian populations. The army's Chemical Warfare Service developed a two-week program, held at seven sites, that taught more than 10,000 citizens to identify and respond to gas and incendiary bomb attacks. Other specialized groups included civilian demolition and clearance crews, decontamination squads, and bomb squads.

Major cities organized civil defense programs for drivers, messengers, canteen workers, hospital aides, and office employees. A week after the war began, 250 teenagers gathered in New York City to begin training as junior air wardens. The very adult Gilda Gray, a Polish Ziegfeld Follies performer known as the "Shimmy Queen," formed the Show Girls Unit of Civilian Defense. "When Hitler sends his blitz to Broadway . . . we'll be ready," she told the United Press. "Many show girls speak several languages, others are mothers and know how to handle children. Most of them drive cars. There are plenty of things we can do in an emergency. . . . I spent a year of air raids in London, and I know how scared you get. I never shook in a shimmy . . . like I shook in my first air raid."

The YMCA and YWCA, the Red Cross, patriotic and veterans clubs, the Boy Scouts and Girl Scouts, and churches and labor unions were among the existing organizations that had members practice first aid and participate in air raid drills. Police departments assigned officers and volunteers to patrol around factories, bridges, railroad crossings, and water and sewer lines. In San Francisco, polo club members guarded beach areas on their own ponies, in the shadow of the Golden Gate Bridge.

Hawaii won praise for its excellent nightly blackout procedures, and blackouts were also frequent on the West Coast. They were ordered along the eastern seaboard in the summer of 1942 to protect ships and coastal targets from German U-boats then ranging through American waters. Other parts of the country, such as the Gulf Coast, went to "grayouts" to reduce visibility and energy consumption. Large windows and skylights were often painted black, and in places susceptible to frequent blackouts, white paint marked roadways for drivers not using their headlights. Flashlights were permitted outdoors as long as "the light is filtered through three thicknesses of newspaper and not pointed above the horizontal," according to the guidebook *Civilian Defense* by C. E. Walton.

Ultimately, civil defense was not needed to defend the United States from attack; its home front never became a battlefront. Only six American civilians were killed by war-related injuries in the 48 states: Elsye Winters Mitchell, a minister's wife, and five children who were with her on a fishing trip at Mount Gearhart near Bly, Oregon, on May 5, 1945; they all died from the explosion of a Japanese balloon bomb that had successfully crossed the Pacific Ocean.

During the Phony War of the winter of 1939–1940 (see Chapter 6), the call for preparing Britain's home front lost much of its urgency. But after Germany invaded Belgium, the Netherlands, and France, the government again asked for Home Guard volunteers on May 14, 1940; in only twenty-four hours, 250,000 people had responded to the call. Civilians aided in the evacuation of Allied armies from Dunkirk in May and June— an event that was both sobering and invigorating. During the Blitz (September–November 1940), British civilians felt fear, but they also demonstrated an energetic will to resist as the Luftwaffe concentrated on bombing British cities. German planes dropped 350 tons of bombs on London on the night of September 18–19 and more than 500 tons on Coventry in November (not the estimated 700 to 3,500 tons that had been feared). On November 14 alone, German bombs destroyed most of the city's medieval center and cathedral and killed 554 people. Instead of demoralizing Britons, the bombing of its cities seemed to unite them.

London observer John Strachey described the explosions of light when bombs dropped and he heard the sounds of incendiaries and sirens. There was a "harsh, rank, raw smell" after an area had been bombed. "Its basis certainly came from the torn, wounded, dismembered houses; from the gritty dust of dissolved brickwork, masonry and joinery. . . . For several hours there was an acrid overtone from the high explosive which the bomb itself had contained; a fiery constituent of the smell. Almost invariably, too, there was the mean little stink of domestic gas, seeping up from broken pipes and leads. But the whole of the smell was greater than the sum of its parts. It was the smell of violent death itself."

Some 60,595 people died in the Blitz and 237,005 were injured. Millions sought refuge every night, some in their own backyards, where they had installed Anderson shelters, named for Britain's Minister of Civil Defense John Anderson. The shelters consisted of two curved steel walls bolted together over a four-foot-deep pit, then covered with dirt.

Others slept in underground subway stations, despite government concerns that this would foster a timid, cave mentality. City-based "trekkers" drove their cars to the countryside each night, slept in them, and returned to work in the morning. Some people sheltered in caves (e.g., those at Chislehurst in Kent) or church halls. Those who lost their homes often lived in the Underground (subway stations) or in "rest centers" (frequently housed in school buildings). Local governments and volunteer agencies made increasingly successful efforts to help the homeless. By August 1941, more than 1.1 million bombed homes throughout Britain had been weatherproofed with boards and tarpaulins so that they were habitable.

Soviet civilians, like the British, demonstrated extraordinary determination and solidarity in resisting the German onslaught that began in June 1941. But while Britons were bombed from the air, the Soviets also faced brutal treatment on the ground, in their own villages, towns, and cities. After German troops had secured an area, often with marked barbarism, the *Einsatzgruppen* and other elements of the *Sicherheitsdienst* (Nazi Security Service, part of the SS) moved in to execute entire Jewish communities and

Britons sleep in a South East London subway shelter to protect themselves from nighttime German bombing raids, 1941–1942. In a West End London shelter, an elderly couple wait patiently while German airplanes bomb the city.

communist functionaries. Slavic peoples were commandeered for forced labor in Germany. German troops confiscated food from peasants and burned buildings; they were particularly ruthless when civilians were suspected of supporting the Soviet partisans who carried on guerrilla actions behind German lines. (See "German War Crimes" in Chapter 8.)

CIVIL DEFENSE, BRITISH STYLE

Having been victims of primitive aerial assaults in World War I, Britain resolutely prepared for the tremendous devastation that likely lay ahead in a second major war with Germany and its allies. Although civil defense authorities were slow to overcome some miscalculations and organizational obstacles, in the face of relentless bombardment that shattered lives, structures, and nerves, the British program improved over time and became a model for the United States.

In June 1940, regular church bell ringing was prohibited, as bells were to be used to warn of impending attacks. That summer, thousands evacuated to the countryside, among them Margaret Kennedy, who in her 1941 book *Where Stands a Winged Sentry* described a civil defense lecture that revealed a few flaws in the system. The lecturer, one Colonel Farraday, "explained how to put up an Anderson steel shelter and said that none were being issued in this part of the country." Plenty of gas masks were available, however (about 5 million more than there were people to use them), and even the littlest Brits were equipped. In March 1939, Sir John Anderson, minister for civil defense, reported to Parliament that 1.4 million baby-size gas helmets were on order.

After the fall of France, street name signs and other identifying markers were removed or painted out all over Britain to confuse Nazi paratroopers or downed air crews as to their whereabouts; on balance, it caused far greater confusion among the native population. Still, Britons were determined to maintain civilized order, as evidenced by a July 1940 *Manchester Daily Dispatch* report: "Though park railings in Manchester are being removed for scrap, the park gates will be retained and locked as usual at night to indicate that the parks are in theory closed."

More than two years later, impatience with unreasonable civil defense measures had begun to build in some quarters. Lord Mottistone, speaking in Parliament's House of Lords, voiced his displeasure with the continued "blacking out of the names of railway stations," calling it a sign of "timidity," and protested the ban on church bell ringing, noting that mute bells had become so rusted they could not sound the alert should the Germans invade. "We need a minister of common sense to do the things which are needful," he said, "and to undo the things which are foolish."

Millions of Soviet civilians also suffered through long-term sieges. The people of Leningrad, including the elderly and children, hastily built 340 miles of antitank ditches and 5,875 miles of open trenches to defend themselves from the German advance in the winter of 1941–1942, but this did not stop German forces from cutting off shipments of food and supplies. The only open route was across the northern and eastern part of Lake Ladoga. One Leningrad inhabitant described the city in January 1942: "30 degrees Celsius below freezing. Piles of snow in the street. Little paths between them, someone on his way to work, another fetching a bucket of water, a third pulling a sledge carrying dead relatives wrapped in sheets. Not everyone has the strength to take them to a cemetery." People burned furniture and houses to stay warm. Through all this, they were continually bombarded by artillery and bombed by German aircraft. Deaths from hunger and cold in the city totaled 632,000—with suburban deaths and those from other war causes added, the death toll during the siege of Leningrad reached 1 million people.

The Germans also laid siege to Moscow from October through December 1942. German troops killed civilians, commandeered their food, and burned buildings in the area surrounding the city. In October 1941, they besieged Sevastopol, on the Black Sea. Civilians lived in basements and caves to protect themselves from bombing, even continuing to manufacture weapons and teach school in these underground spaces. Bombing decreased in the winter, but resumed again in May 1942; Sevastopol was finally taken by the Germans in July. When the Germans penetrated the outskirts of the vital Volga-River city of Stalingrad in September 1942, Stalin would not let the city be evacuated, although buildings were in ruins, and water supplies, telephone, and transportation destroyed. After an epic battle that was one of the turning points of Word War II, Soviet troops were victorious at Stalingrad in February 1943.

To weaken Chinese morale, Japanese aircraft bombed cities in the Nationalist-controlled area, including Kweilin, Kunming, and Sian. Between 1939 and 1941, the Nationalist capital, Chungking, was bombed 268 times, with a death toll in the thousands. In the first two days of May 1939 alone, some 4,400 people were killed. Rather than encourage surrender, the bombings stiffened Chinese civilian resistance. The Japanese also conducted raids in the countryside throughout the war to appropriate or destroy crops. In 1944, the Japanese Ichigo offensive (see Chapter 7) caused most of the civilian war death totals for the entire war in Kwangsi province: 110,000 people and 80,000 oxen (vital to agriculture). Three hundred thousand buildings were also destroyed.

Axis

On August 25, 1940, despite Nazi assurances to the contrary, British air-planes bombed Berlin. However, aerial bombing did not become a major concern until 1942. Allied aircraft bombed seventy-two German cities between 1942 and 1945, the attacks increasing in ferocity each year. The death toll of German civilians increased as well—in the winter of 1942, about 220 people died each month; by the summer, the monthly toll was 750. In 1943, the death toll reached 7,000 per month. In Hamburg alone, 45,000 people were killed in just one week in late July 1943, and the bombing left 900,000 people homeless. The night of July 27 was particularly disastrous, when weather conditions helped to create a massive firestorm that even sucked the air from underground shelters so that the people inside them suffocated. A report from the Police Commissioner of Hamburg, who acted as the local air raid leader, described "an almost utopian picture of a metropolis, suddenly devastated. . . . The streets were covered with hundreds of bodies. Mothers with children, men young and old, burned, charred. . . . Shelters presented the same picture, even more gruesome . . . since it showed here and there the last desperate struggle against a merciless fate." (See also "Bombers" in Chapter 5 and "Hamburg, the First Firestorm" in Chapter 7.)

A large majority of Germans blamed the British, rather than the Nazi government, for destroying German cities; as with Britons in the Blitz, bombing did not weaken civilian morale. The German government had also prepared well against attack—there were enough air raid shelters and equipment to fight fires and immediate help was available with food, clothing, medical care, and shelter after the bombing ended. Nonetheless, Irmgard Marchant, who lived near Hademar, Germany, remembered, "the bombing was terrible. Every night we had alerts at three o'clock, six o'clock and 12 o'clock. . . . Many sleepless nights were spent in the bunkers with our frightened children. My son was born in the bunkers. . . . Shrapnel hit the headboard when my child was born. They were shooting up the whole street."

Despite such massive destruction over the years, Hitler "never did see a city that had been badly bombed," wrote Traudl Junge, one of his secretaries. "We traveled through Germany in the special train with the blinds down and when he reached Anhalter Station in Berlin at night the chauffeur would take the streets that weren't so badly damaged."

Civilians in Italy endured two major periods of aerial bombardment: 1942–September 1943, when bombs were dropped by the Allies, and late

1943 to 1945, after Italy surrendered to the Allies and was occupied by German troops, when both the Allies and the Germans bombed the country. Since many Italian civilians were reluctant to be at war, and there were no significant victories to buoy spirits, the first period of Allied bombing had a profound impact on morale. In Turin alone, 25,000 homes were destroyed in 1942. Twenty-one thousand Italian civilians had been killed during air raids by September 1943. In contrast to civilian populations in all the other major combatant countries, however, the majority of Italians blamed their government (and its wartime alliance with Germany), rather than the British and American enemy, for the destruction.

Popular discontent was a large factor in ousting Mussolini, but even after Il Duce's fall, the Italian home front remained a battlefront. "The little towns of Italy that have been in the path of this war from Salerno northward are nothing more than great rubble heaps," wrote American correspondent Ernie Pyle on December 28, 1943. "There is hardly enough left of most of them to form a framework for rebuilding. When the Germans occupied the towns, we [Allied forces] rained artillery on them. . . . Then after we captured a town, the Germans would shell it heavily. They got it from both sides. Along the road for twenty or thirty miles behind the fighting front, you pass through one demolished town after another." Bombs killed some 64,000 Italian civilians during the course of the war—two-thirds of them (43,000) after the Italian surrender to the Allies.

American planes commanded by Lieutenant Colonel James Doolittle dropped the first Allied bombs on Japan in April 1942—most striking Tokyo, a few Nagoya, in a raid that did little damage but enraged the Japanese government and stunned civilians. Thereafter, the government provided urban air raid shelters that were deemed sufficient to house a city's entire population, but these were not invulnerable to bombs (many were simply open trenches), particularly the incendiary bombs dropped by American planes in 1945, most devastatingly during the March 9–10 raid on Tokyo. An estimated half of Tokyo, Kobe, and Yokohama, 40 percent of Osaka and Nagoya, and 90 percent of Aomori were devastated by bombs. Some 241,000 people were killed in 1945, surpassing the number killed in Hiroshima and Nagasaki by the atomic bomb. (See "The Strategic Bombing Campaign against Japan" in Chapter 7.)

Yoshito Matsushige, a newspaper photographer stationed with the army press unit in Hiroshima, survived the atomic bomb that destroyed the city on August 6, 1945. At his home, approximately four kilometers from the city center, "terrific sparks jumped from the spot where the electric lines entered the house. I heard a tremendous cracking noise, like trees being torn apart, and at the same instant there was a brilliant flash of immaculate white. . . . I sensed an explosive wind like needles striking me. . . . It was absolutely black outdoors. I couldn't see my wife's face even though we were pressed right up against each other." Matsushige walked into the city, where "people's bodies were all swollen up. Their skin, burst open, was hanging down in rags. Their faces were burnt black. . . . They were all barefoot because their shoes had stuck to the asphalt." Later that day he saw "smoldering ruins . . . still sending up plumes of flame. . . . Many people were trapped under the wreckage. . . . This area was hit by winds with a velocity of 440 meters per second and thermal waves of several hundred degrees centigrade. . . . Even had the people gotten out, they couldn't have outrun the flames." Radiation poisoning had long-term effects on people, plants, and animals. An estimated 140,000 people died from the Hiroshima blast by December 1945. On August 9, an atomic bomb dropped on Nagasaki resulted in an estimated 70,000 deaths. (See also "The A-Bomb Decision" in Chapter 2 and "Dropping the A-Bomb" in Chapter 7.)

Mobility/ Evacuations

World War II saw massive movements of population. In the United States and other combatant countries, civilians moved to work in war industries or to be near relatives in the armed forces. In occupied countries, they were relocated by force, often to labor in the country of the occupier. Civilians also were sent to internment and concentration camps (see "The Holocaust" in Chapter 8). In Europe and Asia, bombing raids and food shortages drove urban dwellers into the countryside, and ground combat in countries including the Soviet Union, China, Italy, and France, drove people to relocate. Large-scale evacuations were often organized by governments, but civilians also traveled on their own to safer places.

Wherever people relocated for work or safety, the same issues invariably arose between the newly arrived and longtime residents of a community, or evacuees and the population of reception areas. Differences in class, culture, and income were exacerbated. "They stop and stare in the street, those Muscovite ladies, and laugh out loud at the Shadrinskers, particularly the women . . . who are dressed poorly and tastelessly," read a diary entry from a resident of the town of Shadrinsk in July 1941. "They might well laugh at us, those ladies; they have brought two cooks and wagons full of food with them." The same scenario was repeated in Britain, Germany, Italy, Japan and China, wherever rural and city dwellers were thrown together. Evacuees, in their turn, often felt that local people were charging them outrageous sums for food and shelter.

Allies

"Everybody was crisscrossing the country, riding the rails, thumbing, hoboing, getting where they could, checking to see if they could find a job and moving on to someplace else if they couldn't. . . . I had noticed on packages, most every one I picked up said Made in Chicago. I figured I couldn't help but find a job there," recalled James Majors, who moved from Nashville, Tennessee, to Chicago in 1939 and worked for the Select Novelty Manufacturing Company, which made flower-shaped boutonnieres out of war stamps. Majors was one of some 15 million Americans who relocated during the war, 8 million of them to another state. The majority were people in their twenties and thirties, resilient enough to risk big changes in their lives for the sake of economic opportunity.

Most Americans moved to find better employment near military bases and industrial centers, leaving rural areas to settle in cities, a trend already apparent in the 1920s and 1930s. The sunbelt states of the south Atlantic and Gulf coasts and the Pacific coast states grew significantly. Between 1940 and 1945, the population of California, Oregon, and Washington state increased by 33 percent. The population of Mobile, Alabama, with its active shipyards, jumped from 79,000 in 1940 to some 125,000 in 1943. Such growth fueled another characteristic of the American home front: a shortage of housing. "Entering the city by bus from the east the first thing one sees is a huge trailer camp," wrote Selden Menefee, on assignment to explore the wartime United States in 1943. "Mobile's hotels are perpetually filled, and her rooming houses display 'no room' signs to ward off inquiries. . . . Three downtown buildings have been converted into 'hot-bed' dormitories, with beds available in shifts for 25 cents and up."

Housing was one of the issues raised by the influx of thousands of new people into existing neighborhoods. The National Housing Agency (NHA) was established in 1942 to create new housing, but middle-class residents resisted low-cost housing projects that would change the ethnic and cultural makeup of an area. They also objected to higher taxes for schools to accommodate migrant children. Racial tensions increased as Latinos, American Indians, and African Americans moved into cities; African Americans began arriving in greater numbers after 1942, when the need for even more workers tempered discrimination to some degree. Immigrants and rural white Southerners also encountered prejudice from longtime residents. The mobility of Americans produced complex communities, sometimes in conflict, but also diverse, lively, and dynamic.

Between June and the first week in September 1939, an estimated 3.5 to 3.75 million Britons moved from urban areas to safer sites. Among them were 827,000 schoolchildren, 103,000 teachers, 524,000 younger children and their mothers, and 12,000 pregnant women who evacuated in July 1939. Many of the people who moved on their own were prosperous. One observer in the Thames Valley noted "a constant stream of private cars and London taxis driving up . . . filled with men and women of all ages and in various stages of hunger, exhaustion and fear, offering absurd sums for accommodation in [an] already overcrowded house, and even for food." Most of these evacuees returned home by early 1940.

After the "Phony War" ended with the blitzkrieg attack on the Low Countries and France in May 1940, some 160,000 city children were again sent to the countryside in May and June. A total of 1.25 million people moved over the course of the year. The Children's Overseas Reception Board also arranged for thousands to go to Canada and Australia; by July it had received 200,000 applications. A third major British evacuation took place between June and September 1944, when rockets were fired on London and southern Britain.

After the German invasion, the Soviet Union set in motion large-scale evacuations that included disassembled factories and machinery as well as people. In 1941–1942 alone, 25 million refugees traversed the country. From July to November 1941, 2,600 industrial plants, 10 million people, 800,000 horses, and 2.5 million cows moved from the western part of the country, which was rapidly falling under German occupation, east and south out of enemy range, to as far away as Siberia and Kazakhstan. A Russian later described one evacuation scene: "People were trudging eastward in an unending stream with bundles, traveling on carts with children, old people, and all kinds of cargo. Among the refugees, alone and in small groups, walked wounded soldiers. Here, too, people were driving livestock from the collective farms over the bridge, the cattle plunging, bellowing, into the water, the herders yelling their heads off at the crazed beasts."

Officials of the NKVD, the Soviet internal security organization that had arrested and executed hundreds of people as spies immediately after the invasion, evacuated Kiev in September 1941, as the Germans were surrounding the five Soviet armies that had been ordered to hold the city (all five were smashed later that month). "I saw a truck laden with household effects, as if they were going to their dacha [summer cottage]," observed Naum Korzhavin. "What kind of defense is that if the people who are supposed to form the core are quietly sneaking their families out?" In mid-October, with German troops on the outskirts of Moscow, the diplomatic corps and government officials—except Joseph Stalin and some of his staff—evacuated the city.

The Soviet government was slow in evacuating the civilian population from the besieged cities of Moscow and Leningrad. Between January and April 1942, more than a million people were evacuated from Leningrad. The first to leave Moscow for western Siberia was the chemically preserved corpse of former Soviet leader Vladimir Lenin, seventeen years dead, evacuated in a train complete with an embalming laboratory and mortuary scientists. Ultimately, 1.4 million Muscovites relocated.

The Soviet government also ordered the relocation of suspect ethnic groups within its borders in August 1941. A Decree of Banishment abolished the Autonomous Socialistic Soviet Republic of the Volga Germans, established in 1924. Most of the 400,000 descendants of Germans who had immigrated to Russia in the eighteenth century were deported to Siberia and Kazakhstan in September; the young men were drafted into the Russian army.

China experienced what some scholars call the greatest migration in human history. Japanese aggression in 1937 prompted some 12 million Chinese (along with about 450 disassembled factories and 150,000 tons of machinery) to evacuate from coastal areas to the rural interior during the war. Many of the evacuees were educated and well-to-do government officials, businessmen, and highly skilled workers. Universities and laboratories also relocated to the west or to Hong Kong, with staff and students hauling books and equipment. College groups traveling on foot could cover up to twenty-five miles a day, and some were on the road for months. Later in the war, peasants were among those fleeing the Japanese army, often with no money or belongings.

Local voluntary associations took the lead in assisting refugees, and the Nationalist government gradually assumed greater leadership. The National Relief Commission (NRC) assisted refugees with housing, transportation, medical care and employment, establishing a string of relief stations from the coast to the interior. These stations provided food and other matériel supplied by the government, the Red Cross, and various private agencies, such as the U.S. organization China Relief, Inc. To improve security measures, the

EVACUATION DISASTERS

Dangers threatened evacuees from every country as they traveled toward safety. In 1940, the ocean liner *City of Benares* left Liverpool for Canada with passengers fleeing the Blitz. It carried English, Canadian, Hungarian, French, Indian, and Polish refugees and some 90 British children accompanied by nurses, teachers, and clergymen. After it left its convoy, the liner was torpedoed and sunk on September 13, 1940. Seventy-two adults and 77 children died. The incident led Winston Churchill to tell his cabinet that he was "anxious that the scheme for evacuating children overseas should now be discontinued," and it was.

In August 1941, the Soviet navy evacuated Red Army troops and civilians from Tallinn, Estonia, which was under heavy attack by the Germans. A fifteen-mile convoy, including 67 non-navy ships, headed toward Kronstadt, near Leningrad. Under continuous German attack the convoy lost 38 noncombatant vessels and ten warships; more than 10,000 people lost their lives. On January 30, 1945, a Soviet submarine sank the German cruise liner *Wilhelm Gustloff*, which was carrying about 10,000 German refugees and soldiers who were fleeing Soviet troops. Of this number, 9,343 people were killed.

Escape by land was also dangerous as masses of panicked civilians squeezed into the limited public transportation available or clogged roads on foot. During the major Japanese Ichigo offensive in August and September 1944, a runaway locomotive killed several hundred Chinese refugees as they waited on the tracks. During this time, the railroads stopped selling tickets at regular prices. Passengers could obtain them only at high prices through the black market. Those who boarded the trains were often forced off only a few miles from the station, and the train returned for another group of duped civilians.

NRC implemented a registration policy and issued identification cards to refugees that entitled them to relief station services and discounted boat and bus fares. The NRC also set up dozens of hospitals and developed and marked new travel routes as traditional ones became more dangerous. By the end of 1941, NRC stations had provided assistance to 26 million migrants.

Axis

As early as 1938, the German government made plans to evacuate civilians from the western part of Germany that bordered on France and the Low Countries. Evacuations began when the war did, but were highly disorganized and resisted by the population. A *Sicherheitsdienst* (Nazi Party Security Service) report noted in November 1939 that 80 percent of the evacuees were "leaving the transport without authorization and making their way home or wandering aimlessly." Like Britons, when they seemed to be in no real danger, Germans preferred to live in their own homes. After August 24, 1940, when Allied planes bombed Berlin, women and children were again evacuated to the countryside. Civilian evacuations inevitably sparked doubts among people about the likelihood of victory. Separating families also caused considerable strain and loneliness, lowering morale. Yet continuing Allied bombing raids on Germany from 1942 on prompted more large-scale evacuations from targeted cities on the Rhine and in the Ruhr industrial area to eastern parts of the country, Poland, the Baltic nations, and rural Austria.

A new phase in German evacuations began as the Allies advanced on Germany from both the east and west. In September 1944, German civilians were ordered to leave Aachen (on the German border with the Netherlands) and towns in Belgium. Most had to be forced out by the civil and military police. Some hid in the woods and others barricaded their farms against the Storm Troopers (SA) dispatched to remove them. Many seemed to welcome the Allies. However, the regional German government seemed unprepared when Strasbourg, Austria, fell to the Allies. Alarmed civilians fled toward Germany across the Rhine River before official evacuations were carried out.

On the eastern front, German officials were also slow to evacuate civilian populations. Soviet troops played havoc with transportation, and conditions were so chaotic that Hitler stopped the official flow of refugees. But Germans were terrified of the advancing Soviet army, which brutally slaughtered civilians, including children, and decimated town and countryside. Soviet troops had arrived in Germany primed with hate for the people by bitter experience and a continual flow of propaganda. Soviet military newspapers urged soldiers to record the violence Germans had inflicted on their families in "books of revenge." An army directive issued just before the Soviets entered East Prussia proclaimed, "On German soil there is only one master— the Soviet soldier, . . . he is both the judge and the punisher for the torments of his fathers and mothers. . . . Remember your friends are not there, there is the next of kin of the killers and oppressors."

Some Soviet troops showed exceptional kindness to German civilians, especially children, as they occupied the countryside. But far more often in 1945, Soviets plundered, pillaged, and raped German women on a massive scale. (In Polish Silesia, Poles as well as Soviets raped German women as German troops retreated.) Most women were unable to defend themselves and men who tried to defend them were killed. (See also "Soviet War Crimes" in

Chapter 8.) Frightened Germans improvised what methods they could to leave on foot or using wagons, sleighs, buses, and boats, as the Soviets approached. Those who managed to travel on trains were jammed together, sometimes holding up the dead, who, when discovered, were thrown from the cars to make room for other refugees. When railroad lines to Berlin were cut in January 1945, some Germans crossed a frozen lagoon, the Frisches Haff, to reach the Baltic. Approximately 25,000 died while trying to cross the Baltic Sea, among them the passengers on the *Wilhelm Gustloff* (see box, "Evacuation Disasters").

An Italian girl and her baby brother sit in front of their bombed-out home, October 21, 1943. Many Italian citizens were caught in the fighting between retreating German and attacking American forces.

Cities in northern Italy suffered from Allied aerial bombardment in 1942, causing hundreds of thousands of people to evacuate. These evacuations were disorganized, emphasizing how little control the Fascist government had over civilians and how little it was trusted or respected. After Italy surrendered to the Allies in 1943, German treatment of the Italian population, as well as battles between German and Allied troops, prompted further civilian evacuations. On October 23, 1943, 1.5 million people were evacuated from the city of Naples because of a bomb threat that did not materialize. Also in 1943 in Milan, civilians were caught in the fight between German ground troops and Allied bombers; evacuees left by trains that still managed to operate.

Northern Italian villagers also evacuated to escape German troops, who sometimes executed groups of civilians as retribution for partisan activities.

In Japan, evacuations began in earnest in 1943, starting with wealthier urban civilians who moved on their own to the countryside, partly to avoid air raids but also to be nearer to food supplies. The Japanese government began planning its own evacuations of civilians from major cities late that year, although Prime Minister Hideki Tojo initially worried it would hurt morale. Those not needed for industrial production—primarily senior citizens, mothers, and their young children—were encouraged to move to rural and mountain areas. About 300,000 students were among those who voluntarily evacuated in this first round.

In June 1944, the government announced that children in third to sixth grades would be separated from their families; about 350,000 children were sheltered in country inns, temples, and resorts. In March 1945, some 100,000 first and second graders joined them. By the spring of 1945, about 10 million people overall had fled to the countryside, 2 million of them from Tokyo alone and two-thirds of them women and children.

Japanese Americans on the Home Front

On February 19, 1942, President Roosevelt signed Executive Order 9066, authorizing the creation of U.S. military zones, "from which any or all persons may be excluded." The order ultimately led to the internment of more than 100,000 Japanese and Japanese Americans, about two-thirds of whom were U.S. citizens; they were removed from parts of Washington, Oregon, California, and Arizona. Festering racism spurred partially by economic competition was further inflamed by the Pearl Harbor attack, which raised questions about the loyalty of Japanese American citizens and fears about their possible contribution to the attack. Navy Secretary Franklin Knox, speaking on December 15, 1941, was quoted in *American Magazine:* "I think it may be said that the most effective Fifth Column work [subversion] done in this war was done in Hawaii with the possible exception of Norway."

A heated public debate ensued, with media taking up both sides of the issue. In the Seattle *Post-Intelligencer*, John Boettiger (Franklin Roosevelt's son-in-law at the time) wrote, "Many of the Japanese in America are as loyal as any white Americans, and it would serve only evil purposes to cause them to suffer," while a columnist for the *San Francisco Examiner* wrote, "I am for the immediate removal of every Japanese on the West Coast in a point deep in the interior. Herd 'em up, pack 'em off and give 'em the inside room in the Badlands. Let 'em be pinched, hurt, hungry and dead up against it."

In his final report regarding the Japanese evacuation from the West Coast, Lieutenant General John L. DeWitt, who recommended and supervised the evacuation, argued that internment was a "military necessity," stating that individuals of Japanese heritage were concentrated near many sensitive areas along the West Coast, and were likely implicated in the Pearl Harbor attacks and subsequent incidents off the mainland; he expressed concerns over loyalty, citing numerous organizations and newspapers that, at least prior to Pearl Harbor, had voiced support for Japan and "Emperor-worshiping ceremonies." Of particular interest were the Kibei, Japanese Americans who, although born in the United States, had been educated in Japan. Additionally, he noted that anti-Asian public opinion might constitute danger, and protection should be provided for those of Japanese heritage.

A report by the Japanese American Citizens League (JACL) argued vehemently against DeWitt's explanations, pointing out that though those of Japanese ancestry may have supported Japan in its conflict with China, once the United States, their adopted country, was involved, feelings changed. According to JACL, the number of U.S. residents claiming Japanese ancestry was not large enough to be considered a threat; "Emperor worship" was motivated by religious, rather than political reasons; there was no genuine danger to the safety of the Japanese; and there were never substantiated instances of spying or sabotage carried out by Japanese or Japanese Americans in the United States, only rumors.

Miné Okubo, one of the Japanese Americans held at the Santa Anita racetrack in California before being moved to an internment camp, described her habitation: "The rear room had housed the horse and the front

LOCATION AND POPULATION OF MAJOR RELOCATION CENTERS

Center/Location	Population	Date Opened	Date Closed
Topaz, Utah	8,130	September 11, 1942	October 31, 1945
Poston, Arizona	17,814	May 5, 1942	November 28, 1945
Gila River, Arizona	13,348	July 20, 1942	November 10, 1945
Granada, Colorado	7,318	August 27, 1942	October 15, 1945
Heart Mountain, Wyoming	10,767	August 12, 1942	November 10, 1945
Jerome, Arkansas	8,497	October 6, 1942	June 30, 1944
Manzanar, California	10,056	June 1, 1942	November 21, 1945
Minidoka, Idaho	9,397	August 10, 1942	October 2, 1945
Rohwer, Arkansas	8,475	September 18, 1942	November 30, 1945
Tule Lake, California	18,789	May 27, 1942	March 20, 1946

A Japanese American mother and her four children on Bainbridge Island, Washington, wait for transportation to evacuate them to a U.S. government internment camp, March 30, 1942.

CIVILIAN INTERNMENT IN ASIA

European citizens living in countries throughout the Pacific were also interned, or at least separated into certain areas of various cities, called "protective city blocks," as the Japanese wanted to separate them from the local populace. Men were sometimes kept in separate camps from women and children. Conditions in the civilian internment camps established throughout Asia, altogether holding about 131,000 people, were not as harsh as those in Japanese POW camps, the biggest difference being that the Japanese rarely used European civilians for forced labor on military projects. The internment camp system was chaotic and the running of each camp was largely left to individual Japanese commanders; correspondingly, there were varying degrees of brutality. Civilian internees had to follow confusing and contradictory Japanese rules and were subjected to humiliation and violence by Japanese soldiers, but camp inhabitants were most at risk of malnourishment or disease, as these camps typically provided little or no food and medicine. Occasionally, interned civilians would face reprisals on suspicions of assistance to Japan's enemies, or for disobedience. An estimated 11 percent perished in confinement.

More than 425,000 German and Italian prisoners of war were held in the United States from 1943 to 1945. The location of their camps is given on the map above. Although initially unprepared for the influx of men, the War Department eventually established 141 permanent base camps and 319 branch camps, most of them in the South. American soldiers guarded the prisoners, who were well treated and given the opportunity to study English and take classes in handicrafts and other subjects offered by the YMCA and other civilian charitable organizations. Within the labor restrictions of the Geneva Conventions (see "The Rules of War" in Chapter 8), they could also work for pay at military installations and for private employers. In 1945, nearly 200,000 prisoners of war worked at non-military jobs, largely in agriculture. They helped to make up for the labor shortages the United States experienced during the war.

room the fodder. Both rooms showed signs of hurried whitewashing. Spider webs, horse hair, and hay had been whitewashed with the walls. Huge spikes and nails stuck out. . . . A two-inch layer of dust covered the floor, but on removing it we discovered that linoleum the color of redwood had been placed over the rough manure-covered boards." Etsuko Sunimoto-Mizokuchi, another internee, pointed out "Lots of [Japanese American] men volunteered for the draft. . . . One week after his eighteenth birthday, [my brother] was inducted into the U.S. army. It was when I was saying good-bye to him [that] the impact of his actions really hit me. This is not fair. This is wrong. Hundreds are dying over there and my brother wears a U.S. uniform and [a] guard sits . . . watching us with a gun. I really grew up then."

EDUCATION: TEXTBOOK CASES

The Soviet phrase, *Seichas ne do shkoly idet voina* ("this is no time to think about school, there's a war on") expressed the plight of education during World War II. Even in the United States, where no combat took place on the continental home front, there was a teacher shortage as both men and women joined the military or took more lucrative jobs. By early 1944, 4.6 million U.S. students aged 14 to 19 had farm and factory jobs, while only 1.43 million of these were attending school at the same time. In 1943, 16- and 17-year-old German students were granted "school leaving certificates" without having to pass exams so they could be on air raid duty, and teenage girls served as auxiliary nurses. In Japan, by 1944, children older than 10 were working on farms and in factories almost full time. Bombs destroyed British and Soviet, as well as Axis, school buildings; the ones that remained intact were sometimes appropriated for military or medical use. Paper and textbooks in Japan and the USSR were in short supply.

When children did attend school, they followed curricula and learned from textbooks that expressed war themes. In the United States, Boston twelfth graders learned "defense mathematics," and in Gary, Indiana, wood shop classes produced 1,500 model planes to help the navy identify enemy craft. A 1943 Soviet syllabus linked math to battlefield calculations and agriculture. Students as young as 8 were taught "military studies." Japanese boys in elementary school practiced the art of *kendo* (swords), and girls learned to use *halberds* (spears).

A German children's book, Trau keinem Fuchs auf gruner Heid und keinem Jud bei seinem Eid *("Don't Trust a Fox in a Green Meadow or the Word of a Jew"), published in 1936, includes this illustration of Jewish students and teachers (bottom, left) being expelled from school after passage of anti-Semitic laws in 1933. Such material was typical of many stridently anti-Semitic school lessons and texts that reinforced the Nazi view that Jews were inferior to Aryan Germans and could be subjugated to vile and dehumanizing treatment.*

Students bowed toward the emperor's imperial palace every morning. Where a first-year Japanese reader once had sentences like "Here is a crow, and there also is a sparrow," in the 1930s students read, "Advance, advance, soldier, advance." A typical Italian writing exercise exhorted students "to feel love and gratitude . . . for the Fascism which has saved us." Lessons in Germany followed Hitler's dictate in *Mein Kampf:* "Especially in historical instruction an abridgement of the material must be undertaken." Nazi anti-Semitism and militarism permeated education at every level.

Religion

Allies

The mainstream religions in each of the combatant countries generally supported their governments during the war, but churches could also be a source of patriotic nationalism or dissent. In the United States, most churchgoers were Protestant Christians; political sentiments in these churches leaned toward isolationism before Pearl Harbor, but were prowar afterward.

Americans considered the country to be tolerant of all religions, a characteristic that separated them from the Nazis, who not only "pit race against race, religion against religion, prejudice against prejudice," as Franklin Roosevelt said in 1942, but who denigrated religion in general and curtailed religious expression. Roosevelt made "the freedom of every person to worship God in his own way" one of the four freedoms. One of the fears aroused by communism was its godlessness, but when the United States allied with the Soviet Union, the government and media ignored this faithlessness. Interfaith and interracial U.S. organizations such as the Congress of Racial Equality (CORE) formed during the war. Nonetheless, both religious and racial prejudice still existed, as exemplified by the mass internment of Japanese Americans. A small but virulent conservative Catholic contingent that included Father Charles Coughlin and Edward Lodge Curran remained anticommunist—and consequently profascist—as well as stridently anti-Semitic throughout the war.

During World War I, the Anglican and other churches in Britain had avidly supported both the war and the country's nationalistic goals, but were chastened by the war's devastation. In the 1930s, the British clergy tended toward an attitude of pacifism. However, the Nazi threat, not only to the country and to Europe but to Christianity, made the war seem necessary to most churchpeople. They supported it while being careful not to be too stridently

CONSCIENTIOUS OBJECTORS

During World War II, as many as 100,000 American men were classified as conscientious objectors (COs), a third of one percent of those registered for the draft. Most of them accepted alternative service assignments, under the terms of the Selective Service Act of 1940, which stated that any person who "by reason of religious training and belief is conscientiously opposed to participation in war in any form [could instead be] . . . assigned to work of national importance under civilian direction." Both Mennonites and Quakers felt a strong commitment to do relief work. Some Quakers chose to go to prison instead, as did many Jehovah's Witnesses, believing that even alternative service was a form of conscription that helped the war effort. The Jehovah's Witness claim that each person was a minister was denied by draft boards.

One-quarter to one-half of all conscientious objectors were noncombatants in the armed forces, many of them in the medical corps. Others worked in one of 151 Civilian Public Service Camps, based on the government's Depression-era Civilian Conservation Corps. COs acted as firefighters and served as medical "guinea pigs" for the testing of new medicines. Some three thousand also worked as attendants in forty-one mental institutions and seventeen training schools for "mental deficients"; they drew attention to the plight of mentally ill people by winning a lawsuit against the state of Virginia for inhumane treatment of patients and founding an organization that became the National Mental Health Foundation.

In Britain, 59,192 people claimed to be conscientious objectors: 3,577 were exempted from any duty; 14,691 served in the armed forces as noncombatants; and 28,720 were placed in alternative service, usually in agriculture. Conscientious objector status was denied to 12,204 people. Only a few hundred went to prison. The British government was generally tolerant toward pacifists. When the conscription law was passed in 1939, Neville Chamberlain said, "Where scruples are conscientiously held we desire that they should be respected and that there should be no persecution of those who hold them." With the start of the Blitz, however, the public resented those who refused military service, and many local governments and private employers fired known pacifists.

British COs, like Americans, did not avoid danger. On the home front, they worked in ambulance and bomb disposal units; overseas they worked in medical units—conscientious objectors in the Parachute Field Ambulances, who did not carry weapons, landed with the troops on D-Day.

German pacifists were generally imprisoned in concentration camps, or, like the priest Franz Reinisch in 1942, were executed for undermining military morale.

anti-German. Dr. Cyril Garbett, Bishop of Winchester, expressed the position taken by most clergy in his diary: "Unless we thought that it was God's will that we should war against the Nazis, we ought to have opposed the war; if it is His will, then we must pray for victory."

Under communism before the war, the Russian Orthodox church had been almost completely dismantled, with clergy killed or imprisoned. Only four figurehead bishops existed when Germany invaded the Soviet Union, and one of them, Metropolitan Sergei, broadcast a radio appeal for all Soviet citizens to defend the Russian motherland on the same day as the invasion, while Stalin did not address the people for ten days. The church raised 150 million rubles—enough to buy equipment for an entire tank brigade and a section of the air force. Stalin recognized the importance of the Orthodox church in sustaining civilian morale. In September 1943 he met with Sergei and reinstated the church hierarchy, with Sergei named its Patriarch, or head. The church continued to function in the Soviet Union for several years after the war.

Axis

In a 1941 letter sent to all the regional Nazi leaders in Germany, Martin Bormann, Hitler's influential private secretary, noted the difference between Christianity and National Socialism, the former based on faith and the latter on "scientific foundations." "For the first time in German history the Führer had taken over public leadership," Bormann wrote. "All influences that could impair, or even damage, the Führer's and the Party's rule must be eliminated. More and more the Volk must be wrested away from the Churches and their agents, the pastors."

Hitler endorsed a *Burgfrieden*, or political truce between the government and German churches and supported a "practical Christianity," in which the churches expressed no negative opinions about the Nazi government or the war. In 1933, he reached a Concordat with the Papacy, allowing the Catholic Church to hold Mass and provide Catholic religious education as long as it did not interfere in politics. He tried to bring the Protestant churches under Nazi control in a single Reich Church of "German Christians," espousing a nationalistic, militant religion. However, most Germans practiced their religions as before; in 1939, 95 percent of the population were registered church members.

Clergy, church leaders, and their congregations differed in the degree of their support of the government. Several Protestant leaders, including Martin Niemoller and Dietrich Bonhoeffer, formed a Confessing Church that vocally objected to anti-Semitism and the distortion of Christian values to fit a Nazi worldview. These clergymen were imprisoned; many, including Bonhoeffer, were killed. (See also "Resistance within the Axis" in Chapter 9.) Some Catholics raised objections to the state takeover of church property and the limits placed on religious education, but a large-scale protest never erupted. Despite dissent, the great majority of clergy and their followers, whether Protestant or Catholic, remained loyal to the German state and accepted the war.

The majority of Italians were Catholic, and Mussolini recognized the church's influence on the population. In 1929, he negotiated the Lateran Accords with the Vatican, which received territory to create a small, sovereign Papal State; was allowed to continue religious education through the state schools; and was granted autonomy for Catholic Action, the church's lay organization, as long as it kept out of politics. In turn, the Vatican accepted the Fascist government without criticism. Catholicism, which offered an alternative to Fascist thinking, actually thrived during Mussolini's rule—the number of priests, nuns, and students in religious schools increased. In particular, the Catholic youth organizations competed with Fascist organizations in shaping the social, emotional, and civic life of the next generation.

The religion promoted by the Japanese government was State Shinto, whose traditional warlike gods reinforced Japan's imperial aims and called on individuals to be spiritually and physically fit, values compatible with those of the state. Emperor Hirohito was said to be descended from the Sun Goddess and was Shinto's chief priest. Under the government's bureau of religious ceremonies, organized in November 1940, the various Shinto sects were merged into thirteen groups. Buddhist and Christian denominations were also merged. The government allowed people to practice other religions if they did not express political opinions that challenged the state.

Almost all religious organizations and followers in Japan—Shinto, Buddhist, and Christian—supported the war. People prayed for victory and for the war dead at the great Shinto shrines, including Ise, Meiji, and Yasukuni. Priests from the Buddhist Nishi Honganji temple in Kyoto worked in war industries and raised money to buy airplanes that went into battle bearing the temple's name. Fifty-five women were ordained at the Kongobuji temple to take the places of priests who had joined the military. Pictures of war gods

REHABILITATION ON THE HOME FRONT

Throughout the war, discharged soldiers faced the task of reintegrating into ordinary daily life. Those who were battle casualties, particularly if they were permanently disfigured or disabled, faced an even larger challenge: to retrain their bodies and minds and to build confidence and self-esteem for life in the civilian world. Many combat veterans also had to overcome the debilitating effects of psychological scars before they could fully engage again in work and life.

The idea of psychologically rehabilitating patients, in addition to treating their physical injuries, gained credence during World War II. At Queen Victoria Hospital in East Grinstead (in Britain), Sir Archibald McIndoe treated more than 600 burn victims injured during service with the Royal Air Force and other Commonwealth air forces. McIndoe was experimenting with and developing plastic surgery techniques to deal with severe burns. His patients formed the "Guinea Pig Club," a drinking club whose members had to have served with an air crew and been operated on at least once at the hospital. McIndoe was the first president. The "Guinea Pigs" faced their disabilities with spirit and humor—their anthem began: "We are McIndoe's

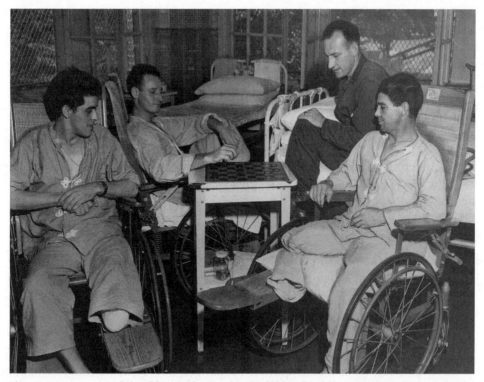

American troops wounded at Normandy convalesce at Walter Reed Hospital in Washington, D.C.

army, / We are his Guinea Pigs. / With dermatomes and pedicles, / Glass eyes, false teeth and wigs. / And when we get our discharge / We'll shout with all our might: / 'Per ardua ad astra' / We'd rather drink than fight." They provided a model for rehabilitation that relied on recognizing the value of common experience and drawing on mutual support.

Beginning in 1943, the American government developed convalescent hospitals, first as annexes to existing general hospitals and then as freestanding centers, to rehabilitate servicepeople sent back to the United States for care. The Old Farms Convalescent Hospital in Avon, Connecticut opened in May 1944, and offered specialized care and equipment to help with the physical and social adjustments necessary for blind people to live on their own. In the same month, the Eyebank for Sight Restoration, the world's first transplant agency, was established in New York. The general hospital in Battle Creek, Michigan, provided training in aviation

and auto mechanics, electronics, printing and other skills for amputees, paraplegics, and those with psychiatric problems. Civilian teachers taught patients, who could earn high school credit for the courses as they recovered.

President Roosevelt strongly favored rehabilitation programs. In 1944, he told Secretary of War Henry Stimson that "no overseas casualty will be discharged from the armed forces until he has received the maximum benefit of hospitalization and convalescent facilities, which must include physical and psychological rehabilitation, vocational guidance, prevocational training, and resocialization." That July, in Hawaii for a meeting with General MacArthur and Admiral Nimitz, the president, who knew the agonies of rehabilitation from hard experience, asked to visit a hospital ward for amputee combat veterans. Smiling, waving, saying little, the wheelchair-bound commander in chief of United States armed forces reminded his wounded soldiers that their lives would go on.

---

hung in classrooms and students visited temples en masse to pray. Their textbooks conveyed a near-mystical relationship between the gods and the aims of the Pacific war that left no room for doubt or failure.

From Home Front to Home

When the Research Branch of the U.S. War Department's Information and Education Division asked a discharged World War II veteran whether he thought the country's war was worth his sacrifice, he replied, "I do, in a way. The whole idea is to gain peace again." In their psychological studies, these researchers found again and again that a combat veteran might have ideological or patriotic reasons to do battle, but that "the desire to be safe, or to be home, or to be free to pursue civilian concerns, was stronger than any motivation to make a further personal contribution to winning the war."

Soldiers fight to end the fight and come home; they also fight to preserve the home they remember. "America has come to mean just this to me . . . a country where I can live the way my folks and I have always lived," wrote one American airman stationed overseas. "A country where there's work to do, . . . where there are no limits on a man's ambition or his opportunity to go as far as ability can take him. Whatever you do, don't change that, ever! I know now—*that's* what I'm fighting for!" The United States this man came back to was in many ways the same country he had left, yet in other ways it had changed significantly. General prosperity and nearly full employment continued; in 1945, Winston Churchill proclaimed, "The United States stand . . . at the summit of the world." But the civil rights movement would soon take off, and the reality of the atomic bomb and Cold War with the Soviet Union would have a sharp impact on American attitudes as well as policies.

In Europe and Asia, the homes soldiers returned to, whether Allied or Axis, were exhausted and physically damaged. They and the civilians of those war-ravaged countries had just survived the most widespread destruction the world had known. Now, it was time to rebuild.

PRINCIPAL SOURCES AND FURTHER READING

Many of the personal quotations in this chapter came from the following books:

Broekmeyer, M. J. *Stalin, the Russians, and Their War, 1941–1945*, translated by Rosalind Buck. Madison: University of Wisconsin Press, 2004.

Cook, Hanuko Taya, and Theodore F. Cook. *Japan at War: An Oral History*. New York: New Press, 1992.

Hoopes, Roy. *Americans Remember the Home Front: An Oral Narrative of the World War II Years in America*. New York: Berkeley Books, 1977.

Other sources include:

Barber, John, and Mark Harrison. *The Soviet Home Front, 1941–1945: A Social and Economic History of the USSR in World War II*. New York: Longman, 1991.

Baudot, Marcel, et al., eds. *The Historical Encyclopedia of World War II*, translated by Jesse Dilson. New York: Greenwich House, 1990.

Beck, Earl. *The European Home Fronts, 1939–1945*. Arlington Heights, IL: Harlan Davidson, 1993.

Briggs, Asa. *Go to It! Working for Victory on the Home Front*. London: Mitchell Beazley, 2000.

Briggs, Susan. *The Home Front: War Years in Britain, 1939–1945*. American Heritage Publishing, 1975.

Budani, Donna M. *Italian Women's Narratives of Their Experiences during World War II*. Lewiston, NY: Edwin Mellen Press, 2003.

Calder, Angus. *The People's War: Britain, 1939–1945*. New York: Pantheon Books, 1969.

Charlot, Monica. *British Civilians in the Second World War*. Paris: Didier Erudition, 1996.

Domenico, Roy Palmer. *Remaking Italy in the Twentieth Century*. Lanham, MD: Rowman and Littlefield, 2002.

Douhet, Giulio. *The Command of the Air*. Dino Ferrari, trans. London: Faber and Faber, 1943.

Fairbank, John, and Albert Feuerwerker, eds. *The Cambridge History of China*. Vol. 13, part 2. New York: Cambridge University Press, 1986.

Fenby, Jonathan. *Chiang Kai-shek: China's Generalissimo and the Nation He Lost*. New York: Carroll & Graf, 2004.

Harrison, Tom and Charles Madge, eds. *War Begins at Home by Mass Observation*. London: Chatto & Windus, 1940.

Hunt, Erling, ed. *America Organizes to Win the War: A Textbook for High Schools*. New York: Harcourt, Brace 1942.

Jeffries, John W. *Wartime America: The World War II Home Front*. Chicago: Ivan R. Dee, 1996.

Kennedy, David M. *Freedom from Fear: The American People in Depression and War, 1929–1945*. New York: Oxford University Press, 1999.

Kennedy, Margaret. *Where Stands a Winged Sentry*. New Haven, CT: Yale University Press, 1941.

Lowe, Roy, ed. *Education and the Second World War*. Washington, D.C.: Falmer Press, 1992.

Mazower, Mark. *Inside Hitler's Greece*. New Haven, CT: Yale University Press, 1995.

Menefee, Selden. *Assignment: USA*. New York: Reynal & Hitchcock, 1943.

Noakes, Jeremy, ed. *The Civilian in War: The Home Front in Europe, Japan, and the USA in World War II*. Exeter, UK: University of Exeter Press, 1992.

Rupp, Leila. *Mobilizing Women for War: German and American Propaganda, 1939–1945*. Princeton, NJ: Princeton University Press, 1978.

Schutz, W. W., and B. De Sevin. *German Home Front*. London: Victor Gollancz, 1943.

Sigaud, Louis. *Douhet and Aerial Warfare*. New York: Putnam, 1941.

Steinert, Marlis G. *Hitler's War and the Germans: Public Mood and Attitude during the Second World War* translated by Thomas De Witt. Athens, OH: Ohio University Press, 1977.

Stouffer, Samuel et al. *The American Soldier: Adjustment during Army Life*. Vol. 1. Princeton, NJ: Princeton University Press, 1949.

Takaki, Ronald. *Double Victory: A Multicultural History of America in World War II*. Boston: Little, Brown, 2000.

Thompson, Doug. *State Control in Fascist Italy: Culture and Conformity, 1925–1943*. New York: Manchester University Press, 1991.

THE AFTERMATH

"The War Is Over!"

The German surrender effective on May 8, 1945, marked the long awaited V-E Day (Victory in Europe), and celebrations broke out across the continent and the British Isles. Huge, jubilant crowds gathered in Moscow's Red Square and in Trafalgar Square and the Mall in London, where a young princess—later, Queen Elizabeth II—joined in knocking the hats off overwhelmed policemen. King George VI, Queen Elizabeth, and Winston Churchill, appearing on the Buckingham Palace balcony, received cheers from more than a million loyal subjects. At the Kremlin, Joseph Stalin ordered a massive victory salute, and one thousand guns fired thirty salvos and pyrotechnics lit up the sky. In Paris, Allied soldiers joined civilians in impromptu parades; warbled "It's a Long Way to Tipperary"; and played the French, American, and British national anthems amid flares, floodlights, and fireworks. Second Lieutenant Mary Catherine McGarr of Carmen, Oklahoma, an army nurse with the 124th Evacuation Hospital, wrote home from Germany, "Today is VE Day in the ETO (European Theater of Operations)—the greatest day of the war so far. I guess maybe we are selfish celebrating it because there are a lot of boys in the Pacific who will die tomorrow, and the next day, and the day after that." Americans at home felt similarly; President Truman issued a proclamation of thanksgiving but stressed that "Our victory is but half won." In recognition of V-E Day, however, the U.S. Capitol dome and other national monuments were lit—for one night only—for the first time since the attack on Pearl Harbor.

Fighting continued in the Far East: the bitter contest for Okinawa was not concluded until June 22, as the strategic bombing campaign against Japan continued. Following the atomic bomb attacks on Hiroshima (August 6) and Nagasaki (August 9), the world anxiously waited through several false news

Massive crowds gathered in London's Trafalgar Square to mark the Allied victory in Europe.

flashes for Japan to accept or reject the Allied demand for surrender. Finally, at noon on August 15, Tokyo time, Emperor Hirohito told his countrymen in a delicately worded radio address that "the war situation has developed not necessarily to Japan's advantage" and that he had accepted the terms. The news set off V-J Day (Victory over Japan) observances worldwide as the last major Axis power succumbed. (In Honolulu, celebrating had begun six days earlier; officials explained, "The war started here and should end here first." Likewise, formerly occupied Manila had two full-scale celebrations before the actual surrender.) Robert Peters Eustace, 19, a navy photographer's mate from Stockton, California, was at Buckner Bay, Okinawa, "sitting at anchor waiting for the invasion of Japan. . . . [T]hey announced . . . some kind of armistice. . . and the island lit up. Everybody fired. Every gun in that island [shot] in the sky. Killed about seven or eight people that night from falling shrapnel." Soldiers in Europe scheduled for deployment to the Pacific received twenty-four-hour leave and led the local celebrations. In heavily bombed Chungking, hundreds of thousands of exuberant Chinese who had

On Mulberry Street in New York's Little Italy, exuberant residents celebrate the Japanese surrender, August 14, 1945.

been displaced by years of fighting were packed and ready to head home. In Australia, the *Sydney Morning News* reported that amid the noisy conga lines and hokey-pokey rings, "grave and reverend seniors acted in a manner that would be deemed incredible in normal life."

A half-million people in New York City's Times Square erupted in joy when the large electric sign flashed the news at 7:03 P.M., August 14, Eastern War Time: "Official—Truman Announces Japanese Surrender." Yeiichi Kelly Kuwayama, a medic wounded in France while serving in the Japanese-American 442nd Regiment, was in the square and decades later said, "It was the happiest day of my life." By 10 P.M., police estimated that 2 million flag-waving, confetti-covered revelers were jammed in the area as the party continued throughout the night. (The next day, sanitation workers collected a record-setting 9.7 million pounds of paper that had been tossed into the streets.) Crowds gathered in Lafayette Square outside the White House and chanted, "We Want Truman!" prompting the president and first lady to make an appearance. Throngs in Chicago jitterbugged in the bumper-to-bumper routes leading to the Loop (downtown), where seven first aid stations and eight ambulances were on hand to treat 250 injuries, faintings, and a few heart attacks. In Los Angeles, motor machinist's mate second class Edgar Buckingham, "who wears the Purple Heart and still uses a cane," said the *Los Angeles Times*, "was kissing women in stalled autos on Hollywood Boulevard. He hit the jackpot when he encountered a stalled bus." Chinatowns in major American cities marked the surrender with fireworks stockpiled for the occasion since the war began. The following day, many businesses closed for festivities and church services, and Truman declared Sunday, August 19, as a Day of Prayer. The U.S. government officially recognized V-J Day as September 2, when Japan formally surrendered, although other nations continue to mark the V-J Day anniversary in August. On September 11, 1945, the U.S. government designated "World War II" as the official name for the just-concluded conflict.

★   ★   ★

As the celebrations died down, hostilities in some areas did not. World War II was over, but it had sprouted civil wars and guerrilla conflicts, some of which had begun well before the German and Japanese surrenders. In China, the communists finally claimed victory over their erstwhile ally, the Nationalists, in 1949. The Soviet Union had subsumed Estonia, Latvia, and Lithuania, but guerrillas continued to battle Soviet forces, and it was not until 1948 that armed resistance ended in Estonia; it continued in Latvia and Lithuania for several more years. Civil war ended in Inner Mongolia when it fell under Chinese rule in 1947, and in Greece, the British and American-backed government battled communists from 1944 to 1949. The weakened state of European colonial powers and a growing sense of nationalism inspired armed challenges to Dutch rule in the East Indies, French control of Indochina, and British power in India and southeast Asia. In Palestine, fighting broke out following the United Nations' adoption of a plan in November 1947 to divide the area into an Arab state and a Jewish state. An Arab-Israeli war began after the Jewish proclamation of the state of Israel, May 14, 1948, the day the British mandate in Palestine ended. That war ended the following year, but hostilities would continue for generations.

In the meantime, authorities made a sobering assessment of World War II's toll. More than 60 million people had perished, tens of millions were uprooted from their homes, hundreds of millions more were wounded physically and emotionally. Poland had lost about 16 percent of its entire population; on a per capita basis, New Zealand had lost the most servicemen among the western Allies. Axis and Allied nations had spent more than a trillion dollars (in 1945 dollars) to prosecute the war; Japan and the USSR each lost about 25 percent of its national wealth, and Japan lost more than a

KEYS TO VICTORY: WHY THE ALLIES WON

Extensive cooperation among the Allies and the successful American Lend-Lease program facilitated victory and were in stark contrast to the Axis partnerships, which were uneven, not efficiently managed, and often more burdensome than helpful to the major Axis nations. By 1943, the Allies were on the offensive in the Pacific and in Europe. That required greater cost and more personnel than holding defensive positions, but the much larger Allied coalition was up to it, having many millions more people than the Axis to serve in the armed forces and in defense work. The Allies also placed greater emphasis on organization, planning, logistics, and supply than did Germany and Japan, which gave more weight to executing combat operations and placed fewer servicemen in critical support roles.

EUROPEAN WAR

Allied Industrial Production. The United States, the Soviet Union, and their many allies as a group significantly outproduced the Axis, giving the Allies much greater air, land, and sea power. Furthermore, the Axis never attacked industrial sites in the United States or deep in the Soviet interior.

Superior Allied Airpower. By dominating the skies with vastly more—and, later, better—aircraft, the Allies knocked out Axis communications, transportation networks, industrial centers, and oil fields. Axis damage to Allied resources was nowhere near as severe.

Intelligence. The Allies outperformed the Axis in collecting and analyzing intelligence; as far as is known, every German agent to reach Britain was "turned" or imprisoned; the Germans never knew that their "impenetrable" Enigma system had been cracked.

British Resolve. The rescue of trapped Allied forces at Dunkirk in May 1940 kept Britain in the war, which might otherwise have ended then; and the country's survival in the Battle of Britain gave the Allies a perfect staging area for the eventual invasion of Europe.

Axis Distractions and Diversions. Continual Italian military failures required Hitler to divert his attention and resources to support his weaker ally. In 1941, this delayed the German invasion of the Soviet Union, one of several important factors that prevented complete success on the Eastern Front before brutal winter weather set in. German failure to achieve quick victory gave Soviets time to regroup. "Anything," said Hitler in April 1945, "would have been better than having [Italians] as comrades in arms."

Battle of the Atlantic. Eventual Allied victory at sea ensured that huge convoys of American Lend-Lease war matériel reached their European destinations.

(continued)

Soviet Military Might. The Germans underestimated Soviet resistance and willingness to sacrifice millions of people in defense of the USSR. Their brutal treatment of Soviet citizens lost Germans the support they had in some areas early in the invasion.

Two-Front War. After the successful D-Day invasion, Germany had neither the manpower nor the resources to survive between the advancing Red Army in the East and Allied forces in the West (including those advancing through Italy, to the south), particularly since the Allied forces acted in concert at an unprecedented level.

Asian-Pacific War

Allied Industrial Production. The United States quickly overcame the damage done to the U.S. Pacific Fleet at Pearl Harbor, while Japan had neither the population nor the resources to match Allied industrial output. The intense rivalry between Japan's army and naval branches greatly limited the country's production capabilities.

Intelligence. Allied intelligence gathering, code breaking, and analysis was far superior; after the war, Japan's chief of army intelligence, Lieutenant General Seizo Arisue admitted, "We couldn't break your codes at all." The Japanese in fact broke some, but to little effect.

Battle of Midway. After the war, all Japanese naval officers questioned by U.S. interrogators cited the defeat at Midway as "the beginning of total failure." Japan could not make up for the tremendous loss of aircraft, warships, or experienced pilots. In 1943–1944, Japan produced seven aircraft carriers; in that same period, the United States produced ninety.

Island Hopping Strategy. By skipping over many fortified Japanese-held islands, the Allies isolated and kept large Japanese forces out of the fight (as at Truk and Rabaul); the strategy also kept the Japanese guessing as to where the Allies would strike next.

Combined Operations and Amphibious Landings. The Allies mastered these techniques to successfully capture the islands necessary for an eventual attack on Japan.

Destruction of the Imperial Navy. At the Battle of Leyte Gulf in October 1944, U.S. forces destroyed nearly all that remained of the Japanese navy, which was "tantamount to the [subsequent] loss of the Philippines," the Japanese naval minister said after the war. "When you took the Philippines, that was the end of our resources."

Conventional and Atomic Bombing of Japan. Bombing from spring 1945 to August destroyed more than 2 million buildings and demolished about 40 percent of the country's urban areas. The destruction and Allied blockades put Japan on the verge of starvation.

third of its industrial fixed assets. It cost billions to rebuild basic infrastructures. In some areas, particularly in Eastern Europe, rubble and gutted buildings remained almost untouched for years, and in the twenty-first century, structures around the globe still bear the scars of bomb and artillery damage. Some places, such as the Prefectural Commercial Exhibition Hall in Hiroshima, St. Nikolai Church in Hamburg, and St. Michael's Cathedral in Coventry, were left deliberately in ruins, as memorials to the dead and reminders to the living.

A New World Landscape

Dramatic postwar changes to the map were inevitable. Japan lost its wartime territorial gains; within a year of its surrender, 6 million Japanese (half of them civilians) had been sent back to the home islands. Almost immediately, the British were back in Hong Kong, and the Russians occupied Manchuria until 1948, when the Chinese communists assumed control. In the West, the USSR incorporated Estonia, Latvia, and Lithuania as Soviet republics and acquired territory from Poland, Germany, Hungary, and Romania. Poland received territory from Germany. Austria was unshackled from Germany but remained under Allied supervision until 1955.

After the Allies refused to recognize the government headed by Admiral Karl Dönitz, Hitler's named successor, the Americans, British, Russians, and French formed the Allied Control Council (or Four Powers) in June 1945 to govern occupied Germany. The country was split into four zones, each under the jurisdiction of one power, as was Berlin, located in the Soviet zone. Later, the American, British, and French zones merged into one, which in May 1949 became the Federal Republic of Germany (West Germany), with Bonn as its capital. Five months later, a new communist nation emerged from the Soviet zone, the German Democratic Republic (East Germany), with East Berlin as its capital. Berlin remained divided: the American, British and French sectors joined together and became West Berlin; the Soviet sector became East Berlin, the oldest and most historic part of the city. West Berlin was culturally, but neither technically nor geographically, part of West Germany, and not until 1972 did the Allies and Soviets sign agreements providing guaranteed access between the two.

Keeping the peace so dearly paid for was a daunting challenge. Although the post-World War I League of Nations had lacked muscle and failed in its mission, optimism remained for a workable international organization. On June 26,

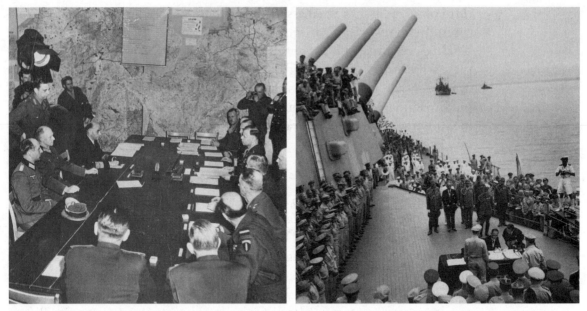

Seated at left, Major Wilhelm Oxenius of the German General Staff, General Alfred Jodl, representing the High Command and the new Dönitz government, and General Hans-Georg von Friedeburg of the navy surrender to Allied officials led by Walter Bedell Smith, chief of staff for General Eisenhower, at Allied headquarters in Reims, France. In a message of remarkable simplicity and punch, Eisenhower duly informed the Allied War Office in London: "The mission of this Allied Force was fulfilled at 0241, local time, May 7, 1945." In a much more formal ceremony in Tokyo Bay, Japan officially conceded defeat on September 2 aboard the battleship USS Missouri as General Douglas MacArthur (behind table, right), American servicemen, and the Japanese emperor's delegation watch Foreign Minister Mamoru Shigemitsu sign the instrument of surrender.

1945, delegates representing fifty countries signed the United Nations (UN) charter in San Francisco. The UN grew out of the Allied coalition of the same name but it incorporated several features that addressed the inherent weaknesses of the League. Most significant was the Security Council, with five permanent powers—China, France, Great Britain, the Soviet Union (replaced by Russia in 1991), and the United States—and originally six temporary members; its purpose was to ensure peace through enforcement of UN resolutions and declarations. Just as important, the United States, which had not joined the League, strongly supported the UN, providing the bulk of its funding and a site in New York City for its deck-of-cards-shaped headquarters, completed in 1952. A spirit of cooperation and the need to help nations rebuild and stabilize in the postwar period prompted the creation of the

World Bank and the International Monetary Fund, which became operational UN agencies in 1945.

★   ★   ★

While new official organizations were taking shape, many of the men and women who had served in uniform were being discharged from service. Between V-E Day and the end of September 1945, the U.S. military discharged more than a million servicemen. With Japan's capitulation, demobilization moved more rapidly, but not fast enough for the troops or their families, and demonstrations broke out at a number of military bases. But as Army Chief of Staff George Marshall pointed out, the military was trying to maintain appropriate staffing levels in occupied areas while mustering out servicemen quickly amid certain complications: those with the most service were usually higher-ranking, and the military could not lose so much experienced leadership so quickly, leaving large numbers of low-ranking men inadequately supervised. In addition, highly trained pilots and captains of transport vessels were generally long-serving veterans and most were eager to leave the military, yet they were essential in bringing home others for discharge. Thousands of Liberty and Victory ships and more than 100 aircraft carriers were used to transport and redeploy 12 million people in just a few months. The United States also provided transport for servicemen's "war brides," 70,000 of them from Britain alone. With increasing efficiency, "Separation Centers" established around the country processed servicemen back into civilians. Discharge involved approval of voluminous paperwork, including service records and financial documents; physical and dental examinations; a review of the GI Bill; and other items. Newly named Secretary of War Robert Patterson, on a round-the-world visit to military theaters in December, was pleased with how well the enormous process of downsizing or closing American installations was actually working. In the meantime, there were other major challenges.

Occupation

Patterson now headed the American occupation of Germany, Austria, Japan, and Korea. He reminded the nation, "We must make sure that the victory that has been won—won by the effort of all the people and at a cost of a million casualties—does not slip from our grasp." Thus, troops in those areas could not leave until fresh new forces arrived to replace them. In the meantime, and even before the Axis surrenders, Allied forces arrested wanted Axis leaders and war crimes suspects, although security was haphazard. Some slipped out of custody, others committed suicide; SS Reichsführer Heinrich Himmler, found disguised as a peasant, killed himself with cyanide in the presence of his British captors. Lower ranking officials and the general public were subject to "denazification," an attempt at reeducating Germans that waned as the Cold War progressed. Allied authorities held unrepentant Nazis in former concentration camps while interviewing and clearing hundreds of thousands of people determined to no longer support Nazi views. Once "denazified," an individual was eligible to obtain work in government and other professions.

Occupation forces were expected to limit their contact with German civilians to maintaining order and conducting business transactions, but the nonfraternization order was routinely ignored. The policy, difficult to enforce among bored GIs, was greatly relaxed by mid-July 1945. Surveys showed that most servicemen liked the German people, who knew their survival depended on good relations with the occupying forces. (For their part, the Germans' view of the Allies strongly depended on what zone they lived in; see box, opposite) Occupation forces also had to adapt to living in devastated Germany. Major Gerald Sullivan of Detroit, Michigan, serving with the 673rd Battalion in Oder-Oberstein wrote home about the hardships of living in damaged buildings, bathing out of his water-filled helmet, and depending on sporadic electricity. He described the foreign refugees who were eager to work for American servicemen as maids, laundresses, and mechanics. The day after the German surrender, Sullivan wrote to his wife that improved supplies were finally becoming available: "We get an amazing variety of rations now. Fresh eggs frequently and chicken about twice a week. They come frozen." Despite the improvements, Sullivan wrote on June 1, he had not "convinced anyone yet that it is time I went home."

Meanwhile, in Japan, occupation went easier than expected for the Allies, as the population obediently followed the emperor's request for cooperation. Unlike the situation in Germany, American officials encouraged socialization between GIs and the Japanese public in the hope of promoting a pro-West, anticommunist ally. Much of the Allied effort went toward facilitating rebuilding and tending to the millions of Japanese rendered homeless. In Hiroshima and Nagasaki, the focus was on coping with the effects of the atomic blasts. In those cities, people who appeared to have survived unscathed or with little injury developed radiation sickness and other excruciating maladies, and the death toll steadily rose through the end of 1945. (See also Chapter 11.)

EYEWITNESS ACCOUNT: LIVING IN OCCUPIED BERLIN

Inge John was a 19-year-old Berliner in 1945 who later married a German American she met during the Allied occupation. Conditions were harsh, especially in the winter: "We used to go through the ruins of the buildings to look for wood and anything we could burn. People went to the parks and took the wood from the trees. After a while, there were no trees left. . . . Oh, we were hungry. . . . I tell you, those days I had to lie down for two hours to be up for three or four hours, I was so weak." Early on, civilians in her neighborhood feared going out and facing Russian soldiers "who kidnapped people every day. . . . And if you were in the wrong place, you got raped. . . . After a while on the streets you would see only [Russian] high brass. I went with my bicycle and a high brass came and took my bicycle—'Just give it to me.' So I had to walk home two hours. They took everything they could. My watch went the first two days. When the British took over, we felt a relief. . . . although the Russians still came over and took things. Soldiers had their time off and would walk around. The French were poor and didn't have anything, but the Americans were all over Berlin in their Red Cross ambulances and their jeeps. . . . They took us to their section and there was a big hall and there was a band and dancing. . . . And then they came around with trays of sandwiches—white bread sandwiches! My gosh, we were so hungry, it was like cake to us. We couldn't believe it that they walked around handing out sandwiches to everybody."

In an attempt to curb Soviet kidnapping raids in the western portions of divided Berlin, British military policemen clearly mark the line between the British and Russian sectors with multilanguage signs and steel barriers. Meanwhile, weary displaced persons (DPs), with their few belongings, wait at Berlin's Anhalter Station for transport out of the city.

JAPAN RECONSTRUCTED

Japan's transition from fanatic enemy of the United States to one of its closest and most reliable allies began during the American postwar occupation. More than 200,000 militarist government officials and other professionals were banned from serving in the new government. General Douglas MacArthur, Supreme Commander of the Allied Powers in Japan, oversaw the occupation and with his staff developed Japan's new constitution. The document went into effect in 1947 and had a profound impact on Japanese culture. It converted the emperor, already stripped of his divinity, into a symbol of democracy, gave women legal equality and the vote, ensured that both houses of the bicameral legislature were popularly elected, and famously renounced "war as a sovereign right of the nation." It was long a state secret that Americans wrote the constitution that Emperor Hirohito promulgated before the Japanese Diet. Even more startling, especially to the handful of Japanese consultants aware of it, was that Beate Sirota, 22, fluent in Japanese and the only woman in MacArthur's "constitutional assembly," researched and wrote groundbreaking Article 24, granting women equality with men. MacArthur

A year after the atomic bomb blast wiped out much of Hiroshima, children attend class in a heavily damaged school building open to the elements.

instituted other significant changes as well. The powerful *zaibatzu* (family-dominated business conglomerates) were split into smaller business entities, and the Americans encouraged new trade unions. Land reform allowed peasants to purchase property at low prices and claim a greater stake in Japan's revival. Demilitarizing national culture and promoting democracy, however, had an unintended effect, as Japan embraced the notion that it was a victim of the war, rather than an instigator and aggressor. Allied occupation ended on April 28, 1952, but Japan maintained its close American ties. It still needed economic assistance, and with a small, 75,000-man military, it relied on U.S. protection. When Tokyo hosted the 1964 summer Olympic Games, Japan was seen as returning to the international community (as was the case with its Axis partners, when Rome held the Olympics in 1960 and Munich in 1972). In the 1970s, Japan renewed relations with China and climbed out of debt. Since military expenditures did not exceed more than 1 percent of government spending, Japan invested heavily in other industries. Its economy flourished and its exports—particularly electronics and automobiles—came to dominate market shares in the free world.

By the end of the twentieth century, three generations removed from the wartime era, Japan had long been prosperous, vibrant, and a major international presence. It could not entirely escape Japan's role in starting the war and its brutal war crimes, however, despite minimizing or ignoring its wartime past in school textbooks and contemporary culture. Japan resisted expressing regret for its actions in World War II and was slow to acknowledge its victims. In the twenty-first century, top Japanese officials continued to visit the Yasukuni Shrine, where military dead, including convicted World War II war criminals, are buried, sparking vehement condemnations from the heads of state representing Australia, China, Indonesia, New Zealand, North and South Korea, and the Philippines.

Refugees and Displaced Persons

Survivors of concentration and work camps, refugees from bombed-out areas, escapees from Russian occupied areas, settlers sent from Germany to Poland, Poles shipped to Russia, and Hungarians moved to Transylvania were among the mass of humanity who ended the war far from where they began it. The Soviets evicted millions from their newly acquired territories; about 7 million civilian refugees were trudging through Russian-held areas and an equal number of them were on the move in western Europe in the summer of 1945. Nearly 10 million more men joined the migratory flow as the Allies released POWs. The United Nations Relief and Rehabilitation Administration (UNRRA) and volunteers distributed tons of food, medicine, and clothing over the next several years, but initially they could meet only a small portion of the demand. With assistance from the International Red Cross, which compiled refugee documents, displaced persons (DPs)

Wartime devastation combined with harsh winter weather caused major food shortages throughout Europe in 1945–1946. A dump site used by American occupation forces drew desperate Berliners, some coming from miles away, scavenging for food.

began to track down the whereabouts of their families, find work, and either make their way back home or create new ones. Many wandered about or languished in grim refugee camps for years. In 1951, West Germany took over operating DP camps—some were actually former concentration camps—and the last camp, Foehrenwald, finally closed in 1957. Those who remained in the country were granted legal equality with German citizens; refugees made up 20 percent of the West German population. About 400,000 people were directly resettled from DP camps to the United States, and another 158,000 to Canada. Many more would follow in the ensuing decades.

SECURING AXIS SCIENTISTS

The Americans and the Soviets were both intent on securing the services and technology secrets of Germany's stellar scientific community as well as its intelligence operatives. The Soviets had captured the Kaiser Wilhelm Institute in Berlin, commandeering the atomic research being done there and would use it to rapidly expand their own nuclear programs. About the same time, the United States confiscated V-2 missiles at Nordhausen before the area fell under Russian jurisdiction. To acquire Nazi intellectual resources before the Soviets did, the United States began Operation Paperclip in August 1945. It involved identifying, interrogating, and slipping key scientists and their families out of Germany. By 1947, more than 450 German scientists were in America and about 100 were working in Britain.

Despite President Truman's order against recruiting active Nazi party members, many of the Paperclip men retained their Nazi views and/or had used slave labor for their projects; some were involved in horrific medical experiments at concentration camps. Perhaps the biggest prize for the United States was Wernher von Braun, head of the V-2 program, whose weaponized rockets were built with slave labor. After he surrendered himself and his colleagues to the Americans in 1945, Von Braun went on to work for the U.S. Army on ballistic missile systems. He later became director of NASA's Marshall Space Flight Center, where he and other Nazi scientists played prominent roles in achieving the moon landing.

Prosecuting War Criminals

As early as December 1942, the United Nations put Axis nations on notice that they would be held responsible for war crimes and atrocities after the war; the Allies reiterated this in the Moscow Declaration released in October 1943. In dealing with the top surviving Nazis, Churchill favored immediate executions, but the Americans insisted on proper legal proceedings as a demonstration of Allied justice. After considerable negotiations in London, the Allies established the International Military Tribunal (IMT) for the major war crimes cases, and it served as a model for the Far East War Crimes Trials that followed. Nazi defendants were not alone in dismissing the legality of the subsequent trials, whose validity was extremely controversial even in Allied legal circles. Critics point out that the judges hailed from Allied—rather than neutral—nations, that the definition of the crimes committed was created after the incriminating events had occurred, and that the Soviets, responsible for innumerable war crimes and atrocities, were immune from prosecution. Thus, it was vital to U.S. Supreme Court Justice Robert Jackson, the Americans' chief prosecutor at the trials of accused Nazi leaders in Nuremberg, that the proceedings be conducted fairly so that the world would accept the IMT's legitimacy, its authority, and its verdicts. There could be no Allied improprieties because, as he explained to Benjamin Ferencz, a young army lawyer who would later prosecute *Einsatzgruppen* (SS death squad) leaders, "To pass these defendants a poisoned chalice is to put it to our own lips as well."

Nazi War Crimes Trials

The best known of the Nuremberg Trials took place between November 1945 and October 1946 and considered the cases against 22 major Nazis. (Martin Bormann, one of Hitler's secretaries, was tried in absentia; Robert Ley, head of the German Labor Front, committed suicide in his cell at Spandau Prison before the trial began; and industrialist Gustav Krupp was ruled incompetent to stand trial.) British Lord Justice Geoffrey Lawrence ran the proceedings with a tribunal comprising judges from the four Allied powers, each of which had a chief prosecutor supported by hundreds of staff members who processed millions of documents and interrogated thousands of witnesses. German lawyers defended the accused against four charges: (1) conspiracy to wage aggressive war, (2) crimes against peace, (3) war crimes, and (4) crimes against humanity. This last count grew out of count 3 and was meant to describe the genocidal and unprecedented nature of Nazi atrocities. The war crimes charge focused more on violations of the Geneva and Hague conventions, such as mistreatment of POWs and civilians in wartime. (See "The Rules of War" and "War Crimes" in Chapter 8.)

In a powerful opening statement, Robert Jackson noted,

> The privilege of opening the first trial in history for crimes against the peace of the world imposes a grave responsibility. The wrongs which we seek to condemn and punish have been so calculated, so malignant and so devastating, that civilization cannot tolerate their being ignored, because it cannot survive their being repeated. That four great nations, flushed with victory and stung with injury, stay the hands of vengeance and voluntarily submit their captive enemies to the judgment of the law, is one of the most significant tributes that Power ever has paid to Reason.

Leading Nazis (seated far left) appear before the International Military Tribunal in Nuremberg, where the Nazi Party once held its massive annual rallies. A group of skilled linguists and a supply of headsets allowed participants to receive simultaneous translations of court proceedings in one of four languages: English, French, German, and Russian.

What followed was a vast amount of evidence from the Nazis themselves—captured documents, photographs, party and government witnesses, as well as Nazi and Allied film footage. Some defendants claimed that they were only following orders, but at Nuremberg, the court did not accept that explanation. Eleven, including Hermann Göring, who killed himself with smuggled cyanide just two hours before his execution, were sentenced to death. Those with prison sentences were sent to Spandau Prison in West Berlin, which the Four Powers managed on a rotating basis. Rudolf Hess (who had been in British custody since 1941) was the only inmate at Spandau for more than twenty years until his death in 1987, and the prison was then demolished. The acquitted—Hjalmar Schacht, Franz von Papen, and Hans Fritzsche—were soon tried by the German government on other charges; Schacht and von Papen spent a short time in prison while Fritzsche received hard labor and was released in 1950.

The first wave of war crimes trials lasted into the 1950s, although trials would continue sporadically into the twenty-first century. Another dozen trials at Nuremberg focused on the Einsatzgruppen leaders, senior military officials, SS officers at concentration and slave labor camps, concentration camp doctors, and German industrialists. More than 20,000 Nazis were convicted in Allied and West German courts, although most received light sentences or early release; another 20,000 Nazis slipped out of the country, many having made arrangements to do so well before the war ended. Belgium and the Netherlands convicted and sentenced about 77,000 and 66,000 Nazis and collaborators, respectively, while

---

RATLINES

Thousands of Nazis—including the Treblinka and Sobibor extermination camp commandants—and other war criminals such as the Ustasha (Croation fascists allied with the Nazis) fled Europe using a network of safe houses and escape routes known as ratlines. Austrian bishop Alois Hudal, the Vatican's representative to Germans held in Allied internment camps in Italy, and Krunoslav Draganovic, a Croatian priest, ran the best known of these lines.

Via the ratlines, war criminals established new lives in Latin America, the United States, the Middle East, and Europe because they were seen as fighters in the war against communism, and some Allies as well as Catholic Church officials believed they would be valuable for intelligence work. From 1949 to 1955, for example, the CIA ran a clandestine network of Germans to report on Soviet activities. However, these and other formerly fascist intelligence operators posed their own security problems and were vulnerable to being recruited by the communists as double agents. In 2004, the Nazi War Crimes and Japanese Imperial Government Records Interagency Working Group, established by the U.S. Congress to declassify and study captured and American World War II documents, concluded in its report, *U.S. Intelligence and the Nazis*, "that American use of actual or alleged war criminals was a blunder in several respects." Among those it cited, "Lack of sufficient attention to history—and, on a personal level, to character and morality—established a bad precedent, especially for new intelligence agencies."

FIRST INTERNATIONAL MILITARY TRIBUNAL TRIAL, AT NUREMBERG

Defendant	Conspiracy to Wage War	Crimes Against Peace	War Crimes	Crimes Against Humanity	Sentence and Fate
	G = Guilty; NG = Not Guilty				
Hermann Göring, Reichsmarshall	G	G	G	G	Death. Committed suicide hours before scheduled execution.
Rudolf Hess, Hitler's deputy	G	G	NG	NG	Life in prison. Death in 1987 at age 93 ruled a suicide.
Joachim von Ribbentrop, foreign minister	G	G	G	G	Death. Hanged October 16, 1946.
Wilhelm Keitel, head of OKW	G	G	G	G	Death. Hanged October 16, 1946.
Ernst Kaltenbrunner, head of the SS RSHA	NG	—	G	G	Death. Hanged October 16, 1946.
Alfred Rosenberg, head of ERR	G	G	G	G	Death. Hanged October 16, 1946.
Hans Frank, head of General Government (Poland)	NG	—	G	G	Death. Hanged October 16, 1946.
Wilhelm Frick, interior minister	NG	G	G	G	Death. Hanged October 16, 1946.
Julius Streicher, editor, *Der Stürmer*	NG	—	—	G	Death. Hanged October 16, 1946.
Walther Funk, economics minister	NG	G	G	G	Life in prison. Released for poor health in 1957. Died in 1960.
Hjalmar Schacht, minister without portfolio	NG	NG	—	—	Acquitted. Died in 1970.

(continued)

FIRST INTERNATIONAL MILITARY TRIBUNAL TRIAL, AT NUREMBERG (CONTINUED)

Defendant	Conspiracy to Wage War	Crimes Against Peace	War Crimes	Crimes Against Humanity	Sentence and Fate
	G = Guilty; NG = Not Guilty				
Karl Dönitz, commander in chief, navy (1943–45)	NG	G	G	—	10 years in prison. Served full term. Died in 1980.
Erich Raeder, commander in chief, navy (1923–43)	G	G	G	—	Life in prison. Released for poor health in 1955. Died in 1960.
Baldur von Schirach, Gauleiter of Vienna	NG	—	—	G	20 years in prison. Served full term. Died in 1974.
Fritz Sauckel, head of Labor	NG	NG	G	G	Death. Hanged October 16, 1946.
Alfred Jodl, chief of operations, OKW	G	G	G	G	Death. Hanged October 16, 1946.
Martin Bormann, Hitler's private secretary	NG	—	G	G	Death. Tried in absentia. Died in 1945; not declared dead until 1972.
Franz von Papen, vice chancellor, ambassador	NG	NG	—	—	Acquitted. Died in 1969.
Artur Seyss-Inquart, commissioner of Holland	NG	G	G	G	Death. Hanged October 16, 1946.
Konstantin von Neurath, governor, Bohemia-Moravia	G	G	G	G	15 years in prison. Released for poor health in 1954. Died in 1957.
Hans Fritzsche, head, German radio	NG	—	NG	NG	Acquitted. Died in 1953.

postwar Austrian and Italian governments proved reluctant to confront war crimes issues. A tormented France, pained by its collaborationist survival strategy, executed 2,000 of its citizens, including Pierre Laval, de facto head of the Vichy government. His superior, Marshal Henri Pétain, died in prison in 1951, having escaped execution by virtue of his advanced age and heroic World War I service. An untold number of other Nazis and collaborators met their fates at the hands of their victims; some Jews took revenge on SS men and camp guards immediately after the war, others tracked them down years later.

Japanese War Crimes Trials

An International Military Tribunal for the Far East, comprising members from various Allied nations, was established in 1946 to try leading Japanese officials for war crimes. Many who might otherwise have been tried had already committed suicide, although General Hideki Tojo, the major figure known to the West, had attempted but failed to kill himself. The Tokyo war crimes trial was similar to the first Nuremberg trial, in that it focused on Japan's leaders; twenty-five men listed as "Class A" defendants went on trial in May 1946 before a court headed by Sir William Webb, an Australian personally selected by MacArthur; President Truman chose the chief prosecutor, Joseph B. Keenan, an American. Charges included crimes against peace, conspiracy to wage aggressive war, permitting war atrocities, and violating traditional laws of war. As at Nuremberg, critics questioned the validity of the trials, especially the meaning of "aggressive war," which the Allies distinguished from war of self-defense, and the legal proceedings were inherently more flawed in Tokyo. (Emperor Hirohito and other notable officials were exempted from charges, as the Allies wanted their cooperation to ensure a smooth occupation of Japan; one of the eleven judges, who was from the USSR, spoke neither Japanese nor English, the two official languages of the trial; another judge was a former POW and survivor of the Bataan Death March.) The trial concluded on April 16, 1948, and in the verdicts given in November, all defendants were found guilty. Seven, including Tojo, were sentenced to death and executed by hanging on December 23. All but two of the remaining eighteen defendants were sentenced to life imprisonment, although those still alive in 1958 were released.

More than 2,000 other trials under the auspices of American, Australian, British, Canadian, Chinese, Dutch, French, and Filipino military courts were conducted for Class B defendants (such as prison guards) and C defendants (usually senior military officers who ordered or failed to prevent crimes), resulting in about 3,000 convicted persons; 920 were executed for war crimes. Many others initially condemned to death later had their sentences commuted to prison terms. In two especially controversial cases involving Generals Tomoyuki Yamashita and Masaharu Homma, each was convicted and executed for not preventing atrocities in the Philippines, despite flimsy prosecutorial evidence. General MacArthur, in his capacity as supreme Allied commander, had prepared the charges against Yamashita and Homma, and he expected—and got—guilty verdicts. Meanwhile, thousands of others responsible for war crimes were never pursued.

General Dwight Eisenhower, left, joined by Generals Omar Bradley and George S. Patton, tours the Merkers salt mine filled with Nazi looted gold and art. The Roberts Commission (1943–1946) and its Monuments, Fine Arts and Archives branch, whose purpose was unprecedented in military history, successfully salvaged and repatriated thousands of cultural treasures.

Allied-run war trials wound down as the Cold War grew frostier. "We had visits from congressmen and senators who favored the rearmament of Germany and who said that we had to get rid of the trials because they're an obstacle," recalled Nuremberg prosecutor William Caming many years later. "Between 1949 and 1958 all of the prisoners had sentences reduced and were then released. . . . It was a political measure. No members of the prosecution staff and none of the judges at Nuremberg were even consulted." The results may not have been satisfactory to all, but the International Military Tribunal set a far-reaching precedent. Since the World War II war crimes trials there has been considerably greater support for holding war criminals to account and pursuing international justice through the IMT's descendants, including international tribunals under the auspices of the United Nations. For example, some persons involved in war atrocities and genocide in the Balkans and Rwanda in the 1990s were later brought before these tribunals and convicted on a charge that was new in the 1940s—crimes against humanity—but has since become a fundamental component of international law.

✶   ✶   ✶

The victors and vanquished had innumerable other issues to settle. Among the most urgent was repatriating prisoners of war. The Soviets had captured 600,000 Japanese soldiers in Manchuria in August 1945, most of whom died in captivity; survivors indoctrinated with communist ideology trickled home in small numbers over the next several years. The Soviets also held German POWs for years, including Luftwaffe ace Erich Hartmann, "the Blonde Knight of Germany," who was not released until 1955. More than 300,000 former POWs released from the USSR between 1946 and 1955 underwent extensive interviews with U.S. Air Force officials, who hoped to gain political or military intelligence the freed POWs might have gleaned as slave laborers. By 1947, the United States had repatriated all its German and Italian POWs. (In some cases, POWs did not return home for decades. In the year 2000, former Hungarian soldier Andras Tama was released from a Russian psychiatric hospital and returned to Hungary when it was discovered who he really was.)

Other issues took more time to settle. Japan paid out reparations in the form of capital goods to the United States until 1949 and lost its assets and industrial property in Manchukuo to the Soviet Union. The Allies officially renounced reparations claims from East and West Germany in 1954, and the latter agreed to make payments to Israel for Jewish losses in the Holocaust. Not until the 1990s would there be large-scale efforts and lawsuits to provide compensation and restitution to former POWs, camp inmates, and other wartime victims.

Postwar America: The United States after V-J Day

The Nation Goes to Peace

Long before the fighting ended, U.S. government officials and business leaders were already planning for demobilization and reconversion, which was hastened with the Japanese surrender. In August, the navy canceled $1.2 billion in contracts, leaving 167 ships partially built (including eleven aircraft carriers); General Motors quickly lost $2 billion in government orders, but by the third week of September, new GM Cadillacs, rather than tanks, were rolling off assembly lines. Other carmakers quickly reconverted to automobile production, turning out the much-delayed 1942 models to meet the huge backlog of orders and current demand. Virginia Shefferly of Detroit, Michigan, whose mother had ordered a Ford before the war, picked up the new vehicle shortly after V-E Day. "I drove it home past a fire station and two firemen dropped what they were doing and stared," she later wrote. "The next night I went by at the same time and they were waiting, the whole fire station was looking to see one of the first new cars off of the line. I felt like I was driving a Rolls Royce. People would come up to me and offer one thousand dollars more than I had paid if I would sell the car to them."

On August 13, the Office of Price Administration (OPA) halted a printing order for 187 million new ration books; gasoline rationing soon ended and luxuries—bubble gum for children, stockings for women—were quickly back on store shelves. Despite the restrictions on consumer goods, U.S. war industries never accounted for more than 40 percent of the nation's production; economically, Americans had not suffered, nor had the country, despite its tremendous output, produced as much as it could have. As Julius Kreg, chairman of the War Production Board, reported to Truman, "Throughout the war, the people at home were subjected to inconvenience, rather than sacrifice." Millions of defense workers were let go by the end of 1945, and within a year of the war's end, more than 99 percent of the War Department's contracts closed. With the return of servicemen and women and laid off war plant workers to a peacetime job market, employers now had their pick of employees. As a result, Paul Henkel, president of the Society of Restaurateurs, predicted notable changes in his industry. "There has been a great deal of discourtesy to patrons on the part of waiters and waitresses," he said. "This should shortly become a thing of the past and the diner can expect and again will receive courteous treatment."

From Serviceman to Civilian

Millions of Chinese, Russian, and Axis servicemen returned home to learn they had lost their families, houses, even their towns, and that they would receive little or no help from the governments they had served. British servicemen were generally much better off; George Cleall, a six-year veteran of the RAF, "returned home with a small amount of money and a new suit of clothing," said his daughter, Betty Hensel. Americans, however, came back to an intact country with a flourishing economy and the GI Bill of Rights, a remarkable piece of legislation Congress passed unanimously in 1944. It funded higher education and vocational training; provided medical benefits and low-interest loans for buying or building a house, new business, or farm; paid up to $1,040 in unemployment for one year; assisted in finding employment; and provided other benefits. By 1954, 8 million veterans had taken advantage of the bill, ensuring that a large portion of the war generation was better educated and more productive than any that had come before it.

No country provided as much for its veterans as the United States, and most U.S. servicemen and women reentered civilian life, married, raised families, and did well for themselves. All were changed by the war, those who had been in the thick of battle the most. Doctors found that readjusting

American postwar prosperity was especially apparent in flourishing suburbia, as standardized housing and government loan guarantees often made it cheaper to buy a home than to rent. New housing developments in Levittown, New York (left), and Park Forest, Illinois, represented a major lifestyle shift away from cities and farms that was accompanied by the Baby Boom, a generation whose first members were born in 1946.

to the freedom and responsibilities of civilian life was a serious challenge for veterans used to following orders and working in tight-knit units, and it could bring to the fore both new and previously latent mental issues. A 1944 *Time* magazine article on the subject inspired producer Samuel Goldwyn to make *The Best Years of Our Lives* (1946). This Academy Award-winning film chronicled the fictional return of three servicemen—one of them played by a veteran who was a double amputee—and gave the public a better understanding of the difficulties veterans faced. Still, well-meaning fellow citizens could not begin to comprehend what veterans had endured and witnessed, or why many found themselves so disillusioned after the thrill of returning home subsided.

What was called "battle fatigue," but later came to be called *posttraumatic stress disorder*, afflicted many veterans: they suffered from occasional to chronic depression, anxiety, lack of concentration, and rage. Most servicemen who saw combat did not talk much about it, if at all, even to their families. (About one out of eight American servicemen engaged in combat, but those in support roles overseas could also come under attack.) Robert Peters Eustace, whose ship lost more than 100 men in a kamikaze strike on October 25, 1944, at Leyte Gulf, said more than fifty years later, "I wasn't ready for civilian life. I thought civilians were a bunch of crud, you know? They didn't appreciate what we did. I did this and they don't think about me now. . . . You realize you weren't appreciated for the sacrifice you had made. And you were kind of jumpy. You were irritable. You were ready to fight at the drop of a hat." While the rest of the country was eager to move forward and return to peacetime life, veterans struggled to cope with, and make sense of, their wartime experiences. The strain of constant peril, intense bursts of violence and confusion, seeing friends killed, and having to kill the enemy took a tremendous emotional toll that did not always ebb with time. Many veterans experienced nightmares and flashbacks into old age, especially those who never sought treatment.

"What kind of war do civilians suppose we fought, anyway?" wrote Edgar Jones, a self-described "ambulance driver, a merchant seaman, an Army historian, and a war correspondent" in the February 1946 issue of *Atlantic Monthly*. "We shot prisoners in cold blood, wiped out hospitals, strafed lifeboats, killed or mistreated enemy civilians, finished off the enemy wounded, tossed the dying into a hole with the dead, and in the Pacific boiled the flesh off enemy skulls to make table ornaments for sweethearts, or carved their bones into letter openers . . . we mutilated the bodies of enemy dead, cutting off their ears and kicking out their gold teeth for souvenirs, and buried them with their testicles in their mouths." Despite great advances in military psychiatric care, for Jones these "flagrant violations of all moral codes reach into still-unexplored realms of battle psychology." A raft of routine injustices fueled other complaints, wrote Jones: thousands of Americans killed by their countrymen in everyday friendly fire incidents; discrimination against reservists by regulars and against black troops who had proved their mettle; the "undemocratic" nature of military life; favoritism of officers over enlisted or drafted men; and "In varying degrees . . . the GI perspective included bitter contempt for the home front's abysmal lack of understanding, its pleasures and comforts, and its nauseating capacity to talk in patriotic platitudes. . . . The majority of the men in uniform hated the Army with a bitterness that made them want to take their misery out on anyone conceivably responsible for their plight."

Meanwhile, the Army's Research Branch found in 1945 that 81 percent of servicemen believed that their army experiences had made them "more nervous and restless," and another survey found that 75 percent of GIs believed the Army had not tried hard enough "to see that men get as square a deal as possible" during their wartime service. To consider these grievances, Secretary of War Patterson formed the Doolittle Board, chaired by Lieutenant General James Doolittle, whose 1942 raid over Japan had made him a national hero. The board's report acknowledged soldiers' complaints, but also pointed out, "When due consideration is given to all the difficulties experienced in preparing for war in a democracy, it becomes obvious that the Army did a truly magnificent job in this Second World War." Some important changes did result, including reforms in officer-enlisted personnel relations and the system of military justice. A single code for all U.S. armed services, the *Uniform Code of Military Justice*, went into effect in May 1951.

On returning home, veterans of the European Theater were generally in better physical shape than those from the Pacific, especially the former POWs. Wounded men went through another round of stateside triage to determine what medical facility could best treat them. Fractures were the most common injury; mine blasts accounted for most of the amputation cases. Doctors rose to the challenge in devising innovative long-term treatment for severe burns, damaged spinal cords, and horrendous abdominal and head wounds. In 1946, the Veterans Administration established the Department of Medicine and Surgery to work in conjunction with hospitals and medical schools in providing care to servicemen nationwide.

Military and Security Reorganization

After the war, American armed forces underwent a radical change as military strength decreased to about 2 million men and women. The wide-ranging National Security Act of 1947 created a new service branch, the United States Air Force, which replaced the U.S. Army Air Force. Each major branch of the armed services—Army, Navy, and Air Force—functioned according to its assigned mission under the new centralized Department of Defense, which replaced the War Department. A new body, the National Security Council, was formed to assist the president in devising foreign policy and in responding to immediate national security issues. The act also created the Central Intelligence Agency, a successor organization to the wartime Office of Strategic Services. The following year, Truman signed Executive Order 9981, which paved the way to ending racial segregation in the military. Five years later, the army announced that 95 percent of its black servicemen were in integrated units.

Balance of Power and the Cold War

When the war ended, London, Paris, and Berlin were no longer capitals of major world powers as they had once been: Britain, virtually bankrupt, endured food rationing and austerity measures that were more severe after the war than during it. France, humiliated by its quick defeat in 1940 but granted postwar status as an Allied power, was burdened by a collaborationist history that it did not acknowledge publicly for decades; and Germany, in utter shambles, under occupation, and damned with the horrific legacy of Nazism, was condemned, once again, for having plunged Europe into a world war. The balance of world power now resided in Washington, D.C., and in Moscow. "[W]e have emerged from this war the most powerful nation in the world," said Truman, "the most powerful nation, perhaps, in all history." "I rejoice that this is so," seconded Churchill. With that power came a sense of international authority and responsibility that prevented a revival of the once prominent isolationist movement. The shift in power also meant that Europe's 300-year-old colonial system could no longer be sustained; subject nations demanded independence, and Britain and France, in particular, were forced to acquiesce. In the twenty-five years following the war, more than fifty countries gained their independence.

By late 1945, Europe fell into essentially two camps (excluding Spain and Portugal, which were governed by rightwing dictatorships): the open West, a

One of the first of many postwar national independence ceremonies began when India and the new state of Pakistan (formed from Indian territory) achieved sovereignty in August 1947. In Karachi, Lord Louis Mountbatten, wearing sash, the last British Governor-General of India, turns ruling authority over to Pakistan's Quaid-i-Azam Muhammad Ali Jinnah.

mix of capitalist and socialist nations, led by the United States; and the repressive Eastern European communist bloc, led by the USSR. All of Eastern Europe except Greece and Turkey fell behind what Churchill in 1946 dubbed "the iron curtain." The Cold War (the chilly-to-frigid relations between East and West) was a principal legacy of World War II and the overarching theme for nearly the rest of the twentieth century in everything from political, military, and economic issues to international sporting events. The close working relationship between Roosevelt and Churchill—the former deceased and the latter out of office from 1945 to 1951—was reflected in the postwar "special relationship" of their two nations, which shared a common language, heritage, and commitment to democracy. The third member of the wartime "Big Three," the USSR, with its vision of an all-communist world, was now the West's chief cold war adversary. Each side feared the expansion and global influence of the other. From 1948, the U.S. Marshall Plan helped fund economic recovery and rebuilding in Western Europe, lest it be drawn into the Soviet orbit (see "The Marshall Plan" box on p. 938).

Naturally, the communist bloc opposed the Marshall plan. In June 1948, the Soviets blockaded West Berlin in an attempt to control the entire city; the Allies responded with the Berlin Airlift, dropping in food and supplies to sustain the western section. The following April, the United States, Belgium, Britain, Canada, Denmark, France, Iceland, Italy, Luxembourg, the Netherlands, Norway, and Portugal founded the North Atlantic Treaty Organization (NATO), headquartered in Brussels, as a bulwark against Soviet aggression, with the underlying principle that an attack on one member was an attack on them all. In May, Stalin called off the Berlin blockade, but in August the Soviets exploded their first atomic bomb, and again the balance of power was altered. After Britain developed its atomic bomb (1952) and West Germany was permitted limited militarization (1954), the USSR established the Warsaw Pact (1955), an alliance among its communist satellite

THE MARSHALL PLAN

Delivering the Harvard University commencement address in June 1947, U.S. Secretary of State George C. Marshall proposed a plan that, when it was established the following year, accomplished a great deal with comparatively little: it saved Europeans in some regions from mass starvation, it facilitated the spread of democratic and free market ideals, and it created a geographic bulwark against Communist states in the east. Congressional opposition to the plan, primarily for economic reasons, ceased when the Soviets backed a successful communist coup in Czechoslovakia, making clear the need to strengthen crumbling Western Europe. The European Recovery Plan (also known as the Marshall Plan) called for continental cooperation in developing a reconstruction program with American financial assistance. From 1948 to 1952, the United States provided $13 billion for new housing projects, industrial revitalization, and massive amounts of machinery and supplies (which were clearly marked on each box and crate as being from the United States of America). The results were astonishing: by 1950, Europe was nearing or at its prewar levels in agricultural production and trade, and industrial output surpassed prewar levels. Britain ($3 billion), France ($2.7 billion), Italy ($1.5 billion), and Germany ($1.4 billion) received the bulk of assistance, with the remainder dispersed to smaller nations. West Germany's "Economic Miracle" in the 1950s was directly traceable to the Marshall Plan. But there was more than that, noted former German chancellor Ludwig Erhard in 1972, on the twenty-fifth anniversary of Marshall's speech. "I have always stressed the fact that it was not the 'money' but rather the spirit in which the aid was given that inspired Germans to make their effort. This spirit gave us hope that we would not be written off but treated as equal partners in the family of civilized nations."

states, Albania, Bulgaria, Czechoslovakia, East Germany, Hungary, Poland, and Romania. Each had either been occupied by or associated with the Axis and had fallen under the Soviet sphere as the Red Army surged toward Berlin in 1945.

The nuclear arms race and competition to purchase the support of unaligned and developing countries in Africa, Asia, and Latin America characterized the Cold War in its middle period, as East and West jockeyed to counteract each other. American foreign policy, in what became known as the Truman Doctrine, was to support foreign nations fighting communism and prevent communism from spreading beyond where it already existed. This policy found military expression in the Korean War (1950–1953), the war in Vietnam (1964–1975), and in numerous covert actions. At the same time, the growing arsenal of American and Soviet nuclear weapons, particularly the advent of intercontinental ballistic missiles, changed fundamental military notions of how a future world war would be fought, if, indeed, it could even be survived. Perhaps the most tangible sign of the Cold War was the Berlin Wall (begun in 1961), a ninety-six-mile-long, twelve-foot-high snake of cement, mortar, and barbed wire that divided the city and was intended to keep those in the east from escaping to the west, as 3 million Germans had already done. Berlin was, indeed, the Cold War writ small: a contrast between the colorful, prosperous western section and the gray and austere eastern portion, where wartime rubble and damaged buildings remained prevalent. When the Soviet Union, outspent by the West and imploding, underwent a period of "perestroika" (restructuring) and "glasnost" (openness) in the late 1980s, the dissolution of the communist bloc swiftly followed. Ecstatic Berliners—from both

In West Berlin, Germans peer over a portion of the Berlin Wall, 1962, during the construction phase. The wall finally came down in 1989.

East and West—struck down the wall and celebrated on its ruins in November 1989; it was a defining moment as the Cold War era drew to a close. In October 1990, fifty-seven years after Hitler came to power and forty-five years after the destruction of the Third Reich, Germany was reunified.

An American Memorial, 2004

In the aftermath of the greatest conflict in human history, thousands of cities and towns in the former Allied countries raised memorials to their men and women who were casualties of the war, and to the bravery and accomplishments of surviving veterans. Many of these memorials were erected throughout the United States. But the country did not have a national commemorative site until the National World War II Memorial, located on the National Mall in Washington, D.C., was dedicated over the Memorial Day weekend in 2004. The dedication was the occasion for a World War II Reunion that brought thousands of veterans to the Mall. For three days, they met one another, described their experiences to eager audiences in thirty hours of programs held in large tents, and recorded their stories for the archives of the Library of Congress Veterans History Project, where recordings and transcriptions are now available to both professional and amateur historians. The celebration culminated in dedication ceremonies attended by 100,000 people. Among the speakers was Senator Bob Dole, who, as a young second lieutenant in the U.S. 10th Mountain Division serving in Italy, was severely wounded while attempting to save a comrade's life:

> What we dedicate today is not a memorial to war, rather it's a tribute to the physical and moral courage that makes heroes out of farm and city boys and that inspires Americans in every generation to lay down their lives for people they will never meet, for ideals that make life itself worth living. . . . In contending for democracy abroad, we learned painful lessons about our own democracy. For us, the Second World War was in effect a second American revolution. The war invited women into the workforce. It exposed the injustice [toward] African Americans, Hispanics and Japanese Americans and others who demonstrated yet again that war is an equal opportunity employer. What we learned in foreign fields of battle we applied in postwar America. As a result, our democracy, though imperfect, is more nearly perfect than in the days of Washington, Jefferson, Lincoln, and Roosevelt. That's what makes America forever a work in progress—a land that has never become, but is always in the process of becoming. And that's why the armies of democracy have earned a permanent place on this sacred ground.

The bodies of soldiers killed in the European Theater began arriving in the United States on October 27, 1945, at Brooklyn Army Base, New York (top); more than 93,000 others were buried overseas in American-run cemeteries. In Arlington, Virginia (bottom), workers install the U.S. Marine Corps Memorial, September 15, 1954. The one-hundred-ton bronze statue depicts the American flag raising on Mount Suribachi, Iwo Jima.

PRINCIPAL SOURCES AND FURTHER READING

Black, Cyril E., et al. *Rebirth: A History of Europe since World War II*. Boulder, San Francisco, Oxford: Westview Press, 1992.

Botting, Douglas. *From the Ruins of the Reich: Germany 1945–1949*. New York: Crown Publishers, 1985.

Buruma, Ian. *Wages of Guilt: Memories of War in Germany and Japan*. New York: Farrar Straus Giroux, 1994.

Chafe, William H. *Unfinished Journey: America since World War II*. 5th ed. New York: Oxford University Press, 2002.

Dower, John. *Embracing Defeat: Japan in the Wake of World War II*. New York: W.W. Norton, 1999.

Eizenstat, Stuart. *Imperfect Justice: Looted Assets, Slave Labor, and the Unfinished Business of World War II*. New York: Public Affairs, 2003.

Gaddis, John Lewis. *The Cold War: A New History*. New York: Penguin Press, 2005.

Harris, Whitney R. *Tyranny on Trial: The Trial of the Major German War Criminals at the End of World War II at Nuremberg, Germany, 1945–1946*. Dallas, TX: Southern Methodist University Press, 1954, revised edition 1999.

Judt, Tony. *Postwar: A History of Europe since 1945*. New York: Penguin Press, 2005.

Nicholas, Lynn. *The Rape of Europa: The Fate of Europe's Treasures in the Third Reich and Second World War*. New York: Random House, 1994.

Schmitt, Hans, ed. *U.S. Occupation in Europe after World War II*. Lawrence, KS: Regents Press, 1978.

Spector, Ronald. *In the Ruins of Empire: The Japanese Surrender and the Battle for Postwar Asia*. New York: Random House, 2007.

Wyman, Mark. *DPs: Europe's Displaced Persons, 1945–1951*. Ithaca, New York: Cornell University Press, 1989.

Information about Images

To order reproductions of Library of Congress images in this book note the negative or digital ID number provided below. Duplicates may be ordered from the Library of Congress, Photoduplication Service, Washington D.C. 20540-4570; (202) 707-5640; fax (202) 707-1771; http://www.loc.gov/preserv/pds. Most images can be viewed and some downloaded from the Library of Congress Prints & Photographs Online Catalog at http://www.loc.gov/rr/print/catalog.html.

Key to Abbreviations

Library of Congress Divisions

GC: General Collections
G&M: Geography & Map Division
RBSC: Rare Book & Special Collections
SGPD: Serial & Government Publications
VHP: Veterans History Project

Other Sources

CMH: Center for Military History- Brochure Series: U.S. Army Campaigns of WWII
IWM: Used with Permission of the Board of Trustees, Imperial War Museum, London
NARA: National Archives and Records Administration
USHMM: United States Holocaust Memorial Museum

p. 95, right	LC-USZ62-96046
p. 98	LC-USZ62-111647
p. 114	LC-USZ62-91957
p. 124	LC-USZ62-114736
p. 132	LC-USZ62-65203

Chapter 3

p. 140	LC-H814-T-1150-071
p. 152	LC-USF34-034116-D
p. 165	Courtesy of Way family
p. 167	LC-USZC4-1652
p. 170	LC-USZ62-92751
p. 173, left	Greenbrier Archive
p. 173, right	Greenbrier Archive
p. 178, top	Lockheed
p. 178, bottom	Lockheed
p. 191	LC-USZ62-105572
p. 193	LC-USE6-D-003761
p. 197	LC-USZ62-121474
p. 205	LC-DIG-ppmsca-13323
p. 211	LC-USW3-024939-C

Chapter 4

p. 226	LC-USZ61-2240
p. 232	LC-USZ61-618
p. 242, row 1:	LC-DIG-ppmsca-13324
	LC-USZ62-102630
	LC-USZ62-105322
	LC-DIG-ppmsca-13325
p. 242, row 2:	LC-DIG-ppmsca-13326
	LC-USZ62-102619
	LC-DIG-ppmsca-13327
	LC-USZ62-122364
p. 242, row 3:	LC-DIG-ppmsca-13328
	LC-USZ62-18014
	LC-DIG-ppmsca-13329
	LC-DIG-ppmsca-13330
p. 255	GC: DS777.53.S395A
p. 263	LC-USZ62-32930
p. 265	LC-DIG-ppmsca-13331
p. 274	LC-USZ62-70810
p. 283, row 1:	LC-DIG-ppmsca-13362
	LC-USZ62-107199
	LC-DIG-ppmsca-13332
	LC-DIG-ppmsca-13363
	LC-USZ62-85201
p. 283, row 2:	LC-DIG-ppmsca-13364
	LC-DIG-ppmsca-13360
	LC-USZ62-44154

	LC-DIG-ppmsca-13359
	LC-USZ62-94366
p. 289	LC-USZ62-121825
p. 296	LC-F9-02-4501-319-10
p. 309	LC-DIG-ppmsca-13333
p. 317, row 1:	LC-USZ62-104296
	LC-USZ62-90331
	LC-USZ62-121096
	LC-USZ62-90028
	LC-USZ62-128510
p. 317, row 2:	LC-USZ62-121098
	LC-USZ62-122229
	LC-USZ62-26014
	LC-USZ62-21027
	NARA: 80-G-424329
p. 317, row 3:	LC-USZ62-97152
	LC-USZ62-121080
	LC-USZ62-84988
	LC-DIG-ppmsca-13365
	LC-USW33-000127-ZC
p. 321	LC-USZ62-98901
p. 323, both	VHP: Mimi K. Lesser (AFC2001/001/11904)

Chapter 5

p. 330, left	LC-USZ62-103751
p. 330, right	LC-USZ62-104100
p. 345	LC-USZ62-132622
p. 348, both	GC: AP2.L547 v.15
p. 351	MSS: Charles Scott Papers, Cont.70, Hains folder
p. 357	LC-USZ62-132598
p. 364	LC-DIG-ppmsca-13334
p. 371	LC-USZ62-99393
p. 382	LC-USZ62-69156
p. 389	LC-USZ62-101012
p. 399	LC-USZ62-99501
p. 402	LC-USZ62-128768
p. 407	LC-USZ62-114866

Chapter 6

p. 414	LC-USZC4-7350
p. 422	LC-USZ62-49065
p. 425	LC-USZ62-132594
p. 431	LC-USZ62-105523
p. 445	LC-DIG-ppmsca-13335
p. 448	LC-USZ62-97495
p. 455	LC-USZ62-95768
p. 471	LC-DIG-ppmsca-13336

p. 812	LC-USZ62-69845
p. 814	TimeLife# 50659710
p. 816, row 1:	LC-USZ62-113325
	LC-USZ62-109633
	LC-DIG-ppmsca-13346
	LC-USZ62-126657
p. 816, row 2:	LC-DIG-ppmsca-13347
	LC-DIG-ppmsca-13348
	LC-USZ62-111077
	LC-USZ62-120968
p. 816, row 3:	LC-USZ62-61128
	LC-USZ62-134505
	U.S. Marine Corps History Division
	LC-DIG-ppmsca-13349
p. 824	LC-USZ62-71874
p. 829	RBSC: N6868.N27
p. 837, left	LC-DIG-ppmsc-03235
p. 837, right	LC-DIG-ppmsc-03236
p. 841, left	LC-DIG-ppmsc-03350
p. 841, right	VHP: Tracy Sugarman (AFC2001/001/05440)

Chapter 11

p. 849	LC-USF34-100226-D
p. 857	LC-USW3-000610-C
p. 859	LC-USZ62-131085
p. 864, top	LC-USZ62-69917
p. 864, bottom	LC-DIG-fsa-8e09323

p. 870, top	LC-USE6-D-008431
p. 870, bottom	LC-USZ62-119160
p. 875, top	LC-USE6-D-010878
p. 875, bottom	LC-USE613-D-004021
p. 884, left	LC-USZ62-112869
p. 884, right	LC-USZ62-112868
p. 895	LC-USZ62-64822
p. 898	LC-USZ62-95995
p. 899	LC Publishing Office
p. 900	GC: DS 145. B35
p. 905	LC-DIG-ppmsca-13351

Chapter 12

p. 910	LC-USZ62-64808
p. 911	LC-USZ62-135620
p. 916, left	LC-USZ62-101110
p. 916, right	LC-DIG-ppmsca-13352
p. 919, top	LC-DIG-ppmsca-13353
p. 919, bottom	LC-USZ62-93707
p. 920	LC-USZ62-127539
p. 922	LC-DIG-ppmsca-13354
p. 925	USHMM: 96326
p. 930	USHMM: 74574
p. 933, left	LC-USZ62-127668
p. 933, right	LC-USZ62-132141
p. 937	LC-USZ62-111689
p. 939	LC-USZ62-122648
p. 941, top	LC-DIG-ppmsca-13355
p. 941, bottom	LC-DIG-ppmsca-13356

INDEX

Page numbers in *italics* refer to captions; page numbers in **bold** refer to principal treatment of a subject.

War Production Board, Chinese, 188
War Production Board (WPB), U.S., 188,
  190, 192, 193, 212, 214
War Refugee Board (WRD), 127, 690, 698,
  699, 701
War Relocation Authority (WRA), U.S.,
  119–20, 134
War Resources Administration, U.S., 189
War Resources Board, U.S., 144, 213
Warsaw, Poland, 424, 426, 571, 602, 617,
  622, 633, 776, 777
  German bombing of, 73
  uprising (1944), 564, 571, **571–72,** 669,
    672, 688, 700
Warsaw Pact, 937–38
War Shipping Administration, U.S., 214
Warspite, 460–61
Wartime (Fussell), 816
Wartime Shipbuilding, Ltd., 199
"War of the Worlds" broadcast, 64
Washington, D.C., 39, 70, 190, 320, *849,*
  875, 905, 936
  air raid drills in, *140,* 141
  Allied conferences in, 113, 115–16, 123
  camouflage measures rejected in, 179
  cultural treasures protected in, 181
  Italian embassy in, 747
  memorials in, 940
  V-J Day celebrations in, 911
Washington, George, 940
Washington, USS, 166
Washington Conference (1921–22), 22
Washington Conference (March 1942),
  321–22
Washington Naval Treaty, 372
Washington Post, 72, 141, 144
Washington State, 164, 890, 896
Wasp, 368
Wasserman, 389–90
Watchtower, Operation, 506, **522–26**
Waterhouse, Alan, 210
Watt, Harry, 826
Wavell, Archibald, 115, 469, 472
WAVES (Women Accepted for Volunteer
  Emergency Service), U.S., *725*
Way, A. L., *165*
weaponry, 220, 246, 409
  aircraft carriers, **368–69**
  aircraft, **328–44**
  antisubmarine, **379–80**
  artillery, **344, 346–48**
  atomic bomb, **401,** *402,* **403**
  balloons, **331–32**
  battleships, **369–70**
  biological weapons, **404–5**
  blimps, **332–33**
  bombers, **333–38**
  chemical weapons, **405–6**
  cruisers, **372–73**
  figures in, **408**
  float planes, **330, 331**
  landing crafts, **370–72**
  land vehicles, **397–98, 400**
  mines, **361–66**
  production of, by country, 1939–1945,
    202–4
  small arms, **380–85**
  submarines, 366–67, **374–77**
  tanks, **349–50,** *351,* **352**
  technological devices, **385–96**
  V-weapons, 387, 403, 404, **406–7,** 408
  see also specific weapons

Weapons and Hope (Dyson), 632
WEASEL, 209, 398
Webb, William, 929
Wedemeyer, Albert C., 168, 266, 300, 578
Wegman, William, 827
Wehrmacht, 144, 185, 246, 248, 325, 348,
  423, 427–29, 436, 438, 440, 441, 444,
  446–47, 462, 469, 481, 484, 494, 497,
  512, 528–29, 535–38, 546–49, *548,*
  552, 554, 567, 571, 580, 604, 657, *657,*
  660, 677, 722, 727, 753, 774, 779, 847
  Army Secret Police of, 658
  Austrian army incorporated into, 61
  collapsing of, 664
  in Czechoslovakia, 293
  development of, 156
  Division for Defense Propaganda under
    control of, 791, 803
  European cable network expanded by,
    717
  in Finland, 129
  horses used by, 397
  in invasion of France, 81
  Maginot Line circumvented by, 357–58
  Mussolini's views of, 244
  North African campaign of, *40*
  Oberkommando der, 658
  partial Jews in, 673
  Polish fortified areas breached by, 358
  pushed out of the Ukraine, *289*
  Rhineland reoccupied by, xv, 19
  Soviet invasion and, 176, 245, 262, 284,
    288
  supreme command of, 745
Weidling, Karl, 618–19
Weimar Republic, *see* Germany, Weimar
Weisskopf, Victor, 403
Weizsäcker, Carl von, 403
Welchman, Gordon, 724
Welles, Orson, 64
Welles, Sumner, 76, 120
Welsh, William, 533
Wenck, Walther, 618
Wenzel, Johann, 745
Weserübung, Operation, **439–41**
West, Horace T., 638–39
West Africa, 282, 268
West Berlin, 915, 925, 937, *939*
West Coast, U.S.:
  blackouts on, 139–42
  defense of, 171
  industrial camouflage on, *178,* 179
  Japanese-Americans on, 207
Western Desert Air Force, British, 470, 472
Western Desert Campaign (Part I, 1941),
  464, **469–72,** 494
Western Desert Campaign (Part II, 1942),
  515–16
Western Front:
  Hitler Youth on, 240
  in World War I, 270, 297
  see also specific places
Western Samoa, 51, 52
Western Task Force, Allied, 533, 534
West Germany, 915, 922, 926, 931, 938
Westindien, Operation, 504
West Wall, 185, 359, 427, 592, 595, 604
Wetzler, Alfred, 697–98
Weygand, Maxime, 334, 443
Weygand Line, *445,* 447–48
What Is to Be Done? (Lenin), 794–95
Wheat and Soldiers (Hino), 835

Wheeler, Keith, 396
Wheeler Air Field, 492
Where Stands a Winged Sentry (Kennedy),
  885
White, Theodore, 867
White, Thomas D., 306
White, Walter, 856–57
White, William Allen, 78, 80
Whitehead, Don, 817
White Rose, 123
White Sulphur Springs, W. Va., 173, *173*
white supremacy, 295
Whithead, Ennis C., 306
Whitworth, W. J., 439
Why We Fight, 828
Wickard, Claude R., *82,* 201, 863
Widder, 373
Wigner, Eugene, 401
Wilhelm Gustloff, 292, 893, 895
Wilhelm II, Kaiser, 3, 7
Wilhelmina, Queen of the Netherlands,
  77–78, 111, 444
Wilhelmshaven naval base, 426, 485
Wilkinson, Charles, 169
Wilkinson, Theodore S., 710
Williams, Francis, 811
Williams, Tennessee, 840
Willkie, Wendell, **85,** 86, 122, 123
Willoughby, Charles A., 711
Willys-Overland, 398
Wilson, Henry Maitland, 475, 566
Wilson, Robert R., 403, 648
Wilson, Woodrow, xvi, 2, 9, 297
Winant, John G., 322
Winchell, Walter, 821–22
WIN code system, 727
Window metallic strips, 553
Wingate, Orde, 342, 542, *543,* 577, 603
Wing and a Prayer, 827
Winkelman, Henri, 443
Winning Your Wings (film), 308
Winter Line, 557, 564
Winter Offensive, Chinese (1939–40),
  438–39
Winter Relief, 148
Winter Storm, Operation, **529–30**
Winter War, 385, 436–38, 466, 481, 485,
  494
Wirth, Christian, 684
Wise, Stephen, 700–701
With the Old Breed at Peleliu and Okinawa
  (Sledge), 616
Wolff, Karl, 131
wolf-pack system, 431–32, 504–5
Wolfschanze (Wolf's Lair), 771
women:
  African American, 857
  in agriculture, 863, *864,* 866, 868, 871,
    872
  Allied countries and role of, 846,
    858–59, **868–71,** 932, 933
  as army nurses, 909
  Axis countries and role of, 847, 854,
    861–62, 866, 868, 869, **872–73,** 900,
    904, 920
  in British war effort, 166, 175, 195, 273,
    276, 278, 279
  in civil defense, 175, 176
  in comfort stations, **649–50,** *650*
  Jewish, 667, *676,* 679, *688*
  in labor and concentration camps, 680,
    686, *688*